Handbook of Cognitive Psychophysiology

Wiley Psychophysiology Handbooks

Series Editor: Anthony Gale
University of Southampton

HANDBOOK OF SOCIAL PSYCHOPHYSIOLOGY
Edited by Hugh Wagner and Antony Manstead

HANDBOOK OF CLINICAL PSYCHOPHYSIOLOGY
Edited by Graham Turpin

HANDBOOK OF PSYCHOPHYSIOLOGY OF HUMAN EATING
Edited by Richard Shepherd

HANDBOOK OF COGNITIVE PSYCHOPHYSIOLOGY
Central and Autonomic Nervous System Approaches
Edited by J. Richard Jennings and Michael G. H. Coles

Handbook of Cognitive Psychophysiology

Central and Autonomic Nervous System Approaches

Edited by

J. Richard Jennings

University of Pittsburgh, USA

and

Michael G. H. Coles

University of Illinois, USA

JOHN WILEY & SONS

Chichester · New York · Brisbane · Toronto · Singapore

Other Wiley Editorial Offices

John Wiley & Sons, Inc., 605 Third Avenue,
New York, NY10158-0012, USA

Jacaranda Wiley Ltd, G.P.O. Box 859, Brisbane,
Queensland 4001, Australia

John Wiley & Sons (Canada) Ltd, 22 Worcester Road,
Rexdale, Ontario M9W 1L1, Canada

John Wiley & Sons (SEA) Pte Ltd, 37 Jalan Pemimpin 05-04,
Block B, Union Industrial Building, Singapore 2057

Library of Congress Cataloging-in-Publication Data:

Handbook of cognitive psychophysiology : central and autonomic nervous system approaches / edited by J. Richard Jennings and Michael G. H. Coles.
p. cm. — (Wiley psychophysiology handbook)
Includes bibliographical references and index.
ISBN 0-471-91613-7 (cloth)
1. Cognition—Physiological aspects. 2. Psychophysiology.
I. Jennings, J. Richard. II. Coles, Michael G. H. III. Series.
[DNLM: 1. Mental Processes—physiology. 2. Nervous System–
–physiology, 3. Psychophysiology. WL 103 H2356]
BF3.H3335 1991
612.8′2—dc20
DNLM/DLC
for Library of Congress 90–13119
CIP

British Library Cataloguing in Publication Data:

Handbook of cognitive psychophysiology: central and autonomic nervous system approaches. – (Wiley psychophysiology handbooks)
1. Man. Cognition. Psychophysiological aspects
I. Jennings, J. Richard. II. Coles, Michael G. H.
153.4

ISBN 0-471-91613-7

Printed and bound in Great Britain by Courier International, East Kilbride

Contents

List of Contributors

Bruno J. Anthony, *Department of Psychiatry, University of Maryland, Baltimore, MD 21201, USA.*

Theodore R. Bashore, *Medical College of Pennsylvania, Philadelphia, PA 19129, USA.*

Jasper Brener, *Department of Psychology, State University of New York, Stony Brook, NY 11790, USA.*

Enoch Callaway, *University of California, San Francisco, CA 94143, USA.*

Michael G.H. Coles, *Department of Psychology, University of Illinois, Champaign, IL 61820, USA.*

Emanuel Donchin, *Department of Psychology, University of Illinois, Champaign, IL 61820, USA.*

Monica Fabiani, *Department of Psychology, University of Illinois, Champaign, IL 61820, USA.*

David Friedman, *Medical Genetics Department, New York State Psychiatric Institute, New York, NY 10032, USA.*

Ira Fischler, *Department of Psychology, University of Florida, Gainesville, FL 32601, USA.*

Frances K. Graham, *Department of Psychology, University of Delaware, Newark, DE 19716, USA.*

Steven A. Hackley, *University of Missouri, Columbia, MO 65211, USA.*

Roy Halliday, *Langley Porter Neuropsychological Institute, University of California, San Francisco, CA 94143, USA.*

J. Richard Jennings, *Department of Psychiatry, University of Pittsburgh, Pittsburgh, PA 15213, USA.*

Arthur Kramer, *Department of Psychology, University of Illinois, Champaign, IL 61820, USA.*

Richard B. Lipton, *Department of Neurology, Albert Einstein College of Medicine, Bronx, NY 10461, USA.*

Jeanette S. Packer, *School of Behavioural Sciences, Macquarie University, Sydney, Australia.*

Gary E. Raney, *Department of Psychology, University of Florida, Gainesville, FL 32601, USA.*

Jean Requin, *Department of Experimental Psychobiology, Inst. Neurophysiol. & Psychophysiol. du CNRS, Marseille Cedex 9, France 13402.*

Christopher Ring, *Department of Psychology, State University of New York, Stony Brook, NY 11790, USA.*

Walter Ritter, *Albert Einstein College of Medicine, Bronx, NY 10461, USA.*

Mary M. Schroeder, *Department of Neurology, Albert Einstein College of Medicine, Bronx, NY 10461, USA.*

David A. T. Siddle, *Department of Psychology, University of Tasmania, Hobart, Tasmania 7001, Australia.*

John Spinks, *Department of Psychology, University of Hong Kong, Hong Kong.*

Maurits W. van der Molen, *Department of Psychology, University of Amsterdam, The Netherlands.*

Nancy Yovetich, *Department of Psychology, University of North Carolina, Chapel Hill, NC 27510, USA.*

Preface by Series Editor

Psychophysiology is still an emerging discipline, even though its key journal *Psychophysiology*, published in North America by the Society for Psychophysiological Research is over twenty-five years of age. One of the editors of the present volume (Michael Coles) has been editor of *Psychophysiology*, and the other (Richard Jennings) is editor of another well-established journal, *Biological Psychology*. More recently, the *Journal of Psychophysiology*, published by European psychophysiological societies, is clearly set to make its mark, with a lively and catholic approach to the discipline, spanning both theory and empirical data. In spite of reductions in research funding, new advances in the discipline continue to emerge and the number of scientists committed to the psychophysiological approach worldwide is increasing. Psychophysiology advances both in the laboratory and in applied contexts.

The very complexity of the subject matter of psychophysiology makes theory building particularly hazardous. Even where a theory has sound formal properties, the move to empirical data is rarely straightforward. The inclusion of variables which are easy to justify from a theoretical point of view in no way guarantees that the outcome of an experiment will be easy to interpret, will relate to previous data, or will settle theoretical issues once and for all. Typically, some of the data can tell one story, while the remainder offer a puzzle. Again, experimentation is a black art, for the researcher seeks to capture in the laboratory a true slice of life, rather than create situationally specific artifacts.

Psychophysiology seeks to integrate data along a bio-social continuum, for physiological data reflect both inherent properties of the nervous system and the impact of extended adaptation to the environment. It therefore has to tackle several major issues, drawing upon a number of separate and even disparate approaches a sub-disciplines. Genetic predisposition is recognized as a source of variance both for general characteristics and for individual variations. Inherent biological characteristics are expressed in terms of the electrophysiology and biochemistry of the nervous system and its functional organization; yet these too are seen to be open to the influence of ontogeny and learning.

The measurement of biological variables has been a major concern in psychophysiology and the development of the laboratory minicomputer and then the microcomputer both revolutionized the acquisition and analysis of data and the sorts of experimental procedure which became feasible. In this sphere of measurement several psychophysiologists have made their mark.

While the burden of experimentation and measurement has fallen on the assessment of central and autonomic system variables, psychophysiologists recognize the need to integrate such data with data describing behaviour, performance, and subjective state. Without reference to observable behaviour and subjective experience, psychophysiology would remain a physiological and not a psychological discipline. It is the measurement of both behaviour and experiential state as well as the non-invasive measurement of physiological change, which marks off psychophysiology from its parent discipline, physiological psychology. Yet measurement in these non-physiological domains creates major problems for a systematic scientist to tackle, even where they are taken separately. The notion that psychophysiology seeks to ***integrate*** data derived from such disparate domains of description distinguishes psychophysiology from most other disciplines of psychology, and the inclusion of experiential data makes psychophysiology unique as a science. It imposes a tremendous intellectual burden on the researcher and of course upon the theorist and the practitioner.

Nor should we believe that measurement of physiological variables themselves is necessarily straightforward. The measures employed vary in their reliability, empirical utility, physiological validity and practical usefulness, particularly in field studies, where there is a need to employ in vivo measurement (Gale, 1987). Moreover, it has been rare for scientists to include more than one physiological measure in their investigations, thus creating a *set* of psychophysiologies, each with its own theoretical interests and research paradigms. It is rare, for example, to read studies which include and integrate both central and autonomic variables.

Given that psychophysiologists employ human subjects as their experimental material the issues of consciousness, self-regulation and self-control must also be handled. As Porges, Ackles and Truax (1983) point out, there are multiple logical relations between the domains of physiology, behaviour, experience and subjective report, and each logical relation in its turn, creates special difficulties for experimental design, measurement, and interpretation of data.

Within psychology at large, cognitive psychology and cognitive science have burgeoned over the last fifteen years. Links between attention, information processing and the creation of cognitive representations of knowledge have been established. The individual is not seen as a passive receptacle of external events, but an active operator, preparing appropriately for action, and storing information derived from feedback.

In this *Handbook* Richard Jennings and Michael Coles bring together recent psychophysiological approaches to cognitive psychology, with particular reference to the processing and storage of information and the changes in the nervous system which accompany them. Unlike many handbooks the aim is not to present all that is known. Rather, the focus is on those areas of psychophysiology which have thrown most light on cognitive processes. Many psychophysiology texts are arranged around systems or measures; the present text is about *processes*. Whereas in the past, central and autonomic measures have been treated separately, they are now brought together where appropriate to illuminate their cognitive correlates. Thus the editors have created collaboration between international authorities working on common processes but with different procedures and laboratory traditions. Several of their chapter authors have neither worked nor written together before. The volume, therefore, represents a considerable editorial feat.

The present *Handbook* is unique in both content and approach. Starting with the long established tradition of research into reaction time and linear models of information processing, the volume addresses issues of capacity, serial and parallel processing and the problem of multiple tasks. Cortical psychophysiological measures are particularly suited to monitoring the direction and allocation of attention and to the identification of stages of processing. Autonomic measures and their relation to energetics enable us to monitor preparation for action; how are mental resources integrated with cognitive and motor functions to yield smooth and integrated performance? Attentional processes may be relatively data-driven, particularly when biological imperatives are built into the system, or centrally controlled as a result of learning. The capacity to scan, store and transmit complex information is clearly limited to human organisms; again, central and autonomic functions may be studied to explain the complexity of human reading. No integrated processing of information is possible without reference to stored information, which enables complex planning and prediction of the environment; thus the volume turns to memorial processes. Finally, insights may be gained by studying both the psychophysiological development of cognitive processes in the infant and the degradation of function associated with aging. Throughout the volume there is concern with both theoretical and empirical research problems, particularly in relation to the integration of data from several sources.

This volume will not only appeal to psychophysiologists but to those concerned with models of cognitive processes; psychophysiology is in the unique position of being able to monitor process and not merely describe inputs and outcomes. Psychophysiologyoffers an additional viewpoint and a key to unsealing the black box.

Other volumes in the series address overlapping concerns in different spheres of theory and application. Volume 1, edited by Hugh Wagner and Antony Manstead, focuses on the fast-growing field of social psychophysiology and, in particular, on biological and socio-psychological aspects of emotion and its expression. Volume 2, edited by Graham Turpin, is devoted to new developments in clinical psychophysiology and behavioioural medicine and is of direct interest to clinical practitioners as well as to basic researchers. Volume 3, edited by Richard Shepherd, novel in the field of psychophysiology, explores the psychophysiology of human eating and nutritional behaviour, demonstrating that human eating behaviour deserves more research interest than it has hitherto attracted. The final volume, edited by Michael Eyseneck and myself, in contrast to the consideration of general processes which are largely the concern of other volumes in the series, focuses on the psychophysiology of individual differences in cognitive and emotional functions.

In inviting world authorities to contribute to the *Wiley psychophysiology Handbooks* series we have encouraged them to offer state-of-the-art reviews. We hope that these well-referenced and timely papers will stand as essential sources for students, advanced researchers and practitioners. We have focused on depth of approach rather than breadth and have encouraged our authors to be critical in evaluating progress in their fields. Researchers seeking a more general introduction to psychophysiological research should turn to other major texts, such as *Psychophysiology: Systems, Processes and Applications*, edited by Coles, Donchin and Porges (1986).

It is clear that psychophysiology raises more questions than answers, but would science be fun or offer a challenge to artistry and ingenuity in experimentation if everything were clear-cut? One advantage of uncertainty is that new discoveries are that much sweeter.

ANTHONY GALE
University of Southampton, October 1990

REFERENCES

Coles, M.G.H., Donchin, E. and Porges, S.W. (1986). *Psychophysiolog: Systems, Processes and Applications*, New York: Guilford.

Gale, A. (1987). The psychophysiological context. In A. Gale and B. Christie (eds), *Psychophysiology and the Electronic Workplace*. Chichester: Wiley.

Porges, S.W., Ackles, P.A. and Truax, S.R. (1983). Psychophysiological measurement: methodological constraints. In A. Gale and J.A. Edwards (eds), *Physiological Correlates of Human Behaviour. Volume 1. Basic Issues*. London: Academic Press.

Preface

Psychophysiology developed along with the capability to electronically probe physiological reactions in humans. The mid-twentieth century timing of this development coincided with the behavioral movement in psychology which had disavowed cognition as a fit object of study. Thus, the application of psychophysiology to the study of cognitive processes had to await the relatively recent cognitive revolution in psychology. The overall aim of the current volume is to show that the tools which have now been developed in psychophysiology have much to offer to the understanding of human cognition.

As illustrated in the accompanying collage (Figure 1), cognitive psychophysiology combines the physiological record—shown as the polygraph tracing—with traditional measures of experimental psychology—such as reaction time—as guided by the cognitive theory—such as the semantic tree depicted. Our goal in assembling this volume is to illustrate how cognitive theory is enriched by psychophysiological measures. Furthermore, it is our contention that measures from both the autonomic and central nervous system will provide that enrichment. Thus, we have asked our authors to address conceptual issues rather than broadly review areas—and to bring to bear both autonomic and central nervous system measures upon the conceptual issues.

As we detail further in our introductory chapter, the volume provides coverage of recent issues upon which psychophysiological measures can be brought to bear. Not all issues or areas relevant to current cognitive psychology can be addressed. We hope, however, that the reader will come away with a clear sense of when and how psychophysiological measures provide critical tools for understanding human information processing. The physiologically oriented reader should also be able to see how cognitive models and performance measures enlighten our understanding of physiology.

We would like to thank a number of individuals at the University of Pittsburgh and the University of Illinois who contributed to this work in important ways that are not otherwise recognized. At Pittsburgh, Kim Novak provided essential clerical and organizational expertise while Kay Brock and Tom Kamarck made much of the work possible by maintaining ongoing research projects. The domestic support of Kay Jennings and Colin, Justin, and Molly Jennings must also be thanked. At the University of Illinois the administrative support of Betty

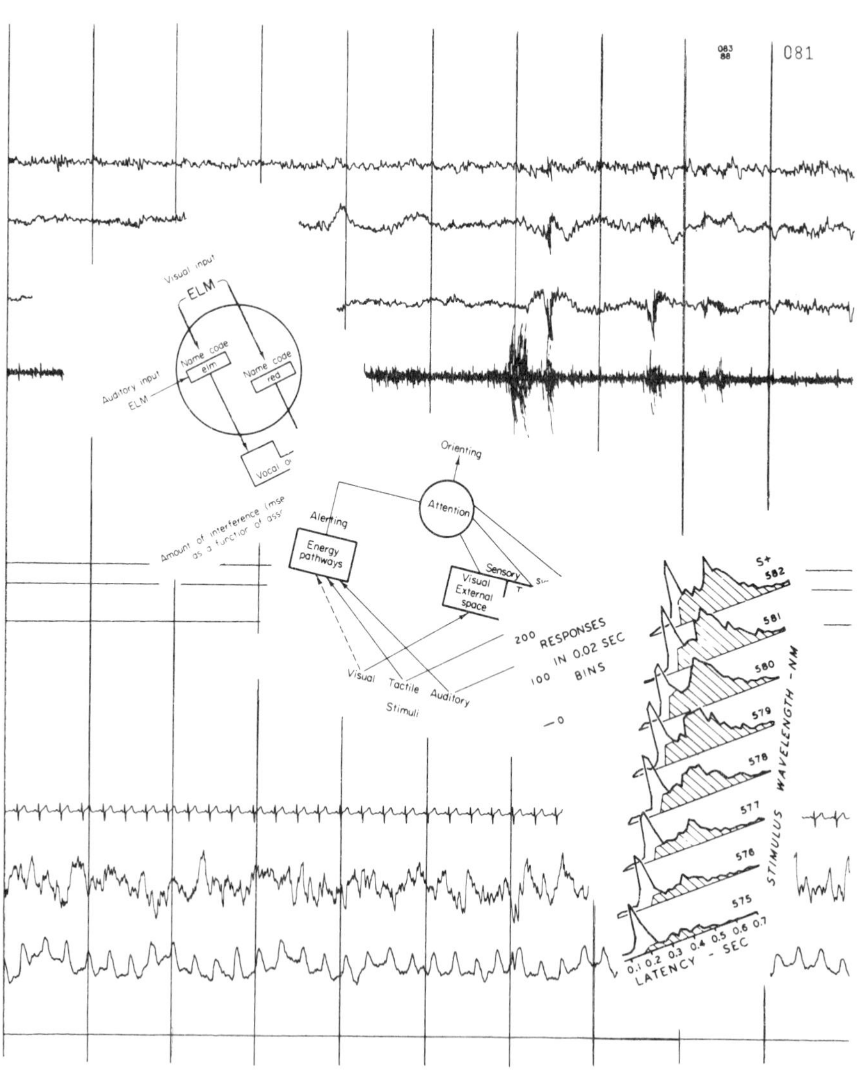
081
Visual input
ELM
Name code
elm
Name code
red
Auditory input
ELM
Orienting
Attention
Alerting
Energy pathways
Sensory
Visual External space
Visual
Tactile
Auditory
Stimuli
200
100
0
RESPONSES IN 0.02 SEC BINS
S+
582
581
580
579
578
577
576
575
STIMULUS WAVELENGTH - NM
0.1 0.2 0.3 0.4 0.5 0.6 0.7
LATENCY - SEC

Figure 1.

Heggemeier was critical; as was the familial support of Pamela and Emily Coles.

We also must thank Michael Coombs and Wendy Hudlass at John Wiley for their patience and support throughout. Tony Gale, the series editor, must be recognized for his support and inspiration at a number of points in the process.

As always for such a book, our gratitude must be extended most significantly to our chapter authors.

J. RICHARD JENNINGS AND MICHAEL G.H. COLES

Introduction

J. Richard Jennings
Department of Psychiatry,
University of Pittsburgh, PA 15213, USA
and
Michael G.H. Coles
University of Illinois, IL 61820, USA

The thesis of this volume is that measures of psychophysiological function can contribute to our understanding of human information processing. Because the information processing system must be implemented in the brain, measures of brain activity have the potential to shed light on information processing activities. Such measures may be relatively direct, as in the case of the event-related brain potential and the electroencephalogram, or more indirect, as in the case of measures of the autonomic nervous system, and the skeletal musculature. In the latter case, the measures can also provide insights into the way in which the outcome of information processing activities is translated into action. Muscular responses must be organized in particular ways for effective behavior and the autonomic nervous system plays a critical role in subserving these responses and, perhaps, their affective context.

This book, then, is not a traditional handbook which seeks to provide a comprehensive review of a field of inquiry. Rather, the purpose of this collection of chapters is to emphasize those instances in which the psychophysiological approach has contributed or may contribute to our understanding of human information processing. In addition, because each section of the book contains contributions dealing both with central and peripheral nervous

Handbook of Cognitive Psychophysiology: Central and Autonomic Nervous System Approaches.
Edited by J. R. Jennings and M. G. H. Coles.

system measures, it is our hope that the book will provide an integrated psychophysiological approach to the issues. For too long, psychophysiologists employing central nervous system and autonomic nervous system measures have proceeded independently without acknowledging the fact that the human organism is comprised of a variety of physiological systems all of which play critical roles in behavior.

The study of human information processing involves both allegiance to a particular conceptual framework and an interest in a particular class of phenomena. The conceptual framework rests on the assumption that the coding and transformation of information is the primary activity of the human brain. The phenomena of interest involve those of concern to traditional experimental psychology—attention, learning, memory, and 'higher' cognitive processes. Early views based strictly on Shannon's information theory (Shannon and Weaver, 1949) examined the brain as an information transmission system and thus focused on variables such as information encoding and the role of redundancy. Later developments included the incorporation of the notion of stages (Sternberg, 1969, Sanders, 1980) each of which is responsible for performing a specific information processing transaction. Questions as to whether these stages operate in parallel or serially, and whether they communicate continuously or discretely, are currently being addressed by researchers in this area (Eriksen and Schultz, 1979; McClelland, 1979; Miller, 1982). Other work has focused more on the limitations in the transmission of information and thus on the notion of capacity. This notion suggests that a limited capacity exists for simultaneously performing certain operations. Where is capacity limited—early in processing at perceptual stages, or at the central stage or later stages (Broadbent, 1958, 1971; Deutsch and Deutsch, 1963)? And are there different kinds of capacities or a single, undifferentiated pool (Kahneman, 1973; Wickens, 1984)? All of these issues will be addressed in the current volume.

The traditional approach to the study of human information processing is limited by the available measures. While the approach emphasizes the internal *covert* processes associated with the transformation of information, measures of *overt* behavior are, in fact, derived—the speed and accuracy of the subject's responses. The occurrence of a particular transform or a series of transformations must be inferred from the pattern of reaction times or errors resulting from task manipulations. This approach can certainly be fruitful given an adequate conceptual model (e.g. Sternberg, 1969; Logan and Cowan, 1984); but different models are often equally able to explain the same data (McClelland, 1979) and precise modeling has tended to focus on simple task performances—for example, choice reaction time. The system could be characterized with much more assurance if measures were available of the time of initiation and completion of specific processes and their magnitude of involvement. Psychophysiology promises to provide such measures. (For further discussion of these issues, see Coles, 1989; Donchin *et al.*, 1986; Hillyard and Hansen, 1986; Jennings, 1986 a,b.) For example, a physiological response associated with the focusing of attention toward sensory input might tell us whether attention is shifted from one of two tasks prior to the completion of a motor response to the first task—that is, whether a form of parallel processing occurred.

In spite of the persuasiveness of the 'psychophysiological argument', cognitive psychologists have been reluctant to incorporate physiological indices into their measurement armamentarium. A prominent example of this neglect is given by the exploration of Kahneman's theory of attention (1973). This theory is widely known, but the primary measure proposed to test the theory—namely, pupillary dilation—has been largely ignored. Kahneman had proposed that this measure could serve as an index of the allocation of processing capacity (attention).

As we have noted above, the theme of the present collection of chapters is that the cognitive psychophysiological approach, involving the non-invasive measurement of physiological function in humans, can contribute to our understanding of the human information processing system. We propose that psychophysiological measures can provide insights into the *timing* of particular information processing activities that are otherwise not directly observable. The measures may also reveal something about the intensity of a particular process. Of course, if it is possible to make these kinds of inferences on the basis of psychophysiological measures, then it is also possible to infer whether or not a particular process is invoked by a particular task or in a particular person. We should hasten to add that not all psychophysiological measures can be used to provide these kinds of precise inferences. This volume will attempt to note our progress in this regard. Our secondary theme will be to show how measures of different physiological systems, particularly those of the central and autonomic nervous systems, may be integrated to provide a more complete understanding of different aspects of information processing than is provided by measures of either system alone.

The cognitive psychophysiological approach has seen increasing acceptance over the last fifteen years. Traditionally, measures of the electrical activity of the brain were associated with neurology and with the problems of identifying the integrity of sensory and motor systems. On the other hand, measures of autonomic function were associated with psychiatry and the concern with identifying the motivational and affective significance of events for an individual. These differences in focus as well as differences in methodologies employed led to relatively independent developments in autonomic and central nervous system psychophysiology. However, in recent times, both areas have actively tried to apply their approaches to understand human information processing.

Non-invasive measurement of electrical brain activity began with Berger's discovery of the electroencephalogram (EEG). The promise of continuously available electrical indices of psychophysiological functioning was quickly recognized. The EEG was characterized in terms of its frequency and amplitude and related to psychological state and concurrent mental activity (Lindsley, 1960). Such relations tended to be rather gross, for example, waveforms in the alpha bandwidth (8–12 Hz) were related to a relaxed non-active mental state while high frequency (beta and above) activity was related to active mental processing. The field soon focused on event-related changes—or event-related potentials (ERPs)—elicited by discrete stimuli that could be identified by ensemble averaging over trials. The initial use of such potentials was to examine elementary sensory processes. In the hands of psychologically oriented physiologists, however, it soon became clear that the potentials could be used to investigate not only sensory systems, but also cognitive phenomena. In particular, identical stimuli present under different task conditions were associated with different ERPs. Thus, these kinds of potentials (the so-called endogenous potentials—see Donchin, Ritter and McCallum, 1978) indexed cognitive processing of the stimulus information rather than the simple sensory processing. Such observations quickly led to a proliferation of clever experiments to identify the functional significance, in cognitive terms, of ERP components (see, for example, Donchin, 1981).

Considerable attention has been paid to the definition of ERP components. The ERP waveform, a voltage versus time function, consists of a number of peaks and valleys. It is proposed that this ERP waveform represents the aggregate of a number of ERP components—that is, different portions of the waveform constitute functionally different entities. These 'entitites' have been dissociated in terms of the latency and polarity of particular peaks or valleys, in terms of portions of the waveform that covary in response to experimental manipulations and/or across subjects, and in terms of portions of the waveform that share the same distribution across the scalp. This latter method of dissociation reflects the belief that an ERP component must arise from the activity of a particular brain system and that such activity would be reflected in a consistent potential distribution on the scalp. (See Coles, Gratton and Fabiani, 1990, and Donchin *et al.*, 1978, for a discussion of these issues.)

Autonomic measures (skin conductance responses) were initially used to identify the arousing effect of certain word associations on psychiatric patients (Boller *et al.*, 1989). Another output measure of central activities, the electromyogram, was developed shortly thereafter and quickly became a tool for examining muscle tension as well as, in the hands of psychologists, motor imagery (Humphrey, 1963). As with the EEG measures, in the 1950s and 1960s, autonomic and motor measures were frequently classified as indices of different arousal states. The measures were related to performance via notions such as the inverted U hypothesis (see Eysenck review, 1977). Tasks were seen as having an optimal level of arousal; arousal above or below this level was deleterious. Concomitant EEG, autonomic, and motor indices identified the arousal state of the individual. Empirical difficulties in the identification of such states led autonomic psychophysiologists like the Laceys (e.g. Lacey, 1967) to question the arousal view. Brief changes in autonomic measures seemed to indicate something about the processing of discrete events rather than about the current state of the individual. In particular, the Laceys (1974) related brief heart rate deceleration to the processing of perceptual input and acceleration to the mental elaboration of such input.

While cognitive research has proceeded independently within each domain (central, myographic, and autonomic), there have been recent attempts to integrate measurement systems within a common conceptual framework. Such models, termed 'cognitive-energetic' models, are relevant to our exploration of the integration of EEG/ERP measures, presumably relatively cognitive, with autonomic/motoric measures, presumable relatively energetic (see Hockey, Coles and Gaillard, 1986). Sanders and Gopher (Sanders, 1983; Gopher, 1986) have presented the most well developed examples of these kinds of models. Their starting points were (a) the desirability of integrating structural theories of stages of processing with relatively functional theories of the limitations of processing capacity, and (b) the need to understand the influence of conditions such as fatigue, excitement, and environmental noise on information processing. They suggest that capacity limitations are due to the availability of energetic support processes that can be organized into three resources—arousal, activation, and effort. These resources have somewhat different properties, but most importantly, they support different stages of information processing; for example, arousal supports and is influenced by perceptual processing. Variables such as fatigue then act on an energetic resource to specifically reduce the efficiency of particular information processes. This cognitive–energetic model thus provides an explanation of why, for example, autonomic variables relate closely both to certain cognitive processes as well as to affective/motivation manipulations. Given that the central nervous system is involved in both information processing and the control of autonomic function, EEG/ERP measures are likely to be related to processes regulating information transformation as well as to energetic support processes. At present, we can hope that cognitive–energetic models represent more than a convenient fiction to integrate diverse areas and methodologies. Again the contributions to this volume, by attempting to integrate central and peripheral physiological indices, provide insights into the viability of cognitive–energetic approaches.

In summary, the theme of this volume is the contribution of the psychophysiological approach to the understanding of human information processing. The volume is unique in showing how the information about cognitive processes from central and peripheral nervous system indices can provide both parallel and complementary information about cognitive function. The content of the volume reflects our attempt to find areas where these themes could be productively developed. Thus, the coverage of human information processing is kaleidoscopic rather than linear and comprehensive. As a result, we suspect that this volume will serve as a supplementary reading for undergraduate courses in information processing, psychophysiology, and motivation and emotion. At the graduate level, it would be an appropriate text for advanced work in any of these areas as well as an interesting theme for a seminar type approach.

A brief overview of the volume may whet the appetite of the reader. The chapters of the book have, in all cases except one (the 'Language by Eye' chapter), been written by an author or authors with a background in central nervous system measures and an author or authors with a background in autonomic or electromyographic measures. In some cases, these authors have written an integrated chapter. In other cases, separate chapter parts have been written and a concluding integration part has been added by the group of authors. Note that in certain cases we have provided, in the list of contents, alternative citations for integrated chapters—this recognizes the primary contribution of each of the authors. The book has been organized to present the reader, first, with a review of general models of information processing (serial versus parallel, continuous versus discrete, and structure versus capacity). Chapters on different aspects of information processing follow. The volume concludes with two developmental chapters—one on child development and one on aging.

Drs van der Molen, Bashore, Halliday, and Callaway review in detail serial stage and related models of information processing. Their chapter has the further advantages for the reader of providing some detail on performance approaches to information processing as well as introductory material on central and autonomic measures. As in all the chapters the primary focus is on the conclusions about information processing which can be drawn from integrating the results from different physiological measures. The next chapter by Drs Kramer and Spinks reviews capacity approaches to information processing. The reader interested in engineering psychology and conditioning will find parts of this chapter of particular interest.

Drs Graham and Hackley next provide an elegant analysis of the available psychophysiological data concerning the influence of attention on the perceptual input to the organism. This chapter makes extensive use of results from studies of the modification of the eyeblink reflex, so readers unfamiliar with this technique may first wish to read Dr Anthony's brief introduction to the techniques (Chapter 7). In Chapter 4, motor preparation is dissected in a thorough fashion by Drs Requin, Brener and Ring. This chapter provides an interesting contrast between metabolic/energetic studies and studies of the functional neural circuitry of motor preparation. So-called higher order functions are next addressed in a chapter on mnemonic function by Drs Siddle,

Packer, Donchin and Fabiani. Autonomic studies based on use of the orienting reflex are related to work on event-related potentials thought to be involved in more specifically cognitive kinds of processes. Drs Fischler and Raney then provide a multi-level analysis of what psychophysiological measures can tell us about how we understand language while reading.

The final two chapters take us from birth to maturity. Drs Anthony and Friedman provide discussions of how peripheral motoric reflexes and event-related potentials index the developing capability of the infant to process information. Drs Schroeder, Lipton, Ritter, Jennings and Yovetich conclude the volume with their analysis of how the psychophysiology of aging may complement current performance analyses of why aging may slow and disrupt the skills we possess.

The volume was conceived as an expedition into a poorly charted wilderness. Few studies are available which concurrently measure and interpret central and peripheral psychophysiological responses during information processing. We have forced our authors to consider multiple-response systems. The results of their efforts have surpassed our expectations. We hope, however, that the reader recognizes the tenuousness of our attempt. More important, we hope that our readers join us in future forays with a multiple-response approach to understanding information processing.

REFERENCES

Boller, F., Galvani, L., Keefe, N.C. and Zoccolotti, P. (1989). Body electricity and the 'galvanic skin response'. *Neurology*, **39**, 868–870.

Broadbent, D.E. (1971). *Decision and Stress*. London: Academic Press.

Broadbent, D.E. (1958). *Perception and Communication*. London: Pergamon Press.

Coles, M.G.H. (1989). Modern mind–brain reading: psychophysiology, physiology and cognition. *Psychophysiology*, **26**, 251–269.

Coles, M.G.H., Gratton, G. and Fabiani, M. (1990). Event-related potentials. In J.T. Cacioppo and L.G. Tassinary (eds), *Principles of Psychophysiology: Physical, Social and Inferential Elements*. New York: Cambridge University Press, pp. 413–455.

Deutsch, J.A. and Deutsch, D. (1963). Attention: some theoretical considerations. *Psychological Review*, **70**, 80–90.

Donchin, E. (1981). Suprise!. . . Surprise? *Psychophysiology*, **18**, 493–513.

Donchin, E., Karis, D., Bashore, T., Coles, M.G.H. and Gratton, G. (1986). Cognitive psychophysiology and human information processing. In M.G.H. Coles, E. Donchin and S. Porges (eds), *Psychophysiology: Systems, Processes and Applications*. New York: Guilford Press, pp. 244–267.

Donchin, E., Ritter, W. and McCallum, C. (1978). Cognitive psychophysiology: the endogenous components of the ERP. In E. Callaway, P. Tueting and S.H. Koslow (eds), *Event-Related Brain Potentials in Man*. New York: Academic Press, pp. 349–411.

Eriksen, C.W. and Schultz, D.W. (1979). Information processing in visual search: continuous flow conception and experimental results. *Perception and Psychophysics*, **25**, 249–263.

Eysenck, M.W. (1977). *Attention and Arousal.* Berlin: Springer-Verlag.

Gopher, D. (1986). In defence of resources: on structures, energies, pools and the allocation of attention. In G.R.J. Hockey, A.W.K. Gaillard and M.G.H. Coles (eds), *Energetics and Human Information Processing.* Dordrecht, Netherlands: Martinus Nijhoff, pp. 353–372.

Hillyard, S.A. and Hansen, J.C. (1986). Attention: electrophysiological approaches. In M.G.H. Coles, E. Donchin and S. W. Porges (eds), *Psychophysiology: Systems, Processes and Applications.* New York: Guilford Press, pp. 227–243.

Hockey, G.R.J., Coles, M.G.H. and Gaillard, A.W.K. (1986). Energetical issues in research on human information processing. In G.R.J. Hockey, A.W.K. Gaillard and M.G.H. Coles (eds), *Energetics and Human Information Processing.*Dordrecht, Netherlands: Martinus Nijhof, pp. 3–21.

Humphrey, G. (1963). *Thinking: An introduction to its Experimental Psychology.* New York: Wiley.

Jennings, J.R. (1986a). Bodily changes during attending. In M.G.H. Coles, E. Donchin and S.W. Porges (eds), *Psychophysiology: Systems, Processes and Applications.* New York: Guilford, pp. 268–289.

Jennings, J.R. (1986b). Memory, thought, and bodily response. In M.G.H. Coles, E. Donchin and S.W. Porges (eds), *Psychophysiology: Systems, Processes and Applications.* New York: Guilford, pp. 290–308.

Kahneman, D. (1973). *Attention and Effort.* Englewood Cliffs, NJ: Prentice-Hall, pp. 1–49.

Lacey, J.I. (1967). Somatic response patterning and stress: some revisions of activation theory. In M.H. Appley and R. Trumbull (eds), *Psychological Stress: Issues in Research.* New York: Appleton–Century–Crofts, pp. 14–42.

Lacey, B.I. and Lacey, J.I. (1974). Studies of heart rate and other bodily processes in sensorimotor behavior. In P.A. Obrist, J. Brener and L.V. DiCara (eds), *Cardiovascular Psychophysiology.* Chicago: Aldine, pp. 538–564.

Lindsley, D.B. (1960). Attention, consciousness, sleep and wakefulness. In H.W. Magoun (eds), *Handbook of Physiology,* Section I: *Neurophysiology,* Vol. 3. Washington: APS, pp. 1553–1593.

Logan, G.D. and Cowan, W.B. (1984). On the ability to inhibit thought and action: a theory of an act of control. *Psychological Review,* **91**, 295–327.

McClelland, J.L. (1979). On the time relations of mental processes: an examination of systems of processes in cascade. *Psychological Review,* **86**, 287–330.

Miller, J. (1982). Discrete versus continuous stage models of human information processing: in search of partial output. *Journal of Experimental Psychology: Human Perception and Performance,* **8**, 273–296.

Sanders, A.F. (1983). Towards a model of stress and human performance. *Acta Psychologia,* **53**, 61–97.

Sanders, A.F. (1980). Stage analysis of the reaction process. In G.E. Stelmach and J. Requin (eds), *Tutorials in Motor Behavior.* Amsterdam: North Holland, pp. 331–354.

Shannon, C.E. and Weaver, W. (1949). *The Mathematical Theory of Communication.* Urbana: University of Illinois Press.

Sternberg, S. (1969). On the discovery of processing stages: some extensions of Donders' method. *Acta Psychologica,* **30**, 276–315.

Wickens, C.D. (1984). Processing resources in attention. In R. Parasuraman and D.R. Davies (eds), *Varieties of Attention.* Orlando, FL: Academic Press, pp. 63–102

Chapter 1

Chronopsychophysiology: Mental Chronometry Augmented by Psychophysiological Time Markers

Maurits W. van der Molen
Universiteit van Amsterdam, The Netherlands

Theodore R. Bashore
The Medical College of Pennsylvania at EPPI, PA 19129, USA

Roy Halliday and Enoch Callaway
University of California, San Francisco, USA
Veterans Administration Medical, San Francisco, USA

ABSTRACT

Mental chronometry is concerned with articulating the temporostructural organization of the human computational mechanisms that mediate speeded task performance. Two broad classes of opposing models have been formulated to delineate these organizational properties—discrete stage and continuous models. Stage models generally assume that information processors are distinct, serially-organized structures whose input is provided by their immediate predecessor. Continuous models, on the other hand, generally assume that information processors are simultaneously active, always passing information on to other processing units. This chapter provides a selective review of the reaction-time methods that have been used to articulate the temporal dynamics of the human information processing system, and a critical evaluation of recent attempts to augment these methods with psychophysiological

Handbook of Cognitive Psychophysiology: Central and Autonomic Nervous System Approaches.
Edited by J. R. Jennings and M. G. H. Coles.

time markers. It is argued that models with reaction-time origins are predominantly computational in nature and, as such, typically do not incorporate into their conceptual framework factors, such as preparation, that may influence computational processes. The case is made that psychophysiological measures can provide insight into the impact of these factors on mental reactions, and can thereby provide an important interface between basic neurocognitive mechanisms and the systematic variables that influence them. Thus, a combined behavioral/psychophysiological methodology is advocated and the term 'chronopsychophysiology' is introduced to denote it.

INTRODUCTION

It is ironic that some 110 years after the founding of experimental psychology we have written a chapter that attempts to bridge a gap in the study of human mental chronometry by integrating psychophysiological and reaction-time (RT) studies. This irony stems from the fact that the first RT studies of mental chronometry (i.e. the structure and timing of mental processing) were undertaken by distinguished nineteenth century scientists whose formal training was in physiology and the recognized beginning of experimental psychology occurred in a laboratory, founded by a physiologist, established to study mental chronometry utilizing rigorous experimental methods adapted from physiology and the natural sciences (Koch and Leary, 1985). Indeed, distinctions between physiology and psychology were blurred throughout most of that century. Textbooks by pioneers in the study of human cognition, like Wundt (1874) and Ladd (1890), included chapters referencing both areas, and the title of Wundt's volume in psychology referred to the field as physiological psychology (*Grundzüge der Physiologischen Psychologie*).

What caused this intimate partnership to dissolve? The dissolution can be attributed, at least in part, to important technological and methodological advances in nineteenth century physiology that produced a growing dissatisfaction among many physiologists with the unreliable behavioral methods they had used in their early research (for example, to estimate human nerve conduction velocity). This dissatisfaction encouraged work that produced refinements in the experimental instrumentation available to physiologists. These refinements, in turn, allowed physiologists to ask questions about fundamental physiological processes that demanded more precise answers than behavioral measures could provide. For many physiologists, this meant the abandonment of interest in human mental reactions. For others, however, the interest remained and was expressed in the new discipline of experimental psychology that had emerged in the last quarter of the nineteenth century. Attempts were made by these investigators to refine the behavioral methodologies that were used to dissect human chronometric processes. These attempts did not produce more reliable behavioral methods, however. This failure, coupled with the contemporaneous ascendancy of the introspectionist criticisms of these behavioral methods, undermined the study of mental chronometry (Boring, 1950). The result was that in the first half of the twentieth century RT studies of mental processing were viewed as having empirical, but little theoretical, import (see, for example, Woodworth, 1938).

Theoretical psychology during this period, exemplified in the learning theoretic work of Clark Hull (1943), was influenced decidedly by logical positivist thinking and, as such, reasoned from empirical observations set in the framework of a hypothetico-deductive system. This framework did not admit recourse to physiological processes in explanation of observable behaviors. As a result, by the middle of this century, the only trace of the original interface between human performance and physiology was restricted primarily to sensory psychology (see, for example, Osgood, 1953). At the same time, however, physiologists were becoming increasingly able to probe systems at microanalytic levels and, consequently, were coming to rely more and more on animal preparations in their research. They also were beginning to use refined quantitative methods to analyze their data and develop formal models. Thus, as physiologists were becoming more able to investigate the infrastructure of physiological systems, psychologists were little interested in research aimed at understanding the relationships between these systems and observable behavioral processes.

It was not until the 1950s that a rapprochement between psychology and physiology began to take place. This process was initiated by the work of scientists like Donald Lindsley who studied the reticular activating system using measures of brain electrical activity, Evgeny Sokolov who sought to explain habituation of the orienting response by recourse to cognitive processes, and John and Beatrice Lacey who conducted research on general autonomic nervous system responsivity to a wide range of psychological variables. Interestingly, unlike the mid-nineteenth century when technological advances contributed to the fractionation of physiology, the advent of new technologies in the last 30 years, in particular the computer and the silicon chip, had the opposite effect; they encouraged the bonding of components of psychology and physiology into the field of psychophysiology. These technologies permitted investigators to record a variety of physiological events, using procedures that were not intrusive, as subjects performed different behavioral tasks. Thus, physiological and behavioral events could be measured concurrently. These new technologies allowed investigators to measure physiological activity that previously had not been accessible to them. Hence, much of the early work in psychophysiology was designed to identify physiological events that co-occurred with well-known behavioral events. Under these circumstances, attention was directed away from hypothesis testing.

Within the past decade, however, as the field has matured, stable empirical relationships have been sought and identified, and theoretical models have been formulated to explain these relationships. Much of the research activity in contemporary psychophysiology is devoted to testing and reformulating these models. Psychophysiological investigations of mental chronometry have evolved as has the field as a whole. Current theoretical models of mental chronometry have developed, by and large, from the research of cognitive psychologists, and the application of psychophysiological measures has been to test components of these models. Only recently, however, have critical communications and collaborations begun between cognitive psychologists and psychophysiologists with the aim of establishing integrated research methodologies and cross-fertilizing theoretical ideas (see, for example, Coles, 1989; Halliday and Bashore, 1988; Stoffels, van der Molen and Keuss, 1990).

Although the initial overtures between the two disciplines are encouraging, representation among psychophysiologists has been confined almost exclusively to those who study event-related brain potentials (ERPs). The link is obvious, but it reflects, in our view, a basic problem in the field; namely, the tendency for investigators to compartmentalize specific physiological systems and, in so doing, to compartmentalize research problems. Thus, psychophysiologists typically restrict their research efforts to the measurement of a single physiologic variable (e.g. electrodermal response, heart rate, event-related brain potentials, pupil dilation, blink rate), to the use of only one or two research paradigms, and to examination of a reasonably narrowly defined hypothesis. In this regard, we resemble our brethren in cognitive psychology who study either RT or speed/accuracy relations, but not both. As psychophysiology has grown, then, we have witnessed a fragmentation of the field in which psychophysiologists who study heart rate (HR), for example, and those who study ERPs use different research paradigms, are interested in different research problems, and in general speak a different language. Ironically, however, many of the major extant physiologically-based theories of behavior were developed on the basis of the integration of recent evidence from several physiological systems (see, for example, McGuinness and Pribram, 1980; Pribram and McGuinness, 1975).

One of our goals in this chapter is to provide a critical account of what is known about the chronometrics of human information processing as they are revealed by both behavioral and a broad range of psychophysiological measures. We take chronometrics to refer to the temporal activation of the components of mental processes that intervene between the presentation of a stimulus and the production of a response. The aim of research in mental chronometry is to articulate the structural organization of the elements of mental processing that are engaged when a stimulus is presented that calls for some type of action, to characterize how information is represented by these elements, to identify the temporal relations among the various elements of processing, and to determine the nature of the output that is transmitted from one processing element to another. Behavioral paradigms have provided considerable insight into these processes. Yet, these methods have important limitations. One of these limitations has been expressed eloquently by Pachella (1974) in his tutorial paper on the use of RT methods in the study of mental chronometry:

> ...modern cognitive psychology can be characterized as the study of events that cannot be directly observed. The events of interest to a cognitive psychologist usually take place when the subject is not engaged in any overt activity. They are events that often do not have any overt behavioral component. Thus, RT is often chosen as a dependent variable by default: there simply isn't much else that can be measured. (p. 43)

Unlike RT, psychophysiological activity can be measured when 'the subject is not engaged in any overt activity'. As early as 1938 Woodworth had speculated on the possibility of using psychophysiological response systems to supplement behavioral measures of the temporostructural characteristics of mental events:

> Time as a dimension of every mental or behavioral process lends itself to measurement, and can be used as an indicator of the complexity of the performance or of the subject's readiness to perform. A technical difficulty at once suggests itself. 'The speed of thought,' we say; but as soon as we set about measuring the time occupied by a thought we find that the beginning and end of any measurable time must be external events. We may be able in the future to use 'brain waves' as indicators of the beginning and end of a mental process, and even now muscle currents enable us to penetrate the organism a little way with our timing apparatus. ... (p. 238)

The contributions that a combined psychophysiological/behavioral approach can make to our understanding of human mental chronometry are just beginning to be explored, however. Accordingly, firm conclusions cannot be drawn about the value of this approach. In the sections that follow we review studies of mental chronometry in which psychophysiological measures have been used to augment behavioral measures. They suggest that the promise of this combined approach is sufficient to encourage continued systematic research. In anticipation of this discussion, we begin with a selective review of RT methods that have been used to examine the temporal dynamics of the human information processing system.

STAGE MODELS DERIVED FROM RT

In the first half of the nineteenth century physiologists were interested in the problem of variation in human nervous system transmission, but they were bound to the view that its speed was instantaneous (Boring, 1950; Woodworth, 1938). It was not until the distinguished physiologist Helmholtz (1850) published his studies on nerve conduction velocity that this notion was challenged. He estimated nerve conduction velocity in the frog by stimulating a nerve in its leg, as far away from and as close as possible to the muscle. In each case, the time was measured that elapsed between stimulation of the nerve and contraction of the muscle. The difference in time between the two measurements was used to derive an estimate of nerve conduction velocity. His estimates were about 26 m/s, a surprisingly slow rate given the belief that transmission was so rapid it could probably never be measured. Helmholtz then conducted similar studies with humans that represent the first systematic studies of human RT. In these studies, a slight electrical shock was applied to different parts of the skin of his subjects and they were required to respond to it as quickly as possible with a movement of the hand or jaw. RTs were found to increase as the distance of the site of stimulation increased from the brain. The estimated human nerve conduction velocity was calculated to be about 60 m/s. However, there was so much variability in the results—not only from one individual to another but also from one trial to another for the same individual—that Helmholtz concluded that the RT method was too unreliable to determine the speed of neural transmission and abandoned its use. Indeed, within the next 30 years use of the RT experiment was discouraged further by about another dozen studies, designed to replicate Helmholtz's findings, in which even greater variability was reported (Murphy and Kovach, 1972).

SUBTRACTING OUT MENTAL STAGES FROM PHYSIOLOGICAL TIME

Despite the general pessimism about the utility of the RT method in measuring simple mental reactions, the Dutch physiologist Donders (1868a) grasped the psychological significance of the procedure. His work marked the beginning of the use of RT measures to infer the timing of mental processes. Indeed, it helped usher into the late nineteenth century, under the leadership of psychology's founding father Wilhelm Wundt, what has been called the period of *mental chronometry* (Boring, 1950). Donders' thinking was influenced not only by Helmholtz' work, but also by the research of the Swiss astronomer Hirsch (1862) who conducted a series of studies between 1861 and 1864 aimed at measuring what he called 'physiological time' in the auditory, visual, and somatosensory modalities. His own times were respectively 149, 203, and 182 ms; a pattern that would prove to be remarkably consistent in future research. Donders and his doctoral student, De Jaager, reasoned that the physiological times of more complicated mental acts, such as discrimination and choice, could be determined by systematically adding these processes to the simple reactions studied by Helmholtz and Hirsch.

They performed a series of experiments to estimate human nerve conduction velocity, as did Helmholtz, and physiological time, as did Hirsch. Like Helmholtz, they found substantial variability among their subjects that precluded any firm estimate of conduction velocity. Like Hirsch, they were able to estimate physiological times in the three sensory modalities and, indeed, replicated his basic pattern of times. The uninterpretable variability Donders and De Jaager found in their estimates of human nerve conduction velocity did not dissuade them from pursuing their work. They assumed that only a small amount of the time taken by a mental action could be ascribed to nerve conduction velocity and that the durations of mental acts could be calculated by measuring increases in physiological times that were produced by the systematic introduction of more complex reactions (De Jaager, 1865; Donders, 1868a). They assumed further that the physiological time taken from the stimulus input to the response output was the sum of the times taken at each level of processing in the nervous system. Thus, they reasoned that by starting with the simple reaction of Helmholtz and Hirsch and progressively adding complexity to this reaction they could infer the durations of the inserted mental processes from the increases in the resultant physiological times. This experimental approach assumed, therefore, not only that processes were *additive*, but also that the addition of a new process to a reaction did not alter the durations of the other processes. The latter assumption, known as *pure insertion*, in combination with the assumption of additivity, led to their development of the *subtraction method* to infer the duration of mental processes.

Donders and De Jaager assumed the existence of a three-level hierarchy of mental reactions, identified by them as the a-, b-, and c-reactions. The *a-reaction* is a simple reaction that requires no stimulus discrimination or response selection decisions. Subjects were presented a random series of two different stimuli, each of which signaled a different response, and were informed which stimulus would be presented prior to each trial. By being given a forewarning, they did not have to discriminate the stimulus or select the response it signaled. Hence, subjects were required only to detect the onset of the stimulus and make the designated response to it. The *b-reaction* is a choice reaction that required both a stimulus discrimination and a response choice. In the task designed to engage this reaction, subjects were presented a random series of two stimuli, each of which signaled a specific response. However, unlike the a-task there was no forewarning of the impending stimulus. The *c-reaction* was elicited in a task in which the subject was presented with two or more stimuli and was required to make a fixed response to only one of them. Like the b-task, the subject was not informed of the stimulus prior to its occurrence. This task was assumed to require stimulus discrimination, but not response choice. The assumptions of additivity and pure insertion led Donders and De Jaager to assert that the difference in physiological times between the a- and c-reactions provided a measure of stimulus discrimination time and the difference in times between the b- and c-reactions gave an estimate of response selection time.

In their first study, Donders and De Jaager (De Jaager, 1865) attempted to measure the duration of well-defined mental events in a series of experiments in which a mild electrical shock was applied to the left or right foot of a subject whose task was to respond to this stimulation by pressing a key with the ipsilateral hand. There were two experimental conditions. In one, the subject knew which foot would be stimulated; in the other, he was uninformed. In Donders' terminology, the first condition produced an a-reaction, whereas the latter produced a b-reaction. The 'physiological time' was about 66 ms longer in the b-reaction. Donders and De Jaager concluded that this added time resulted from the insertion of stimulus discrimination and response choice into the a-reaction. This finding encouraged them to pursue other studies to estimate the durations of stimulus discrimination and response choice processes by subtracting a-reactions from c-reactions and c-reactions from b-reactions, respectively. The results of their studies indicated that the times needed to discriminate the stimulus and to select the response are about equal.

Criticisms and Empirical Tests of the Subtraction Method

The earliest criticisms focused on Donders' conceptualization of the mental processes subserving the various reactions. Wilhelm Wundt, founder of the first psychological laboratory at Leipzig University in 1879, was among the first to criticize it. He argued that the c-reaction did indeed include a response choice, to respond or not to respond (see Welford, 1980, for a recent variety of this criticism). But the near fatal criticism of the very foundation of Donders' theory and experimental method was made by Külpe (1895) and his coworkers Ach (1905) and Watt (1905). Rather than accepting the fundamental assumptions of Donders' model (additivity and pure insertion), and attempting to refine his conceptualization of the various types of reactions, Külpe and his associates evaluated these assumptions. Subjects in their studies gave introspective reports of their experiences as they performed the various tasks. These introspections revealed that the different reactions invoked very different experiences. For example, the a-reaction was reported to be associated with a higher state of motor preparedness than the b-reaction. On the basis of these and related findings, Külpe argued that changing a task generally implies changing the process. Thus the change from an a-reaction to a c-reaction does not simply involve adding stimulus discrimination to stimulus perception and response actualization; it means that the more complicated reaction process is substituted for the simple reaction process.

The original criticisms of the subtraction method derived largely from introspective reports. In recent years, however, strong empirical support has been provided for the assumptions underlying this method in two experimental tests. Taylor (1966) tested the assumption of additivity using two tasks he developed to assess the durations of stimulus discrimination and response choice. Performance on these tasks was compared with that on two traditional Donders' tasks. In both traditional tasks, his subjects were shown a red or a green light that was preceded by an auditory warning stimulus. In one, the b-reaction, each color indicated a different response. The colors were presented in a random, but equiprobable, sequence. According to Donders, the processes engaged in this reaction comprise three additive stages—stimulus discrimination, response choice, and response execution. In the other, the c-reaction, only one of the two lights signaled a response; no response was made to the other light. According to Donders, this reaction includes stimulus discrimination and response execution, but not response choice, processes. To these traditional tasks, Taylor added two new tasks, he called the b′- and c′-reactions. In the b′-reaction, the warning stimulus was followed at a fixed interval by either the onset or the absence of the onset of a colored light. Either occurred randomly, but equiprobably, in a block of trials. The subject was required to make one response to the onset of the light and another to its absence at the anticipated time. Taylor assumed that this reaction required response choice and response execution, but little or none of what is ordinarily meant by stimulus discrimination. In the c′-reaction, subjects again saw a random sequence of light flashes or their omission, but were required to respond only to the occurrence of the light. In Taylor's view, this reaction engages response execution processes, but not stimulus discrimination or response selection processes. Donders' assumptions of pure insertion and additivity led Taylor to predict that $(b - c') = (c - c') + (b' - c')$. Thus, the difference in latency of the traditional b-reaction (stimulus discrimination, response selection, response execution) and the newly devised c′-reaction (response execution) was assumed to equal the difference of the traditional c-reaction (stimulus discrimination, response execution) and the c′-reaction (response execution) plus the difference of the newly devised b′-reaction (response selection, response execution) and the c′-reaction (response execution). Although a bit noisy, Taylor's data did conform to the additivity hypothesis, not only for the means but also for the higher moments of the RT distributions.

The second test of the subtraction method was performed by Gottsdanker and Shragg (1985). They argued that Donders' notion of pure insertion implies that in the b-reaction the stimulus provides information that is essential both in discriminating the stimulus and in executing the appropriate response. That is, it makes distinct contributions to the reaction that are both informative and imperative. According to this view, the informative contribution made by the stimulus is to permit it to be discriminated from other stimuli and the response to it to be selected from among the response choices, whereas the imperative contribution is to activate execution of the selected response. Thus, the effect of the imperative contribution is delayed until a response has been selected. To test this hypothesis, they performed an experiment in which informative and imperative contributions made by the choice stimulus were dissociated temporally. This was achieved by presenting an informative visual stimulus as precue and then following it after very brief intervals by an auditory imperative stimulus. Following Donders, they assumed first that response execution does not begin until the stimulus has been discriminated and selection of the appropriate response has been completed. From this reasoning it follows that during the interval occupied by these two processes the imperative stimulus can trail the precue without affecting the overall response latency. Gottsdanker and Shragg assumed further that when stimulus discrimination and response selection have been completed, the remaining portion of the choice reaction is identical to the simple reaction. Thus, they claimed that if, over very brief precue-to-stimulus intervals the latency between the precue and the response is invariant, and if, for somewhat longer intervals, the latency of the response to the imperative stimulus is equal to simple RT, the assumptions of the subtraction method are supported.

Their subjects were required to perform two tasks; a warned simple RT task and a precued choice RT task in which the interval between the precue and the imperative stimulus varied from 0 to 150 ms in steps of 30 ms. The pattern of results was in perfect agreement with the assumption that inserted operations (in this case stimulus discrimination and response selection) do not overlap in time with the execution of the response. Simple RT varied between 148 and 154 ms as a function of the interval between the warning and imperative stimuli. The latencies of the responses to the imperative stimulus in the choice RT task were 235, 204, 174, 159, 155, and 153 ms for the 0 to 150 ms precue intervals, respectively. Thus, there is a precise ordering of these times that is consistent with the expectations of the additivity assumption when the precue interval is added to the choice RT: 235 ms for the 0 ms interval, 204 ms for the 30 ms interval, 174 ms for the 60 ms interval, and for the longer intervals RTs that are comparable to those obtained in the simple reaction. This latter finding supports the assumption that the simple reaction is identical to the choice reaction after the stimulus discrimination and response selection stages have been deleted. These findings, then, lend very strong empirical support to the assumptions that led Donders to develop the subtraction method. The finding that response execution does not begin before response selection has been completed is of particular interest to the present discussion of serial stage versus continuous flow models of information processing (e.g., Miller, 1988; Stoffels, van der Molen, and Keuss, 1990).

THE DISCOVERY OF PROCESSING STAGES USING THE ADDITIVE FACTORS METHOD

Külpe's attack on Donders' 'pure insertion' assumption struck a near-fatal blow to the subtraction method in particular and to RT methods in general. During the first few decades of this century, the RT method was not used to measure the duration of mental processes. Indeed, it was not even discussed in the most influential experimental psychology textbooks of the 1950s (Osgood,

1953; Stevens, 1951; Woodworth and Schlossberg, 1954). Quite surprisingly, in a recently edited volume commemorating the first 100 years of scientific psychology, dating to the founding of Wundt's laboratory, there is not a single reference to the RT method in the subject index (Koch and Leary, 1985).

In contrast to the first 70 years of this century, the last 20 years have seen a dramatic renaissance in the RT method. Much of the credit for this rebirth can be attributed to Saul Sternberg. In the centennial tribute to Donders in 1969, he articulated his model of human information processing and described the experimental method he developed to test it, the additive factors method (AFM). It is not unreasonable to assert that Sternberg's ideas have been as important as any in modern cognitive psychology. We now turn to a discussion of his work.

Like Donders, Sternberg (1969) assumed that human information processing, from stimulus input to response output, was achieved via a series of non-overlapping stages whose durations were stochastically independent. Unlike Donders, however, he did not assume that experimental tasks could be devised that would insert or delete stages of processing. Rather, Sternberg assumed that the existence of a stage could be inferred and the amount of information processed by it could be manipulated by judicious selection of experimental factors. That is, he assumed that factors could be identified that have a *selective influence* on information processing. Further, he assumed that the pattern of statistical effects produced by these manipulations supported specific conclusions about the stage or stages of processing being influenced. Inferences could thus be drawn about the structure of mental processing, but not about its timing.

Sternberg illustrated the basic idea underlying his new method with the following example. Suppose that the RT interval consists of three stages, *a*, *b*, and *c*. Suppose further that the duration of stage *a* is influenced only by factor F, of stage *b* by factor G, and of stages *b* and *c*, but not *a*, by factor H. From Sternberg's assumptions that stages are temporally discrete and stochastically independent, it follows that (i) experimental factors that influence the durations of different stages will produce additive effects on RT; and (ii) experimental factors that influence the same stage will produce interactive effects on RT. Thus, in this example, factors F and G will have additive effects on RT (i.e. the effects of F will not vary as a function of the level of G or vice versa), but factors G and H will have interactive effects on RT.

Rather than postulating the existence of stages of processing *a priori*, as did Donders, Sternberg inferred processing stages from the pattern of statistical effects produced by the experimental factors he manipulated. He used the following criteria to define a stage. First, a stage has single-channel capacity in that it can process no more than one signal at a time (Welford, 1960). Second, the durations of stages are stochastically independent. Although not required to meet the assumption of additivity, stochastic independence implies not only additivity of factor effects on variance, but also on all higher cumulants of the RT distribution. Third, and most importantly, the output of a stage is hypothesized to be independent of factors that influence its duration. Experimental manipulations must influence only processing duration, not processing quality. If processing quality is changed, it is not possible to draw consistent inferences about the structure of the reaction process from the pattern of experimental effects on RT.

Sternberg pointed out that additivity and independence may not co-occur; that is, there may be additivity without stochastic independence. Thus, the assumptions of additivity and independence should be tested separately. Of course, the strongest version of Sternberg's model incorporates both assumptions because independence implies additivity of variances as well as other higher cumulants of the RT distribution. Hence, consistent experimental demonstrations of stochastic independence in the durations of stages would offer strong support for the hypothesized serial model, whereas repeated failures would cast doubt on both the hypothesis and on the AFM.

Thus, the AFM would seem to provide a powerful tool for inferring mental processes from total RT. This method has several limitations, however, that Sternberg enumerated. First, the AFM cannot determine the absolute duration of a stage. It can be used to delineate a set of stages, but not to specify their timing within the RT interval. Second, this method can only distinguish stages, it cannot distinguish processes within a stage. An interaction may therefore allow one to reject separate stages, but not separate processes. Within a stage, two distinct processes, separately affected by two experimental factors, might occur in parallel and produce the interaction. Third, violations of the assumptions underlying the AFM may easily lead to erroneous conclusions. When stage durations are not additive and independent, an interaction between two factors can be mistakenly interpreted as reflecting a common influence on a single stage. This could occur, for example, when two stages have a capacity-sharing relationship. Indeed, Sternberg suggested that information processing views that assume allocation of limited processing capacity are antithetical to the basic tenets of his model. Similarly, an observed interaction between two experimental factors can lead to the erroneous conclusion that a single stage has been affected when the single-channel assumption is violated. For example, if the processing of one stage cannot begin until the processing of two independent, but simultaneously operating, stages is completed, then two experimental factors that influence these two stages may produce an underadditive effect on RT. Sternberg cautioned that under these circumstances blind adherence to the additive factors logic could very easily lead to the incorrect conclusion that one stage was being influenced. Fourth, he recommended against drawing inferences about the stage structure of a mental process on the basis of only one experiment. If a new factor is found to have additive effects with other factors in a series of experiments, then it is justified to hypothesize that another stage may exist. Likewise, if a factor is found to have interactive effects with other factors over a number of experiments, then one can legitimately develop an hypothesis that redefines or further articulates the stage's functions. Thus, additivity is used to decompose stage structure and interaction to infer the functions subserved by a stage. Lastly, considerations other than additivity must be used to determine the proper sequencing of stages.

Application of the Additive Factors Method to Memory Scanning

Sternberg first used the AFM in a series of experiments with a memory scanning task that is perhaps best associated with his work. In the memory scanning task, the subject had to determine on each trial whether or not a stimulus was a member of a previously presented list. The list, or memory set, consisted of the digits 0 through 9 and varied in length from 1 to 6 digits. The memory set items were presented in sequence to the subject. Shortly after the offset of the last digit a single digit, or test item, was presented and the subject was required to make a button press indicating whether or not it was in the memory set. Stimulus quality (normal, degraded), memory set size (one to six items), response type (positive, negative), and frequency of response type (0.25, 0.50, 0.75) were varied. These factors were found to have additive effects on RT, with no significant interactions. Stimulus quality and response frequency were examined in separate experiments so their relation was not examined directly. Sternberg also found that the effect of memory set size on mean RT was linear (i.e. the addition of one item to the memory set produced the same increment in RT regardless of the set size). Thus, the effect of memory set size on mean RT can be described by the linear regression function $\mathrm{RT} = a + bM$, where a refers to the Y-intercept, b to the slope of the regression line, and M to the number of items in the memory set. We should note here that dozens of studies of memory scanning have reported this same pattern of results.

From this data pattern, Sternberg inferred the following stage structure. The initial processing of the test stimulus occurs at the *stimulus encoding* stage, the duration of which is influenced by the quality of the stimulus. The output of this stage is passed to a *serial comparison* stage where the test stimulus is compared with the items in the memory set. The comparison process was postulated to be accomplished one item at a time, in the order in which the memory set items were presented. Thus, the duration of this stage is determined by the number of items that must be compared with the test item. Sternberg speculated that the memory set was scanned in its entirety, irrespective of the location of the (positive) test item in the list (in his words, the scan was exhaustive). The outcome of this comparison process is passed to the *binary decision* stage where the 'yes' or 'no' response choice is made. The duration of this stage is influenced by the type of choice made; negative responses take longer than positive responses. Once the positive or negative decision is made, it is passed to the *response translation and organization* stage where the response is selected for execution. The duration of this stage varies with the relative frequency of the response type (i.e. of positive or negative responses). Where serial comparison processes were inferred from the slope of the RT versus memory set regression line, effects on the other stages were inferred from changes in the intercept of this line.

Sternberg's ideas have been almost singlehandedly responsible for catalyzing a substantial research effort in cognitive psychology, that is thriving today, whose aim is to articulate mental chronometric processes. A number of refinements to his stage model have been proposed, as have alternatives to it. Among the most elaborate versions of Sternberg's four-stage model is that developed by Briggs and colleagues (Briggs and Blaha, 1969; Briggs and Swanson, 1969, 1970; Swanson and Briggs, 1969) in the late 1960s and early 1970s (see review in Mudd, 1983). The starting point for Briggs' work on stage decomposition was Sternberg's model of memory scanning. A distinctive feature of Briggs' work is the focus on interactions between task variables to specify the nature of the processes involved in the various stages that have been established by the additive factors pattern. We will not review this work. The interested reader is referred to the original papers and to Mudd's review.

Another interesting elaboration of the memory scanning process has been developed recently in research by Lewine (1989) in which the performance of humans was compared with that of non-human primates (macaques) on a variant of the Sternberg task. Seven humans and six macaques completed a version of the task that required them to indicate whether or not a probe stimulus belonged to a memory set that varied from one to seven items in length. The pattern of results Lewine obtained for the humans replicated the pattern seen generally on this task: RT increased monotonically with increases in memory set size and the increase in RT associated with each additional memory set item was about 24 ms. A similar pattern was observed for the macaques, with one important exception. They were able to respond as accurately as humans, but each additional memory set item only added about 7 ms to the overall RT. To explain this difference between the two species, Lewine analyzed the statistical properties of the individual RT distributions for each subject in each group. This analysis of the RT distributions led him to propose a memory search that consists of two sequential substages, one associated with a trace-evaluation mechanism and the other similar to the serial-exhaustive search element of Sternberg's model.

Lewine speculated that when the probe item is presented the critical task at the first substage is not to determine its identity, but rather to determine if the trace strength of the memory engram is sufficiently greater than some criterion to warrant a judgment that the engram had previously been activated when the memory set items were presented. Immediately following completion of this substage, macaques apparently make a response decision, whereas humans engage in an exhaustive serial search before making a response decision. Given that the trace-strength evaluation process appears to be sufficient for adequate performance, it must be explained why humans delay their response. Lewine hypothesized that even though activation of the search mechanism does not benefit performance on the memory scanning task, it either serves to check the outcome of processing at the previous substage or it allows humans to access associative, contextual information that may or may not be necessary for performance of the task. Lewine's work is of interest from at least two perspectives. First, it suggests, as does the work of Briggs, that the memory scanning process is more complicated than originally proposed by Sternberg. And, second, it suggests that studies of differences in the cognitive functions of human and non-human primates may shed light on the temporal dynamics of information processing in both groups.

Application of the Additive Factors Method to Choice Reactions

Sternberg's model and method were developed to provide a general model of mental reactions and a general method by which the model could be tested. Accordingly, as we noted above, in Sternberg's tribute to Donders he also described the application of his experimental method to test the stage model in a standard two-choice RT task. In this task the subject was required to make a verbal response to a visually presented numeral. Three factors were manipulated, each at two levels. Stimulus quality was varied by presenting the numeral intact or degraded; S–R compatibility was varied by requiring the subject to respond either by naming the numeral or by saying the name of the numeral that was one value larger; and the number of equally likely stimulus–response alternatives was varied by having the subject respond to a numeral selected from a set of either two or eight numerals. The effects of stimulus quality and S–R compatibility were perfectly additive, but both of these factors interacted with the third factor, number of alternatives. When the numerals were intact and easily discriminable, the time taken to name the numeral (i.e. make a compatible response) was increased a negligible amount by an increase in the number of alternatives. When the numerals were degraded, a slight increase in vocal naming time was produced by increasing the number of alternatives. However, when the subject had to make the less compatible response (name the numeral plus one), there was a substantial increase in RT to the intact stimulus that was even greater when the stimuli were degraded. It should be pointed out that the interaction between stimulus quality and number of alternatives was weak, whereas that between S–R compatibility and number of alternatives was strong (respectively, 35% and 141% greater than the simple main effects). Sternberg interpreted this pattern of results as follows. The additive effects of stimulus quality and S–R compatibility imply that the task is mediated by at least two distinct stages, stimulus encoding and response translation and organization. The interaction of both these factors with the number of alternatives factor suggests that this latter factor influences both stages of processing. However, the weakness of the interaction with stimulus quality, mediated presumably at the stimulus encoding stage, suggests further that encoding processes are less affected than are response choice processes by varying the number of stimulus–response alternatives. Sternberg cautioned that his interpretations were quite tentative and that no firm conclusions could be drawn on the basis of this one experiment.

In fact, recent work suggests that more stages of processing exist in choice reactions than was suggested by this early work. Evidence has been presented for the existence of at least six processing stages: three perceptual stages, a response selection stage, and two motor stages (see Figure 1.1; Frowein, 1981; Sanders, 1990). A number of studies have shown that stimulus quality has additive effects with other variables that are likely to affect the perceptual side of the reaction process, such as stimulus intensity (e.g. Sanders, 1980) and stimulus discriminability (e.g. Schwartz, Pomerantz and Egeth, 1977). From these findings, a stimulus preprocessing stage has been hypothesized in which sensory input undergoes a 'perceptual clean-up' in preparation for subsequent processing. Stimulus intensity has been assumed to affect the duration of this stage. Once this preprocessing is completed, the output is then fed into a second stage where feature analysis occurs. The duration of this stage is thought to be affected by stimulus quality. Output from this feature analysis stage is passed to a third stage in which the analysis of the entire stimulus takes place. The duration of this stage is determined by the ease with which the different stimuli can be discriminated into the various relevant classes.

The response end of processing may include at least three distinct stages:

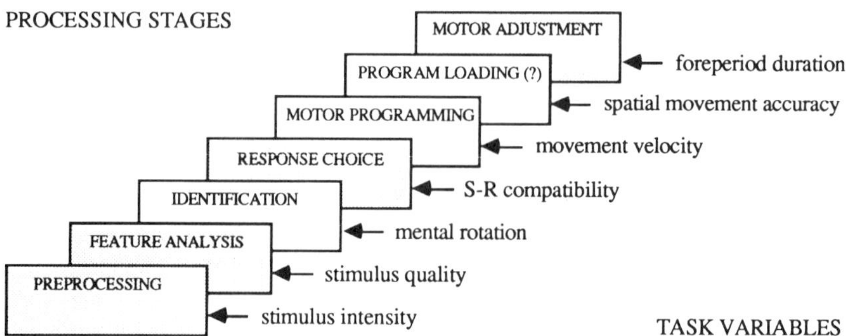

Figure 1.1. Processing stages established by the additive factors method and task variables that are typically used to influence these stages (after Sanders, 1990). The shaded boxes refer to stages that are well established, whereas the unshaded boxes refer to stages for which there is only preliminary evidence.

response selection, motor programming, and motor adjustment. Support for the existence of a response selection stage that is distinct from the perceptual stages comes from the persistent observations of non-zero, but statistically non-significant, interactions between the effects of S–R compatibility and stimulus quality (e.g. Blackman, 1975). Support for the existence of motor stages that are distinct from not only the perceptual stages, but also from the response selection stage comes from numerous studies in which additive effects have been observed between stimulus quality, S–R compatibility, and time uncertainty—usually manipulated by varying the interval between a warning stimulus and the stimulus that calls for a response (Stoffels, van der Molen and Keuss, 1985). In addition, time uncertainty and movement velocity have been reported not to interact. Spijkers and Walters (1985), for example, reported additive effects of S–R compatibility, time uncertainty, and movement velocity. These authors assumed that after the selection of a response, specific motor features of the response are elaborated during a stage that they labeled as 'motor programming'. This stage is then distinguished from a stage they denoted as 'motor adjustment' that is influenced by a general process of response readiness. Further support for the existence of a separate programming stage is found in the reported interaction of movement velocity and movement direction, and additivity of movement direction and time uncertainty (Spijkers and Steyvers, 1984). It is assumed that during the motor adjustment stage, the readiness to respond approaches the motor action limit and once this limit is exceeded a response is produced automatically (cf. Näätänen and Merisalo, 1977).

Challenges to the Additive Factors Method

Our selective review of applications of the AFM in studies of memory scanning and choice reactions following Sternberg's classic research has revealed that processing is more finely articulated than he hypothesized. We do not want this brief review to create the impression, however, that by using the AFM it is possible to relate any pattern of factor effects to a corresponding set of stages. There are numerous challenges to this straightforward linkage, starting with that of Sternberg himself in his 1969 paper. Using the logic of additive factors, it would be difficult, for example, to interpret the absence of a lower order interaction between two or more factors in the presence of a higher order interaction between these factors and one or more other factors. The former suggests separate stages of processing, whereas the latter suggests a common stage. Sternberg (1969) has argued that in order to retain a stage model for such a data pattern it would have to be assumed that two or more factors influencing the same stage do not interact. Of course, the implausibility of this situation is one of the cornerstones of the AFM.

The opposite pattern, an interaction between factors assumed to affect different stages, is also considered to be inconsistent with additive factors logic. The logic of the AFM does not permit a typical input variable, like stimulus intensity, and a typical output variable, like foreperiod duration, to interact. Strong signals, however, seem to counteract the detrimental effect of long foreperiods. The effect appears to be modality-specific. It is evident in the auditory and somatosensory modalities, but not in the visual modality, at least for stimuli within the usual intensity limits. Sanders (1977, 1980) assumed that stimulus intensity might influence motor adjustment as well as stimulus preprocessing. He speculated that changes in stimulus intensity may serve to modulate motor adjustment through a process he called 'immediate arousal'. According to this view, increases in immediate arousal produced by strong signals serve to directly facilitate motor activation such that the motor action limit (i.e. response threshold) is achieved sooner than when weak signals are presented. The result is faster responses. Support for this hypothesis can be found in studies by van der Molen and Keuss (1979, 1981) and Keuss and van der Molen (1982).

If there is indeed this type of immediate arousal produced by strong stimulation, then the assumption made by Sternberg that stages are sequenced in a single dimension is violated. The intensive and informative aspects of the stimulus are processed along separate routes. A similar violation may occur when the stimulus contains task-irrelevant location information besides the task-relevant information signaling the response (Stoffels, van der Molen and Keuss, 1985, in press). It is a well-established finding that RT to the informative aspect of the stimulus is considerably prolonged when the response direction does not correspond to the location of the stimulus (see review in Simon, 1990). This finding has been interpreted to suggest that the location of the stimulus source elicits a natural tendency to respond in that direction; and this tendency must be suppressed when the direction of the correct response and the location of the stimulus do not correspond. The effect of this suppression is to prolong response latency. This phenomenon has been explained by postulating a model in which the location and informative aspects of the stimulus are processed in parallel up to the response decision stage, at which point they interfere with each other in selecting a response.

Another example of an unwanted interaction is provided by Stanovich and Pachella (1977). They obtained a significant underadditive interaction between the effects of stimulus quality and S–R compatibility. In their study, the effect of reducing the contrast of a visual stimulus was less when it called for an incompatible than when it called for a compatible response. Stanovich and Pachella suggested that when the contrast is reduced between the stimulus and its background, information about the stimulus is passed to the response selection stage before processing is completed in the perceptual stage. If so, the response selection stage would be enabled earlier to dim than to bright stimuli and this gain would be reflected in the underadditive interaction.

Basically, this interpretation suggests that underadditive interactions might be disguised additive effects resulting from the temporal overlap of processing at two or more stages. Sanders (1980) has questioned the notion of stage overlap and raised the possibility that in the Stanovich and Pachella (1977) experiments contrast reductions may have been near threshold. In dim conditions, therefore, the response selection stage may have received distorted outputs. He reasoned that production of a compatible response would suffer in particular from such distortions because the 'natural' stimulus–response relationship is altered (p. 340). Sanders' interpretation preserves the additive factors logic, whereas Stanovich and Pachella's rejects the method's assumption of non-overlapping stages.

A more telling problem concerns the speed/accuracy tradeoff. In presenting the AFM, Sternberg focused entirely on RT and ignored errors. Indeed, his tasks were designed to be sufficiently easy for subjects to perform at near perfect accuracy (about 1–2% errors). The usual reasoning is that subjects would probably never make errors if they were not making a timed response. But errors do occur occasionally, particularly when the memory set is four or five items. These errors probably result from subjects responding prematurely. The common procedure is to discard error trials from the analysis or to demonstrate that the proportion of errors does not vary with experimental condition. If error rates were found to correlate with experimental condition, it would be quite difficult to infer the underlying cognitive structure from response latencies alone. Moreover, the function relating speed to accuracy is negatively accelerating, therefore small differences in error may be associated with large differences in RT (Wickelgren, 1977). This is particularly true for the error rates typically obtained in additive factors designs (about 5–10%). For some investigators this has been the principal reason for discrediting the AFM (e.g. Wickelgren, 1977). In their view, the only acceptable approach is to examine both response time and accuracy.

The problem of variable error rates can be prevented from happening by standardizing procedures and using well-trained subjects (Sanders, 1980). Another way to deal with this variability is to correct for it by analyzing RTs as predicted by a regression analysis for some constant level of error rate. Yet another possibility is to treat RTs and errors as bivariate dependent variables and submit them to a multivariate analysis of variance (Pachella, 1974). A more drastic approach is to focus on the speed/accuracy tradeoff itself by having subjects respond at different speed levels. This means adding another variable to the multifactor, multilevel design of the AFM, and necessitates the collection of about five times as much data as in the standard RT design. It is not surprising, therefore, that speed/accuracy manipulations have not been applied routinely in additive factors studies. Moreover, as Luce (1986) pointed out, it should be established first that the speed/accuracy model is compatible with the additive factors model. Other models assume that subjects accumulate information about the stimulus over time and that they respond, complying with time pressure, on the basis of what information is available at that moment. The constant stage output assumption of Sternberg's model does not permit a premature cutoff of perceptual analysis before a response can be selected and executed, as is implied in the speed/accuracy tradeoff. Hence, the assumption of a constant stage output is incompatible with the notion of a speed/accuracy tradeoff.

A more fundamental criticism of Sternberg's model and experimental method is reminiscent of the challenge made by Külpe against Donders' ideas. Pachella (1974) argued that the manipulation of factor levels may cause a fundamental change in the processing sequence (as did Külpe in challenging Donders' idea of pure insertion). Indeed, the difference between manipulating the number of overt responses (c- vs b-reaction), as did Donders, and varying a factor such as stimulus quality, as did Sternberg, seems to be quite subtle. Sternberg's assumption that manipulations of stimulus quality selectively influence the processing of only one stage may be prey to the same criticism that Külpe raised of Donders' notion of pure insertion; namely, the nature of the task changes when stimulus quality is changed as it does when a new response requirement is instituted. Pachella went so far as to suggest that, in a certain sense, construction of a comparison task in the subtraction method could be considered as a limiting case of a factor manipulation (p. 54). This criticism has usually been countered by pointing to the assumptions underlying the AFM. Factor levels are not allowed to change the quality of stage output, only stage duration. The problem is that on the basis of the pattern of factor effects it is difficult to assess whether the assumption of constant stage output has been violated. The appropriate research strategy would be to conduct multilevel rather than two-level experiments, and examine whether the pattern of factor effects changes across the level range of the factor of interest.

If one allows the possibility that a change in factor level induces a change in strategy, which in turn produces a correlation in stage durations, stages may remain additive but no longer stochastically independent. This possibility led Taylor (1976) to propose an alternative method for decomposing the RT process which allows for interdependence and temporal overlap among stages. His method is a modification of the AFM in that it relies on conducting multifactorial experiments to reveal patterns of factor effects that are used to infer stages. Unlike Sternberg's method, however, Taylor's relies on interaction rather than additivity as the informative outcome. Following Taylor, a significant interaction between one or more factors implies that these factors influenced one or more stages in common. However, a failure to obtain such an interaction does not imply that these factors affected separate stages; factors might influence the same stage but in an additive way. Moreover, the effects of an interaction may be masked by overlapping or dependent stages. Thus, factor effects become virtually uninterpretable.

The strategy proposed by Taylor to handle this problem consists of conducting multifactorial experiments which combine factors that are expected to influence common stages. The patterns of interactions that emerge from a series of such experiments should provide a picture of how many stages are involved in the reaction process and which factors influence which stages. It is important to bear in mind that this strategy implies an *a priori* model of the RT process and how factors should be assigned to stages. The assignment of factors to stages can then be used for the interpretation of factor interactions. However, if the initial mappings are incorrect, then further assignments based on interactions of factor effects will also be wrong (Taylor, 1976; p. 182).

INTERIM CONCLUSIONS ON DISCRETE STAGES AND REACTION TIME METHODS

At this point it can be concluded that Donders' subtraction method might be conceptualized as a limiting case of Sternberg's AFM (cf. Pachella, 1974). The advantage of the AFM is that it is not limited to the special case where experimental manipulations add or delete entire stages. This advantage is gained at high cost. It is no longer possible to obtain estimates of stage durations. Similarly, Sternberg's AFM might be conceived of as a limiting case of Taylor's interactive factor method. In contrast to Sternberg's method, the interactive factor method does not require the assumption that stages are additive or stochastically independent. Stage durations may overlap or have compensatory relationships with each other. Again, a high price is paid for relaxing assumptions. Sternberg proposed his method for the 'discovery' of stages. In contrast, Taylor's method requires a working model of the RT process, on the basis of which factors are assigned to *a priori* stages. Obviously, the dilemma is between strict assumptions allowing strong predictions, but a limited scope of applicability, and relaxed assumptions with a wider scope. The problem here is not so much as to determine which model is 'true' but to define the limiting conditions for the model's application. Advocates of the AFM (e.g. Sanders, in press) claim that stage robustness can be used as a built-in criterion for deciding whether the method has been applied properly. The stages inferred from the mutual relations between factors should not change easily when an additional factor is added to the design. If this would occur, the model can be rejected. In that case, the models we discuss in the following sections may prove to be viable alternatives. These models do not require constant stage output or non-overlapping stage durations, and some of the models even discard the notion of processing stages altogether.

TEMPORAL OVERLAP BETWEEN PROCESSING STAGES

One of the elegant features of Sternberg's work is that the theoretical component, stages of processing, is connected directly to a methodological and a statistical component, additive factors and statistical patterns of factor effects. As we have seen, this is both a strength and a weakness of his work. Violations of the assumed linkage between factor effects and stages of processing can be difficult to reconcile, as was the case, for example, in the Stanovich and Pachella (1977) study. In 1975, Meyer, Schvaneveldt and Ruddy published an additive factors study of the effects of priming on the speed of lexical decision-making that provides another example of this difficulty. Subjects were presented letter strings and had to decide whether they were words or non-words. These letter strings were either degraded or intact, and were preceded by a prime that was either related or unrelated to it. The results of interest were obtained when words were presented. Both the quality of the stimulus and the type of prime preceding the target word affected RT and their effects interacted. The logic of the AFM led these authors to conclude, therefore, that stimulus quality and lexical context must influence a common processing stage. To McClelland (1978), however, 'This conclusion just never seemed right. ... Degrading ought to affect some relatively early level, such as feature extraction, and priming ought to affect a later level, such as activation of a representation in memory corresponding to the word' (pp. 5–6).

From results like these, the seeds were sown for McClelland's theoretical work on an alternative to the Sternberg's model, the 'cascade model'. In contrast to the stage model, the cascade model hypothesizes the simultaneous activation of several levels of processing. The assumption that mental operations follow one another in strictly temporal, non-overlapping succession, however, has been challenged by several investigators in addition to McClelland (e.g. Eriksen and Schultz, 1979; Miller, 1982, 1983), and the result of these challenges is the formulation of a number of alternatives to a strictly discrete serial stage model that can be conceptualized as falling on different points along a discrete–continuous continuum. In the next three sections we shall describe two representatives from these alternatives. First, we describe parallel models, as embodied in the work of McClelland (1979) and C.W. Eriksen (Eriksen, B.A. and Eriksen, C.W., 1974; Eriksen, C.W. and Schultz, 1979). McClelland's work was selected because it represents an important attempt to provide a general model of information processing as an alternative to Sternberg's model, and C.W. Eriksen's work was selected not only because it also attempts to provide an alternative to the discrete serial stage model, but also because his model has been investigated in a number of psychophysiological studies. After this discussion, we then discuss a model formulated by Miller (1982, 1983) that combines features of both serial discrete and continuous models.

Reaction Processes in Cascade

At the time McClelland (1979) presented his cascade model, a number of theorists had questioned Sternberg's model and some extant models postulated parallel mechanisms in certain perceptual and cognitive processes (see discussion in McClelland's paper). Yet, as McClelland noted, there was no general model for representing these processes. His model was an attempt to 'bridge this gap'. He hypothesized that all the stages of an information processing system make their output continuously available to subsequent stages of the system until the information flow enters the response execution stage. Specifically, his model attempts to characterize the properties of systems that (i) consist of several processing levels, each of which is continuously active and working to optimize its output to the next level; (ii) pass the output from one level to another in one direction only, with no skipping or bypassing of processing levels, in the form of continuous quantities that are always available for processing at the next level; (iii) identify the response as the output of a final continuously active process, response activation, where the response choice is selected from among the alternatives; and (iv) pass this output to the response execution level, the only discrete stage in the model, at which point the response is executed and the duration of this single stage is added to the processing sequence.

Thus, McClelland retained the basic idea of a system in which information processing is accomplished via the unidirectional activation of processors at different stages. In contrast to the discrete stage model, and with the exception of the response execution stage, component processes in the cascade model are not conceived of in terms of finite durations. Rather, the parameters of significance are the relative asymptotic activation of processing units and the rate at which this activation occurs. McClelland assumed that each component process consists of a number of processing units, each of which is a linear integrator that accumulates information (i.e. is activated) at a particular rate and to a certain asymptotic level. Thus, the input to each unit that drives it to its asymptotic level of activation is simply a weighted sum of a subset of the outputs of units at the preceding level. He assumed further that the rate and asymptote were independent, and that all of the processing units at the same level had the same activation function for every possible stimulus. Only the asymptotic level of activation is assumed to vary across processing units and stimuli. The slope (i.e. rate) of the activation function is also assumed to be determined by the relatively slow or rate-limiting processes of the system, whereas the point at which the function begins to rise is determined by the relatively fast processes. A central assumption of the cascade model is that the rate of activation of a unit at a particular processing level depends on the difference between the amount of activation the unit has already attained and the value to which it is being driven by its inputs. When the discrepancy is large the change will be rapid, when it is small the change will be slow. Thus, the rate at which the activation function achieves its asymptote for a processing unit refers to the dynamics of that component process. The activation function of processes in cascade usually begins with a slow rise that is followed by an exponential approach to asymptote. It is important to note that the shape of the activation function of a unit tells nothing about the temporal arrangement of processes in the system or about the number of processes in the system.

McClelland provided support for his model in the form of simulation studies and re-analyses of a number of additive factors studies. In these re-analyses he enumerated sets of specific predictions and determined the extent to which they were supported in the data. McClelland noted the similarity of the activation function and the shape of the function typically obtained in speed/accuracy tradeoff experiments. Those functions show accuracy to stay at a chance level for the initial portion of the curve and then to increase rapidly over a short time period before leveling off in the final portion of the curve. He then re-interpreted speed/accuracy findings in terms of the cascade model; that is, in terms of the asymptotic and dynamic parameters of the activation function. To do so, he examined the results of an experiment by Reed (1976) in which speed/accuracy functions were analyzed in a Sternberg memory scanning task. As in the standard Sternberg task, letters served as the stimuli and the primary manipulation was memory set size. McClelland hypothesized that the set size effect might consist of a lowering of memory inputs to the comparator units which compute the product of their inputs from the memory set and the test stimulus. The more closely the correspondence between the inputs from the memory set and the test stimulus to a comparator unit, the larger the asymptotic output of the comparator. Lower correspondence results in lower comparator outputs and, consequently, in lower asymptotic outputs of the response units. Alternatively, an increase in set size might result in a slowing of the rate of the comparison process. McClelland's analysis indicated that set size might have both effects; a small asymptotic effect and a rate effect. He also provided examples, however, of experimental manipulations which affect the dynamics of the system, but not the asymptote and vice versa.

Before applying the cascade model to results obtained in standard RT experiments, McClelland made two additional assumptions. In contrast to speed/accuracy experiments, subjects in standard RT experiments have no external reference (e.g. a deadline or response signal) for determining the instant in time when a response has to be emitted. Subjects are typically instructed to respond as quickly and as accurately as possible. A serial stage model permits the response to be executed only after the output of the response selection stage becomes available. Prior to that, the subject must guess. Thus, there should be a discrete step from guessing to near perfect accuracy. In contrast, however, because response units are being continuously activated as information accumulates about the stimulus, the potential for making an accurate response grows concurrently. In this context, McClelland proposed that subjects adopt a fixed response criterion and he assumed that they make very few errors. These additional assumptions were used to examine Donders' (1868a; 1969) subtraction method for a system of processes in cascade. As we discussed earlier, Donders assumed that the insertion of one processing component does not alter the duration of other stages and, consequently, increases RT by a fixed amount. It turns out that insertion of a processing component into a system of processes in cascade can also produce an invariant effect on RT if, and only if, the inserted process does not alter the asymptotic activation level of the response units and is not a rate-limiting process. When these conditions hold, the activation function is simply shifted to the right so that it takes longer to reach the response criterion. Otherwise, the effect of the inserted process may vary with the other parameters of the activation function or the setting of the response criterion relative to the asymptote. McClelland did a similar analysis of the AFM for interpreting factor effects on RT. Recall, the logic of this method necessitates concluding that factors that have additive effects on RT affect different stages of processing and those that have interactive effects affect at least one stage in common. First, McClelland assessed the validity of additivity and the range of variation over which it applies. His assessment led him to conclude that it is an extremely valid conception of processing, even for systems in cascade, as long as the experimental factors affect only the rate parameter. However, its validity diminishes when the experimental factors include those that affect the rate and those that affect the asymptote parameters. For example, when a factor affecting the relative asymptotic output levels is combined with a factor influencing the rate of a relatively fast processing stage, an additive pattern will result. However, when the same factor is combined with a factor influencing a relatively slow or rate-limiting processing stage the outcome will be an overadditive interaction. A similar result will be obtained when both factors influence the asymptote. Thus, as soon as experimental manipulations affect the asymptote, serial stage and cascade models diverge. McClelland's analysis suggests that the critical difference between serial stage and cascade models lies in the idea that the output of a processing stage is either a discrete code, as Sternberg and Sanders assume, or a continuous quantity, as McClelland proposes. As we have seen, Sternberg is quite clear on this point: when an experimental factor affects both the duration and the output of a stage, the additive factors logic no longer applies.

The predictions McClelland derived from the cascade model must be qualified in light of a point first made by Ashby (1982). He observed that for the parameter values typically used in McClelland's simulation studies there is a 4% probability that a response never occurs. He then conditioned the cascade model on the event that a response does occur eventually and calculated the means and variances of the model's RTs over a wide range of parameter values. He found that when an additional stage is inserted in the system, mean RT additivity is obtained for virtually all values of the rate parameter. Thus, subject to the condition that a response will be emitted, the model predicts that additivity does not simply depend on the relative rate of the inserted stage and the rate of the slowest stage of the system, as suggested by McClelland's rule of thumb for the interpretation of results obtained using Donders' subtraction method.

Ashby made a second observation that pertains to the validity of inferences derived from the additive factor logic when the processing system is in cascade. He confirmed McClelland's claim that additivity is virtually exact as long as experimental manipulations have a selective affect on the rates of stages. But he pointed out that the large standard deviations produced by the model will make it extremely difficult to detect non-additivity. For typical values used in McClelland's simulation studies, a true deviation from additivity would require about 2000 trials for each experimental condition. Hence, the most important drawback of the cascade model is its unrealistically large standard deviations. As Ashby indicated, the surprisingly large standard deviations by the model increase too slowly with the mean to account for the findings obtained in the empirical literature. He pointed out that this failure is due to the *post hoc* way in which variability is introduced into the cascade model. In the model, activation basically grows in a deterministic fashion; it has no inherent variability. Ashby suggested that one way to deal with this problem might be to let the cascade rates vary from trial to trial so that inserting a stage would increase variability because it adds another source of variation to the system (cf. Ashby, 1982; p. 603).

A version of the cascade model with more stochastic elements has been proposed recently by Molenaar and van der Molen (1986). Ashby had indicated that the price paid for a truly stochastic version of the cascade model is greatly increased analytical complexity. In fact, he suggested that derivation of the exact RT distribution for such a model might prove to be intractable, although computer simulation might provide some insight into the behavior of the model. This is exactly what Molenaar and van der Molen did. They considered a system of processing stages as a special instance of Grossberg's (1982) functional–differential network. In this neural network, the activity of each of the stages of processing is represented by a differential equation (see the next subsection for a more detailed exposition of this approach). An important property of the neural network is that its rate parameters vary randomly from trial to trial, whereas the original cascade model contains fixed rate parameters. Moreover, the differential equations contain a threshold parameter which serves to gate the input from one processing stage to the next. This parameter endows the neural network representation of the processing system with its discrete stage structure. Input from one component to the next is delayed until the first component generates sufficient activity. If the system's thresholds are fixed at zero, all stages will be continuously active. This has the effect of transforming the discrete stage character of the network into a system of processes in cascade. Thus, discrete stage and cascade models are qualitatively similar instances of the same neural network. This allows for an assessment of the results arising from equivalent simulations of both models.

An initial simulation study was conducted in which the two factors influenced couplings between consecutive stages. The simulation was performed once using the discrete stage variety of the network and repeated using the cascade version (i.e. in the latter case all thresholds were fixed at zero). Each simulation produced interactions. These interactions are consistent with both models because both factors affected the relative asymptotic activation (see McClelland, 1979; p. 314). A second simulation study was then conducted in which two factors influenced the rates of different processing stages, one being the rate-limiting process. Again, the simulation was performed for both the discrete stage and the cascade versions of the neural network. The results of the simulation for the serial stage model were consistent with the predictions of the additive factors logic in showing additive effects. The results from the simulation for the cascade model did not show the interaction anticipated on the basis of McClelland's predictions, however (see McClelland, 1979; p. 311). The two factors produced additive effects. What is important about this observation is that it suggests that serial stage and cascade models may be two instances of a variety of models ranging along a single continuum that differ only in the value of the threshold parameters (non-zero for the stage model and zero for the cascade model). This work suggests, therefore, that the differential neural network approach might prove to be a useful tool in studying the temporal organization of stages of complex information processing systems (see also Molenaar, 1990).

Continuous Flow Conception of the Reaction Process

Unlike McClelland's cascade model that was built on a foundation of mathematical formalisms and tests of simulated data, the foundation for C.W. Eriksen's 'continuous flow model' was constructed from empirical findings generated in a series of experiments by his research group. These studies were designed to disentangle the contributions of stimulus and response processing variables in determining the speed of visual search by providing a baseline condition against which to make comparisons. C.W. Eriksen and his colleagues argued that the focus of previous research on visual search had been to characterize the effects of variations in the noise elements of a display on the speed with which a target element could be identified, and that the very nature of the search tasks used to achieve this end necessitates confounding the effects of noise with the process by which a visual display is searched. They reasoned that in order to understand the search process with more clarity the effect of noise elements on the identification of a target must be understood when no visual search is required. This would provide the baseline task for characterizing the contribution of target identification itself to the visual search process.

Previous work from C.W. Eriksen's laboratory had demonstrated that even when the location of the target stimulus in a stimulus array is signaled in advance of the array's presentation, the presence of noise elements in the display prolongs the search time (Colegate, Hoffman and Eriksen, C.W., 1973; Eriksen, C.W. and Collins, 1969; Eriksen, C.W. and Hoffman, 1973; Eriksen, C.W. and Rohrbaugh, 1970). This research revealed three major findings: (i) Proximal extraneous stimuli cannot be selectively disattended, even when the location of the critical stimulus is forewarned. (ii) The extent to which the presence of noise elements slows RT to the target element is a non-linear function of the spacing of these elements. (iii) Noise effects vary as a function of their relationship to the response output; that is, if the noise elements are associated with the same learned response as the target element they produce little effect on RT, even if they are physically quite dissimilar to the target, but if the noise elements are associated with a response that is opposite or incompatible with that of the target they produce a significant slowing of RT. C.W. Eriksen and his colleagues inferred from this that the locus of the effect of the noise elements is at the response selection level of processing, and the prolongation of RT is produced by a process of response competition that is established as the result of the simultaneous activation of mutually incompatible responses by the target and noise elements in the display. As we shall see, this concept of response competition lies at the heart of the continuous flow model.

In this early work, circular stimulus displays were used and the location of the target was precued by an indicator that preceded the display by varying intervals. B.A. Eriksen and C.W. Eriksen (1974) introduced the task that has come to be identified as the paradigmatic task in testing the continuous flow model (see also Eriksen, C.W., Hamlin and Daye, 1973). Indeed, the findings they reported have now been replicated numerous times by the Eriksen group as well as by other investigators, and variants of this paradigmatic task have been used most often in psychophysiological studies of the model (see below). The Eriksens required their subjects (all dextrals) to move a response lever (with the right hand) to the right or to the left in response to the presentation of a target letter that designated the direction of the movement. Four letters were used as targets (H,K,S,C), with H and K indicating one movement and S and C indicating the opposite movement. The target letters were presented (for 1000 ms) alone or flanked by three letters on each side of a horizontal display. These flankers provided the noise elements in the display. Subjects were instructed, however, to fixate a point above which the center target would always appear and to ignore the flanking letters. Thus, visual search was not required to locate the target stimulus. Six different displays were used, examples of which are shown in Table 1.1.

The featural complexity of the angular and curved stimuli was matched using Gibson's system (Gibson, 1969). When targets appeared alone, they were presented either in blocked trials with no other displays or mixed with the other

Table 1.1. Experimental conditions and representative displays (B.A. Eriksen and C.W. Eriksen (1974)).

Condition	Example						
1. Noise same as target	H	H	H	H	H	H	H
2. Noise response compatible	K	K	K	H	K	K	K
3. Noise response incompatible	S	S	S	H	S	S	S
4. Noise hetergeneous–similar	N	W	Z	H	N	W	Z
5. Noise heterogeneous–dissimilar	G	J	Q	H	G	J	Q
6. Target along				H			

displays. The spacing between the letters was also varied (0.06, 0.5, or 1 degree of visual angle). The pattern of responses observed by the Eriksens is shown in Figure 1.2. As is apparent, RT to the target stimulus varied as a function of the type of flankers and their spacing, and the effect of the spacing varied with the type of flanker. Specifically, RT decreased as spacing increased for each type of flanker and the difference in RT among the various flankers was greatest at the closest spacing. Indeed, response latencies were comparable among those arrays with flankers that were identical to the target ('noise same as target'), that were physically dissimilar to the target but signaled the same response ('noise response compatible'), and that shared featural properties with the target but were not associated with a response ('noise heterogeneous—similar) at the widest spacing, 1 degree of visual angle separating the letters. Across all spacings, RTs were slowest when the flankers signaled the opposite response ('noise response incompatible') and fastest when they were identical to the target ('noise same as target').

Of particular interest was the finding that when the flankers were not physically identical to the target stimulus, but signaled the same response (i.e. the 'noise response compatible' condition), RT did not differ from when the flankers were identical to the target (the 'noise same as target' condition). The fastest RTs were evident, however, when the target letters were presented alone in blocked trials. When they were presented alone in mixed trials containing the other arrays, they elicited RTs that were comparable to those seen to the 'noise same as target', 'noise response compatible', and 'noise heterogeneous—similar' displays at 1 degree of spacing. The pattern of errors paralleled the RT data and did not suggest variations that could be attributed to speed/accuracy tradeoffs.

From these findings, the substance of the continuous flow model began to emerge. In reviewing the 1974 study, C.W. Eriksen and Schultz (1979) concluded that the two most important findings were that attention cannot be restricted to the single target letter and that the flankers are processed along with the target to the level of 'incipient response activation'. Reasoning from these findings, from the known temporal summation of energy in the visual system (of the order of 100–200 ms;

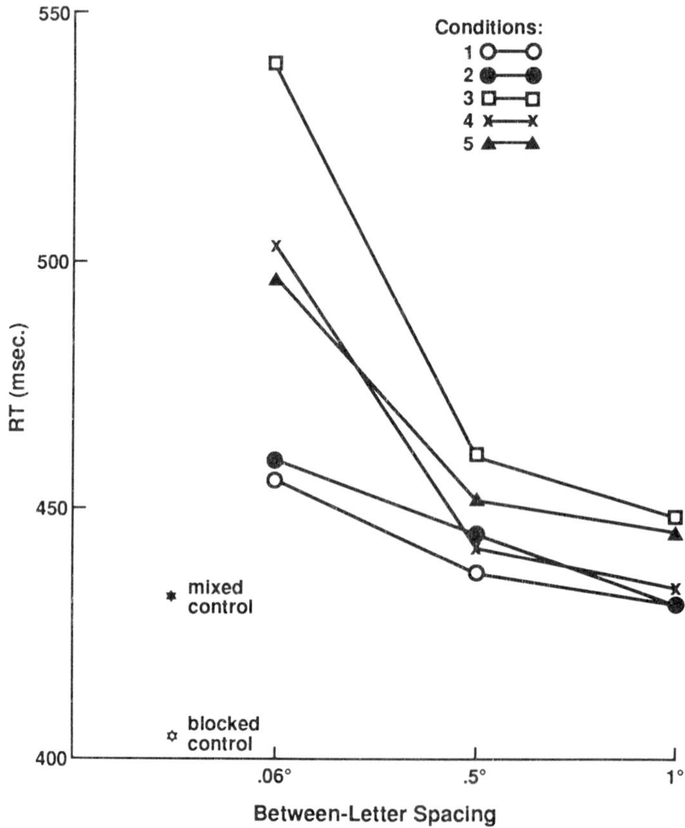

Figure 1.2. Data from Eriksen, B.A. and Eriksen, C.W. (1974) that revealed the effect of incompatible noise on mean reaction time. This figure shows the effect of spacing as well as of noise. There were five experimental conditions and two control conditions. The experimental conditions were: (1) noise same as target; (2) noise response compatible; (3) noise response incompatible; (4) noise heterogeneous similar; (5) noise heterogeneous dissimilar. (Reprinted with permission of the authors and publisher. © 1974 Psychonomic Society Inc.)

Eriksen, C.W. and Schultz, 1978; Ganz, 1975; Kahneman and Norman, 1964; Kahneman, Norman and Kubovy, 1967), and from the known falloff in visual acuity with retinal eccentricity (Eriksen; C.W. and Schultz, 1977; Lefton and Haber, 1974), C.W. Eriksen and Schultz (1979) proposed what they called the *continuous flow conception* of visual information processing that merged the concept of the temporal distribution of stimulus processing in the visual system with that of response competition produced by the concurrent activation of incompatible responses:

> In this conception, information about stimuli accumulates gradually in the visual system, and as it accumulates, responses are concurrently primed or partially activated. We conceive of several processes or levels comprising the events from stimulation to response activation. With the onset of stimulation, input channels begin to feed a continuous output to feature detectors which, in turn, continuously feed form units. The output from the form units is a priming or activation flow to the response system. The output from each process becomes increasingly more detailed or exact over time as energy is integrated in the visual sense organ. The effect at the response level, with this continuous flow, is an initial priming of a wide range of responses. But as the processing at lower levels proceeds in time, the priming flow becomes increasingly restricted to fewer and fewer responses, namely, those that are still viable alternatives in terms of the increasingly more exact or complete output of the lower processes. (p. 252)

C.W.Eriksen and Schultz (1979) tested this model in a series of three experiments. In the first experiment, they varied the relative processing times of the target and flanking letters by manipulating the size and figure–ground contrast of the target. The letters A and H served as the stimuli, and they were flanked either by two repetitions of themselves (on each flank) or by the other letter. There were five experimental conditions: (1) Baseline, in which all of the stimuli were the same size and intensity; (2) Size, in which the target was twice as large as the noise letters; (3) Contrast, in which the target had a much lower contrast with the ground than did the flankers; (4) Size-contrast, in which conditions 2 and 3 were combined; and (5) No-noise control, in which the target appeared alone. Trials were presented either with the flanking letters blocked (e.g. all As) and the targets varying randomly or with targets and flankers mixed randomly. Again, the subject was instructed to ignore the flankers and to move a lever to the left or right in response to the target letter.

A number of predictions were derived from the model, most important among which were that incompatible noise would have its smallest effect when the target was larger than the noise and its largest effect when the target contrast was low. These predictions derive from the combined notion of temporal energy summation as stimulus processing emerges and the concurrent activation of competing responses by the noise as partial stimulus information is passed to response activation channels. Thus, the higher energy in the large target should produce a faster rate of summation of the target *vis-à-vis* the noise, where the opposite should obtain when the figure–ground contrast of the target is lower than that of the noise. These predictions were supported, as indicated in Figure 1.3. Incompatible noise produced the longest RTs and its dilatory effect on RT varied with differences in the target and in blocking. When the type of flanker was blocked, the influence of incompatible noise was reduced compared with mixed trials and, indeed, doubling the size of the target eliminated the effect of incompatible noise completely. Note that even though the effect of incompatible noise was reduced in the non-blocked

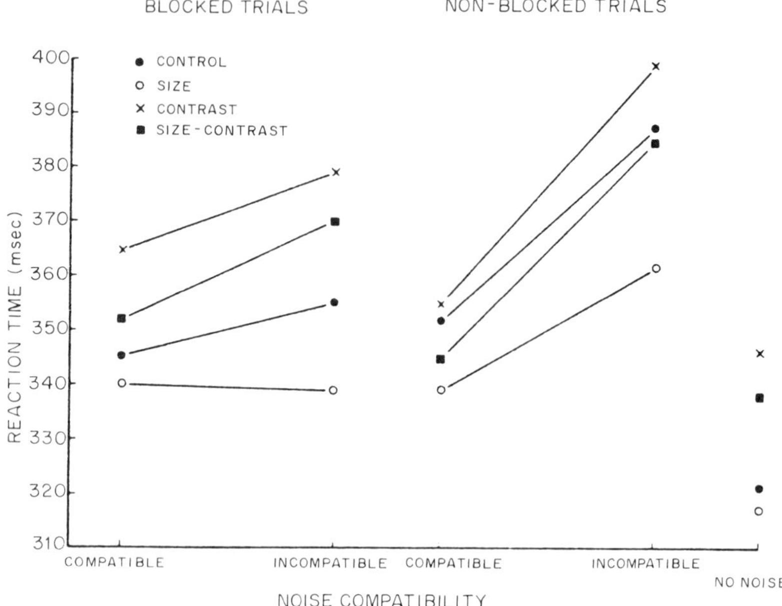

Figure 1.3. Data from C.W. Eriksen and Schultz (1979) in which the influence of flanking noise in blocked versus mixed presentations of the stimulus arrays is revealed. (Reprinted with permission of the authors and publisher. © 1979 Psychonomic Society Inc.)

condition when the target was larger than the noise, it persisted in delaying response time, albeit to a lesser extent then in the low-contrast and baseline conditions.

In the second experiment, C.W. Eriksen and Schultz evaluated the effect of increasing the energy in the noise level on the compatibility effect. To do so, they varied the flanker to target ratio (2:1 and 4:1), the latter being selected to determine if there was a limit in size beyond which interference did not occur. They found that the effect of incompatible flanking noise was greatest when the ratio was 2:1, and that the baseline and the largest noise conditions did not differ in their effect on RT. This pattern of results was interpreted in terms of varying degrees of energy summation between the target and the noise and the partial recession of the larger noise into the ground (from which the target emerged).

The third experiment was designed to assess the temporal nature of the energy summation for the flanking stimuli and its effect on the production of response competition. Here, the flankers were presented at varying intervals before (what the authors called 'foreward masking') or after ('backward masking') the target. It was predicted that compatible noise would produce little or no effect on RT, whereas the effect of incompatible noise would be more apparent for forward than for backward masking. The latter prediction followed from the notion that presentation of the target before the noise allows target priming of the correct response (and summation of the energy in the stimulus) to gain an advantage on the noise elements, thereby delaying their competitive response priming effects. With a sufficient delay, the target will have been recognized before the noise is presented. When the noise precedes the target by a long interval, response competition produced by the noise is expected to have dissipated before the target is presented and therefore should produce little or no effect on RT. As the interval is shortened, however, the response competition effects should emerge because they have not had time to dissipate. At sufficiently short intervals, incompatible noise may produce effects that are even greater than those seen with simultaneous onset because the competitive response may have been primed to a peak. In addition to these manipulations, they looked at competition effects among internal recognition responses hypothesized to be engaged when physically dissimilar stimuli are associated with the same response (recall Eriksen, B.A. and Eriksen, C.W., 1974). Four stimuli were used, two of which (W,T) signaled one response and two of which (A,M) signaled the alternative response. Under these conditions, comparisons could be made of stimuli whose physical properties differed and thereby elicited different recognition responses, but whose response-related significance was identical. Their results supported the predictions for the effects of forward and backward masking, and replicated the earlier finding of the 1974 study that RT was impaired when the target and flankers belonged to incompatible response categories but not when they belonged to the same response category.

The continuous flow model was formulated on the basis of two critical assumptions and one important claim. One assumption is that there is a gradual, cumulative development of stimulus information in the visual system. C.W. Eriksen and Schultz (1979) likened the process to the immersion of photographic film in developer. Information on the film becomes available first as gross differentiations of figure and ground. As the developer acts upon the film, increasingly finer details of the photograph become discernible. Thus, when a visual stimulus contains information that is both relevant and irrelevant to the production of a response, discriminations of the relevant component will take longer when it is more difficult to distinguish the two elements of the stimulus. This inference derives from research that suggests information is integrated over time in the visual system. The second assumption is that when the stimulus is first presented all of its elements are processed simultaneously and the output of this processing is transmitted continuously to the response system where a wide array of responses are primed. As more information about the percept accumulates, however, the output from the visual system becomes restricted to fewer and fewer responses until the activation of the correct response reaches its evocation limit and is executed. Hence, there is an hypothesized concurrent global activation of both systems in response to the stimulus input that is thought to become increasingly focused as information accumulates in the visual system. This assumption is based on the findings that the effect of the irrelevant elements of a visual display vary on the basis of their experimentally-defined relationship to the relevant element and on the basis of the relative timing of the onset of the relevant and irrelevant elements. A corollary to this assumption is that instructions, psychological set or expectancy may act to differentially prime certain responses over others. As a consequence, a preferentially primed response will reach the evocation threshold earlier than if it were not (Eriksen, C.W. and Schultz, 1979; p. 252).

In addition to these two assumptions, an important claim made by the Eriksen group is that the graded effect of the irrelevant flankers on the processing duration of the relevant target is difficult to reconcile with a discrete serial stage model of RT. Thus, according to this view a central decision stage that isolates perceptual processes from later response activation would block the access of the irrelevant stimulus information to the response system. Under these circumstances, the irrelevant information could affect the speed with which relevant information becomes available to the decision process and perhaps determine the duration of the decision process, but the irrelevant information would no longer have an effect once a decision is reached and a response is activated.

Can the assumptions of the continuous flow conception be challenged and its claim refuted? Our response to this question follows. The assumption that stimulus information accumulates continuously in the visual system derives from the work of Ganz and others (see references in C.W. Eriksen and Schultz, 1979) in the 1960s and 1970s. Research subsequent to that time indicates, however, that the accumulation of information in the visual system may be more complicated than was suggested by this early work. For example, Laming (1986) presents a very cogent argument for the existence of three distinct stages in perceptual analysis. His model is based on research in psychophysics whose aim is to characterize threshold properties for luminance and sound pressure. In the first stage of the perceptual process, sensory analysis, primitive features of the stimulus are hypothesized to be differentiated from the random physical and neural flux that characterizes initial sensory stimulation. These primitive features are then synthesized into a perceptual experience in the subsequent two stages. Laming proposed that sensory analysis begins with a primary response that is Poisson in nature. In the visual system, this process refers to the absorption of light quanta in the photopigments of the retina that produces small perturbations in cellular potential at the next retinal level. These quantal absorptions first pass through a stage of exact differential coupling (Stage 1). At the physiological level, this process might reveal itself as the response of retinal ganglion cells. The output of Stage 1 processing provides the input to the next stage, where dispersed differential coupling is assumed to occur. At this stage, the positive and negative inputs from Stage 1 are characterized by different dispersal distributions such that brief increments are transmitted as detectable pertubations of the mean. Stage 2 comprises two substages, one for monocular (2A) and the other for binocular (2B) dispersed coupling. This second stage is thought to realize the square-law phenomena of psychophysics (detectability function, threshold summation, and negative masking). Laming assumed that Stage 2A processing takes place in the visual pathway from the ganglion cells to the simple cells in layer IVb of the striate cortex, and that Stage 2B processing occurs in the complex cells. Small, brief discrete stimuli are thought to require an additional stage, Stage 3, in which exact differentiation of the stimulus occurs. Stage 3 passes on only the noise component of the Poisson samples as a basis for discrimination.

Laming used this model to develop a successful account of the detection and discrimination of simple stimuli as well as of more complicated perceptual processing such as the discrimination of contrast. Thus, his work suggests that the transmission of stimulus information may be serial, rather than continuous, even at the most primitive levels of sensory processing. Indeed, evidence from neurophysiological studies of the visual system is consistent with this conclusion (see review in Ungerleider and Mishkin, 1982). Moreover, neurotransmission in the somatosensory system, as revealed in studies of single unit activity, appears to be organized in series (Pons *et al.*, 1987). Findings of this sort have led some investigators to conclude that the transmission of information in all sensory modalities is accomplished by serially organized multisynaptic processing pathways (Mishkin, 1979; Mishkin, Ungerleider and Macko, 1983; Turner, Mishkin and Knapp, 1980). It should be noted as well that, even if there were a gradual accumulation of information in the visual system, this does not necessarily preclude a serially organized system. Proponents of serial stage models generally do not assert that the reaction process is discrete in every respect. Rather, their position is that, whereas transmission between information processing stages must be serial and discrete, it can be overlapping, parallel, or connected through feedback loops within an information processing stage (Sanders, 1980). Thus, discrete models have no difficulty with gradually accumulating stimulus information within the visual system as long as it occurs within a stage (see also Miller, 1988, and later under 'More Thoughts...', for a more elaborate discussion of this point).

The second assumption of the continuous flow model suggests that the presence of conflicting information in the stimulus array prolongs RT by priming both the correct and the incorrect responses (i.e. by producing response competition). Thus, initiation of the overt response takes longer when there is concurrent activation of the other response alternative. The point at which initiation of the overt response to the stimulus takes place is also thought to depend on a process called 'aspecific priming' (Coles *et al.*, 1985). In contrast to response competition processes that are driven by the content of the stimulus, aspecific priming is considered to be independent of the stimulus content. That is, a particular response may be activated even though there is nothing in the stimulus associated with that response. Thus, if a specific task manipulation leads to an increase in the level of aspecific priming of a response, less additional activation is required to reach the response evocation threshold. From these assumptions a set of specific predictions can be derived and tested. First, consider an experiment in which the discriminability of the stimulus is manipulated by varying its contrast and the relative frequency of responses associated with the different levels of contrast. If the rate of response activation is slower for dim than for bright stimuli and the distance to the response evocation threshold is shorter for the high than for the low response frequency, the prediction is that the effect of stimulus contrast will be more pronounced for the low than for the high response frequency. Figure 1.4 presents a graphic illustration of this prediction.

Consider now a second experiment in which the subject must make the appropriate response to the center stimulus in a typical Eriksen display (e.g. SSSSS, HHSHH, HHHHH, SSHSS), the onset of which is preceded either by a warning stimulus (e.g. a tone) or by no warning stimulus. If we assume, as does C.W. Eriksen and his colleagues, that the rate of response activation to the target is slower when the flankers signal the incorrect response and that the distance to the response evocation thresholds is greater when a warning stimulus is not given than when it is, the prediction follows that the effect of the incompatible flankers will be greater in the absence of a warning than in its presence. This prediction is also illustrated in Figure 1.4.

Finally, consider an experiment that is similar to the previous experiment in all details except that an alerting stimulus is presented at the onset of, rather than before, the stimulus array. The alerting tone is presented randomly to either the left or the right ear, thereby permitting two types of trials to be distinguished, corresponding and non-corresponding. On corresponding trials, the tone is presented on the same side as the correct response (e.g. left ear, left-hand button press); on non-corresponding trials, the tone is presented to the side opposite the correct response (e.g. left ear, right button press). A large body of literature has revealed that responses are considerably slower under these conditions when the directional information provided by the imperative and alerting stimuli do not correspond (see above under 'Challenges to the Additive Factors Method'). If we assume, as does C.W. Eriksen and coworkers, that the rate of response activation to the target is slower for arrays that contain information signaling both responses and, further, that the distance to the response evocation is longer when directional information provided in the alerting and imperative stimuli is conflicting, it follows that the effect of the incompatible flankers on RT will be greater when the alerting stimulus is presented to the ear opposite the correct response hand than when it is presented to the ear on the same side (see Figure 1.4).

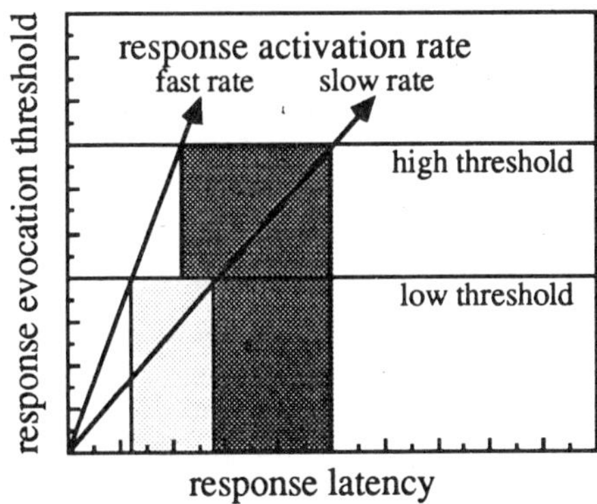

Figure 1.4. Schematic representation of a model in which reaction time is assumed to depend on the setting of a response evocation limit and the rate this level is attained. Note that the effect of the response activation rate on response latency will increase with higher settings of the response evocation limit. This combined effect on reaction time can be evaluated by comparing the light and dark shaded areas along the abscissa of the diagram. In the first hypothetical experiment, the response evocation limit is manipulated by varying S–R frequency (low S–R frequencies are assumed to induce higher thresholds than high frequencies), and the rate of response activation is varied by changing stimulus quality (bright stimuli are assumed to produce faster rates than dim stimuli). In the second hypothetical experiment, the response evocation limit is manipulated by an alerting stimulus (unsignaled trials are thought to be associated with higher thresholds than signaled trials), and the rate of response activation is assumed to be affected by stimulus compatibility (incompatible arrays produce slower rates than compatible arrays). In the third hypothetical experiment, the response evocation limit is varied by changing the location of an auditory noise stimulus (non-corresponding trials have higher thresholds than corresponding trials), and the rate of response activation is manipulated by stimulus compatibility, as in the second experiment. (See text for further details.)

All three experiments have been conducted and in each one additive, as predicted by a stage model, rather than interactive, as predicted by the continuous flow model, effects have been observed. In the first experiment, conducted by Miller and Pachella (1973; Experiment 1), variations in stimulus contrast and S–R frequency (for probabilities varying between 0.125 and 0.275) were found to produce additive effects on RT. This finding was confirmed in a second study by Miller and Pachella (1976; Experiments 2 and 3). In the second experiment, conducted by Coles *et al.* (1985), the influence of variations in the compatibility of the flankers in the stimulus array was not altered by the presence or the absence of a warning stimulus. And, in the third experiment, conducted by Stoffels and van der Molen (1988; see also Stoffels, 1988), the effect of changes in the compatibility of the flankers in the stimulus array was not affected by presenting the alerting tone in the ear on the same or opposite side of the response signaled by the target element. Stoffels and van der Molen discussed, but rejected, the hypothesis that this additive effect represented the influence of these variables on a common process—response competition—so that the increases in RT produced by both factors were simply added to one another. As an alternative, they proposed that the two variables affect different processes. Similarly, the findings of Miller and Pachella and of Coles *et al.* are explained more parsimoniously by a discrete stage than by a continuous flow conception. The basic difference between the two conceptions is that stage models assume a reaction process composed of discrete perceptual and motor stages separated by a response selection stage, whereas continuous flow models assume no such distinctions. In effect, the latter posits one stage comprising stimulus and responses processes. These differences are expressed in predictions of additive effects by stage models, but interactive effects by continuous flow models, when factors affecting stimulus and response processes are varied. Additive effects are difficult to interpret within the constraints of a continuous flow model unless they are viewed as the influence of two task variables on the same process. If so, the continuous flow model is reduced to a position of being compatible with any finding and this would dissipate any of its predictive power (see Sanders, 1977, for a related criticism of Grice's 'variable criterion model'; Grice, Nullmeyer and Spiker, 1982).

Finally, the claim by C.W. Eriksen and Schultz (1979) that their findings are difficult to reconcile with a discrete serial stage model has been challenged by Miller (1988). He argued that the graded flanker effect provides evidence, at most, for models in which at least one stage carries out its transformation relatively continuously. Thus, he proffered a model that is continuous only at the response activation level in the choice reaction process. In this model, stimulus letters in the array are identified in parallel across the different display positions by mechanisms tied to the individual letter positions. Each mechanism performs a discrete transformation leading to the selection of a discrete code for the name of the letter in its position, and no information about any letter is transmitted to the decision stage until identification of the letter is complete. In the decision stage, each letter is evaluated with respect to its relevance (i.e. position) and its response assignment. Letters are evaluated one at a time, in the order of arrival from letter identification mechanisms, with queuing if one letter arrives before the previous one has been processed completely. After each letter had been analyzed, the decision stage sends a discrete output to the motor system. This output indicates a response to be activated (left or right) and a degree of activation (large or small), depending on the relevance of the letter. The motor system activates the designated response to the specified degree, but does so with a gradual transformation, initiating a response when a threshold level of activation has been achieved. The build-up of motor activation is hypothesized to be slow enough, relative to letter identification and decision times, to permit information about several different letters to be received during activation—not just information about the target. When more than one transmission has been received from the decision stage, motor activation builds at a rate proportional to the sum of the activations. Thus, flankers influence the rate at which activation of the correct response builds and produce the stimulus compatibility effect by weakly activating motor responses at the end of their discrete journey through the information processing system (cf. Miller, 1988, p. 223–224).

In a recent paper, Molenaar (1990) examined the validity of Miller's explanation of the flanker effect using a test based on a neural network representation of the model. This representation allowed him to simulate the model under various conditions and to compare its quantitative behavior with experimental results cited in the literature as support for the continuous flow model. Molenaar tested the model using a non-committal mathematical description of the information flow. That is, the time-dependent behavior of each of the processing components in a given structural model was represented by a simple, non-informative dynamic equation that had no affect on the theoretical structure of the model. He derived a mathematical specification of each processing component from Grossberg's (1982) differential neural network approach. In this approach, processing components are represented as input–output devices in which the input of each device, apart from optional external sources, originates from the other processing components in the model and the output is delayed owing to the presence of a threshold. To obtain a stable network, the activation of each component must decay to zero in case the input is vanishing. Hence, each component in the network involves two basic types of parameters, thresholds and decay rates. The dynamics of each processing component in the system is represented by a differential equation in which the stochastic nature of RTs is incorporated by defining the rate of decay parameters as random variables with some time-independent distribution, rather than by adding noise to the output as did McClelland (1979) in the pseudostochastic equations he used in the cascade model. The stochastic differential equations were used by Molenaar to represent the component processes at the stimulus identification level of Miller's model. The limited capacity decision stage, where the outputs of the stimulus identification stage are evaluated sequentially in the order of arrival, was represented by a system of differential equations involving inhibitory couplings. The two components of the motor stage, one associated with the correct response and the other with incorrect response, were represented by assigning a higher weight to the coupling between the decision stage and the component of the motor stage associated with the correct response. Using these parameters, Molenaar completed a simulation study in which distinct stages of the Miller model were perturbed in a factorial design. His results were consistent with the predictions from Miller's model. RTs were faster for compatible than for incompatible stimulus arrays and, most importantly, manipulations affecting stimulus identification, decision, and motor activation produced significant main effects but no significant interactions.

In conclusion, the critical assumptions on which the continuous flow conception is based may be in need of revision. Thus, the assumption that information accumulates gradually in the visual system may be in need of modification to include sequential processing, even at the earliest levels of processing. Moreover, the assumption that the gradual accumulation of stimulus information is associated with the concurrent continuous transmission of this information to the motor system where responses are primed may be in need of revision to account for the additive relations between experimental factors that are assumed to influence only this aspect of processing. Finally, despite the claim of Eriksen and his colleagues to the contrary, a serial model with only one continuous component can explain the effect of the flankers on RT.

The Asynchronous Discrete Coding Model

The cascade and continuous flow models offer alternatives to Sternberg's stage model that eschew discrete processing in favor of the continuous transmission of information (save the response output component of the cascade model). In essence, these models postulate infinitely small units of information transmission. A model proposed recently by Miller (1982) represents an intermediate between the two extremes of discrete and continuous information transmission. It evolved from a series of experiments performed to determine if responses can be prepared before stimulus processing has been completed (reported originally in Miller 1982, 1983, and summarized in Miller, 1988). If so, the possibility would be raised that the preliminary output of a stage is transmitted to a subsequent stage before the previous stage has finished its operations. This, in turn, would necessitate loosening the strict assumption of discrete stages and would mean that the total RT is not simply the sum of the durations of the individual stages it comprises. It would suggest, therefore, that an experimental manipulation that prolongs the duration of one stage may not necessarily change the total RT by the same amount because a subsequent stage may start working with the preliminary output of the affected stage and thereby compensate for the delay of the previous stage. Miller (1982) reasoned that the crux of the dispute between discrete and continuous models concerns the fate of information that becomes available relatively early in the course of processing done by a particular stage. According to discrete models, such preliminary information is simply held until full stimulus information is available (e.g. Sternberg, 1969). Continuous models, however, assume that preliminary information is used by the subsequent processes to accomplish some 'preparation' or 'priming' (e.g.

Eriksen, C.W. and Schultz, 1979). This preparation is believed to heighten readiness for a set of stimuli suggested by the preliminary information, generally facilitating the processing that is done when full information becomes available. To test the differences between these two models, Miller (1982, 1983) designed a series of experiments to determine if information available early in the processing of a stimulus can be used to activate a response before the perceptual analysis of the stimulus has been completed. To do so, he varied properties of the stimuli (identity and/or size) as well as the efficiency with which the responses they signaled could be prepared (same versus different hand responses). The experimental tasks were designed to ensure that partial information about the stimulus was available well before the stimulus had been recognized completely and therefore could be used to facilitate preparation of the correct response (what Miller, 1982, referred to as the *response preparation effect*).

This design and the interpretations that derive from it are grounded on the assumption that preparation of responses on one hand is more efficient than preparation of responses on different hands and, therefore, that the response preparation effect is revealed in the difference in RTs between responses made on the same hand and those made on different hands. The corollary to this assumption is that the response preparation effect will be larger for responses that are prepared efficiently than for responses that are prepared less efficiently. Discrete and continuous models make different predictions about the response preparation effect. Classical discrete models predict no response preparation effect because responses are hypothesized to be prepared only after the stimulus is evaluated completely. Continuous models, on the other hand, predict such an effect because they assume that the processing system can take advantage of the availability of preliminary information.

Miller (1982, 1983) constructed stimulus sets consisting of four stimuli that signaled responses by separate digits on each hand (i.e. the typical task was a four-choice reaction). These stimuli were grouped into pairs that signaled responses by digits either on the same or different hand. The stimuli could be distinguished on the basis of characteristics that were either easy (letter identity) or difficult (letter size) to discriminate. Thus, preliminary information about a stimulus came from a discrimination that was relatively easy to make and secondary information from a discrimination that was relatively difficult to make. Miller's procedure for manipulating preparation efficiency was suggested by findings that indicated that responses made by the same arm are prepared more efficiently than are responses by different arms (e.g. Rosenbaum, 1980) and from his replication of this effect (see Miller, 1982, Experiment 1). His subjects were required to make a single key press response with the middle or index finger of the left or right hand. Miller assumed that advance preparation of fingers on the same hand would reduce RT more than advance preparation of two fingers on different hands. His basic idea was that if preliminary information is used for response preparation, preparation efficiency should produce a main effect. If not, it should produce no effect (cf. Miller, 1982; p. 276).

Miller (1982) completed a series of experiments to test this idea using the aforementioned paradigm. For example, he used a stimulus set that consisted of four characters: S, T, T, T. A pilot study indicated that letter information (S versus T) was recognized much faster than size information, so in the perceptual analysis of the stimulus, letter information was expected to become available before size information. For subjects in the 'same hand' condition, the preliminary letter information determined which hand would make the response (e.g. SSTT or TTSS was mapped to response keys for the left middle (S, T), left index (S, T), right index (T, S), right middle (T, S) fingers). Subjects in the 'different hand' condition received assignments such as STST or TSST that determined which finger would respond. Recall, Miller reasoned that discrete stage models predict equally fast responses in both conditions because these models deny the possibility of preliminary information about the stimulus being transferred between stages prior to a complete analysis of the stimulus. His results indicated, however, that responses could be prepared more efficiently by digits on the same hand than by digits on different hands, suggesting that preliminary letter information is used for response preparation.

That partitioning the target stimuli into multiple codes (letter, size) may be essential to producing the response preparation effect was suggested in experiments by Miller in which it was found that stimuli distinguishable only on the basis of a single code, letter identity, did not produce a response preparation effect nor did the availability of a second code, digit identity, when the featural discrimination between letters and digits was difficult to make. Miller (1982) argued that a continuous model would predict an effect under both conditions because priming is hypothesized to occur under all stimulus conditions. Hence, neither classically discrete nor continuous models could explain either the presence or the absence of the response preparation effects he obtained.

Miller (1983) developed a second paradigm to provide a set of converging results for the response preparation effect. In this paradigm, stimulus sets were used in which preliminary information was available from the early perceptual analysis of the stimulus (given by the name of the letter), and secondary information was available only after a more complete analysis of the stimulus (given by the size of the letter). The ease with which the secondary information became available was varied by making the difference in the size of the letters either easy or difficult to discriminate. This manipulation was assumed to influence the amount of time available for preparing responses on the basis of the preliminary stimulus information provided by the letter's identity. According to Miller (1983), difficult secondary discriminations allow more time for preliminary information to activate the response preparation process. He argued that continuous flow and serial stage models make different predictions about the effect of variations in the difficulty of the secondary discrimination: continuous models predict that increases in the difficulty of the discrimination will increase the total RT by an amount that is less than the time needed for the recognition process, but serial models predict no effect on response preparation because it cannot begin until stimulus recognition has been completed. An important test of these predictions, in Miller's view, is accomplished by examining the extent to which informative (i.e. directional) hints versus uninformative hints benefit RT when the secondary discrimination is difficult or easy to make. His rationale was that informative hints provide the opportunity for responses to be prepared before the stimulus is presented. Under these circumstances, continuous and serial models again make different predictions about the effect of an informative hint. Continuous models predict that such a hint would be more helpful when the secondary discrimination is easy (i.e. allows little or no time for response preparation), whereas serial models predict that the effect of the hint would be comparable for both difficult and easy secondary discriminations. Hence, continuous models predict an underadditive interaction between the discriminability and hint manipulations, where serial models predict that the informative hint will be of equal benefit for easy and difficult size discriminations.

Consider the following experiment using the letters T, T, N, N, E, E, A, and A, each letter signaling a response with a different finger. (In this letter set the difference in size between large and small Ts and Es is less than that between large and small Ns and As.) Each trial begins with either an informative (arrow pointing to the left or to the right) or an uninformative (diamond) hint that is followed by the presentation of one of the letters. The subject must then press the response key designated by this letter (with the appropriate middle or index finger on the left or right hand). Differences in the size and the identity of the letter determine the digit and hand that will be used. The assumption underlying this design is that preliminary information about the identity of the letter can be used to initiate preparation of the response before the analysis of the size difference is completed. Therefore, responses to Ts and Ns are mapped on to fingers on the left hand, whereas responses to Es and As are mapped on to fingers on the right hand. Thus, letter identity can be used to prepare the appropriate response hand. Smaller letters are mapped on to the left middle and right index fingers and larger letters are mapped on to the left index and right middle fingers. For two letters, T and E in this example, there is little variation in size, making the secondary size discrimination difficult and allowing more time for preliminary letter identity information to initiate response preparation processes. The other two letters, N and A, differ more in size, making the size discrimination relatively easy and permitting less time for letter identity to prepare the response. Given the aforementioned assumptions, the expectation is that the effectiveness of the hint will be greater for letters whose size difference is easily discriminated than for letters whose size difference is difficult to discriminate. This is precisely the task used by Miller (1983) in his first experiment and he found the expected underadditive interaction. Support was thus given for the inference that response preparation can begin on the basis of partial stimulus information (letter identity) and can proceed in parallel with other stimulus processes (size discrimination) until they are completed.

In a second experiment, he changed the design to rule out the possibility that the underadditive interaction arose because of some process other than response preparation. In this experiment, the same letter set was used except that the letters were presented in the upper or lower left or right quadrants of the visual field and signaled only a left or a right key press with the left or the right index finger. Letters to the left signaled a left button press and those to the right signaled a right button press. Informative or uninformative hints were presented before each letter. However, the informative hint provided up/down information, not left/right (i.e. the arrow pointed up or down). Small and large versions of each letter were always associated with different response keys. Thus, both the informative hint and the preliminary stimulus information could provide no useful information for response preparation. Under these conditions, the underadditive interaction was abolished. Next, in two experiments analogous to the first two in this series, Miller examined the relationship between the type of hint and the discriminability of the letter sets when they consisted of pairs of visually similar (e.g. UVMN) or dissimilar (e.g. CVEM) letters. Recall that the results from his previous series of experiments suggested that subjects do not use preliminary information about the visual similarity of the two letters (e.g. stimulus is either U or V) to initiate response preparation before their identification is completed, even though they call for a response on the same hand. Thus, he was interested initially in determining if the underadditive interaction he obtained in the first experiment using a hint and four response choices would be evident when the informative hint indicated the response hand but the stimulus choices mapped to that hand had only one discrete code (identity). He failed to obtain an underadditive effect in either this experiment or the next experiment in which two response choices were made and the informative cue provided up/down information (as in Experiment 2). Both failures are inconsistent, of course, with models that postulate the continuous accumulation and transmission of all elements of stimulus information. Thus, the conclusion is supported in both series of experiments that preliminary information indicating the letter pair cannot be used to prepare responses before the full analysis of the identity of the letter has been completed. For this stimulus set, then, the transmission of perceptual information to response preparation processes appears to be discrete.

The fundamental assumption in Miller's experimental method, and the assumption on which the response preparation effect is interpreted, is that responses are prepared more efficiently by stimuli mapped on the same hand than they are by stimuli on different hands. He tested this assumption in the first experiment of the series (Miller, 1982, Experiment 1). In this experiment, pairs of response effectors (i.e. index and middle fingers) on the same hand or on different hands were precued. The hands were placed with the fingers on four response keys assigned compatibly to four equally spaced horizontal locations on a visual display, indicated by a warning stimulus consisting of four plus (+) signs. Precues consisted of plus (+) signs being presented in either two (the prepared conditions) or four (the unprepared condition) positions. When only two precues were presented, they corresponded either to the middle and index fingers of the same hand (prepared: hand condition), the same fingers on different hands (prepared: finger condition), or to different fingers on different hands (prepared: neither condition). The target stimulus was a single plus sign that occurred below one of the positions of the precue signs following a variable interval less than or equal to 1 s. Response latencies were found to be fastest when the precue permitted digits on the same hand to be prepared and slowest when the precue did not permit any specific finger or hand preparation. Intermediate, and comparable, RTs were obtained when the same fingers were prepared on different hands, or when different digits on different hands were prepared.

The generality of this finding has been challenged, however, by a number of investigators. Reeve and Proctor (1984) replicated Miller's Experiment 1 and added precuing intervals up to 3 s. Like Miller, these investigators found an advantage for preparation of digits on the same hand over digits on different hands at precuing intervals less than 1.5 s. However, at longer intervals they found no difference among the various preparation conditions, all being faster than the unprepared condition. More importantly, Reeve and Proctor showed that responses were always fastest when the precue consisted of the two leftmost or two rightmost '+' signs, independent of the finger placement (i.e. whether the placement was of adjacent fingers—left middle, left index, right index, right middle—or of overlapping fingers—right index, left middle, right middle, left index). They suggested that the leftmost or rightmost precue placement constituted a more compatible relationship with the leftmost and rightmost response keys than any other precue–response key relationship, and that this relationship was more influential in determining response latency differences than was specific activation of the motor system mediating the response output. Thus, they argued that the mapping of the stimulus on to the response (i.e. S–R compatibility) and not the efficiency of motor preparation was the determining factor in producing Miller's 'response preparation effect'.

Compatibility effects were found in later work by these investigators to be prepotent not only for the display used in Miller's 1982 Experiment 1, but also for displays containing symbolic stimuli (Proctor and Reeve, 1985). We should note that Miller (1982) had dismissed S–R compatibility effects in his experimental design by referring briefly to two unpublished experiments he conducted in which same hand responses were superior, irrespective of variations in S–R compatibility. This observation is not consistent, however, with the bulk of the S–R compatibility literature (see reviews in Bashore, 1981, 1990a). Thus, the response pattern reported in Experiment 1 by Miller (1982) may reflect insufficient preparation and S-R compatibility effects, rather than fundamental differences in response preparation. Perhaps even more troubling to Miller's experimental method is that, in contrast to his 1982 assertion, the literature on human motor behavior indicates that in choice reactions response selection decisions are made more efficiently by digits on different hands than by digits on the same hand (Kornblum, 1965; Rosenbaum and Kornblum, 1982; Shulman and McConkie, 1973).

From the above discussion, it is apparent that the locus of the response preparation effect reported by Miller (1982) is controversial. It is therefore questionable if Miller's paradigm can be used to differentiate discrete from continuous flow models of human information processing. Suppose that the manipulation of pairwise discriminability and response preparation results in an equivalent RT pattern (i.e. no differences between same and different hand conditions). What does this mean? According to Miller's reasoning, this finding supports a discrete model which assumes that information is transmitted from perceptual to motor stages only after the stimulus has been identified completely. Note that this conclusion involves accepting the null hypothesis, dangerous ground on which to tread. Alternatively, an equivalent RT pattern might suggest that there were simply no codes available which could be activated by preliminary stimulus activation, an alternative fully appreciated by Miller.

The findings from the hint paradigm concur, however, with those of the same-hand paradigm. This is important because the effects are not dependent on the assumption that responses on the same hand can be prepared more efficiently than can those on different hands. The findings from this second set of experiments indicate, as did those in the first set, that response preparation processes can be activated by partial stimulus information if that information constitutes an internal code (e.g. letter identity). Miller's findings would have been more convincing, of course, if they had been obtained with hints to the same fingers on different hands. The fact that the same-hand and hint paradigms produced similar findings poses interesting questions. For example, is there a hidden artifact in the discrimination task? Does the same-hand paradigm produce reliable results if certain design constraints are met? We will not attempt to answer these questions here. The important point is that Miller's formulation presents a challenging conceptualization of human information processing that, at the very least, widens the scope of serial stage models that heretofore were only able to accommodate single-feature stimuli.

MORE THOUGHTS ON DISCRETE STAGES AND CONTINUOUS FLOW

Our discussion has focused thus far on two broad classes of models of mental chronometry, discrete stage and continuous flow. As we have seen, stage models conceptualize the reaction process as a series of processing stages in which the output of one stage serves as the input to the next stage. Moreover, output from the first stage occurs only after it has finished its processing. In contrast, continuous flow models assume a gradual accretion of information in the visual system that is continuously transmitted to the motor system, where responses are primed as perceptual evidence accumulates in support of them.

In a recent article that is obligatory reading for everyone in the field, Miller (1988) has argued that discreteness and continuity do not constitute a simple dichotomy of mutually exclusive and exhaustive classes, but represent two ends of a continuum that he conceptualizes on the basis of grain size. Within this view, at the extreme continuous end the grain size is zero and at the extreme stage end the grain size is one. Models that combine stage and continuous elements fall at points along the continuum on the basis of the grain sizes they comprise. In developing his position, Miller discussed three properties (what he referred to as 'senses') of RT models of mental chronometry that can combine in a variety of ways to produce organizational characteristics that are relatively discrete or relatively continuous. In his view, an adequate model must account for the representation, transformation, and transmission of information from stimulus input to response output. Representations refer to passive codes that store information that is processed at a particular stage. Thus, representations serve both as inputs to and outputs from a stage. As input, the representation is passed to a stage where it is transformed to an output representation that is suitable for transmission to the subsequent stage. A stage is then characterized as (relatively) discrete or (relatively) continuous on the basis of the information it receives as input, the type of transformation it makes on this input, the output it produces in consequence, and how that output is transmitted to the next stage. Discrete representations (i.e. inputs and outputs) are composed of highly distinct information codes (i.e. have a large grain size), whereas continuous representations consist of highly similar codes (i.e. their grain sizes are very small). Of course, intermediate representations are neither highly distinct nor arbitrarily similar. Transformations of input can be abrupt (i.e. discrete) or gradual (i.e. continuous). A completely discrete transformation would occur in a single step, whereas a completely continuous transformation would occur in infinitely small steps. An intermediate transformation would be performed in several steps, not just one or infinitely many. Finally, information can be transmitted from one stage to another in a single discrete output that must be received by the next stage before its processing can begin, in a continuous stream of partial information, or in some intermediate of several sequential quanta.

Miller argued that these three elements of discreteness/continuity are almost completely independent so that, in principle, almost all combinations are possible. One exception is the case in which a transformation in a stage is completed in one step. In this instance, no preliminary information can be transmitted to the next stage. Thus, the combination of a single discrete transformation of a representation and its continuous transmission is logically impossible. Miller pointed out that a discrete representation of information and its continuous transmission are not incompatible. In justification of this position, he argued that continuous transmission requires only that preliminary information is transmitted to the next stage, not that it transmits small, partial units of information. Thus, a stage may transmit its best guess at several points in time before it completes its processing. At each point in time, the best guess would be a discrete output representation to the next stage that it would begin to process while being sensitive to the possibility that the guess might change. The variety of combinations of discreteness and continuity that are possible for a single stage can then be extended to systems with several distinct stages. In such a system, the different stages need not all be equally discrete or continuous in their representations, transformations, and transmissions (cf. Miller, 1988; pp. 205–209).

This conceptual analysis was then used by Miller to provide the framework for a critical evaluation of the evidence that is most frequently cited in support of continuous models. This evidence typically refers to graded effects on performance produced by gradual changes in an experimental variable. The most notable example of that effect is found in the work of C.W. Eriksen and Schultz (1979). We earlier discussed Miller's criticism of the conclusions drawn from this work—a discrete model that is continuous only in the transformation of the response activation stage can also explain the effect of incompatible flankers on RT. Another example of graded effects on RT is found in studies of the speed/accuracy tradeoff. They show that the percentage of correct responses increases gradually as the time taken to produce the response is lengthened (see earlier). This gradual increase is easily equated with continuous processing. Miller suggested, however, that this function may be produced by a discrete information processing system that has only two possible outcomes. One outcome is a response with maximal accuracy that is generated only after the system has finished its stimulus processing, and the other outcome is a complete guess. A gradual increase in the time taken or available for analyzing the stimulus will result in a greater proportion of trials on which processing finishes, and thus in an increase in the proportion of correct responses. Some studies suggest, however, that responses can be based on partial information as well. Miller's position is that even in this case only information transmission must be continuous. A discrete code can be selected just as easily on the basis of partial information as it can on the basis of complete processing or guessing. Similarly, information need not be transmitted until a stage has completed its processing, whether it performs a cursory analysis or something in between. Miller argued that responses based on partial output require only that a stage performs its transformation in steps. When processing time expires owing to experimenter-imposed limitations, this stage simply produces its single best guess based on the information then available. He pointed out that most stochastic decision models are compatible with a stage model that is continuous only in transformation, not representation or transmission. Finally, Miller discussed the implications of continuous information transmission for discrete models. In this discussion, he introduced two auxiliary criteria. One is the contingency criterion. This criterion states that the temporal sequencing of stages must be such that one stage begins processing earlier than another stage and the output of the earlier stage provides the input to the later stage. If the later stage can begin processing without this input, then stage overlap is irrelevant to the question of information transmission between stages. For example, discrete models allow motor preparation to begin at the same time as the transformation of stimulus information is occurring at the perceptual analysis stage (see Sanders, 1990). Thus, the activity of the information processing system is always a joint function of the operations performed on stimulus input and the presetting of stages produced by expectancies, instructions, and, perhaps, the state of the organism. The second criterion concerns the range over which processes overlap. Discrete models do not deny overlapping processes within stages (e.g. Sanders, 1980) and overlap between adjacent stages does not imply that information processing is continuous throughout the entire sequence of processing stages. Miller claimed that in some cases it can be questioned whether overlapping stages are contingent and in other cases the two overlapping stages may perform such closely related functions that it is doubtful whether or not they are distinct stages. Overall, Miller concluded that the evidence for overlapping stages is remarkably weak and, similar to the observation of graded effects, does not qualify as a serious challenge to discrete stage models.

One important conclusion to be drawn from Miller's discussion is that the three senses of discreteness/continuity he elaborated define a model space with a wide variety of possible combinations. The task of mental chronometry, then, is to identify the combination(s) that most accurately describe the human information processing system. An immediate difficulty in achieving this end, however, is that the most powerful tool for drawing inferences about the timing and organization of mental processes from the total RT—the AFM—is derived from a stage model that is based on a number of strong assumptions of discrete processing (see earlier). Miller's conceptual analysis compels us to be more precise in defining discrete processing in our application of the AFM. Miller addressed this issue, as did Sanders (1990). They agree in suggesting that continuous information transformation would not be harmful to the additive factors logic. Information transformation is an operation that takes place within a stage and the AFM does not require within-stage assumptions, only between-stage assumptions. They disagree, however, as to the most important criterion for applying the AFM. Miller asserted that the transmission of information is decisive for the validity of the method, since it relies on the assumption that the total RT is the sum of the times taken for the stages involved in the task. Thus, overlapping stages would invalidate the additive factors logic. In contrast, Sanders (1990) argued that discrete internal codes (i.e. representations) are most important. Task variables, in his view, can influence stage duration but not the quality of stage output without violating additive factors logic. To support this position, he pointed to McClelland's (1979) simulation study (discussed earlier) in which it was shown that the additive factors logic was invalidated when task manipulations influence asymptotic activation. A prudent conclusion, then, is that the validity of the method depends on both discrete information representation and discrete information transmission.

The second major conclusion we have drawn from Miller's presentation is that it is extremely difficult to discriminate between discrete and continuous models on the basis of RT measures alone. In this respect, the distinction between discrete and continuous strongly resembles the serial–parallel distinction. In a mathematical analysis, Townsend (1971) has shown that virtually any parallel model can be translated into a serial model and most parallel models can predict results that are compatible with serial models. It should be noted, however, that the serial–parallel distinction differs from the discrete–continuous distinction in that the former is applied to independent processes within a stage whereas the latter is applied to different, but logically contingent, stages (cf. Miller, 1988). Townsend's proof is therefore not necessarily valid for discrete stage models.

Early in the rebirth of interest in mental chronometry in the 1960s, some investigators also concluded that RT measures alone were unable to articulate the structure and timing of mental processing. They turned to measures of physiological response systems to supplement behavioral measures (see review by Hohle, 1967). These investigators dissected the choice reaction process into a set of hypothetically distinct components: stimulus–afferent events–central sensory events–central decision events–central motor events–efferent events–motor response. Their goal was to identify those component latencies that were directly measurable and those that were not. The measurable portions can then be subtracted out from total RT to obtain an estimate of the 'unmeasurable' portion. Two portions of RT are relatively easily accessible. At the perceptual side, the duration between stimulus onset and the initial evoked potential in the cortex was estimated to be about 50 ms, depending upon stimulus modality and intensity. At the motor side, the interval between the first muscle action potentials recorded from the effector (e.g. forearm) and the overt response (e.g. finger closure of a switch) was found to be also of the order of 50 ms. Hohle reasoned that, if we allow about 20 or 30 ms for efferent nerve conduction, there is not much time available for central processing. In simple RT tasks, yielding an average response speed of about 180 ms, the time left for central processing would be only 50–60 ms. In choice RT tasks, however, total RT is increased by at least another 100 ms. Hohle concluded that it would be unreasonable to attribute this increase to effects on peripheral events. Hence, the more interesting task variables have an effect on central perceptual, decision making, and motor processing. Thus, the processes underlying RT that are of greatest interest to the chronometrician are also the least accessible to direct observation (cf. Hohle, 1967; p. 232).

Recent refinements in psychophysiological theory and methodology suggested to cognitive psychologists that it would now be possible to measure the timing of peripheral and central physiological events during the foreperiod of an RT task and as a mental reaction evolves. This offers an obvious benefit to the mental chronometrician—a physiological record is provided of mental events as they emerge, unlike measures of response latency and accuracy that represent the final common output of the reaction. Quite simple reasoning has motivated the use of one set of psychophysiological measures, ERPs, in studies of mental chronometry: Since cognitive processing is implemented in the brain and this processing is manifested by brain events that are recorded on the scalp, it makes sense to examine these scalp signals in chronometric paradigms (cf. Coles, 1989). To arrive at this point, however, required several years of research establishing the experimental factors that affect the properties of these signals. The nexus between mental chronometry and other psychophysiological measures is less obvious, however. In the remainder of this chapter, we shall first review research that provided the essential validation for the application of psychophysiological measures into the domain of mental chronometry, then discuss studies in which psychophysiological measures have been used to augment behavioral measures of mental chronometry, and last discuss the problems and prospects of chronopsychophysiology.

ANTECEDENTS OF PSYCHOPHYSIOLOGICAL TIME MARKERS

The point should be made at the outset of this section that psychophysiologists have not been responsible for formulating models of mental chronometry. All of the models they have studied to date are those that have been developed on the basis of reaction time studies. Recent contributions from psychophysiologists have been tests of these models. This can be explained in large part by the fact that, following the discovery of non-invasive methods for obtaining physiological measures, much of the early and ongoing work has been to determine the factors that control variability in the measures. This in turn has led to research whose aim is to determine the cognitive functions indexed by these various psychophysiological measures, and to psychophysiological studies of mental chronometry. We turn our attention to the former two types of studies in this section. In the next section we address the question of how these various psychophysiological measures can be used to test models of mental chronometry or to provide converging evidence for these models.

Our discussion focuses on three types of psychophysiological measures; two from the autonomic nervous system (heart rate and pupil dilation) and one from the central nervous system (ERPs). ERPs provide obvious manifestations of mental processing whose temporal resolution satisfies the needs of chronometric analyses. Thus, reasonably precise inferences can be drawn about the temporal organization of the components of a mental reaction and the influences of experimental factors on this timing. Measures of heart rate (HR) response and pupil dilation do not provide the same degree of temporal resolution, but they may provide information about the activation level of processing elements when the subject is preparing for the arrival of a stimulus and executing a response to it. We shall begin by presenting a brief history of these measures and their antecedents in the RT paradigm.

HEART RATE

The heart provides muscle to the cardiovascular system. It is responsible for pumping blood through an organism whose need for fresh blood may be changing constantly. To perform its task efficiently, the heart receives information from chemical and pressure receptors that it uses to adjust its rate, contractile force, output, and blood flow to the vascular networks. From a chronometric perspective, our primary interest is in heart rate. An obvious advantage of measuring changes in HR is that it is very easy to do. Thus, it is not surprising that HR is undoubtedly the most widely used of all psychophysiological measures. But the reader should bear in mind that changes in rate provide only a very limited view of the complexities of the cardiovascular–behavioral interaction.

When HR is used as a physiological marker of information processing activity, it is important to understand how the cardiovascular control systems interact with brain regions. Korner's (1979) excellent review suggests that projections from relatively autonomous cardiac control systems innervate various sites in the brain and in turn receive innervation from a number of brain regions. The main inputs for the cardiovascular regulatory center in the medulla are the primary afferents from the baroreceptors, chemoreceptors and lung inflation receptors that enter the medulla through the ninth and tenth cranial nerves. After entering the medulla, the nerves relay through the nucleus of the tractus solitarius, a complex integrative zone and the major site for receiving arterial baroreceptor afferents. Although the exact course of the ascending projections of the cardiorespiratory receptors is not known, several units in the hypothalamus have been identified that respond to baroreceptor stimulation. Conversely, rises in HR have been elicited by stimulating many discrete regions in the hypothalamus—this effect is more pronounced for right-side stimulation. A marked slowing in HR can be elicited by stimulating the anterior part of the hypothalamus, an area that receives arterial baroreceptor inputs. At still higher levels, stimulation of the carotid sinus nerve and vagal afferents has been found to alter the EEG. Conversely, electrical stimulation of different cortical areas—sensorimotor, orbital, and temporal sites—produces reliable changes in blood pressure and HR. The cerebellum is also involved in cardiovascular control. After cerebellectomy, baroreflexes and HR have been observed to change dramatically. Korner's overview of the heart–brain interaction indicates that HR can be influenced by a variety of inputs from different levels of the brain. It should be noted that simultaneous changes in the activity of two or more inputs to the central nervous system can elicit an HR pattern through the activation of relatively independent pathways or through the interactions between two or more pathways. Thus, under virtually all real life conditions HR responses are not simply mediated by autonomous reflexes, but are often nonlinear reactions due to the interactions arising from the complexity of peripheral and central afferents involved in cardiovascular control.

The measurement of HR is based upon the fact that an electrical event is the origin of the heart beat (Noble, 1979). A non-invasive record of the bioelectrical activity in the pumping cardiac muscle is provided by the electrocardiogram (ECG). The electrical impulse that is conducted across the myocardium spreads to the tissue surrounding the heart and then to the body surface. Electrodes properly attached to the body record these currents and translate them in the ECG. The normal ECG consists of waves and intervals. The waves are given a letter designation for uniform identification. The cardiac cycle is initiated by the P-wave that is produced by atrial depolarization and occurs prior to atrial contraction. Ventricular excitation is recorded as the QRS complex, whereas the subsequent T-wave signifies ventricular repolarization. In principle, the ECG may be recorded by measuring the potential differences between any two sites on the body surface.

Computerized HR measurement typically involves the use of a Schmitt trigger to produce an output whenever the voltage of the cardiac signal exceeds a predetermined level. This level is adjusted so that the amplitude discriminator will trigger at the upgoing flank of the R-wave but not at the T- or P-wave. In order to prevent triggering twice during one cardiac cycle, one may use a one-shot trigger set for a delay period greater than the R–T interval. Occasional errors will occur, however. These errors must be detected and trials including errors must be edited or removed (see Weber, Molenaar and van der Molen, in press, for a computer editing technique). After editing the data, the investigator must decide between HR or heart period as the dependent variable. The most common choice is HR measured in real-time units such as seconds or half-seconds. The mean values of all full or partial interbeat intervals (IBIs) during a fixed time interval are weighted according to the fraction of that interval occupied by each and are standardized in terms of beats per minute (bpm). The other cardiac score is heart period which is defined as the length of the IBI and is measured in cardiac-time units (beat-by-beat). Although there may appear to be little difference between HR and heart period, it should be noted that the transformation of heart period to HR is nonlinear. There is some debate about how this transformation might affect the data, but as yet statistical considerations have produced no consensus favoring one cardiac score over another (see Richards, 1980, for a full discussion). For our purposes, the real-time HR measure is more appropriate than the organismic beat-by-beat measure. First, the real time measure ensures that the time of a relevant event—stimulus or response onset—can be referenced as zero. Second, the real-time measure allows comparisons across timed events and other psychophysiological response systems.

The cardiac response is usually examined by event-related averaging. In this procedure, single-trial cardiac activity is averaged across trials and it is assumed that activity not systematically related to the critical processing event (i.e. noise) will average to zero. A straightforward procedure for defining the event-related cardiac response is to take a difference score relative to a pre-event baseline. A wide variety of descriptors of the event-related HR response is possible. One is to take the whole waveform into account—either in second-by-second or beat-by-beat format. Other measures that can be considered are peak and trough magnitudes and latency to peak or trough magnitudes. It should be noted, however, that results from a single response measure may be quite misleading and may generate the wrong conclusions. A simple recommendation is that the researcher should not blindly look for peaks or troughs, but first should explore the individual beat-by-beat responses before deciding upon a particular response parameter.

HR responsivity is frequently expressed in difference scores. Although computing difference scores relative to a pre-event baseline seems to be a reasonably straightforward procedure for characterizing event-related HR change, the investigator must be aware of the fact that change scores may be related to the pre-event baseline. That is, post-event HR may contain variance due not only to the experimental manipulations, but also to the HR level prior to the stimulus or response. Several procedures have been proposed to deal with this problem. One is experimental control of the baseline HR. The experimenter simply waits for the HR to reach a certain intermediate level before presenting the stimulus. However, the baseline may drift slowly to higher or lower levels as the experiment proceeds. Moreover, the initial HR level does not provide a stable baseline but shows considerable variability inherent to the cardiac activity itself. In the resting subject, the HR signal shows cyclic trends, the most important of which is associated with the respiratory cycle. HR decelerates during an expiratory phase and quickens again during inspiration. The event-related cardiac response will be superimposed upon this respiratory sinus arrhythmia. Several methods have been proposed for removing pre-event cyclic trends that may continue during the post-event period. One approach utilizes time series analysis to predict post-event cardiac activity on the basis of pre-event activity, and the event-related cardiac response is then obtained by comparing predicted and observed values. These and other techniques have been discussed in Siddle and Turpin (1980). An even more important concern is that event-related cardiac responses are modulated directly by respiratory activity. This is particularly true for the short latency responses that are observed in the standard reaction time paradigm and are mediated by the vagus. Physiological investigations have demonstrated that cardiac deceleration elicited by baro- or chemoreceptor stimulation depends on the phase of the respiratory cycle; stimulation during early or mid-inspiration does not elicit cardiac slowing, whereas stimulation during expiration produces pronounced decelerations. It has been hypothesized that the vagal influence on the cardiac pacemaker is either gated or modulated by respiration (see for a review Turpin, 1986).

An Historical Overview of Heart Rate Research

The psychophysiological interest in HR can be traced to the work of the Italian physiologist Angelo Mosso (1881) who, in both clinical and experimental studies, tried to establish the relation between organic processes and consciousness. He observed that HR increased during various forms of mental effort and that almost every kind of psychic activity he studied increased blood flow to the brain and decreased it to the periphery. Yet, he did not think that cerebral circulation and psychological processes were closely related. He reasoned that while blood sustains cells its mere presence is not sufficient to sustain their activity. HR acceleration was also reported by other investigators to occur in the presence of intellectual effort as well as with changes in emotional state (Angell and McLennan, 1896; Angell and Thompson, 1899; Binet and Courtier, 1896, 1897; Binet and Sollier, 1895; Binet and Vaschide, 1897). Both Angell and Binet assumed that the intensity of the psychological state, rather than its quality, determined the pattern of autonomic responses. Angell concluded, for example, that classification of psychological states on the basis of their autonomic response patterning was pointless given that all psychological states produce similar autonomic patterns in response to both agreeable and disagreeable stimuli.

Research contemporary with that of Binet and Angell revealed, however, that autonomic reactions to simple stimuli were more variable than those produced by general psychological states. Indeed, some stimuli were observed to elicit an increase in HR while others exerted either the opposite or no effect at all (MacDougall, 1896). Work by Mentz (1895) demonstrated that HR responses varied with the intensity of the stimulus and with the subject's level of attention to the source of stimulation. For example, he reported that HR decreased when the intensity of an auditory stimulus changes from weak to moderate levels, but increased if the transition was from moderate to high intensity. He also observed, however, that this effect was modulated by the subject's attention—these relations held only when the subject's attention was captured involuntarily by the auditory stimulus. With voluntary attention, the stimulus produced accelerations in HR, without exception. Mentz also replicated the finding that HR varies with changes in the respiratory cycle; HR accelerates with inspiration and decelerates with expiration. This relationship was first established by Donders (1868b), who demonstrated that respiratory sinus arrhythmia is mediated by the vagus nerve and established that vagal input to the heart depends critically on the timing of the cardiac cycle.

While most of the psychophysiological studies done at this time were aimed at classifying mental states on the basis of differential autonomic patterns, some investigators examined the relation between RT performance and natural variations in cardiovascular functioning. Van Biervliet (1894), for example, reported that RT shortened in some individuals when heart period lengthened, but that in general there was considerable variability among individuals. Similarly, Patrizi (1896) investigated the relation between response speed and cerebral perfusion and found only a 12 ms difference in RT between minimum and maximum perfusion. He concluded from this that such a small difference provided little support for a close relation between cerebral perfusion and attention, if there is any relation at all.

Darrow's (1924) frequently cited review of the early literature suggested a basic dichotomy underlying HR changes in attention-demanding tasks. Ideational stimuli would produce HR speeding, whereas sensory stimuli were assumed to elicit HR slowing (see also Eng, 1925, cited in Svebak, 1983). This conclusion is based, however, on findings that are inconsistent. Although mental elaboration of stimuli might consistently produce HR acceleration, the cardiac response to sensory stimuli is unpredictable. Thus, most investigators followed in the footsteps of Binet. Their investigations aimed at describing the relation between physiological response patterning and the intensity of psychic states, not their quality. Indeed, Cannon (1915) suggested that a general energy dimension underlies the physiological response patterns associated with emotions. Davis and coworkers, for example, described a general response pattern elicited by sensory stimuli that consists of an increase in muscle tension, HR, sweat gland activity, respiration rate, and vasoconstriction (see for an overview Davis, Buchwald and Frankman, 1955). They noted that this pattern is almost identical to the response complex that can be observed in emergency reactions and during exercise.

These and similar findings led to the formulation of the concept of activation (see Duffy, 1972, for a review). The activation concept was proposed to provide a unified framework for explaining the effects of simple stimuli, emotional states and mental work on physiological response systems. The activation concept refers to a generalized response of the individual, independent of the nature of the stimulation and the uniqueness of the individual. Activation was thought of as the 'energizer' of behavior and was described as a massive response of the sympathetic branch of the nervous system. HR, along with other peripheral measures, was considered an index of the degree of activation. The concept of activation led to a reformulation of Patrizi's and Biervliet's prediction. It was assumed that RT would vary as a function of the subject's state of activation. Duffy (1972; p. 602) referred to a study performed by Atkins (1964) showing that oscillations in response speed directly follow diurnal variations in pulse rate—slower responses being associated with lower pulse rates.

A continuing problem for activation theory was the recurrent finding of poor correlations among peripheral measures assumed to index the same general arousal state. At first, low or non-significant correlations were attributed to imperfect measurement (e.g. Duffy, 1972). Lacey (1959), however, noted examples of what he called 'directional fractionation of response' in which the direction of change in one physiological system is contrary to what might be expected from unidimensional activation theory. Specifically, the directional fractionation consisted of instances in which skin conductance increased but HR decreased. A speeding of HR occurred under conditions that required mental elaboration, whereas slower HRs were typically observed when the subject paid attention to external stimuli. (Note the resemblance between the Lacey hypothesis and both Darrow's ideational and sensory conditions and the early pioneers' distinction between voluntary and involuntary attention.) Skin conductance increased independent of the task requirements. Lacey claimed that activation theory cannot account for this disparity. Activation should produce palmar sweating and HR acceleration in both conditions. According to Lacey, the basic dimension underlying HR changes in attention-demanding tasks is 'intake-rejection', not activation. Lacey's claim was supported by subsequent studies that led him to hypothesize that HR acceleration accompanies and perhaps even facilitates mental work, whereas cardiac slowing is associated with the intake of sensory information and might perhaps facilitate the detection of simple stimuli (e.g. Lacey *et al.*, 1963).

In their early studies (e.g. Lacey, J.I. *et al.*, 1963), the Laceys averaged across consecutive IBIs so that the reference time base was at least a minute. In later studies, the focus of the analyses shifted from tonic to phasic measures. Typically, the relation between HR and psychic state was examined by employing a signaled RT task, wherein a first stimulus acts as a warning signal for the second, imperative stimulus. The HR response occurring in this paradigm was analyzed on a beat-by-beat basis and was observed to consist of three components (see Figure 1.5 for a prototypical response): a small and brief deceleration following the warning stimulus; a more pronounced and longer-lasting deceleration reaching its nadir at some point in time near the onset of the imperative stimulus; and an acceleratory recovery following the subject's motor response to the second stimulus (e.g. Lacey, J.I. and Lacey, B.C., 1970). When the time interval between the first and the second stimulus was lengthened, the second deceleration continued to be time-locked to the imperative stimulus. This finding is important in suggesting that the second deceleratory component is an anticipatory response to the imperative stimulus, not a reflex-like response to the warning stimulus. Accordingly, the Laceys associated the time-locked deceleratory cardiac response with the subject's intention to note and detect environmental input.

In a series of subsequent studies, the Laceys observed that the depth of anticipatory deceleration preceding the imperative stimulus was positively related to the speed of the subject's motor response to the stimulus (e.g. Lacey, B. C. and Lacey, J.I., 1974). They interpreted this finding in terms of the intake-

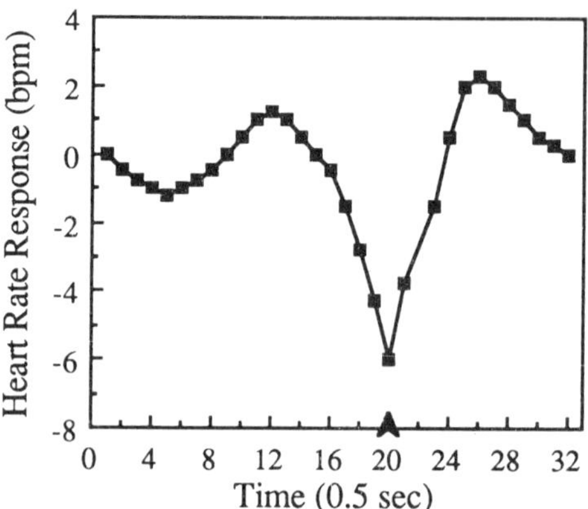

Figure 1.5. Prototypical heart rate response as it occurs during the foreperiod of a signaled reaction-time task. The warning signal elicits a small heart rate deceleration that is followed by an increase in heart rate and then a second deceleration that reaches its nadir at about the time at which the imperative stimulus is presented (indicated by the arrowhead). The heart rate response is expressed in difference scores relative to a pre-warning baseline.

rejection hypothesis they had formulated previously to explain their tonic HR findings (e.g. Lacey, J.I., 1967). This hypothesis suggests that HR slowing directly influences attention through the effect of baroreceptor changes on cortical arousal. More specifically, heart rate decreases in anticipation of the RT stimulus, and this slowing reduces the pressure on the baroreceptors, decreasing their rate of firing. This decrease results in a lowering of sensory thresholds, a prolongation of the impact of stimuli, and an increase in spontaneous activity. The Laceys assume that this state of cortical activation facilitates the sensorimotor integration that is required in the typical RT task.

The Laceys suggested that averaging across several heart beats, as was done in their earlier studies, might conceal important phenomena. They observed that it is the HR at, or immediately prior to, the imperative stimulus that is most closely associated with response speed. With increasing remoteness, the HR–response speed relationship breaks down. This principle of 'temporal proximity' made the Laceys focus on a single cardiac cycle. In one of their studies (Lacey, B.C. and Lacey, J.I., 1974), they analyzed the effect of the relative timing of presentations of the imperative and the warning stimuli in the cardiac cycle *vis-à-vis* a control point. They observed that imperative stimuli occurring early in the cycle (i.e. stimuli close to the R-wave initiating the cardiac cycle of their occurrence) seem to prolong the IBI during which they occurred. Late stimuli, in contrast, exerted their effect on the subsequent IBI, not on the concurrent IBI. This 'cardiac-cycle-time-effect' they called 'primary bradycardia', and was absent for warning stimuli and no significant trends were observed for the control point (see Figure 1.6). In seeking an explanation for these cardiac cycle time dependencies, the Laceys assumed that early stimuli lengthen their cycle more rather than shorten it less. This would be congruent with the idea that stimulus intake is associated with HR deceleration. It would also be in accordance with evidence from cardiovascular physiology that implicates the vagal nerve as the final common pathway for cardiac cycle time effects. On the basis of animal work, the Laceys submitted that in RT tasks vagal control is prepotent over sympathetic control, and that vagal, but not sympathetic, control can produce such prompt changes in HR (see the next section for a more detailed exposition of the neural control of HR).

In one of their later studies (Lacey, B.C. and Lacey, J.I., 1980), the Laceys presented a graph depicting the results of an earlier RT experiment (see Figure 1.7). In this study, imperative stimuli were presented either at the R-wave or 350 ms later. Their figure shows that prolonging the cycle time of the imperative stimulus by 350 ms results in a lengthening of the concurrent IBI. On the face of it, these results seem inconsistent with their findings indicating longer cycles with earlier stimuli. The Laceys pointed out, however, that the morphology of the cardiac cycle time function is critically dependent on the length of the cycle. Subjects with a fast pulse will show a linear trend, whereas subjects with a slow HR usually produce the bitonic trend.

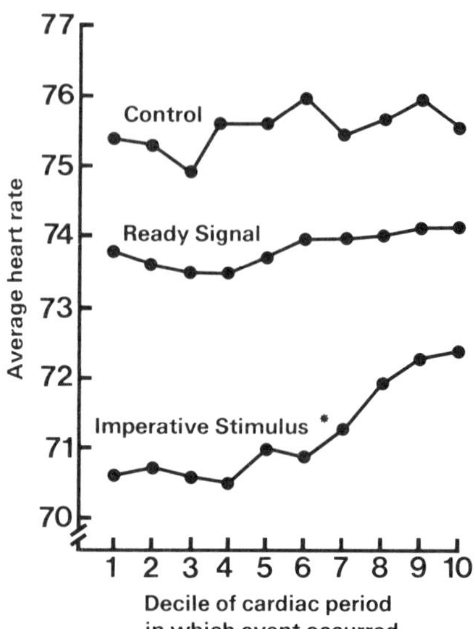

Figure 1.6. The relationship of momentary heart rate level to the cardiac cycle time of event occurrence (i.e. R-wave-to-event interval) reported by Lacey, B.C. and Lacey, J.I. (1974). The asterisk indicates that significance was obtained for imperative stimuli only. Reprinted with permission of the authors and publisher. Copyright 1974 Aldine Publishing Co.

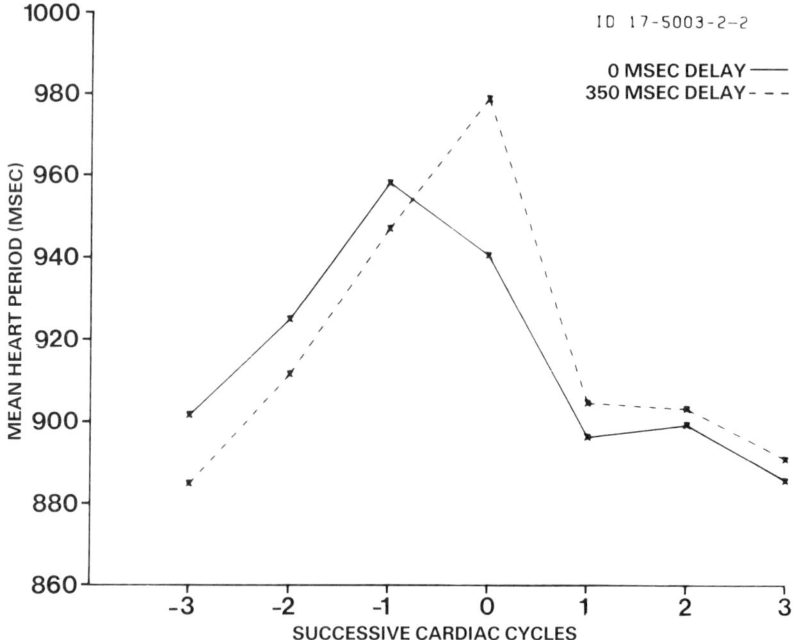

Figure 1.7. Mean heart period from three cardiac cycles before to three cycles after an auditory imperative stimulus for a single subject in a study by Lacey, J.I. and Lacey, B.C. (1980). The cycle in which the stimulus fell is labeled 0. (Reprinted with permission of the authors and publisher. © 1980 Academic Press.)

Jennings and Wood (1977) offered an alternative explanation. They reasoned that in RT tasks early stimuli are typically associated with early motor responses and late stimuli with late motor responses. It could be possible, then, that responses exert an effect of their own in addition to the effect elicited by stimuli. They addressed this possibility by performing an experiment in which the cycle times of stimuli and responses were varied independently. Stimuli were presented at the R-wave or 350 ms later, as in the Laceys' study, but, in contrast to the Laceys' study, subjects were instructed to carefully time their responses to the stimuli according to five time bands, ranging from 150 to 350 ms in steps of 50 ms. Thus, the cardiac cycle time of the response was controlled at ten different points, ranging from 150 to 700 ms after the R-wave. They analyzed their data first for stimulus timing and then for response timing *vis-à-vis* the cardiac cycle. Their stimulus analysis showed a bitonic trend similar to the findings obtained by the Laceys. However, when they analyzed response timing and kept stimulus time constant, they observed that early responses (i.e. responses occurring within 350 ms after the R-wave) were associated with a shortening of the IBI, whereas later responses were associated with a lengthening of the cardiac cycle. Jennings and Wood offered a 'vagal inhibition' hypothesis to explain their findings. The hypothesis assumes that vagal discharges to the cardiac pacemaker are not uniformly distributed across the time interval of the cardiac cycle. Based on the animal literature, it was suggested that the bulk of vagal activity occurs around 300 ms post R-wave. The hypothesis further assumes that task termination occurring early in the cardiac cycle 'inhibits' the vagal input to the heart and in so doing prevents HR slowing. For later responses, the vagal discharges leading to cardiac slowing have already occurred; the effect of these responses will be observed during the subsequent beat.

In sum, in the HR literature three measures have been developed that may be of potential value in chronometric analyses of mental events: (1) anticipatory HR deceleration; (2) primary bradycardia (a stimulus-related cardiac-cycle time effect); and (3) vagal inhibition (a response-related cardiac-cycle time effect). It should be noted, however, that these measures evolved from research that was directed primarily at the issue of how directional HR changes might differentiate among attentional states along the 'intake-rejection' dimension (Lacey, B.C. and Lacey, J.I., 1974), or, in the language of the early pioneers, along the 'involuntary–voluntary attention' dimension (e.g. Mentz, 1895). It remains to be seen whether the chronometrician interested in speeded performance will be able to gain useful insights from a psychophysiological measure that (a) is more compatible with a capacity than a chronometric view of the mind; and (b) has a resolution of seconds rather than milliseconds. These issues will be addressed later in this chapter. We now briefly summarize the antecedents of HR change in the RT paradigm.

Antecedents of Heart Rate Change in the Reaction Time Paradigm

The Laceys' hypothesis, that HR changes differentially on the basis of whether subjects prepare for stimulus intake or for stimulus rejection, promoted the use of differential HR change as an indicator of attention in areas as divergent as orienting (Kimmel, Van Olst and Orlebeke, 1979), infancy research (e.g. Richards, 1988), individual differences and psychopathology (e.g. Gale and Edwards, 1986), stress and performance (e.g. Orlebeke, Mulder and Van Doornen, 1985), and information processing (e.g. Kahneman, 1973). In this subsection we will focus on HR changes typically observed in speeded performance tasks. Our goal is to illustrate the effects of RT task variables on cardiac activity, not to present an extensive review. The recent literature on HR changes during information processing has been discussed in two excellent reviews by Jennings (1986a,b).

We saw in Figure 1.5 that in a signaled RT task, HR decelerates, accelerates again, and then shows a beat-by-beat deceleration that reaches its nadir at the time of the stimulus and response. If the foreperiod is lengthened, HR continues to slow down until the presentation of the imperative stimulus (cf. Bohlin and Kjellberg, 1979). This finding was taken to suggest that HR deceleration prior to the imperative stimulus is not a reflex elicited by the warning stimulus, but reflects the subject's preparation to detect the stimulus and to execute a speeded motor response (Lacey, B.C. and Lacey, J.I., 1974).

The effect of perceptual task demands on anticipatory HR deceleration has been assessed in a number of studies. Unfortunately, however, these studies have yielded inconsistent results. Some suggest a positive relation between the depth of anticipatory deceleration and the difficulty of perceptual analysis, but others do not. In a series of experiments, Coles and Duncan-Johnson reported that anticipatory cardiac deceleration increased as discriminability of the imperative stimulus decreased, but that this effect was not apparent when the levels of difficulty were blocked (Coles, 1974; Duncan-Johnson and Coles, 1974; Coles and Duncan-Johnson, 1977). Also, deeper decelerations may be produced by short than by long duration stimuli (Simons, Ohman and Lang, 1979) and may be associated with correct detections of visually faint stimuli (Schell and Catania, 1975). In contrast, anticipatory HR deceleration has been reported not to be affected by stimulus discrimination in RT tasks (Connor and Lang, 1969; Higgins, 1971; Meyers and Obrist, 1973). Indeed, greater decelerations have been reported in RT tasks when there was no need for discrimination as opposed to when discrimination was required (Lawler, Obrist and Lawler, 1976).

Heart rate studies manipulating response selection are relatively scarce. An early study by Walter and Porges (1976) varied the number of response alternatives (no choice, three or five choices). They found a greater anticipatory deceleration for the simple task than for the choice tasks. The effect of variation in response output requirements has been investigated most often. These studies have produced inconsistent results. In an early study, Chase, Graham and Graham (1968) found that HR acceleration occurred prior to the production of a leg lift or a button press in a choice reaction, but that deceleration occurred prior to the button press only. Graham (1979) later interpreted the effect of motor requirements on the acceleratory HR component as support for the hypothesis that anticipatory acceleration facilitates motor preparation, whereas anticipatory deceleration facilitates sensory intake. Brunia and Damen (1985) failed, however, to find an effect of response type (finger, foot, eyelid or verbal response) on the preparatory response. They suggested that the deceleration prior to the response reflects response intention and is not related to the particular response to be made. Similarly, van der Molen *et al.* (1985) failed to obtain an effect of response complexity (straight tracing versus maze tracing response) while it was expected, following the Laceys' hypothesis, that preparing for a complex movement would contribute a strong deceleratory trend in the cardiac response. Finally, in a recent study, Jennings *et al.* (1990) found that variations in response force requirements did not affect the preparatory cardiac response.

Numerous studies have been performed that manipulated the time interval between the warning stimulus and the imperative stimulus. Time uncertainty was considered a powerful manipulation of attention and HR changes during the foreperiod and were assumed to covary with the time course of attention. Typically, greater decelerations have been observed when the foreperiod is lengthened (e.g. van der Molen *et al.*, 1985). These findings have been interpreted to suggest that the magnitude of anticipatory deceleration provides an index of expectancy; the greater uncertainty about the time of stimulus occurrence or stimulus type, the greater the HR deceleration preceding the stimulus (cf. Bohlin and Kjellberg, 1979). This interpretation has been questioned by results reported by van der Molen, Somsen and Orlebeke (1983). They varied the length of the foreperiod but presented a leading stimulus, providing an extra time-cue, just prior to the imperative stimulus. Thus, the time interval was lengthened while time uncertainty remained constant. RT did not differentiate between foreperiod conditions, suggesting that foreperiod lengthening did not substantially increase the subject's uncertainty. HR deceleration was considerably greater, however, in longer than in shorter foreperiod conditions. This finding indicates that lengthening the foreperiod has at leasts two effects: (1) it may increase temporal uncertainty and this may be associated with HR deceleration; (2) it simply makes more time available for the cardiac response to develop. Thus, a confounding is likely to occur in the typical foreperiod study. One remedy would be to present foreperiod durations in blocked series (inducing relatively little uncertainty) and mixed series (inducing greater uncertainty) and to compare foreperiods of equal length (e.g. van der Molen *et al.*, 1987).

The Laceys' hypothesis assumed that anticipatory HR deceleration facilitates sensorimotor integration in RT tasks. Best–worst analysis has been frequently employed in the HR literature to examine the relation between HR change and response efficiency. A best–worst analysis is a *post hoc* procedure that compares the HR curves obtained on the fastest and slowest response trials. Some studies report greater decelerations preceding faster responses, whereas other studies fail to observe this relationship (e.g. van der Molen *et al.*, 1985). Other investigators have used a reverse procedure. They first manipulated the subject's speed of responding and then compared the HR curve for the different speed conditions employed. Jennings and Wood (1977) obtained greater anticipatory decelerations under speed conditions and a smaller response when instructions emphasized a more relaxed attitude. The Laceys (Lacey, J.I. and Lacey, B.C., 1970) obtained similar effects. On the other hand, Schwartz and Higgins (1971) did not find an effect on anticipatory deceleration by changing speed instructions. Moreover, the opposite relation has been reported by Somsen *et al.*, 1985). These findings exemplify the inconsistent relation between response efficiency and anticipatory cardiac deceleration typically reported in the literature.

When the IBI of stimulus occurrence is selected as the criterion measure for anticipatory deceleration, the researcher should be aware of the fact that this IBI is likely to be determined both by preparatory processes and processing elicited by the stimulus (e.g. Coles and Duncan-Johnson, 1977). To differentiate these two effects, investigators began to select the prestimulus IBI as a measure of anticipatory deceleration and to look at the IBI of the stimulus for stimulus-induced effects. A series of RT studies focused on the IBI of the stimulus and observed that the cycle time of the stimulus (i.e. delay from the R-wave that initiates the stimulus beat) exerts an immediate effect on that same IBI. Early occurring stimuli produce a greater lengthening of the IBI than do later stimuli (see, for example, the van der Molen *et al.*, 1985, review). Coles, Pellegrini and Wilson (1982) tested the Laceys' hypothesis that only information-bearing stimuli elicit primary bradycardia. They varied the degree to which warning and imperative stimuli delivered information about response choice in a signaled choice reaction task and observed that only warning and imperative stimuli delivering information elicited primary bradycardia. The effect was somewhat stronger for imperative than for warning stimuli (a 30 versus 20 ms lengthening). Van der Molen *et al.* (1983) used a choice reaction task in which the warning stimulus provided information about the imperative stimulus. There were three types of trials. On NoGo trials subjects knew in advance that no response was required to the forthcoming imperative signal. On the other trials, this information was delivered at the onset of the

imperative stimulus. On some trials, subjects were required to execute a motor response to the stimulus (Go trials), whereas on other trials they had to refrain from responding (Catch trials). Primary bradycardia was observed on Go and Catch trials but not on NoGo trials. Thus, available primary bradycardia results indicate that the coupling of a motor response to the stimulus is not a critical determinant of primary bradycardia. It seems to be the information that a stimulus conveys which determines whether or not primary bradycardia will be elicited.

Anticipatory HR deceleration and stimulus-elicited primary bradycardia are not the only determinants of the IBI of stimulus occurrence. Acceleratory changes related to the motor response may also contribute to determining the length of the cardiac cycle. Jennings and Wood (1977) observed that early responses (i.e. responses occurring not later than 350 ms after the R-wave initiating the cardiac cycle of stimulus occurrence) result in a shortening of the IBI. In subsequent studies, Jennings and colleagues (e.g. Jennings, van der Molen, and Brock, 1988) demonstrated that the acceleratory change induced by the response prevents the stimulus-elicited primary bradycardia from occurring. It should be noted that the execution of a motor response is not necessary for the occurrence of the shift from anticipatory deceleration to acceleration. The shift also occurs when subjects are instructed to give 'thought' responses, and even when they are not responding at all, on a catch trial or when the reaction stimulus is omitted (see van der Molen *et al.*, 1985, review). Hence, Jennings and Wood proposed that the timing of the shift from anticipatory deceleration to acceleratory recovery is related to task completion *vis-à-vis* the cardiac cycle. Jennings (1985, 1986a,b) proposed a capacity view of the initiation and termination of anticipatory HR deceleration. According to this view, anticipatory deceleration is a manifestation of holding processing capacity available. During focused temporal anticipation—such as that produced by the foreperiod of an RT task—efficient performance requires that the subject gets ready to receive and act upon task relevant information at the appropriate time. Competing processes must be inhibited. This requires establishing a priority of one set of processes over another. Thus, the initiation and termination of HR deceleration is assumed to reflect a shift in attentional priorities. It is argued that the precise timing of the termination of anticipatory deceleration may be useful in timing the regulation of attention during information processing. Note that Jennings' capacity formulation emphasizes the time course of phasic HR change rather than the amplitude of these changes, as do most other psychophysiological interpretations of HR change. In this respect, Jennings' view is more compatible with the goal of mental chronometry. If the analysis of HR change would provide a continuous measure of the deployment of information processing mechanisms, then the investigator would be able to gain insights that cannot be gained from the latency and accuracy of button press responses. In the next subsection, we will develop in more detail how the analysis of phasic HR change may supplement RT and error measures in the study of mental chronometry.

Preliminary Steps to a Mental Chronometry using Heart Rate

In a recent review of cardiac-cycle time effects, Coles and Strayer (1985) proposed a model which relates cardiac-cycle time effects and other phasic HR changes to information processing activity that is believed to occur in signaled choice RT tasks. In such tasks, the warning stimulus has to be encoded first, followed by a period of subsequent elaboration of the information conveyed by the warning stimulus. Next, the subject prepares for the imperative stimulus. When the imperative stimulus arrives, it must be encoded and its features analyzed. After the stimulus has been identified, the response it signals must be selected and then executed. The flow of information processing activities is depicted in the upper part of Figure 1.8. In the lower part of the figure, the HR

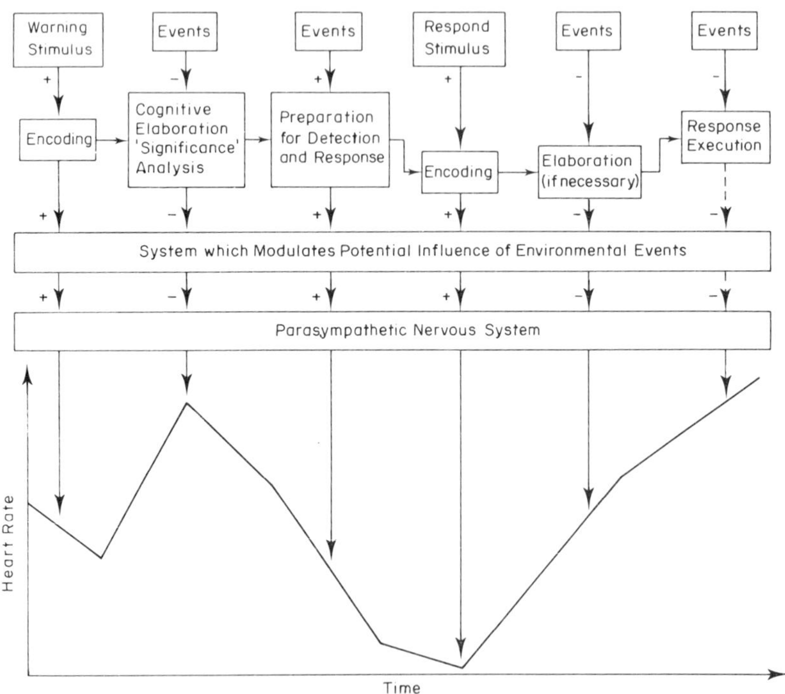

Figure 1.8. The Coles and Strayer (1985) model relating environmental events, information processing activity, vagal activity, and phasic heart rate changes to a system that modulates the potential influence of environmental events on the information processing structure. (Reprinted with permission of the authors and publisher. © 1985 Plenum Publishing Co.)

changes are depicted that are typically observed when subjects are performing a signaled-choice RT task. Encoding of the warning stimulus is associated with a brief slowing of HR, followed by HR speeding which is assumed to be associated with subsequent analysis of the significance of the signal. HR acceleration is then followed by a more pronounced deceleratory component associated with the subject's readiness to detect and to respond to the imperative signal. The respond signal is encoded, accompanied by a brief deceleratory trend, and then analyzed, perhaps contributing an acceleratory response. The execution of the motor response is associated with an acceleratory response to baseline.

The middle part of the panel contains two systems relating information processing activities to HR changes. The lower system refers to the physiological mechanism underlying the HR changes observed in RT performance. As indicated later in our discussion of the validation of pupil dilation, the phasic HR responses observed in signaled RT tasks are relatively insensitive to sympathetic blocking agents while their sensitivity to respiratory influences makes it reasonable to assume that they are all under vagal control. The second system is proposed to modulate environmental influences on the information processing structure. This system is the most distinctive feature of the Coles and Strayer model. It is a reformulation of Donchin's (1981) 'subroutine' metaphor that incorporates the Laceys' (Lacey, J.I. *et al.*, 1963) intake-rejection hypothesis. Donchin proposed the 'subroutine' metaphor to explain the consistent effects of certain experimental manipulations on certain components of the ERP. He assumed that the consistent response of a component to a class of experimental manipulations reflects the fact that it is invoked only when a distinct element—'subroutine'—of the information processing system is engaged. (For a full discussion of the subroutine metaphor and its more recent successor, the 'whirring noise' analogy, the interested reader is referred to Donchin *et al.* (1986) and Donchin and Coles (1988), respectively.) Coles and Strayer adopted the subroutine metaphor to propose that positive or negative changes in vagal influence occur when positive or negative calls are made to the subroutine that modulates the potential influence of environmental events on the information processing structure (cf. Coles and Strayer, 1986; p. 531). For example, when encoding or preparatory processes are activated, a positive call is made to the subroutine (manifested by HR deceleration) and an increase in sensitivity to external events results. During periods of cognitive elaboration, a negative call is made to the subroutine (manifested by HR acceleration) and this produces an increase in sensory thresholds to protect the system from environmental interference.

The Coles and Strayer model provides an elegant framework for interpreting HR changes as they occur during the performance of speeded RT tasks. The charm of the model, however, does not exempt it from a critical analysis. Thus, we offer a caveat concerning the linkage of the subroutine metaphor to the Laceys' intake-rejection hypothesis. This caveat extends beyond the HR literature to include cognitive psychophysiology as a whole. It should be stressed that Donchin and his colleagues proposed the subroutine metaphor because of their objections to attempts to explain the functional significance of ERP components by recourse to broad psychological constructs such as 'attention', 'decision' or 'surprise' (cf. Donchin *et al.*, 1986). The naivete of correlating psychophysiological responses with global descriptions of the information processing apparatus like these is not very different from the proposal that RT is, for example, a measure of fatigue when it is observed to slow at the end of a day's testing or that error rate is an index of distractibility when it is seen to increase when stimulus displays are noisy. To lend more precision to their theory building, Donchin and his coworkers used the metaphor of the subroutine to refer to the specific functional activities reflected in an ERP component. Within this context, an individual component is the expression of the activity of a specific information processor, not of its output. The outputs of each subroutine are viewed by these investigators as being framed in the internal codes of the information processing system. Likewise, and perhaps even more obviously for HR, the electrical activity that is measured at the surface of the body may reflect the invocation of a particular subroutine, not its output. According to Donchin and colleagues, the cognitive psychophysiologist's task is to provide a parsimonious summary of the antecedent conditions that elicit the component (i.e. discover the factors that invoke the hypothesized subroutine), to characterize the functional significance of the component (i.e. determine the transactions performed by the subroutine) and link the production of the component on the scalp to the activation of specific neural structures, and to articulate the consequences of the invocation of the processes that produce the component.

Considerable effort in psychophysiology has been expended to identify the antecedent conditions that produce a particular electrical response. And, this has proven to be a formidable challenge. In the ERP literature, for example, the conditions controlling the activation of the hypothetical subroutine that is manifested by the P300 have been summarized by Donchin and his colleagues under the broad and reasonably abstract category of 'context updating' (Donchin and Coles, 1988). They have grouped the perplexing variety of task manipulations that elicit the P300 on the basis of stimulus significance. Stimuli thus defined elicit the P300 and the subroutine it manifests is invoked only when the significant stimulus has been adequately categorized. Once categorized, the stimulus information is then used to '...update the mental model (or schema) that humans maintain of the environment' (Donchin *et al.*, 1986; p. 256). For HR changes observed in RT tasks, Coles and Strayer partitioned the antecedent conditions into a simple dichotomy: conditions of external- versus internal-directed attention. Our caveat is directed at the danger inherent in summarizing the antecedents of psychophysiological responses. The obvious danger is that global categories may obscure important between-task differences. There is always the possibility that in going from one task to another, the subroutine does not remain the same.

The following example can be used to illustrate this point. The paradigm that has been used most frequently to elicit anticipatory HR deceleration is the so-called 'two-stimulus' or 'S1–S2' paradigm, in which S1 acts as a warning for S2. This paradigm has been used in conjunction with a great variety of tasks ranging from conditioning to information processing. Without exception, anticipatory HR deceleration has been observed to occur prior to S2, whether it is an electric shock or an imperative stimulus, and this has been taken to suggest that anticipatory HR deceleration is associated with 'expectancy' (e.g. Bohlin and Kjellberg, 1979). Thus, invocation of the subroutine whose activities are expressed by a deceleration in HR appears to play a role whenever subjects are preparing for a significant stimulus. Indeed, it seems reasonable to assume commonality of processing during the S1–S2 interval in a wide range of tasks. It seems less reasonable, however, to assume that only common features, but no differences, exist between tasks. Previously, we have shown that in going from an unavoidable shock task to a conventional RT task (with two intermediate tasks), the pattern of HR changes observed during the S1–S2 interval changed (Somsen, van der Molen and Orlebeke, 1983). Although all of the tasks showed the prototypical triphasic HR response, the unavoidable shock task elicited a more pronounced anticipatory deceleration than did the conventional RT task, apparently at the cost of the preceding acceleratory trend. The intermediate tasks produced intermediate patterns.

Our point in stressing differences in psychophysiological responses between tasks, and the importance of those differences *vis-à-vis* summary statements regarding the functional significance of the subroutine that might have been implemented in all of the different tasks, may be understood best by recalling Külpe's criticism of Donders' subtraction method—when using the subtraction method to estimate the duration of a particular processing stage the investigator runs the risk that the mental reactions engaged by two comparison tasks do not differ simply on the basis of an added or deleted stage, but may be fundamentally different reactions. Here we are arguing that in reducing the multiplicity of conditions eliciting a particular psychophysiological response the investigator runs the risk of overemphasizing task similarities at the expense of task differences.

In the RT literature, the AFM has been proposed as an alternative to subtracting mean RTs obtained in different tasks. The AFM involves a factorial combination of different task variables, not a comparison of different tasks. In previous work, we took Külpe's lesson seriously and proposed a similar strategy to avoid unjustified generalizations in interpreting the functional significance of psychophysiological responses (van der Molen *et al.*, 1985). In the reaction time literature, the AFM has been used not only to discover new processing stages, but also to determine the stages affected by the introduction of new task variables. It is in the latter sense that we suggested using the AFM in cognitive psychophysiology. Consider an experimental design comprising a factorial combination of two variables in a choice RT task. Suppose that these two factors have additive effects on mean RT. According to the additive factors logic, this pattern of results indicates that the two factors influence the duration of different stages. Let us assume further that, in addition to RT, the investigator obtained a psychophysiological measure that was influenced by one, but not the other task variable. This finding would strongly suggest that the psychophysiological measure is sensitive to the activity of the processing stage influenced by that particular task variable, but not to the activity of the processing stage affected by the other task variable. Thus, the AFM allows more precise inferences about the critical task variables for particular changes in psychophysiological response systems. Moreover, the choice reaction domain of the AFM also provides interpretations of the functional significance of psychophysiological responses in terms that have direct links to information processing concepts (see McCarthy and Donchin, 1981, for an example of this reasoning applied to P300 latency and RT). In contrast, unwarranted generalizations across tasks in an attempt to reduce the multiplicity of conditions eliciting a particular psychophysiological response might easily lead to global concepts that have no relation whatsoever with information processing constructs. This criticism has been directed at the concept of 'stimulus evaluation' formulated to account for changes in the timing of the P300 component of the ERP (e.g. Sanders, 1990).

The Somsen *et al.* (1983) results can also be used to make a related point. They indicate that focusing analytic attention on single peaks and troughs of the HR response may only be of limited value. The increase in anticipatory deceleration observed on the shock tasks was associated with a reduction of the preceding acceleratory response. Thus, HR patterns should be examined in the context of the total pattern of the cardiac response evoked by the processing demands of the task. In the Coles and Strayer (1985) scheme, information processing elements such as the preparation for stimulus detection and response preparation, stimulus encoding, and further elaboration of the stimulus, are organized serially, as are the HR changes that accompany the activity of the different processing elements. Positive and negative calls to the subroutine are scheduled in a strict sequence. It may be, however, that information processing components are implemented simultaneously and induce opposing changes in HR. The Laceys (1974) observed vectorial response patterns when a task induced opposing HR trends. Others have observed dominance of one trend over the other (e.g. Jennings, 1975; Somsen *et al.*, 1985). The problem of component mixtures is of course by no means unique for the HR literature. Similar problems confront investigators in event-related brain research. Donchin and Heffley (1978) proposed a combined statistical–experimental approach to identify uncorrelated components in psychophysiological waveforms. According to their procedure, the investigator should subject the waveforms to principal component analysis and determine the sensitivity of each of the statistically derived components to experimental task manipulations. Unfortunately, attempts to get around the problem of hybrid response patterns are virtually absent in the HR literature. (But see Siddle and Turpin (1980) who used a time series approach to deal with overlapping long latency HR components, and Jennings *et al.* (in press) who used a technique for differentiating between pre- and poststimulus effects on a single IBI.)

The Somsen *et al.* data were used to illustrate two basic problems that must be solved by psychophysiologists—formulating operational definitions of psychophysiological response components and determining their functional significance. Unfortunately, their data also suggest that psychophysiology has a long way to go before it can provide the mental chronometrician with a set of HR measures that can be used in the stage analysis of speeded performance. Moreover, the time constant of HR changes is relatively slow. The mental chronometrician must resolve processing time in speeded decision-making tasks to the nearest millisecond or, at most, tens of milliseconds. In contrast, in order to detect a change in phasic HR we need at least three IBIs (approximately 2–3 s). Although, cardiac cycle time effects have a better resolution, it is of the order of about 100 ms. Thus, in view of the operational and definitional problems and the tick count of the heart beat, the question may arise whether there is anything the mental chronometrician can learn from measuring HR. We shall return to this issue later.

PUPIL DILATION

The pupil is nothing but a hole. It is the area surrounded by the iris that is composed of two groups of smooth muscle under autonomic nervous system control. One group, the pupillary sphincter, circles the pupil and is activated by parasympathetic fibers originating from the Edinger–Westphal nucleus located in the central core of the midbrain. The other group, the pupillary dilator, is oriented radially in a spoke-like fashion and is activated by sympathetic fibers originating in the superior cervical ganglion that receives its input from a number of autonomic structures via the cilio-spinal center of Budge located in the lower cervical and upper thoracic regions of the spinal cord. The pupillary sphincter and dilator form an antagonistic pair of smooth muscles; the sphincter contracts and the dilator expands the pupillary opening. It is commonly held that pupil diameter is the reflection of the balance of activity between these two muscles. Under most conditions, however, the activity of the pupillary sphincter seems to dominate pupil size (cf. Beatty, 1986).

The use of pupil size in the study of information processing is based on the assumption that pupillary movements reflect more than the reflexive activation of the oculomotor system by the autonomic nervous system, but may also reflect the influences of higher-order central nervous system functions. Although central nervous system contributions to pupillary control have not yet been fully delineated, there are ample connections with hypothalamo-thalamo-cortical centers to suggest that they may be important. Hess (1972), for example, reviewed Russian work showing inextinguishable pupillary dilation in response to repeated stimulation in decorticated animals. He interpreted this to suggest that pupillary dilation has its executive mechanism located at the subcortical level, whereas its regulatory mechanism is located in cortical structures. For a more extensive description of the physiology and innervation of the pupillary system the interested reader is referred to Lowenstein and Loewenfeld (1969). Here it suffices to say that neural traffic moving up and down the reticular formation is likely to have an effect on the autonomic periphery (cf. Beatty, 1982; p. 290).

The measurement of pupil size seems easy. It is one of few psychophysiological indices that is open to unaided observation. However, in his 1975 survey of sources of variation, Tyron listed over 20 sources of error variance in pupillary experiments, the most important being the light- and near-reflex elicited by visual stimuli. An increase in luminance results in constriction, while a decrease causes dilation. Consequently, any pupillary research must control for the light reflex. Thus, it is essential to control both the overall luminance of the experimental chamber and the luminance of the stimulus when visual stimuli are used. The experimental room should have a constant illumination with the intensity level set at a value resulting in an average pupil size between 4 and 6 mm (i.e. the medium range of pupil size of most people). Failure to control differences in luminance has been a central criticism of research that claimed attitudes and emotions were reflected in the pupillary response. In one of his early studies, Hess (1965) observed that a pleasant stimulus elicited dilation, whereas a negative stimulus produced constriction. This led Hess (1968) to propose that pupillary response could be used in the marketing of consumer goods. Many authors, however, proffered severe criticisms of Hess' attraction-dilation/aversion-constriction hypothesis because emotional valence and luminance might have been confounded in Hess' marketing studies (see Janisse, 1977, for a review).

The measurement of pupil size consists basically of tracking the pupillary movements by an optical device to collect a series of pupillary images. These images are then quantified by taking pupil diameter or area to obtain values of peak amplitude and latency with reference to a predetermined baseline. Most laboratories are now using electronic video based systems. These pupillometer systems use a high-resolution linear infrared video camera to obtain a visual image of the iris and the pupil. They provide analog output as well as digital values at a sampling rate of about 60 Hz. Pupil area or pupil diameter are then computed electronically with a resolution of 0.01 mm for a range extending from 2 to 10 mm. The simpler systems require a head rest to fix the position of the eye relative to the video camera. More expensive systems permit free eye and head movements by using eye- and head-tracking systems. The digitized output of the pupillometer is stored in a computer for further analysis.

The first step in the analysis of pupillary data consists of removing artifacts such as those produced by eye blinks. Most investigators use an algorithm for automatic artifact detection. Trials containing artifacts are then corrected by interpolation, but trials containing major artifacts or artifacts occurring at critical moments during a trial are discarded from further analysis. In RT experiments, artifacts result in a loss of about 30–40% of the pupillary data (e.g. Richer, Silverman and Beatty, 1983; van der Molen *et al.*, 1989). It should be noted that the magnitude of the pupillary response typically observed in RT experiments is quite small compared with the changes induced by variations in ambient illumination or accommodation, ranging from 0.1 to 0.2 mm. Under most conditions, these effects are not detectable unless special techniques are employed. These techniques are the same as the procedures used to extract the ERP from the background EEG. Thus, in order to increase the signal-to-noise ratio, artifact-free data are first averaged across trials relative to a task relevant temporal marker (e.g. stimulus onset or response switch). Changes in pupil dilation are then plotted against time. Figure 1.9 presents one such plot of a typical pupil response obtained in an RT task. The latency and amplitude of the averaged pupillary response are determined by peak-picking procedures. These data are then subjected to standard procedures for the analysis of task effects on the pupillary response.

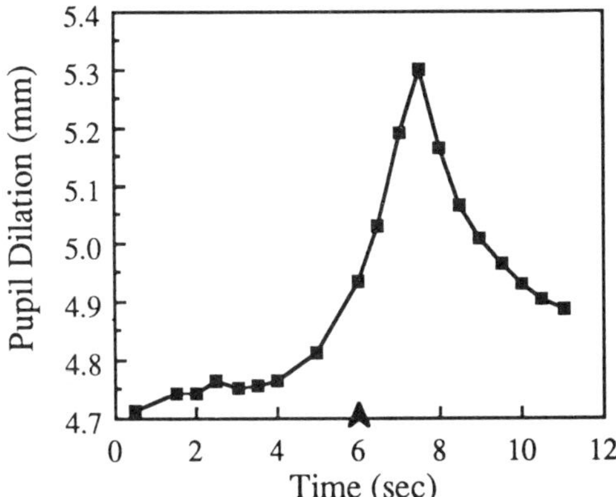

Figure 1.9. Prototypical pupillary dilation response as it occurs during the foreperiod of a signaled reaction-time task. The dilation starts well before the presentation of the imperative stimulus (indicated by the arrowhead) and reaches its peak amplitude about 1.5 seconds after response execution.

A Short History of Pupillography

Studies of the pupil can be traced to Archimedes who apparently developed a device to measure its size (see Hakerem, 1967). More recent investigations have concentrated on the pupillary light reflex. Janisse (1977) reported that Loewenfeld, a distinguished pupillographer, possessed a file of over 10 000 references. She also published an excellent review on the physiology of the pupillary dilation reflex (Loewenfeld, 1958). An important issue in the older literature concerned the relation between certain diseases and abnormalities in the pupillary reflex. In fact, pupil size became an important diagnostic indicator in clinical medicine (e.g. Bumke, 1911). In catatonic schizophrenics, for example, a pupillary response could be observed that was so typical for these patients it was called the 'catatonic pupil'. A characteristic feature of this response was reduced pupillary constriction to light and slow redilation after cessation of the stimulus (cf. Hakerem, Sutton and Zubin, 1964).

Much less was known about the relation between pupil size and mental functioning. One of the first studies investigating the relation between pupil size and attention was conducted by Heinrich (1896) in Exner's laboratories at Vienna. Heinrich addressed the claim made by Helmholtz (1867) of the relative independence between changes in attention and the functioning of the oculomotor system. In a first series of experiments, Heinrich asked his subjects to direct their attention either to visual stimuli that could be presented at central or peripheral locations or to the solution of difficult mental arithmetic problems. He observed that pupil size increased as a function of visual angle between the central fixation point and the location of the visual stimulus; but pupil size was greatest during mental arithmetic. In subsequent experiments, Heinrich tried to determine whether the pupillary response was due to variations in accommodation or to another source of change. He systematically varied the distance at which the stimuli were presented and, in addition to pupil size, measured the radius of the eye lens. He observed that when attention was directed to a laterally presented stimulus, with distance kept constant, accommodation decreased and pupil dilation increased compared with centrally presented stimuli. As in the previous experiments, pupil dilation further increased during mental arithmetic. Heinrich noted that in this condition accommodation of the eye was virtually absent. In contrast to Helmholtz, Heinrich concluded that attention is intimately related to the oculomotor system. His findings led him even to suggest that fluctuations in attentional state, as observed in signal detection tasks, are due to momentary changes in the accommodation of the eyes.

The first systematic investigation of the relation between pupil size and mental functioning was performed by Hess and Polt (1964). They presented multiplication problems with increasing difficulty to their subjects and observed that pupil size gradually increased during problem presentation, reached a peak just before a solution was given, and then returned to baseline. It was found that the amplitude of the pupillary response varied directly with the difficulty of the multiplication problem. The pupillary response was absent when the problem was either too easy or too difficult to solve. These findings suggested to Hess and Polt that pupil size could be used as a direct measure of mental activity. This report prompted many experimenters to explore further the relation between pupil size and mental functioning. The measurement of pupillary movements undoubtedly received its main impetus from the work of Kahneman (1973). He presented a theory of mental effort suggesting that variations in mental effort are related directly to variations in physiological arousal. Because of the connection between mental effort and arousal, physiological measures can be used to measure the exertion of effort. Kahneman proposed pupil dilation as the prime measure of mental effort. Pupil size is sensitive to between-tasks variations (i.e. it orders tasks by their difficulty). Pupil size is sensitive to between-subjects differences (i.e. it reflects differences in the amount of effort people invest in a given task). Finally, pupil size is sensitive to within-task variations (i.e. it reflects the momentary involvement in the task). Furthermore, Kahneman (1973) was able to demonstrate that neither anxiety nor muscular strain could account for the pupillary responses observed during mental task performance (pp. 17–27).

The work relating pupillary movements to mental activity has been reviewed by Hess (1972), Janisse (1977) and, more recently, by Beatty (1982, 1986). These reviews underscore Bumke's (1911) observation that for normal subjects '...in general every active intellectual process, every psychical effort, every exertion of attention, every active mental image, regardless of content, particularly every affect just as truly produces pupil enlargement as does every sensory stimulus' (p. 60). This broad claim justifies the measurement of pupil dilation in RT paradigms. We will now turn to a discussion of this work.

The Psychophysiological Validation of Pupil Dilation

The bulk of pupillary studies of information processing address the issue of information processing capacity rather than speed. The pupillary response has been investigated using a wide array of information processing tasks, ranging from simple perceptual discrimination to complex language processing tasks. Beatty's (1982) review of the available literature suggests that the pupil response does a fair job as a measure of processing load or mental effort. He claimed that the pupil response provided a global indication of task-induced processing load even when tasks differed in the processing resources involved in task performance. Moreover, the pupillary response may also provide an indication of the joint demands for processing resources in dual-task interactions. Thus, the use of the pupillary response as a measure of processing load is not restricted to general capacity theories, such as Kahneman's (1973), but may augment behavioral measures of processing load used in experiments based on multiple resource theories (e.g. Navon and Gopher, 1979; Wickens, 1980).

The number of pupillary RT studies is small. In a series of studies, Bradshaw (e.g. 1968, 1969, 1970) examined the pupillary response in RT tasks. In one study, Bradshaw (1969) addressed the methodologically relevant issue of how background illumination might affect the pupillary movements during RT performance. He employed a signaled simple RT task with a random presentation of 2.75 and 5.50 s warning intervals. The background illumination was varied across a wide range, but extreme values were not included. Bradshaw's results indicated that pupillary diameter increased 33% going from the bright to the dark condition (from about 4.2 to 5.5 mm), but the change in illumination did not affect the amplitude of the pupillary response to the imperative stimulus. Thus, the pupillary measure might be more resistent to illumination artifacts than initially thought. The pupil began to dilate just prior to the imperative stimulus and peaked shortly after the response had been executed. Bradshaw observed that for long foreperiods the pupillary trace showed two dilations; a small dilation that peaked at 2.75 s after the warning signal (i.e. at the anticipated time of the stimulus for the short foreperiod) and a larger dilation at the time of the stimulus and response (i.e. at about 5.50 s after the stimulus). The initial response indicates that the execution of a motor response is not necessary for a dilation to occur. This is consistent with Simpson's (1969) finding of a dilation on NoGo trials. The larger amplitude at the time of the stimulus and response suggests that the actual execution of the motor response may contribute considerably to the dilatory trend.

In a second experiment, Bradshaw (1968) pursued the uncertainty issue further. In this experiment, he compared the effects of time- and stimulus-uncertainty. Stimulus-uncertainty was varied by presenting visual and auditory respond stimuli in a random fashion or by presenting only auditory signals. As in the previous experiment, time-uncertainty was manipulated by presenting fixed or variable warning intervals. Both stimulus- and time-uncertainty prolonged RT to a considerable extent. The pupillary response, however, was only affected by stimulus-uncertainty, not by time-uncertainty. When the subject was kept uncertain about the modality of the stimulus the pupillary response showed an increased baseline and a lower amplitude than in the certain condition. Bradshaw suggested that the elevated baseline could be a correlate of cognitive load, while lower peaks could reflect a decrease in response readiness. Thus, these findings indicate a dissociation between RT and pupil dilation; the former is sensitive to both stimulus- and time-uncertainty, whereas the latter is only affected by stimulus-uncertainty manipulations. An alternative interpretation would be that the dilation amplitude is smaller because the pupil is so large in the uncertain condition that it cannot dilate any further.

This interpretation is incompatible with the results of his illumination study, however.

Bradshaw (1970) explored the relation between pupillary baseline and peak amplitude more fully by using drugs. His subjects performed the standard simple RT task, including variable foreperiods, under three conditions: no drug, alcohol treatment, and amphetamine treatment. Alcohol was chosen because of its apparent detrimental effects on performance and amphetamine was selected because of its sympathometic effects that resemble the effect of adrenaline on the reticular formation. Response speed was somewhat faster for long compared with short foreperiods. Amphetamine did not significantly affect response speed, but alcohol did. The drugs affected the pupillary response in a very dissimilar way. Amphetamine had an effect comparable to a darkening of the room (i.e. a dilatory baseline shift but no effects on the peak amplitude). By contrast, alcohol exerted its effect on the amplitude of the response—a considerable reduction—but not on the baseline. The importance of the results obtained by the illumination and drug manipulations is that they demonstrate that phasic pupillary dilations at the time of the stimulus and motor response are relatively insensitive to changes in pupillary baseline. From a methodological point of view, Bradshaw's findings are important because they suggest that pupillary baseline shifts do not dramatically alter the magnitude of phasic dilations.

Bradshaw's suggestion that pupil size might be a sensitive indicator of stimulus-uncertainty has been addressed more recently by Van Olst, Heemstra and Ten Kortenaar (1979). Their subjects were presented sequences consisting of two tones of the same duration (5 s), but different frequencies. They were asked to respond to the offset of one tone (Go trial) and to withhold their motor response to the offset of the other tone (NoGo trial). Thus, subjects performed a disjunctive RT task. One group of subjects received the tones in an alternating sequence and they were told about the alternating nature of the sequence prior to receiving the tones. Another group of subjects received the tones in a pseudorandom order and were told in advance that the same tone would never be presented more than three times in a row. The pupillary response to the reaction stimulus showed two peaks, a small peak to the onset of the tone and a larger peak at its offset. The NoGo stimulus showed only the pupillary peak at stimulus onset and no response at stimulus offset. The amplitude of the pupillary responses to stimulus onset was larger for the uninformed group than for the informed group. Stimulus uncertainty did not affect the pupillary response to stimulus offset. The difference in pupillary response at stimulus onset was interpreted to suggest that pupil dilation is sensitive to manipulations of stimulus-uncertainty, while the marked dilation on Go trials, and its notable absence on NoGo trials, was assumed to reflect response preparation. The authors attributed the different amplitudes at stimulus onset to differences in response uncertainty. The latter claim must be questioned given the relatively long foreperiod of 5 s. With a time interval of this length, one cannot seriously entertain the idea that subjects are unprepared, no matter how irregular the series of tones.

Our brief selection of pupillary RT studies makes three important points. From a methodological perspective, the majority of the results demonstrate a relative independence of baseline shifts and response morphology. This finding provides the experimenter with considerably more degrees of freedom than could be expected from the initial concerns with baseline effects (e.g. Janisse, 1977). Second, and more importantly, the morphology of the pupillary response obtained in RT tasks consists of a gradual rise prior to an expected stimulus that attains its peak shortly after the response has been executed. The amplitude of the pupillary response is sensitive to manipulations of response preparation. Thus, this autonomic nervous system measure may be particularly well suited for the analysis of covert aspects of behavior as subjects prepare for stimulus detection and subsequent action. Third, it is also clear that the pupillary response does not provide the chronometrician with a high-resolution technique for assessing the temporal dynamics of processing stages. This latter deficiency does not characterize the event-related potential, to which we now turn our attention.

EVENT-RELATED BRAIN POTENTIALS

ERPs represent changes in electrophysiological activity generated in the brain in response to a stimulus event or in association with a movement that can be recorded on the scalp. In both cases, the ERP is manifest as a series of time-dependent changes in voltage that are most apparent in averages of the electroencephalographic (EEG) activity derived from repeated occurrences of the critical event. These voltage–time fluctuations exhibit a typical series of peaks and valleys (known separately as components) that represent positive and negative changes in the electrical polarity of the EEG signal. A considerable body of research now demonstrates that the amplitude and timing of these components are quite sensitive to variations in the physical properties of the eliciting stimulus and to the psychological demands of an information processing task. This activity has been categorized by investigators in the field into two broad types, exogenous and endogenous. The presence of exogenous components in the ERP reflects the obligatory activation of neuroanatomical structures in the stimulated primary sensory pathways. These components are sometimes referred to as sensory evoked potentials or EPs. Typically, the amplitude and latency of these components vary with changes in the physical parameters of a stimulus (e.g. intensity). Exogenous components usually occur within the first 80–100 ms after stimulus onset and can be detected within a few milliseconds after stimulation (e.g. the brain stem auditory evoked response, a series of components manifest within the first several milliseconds after presentation of a click). They have characteristic distributions on the scalp that vary with the source of stimulation. For example, a component whose amplitude is maximal at central electrode sites for somatosensory stimulation will be maximal at occipital sites for visual stimulation. The activity of exogenous components is often deduced from knowledge of the structural and functional neuroanatomy of primary afferent pathways. An important property of the exogenous components is that their elicitation is not dependent upon the subject performing some type of decision-making task on the stimuli that produce them. That is, they can be recorded under conditions of passive stimulation during which the subject is instructed to just let his/her mind wander. Indeed, these components can be evoked in comatose patients whose primary sensory pathways are intact.

In contrast to the exogenous components, the emergence of endogenous components in the ERP is dependent on the subject being actively engaged in an information processing task. In fact, the latency and amplitude of these components of the ERP are sensitive to variations in the stimulus and response processing demands of a task, while being relatively insensitive to changes in the physical properties of the stimulus. Indeed, the appearance of these components in the ERP in response to a particular stimulus may vary as a function of the presence or absence of critical processing demands associated with its presentation. In addition, the same stimulus may elicit an endogenous component under some task conditions, but not under others. The exogenous components will be present, however, in response to each presentation of the stimulus, irrespective of the processing demands associated with it. Unlike the exogenous components of the ERP, endogenous components are usually thought to occur late in the ERP (beyond 150–200 ms poststimulus) and to have a reasonably invariant scalp distribution across stimulus modalities. It has been known for some time that there is temporal overlap among certain exogenous and endogenous components, particularly in the time period spanning 100–200 ms after stimulation (Näätänen and Picton, 1987). These components have been referred to as middle latency by some investigators (e.g. Buchsbaum, 1977). Recent evidence suggests, however, that the influence of cognitive processes may be present as early as 40 ms after stimulation in a selective attention task (e.g. Desmedt, Huy and Bourguet, 1983).

The orderly temporal structure of endogenous components and their sensitivity to variations in task demands suggest that changes in the amplitude and timing of these components may be associated with the onset and offset of specific information processing activities. These observations provide the empirical justification for using the ERP as a tool to study the chronometric properties of human information processing in conjunction with traditional behavioral measures. An important property of these signals for studies of human information processing is that the eliciting event can be a simple stimulus with minimal psychological meaning, such as a brief tone, or a complex event, such as the identification of a word from a specific grammatical class (see Donchin *et al.*, 1986, and Picton and Stuss, 1980, for reviews) so long as the subject must make decisions about these stimuli. Thus, the appearance of endogenous components appears to be related closely to the abstract properties of a stimulus, rather than simply to its physical properties.

ERP components are most often referred to on the basis of their electrical polarity and the minimum latency at which their maximum amplitude is achieved. Thus, the N100 component has a negative polarity whose maximum occurs about 100 ms after the stimulus has been presented, while the P300 has a positive polarity that attains its maximum amplitude around 300 ms (in simple information processing tasks). These designations are approximate since the actual latency will vary with stimulus modality, processing load, and other factors such as age and psychopathology. This is particularly true for later components like the P300, whose latency can range from 250 ms (in 15-year-olds doing a simple tone discrimination task) to 800 or 900 ms (in 70-year-olds doing a difficult visual discrimination task) (Bashore, 1990b; Bashore, Osman and Heffley, 1989). The fact that some components cannot be identified strictly on the basis of time has led to the use of other criteria for identifying them. Two such criteria are the component's distribution over the scalp and its response to task manipulations.

The most thoroughly studied components are the N100, P200, N200, P300, and N400. In addition, a number of components with slower frequencies have been implicated in information processing. These include a slow negative-going potential, termed the contingent negative variation (CNV), that occurs in the foreperiod between the presentation of a warning stimulus and an imperative stimulus calling for some response; a similar negative-going potential that precedes the initiation of an unwarned, spontaneous movement, the readiness potential (RP); another negative component that occurs in the same time period as the N100 and N200, the processing negativity (Nd); and a slow positive component, called the slow wave, that overlaps the P300.

Examples of ERPs recorded from subjects as they performed cognitive tasks in the visual or somatosensory modality are shown in Figure 1.10. The ERPs shown on the left were recorded by Bashore and Osman (1987) in a variant of the Eriksen task. A visual warning stimulus, the word READY, was presented 1000 ms before an imperative stimulus, an arrow array that contained five arrows that pointed in the same direction (left or right) or that contained a center arrow that pointed in one direction and two flankers on each side that pointed in the opposite direction. The subject was required to move a lever with the left or right hand in the direction of the center arrow. Note that during the foreperiod there is activity that resembles the contingent negative variation or CNV (i.e. an early positivity to the warning stimulus followed by a slow ramp-like negativity preceding the imperative stimulus). This activity has the form of the classic CNV which is largest at frontocentral electrode sites. In evidence after

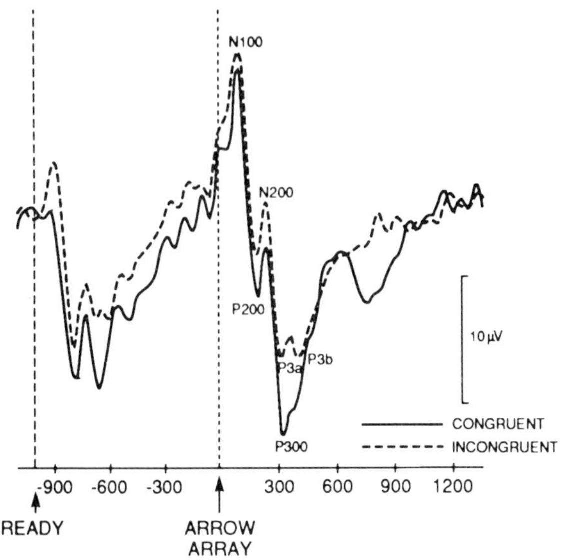

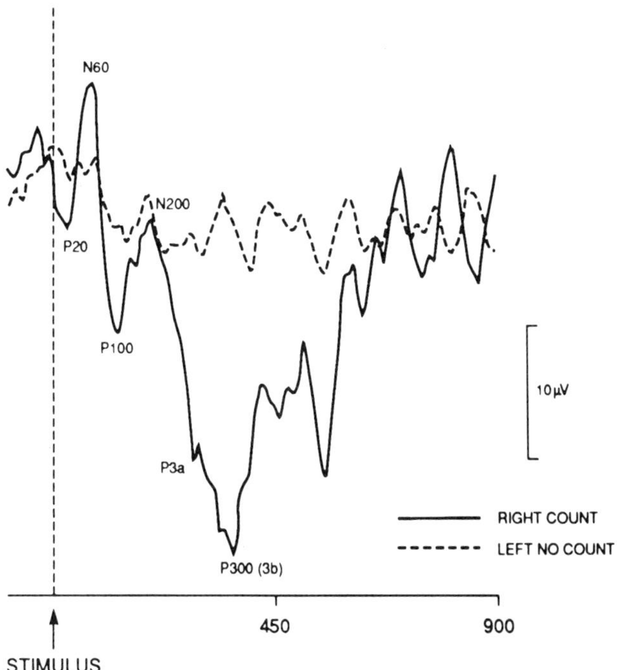

Figure 1.10. Examples of ERPs recorded from individual subjects at Pz as they performed cognitive tasks in the visual and somatosensory modalities (see text).

the imperative stimulus has been presented is a series of positive and negative deflections (i.e. components) that are labeled on the basis of electrical polarity (positive, P, or negative, N) and modal peak latency in milliseconds. The solid and dashed lines depict the activity recorded following either an array of arrows that pointed in the same direction or a mixed array, respectively. Note that the broad positive sweep of activity seen after the imperative stimulus may include multiple constituents, hence it is often called the 'late positivity'. In this example, when the array was mixed, the late positivity includes the P3a and P3b (Squires, Squires and Hillyard, 1975). The latter is identified with the traditional P300.

The ERPs shown on the right were recorded in an ongoing study by Bashore, Josiassen and Guterman as the subject received mild electrical pulses to the left or right index finger. Her task was to keep a running mental count of the number of times the right finger was stimulated and to refrain from counting the pulses to the left finger. A pulse was delivered randomly to the right finger on 20% of the trials. Thus, this is an example of the classic 'oddball' task in which the P300 is elicited. The responses to the counted and uncounted pulses are shown as solid and as dashed lines, respectively. Note the presence of a large late positive complex in response to the counted pulse that contains a P3a and P3b. Note further that the effects of directed attention appear to be manifest at least as early as the N60 component, and perhaps as early as the P20.

The core problem confronting the cognitive psychophysiologist who utilizes the timing of components of the ERP to infer mental chronometric processes is signal analysis. The first step in this process is signal acquisition. Signals must be recorded with the appropriate filter settings on the amplifiers so that distortion of the signal is minimized. Scalp recordings are typically referenced to a cephalic or non-cephalic site that is presumed to be 'neurologically quiet'. A variety of different references, both cephalic and non-cephalic, are used across laboratories and this can influence estimates of component parameters (e.g. Naylor, Halliday and Callaway, 1985). Explanations for conflicting findings in similar paradigms are typically not sought, however, in variations in reference sites. Once recorded, components of the event-related brain potential are concealed within a background of EEG activity that is usually many times larger than the components themselves and is considered by the investigator to be noise. The historical definition of noise is any constituent frequency of the EEG that does not respond systematically to the stimulus or is not time-locked to the execution of a movement. This assumption provided the rationale for averaging a large number of trials and estimating component parameters from the average. Thus, it was assumed that the non-systematic background EEG or noise would average to zero.

In the 1970s methods began to be explored that permitted extraction of the signal from the background EEG on a single-trial basis. These procedures involve digital filtering to reduce noise (Ruchkin and Glaser, 1978) and analytic procedures to identify component latencies and amplitudes on single trials (Donchin and Heffley, 1978; Callaway and Halliday, 1973). These efforts continue (Gratton, Coles and Donchin, 1989; Gratton *et al.*, 1989; Möcks, 1988). Thus, the problem of extracting the ERP component from the background EEG must be confronted, a problem that is compounded when task processing demands increase and produce a concomitant increase in the complexity of the event-related brain potential. The most appropriate digital filtering technique has not yet been determined, however. Recent work by Möcks *et al.* (1988), Pham *et al.* (1987), Raz, Turetsky and Fein (1989), and Turetsky, Raz and Fein (1989) provide examples of attempts to improve these procedures.

Once the signal is extracted from the noise, the component latency must be estimated on the single-trial ERP. A variety of procedures have been used to derive these estimates, including simply identifying the maximum value within a specified time window, lag cross-correlations, and discriminant functions. Recent efforts by Fabiani *et al.* (1987), Gratton, Coles and Donkin (1989), and Gratton *et al.* (1989) have been directed at developing new methods to estimate component latency and on evaluating the reliability of the various choices. Thus, any factor effect on component latency may be influenced by the procedures used to derive the estimate. It should also be noted that the component recorded on the scalp as a single event may in fact comprise a number of independent, but temporally overlapping, signals with different neural origins and cognitive significance. Articulation of these constituent signals may be intractable for current analytic techniques such as the most commonly used procedure for achieving this end, principal components analysis (Möcks, 1986). Alternatives have been suggested (Möcks, 1988). Here, the dipole component modeling procedures of Turetsky, Raz and Fein (in press) may prove to be quite powerful because they link component activity measured on the scalp to underlying neural generators (see also our discussion of these issues in the final main section of this chapter).

A Brief History of Event-related Brain Potentials

The electrical nature of the brain has been known for some time (see reviews in Boring, 1950; Lindsley, 1969; Donchin, 1979). Early studies by Fritsch and Hitzig (1870) revealed that electrical stimulation of the dog's cortex, in what is now known as the motor area, produced movements that were dependent upon the current of the stimulating electrode. This work was soon extended by the English investigator, David Ferrier (1876), who produced a fairly detailed map of the motor cortex. In 1875, Caton reported the production of an evoked potential in rabbit brain that resembles what today is called the CNV. It was not until the 1920s, however, that Hans Berger (1929), a German psychiatrist, discovered that ongoing human brain electrical activity, what he named the electroencephalogram (EEG), could be measured at the scalp. The EEG represents the spontaneous electrical activity of the brain that varies continuously over time. Berger thought that the EEG would provide a sensitive method for measuring consciousness in general and different elements of cognition in particular, and would be useful in understanding psychiatric disorders. The EEG has proved helpful in understanding certain neurologic disorders such as epilepsy and some organic brain disorders, but it has not contributed to our understanding of psychiatric disorders and has had only limited success in improving our understanding of higher mental processes.

The spontaneous and general nature of the EEG does not make it suitable to study the chronometric aspects of human information processing. By definition, mental chronometry is the study of the timing of mental events that are activated by a stimulus and culminate in the execution of some type of response, be it overt or covert. The mere presentation of the stimulus produces a transient change in the EEG that is the ERP. In the 1930s there were observations that specific stimuli could elicit small voltage shifts in the EEG that were distinguishable from the background EEG. This activity was reported for visual stimuli by Cruikshank (see Donchin, 1979) and for auditory stimuli by Davis (1939). In the latter case, intense auditory stimuli produced a large negative deflection at approximately 100 ms after the stimulation that was largest at the geometric center of the top of the head (known as the vertex or Cz in the most widely used electrode placement system, the 10–20 system). Davis (1939) was able to enhance the signal-to-noise ratio by increasing the intensity of the auditory stimulus and to observe evoked responses on single trials for the higher intensities.

The initial application of ERPs in the study of cognitive processes occurred in the 1960s. This early period is distinguished by astonishing progress. Most of the major ERP components were discovered in the span of a few years, and from the outset this research has involved an international community of scholars. For example, in 1964 the US investigators Haider, Spong and Lindsley reported that the amplitude of the N100–P200 complex was increased when the subject monitored visual events in a vigilance task. These studies led to the discovery of negative components, now called processing negativities, that develop early in the ERP and appear to index selective attention mechanisms (for a review see Näätänen, 1975). In the same year, Walter and his colleagues at the Burden Neurological Institute in Bristol, England, reported that a slow, ramp-like negative wave was elicited in a warned RT task between the presentation of a warning and an imperative stimulus (Walter *et al.*, 1964). They suggested that this component reflected the development of a subject's expectancy for the imperative stimulus during the preparatory interval, and named it the *contingent negative variation* (CNV). In 1965, Kornhuber and Deecke in Germany reported that a slow negative potential could be observed to develop over a period of 1000–1500 ms preceding the execution of a spontaneous unsignaled movement. They labeled it the *Bereitschaftpotential* or readiness potential (see also Vaughan *et al.*, 1968). This movement-related potential has begun to play an important role in attempts to understand how information is used in preparing and executing a response, and is discussed at more length in the section on mental chronometry and ERPs.

Perhaps the most studied ERP component in the cognitive psychophysiological literature, the P300, was first observed by Samuel Sutton and his colleagues at the New York State Psychiatric Institute (see Donchin, 1984, for a personal view of the history of P300; for other excellent reviews see Duncan-Johnson and Donchin, 1982, and Pritchard, 1981). They reported their findings at a symposium of the 1964 convention of the American Psychological Association, and published their first paper the next year in *Science* (Sutton *et al.*, 1965).

In Figure 1.11 we show the first P300s published by the Sutton group. They were recorded in a task that required the subject to guess which of two stimuli (a click or brief light flash) would be presented on a given trial. A trial consisted of the presentation of a temporally sequenced pair of stimuli, designated as the cueing stimulus and the test stimulus. In one condition, the cueing stimulus always indicated that a particular test stimulus, either the click or the light flash, would follow. In the second condition, the cueing stimulus could be followed

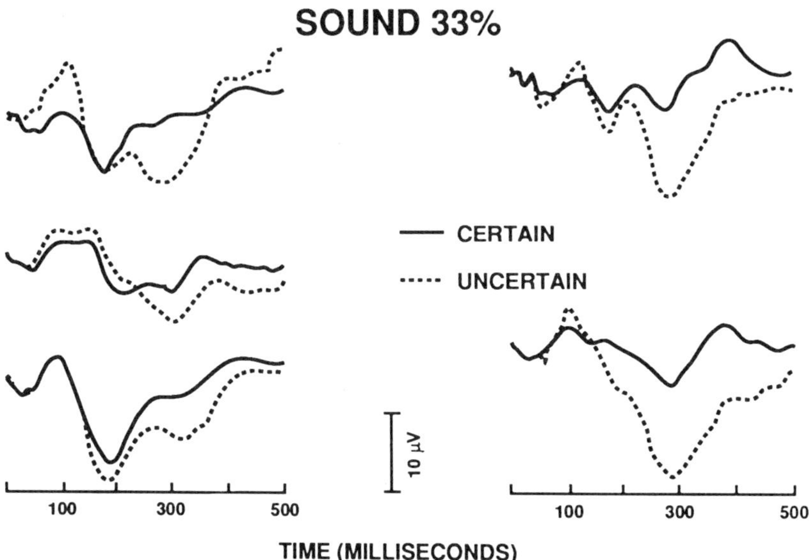

Figure 1.11. The first P300s published in the cognitive psychophysiological literature by Sutton *et al.* (1965). These ERPs were elicited by an auditory stimulus. Each ERP is for an individual subject. (Reprinted with permission of the publisher. © 1965 American Association for the Advancement of Science.)

unpredictably by either a click or a flash. The interval between the cue and test stimuli varied randomly between 3000 and 5000 ms. It was during this interval that the subject guessed which test stimulus would be presented. Figure 1.11 shows the ERPs elicited by sound stimuli when their occurrence was certain (the solid line) and when it was uncertain ($p = 0.33$, dashed line). They reveal the appearance of a late positive wave (or P300) under conditions of stimulus uncertainty and provide classic examples of the effect of this factor on brain electrical activity.

In other experiments described in this report, Sutton *et al.* also demonstrated that the amplitude of the late positive wave varied with the probability of occurrence of the test stimulus, irrespective of the type of stimulus. Thus, in general the largest P300 was elicited by the lower probability stimulus (0.33 versus 0.66), be it a click or a flash. In ending their paper, Sutton *et al.* summarized the significance of their findings as follows:

> These data. . .indicate that the evoked-potential waveform recorded from the scalp of human subjects may reflect two kinds of influences. One of these is largely exogenous and related to the character of the stimulus. The other is largely endogenous and related to the reaction, or attitude, of the subject to the stimulus. The reaction of the subject is at least in part amenable to quantitative manipulation. (p. 1188)

Identification of the P300 could not have occurred at a more propitious time. After a half century of neglect, the psychology of human performance was becoming a central topic in psychology, recast in the newly emerging field of cognitive psychology. In contrast to the predominant behaviorist philosophy, cognitive psychology appealed to a wide variety of disciplines including psychology, computer science, psychophysiology, psychiatry, and neurology. Sutton's discoveries that the same sensory events could generate a very different P300 depending on what the subject was instructed to do, and in later work that the P300 could be generated in the absence of an external stimulus event (Sutton *et al.*, 1967), became rallying points for investigators with an interest in bringing the brain back into psychology. These discoveries demonstrated quite dramatically that human cognitive activity does not simply entail the connection of stimulus input to response output. Within the first few years of Sutton's discoveries his findings were corroborated and extended by other investigators, most notably Emanuel Donchin and his colleagues at the University of Illinois, and Herbert Vaughan and Walter Ritter and their colleagues at the Albert Einstein Medical College.

P300—A Case Study in Hypothesis Testing

Ritter and Vaughan (1969) and Ritter, Simson and Vaughan (1972) first suggested that the latency to the peak of the P300 reflected the time taken by central mechanisms mediating cognitive stimulus evaluation. This inference was suggested to them by findings that changes in RT and in P300 latency following manipulations of stimulus discriminability were highly correlated. These observations were followed by several others, however, that either did or did not verify this correlation. These negative findings were important because they demonstrated that the processes manifested by P300 latency and RT did not overlap completely and thereby suggested the former comprised a subset of the latter (Donchin, 1979; Kutas, McCarthy and Donchin, 1977). If the two sets of processes overlapped completely, P300 would be a far less interesting component to study. Indeed, it might be meaningless to the mental chronometrician. The task, therefore, was to determine the subset of processes manifest by the P300.

The seminal study demonstrating the importance of the dissociation between P300 latency and RT was by Kutas *et al.* (1977). Their subjects were presented three randomly mixed series of words. One series of words included only the female name Nancy (on 20% of the trials) and the male name David (on 80% of the trials); another series was composed of several female names (presented on 20% of the trials) and several male names (presented on 80% of the trials); and the third series consisted of synonyms for the word 'prod' (on 20% of the trials) and words unrelated to it (on 80% of the trials). Each series was presented under three different response requirements. In one, subjects were required to keep a running mental count of the infrequent stimulus (e.g. Nancy) and to refrain from counting the other stimulus (e.g. David); in another, they were required to make a choice reaction indicated by a button press (e.g. left button to Nancy, right button to David) under speed instructions; and in another they made a choice reaction under accuracy instructions. Comparisons of trial-by-trial estimates of P300 latency and RT revealed that the correlations between these two measures varied with the instructional set. When speed was emphasized, the correlation between P300 latency and RT was 0.48, but when accuracy was emphasized the correlation increased to 0.66 for correct responses. Of particular interest was the finding that the temporal relation of these two measures varied with the accuracy of the subject's response. When a correct response was made, the peak of the P300 usually preceded the response (by 91 ms±88 ms). However, when an incorrect response was made the response preceded the peak of the P300 (26 ms±88 ms). In addition to the relation of RT and P300 latency to response output accuracy, Kutas *et al.* found that P300 latency increased as the stimulus processing demands increased across tasks (from discriminating two names, to discriminating two classes of names, to identifying synonyms). Kutas *et al.* concluded from these findings that the timing of stimulus processing is indexed by P300 latency, that reactions to a stimulus often precede the complete evaluation of that stimulus when speed of responding is emphasized, and this in turn increases the likelihood of an error being emitted. A similar pattern of relations among instructional set, RT, P300 latency, and response output accuracy has been reported by Pfefferbaum *et al.* (1983).

The most convincing early demonstration of the differential sensitivity of P300 latency and RT to stimulus and response factors was by McCarthy and Donchin (1981). They varied stimulus discriminability and S–R compatibility in a choice RT task. The subject's task was to press a left or a right button in response to brief presentations of the word LEFT or RIGHT. Stimulus discriminability was varied by placing the word in a matrix of number signs (#) or of letters chosen randomly from the alphabet. The row and starting column of the target word varied randomly within a block of trials. S–R compatibility was varied by requiring subjects to make either compatible (e.g. LEFT calls for a left button press) or incompatible (e.g. LEFT calls for a right button press) responses. This mapping was indicated to the subject by the presentation of a cue word, SAME or OPPOSITE, that preceded the onset of the matrix. These experimental factors were mixed randomly within a block of trials.

The results of this experiment, shown in Figure 1.12, revealed the dissociation predicted by McCarthy and Donchin. RT was found to increase when the target word was surrounded by letters and when an incompatible response was made, and these effects were additive. However, P300 latency was affected only by the ease with which the target could be identified. Moreover, the magnitude of this effect varied as a function of the row in which the target was presented. P300 latency was shortest when the target word appeared in the middle rows. This pattern of findings led McCarthy and Donchin to conclude that P300 latency is sensitive to variations in the timing of stimulus evaluation processes, while being relatively insensitive to changes in the timing of response-related processes, whereas RT is sensitive to variations in the timing of both stimulus and response processes. This experiment provided an elegant demonstration of the experimental dissociation of P300 latency and RT, and as such suggested quite forcefully that these measures are manifestations of separable processes.

These findings were replicated and extended by Magliero *et al.* (1984). Their work demonstrated not only that P300 latency was reasonably insensitive to manipulations of S–R compatibility, but also that it increased in a systematic fashion with increases in the difficulty of discriminating the target word in the matrix. Moreover, it has been demonstrated in several studies by Callaway and associates (see review in Callaway, 1983) that S–R compatibility is not the only response manipulation that fails to change P300 latency while changing RT. They varied the number of response alternatives (two versus four) and found that P300 latency was not altered by the additional response choices, but RT was prolonged. The consistent dissociation of P300 latency and RT revealed in these studies has encouraged investigators to use P300 latency and RT to infer the relative contributions of stimulus and response processes to the Stroop effect (Duncan-Johnson and Kopell, 1981), the stages of processing

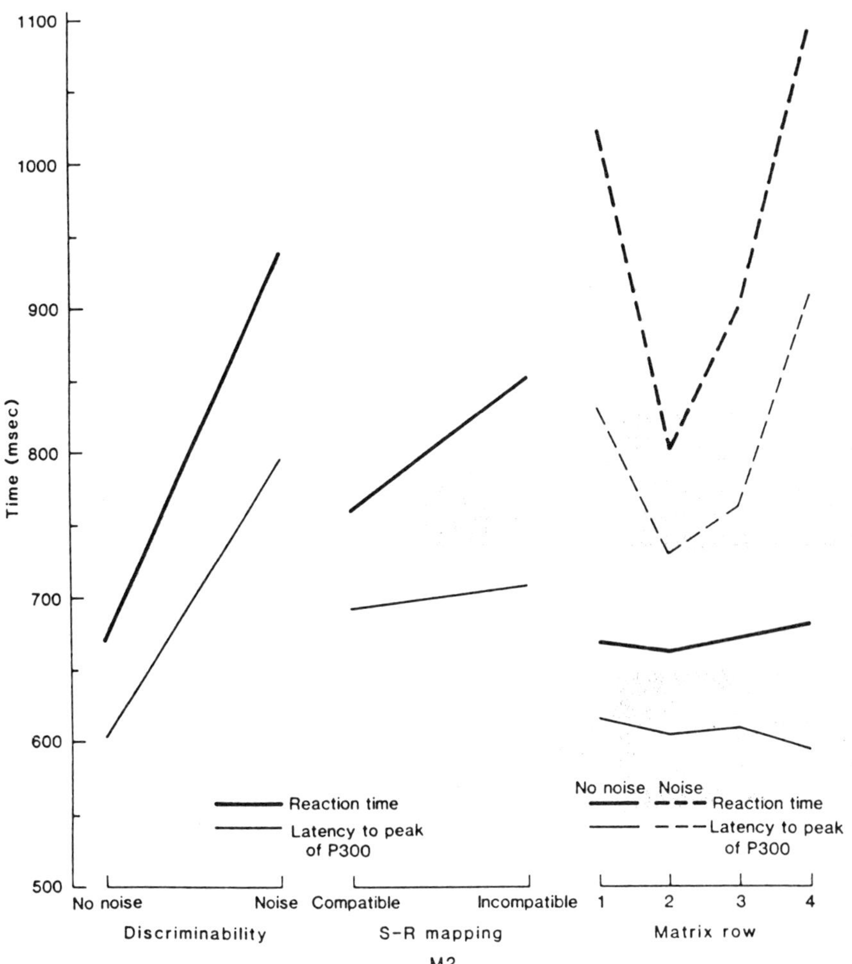

Figure 1.12. Mean RTs (thick lines) and P300 latencies (thin lines) obtained by McCarthy and Donchin (1981) for each experimental factor left panel—stimulus discriminability; middle panel—S-R compatibility; right panel—matrix row by noise interaction. (Reprinted with permission of the authors and publisher. © 1981 American Association for the Advancement of Science.)

that slow differentially with age in memory scanning (e.g. Ford *et al.*, 1979), and the cognitive effects of psychotropic medication (e.g. Callaway, 1983). There remains some controversy, however, about the relative influence of response factors in determining P300 latency. Ragot's group (e.g. Ragot, 1984; Ragot and Lesevre, 1986) has shown that spatial incompatibility prolongs P300 latency, and Pfefferbaum *et al.* (1986) have reported that the influence of S–R compatibility on P300 latency varies as a function of task demands.

In summary, the research demonstrates that P300 latency and RT can be dissociated experimentally, and that this dissociation derives to a large extent from the differential sensitivity of P300 latency to variables that influence stimulus processing time. These findings provide a strong rationale for evaluating variations in the timing of this component in studies of mental chronometry.

PSYCHOPHYSIOLOGICAL STUDIES OF MENTAL CHRONOMETRY

The issues we have addressed fall into two broad categories, the temporal organization of the microstructure of speeded mental reactions and the influence of presetting mechanisms on the temporal properties of these reactions. With regard to the former, we have argued that the additive factors method is the chronometrician's most powerful tool for inferring the timing of processing stages from RT data. We have also pointed out, however, that the validity of this method depends critically on the assumption that stages are discrete in at least two ways: (i) their activation does not overlap in time (Miller, 1988), and (ii) they have a constant output (Sanders, in press). Event-related brain potentials have been used to examine the temporal relations among stages. Later in this section we shall discuss recent examples of attempts in which these measures have been utilized to chart the time course of stage communications. Unfortunately, to our knowledge, similar studes are not extant that address the issue of constant stage output. With regard to the issue of stage duration, we have pointed out that it is determined not only by stimulus input, but also by presetting processes that are activated prior to the arrival of the stimulus and execution of the response. Psychophysiologists have tried to identify these preparatory processes using autonomic and central nervous system measures. In the following two subsections, we discuss how heart rate and pupillary measures have been used to augment behavioral measures of mental chronometry.

HEART RATE AND THE ADDITIVE FACTORS LOGIC

When studying mental reactions, two major approaches are commonly distinguished (see discussion in Sanders, 1977). One approach emphasizes the structural aspects of the reaction process. Investigators who adopt this approach examine the flow of information processing through hypothetical mechanisms like those we have described in our discussion of RT studies of mental chronometry. Structural models have derived typically from behavioral studies. The other approach emphasizes the functional aspects of the reaction process. Adherents of this approach have a primary interest in issues such as the effect of changes in alertness on the efficiency of performance. Traditionally, this approach has attracted greater interest among psychophysiologists, particularly those studying the dynamics of the heart rate response, because of the intimate relation between attention and physiological arousal or activation (e.g. Duffy, 1972; Lacy, J.I. *et al.*, 1963).

Only recently have theorists such as Sanders (1983) and Mulder (1986) proposed a rapprochement. Figure 1.13 puts in diagrammatic form the position taken by Sanders (1983; see also Chapter 8 in this volume). It includes three aspects of information processing: (i) a cognitive level with stages of processing; (ii) an energetic level that allocates processing resources; and (iii) an evaluative level that corresponds to an executive process. The processing stages at the cognitive level are established for the most part using the additive factors method. At the energetic level, there are three supply mechanisms, two of which are basal—arousal and activation—that are coupled to input and output processing stages, respectively. The basal mechanisms are coordinated and supervised by an effort mechanism that is linked directly to the central stage of response choice. In addition, the effort mechanism serves the function of keeping the basal resources at an optimal level. The basal resources bear a close resemblance to mechanisms proposed by Pribram and McGuinness on the basis of neurophysiological evidence (Pribram and McGuinness, 1975; McGuinness and Pribram, 1980). In order to be informed about the state of

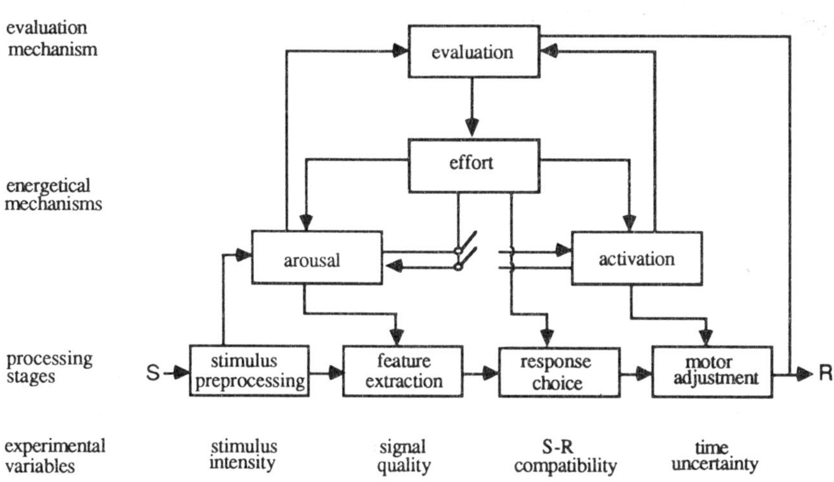

Figure 1.13. Sanders' (1983) cognitive–energetic model of human information processing. (Reprinted with permission of the author and publisher. © 1983 Elsevier Science Publishers B.V.)

arousal and activation, their functioning must be monitored. The evaluative mechanism receives at least two types of feedback information to achieve this end. In one, direct feedback reflecting the physiological state of the system is provided that guarantees intervention by the effort mechanism if there is an imbalance. In the other, evaluative feedback on the adequacy of the performance is given on a cognitive level so that performance can be monitored. Evaluation of the state of the organism as well as of the adequacy of the performance were important elements in Kahneman's (1973) capacity model of attention as well.

In Sanders' model, processing time is determined by the allocation of processing capacity as well as by the computations accomplished at each of the processing stages. It should be noted that the serial stage dimension of the model imposes an important constraint on its capacity dimension. Capacity cannot be distributed freely over stages so that allocation to one stage may lead to shortage of capacity at the next stage. This state of affairs would lead invariably to interactions that are incompatible with the assumptions underlying the additive factors method (Sanders, 1983). Hence, specificity of cognitive–energetic relations is the essential assumption of Sanders' model. In other words, functional factors have a selective, rather than a global, influence on RT. This assumption poses a difficult problem, however. It is difficult to determine how the effects of variations in functional and structural task variables can be distinguished with respect to their relation to changes in the allocation of processing capacity and in the rate of computations. The complex arrangement of the components in the flow diagram does not reveal the different consequences of variations in the linked computational and energetical mechanisms.

In presenting his model, Sanders outlined two research strategies for discriminating between functional and structural effects on the reaction process. The first is based on properties of the RT distribution. Sanders argued that structural variables would have their effect on all individual trials and, hence, on the entire RT distribution. In contrast, he argued that functional effects would vary strongly across individual trials so that their effect would be seen primarily at the tails of the RT distribution. The second strategy concerns the distinction between effects on arousal, activation, and/or effort. First, an interaction between a structural and a functional variable is to be interpreted as an effect of that functional variable on the energetic mechanism that supplies capacity to the processing stage affected by the structural variable. Thus, an interaction between a functional variable and stimulus degradation, for example, is interpreted as indicating that the functional variable exerted its influence on arousal, not on activation. Second, the principal way of deciding between effects on either arousal or activation as opposed to those on effort is to consider the effects of motivational variables. Such variables are strongly related to effort allocation and, hence, their effects provide the tools for distinguishing between the more basal mechanisms of arousal and activation and the more voluntary mechanism of effort. Additional criteria for distinguishing these processes are that influences on the effort mechanism would (1) produce an equal effect on the supply of capacity to the arousal and the activation systems, and (2) have an effect on response choice variables (cf. Sanders, 1983).

Sanders and his colleagues illustrated these research strategies in a series of studies on the effects of barbiturates, amphetamine, and sleep loss on choice RT. One such illustration is given in Frowein (1981). He found that treatment with a barbiturate and variations in stimulus quality produced interactive effects on RT, but that manipulations of S–R compatibility and foreperiod duration produced additive effects. Similar findings have been reported by Logsdon *et al.* (1984) in their examination of the effects of secobarbital on perceptual processing (i.e. the drug effect interacted with the quality of the stimulus). According to Sanders, these findings suggest that barbiturates have a negative effect on the state of the arousal system, which in turn produces a detrimental effect on the stimulus encoding stage. Amphetamine, on the other hand, seems to have its predominant effect on the activation mechanism. This drug has additive effects with perceptual or decisional variables, but interacts with time uncertainty (e.g. Frowein, 1981). Finally, sleep loss has been found to interact with signal degradation (Sanders, Wijnen and van Arkel, 1982) and time uncertainty (Frowein, Reitsma and Acquarius, 1981). Thus, sleep deprivation may have a negative effect on both the arousal and activation systems.

Steyvers (1987) examined the effect of sleep loss in combination with knowledge-of-results, a variable assumed to affect the effort system. He expected the detrimental effect of sleep loss to be mitigated by the effect of performance feedback on the effort system. His results replicated the interaction of stimulus quality and sleep loss and revealed that the detrimental effect of sleep loss was lessened by performance feedback. The predicted second-order interaction of these three variables did not occur, however. Apparently, the effect of performance feedback does not influence arousal. Steyvers concluded that the locus of the combined effect of sleep loss and performance feedback is at a stage other than stimulus encoding. Possibly, the ameliorative effect of performance feedback is by way of the activation mechanism. An experimental test of this interpretation would be to combine sleep loss and performance feedback with a task variable that affects the motor side of the reaction process (e.g. foreperiod duration).

Van der Molen and coworkers reasoned that psychophysiological analysis may constitute an additional means by which to test a model like Sanders' (van der Molen *et al.*, 1987b). They used components of the HR response to complement performance measures in distinguishing functional from structural effects on the choice reaction process. To derive a set of specific predictions concerning the relation between HR and the state of energetic components in Sanders' model, they used Pribram and McGuinness' (1975) conceptualization of arousal, activation, and effort. But, as we shall see shortly, they deviated from it in a number of important respects. For Pribram and McGuinness, any information input triggers a response from the arousal system that is reflected in changes of sympathetic nervous system activity that induces HR deceleration. The activation system is involved when the subject maintains a set to respond to external events. They suggested that a state of readiness will be reflected in HR deceleration. Conversely, when problem solving takes place, HR acceleration is postulated to occur that reflects the task demands on the effort system (see also McGuinness and Pribram, 1980).

It has been pointed out by van der Molen and colleagues that the change in HR that Pribram and McGuinness associated with the three systems of attention may not be related directly to the typical pattern of HR change observed during performance of a signaled choice RT task (cf. van der Molen *et al.*, 1987b; p. 255). In the time interval between the warning stimulus and the imperative stimulus a triphasic HR response is usually observed that consists of an initial deceleration, then an acceleration, and, finally, a more pronounced deceleration that reaches its nadir at some point in time near the response to the imperative stimulus. Thus, van der Molen *et al.* reasoned that the deceleration preceding the imperative stimulus may be a manifestation of the coordinating and supervising role played in the choice reaction process by the effort mechanism. During focused temporal anticipation—as in the signaled choice RT task—the voluntary effort mechanism may maintain the basal mechanisms in states of readiness to receive input and this, in turn, facilitates performance of the anticipated action. In contrast to Pribram and McGuinness, van der Molen *et al.* pointed out that the phasic response to input is cardiac deceleration, not acceleration. This position is supported by the demonstration in the cardiac-cycle time literature that information input elicits primary bradycardia in association with the allocation of capacity to the early perceptual stages of information processing (Coles and Strayer, 1985). Finally, van der Molen *et al.* suggested that there is a transition from anticipatory HR deceleration to acceleration when response initiation mechanisms are engaged.

They performed two experiments to test these notions. In both experiments the structural task variables they manipulated were the quality of the stimulus (intact versus degraded), the number of response alternatives (two versus four), and the duration of the foreperiod (short—4 s—versus long—12 s—in the first experiment; and fixed—6 s—and variable—6, 9, or 12 s—foreperiods in the second experiment). As we reviewed earlier, these factors are commonly observed to have additive relations, suggesting that they influence different stages of processing—stimulus encoding, response choice, and motor adjustment, respectively. In addition, both experiments included a functional task variable van der Molen *et al.* labeled as 'task involvement'. This variable was not manipulated. It was inferred from a *post hoc* analysis of trial-to-trial fluctuations in the best (fastest) and the worst (slowest) reactions (defined as the first and fourth quartiles of the RT distribution). In the heart rate literature, this type of comparison is often used to assess the relation between anticipatory deceleration and the efficiency of sensorimotor performance (van der Molen *et al.*, 1985). In the RT literature, this comparison is often made in speed/accuracy tradeoff analyses (Wickelgren, 1977), and is referred to as a microanalyis, as opposed to a macroanalysis (that involves the use of response deadlines, response signals, or variations in response speed instructions), of the speed/accuracy function. Van der Molen *et al.* assumed that this analysis would reveal effects on the effort mechanism as it coordinated the activity of the basal mechanisms, arousal and activation. To further engage the effort mechanism in its coordinating and supervising role, performance feedback was provided after each trial.

In the first experiment, the threat of shock was used as an additional functional task variable. Following Sanders (1983; p. 81), anticipation of a threatening stimulus was expected to induce a pattern of stress dominated by overactivation. The shock was presented randomly in lieu of the imperative stimulus on 0, 1, 2, or 3 trials in a block of 42 trials. The experimental factors were blocked in Experiment 1, but mixed randomly within a block in Experiment 2. The mixed presentation was designed to enhance the effects of the task variables on heart rate and to place a greater task load on the effort system.

The performance data from both experiments revealed a pattern that is at the same time compatible and at variance with the additive factors literature. When the experimental factors were blocked and there was no threat of shock, the structural task variables contributed additively to mean RT. This finding is consistent with previous research and suggests that the three variables (stimulus quality, number of response choices, foreperiod duration) affect three different stages of processing (stimulus encoding, response choice, motor adjustment). The threat of shock prolonged RT considerably, as it has been shown to do in previous reports (e.g. Jennings *et al.*, 1971; Somsen *et al.*, 1983). In contrast to Sanders' prediction, however, the threat of shock interacted weakly with the duration of the foreperiod but strongly with the quality of the stimulus. Thus, following Sanders' criterion, anticipation of the threatening stimulus seems to have its predominant effect on the state of the arousal mechanism. Finally, the functional task variable, task involvement, interacted with all of the structural variables, as well as with the threat of shock. By and large, the effects of these variables were half the size for the fastest quartile of RTs as compared with the slowest quartile. This pattern was interpreted to reflect the working of a central mechanism that counteracts the detrimental effects of degraded stimuli, an increased load on the response choice stage, time uncertainty, and the anticipation of a threatening stimulus.

Thus, dichotomizing the RT distribution into its best and the worst times may permit the compensatory activities of the effort mechanism to be revealed.

The interpretation of the results was complicated, however, by the finding that the serial stage structure of the reaction process obtained under blocked conditions with no threat of shock was destroyed by the threat of shock. Thus, the entire pattern of results did not conform to the 'stage robustness' criterion of the additive factors method. The relation between two factors should not change when a third factor is added to the design. The results from the van der Molen *et al.* study showed, however, that the additive relation between the quality of the stimulus and the number of response choices turned into an overadditive interaction when subjects were faced with the threat of shock. Interestingly, a similar pattern emerged when RTs were dichotomized into fastest and slowest quartiles. An additive relation was found between the quality of the stimulus and the number of response choices for the response latencies in the fastest quartile of the RT distribution, but an interactive relation was found for the responses in the slowest quartile. This pattern was replicated in the second experiment. Van der Molen *et al.* suggested that the overadditive interaction (between stimulus quality and response choices) reflected a malfunctioning of the arousal system when task involvement was low and there was the threat of shock. More specifically, they assumed that (1) efficient stimulus encoding requires the preactivation of internal codes when the stimuli are degraded, and (2) under suboptimal conditions the state of the arousal mechanism is lowered to prevent adequate preactivation, particularly when a number of stimulus alternatives are involved. Thus, it could well be possible that the output of the stimulus encoding stage was not identical in the two- and four-choice conditions. An overadditive interaction would be expected if in the four-choice condition the response choice stage received a more distorted output than in the two-choice condition. Note from our earlier discussion that Sanders (1980) made a similar suggestion in explaining the underadditive relation obtained by Stanovich and Pachella (1977) between signal contrast and S–R compatibility.

For the present discussion, it is important to determine if the analysis of HR changes during the reaction process can contribute to a deeper understanding of the cognitive–energetic relations. Figure 1.14 illustrates the HR responses obtained by van der Molen *et al.* in the second experiment. Recall that in this experiment time uncertainty was varied by comparing responses in a fixed foreperiod reaction (6 s) with those in a variable foreperiod reaction (6, 9, or 12 s). The morphology of the heart rate response observed under these conditions indicates that the subject did not wait passively for the imperative stimulus to arrive, but made active attempts to predict the time of its occurrence. With a fixed foreperiod, the deceleratory response showed a steep trend that reached its nadir at the time at which the stimulus occurred. With variable foreperiods, HR responses did not differ for the first six seconds. In this

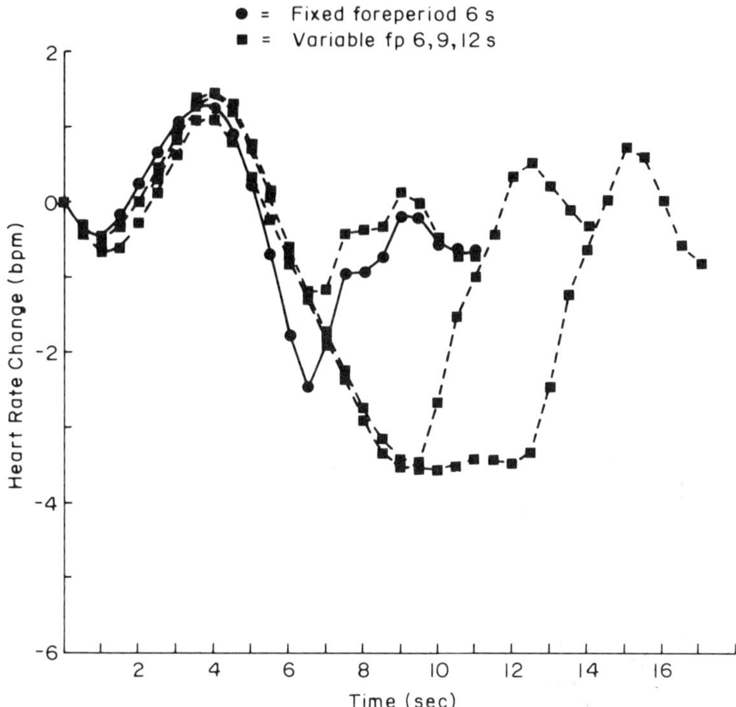

Figure 1.14. Data from van der Molen, *et al.* (1987b). The effect of foreperiod on the heart rate response. The solid line represents the response obtained by using a fixed 6 s interval, whereas the dashed lines represent the responses occurring under variable 6, 9, or 12 s intervals. (Reprinted with permission of the authors and publisher. © 1987 Elsevier Science Publishers B.V.)

condition, subjects seemed to set their response to the medium length of the foreperiod alternatives. At the shorter length, the response was interrupted by the early presentation of the imperative stimulus, whereas at the longer length it leveled off beyond the medium length until the stimulus was presented. The dynamic nature of the anticipatory HR response led van der Molen *et al.* to suggest that this response reflects voluntary tuning of the basal mechanisms by the effort system.

A second important finding was that there was a pronounced increase in the anticipatory deceleration just prior to or at the moment of stimulus occurrence when the foreperiod was fixed (i.e. time uncertainty was low). This cardiac response must be differentiated, however, from that seen when the foreperiod is variable but an external cue is presented that enables the subject to predict the exact time when the stimulus will occur (Jennings, van der Molen and Terezis, 1988). Under these conditions, the commonly observed triphasic HR response is absent and there is only a deceleration immediately prior to the stimulus occurrence. This pattern is consistent with the suggestion of van der Molen *et al.* that the deceleration they observed actually consists of two components, one associated with temporal prediction and the other with processing capacity becoming available just prior to the arrival of the stimulus. Also in accord with this speculation is their finding that the length of the foreperiod exerted an effect on primary bradycardia and vagal inhibition. The cardiac-cycle time effect seen at the time the stimulus was presented was stronger when the length of the foreperiod was fixed than when it was variable. This finding suggests that when the subject is able to predict the time of stimulus onset processing capacity can be allocated to the perceptual stages of the reaction in a timely fashion. This interpretation requires that either the threat of shock or variations in the quality of the stimulus influence primary bradycardia as well. However, neither factor modified the magnitude of primary bradycardia. Finally, time uncertainty affected vagal inhibition. The response-related cardiac-cycle time effect was more pronounced when the length of the foreperiod was fixed (i.e. time uncertainty was low) than when it was variable (i.e. time uncertainty was high), suggesting that heart rate deceleration shifts from deceleration to acceleration when the response initiation stage is engaged.

In discussing the relation between RT and HR changes, van der Molen *et al.* pointed out that Sanders' cognitive–energetic model offers a more complete explanation than other serial stage models because it attempts to explain processes that occur prior to the arrival of the imperative stimulus. Sanders' conceptualization emphasizes presetting mechanisms and their influence on processing stages in anticipation of the occurrence of the imperative stimulus (cf. Gopher and Sanders, 1984). Van der Molen *et al.* suggested that measures derived from the ECG are particularly useful in studying covert behavior during the preparatory interval. They summarized the changes in heart rate during the foreperiod as follows (pp. 284–286):

(1) The first manifestation of preparation during the foreperiod is cardiac slowing. This response disappears when there is no need for temporal prediction (e.g. Jennings *et al.*, 1988).
(2) Subsequently, deceleration is added just prior to the stimulus. The amplitude of this response increases with the likelihood of a motor response (van der Molen *et al.*, 1987b).
(3) The imperative stimulus elicits 'primary bradycardia'. The amplitude of this phase-dependent cardiac slowing increases with stimulus significance (Coles *et al.*, 1982) and decreases with increases in time uncertainty (van der Molen *et al.*, 1987b).
(4) Finally, initiation of the motor response induces 'vagal inhibition'. That is,

the timing of the cardiac shift from deceleration to acceleration depends on the cycle time of response initiation (Somsen *et al.*, 1985).

To explain this pattern of results, van der Molen *et al.* proposed an integration of Niemi and Näätänen's conception of the foreperiod effect with Sanders' cognitive–energetic model. Niemi and Näätänen argued that the preparatory phase of a mental reaction that takes place during the foreperiod includes both perceptual and motor components. Perceptually, preparation is assumed to consist of a process whereby a mental image of the stimulus is retained and rehearsed, a process that facilitates its subsequent identification. Motor preparation, in their view, consists of a priming-like activation of the response system toward the 'motor action limit' that facilitates the attainment of this limit when a particular response is engaged. Given this combination of intensive processes, it is not surprising that it is difficult and energy-consuming to maintain a constant, high state of preparation (Gottsdanker, 1975).

Niemi and Näätänen's conceptualization of the processes engaged during the foreperiod of a mental reaction and their effect on the speed of the reaction can be incorporated into Sanders' framework. Following Sanders' colleague Frowein (1981), at the input side of the reaction there are three hypothesized stages: stimulus preprocessing, stimulus encoding, and stimulus identification. Frowein hypothesized that the initial peripheral processing of a stimulus occurs in the preprocessing stage. Here, extraneous stimulus information is eliminated from further analysis (e.g. the noise elements in a degraded stimulus). The output of this stage is then passed to the more central stimulus encoding stage where the feature analysis of the stimulus takes place. The output of this analysis is then passed to the stimulus identification stage where the final integration and selection of the stimulus from a set of alternatives is made. Following Sanders, van der Molen *et al.* assumed that the two more central stages, stimulus encoding and identification, receive energetic support from the 'arousal' system, the temporary state of which might be altered by input from the early preprocessing stage.

It was also assumed that the output of the stimulus identification stage might elicit a phasic response by the arousal system. Van der Molen *et al.* suggested that the effect of perceptual preparation on speeded RT tasks consists primarily of more effective processing of sensory input at the preprocessing stage. Thus, when the subject is prepared at the optimal level, stimulus preprocessing exerts a stronger effect on the arousal system. They pointed out that the active processes involved in perceptual preparation may be similar to the notion of selective attention offered by Posner and Boies (1971). Consider a subject who is instructed to attend to one set of stimuli and to ignore another. When a designated stimulus is presented, the output of the identification process may trigger a response from the arousal system, the magnitude of which is proportional to the significance of the stimulus. Van der Molen *et al.*

hypothesized that primary bradycardia is the autonomic component of this arousal response to significant stimuli.

The response end of the reaction (i.e. the motor adjustment or initiation stage; Frowein, 1981) can be viewed as the stage at which the motor action limit is exceeded and motor readiness automatically engages response execution processes. During the foreperiod, the subject attempts to maintain an optimal level of response readiness to minimize the amount of activation required to attain the motor action limit. To do so, however, consumes energy. Therefore, the call for energetic support occurs only when the subject expects the stimulus to occur. Van der Molen *et al.* suggested that the sudden enhanced deceleration of HR immediately prior to the arrival of the imperative stimulus reflects energetic support provided by the activation system. When motor initiation processes are completed, response execution begins (i.e. the muscular processes that are necessary to execute the response). They suggested that the timing of these processes is reflected in the timing of the shift from HR deceleration to acceleration.

An important element in Sanders' cognitive–energetic framework is the evaluation mechanism, a system that acts as a governor to determine the amount of energetic support needed to satisfy the demands of the task or to titrate the basal arousal and activation systems. Van der Molen *et al.* noted that this formulation bears a strong resemblance to the concept of expectancy that Niemi and Näätänen invoked to explain the effects of time uncertainty on response latency. Accordingly, they assumed that during the preparatory period in an RT task evaluation consists of an active prediction of the arrival time of the stimulus. They assumed further that expectancy exerts its influence on preparation via a mechanism they called 'effort', which in turn coordinates engagement of the arousal and activation systems. Van der Molen *et al.* suggested that anticipatory HR deceleration associated with the need for temporal prediction reflects a specific pattern of coordination by the effort system; namely, holding available processing capacity in anticipation of subsequent action.

The attentive reader will have noticed that in the van der Molen *et al.* conceptualization of the influence of presetting on processing stages and its cardiac concomitants, the processes related to response choice are strikingly absent. This omission may result from the fact that Niemi and Näätänen's discussion of the foreperiod effect is restricted to simple reactions, while most additive factor studies of choice reaction processes use highly overlearned or natural stimulus–response relations. In the van der Molen *et al.* study, for example, response choice was manipulated by varying the number of response choices while keeping the S–R mappings constant. According to Sanders, active processes involved in presetting response choices can profit from energy supplied by the effort system and this is used for handling incompatible S–R mappings or, in a more general sense, is needed for an adequate functioning of the response choice stage. In Sanders' view, processing at this stage can be considered to be 'conscious', thus constituting one of Posner's (1978) components of attention. On the basis of Pribram and McGuinness' (1975) neurophysiological review, one would predict that whenever the effort system is invoked for handling incompatible S–R mappings the direct connection between arousal and activation is uncoupled, and this would be associated with HR acceleration.

The prediction that incompatible S–R mappings elicit HR acceleration was tested recently by Jennings *et al.* (1988). They manipulated compatibility by varying the spatial mapping between stimuli and responses in a four-choice reaction time task. For simple mapping, stimuli were mapped from left-to-right on to response keys that were aligned similarly. For complex mapping, the spatial relations between the stimuli and responses were randomized. HR responses differed from the triphasic pattern seen typically in choice RT tasks. Deceleration was maximal during the second interbeat interval after the stimulus. For the complex, but not for the simple, mapping a brief secondary deceleration occurred during the interbeat interval after the imperative stimulus. The secondary deceleration was stronger for short interstimulus intervals and slower responses than for long interstimulus intervals and faster responses. Jennings *et al.* concluded that these findings suggest that effortful mapping of a stimulus on to a response may induce transient deceleration rather than HR acceleration. In terms of the Sanders' model, this transient deceleration might reflect the uncoupling of the arousal and activation mechanisms or, in other words, the active inhibition of overlearned or natural stimulus–response relations.

This brief review suggests that changes in HR can be used to assess the extent to which an individual prepares for a stimulus and how this relates to response time. Next we turn to a discussion of the contribution that systematic changes in pupil dilation can make to furthering our understanding of chronometric processes.

PUPIL DILATION AND THE SUBTRACTION METHOD

Validation studies of changes in pupil size that accompany information processing suggest that they reflect a common factor related to the processing demands of a wide array of tasks ranging from simple perceptual tasks to more complex problem solving tasks. That is, this research indicates that variation in the size of the pupil is related to the allocation of resource capacity to information processors, rather than to the precise timing of their activation. Thus, pupil dilation, like HR, is associated with the functional, rather than the structural, elements of human information processing. However, in contrast to HR, there is no extant model that relates pupil responses to RT in the context of cognitive–energetic processes—although the first steps have been taken in its development.

Richer, Silverman and Beatty (1983) claimed that the pupil response can be used as a measure of both the time course and the amount of processing demands involved in the performance of RT tasks. The advantage of the pupil response, according to Richer *et al.*, is that it provides a continuous index of phasic changes in processing demands for the complete duration of the task without requiring the production of overt responses or the use of experimental manipulations that alter performance in any way. They attempted to substantiate this claim by applying the subtraction method to examine the relation between pupil dilation and RT. First, they tried to establish a proper baseline response pattern by recording pupillary responses in subjects during the foreperiod of a Donders' a-reaction (simple RT task). The length of the foreperiod was either 1 or 3 s, and was fixed within a block of trials. Both the warning and imperative stimuli were clearly distinguishable tones. As expected, RTs were longer for the 3 s than for the 1 s foreperiod. The pupil exhibited a steady dilation during both foreperiods that was greatest (0.34 mm) at about 900 ms after the imperative stimulus was presented. Analyses of the pupillary response time-locked to the manual response revealed that the dilation began at about 990 ms before the overt response when the foreperiod was short and at about 1340 ms when the foreperiod was long. This pattern of activation closely resembled the pattern they had observed in a previous study of unsignaled, spontaneous movements (Richer and Beatty, 1982; cited in Richer *et al.*, 1983). Since both the simple reaction and the unsignaled movement share a common process, execution of a motor output, Richer *et al.* concluded that the slow dilation of the pupil that is evident in the foreperiod of the simple reaction reflects response preparation, as opposed to stimulus anticipation, processes.

Following in the tradition of the subtraction method, they then complicated the simple reaction by inserting stimulus discrimination into the reaction, making it a disjunctive (or, in Donders' terminology, c-) reaction. Subjects were presented a warning stimulus that was followed by one of two stimuli, one of which signaled an overt response (the Go stimulus) and the other of which required no response (the NoGo stimulus). This reaction was performed under two conditions, immediate and delayed response. In the former, the subject was required to respond to the Go stimulus as quickly as possible after its onset. In the latter, the subject had to postpone execution of the response to the Go stimulus until a third (the Delayed Go) stimulus was presented. Richer *et al.* considered the reaction to be a b-reaction and reasoned, accordingly, that the delayed response condition allows response selection and response production processes to be separated. They assumed that the pupillary response to the third signal (Delayed Go stimulus) reflects response production processes; while the pupillary response to an imperative stimulus (NoGo) when it requires a Go/NoGo decision reflects the response selection process.

Richer *et al.* argued that these experimental conditions provide three pupillary estimates of response selection. First, assuming that only Go/NoGo decisional processes occur to NoGo stimuli, the pupil response to these stimuli in the immediate response condition provides a direct estimate of response selection. Second, subtraction of the pupillary response obtained in the delayed response condition from that obtained in the immediate response condition provides an estimate that is analogous to subtracting simple RT from choice RT. Third, the pupillary response to either the Go or NoGo stimulus in the delayed condition also provides an estimate of the Go/NoGo decisional process, if it is assumed that both stimuli are related only to response selection processes when response execution is postponed. Richer *et al.* made an important point about the validity of their estimates. It is based on the assumption that the pupillary response is an interval scale measure. They argued that Beatty's (1982) review demonstrating a marked regularity in the relationship of pupil dilation to information processing variables suggests that this assumption may well be met (p. 365).

It should be noted, however, that the reasoning followed by Richer *et al.* in deriving their estimates departs from the classic logic of Donders' subtraction method. They claimed that subtraction of the delayed response from the immediate response is tantamount to subtracting a simple (a-reaction) from a choice (b-reaction) reaction and, therefore, provides an estimate of response selection. Donders reasoned differently, however. In his view, the difference yielded in this subtraction represents the summed value of response selection and stimulus discrimination processes. According to Donders, response selection time is estimated by subtracting a c- from a b-reaction (i.e. a disjunctive from a choice reaction). In contrast, subtraction of the delayed response time from the immediate response time involves a simple and a disjunctive, not a choice, reaction. This subtraction (c-reaction minus a-reaction) provides an estimate of stimulus discrimination, not response selection, time.

With these provisions in mind, the results of this study can be evaluated. Richer *et al.* observed that RTs were longer in the immediate response than in the delayed response condition (333 ms versus 279 ms). They noted that this difference is in accord with previous observations of the difference in speed between simple and choice reactions (p. 364). The reader should bear in mind, however, that the difference is actually between simple and disjunctive reactions. The left panel of Figure 1.15 presents the pupil responses obtained in the four types of trials. It is evident that a larger response was elicited by the Go stimulus than by the NoGo stimulus. In the delayed response condition, the pupillary response to the Delayed Go stimulus began after the peak of the response to the Go stimulus and is superimposed on it. Differences in the amplitude of the peaks in the pupillary response elicited by Go and NoGo stimuli (i.e. S2 in Figure 1.15) were statistically significant, but smaller in

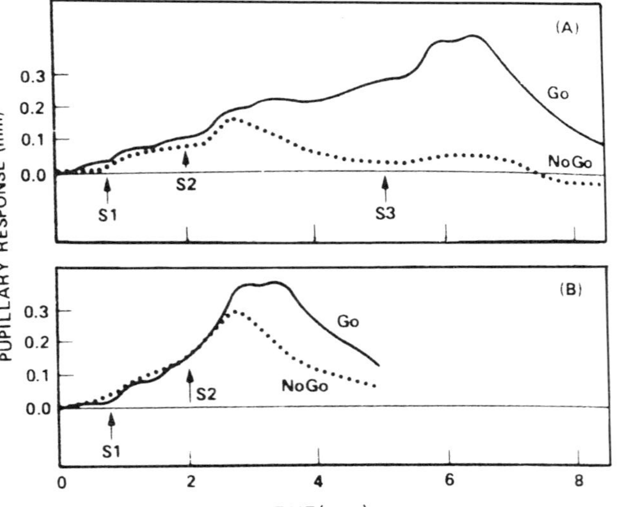

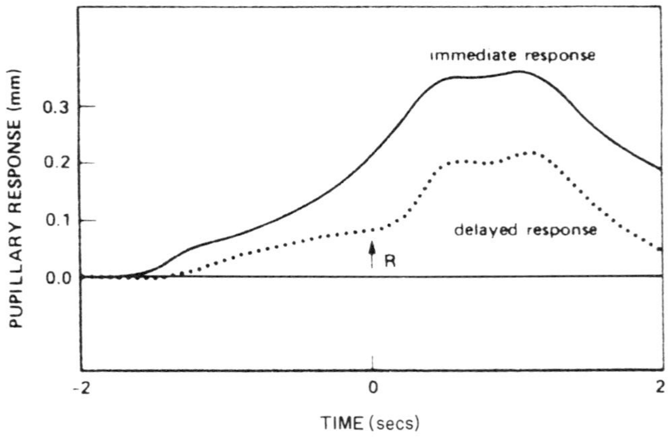

Figure 1.15. Data from Richer, Silverman and Beatty (1983). Stimulus-locked averaged pupillary responses obtained in immediate (left panel A) and delayed (left panel B) response conditions in disjunctive (Go/NoGo) reactions. The response-locked waveforms obtained for Go trials in immediate and delayed response conditions are depicted in the right panel of the figure. (Reprinted with permission. © 1983 by the American Psychological Association.)

magnitude, in the delayed than in the immediate response condition. The right panel of Figure 1.15 presents the pupillary response measured back in time from the overt response. It can be seen that the amplitude of the pupillary response is larger in the immediate than in the delayed response condition (0.42 versus 0.25 mm).

Richer *et al.* interpreted this pattern of findings in terms of response preparation and response selection processes. They pointed out that the main component of the pupillary response in disjunctive reactions is a slowly developing dilation that has a phasic response associated with the presentation of the discriminative stimulus superimposed on it. They identified the pupillary response to the Go and NoGo stimuli with response preparation. This conclusion was based on the observation that the phasic component of the pupillary response was present in the immediate but absent in the delayed response condition.

To obtain a pupillary marker of response selection, they first measured the dilation produced by the NoGo stimulus in the immediate response condition, believed by them to provide a direct estimate of this process. The amplitude of the response to the NoGo stimulus was 0.31 mm, a value that is considerably larger than their second estimate of response selection. Their second estimate was obtained by subtracting the pupillary response to the Delayed Go stimulus from the response elicited by the Immediate Go stimulus. It yielded a value of 0.17 mm. Next, they measured the amplitudes of the pupillary responses to the Go and the NoGo stimuli in the delayed response condition, assumed by them to provide a third estimate of response selection. These measurements yielded values of 0.21 mm for Go stimuli and 0.17 mm for NoGo stimuli. The reader should note that the latter value (0.17 mm) agrees with the value obtained using the second estimation procedure. Last, they measured the dilation produced by the Go stimulus (0.25 mm). Richer *et al.* interpreted this response as an index of the processing demands made on response preparation and execution processes, and the dilation produced by the NoGo stimulus in the delayed condition (0.17 mm) as an index of processing demands on response selection. The difference in dilation they observed in response to NoGo stimuli in the delayed and immediate response conditions (0.17 versus 0.31 mm), both of which they assumed to be indices of response selection processes, was attributed to the increase in processing demands imposed on the subject by the need to withhold the response in the immediate response condition.

Richer *et al.* performed a third experiment to clarify the role of response-related processes to the pupil responses seen to NoGo stimuli. They reasoned that response-related processes are related to the probability of occurrence of Go stimuli. Thus, by increasing the probability of occurrence of overt responses a bias toward preparing the response is achieved and dilation to presentations of the NoGo stimulus should be more similar to that of the Go stimulus. They assumed that this manipulation would only affect responses to the NoGo stimulus because execution of the motor response to the Go stimulus saturates the motoric processing demands of the task. They used a task that is very similar to the disjunctive RT task (immediate response condition) in the previous experiment, with the exception that the second stimulus could be one of three tones that differed only in pitch. The experiment included high- and low-probability conditions. In the high-probability condition, subjects were instructed to respond to the high- and the medium-pitched tones, but to refrain from responding to the low-pitched tone. In the low-probability condition, they were instructed to respond only to the high-pitched tone.

Reaction time did not vary as a function of probability. As expected, pupil dilation to the Go stimulus was not affected by changes in the probability of making an overt response, whereas dilation to the NoGo stimulus was influenced. When the probability of making a response was increased, dilation of the pupil to the Go and NoGo stimuli was comparable. This finding was taken to provide strong support for the suggestion that NoGo reactions include non-decisional processes related to the imminence of a motor response.

The interpretation of pupil dilation as an index of response preparation processes led van der Molen *et al.* (1989) to complete a cross-validation study in which they examined the relation between pupil dilation, HR deceleration, and RT in a Go/NoGo task in which the probability of a Go stimulus being presented was varied across three levels. The task required a signaled choice reaction in which a high-frequency tone indicated a response with the left hand, a low-frequency tone indicated a response with the right hand, and a medium-frequency tone indicated that no response should be made. The probability of a Go stimulus was 0.25, 0.50, or 0.75. The effect of probability on pupil dilation obtained by Richer *et al.* was replicated; that is, pupil dilation was made comparable to Go and NoGo stimuli by increasing the probability of the Go stimulus. In addition, the amplitude of the HR response at the time of the stimulus presentation paralleled the pupil findings; a more pronounced deceleration was observed as the relative probability of the Go stimulus increased from 0.25 to 0.50 to 0.75. These findings support the hypothesis that pupil dilation and HR deceleration provide converging measures of response preparation. This hypothesis must be qualified by the following observations, however. Van der Molen *et al.* observed that for HR, in contrast to pupil dilation, the probability effect was the same for decelerations to Go and for NoGo stimuli. The computed correlations between either amplitudes or latencies of the physiological responses were low, in different directions, and non-significant. Thus, both the heart and the pupil are sensitive to response preparation, but they may provide different windows on this activation process. This conclusion emphasizes the need for multi-measure analyses of reaction processes. For the mental chronometrician, the important finding is that there are, in fact, motor processes associated with not responding to the NoGo stimulus. Thus, Richer *et al.* provided empirical support for Wundt's (1874) claim, based on introspective reports, that disjunctive reactions also involve a kind of response selection. We now turn our attention to ERPs.

EVENT-RELATED BRAIN POTENTIALS AND EARLY COMMUNICATION

Perhaps the first cognitive psychophysiological test of a model of human information processing was published by Coles *et al.* (1985). These investigators used measures of RT, P300 latency, and electromyographic (EMG) and response device activation to test the continuous flow model. They were interested specifically in assessing the relative contributions of stimulus evaluation (assumed to continuously supply information to the response channels), response competition (assumed to be activated by stimuli that are associated with different responses), and aspecific priming (assumed to be produced by the activation of a particular stimulus-related response channel prior to the presentation of the stimulus) to the total time of a choice reaction.

Subjects completed a variant of the Eriksen task. They were trained to respond to one letter (e.g. H) by squeezing a dynamometer with one hand (e.g. left hand) and to respond to a second letter (e.g. S) by squeezing another dynamometer with the other hand (e.g. right hand). The letter was presented in a five element horizontal array flanked either by two repetitions of itself on both flanks (e.g. HHHHH) or by two repetitions of the other letter on each flank (e.g. SSHSS). These arrays were referred to as compatible or incompatible, respectively, by Coles *et al.* Presentation of an array was either warned (a tone) or unwarned, and the type of flanker was either fixed within a block of trials or mixed randomly. Subjects were instructed to ignore the flankers and to make their response decisions exclusively on the basis of the letter in the center position. In addition, they were instructed to favor speed over accuracy in their decision-making. The authors encouraged speed to increase the likelihood of false starts being made, detected, and corrected. The dynamometers were set with a threshold for response activation (25% of the standard squeeze force) that permitted subjects to detect an incorrect response and stop it before the threshold was achieved. To identify error detection and correction, EMG activity was recorded and the voltage output of the dynamometers was digitized. Recordings of EMG activity were made so that the time course of EMG activation could be followed and estimates of its onset derived. Likewise, the output of the dynamometers was digitized so that the time course of its activation could be analyzed. These two measures could then be used to classify responses into a variety of activation categories.

Some reasonably straightforward predictions could be tested under these experimental conditions. A strict serial model would assert that errors cannot be detected, and therefore only two classes of response should emerge, correct and incorrect. That is, there should be no evidence of error detection and correction in the EMG or voltage output from the dynamometers because information about the stimulus is not passed to the response output stages until the stimulus is evaluated completely. Thus, in those instances where errors are made, the stimulus has been evaluated completely, but incorrectly. (Note that a model like Miller's permits error detection and correction because of the assumed temporal overlap of stage processing.) In contrast, the continuous flow model asserts that stimulus information is being passed to response channels as it accumulates, the effect of which is to prime these response channels for responding as the stimulus is being evaluated. Once this priming effect achieves a critical threshold on either channel, the response is initiated. However, since response activation is presumed to be continuous as well and stimulus information continues to be passed to the response channels after a response has been initiated, initiation of an incorrect response can be detected and corrected before the point at which a response has been attained (i.e. the point of no return). This notion distinguishes the continuous flow model from the cascade model which postulates a discrete response output. Like the serial stage model, the cascade model predicts that once a response has been initiated it cannot be stopped.

Onset of EMG and response device activation provided indices of the response activation process. The authors' choice of P300 latency was based on the results of the aforementioned studies that suggested its differential sensitivity to stimulus factors. It could therefore be used in conjunction with the other measures to infer the relative timing of stimulus and response processes. Thus, response-related activity could be inferred from EMG and dynamometer activation, and stimulus-related activity from P300 latency. Presentation of the flanking letters was presumed to concurrently activate stimulus- and response-related processes. This would be evident in both P300 latency and the measures of response channel activation. When the flankers were associated with a different response from the center letter, they were assumed to produce response competition via the simultaneous activation of response channels associated with both stimuli consequent to the transmission of continuously accumulating stimulus information. The presence of a warning stimulus was presumed to facilitate response-related processes, in particular aspecific priming. This would be manifest as variation in the measures of response system activation, with P300 latency remaining relatively unchanged. And, the blocked presentation of an array type (either center letter flanked by itself or by the other letter) was presumed to facilitate the stimulus evaluation process. This would be revealed in variation in P300 latency.

Like C.W. Eriksen and others have found (see earlier in this chapter), RT and error rate varied in this study as a function of the type of flanker. RT was prolonged and more errors (defined as squeezes above the 25% response threshold) were made across conditions when the center letter and flankers signaled the opposite response (397 versus 444 ms, about 8 versus 17% error rates). The presentation of a warning tone in advance of the array reduced

RT (410 versus 430 ms), as did fixing the type of flanker within a block (413 versus 428 ms). The advantage of blocking was more pronounced, however, for incompatible than for compatible arrays (19 versus 11 ms). For errors, fixing the flanker type resulted in a decrease in errors in the incompatible condition, but an increase in the compatible.

This pattern of behavioral results is certainly consistent with what had been reported in the literature. A closer look at the response output associated with this task was afforded, however, by the addition of the EMG and response device measures. Use of these measures permitted Coles *et al.* to identify four categories of response channel activation. In the first, activity was present only on the correct side for both EMG and dynamometer activation (the N category); in the second, EMG activity was apparent in both the incorrect and correct arms, but dynamometer activity occurred only on the correct side (the E category); in the third, EMG and response device activity were identified on both the incorrect and correct sides, and the incorrect squeeze may or may not have reached the response threshold (the S category); and in the fourth, EMG and squeeze activity was apparent on the incorrect side, with EMG activity either present or absent on the correct side (the Error category).

This response classification system discriminated among ordered classes of responses. Coles *et al.* found that correct activation at both the EMG and response device levels was associated with monotonic increases in onset latency from N to E to S categories, whereas incorrect activation at both levels was associated with monotonic decreases in onset latency from E to S to Error categories. Thus, for both correct and incorrect response channels onset activation of both the EMG and response device was delayed when activation occurred in the other response arm. In addition, the interval between the initiation of a correct response (indexed by EMG onset) and its execution (indexed by activation of the response device) varied with the response category. The interval was longer for the S (80 ms) than for the E (53 ms) and N (57 ms) responses. This pattern suggests that the execution of the correct response slows as the amount of response channel activation increases in the opposite channel. Coles *et al.* also reported that when squeeze activity occurred on both sides (the S category) the onset of the incorrect squeeze was always shorter than that of the correct squeeze (396 versus 501 ms).

These findings led the authors to conclude that: (a) both response channels may be activated on the same trial; (b) if this activation reaches the level of a squeeze, the two response channels inhibit each other (response competition); (c) response activation is not an all-or-none phenomenon—rather, several levels of activation are possible; (d) activation of the correct response to the threshold for squeeze emission may occur after the emission of an incorrect squeeze, but the converse is not true (p. 543).

P300 latency was also found to increase monotonically with increases in the degree of activation of the incorrect response channel (from N, to E, to S,

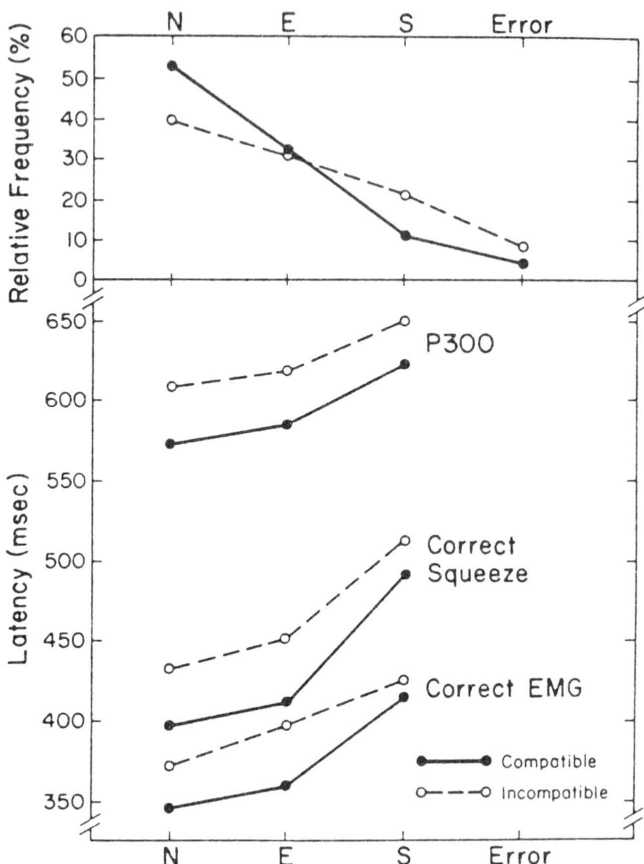

Figure 1.16. Mean onset times for correct electromyographic and squeeze activity and mean P300 latency as a function of response category for compatible and incompatible stimulus arrays reported by Coles *et al.* (1985). Shown in the upper panel are the relative frequencies for each type of response in each response category. (Reprinted with permission. © 1985 American Psychological Association.)

to Error). If P300 latency is associated with the timing of stimulus evaluation processes, then the suggestion is that when these processes are slowed there is a greater likelihood that the incorrect response channel will be activated. This entire pattern of findings is shown in Figure 1.16.

This figure also reveals that the proportion of trials in each response category varied as a function of the type of flanker. A greater number of trials with no incorrect motor activity (N responses) and a fewer number of trials with incorrect EMG and squeeze device (E and Error responses) activation occurred when compatible arrays were presented. This suggests, of course, that responses to incompatible arrays not only include a larger number of errors (as traditional RT analyses indicate), but also that bimanual responses are more frequent and may occur before the correct response is executed.

Coles *et al.* then used the psychophysiological measures to infer the relative contributions of stimulus and response processes to the 47 ms difference in RT revealed in the traditional analysis between compatible and incompatible arrays. They deduced the presence of response competition from the prolongation of EMG and response device activation in the correct arm when activation occurred in the incorrect arm and from the concurrent prolongation of the execution of the correct response itself on these trials. By weighting the mean RTs in three response categories (N, E, S) on the basis of the proportion of trials in each category for both compatible and incompatible arrays, they arrived at a value of 10 ms for the contribution of the S response to the overall cost of incompatibility. By using response category as a factor in an analysis of variance and doing the appropriate weighting, they were able to determine that response execution was delayed for correct responses to incompatible arrays (i.e. when there was no evidence of incorrect activation) by an additional 12 ms. Thus, they suggested that 22 ms of the 47 ms compatibility effect could be accounted for by response competition effects associated both with threshold and subthreshold activation of the incorrect response channel. Similarly, the weighted P300 latency was determined to account for the rest of the time added by the presence of incompatible noise in the array. Hence, the relative contributions of stimulus evaluation and response competition processes to the 47 ms effect of flanker incompatibility could be inferred.

However, activation of the incorrect response channel also occurred in the absence of any stimulus input associated with that response (i.e. on compatible trials). To explain this, the authors invoked the notion of aspecific priming. This process was inferred from the observations that EMG and squeeze device activation occurred earlier when a warning tone preceded the arrays than when it did not on both correct and incorrect responses but that P300 latency was unchanged. This pattern suggests that stimulus evaluation time remains relatively invariant as the threshold for a motor response is reduced when a warning tone is presented. In contrast to the effect of a warning stimulus on the reaction process, EMG and squeeze device activation, as well as P300 latency, were earlier when the type of array was fixed within a block of trials. However, the proportion of S trials increased (and N decreased) for compatible trials but not for incompatible trials when the type of array was fixed. Thus, where stimulus evaluation processes may have been speeded for both arrays, the response strategy may have changed (become less conservative) for compatible arrays.

An especially interesting component of their analysis was the speed/accuracy analyses they did using P300 latency as the index of stimulus evaluation time. Traditional speed/accuracy analyses use response latency as an

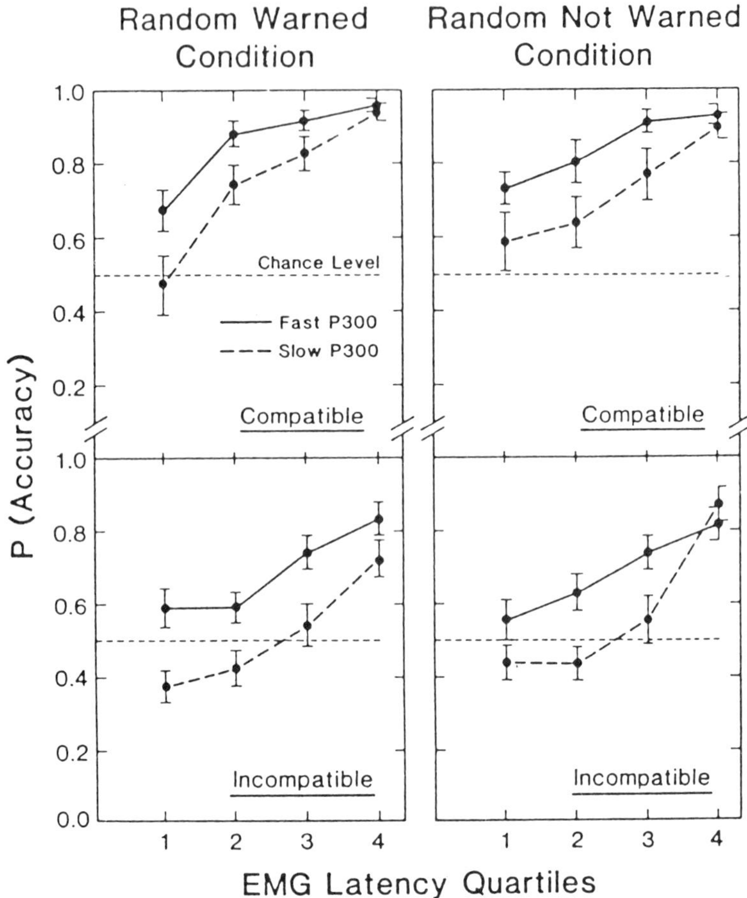

Figure 1.17. Speed/accuracy tradeoff curves calculated by Coles *et al.* (1985) for compatible and incompatible noise arrays, with P300 latency as the dependent variable. Shown in the two panels on the left are the functions obtained when noise was mixed randomly within a block of trials and the subject either did or did not receive a warning tone. The two panels on the right show these functions when the noise was fixed within a block of trials. (Reproduced with permission. © 1985 American Psychological Association.)

experimental factor to provide an unbiased estimate of stimulus evaluation processes (Pachella, 1974). This method assumes, however, that stimulus evaluation processes are constant at a particular response latency. Since this assumption may not be valid (Meyer and Irwin, 1982), Coles *et al.* computed speed/accuracy functions for trials with different durations of stimulus evaluation using P300 latency as the index of this variation. In addition, rather than using RT (i.e. time to achieve the 25% criterion on the

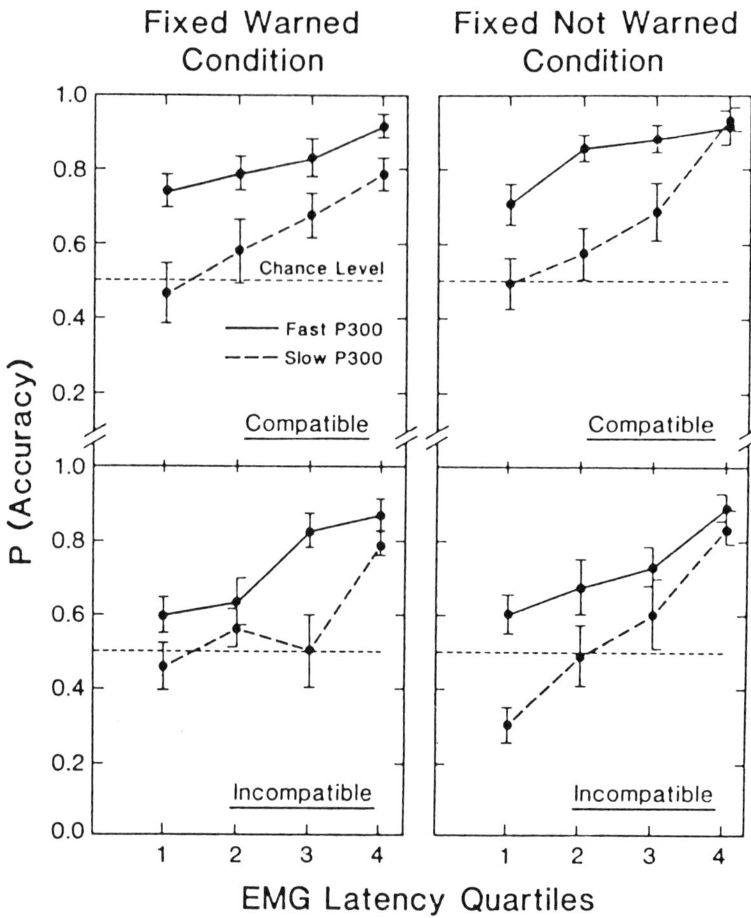

Figure 1.17. (*continued*)

response device) as the measure of response latency, they used EMG onset. Single-trial P300 latencies were sorted into those that were fast and those that were slow (defined as being below or above the median for the subject and condition), and were classified into quartiles on the basis of EMG onset latency. Thus, trials were sorted into eight groups (fast/slow P300 by four EMG latencies). Accuracy was computed by determining the percentage of correct trials for each of the eight groups.

The pattern revealed in this analysis is shown in Figure 1.17 for all of the experimental conditions. First, it is apparent that accuracy increases as EMG onset latency increases, irrespective of the speed of the P300. Second, when subjects responded to either a compatible or an incompatible array, in all conditions, accuracy levels were higher when the P300 was fast than when it was slow. Third, accuracy levels are similar when either the P300 is fast and the EMG onset is early, or the P300 is slow and the response is slow. Together, these findings suggest that response accuracy is tied very closely to the timing of the stimulus evaluation process. Note, however, that the functions for compatible and incompatible arrays differ in some fundamentally important ways. Accuracy is lower at all levels of response speed for incompatible arrays, and if a fast response is emitted when the P300 latency is slow accuracy falls below the chance level for these arrays. This suggests that the flankers may be driving the decision process on these trials. Coles *et al.* interpreted this pattern as reflecting a two-step process in which the salient features of the stimulus array are identified before the location of the target is identified. Their data did not allow them to speculate on the relative timing of these processes (i.e. serial versus parallel), but the authors did suggest that the results indicated that the feature analysis occurred at a faster rate than the location analysis.

This experiment was followed by a study designed to look specifically at the response mechanisms engaged in the Eriksen task (Gratton *et al.*, 1988). The authors were especially interested in assessing the relative and varying contributions of differences in levels of response preparation and response competition on the final response latency. They conceptualized the choice reaction as comprising two main constituents, response channel and stimulus evaluation processes. The former was assumed to include all of the processing related to the production of the overt response, and the latter all of the processing involved in analyzing the stimulus content and passing the results of this processing to the appropriate response channel. Within this context, response preparation is viewed as an increase in the level of activation of a response channel and response competition as a decrease in the level of activation of one channel as a result of the concurrent activation of a second channel. As in the Coles *et al.* study, these levels of activation were inferred in part from the peripheral activation of the muscles and response devices involved in the execution of the overt response.

In this study, Gratton *et al.* added a central analog measure of the activation of the response system, the lateralized readiness potential. This movement-related potential is a derivative of the readiness potential we described earlier. Recall, the readiness potential was first identified in association with unsignaled movements as a slow negative-going change in brain electrical activity in the period preceding the movement, that became larger at the central scalp site overlying the motor area controlling the movement about 400 ms before its execution (Kornhuber and Deecke, 1965). Subsequent work has revealed that a similar pattern of activity occurs in the foreperiod of signaled RT tasks (Kutas and Donchin, 1980; Rohrbaugh and Gaillard, 1983; Rohrbaugh, Syndulko and Lindsley, 1976). The timing of the relative lateralization of this activity varies in a choice reaction, however, as a function of the information conveyed by the warning stimulus *vis-à-vis* the imperative stimulus (Kutas and Donchin, 1980).

When the warning stimulus provides information critical to the choice signaled by the imperative stimulus the negativity lateralizes during the foreperiod; when the warning stimulus does not provide such information, the negativity does not lateralize until after the imperative stimulus has been presented. This pattern suggests that activation of specific motor systems is manifest in the activity of the readiness potential. The lateralized readiness potential is computed by subtracting the activity recorded at the scalp site over the motor area ipsilateral to the (incorrect) movement from the activity at the scalp site over the motor area contralateral to the (correct) movement for both hands, summing the values thus derived and dividing this sum by two. The assumption is that all lateralized activity not associated with the movement will average to zero (see discussion in Coles, 1989).

Gratton *et al.* distinguished motor activity in the prestimulus period from that in the poststimulus period. It was their contention that activation of response channels during these two periods could be deduced from the lateralized readiness potential and, in turn, variation in this activation could be used to test hypotheses about the factors involved in establishing response output thresholds. According to the variable baseline hypothesis (Posner, 1978), for example, differential preparation of one response channel during the prestimulus period would be revealed in an asymmetry in activity consistent with this preparation. The effect of this differential preparation would be to move the level of activation of the response channel closer to the threshold for a response. This process would be revealed in the amplitude of the lateralized readiness potential during the foreperiod. When the warning stimulus provides no information about the imperative stimulus, as in this study, then any directional preparation is a guess. If the imperative stimulus happens to match the guess, a fast and accurate response will ensue. If not, a fast error will be produced. Hence, the production of responses will vary on a trial-to-trial basis as a consequence of shifts in the prestimulus baseline activation of the response channels (but the response threshold will remain constant).

Response channel activation following the imperative stimulus is presumed to be driven by the content of the stimulus array. Recall that the speed/accuracy analysis Coles *et al.* did on P300 latency revealed that the combination of a fast response output and a slow P300 resulted in below-chance levels of accuracy when an incompatible array was presented (where all other combinations resulted in chance or above-chance levels). This pattern was used to support the conclusion that the flanking letters drove the response on these trials and led to the speculation that processing of the letter array had two components, feature and location analysis, and that the feature analysis occurred at a faster rate than did the location analysis. Gratton *et al.* suggested, therefore, that partial information about the stimulus array could be used to activate response channels and that this influence would be revealed in the lateralized readiness potential by the activation of the response channel associated with the flankers on incompatible trials. Here they proposed to test the notion that, in contrast to the variable baseline hypothesis, response latency on any given trial is determined by variation in a response criterion threshold (Grice *et al.*, 1982).

To test these two hypotheses, Gratton *et al.* replicated the basic design used by Coles *et al.* All of their response latency measures were done on EMG and response device onset latencies. They derived conditional accuracy functions for these measures on compatible and incompatible trials that revealed a pattern similar to what Coles *et al.* had observed; response accuracy increased with increases in onset latency for both measures, compatible trials were associated with above-chance levels of performance for all response latencies except those less than 150 ms, and incompatible trials were associated with chance levels of accuracy at very fast latencies (<150 ms), below-chance levels of performance at fast response latencies, but above-chance levels of performance at slower latencies (>300 ms). Indeed, the latter responses tended to be correct regardless of the compatibility of the array. Chance levels of performance for both compatible and incompatible arrays when response latencies were very fast suggested to the authors that these responses were fast guesses that bore no relationship to the content of the array. These results are shown in Figure 1.18.

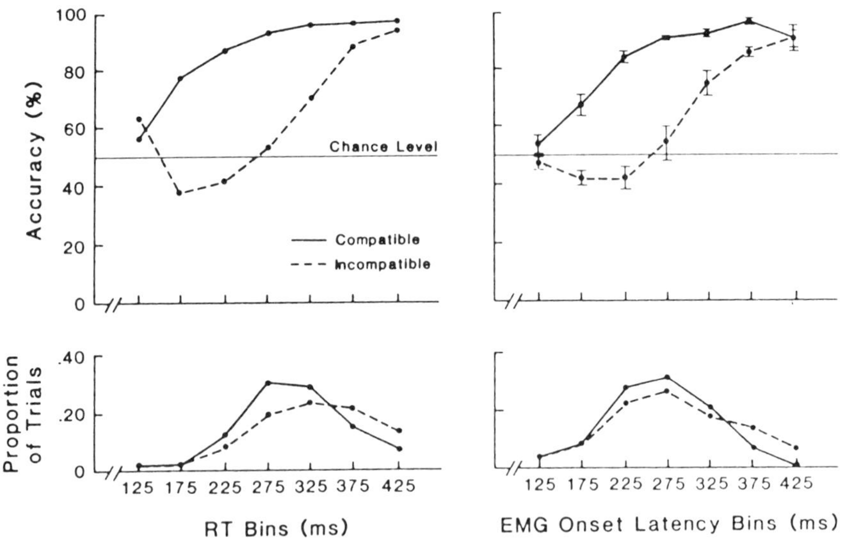

Figure 1.18. Conditional accuracy functions (upper panel) derived by Gratton *et al.* (1988) and associated proportions of trials for each response latency bin (lower panel) for compatible and incompatible noise. On the left are response bins determined on the basis of squeeze activity and on the right are those based on EMG activation. The response latency values represent the midline for each bin. Standard errors are indicated in the EMG plots by vertical lines. (Reprinted with permission. © 1988 American Psychological Association.)

To determine if changes in prestimulus baseline activity were associated with the accuracy of the response to the imperative stimulus, they calculated lateralized readiness potentials for correct and incorrect trials from the activity recorded at lateral electrodes placed over the motor areas. Negative values in these calculations indicated that the activation was at the site overlying the motor area contralateral to the correct responding hand, and positive values that the activation was contralateral to the incorrect hand. They then determined the extent to which this activity varied as a function of response speed (i.e. EMG onset). Their analyses revealed that (i) there is a linear relationship between response speed and the degree of lateral activation—fast responses have a greater degree of laterality than do slow responses; (ii) the direction of the lateralized readiness potential is related to the correctness of the response—fast correct responses are associated with a contralateral asymmetry in activity in the direction of the correct response, whereas incorrect responses are associated with an asymmetry that is contralateral to the incorrect response (this relationship is shown in Figure 1.19 for incompatible trials, for which the analysis was restricted since too few trials were available for compatible trials); (iii) the conditional accuracy of responses varied as a function of the asymmetry of the prestimulus readiness potential in that it was highest for fast responses when the asymmetry was opposite the correct response arm, lowest (and below-chance) when it was opposite the incorrect arm, and intermediate when there was no asymmetry in the prestimulus period. This pattern is shown in Figure 1.20 for six response speed groups.

Poststimulus motor system activation revealed in the lateralized readiness potential for compatible and incompatible trials indicated that response channels are engaged before stimulus processing is complete. This activation is evident in the lateralized readiness potential for incompatible trials. On these trials, a slight positive-going deflection of short duration between 150 and 250 ms is apparent in the poststimulus activity, suggesting that the incorrect response channel was activated early in the reaction. This pattern is shown in Figure 1.21 for all of the trials (middle panel) and for correct trials with response latencies between 300 and 349 ms (bottom panel). Included in the top panel of the figure is the conditional accuracy function for compatible and incompatible trials. Note the striking resemblance between this function and the difference waves in the bottom two panels.

Here it is important to note that, although the conditional accuracy functions and lateralized readiness potentials for all of the trials suggest a cumulative accretion of stimulus information that is passed continuously to the response channels, these smooth functions are averages and may result from latency variability across trials in a discrete process. The likelihood that this explanation is correct is argued against, however, by the activity shown in the bottom panel. Here only correct responses (i.e. no evidence of EMG activation on the incorrect side) that were relatively slow are depicted. Again, the brief negative

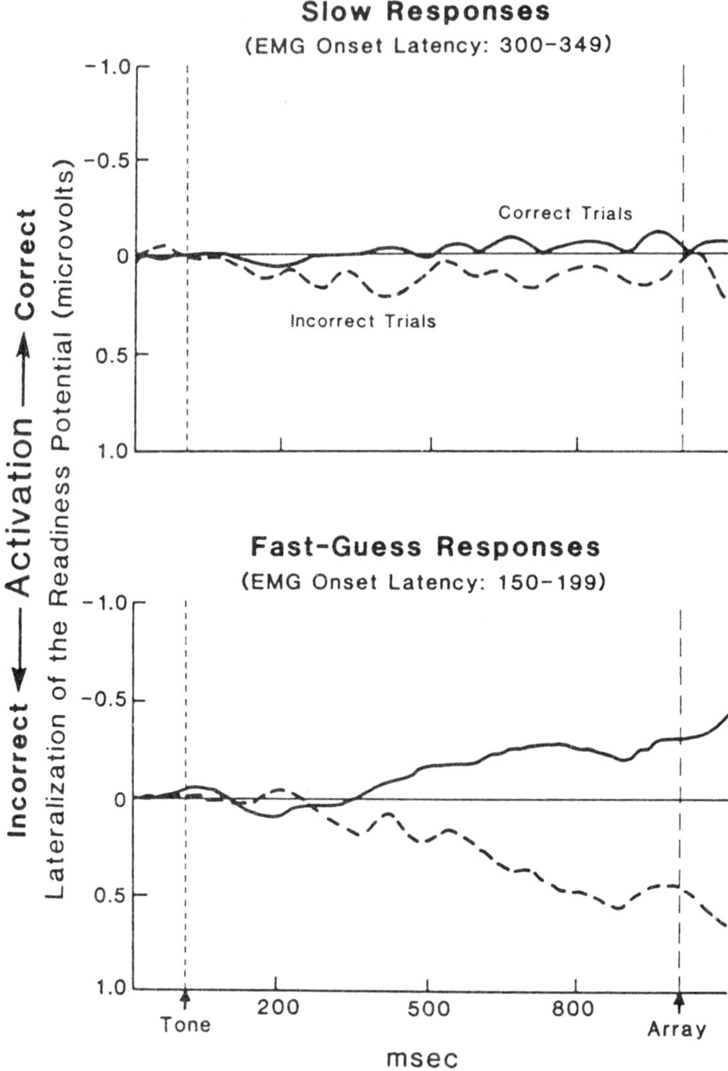

Figure 1.19. Grand average lateralized readiness potential activity recorded in the foreperiod of the Eriksen task by Gratton *et al.* (1988) for correct (solid lines) and incorrect (dashed lines) responses when the target was flanked by incompatible noise. Response latency is based on EMG onset. In the upper panel are responses with latencies between 300 and 349 ms, and in the bottom panel are those with latencies between 150 and 199 ms. Greater activation at the contralateral electrode site is indicated by a negative (upward) deflection, whereas greater activation at the ipsilateral site is indicated by a positive (downward) deflection. (Reprinted with permission. © 1988 American Psychological Association.)

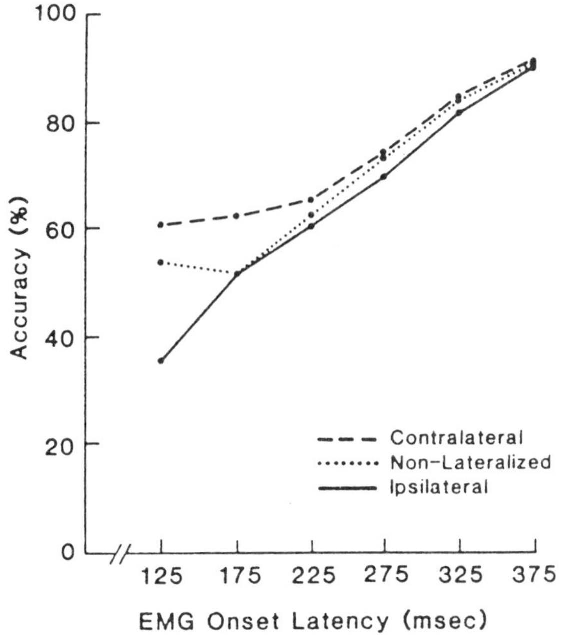

Figure 1.20. Conditional accuracy functions derived by Gratton *et al.* (1988) for different directions of lateralization of the readiness potential in the last 100 ms of the foreperiod. (Reprinted with permission. © 1988 American Psychological Association.)

deflection is evident. This suggests that the incorrect response channel was activated early on by the flanking incompatible noise without producing any consequent peripheral activation. The fact that slow, correct responses were typically associated with symmetric prestimulus activation suggests further that this early incorrect response activation occurs even when there is little or no aspecific priming. Recall that the variable criterion hypothesis assumes that the response criterion varies on a trial-by-trial basis. This assumption was not supported in the lateralized readiness potential. Irrespective of the speed of the response and the associated motor activation, the value of the lateralized readiness potential was unchanged at the time of EMG onset. Thus, the findings from this study suggest that variations in prestimulus activation of the response channels are associated with variations in response latency and accuracy, not changes in response criterion levels.

The work of Coles, Gratton, Eriksen and colleagues provides elegant examples of the use of psychophysiological measures in studies of mental chronometry (for a detailed discussion of this research and its rationale see Coles, 1989). In particular, it has given us insights into the role of aspecific priming, response competition, and stimulus evaluation processes in choice

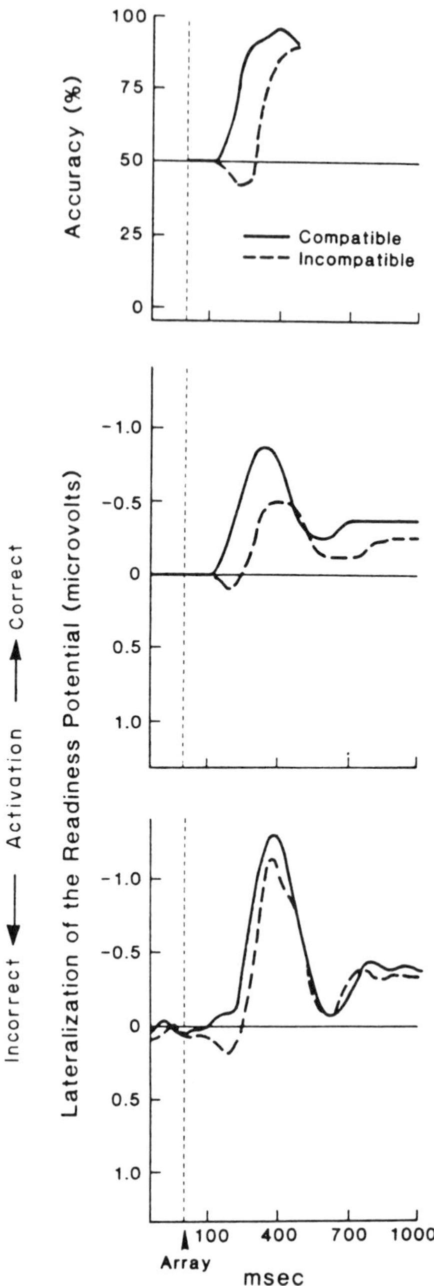

Figure 1.21. Conditional accuracy function (top panel) and lateralized readiness potentials (bottom two panels) for compatible and incompatible responses reported by Gratton *et al.* (1988) for poststimulus activity. The middle panel shows LRP activity for all compatible and incompatible trials, and the lower panel shows this activity for correct trials with response latencies between 300 and 349 ms. (Reprinted with permission. © 1988 American Psychological Association.)

reactions, and has provided a test of the variable baseline and variable criterion hypotheses of response latency and accuracy. However, although the results of these studies are not consistent with a strictly serial model, they do not permit stage models with temporal overlap among stages, like Miller's ADC model, to be rejected. Next, we turn to a cognitive psychophysiological test of this model.

De Jong *et al.* (1988) tested the ADC model directly utilizing what they referred to as the corrected motor asymmetry (CMA), a measure that is derived from lateral scalp sites overlying the motor cortex and is functionally equivalent to the lateralized readiness potential of the Coles' group. They demonstrated first that differences in the onset time of this motor asymmetry could differentiate response hand preparation when a precue signaling which response hand is to be used provided only partial response information. In previous research, including that of the Coles group, subjects were required only to make response hand decisions in two-choice reactions. That is, a further choice of response digits was not required. Thus, the precue provided complete response information. De Jong *et al.* added a response digit selection requirement to determine if lateralized motor activity were still evident under these circumstances. Subjects were presented a precue, the letter L, R, or U, that was followed by an imperative stimulus shown to the left or to the right of fixation. The precue either specified the required response hand (L = left, R = right) or was uninformative (U). The imperative stimulus consisted of two letters that indicated the response hand (L or R) and the response digit (I = index, M = middle). Subjects were informed that the precue would always be accurate and were instructed to balance speed with accuracy in their responding. A foreperiod of 500 ms was given between the onset of the precue and the onset of the imperative stimulus.

Replicating previous research, De Jong *et al.* found that RTs were faster when the precue was informative than when it was uninformative. Most important for their purposes, however, was their finding that an asymmetry in motor activity occurred in the foreperiod following an informative, but not an uninformative, precue. With an uninformative precue, the asymmetry did not emerge until after the imperative stimulus was presented. This difference is shown in Figure 1.22. This pattern of results corroborates the work of Gratton *et al.* and suggests further that activation of response channels does occur when only partial response information is provided in a precue.

In their second experiment, De Jong *et al.* tested the ADC model using a variant of the tasks developed by Miller (1982) to determine if partial stimulus information could be used to prepare responses. The imperative stimuli were the letters N and S, presented at fixation in two slightly different sizes and with no precue. In separate conditions, subjects were required to make two-choice or four-choice reactions. There were two two-choice conditions. In one, the name of the letter distinguished the response hand and in the other the size of the letter determined the response hand (in both conditions only one digit on

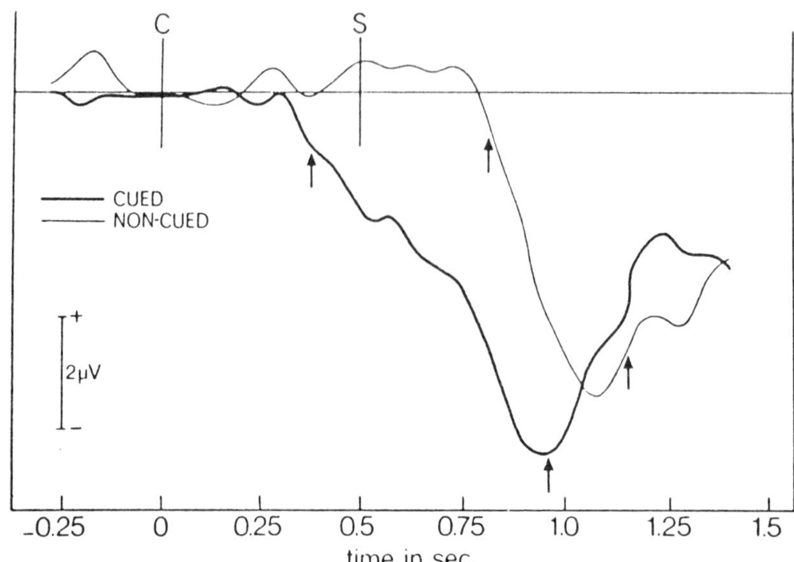

Figure 1.22. Lateralized readiness potential activity recorded by De Jong *et al.* (1988) for the two precue conditions. C and S indicate the presentation of the precue and the imperative stimulus, respectively. The first arrow signifies the onset of the lateralized readiness potential and the second identifies the mean reaction time. (Reprinted with permission. © 1988 American Psychological Association.)

each hand was used to respond). There were three four-choice conditions. In the first, the name of the letter indicated the response hand (and the size of the letter determined the digit on the hand); in the second, the size of the letter signaled the response hand (and the name of the letter determined the digit on the hand); and, in the third, neither the name of the letter nor its size distinguished the response hand (but the name of the letter signaled the digit on the response hand).

Recall from our earlier discussion that under similar experimental conditions both Miller (1982) and Proctor and Reeve (1985) found an advantage in RT when the salient stimulus attribute (letter name) indicated the response hand. They interpreted the advantage differently, however. Miller interpreted it to reflect differences in the efficiency of response preparation processes that can capitalize on the presence of partial stimulus information. In contrast, Proctor and Reeve suggested that the benefit lies at the level of stimulus–response translation (i.e. response selection), which may or may not benefit from partial stimulus information. Each of these interpretations would predict both an RT advantage and an asymmetry in the poststimulus motor activation whose onset would occur earliest when the letter name signifies the response hand in both the two- and four-choice reactions. Moreover, P300 latency would be expected to be slower for letter size than for letter name discriminations in both types of reactions.

The behavioral predictions were supported. RT was found to be faster for two-choice reactions when the name of the letter distinguished the response hand than when the size of the letter did for both fast and slow responses (below or above the median for each experimental condition). Importantly, error rates did not differ in the two conditions. When making a four-choice reaction, subjects were significantly faster when the letter name signaled the response hand than when letter size did or neither dimension signaled the response hand. This effect was greater, however, for slow than for fast responses. The latter two conditions did not differ in RT, and error rates were comparable across all three conditions. The finding of an RT advantage when the letter name signaled the response hand is consistent with the research we reviewed earlier, and the observation that this effect is most evident for relatively slow responses is consistent with the findings of the Stoffels and van der Molen (1988) studies we also reviewed earlier.

Analyses of the poststimulus motor activity revealed that in the two-choice reaction the onset of the motor asymmetry occurred earlier when the name of the letter indicated the response hand than when its size did, and when fast as opposed to slow responses were made. As was found for RT, the magnitude of the differences in onset latencies between the name and the size conditions was comparable for fast and slow responses. P300 latency was observed to be shorter when the letter name indicated the response hand than when the letter size did. This pattern is consistent with the RT findings and with the predictions that derive from the work of both Miller and of Proctor and Reeve.

When a four-choice reaction was made, however, the onset of the motor asymmetry differed among the three conditions only for slow responses. Here, though, onset latencies were longest if the letter name indicated the response digit (i.e. neither dimension specified the response hand), but were comparable for the other two conditions (letter name–response hand; letter size–response hand). Moreover, P300 latency did not differ among the four-choice conditions for fast or for slow responses. The results of this experiment are shown in Table 1.2. These findings do not support the predictions by either Miller or Proctor and Reeve.

The pattern of results reported by De Jong *et al.* suggests that the two- and four-choice reactions differ with respect to the mechanisms they engage and/or to the strategies employed by the subjects. The electrophysiological data indicate that in a two-choice reaction the behavioral advantage seen when the response hand is signaled by the letter name (*vis-à-vis* letter size) results from influences in both stimulus- and response-related processes. Thus, both P300 latency and the onset of the motor asymmetry occurred earlier in this condition. This is precisely what would be predicted by Miller's model. However, De Jong *et al.* asserted that this result is not diagnostic of the use of

Table 1.2. Experiment 2: mean latencies for correct trials (De Jong *et al.*, 1988).

Condition	Reaction time Fast	Reaction time Slow	LRP onset latency Fast	LRP onset latency Slow	P300 latency Fast	P300 latency Slow
Two-choice						
Name:only	311	440	126	220	405	411
p=0.01			128	236		
Size:only	390	507	201	213	452	464
p=0.01			215	320		
Four-choice						
Hand:name	491	625	232	324	521	528
p=0.01			265	355		
Hand:size	510	677	224	340	517	518
p=0.01			260	369		
Hand:neither	523	690	230	413	528	530
p=0.01			240	430		

Note: LRP=lateralized readiness potential. The label 'p=0.01' refers to the point at which the onset achieved signifance at 0.01 according to a combined Wilcoxin rank sum and t test. De Jong *et al.* referred to the motor activity as the 'correct motor asymmetry' or CMA.

partial stimulus information in preparing responses because the same pattern would be expected if, as suggested by Proctor and Reeve, response translation processes, beginning after stimulus processing is completed, are more efficient since response preparation cannot begin until a response has been selected.

For them, the most informative comparison is between the two-choice reaction in which the size of the letter indicates the response hand and the four-choice condition in which the name of the letter indicates the response hand. They reasoned that if response preparation can begin on the basis of partial information, then the onset of the motor asymmetry should be earlier for the easier letter name–response hand condition than for the more difficult letter size–response hand condition even when the comparison is between two- and four-choice reactions. However, they reasoned further that if response preparation is contingent upon the completion of stimulus recognition processes, then the onset of the motor asymmetry in the four-choice reaction would be expected to be slower than in the two-choice reaction because the addition of stimulus–response alternatives is thought to affect stimulus recognition and response translation processes primarily and, as such, would delay response preparation (Sanders, 1980).

In contrast to the first prediction, the onset of the motor asymmetry occurred earlier in the two-choice reaction when letter size indicated the response hand than it did in the four-choice reaction when letter name indicated the response hand. According to the authors, the direction of this effect is inconsistent with Miller's model in specific and with continuous models in general. In accord with the second prediction, the onset latencies of the motor asymmetry in the four-choice reactions were longer than those in the two-choice reaction.

However, with the exception of slow responses, the difference in onset latencies was only a fraction of the difference in RTs. De Jong *et al.* argued, therefore, that this difference was sufficiently small to reject the conclusion that response preparation had not begun until stimulus recognition and response selection had been completed (i.e. a strictly serial interpretation). Thus, they argued that their data are inconsistent with discrete, continuous, or ADC models. Accordingly, they interpreted their findings as being consistent with models that postulate a continuous relationship between stimulus recognition and decision processes and a serial relationship between these processes and response preparation (e.g. McClelland's cascade model). This interpretation was based on the observation that in two-choice reactions the interval between the onset of motor system activation and of response latency did not differ between fast and slow responses, nor did P300 latency. The suggestion, then, is that intermediate response selection processes are the main determinant of trial-to-trial variability in RT.

It may be, however, that the two- and four-choice reactions are sufficiently different that interpretations based on comparisons between them are spurious. To reconcile the difference between their findings, which do not support the activation of response channels by partial stimulus information in the four-choice reaction, and those of Coles *et al.* which do support this activation in two-choice reactions, De Jong *et al.* suggested that variations in subject strategy may have produced the discrepancy. This is suggested in the four-choice reactions by the observations that (i) the onset latencies of the motor asymmetries did not vary with changes in stimulus feature–response hand mapping, (ii) the interval between onset of the motor asymmetry and response latency was greater than in the two-choice reaction, and (iii) P300 latency was comparable across conditions.

If different strategies are used by subjects in the four- and two-choice reactions, this may reflect differences in the difficulty of the two tasks. It is also conceivable, however, that the addition of a response digit selection in the four-choice reaction does not simply result in the insertion of this selection process into the reaction. Rather, the temporal relations among the various elements engaged may be altered as well or new elements may be activated. A simple extrapolation from the two-choice to the four-choice reaction to draw comparisons and make inferences assumes that processing elements are inserted in the more complicated reaction or that the same elements are engaged but their durations are changed. Both assumptions may be false. In addition, although Experiment 1 demonstrated that a precue that provides only partial information can induce an asymmetry in the preparatory period, this finding is not surprising. Even though the precue did not specify the entire response, it provided lateral information which should produce asymmetrical preparation in the foreperiod. One needs to determine if the presentation of a precue that provides partial, bilateral information (e.g.

the response digit) is associated with symmetric activation in the foreperiod that lateralizes after the stimulus, indicating the response hand, is presented. Under these circumstances, the time course of the lateralized motor activation can be estimated. This can then be used for comparisons with the two-choice reaction in which the imperative stimulus provides hand information. However, for comparisons with the four-choice reaction, a more appropriate comparison may be with a four-choice reaction in which the imperative stimulus provides the response hand and response digit information (e.g. LI). Again, the emergence of the lateralized motor activation can be monitored after stimulus onset.

Thus, the test of Miller's model using lateralized motor activity has produced an interesting mosaic of results. These results cast doubt on Miller's model, as well as on models that posit completely continuous stimulus and response activation. They are consistent with a model such as McClelland's which combines continuous stimulus processing with discrete response selection. These conclusions were drawn to a large extent, however, from comparisons of two different mental reactions. Thus, the pattern of results may reflect shifts in subject strategy between reactions that make it difficult to determine the temporal ordering of activation, or it may reflect the fact that comparisons were made between reactions that are fundamentally different. This study provides the starting point from which these issues can be addressed.

In summary, the studies we have reviewed in this section suggest that the time course of the lateralized readiness potential and the latency of P300, measured in conjunction with response speed and accuracy, may offer insights into elements of mental processing that are not accessible to behavioral measures alone. In particular, the work of Coles, Gratton, Eriksen and colleagues has provided strong tests of the variable baseline and variable criterion hypotheses of response speed and accuracy, as well as some elucidation of the roles of certain aspects of stimulus and response processing in the mental reaction induced by the Eriksen task. The work of De Jong and his colleagues reveals further the potential contributions that cognitive psychophysiological measures can make to tests of models of mental chronometry derived from reaction time studies. Examples of a research approach that bears a strong resemblance to the studies reviewed in this section can be found in Wijers *et al.* (1989a,b,c). In the concluding section, we shall return to a discussion of the lateralized readiness potential and its role in studies of mental chronometry.

CHRONOPSYCHOPHYSIOLOGY AND BEYOND

In this chapter, we have introduced the term chronopsychophysiology to refer to investigations of mental chronometry in which traditional behavioral measures are supplemented by psychophysiological measures. The basic assumptions of traditional mental chronometry are that (i) the completion of mental processes takes time, (ii) different paths through the information processing system require different periods of time, and (iii) inferences can be made back from the pattern of RTs obtained under different experimental conditions to the processing structures involved (cf. Luce, 1986). The fundamental impediment to this inferential enterprise is that the chronometrician must rely on an overt response (e.g. button press), the end point in the processing sequence, to infer the entire sequence of mental transactions that precedes it. Indeed, this dependence led Woodworth (1938) to speculate that future technological developments might one day permit the use of brain waves to signal the beginning and the end of a mental reaction. Within the past 15 years, we have begun to see this speculation become a reality. In the same spirit as Woodworth, Posner and McLeod (1982) have recently advocated a union between cognitive psychology and the neurosciences in which the contemporary mental chronometrician searches for the neural substrates where elementary mental operations established by reaction time methods are implemented (also see discussions in Posner, 1986, and Posner and Petersen, 1990). Indeed, over the past several years a new discipline, cognitive neuroscience, has emerged with the aim of characterizing the functional neuroanatomy of human information processing.

Our review has focused on Woodworth's call for the use of psychophysiological measures in the study of mental chronometry. It has covered aspects of the construction of these measures and their application in the stage analysis of the reaction process. Much of our review of traditional mental chronometry has focused on the application of Sternberg's AFM to infer the constituents of a mental reaction. As we discussed, provided a number of strong assumptions are satisfied, this method can be used to infer (i) the existence of processing stages that are activated between the stimulus input and the response output, and (ii) the locus of task effects in the chain of information processing. However, these inferences derive from the assumption that stages are activated in a serial and contingent fashion. If this assumption is violated, serious inferential errors may result. Cognitive psychologists have proposed a criterion of 'stage robustness' for deciding whether the AFM can be applied properly (e.g. Sanders, 1983). It states that the pattern of factor effects should not change when another factor is added to the design. Basically, the principle expressed in this criterion is that strong conclusions should never be made on the basis of the results from one experiment. This same position was taken by Sternberg (1969). While adherence to this principle may protect the investigator against injudicious interpretations of factor effects, it does not provide a direct means by which to infer stage overlap. To do so, objective measures must be available that index the relative timing of the offset of stage n and the onset of stage $n+1$. These measures would permit strong inferences to be drawn about the temporal overlap of two stages. Behavioral measures alone cannot achieve this degree of precision. Can it be achieved by supplementing them with psychophysiological measures? In this section, we shall attempt to answer this question by considering several important issues that confront the chronopsychophysiology of the reaction process.

A second class of issues identified in our review pertains to Sternberg's (1969) assertion that the assumptions on which the stage concept are based, independent and additive processing stages, are incompatible with views that assume the differential allocation of limited processing resources to the components of a mental reaction. In the stage analysis, the constructs of theoretical concern all relate to the computational aspects of the reaction process (e.g. the noise of processing stages, the accumulation of information within a processing stage, the transmission of information from one stage to another), and little attention is given to capacity limitations of the information processing system. We have argued, in agreement with the position taken by Sanders (see also Mulder, 1986), that stage and capacity models may not be mutually exclusive. Hybrid models like that of Sanders gain their inspiration in part from the classic work of Kahneman (1973).

The position he formulated assumes that mental processing is driven by two types of input—information and resource. The duration of any particular element in a mental reaction depends, then, on not only the characteristics of the stimulus input and the response output (i.e. the processing demands), but also on the amount of processing capacity (i.e. resources) allocated to that element. Kahneman's model attempted to integrate computational constructs (e.g. the sequence of information processing units engaged in the performance of particular tasks) and state constructs (e.g. resource allocation and physiological arousal). Thus, Kahneman's model provides a powerful entrée into the study of the influence of presetting (or other state) processes on human mental reactions that is not afforded by traditional stage models. At the same time, the complexities and subtleties of hybrid stage–state models are difficult to assess by empirical tests that rely upon performance measures alone. Can they be assessed in greater detail by judicious addition of psychophysiological measures? In this section we shall attempt to answer this question by discussing the role of preparatory factors in the timing of processing stages and by illustrating how chronopsychophysiology may contribute to a more complete characterization of stage–state formulations of the reaction process.

CHRONOPSYCHOPHYSIOLOGY OF STAGE TIMING

By design, our review of the psychophysiological literature has been quite selective. We have attempted to identify and underscore the issues we think are most important in (i.e. reaction time) mental chronometry and to provide specific exemplars of efforts to test certain of these issues. Our choice of the autonomic literature has been produced by necessity, however, rather than by the inspiration of strict model testing criteria. As we have asserted, the reaction time paradigm has been used to study autonomic responsivity, not mental chronometry. Indeed, in this type of study, it is not unusual for analyses to be done only on the physiological measures. Hence, there are few studies in which performance and autonomic measures have been used conjointly to study mental chronometry. The dearth of such studies may not simply reflect an absence of interest in mental chronometry among autonomic psychophysiologists. It may reflect a deeper problem: inherent deficiencies in this approach. Thus, legitimate questions can be raised about the extent to which these distant autonomic measures can inform us about the time course of mental events. It is not unreasonable to suggest, for instance, that if psychophysiological measures are to provide a window through which the elements of mental processing can be viewed, the only perspicacious view will be afforded by measures derived from activation of the brain, not of the heart or of the eye.

Indeed, appreciably more ERP than autonomic studies of mental chronometry have been done. Yet, we have not included a fair number of these studies in the present review. In many cases, studies were not included because in our view their intent was to add ERP measures (e.g. P300 latency) presumed to reflect certain cognitive processes (e.g. stimulus evaluation) to behavioral measures and, in so doing, to articulate parameters of a model not accessible to behavioral measures alone. As such, they were designed to refine the model, not to test it. Thus, in these studies experimental procedures (e.g. AFM) and the theoretical model on which they are based (e.g. stages of processing) were not evaluated. Examples of this approach can be found in studies of memory scanning by Ford, Pfefferbaum and colleagues (Ford *et al.*, 1979, 1982).

Still other studies have used a particular experimental methodology to help elucidate the cognitive processes manifest by a particular ERP component. They, too, were not designed to evaluate the method or its theoretical foundations. Examples of this approach can be found in the work of McCarthy and Donchin (1981), Magliero *et al.* (1984), Callaway (1983), Pfefferbaum *et al.* (1986), Mulder *et al.* (1984), and Ragot (1984). Yet other studies have utilized a certain experimental methodology to help isolate factor effects like age (Callaway, 1983; Ford *et al.*, 1979, 1982; Ford and Pfefferbaum, 1985; Pfefferbaum *et al.*, 1980) and/or pharmacologic treatment (Callaway, 1983; Halliday *et al.*, 1986). In these studies, ERP components are assumed to manifest particular aspects of mental processing, and the theoretical assumptions underlying the experimental method provide the inferential framework for interpreting the factor effects of interest on component latency and reaction time.

In a last set of studies, inferences are drawn about mental chronometry on the basis of the temporal sequencing among ERP components and their relationship to reaction time, but effort is directed less at testing a specific model of information processing than it is at characterizing the general nature of information processing. Thus, once the timing parameters are established they are interpreted as providing support for serial, parallel, or hybrid models. Examples of this approach are found in the work of Ritter, Vaughan and colleagues (Ritter, Simson and Vaughan, 1983; Ritter *et al.*, 1982; Ritter, Vaughan and Simson, 1983), Renault and colleagues (Renault, Fiori and Giami, 1988; Renault *et al.*, 1982), and Mulder and colleagues (see Wijers et al., 1989a,b,c). This work comes closest to the studies we have reviewed in this chapter.

Critical Issues in the Chronopsychophysiology of Stimulus Processing

The rationale for adding measures of event-related brain potential activity to behavioral measures is that they provide new sources of information. The power of this methodology is expressed best when factor effects on RT and on component latency are dissociated, thereby demonstrating that more than redundant information is being provided by the psychophysiological measures. Opportunities then emerge to evaluate differential higher-order factor effects on the multiple dependent measures, and to draw inferences about the elements of processing revealed by the ERP component. A case in point is the McCarthy and Donchin (1981) study we described earlier in which it was demonstrated that P300 latency was affected by stimulus discriminability, but not by response compatibility, whereas reaction time was influenced by both factors. This was interpreted as support for the view that P300 latency reflects stimulus evaluation, but not response selection/execution, processes. Thus, the cognitive significance of P300 latency was inferred from this differential factor effect. Indeed, the search for such dissociations has motivated much of the research in psychophysiology for the last decade.

The McCarthy and Donchin (1981) study provides a classic example of this research. A number of objections can be raised to their conclusion of the functional significance of P300, however. The first objection is with the construct of stimulus evaluation. It has no parallel in the traditional mental chronometry literature and therefore is difficult to translate into terms that are meaningful to cognitive psychologists (Sanders, 1990). This illustrates a basic problem between chronopsychophysiology and cognitive psychology. While investigators in both fields share a common interest in human information processing, they often use different concepts to infer the constituents of a mental reaction and these concepts often have no formal relationship to each other. Another problem with the construct is that the range of manipulations used to refine the theoretical connection between P300 latency and the timing of stimulus-related processing has been relatively small. Within this small body of literature, there are important contradictions to the assumption that P300 latency is refractory to response manipulations, and this evidence persists (e.g. see Ragot, 1984; Ragot and Lesevre, 1986). The core problem is that differences between paradigms may be important in delineating the boundary conditions for the theoretical formulations. For example, Pfefferbaum *et al.* (1986) have demonstrated that response compatibility may affect P300 latency (observed to be a small effect by McCarthy and Donchin and Magliero *et al.*, 1984) when the stimulus array contains information about both the stimulus and the compatibility of the response to be made (for a related discussion, see McCarthy and Donchin, 1983). Bashore and Osman (1987) have suggested further that S–R compatibility may influence P300 latency when noise elements in a visual display contain response-relevant information but not when they are neutral (as in the McCarthy and Donchin, 1981, study). To date, hypotheses that explain these task effects have not been proposed.

A second objection raised against using P300 latency as an index of stimulus processing time is that in some paradigms it occurs after the overt response (e.g. Coles *et al.*, 1985; Kutas *et al.*, 1977; Pfefferbaum *et al.*, 1983; Ritter, Vaughan and Simson, 1983). Meyer *et al.* (1988b) offered a simple interpretation for this relative delay. They suggested that some residual delay could intervene between the termination of the processing stage and the occurrence of the component associated with the event. As long as the factor effects on stage duration appear fully in the latencies of the selected component, there need be no problem. While this may be true for interpreting task effects on P300 according to the additive factors logic, it is not true for using P300 in determining the time course of processing stages (see Ritter, Vaughan and Simson, 1983, for a similar argument). In that case, we need to have experimental operations that distinguish between stage processing and ancillary processing. A similar point was made by Miller (1988) when he criticized the inference that overlapping component activity implies continuous transmission. Recall, he argued that the activities of a later stage might be contingent upon only a subset of the processing activities of an earlier stage. That is, component overlap does not tell us whether the activity of a later stage is contingent upon *all* of the activity carried out by an earlier stage or by just the early portions of that activity. Thus, response generation might be contingent upon the first part of stimulus processing, where P300 generation is contingent upon all of the stimulus processing activities and perhaps even some ancillary processing.

Donchin and Coles (1988) provided alternative interpretations of fast button presses and slow P300 latencies. First, they suggested that a button press response might be executed before a full analysis of the stimulus has been completed (see also Kutas *et al.*, 1977). Thus, button press latencies shorter than P300 latencies would indicate fast guesses. With this interpretation in mind, the interested reader should consult Figure 5 of the Coles *et al.* (1985) paper (see Figure 1.16, p. 118 above). This figure shows that response latencies (squeeze responses) are between 300 and 500 ms, whereas P300 latencies are about 600 ms. If, indeed, the relative timing of P300 latency and RT can be used to infer fast guessing, these values suggest that the subjects were guessing on virtually every trial. Under these conditions, we would expect accuracy levels to approximate chance. However, the actual error rates were of the order of 5–21%. In addition, P300 latencies are slower on error than on correct trials. This difference is not inconsistent with the inference that the stimulus was processed less efficiently when the subject made an error than when he made a correct response. This may have nothing to do with guessing—it may represent normal variation in the engagement of processing mechanisms. Thus, a fast guess interpretation is difficult to entertain.

Apparently, Donchin and Coles arrived at the same conclusion when they referred to a study in which P300 latency on errors was about 100 ms longer than on correct trials. They then suggested that this extra period is used to assess the consequences of the error trial so that proper adjustments can be made to avoid errors in the future. They assumed that P300 is a manifestation of adjustment-related processing (Donchin and Coles, 1988; p. 371). Thus, in addition to stimulus evaluation, the processes indexed by P300 may include evaluation of the response consequences, as well as evaluation of S–R mapping rules (also see Magliero *et al.*, 1984). This interpretation implies that the P300 may be generated by processes that monitor the entire mental transaction rather than by the activation of a single processing stage, thus rendering questionable the value of P300 latency as a tool for stage analysis. It would not be surprising if such were the case, given that the late positive complex may contain not only the P300 (or P3b) but also other components such as the P3a (Squires *et al.*, 1975), P3e and P3x (Ruchkin, Sutton and Mahaffey, 1987) that reflect different cognitive processes (see also Turetsky *et al.*, in press). Thus, the distinction between P300 as a reflection of a transcendant monitoring process or the activation of a single stage of processing must be clarified.

Cognitive psychologists have added to these concerns. Both Miller (1988) and Meyer *et al.* (1988b) have expressed a particular interest in the potential of a combined ERP/RT approach to the analysis of mental chronometry. In so doing, they have argued that a number of issues must be resolved before this potential can be realized. These issues relate both to the measurement parameters of the ERP component that are used as indices of the timing of specific cognitive operations and to the empirical/theoretical framework within which inferences are then drawn from these timing parameters. Of particular concern to these investigators are two assumptions used by many cognitive psychophysiologists to infer temporostructural relationships in mental processing. The first is that the time to the maximum amplitude of a component represents the end of a specific type of processing, and the second is that the continuous transmission of information in a mental reaction is manifest at the scalp by overlapping component activity. Miller (1988) has argued, and Meyer *et al.* (1988b) have concurred, that it is extremely difficult to determine if a particular component represents processing of a particular kind or if it is merely the consequence of that processing (a similar concern has been raised by cognitive psychophysiologists such as Ritter, Vaughan and

Simson, 1983). The difficulty in establishing a theoretical link between the timing of a mental operation and of an ERP component is exacerbated, in their view, by uncertainty over the parameters of the ERP component that should be selected for measurement. Thus, as Meyer *et al.* asserted, there is no strong theoretical justification for the assumption that the most commonly used measure, peak latency of a component, reveals the completion of a specific mental operation.

Further, they argued that use of the peak latency assumes that even if it does not represent the end point of a particular operation, it does vary in a constant fashion with the actual termination of that operation. This may not be true. Thus, alternative measures would be onset and offset times of the component. In their view, the selection of peak latency as the measurement of choice is more a matter of convenience than of sound deductive reasoning. Related very closely to the assumption that links component latency to the termination of a specific mental operation is the assumption that overlapping components imply continuous processing. According to Miller (1988), this assumption fails to appreciate that the overlap does not inform us of the temporal contingencies of information transfer from one processor to another. That is, we are not informed by this overlap as to whether the activity of a later stage of physiological processing is contingent upon all of the activity carried out by an earlier stage or by just the early portions of that activity. Thus, in the view of these investigators, not only is there conceptual uncertainty about the cognitive significance of the time course of an individual ERP component, there is an absence of clarity as to the implications of component overlap for the timing of mental processing.

Meyer *et al.* also pointed out that strong theoretical models of mental chronometry must include specification of the relations among specific elements of mental processing, specific ERP components, and the neural generators for these components; and must account for the inherent stochastic variability in the activation (e.g. start/stop times, output) of specific information processors and link it to the variability evident in the behavioral and psychophysiological measures. These theoretical ends cannot be achieved, however, according to Meyer *et al.* (1988b), utilizing 'current techniques for analyzing psychophysiological data' because they 'tend to be somewhat inadequate, given the substantial complexity and variability inherent in patterns of ERPs and RTs' (p. 46). In particular, they asserted that the component parameters of interest should be measured on single trials, not on the averaged ERP. They contended that the methods currently being used to estimate component latencies do not permit single-trial estimates that are sensitive to stochastic fluctuations in both the shape and the timing of the component or to the contribution of noise to the morphology of the component. This is a problem long appreciated by cognitive psychophysiologists (e.g. Donchin and Heffley, 1978; Ruchkin and Glaser, 1978) and attempts to solve it are ongoing (e.g. Gratton *et al.*, 1989;

Gratton, Coles and Donchin, 1989; Raz *et al.*, 1989; Turetsky *et al.*, 1989).

However, the first, and still most common, method used to handle these problems is to assume that averaging reduces the contribution of noise or stochastic variability to the signal. Meyer *et al.* argued, however, that averaging can introduce biases that would produce artifactual interactions and, as a result, compromise inferences about the dynamics of mental processing. Their recommendation is to '. . .first measure peak latencies and then average, not the reverse' (p. 47). They also suggest that when values are being estimated on single-trial ERPs, variability in both component timing and reaction time must be considered in the analytic process because an artifactually smooth curve may result from these measures when, in fact, the underlying process is a discrete, but variable, step function. (See the discussion by Meyer *et al.* of the use of an RT/P300 latency ratio measure by Coles and Gratton (1986) to deal with this problem; and see Gratton *et al.* (1988) for further discussion of this issue.) Thus, experimental and analytic techniques must be identified or developed to tease apart these factors.

The aforementioned concerns are expressed about P300 latency as the dependent measure in chronometric studies. It may be, however, that other timing parameters for P300 are more appropriate. The important comparisons in mental chronometry experiments are the between-task (subtraction method) or between-condition (AFM) effects on RTs. Such comparisons are allowed only if (i) the insertion of a processing stage does not alter the nature of the reaction (Külpe's lesson), and (ii) the task manipulation affects only the duration of processing stages, not the quality of their output (Sternberg's and Sanders' lesson). From RT alone, it is difficult to determine whether the experimental design meets these requirements. Recall, for example, the difficulty in interpreting the underadditive interaction obtained by Stanovich and Pachella (1977). The time course of the P300 might provide additional information. Mental chronometricians have focused their attention almost exclusively on P300 latency. But there is more information in P300 than the time it takes to achieve its peak. For example, if P300 latency is assumed to provide an index of the duration of a subset of processes, then the effects of task variables on spatial–temporal maps (chronotopograms) can be examined. That is, both the timing of the component and its distribution on the scalp are evaluated. Thus, if the effect of an experimental manipulation is to increase the duration of processing by changing peak latency, then the distribution of the component in the spatial–temporal map will be displaced in time, but the map will continue to show the same general spatial configuration. In contrast, if the effect of the task variable is to change the manner of processing by introducing new components, then changes in the spatial distribution of the map may result (e.g. Brandeis *et al.*, 1988).

Turetsky *et al.* (in press) have recently developed a procedure for decomposing an ERP into its constituent components, the dipole component model, that permits inferences to be drawn about both the neural origin of a component like the P300 and the onset/offset times of the dipole or dipoles generating it. In this procedure, spatial–temporal properties of the ERP components are analyzed on the basis of assumptions about the dynamics of aggregates of neuronal masses (i.e. the dipole sources) that generate them and the electrostatic processes that conduct their activity to the scalp. Turetsky *et al.* were able to model the ERP elicited in an auditory target detection task. Subjects were required to press a button to a rare target tone (0.15 probability of occurrence), and to refrain from responding to a rare non-target tone (0.15 probability) or a frequent standard tone (0.70 probability). The model they derived contained four dipoles that conform to the N100, P200, N200, and P300 components typically elicited in this type of task. Further, it revealed that three of these dipoles contributed to the P300 component, and the onset and offset times of these dipoles could be specified. This procedure has the potential, then, to estimate the entire time course of activation of the processes producing the P300, as well as other components. Successful utilization of P300 in studies of mental chronometry thus entails the resolution of important methodological and theoretical issues.

Suggestive Research Findings—the Chronopsychophysiology of Response Preparation

Our review of investigations in chronopsychophysiology suggests that earlier theoretical gains may be achieved utilizing measures of lateralized readiness potential (LRP) activity in conjunction with P300 and reaction time than by using the latter two measures in combination. The motivation for making this assertion stems from our basic agreement with the position of Meyer *et al.* (1988b) that the strongest theoretical positions will emanate from formulations that link specific mental operations to specific ERP components to specific neural generators. In that regard, the lateralized readiness potential is currently the strongest candidate from among the endogenous components to advance our theoretical understanding of mental chronometry. Unlike other endogenous components, such as the P300, where we have little understanding of the generators (Wood *et al.*, 1984) and have conceptualized the mental operations they manifest in relatively general terms (e.g. stimulus evaluation), reasonably strong connections have been established between neurophysiological activity in motor cortex, the potentials measured at the scalp, and the neurocognitive functions they manifest. There is compelling evidence that the scalp potentials associated both with preparation and execution of a movement originate in motor cortex (see discussions in Coles, 1989, and Bashore *et al.*, 1982). Moreover, this activity appears to meet the standard set by Miller (1982) when he described the rationale underlying the development of his technique:

> (It) overcomes the serious problem of finding a dependent variable that accurately reflects continuous response preparation. Making a response in an information-processing task is, for all practical purposes, a discrete process. Given the discreteness of the response, it is hard to determine whether processes prior to the response are also discrete, or whether there is simply a discrete criterion at the end of a continuous system (e.g. McClelland, 1979). The method proposed here circumvents this problem by looking at a variable that need not reach a discrete threshold on each trial: the efficiency of response preparation. (p. 277)

As we have seen, however, the Miller paradigm may not provide an uncontaminated measure of the efficiency of response preparation. That is, the effects on reaction time observed by Miller (1982, 1983) may include the contribution of S–R compatibility.

Meyer *et al.* (1985; see also the review in Meyer *et al.*, 1988a) have evaluated response preparation processes under conditions in which a prime stimulus (word or non-word) precedes an imperative stimulus (left- or right-pointing arrow) by varying intervals (0, 200, 700 ms) and provides directional information for the subject. Thus, when the imperative stimulus was presented subjects were unprimed (0 ms), partially primed (200 ms), or completely primed (700 ms) for its arrival. Analyses were then done in which the obtained reaction time distributions were compared with hypothetical distributions derived from discrete or continuous formulations of the preparation process. The results indicated that response preparation is tied intimately to the number of stimulus–response alternatives, to the complexity of the mapping of stimuli on to responses, and to the type of response output required of the subject. Meyer *et al.* (1985) suggested that as the number of stimulus–response choices increases and the stimulus–response mapping becomes more complex, increasingly finer gradations in preparation may be required. With simple stimulus and response processing demands preparation may involve nothing more than a discrete step from unprepared to prepared. Intermediate demands may involve a concatenation of discrete preparatory steps. And, of course, as processing demands increase, there may be a transition from discrete to continuous preparation. Insight into these processes may be provided by studies of the effects of variables such as priming and S–R compatibility on the lateralized readiness potential, as it provides an apparently continuous record of motor system activation.

It may be a serious error to assume, however, that because the activity measured at the scalp provides a continuous record the processes it manifests are likewise continuous. Thus, although we see a smooth transition in the pre- and poststimulus lateralized readiness potential, this continuity may reflect nothing more than the serial, but temporally variable, recruitment of different motor neuron populations as responses are being prepared and selected for execution. Variability in their recruitment time may produce an artifactually smooth signal, as can happen in a reaction time function generated by variable transition times between discrete processes (Meyer *et al.*, 1988b). The final functional motor pathway in cortex (supplementary motor area, premotor area, and precentral or primary motor area) for distal limb movements includes classes of neurons that are differentially distributed across its divisions, are active at different times in the course of the preparation and execution of a movement, and are activated preferentially by contralateral, ipsilateral or bilateral movements of varying complexity and the instructional signals that permit preparation of these movements (see references below for work by Requin and colleagues, and Tanji and colleagues).

For example, it has been reported that immediately before and after a reasonably complicated movement of the contralateral hand a preponderance of neurons in primary motor cortex (85%) of non-human primates was activated, whereas much smaller proportions of neurons were activated in the premotor (13%) and supplementary motor (31%) areas (Tanji, Okano and Sato, 1988). In contrast, only a small proportion of neurons in precentral cortex (16%) changed their activity in response to a warning stimulus that provided perfectly accurate directional information for the response to the imperative stimulus, but larger proportions were activated by this stimulus in the premotor (28%) and supplementary motor (41%) areas. Note, however, that contralateral preparation was most evident in the precentral area (13% out of the total 16%) and that bilateral activation was most evident in the other two areas (14% of 28% in premotor cortex and 24% of 41% in supplementary motor cortex). The suggestion is that there is a convergence of activation from higher-order motor areas to the specific primary area where the final output command is initiated (Goldberg, 1985; Lecas *et al.*, 1986; Tanji, Okano and Sato, 1987). However, when simpler movements are made, most neurons in supplementary motor cortex respond to the warning stimulus when it signals preparation of the contralateral limb (Tanji and Kurata, 1981).

The timing parameters of the activation of motor neurons in these areas during preparation of the movement, the transition to execution of the movement, and its actual execution are not well specified. However, the available research is not inconsistent with a temporally discrete pattern of activation in response to the warning stimulus (Kurata and Tanji, 1986; Tanji and Kurata, 1982), during preparation of the response, particularly if both the direction and the extent of the movement must be prepared (Riehl and Requin, 1989), and in the transition to activation of the primary motor cortex (Requin, 1985; Riehl and Requin, 1989; Tanji *et al.*, 1988; Tanji and Kurata, 1982). If the motor system is organized like sensory systems appear to be, especially the visual and somatosensory systems, then discrete transitions in the activation patterns of these motor areas are certainly quite possible. There is growing evidence from electrophysiological studies of single and multiple unit activity that information processing is serial within these systems (Ungerleider and Mishkin, 1982; Pons *et al.*, 1987). This possibility suggests that inferences about the accumulation of information in the nervous system from output measures such as reaction time or the timing of an ERP component may be problematic without theoretical links to the underlying neurophysiology (see Deecke, 1987, for an example of this type of theoretical integration in the motor system).

A rather simplistic view of the time course of an ERP component, for example, is that its onset represents the initial engagement of a specific processor, its peak the termination of processing at that level, and its offset the time at which output is passed to the next level. Of course, this simple notion may conform to reality. To test this, one might present an imperative stimulus that calls for some response followed by another (to be ignored) distractor stimulus at varying points in the stream of information and determine the extent to which ERP component structure is altered and performance affected. For example, distractors generating noise, conflicting location or symbolic information, or facilitating information related to the imperative stimulus, could be presented and variations in the timing and morphology of critical ERP components could be evaluated along with changes in performance. Alternatively, response signals could be presented at varying intervals after the imperative stimulus to determine their impact on component characteristics as well as on response speed and accuracy. Indeed, one version of the latter would be a direct application of the Meyer *et al.* (1988a) speed–accuracy decomposition technique to ERPs. How might this enlighten us?

An interesting parallel emerges here between ERP measures and reaction time that illustrates the difficulties in articulating chronometric processes. The speed–accuracy decomposition technique was designed to determine the extent to which stimulus discrimination and evaluation are discrete or continuous processes. Subjects are presented with a warning stimulus (a fixation mark) followed shortly thereafter by an imperative stimulus (e.g. a word or a non-word; a pair of words or non-words, or a word and a non-word) that calls for a lexical decision (Yes to a word or No to a non-word) to a single word, or a same–different decision to a pair (Same to a pair of word or non-words, Different to a word/non-word pair), that is indicated by a key press. There are two types of randomly interspersed trials, regular and signal. On regular trials the sequence (warning stimulus, imperative stimulus, subject's response) is uninterrupted. On signal trials, however, a response signal (tone) is presented at varying intervals after the imperative stimulus. If the subject has not yet responded, he/she is instructed to respond immediately with a best guess. Since the two trial types are mixed, subjects are instructed to treat the beginning of each trial as if it is a regular trial. In brief, Meyer *et al.* (1988a) found what they considered to be evidence for continuous accumulation of stimulus information when the decision was made to a single stimulus, but evidence for a discrete process when the decision was made to stimulus pairs. This method assumes that subjects approach each trial with a consistent mental set and that the presentation of a response signal does not alter the normal processing of a stimulus. Rather, presentation of the response signal is thought to engage a guessing process that is independent of the normal process.

The power of this technique rests on the assumption that the two processes are, in fact, independent. De Jong (unpublished manuscript) has challenged this assumption in a manner reminiscent of the criticism leveled against Donders by Külpe at the end of last century. That is, he challenges the assumption that the normal process is not changed by the presentation of the response signal. His analyses of both experimental data from a lexical decision task and simulated data from a Monte Carlo study suggest that facilitation of normal processing, rather than activation of an independent process, occurs with the presentation of a response signal. De Jong's analysis suggests an historically important principle: With each addition of an independent variable to an information processing task, the nature of the task and the processes it engages may be transformed in subtle but important ways. That is, the task may change and with it information processing demands may change as well. These changes may be sufficient, although subtle, to subvert the assumptions of a theoretical model and to invalidate the method derived to test it. It follows from this that the most powerful procedures for evaluating chronometric processes will not involve intrusions into the information processing sequence to infer how that sequence is structured. What may be measured under circumstances in which intrusive stimuli are presented is how the information processing system responds to these intrusions, not how the normal processes emerge (for example, see the recent cognitive psychophysiological study by De Jong *et al.*, 1990, of response inhibition processes activated by a 'stop' signal). Here, psychophysiological measures offer their promise. That is, as we have asserted at various points in this chapter, in contrast to behavioral measures, psychophysiological measures permit access to the activation of information processing elements that are engaged between the stimulus input and the response output. In principle, the investigator is no longer shackled by the necessity to introduce intervening stimuli to infer normal, uninterrupted mental processing.

CHRONOPSYCHOPHYSIOLOGY OF STAGE PRESETTING

Our focus in this chapter has been on information processing models that conceptualize the reaction process in terms of a limited set of processing elements, be they distinct stages of processing or continuously activated processors. In the stages of processing conception, each stage is hypothesized to receive an input representation, to perform some transformation on that representation, and to produce an output representation that is transmitted to the next stage (cf. Miller, 1988). Thus, stage models have been characterized as bottom-up, stimulus-driven processing models that stand in contrast to top-down, resource-driven processing models. The latter are thought by some to be more representative (i.e. ecologically valid) of human information processing than the former (e.g. Rabbitt, 1979). The continuous flow conception can be characterized in much the same way.

How might the distinction between stimulus- and resource-driven processing express itself in a typical choice reaction time task? In a common variant of the choice reaction, a trial is structured such that a warning stimulus precedes the discriminative stimulus by some fixed interval. The subject is instructed to respond quickly to the discriminative stimulus while at the same time making relatively few errors (i.e. balance speed with accuracy). Stimulus-driven conceptions of this reaction emphasize its computational requirements and develop models that express input–output relations using the computer as their metaphor. But the subject is not waiting passively for the stimulus to arrive on any given trial to begin processing it. During the preparatory period, we can infer that the subject readies himself or herself to process the stimulus and respond appropriately to it. This is particularly evident when the task is changed in a relatively subtle way—the preparatory interval is varied randomly within a block of trials such that there is a brief interval (e.g. 250 ms) as well as a long interval (e.g. 1000 ms). The degree of readiness varies as a function of the preparatory interval (see reference above to Meyer *et al.*, 1985; and see Posner, 1978). This variation is inferred from associated changes in reaction time and response accuracy. Thus the degree of stimulus–response preparedness is influenced importantly by the length of the preparatory interval, and this differential preparedness is expressed in performance measures (again, see Posner, 1978, for an important discussion of this relationship).

Similar effects on performance can be achieved by varying the instructional set, as is done in studies of the speed/accuracy tradeoff. If the subject is instructed to respond as quickly as possible and have little concern for accuracy, response latencies decrease but error rates increase relative to when balance is encouraged. It can be inferred from this pattern that during the foreperiod response systems are activated to a higher state of preparation and processing of the stimulus content assumes less salience when speed is emphasized in the instructions than when speed/accuracy instructions are given. In turn, instructions that emphasize accuracy may reduce response system activation and enhance stimulus processing preparation *vis-à-vis* speed/accuracy instructions. As we discussed above, a fundamentally similar assumption was tested by Külpe when he challenged Donders' notion of pure insertion. He concluded from the introspective reports of his subjects that preparation varied with the type of reaction and, as a result, the assumption was not justified that processes can be added or deleted from a reaction without changing its fundamental nature. As we know, a vast behavioral literature has emerged since Külpe's research that documents the effects of instructions, foreperiod duration, and a wide array of other state variables on response latency and accuracy and, inferentially, on response preparation and activation. Stimulus-driven models have not successfully explained these effects. This inability may be explained in part by their failure to incorporate non-computational variables.

Conceptual efforts by some stage and continuous flow theorists have been directed recently, however, at achieving this end by integrating resource-driven constructs into the stimulus-driven models. Within the stages of processing conception, for example, Sanders (1980) has distinguished two types of task variables—computational and state—that influence mental reactions. According to this view, computational variables (e.g. stimulus contrast, stimulus quality) exert their effect on a reaction after the stimulus has been presented, whereas state variables (e.g. preparatory interval, relative S–R frequency) exert their effect largely prior to the arrival of the stimulus. State variables are hypothesized to mediate what Sanders refers to as 'presetting' processes. These processes are presumed to alter the activity of certain stages in anticipation of the stimulus input, rather than to influence 'computing' as it occurs during stimulus processing. Thus, he suggested that 'state' variables are motor rather than perceptual variables (cf. Sanders, 1980; p. 349). He reasoned that the effect of state variables is strongly determined by instruction and motivation. For example, their effect may disappear when instructions emphasize accuracy over speed. Thus, the effects of state variables may be more variable and general than those of the 'computational' variables. The concept of 'aspecific priming' proposed by Coles *et al.* (1985) within the conceptual framework of the continuous flow model that we discussed earlier represents an integration that is similar to Sanders'. Recall that they distinguished between stimulus-related response activation and response activation that is independent of the stimulus and may occur prior to its presentation (i.e. aspecific priming). This type of response activation is thought to be triggered by variables such as instructional set, expectancy, and payoff schedule (cf. Eriksen, C.W. and Schultz, 1979).

Thus, recent theoretical efforts by both serial stage and continuous flow theorists have assumed that response latency is influenced not only by stimulus-driven processes, but also by presetting processes that are activated before the stimulus arrives. In Sanders' terms, mental reactions are influenced by at least two broad classes of variables, computational and state. Of concern to our discussion here is how cognitive psychologists have attempted to conceptualize the processes that mediate the effects of state variables on the reaction process. However, it is exceedingly difficult to infer these processes from performance measures alone (recall from our earlier discussion that Coles *et al.*, 1985, formulated their construct on the basis of combined performance and electrophysiological data).

Problems in the Behavioral Analysis of Presetting

Illustrative examples of the difficulty of inferring the effects of presetting are to be found in behavioral studies of sequential effects on response latency and accuracy. This research has demonstrated that response latency on a given trial varies as a function of the sequence of trials in which it is embedded. To this point, our discussion has not considered the extent to which mean reaction time for a block of trials varies as a function of trial sequencing within that block. On many occasions, however, trials are not independent and cognitive psychologists have tried to account for these dependencies. Sequential effects refer to the finding that in a subset of trials within a block each trial has a particular relationship with its predecessor(s) that may distinguish these trials and be expressed in RTs that differ from the mean reaction time for the entire block of trials.

Two basic explanations have been offered to explain this sequential effect. The first assumes that it is mediated by activity at the primary sensory level: a stimulus is thought to leave a sensory trace that facilitates the processing of the succeeding stimulus or that eliminates the need to activate certain processing elements that normally intervene between the stimulus and the response. The second explanation invokes a mechanism that has been conceptualized in terms of 'strategies', some of which may be implemented prior to the arrival of the stimulus (e.g. the expectancy of a particular stimulus–response pair formulated on the basis of previous pairings) and others of which may be activated after the stimulus has been presented (e.g. inspection of a stimulus array in a particular order because the stimulus is expected to appear only in certain locations). Neither explanation is sufficiently powerful to account for the range of sequential effects reported in the literature, however. Moreover, it is extremely difficult to formulate operational distinctions among the different explanations (for a more detailed discussion of this issue, see Kirby, 1980, and Luce, 1986).

Numerous investigators have attempted to isolate the specific information processing elements where sequential effects are mediated. These attempts have exploited three different experimental methodologies: subtraction, additive factors, and speed/accuracy tradeoff. An example of the application of a variant of Donders' subtraction method to this problem is found in the work of Bertelson (1965). He developed the information-reduction paradigm, used perhaps more frequently than any other paradigm to evaluate sequential effects. It is structured as follows. Four equiprobable stimuli are mapped to two different responses, two stimuli per response. Three different reaction time categories are created from this combination: (1) 'identical'—the stimulus and response on a given trial are identical to the pair on the previous trial; (2) 'equivalent'—the response on a given trial is identical to the response on the previous trial, but the stimuli are different; (3) 'different'—both the stimulus and the response on a given trial differ from the stimulus and the response on the previous trial. The contributions of stimulus and response factors to the response latency are then estimated using a subtraction procedure. By subtracting the 'identical' RT from the 'equivalent' RT an estimate of the stimulus contribution is derived, and by subtracting the 'equivalent' RT from the 'different' RT an estimate of the response contribution is provided. Bertelson's work revealed important latency differences between 'different' RT and 'equivalent' RT types, suggesting that sequential effects are due primarily to response, rather than to stimulus, repetition.

A more elaborate taxonomy of repetition effects has been developed by Rabbitt and Vyas (1973). They provided evidence suggesting that repetition effects influence central stages of processing without simultaneously affecting peripheral stages of processing. Specifically, they observed that variations in S–R compatibility interacted with repetition, even when neither a particular response nor a particular signal is repeated immediately. Thus, repetition effects may also be mediated by the repetition of coding rules. Such repetition need not entail the repetition of particular signals or responses, but may affect the time taken for the mapping of a stimulus on to a response. Their findings and the diversity of results previously reported in the literature led them to suggest that repetition effects could occur at any one of six processing stages intervening between the presentation of the stimulus and the execution of a response. According to Rabbitt and Vyas, repetition effects have been found to affect at least five of the hypothesized processing stages; (i) perceptual identification, in cases when successive signals are physically identical and require the same response; (ii) stimulus coding, when successive signals are physically distinct but require the same response; (iii) stimulus–response mapping, when a spatial rule to map stimuli to responses is the same across successive trials; (iv) response selection, when responses are physically distinct but are made from a common semantic category; and (v) response programming—certain sequences of physically different motor responses are easier to make than others (e.g. some sequences of finger movements are made faster and more accurately than others, cf. Rabbitt and Vyas, 1973, p. 340).

Attempts to isolate the loci of sequential effects have also been made using speed/accuracy tradeoff procedures. From this perspective, the issue of concern is the effect of an error on response latencies and accuracies on the immediately subsequent trials. This research has revealed that both reaction time and accuracy increase, but that response latencies return to pre-error rates more rapidly than do accuracy levels. According to some theorists, this pattern suggests the existence of two types of preparation, one that is brief in duration and non-selective and another that is longer in duration and selective (cf. Luce, 1986). The former is hypothesized to be associated with time estimation and the latter with implementation of the speed–accuracy relationships.

The explanations sought for sequential effects in each of these experimental approaches are computational in nature. That is, they derive from the same stimulus-driven models and assumptions on which they are based as do interpretations of performance effects in traditional behavioral research on mental chronometry. In particular, they are influenced by the serial stage assumptions of additivity and functional independence even though there is no *a priori* reason to believe these assumptions are appropriate to the task of explaining sequential effects. There is a parallel here to Miller's work testing the assumption of serial stage models that response preparation cannot begin until stimulus processing is complete. In the sequential effects literature, it is assumed that the presetting of processing stages on the basis of previous history affects the entire sequence of stages, both before and after signal presentation. Thus, it is essential to determine not only the time course of stimulus and response processing after a stimulus is presented, but also the degree to which these temporal parameters are changed by variations in response system preparation that vary within small subsets of trials. Performance measures alone are hard pressed to achieve this end.

Suggestive Research Findings—The Chronopsychophysiology of Presetting

At the outset, it should be made clear that we shall not claim that batteries of psychophysiological measures will provide the panacea for all problems encountered in the study of presetting processes. We do want to assert, however, that measures of central and autonomic activity can enrich the behavioral analysis of presetting processes. We will illustrate this assertion in a brief review of recent neurophysiological and psychophysiological investigations of the probability effect (i.e. the observation that more probable stimuli are responded to more rapidly and more accurately than less probable ones). This effect has been suggested by Laming (1969), for example, to be a special kind of sequential effect, with both effects being mediated by the same mechanisms. Evidence from a wide variety of sources, including single-neuron and scalp-recorded measures of nervous system activity, converges to suggest that presetting processes, inferred from the effects of probability manipulations, are associated with a rich pattern of activation as preparation for a stimulus occurs and execution of a response to that stimulus takes place.

Studies of single cell activity in monkeys as they performed a pointing task have revealed that unit activity varies in motor cortex as a function of response probability (Requin, Lecas and Bonnet, 1984). The pointing task required the monkey to initiate a trial by pressing a lever simultaneously with the left and right hands. After a variable wait, a warning tone was presented signaling a fixed 1 s foreperiod that ended with the onset of a light above one of the levers. The monkey was trained to release the corresponding lever and point to the light as quickly as possible. The response probability of the arm contralateral to the recording site was varied systematically from 0 to 1.00 in steps of 0.25. When response probabilities were identical for movements of the left or right arm, cells identified as controlling the bicep muscle in the arm contralateral to the movement discharged slightly during the preparatory period and increased their firing rates when the monkey moved the lever. Importantly, changes in cell activity during the foreperiod were not accompanied by any appreciable change in EMG activity. Thus, the suggestion is that this activity is associated with response preparation, not response execution (see also the work reviewed in the earlier subsection 'Suggestive Research Findings...'). Additionally, the presetting activity was unrelated to response speed in the ipsilateral arm, suggesting that this activity does not reflect general arousal. Subsequently, two groups of cells were identified in the motor cortex whose firing rates increased similarly during the 250 ms period preceding the movement, but whose pattern of activity differed during the movement itself. The firing rates of cells in one group increased during the movement, while those in the other group decreased. Importantly, the degree of increase or decrease in this movement-related activity was affected by the probability that a response would be made. An increase in response probability (from 0.50 to 1.0) produced a significant decrease in reaction time that was accompanied by further decreases in activity of the inhibited cells but increases in activity of the excited cells during the movement (see Figure 13.6 in Requin, Lecas and Bonnet, 1984). Thus, changes in the firing rates of motor neurons associated both with preparation of a movement and its execution may vary systematically with changes in the probability that a particular response is to be emitted.

Not surprisingly, a similar type of selectively may occur in the reflex components of a movement. Brunia and his coworkers have studied the selective aspects of motor preparation as they are expressed in the tendon reflex (see Brunia and Boelhouwer, 1988, for a review). Their procedure is to elicit tendon reflexes during each trial in a warned Go/NoGo reaction time task as the subject prepares a unilateral plantar flexion of the foot. Changes in reflex amplitude on the side ipsilateral to the movement should reflect the selective aspects of motor preparation, whereas changes on the side contralateral to the movement should reflect the non-selective aspects of preparation. Brunia and Boelhouwer observed an increase in reflex amplitude for both the responding and non-responding legs shortly after the warning stimulus was presented. This bilateral increase was followed during the rest of the foreperiod by a reduction in reflex amplitude in the responding limb and an increase in the non-responding limb when subjects were biased toward responding (warning stimulus signaled a response was to be executed with a probability of 0.80) but not when they were unbiased (i.e. response probability was 0.50). This differential effect suggests that selective preparation was induced by the probability manipulation (see Brunia and Boelhouwer, 1988, Experiment 20).

The single-unit studies of Requin and coworkers and the reflex studies of Brunia and his colleagues suggest that variations in response probability manifest themselves at very primitive levels of nervous system processing. Examples of the effect of changes in response probability are abundant in the event-related brain potential literature. Two such examples that are pertinent to our interest in presetting can be found in the work of Gaillard (1977) and Roth *et al.* (1976) on the contingent negative variation (CNV; a slow negative brain potential seen during the preparatory period of a warned reaction time task). Gaillard was interested in evaluating changes in response preparation, expressed in variation in the CNV and in performance, as response probability and speed/accuracy instructions were varied factorially in a warned two-choice reaction time task. Variations in the probability that a certain stimulus would be presented occurred on a trial-by-trial basis and were indicated by changes in the pitch of the warning tone (0.9, 0.5, or 0.01). The length of the foreperiod was fixed at 3 s. Subjects performed the task under three levels of speed/accuracy instructions: speed, accuracy, and 'detection'. The 'detection' condition required subjects to postpone their responses until approximately 1 s after the stimulus had been presented. Gaillard observed an early CNV component with a latency of 700 ms under all experimental conditions. More importantly, he found a gradually increasing late CNV component that was largest when the subject was biased towards responding (i.e. probability of making a response was highest) and response speed was emphasized. This component was absent when subjects were biased towards non-responding (either by low response probabilities or under detection instructions).

Effects similar to those reported by Gaillard were obtained by Roth et al. (1976) in an experiment in which subjects were required to make a Go/NoGo response choice. Subjects heard a series of tone pips whose pitch changed occasionally. These changes in pitch served as a warning to the subject that a noise burst might occur 1 s later. The probability that a noise burst would follow was either 1.0 or 0.1. Subjects completed two conditions. In one condition, they were instructed to depress a response button throughout the duration of the experimental session to prove that they were awake, but they were not required to pay attention to the auditory stimulation. In the other condition, they were asked to respond to the noise bursts by pressing the button as quickly as possible. As in Gaillard's study, they found that CNV amplitudes were larger for the high than for the low probability stimuli that signaled a response and they were higher when subjects were required to respond with a button press response to the noise bursts. As we reviewed in the previous main section, this probability effect is expressed at the autonomic level as well by changes in HR activity and pupil dilation. High-probability stimuli are associated with lower anticipatory HRs and larger pupillary dilations compared with low-probability stimuli. Findings of this type suggest that presetting involves widespread activation of the nervous system. This activation is not revealed, however, in straightforward fashion by behavioral measures alone.

How can psychophysiological measures help to articulate this activation? In our view, they may supplement performance measures of presetting in at least four different respects. First, they can make a methodological contribution. The continuous character of psychophysiological measures such as HR, pupil dilation and measures of brain electrical activity allow the investigator to chart the time course of general and selective preparation in the absence of overt responding without resorting to the use of intrusive probe stimuli. Second, psychophysiological measures can be used to disentangle the relative contributions of peripheral, central, stimulus, and response factors to the preparation process. It should be noted that these measures all appear to be sensitive to changes in the functional state of the nervous system, but that their intercorrelations are low. Of course, low intercorrelations might be due to poor measurement. Alternatively, they may reflect a process of preparation in which the recruitment and activation of different components of the nervous system is temporally sequenced. Third, if we can link changes in these psychophysiological measures to changes in single neuron activity, we can then examine how the mechanisms involved in preparatory activities are implemented in the brain. Results available to date suggest that a wide array of neurophysiological mechanisms are very sensitive to changes in an organisms' preparatory state (cf. Evarts, 1984). Finally, psychophysiological measures provide at least two types of information, latency and amplitude. The latency of a psychophysiological response may index the timing of processing elements, while its amplitude may index changes in the state of the processing element. Thus, multiple measures of psychophysiological activity may reveal the complexities of the interaction between the time of engagement of a processing stage and fluctuations in the state of activation of the subject.

CHRONOPSYCHOPHYSIOLOGY: FUTURE DIRECTIONS

In a strict sense, we have defined chronopsychophysiology as the augmentation of classical mental chronometry by psychophysiological time markers. Our discussion has focused on the extent to which measures of event-related brain potential, pupil, and HR activity can serve, with performance measures, as probes of the information processing apparatus to attain greater depths than would be possible using the single probe of overt behavior. Thus, the task as we see it is to evaluate the potential of these psychophysiological measures as online indices of the temporal activation of processing stages. Our discussion turned necessarily on two broad areas of concern, methodological and theoretical. It has led to the conclusion that, although the research that has been done to date is promising, much more research must be done to determine the value of these measures for the mental chronometrician. Nonetheless, we are reasonably enthusiastic about the prospects for important insights to emerge. Advances in chronopsychophysiology, however, will entail the refinement of measurement procedures and data analytic techniques, articulation of the cognitive processes manifest by the various measures, and the investment of considerable effort in demonstrating the validity of psychophysiological techniques in chronometric paradigms. If successful, chronopsychophysiological studies may produce new theoretical insights that eventuate in a reconceptualization of mental chronometry. Among these may be a deeper understanding of how the temporal activation of information processing elements and the state of the organism interact to produce (systematic) variability in the manifest output, and how these processes are implemented in the nervous system. We shall conclude with brief discussions of measurement and validation issues, and of the theoretical promise that may be realized if the endeavor succeeds.

The empirical success of any research effort in psychophysiology, and ultimately any theoretical developments that emerge from it, is linked inextricably to the resolution of critical technical and methodological problems. In chronopsychophysiology, a number of unresolved measurement problems abound that compromise the efficacy of the measures we have proposed as markers of the temporal organization of elementary mental processes (again, the reader is referred to Coles *et al.*, 1986, for a detailed review of these issues). At the most fundamental level, there is the problem of defining a psychophysiological component, determining its time course, and identifying the time points in the component that manifest the elementary mental process of interest. Clearly, this problem is both conceptual and methodological. The former includes establishing universal definitions of components and specifying how the timing of a component conforms to the timing of a particular mental operation. The latter includes technical issues related to the selection of filters and of the methods for identifying the time points for analysis. Again, universal standards have not been established. Current practice is for individual investigators to make rational choices. The consequence is a reasonably high degree of variability that can express itself in contradictory results from one laboratory to another.

Definition and measurement issues are bound tightly together. It should be pointed out that the psychophysiologist typically applies a relatively small set of analytic techniques to the data, most of which are not tailored specifically for psychophysiological signals. Molenaar and van der Molen (1985) have distinguished three types of models that guide decisions about the analysis of cardiac activity. They aligned these models along a dimension of content specificity. At one extreme are black box models, such as those underlying principal components and spectral analysis, that are almost completely uninformative about the dynamics of cardiac activity (i.e. they are content-free). At the other extreme are content models in which great specificity is provided. These models, although conceptually rich, are considered impractical in psychophysiological research settings because not enough is known about the functional significance of the measures to connect them to the specifics of the model. Between these two extremes are what Molenaar and van der Molen called global models. These models have sufficient content to make them of theoretical interest, but not too much to render them impractical in application. Their content is expressed in mathematical expressions that have been derived from theoretical principles concerning a particular qualitative aspect of the physiological signal. They are invoked in research designed to evaluate the effects of experimental manipulations on processes the electrophysiological signal is hypothesized to reveal. This type of reasoning has also guided decision-making in the analysis of brain electrical activity as well (Molenaar, 1990). Mental chronometry has obviously evolved into a rich content area, and the task of the chronopsychophysiologist is both to take advantage of this endowment and to enrichen it further.

To achieve these ends, the cognitive significance of psychophysiological components must be delineated. That is, content-rich, articulated models of the mental operations manifest by the components must be developed, and these models must be validated. The problematic status of P300 in the context of mental chronometry is due in large measure to failings on both of these counts. Among other things, this requires replication of well-established chronometric experiments using psychophysiological batteries (as have the investigators whose work we have reviewed). The additive factors approach provides a very reasonable organizational framework for initiating this process. (See van der Molen, Somsen and Orlebeke (1985) for advocacy of this approach in HR studies; see also Townsend (1990) for discussion of a related methodology he calls factorial interaction.)

Meyer *et al.* (1988b) educed six inference rules that they believe have provided the conceptual framework in which chronopsychophysiologists interpret results. In this context, chronopsychophysiologists are presumed to evaluate joint factor effects on the latencies of components of interest and on reaction time. These rules are essentially expressions of Sternberg's additive factors/stages of processing perspective translated into the language of chronopsychophysiology; that is, component latency is merely an added dependent variable in an additive factors design. The inference rules can be summarized as follows:

(1) The mental operations indexed by a particular ERP component are revealed when manipulations of an experimental factor thought to influence a particular mental process produce systematic effects on its timing parameters (i.e. Sternberg's selective influence).

(2) When the mental operations of an ERP component are inferred as in (1) and an experimental factor has equivalent effects on the timing of this ERP component and reaction time, it can be concluded that the factor effect is restricted to a subset of the processing elements that mediate the production of overt responses.

(3) When the mental operations of an ERP component are inferred as in (1) and an experimental factor has a larger effect on reaction time than on the component's timing, it can be concluded that the factor effect includes processes manifest by the ERP component as well as subsequent additional processes that mediate production of overt responses but not generation of the component.

(4) When the mental operations of an ERP component are inferred as in (1) and two experimental factors have additive effects on its timing, it can be concluded that the factors influence two distinct processing stages, either the stage associated with the component and a preceding stage or another earlier stage. If the two factors have interactive effects on a component's timing, the conclusion is that these factors both influence either the process manifested by the component or some prior process.

(5) When two temporally non-overlapping ERP components are thought to manifest two distinct mental processes and an experimental factor has equal effects on the timing of each component, it can be concluded that the processes are mediated at two non-overlapping stages and that the factor effect is at the first or some earlier stage.

6) When an ERP component is thought to manifest a distinct mental process and an experimental factor affects its peak latency but not its onset time, it can be concluded that the factor effect is restricted to the stage mediating the mental process and not to any earlier stages.

As is apparent, and as Meyer *et al.* argued, this conceptual framework derives directly from the experimental methods and theoretical formulations of Donders and Sternberg. Thus, it is a direct extension of their approach to event-related brain potentials. We agree. Indeed, we agree with the general characterization by these authors that cognitive psychophysiological studies of mental chronometry have been guided to a large extent by these tenets. In our view, this reflects not only the intellectual appeal of this approach, but also the relative infancy of the field; and parallels the history of contemporary mental chronometry. Recall that for at least a decade after Sternberg published his seminal papers in the late 1960s, the AFM was the predominant methodology for studying chronometric processes, and the inference rules derived from it were used to interpret findings (in the context of stages of processing). As we have seen, it was not until the late 1970s that serious challenges began to emerge (e.g. McClelland, 1979; Ratcliff, 1978). The issue then is not where chronopsychophysiologists have been, but where they can go.

In our view, the ultimate destination is the brain. Initiating this journey by applying Sternberg's method and the theoretical assumptions on which it is based has not misdirected us. It may be premature, however, to attempt to link specific components of psychophysiological signals to the activation of specific stages of processing. The relevant parametric studies have not yet been done. Under these circumstances, indices derived from psychophysiological measures can be used in an 'agnostic' way. That is, they can be used as time markers, like the button press, that have the advantage of occurring during the information transmission process itself. However, because these signals are measured at sites of varying distance from their physiologic sources and these sources are usually components of larger physiologic systems, there may be a loss as well as a gain in the information they transmit. For example, measures of HR change may be more closely linked to effects of respiration on cardiac activity that are irrelevant to the task being performed than to the demands imposed by the task itself (for a detailed discussion of this issue, see Jennings, 1986a). Components of the event-related brain potential measured at the scalp, like the P300, are probably aggregates of activity generated from multiple sources in the brain that is passively conducted through neural tissue, the calvarium, and the scalp. Each of these sources may in turn be constituents of a larger system or systems that multiply influence them. Some of these influences may be relevant, others irrelevant to the emergence of the mental reaction. This conundrum leads paradoxically to the promise of making theoretical strides using psychophysiological time markers that cannot be attained using behavioral time markers alone: we can descend from the scalp, the eye, and the chest to the brain and perhaps be able to offer clues as to how cognitive systems are implemented in brain systems.

It is there where we may be able to speculate on the contents of specific elements of processing (e.g. stages) and how they are organized. Stage analyses of mental processing using performance measures permit global conclusions about overall organization but not about the specific details of implementation (cf. Luce, 1986; p. 1). Here it is important to recall that the notion of stage is an operational rather than a theoretical construct. The consequence of this is that it may provide nothing more than a convenient shorthand for conceptualizing the effects of experimental variables (cf. Pachella, 1974; p. 57). In this chapter, we have reviewed evidence which suggests that studies of the lateralized readiness potential may provide insight into the neurocognitive mechanisms associated with the engagement of response processors by revealing activity originating from brain regions that mediate movement. Other examples, perhaps more convincing, can be found in this volume and elsewhere (e.g. Graham and Hackley, this volume; Posner, 1986). The measures we have proposed in this chapter can be augmented as well with other methods for evaluating neural activation, in particular, magnetoencephalograms (MEG) (e.g. Okada, Kaufman and Williamson, 1983) and cerebral blood flow (Posner *et al.*, 1988).

While measures of cerebral blood flow do not provide the temporal resolution of the ERP or the MEG, they do provide information about changes in circulation in specific parts of the brain that permit inferences about their relative activation that cannot be extracted from brain electrical or magnetic activity. These studies might provide insight into the distribution of resources among neural systems and permit the development of hypotheses about the organization of systems mediating mental chronometric processes. An additional source of information about the organization of these systems and the distribution of resources among them may be derived from studies of patients with localized brain lesions (e.g. Johnson, 1989; Knight, 1984; Smith Stapleton and Halgren, 1986).

The impetus for undertaking this journey is given, however, by an early enthusiasm that the marriage between mental chronometry and psychophysiology will unite structural and energetic processes, and in so doing will produce a synergism absent when the two are studied alone. The mental chronometrician brings into this marriage a taxonomy of task variables that can be used to detail the structure and timing of the information processing system, whereas the psychophysiologist's dowry is a set of measurement techniques that permit examination of this aspect of mental processing and of the changing patterns of physiological responses associated with changing states of the organism. Thus, chronopsychophysiology may contribute not only to the analysis of the organizational and temporal aspects of mental processing by providing more detailed information about elementary mental operations and their implementation in the brain, but also by providing the possibility of examining variations in mental reactions under a wide range of conditions that have been referred to as 'energetical' states. In the stage analysis of the reaction process, for example, conditions are established to encourage optimal performance (e.g. subjects are rested and well-trained, performance incentives are given). In principle, then, the operating characteristics of the information processing system are invariant. That is, performance variability within and between subjects is attributed to normal fluctuations and individual differences, not to systematic changes in internal and environmental processes that influence the subject's performance. This may be something of a caricature, but it is not unfair to argue that the perspective of the stage analysis is computational.

Of course, as originally argued by Sternberg (1969), the position can be taken that energetical concepts are beyond the purview of stage models. We used the example of 'presetting' to suggest that these models cannot neglect such concepts, however. They are too pervasive and influential. We suggested as well that psychophysiology can make important contributions in this effort, but must overcome a large obstacle. Namely, current state models of energetical processes and stage models of computational processes cannot be integrated readily. We pointed to Sanders' (1983) cognitive–energetic model as an example of current attempts to assimilate state variables into stage concepts. One problem with his approach is that the components of the energetic level of the model are postulated to influence the computational levels, but there is no clear description of how the two levels interact. A strong case can be made that the influences are bidirectional and thus must be specified in the model. So, at this point, the integration is more apparent than real. A related problem is that the model lacks manifest content. In its present form it provides a taxonomy of state and computational variables, but does not provide theoretical substance by defining the processing characteristics of its constituents. In the end, this is an essential desideratum in the formulation of cognitive–energetic models of human mental reactions.

The work is just beginning that may accomplish this end. To achieve it, a concerted effort must be mounted in the four areas we discussed above. (i) Measurement techniques must be improved. (ii) The measures thus selected must be validated in chronometric paradigms, and the work extended to incorporate cognitive–energetic paradigms. (iii) Processing models must be developed that incorporate cognitive and energetic postulates. At the behavioral level, processing models can be advanced by concentrating on task variables *per se*, on interactions between task variables, and on interesting deviations from the usual patterns of additivity and interaction (cf. Sanders, 1980). At the psychophysiological level, characterization of the interactions between cognitive and energetic processes will depend on resolution of the technical, methodological, and conceptual issues we enumerated above, as well as taking the combined approach further to include techniques such as the magnetoencephologram, cerebral blood flow, and studies of patients with brain lesions. (iv) The marriage will succeed to the extent that each partner makes sufficiently specific contributions. Perhaps, a useful starting point to respond to the challenge of chronopsychophysiology is Sanders' model. We regard it, however, as a heuristic tool, not as a well-articulated theory; as a prototheory in the sense meant by the famous jazz composer George Russell:

> A useful theory of any kind demands obedience at first in order to master it. However, a really useful theory doesn't enslave one without making the period of servitude interesting and worthwhile and without eventually freeing its subscribers through its own built-in liberation apparatus. (quoted in Simpkins, 1975)

ACKNOWLEDGEMENTS

Preparation of this chapter and parts of the research described were supported by NWO grants 153209, 560–263–023 and 560–265–026, and NIMH grant 40418 to Dr van der Molen; by NIA grant AG04581 and a grant from the Allegheny–Singer Research Foundation to Dr Bashore; by an Academic Senate grant from UCSF to Dr Halliday; and by a Veterans Administration Merit Review grant, NIMH grants MH2219 and MH3869, and Biomedical Research Support (Department of Psychiatry, UCSF) to Dr Callaway.

We are indebted to our colleagues Peter Molenaar, Riek Somsen, Evert-Jan

Stoffels and Dick Jennings: without their help the 'Amsterdam' part of the chapter would not have been possible. Hilary Naylor, Bruce Turetsky, Lovelle Yano, George Fein, and in particular Craig Van Dyke, greatly facilitated the 'San Francisco' contribution to the chapter. Finally, special thanks are due to Marsha Tatipikalawan (in Amsterdam) and Laura Chilinskas (in Philadelphia) for helping us put the chapter together.

REFERENCES

Ach, N. (1905). *Über die Willenstä tigkeit und das Denken*. Göttingen: Vandenhoeck.

Angell, J.R. and McLennan, S. (1896). The organic effects of agreeable and disagreeable stimuli. *Psychological Review*, **3**, 371–377.

Angell, J.R. and Thompson, H.B. (1899). Organic processes and consciousness. *Psychological Review*, **6**, 32–69.

Ashby, F.G. (1982). Deriving exact predictions from the cascade model. *Psychophysiological Review*, **89**, 599–607.

Atkins, S. (1964). Performance, heart rate, respiration rate and the day–night continuum. *Perceptual and Motor Skills*, **18**, 409–412.

Bashore, T.R. (1981). Vocal and manual reaction time estimates of interhemispheric transmission time. *Psychological Bulletin*, **89**, 352–368.

Bashore, T.R. (1990a). Stimulus–response compatibility viewed from a cognitive psychophysiological perspective. In R.W. Proctor and T.G. Reeve (eds), *Stimulus–Response Compatibility: An Integrated Perspective*. Amsterdam: North-Holland, pp. 183–223.

Bashore, T.R. (1990b). Age-related changes in mental processing revealed by analyses of event-related brain potentials. In J. Rohrbaugh, R.Parasuraman and R. Johnson (eds), *Event-Related Potentials: Basic Issues and Applications*. New York: Oxford University Press, pp. 242–278.

Bashore, T.R., McCarthy, G., Heffley, E.F., Clapman, R.C. and Donchin, E. (1982). Is handwriting posture associated with differences in motor control? An analysis of asymmetries in the readiness potential. *Neuropsychologia, 20*, 327–346.

Bashore, T.R. and Osman, A. (1987). On the temporal relation between perceptual analysis and response selection: a psychophysiological investigation of stimulus congruency and S–R compatibility effects on human information processing. Poster presented at the Fourth International Congress of Cognitive Neuroscience, Dourdan, France.

Bashore, T.R., Osman, A. and Heffley, E.F. (1989). Mental slowing in elderly persons: a cognitive psychophysiological analysis. *Psychology and Aging*, **4**, 235–244.

Beatty, J. (1982). Task-evoked pupillary responses, processing load and the structure of processing demands. *Psychological Bulletin*, **91**, 276–292.

Beatty, J. (1986). The pupillary system. In M.G.H. Coles, E. Donchin and S.W.Porges (eds), *Psychophysiology: Systems, Processes and Applications*, New York: Guilford Press, pp. 43–50.

Berger, H. (1929). Über das elektrenkphalogramm des Menschen. *Archiv für Psychiatrie Nervenkrankheiten, 87*, 527–570.

Bertelson, P. (1965). Serial choice reaction-time as a function of response versus signal-and-response repetition. *Nature*, **206**, 217–218.

Biervliet, Van, J.J. (1894). Ueber den Einfluss der Geschwindigkeit des Pulses auf die Zeitdauer der Reaktionszeit bei Schalleindrüken. *Philosphische Studien*, **10**, 161–168.

Binet, A. and Coutier, J. (1896). La circulation capillaire dans ses rapports avec la respiration et les phnomenes psychiques. *L'Anné Psychologique, II*, 87–167.
Binet, A. and Coutier, J. (1897). Les changements de forme du pouls capillaire a ux diffrentes heures de la journe. *L'Anné Psychologique, III*, 10–126.
Binet, A. and Sollier, P. (1895). Recherches sur le pouls cerebral dans ses rapports avec les attitudes du corps, la respiration et les actes psychiques. *Archives de Physiologie*, **4**, 719–734.
Binet, A. and Vaschide, N. (1897). Influence du travail intellectuel des motions et du travail physique sur la pression du sang. *Anne Psychologique, III*, 127–183.
Blackman, A.R. (1975). Test of the additive-factor method of choice reaction time analysis. *Perceptual and Motor Skills*, **41**, 607–613.
Bohlin, G. and Kjellberg, A. (1979). Orienting activity in two stimulus paradigms as reflected in heart rate. In H.D. Kimmel, E.H. van Olst and J.F. Orlebeke (eds), *The Orienting Reflex in Humans*. Hillsdale, NJ: Lawrence Erlbaum Associates, pp. 169–197.
Boring, E.G. (1950). *A History of Experimental Psychology*. New York: Appleton–Century–Crofts Inc.
Bradshaw, J.H. (1968). Pupillary changes and reaction time with varied stimulus uncertainty. *Psychonomic Science*, **13**, 69–70.
Bradshaw, J.H. (1969). Background light intensity and the pupillary response in a reaction task. *Psychonomic Science*, **14**, 265–271.
Bradshaw, J.H. (1970). Pupil size and drug state in a reaction time task. *Psychonomic Science*, **18**, 112–113.
Brandeis, D., Callaway, E., Naylor, H. and Yano, L. (1988). Cholinergic control of stimulus and attentional processing. *Psychophysiology*, **25**, 425 (abstract).
Briggs, G.E. and Blaha, J. (1969). Memory retrieval and central comparison time in information processing. *Journal of Experimental Psychology*, **79**, 395–402.
Briggs, G.E. and Swanson, J.M. (1969). Retrieval time as a function of memory ensemble size. *Quarterly Journal of Experimental Psychology*, **21**, 185–191.
Briggs, G.E. and Swanson, J.M. (1970). Encoding, decoding, and central functions in human information processing. *Journal of Experimental Psychology*, **86**, 296–308.
Brunia, C.H.M. and Damen, E.J.P. (1985). Evoked cardiac responses during a fixed 4 sec foreperiod preceding four different responses. In J.F. Orlebeke, G. Mulder and L.J.P. van Doornen (eds), *Psychophysiology of Cardiovascular Control: Models, Methods, and Data*. New York: Plenum Press, pp. 613–620.
Brunia, C.H.M. and Boelhouwer, A.J.W. (1988). Reflexes as a tool: a window in the central nervous system. In P.K. Ackles, J.R. Jennings and M.G.H. Coles (eds), *Advances in Psychophysiology*, Vol. 3, Greenwich, CT: JAI Press, pp. 1–67.
Buchsbaum, M. (1977). The middle evoked response components and schizophrenia. *Schizophrenia Bulletin*, **3**, 93–104.
Bumke, O. (1911). Die Pupillenstorungen, bei Geistes- und Nervenkrankheiten (*Physiologie und Pathologie der Irisbewegungen*). Jena: Fischer Verlag.
Callaway, E. (1983). The pharmacology of human information processing. *Psychophysiology*, **20**, 359–370.
Callaway, E. and Halliday, R. (1973). Evoked potential variability: effects of age, amplitude and methods of measurement. *Electroencephalography and Clinical Neurophysiology*, **34**, 125–133.
Cannon, W.B. (1915). *Bodily Changes in Pain, Hunger, Fear and Rage*. New York: Appleton.
Caton, R. (1875). The electric currents of the brain. *British Medical Journal*, **ii**, 278.
Chase, W.G., Graham, F.K. and Graham, D.T. (1968). Components of HR response in anticipation of reaction time and exercise tasks. *Journal of Experimental Psychology*, **76**, 642–648.

Colegate, R.L., Hoffman, J.E. and Eriksen, C.W. (1973). Selective encoding from multielement visual displays. *Perception and Psychophysics*, **14**, 217–224.

Coles, M.G.H. (1974). Physiological activity and detection: the effects of attentional requirements and the prediction of performance. *Biological Psychology*, **2**, 113–125.

Coles, M.G.H. (1982). Respiration phase and the cardiac cycle effect. *Biological Psychology*, **15**, 273 (abstract).

Coles, M.G.H. (1989). Modern mind–brain reading: psychophysiology, physiology, and cognition. *Psychophysiology*, **26**, 251–269.

Coles, M.G.H. and Duncan-Johnson, C.C. (1977). Attention and cardiac activity: heart rate responses during a variable foreperiod, disjunctive reaction time task. *Biological Psychology*, **5**, 151–158.

Coles, M.G.H. and Gratton, G. (1986). Cognitive psychophysiology and the study of states and processes. In G.R.J. Hockey, A.W.K. Gaillard and M.G.H. Coles (eds), *Energetics and Human Information Processing*. Dordrecht, Netherlands: Nijhoff, pp. 409–424.

Coles, M.G.H. and Strayer, D.L. (1985). The psychophysiology of the cardiac cycle time effect. In J.F.Orlebeke, G. Mulder and L.J.P. van Doornen (eds), *Psychophysiology of Cardiovascular Control: Models, Methods, and Data*. New York: Plenum Press, pp. 517–534.

Coles, M.G.H., Pellegrini, A.M. and Wilson, G.V. (1982). The cardiac cycle time effect: influence of respiration phase and information processing requirements. *Psychophysiology*, **19**, 648–657.

Coles, M.G.H., Gratton, G., Bashore, T.R., Eriksen, C.W. and Donchin, E. (1985). A psychophysiological investigation of the continuous flow model of human information processing. *Journal of Experimental Psychology: Human Perception and Performance*, **11**, 529–553.

Coles, M.G.H., Gratton, G., Kramer, A.F. and Miller, G.A. (1986). Principles of signal acquisition and analysis. In M.G.H. Coles, E. Donchin and S.W. Porges (eds), *Psychophysiology: Systems, Processes, and Applications*. New York: The Guilford Press, pp. 183–221.

Connor, W.H. and Lang, P.J. (1969). Cortical slow wave and cardiac rate responses in stimulus orientation and reaction time conditions. *Journal of Experimental Psycholgy*, **82**, 310–320.

Darrow, C.W. (1924). Differences in the physiological reactions to sensory and ideational stimuli. *Psychological Bulletin*, **26**, 185–201.

Davis, P.A. (1939). Effects of acoustic stimuli on the waking human brain. *Journal of Neurophysiology*, **2**, 494–499.

Davis, R.C., Buchwald, A.M. and Frankman, R.W. (1955). Autonomic and muscular responses and their relation to simple stimuli. *Psychological Monographs: General and Applied*, **69**, 1–71.

Dawson, G.D. (1947). Cerebral responses to electrical stimulation of peripheral nerves in man. *Journal of Neurology and Neurosurgical Psychiatry*, **10**, 134–140.

De Jaager, J.J. (1865). De Physiologische tijd bij psychische processen. In J. Brözek and M.S. Sibinga (eds), *Origins of psychometry: Johan Jacob de Jaager, Student of F.C. Donders*. Nieuwkoop: B. de Graaf.

De Jong, R. (unpublished manuscript). Partial information or facilitation? A caution on the speed–accuracy decomposition technique.

De Jong, R., Coles, M.G.H., Logan, G.D. and Gratton, G. (1990). In search of the point of no return: the control of response processes. *Journal of Experimental Psychology: Human Perception and Performance*, **16**, 164–182.

De Jong, R., Wierda, M., Mulder, G. and Mulder, L.J.M. (1988). Use of partial stimulus information in response processing. *Journal of Experimental Psychology: Human Perception and Performance*, **14**, 682–692.

Deecke, L. (1987). Bereitschaftspotential as an indicator of movement preparation in supplementary motor area and motor cortex. In G. Bock, M. O'Connor and J. Marsh (eds), *Motor Areas of the Cerebral Cortex*. New York: John Wiley, pp. 231–245.

Desmedt, J.E., Huy, N.T. and Bourguet, M. (1983). The cognitive P40, N60, and P100 components of somatosensory evoked potentials and the earliest signs of sensory processing in man. *Electroencephalography and Clinical Neurophysiology*, **56**, 572–582.

Donchin, E. (1979). Event-related brain potentials: a tool in the study of human information processing. In H. Begleiter (ed.), *Evoked Potentials and Behavior*. New York: Plenum Press, pp. 13–75.

Donchin, E. (1981). Surprise!. . .Surprise? *Psychophysiology*, **8**, 493–513.

Donchin, E. (ed.) (1984). *Cognitive Psychophysiology*, vol. 1. Hillsdale, NJ: Erlbaum.

Donchin, E. and Coles, M.G.H. (1988). Is the P300 component a manifestation of context updating? *Behavioral and Brain Sciences*, **11**, 357–374.

Donchin, E. and Heffley, E.F. (1978). Multivariate analysis of event-related potential data: a tutorial. In D. Otto (ed.), *Multidisciplinary Perspectives in Event-Related Brain Potential Research*. Washington, DC: US Government Printing Office, pp. 555–572.

Donchin, E., Karis, D., Bashore, T.R., Coles, M.G.H. and Gratton, G. (1986). Cognitive psychophysiology and human information processing. In M.G.H. Coles, E. Donchin and S.W. Porges (eds), *Psychophysiology: Systems, Processes, and Applications*. New York: Guilford Press, pp. 244–267.

Donders, F.C. (1868a). On the speed of mental processess. In W.G. Koster (ed.), *Attention and Performance*, vol. II (*Acta Psychologica*, **30**, 1969). Amsterdam: North-Holland, pp. 412–431.

Donders, F.C. (1868b). Zur Physiologie des Nervus Vagus. *Plugers Archiv fur die gesammte Physiologie*, **1**, 331–361.

Duffy, E. (1972). Activation. In N.S. Greenfield and R.A. Sternbach (eds), *Handbook of Psychophysiology*. New York: Holt, Rinehart and Winston, pp. 577–622.

Duncan-Johnson, C.C. and Coles, M.G.H. (1974). Heart rate and disjunctive reaction time: The effects of discrimination requirements. *Journal of Experimental Psychology*, **103**, 1160–1168.

Duncan-Johnson and Donchin, E. (1982). The P300 component of the event-related brain potential as an index of information processing. *Biological Psychology*, **14**, 1–52.

Duncan-Johnson, C.C. and Kopell, B.S. (1981). The Stroop effect: brain potentials localize the source of interference. *Science*, **214**, 938–940.

Einthoven, W. (1913). Über die Deutung des Elektrokardiograms. *Pflügers Archiv*, **149**, 65–86.

Eriksen, B.A. and Eriksen, C.W. (1974). Effects of noise letters upon the identification of a target letter in a nonsearch task. *Perception and Psychophysics*, **16**, 143–149.

Eriksen, C.W. and Collins, J.F. (1969). Temporal course of selective attention. *Journal of Experimental Psychology*, **80**, 254–261.

Eriksen, C.W. and Hoffman, J.E. (1973). The extent of processing of noise elements during selective encoding from visual displays. *Perception and Psychophysics*, **14**, 155–160.

Eriksen, C.W. and Rohrbaugh, J. (1970). Visual masking in multielement displays. *Journal of Experimental Psychology*, **83**, 147–154.

Eriksen, C.W. and Schultz, D.W. (1977). Retinal locus and acuity in visual information processing. *Bulletin of the Psychonomic Society*, **9**, 81–84.

Eriksen, C.W. and Schultz, D.W. (1978). Temporal factors in visual information processing. In J. Requin (ed.), *Attention and Performance*, vol. VII. New York: Academic Press.

Eriksen, C.W. and Schultz, D.W. (1979). Information processing in visual search: a continuous flow conception and experimental results. *Perception and Psychophysics*, **25**, 249–263.

Eriksen, C.W., Hamlin, R.M. and Daye, C. (1973). The effect of flanking letters and digits on speed of identifying a letter. *Bulletin of the Psychonomic Society*, **2**, 400–402.

Evarts, E.V. (1984). Neurophysiological approaches to brain mechanisms for preparatory set. In S. Kornblum and J. Requin (eds), *Preparatory States and Processes*. Hillsdale, NJ: LEA, pp. 137–153.

Fabiani, M., Gratton, G., Karis, D. and Donchin, E. (1987). Definition, identification, and reliability of the P300 component of the event-related brain potential. In P.K. Ackles, J.R. Jennings and M.G.H. Coles (eds), *Advances in Psychophysiology*, vol. 2. Greenwich, CT: JAI Press, pp. 1–78.

Ferrier, D. (1876). *The Functions of the Brain*. London: Smith and Elder.

Ford, J.M. and Pfefferbaum, A. (1985). Age-related changes in event-related potentials. In P. Ackles, J.R. Jennings and M.G.H. Coles (eds), *Advances in Psychophysiology*, vol. 3. Greenwich, CT: JAI Press, pp. 301–339.

Ford, J.M., Pfefferbaum, A., Tinklenberg, J.R. and Kopell, B.S. (1982). Effects of perceptual and cognitive difficulty on P3 and RT in young and old adults. *Electroencephalography and Clinical Neurophysiology*, **54**, 311–321.

Ford, J.M., Roth, W.T., Mohs, R.C., Hopkins, W.F. and Kopell, B.S. (1979). Event-related potentials recorded from young and old adults during a memory retrieval task. *Electroencephalography and Clinical Neurophysiology*, **47**, 450–459.

Fritsch, G. and Hitzig, E. (1870). Über die elektrische Erregbarkeit des Grosshirns. *Archiv für Anatomie, Physiologie, und wissenschaftliche Medicin*, **8**, 300–332.

Frowein, H.W. (1981). Selective drug effects on information processing. Doctoral Dissertation, Catholic University of Brabant, Tilburg, Netherlands.

Frowein, H.W., Reitsma, D. and Acquarius, C. (1981). Effects of two counteracting stresses on the reaction process. In J. Long and A. Baddely (eds), *Attention and Performance*, vol. IX. Hillsdale, NJ: Lawrence Erlbaum Associates.

Gaillard, A.W.K. (1977). The late CNV wave: preparation versus expectancy. *Psychophysiology*, **14**, 563–568.

Gale, A. and Edwards, J.A. (1986). Individual differences. In M.G.H. Coles, E. Donchin and S.W. Porges (eds), *Psychophysiology: Systems, Processes, and Applications*. New York: Guilford Press, pp. 431–507.

Ganz, L. (1975). Temporal factors in visual perception. In E.C. Carterette and M.P. Friedman (eds), *Handbook of Perception*, vol. V. New York: Academic Press.

Gibson, E.J. (1969). *Principles of Perceptual Learning and Development*. New York: Appleton–Century–Crofts.

Goldberg, G. (1985). Supplementary motor area structure and function: review and hypotheses. *The Behavioral and Brain Sciences*, **8**, 567–588.

Gopher, D. and Sanders, A.F. (1984). S-Oh-R: Oh stages! Oh resources!. In W. Prinz and A. Sanders (eds), *Cognition and Motor Behavior*. Heidelberg: Springer Verlag.

Gottsdanker, R. (1975). The attaining and maintaining of preparation. In P.M.A. Rabbit and S. Dornic (eds), *Attention and Performance*, vol. V. London: Academic Press, pp. 33–49.

Gottsdanker, R. and Shragg, G.P. (1985). Verification of Donders' substraction method. *Journal of Experimental Psychology: Human Perception and Performance*, **11**, 765–776.

Graham, F.K. (1979). Distinguishing among orienting, defense, and startle reflexes. In

H. D. Kimmel, E.H. van Olst and J.F. Orlebeke (eds), *The Orienting Reflex in Humans.* Hillsdale, NJ: Erlbaum, pp. 137–168.

Gratton, G., Coles, M.G.H. and Donchin, E. (1989). A procedure for using multi-electrode information in the analysis of components of the event-related potential: vector filter. *Psychophysiology*, **26**, 222–232.

Gratton, G., Coles, M.G.H., Sirevaag, E.J., Eriksen, C.W. and Donchin, E. (1988). Pre- and poststimulus activation of response channels: a psychophysiological analysis. *Journal of Experimental Psychology: Human Perception and Performance*, **14**, 331–344.

Gratton, G., Kramer, A.F., Coles, M.G.H. and Donchin, E. (1989). Simulation studies of latency measures of components of event-related brain potentials. *Psychophysiology*, **26**, 233–248.

Grice, R.G., Nullmeyer, R. and Spiker, V.A. (1982). Human reaction time: toward a general theory. *Journal of Experimental Psychology: General*, **111**, 135–153.

Grossberg, S. (1982). *Studies of Mind and Brain: Neural Principles of Learning, Perception, Development, and Motor Control.* Dordrecht, Holland: D. Reidel.

Haider, M., Spong, P. and Lindsley, D.B. (1964). Attention, vigilance and cortical evoked potentials in humans. *Science*, **145**, 180–182.

Hakerem, G. (1967). Pupillography. In P.H. Venables and I. Martin (eds), *Manual of Psychophysiological Methods.* Amsterdam: North-Holland.

Hakerem, G. Sutton, S. and Zubin, J. (1964). Pupillary reactions to light in schizophrenic patients and normals. *Annals of the New York Academy of Science*, **105**, 820–831.

Halliday, R. and Bashore, T. (1988). How times have changed: advances in event-related potential chronometry. *Psychophysiology*, **25**, 425 (abstract).

Halliday, R., Callaway, E., Naylor, H., Gratzinger, P. and Prael, R. (1986). The effects of stimulant drugs on information processing in elderly adults. *Journal of Gerontology*, **41**, 748–757.

Heinrich, W. (1896). Die Aufmerksamkeit und die Funktion der Sinneorgane. *Zeitschrift für Psychologie und Physiologie der Sinne*, **IX**, 342–388.

Helmholtz von H. (1850). Messungen er den zeitlichen Verlauf der Zuckung animalischer Muskeln und die Fortpflantzungsgeschwindigkeit der Reizung in den Nerven. *Archiv fur Anatomoie, Physiologie und wissenschaftliche Medicin*, 276–364.

Helmholtz von H. (1867). *Handbuch der Physiologischen Optik.* Leipzig: Voss.

Hess, E.H. (1965). Attitude and pupil size. *Scientific American*, **212**, 46–54.

Hess, E.H. (1968). Pupillometrics. In F.M. Bass and E.A. Passemeier (eds), *Applications of the Sciences in Marketing Management.* New York: Wiley.

Hess, E.H. (1972). Pupillometrics: a method of studying mental, emotional, and sensory processes. In N.S. Greenfield and R.A. Sternbach (eds), *Handbook of psychophysiology.* New York: Holt, Rinehart and Winston, pp. 491–534.

Hess, E.H. and Polt, J.M. (1964). Pupil size in relation to mental activity during simple problem solving. *Science*, **143**, 1190–1192.

Higgins, J.D. (1971). Set and uncertainty as factors influencing anticipatory cardiovascular responding in humans. *Journal of Comparative and Physiological Psychology*, **74**, 272–283.

Hirsch, A. (1862). Experiences chronoscopiques sur la vitesse des differentes sensations et de la transmission nerveuse. *Bulletin de la Société des Sciences Naturelles de Neuchatel*, **6**, 100–114.

Hockey, G.R.J., Gaillard, A.W.K. and Coles, M.G.H. (eds) (1986). *Energetics and Human Information Processing.* Dordrecht, The Netherlands: Nijhoff.

Hohle, R.H. (1967). Component process latencies in reaction times of children and adults. In L.P. Lipsitt and C.C. Spiker (eds), *Advances in Child Development and Behavior*, vol. 3. London: Academic Press, pp. 225–261.

Hull, C.L. (1943). *Principles of Behavior: An Introduction to Behavior Theory*. New York: Appleton–Century–Crofts.

Jannisse, M.P. (1977). *Pupillometry, The Psychology of the Pupillary Response*. New York: Wiley.

Jennings, J.R. (1975). Information processing and concomitant heart rate changes on the overweight and underweight. *Physiological Psychology*, **3**, 290–296.

Jennings, J.R. (1986a). Bodily changes during attending. In M. G. H. Coles, E. Donchin and S.W. Porges (eds), *Psychophysiology: Systems, Processes and Applications. New York: Guilford Press, pp. 268–289.*

Jennings, J.R. (1986b). Memory, thought, and bodily response. In M. G. H. Coles, E. Donchin and S.W. Porges (eds), *Psychophysiology: Systems, Processes and Applications*. New York: Guilford Press, pp. 290–308.

Jennings, J.R. and Wood, C.C. (1977). Cardiac cycle time effects on performance, phasic cardiac responses and their intercorrelation in choice reaction time. *Psychophysiology*, **14**, 297–307.

Jennings, J.R., Averill, J.R., Opton, E.M. and Lazarus, R.S. (1971). Some parameters of heart rate change: perceptual versus motor requirements, noxiousness and uncertainty. *Psychophysiology*, **7**, 194–212.

Jennings, J.R., van der Molen, M.W. and Brock, K. (1990). Forearm, chest, and skin vascular changes during simple performance tasks. *Biological Psychology*, in press.

Jennings, J.R., van der Molen, M.W., Somsen, R.J.M. and Brock, K. (1988). Response preparation effort induces cardiac deceleration: evidence from a perceptual-motor compatibility experiment. *Psychophysiology*, **25**, 457 (abstract).

Jennings, J.R., van der Molen, M.W., Somsen, R.J.M. and Terezis C. (1990). On the shift from anticipatory heart rate deceleration to acceleratory recovery: Revisiting the role of response factors. *Psychophysiology*, **27**, 385–395.

Jennings, J.R., van der Molen, M.W., Somsen, R.J.M. and Ridderinkhof, K.R. (1990). Graphical and statistical techniques for cardiac cycle (phase) dependent changes in inter-beat interval. *Psychophysiology*, **27**, 385–395.

Jennings, J.R., van der Molen, M.W. and Terezis, C. (1987). Primary bradycardia and vagal inhibition as two manifestations of the influence on the heart beat. *Journal of Psychophysiology*, **4**, 361–374.

Johnson, R. (1989). Auditory and visual P300s in temporal lobectomy patients: evidence for modality-dependent generators. *Psychophysiology*, **26**, 633–650.

Kahneman, D. (1973). *Attention and Effort*. Englewood Cliffs, NJ: Prentice-Hall.

Kahneman, D. and Norman, J. (1964). The time–intensity relation in visual perception as a function of the observer's task. *Journal of Experimental Psychology*, **68**, 215–220.

Kahneman, D., Norman, J. and Kubovy, M. (1967). The critical duration for the resolution of form: centrally or peripherally determined? *Journal of Experimental Psychology*, **73**, 323–327.

Keuss, P.J.G. and van der Molen, M. W. (1982). Positive and negative effects of stimulus intensity in auditory reaction tasks: further studies on immediate arrousal. *Acta Psychologica*, **52**, 61–72.

Kimmel, H.D., Van Olst, E.H. and Orlebeke, J.F. (1979). *The Orienting Reflex in Humans*. Hillsdale, NJ: Erlbaum.

Kirby, N. (1980). Sequential effects in choice reaction time. In A.T. Welford (ed.), *Reaction Times*. London: Academic Press, pp. 129–172.

Knight, R. (1984). Decreased response to novel stimuli after prefrontal lesions in man.

Electroencephalography and clinical Neurophysiology, **59**, 9–20.
Koch, S. and Leary, D.E. (eds), (1985). *A Century of Psychology as Science*. New York: McGraw-Hill.
Kornblum, S. (1965). Response competition and/or inhibition in two choice reaction time. *Psychonomic Science*, **2**, 55–56.
Korner, P.I. (1979). Central nervous control of autonomic cardiovascular function. In R.M. Berne, J.S. Geisser and N. Sperelakis (eds), *Handbook of Physiology*, sect. 2, vol. 1. Maryland: Am. Physiol. Soc., Bethesda.
Kornhuber, H.H. and Deecke, L. (1965). Hirnpotentialanderungen bei Willkurberegungen des Menschen: Bereitschaftspotential und reafferente Potentiale. *Pflügers Archiv für die Gesammte Physiologie des Menschen und der Tier*, **47**, 229–238.
Külpe, O. (1895). *Outlines of Psychology*. New York: Macmillan.
Kurata, K. and Tanji, J. (1986). Premotor cortex neurons in macaques: activity before distal and proximal forelimb movements. *Journal of Neuroscience*, **6**, 403–411.
Kutas, M. and Donchin, E. (1980). Preparation to respond as manifested by movement-related brain potentials. *Brain Research*, **202**, 95–115.
Kutas, M., McCarthy, G. and Donchin, E. (1977). Augmenting mental chronometry: the P300 as a measure of stimulus evaluation time. *Science*, **197**, 792–795.
Lacey, B.C. and Lacey, J.I. (1974). Studies of heart rate and other bodily processes in sensorimotor behavior. In P.A. Obrist, A.H. Black, J.Brenner and L.V. DiCara (eds), *Cardiovascular Psychophysiology*. Chicago: Aldine, pp. 538–564.
Lacey, B.C. and Lacey, J.I. (1980). Cognitive modulation of time-dependent primary bradycardia. *Psychophysiology*, **17**, 209–221.
Lacey, J.I.(1959). Psychophysiological approaches to the evaluation of psychotherapeutic process and outcome. In E.A. Rubinstein and M.B. Parloff (eds), *Research in Psychotherapy*. Washington, DC: National Publishing Co.
Lacey, J.I. (1967). Somatic response patterning and stress: some revisions of activation theory. In M.H. Appley and R. Trumbull (eds), *Psychological Stress: Issues in Research*. New York: Appleton–Century–Crofts.
Lacey, J.I. and Lacey, B.C. (1970). Some autonomic–central nervous system interrelationships. In P. Black (ed.), *Physiological Correlates of Emotion*. New York: Academic Press.
Lacey, J.I. and Lacey, B.C. (1980). The specific role of heart rate in sensorimotor integration. In R.F. Thompson, L.H. Hicks, and V.B. Sharkov (Eds), *Neural Mechanisms of Behaviour and Learning*, New York: Academic Press, p. 499.
Lacey, J.I., Kagan, J., Lacey, B.C. and Moss, H. (1963). The visceral level: situational determinants and behavioral correlates of autonomic response patterns. In P.H. Knapp (ed.), *Expression of the Emotions in Man*. New York: International Universities Press, pp. 161–197.
Ladd, G.T. (1890). *Elements of Physiological Psychology*. London: Longmans Green.
Laming, D.R. (1969). Subjective probability in choice reaction time experiments. *Journal of Mathematical Psychology*, **6**, 81–120.
Laming, D.R. (1986). *Sensory Analysis*. New York: Academic Press.
Lawler, K.A., Obrist, P.A. and Lawler, J.E. (1976). Cardiac somatic response patterns during a reaction time task in children and adults. *Psychophysiology*, **13**, 448–455.
Lecas, J.-L., Requin, J., Anger, C. and Vitton, N. (1986). Changes in neuronal activity of the monkey precentral cortex during preparation for movement. *Journal of Neurophysiology*, **56**, 1680–1702.
Lefton, L.A. and Haber, R.N. (1974). Information extraction from different retinal locations. *Journal of Experimental Psychology*, **102**, 975–980.

Lewine, J.D. (1989). The temporal dynamics of event memory: a stage analysis of mnemonic processing by man and macaque. *Journal of Cognitive Neuroscience*, **1**, 356–371.

Lindsley, D. B. (1969). Average evoked potentials—achievements, failures and prospects. In E. Donchin and D.B. Lindsley (eds), *Averaged Evoked Potentials: Methods, Results, and Evaluations*. Scientific and Technical Information Divisions, Office of Technology Utilization, National Aeronautics and Space Administration, pp 1–43.

Loewenfeld, I.E. (1958). Mechanisms of reflex dilation of the pupil; historical and experimental analysis. *Documenta Ophthalmologica*, **12**, 185–448.

Logsdon, R., Hochhaus, L., Williams, L., Rundell, H.L. and Maxwell, D. (1984). Secobarbital and perceptual processing. *Acta Psychologica*, **55**, 179–193.

Lowenstein, O. and Loewenfeld, I.E. (1969). The pupil. In H. Davidson (ed.), *The Eye*, vol. 3. New York: Academic Press.

Luce, R.D. (1986). *Response Times: Their Role in Inferring Elementary Mental Organization.* New York: Oxford University Press.

MacDougall, R. (1896). The physical characteristics of attention. *Psychological Review*, **11**, 158–180.

Magliero, A., Bashore, T.R., Coles, M.G.H. and Donchin, E. (1984). On the dependence of P300 latency on stimulus evaluation processes. *Psychophysiology*, **21**, 171–186.

McCarthy, G. and Donchin, E. (1981). A metric for thought: A comparison of P300 latency and reaction time. *Science*, **211**, 77–80.

McCarthy, G. and Donchin, E. (1983). Chronometric analysis of human information processing. In A.W.K. Gaillard and W. Ritter (eds), *Tutorials in Event-Related Potential Research: Endogenous Components*. Amsterdam: North-Holland, pp. 251–268.

McClelland, J.L. (1978). On the time relations of mental processes: theoretical explorations of systems of processes in cascade. Paper presented at the Sixteenth Annual Meeting of the Psychonomics Society, San Antonio, Texas.

McClelland, J.L. (1979). On the time relations of mental processes: an examination of processes in cascade. *Psychological Review*, **86**, 287–330.

McGuinness, D. and Pribram, K (1980). The neuropsychology of attention: emotional and motivational controls. In M.C. Wittrock (ed.), *The Brain and Psychology*. New York: Academic Press, pp. 95–140.

Mentz, P. (1895). Die Wirkung akustischer Sinnesreize auf Puls und Atmung. *Philosophische Studien*, **11**, 61–131.

Meyer, D.E. and Irwin, D.E. (1982). *On the Time Course of Rapid Information Processing*. Ann Arbor: University of Michigan, Cognitive Science Program Technical Report 43).

Meyer, D.E., Irwin, D.E., Osman, A.M. and Kounios, J. (1988a). The dynamics of cognition and action: mental processes inferred from speed–accuracy decomposition. *Psychological Review*, **95**, 183–237.

Meyer, D.E., Osman, A.M., Irwin, D.E. and Yantis, S. (1988b). Modern mental chronometry. *Biological Psychology*, **26**, 1–58.

Meyer, D.E., Schwaneveldt, R.W. and Ruddy, M.G. (1975). Loci of contextual effects on visual word-recognition. In P.M.A. Rabbitt and S. Dornic (eds), *Attention and Performance*, vol. V. London: Academic Press, pp. 98–118.

Meyer, D.E., Yantis, S., Osman, A.M. and Smith, J.E.K. (1985). Temporal properties of human information processing: tests of discrete versus continuous models. *Cognitive Psychology*, **17**, 445–518.

Meyers, K.A. and Obrist, P.A. (1973). Psychophysiological correlates of attention in children. *Psychophysiology*, **10**, 210.

Miller, J. (1982). Discrete versus continuous stage models of human information processing: in search of partial output. *Journal of Experimental Psychology: Human Perception and Performance*, **8**, 273–279.

Miller, J. (1983). Can response preparation begin before stimulus recognition finishes? *Journal of Experimental Psychology: Human Perception and Performance*, **9**, 161–182.

Miller, J.O. (1988). Discrete and continuous models of human information processing: theoretical distinctions and emperical results. *Acta Psychologica*, **67**, 191–257.

Miller, J.O. and Pachella, R.G. (1973). Focus of the stimulus probability effect. *Journal of Experimental Psychology*, **101**, 227–231.

Miller, J.O. and Pachella, R.G. (1976). Encoding processes in memory scanning tasks, *Memory and Cognition*, **4**, 501–506.

Mishkin, M. (1979). Analogous neural models for tactual and visual learning. *Neuropsychologia*, **17**, 139–152.

Mishkin, M., Ungerleider, L.J. and Macko, K.E. (1983). Object vision and spatial vision: two cortical pathways. *Trends in Neurosciences*, **6**, 414–417.

Möcks, J. (1986). The influence of latency variations in principal components analysis of event-related potentials. *Psychophysiology*, **23**, 480–484.

Möcks, J. (1988). Decomposing event-related potentials: a new topographic components model. *Biological Psychology*, **26**, 199–215.

Möcks, J., Kohler, W., Gasser, T. and Pham, D.T. (1988). Novel approaches to the problem of latency jitter. *Psychophysiology*, **25**, 217–226.

Molenaar, P.C.M. (1990). Neural network simulation of a discrete model of continuous effects of irrelevant stimuli. In E.J. Stoffels, M.W. van der Molen and P.J.G. Keuss (eds), *Stage Analysis of the Reaction Process: Models, Methods, and Applications. Acta Psychologica*, **74**, 237–258.

Molenaar, P.C.M. (in press). Dynamic factor analysis of psychophysiological signals. In J.R. Jennings, P. Ackles, and M.G.H. Coles (eds) *Advances in Psychophysiology*. London: Jessica Kingsley Publishers.

Molenaar, P.C.M. and van der Molen, M.W. (1986). Steps to a formal analysis of the cognitive–energetic model of stress and human performance. *Acta Psychologica*, **62**, 237–261.

Molenaar, P.C.M. and van der Molen, M.W. (1985). Global models: a viable compromise between content specificity and ease of application to heart rate change. In J.F. Orlebeke, G. Mulder and L.J.P. van Doornen (eds), *Psychophysiology of Cardiovascular Control: Models, Methods and Data*. New York: Plenum Press, pp. 375–390.

Mosso, A. (1881). *Über den Kreislauf des Blutes im menschlichen Gehirn*. Leipzig: Vert und Comp.

Mudd, S. (1983). *Brigg's Information Processing Model of the Binary Classification Task*. London: Lawrence Erlbaum Associates.

Mulder, G. (1986). The concept and measurement of mental effort. In G.R.J. Hockey, A.W.K. Gaillard and M.G.H. Coles (eds), *Energetics and Human Information Processing*. Dordrecht: Martinus Nijhoff, pp. 175–198.

Mulder, G., Gloerich, A.B.M., Brookhuis, K.A., Van Dellen, H.J. and Mulder, L.J.M. (1984). Stage analysis of the reaction process using brain-evoked potentials and reaction. *Psychological Research*, **46**, 15–32.

Murphy, G. and Kovach, J.K. (1972). *Historical Introduction to Modern Psychology*. New York: Harcourt, Brace and Janovich.

Näätänen, R. (1975). Selective attention and evoked potentials in humans—a critical review. *Biological Psychology*, **2**, 237–307.

Näätänen, R. and Picton, T. (1987). The N1 wave of the human electric and magnetic response to sound: a review and an analysis of the component structure. *Psychophysiology*, **24**, 375–418.

Näätänen, R. and Merisalo, A. (1977). Expectancy and preparation in simple reaction time. In S. Dornic (ed.), *Attention and Performance*, vol. VI. Hillsdale, NJ: Lawrence Erlbaum Associates, pp. 115–139.

Navon, D. and Gopher, D. (1979). On the economy of the human information processing system. *Psychological Review*, **33**, 177–184.

Naylor, H., Halliday, R. and Callaway, E. (1985). The effect of methylphenidate on information processing. *Psychopharmacology*, **86**, 90–95.

Noble, D. (1979). *The Initiation of the Heartbeat*. Oxford: Clarendon Press.

Okada, Y.C., Williamson, S.J. and Kaufman, L. (1983). Magnetic field of the human somatosensory cortex. *International Journal of Neuroscience*, **17**, 33–38.

Orlebeke, J.F., Mulder, G. and Van Doornen, L.J.P. (1985). *Psychophysiology of Cardiovascular Control: Models, Methods, and Data*. New York: Plenum Press.

Osgood, C.E. (1953). *Method and Theory in Experimental Psychology*. New York: Oxford University Press.

Pachella, R.G. (1974). The interpretation of reaction time in information processing research. In B. Kantowitz (ed.), *Human Information Processing: Tutorials in Performance and Cognition*. Hillsdale, NJ: Lawrence Erlbaum Associates.

Patrizi, M.L. (1896). Primi Esperimenti intorno all'influenza della musica sulla circulazione del sangue nel cervello umano. Reprinted from *Archivi di Psichiatri*, **XVII**, 390–406.

Pfefferbaum, A., Christensen, C., Ford, J.M. and Kopell, B.S. (1986). Apparent response incompatibility effects on P3 latency depend on the task. *Electroencephalography and Clinical Neurophysiology*, **64**, 424–437.

Pfefferbaum, A., Ford, J., Johnson, R., Wenegrat, B. and Kopell, B.S. (1983). Manipulation of P3 latency: speed vs. accuracy instructions. *Electroencephalography and Clinical Neurophysiology*, **55**, 188–197.

Pfefferbaum, A., Ford, J.M., Roth, W.T. and Kopell, B.S. (1980). Age diffrences in P3-reaction time associations. *Electroencephalography and Clinical Neurophysiology*, **49**, 257–265.

Pham, D.T., Möcks, J., Kohler, W. and Gasser, T. (1987). Variable latencies of noisy signals: estimation and testing in brain potential data. *Biometrika*, **74**, 55–533.

Picton, T.W. and Stuss, D.T. (1980). The component structure of the human event-related potentials. In H.H. Kornhuber and L. Deecke (eds), *Motivation, Motor, and Sensory Processes of the Brain* (*Progress in Brain Research*, vol. 54). Amsterdam: Elsevier/North -Holland, pp. 17–49.

Pons, T.P., Garraghty, P.E., Friedman, D.P. and Mishkin, M. (1987). Physiological evidence for serial processing in somatosensory cortex. *Science*, **237**, 417–420.

Posner, M.I. (1978). *Chronometric Explorations of Mind*. Hillsdale, NJ: Lawrence Erlbaum Associates.

Posner, M.I. (1986). A framework for relating cognitive to neural systems. In W.C. McCallum, R. Zappoli and F. Denoth (eds), *Cerebral Psychophysiology Studies on Event-Related Potentials* (*EEG*, Suppl. 38). Amsterdam: Elsevier Science Publishers B.V., pp. 155–166.

Posner, M.I. and Boies, S.J. (1971). Components of attention. *Psychological Review*, **78**, 391–408.

Posner, M.I. and McLeod, S. (1982). Information processing models—in search of elementary operations. *Annual Review of Psychology*, **30**, 363–396.

Posner, M.I. and Petersen, S.E. (1990). The attention system of the human brain. In W.M. Cowan, E.M. Shooter, C.F. Stevens and R.F. Thompson (eds), *Annual Review of Neuroscience*. Palo Alto: Annual Reviews, pp. 25–42.

Posner, M.I., Petersen, S.E., Fox, P.T. and Raichle, M.E. (1988). Localization of cognitive operations in the human brain. *Science*, **240**, 1627–1631.

Pribram, K.H. and McGuinness, D. (1975). Arousal, activation and effort in the control of attention. *Psychological Review*, **82**, 116–149.

Pritchard, W. (1981). The psychophysiology of P300. *Psychological Bulletin*, **89**, 506–540.

Proctor, R.W. and Reeve, T.G. (1985). Compatibility effects in the assignment of symbolic stimuli to discrete finger responses. *Journal of Experimental Psychology: Human Perception and Performance*, **11**, 623–639.

Rabbitt, P.M.A. (1979). Current paradigms in human information processing. In V. Hamilton and D.M. Warburton (eds), *Human Stress and Cognition*. New York: Wiley.

Rabbitt, P.M.A. and Vyas, S. (1973). What is repeated in the 'repetition effect'? In S. Kornblum (ed.), *Attention and Performance*, vol. IV. London: Academic Press, pp. 327–342.

Ragot, R. (1984). Perceptual and motor space representation: an event related potential study. *Psychophysiology*, **21**, 159–170.

Ragot, R. and Lesevre, N. (1986). Electrophysiological study of intrahemispheric S–R compatibility effects elicited by visual directional cues. *Psychophysiology*, **23**, 19–27.

Ratcliff, R. (1978). A theory of memory retrieval. *Psychological Review*, **85**, 59–108.

Ratcliff, R. and Murdock, B.B. (1976). Retrieval processes in recognition memory. *Psychological Review*, **91**, 190–204.

Raz, J., Turetsky, B. and Fein, G. (1989). Selecting the smoothing parameter for estimation of slowly changing evoked potential signals. *Biometrics*, **45**, 745–762.

Reed, A.V. (1976). List length and the time course of recognition in immediate memory. *Memory and Cognition*, **4**, 16–30.

Reeve, T.G. and Proctor, R.W. (1984). On the advance preparation of discrete finger responses. *Journal of Experimental Psychology: Human Perception and Performance*, **10**, 541–553.

Renault, B., Fiori, N. and Giami, S. (1988). Latencies of event related potentials as a tool for studying motor processing organization. *Biological Psychology*, **26**, 217–230.

Renault, B., Ragot, R., Leserve, N. and Remond, A. (1982). Onset and offset of brain events as indices of mental chronometry. *Science*, **215**, 1413–1415.

Requin, J. (1985). Looking forward to moving soon: ante factum selective processes in motor control. In M.I. Posner and O.S.M. Marin (eds), *Attention and Performance*, vol. XI. Hillsdale: Lawrence Erlbaum, pp. 147–167.

Requin, J., Lecas, J-C. and Bonnet, M. (1984). Some experimental evidence for a three-step model of motor preparation. In S. Kornblum and J. Requin (eds), *Preparatory States and Processes*. Hillsdale, NJ: LEA, pp. 259–284.

Richards, J.E. (1980). The statistical analysis of heart rate data: a view emphasizing infancy data. *Psychophysiology*, **17**, 153–166.

Richards, J.E. (1988). Heart rate responses and heart rate rhythms: infant sustained attention. In P.K. Ackles, J.R. Jennings and M.G.H. Coles (eds), *Advances in Psychophysiology*, vol. 3. Greenwich, CT: JAI Press, pp. 189–222.

Richer, F., Silverman, C. and Beatty, J. (1983). Response selection and initiation in speeded reactions: a pupillometric analysis. *Journal of Experimental Psychology: Human Perception and Performance*, **9**, 360–370.

Riehl, A. and Requin, J. (1989). Monkey primary motor and premotor cortex: single cell activity related to prior information about direction and extent of an intended movement. *Journal of Neurophysiology*, **61**, 534–549.

Ritter, W. and Vaughan, H.G. (1969). Averaged evoked responses in vigilance and discrimination: a reassessment. *Science*, **164**, 326–328.

Ritter, W., Simon, R. and Vaughan, H.G. (1972). Association cortex potentials and

reaction in auditory discrimination. *Electroencephalography and Clinical Neurophysiology*, **33**, 547–555.
Ritter, W., Simson, R. and Vaughan, H.G. (1983). Event-related potential correlates of two stages of information processing in physical and semantic discrimination tasks. *Psychophysiology*, **20**, 168–179.
Ritter, W., Simson, R., Vaughan, H.G. and Macht, M. (1982). Manipulation of event-related potential manifestations of information processing stages. *Science*, **218**, 909–911.
Ritter, W., Vaughan, H.G. and Simson, R. (1983). On relating event-related potential components to stages of processing. In A.W.K. Gaillard and W. Ritter (eds), *Tutorials in Event-Related Potential Research: Endogenous Components*. Amsterdam: North-Holland, pp. 143–159.
Rohrbaugh, J.W. and Gaillard, A.W.K. (1983). Sensory and motor aspects of the contingent negative variation. In A.W.K. Gaillard and W. Ritter (eds), *Tutorials in Event-Related Potential Research: Endogenous Components*. Amsterdam: North-Holland, pp. 269–310.
Rohrbaugh, J.W., Syndulko, K. and Lindsley, D.B. (1976). Brain components of the contingent negative variation in humans. *Science*, **191**, 1055–1057.
Rosenbaum, D.A. and Kornblum, S. (1982). A priming method for investigating the selection of motor responses. *Acta Psychologica*, **51**, 223–243.
Rosenbaum, D.A. (1980). Human movement initiation: specification of arm, direction, and extent. *Journal of Experimental Psychology: General*, **109**, 444–474.
Roth, W.T, Ford, J.M., Lewis, S.J. and Kopell (1976). Effects of stimulus probability and task-relevance on event-related potentials. *Psychophysiology*, **13**, 311–317.
Ruchkin, D.S. and Glaser, E.M. (1978). Simple digital filters for examining CNV and P300 on a single trial basis. In D. Otto (ed.), *Multidisciplinary Perspectives in Event-Related Potential Research* (EPA-600/9–77–043). Washington DC: US Government Printing Office.
Ruchkin, D.S., Sutton, S. and Mahaffey, D. (1987). Functional differences between members of the P300 complex: P3e and P3b. *Psychophysiology*, **24**, 87–103.
Sanders, A.F. (1977). Structural and functional aspects of the reaction process. In Dornic, S. (ed.), *Attention and performance*, vol. V. Hillsdale, NJ: Lawrence Erlbaum Associates, pp. 3–26.
Sanders, A.F. (1980). Stage analysis of reaction processes. In G.E. Stelmach and J. Requin, (eds), *Tutorials in Motor Behaviour*, vol. 20. Amsterdam: North-Holland, pp. 331–353.
Sanders, A.F. (1983). Towards a model of stress and human performance. *Acta Psychologica*, **53**, 61–97.
Sanders, A.F. (1990). Some issues and trends in the debate on discrete *vs* continuous processing of information. In E.J. Stoffels, M.W. van der Molen and P.J.G. Keuss (eds), *Stage Analysis of the Reaction Process: Models, Methods, and Applications*. *Acta Psychologica*, **74**, 123–169.
Sanders, A.F., Wijnen, J.L.C. and Van Arkel, A.E. (1982). An additive factor analysis of the effects of sleep-loss on reaction processes. *Acta Psychologica*, **51**, 41–59.
Schell, A.M. and Catania, J. (1975). The relationship between cardiac activity and sensory acuity. *Psychophysiology*, **12**, 147–151.
Schwartz, G.E. and Higgens, J.D. (1971). Cardiac activity preparatory to overt and covert behavior. *Science*, **173**, 1144–1146.
Schwartz, S.P., Pomerantz, J.R. and Egeth, H.E. (1977). State and process limitations in information processing: an additive factors analysis. *Journal of Experimental Psychology: Human Perception and Performance*, **3**, 402–410.

Shulman, H.G. and McConkie, A. (1973). S–R compatability, response discriminability and response codes in choice reaction tasks. *Journal of Experimental Psychology*, **98**, 375–378.

Siddle, D.A.T. and Turpin, G. (1980). Measurement, quantification and analysis of cardiac activity. In I. Martin and P.H. Venables (eds), *Techniques in Psychophysiology*. New York: Wiley.

Simon, J.R. (1990). The effects of an irrelevant directional cue on human information processing. In R.W. Proctor and T.G. Reeve (eds), *Stimulus–Response Compatibility: An Integrated Perspective*. Amsterdam: North-Holland, pp. 31–86.

Simons, R.F., Ohman, A. and Lang, P.J. (1979). Anticipation and response set: cortical, cardiac, and electrodermal correlates. *Psychophysiology*, **16**, 222–233.

Simpkins, C.O. (1975). *Coltrane: A Biography*. Pert, Amby, NJ: Herndon House Publishers.

Simpson, H.M. (1969). Effects of task relevant response on pupil size. *Psychophysiology*, **6**, 115–121.

Smith, M.E., Stapleton, J. and Halgren, E. (1986). Human medial temporal lobe potentials evoked in memory and language tasks. *Electroencephalography and Clinical Neurophysiology*, **63**, 145–159.

Somsen, R.J.M., van der Molen, M.W. and Orlebeke, J.F. (1983). Phasic heart rate changes in reaction time, shock avoidance and unavoidable shock tasks: are hypothetical generalizations about different S1–S2 tasks justified? *Psychophysiology*, **20**, 88–94.

Somsen, R.J.M., van der Molen, M.W., Boomsma, D. and Orlebeke, J.F. (1985). Phasic cardiac responses in reaction time and mental arithmetic tasks: the dominant influence of mental task performance on heart-rate in adolescents. In J.F. Orlebeke, G. Mulder and L.J.P. van Doornen (eds), *Psychophysiology of Cardiovascular Control, Models, Methods and Data*, New York: Plenum Press, pp. 583–598.

Somsen, R.J.M., van der Molen, M.W., Jennings, J.R. and Orlebeke, J.F. (1985). Response initiation not completion seems to alter cardiac cycle length. *Psychophysiology*, **22**, 319–325.

Spijkers, W.A.C. and Steyvers, F. (1984). Specification of direction and duration during programming of discrete sliding movements. *Psychological Research*, **46**, 59–71.

Spijkers, W.A.C. and Walters, A. (1985). Response processing stages in choice reactions. *Acta Psychologica*, **58**, 191–204.

Squires, N.K., Squires, K.C. and Hillyard, S.A. (1975). Two varieties of long-latency positive waves evoked by unpredictable auditory stimuli in man. *Electroencephalography and Clinical Neurophysiology*, **38**, 387–401.

Stanovich, K.E. and Pachella, R.G. (1977). Encoding, stimulus–response compatibility and stages of processing. *Journal of Experimental Psychology: Human Perception and Performance*, **3**, 411–421.

Sternberg, S. (1969). The discovery of processing stages: extensions of Donders' method. In W.G. Koster (ed.), *Attention and Performance*, vol. II. (*Acta Psychologica*, **30**). Amsterdam: North-Holland, pp. 276–315.

Stevens, S.S. (ed.) (1951). *Handbook of Experimental Psychology*. New York: Wiley.

Steyvers, F.J.J.M. (1987). The influence of sleep deprivation and knowledge of results on perceptual encoding. *Acta Psychologica*, **66**, 173–188.

Stoffels, E.J. (1988). *Reactions Toward the Stimulus Source: The Locus of the Effect*. Doctoral thesis, Free University, Amsterdam, The Netherlands.

Stoffels, E.J. and van der Molen, M.W. (1988). Effects of visual and auditory noise on choice reaction time in a continuous flow paradigm. *Perception and Psychophysics*, **44**, 7–14.

Stoffels, E.J., van der Molen, M.W. and Keuss, P.J.G. (1985). Intersensory facilitation and inhibition: immediate arousal and location effects of auditory noise on visual choice reaction time. *Acta Psychologica*, **58**, 45–62.

Stoffels, E.J., van der Molen, M.W. and Keuss, P.J.G. (eds), (1990). Stage analysis of the reaction process: models, methods, and applications. *Acta Psychologica.*

Sutton, S. and Ruchkin, D.S. (1984). The late positive complex: advances and new problems. In R. Karrer, J. Cohen and P. Tueting (eds), *Brain and Information: Event-Related Potentials*. New York: Annals of the New York Academy of Sciences, pp. 1–23.

Sutton, S., Braren, M., Zubin, J. and John, E.R. (1965). Evoked potential correlates of stimulus uncertainty. *Science*, **150**, 1187–1188.

Sutton, S., Tueting, P., Zubin, J. and John E.R. (1967). Information delivery and the sensory evoked potential. *Science*, **155**, 1436–1439.

Svebak, S. (1983). Helga Eng: a Norwegian precursor to Darrow and Lacey. *Psychophysiology*, **12**, 600–601.

Swanson, J.M. and Briggs, G.E. (1969). Information processing as a function of speed versus accuracy. *Journal of Experimental Psychology*, **31**, 223–229.

Tanji, J. and Kurata, K. (1981). Contrasting neuronal activity in the ipsilateral and contralateral supplementary motor areas in relation to a movement of monkey's distal hind limb. *Brain Research*, **222**, 155–158.

Tanji, J. and Kurata, K. (1982). Contrasting neuronal activity in supplementary and precentral motor cortex of monkeys. I: Responses to instructions determining motor responses to forthcoming signals of different modalities. *Journal of Neurophysiology*, **53**, 129–141.

Tanji, J., Okano, K. and Sato, K.C. (1987). Relation of neurons in the nonprimary motor cortex to bilateral hand movement. *Nature*, **327**, 618–620.

Tanji, J., Okano, K. and Sato, K.C. (1988). Neuronal activity in cortical motor areas related to ipsilateral, contralateral, and bilateral digit movements of the monkey. *Journal of Neurophysiology*, **60**, 325–343.

Taylor, D.H. (1966). Latency components in two-choice responding. *Journal of Experimental Psychology*, **72**, 481–487.

Taylor, D.A. (1976). Stage analysis of reaction time. *Psychological Bulletin*, **83**, 161–191.

Townsend, J.T. (1971). A note on the identifiability of parallel and serial processes. *Perception and Psychophysics*, **10**, 161–163.

Townsend, J.T. (1990). Serial *vs.* parallel processing: sometimes they look like tweedledum and tweedledee but they can (and should) be distinguished. *Psychological Science*, **1**, 46–54.

Turetsky, B.I., Raz, J. and Fein, G. (1989). Estimation of trial-to-trial variation in evoked potential signals by smoothing across trials. *Psychophysiology*, **26**, 700–712.

Turetsky, B.I., Raz, J. and Fein, G. (1990). Representation of multi-channel evoked potential data using a dipole component model of intra-cranial generators: application to the auditory P300. *Electroencephalography and Clinical Neurophysiology*, **76**, 540–556.

Turner, B.H., Mishkin, M. and Knapp, M. (1980). Organization of the amygdalopetal projections from modality-specific cortical association areas in the monkey. *Journal of Comparative Neurology*, **191**, 515–543.

Tyron, W.W. (1975). Pupillometry: a survey of sources of variation. *Psychophysiology*, **12**, 90–93.

Ungerleider, L.G. and Mishkin, M. (1982). Two cortical visual systems. In D.J. Ingle, M.A. Goodale and R.J.W. Mansfield (eds), *Analysis of Visual Behavior*. Cambridge, MA: MIT Press, pp. 549–586.

Van der Molen, M. W., Somsen, R.J.M. and Orlebeke, J.F. (1985). The rhythm of the heart beat in information processing. In P. Ackles, J. R. Jennings and M.G.H. Coles (eds), *Advances in Psychophysiology*, vol. 1. Greenwich, CT: JAI Press, pp. 1–88.

Van der Molen, M.W. and Keuss, P.J.G. (1979). The relationship between reaction time and auditory intensity in discrete auditory tasks. *Quarterly Journal of Experimental Psychology*, **31**, 95–102.

Van der Molen, M.W. and Keuss, P.J.G. (1981). Response selection and the processing of auditory intensity. *Quarterly Journal of Experimental Psychology: Human Experimental Psychology*, **33**, 177–184.

Van der Molen, M.W., Boomsma, D.I., Jennings, J.R. and Nieuwboer, R.T. (1989). Does the heart know what the eye sees? Cardiac pupillometric analysis of motor preparation and response execution. *Psychophysiology*, **26**, 70–80.

Van der Molen, M.W., Somsen, R.J.M. and Orlebeke, J.F. (1983). Phasic heart rate responses and cardiac cycle time in auditory choice reaction time. *Biological Psychology*, **16**, 255–272.

Van der Molen, M.W., Somsen, R.J.M., Jennings, J.R. and Orlebeke, J.F. (1985). Sensorimotor integration and the timing of the heart rate deceleration. In J.F. Orlebeke, G. Mulder and L.J.P. van Doornen (eds), *Psychophysiology of Cardiovascular Control: Models, Methods and Data*. New York: Plenum Press, pp. 565–582.

Van der Molen, M.W., Somsen, R.J.M., Jennings, J.R., Nieuwboer, R.T. and Orlebeke, J.F. (1987). A psychophysiological investigation of cognitive–energetic relations in human information processing: a heart rate/additive factors approach. *Acta Psychologica*, **66**, 251–289.

Van Olst, E.H., Heemstra, M.L. and Ten Kortenaar, T. (1979). Stimulus significance and the orienting reaction. In H.D. Kimmel, E.H. van Olst and J.F. Orlebeke (eds), *The Orienting Reflex in Humans*. Hillsdale, NJ: Lawrence Erlbaum Associates, pp. 521–548.

Vaughan, H.G., Costa, L.D. and Ritter, W. (1968). Topography of the human motor potential. *Electroencephalography and Clinical Neurophysiology*, **25**, 1–10.

Walter, G.F. and Porges, S.W. (1976). Heart rate and respiratory responses as a function of task difficulty: the use of discriminant analysis in the selection of psychologically sensitive physiological responses. *Psychophysiology*, **13**, 149–154.

Walter, W.G., Cooper, R., Aldridge, V.J., McCallum, W.C. and Winter, A.C. (1964). Contingent negative variation: an electric sign of sensorimotor association and expectancy in the human brain. *Nature*, **203**, 380–384.

Watt, H.J. (1905). Experimentelle Beitrge zu einer Theorie des Denkens. *Archiv fur Psychologie*, **4**, 289–463.

Weber, E.J.M., Molenaar, P.C.M. and van der Molen, M.W. (in press). PSPAT: a program for spectral analysis of point events particularly for cardiac inter-beat intervals, including a test and selection procedure for stationarity. In L.J.M. Mulder, F.J. Maarse, W.B.B. Sjouw and A.E. Akkerman (eds), *Computers in Psychology: Applications in Education, Research, and Psychodiagnostics*. Lisse: Swets and Zeitlinger.

Welford, A.T. (1960). The measurement of sensory-motor performance: survey and reappraisal of twelve years' progress. *Ergonomics*, **3**, 189–230.

Welford, A.T. (1980). *Reaction Times*. London: Academic Press.

Wickelgren, W.B. (1977). Speed–accuracy tradeoff and information processing dynamics. *Acta Psychologica*, **41**, 67–85.

Wickens, C.D. (1980). The structure of attentional resources. In R.S. Nickerson (ed.), *Attention and Performance*, vol. VIII. Hillsdale, NJ: Lawrence Erlbaum Associates.

Wijers, A.A., Mulder, G., Okita, T. and Mulder, L.J.M. (1989a). Event-related potentials during memory search and selective attention to letter size and conjunctions of letter size and color. *Psychophysiology*, **26**, 529–547.

Wijers, A.A., Mulder, G., Okita, T., Mulder, L.J.M. and Scheffers, M.K. (1989b). Attention to color: an analysis of selection, controlled search, and motor activation, using event-related potentials. *Psychophysiology*, **26**, 89–109.

Wijers, A.A., Otten, Feenstra, S., Mulder, G. and Mulder, L.J.M. (1989c). Brain potentials during selective attention, memory search, and mental rotation. *Psychophysiology*, **26**, 452–468.

Wood, C.C., McCarthy, G., Squires, N.K., Vaughan, H.G. and McCallum, W.C. (1984). Anatomical and physiological substrates of event-related potentials. In R. Karrer, J. Cohen and P. Tueting (eds), *Brain and Information: Event-Related Potentials*. New York: NY Academy of Sciences, pp. 681–721.

Woodworth, R.S. (1938). *Experimental Psychology*. New York: Holt.

Woodworth, R.S. and Schlosberg, H. (1954). *Experimental Psychology*. New York: Henry Holt and Co.

Wundt, W. (1874). *Grunzuge der Physiologischen Psychologie*. Leipzig: W. Engelmann.

Chapter 2

Capacity Views of Human Information Processing

Arthur Kramer
Department of Psychology, University of Illinois, IL 61820, USA
and
John Spinks
Department of Psychology, University of Hong Kong, Hong Kong

ABSTRACT

The concept of 'capacity' in human information processing is examined as a contrast to the structural approach reviewed in the preceding chapter. After describing the differences between structural and capacity models, we provide a brief historical overview of both undifferentiated and multiple capacity models, indicating how these models have guided research in the areas of dual-task performance, workload and skill acquisition. Recent controversies concerning the viability of capacity models are examined prior to the description of how psychophysiological measures have been used to resolve a number of issues concerning capacity. Although this chapter is jointly authored, authorship of major sections is noted to reflect primary contributions.

Handbook of Cognitive Psychophysiology: Central and Autonomic Nervous System Approaches.
Edited by J. R. Jennings and M. G. H. Coles.

STRUCTURE VERSUS CAPACITY

A number of attributes have been ascribed to the concept of processing capacity despite the absence of a definition that is universally agreed upon. The notion of capacity has usually been treated as a hypothetical construct accounting for variation in the efficiency of processing, particularly in the case in which several tasks are performed concurrently (Gopher and Donchin, 1986; Wickens, 1986). The limited nature of processing capacity is often said to account for changes in performance efficiency. Thus, if a number of concurrently performed tasks demand more capacity than is available in the system, performance on one or more of the tasks will decline. The fact that several tasks can take place simultaneously suggests a second attribute of capacity, that it is shareable. A third attribute of capacity, its flexibility, suggests that humans may strategically allocate capacity to tasks, thereby protecting performance on one task to the detriment of performance on another task. Finally, the operation of a limited-capacity processing system has been related to consciousness (Posner and Klein, 1973). Note also that the construct of capacity has been used interchangeably with a number of other terms such as resources, effort, energetics and attention (Mulder, 1979a; Wickens, 1980).

A few additional aspects of capacity-based models are worth noting. First, implicit in pure capacity models is the assumption of non-specific interference. Under this assumption two difficult tasks should compete for processing capacity regardless of their structure. For example, if one task involves the processing of spatial material while another task requires transformations of verbal information, this should have no effect on the degree of interaction of either task with a third task which entails spatial processing. This assumption of non-specific interference is related to the search for a 'general measure' of processing capacity that could be applied across a wide variety of task settings (Brown, 1978; Kahneman, 1973; Wickens and Kramer, 1985). In fact, Norman and Bobrow (1975) asserted that one strength of the capacity approach is that, 'it requires only weak assumptions about the mechanisms that underlie initial stages of information processing' (p. 62).

Parallel processing is a second implicit assumption of pure capacity models. Thus, when two tasks are performed together it is assumed that they are timeshared rather than multiplexed or switched. Although the distinction between sharing and switching is dependent on the level of analysis of the tasks (e.g. tasks that appear to be timeshared when the temporal resolution is a few milliseconds may, in fact, be switched at the nanosecond level), a number of mathematical techniques have been proposed to test this assumption (Falmagne, 1968; Ratcliff, 1979; 1985; Sperling and Melcher, 1978). A description of how physiological measures have been used to augment these techniques will be provided below. A third assumption of pure capacity models is task independence. The capacity approach assumes that two tasks maintain their independent identities when performed concurrently. It is asserted that the only difference between single and dual task conditions is the resource allocation policy. However, theoretical arguments as well as empirical evidence have suggested that humans can modify their processing strategies in multitask situations to 'coordinate' or 'conjoin' tasks (Allport, 1987; Hirst, 1987; Neumann, 1987; Spelke *et al.*,1976). In later sections we will suggest how physiological measures may be used to shed some light on the mechanisms responsible for the transition from single to dual-task performance.

Capacity-based models have proven useful in describing and predicting changes in the efficiency of performance with variations in task demands and practice. However, these models provide only a limited view of the human information processing system. Another class of models, described in Chapter 1, describe the processing system from a different perspective variously labeled as 'structural', 'process', or 'computational'. Structural models of information processing focus on explicating the mechanisms responsible for the transformation of information as it flows through the processing system. Thus, rather than describing performance variability in terms of the efficiency and amount of capacity devoted to a task, structural models describe this variability in terms of changes in the number and nature (e.g. duration) of the processes that occur between the encoding of a stimulus and the execution of a response (McClelland, 1979; Miller 1988; Sternberg, 1969). Within a dual-task setting, performance decrements are proposed to occur when the processes or mechanisms are required to carry out incompatible operations. The methodologies and paradigms that have been employed to examine the structural basis of information processing have emphasized the timing and sequencing of these hypothetical mental operations (see Meyer *et al.*, 1988, and Chapter 1 in this volume for in-depth descriptions of structural models).

Capacity and structural models may not be mutually exclusive. Although the models have different attributes and emphasize different aspects of information processing, in practice few information processing tasks are described completely by either of these models. Instead, such tasks can be described within a multidimensional space that includes vectors for both capacity and structure. For example, Broadbent's (1958) early filter model included both structural and capacity components. According to this model, environmental information is passed through a number of stages, each of which completes specific operations on the information. The notion of capacity or resources is found in the model in the form of a bottleneck in processing that occurs when the human information processing 'channel' narrows from a parallel to a serial processor.

HISTORICAL OVERVIEW OF THE CONCEPT OF CAPACITY

Early 'bottleneck' models of attention (e.g. Broadbent, 1958) outlined the concept of a limited-capacity channel which could only cope with restricted, and probably fixed, amounts of information. The rich array of sensory information had to be severely attenuated or filtered prior to entry to such a channel. The exact point of the capacity limitation or bottleneck varied from model to model—Broadbent suggested that it was early in the sensory processing of the stimulus, whereas Deutsch and Deutsch (1963) preferred a later selection. As models developed, theorists came to prefer more flexible accounts of selectivity, with Johnston and Heinz (1978) arguing that the bottleneck could occur at any stage of the linear process.

Moray (1967) proposed a capacity-based model in which the human information processing system was likened to the central processing unit of a computer. This analogy served to emphasize both the limited nature of the processing system as well as its flexibility in strategically allocating capacity among concurrently performed tasks. This model can account for the effects of task difficulty and task interactions on performance. It can also account for practice effects by assuming that humans discover less capacity-demanding strategies during learning.

In an attempt to integrate psychological and physiological research on attention, Kahneman (1973) proposed that the amount of available processing capacity could be influenced by the arousal level of the organism. As task demands increased, arousal mechanisms would increase the supply of capacity. However, with large increases in task difficulty or the addition of several tasks, the supply would be insufficient to meet the processing demands and performance would deteriorate. Kahneman also suggested that the allocation policy was governed by both strategic factors and automatic responses (i.e. orienting response, defense reaction). These concepts are summarized in greater depth prior to our review of the relation of autonomic changes to capacity allocation.

Although both Moray and Kahneman provided detailed accounts of the role of capacity in human information processing, the mapping between capacity and performance required further delineation. Norman and Bobrow (1975) introduced the concept of the *performance resource function* (PRF) in an effort to relate capacity/resources and performance. PRFs for two hypothetical tasks are presented in Figure 2.1. Two distinct regions can be observed in the PRF in Figure 2.1 (a). The initial portion of the function indicates a monotonic relation between performance and resources. This region is said to be 'resource-limited'. The asymptotic portion of the function is said to be 'data-limited'. Data limits can occur at any level of performance and are the result of either signal limits (i.e. the S/N ratio) or memory limits (i.e. memory span). For example, a data limit may be produced by poor contrast between the foreground and background in a visual display. In this case performance will not change with the allocation of additional resources. Improvements in performance will only occur with enhanced contrast. The PRF in Figure 2.1(b) indicates a purely resource-limited task. It is important to note that the PRF is a hypothetical function since only one of the variables is actually observed.

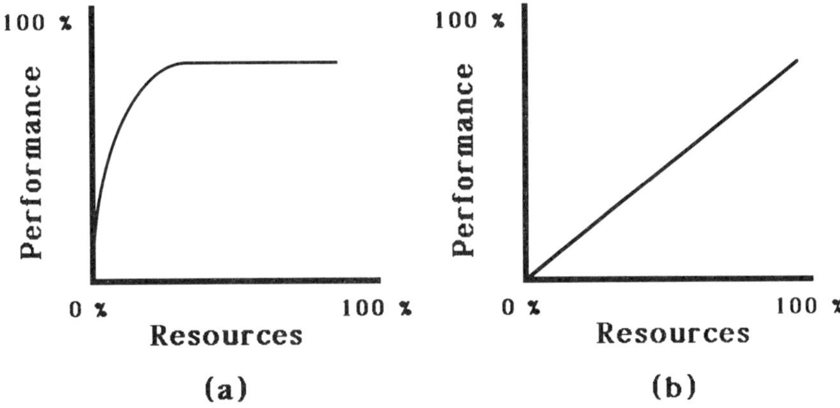

Figure 2.1. PRFs for two hypothetical tasks.

Norman and Bobrow (1975) introduced another graphical technique, the *performance operating characteristic* (POC), to illustrate performance tradeoffs between tasks (see Sperling and Melcher, 1978, for a similar concept). Although POCs can be used in a purely descriptive manner to indicate changes in the performance of one task as a function of the level of performance on another task, they are usually used to infer the underlying resource structure of the tasks. Figure 2.2 presents POCs for three pairs of tasks. Several aspects of the POC space are noteworthy. First, single-task performance levels are indicated on the abscissa and the ordinate. These points provide a baseline against which dual-task performance can be compared. Second, the efficiency of dual-task performance is represented by the distance of the POC functions from the intersection of the ordinate and the abscissa. Thus, the two tasks represented by POC I are more efficiently timeshared than the tasks represented by POC II, which in turn are more efficiently timeshared than the task pair represented by POC III.

A third important aspect of POCs is their shape. POC I represents task independence since changes in the performance in one task has no effect on the performance exhibited in the other task. The PRFs for these tasks would be highly data-limited. POC III represents a case of complete overlap

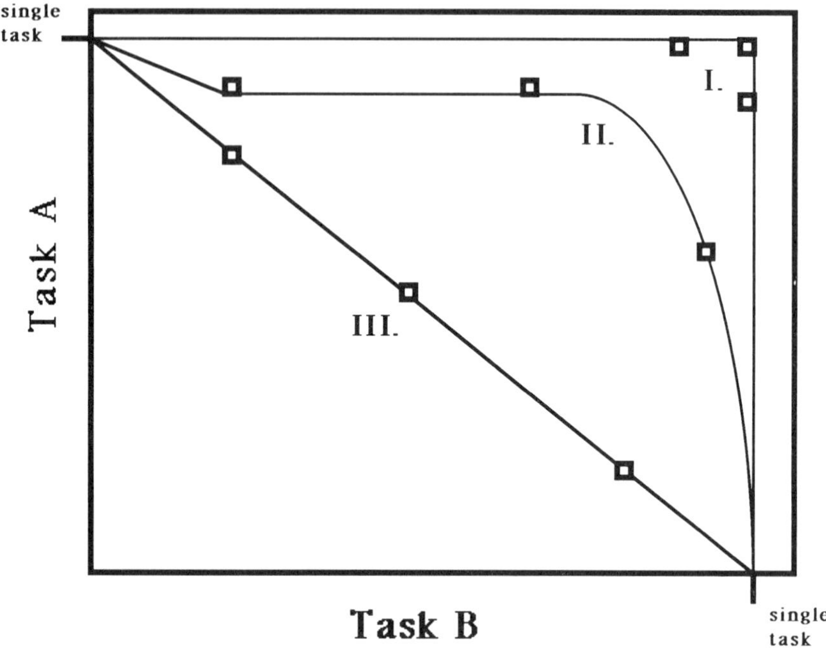

Figure 2.2. POCs for three pairs of tasks.

since a change in performance in one task represents an equivalent change in performance in the other task (e.g. a 1:1 ratio). The PRFs for these tasks would be completely resource-limited. Given the perfect symmetry of POC III, the PRFs would also be identical (the same is true for POC I). POC II is produced by the PRFs in Figure 2.1 and reflects partial overlap in resource demands. The asymmetric shape of the POC is the result of the different shapes of the PRFs. Finally, the difference between single- and dual-task performance is represented in the POC and is usually referred to as the 'cost of concurrence'. This concurrence cost is said to reflect the costs incurred in the management of two tasks (Navon and Gopher, 1979).

A few additional caveats concerning PRF/POC methodology are noteworthy. First, the determination of the shape of the underlying PRFs requires that the entire range of the POC is examined. Thus, the relative emphasis on the tasks must be manipulated so as to produce a number of different dual-task conditions. Second, POCs are only valid if subject–task factors are held constant while task emphasis is varied. Subject–task factors include: S/N ratio of display items, S–R compatibility, task difficulty, arousal level of the subject, etc. Although these factors must be held constant when deriving a POC, the resource tradeoffs for different values of these parameters can be examined by deriving a 'family of POCs'. Third, there is no generally agreed method of scaling different dependent variables and tasks (Kantowitz and Weldon, 1985). Thus, the question of how many milliseconds of RT are equivalent to a 1% change in accuracy or 1 unit of root-mean-square tracking error remains unanswered. A number of different transformations have been suggested to normalize these dependent measures (Colle *et al.*, 1988; Mountford and North, 1980; Wickens, Mountford and Schreiner, 1981; Wickens and Yeh, 1985). However, since different transformations differentially affect the slope of the POC, which in turn has implications for the shape of the underlying PRFs, it would be preferable to use a single measure that could be compared across different tasks. Psychophysiological indices of capacity may provide such a measure. A number of other assumptions of POC methodology can be added to those described above. These assumptions include: (a) sensitivity of performance to resources, (b) control of resource allocation, (c) fixed quantity of resources, (d) task independence, and (e) the principle of complementarity (the sum of capacities for each task is the total capacity). Kahneman's (1973) model clearly violates assumption (c) since the model suggests that capacity varies with arousal. However, this problem can be dealt with by controlling for arousal level within a POC. Problems can also be encountered for assumptions (d) and (e) (e.g. tasks can be integrated, concurrence costs violate the principle of complementarity). However, although these problems can occur when comparing single and dual tasks, they generally do not exist when comparing different dual-task conditions.

The capacity-based models and PRF/POC methodologies discussed thus far were developed under the assumption that capacity or resources could be represented as a single undifferentiated commodity. However, it soon became apparent that task structure had an important influence on the pattern of dual-task decrements that was observed. For example, a number of studies have been reported in which increases in the difficulty of one task failed to influence the performance of a concurrent task (Isreal *et al.*, 1980a; Kantowitz and Knight, 1976). North (1977) found that increasing the difficulty of a digit processing task had no influence on a concurrently performed tracking task. However, the manipulation of difficulty in the digit processing task did influence single-task performance levels in the task and also influenced performance in a digit cancellation task. This phenomenon has been labeled 'difficulty insensitivity' (Wickens, 1980). Given that tasks are not data-limited, examples of perfect timesharing also appear to be problematic for undifferentiated capacity models (Allport *et al.*, 1972; Shaffer, 1975). Kahneman (1973) dealt with instances of task-specific interactions by suggesting that in addition to capacity, tasks could also compete for perceptual and response-related processing structures. However, unlike resources, these structures could not be voluntarily allocated among tasks, and therefore functioned in an all-or-none manner.

An alternative to the capacity/structural interference models discussed above is a class of multiple resource models. Adherents of this view propose that structure-specific task interactions can be accounted for by postulating a small set of resources. Each of these resources can be voluntarily allocated among concurrently performed tasks. Within this framework two tasks will be efficiently timeshared to the extent that they demand separate resources. Thus, boxlike POCs (i.e. POC I in Figure 2.2) can occur either (a) because both tasks possess relatively large data-limited regions, or (b) because the tasks do not compete for common resources.

A number of different multiple resource models have been proposed. However, in each case the major goal has been to account for the most variance in dual-task performance with the fewest resource types. The most detailed multiple resource model is that of Wickens (1980, 1984a). The model divides information processing into three dichotomous dimensions with each level of a dimension representing a separate resource. Dimensions include: stages of processing (perceptual/central and response), codes of processing (verbal and spatial), and modalities of input and output (input: visual and auditory, output: speech and manual). Other multiple resource models have defined resources in terms of cerebral hemispheres (Freidman and Polson, 1981; Polson and Freidman, 1988), distance in functional cerebral space (Kinsbourne and Hicks, 1978), and arousal, activation and effort (Sanders, 1981; see also Baddley and Hitch, 1974; Navon and Gopher, 1979; Sanders, 1979). The contribution of psychophysiological techniques to the validation of these resource dimensions will be discussed below.

APPLICATIONS OF THE CONCEPT OF CAPACITY

The development of capacity-based theories of human information processing has had important implications for a number of other domains, including mental workload assessment, models of skill acquisition and training, and individual differences. In this section we will briefly illustrate how capacity notions have impacted these domains and how these interactions have provided insights into the utility of capacity models of information processing.

The concept of mental workload has been defined in terms of the 'costs' a human operator incurs as tasks are performed (Gopher and Donchin, 1986; Wickens and Kramer, 1985). Unlike physical workload, however, these 'mental costs' cannot be readily observed. Fortunately, a number of measurement techniques have been designed to enable researchers and human factors practitioners to infer changes in mental capacity with variations in task demands and operator state. One of these measurement procedures is referred to as the 'secondary-task technique'. The technique functions in the following manner. A subject/operator performs the task of interest both separately as well as concurrently with another task. When the two tasks are performed together the task of interest is assigned primary emphasis and the other task is designated as secondary. An assumption of the secondary-task technique is that variations in primary-task demands will be reflected in secondary-task performance. Thus, secondary-task performance is used to infer the amount of residual resources remaining after the performance of the primary task. Many of the studies reviewed use a dual-task paradigm. Furthermore, Siddle and Spinks (1979) argued that future research strategies in the psychophysiology of information processing should employ more dual-task designs, in which inferences concerning the processing of one task or stimulus could be gleaned by the examination of the other task.

The method can be traced back to before the beginning of this century, when Welch assessed the attention allocated to (primary) cognitive tasks by measuring the maximal hand-grip exerted (study cited by Eysenck, 1982, p.43). A secondary task which has been adopted by a number of psychophysiological researchers (e.g. Jennings, Lawrence and Casper, 1978) is the probe reaction time (RT) task (Posner and Boies, 1971). In these studies, stimuli, which may be auditory or visual, are introduced at infrequent intervals during the execution of a primary task, the subjects having been instructed to react to the stimuli as quickly as possible by pressing a response key. The assumptions related to this particular technique can be developed rather specifically following the general assumptions related to dual-task techniques just developed *vis-à-vis* the POC.

The assumption of this method is that an increase in the limited capacity used by a primary task will result in a decrease in the capacity available for other tasks, which will, in turn, lead to an increase in probe RT. It is pertinent to point out at this stage, however, that despite the extensive use of this measure over the last two decades, its relationship to the allocation of capacity should not be accepted uncritically, for a number of reasons. First, there are difficulties in justifying the assumption that a temporal measure (such as RT) should be linearly related to a structural or process-related state (capacity availability), although this is an assumption which researchers seem willing to make. Second, it must be remembered that changes in subject strategy will affect the allocation of capacity, with consequent changes to the probe RT measures. In this respect, it is often assumed that subjects pay heed of instructions to concentrate on the primary task, but this is not necessarily warranted, given the difficulty in precisely stating to the subject what is meant by such instructions, and given the subjects' noted lack of compliance (O'Connor, 1981). Few subjects can be expected to refrain from engaging in tertiary, private tasks. It might be more parsimonious to employ the concept of processing priority to describe the processes indexed by probe RT.

Related to this, it is often assumed, again perhaps incorrectly, that the secondary task uses all of the spare capacity available at that moment in time. In relation to the undifferentiated capacity models at least, there is a problem if subjects modify the capacity available by altering the effort invested in the experimental situation (Kahneman, 1973). Both Benson, Huddleston and Rolfe (1965) and Corcoran (1964) have argued that subjects compensate for a deterioration in performance by increasing effort. In this respect, it should be noted that the capacity available for the probe RT task is not necessarily the inverse of capacity or resources employed on the primary task. Capacity theorists such as Kahneman (1973) have argued that the total amount of resources available for processing expands with an increase in arousal. Taking account of Easterbrook's (1959) hypothesis that arousal is also associated with a restriction in attentional focus, this suggests that responses to probes, which form part of a secondary task, would become less efficient as arousal (and capacity) increases, contrary to the usual assumption. This is not a problem if capacity only increases as a result of an increase in the information processing demands, as Kahneman has suggested. However, if arousal and capacity can vary independently of these demands (owing to variations in motivation or strategy), then the relationship between the available capacity and probe RT becomes more complicated.

Therefore, while there seem to be a number of potential difficulties with the use of secondary-task measures such as probe RT, it is difficult to evaluate their practical effect. The difficulties may not vitiate the technique when the subject is (it is hoped) attending to instructions, and when motivation levels do not vary from one condition to another. These issues should, however, serve as a warning to researchers not to use such techniques indiscriminately, and perhaps as an incentive to others to evaluate such effects, for example by employing different secondary tasks along with the same primary task. Indeed the researcher can look to workload measurement techniques which have been designed to account for the issues raised by the theoretical and empirical suggestion of more than one limited-capacity resource. Thus, while the initial goal in the workload assessment field was the discovery of the 'best' measure of capacity allocation (Knowles, 1963), more recent workload measurement reviews and taxonomies have emphasized the importance of designing a battery of measures that would tap different dimensions of mental workload (Leplat, 1978; O'Donnell and Eggemeier, 1986; Ogden, Levine and Eisner, 1979; Wickens, 1979). The sensitivity of psychophysiological measures to different aspects of workload will be described below.

This emphasis on the relationship between capacity and mental workload has also led to the development of a number of predictive models which incorporate notions of demand levels and task structure (McCracken and Aldrich, 1984; Aldrich, Szabo and Bierbaum, 1988; Laughery, Drews and Archer, 1986; Parks and Boucke, 1988). For instance, Wickens's (1980, 1984) three-dimensional representation of the capacity space serves as the core of the WINDEX workload predictive model (North, 1985; North and Riley, 1988). Although the validity of these models for the prediction of workload in operational settings has not yet been established, preliminary investigations in quasi-real-world environments have provided encouraging results (Wickens *et al.*, 1988).

Traditionally, capacity-based models of information processing have not dealt with the relationship between capacity and learning. However, learning theorists have often invoked the concept of capacity when describing changes in information processing that accompany practice (Crossman, 1959; LaBerge, 1973; Logan, 1979; Newell and Rosenbloom, 1981). For example, Schneider and Shiffrin (1977; also Shiffrin and Schneider, 1977) have included differences in capacity or resource allocation as a defining characteristic of automatic and controlled processing (see also Schneider, 1985; Schneider and Detweiler, 1988). Controlled processing represents a temporary sequence of operations which are under the control of the subject, require active attention, and are capacity-limited. Controlled processing is used in novel situations or in situations in which stimulus–response relations are varied over time. Automatic processing, which develops as a result of extensive practice with consistent stimulus–response relations, is fast, often insensitive to capacity limits, and is difficult to modify once initiated.

A derivative of the Schneider–Shiffrin theory is Öhman's (1979) information processing model which postulates a call for central channel capacity following the classification of the evoking stimulus on the basis of a preattentive analysis. However, Öhman also (a) develops an explanation of skin conductance response conditioning data within this model, and (b) explains how learning is related to central channel processing. A UCS is, almost by definition, processed within the central channel. This processing will call up the contents of the short-term store, which will contain information about any CS. Build-up of expectations concerning the occurrence of a UCS following a CS is assumed to involve transfer from processing routines demanding capacity to those involving only preattentive control (i.e. automatic processing). Capacity is only called again when there is a deviation from expectation. Thus, from Öhman's and Schneider and Shiffrin's perspective, learning is assumed to be dependent on controlled processing, which, in turn, requires information processing capacity. As we will see later in this chapter, researchers have studied the conditioning process, using psychophysiological and behavioral evidence to provide interesting insights into the dependence of the learning process upon available capacity.

Although the concept of capacity provides a reasonable account of a subset of the changes that accompany skill development, a number of questions remain unanswered. For instance, do resource demands decrease with the development of expertise and/or do resource supplies increase? Rather than a decrease in resource demands with practice, could it be instead that there is a shift in the types of resources consumed? What implications do changes in strategies and task organization have on the types and amounts of resources required for successful performance? Although the answers to many of these questions remain unresolved, in later sections we will describe how psychophysiological approaches to these problems have provided some intriguing insights.

Another domain in which the concept of capacity has proven useful is the assessment of individual differences in divided attention, focused attention, and the rapid reorientation of attention. These differences have been examined with regard to their relevance to operator performance in complex, real-world tasks. Several assumptions underlie this research. First, it is assumed that individuals differ in the amount of 'residual' resources they retain during the performance of tasks. Second, it is assumed that increased skill levels lead to decreased capacity demands. Finally, it is assumed that measures of residual capacity can account for variance in criterion task performance not accounted for by single-task measures.

An example of the use of this logic is provided by a study of bilinguals using their non-dominant language (Dornic, 1980). Although no differences between first- and second-language speakers could be discerned by tests of speaking ability, individuals using their non-dominant language performed significantly worse on a secondary task than did native speakers. In another setting North and Gopher (1976, see also Damos, 1978) found that, while instructor and student pilots were indistinguishable on single-task measures of digit cancellation and tracking performance, the instructors performed significantly better than the students in the dual-task condition. The dual-task measures also discriminated between student pilots who passed and those who failed a flight examination. In yet another setting, Lansman and Hunt (1982) found that performance on a secondary task was a better predictor of performance on a difficult primary task than single-task performance on the easy version of the primary task. This set of studies suggests that (a) skills of timesharing are distinct from skills on the composite tasks, and (b) timesharing skills are relevant to real-world performance.

The individual differences described above are relevant to situations that require the division of attention among several tasks. However, other studies have found that humans also differ in their ability to focus attention and to reorient attention quickly to relevant information. Such skills appear to be important in professions that require the monitoring of sources of information that vary in importance. A series of studies have employed a dichotic listening task developed by Gopher and Kahneman (1971) to examine the relevance of focusing and switching skills to performance in real-world tasks.

Two different phases of the dichotic listening task can be distinguished. In the first phase, subjects are instructed to repeat digits presented to the cued ear while ignoring information presented to the uncued ear. The digits are presented at a rapid pace and are interspersed with words. In the second phase, subjects receive a cue which either indicates that they should maintain their attention on the same ear or switch attention to the other ear. Omission errors in phase I and performance in phase II discriminate between automobile and bus drivers with good and poor safety records (Avolio, Kroeck and Panek, 1985; Kahneman *et al.*, 1973), flight cadets who later fail or succeed at initial flight training (Gopher, 1982), and flight cadets who are later assigned to transports or high-performance jets (Gopher and Kahneman, 1971). Furthermore, in the assessment of success of flight training, performance in the dichotic listening task was not significantly correlated with other items in a prediction battery. Thus, like measures of divided attention, the assessment of focused attention and switching appears both to extend the notion of capacity beyond laboratory tasks and to provide a useful tool for the prediction of complex task performance. The utility of psychophysiological measures for the assessment of individual differences in timesharing and focused attention will be examined below.

CAPACITY REVISITED: A FEW CAVEATS

In recent years the notion of capacity has been challenged on several fronts. A number of authors have re-emphasized the methodological pitfalls encountered in the examination of capacity models of human information processing (Kantowitz, 1985; Kantowitz and Weldon, 1985; Navon, 1984). However, since the majority of these issues were described by early capacity theorists (Kahneman, 1973; Norman and Bobrow, 1985) and were discussed in previous sections of the present review, they will not be reiterated here.

We will, however, briefly describe a novel methodological problem discussed by Navon (1984). In his description of traditional POC methodology, Navon has suggested that:

> Performance tradeoffs that are exhibited when minimal performance requirements are set by the experimenter may not be due to any limit on joint performance but rather to some sort of compliance of the subjects with what they figure are the objectives of the experimental situation. (p. 228)

In the case of POC methodology this compliance may take the form of probability-ratio matching. Thus, subjects may produce performance tradeoffs in the specified ratios even when their performance could be better. In an effort to examine this potential artifact, Navon (1984) has suggested the method of twin POCs. With this technique, performance levels are designated for only one task while performance on the other task is to be maximized. This procedure is carried out so that in different conditions performance is maximized for each of the tasks. If this method produces a more 'box like' POC than the traditional method, it would suggest that subjects are probability-ratio matching, which in turn would underestimate the quantity of capacity available.

In addition to the methodological problems that have been outlined, a number of serious theoretical challenges have also been posed. The general argument is that capacity models have been oversold since, at best, they account for only a small subset of multitask interactions (Allport, 1987; Hirst, 1987; Hirst and Kalmar, 1987; Kantowitz, 1985; Neumann, 1987). Furthermore, it has been asserted that alternative models of dual-task performance are both more parsimonious and more easily tested than capacity models.

Addressing the general criticism first, that capacity models have been oversold, it would appear that even the early capacity theorists were cognizant of the limits of their models. For instance, Kahneman (1973) acknowledged the importance of both structure and capacity, suggesting that perceptual and response interactions could be accounted for by structural rather than resource factors. Norman and Bobrow (1975) carefully distinguished between performance decrements due to data limits and those that could be attributed to resource limits. Other theorists asserted that resource explanations could only be invoked given constant subject–task factors and evidence that subjects were timesharing rather than task switching (Navon and Gopher, 1979; Wickens, 1980).

More recent research has suggested further qualifications of capacity models. For example, Wickens, Mountford and Schreiner (1981) found that stimulus–central-processing–response (S–C–R) compatibility and resource competition interact such that greater competition is experienced with tasks of lower compatibility and increases in timesharing efficiency are obtained when compatibility is increased. Wickens and Boles (1983) suggested further limits on resource models by proposing that some tasks can actually benefit by sharing the same resources. Thus, tasks that involve the integration of information or response sequences will benefit from similar resource requirements while tasks that involve separate processing and response components will be performed most successfully when they require separate resources.

In summary, it appears that both early as well as recent resource theorists have acknowledged the limitations of capacity models of information processing. The relevance of psychophysiological data for defining the boundary conditions of resource models will be described below.

The second major criticism concerns the degree to which alternative models provide a better account of task interactions than resource/capacity models. The small number of alternative models that have been proposed thus far are based on empirical results which suggest that task interference may be both more and less specific than suggested by multiple resource models. For example, Hirst and Kalmar (1987) found that subjects had more difficulty monitoring for spelling errors in separate messages presented simultaneously to the two ears than monitoring for spelling errors and arithmetic errors. Navon and Miller (1987) found that the degree of interaction between two concurrently presented visual detection tasks depended upon the semantic similarity of the items in the two tasks. Finally, Hatano, Miyake and Binks (1977) found that, while expert abacus users could answer non-mathematical questions while performing abacus calculations, they were unable to answer mathematical questions. Thus, these results suggest that interference is more specific than would be predicted by multiple resource models. Other studies suggest that task interference can also be quite diffuse. The detection of the occurrence of probes has been found to produce equivalent interference in other tasks regardless of input and output modalities (Posner, 1982; Proctor and Proctor, 1979).

Two classes of alternative models have been proposed to account for these patterns of dual-task performance. Navon (1984) and others (Allport, 1980; Hirst and Kalmar, 1987; Navon and Miller, 1987) have suggested that dual-task interference can be explained in terms of different forms of crosstalk or outcome conflicts that occur between parallel processes. It is asserted that crosstalk occurs as a result of the 'confusability' of similar types of stimulus materials, similar transformations or similar response patterns. For example, crosstalk will occur when non-targets in one task belong to the same semantic category as targets in the other task. Thus, within this framework the emphasis is on explicating the nature and breadth of processing that takes place in different processing mechanisms.

Navon and Miller (1987) suggest that, in order to discriminate between resource and outcome conflict explanations,

> ... one may vary experimental factors that are thought to affect the likelihood of outcome conflict without affecting the complexity of each task performed alone. Since such variables do not change the resource demands of individual tasks, an effect on task interference must be ascribed to some interaction between the tasks other than their competition for common resources. (p. 437)

While this statement is intuitively appealing, in practice it might be quite difficult to ensure that single-task resource demands do not change when task parameters are modified.

The other class of alternative models argues that tasks are performed by executing perception–action rules (Allport, 1987; Neumann, 1987). Therefore, increasing the difficulty of one task should affect the other task, if and only if the difficulty manipulation has its effect on the number and/or complexity of the perception–action rules. Thus, like the crosstalk models, the perception–action models argue that performance decrements are due to interference between parallel processes. The difference between these models is in the nature of the representation. Within the perception–action framework, concurrent activities should be possible during initial levels of learning only to the degree that the tasks require different components of perception and action. However, with practice it is suggested that the tasks will be integrated into a 'meta' perception–action rule and therefore the tasks will no longer interfere with each other.

It is obvious from our review that a number of different factors have been proposed to account for patterns of dual-task performance. It also seems to be the case that each of these factors can account for a portion of the variance in dual-task interactions. While the influence of these different factors can be difficult to disentangle, we have described a number of tools that can aid the researcher in this process. In the next section, we discuss how psychophysiological methods can be used to further explore the resources, structures and mechanisms responsible for single- and multi-task performance.

CENTRAL NERVOUS SYSTEM MEASURES OF CAPACITY

ARTHUR KRAMER AND JOHN SPINKS

This section will focus on the contribution of central nervous system (CNS) measures to the examination of resource models of human information processing. More specifically, we will concentrate on three distinct classes of CNS measures; event-related brain potentials (ERPs), electroencephalographic (EEG) activity, and measures of metabolic activity (e.g. glucose utilization, regional cerebral blood flow). The magnetic counterparts of ERPs and the EEG will also be briefly discussed. Although each of these techniques provides insights into the changes in resource allocation that accompany performance and learning, ERPs have, thus far, been most extensively employed. Therefore, our discussion of the relevant issues will be necessarily biased towards ERPs.

CHARACTERISTICS OF THE MEASUREMENT TECHNIQUES

Given that each of the CNS measures provides a distinctive view of the changes in nervous system activity that accompany human information processing, we will briefly describe the important characteristics of each class of measures. EEG has the longest history of any of the measures that will be discussed (Berger, 1929). The EEG is traditionally recorded from the scalp and is composed of a composite of waveforms with a frequency range of between 1 and 40 Hz and with a voltage range of 10–200 microvolts. The voltage × time vector is usually decomposed into a number of constituent frequency bands including: delta (up to 2 Hz), theta (4–7 Hz), alpha (8–13 Hz) and beta (14–25 Hz). The characteristics of the EEG that make it a useful variable in research on human information processing include: (a) it does not require the presentation of extraneous stimuli, (b) it is a multivariate measure (e.g. different frequency bands and recording sites), (c) it can be sampled continuously, (d) it can be recorded in laboratory and field environments, (e) it is relatively non-invasive, and (f) it offers both tonic and phasic measures.

The ERP is a transient series of voltage oscillations in the brain that can be recorded from the scalp in response to the occurrence of a discrete event. This measure has been described in Chapter 1 (pp. 86–98).

The recording of magnetoencephalographic (MEG) activity during active task performance has begun only recently and therefore has not yet produced much information concerning capacity aspects of information processing. However, since the MEG technique provides information that complements that obtained from EEG and ERPs, it offers the potential of enhancing our understanding of the relationship between the neurophysiological and psychological concepts of capacity. In particular, since MEG activity is relatively immune to 'spatial smearing' that plagues the recording of electrical activity, it may be quite useful in localizing the scalp-recorded magnetic fields that are sensitive to changes in processing capacity (Cuffin and Cohen, 1979; Williamson and Kaufman, 1981). However, at present the painstaking data recording-techniques required to 'localize' the source of MEG activity make it an impractical tool for the analysis of complex multitask designs. This methodological limitation should be overcome in the near future with the development of large-array recording devices.

The measurement of cerebral blood flow and the metabolic activity of the brain has recently been applied to issues of human information processing (Phelps and Mazziotta, 1985; Posner *et al.*, 1988; Risberg and Prohovnik, 1983). Although these techniques are 'non invasive' in the sense that they do not require surgical intervention, the need to employ radioisotopes necessitates that the techniques be restricted to medical settings. Perhaps the best known of this class of techniques is positron emission tomography (PET). The PET technique involves three major components. First, the compound of interest is labeled with a radioisotope such as oxygen-15 or fluorine-18. These isotopes decay with the emission of positrons that combine with electrons to produce two gamma rays. The gamma rays are emitted 180 degrees apart from the head. The second component of the PET technique, the positron tomograph, records the gamma ray activity and constructs a series of cross-sectional maps of the distribution of radioactivity in the tissue. Finally, tracer kinetic models are used to provide a mathematical description of the transport and biochemical reaction sequences of the labeled compounds.

Techniques such as PET complement the information derived from the recording of electroencephalographic activity since, while ERPs can provide precise temporal localization of different aspects of information processing, spatial resolution is quite limited. On the other hand, while the temporal resolution of PET is limited by the decay rate of the radioisotopes (e.g. it takes at least 30 s to produce a PET map), spatial resolution of the metabolic activity can be quite precise. Thus, the relative strengths of electrical/magnetic and metabolic measurement techniques suggest that their joint use should provide a detailed view of the changes in brain activity that accompany variations in human information processing.

VARIETIES OF CAPACITY: SENSITIVITY AND DIAGNOSTICITY OF CNS MEASURES

Each of the capacity models predicts a monotonic relationship between performance efficiency and capacity for resource-limited tasks. Thus, a reasonable initial question is whether this relationship is reflected in one or more of the CNS measures. Consider the following paradigm as an example of how this question might be addressed. Subjects are seated in front of a CRT and instructed to fixate a centrally located marker. As subjects are fixating the marker, stimuli are presented in a random fashion to the right and left visual fields. Subjects are instructed to 'attend' to either the right or left or both visual fields and respond to the occurrence of an infrequent target event (e.g. a dim flash presented in a series of bright flashes). An analysis of the processing requirements of such a task would suggest that the largest amount of capacity could be allocated to the attended field items in the focused attention condition. It would also be predicted that little capacity would be allocated to events in the unattended visual field. Finally, since in the divided attention condition subjects must process events in both visual fields, the capacity available for events in this condition would fall between the focused and ignore conditions.

Van Voorhis and Hillyard (1977) employed the paradigm described above and found that the N100 component of the ERP was largest when elicited by attended events in the focused attention condition, intermediate in amplitude when elicited by events in the divided attention condition, and smallest when elicited by unattended events in the focused attention condition. Thus, changes in the amplitude of the N100 appear to reflect the distribution of capacity to events in the visual field (see Hink, Van Voorhis and Hillyard, 1977; Kramer, Sirevaag and Braune, 1988; Okita, 1979; Parasuraman, 1978, for similar effects in visual and auditory modalities).

In addition to finding that N100 was sensitive to the processing demands in focused and divided attention conditions, Van Voorhis and Hillyard obtained evidence that indicated the limited nature of this capacity. Given that (a) a finite supply of capacity is available for the processing of events in the visual field, and (b) that capacity is fully allocated in focused and divided attention conditions, it would be predicted that the total amount of capacity expended in the focused and divided attention condition should be equivalent. Thus, assuming that N100 is sensitive to the distribution of capacity, the sum of the amplitude of the N100s elicited by events in the attended and unattended fields in the focused attention condition should equal the sum of the amplitudes of the events in both fields in the divided attention condition. This equivalence was obtained by Van Voorhis and Hillyard.

Thus far we have seen the sensitivity of N100 to changes in the distribution of capacity by comparing focused and divided attention conditions. While these conditions differ in the amount of processing required for different events they also differ in the number of 'channels' a subject must monitor. In the Van Voorhis and Hillyard example, one channel (e.g. visual field) must be monitored in the focused attention condition while two channels (e.g. right and left visual fields) are monitored in the divided attention condition. A paradigm employed by Parasuraman (1985) avoided this confound between the number of channels to be monitored and the distribution of processing capacity. Subjects were required to monitor trains of auditory and visual stimuli and to detect tones and circles that were presented for a slightly longer duration than the frequently presented standard stimuli. Unlike the divided and focused attention paradigm described above, subjects always monitored both streams of stimuli. Thus, the number of channels was equated in different conditions. Processing demands were manipulated by instructing subjects to maximize their performance on either the auditory or the visual task or to treat both tasks as equally important. The performance data obtained with a fast presentation rate was plotted in a POC space and indicated a tradeoff between the tasks as a function of priority. Detection performance was best when the task was emphasized, intermediate when both tasks were treated equally, and poorest when the other task was emphasized. The early negativities obtained in the visual (N160) and auditory (N100) tasks showed a reciprocity as a function of priority. N100s increased in amplitude with increasing emphasis on the task while N100s decreased in the other task.

Based on the studies described above, the early negative-going component(s) of the ERP appear to reflect a number of characteristics that have been attributed to processing capacity: they show a graded sensitivity to processing demands, they reflect the limited nature of capacity, and they suggest that the limited commodity can be flexibly allocated among different events. Another characteristic of recent capacity models is the multidimensional nature of capacity (Freidman and Polson, 1981; Sanders, 1979; Wickens, 1980, 1984). An important question is whether CNS measures are selectively sensitive to different types of capacity. The question can be answered in the affirmative for the early negative components. In variants of the focused attention conditions described above, target and non-target events are presented to both the attended and unattended fields. Subjects are instructed to respond to the target events in the attended field. However, large negativities are elicited by both the target and non-target events only in the attended field. Patterns of results such as these have been interpreted to be consistent with Broadbent's (1970) stimulus set model of selective attention in which two different channels of information are distinguished early in processing on the basis of physical characteristics of stimuli such as space, time, frequency, color, etc. (Hillyard, Munte and Neville, 1985; Näätänen, 1988). Thus, within a capacity framework these early negative-going components appear to reflect the distribution of perceptual resources.

Within the same focused attention condition described above, a second component of the ERP is elicited by the occurrence of the target events in the attended field. Unlike the early negativities, this component is not elicited by the non-targets in the attended field. This component is referred to as the P300 and occurs with a parietally maximal scalp distribution and a minimum latency of 300 ms post-stimulus. Within Broadbent's attention model the P300 has been likened to response set filtering. This form of filtering is said to occur later in the processing stream than stimulus set filtering and depends on higher-order characteristics of the stimuli. Thus, as in the case of the N100 and P300 components of the ERP, there is a hierarchical relationship between stimulus set and response set filtering.

It is important to note that, although changes in P300 have been associated with response-set filtering, this does not imply that P300 is sensitive to response or motor processes. On the contrary, a number of studies have demonstrated that, while P300 is influenced by manipulations that affect stimulus evaluation processes, it is relatively insensitive to factors that influence response selection and execution processes (Isreal *et al.*, 1980a; Kutas, McCarthy and Donchin, 1977; McCarthy and Donchin, 1981; Ragot, 1984). Thus, within a multiple resource framework it appears that P300 is primarily sensitive to factors that influence perceptual/central processing resources.

The sensitivity of the P300 component to processing resources has also been investigated extensively in multitask paradigms (Donchin, Kramer and Wickens, 1986; Kramer, 1987). For example, Isreal *et al.* (1980a) required subjects to perform a simulated air traffic control (ATC) task concurrently with a visual discrimination task. Subjects were instructed to treat the ATC task as primary and the visual discrimination task as secondary. ERPs were elicited by secondary-task events. The amplitude of the P300 component decreased with increases in the number of elements to be monitored in the ATC task.

Other studies have also found decreases in the amplitude of P300s elicited by secondary-task events with increases in the difficulty of a primary task. These studies have employed a variety of primary tasks, including pursuit and compensatory tracking, flight control and navigation, and memory/visual search as well as both visual and auditory secondary tasks (Hoffman *et al.*, 1985; Kramer and Strayer, 1988; Kramer, Sirevaag and Braune, 1987; Kramer, Wickens and Donchin, 1983, 1985; Lindholm *et al.*, 1984; McCallum, Cooper and Pocock, 1987; Natani and Gomer, 1981; Strayer and Kramer, 1990). Capacity models predict that as the difficulty of a primary task increases, fewer resources should be available for the performance of a secondary task. The studies described above suggest that the P300s may reflect the residual resources available for secondary-task performance.

Given that P300s reflect the distribution of processing resources in a dual-task situation, P300s elicited by primary task events should increase in amplitude with increases in the difficulty of the primary task. Thus, capacity models predict a reciprocal relationship between the resources allocated to one task and the residual resources available to another, concurrently performed task. The question of whether P300 would reflect this reciprocity was addressed in a study conducted by Wickens *et al.* (1983). ERPs were elicited by events in both the primary and secondary tasks. In the primary task, pursuit step tracking, ERPs were elicited by changes in the spatial position of the target, while in the secondary task, auditory discrimination, ERPs were elicited by the occurrence of high- and low-pitched tones.

Difficulty was varied by manipulating two variables in the tracking task: the predictability of the positional changes of the target, and the control dynamics. The ordering of difficulty was validated by measures of tracking performance and subjective ratings of tracking difficulty. Consistent with previous results, P300s elicited by discrete secondary-task events decreased in amplitude with increases in the difficulty of the primary task. On the other hand, increasing the difficulty of the tracking task by decreasing the stability of the control dynamics and the predictability of the target resulted in a systematic increase in primary-task P300 amplitude. The reciprocal relationship between P300s elicited by primary- and secondary-task stimuli as a function of primary-task difficulty is consistent with the resource tradeoffs presumed to underlie dual-task performance decrements (see also Sirevaag *et al.*, 1989).

Other demonstrations of the P300 reciprocity effect have been provided in paradigms in which priority rather than difficulty was manipulated. For example, Strayer and Kramer (1990) instructed subjects to perform two tasks concurrently: recognition running memory and memory search. In different conditions subjects were to emphasize the performance of one task or the other or treat both tasks equally. The amplitude of the P300s reflected task priority. P300s increased in amplitude with the priority of one task while simultaneously decreasing in amplitude in the other task. Thus, the demonstration of reciprocity effects with both difficulty and priority manipulations provides strong support for the argument that P300 amplitude reflects the distribution of perceptual/central processing resources among concurrently performed tasks.

In our initial description of capacity models, we discussed the difficulty of assessing the allocation of capacity within a single task. This difficulty arises because in the single-task conditions there is no measure of secondary-task performance from which to infer the allocation of resources to a primary task. The problem can be illustrated with the following example. Assume that two different air traffic controllers are monitoring their respective displays for aircraft traffic. One of the controllers has 15 years of experience while the other controller has just completed his fifth year. Furthermore, assume that under normal conditions it is impossible to distinguish between the two controllers on the basis of their handling of the aircraft. However, once the airspace becomes crowded the senior controller is able to cope adequately with the additional processing load while the junior controller must request assistance. This simple example illustrates the distinction between performance and workload. Capacity theorists would argue that while the performance of the controllers was equivalent in the low-load situation, the senior controller possessed more residual capacity that enabled her to handle additional aircraft in the crowded sky situation. An important question is whether physiological measures might provide insight into the residual resources available to individuals during single-task performance.

Given that P300 provides a measure of resource allocation in dual-task situations, it would appear to be a good candidate measure of single-task resource demands. Ullsperger, Metz and Gille (1988) investigated whether P300 would reflect processing demands in a single task by instructing subjects to detect omitted digits in a train of randomly ordered digits varying in number. The ordering of difficulty, as validated by measures of reaction time and subjective effort, increased with the number of digits presented in the display. P300 amplitude tracked the changes in difficulty. The amplitude of the P300 increased with increasing task difficulty. Horst *et al.* (1984) also found increases in a late positive component of the ERP with increases in the number of gauges that subjects were instructed to monitor (see also Sirevaag *et al.*, 1988). Thus, the empirical evidence suggests that P300 provides a sensitive measure of resource allocation in both single- and multitask situations.

Thus far we have confined our discussion of physiological metrics of resource allocation to two different components of the ERP: the early negativities (i.e. N100) and the P300. There is, however, some evidence to suggest that other ERP components may also be sensitive to variations in capacity in single- and dual-task conditions. For example, McCallum, Cooper and Pocock (1987) found that a slow negative wave distinguished between levels of tracking difficulty. This negative-going wave was detected only with DC amplifiers and extended over most of a 20 s tracking period. In a series of simulated flight maneuvers, Lindholm *et al.* (1984) found that the amplitude of the N200 component discriminated between different levels of single and dual task demands. Finally, Horst *et al.* (1987) observed an increase in negativity with increasing monitoring demands. This increased negativity occurred at both 200–300 ms and 400–500 ms following the presentation of a bank of gauges. While the results of these studies are potentially important, additional research will be necessary to determine the sensitivity and diagnosticity of these components to varieties of capacity.

In addition to ERPs, several other CNS measures have been associated with processing demands and capacity. For example, Berger (1929) was one of the first investigators to observe changes in the frequency spectra of EEGs with variations in mental load. These changes have generally taken the form of decreases in alpha and increases in beta with more difficult mental processing (Gale and Edwards, 1983). Decreases in theta power with increased task difficulty has also been observed in both single- and dual-task conditions (Lang *et al.*, 1987; Natani and Gomer, 1981). In general, it appears that while changes in EEG spectra may provide an index of general processing capacity they are not selectively sensitive to changes in the demands for different varieties of capacity. However, more diagnostic information may be available in the dynamic changes in EEG spectra across time and scalp sites than has been obtained from traditional frequency decomposition techniques (Gevins *et al.*, 1979, 1987).

Another class of techniques that offers the potential to provide insights into capacity changes during human information processing includes the measurement of cerebral blood flow and the metabolic activity of the brain. As we have noted these techniques do not permit a precise temporal analysis of the changes in brain function that accompany cognitive processing. However, they do provide a much finer spatial resolution than electrical measures.

A number of recent studies have obtained systematic relationships between measures of blood flow and task complexity in single- and dual-task settings (Gur *et al.*, 1988; Phelps and Mazziotta, 1985). In one such study, Risberg and Prohovnik (1983) instructed subjects to view a stationary spiral, view a rotating spiral, or perform a spatial after-effects test. Average cerebral blood-flow increases in these conditions compared with a resting baseline were 5%, 7% and 12%, respectively. Furthermore, the conditions were also distinguished on the basis of increases in blood flow in different brain regions.

A clever use of measures of cerebral blood flow and Donder's subtractive logic has been reported by Posner *et al.* (1988). In their study subjects participated in a number of different conditions including: fixating a central marker, passively viewing visually presented words, repeating visually presented words, generating uses of words, and monitoring for words from specific semantic categories. Blood flow maps were obtained for each of the conditions. Assuming that each of the conditions required different forms of processing, the authors performed a number of subtractions to isolate the brain regions that were active during simple word reading. For instance, it was suggested that the processes of semantic association and attention could be isolated by subtracting the map obtained in the repeat word condition from the map obtained in the generate word use condition. While the Posner *et al.* (1988) study does not address capacity issues *per se*, the joint use of cerebral blood-flow measures and subtractive logic might prove useful in examining the type and magnitude of resources utilized during single- and dual-task performance.

BEYOND CAPACITY: THE OBJECT FILE MODEL OF ATTENTION

Earlier, under 'Capacity Revisited: A Few Caveats', we discussed a number of modifications and challenges to the concept of capacity in human information processing. One important modification has been suggested by Kahneman and colleagues in their 'object file' model of attention (Kahneman and Henik, 1981; Kahneman and Treisman, 1984; Kahneman, Treisman and Burkell, 1983; also see Duncan, 1984). The object file model underscores the importance of objects in the control of attention by suggesting that attentional competition arises between, not within, objects. This proposal implies that tasks requiring the processing of different dimensions of the same object will be processed within the same resource framework. Thus, the degree to which two separate tasks can be integrated into a single object will presumably determine the resource competition between the tasks.

Capacity models suggest that performance decrements in dual-task situations depend on the overlap in the resource demands of two tasks. Tasks that require the same type of resources will be more poorly timeshared than tasks that require different resources. The object file model suggests that the magnitude of the dual-task decrement can be influenced by the configuration of the displays. Assuming that the two tasks do not require incompatible responses, the object file model would predict that dual-task performance can be enhanced by integrating the tasks into a single object. Thus, when viewed together, capacity and object file models suggest that dual-task performance is influenced by both the types of resources required by the tasks and the configuration of the task-related displays.

The predictions of the object file model were tested by Kramer, Wickens and Donchin (1985). Subjects were required to perform concurrently two tasks: a pursuit step tracking task and a visual discrimination task. In different conditions subjects performed the tasks with (a) two different objects, or (b) two different dimensions (i.e. spatial position and brightness) of a single object. ERPs were elicited by events in both tasks. Consistent with the predictions of the object file model, measures of root-mean-square (RMS) tracking error and reaction time to the visual probes indicated that performance was superior when a single object was employed.

In the different object conditions, P300 amplitude showed a reciprocity effect compatible with a tradeoff in resources between the tasks. P300s elicited in the tracking task increased in amplitude with increases in tracking difficulty while P300s elicited by events in the visual discrimination task decreased with increases in tracking difficulty. However, in the same object conditions, P300s in both the tracking and visual discrimination tasks increased in amplitude with increases in tracking difficulty. These changes in P300 amplitude are consistent with the resource allocation policy predicted by the object file model; attentional competition arises between, not within, objects (Kahneman and Henik, 1981).

This study illustrates how the joint use of performance and physiological measures can provide insights into cognitive processes that are unavailable to either measure when used alone. While measures of RMS tracking error and reaction time established the performance superiority for the single-object condition, an analysis of the pattern of P300s was required to document changes in the resource allocation policy in the two conditions.

LEARNING AND AUTOMATICITY

A number of theories of skill acquisition associate the development of highly skilled behaviors with a diminished requirement for processing resources (Crossman, 1959; LaBerge, 1973; Schneider and Detweiler, 1988). Within Norman and Bobrow's (1975) PRF, performance transitions were from resource-limited to data-limited with practice. Thus, the failure to find performance tradeoffs in a POC space can be due to at least two different factors. First, the two tasks could require different types of resources. In this case, the release of resources from one task could not be used to improve performance in the other task. Second, the tasks could be sufficiently well learned so that they both possess large data-limited regions. In this situation, only a small quantity of resources may be required for the performance of the tasks, with the result that timesharing performance would be unaffected by changes in processing priority.

Given that CNS measures have been shown to be sensitive to the allocation of resources within and between tasks, it would be expected that these measures should reflect the changing resource demands during learning. Such effects have been obtained for a number of CNS measures. For instance, P300 amplitude has been found to increase during practice in a variety of tasks such as probability learning (Johnston and Holcomb, 1981), paired-associate learning (Peters, Billinger and Knott, 1977), pattern discrimination (Poon *et al.*, 1974) and maze learning (Roth *et al.*, 1987). Interestingly, P300s have also been found to decrease in amplitude for irrelevant stimulus attributes during learning and with increased practice once a task has become well learned (Mantysalo and Gaillard, 1986; Poon *et al.*, 1974; Rosler, 1981).

The results of these studies can be interpreted within a resource framework. During practice it would be predicted that subjects learn to allocate their resources to the important aspects of the tasks, thereby reducing the resources that they dedicate to extraneous events. Once the task is well learned a portion of the resources could again be reallocated, in this case to the performance of other functions or tasks. This prediction implies that in a dual-task situation resources could be increasingly reallocated from a primary to a secondary task with practice.

Kramer, Wickens and Donchin (1983) examined the effects of practice on resource allocation in a dual-task paradigm (see also Natani and Gomer, 1981). Subjects concurrently performed two different tasks throughout training. The primary task required subjects to track a spinning target in two-dimensional space. Once the subjects locked-on to the target they began to rotate their cursor at the same velocity and the same orientation as the target. The trial ended when the target and cursor were matched in x and y positions, orientation direction, and orientation velocity. Difficulty was manipulated by varying the control dynamics in the target acquisition task. The secondary task required the discrimination between two tones of different frequency.

Early in training there was a large performance difference between the first- and second-order versions of the target acquisition task. This difference was also reflected in the amplitude of the P300s elicited by the secondary task. P300s decreased in amplitude with increases in the difficulty of the primary task. Thus, it appeared that the P300s were reflecting the residual resources remaining for the performance of the secondary task. After a significant amount of training, the P300s elicited in the first- and second-order versions of the dual tasks no longer discriminated between conditions. The P300s in the more difficult task combination were now the same size as the P300s elicited in the easy dual-task condition. Such a pattern of results appears to be consistent with the predictions of resource models: with training, more resources should be available for secondary-task performance. Thus, the equivalent-amplitude P300s could be taken as evidence that both versions of the target acquisition task required the same quantity of resources.

However, there was an interesting twist to the story. Even after substantial practice, performance measures still distinguished between the two versions of the target acquisition task. Root mean tracking error was higher in the second-order condition. Why, then, did P300 fail to reflect this difference? One possibility was that the P300 was less sensitive than the performance measures. Thus, although P300 might provide a sensitive measure of resource demands at low and intermediate levels, it might saturate when demands are high. However, this possibility seems unlikely given the substantial literature on the sensitivity of P300 to a wide range of processing demands (Donchin, Kramer and Wickens, 1986; Kramer, 1987).

A second reason for the dissociation of P300 and performance measures relates to the structure of processing resources. It is possible that the second-order control may still demand greater resources than first-order control after practice but the resources may not be of the perceptual/central variety indexed by P300. An analysis of subjects' tracking strategies suggested that this was the case. Subjects shifted from smooth pursuit tracking early in training to a double impulse strategy later in training. The double impulse strategy is characterized by a few rapid movements that places the cursor on the target trajectory thereby diminishing the need for the perceptual/anticipatory processing indexed by P300 (Sheridan and Ferrell, 1974). Thus, P300 in conjunction with performance measures provided insights into the resource costs of strategic shifts with practice that could not be gleaned from either of the measures used in isolation.

A number of studies have employed CNS measures to examine the degree to which resources are utilized during automatic processing (Hoffman, Nelson and Houck, 1983; Kramer *et al.*, 1986; van Dellen *et al.*, 1984). In one such study, Hoffman *et al.* (1985) examined the tradeoffs in P300 amplitude in a dual-task paradigm as subjects shifted their priorities between two well-practiced tasks. The tasks were a consistently mapped memory search task and a dot detection task. The processing priority was manipulated by instructing subjects to emphasize one or the other task or treat them equally. P300 amplitude and performance measures showed a tradeoff as a function of processing priority, suggesting that with this particular task combination resources were employed during automatic processing.

It is interesting to note that in the Hoffman *et al.* study two different criteria were used to ensure that automatic processing was occurring: a non-significant memory search slope and the intrusion of the CM target into dot detection performance. However, one additional criterion, perfect timesharing, was not attained prior to examining the resource costs of automatic processing. Given that automatic processing varies in magnitude as a function of practice and that perfect timesharing indicates a greater degree of automaticity than the reduced slope and intrusion criteria, it might be expected that P300 tradeoffs will not occur when all three criteria have been achieved.

Strayer and Kramer (1990) examined the resource costs of automatic processing in a paradigm in which all three criteria were met. Subjects performed a consistently mapped memory search task concurrently with a running memory task. Neither processing priority nor memory load had a significant effect on performance. Therefore, on the basis of performance measures it appeared that resources were not necessary for automatic processing. However, the P300 data tell a different story. As predicted, P300 tradeoffs did not occur in this paradigm. On the other hand, P300s were large and of uniform size in all dual-task conditions. Given that P300s reflect resource allocation it might seem paradoxical that large P300s were obtained during automatic processing. However, while it has been asserted that automatic processing is not effortful, it has also been suggested that: 'Any process that always uses general resources and decreases general processing capacity whenever a given set of external initiating stimuli are presented, regardless of the subject's attempt to ignore or bypass the distinction, is automatic' (Shiffrin and Dumais, 1981; pp. 116–117). This mandatory activation or call for resources has been referred to as the ***automatic attention response*** (AAR).

Strayer and Kramer (1990) obtained additional evidence for the AAR by examining the 100/0 dual-task condition. In this condition, subjects were to perform only the running memory task and ignore the memory search stimuli. Thus, responses were not required for the memory search task. However, the P300s elicited by the target stimuli from the memory search task were significantly larger than the P300s elicited by other 'ignore' stimuli. Thus, it appears that P300 reflected the automatic call for attention by the well-practiced target stimuli even when they were irrelevant.

While the P300 component of the ERP has been the most extensively investigated metric of resource allocation strategies during learning, other measures have also been examined. A number of studies have reported decreases in the CNV component of the ERP with practice in paired associate and pattern recognition tasks (Donald, 1980; Peters, Billinger and Knott, 1977; Poon *et al.*, 1974). Rosler (1981) found that the P160 component of the ERP decreased with learning for both relevant and irrelevant stimulus attributes in a paired associate task. However, the decrease was larger for the irrelevant than the relevant attributes. Finally, a number of EEG studies have reported decreases in power in the theta band during learning in both single and dual tasks (Lang *et al.*, 1987; Natani and Gomer, 1981).

MENTAL WORKLOAD ASSESSMENT

The research reviewed thus far suggests that CNS measures have provided important insights into a number of theoretical and methodological issues relevant to capacity views of human information processing. However, in addition to providing a theoretical structure for information processing, capacity models have also served as a framework for application, particularly in the domain of mental workload assessment. The concept of mental workload has been defined in terms of the 'costs' incurred by a human operator as tasks are performed (Wickens and Kramer, 1985). In turn, these mental costs have been described in terms of resources or capacities (Freidman and Polson, 1981; Sanders, 1979; Wickens, 1980).

Although the resources expended during task performance cannot be directly observed, measurement techniques have been developed that enable investigators and practitioners to infer the processing demands imposed upon human operators. For instance, the secondary-task technique assumes that fluctuations in primary-task demands will be reflected in secondary-task performance. CNS measures such as the P300 component of the ERP have been used to augment secondary-task measures in the assessment of primary-task demands (Kramer, Wickens and Donchin, 1983, 1985).

While the secondary task techniques are useful in the laboratory environment, the imposition of an additional task is often unacceptable in operational settings. An alternative technique is to elicit ERPs from events in the primary task. As previously described, early negativities and the P300 component show a systematic relationship to processing demands in both single- and dual-task conditions. Thus, although performance measures alone are insufficient for the measurement of mental workload in single tasks the joint use of psychophysiological and performance measures provides an index of resource allocation.

The irrelevant probe technique has also been proposed in an effort to eliminate the additional processing demands imposed on the operator by secondary-task measures (Bauer, Goldstein and Stern, 1987; Papanicolaou and Johnstone, 1984). In this technique, irrelevant auditory or visual probes are occasionally superimposed on the subject's task. However, unlike the secondary-task technique subjects are not required to respond to the probes. In spite of this difference the theoretical assumptions underlying the secondary-task and irrelevant-probe techniques are quite similar. It is assumed that the size of the P300s elicited by the irrelevant probes will be inversely proportional to the difficulty of the subject's task. Thus, variations in the amplitude of the P300 is taken as evidence of changes in resource demands.

Although the irrelevant probe technique eliminates the problem of additional demands that are associated with the secondary-task measures, it does suffer from other problems. In particular, it is necessary to assume that, as in the secondary-task technique, residual resources that are not used in the 'primary' task are devoted to the processing of the irrelevant probes. However, unlike the secondary-task method, there are no performance data to corroborate this assumption. Thus, while subjects could devote additional processing capacity to the irrelevant probes, it is equally plausible that they either do not use the excess capacity or that they devote it to other functions (e.g. planning dinner).

The workload assessment techniques that utilize ERPs require the presence of discrete events; either within the primary task, within a secondary task, or presented as extraneous probes. However, many operational settings possess few such events (e.g. monitoring a continuously changing process). An alternative in these situations is to record CNS measures that do not require the occurrence of discrete stimuli and responses. EEG has served such a function in the assessment of mental workload (Wierwille, 1979). However, while EEG measures enable the investigator to evaluate workload in continuous tasks, they do not allow for the temporal precision or diagnosticity available with ERPs.

While we have described a number of psychophysiologically based methods that can be used in the measurement of mental workload, we have yet to indicate how these techniques fare in extra-laboratory environments. In fact, CNS measures have been employed in operational settings since the early 1960s. Sem-Jacobsen and Sem-Jacobsen (1963) described a series of studies in which EEG was used to assess pilots' tolerance for high-G maneuvers. More recently, a number of studies have examined the utility of ERP-based workload metrics in high-fidelity aircraft simulators (Natani and Gomer, 1981; Lindholm *et al.*, 1984). Kramer, Wickens and Donchin (1987) found that P300s elicited by secondary-task probe stimuli discriminated among flights differing in the degree of turbulence and the presence of subsystem failures.

In addition to offline assessments of mental workload, several investigators have suggested that physiological measures might be useful in online evaluations of the moment-to-moment fluctuations in operator state and processing demands (Defayolle, Dinand and Gentil, 1971; Gomer, 1981; Groll-Knapp, 1971; Sem-Jacobsen, 1981). While research in this area is still in its infancy, a few recent studies suggest that online assessment might be feasible, at least in restricted settings.

For instance, Farwell and Donchin (1988) demonstrated that ERPs can be used to communicate selections from a 6 × 6 menu. In their task subjects were instructed to attend to one item from a 6 × 6 matrix of items. The rows and columns of the matrix flashed randomly and the ERPs elicited by the flashes were used to discriminate attended from unattended items. A communication accuracy of 95% was achieved with 26 s of data. Kramer *et al.* (1989) found that variations in mental workload can also be discriminated with a high degree of accuracy with a relatively small amount of ERP data. Subjects were required to perform two tasks, monitoring and mental arithmetic, both separately and together. Differences in workload among experimental conditions was indexed by secondary-task and subjective measures. Discriminations between easy and difficult versions of the dual-task conditions were achieved with greater than 90% accuracy with less than 30 s of ERP data.

AUTONOMIC MEASURES

JOHN SPINKS AND ARTHUR KRAMER

This section will survey psychophysiological studies which have investigated aspects of capacity using autonomic indices, complemented in many cases by concurrent behavioral measurement. In some of the studies in this area, the physiological measures have been taken to help elucidate the nature and extent of capacity allocation, while, in other cases, behavioral measures (e.g. probe RT) have been used to illuminate the capacity changes that take place during a process of interest to psychophysiologists (e.g. electrodermal conditioning, orienting). The section will also cover, in more detail, some recent studies by one of the present authors (JAS) which examine the relationships among physiological measures, capacity and resource allocation.

Perhaps the most interesting theoretical exposition linking capacity with autonomic indices was that of Kahneman (1973). In this treatise, Kahneman presented a theory of information processing based on a framework of motivational, attentional and arousal factors. According to this theory, as information processing demands of a task increase, subjects increase the mental effort they invest in the task. This mental effort is equated with information processing capacity.

Because there is an upper limit to the available capacity, the difference between the capacity required by the task and the capacity supplied to deal with it increases as the task becomes more difficult. However, Kahneman also suggested that the total amount of capacity available increases with effort, again, of course, only up until some asympototic level. These relationships are more easily seen in Figure 2.3. As can also be seen, the spare capacity decreases as task demands rise, despite the increases in total capacity.

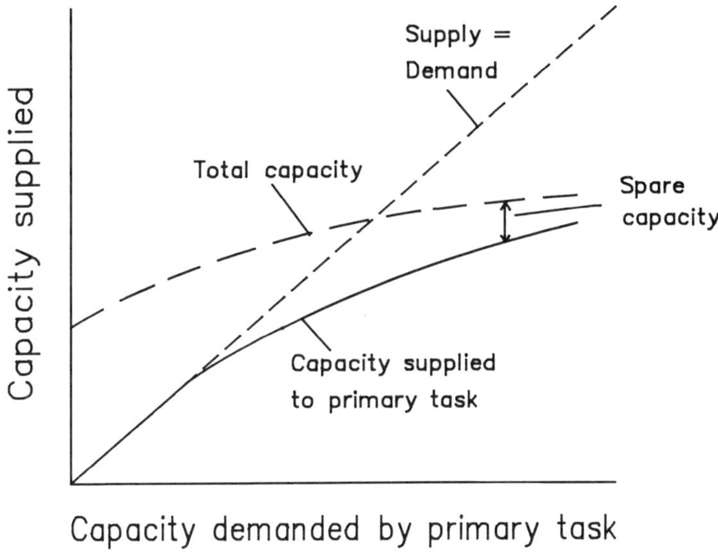

Figure 2.3. The hypothesized relationship between capacity supply and demand. (Redrawn from Kahneman (1973) with permission. © Prentice-Hall.)

The specific relevance of this theory to the present chapter is that Kahneman suggested that the effort invested in a task, and therefore the capacity available for task processing, is indexed by physiological measures of arousal (Figure 2.4). It should be noted that effort and capacity are determined by the subject's evaluation of the demands of the task; arousal, however, is determined by both these internal demands and other miscellaneous factors, such as motivational or drug influences. Since this view provides a very strong link between the autonomic nervous system and information processing capacity, we will review, in the sections that immediately follow, concepts intimately related to capacity using Kahneman's theory as the basis for much of the discussion. We will see how autonomic measures have been used to help in the formulation of views concerning concepts of capacity and resource allocation, and we will look at some of the problems which have resulted from these studies. We will also discuss the theoretical issues that have been illuminated by the studies.

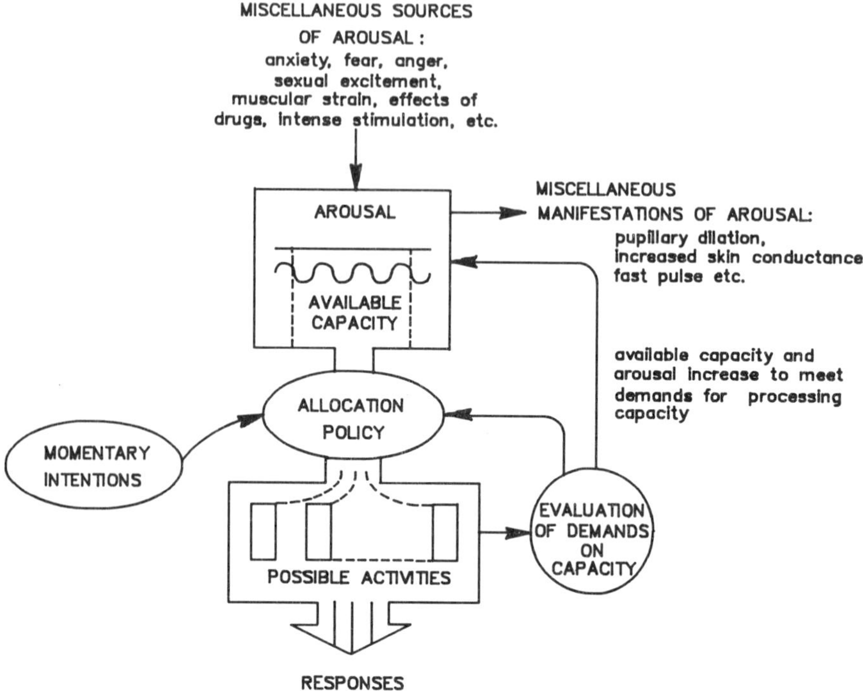

Figure 2.4. Kahneman's model of effort, attention and arousal. (Redrawn from Kahneman (1973) with permission. © Prentice-Hall.)

ATTENTION AND AROUSAL

The proposed relationship between capacity and attention derives from a number of sources in addition to Kahneman's work. Some have been mentioned at the beginning of this chapter (e.g. Johnston and Heinz, 1978). There are a number of theorists who view the processing of material in a limited-capacity channel as equivalent to being aware of such processing. The automatic attention response (Shiffrin and Schneider, 1977) also suggests a close link between the capacity required for controlled processing and the direction of attention. Öhman's (1979) information-processing model identifies reflexive and voluntary attention with a call for processing capacity. The role of the orienting response (OR), and its measurable indices, is the subject of some discussion later in this chapter (see also Spinks and Siddle, 1983, and Chapter 3 of this volume). Let us first return, however, to Kahneman's conception.

Physiological arousal is an important component of Kahneman's (1973) theory of information processing, in part because it can be easily and objectively measured. Kahneman has thus reviewed a considerable amount of literature on psychophysiological indices of arousal and effort. As has been described above, his theory suggests that an increase in processing load leads to a rise in arousal, and, concomitantly, an increase in the capacity available for processing the extra workload. Within limits, this capacity and the resultant resources are thus matched to the demands imposed on the organism.

There are, of course, many psychophysiological indices of different types of arousal, with skin conductance level, a number of non-specific electrodermal fluctuations, T-wave amplitude, heart rate variability, peripheral vasoconstriction, pupil dilation, eye blinks and eye movements each having at least empirical justification for their use. It is now generally accepted that arousal is, like attention, not a unitary concept. The concept can be traced to its physiological basis, and the term is restricted to this usage in Pribram and McGuinness' (1973) and, to a lesser extent, Kahneman's (1973) theories discussed elsewhere in this chapter. In some circles, however, it has assumed a more cognitive, or, occasionally, behavioral orientation.

With this broadened perspective, in particular, it is hardly surprising that some subcomponents may be relatively independent of other subcomponents. The seminal paper here is that of Lacey (1967), mentioned above, in which it was argued that autonomic, central and behavioral measures could be dissociated under a variety of conditions (e.g. by certain drugs). Differentiation of threat-oriented and task-oriented arousal has been discussed by Edelberg (1972). Kahneman summarizes this area by distinguishing two or three states of heightened arousal, a state of motor inhibition coupled with expectant alertness, a pattern of sympathetic dominance accompanying physical or mental effort, and, possibly, a state of relaxed acceptance of external stimulation. More will be said of this differentiation within the concept of arousal later in this section.

Perhaps the most well-known relevant literature that relates attention to a particular form of psychophysiological response is the Lacey hypothesis. In the Laceys' intake-rejection hypothesis, heart rate (HR) deceleration is seen as an index of attention to environmental events and HR acceleration as an index of attention to mental processing (Lacey, 1967). The HR response is seen by the Laceys as being functionally significant in altering sensory sensitivity. This position has received a respectable amount of academic scrutiny, with the most influential criticism stemming from papers by Obrist (e.g. Obrist *et al.*, 1970) suggesting that HR deceleration is merely a consequence of the general motor inhibition that accompanies attention to external stimuli. The interested reader should also consult Graham and Clifton (1966) and Bohlin and Kjellberg (1979) for reviews of the relationship between HR changes, orienting and attention.

A plethora of studies in addition to those just noted have linked the concepts of attention to autonomic measures. The plural of 'concept' is purposely used here, because of the multidimensional or multipartite nature of what is currently subsumed under the term 'attention'. The breadth of the concept of attention suggests that it would not be sensible at this level to employ the term as an explanatory concept in studying the relationship between autonomic indices and capacity, and we will therefore go no further than the introductory remarks made above. However, it is possible for readers to reinterpret many of the areas reviewed below as providing evidence for links between psychophysiological indices and attention.

EFFORT, COGNITIVE LOAD AND WORKLOAD

Since Kahneman has suggested that exerting mental effort and investing capacity in the processing of a stimulus are, as far as can be ascertained, the same processes, it is pertinent to comment on the effort literature. Early work suggested a variety of indices of effort. Benson, Huddlestone and Rolfe (1965) employed HR, EMG, electrodermal and respiratory measures as indices of the effort allocated to a task. Corcoran (1964) argued specifically that such indices reflected effort rather than arousal. Subjective reports of 'effort' have been shown to be significantly related to HR changes and level (e.g. Vicente, Thornton and Moray, 1987).

However, Janisse and Kuc (1977) argued that pupil dilation is more sensitive to cognitive variables than is HR. The pupil dilation literature has been reviewed by Goldwater (1972) and Kahneman (1973) who noted that it covaried with cognitive load under a wide variety of circumstances (arithmetic tasks, memory load, perceptual discrimination, learning, problem solving, imagery, motor activity). As was pointed out above, Kahneman's (1973) theory suggested that mental effort, or capacity, could be inferred from autonomic measures of arousal. However, he noted that these measures were also determined, in part, by extraneous variables (such as drug or motivational states). In a search for indices of arousal minimally affected by the latter, Kahneman (1973) suggested that pupil dilation was the most appropriate, being sensitive to cognitive load and to task difficulty across tasks, and to the subject's moment-to-moment involvement within a task.

In studies (Kahneman, 1973) somewhat akin to the dual-task paradigm (e.g. Posner and Boies, 1971), pupil dilation changes closely paralleled the efficiency of processing in a discrete, secondary, perceptual task that was assumed to tap spare capacity. According to Kahneman, the two were closely related because they both measure effort, or capacity allocated. Although Kahneman claimed this finding could not be attributed to muscle activity, it is possible that such activity increases with increased attention (Berdina *et al.*, 1972; Wilkinson, 1962; but see also Eason and Banks, 1963) perhaps giving rise, in part at least, to the increase in physiological arousal (see also Pribram and McGuinness, 1975).

Kahneman's conclusion is that effort, as a concomitant of capacity available or allocated, is best reflected in either pupil dilation or skin conductance (e.g. Kahneman *et al.*, 1969). Certainly, there is evidence (Coles, 1972) that tonic HR is lower and cardiac deceleration is greater during high-, compared with low-discriminability tasks. As Coles pointed out, however, these findings are more in accordance with the Laceys' position outlined earlier, than with a hypothesis that such variables reflect undifferentiated cognitive effort. We will return to the issue of specificity of concepts, particularly those of arousal and capacity, later in this chapter.

Two concepts related to effort are cognitive load and workload. As might be expected from the above, cognitive load has been used to explain changes in pupil dilation (e.g. Beatty, 1982), heart rate (e.g. Boyce, 1974) and sinus arrhythmia (e.g. Firth, 1973). The interested reader is directed to Moray's (1979) review of this field.

One physiological measure that has received considerable attention in connection with mental effort or workload is that of sinus arrhythmia (SA) or heart rate variability (HRV) (Corlett, 1973; Firth, 1973; Sayers, 1973; Zwaga, 1973). There is evidence from a number of studies (e.g. Kalsbeek and Sykes, 1976; Porges, 1972) that decreases in SA accompany increases in processing rates. Kalsbeek and Sykes (1976) reported respectable correlations between channel capacity (calculated using dual-task behavioral measures) and SA scores when the degree of subject effort or motivation was allowed to vary. The measure appears to be more sensitive to the total processing demand imposed upon the system than the amount of resource competition, or dual-task decrement (Wickens, 1984b).

Other studies (Aasman, Mulder, and Mulder, 1987; Sayers, 1973; Vicente *et al.*, 1987) have shown that effort, assumed to be a function of the total amount of controlled processing (but measured in the latter study on a subjective rating scale) was accurately indexed by a spectral analysis of HRV, using power in the 0.06 Hz to 0.14 Hz band. This frequency band carries variation due primarily to mechanisms regulating arterial pressure, in contrast to bands of higher frequencies reflecting the influence of respiratory activity (Sayers, 1971; see Mulder, 1979b, for a physiological model). In this regard, the term HRV is preferred to the term SA, which suggests respiratory covariability. Aasman *et al.*, following up earlier studies by Mulder showing a strong relationship between the amplitude of the 0.1 Hz band and memory load, found that, additionally, the HRV was only sensitive to changes in the use of resource-limited (effortful) operations, but not to those involving data-limited operations (e.g. degraded display), a necessary feature of any metric of capacity or resource utilization (cf. task difficulty). The extent to which the reduction in HRV with effort may be just one example of what is a general effect of a reduction in autonomic variability with increased capacity remains to be seen.

As capacity limitations are exceeded, there must be a resultant increase in performance errors on the task. The 0.1 Hz HRV component is markedly reduced at this time (Sayers, 1975), while there is a leveling out, or drop, in pupillary dilation (Peavler, 1974; Poock, 1973). One interpretation of this pupil dilation data suggests that processing activities may be suspended. However, given the apparent asymptote in the data, another interpretation suggests that it indexes capacity availability or capacity employed on the task (cf. Figure 2.3). The HRV data, on the other hand, seem to fit a mental effort or perceived workload concept somewhat better.

Mulder and colleagues have argued that mental workload should be explicitly distinguished from mental effort. The former should refer to the stimulus characteristics, such as memory set-size or stimulus discriminability (in which case the hypothetical construct could perhaps be dropped altogether in favour of a description of task parameters), whereas the latter should be related to the subject's cognitive response in terms of the amount of capacity devoted to cope with the task demands. The research cited above suggests that the 0.1 Hz component of HRV is a sensitive index of mental effort, or, at low to medium levels of effort at least, of the amount of controlled processing invested in a task. On the other hand, some authors have argued that mean HR scores are more sensitive than SA scores to varying informational load (Sharit and Salvendy, 1982). More recently, Mulder (1986) has distinguished between two types of effort. The first relates to task difficulty or processing complexity and is indexed by pupil dilation or HRV. If the comments above concerning the differentiation of HRV and pupil dilation are accepted, then this first type of effort can be further subdivided. The other type of effort discussed by Mulder is related to subjects' efforts to arouse themselves to a state capable of complex processing, indexed by muscular activity (Wilkinson, 1962) or beta-adrenergically mediated cardiovascular changes, such as pulse transit time or pre-ejection period (Light and Obrist, 1983). These two types of effort may be seen to be rather similar to Kahneman's distinction between task-driven arousal and miscellaneous sources of arousal (see Figure 2.4).

The other component of the cardiovascular system that has been linked to mental effort is T-wave amplitude (TWA). Part of the rationale behind the use of this measure is that it is a measure of sympathetic influence, although the physiological mechanisms involved in this linkage are not clear at present. The sympathetic influence is, in turn, assumed to be an important component of mental effort. Furedy (1987) has recently reviewed a number of studies in this area by Furedy, Heslegrave and others, in which support is found for a relationship between mental effort and TWA. Although the research in this area is at a more exploratory stage than is the case for HR changes, TWA could, arguably, have a greater potential. Joint use of heart rate and T-wave amplitude measures may make it possible to independently analyze sympathetic and parasympathetic activity. Given the rather non-specific nature of autonomic nervous system responses as indices of cognitive processes (the HRV work described above being a notable exception), this development (which is not limited strictly to just TWA) would be highly desirable.

TASK DIFFICULTY

Much of the literature reviewed above can be related to the dimension of task difficulty, higher levels of which would initiate, within limits, an increase in arousal or the pool of processing resources, according to Kahneman. The HR literature reveals evidence for a direct relationship between HR acceleration and task difficulty (e.g. Kahneman *et al.*, 1969) and between HR deceleration and task difficulty (e.g. Duncan-Johnson and Coles, 1974), depending upon the nature of information processing required in the task. This, of course, would be expected if the direction of attention is important in determining the nature of HR responses (Lacey, 1967). Skin conductance responses (SCRs) (e.g. Kaiser and Sandman, 1975) and pupil dilation (e.g. Kahneman *et al.*, 1969) have both been shown to be consistently related to task difficulty, as well as to task complexity. However, as Kahneman (1973) noted, task difficulty and task complexity are not always correlated with effort. An apparently easy task, choice reaction time, may involve complex processing that may evoke a large pupillary dilation relative to an apparently difficult associative learning task.

MEMORY TASKS

The workload/heart rate relationship has also been examined within the field of memory research, although the concept of workload itself has to be modified slightly within this context. One of the most impressive papers here was a study by Jennings, Lawrence and Kasper (1979). This was one of the first studies to use probe RT and autonomic measures within the same paradigm, predating the important work on orienting and conditioning discussed below. Jennings *et al.* showed that, in a serial learning task, subjective reports of mental effort were not correlated with either RT or HR measures. Of more interest, however, was the significant slowing of probe RT at the time of occurrence of the to-be-learnt items, particularly when subjects were trying to recall (anticipate) the items. Across time within trials, and across conditions, the HR was generally higher as probe RT increased. These authors suggested that HR change indexed the availability of capacity for perceptual processing—an increase reflected unavailability, since the central channel was occupied, a decrease reflected available capacity (cf. the Laceys' hypotheses). There were interesting relationships with learning and performance, probe RTs being slowed during correct recall (anticipation), as one might expect if this measure reflects allocation of capacity, and HR being slower during the learning phase (although not during recall) of subsequently correctly recalled items, a phase which would clearly require perceptual input. A number of these findings have been replicated in subsequent studies (Jennings and Hall, 1980; Kribbs, Shaffer and Muswick, 1984).

It might be noted that Sharit, Sálvendy and Deisenroth (1982) prefer to use the dimension of uncertainty (about future environmental events) to explain the mental workload apparently indexed by HR changes. According to a capacity view, memory load (set-size) might be expected to influence autonomic components, although there is, at most, weak support for a relationship with HR (Bauer, Goldstein and Stern, 1987; Jennings and Hall, 1980). Bauer *et al.* (1987), however, reported a significant effect of memory set size on eye blink rate, with an initial depression of blink rate for high-memory-load items, reflecting the larger perceptual load in this condition, and a subsequent elevated blink rate, interpreted as indicating an enhanced effort during rehearsal. By placing probes at different time points during cue, memory and test intervals, and measuring ERPs to these probes, Bauer *et al.* were able to obtain evidence for functionally independent processing resources being brought in and out of play as the information processing requirements changed from moment to moment. This kind of specificity is clearly more difficult to identify using measurement of autonomic responses which are typically slower to respond.

CONCEPTUAL DIFFERENTIATION

It might be useful at this point to summarize the work discussed so far in this section, by evaluating Kahneman's theory. His conceptual relationship between effort, capacity and arousal was used as the starting point for the discussion of work relating capacity to autonomic measures, and it is probably fair to say that the theory has promoted a great deal of useful research. However, the concepts used by Kahneman are very broad, to the extent that it is somewhat difficult to distinguish between arousal, effort, allocation of capacity and attention. Other authors have been critical of his theory for failing to adequately define concepts to allow for testable hypotheses (Eysenck, 1982; Pribram and McGuinness, 1975; Spinks and Siddle, 1983). Some have tried to explicitly distinguish between some of these terms on conceptual grounds.

For example, Pribram and McGuinness (1975) have argued that, while phasic physiological arousal responses (the 'arousal' system) are usually yoked to perceptual and motor readiness (the 'activation' system), these two systems can be uncoupled by an increase within an 'effort' system. Effort is then defined as a measure of attention paid to increase the competency within information processing channels, the result of which is to effectively increase the organism's capacity to deal with information (much like 'chunking' effectively increases memory capability).

Pribram and McGuinness provide neurophysiological and neuropsychological data to support this scheme. However, although the three systems are also differentiated by Pribram and McGuinness in terms of autonomic indices as well, the support for this is less than impressive. On the other hand, the autonomic research discussed so far has provided a firm basis for the further differentiation within some of Kahneman's concepts as well as between the concepts. It has been shown above that effort can be subdivided into perhaps three components, as revealed by the fractionation shown by HRV, pupil dilation and beta-adrenergically mediated cardiovascular changes. The Laceys' work, supported by a number of studies discussed above, indicates that the arousal concept should not be treated as unitary. Attention has, of course, been differentiated by many authors over the years. In another sense of differentiation, capacity is seen as primarily undifferentiated by Kahneman, in contrast to the independent resource pool theorists discussed in the Introduction (e.g. Wickens, 1980). These latter two concepts, however, owe their further development to research which is mainly outside the domain of autonomic research. Thus, a number of the key concepts within Kahneman's approach seem to suffer from serious difficulties when evaluated against the subsequent literature. More recent work also uses Kahneman's concepts, but applies them within more developed models of specific learning/performance problems. We will next turn to these in an examination of associative learning and orienting.

ASSOCIATIVE CONDITIONING

The effect of omitting an expected stimulus has been investigated in a number of studies (Siddle, 1985; Siddle and Hirschhorn, 1986; Siddle *et al.*, 1983), since it provides a well-controlled test of a number of theories of orienting and habituation. These early experiments had consistently shown that the omission of an expected stimulus in an associative conditioning paradigm, as well as the re-presentation of this omitted stimulus later, leads to enhanced SCRs. Siddle and his colleagues interpreted these results as indicating that such events command an increase in the allocation of processing resources. Siddle and Packer (1987) used a probe RT technique to support this interpretation, showing that both omission of an expected stimulus, and its later re-presentation, result in longer RTs.

Further studies (Siddle and Packer, in press) have extended these findings to show that a miscued stimulus (i.e. a stimulus S2, which followed a stimulus S1 during training, but unexpectedly followed a stimulus S3 during miscuing trials) evokes a larger SCR and retards probe RT, in comparison with a control stimulus. Much of this recent work has been based on Pearce and Hall's (1980) model of associative conditioning, in which it is argued that stimuli which are poor predictors of future events (high associability) are processed in the controlled mode, whereas good predictors demand only automatic processing. Associability is indexed by the OR (Kaye and Pearce, 1984). One of the most theoretically interesting effects (Packer and Siddle, 1989; Siddle, Broekhuisen, and Packer, 1988; Siddle and Packer, in press) was that enhanced SCR-ORs were found to S2 on the S1–S2 trial following a miscuing trial, probe RTs also being slowed at this time. This finding is not predicted by theories of associative conditioning which assume that changes in associative strength are determined by the history of CS reinforcement or non-reinforcement. In these studies, the SCR-OR seems to be consistently evoked concomitantly with a slowing of probe RTs, adding further weight to those who see the physiological response as an indication of resources or capacity allocated.

Dawson and his colleagues (Dawson *et al.*, 1982; Dawson, Schell and Munro, 1985; Filion, Dawson and Schell, 1986, 1988) have examined resource allocation within conditioning and, more recently, orienting paradigms, in a series of innovative studies. The results of the first two experiments (Dawson *et al.*, 1982) are presented in Figure 2.5. The CS+ and CS– were colored lights, and the UCS, which always followed the CS+, was an electric shock. Subjects were instructed that the primary task was to pay attention to the colored lights and shock, but that they should also depress an RT key as quickly as possible upon hearing the probe tone. The data imply that there is a

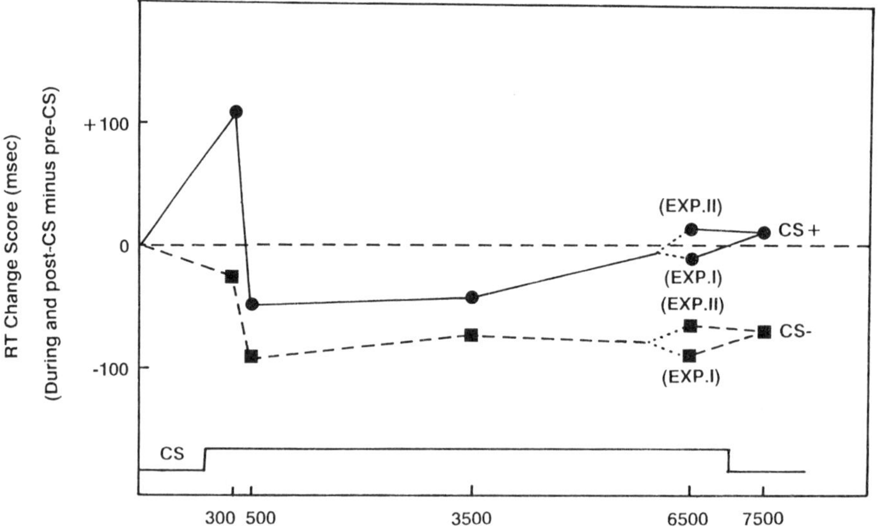

Figure 2.5. Summary of probe reaction time (RT) data from two experiments during and after presentation of conditioned stimuli CS+ and CS–. (Redrawn from Dawson *et al.* (1982) with permission. © American Psychological Association.)

differential allocation of processing resources at the time of CS+ occurrence, compared with CS– presentation, indicating that build-up of expectancy of the UCS during the conditioning process is not automatic. However, perhaps of more interest to this chapter is the finding that the resource allocation seems to differ between subjects who show large responses to the CS (first interval responses—FIRs) and those who show small responses. Processing demands as the CS is being analyzed appeared to be greater, but concentrated closer in time to CS onset, for those subjects who showed large FIRs. These subjects also showed earlier differential resource allocation as the time of UCS occurrence approached. On the basis of comparisons with ORs during the preconditioning adaptation period, Dawson *et al.* proposed that those individuals who show larger SCR-ORs during adaptation expend greater capacity allocation in the processing of environmental stimuli.

The relationship between different aspects of autonomic conditioning and capacity allocation has been reviewed in Dawson and Schell (1985). Their conclusions are generally in line with Öhman's (1979) model, autonomic CRs being elicited, it is argued, on the basis of a call for central channel resources, regardless of whether there are resources available for the call to be answered. On the basis of many studies, they conclude that the acquisition of autonomic CRs cannot occur in the absence of awareness, or central channel capacity allocation. On the other hand, performance of previously acquired CRs can take place in an automatic mode, as Öhman has argued.

ORIENTING AND CAPACITY

The orienting response (OR) is a complex of autonomic, central and behavioral components thought by early theorists (Sokolov, 1963; Graham and Hackley, this volume) to indicate attentional responses to environmental information. Both Sokolov and Berlyne (e.g. Berlyne, 1960) proposed three classes of stimulus attributes as being primary determinants of the OR. These were the physical properties of the stimulus, particularly its intensity; the signal value or significance of the stimulus; and collative properties, in particular, the conflict between expectation and actual stimulus input, as in the case of novel or unexpected stimuli. While early studies adopted an approach which placed the OR within an involuntary, reflexive class of responses, more contemporary views incorporate the OR as an integral part of an information processing system, linked closely to the concept of either selective attention, or, more often, generalized attention (alertness, arousal, or intensive attention). The OR has also been traditionally defined in terms of response decrement (habituation) across repeated presentations of a stimulus, and response recovery when a change stimulus is introduced. Kahneman's book was one of the first to examine the relationship between information processing capacity and the OR. The OR might, within this theory, reflect a transient and involuntary effort to process and analyze an alerting stimulus. There could at the same time be a reallocation of the available capacity, so that the stimulus, or whatever might be predicted to follow it, could be more intensively analyzed. Earlier theoretical positions (Sokolov 1966, 1969) could also be seen, in retrospect, to have made similar statements, but using somewhat different terms. These positions are central to this chapter, since they provide the basis for a number of psychophysiological investigations of capacity.

Siddle and Spinks (1979) similarly argued that, if the OR represented an active, alerting process that is important for the analysis of the eliciting stimulus, as suggested by Sokolov and others, then it has logically to be evoked following a preliminary analysis of this stimulus. Otherwise, the OR would be evoked to analyze a stimulus that had already been analyzed.

However, Öhman (1979) admitted to the possibility that the OR may reflect the actual activity in the central channel, as much as the call for central channel capacity, and there is certainly evidence from a number of studies from one of the present authors (JAS) that suggests that the OR is more sensitive to the actual resources allocated. Because the findings of these studies are central to the relationships between the OR, arousal, effort, and capacity allocation, they will be reviewed in more detail here.

Two studies (Spinks and Siddle, 1985; Spinks *et al.*, 1985) had shown that SCRs, evoked in the interval between a warning stimulus and a subsequent imperative stimulus which the subject had to identify, were larger when a more informationally complex imperative stimulus was expected. It was argued in these papers that the OR, at least as reflected by the SCR component, was best seen as 'part of an activational mechanism, initiated whenever extra information processing capacity is required or anticipated' (Spinks *et al.*, 1985, p.390). Later work confirmed that similar effects could be seen with the P300 response (Blowers, Spinks and Shek, 1986). More recent work (van der Molen *et al.*, 1989) has looked at preparation processes, where HR deceleration prior to stimulus occurrence is seen as indexing a mechanism that allocates processing resources to stimulus encoding, and motor preparation (see also the review by Bohlin and Kjellberg, 1979). However, Bauer, Goldstein and Stern (1987) had earlier reported that anticipated cognitive load was reflected by neither heart rate (as Spinks and Siddle, 1985) nor eye-blink rate.

In two further studies, however (Spinks, Chan and Chan, 1985; Spinks, 1987a), no support was found for the proposal that the SCR indexes a call for capacity as a result only of a preattentive analysis. In these studies, each trial consisted of two stimuli (Figure 2.6), a warning stimulus and an imperative stimulus. The imperative stimulus could be simple (one letter) or complex (six letters) and the subjects' task was to identify as many of the letters as was possible in the short time for which the stimulus was displayed. Eight seconds prior to the imperative stimulus, a warning stimulus was presented, this giving information about which of the two types of imperative stimuli would follow.

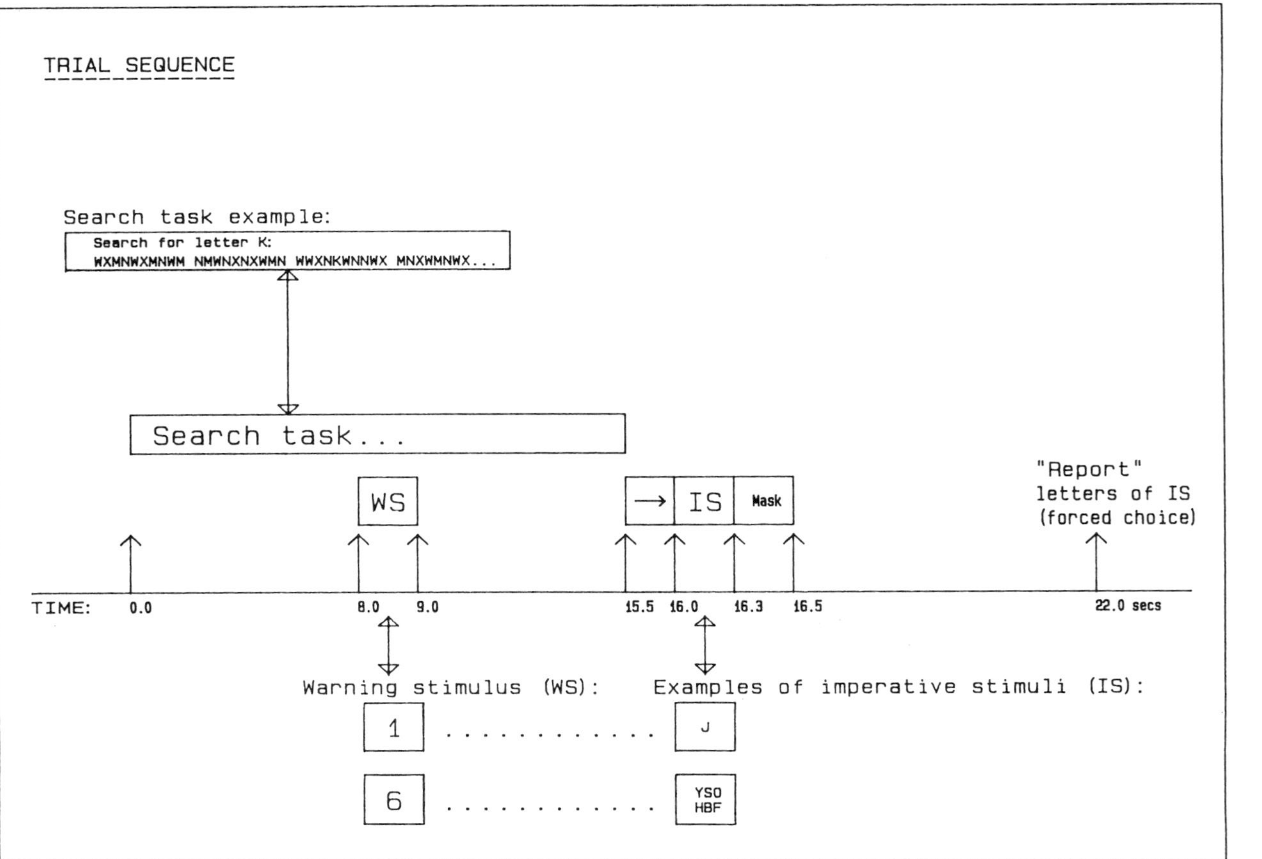

Figure 2.6. Sequence of events on each trial of the experiment. (Reprinted from Spinks (1989) with permission. © Elsevier Science Publishers B.V.)

However, at the time of presentation of this warning, and during most of the rest of the interval between warning stimulus and imperative stimulus, the subjects were engaged in another task. This was a letter search task, which could vary in difficulty, employing different amounts of information processing resources. The difficult search task condition was actually similar to the 'varied mapping' condition of Shiffrin and Schneider (1977), which was presented there to typify a task requiring controlled processing (i.e. employing limited capacity resources).

If the OR reflects the results of a preattentive process, then it should not be affected by the amount of capacity available at any moment in time, since preattentive processing is, by most definitions, automatic or capacity independent. However, the results showed that this was not the case. The SCRs evoked by the warning stimulus were larger when the warning stimulus indicated that a complex imperative stimulus was to follow, compared with when it signaled a simple imperative stimulus. But, more importantly, in both the studies, there was a significant interaction between the complexity of the warned imperative stimulus and the difficulty of the background task (the results of the first study are summarized in Table 2.1). Clearly, the data support the contention that the SCR is sensitive to the amount of processing capacity available for allocation. The SCR, according to these findings, appears to index the actual allocation of resources, rather than the 'call' for processing resources following a preattentive analysis as Öhman (1979) had suggested.

Table 2.1. Magnitude (range-corrected change in ms) of SCRs evoked by the warning stimulus.

	One letter	Six letters	Mean	p
No task	0.111	0.200	0.156	
Easy	0.092	0.121	0.107	<0.01
Difficult	0.067	0.079	0.073	
	$p<0.01$		(Interaction $p < 0.05$)	

Further work (Spinks, 1989) has confirmed that the capacity allocation during the interval between the warning stimulus and the imperative stimulus does depend on the anticipated informational content of the forthcoming imperative stimulus. Figure 2.7 shows some performance data from a similar experiment to that reported above, except that there was no background search task. On random trials, but at a time point 3 s prior to the warning stimulus (control period), or at three time points during the warning-stimulus–imperative-stimulus interval, probe stimuli were presented to which the subject had to make reaction time (RT) responses. The rationale behind this 'probe RT' method, as well as the possible limitations of the technique, have been

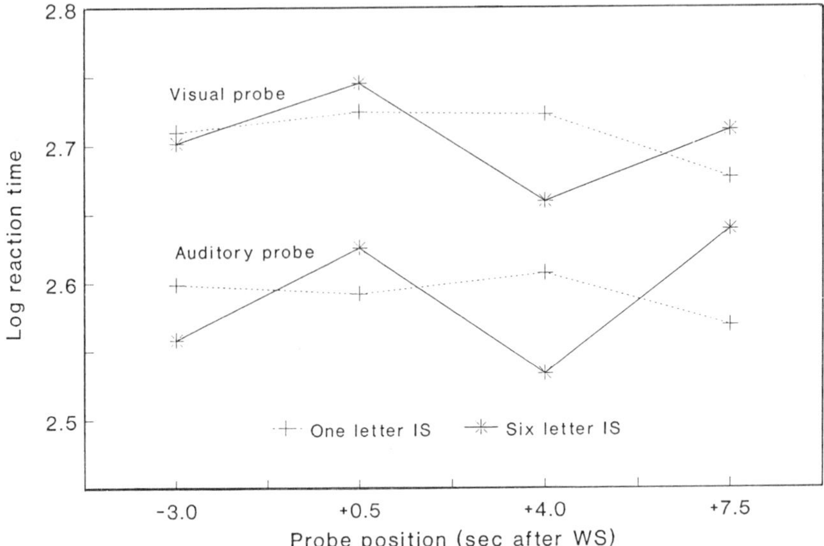

Figure 2.7. Mean reaction time to probe stimuli presented before and after the warning stimulus. (Reprinted from Spinks (1989) with permission. © Elsevier Science Publishers B.V.)

discussed above. If the rationale is accepted, then the data shown in Figure 2.7 suggest that there is little change in the availability of resources during the one-letter imperative stimulus trials. However, there are fewer resources available just prior to the complex imperative stimulus (compared with the period just prior to the simple imperative stimulus, or compared with a time earlier in this interval), presumably as subjects reallocate resources to the anticipated requirements of the more difficult identification task. A similar drop in available resources can be seen at the time of presentation of the warning itself, when the warning message is that a complex imperative stimulus will follow. The data generally support the inferences about the relationship between the OR and capacity allocation from the study previously described.

An explanation of the faster probe RT (in the six-letter condition 4 s after the warning stimulus) within a resource allocation framework would involve the concept of a generalized arousal response following this warning stimulus. According to Kahneman (1973), this would lead to an increase in the amount of capacity available to the organism, which would, in turn, be reflected by shorter probe RTs. As had been shown in earlier studies, in the period 4 s to 8 s following the warning stimulus, SCRs are larger and spontaneous electrodermal fluctuations are more frequent in the six-letter condition compared with the one-letter condition, thus providing support for this explanation of the probe RT data. As noted above, however, the increase in speed of responding to the probe may well be limited by the attentional narrowing that may result from such increases in arousal.

The probe reaction time study also attempted to address another issue. The warning and imperative stimuli in this study were both presented in the visual modality, via a visual display unit in front of the subject. Proponents of structure-specific resource pools have argued that the visual and auditory analysis systems are reasonably independent of each other (e.g. Wickens, 1979). Thus, a change in the allocation of resources in one modality should not affect the availability of resources in the other—changes in probe reaction time should only have been seen in this task in the visual modality. However, Figure 2.7 shows that this was clearly not the case. No statistically significant interactions were found with modality. Wickens (1980, 1984a) has argued that there are cases where interference between modality-specific resource pools can occur; for example, when the task is so difficult that not only do all available resources in that modality have to be employed, but resources have to be 'borrowed' from the pool normally allocated to the other modality. However, in this task, it is very unlikely that this level of difficulty, or such high task motivation, could have occurred.

AUTOMATIC VERSUS CONTROLLED PROCESSING

The basis of Öhman's (1979) position that the OR reflected a call for capacity based on the outcome of earlier preattentive processing was a number of dichotic listening studies (Corteen and Wood, 1972; Corteen and Dunn, 1974; von Wright, Anderson and Stenman, 1975; see also Forster and Govier, 1978). These are of additional relevance to this chapter, however, because of the equation of capacity with consciousness (e.g. Posner and Boies, 1971). The studies claimed that the SCR is an index of processing of which we may not be consciously aware. Their authors reported evidence that, after pairing the presentation of a word with shock, this word and semantically related words evoked SCRs even when they were apparently unattended.

Although there have been some failures at replication (Wardlaw and Kroll, 1976), more recent work seems to have confirmed that previously conditioned electrodermal responses may occur without measurable capacity allocation to the processing of the evoking stimulus (Dawson and Schell, 1982). Analyzing only responses to stimuli in the unattended channel, Dawson and Schell reported larger and more frequent SCRs to words from a category previously associated with shock, compared with no-shock category words, when there was no behavioral evidence (shadowing errors in attended channel; recognition of, or key presses to words in unattended channel) to indicate any reallocation of resources. Although, as in the earlier studies, it is possible that the reorientation of attention occurs so quickly that behavioral evidence is insensitive to such changes, the most interesting finding from this study was that the effect was lateralized, only occurring when the unattended words were presented in the left ear. One explanation they present for this finding (Dawson and Schell, 1983) is that the left hemisphere in these subjects was incapable of unaware semantic analysis, since the resources were being heavily utilized by the verbal shadowing of material presented in the attended channel. This particular line of reasoning implies that processing of material of which we are unaware does require limited-capacity resources.

This is a line which is also taken by Öhman (1988). The most relevant studies of Öhman that are covered in this review are those that have used a backward masking paradigm to examine responses to stimuli that are only preattentively processed (Marcel, 1983). In a number of experiments (Öhman, 1986; Öhman, Dimberg and Esteves, 1989), Öhman has found reliable evidence that previously shock-associated faces (CS+) elicit larger SCRs than do faces not associated with shock, even when the presentation duration is short and the stimulus is masked to preclude conscious awareness. Interestingly, in view of the comments above about lateralization, Öhman also found that the effect was strongest when stimuli were initially presented to the right hemisphere. Clearly, there are alternative explanations for this effect within this particular paradigm, in view of the nature of the stimuli employed and the fact that the same duration was used for stimuli presented to either hemisphere. However, there is also evidence that the discriminative electrodermal responding is more easily seen on the left hand than on the right (Öhman *et al.*, 1988). In reviewing the backward masking and dichotic listening studies, as well as some on prosopagnostic patients, Öhman (1988) concludes that autonomic responses, learned or unlearned, can be elicited by stimuli about which the person remains unaware. How might the results of the Spinks studies, which indicate that the magnitude of the SCR-OR is dependent upon available processing resources, be reconciled with this position?

Some explanations might be based on technical features, such as possible response overlap in some of the studies. A somewhat higher level of explanation might consider the different stimuli in the studies (the Spinks studies employing neutral cognitive stimuli, other studies cited above using emotional stimuli, previously shock-associated stimuli or stimuli for which, it could be argued, subjects are biologically prepared). There is little evidence for SCRs being elicited as a result of preattentive or non-conscious processing of stimuli which are merely informative, as in the Spinks studies. Given Sokolov's (1966, 1969) views about the OR as a regulator of information during cognitive processing, this is somewhat surprising. An exception is the study reported by Bauer (1984), who examined SCRs in prosopagnostic patients to famous faces. But, even here, there is evidence to suggest that recognition of human faces has some degree of biological preparedness. That this distinction between types of stimuli is important is supported by the different preattentive effects that exist when faces on the one hand and geometric figures on the other are employed (Öhman, 1988).

A better, and simpler answer, however, is that the autonomic nervous system (ANS) is not as specific as is implied by those who advocate that the SCR is an index of only preattentive processing. Although there are aspects of the ANS that are likely to be far more complex than the traditional 'vegetative nervous system' label would imply, the fact remains that it is a phylogenetically old system (van Toller, 1979). One of its primary roles is to prepare the organism for anticipated consequences (Cannon, 1930; Brooks, 1979). It is unlikely that the inputs to such a system would be limited to only those processes which occur preattentively. There are many consequences of controlled processing that might be expected to result in a number of ANS changes, particularly those related to anticipated motor activity. The work on ANS concomitants of effort supports this position. A counterargument to this view might be that these changes do not constitute components of the OR, which involves only a particular subset of ANS responses. However, even at this level of specificity, it is difficult to see how such peripheral components as those measured as OR components could be related to the major function of the OR, which, it is argued, is primarily a cognitive enhancement (Spinks and Siddle, 1983). Also, much of the work on the OR itself can be organized around the concept of preparing for anticipated consequences of stimulation.

It would therefore seem sensible to suggest that the OR is evoked in relation to processing which is capacity-independent (preattentive) as well as resource-limited (controlled). Of course, under cleverly controlled conditions, it may be possible to eliminate controlled processing, or at least hold such processing constant, which would then allow the examination of the effects of capacity-independent preattentive processing on OR parameters. However, it is clear from recent reviews of automaticity that the automatic and controlled processing constructs overlap, with different levels of automaticity suggested by Kahneman and Treisman (1984).

Within the more recent revisions of Öhman's theory (Öhman, 1986; 1987), it can be seen that controlled processing has influences on response mobilization (see Figure 2.8). Since the ANS is particularly concerned with advance mobilization of motor resources, it would seem sensible to include OR components within this category. It might also be noted that the concept of response mobilization accords well with ideas currently being developed concerning the relationship between the ANS, OR and the evaluation of consequences (Lyytinen and Spinks, 1988).

There is one other possible explanation that deserves comment. Looking particularly to the findings of Mathews and MacLeod (1986) and de Haan, Young and Newcombe (1987), Öhman (1988) has argued that there can be resource limiting processing even when subjects are unaware of the stimuli being processed. Conscious awareness is seen as being part of much later

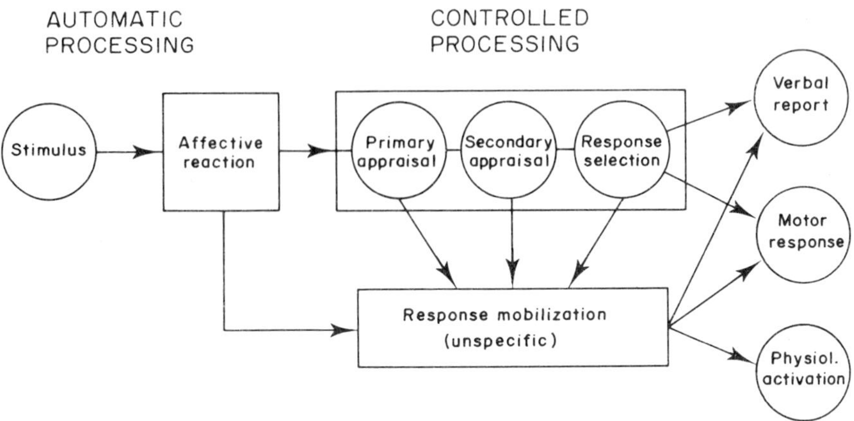

Figure 2.8. Öhman's model of information processing. (Reprinted from Öhman (1987) with permission. © JAI Press.)

controlled processing, perhaps related to the response selection mechanisms, since it is often linked to verbal reports. While this view adds further weight to the arguments against using behavioral measures as indices of capacity allocation, it also opens up the possibility that preattentive processing may require resources or capacity, thus providing another explanation of the Spinks data described above. As has been seen above, current views suggest that there are different levels of automaticity, some of which occasionally require, or are speeded by, attention or capacity allocation (Kahneman and Treisman, 1984). However, there are problems with this position. First, it indicates a processing system which would reveal severe deficiencies under high workload—the cocktail party phenomenon would not exist if the ongoing conversation took up large amounts of capacity. Second, it is difficult to see specifically why the difference in SCR magnitude between the one-letter and six-letter warning stimulus (Figure 2.6) should be a graded value, directly related to the resources available. The above reasoning suggests that this difference should only depend on whether the warning stimulus is identified, which would depend, in turn, on whether enough capacity was available for such processing (at a preattentive level). This is more a binary outcome than a graded outcome, and it is likely that such spare capacity would easily be available in both the 'No Task' and 'Easy' conditions.

Although these two points could evoke some counterarguments (e.g. graded group means may obscure individual binary data), the explanation that the SCR reflects the actual allocation of capacity to the processing of information (of which we may be aware or unaware) seems to result in fewer difficulties in interpretation. To be more exact, the SCR, being a phasic response to a change in circumstances, should be said to reflect a change in the allocation of capacity, a view supported by recent work by Dawson's group. These studies have revealed some particularly interesting findings relating ORs to capacity allocation. In the first of these (Dawson, Schell and Munro, 1985), there was a significant increase in probe RT during the first 600 ms of the presentation of orienting stimuli. In support of the individual difference data from the earlier report, Dawson *et al.* also found significantly longer probe RTs in subjects who showed larger ORs to the stimuli.

In this and subsequent studies (Filion, Dawson and Schell, 1986, 1988; Dawson, Filion and Schell, in press), evidence was reported to support an association between OR elicitation and resource allocation. The latter was shown to be greater during presentations of orienting stimuli early in an habituation series compared with later stimuli, and greater to novel than to familiar orienting stimuli. There were significant correlations between SCR-OR magnitude and probe RT slowing 150 ms after the presentation of orienting stimuli, at least early in the habituation series. However, perhaps the most interesting finding was a consistent dissociation between SCR magnitude and resource allocation (as indexed by probe RT). Unexpectedly, stimuli which the subject was told to ignore were accompanied by a greater increase of probe RTs than stimuli that the subject was told to attend to, at least on early trials. One could argue that these data highlight the problems of giving instructions to subjects and expecting them to follow exactly the wishes and intentions of the experimenter (O'Connor, 1981). However, SCR magnitude was greater to the to-be-attended stimulus than to the to-be-ignored stimulus. Clearly, Dawson's findings argue against a simple equation of SCR magnitude with resource allocation.

One possible explanation of the data involves the specification of the goals of the resource allocation. A traditional view was that resources are allocated in order to further process the alerting stimulus, and that this is exactly the function of the OR. However, it has been argued above that the OR is as sensitive to anticipated information processing as to characteristics of the eliciting stimulus itself. Lyytinen and Spinks (1988) have argued that the main determinant of observable orienting activity is the anticipated consequences of stimulation. The to-be-attended stimuli in Dawson's experiments have consequences in that they should be remembered or counted, or whatever the subject associates with 'attention'. The to-be-ignored stimuli have no consequences (once the subject has learnt that the instructions can be trusted!). Thus, differential SCR elicitation would be expected. But the stimulus itself does not have to be analyzed in any great depth—it is a simple tone, whose characteristics can be ascertained, to a level acceptable to undergraduate subjects, in a trial or two. One could argue that it is the to-be-ignored tone which continues to have processing resources allocated to its analysis, since it is not fully analyzed on earlier trials, because of the experimenter's instructions to ignore it.

There is evidence from Stenfert Kroese and Siddle (1983) which supports this view. In this study, SCRs to task-irrelevant stimuli were larger and more resistant to habituation, when the task occupied more processing resources. The interpretation of these data was that the task-irrelevant stimuli are processed less when there is little capacity available as a result of the more difficult primary task, and there is therefore a continued 'call' for attention or processing resources when these tones are repeatedly presented. This inference would have to be modified, however, to fit in with the explanation of the Dawson *et al.* data. A possible alternative explanation would be that the irrelevant tones initially elicit larger ORs in the difficult task condition because subjects have to find a way of cognitively coping with the intrusion (Kahneman would prefer recourse to the concept of mental effort). It could be argued that it is the resources required to deal with the cognitive complexity of dealing with the two sets of stimuli, rather than the resources required for identification of the stimulus (a simple tone), which determines SCR magnitude.

Dawson *et al.* argue that probe RT slowing is not so much a measure of capacity allocation, but rather an index of attentional switching (see earlier). In many cases, those two would be closely yoked, but under certain situations can be separated. There are, however, some difficulties to be overcome in fitting the data on stimulus omission within this explanation. The SCR-OR obviously indicates a different process if the two measures can be dissociated under certain circumstances. This is another of the very interesting findings in this area, and one that is likely to lead to some reconceptualization of the relationship between capacity and orienting.

INTEGRATIVE SUMMARY: AUTONOMIC AND CENTRAL NERVOUS SYSTEMS MEASURES

JOHN SPINKS AND ARTHUR KRAMER

ACCOMPLISHMENTS AND CHALLENGES

One goal of psychophysiological research is a correlative one, to investigate the extent and degree of relationships between cognitive constructs and physiological measures. It has been shown that there is a reasonable literature linking the concept of effort (or capacity invested) to autonomic measures such as pupil dilation, skin conductance and heart rate variability as well as to central nervous system measures such as the N100 and P300 complexes of the ERP and measures of metabolic activity of the brain (e.g. rCBF, PET). Cognitive load also appears to be closely linked to heart rate variability parameters. The heart rate literature has gone one step beyond the simple correlative stance by dissociating capacity used for perceptual purposes from that used for cognition, thereby predating the structure-specific theories. Similarly, ERP components have been found to be differentially sensitive to perceptual and central processing dimensions of resource allocation. The work on conditioning and orienting is an example of later stages of the evolution of psychophysiological research, in that it is based on earlier correlative data. Psychophysiological measures have clearly aided the development of ideas about aspects of information processing, although it is probably true to say that they have been more frequently used to test ideas developed from other sources. An example of psychophysiological data that might be expected to result in some rethinking of our current ideas is given below.

Although the emphasis in the discussion of autonomic measures has been to review the empirical data from a theory development point of view, autonomic measures have been used extensively in applied settings. This work is usually, of course, based on earlier correlative data—in particular, reports of relationships between autonomic measures and workload. Indeed, a number of the studies cited above have applied goals, although they have been purposely viewed from a different perspective (e.g. Sharit and Salvendy, 1982). As described above, numerous central nervous system measures have also been examined within applied contexts such as simulated flight missions and air traffic control scenarios. The applied research has been primarily focused on two issues: the assessment of mental workload (Kramer, 1987) and the detection and communication of task-relevant events (Farwell and Donchin, 1988; Kramer *et al.*, 1989). The examination of both of these issues has arisen as a result of developments in basic psychophysiological research on selective and divided attention. However, it is interesting to note that while basic research is usually viewed as providing information of use in applied settings, the development and utilization of psychophysiological metrics of mental workload has uncovered issues such as the strategic control of behavior in high-workload situations that have suggested a reconceptualization of models of capacity allocation (Hart, 1989).

There are a number of advantages that accrue from using physiological measures to elucidate the nature of capacity changes. They are usually measured along a parametric scale, are often continuous, and they are not as intrusive as behavioral measures, at least once the electrodes have been attached. In addition, while it is often advisable to collect performance data along with physiological data, the fact that psychophysiological data can be collected in the absence of behavior makes it particularly useful when it is either impossible or undesirable to impose response demands on subjects. In some cases, the experimental demands make behavioral (e.g. verbal) responding awkward, while in other cases subjects may be unable to verbalize or the behavioral measures may be insensitive to the rapid cognitive changes that are taking place.

There are also a number of disadvantages. As many authors have noted, physiological measures are an extra step removed from the conceptual systems that interest psychologists. One must be willing to make an assumption that physiological system X is a reasonable measure of a conceptually distant cognitive parameter Y, an assumption that is often based on earlier empirical work. There are two problems that follow from these assumptions. The simple problem is one of heterogeneity of results—measures investigated only show, at best, an imperfect correlation with a cognitive activity of interest, and then often only under certain conditions. Evolution has failed abysmally in that it has only provided psychophysiologists with very poor quality indices—a situation that is even less surprising given that the cognitive schemata have been generated within the fertile minds of psychologists. One solution to this problem might be to develop concepts around a measure, rather than the other way round, if researchers feel confident that a particular excursion of the polygraph pen reflects some heuristically useful central process (some difficulties with this solution should be readily apparent). The second problem is that rampant empiricism fails to deal with the issue of why a particular physiological system should reflect cognitive actions. Since this is a more important issue in any discussion of physiological indices, particularly those within the autonomic system, a few comments will be made here.

There are two main reasons why a psychophysiological metric might be correlated with aspects of capacity or resources. The first, as the Laceys have advocated in their baroreceptor feedback hypothesis, is that the biological change is causally responsible for changes at a cognitive level. For example, pupil dilation may increase the sensitivity of the visual system, while decreasing the width of the field of acute vision.

Historically, one scheme even suggested that the autonomic responses reflected the activity of specific muscle groups which were causally related to changes in sensitivity (Ruttkay-Nedecky, 1967). Alternatively, general activity in the autonomic and central nervous systems, activation, may lead to (and might be necessary for) an increase in cognitive activity. Individual responses would then be seen as part of this general action, which might correspond to what researchers have called 'mental effort'.

The second reason for covariation might stem from an evaluation of the consequences of cognitive processing. Certain types of stimuli will be evaluated by the system as having particular expected consequences, as, for example, warning stimuli, or unexpected stimuli. Autonomic and central nervous system activity in this case may be based upon the upper limits of the anticipated metabolic requirements (Cannon, 1930; Lyytinen and Spinks, 1988). Perhaps all human information processing can be seen from this perspective (Germana, 1969), since it always has, at least, potential behavioral consequences. One of the most satisfying aspects of a recent reconceptualization of both central and autonomic data in terms of a much older concept—that of energetics—

has been the attempt by a number of the contributing authors to justify psychophysiological measurement along these lines (Hockey, Gaillard and Coles, 1986). Notwithstanding these developments, there is clearly a need to continually confront the issue of the logical status of psychophysiological responses in the information processing system.

DIAGNOSTICITY AND SENSITIVITY

In comparison with behavioral measures of secondary task performance, autonomic nervous system measures are generally less diagnostic, since they are rarely associated with specific types of resources. However, this lack of specificity is compensated by an increase in the sensitivity to the total resource demands or allocation (Wickens, 1984b). On the other hand, a number of measures of CNS activity have proven to be uniquely sensitive to perceptual (N100 complex), central processing (P300, slow wave) and response (readiness potential) dimensions of capacity. As has been pointed out in earlier sections, ERPs to probes can be used to discriminate moment-to-moment changes in processing resources more accurately than slower autonomic responses (e.g. Bauer, Goldstein and Stern, 1984). Furthermore, measures of glucose metabolism and cerebral blood flow appear to be sensitive to distinctions between verbal and spatial processing as specified by Wickens' (1980, 1984) codes of processing dimension.

Models of information processing have been described in the introduction to this chapter. It is clear that the specificity described in these views is not yet matched by the availability of physiological measures shown to be reliably correlated with information processing system components. Apart from the goal of providing such metrics, psychophysiology could be asked to elucidate the ways in which subject strategies or external factors, such as stress, have influenced information processing changes. It could be argued that control systems, determining, for example, the extent to which processing is to be resource- or data-driven, might have psychophysiological correlates which are essentially epiphenomenal in nature.

An example of how psychophysiological measures might be used to elucidate processing strategies that develop with practice was illustrated by the Kramer *et al.* studies described above. Briefly, in those studies, the P300s elicited by secondary-task events discriminated between a first- and a second-order version of an unpracticed tracking task. However, with practice, P300s elicited in the second-order tracking conditions increased in amplitude, presumably reflecting reduced demands for resources in the difficult version of the tracking task. After substantial practice, secondary task P300s were as large in the second-order tracking conditions as they were in the first-order conditions. Given that P300s are sensitive to perceptual/central processing demands but are relatively insensitive to motor demands, the changes in

P300s with tracking practice suggested a resource-specific improvement in task performance. Equivalent amplitude P300s along with differences in root-mean-square tracking error in the first- and second-order conditions pointed towards improvements in the perceptual/central processing aspects of performance but continued deficiencies in the response aspects of processing in the second-order conditions. An examination of tracking strategies confirmed these hypotheses. During training, subjects had transitioned from a tracking strategy that relied on perceptual anticipation (e.g. smooth pursuit control) to a strategy that involved a few rapid movements (e.g. double impulse control). ERPs have also been employed successfully to 'decompose' strategy shifts during the development of automatic processing (Buckley, Kramer and Strayer, 1988; Hoffman *et al.*, 1985; Kramer *et al.*, 1986; Kramer and Strayer, 1988; van Dellen *et al.*, 1984).

Some authors (e.g. Näätänen, 1986) have similarly argued that autonomic responses are less discriminating than central measures in what they reveal about cognitive processing. As will have been made clear from the earlier sections, autonomic responses are not merely epiphenomenal byproducts of some general state of the organism, such as arousal or activation. At one level, different effects would be expected, and are found, between measures primarily controlled by sympathetic and those controlled by parasympathetic influences. There is evidence that heart rate responses distinguish between qualitatively different types of arousal (Furedy, 1987), and that pupil dilation is differentially affected by presentation, storage and retrieval stages of a digit-span task (Kahneman and Wright, 1971). Pribram and McGuinness (1975) have argued for a distinction between arousal and activation, these systems being reflected in the phasic electrodermal and heart rate responses respectively. A third system, that of effort, which allows the arousal and activation systems to be uncoupled in non-automatic processing, may possibly be indexed by muscular activity. This conceptual system has been developed by Mulder (e.g. Mulder, 1986), who has attempted to link it with a linear process model of information processing (preprocessing—feature extraction—identification—controlled processing), stages of which are indexed by ERP components (NaPa—N1—P2N2—P375/P550/SW respectively). It might be appropriate at this point to comment on the linear process (stage) view of processing, since this is a major issue in any work using temporally locked measures. One can argue from two standpoints that such a paradigmatic influence is heuristically undesirable. First, stimulus input rarely arrives as a discrete physical entity surrounded by total silence. Monitoring the environment on a continuous (and varying) basis is a more ecologically valid (Petrinovich, 1979) paradigm, although there are obvious counterarguments to this position. Second, many authors have argued that activity in the perceptual system alone is dependent on a large number of top-down influences, to the extent that processing of any stimulus must be considered as merely a part of a series of feedback loops and processing (system) circuits. Capacity views of information processing systems can be, but are certainly not necessarily, linked to linear processing models. It might be expected, however, that ERP measures are more suitable for testing linear processing models than autonomic responses, by virtue of the information available about time sequencing in ERPs. Autonomic measurement, however, might well prove to be particularly valuable in research into models that have capacity-based concepts as the primary components.

AUTOMATICITY AND ATTENTION

As has been noted above, one of the areas of psychophysiology that has seen the greatest conceptual development has been that of the OR. Traditionally, this has been investigated using autonomic measurements, a feature which no doubt stems from the work of Sokolov (1963). Given the rich array of theoretical structures that have been built around this concept, it is not surprising that authors have attempted to integrate CNS findings with those from studies employing autonomic measurement (e.g. Loveless, 1983; Näätänen, 1986; Rohrbaugh, 1984; Roth, 1983). There have been a number of papers which have suggested that the P300 response is closely related to the OR as measured by autonomic components (e.g. Blowers, Spinks and Shek, 1986). It was pointed out earlier in this chapter that P300 amplitude can be viewed as reflecting processing priority, responses to secondary stimuli decreasing as fewer resources become available through the manipulation of primary task difficulty (Isreal, *et al.*, 1980a,b; Kramer, Wickens and Donchin, 1983, 1985; Kramer, Sirevaag and Braune, 1987).

Isreal *et al.* (1980a) had reported that the amplitudes of P300 responses to tones was reduced when a second task (tracking) was introduced. These results seem to be contrary to those found for SCRs in the Stenfert Kroese and Siddle (1983) study described in the 'Autonomic' section. However, it should be remembered that the subjects in the latter study were instructed to ignore the tones, whereas in Isreal's study they were required to count the tones for later report. That this is a critical difference in design is supported by Spinks' data (Figure 2.6) where relevant stimuli evoked smaller SCR-ORs when presented during a more difficult primary task. However, the Isreal study showed that additional increments in the difficulty level of the primary tracking task did not lead to any further attenuation of amplitudes of P300s to the tones. Ruling out a number of possible explanations, they opt for a conclusion which accepts the P300 as a measure of resources allocated, but suggest that it is insensitive to further variations in the tracking difficulty level because the perceptual processing indexed by the P300 used resources independent of those used up by changes in the tracking task. This interpretation is supported by a number of additional studies using ERPs (e.g. Kramer, Wickens and Donchin, 1983, 1985; Sirevaag *et al.*, 1989).

Some authors have been particularly successful in providing new insights into the concept of the OR through ERP measurement. In a series of studies, Näätänen (e.g. 1986; in press) examined the OR and related concepts, focusing particularly on early ERP components. One of these, the mismatch negativity (MMN), which peaks at around 170 ms following stimulus onset, seems to reflect a preperceptual response to change in a repeated series of auditory stimuli (see Chapter 1). Näätänen has proposed that the elicitation of the MMN is the result of a detection of a mismatch from a neuronal model of the physical characteristics of the stimulus. Although conceptually this seems similar to Sokolov's original neuronal model idea, it is different from the scheme of response generation developed around the OR.

According to Näätänen (1979), however, the cognitive process underlying the MMN may initiate elicitation of the OR (or may, indeed, reflect an 'involuntary OR'). He has therefore suggested that the MMN represents a process which may alert, or call, the limited-capacity system (Näätänen, 1985, 1986; cf. Öhman, 1979). This call may be answered, and an attentional switch will then take place. It is suggested that this intrusion of the stimulus into awareness is marked by the occurrence of a P3a (Sams *et al.*, 1985). It is possible that the attentional switch may be further differentiated by examining the N2 wave, which precedes P3a when subjects are asked to pay attention to the deviant stimuli (Näätänen and Gaillard, 1983).

Recent research by Lyytinen has looked at ANS–CNS integration, with particular reference in current work to the OR (Lyytinen, Bloomberg and Näätänen, submitted). In this paper, deviant auditory stimuli evoked MMN even when no autonomic (SCR, HRR) response was evident. On the other hand, P3 amplitudes were greater on trials evoking SCRs. It might be concluded that the MMN, reflecting, as accumulating evidence suggests, a preattentively detected physical mismatch, is a necessary but not sufficient precursor of the OR within short ISI oddball paradigms. The P3a (and SCR), as Lyytinen points out, indexes perhaps an intrusion of the stimulus into conscious awareness, after this automatic stage reflected by the MMN has passed.

Näätänen's (not altogether unreasonable) view is that the concept of the OR has become too large to be of great predictive value (see also Spinks, 1987b; Spinks and Siddle, 1983). He infers from his work that the OR concept can be usefully split into arousal and attentional components, indexed by non-specific and specific N1 components respectively, and an attentional component to deviant stimuli, indexed by the MMN. The multidimensional nature of these concepts suggests that research in this area will generate further refinement in our understanding of orienting and related processes. Following on from Näätänen's work, there has been a move by ERP researchers to view ORs to the initial presentation of a stimulus series as conceptually different from those to stimulus change, and to structurally distinguish between responses to neutral and responses to significant stimuli, using single-trial ERPs (Kenemans *et al.*, 1988). Although this research has not specifically addressed the issue of capacity and resources, one could, with a few extra assumptions, infer from the CNS and ANS literature that the OR has two components to it. First, there are shifts in the allocation of resources from an ongoing analysis to a new set, these shifts resulting from preattentive or more prolonged controlled processing. Second, there is a physiological arousal response, which (in contrast to Pribram and McGuinness, 1975) is probably related to anticipated metabolic requirements. Whether components of this physiological arousal are directly and causally related to future anticipated cognitive processing is less well established. However, one possibility outlined in this chapter has been that there is an increase in capacity available for processing generally, as Kahneman (1973) has suggested.

While ERPs have not been traditionally used to examine the OR, they have been recently employed in the study of a related phenomenon, the *automatic attention response* (AAR). The AAR which develops as a function of consistent practice has been described as 'any process that always uses general resources and decreases general processing capacity whenever a given set of external initiating stimuli are presented, regardless of the subject's attempt to ignore or bypass the distraction' (Shiffrin and Dumais, 1981; pp. 116–117). In a series of studies, Kramer and Strayer (1988, see also Strayer and Kramer, 1990) have found that the P300 provides a sensitive index of the mandatory allocation of resources that characterizes the AAR. In their studies, automatically processed stimuli elicited large and invariant P300s regardless of task difficulty, number of tasks performed simultaneously, or processing priority (e.g. concentrate on one task or the other in dual-task conditions).

It must be borne in mind that the research outlined here on the OR is attacked from a quite different perspective in current ERP research, where the emphasis is more on short-duration, frequent, physical stimuli which do not carry much in the way of semantic content. ANS researchers, on the other hand, are developing models around research using stimuli that might be subjected to a very prolonged analysis, or research on processing of information that is very difficult to break up into discrete stimuli, or which may only be based upon internal representations. These differences, together with the more practical problems (e.g. the necessity for time locking in ERP research) has hampered the quest for integration in the past. Research on the OR and the AAR illustrates that CNS and ANS measures can be used to provide different but overlapping views of a set of complex, psychological phenomena. Furthermore, the joint use of ANS and CNS measures has provided conceptual enhancement to an area which might not have come about by looking only at a single system, as in the above example, where it could be argued that recent ERP research has resulted in a narrowing of the range of applicability of a conceptual area, by sharpening the defining characteristics of the OR.

ACKNOWLEDGEMENTS

The preparation of this chapter was supported by grants from NASA Ames Research Center (NAG-2-308) and the Office of Naval Technology (RS34H21) to Arthur Kramer, and by funding from the Committee on Research and Conference Grants of the University of Hong Kong to John Spinks.

The authors wish to thank Michael Coles, Richard Jennings, Heikki Lyytinen and Susanna Yip for their helpful comments on an earlier draft of this chapter.

REFERENCES

Aasman, J., Mulder, G. and Mulder, L.J.M. (1987). Operator effort and the measurement of heart-rate variability. *Human Factors*, **29**, 161–170.

Aldrich, T., Szabo, S. and Bierbaum, C. (1988). The development and application of models to predict operator workload during system design. In G. McMillian (ed.), *Human Performance Models*. Orlando, Florida: NATO AGARD.

Allport, A. (1980). Attention and performance. In G. Claxton (ed.), *Cognitive Psychology*. London: Routledge.

Allport, A. (1987). Selection for action: some behavioral and neurophysiological considerations of attention and action. In H. Heuer and A. Sanders (eds), *Perspectives On Perception and Action*. Hillsdale, NJ: Erlbaum.

Allport, A., Antonis, B. and Reynolds, P. (1972). On the division of attention: a disproof of the single channel hypothesis. *Quartely Journal of Experimental Psychology*, **24**, 225–235.

Avolio, B., Kroeck, K. and Panek, P. (1985). Individual differences in information processing ability as a predictor of motor vehicle accidents. *Human Factors*, **27**, 577–588.

Baddeley, A. and Hitch, G. (1974). Working memory. In G. Bower (ed.), *Recent Advances in Learning and Motivation*. New York: Academic Press.

Bauer, L., Goldstein, R. and Stern, J. (1987). Effects of information processing demands on physiological response patterns. *Human Factors*, **29**, 213–234.

Bauer, R.M. (1984). Autonomic recognition of names and faces in prosopagnosia: a neuropsychological application of the Guilty Knowledge Test. *Neuropsychologica*, **22**, 457–469.

Beatty, J. (1982). Task evoked pupillary responses, processing load and the structure of processing resources. *Psychological Bulletin*, **91**, 276–292.

Benson, A., Huddleston, J. and Rolfe, J. (1965). A psychophysiological study of compensatory tracking on a digital display. *Human Factors*, **7**, 457–472.

Berdina, N., Kolenko, O., Kotz, I., Kuzetzov, A., Rodinov, I., Savtchencko, A. and Thorevsky, V. (1972). Increase in skeletal muscle performance during emotional stress in man. *Circulation Research*, **6**, 642–650.

Berger, H. (1929). On the electroencephalogram of man. *Archives of Psychiatry and Nervous Diseases*, **87**, 511–570.

Berlyne, D.E. (1960). *Conflict, Arousal and Curiosity*. New York: McGraw Hill.
Blowers, G.H., Spinks, J.A. and Shek, D.T.L. (1986). P300 and the anticipation of information within an orienting response paradigm. *Acta Psychologica*, **61**, 91–103.
Bohlin, G. and Kjellberg, A. (1979). Orienting activity in two stimulus paradigms as reflected in heart rate. In H.D. Kimmel, E.H. van Olst and J.F. Orlebeke (eds), *The Orienting Reflex in Humans*. Hillsdale, NJ: Erlbaum, pp. 169–198.
Boyce, P.R. (1974). Sinus arrhythmia as a measure of mental load. *Ergonomics*, **17**, 177–183.
Broadbent, D. (1958). *Perception and Communication*. London: Pergamon Press.
Broadbent, D.E. (1970). Stimulus set and response set: two kinds of selective attention. In D.I. Mostofsky (ed.), *Attention: Contemporary Theory and Analysis*. New York: Appleton–Century–Crofts.
Brooks, C.M. (1979). The development of our knowledge of the autonomic nervous system. In C.M. Brooks, K. Koizumi and A. Sato (eds), *Integrative Functions of the Autonomic Nervous System* Amsterdam: Elsevier, pp. 473–496.
Brown, I. (1978). Dual task methods of assessing workload. *Ergonomics*, **21**, 221–224.
Buckley, J., Kramer, A. and Strayer, D. (1988). Component task consistency and automatic processing. *Psychophysiology*, **25**, 437–438.
Cannon W.B. (1930). The autonomic nervous system: an interpretation (The Linacre lecture). *Lancet*, 1109–1115.
Coles, M.G.H. (1972). Cardiac and respiratory activity during visual search. *Journal of Experimental Psychology*, **96**, 371–379.
Colle, H., Amel, J., Ewry, M. and Jenkins, M. (1988). Capacity equivalence curves: a double trade-off curve method for equating task performance. *Human Factors*, **30**, 645–656.
Corcoran, D.W.J. (1964). Changes in heart rate and performance as a result of loss of sleep. *British Journal of Psychology*, **55**, 307–315.
Corlett, E.N. (1973). Cardiac arrhythmia as a field technique: some comments on a recent symposium. *Ergonomics*, **16**, 3–4.
Corteen, R.S. and Dunn, D. (1974). Shock associated words in a nonattended message: a test for momentary awareness. *Journal of Experimental Psychology*, **102**, 1143–1144.
Corteen, R.S. and Wood, B. (1972). Autonomic responses to shock-associated words in an unattended channel. *Journal of Experimental Psychology*, **94**, 308–313.
Crossman, E. (1959). A theory of acquisition of speed skill. *Ergonomics*, **2**, 153–166.
Cuffin, B. and Cohen, D. (1979). Comparison of the magnetoencephalogram and electroencephalogram. *Electroencephalography and Clinical Neurophysiology*, **47**, 132–146.
Damos, D. (1978). Residual attention as a predictor of pilot performance. *Human Factors*, **20**, 435–440.
Dawson, M.E. and Schell, A.M. (1982). Electrodermal responses to attended and nonattended significant stimuli during dichotic listening. *Journal of Experimental Psychology: Human Perception and Performance*, **8**, 315–324.
Dawson, M.E. and Schell, A.M. (1983). Lateral asymmetries in electrodermal responses to nonattended stimuli: a reply to Walker and Ceci. *Journal of Experimental Psychology: Human Perception and Performance*, **9**, 148–150.
Dawson, M.E. and Schell, A.M. (1985). Information processing and human autonomic classical conditioning. In P.K. Ackles, J.R. Jennings and M.G.H. Coles (eds), *Advances in Psychophysiology*, vol I. Greenwich, CT: JAI Press, pp. 89–165.
Dawson, M.E., Filion, D.L. and Schell, A.M. (in press). Is elicitation of the autonomic orienting response associated with allocation of processing resources? *Psychophysiology*.

Dawson, M.E., Schell, A.M., Beers, J.R. and Kelly, A. (1982). Allocation of cognitive processing capacity during human autonomic classical conditioning. *Journal of Experimental Psychology: General*, **11**, 273–295.

Dawson, M.E., Schell, A.M. and Munro, L.L. (1985). Autonomic orienting, electrodermal lability, and the allocation of processing resources. *Psychophysiology*, **22**, 587.

Defayolle, M., Dinand, J. and Gentil, M. (1971). Averaged evoked potentials in relation to attitude, mental load and intelligence. In W.T. Singleton, J.G. Fox and D. Whitfield (eds), *Measurement of Man at Work*. London: Taylor and Francis.

de Haan, E.H.F., Young, A. and Newcombe, F. (1987). Face recognition without awareness. *Cognitive Neuropsychology*, **4**, 385–415.

Deutsch, J.A. and Deutsch, D. (1963). Attention: some theoretical considerations. *Psychological Review*, **70**, 80–90.

Donald, M. (1980). Memory, learning and event-related potentials. In H. Kornhuber and L. Deecke (eds), *Motivation, Motor and Sensory Processes of the Brain: Electrical Potentials, Behavior and Clinical Use*. Amsterdam: Elsevier.

Donchin, E., Kramer, A.F. and Wickens, C.D. (1986). Application of brain event-related potentials to problems in engineering psychology. In M.G.H. Coles, S. Porges and E. Donchin (eds), *Psychophysiology: Systems, Processes and Applications*. New York: Guilford Press.

Duncan, J. (1984). Selective attention and the organization of visual attention. *Journal of Experimental Psychology: General*, **113**, 501–517.

Duncan-Johnson, C.C. and Coles, M.G.H. (1974). Heart rate and disjunctive reaction times: the effects of discrimination requirements. *Journal of Experimental Psychology*, **103**, 1160–1168.

Eason, R.G. and Banks, J. (1963). Effect of level of activation on the quality and efficiency of verbal and motor tasks. *Perceptual and Motor Skills*, **16**, 525–543.

Easterbrook, J.A. (1959). The effect of emotion on cue utilization and the organization of behavior. *Psychological Review*, **66**, 183–201.

Edelberg, R. (1972). Electrodermal recovery rate, goal orientation and aversion. *Psychophysiology*, **9**, 512–520.

Eysenck, M.W. (1982). *Attention and Arousal*. New York: Springer-Verlag.

Falmange, J. (1968). Note on a simple fixed-point property of binary mixtures. *British Journal of Mathematical and Statistical Psychology*, **21**, 131–132.

Farwell, L. and Donchin, E. (1988). Talking off the top of your head: toward a mental prosthesis utilizing event-related brain potentials. *Electroencephalography and Clinical Neurophysiology*, **70**, 510–523.

Filion, D.L., Dawson, M.E. and Schell, A.M. (1986). Autonomic orienting and the allocation of processing resources. *Psychophysiology*, **25**, 435–436.

Filion, D.L., Dawson, M.E. and Schell, A.M. (1988). Dissociation between autonomic orienting and resource allocation. *Psychophysiology*, **25**, 445.

Firth, P.A. (1973). Psychological factors influencing the relations between cardiac arrhythmia and mental load. *Ergonomics*, **16**, 5–16.

Forster, P.M. and Govier, E. (1978). Discrimination without awareness? *Quarterly Journal of Experimental Psychology*, **30**, 282–295.

Freidman, A. and Polson, M. (1981). Hemispheres as independent resource systems: limited capacity processing and cerebral specialization. *Journal of Experimental Psychology: Human Perception and Performance*, **7**, 1030–1058.

Furedy, J.J. (1987). Beyond heart rate in the cardiac psychophysiological assessment of mental effort: the T-wave amplitude component of the electrocardiogram. *Human Factors*, **29**, 183–194.

Gale, A. and Edwards, J. (1983). The EEG and human behavior. In A. Gale and J. Edwards (eds), *Physiological Correlates of Human Behavior*. New York: Academic Press.
Germana, J. (1961). Central efferent processes and autonomic–behavioral integration. *Psychophysiology*, **6**, 78–90.
Gevins, A., Morgan, N., Bressler, S., Cuttillo, B., White, R., Illes, J., Greer, D., Doyle, J. and Zietlin, G. (1987). Human neuroelectric patterns predict performance accuracy. *Science*, **235**, 580–585.
Gevins, A., Zeitlin, G., Yingling, J., Doyle, J., Dedon, M., Schaffer, R., Roumasset, J. and Yeager, C. (1979). EEG patterns during cognitive tasks: I. Methodology and analysis of complex behaviors. *Electroencephalography and Clinical Neurophysiology*, **47**, 693–703.
Goldwater, B.C. (1972). Psychological significance of pupillary movements. *Psychological Bulletin*, **77**, 340–355.
Gomer, F. (1981). Physiological monitoring and the concept of adaptive systems. In J. Morael and K.F. Kraiss (eds), *Manned Systems Design*. New York, Plenum Press.
Gopher, D. (1986). In defense of resources: on structures, energies, pools and allocation of attention. In G. Hockey, A. Galliard and M. Coles (eds), *Energetics and Information Processing*. Netherlands: Martinus Nijhoff.
Gopher, D. and Donchin, E. (1986). Workload—An examination of the concept. In K. Boff, L. Kaufman and J. Thomas (eds), *Handbook of Perception and Performance: Cognitive Processes and Performance*. New York: Wiley, pp.41.1–41.49.
Gopher, D. and Kahnemen, D. (1971). Individual differences in attention and the prediction of flight criteria. *Perceptual and Motor Skills*, **33**, 1335–1342.
Graham, F.K. and Clifton, R.K. (1966). Heart rate change as a component of the orienting response. *Psychological Bulletin*, **65**, 305–320.
Groll-Knapp, E. (1971). Evoked potentials and behavior. In W.T. Singleton, J.G. Fox and D. Whitfield (eds), *Measurement of Man at Work*. London: Taylor and Francis.
Gur, R., Gur, R., Skolnick, B., Resnick, S., Silver, F., Chawluk, J., Muenz, L., Obrist, W. and Revich, M. (1988). Effects of task difficulty on regional cerebral blood flow: relationships with anxiety and performance. *Psychophysiology*, **25**, 392–399.
Hart, S. (1989). Crew workload management strategies: a critical fact of system performance. Paper presented at the Fifth International Symposium on Aviation Psychology, Dayton, Ohio.
Hatano, G., Miyake, Y. and Binks, M. (1977). Performance of expert abacus operators. *Cognition*, **5**, 57–71.
Hillyard, S.A., Munte, T. and Neville, H. (1985). Visual spatial attention, orienting and brain physiology. In M. Posner and O. Marin (eds), *Attention and Performance*, vol. XI. Hillsdale, NJ: Erlbaum.
Hink, R., Van Voorhis, S. and Hillyard, S. (1977). The division of attention and the human auditory evoked potential. *Neuropsychologica*, **15**, 597–605.
Hirst, W. (1987). The psychology of attention. In J. LeDoux and W. Hirst (eds), *Mind and Brain*, New York: Cambridge University Press.
Hirst, W. and Kalmar, D. (1987). Characterizing attentional resources. *Journal of Experimental Psychology: General*, **116**, 68–81.
Hockey, G.R.J., Gaillard, A.W.K. and Coles, M.G.H. (eds) (1986). *Energetics and Human Information Processing*. Dordrecht: Martinus Nijhoff.
Hoffman, J., Houck, M. MacMillian, F., Simons, R. and Oatman, L. (1985). Event-related potentials elicited by automatic targets: a dual-task analysis. *Journal of Experimental Psychology: Human Perception and Performance*, **11**, 50–61.
Hoffman, J., Nelson, B. and Houck, M. (1983). The role of attentional resources in automatic detection. *Psychophysiology*, **20**, 625–632.
Horst, R., Munson, R. and Ruchkin, D. (1984). Event-related potential indices of

workload in a single task paradigm. In *Proceedings of the 28th Annual Meeting of the Human Factors Society*. Santa Monica, CA: Human Factors Society.

Horst, R., Ruchkin, D., Munson, R. (1987). Event-related potential processing negativities related to workload. In R. Johnson, J. Rohrbaugh and R. Parasuraman (eds), *current Trends in Event-Related Potential Research*. Amsterdam: Elsevier.

Isreal, J., Chesney, G., Wickens, C. and Donchin, E. (1980). P300 and tracking difficulty: evidence for multiple resources in dual task performance. *Psychophysiology*, **17**, 259–273.

Isreal, J., Wickens, C., Chesney, G. and Donchin, E. (1980b). The event-related brain potential as an index of display monitoring workload. *Human Factors*, **22**, 211–224.

Janisse, M.P. and Kuc, S.G. (1977). The cognitive–emotional arousal distinction as assessed by pupil size and heart rate. *Psychophysiology*, **14**, 80.

Jennings, J.R. and Hall, W.S. (1980). Recall, recognition and rate: memory and the heart. *Psychophysiology*, **17**, 37–46.

Jennings, J.R., Lawrence, B.E. and Kasper, P. (1979). Changes in alertness and processing capacity in a serial learning task. *Memory and Cognition*, **6**, 43–53.

Johnston, W.A. and Heinz, S.P. (1978). Flexibility and capacity demands of attention. *Journal of Experimental Psychology: General*, **107**, 420–435.

Johnston, V. and Holcomb, P. (1980). Probability learning and the P3 component of the visual evoked potential in man. *Psychophysiology*, **17**, 396–400.

Kahneman, D. (1973). *Attention and Effort*. Englewood Cliffs, NJ; Prentice-Hall.

Kahneman, D., Ben-Ishai, R. and Lotan, M. (1973). Relation of a test of attention to road accidents. *Journal of Applied Psychology*, **58**, 113–115.

Kahneman, D and Henik, A. (1981). Perceptual organization and attention.. In M. Kubovy and J.R. Pomerantz (eds), *Perceptual Organization*. Hillsdale, NJ: Erlbaum.

Kahneman, D. and Treisman, A. (1984). Changing views of attention and automaticity. In R. Parasurman and R. Davies (eds), *Varieties of Attention*. New York: Academic Press, pp. 29–62.

Kahneman, D., Treisman, A. and Burkell, J. (1983). The cost of visual filtering: a new interference effect. *Journal of Experimental Psychology: Human Perception and Performance*, **9**, 510–522.

Kahneman, D., Tursky, B., Shapiro, D. and Crider, A. (1969). Pupillary, heart rate and skin resistance changes during a mental task. *Journal of Experimental Psychology*, **79**, 166–167.

Kahneman, D. and Wright, P. (1971). Changes of pupil size and rehearsal strategies in a short-term memory task. *Quarterly Journal of Experimental Psychology*, **23**, 187–196.

Kaiser, D.N. and Sandman, C.A. (1975). Physiological patterns accompanying complex problem solving during warning and nonwarning conditions. *Journal of Comparative and Physiological Psychology*, **89**, 357–363.

Kalsbeek, J.W.H. and Sykes, R.N. (1976). Objective measurement of mental load. *Acta Psychologica*, **27**, 253–261.

Kantowitz, B. (1985). Channels and stages in human information processing: a limited analysis of theory and methodology. *Journal of Mathematical Psychology*, **29**, 135–174.

Kantowitz, B. and Knight, R. (1976). Testing tapping and timesharing. II: Use of auditory secondary tasks. *Acta Psychologica*, **40**, 343–362.

Kantowitz, B. and Weldon, M. (1985). On scaling performance operating characteristics: caveat emptor. *Human Factors*, **27**, 531–548.

Kaye, H. and Pearce, J.M. (1984). The strength of the orienting response during Pavlovian conditioning. *Journal of Experimental Psychology: Animal Behavior Processes*, **10**, 90–109.

Kenemans, J.L., Verbaten, M.N., Sjouw, W. and Slangen, J.L. (1988). Effects of task relevance on habituation of visual single-trial ERPs and the skin conductance orienting response. *International Journal of Psychophysiology*, **6**, 51–63.

Kinsbourne, M. and Hicks, R. (1978). Functional cerebral space. In J. Requin (ed.), *Attention and Performance*, vol. VII. Hillsdale, NJ: Erlbaum, pp. 345–362.

Knowles, W. (1963). Operator loading tasks. *Human Factors*, **5**, 155–161.

Kramer, A.F. (1987). Event-related brain potentials. In A. Gale and B. Christie (eds), *Psychophysiology and the Electronic Workplace*. Chichester: Wiley, pp. 177–222.

Kramer, A.F., Humphrey, D., Sirevaag, E. and Mecklinger, A. (1989). Real-time measurement of mental workload: a feasibility study. In *Proceedings of the Third Annual Workshop on Space Operations, Automation and Robotics*. Houston, Texas: NASA Johnson Space Center.

Kramer, A.F., Schneider, W., Fisk, A.D. and Donchin, E. (1986). The effects of practice and task structure on components of the event-related brain potential. *Psychophysiology*, **23**, 33–47.

Kramer, A.F., Sirevaag, E. and Braune, R. (1987). A psychophysiological assessment of operator workload during simulated flight missions. *Human Factors*, **29**, 145–160.

Kramer, A.F., Sirevaag, E. and Hughes, P. (1988). Effects of foveal task load on visual–spatial attention: event-related brain potentials and performance. *Psychophysiology*, **25**, 512–531.

Kramer, A.F. and Strayer, D. (1988). Assessing the devlopment of automatic processing: an application of dual-task and event-related brain potential methodologies. *Biological Psychology*, **26**, 231–268.

Kramer, A.F., Wickens, C.D. and Donchin, E. (1983). An analysis of the processing demands of a complex perceptual-motor task. *Human Factors*, **25**, 597–621.

Kramer, A.F., Wickens, C.D. and Donchin, E. (1985). Processing of stimulus properties: evidence for dual-task integrality. *Journal of Experimental Psychology: Human Perception and Performance*, **11**, 393–408.

Kribbs, N.B., Muswick, G. and Shaffer, J.J. (1984). Cognitive processing capacity and heart rate in recognition memory for numbers and random shapes. *Perceptual and Motor Skills*, **59**, 241–242.

Kutas, M., McCarthy, G. and Donchin, E. (1977). Augmenting mental chronometry: the P300 as a measure of stimulus evaluation time. *Science*, **197**, 792–795.

LaBerge, D. (1973). Attention and the measurement of perceptual learning. *Memory and Cognition*, **1**, 268–276.

Lacey, J.I. (1967). Somatic response patterning and stress: some revisions of activation theory. In M.H. Appley and R. Trumbull (eds), *Psychological Stress: Issues in Research*. New York: Appleton–Century–Crofts.

Lang, W., Lang, M., Diekmann, V. and Kornhuber, H. (1987). The frontal theta rhythm indicating motor and cognitive learning. In R. Johnson, J.W. Rohrbaugh and R. Parasuraman (eds), *Current Trends in Event-Related Potential Research*. Amsterdam: Elsevier.

Laughery, R. Drews, C. and Archer, R. (1986). A micro SAINT simulation analyzing operator workload in a future helicopter. In *Proceedings of NAECON*. New York: IEEE.

Leplat, J. (1978). Factors determining workload. *Ergonomics*, **21**, 143–149.

Light, K.C. and Obrist, P.A. (1983). Task difficulty, heart rate reactivity, and cardiovascular responses to an appetitive reaction time task. *Psychophysiology*, **20**, 301–312.

Lindholm, E., Cheatman, C., Koriath, J. and Longridge, T. (1984). *Physiological Assessment of Aircraft Pilot Workload in Simulated Landing and Simulated Hostile Threat Environments*. Air Force Systems Command, Technical Report AFHRL-TR-83-49.

Logan, G. (1979). On the use of a concurrent memory load to measure attention and automaticity. *Journal of Experimental Psychology: Human Perception and Performance*, **5**, 189–207.

Loveless, N. (1983). The orienting response and evoked potentials in man. In D. Siddle (ed.), *Orienting and Habituation: Perspectives in Human Research*. Chichester: Wiley, pp. 71–108.

Lyytinen, H., Bloomberg, A.P. and Näätänen, R. (submitted). Event-related potentials and autonomic responses to a change in unattended auditory stimuli.

Lyytinen, H. and Spinks, J.A. (1988). Consequentiality as an explanatory construct in psychophysiology. In V.B. Shvyrkov, R. Naatanen, M. Sams, I.O. Alexsandrov and N.E. Maksimova (eds), *Psychophysiology of Cognitive Processes*. Moscow: Institute of Psychology, Academy of Sciences of the USSR, pp. 39–43.

Mantysalo, S. and Gaillard, A. (1986). Event-related potentials (ERPs) in a learning and memory test. *Biological Psychology*, **23**, 1–20.

Marcel, A. (1983). Conscious and unconscious perception: an approach to the relations between phenomenal experience and perceptual processes. *Cognitive Psychology*, **15**, 238–300.

Matthews, A. and MacLeod, C. (1986). Discrimination of threat cues without awareness in anxiety states. *Journal of Abnormal Psychology*, **95**, 131–138.

McCallum, C., Cooper, R. and Pocock, P. (1987). Event-related and steady state changes in the brain related to workload during tracking. In K. Jessen (ed.), *Electric and Magnetic Activity of the Central Nervous System: Research and Clinical Applications in Aerospace Medicine*. France: NATO AGARD.

McCarthy, G. and Donchin, E. (1981). A metric for thought: a comparison of P300 latency and reaction time. *Science*, **211**, 77–80.

McClelland, J. (1979). On the time relations of mental processes: an examination of systems of processes in cascade. *Psychological Review*, **86**, 287–330.

McCracken, J. and Aldrich, T. (1984). *Analysis of Selected LHX Mission Functions*. Technical Note ASI 479–024–84, Anacapa Sciences.

Meyer, D., Osman, A., Irwin, D. and Yantis, S. (1988). Modern mental chronometry. *Biological Psychology*, **26**, 3–67.

Moray, N. (1967). Where is capacity limited? A survey and a model. *Acta Psychologica*, **27**, 84–92.

Moray, N. (ed.) (1979). *Mental Workload: Its Theory and Measurement*. New York: Plenum Press.

Mountford, J. and North, R. (1980). Voice entry for reducing pilot workload. In *Proceedings of the 24th Annual Meeting of the Human Factors Society*. Santa Monica, CA: Human Factors Society.

Mulder, G. (1979a). Mental load, mental effort and attention. In N. Moray (ed.), *Mental Workload: Its Theory and Measurement*. New York: Plenum Press, pp. 299–325.

Mulder, G. (1979b). Sinus arrhythmia and mental workload. In N. Moray (ed.), *Mental Workload: Its Theory and Measurement*. New York: Plenum Press, pp. 327–343.

Mulder, G. (1986). The concept and measurement of mental effort. In G.R.J. Hockey, A.W.K. Gaillard and M.G.H. Coles (eds), *Energetics and Human Information Processing*. Dordrecht: Martinus Nijoff, pp. 91–111.

Näätänen, R. (1979). Orienting and evoked potentials. In H.D. Kimmel, E.H. van Olst and J.F. Orlebeke (eds), *The Orienting Reflex in Humans*. Hillsdale, NJ: Erlbaum, pp. 61–75.

Näätänen, R. (1985). Selective attention and stimulus processing: reflections in event-related potentials, magnetoencephalogram, and regional cerebral blood flow. In M. Posner and O. Marin (eds), *Attention and Performance*, vol. XI. Hillsdale, NJ: Erlbaum, pp. 355–373.

Näätänen, R. (1986). The orienting response theory: an integration of informational and energetical aspects of brain function. In R.G.J. Hockey, A.W.K. Gaillard and M.G.H. Coles (eds), *Energetical Aspects of Human Information Processing*. Dortrecht: Martinus Nijhoff.

Näätänen, R. (in press). The role of attention in auditory information processing as revealed by event-related potentials and other brain measures of cognitive functon. *Behavioral and Brain Sciences*.

Näätänen, R. and Gaillard, A.W.K. (1983). The orienting reflex and N2 deflection of the event-related potential (ERP). In A.W.K. Gaillard and W. Ritter (Eds), *Tutorials in ERP Research: Endogenous Components*. Amsterdam: North-Holland, pp. 119–141.

Natani, K. and Gomer, F. (1981). *Electrocortical Activity and Operator Workload: A Comparison of Changes in the Electroencephalogram and in Event-Related Potentials*. Technical Report MDC E2427, McDonnell Douglas Corp.

Navon, D. (1984). Resources—a theoretical soup stone? *Psychological Review*, **91**, 216–234.

Navon, D. and Gopher, D. (1979). On the economy of the human processing system. *Psychological Review*, **86**, 214–255.

Navon, D. and Miller, J. (1987). The role of outcome conflict in dual-task interference. *Journal of Experimental Psychology: Human Perception and Performance*, **13**, 435–448.

Neumann, O. (1987). Beyond capacity: a functional view of attention. In H. Heuer and A. Sanders (eds), *Perspectives on Perception and Action*. Hillsdale, NJ: Erlbaum.

Newell, A. and Rosenbloom, P. (1981). Mechanisms of skill acquisition and the law of practice. In J. Anderson (ed.), *Cognitive Skills and their Acquisition*. Hillsdale, NJ: Erlbaum.

Norman, D. and Bobrow, D. (1975). On data-limited and resource-limited processes. *Cognitive Psychology*, **7**, 44–64.

North, R. (1977). Task functional demands as factors in dual task performance. In *Proceedings of the 21st Meeting of the Human Factors Society*. San Francisco, CA: Human Factors Society.

North, R. (1985). WINDEX: a workload index for interactive crew station evaluation. In *Proceedings of NAECON*. New York: IEEE.

North, R. and Gopher, D. (1976). Measures of attention as predictors of flight performance. *Human Factors*, **18**, 1–14.

North, R. and Riley, V. (1988). WINDEX: a predictive model of operator workload. In G. McMillian (ed.), *Human Performance Models*. Orlando, Florida: NATO AGARD.

Obrist, P.A., Webb, R.A., Sutterer, J.R. and Howard, J.L. (1970). The cardiac–somatic relationship: some reformulations. *Psychophysiology*, **6**, 569–587.

O'Connor, K.P. (1981). The intentional paradigm and cognitive psychophysiology. *Psychophysiology*, **18**, 121–128.

O'Donnell, R. and Eggemeier, F.T. (1986). Workload assessment methodology. In K. Boff, L. Kaufman and J. Thomas, (eds), *Handbook of Perception and Human Performance*. New York: Wiley, pp. 42.1–42.49.

Ogden, G., Levine, J. and Eisner, E. (1979). Measurement of workload by secondary tasks. *Human Factors*, **21**, 529–548.

Öhman, A. (1979). The orienting response, attention and learning: an information processing perspective. In H.D. Kimmel, E.H. van Olst and J.F. Orlebeke (eds), *The Orienting Reflex in Humans*. Hillsdale, NJ: Erlbaum.

Öhman, A. (1986). Face the beast and fear the face: animal and social fears as prototypes for evoluntionary analyses of emotion. *Psychophysiology*, **23**, 123–145.

Öhman, A. (1987). The psychophysiology of emotion: an evolutionary cognitive perspective. In P.K. Ackles, J.R. Jennings and M.G.H. Coles (eds), *Advances in Psychophysiology*, vol. 2. Greenwich, CT: JAI Press, pp. 79–127.

Öhman, A. (1988). Nonconscious control of autonomic responses: a role for Pavolian conditioning? *Biological Psychology*, **27**, 113–135.

Öhman, A. Dimberg, U. and Esteves, F. (in press). Preattentive activation of aversive emotions. In T. Archer and L.G. Nilsson (eds), *Aversion, Avoidance and Anxiety: Perspectives on Aversely Motivated Behavior*. Hillsdale, NJ: Erlbaum.

Öhman, A. Esteves, F., Parra, C. and Soares, J. (1988). Brain lateralization and preattentive elicitation of conditioned skin conductance responses. *Psychophysiology*, **25**, 473.

Okita, T. (1979). Event-related potentials and selective attention to auditory stimuli varying in pitch and localization. *Biological Psychology*, **9**, 271–284.

Packer, J.S. and Siddle, D.A.T. (1989). Stimulus miscuing, electrodermal activity, and the allocation of processing resources. *Psychophysiology*, **26**, 192–200.

Papanicolaou, A. and Johnstone, J. (1984). Probe evoked potentials: theory, method and applications. *International Journal of Neuroscience*, **24**, 107–131.

Parasuraman, R. (1978). Auditory evoked potentials and divided attention. *Psychophysiology*, **15**, 460–465.

Parasuraman, R. (1985). Event-related brain potentials and intermodal divided attention. In *Proceedings of the 29th Annual Meeting of the Human Factors Society*. Santa Monica, CA: Human Factors Society.

Parks, D. and Boucek, G. (1988). Time-line analysis. In G. McMillian (ed.), *Human Performance Models*. Orlando, Flordia: NATO AGARD.

Pearce, J.M. and Hall, G. (1980). A model of Pavlovian learning: variations in the effectivness of conditioned but not unconditioned stimuli. *Psychological Review*, **87**, 532–552.

Peavler, W.S. (1974). Pupil size, information overload, and performance differences. *Psychophysiology*, **11**, 559–566.

Peters, J., Billinger, T. and Knott, J. (1977). Event related potentials of brain (CNV and P300) in a paired associate learning paradigm. *Psychophysiology*, **14**, 579–585.

Petrinovich, L. (1979). Probabilistic functionalism. *American Psychologist*, **34**, 373–390.

Phelps, M. and Mazziotta, J. (1985). Positron emission tomography: human brain function and biochemistry. *Science*, **228**, 799–809.

Polson, M. and Freidman, A. (1988). Task sharing within and between hemispheres: a multiple resource approach. *Human Factors*, **30**, 633–643.

Poock, G.K. (1973). Information processing vs pupil diameter. *Perceptual and Motor Skills*, **37**, 1000–1002.

Poon, L., Thompson, L., Williams, R. and Marsh, G. (1974). Changes of antero-posterior distribution of CNV and late positive component as a function of information processing demands. *Psychophysiology*, **11**, 660–673.

Porges, S.W. (1972). Heart rate variability and deceleration as indexes of reaction time. *Journal of Experimental Psychology*, **92**, 103–110.

Posner, M. (1982). Cumulative development of attentional theory. *American Psychologist*, **37**, 168–179.

Posner, M. and Boies, S.J. (1971). Components of attention. *Psychological Review*, **78**, 391–408.

Posner, M. and Klein, R. (1973). On the functions of consciousness. In S. Kornblum (ed.), *Attention and Performance*, vol. IV. New York: Academic Press.

Posner, M., Petersen, S., Fox, P. and Raichle, M. (1988). Localization of cognitive operations in the human brain. *Science*, **240**, 1627–1631.

Pribram, K.H. and McGuinness, D. (1975). Arousal, activation and effort in the control of attention. *Psychological Review*, **82**, 116–149.

Proctor, R. and Proctor, J. (1979). Secondary task modality, expectancy, and the measurement of attention capacity. *Journa of Experimental Psychology: Human Perception and Performance*, **5**, 610–624.

Ragot, R. (1984). Perceptual and motor space representation: an event related potential study. *Psychophysiology*, **21**, 159–170.

Ratcliff, R. (1979). Group reaction time distributions and an analysis of distribution statistics. *Psychological Bulletin*, **86**, 446–461.

Ratcliff, R. (1985). Theoretical interpretations of the speed and accuracy of positive and negative responses. *Psychological Review*, **92**, 212–225.

Risberg, J. and Prohovnik, I. (1983). Cortical processing of visual and tactile stimuli studied by non-invasive rCBF measurements. *Human Neurobiology*, **2**, 5–10.

Rohrbaugh, J.W. (1984). The orienting reflex: performance and central nervous system manifestations. In R. Parasuraman and D.R. Davies (eds), *Varieties of Attention*. New York: Academic Press, pp. 323–373.

Rosler, F. (1981). Event-related brain potentials in a stimulus discrimination learning paradigm. *Psychophysiology*, **18**, 447–455.

Roth, N., Leubuscher, H.J., Pogelt, A., Bergmann, R. and Pogelt, B. (1985). Cortical ERP in man and processing of feedback information during maze learning. In F. Klix, R. Näätänen and K. Zimmer (eds), *Psychophysiological Approaches to Human Information Processing*. North-Holland: Elsevier, pp. 257–268.

Roth, W.T. (1983). A comparison of P300 and skin conductance response. In A.W.K. Gaillard and W. Ritter (eds), *Tutorials in ERP Research: Endogenous Components*. Amsterdam: North Holland, pp. 177–200.

Ruttkay-Nedecky, I. (1967). Outline of a general scheme of physiological changes during the orienting reaction in man. In I. Ruttaky-Nedecky, L. Ciganek, V. Zikmund and E. Kellerova (eds), *Mechanisms of the Orienting Reflex in Man*. Britislava: Slovak Academy of Sciences, pp. 187–197.

Sams, M., Paavilainen, P., Alho, K. and Naatanen, R. (1985). Auditory frequency discrimination and event related potentials. *Electroencephalography and Clinical Neurophysiology*, **62**, 437–448.

Sanders, A. (1979). Some remarks on mental load. In N. Moray (ed.), *Mental Workload: Its Theory and Measurement*. New York: Plenum Press, pp. 41–78.

Sanders, A. (1981). Stress and human performance: a working model and some applications. In G. Salvendy and E. Smith (eds), *Machine Pacing and Occupational Stress*. London: Taylor and Francis.

Sayers, B. (1971). The analysis of cardiac interbeat interval sequences and the effects of mental workload. *Royal Society of Medicine*, **64**, 707–710

Sayers, B. (1973). Analysis of heart rate variability. *Ergonomics*, **16**, 17–32.

Sayers, B. (1975). Physiological consequences of informational load and overload. In P.H. Vernables and M.J. Christie (eds), *Research in Psychophysiology*. London: Wiley.

Schneider, W. (1985). Towards a model of attention and the development of automatic processing. In M. Posner and O. Marin (eds), *Attention and Performance*, vol. XI. New York: Erlbaum, pp. 475–492.

Schneider, W. and Detweiler, M. (1988). The role of practice in dual-task performance: toward workload modelling in a connectionist/control architecture. *Human Factors*, **30**, 539–566.

Schneider, W. and Shiffrin, R. (1977). Controlled and automatic information processing. I: Detection, search and attention. *Psychological Review*, **84**, 1–66.

Sem-Jacobsen, C.W. (1981). Brain/computer communication to reduce human error: a perspective. *Aviation, Space and Environmental Medicine*, January, 31–38.

Sem-Jacobsen, C.W. and Sem-Jacobsen, I.E. (1963). Selection and evaluation of pilots for high performance aircraft and spacecraft by inflight EEG study of stress tolerence. *Aerospace Medicine*, July, 603–609.

Shaffer, L. (1975). Multiple attention in continuous tasks. In P. Rabbitt and S. Dornic (eds), *Attention and Performance*, vol. V. London: Academic Press.

Sharit, J., Salvendy, G. and Deisenroth, M.P. (1982). External and internal attentional environments. I: The utilization of cardiac deceleratory and acceleratory response data for evaluating differences in mental workload between machine-paced and self-paced work. *Ergonomics*, **25**, 107–120.

Sharit, J. and Salvendy, G. (1982). External and internal attentional environments II. Reconsideration of the relationship between sinus arrhythmia and information load. *Ergonomics*, **25**, 121–132.

Sheridan, T, and Ferrell, W. (1974). *Man–Machine Systems: Information, Control and Decision Models of Human Performance*. Cambridge, MA: MIT Press.

Shiffrin, R. and Dumais, S.T. (1981). The development of automatism. In J.R. Anderson (ed.), *Cognitive Skills and Their Acquisition*. Hillsdale, NJ: Erlbaum.

Shiffrin, R. and Schneider, W. (1977). Controlled and automatic human information processing. II: Perceptual learning, automatic attending and a general theory. *Psychological Review*, **84**, 127–190.

Siddle, D.A.T. (1985). Effects of stimulus omission and stimulus change on dishabituation of the skin conductance response. *Journal of Experimental Psychology: Learning, Memory and Cognition*, **11**, 206–216.

Siddle, D.A.T. and Hirschhorn, T. (1986). Effects of stimulus omission and stimulus novelty on dishabituation of the skin conductance response. *Psychophysiology*, **23**, 309–314.

Siddle, D.A.T. and Packer, J.S. (1987). Stimulus omission and dishabituation of the electrodermal orienting response: the allocation of processing resources. *Psychophysiology*, **24**, 181–190.

Siddle, D.A.T., Broekhuizen, D. and Packer, J.S. (1988). Stimulus miscuing and dishabituation: electrodermal activity and resource allocation. *Psychophysiology*, **25**, 481.

Siddle, D.A.T. and Packer, J. (in press). Orienting, habituation and the allocation of processing resources. In N.W. Bond and D.A.T Siddle (eds), *Psychobiology: Issues and Applications*. (Proceedings of the 24th International Congress of Psychology, Sydney, Australia, vol. 5). Amsterdam: Elsevier, pp. 104–113.

Siddle, D.A.T., Remington, B., Kuiack, M. and Haines, E. (1983). Stimulus omission and dishabituation of the skin conductance response. *Psychophysiology*, **20**, 136–145.

Siddle, D.A.T. and Spinks, J.A. (1979). Orienting response and information processing. some theoretical and empirical problems. In H.D. Kimmel, E.H. van Olst and J.F. Orlebecke (eds), *The Orienting Reflex in Humans*. Hillsdale, NJ: Erlbaum.

Sirevaag, E., Kramer, A., Coles, M. and Donchin, E. (1989). Resource reciprocity: an event-related brain potentials analysis. *Acta Psychologica*, **70**, 77–97.

Sirevaag, E., Kramer, A., de Jong, R, and Mecklinger, A. (1988). A psychophysiological analysis of multi-task processing demands. *Psychophysiology*, **25**, 482.

Sokolov, E.N. (1963). *Perception and the Conditioned Reflex*. Oxford: Pergamon.

Sokolov, E.N. (1966). Orienting reflex as information regulator. In A. Leontiev, A. Luria and A. Smirnov (eds), *Psychological Research in the USSR*, vol. I. Moscow: Progress Publishers, pp. 334–360.

Sokolov, E.N. (1969). The modeling properties of the nervous system. In M. Cole and I. Maltzman (eds), *A Handbook of Contemporary Soviet Psychology*. New York: Basic Books, pp. 671–704.

Spelke, E., Hirst, W. and Neisser, U. (1976). Skills of divided attention. *Cognition*, **4**, 215–230.

Sperling, G. and Melchner, M. (1978). The attention operating characteristic: examples from visual search. *Science*, **20**, 315–318.

Spinks, J.A. (1987a). Switching of attentional resources: ERP correlates. *Psychophysiology*, **24**, 613.

Spinks, J.A. (1987b). Paradigms and problems in psychophysiology. *Journal of Psychophysiology*, **1**, 17–20.

Spinks, J.A. (1989). The orienting response in anticipation of information processing demands. In N.W. Bond and D.A.T. Siddle (eds), *Psychobiology: Issues and Applications* (Proceedings of the 24th International Conference of Psychology, Sydney, Australia, vol. 6).. Amsterdam: Elsevier, pp. 138–150.

Spinks, J.A., Blowers, G.H. and Shek, D.T.L. (1985). The role of the orienting response in the anticipation of information: a skin conductance response study. *Psychophysiology*, **22**, 385–394.

Spinks, J.A., Chan, T.C. and Chan, K.K. (1985). Orienting and anticipation in a two-stimulus, dual-task paradigm. *Psychophysiology*, **22**, 614.

Spinks, J.A. and Siddle, D.A.T. (1983). The functional significance of the orienting response. In D. Siddle (ed.), *Orienting and Habituation: Perspectives in Human Research*. Chichester: Wiley, pp. 237–314.

Spinks, J.A. and Siddle, D.A.T. (1985). The effects of anticipated information on skin conductance and cardiac activity. *Biological Psychology*, **20**, 39–50.

Stenfert-Kroese, B. and Siddle, D.A.T. (1983). Effects of an attention-demanding task on amplitude and habituation of the electrodermal orienting response. *Psychophysiology*, **20**, 128–135.

Sternberg, S. (1969). On the discovery of processing stages: some extensions of Donder's method. *Acta Psychologica*, **30**, 276–315.

Strayer, D. and Kramer, A.F. (1990). Attentional requirements of automatic and controlled processes. *Journal of Experimental Psychology: Learning, Memory and Cognition*, **16**, 67–82.

Ullsperger, P., Metz, A. and Gille, H. (1988). The P300 component of the event-related brain potential and mental effort. *Ergonomics*, **31**, 1127–1137.

Van Dellen, H., Brookhuis, K., Mulder, G., Okita, T. and Mulder, L. (1984). Evoked potential correlates of practice in a visual search task. In D. Papakostopoulos *et al.* (eds), *Clinical and Experimental Neuropsychophysiology*. Beckenham, UK: Croom Helm.

Van der Molen, M.W., Boomsma, D.I., Jennings, J.R. and Nieuboer, R.T. (1989). Does the heart know what the eye sees? A cardiac/pupillometric analysis of motor preparation and response execution. *Psychophysiology*, **26**, 70–80.

Van Toller, C. (1979). *The Nervous Body*. Chichester: Wiley.

Van Voorhis, S. and Hillyard, S. (1977). Visual evoked potentials and selective attention to points in space. *Perception and Psychophysics*, **22**, 54–62.

Vicente, K.J., Thornton, D.C. and Moray, N. (1987). Spectral analysis of sinus arrhythmia: a measure of mental effort. *Human Factors*, **29**, 171–182.

von Wright, J.M., Anderson, K. and Stenmen, U. (1975). Generalization of conditioned CSRs in dichotic listening. In P.M.A. Rabbitt and S. Dornic (eds), *Attention and Performance*, vol. V. London: Academic Press.

Wardlaw, K.A. and Kroll, N.E.A. (1976) Autonomic responses to shock associated words in a non-attended message: a failure to replicate. *Journal of Experimental Psychology: Human Perception and Performance*, **2**, 357–360.
Wickens, C.D. (1980). The structure of attentional resurces. In R.S. Nickerson (ed.) *Attention and Performance*, vol. VIII. Hillsdale, NJ: Erlbaum, pp. 239–257.
Wickens, C.D. (1984a). Processing resources in attention. In R. Parasuraman and D. Davies (eds), *Varieties of Attention*. New York: Academic Press, pp. 63–102.
Wickens, C.D. (1984b). *Engineering Psychology and Human Performance*. Columbus, Ohio: Merrill.
Wickens, C.D. (1986). Gain and energetics in information processing. In G. Hockey, A. Gaillard and M. Coles (eds), *Energetics and Information Processing*. Netherlands: Martinus Nijhoff.
Wickens, C.D. and Bowles, D. (1983). *The Limits of Multiple Resource Theory: The Role of Task Correlation/Integration in Optimal Display Formatting*. Technical Report EPL-83-5, Engineering Psychology Research Laboratory, University of Illinois, Champaign, IL.
Wickens, C.D., Harwood, K., Segal, L., Tkalcevic and Sherman, B. (1988). TASKILLAN: a simulation to predict the validity of multiple resource models of aviation workload. In *Proceedings of the 32nd Annual Meeting of the Human Factors Society*. California: Human Factors Society.
Wickens, C.D. and Kramer, A.F. (1985). Engineering Psychology. In *Annual Review of Psychology*. New York: Annual Reviews Inc.
Wickens, C.D., Kramer, A.F., Vanasse, L. and Donchin, E. (1983). The performance of concurrent tasks: a psychophysiological analysis of the reciprocity of information processing resources. *Science*, **221**, 1080–1082.
Wickens, C.D., Mountford, J. and Schreiner, W. (1981). Multiple resources, task-hemispheric integrity, and individual differences in time-sharing. *Human Factors*, **23**, 211–229.
Wickens, C.D. and Yeh, Y. (1985). POCs and performance decrements: a reply to Kantowitz and Weldon. *Human Factors*, **27**, 549–554.
Wierwille, W. (1979). Physiological measures of aircrew mental workload. *Human Factors*, **21**, 575–594.
Wilkinson, R.T. (1962). Muscle tension during mental work under sleep deprivation. *Journal of Experimental Psychology*, **64**, 565–571.
Williamson, S. and Kaufman, L. (1981). Biomagnetism. *Journal of Magnetism and Magnetic Materials*, **22**, 129–201.
Zwaga, H.J.G. (1973). Psychophysiological reactions to mental tasks: effort or stress? *Ergonomics*, **16**, 61–67.

Chapter 3

Passive and Active Attention to Input

Frances K. Graham
Department of Psychology, University of Delaware, Newark, DE 19716, USA.
and
Steven A. Hackley
Department of Psychology, University of Missouri, Columbia, MO 65211, USA.

ABSTRACT

Passive and active attention to input induces a number of changes in brain activity, reflex sensitivity, and autonomic activity. Passive attention is reviewed with an emphasis on the generalized orienting reflex (OR). The review of active attention focuses on the locus of attentional filtering, its automaticity, and the representation of the attended information. Although this chapter is jointly authored, authorship of major sections is noted to reflect primary contributions.

INTRODUCTION

The term 'attention' commonly refers to an internal, central process that benefits sensory reception and perception. It is a fuzzy construct whose

Handbook of Cognitive Psychophysiology: Central and Autonomic Nervous System Approaches.
Edited by J. R. Jennings and M. G. H. Coles.

history has included banishment and resurrection, and its ultimate place in any comprehensive theory of human information processing is by no means secure. The current resurrection beginning in the fifties appears to have arisen independently from two main sources: one, the development of information processing concepts in response to the practical problems of characterizing observer behavior in industrial and military situations; the other, the development of 'orienting' theory which appeared to offer an objective physiological measure of an attentional process.

These two sources differ in the type of attention emphasized: active, voluntary attention or passive, involuntary attention. The psychological/behavioral literature on observer behavior has dealt primarily with active attention and with theories of when and how input processing becomes selective and limited. In contrast, orienting theory has been concerned mainly with passive attention. Psychophysiology has contributed to research on both types of attention, but more or less segregated by the physiological measures employed: research on responses of the autonomic nervous system (ANS) has concentrated on a particular form of passive attention, the generalized 'orientation reflex' (OR), while research on evoked and emitted brain potentials, collectively termed 'event-related potentials' (ERPs), has emphasized active attention. However, in the last decade, there has been considerable interest in integrating the two approaches, as evidenced by a panel report (Donchin *et al.*, 1984) which discussed a possible integrated theory of the organism's reaction to novelty based on both the ANS and ERP literature. Another recent development in psychophysiology has exploited the malleability of somatic reflexes as a means of investigating both active and passive attention.

The first part of this chapter reviews passive attention with emphasis on the generalized OR. The major question is whether response to novel change requires a cognitive model-comparison process or can be explained by a non-cognitive theory on the basis of the pattern created by differential habituation of elements and a general sensitization process. A second concern is the role of preattentive processes in transmitting information about the transient and sustained characteristics of stimuli. The chapter then goes on to review active attention and, specifically, three questions that are important for a general theory of information processing: (1) the initial divergence in processing of attended and ignored stimuli; (2) levels of automaticity; (3) some implications of the question of continuous versus discrete representation and transmission of input information. Autonomic, ERP, and somatic reflex evidence are considered in both sections.

Both types of attention may act peripherally as well as centrally, and on decisions and responses as well as on sensory–perceptual processes. The question of how to infer effects on input uncontaminated by other effects is in essence the question of the locus of effects, which may be answered not only in terms of psychological concepts but also in terms of the chronometric and anatomic loci. The debates about intraperceptual versus extraperceptual effects (Johnston and Dark, 1986) and about early versus late selection are variants of this fundamental issue, as is the controversy concerning automaticity in perception (Schneider and Shiffrin, 1977; Kahneman and Treisman, 1984). These questions are often discussed in terms of an additive-factors, discrete-stage theory in which one stage must be completed before the next stage can begin (Sternberg, 1969). However, newer theories, hypothesizing parallel distributed processing and continuous outputs of partially analysed information, may offer a better possibility for integrating psychological and psychophysiological findings and of illuminating differences between various types of attention (Livingstone and Hubel, 1988; Posner *et al.*, 1988).

PASSIVE ATTENTION AND GENERALIZED ORIENTING

F.K. GRAHAM AND S.A. HACKLEY

Sokolov's writings (e.g. Sokolov, 1963) describe the generalized OR as a response elicited by any discriminable change in 'non-signal' stimuli; that is, stimuli incapable of reinforcing other responses and not associated with reinforcing stimuli either through conditioning procedures or instructions. Although, in theory, generalized orienting benefits sensory analysis, the benefits are assumed to be non-selective and, thus, are unlike the selective benefits conferred by active attention or the 'localized' OR. The localized OR is a response akin to active selective attention in that it occurs to 'signal' stimuli, such as warning and conditioned stimuli, which provide information about subsequent stimuli for voluntary or unconditioned responses.

Sokolov's theory of orienting is an information-processing conceptualization. Stimuli elicit an OR, independent of specific qualities of the stimuli, when they carry information that a change has occurred or that a significant stimulus will follow. The mechanism for recognizing change or novelty is detection of a discrepancy between the current stimulus and a neuronal model of past and expected stimulation. The model, consisting of internal representations of the characteristics of prior stimulation, includes not only simple qualitative, intensive, and temporal characteristics, but also more complex relationships such as the sequence or pattern of stimuli, the meaning of words, and the probability of occurrence (Sokolov, 1963; pp. 286–289). Any deviation of current stimulation from the model leads to an OR whose size is proportional to the degree of discrepancy (Sokolov, 1969; p.674). Because the model is continually updated as a stimulus is repeated, it incorporates additional information so that the discrepancy lessens until, with information extraction complete, the OR is completely habituated.

A further step in developing an information-processing theory of orienting was taken by Öhman (1979) in his proposal that an OR is elicited under two sets of conditions: (1) when a stimulus occurs that cannot be matched by preattentive mechanisms to representations in short-term memory; (2) when the stimulus matches a representation primed as significant. The latter proposition is a considerable revision of Sokolov's formulation which did not deal explicitly with how a signal stimulus elicited a localized OR. By implication from Sokolov's discussions of how a localized OR develops from a generalized OR in the course of acquiring a conditioned response, it could be assumed that incorporating the information of stimulus association requires more repetitions than are needed when the same stimulus is not a signal. Discrepancies would, therefore, continue to be detected and the OR to be elicited. However, once the current stimulus matched the neuronal model, OR elicitation would be blocked. In contrast, Öhman's formulation allows a stimulus matching a representation primed as significant to continue to elicit an OR until, through the resulting attentional processing, automatic routines for appropriate responding are established.

Öhman's (1979) formulation also substitutes for the neuronal model, two types of memory store, short-term and long-term, which function similarly to the memory stores in such information-processing theories as those of Wagner (1976) and Shiffrin and Schneider (1977). Such theories assume that information can be stored in long-term memory only through processing in a central, or limited-capacity channel which is equated with attentional processing. In adopting the idea of limitations in processing, whether of resources or capacity (e.g. Kahneman, 1973), Öhman has aligned OR theory with the mainstream of cognitive theory. In Öhman's view, the OR is a physiological indicant that a call has been made for controlled resource-limited processing, but the call may not be answered if resources are fully engaged. Others view the OR as a sign that resources have already been allocated to the OR-eliciting stimulus (Dawson, Filion and Schell, 1989; Posner, 1978).

Historically, the idea of passive attention encompassed conditions which are excluded from the Sokolovian idea of generalized orienting. William James (1890), in describing stimuli eliciting 'passive, reflex, non-voluntary, effortless' sensory attention, included stimuli which were very intense or sudden or else were 'instinctive'; that is, intrinsically salient or prepotent for a particular species. It is now known that such stimuli also elicit other responses which can distort measures of the OR; thus, their specific effects need to be distinguished from those of the OR *per se*.

DISTINGUISHING CHARACTERISTICS

There are several excellent recent reviews on orienting (Kimmel, van Olst and Orlebeke, 1979; Rohrbaugh, 1984; Siddle, 1983), in addition to Sokolov's writings (see the English language bibliography in Graham, 1989). Our discussion is largely restricted to problems in distinguishing the generalized OR from reactions with which it has been confused, and to problems important for relating research from different areas.

Eliciting Stimuli and Functional Effects

The main feature of Sokolov's generalized OR, a widespread reaction consisting of ANS as well as electroencephalographic (EEG) components, is that it is elicited by a non-specific stimulus characteristic; that is, by any change in stimulation with a low probability of occurrence, rather than by some specific stimulus quality. A number of terms have been employed to describe this characteristic—for example, novel, surprising, unexpected, or incongruous (Berlyne, 1969; Lynn, 1966)—but they all connote an improbable stimulus. Although questions about the role of stimulus 'significance' remain, and were argued in 1979 in a series of papers in *Psychophysiology*, we adopt the view that many significant stimuli are signals and should elicit a localized rather than a generalized OR.

Sokolov distinguished the OR from a second generalized system, the '*defense* reflex', which was also elicited independent of specific quality and occurred in response to any stimulus of high intensity. The term 'defense' seems to be a misnomer because eliciting stimuli need not be sufficiently painful or dangerous to require protective reactions although, with repetitive presentation, they might become mildly noxious. Sokolov (1963) reported defense responses to acoustic stimuli as low as 70 dB (pp.47, 184) or even 60 dB (p.177). The concept has also been extended to include stimuli which evoke negative affect (e.g. Hare and Blevings, 1975). Despite ambiguity in specifying how intense or noxious an elicitor must be, it is clear that a decrease in stimulus intensity or the offset of a stimulus is a stimulus change which is appropriate for eliciting an OR, but not a defense reflex.

A major premise of Sokolov's orienting theory is that the generalized OR and defense reflex have opposite effects on the sensitivity to sensory input: while the OR is assumed to lower absolute thresholds and enhance the ability to discriminate stimulus characteristics, the defense reflex is assumed to reduce sensitivity to sensory inputs. Improved ability to discriminate stimulus qualities does not, however, imply an increased ability to experience the subjective sensation of pain. Sokolov (1963; pp.15, 183) described the two types of sensitivity as inversely related with 'each having an inhibitory effect on the other'.

Sokolov also distinguished the generalized OR and defense reflexes from a class of specific *adaptive* reflexes which react to the particular characteristics of a stimulus and serve a variety of specific homeostatic functions. Examples include vasomotor responses to heat and cold, pupillary responses to light and dark, and digestive responses to specific types of taste stimuli. Sokolov did not discuss the class of stimuli referred to as 'instinctive' by James (1890). Except when they are intense or signal potentially damaging stimulation, and thus elicit a defense reflex, these emotion-engaging stimuli do not fit well into Sokolov's three-category system.

Another class of generalized reflexes can also be distinguished, namely, reflexes elicited solely by transient characteristics of stimuli. Although Sokolov (1963) did not make the distinction explicit, he noted that the onset of stimulation signaled only the presence of a stimulus, and provided different information than that of stimulus prolongation (p.68). Other research shows that onsets reaching a sufficiently high intensity in a sufficiently brief time, of the order of 10–30 ms (Berg, 1973; Blumenthal and Berg, 1986), elicit a *startle* reflex. In its full form, the primary startle reaction consists of widespread flexor contractions beginning with the eyeblink, the most persistent component, and spreading caudally. Secondary, longer-lasting and variable reactions may follow, but these apparently depend on later controlled processing (Landis and Hunt, 1939). When the stimulus is novel as well as sudden, both startle and an OR may occur; similarly, if the novel sudden stimulus is intense and lasts longer than 10–30 ms, both startle and defense may be elicited in addition to an OR. Landis and Hunt pointed out that the startle response is non-directional with respect to the eliciting stimulus and, thus, is not a protective reflex like the flexor withdrawal to painful stimuli.

Graham (1979) suggested that startle may best be described as an interrupt of ongoing activity. She left open the question whether it should be viewed simply as the high-intensity extreme of a preattentive transient-detecting system or a separate interrupt system, but later proposed (Graham, 1984; Graham, Anthony and Zeigler, 1983; pp.392ff.) that there were adequate grounds for distinguishing the startle reaction from the reaction elicited by low-intensity transients. Although all transient information may be transmitted rapidly to higher levels, effects of high- and low-intensity transients may be transmitted via distinct neural paths (Lundberg, 1966). More important, effects of intensity extremes differ in the direction of the short-latency heart rate changes they produce (see following subsection), in their early maturation and rates of habituation (Graham, 1984; Graham, Anthony and Zeigler, 1983), and in effects on the dissociable latency and amplitude of the response to a shortly-following high-intensity transient (Stitt *et al.*, 1976). The responses to low-intensity transients were called *transient-detecting responses*. It has been suggested that these may affect the processing of additional information about sustained stimulus characteristics (see 'Preattentive Transient Processing' below). They may also signal the spatial location, as well as the presence of a stimulus, and thus underlie the non-habituating facilitation of reaction time by a lateralized, transient 'accessory' stimulus (Faber *et al.*, 1986) or the facilitating or inhibiting effects of irrelevant transients on the response to imperative or target stimuli (e.g. Jonides, 1981; Muller and Rabbitt, 1989).

Response Characteristics

The four generalized (modality non-specific) reflexes of orienting, defense, startle, and transient-detecting are, thus, distinguishable in terms of the stimulus characteristics which elicit them; that is, low probability change, sustained high intensity, and high-intensity and low-intensity rapid transients, respectively. The four reflexes also have distinguishing as well as overlapping response components. In general, the overlapping components are those which have been associated with heightened arousal or effort (Berlyne, 1969; Kahneman, 1973), and include sympathetic adrenergic reactions, a sympathetic but cholingergic reaction (the electrodermal response), EEG desynchronization, and non-specific electromyographic (EMG) activity. Several ERP components have also been associated with generalized and/or localized orienting as well as with defense, startle, and transient-detection. The question of which ERP components might be functionally related to these reflexes is addressed later in the present chapter.

Those ANS components that have been identified as non-overlapping and distinguishing are components that change bidirectionally as a function of intensity. Thus, the OR differs from both startle and defense in showing prolonged heart rate deceleration rather than acceleration (Graham, 1979), and in showing cephalic vasodilitation rather than constriction (Sokolov, 1963). However, the latter response has proven difficult to record reliably (e.g. Graham, 1979; Skolnick, Walrath and Stern, 1979). Changes in muscle activity that are non-specific with respect to locating a stimulus are also distinguishing. Reductions rather than increases in general motor activity, and slowing rather than speeding of respiration, may separate the OR from defense and startle (Graham, Anthony and Zeigler, 1983; Lynn, 1966). Startle, in addition, is manifested in the distinctive flexor-contraction pattern. Separation of transient-detection from the other reflexes has been studied mainly via its effect in attenuating the startle blink to a subsequent stimulus (Anthony, 1985; Graham, 1979). Unless the detected transient is itself capable of eliciting startle, transient-detecting responses are also reflected in a brief 1 or 2 s heart rate deceleration (Barry, 1987; Graham, 1979, 1984), which was described as a 'subcortical OR' by Graham and Jackson (1970).

Many writers have associated orienting with receptor-directing movements towards the location of a novel stimulus, as in Pavlov's 'orienting–investigatory' reaction or the alignment of peripheral systems to an input pathway (Posner, 1978). Such movements are not a necessary concomitant of orienting and are often excluded by experimental controls. Sokolov (1963; p.11) stated explicitly that the Pavlovian definition was 'too wide' and, consequently, he excluded directed motor/postural reactions which bring the receptors into better alignment with a stimulus. According to Berlyne (1969), who cited the Russian language publication of Sokolov's 1963 book, Pavlov in his later work also separated receptor-adjusting acts from orienting. The classification system proposed by Graham (1984) maintains a distinction between orienting and both high-intensity transient-detecting startle and low-intensity transient-detecting responses. If transient detection reflexly elicits directed responses such as saccadic eye movements—a debated issue, briefly reviewed by Muller and Rabbitt (1989)—their occurrence would be a further means of distinguishing transient detection from orienting.

Finally, although each of the generalized reflexes can be considered a distinct 'system' in the sense of serving a common function in response to a common aspect of stimulation, the degree of covariation among a system's components is not high (Barry, 1987; Voronin and Sokolov, 1960). As with biological systems in general—digestive, auditory, sympathetic, and so on—components have different thresholds for elicitation, are measured with differing sensitivity over backgrounds of greater or lesser 'noise', and participate to differing degrees in other systems. Components of the OR which overlap with defense or startle might be expected to covary more highly with one another than with non-overlapping components, and components which play a major role in the bodily economy (for example, the cardiovascular components) might be expected to show a poorer signal/noise ratio as measures of orienting than a component like the electrodermal response which has a relatively limited role.

Methodological Considerations

In order to study processes within the central nervous system that underlie attention, whether passive or active, it is necessary to control for *confounding peripheral factors*. These include changes in proximal stimulus intensity, response contamination, sensory receptor adaptation, and effector fatigue. Although instructions and restraining devices may reduce or prevent the head, eye, and other muscle movements that can change the intensity of stimulation reaching a receptor or contaminate measures of dependent response variables, the addition of adequately sensitive monitoring allows for trial exclusion and statistical adjustment if movement is present. Receptor effects are avoided by stimulating at rates within which response of the first-order sensory nerve remains flat. Rates no faster than 100 per second have been suggested for acoustic and somatosensory stimuli (Davis, 1976; Thompson and Spencer, 1966), but 10 per second is a safer cutoff point (Picton, Stapells and Campbell, 1981; Worden, 1973) and should also avoid striate muscle fatigue if the total period of stimulation is not longer than several minutes (Goodgold and Eberstein, 1977). In practice, slower rates may be required for the study of long-latency ERP components and electrodermal responses which would otherwise be lost or obscured due to the overlap of responses to successive stimuli. The most important control is provided by randomizing or balancing stimulus presentations. The second part of this chapter starts with a discussion of useful design features.

The phasic responses that index attention can also be affected by changes in *tonic state* if ambient temperature, noise levels, or illumination vary during a session, or if sessions begin before subjects adapt to differences between the external and laboratory environments. Constancy in the general state of alertness is critically important. The problems have been dealt with variously, as by monitoring tonic physiological levels, by attempting to control state through increasing interest value and demand characteristics of the situation and, again, by using random or balanced presentation of stimulus conditions.

The *standard paradigm* for studying orienting includes a series of repetitions of one stimulus (S1), leading to response decrement or habituation, and a change stimulus (S2), which may lead to *recovery* of the decremented response. In ANS research, S2 is usually substituted for an S1 without a break in delivery rate; but Groves and Thompson (1970), in startle studies, inserted S2 within an interstimulus interval (ISI) and measured its effect on *dishabituation* of response to re-presentation of S1. Although the term 'dishabituation' has also been applied to the recovered response elicited by S2, we will preserve the distinction: that is, 'recovery' for enhanced response to S2 and 'dishabituation' for enhanced response to re-presentation of S1.

Non-standard paradigms have also been used. Repeated blocks of stimuli, with each block including all of several different stimuli, allows balanced presentation but, owing to generalization of incrementing and decrementing effects, is an insensitive, difficult-to-interpret procedure for testing repetition and change effects. Variants used in ERP research, to overcome poor signal-to-noise ratios, include averaging by ordinal position across a number of runs or trains of stimuli (Ritter, Vaughan and Costa, 1968) or, in the 'oddball' paradigm, averaging standard (habituating) stimuli and, separately, rare (change) stimuli interspersed among standards. In any design to study the OR, it is critical that response averages include only a few trials. Otherwise, the rapid habituation characterizing the generalized OR—which may occur in as few as two or three trials (e.g. Voronin and Sokolov, 1960)—can be missed altogether.

Typically, the procedures used in OR research have *low demand characteristics*. Subjects are given little information except to relax while stimuli are presented, and are assured that no response is required. Iacono and Lykken (1983) noted that such vague instructions may increase variability because subjects will decide for themselves whether to attend or ignore the stimuli. They suggested that it is preferable to provide explicit attend–ignore instructions or a task, which may either direct attention to the habituation stimuli (e.g. counting habituation stimuli) or direct attention to other stimuli (e.g. reading during presentation of auditory stimuli).

In discussing passive attention, we report only findings obtained when there is no explicit task involving the modality of novel/rare stimuli, that is, the stimuli of interest in understanding passive attention. We assume that even such low-demand tasks as counting or attending selectively to a specified rare stimulus and ignoring a different stimulus in the same modality requires discrimination and may involve active attention. However, we do consider studies in which effects of rare stimuli in one modality were obtained while a task directed attention to stimuli in a different modality. Although requirements of a task, such as reading during the presentation of auditory stimuli, may leave fewer resources available for processing the non-signal auditory stimuli, any novel/rare change in the auditory stream could potentially elicit passively, via the detection of mismatch, a call for processing resources.

COGNITIVE AND NON-COGNITIVE THEORIES

Two general classes of theory have developed to account for effects of stimulus change and its opposite, stimulus repetition. They can be broadly characterized as non-cognitive–non-associative, based on temporal and spatial contiguity of stimulus representations, or cognitive–associative, based on associative contingency relations among stimuli. The cognitive theory treats a novel or improbable stimulus as a special case which elicits a complex of responses qualitatively different from those elicited by a familiar stimulus. Both types of theory view stimulus repetition as a manipulation which leads to the decrementing of stimulus-evoked response by a central habituation process.

Model-Comparator Theory

Sokolov (1960) introduced the first detailed cognitive theory of habituation and dishabituation. His premise, that orienting is a response to information, implies that, as the information supplied by a stimulus is reduced by its incorporation into a neuronal model, the OR will also be reduced. Following a low-level analysis of stimulus properties, information is relayed to OR efferents both relatively directly via collaterals to interneurons in the reticular system and, relatively indirectly, via higher-level sensory analyzers in the cortex and, especially, in the hippocampus (Sokolov, 1975). In the hippocampus, 'novelty detectors' or 'attention units' presumably provide mismatch signals for amplifying the output to OR effectors or, through parallel inhibitory paths, for blocking OR expression. Units that are sensitive to attention and to violations of expectancy are probably widely distributed among cortical areas. However, the hippocampus and the associated amygdala are known to have connections with all sensory areas, to be involved in memory, and, probably, to play a role in attaching emotional significance to stimuli (Mishkin and Appenzeller, 1987). They seem well designed, therefore, to detect divergence between any type of current input and short-term memory patterns, and to detect matches between current input and memory nodes primed as significant. Thus, for the response class of OR components, both habituation and amplification are assumed to be due to extrinsic effects; that is, to inhibition or excitation not originating in the reflex path itself (Davis and File, 1984).

It follows from Sokolov's theory that, if the rate of OR habituation reflects the rate of adding information to the model, then OR habituation should be rapid with simple non-signal stimuli. By contrast, habituation should be slower to stimuli which are more difficult to model or discriminate, such as near-threshold stimuli or complex stimuli, and should also be slow to signal stimuli, which require a model of the association between stimuli. Habituation of an OR to novel, brief, startle-eliciting stimuli might also be expected to occur rapidly if the stimuli are simple, but the reflection of orienting by such bidirectional components as heart rate deceleration may be obscured initially or completely by the occurrence of heart rate acceleration in conjunction with the widespread flexor movements of startle. The defense, low-intensity transient-detecting, and adaptive reflexes that, except for overlapping components, are not affected by the model-comparison process, should show the relatively slow habituation which may be accounted for by non-cognitive theories. Overlapping components may even be intensified over the first few trials as orienting constituents of opposite directionality become extinguished.

Dual-Process Theory

The prevailing non-cognitive account of habituation and dishabituation does not treat the OR as being a response complex particularly sensitive to change. The theory was introduced in two influential articles by Thompson and Spencer (1966) and Groves and Thompson (1970). The former article summarized nine characteristics, abstracted from the literature on behavioral response habituation, that were proposed as an operational definition of habituation: decrements with stimulus repetition should (1) be progressive within series, (2) be progressive between series, (3) increase with faster repetition rates (later modified), (4) relate inversely to intensity (later modified), (5) generalize to other stimuli, (6) recover spontaneously with time, (7) recover more slowly if repetitions continue beyond zero responding (later modified), (8) dishabituate after insertion of another, usually strong, stimulus, and (9) reappear with repetition of a dishabituating stimulus (habituation of dishabituation).

In contrast to cognitive theory, dual-process theory accounts for the decrementing effect of repetition in terms of intrinsic habituation, that is, synaptic depression in interneurons of the reflex path itself. Thompson *et al.* (1979) point out that homosynaptic depression can also account for the generalization of habituation to other stimuli which share some but not all neuronal elements, the number shared probably being a function of the difference between the habituating stimulus and the stimulus to which habituation is generalized. They further note that the pattern created in the direct reflex path by completely habituated, partially habituated, and unaffected elements could provide, as well, the mechanism for formation of a stimulus model, thereby suggesting a basis for reconciliation with cognitive theory.

Dual-process theory also assumes that every stimulus, including the first in an habituation series, activates both the specific response-eliciting path, and an extrinsic 'sensitization' process in the non-specific or general state system (Groves and Thompson, 1970; Thompson *et al.*, 1979). Sensitization is a transitory independent process and its amplitude and duration are a direct function of stimulus intensity; it combines with the decremental process to produce the response output. Because the temporal course of the behavioral response depends on the relative contributions of the decrementing and incrementing processes, it may take any form including an initial period during which stimuli elicit larger responses before decrementing (Groves and Thompson, 1970; Figure 1).

Theory Differences

Both types of theory thus propose both incrementing and decrementing processes, but they differ in at least three main respects. First, in dual-process theory, modeling of the stimulus takes place entirely in the intrinsic path, that is, the most direct stimulus–response path. Second, the amplifying system in dual-process theory is non-specific, dependent on dynamogenic/energetic characteristics of stimuli, and independent of modeling in the intrinsic path. In contrast, amplification in model-comparator theory depends on the outcome of the comparison of past and expected stimulation with current stimulation, and, therefore, is a function of stimulus change *per se*. The third major difference between theories is that model-comparator theory is concerned with a special class of responses, the OR, while dual-process theory is concerned with any reflex response, including the OR.

Habituation Versus Refractoriness

Some writers have expressed concern that habituation be distinguished from refractoriness even in structures beyond the receptor and first-order sensory nerve and have cautioned that response decrements might be due 'simply' to refractoriness unless they can be shown to meet each of the Thompson and Spencer (1966) criteria for habituation. There appear to be two main arguments for making the distinction.

The first argument treats all repetition rate effects as refractory effects, and applies the term 'habituation' only when decrements are due to learning that a stimulus is without biological significance (Worden, 1973). Under this definition, the critical test for habituation is that dishabituation can be produced by both rate increases and decreases: because both changes are novel, they provide an opportunity for learning about stimulus significance. In contrast, effects due solely to temporal characteristics of neural mechanisms would show enhanced response (dishabituation) only with decreases in rate. Model-comparator theory would also predict dishabituation independent of direction of a rate change. However, dual-process theory would not. Therefore, under Worden's definition, a decremented response showing all of the properties of habituation described by dual-process theory, but not meeting the rate test, would be termed a refractory effect. Because the processes hypothesized by the two types of theory may indeed be different, the distinction Worden proposes is an important one that we acknowledge, but without adopting his terminology.

The second argument applies mainly to ERPs. Roemer, Shagass and Teyler (1984) pointed out that habituation studies measure some type of effector activity and suggested that ERPs 'are not, by and large, mediators of effector activation but of hypothetical intermediate processes: sensory encoding, stimulus evaluation, and so forth'. In reviewing the nine criteria of habituation proposed by Thompson and Spencer (1966), Roemer *et al.* described two effects, both requiring sensitization, that would distinguish habituation from refractoriness: (1) if, at some ISI greater than 0.5 s, repetition of high-intensity stimuli did not produce decrement (Roemer *et al.*; Criterion 5); (2) if the response could be dishabituated following a change stimulus (Criterion 8). According to dual-process theory, both of these criteria require that sensitization effects be present and, thus, if not present, would imply solely refractory effects. However, an absence of sensitization effects could still be consistent with dual-process theory if the hypothesized, but independent, incrementing sensitization and decrementing habituation did not converge at a locus which could influence the area generating a given ERP component. In fact, Thompson and Spencer commented explicitly that distinctions in terms of recovery time, the opposite of refractory period, seemed 'somewhat arbitrary'. This observation also applies to the assumption, sometimes made, that refractoriness yields a step-function decrement, while habituation yields an exponential decline.

Roemer *et al.* (1984) also commented that it was not apparent how refractory processes could contribute to a more rapid response decrement over repeated habituation series. Although transitory decrements may be due to a process different from those producing more permanent decrements (e.g. Kandel, 1985), the effect is compatible with both cognitive and non-cognitive theories and we will not discuss it further.

THEORY-DIFFERENTIATING PREDICTIONS: ANS AND STARTLE

Many apparently opposed predictions have been generated from cognitive and non-cognitive theories; but, as Stephenson and Siddle (1983) comment in an extensive review of possibly differentiating effects on ANS–OR phenomena, it has not always been clear either that the predictions follow from the theories or that, lacking quantitative precision, they generate answerable questions. A major source of confusion in evaluating cognitive theories is to determine whether they substitute for or add to non-cognitive theory. However, Sokolovian theory was built upon Pavlovian principles and specifically incorporated both generalization of habituation (e.g. Voronin and Sokolov, 1960; p.338) and the 'law of strength', that is, a stronger stimulus produces a stronger response (Sokolov, 1963; p.41). Thus, it is fallacious to argue, for example, that because stimulus repetition improves the neuronal model, Sokolov's theory *requires* that repetition also increase the response to a change stimulus (S2): it is necessary as well to subtract the effects of simultaneously increasing and generalizing habituation. Similarly, given the differing dynamogenic effects of weaker and stronger stimuli, equal increases and decreases of intensity would not be expected to produce equal response recovery.

Another source of confusion is that the theories have undergone development since they were introduced. Sokolov's 1966 and 1969 papers stress information more than the 1960 and 1963 publications. Dual-process theory, as presented by Groves and Thompson (1970), included major changes in the Thompson and Spencer (1966) assumption of an inverse relation between intensity and habituation, and was further modified by Thompson *et al.* (1973) and Thompson *et al.* (1979). Thus, some predictions derived for early versions of either theory may not hold for later versions.

Intensity Effects

Dual-process and Sokolovian theory both predict increasing response with stimulus intensity increases in the moderate range for responses that are not bidirectional. However, Sokolov (1963) found that near-threshold stimuli elicited relatively larger electrodermal ORs than moderately intense stimuli and ascribed the effect to difficulty in forming a model of such stimuli. Jackson (1974) did not replicate the effect on electrodermal ORs, but it has been found with both respiration (Rousey and Reitz, 1967) and heart rate deceleration (Jackson, 1974). Sokolov also showed that intensity had non-monotonic effects on the bidirectional vasomotor responses. As intensity increased into the range which elicits defense, the previously increasing dilitation characteristic of the OR began to decrease and then gave way to the defense response of constriction. As reviewed in Graham (1979), several studies have shown a similar non-monotonic change in the OR component of heart rate deceleration and a shift to acceleration as intensity increased (see also Turpin and Siddle, 1983).

Modality Change Following Habituation

Several studies have reported larger electrodermal response to light following an habituation series with tone, and of larger response to tone following an habituation series with light. The response in each case was larger than the response on the last habituation trial, and larger than the response elicited when the change stimulus was the first stimulus of an habituating series (Furedy and Ginsberg, 1975; Ginsberg and Furedy, 1974; Houck and Mefferd, 1969). Model-comparator theory can accomodate these findings on the grounds that the neuronal model after repeated presentations of an habituating stimulus reflects decreased subjective probability of a stimulus change; that is, given that total probability can not exceed 1.0, as the probability of a repeated stimulus increases, probabilities of other stimuli decrease. Thus, when a change stimulus is presented, mismatch is greater than on initial trials and elicits a larger OR. This assumes that there is little generalization of habituation with a change in modality. Dual-process theory contains no provision for explaining an increase greater than control levels of a given stimulus, except through sensitization. Because sensitization increases only transiently, unless a different-modality stimulus were introduced into an habituation series during the period of initial increase in sensitization, it should not elicit a response larger than it elicits on initial presentation as an habituating stimulus. Although it is unlikely that sensitization of electrodermal activity would persist through 14 to 15 habituation trials, the possibility could be tested by presenting the habituating stimulus twice, separated by an ISI equal to the time between initial and change trials (about 10 minutes).

Non-Arousing Stimulus Change

An important distinction between model-comparator and dual-process theories is how they account for recovery and dishabituation induced by a non-arousing stimulus change (e.g. an intensity decrease) following an habituation series. Sokolov (1963) assumed that OR components recover in such a case because the eliciting stimulus fails to match the neuronal model. If the habituating stimulus is re-presented following a change stimulus, the response might also be dishabituated because the neuronal model was updated to include the change. Both recovery and dishabituation are, thus, due to extrinsic amplifying effects and the extrinsic removal of inhibition, and depend on the degree of discrepancy between the model of expected stimulation and the current stimulus.

Dual-process theory, on the other hand, allows only stimulus changes coded by elements in the intrinsic path to produce *recovery* in the absence of sensitization. Recovery would depend on (1) how many fresh elements, not shared with S1, were activated by S2, and (2) how habituation effects were distributed between shared and unshared elements activated by S1. The theory does not provide for elements coding rate or stimulus duration so that neither an increase in rate or decrease in stimulus duration would be expected to produce recovery when low-intensity, non-arousing stimuli are employed; that is, in the absence of sensitization. Faster rates (shorter ISIs) produce increased refractoriness, and briefer stimuli would presumably activate fewer (but not different) elements than longer stimuli. If high and low intensity are coded by separate elements (Thompson and Spencer, 1966; p.33), response recovery could be predicted for both increases and decreases of intensity, but if intensity is coded by the number of elements activated (Thompson *et al.*, 1973; p.259), it is not clear that a change from high to low would activate fresh elements and, thus, produce recovery.

Dual-process theory was developed from research on the spinal flexor and startle reflexes, but effects of non-arousing changes on recovery of these reflexes were apparently not tested. Thompson *et al.* (1979) did note, without specifying the response, that dishabituation by stimulus omission is 'often difficult to obtain in animals'. Further, a study of humans, using the acoustic blink reflex as a measure of startle, did not find blink recovery or dishabituation following either an intensity decrease of 44 dB or a spectral change from white noise to tone or vice versa. In contrast, these changes did elicit an OR component, cardiac deceleration (Clarkson and Clifton, 1983; and personal communication). Other OR studies have also found recovery of habituated components to S2s that decrease stimulation without changing its quality. Literature reviews (Graham, 1973; Siddle, Stephenson and Spinks, 1983; Stephenson and Siddle, 1983) indicate that, although negative findings have been obtained, reliable enhancement has been demonstrated for the electrodermal response and, in occasional tests, for cardiac deceleration and alpha blocking, in response to decreases in stimulus intensity, decreases in stimulus duration, and the omission of stimuli. The test for response enhancement following shortened ISIs appears not to have been made with ANS components but has been applied to ERP measures (see later).

Although dual-process theory allows for recovery with some types of non-arousing changes that activate fresh elements, it predicts *dishabituation* only following arousing S2s. As noted above, startle blink was not dishabituated following an intensity decrease. However, ORs have been dishabituated following intensity decreases of 20 or 30 dB when arousal, measured by tonic change in skin conductance levels, remained constant (Magliero, Gatchel and Lojewski, 1981; Rust, 1976).

The strongest evidence that dishabituation cannot be due solely to a non-specific arousal or sensitization process comes from findings of selective dishabituation. Selectivity was first demonstrated by the vasomotor response of rabbits following a dishabituating stimulus interspersed between members of a pair of identical or non-identical stimuli (Whitlow, 1975). The dishabituating stimulus restored the depressed response to the second of identical stimuli but did not enhance response to the non-identical stimulus. Krasne (1976), in discussing an invertebrate study showing such selective enhancement, described the selective effect as 'true dishabituation' which appears to involve the 'erasure of an engram'. Siddle *et al.* (1983) found a similar enhancement of the electrodermal OR in human subjects: on the trial following omission of the second of a pair of habituating stimuli, dishabituation was specific to re-presentation of the omitted second stimulus and did not occur with re-presentation of S1 nor as a function of the longer ISI resulting from omission. Later work replicated the selective effects of S2 omission and found specific dishabituation when S2 was changed in modality or was miscued (Siddle, 1985; Siddle and Hirschhorn, 1986).

Length of Habituation Series

Cognitive and non-cognitive theories also differ in accounting for the effects of length of habituation series on the response to stimulus change. Dual-process theory, as amended (Thompson *et al.*, 1979), predicts a non-monotonic effect for responses, such as electrodermal activity, that habituate to zero: namely, decrementing until zero responding is reached; then incrementing, because failure to fire the first neuron in a chain allows later neurons to recover. In contrast, cognitive theory is compatible with a monotonic, increasing response to change, as long as the excitation due to mismatch is sufficiently large to overcome generalized habituation. Several studies of electrodermal activity have shown the monotonic increase in response to change that is predicted from cognitive theory (Edwards, 1975a,b; Magliero, Gatchel and Lojeski, 1981; O'Gorman and Lloyd, 1984; Siddle and Heron, 1977).

Change in Pattern, Sequence, and Word Meaning

The strongest evidence supporting a cognitive model comes from studies of change in pattern, sequence, and word meaning. Such changes as insertion of an out-of-sequence digit or a change from an alternating to a repeated pattern can produce recovery of habituated OR components (Berlyne, 1961; Unger, 1964; Yaremko, Blair and Leckart, 1970; Yaremko and Keleman, 1972). So also can differences in word meaning (see the review by Siddle *et al.*, 1983). Findings reported by Siddle *et al.* (1979) were particularly interesting. In three experiments, between-category changes in visually displayed words produced greater recovery than within-category changes. The change was introduced after the twelfth habituation trial, when curves were not yet asymptotic, and in two groups the recovered electrodermal response was approximately as large as response on the initial trial. Thus, semantic change appears to have an unusually robust effect compared with other non-arousing, within-modality changes in simple physical characteristics.

Summary

The occurrence of change in simple physical characteristics, whether or not arousing, can probably be detected at subcortical relays (Buchwald and Humprey, 1974; Sokolov, 1975) and so, potentially, could be modeled by either dual-process or model-comparator theory. In many instances, this appears to be the case, but dual-process theory has not, to date, accounted for recovery of habituated ORs to decreases in stimulus intensity and duration, and to non-arousing changes in acoustic spectra which have occurred prior to asymptotic levels and have apparently increased monotonically with length of the habituation series. The theory has also not accounted for dishabituation of the S1 response following a non-arousing S2 and the evidence that, with paired stimulation, dishabituation may be selective rather than generalized.

The two types of theory also differ with respect to the responses assumed capable of reflecting such effects. Sokolovian theory predicts that only OR components respond to novel change, while dual-process theory does not distinguish effects on ORs from effects on startle, defense, or other low-level responses. Although few studies have investigated the effects of non-arousing change on startle, startle was found to differ from OR components in response to intensity decreases and spectral change, and in recovery as a function of the length of habituating series. Thus, both the OR findings which are not consistent with dual-process theory and the findings of different effects on low-level reflexes and OR components suggest that dual-process theory can adequately account for a variety of findings with low-level reflexes, but a full account of the generalized orienting reflex will likely require cognitive conceptions of representation and processing.

PREATTENTIVE TRANSIENT PROCESSING: REFLEX MODULATION AND EXOGENOUS ERPS

Our review of findings obtained with the traditional habituation–dishabituation paradigm suggests that certain non-arousing stimulus changes affect startle and ANS–OR components differently and that the OR findings are more readily explained by a model-comparator theory than by the pattern of differential habituation among elements. Öhman (1979), in extending model-comparator theory, hypothesized that the generalized OR reflects a call for controlled processing, issued when preattentive mechanisms detect a mismatch between current input and short-term-memory representations of prior and expected stimulation. If the call is answered, the current stimulus undergoes additional processing which includes searching the larger long-term store for associated representations and encoding the new information into long-term memory. It is assumed that information can be stored in long-term memory *only* through controlled processing.

A disadvantage in using ANS responses to test Öhman's hypothesis is that they occur too slowly to distinguish between a call and its answer. As he notes, electrodermal responses are good indicants of mismatch detection, but they are also sensitive to the cognitive effort involved in controlled processing (Kahneman, 1973). The direction of heart rate changes is potentially capable of making the discrimination because, while a brief heart rate deceleration has been identified with transient-detection and longer-lasting deceleration with the OR, heart rate acceleration has been related to cognitive elaboration, including memory search and decision-making (e.g. Coles and Duncan-Johnson, 1975; Jennings and Hall, 1980; Tursky, Schwartz and Crider, 1970). Presumably, acceleration occurs only with an effortful search of long-term memory under controlled processing, and not with a search of short-term memory which is assumed to be carried out effortlessly by preattentive processes.

In this section, we consider preattentive processes that are sensitive only to transient characteristics of stimulation, such as onset or offset of a stimulus; the processing of sustained characteristics is discussed in the following section. It is assumed that information about transient and sustained characteristics is transmitted in parallel by systems with different filtering and conduction characteristics (e.g. Gersuni, 1965; LaMotte, 1977; Livingstone and Hubel, 1988), subserving different psychological functions (e.g. Burbeck and Luce, 1982; Keesey, 1972; Poulsen, 1981; Watson, 1986). Specifically, a short-time-constant, rapidly-conducting system is well-designed for detecting, localizing, and alerting to stimulus change; a system with lowpass filtering and slow conduction may allow more extensive analysis.

We review two classes of transient-detecting response–reflexly inhibited startle and obligatory ERPs–which do not *require* attention but may be affected by it (see the second part of this chapter). Evidence is presented for their obligatory and transient-detecting nature, their neuroanatomical source when known, and their sensitivity, compared with that of psychophysical measures, to differences along physical dimensions such as intensity and frequency. Our interest is in inferring preattentive processes that may serve as gating mechanisms, either to affect the information transmitted to later analyzers or to detect types of mismatch requiring a model-comparison process and that might, therefore, lead to a call for controlled processing.

Prepulse Inhibition of Reflex Startle

In one type of reflex modulation, prepulse inhibition, startle amplitude is markedly reduced by a weak transient change shortly-preceding a startle-eliciting stimulus. As described in reviews of animal research on whole-body startle (Hoffman and Ison, 1980) and human research on the startle blink (Anthony, 1985; Graham, 1975), prepulse inhibition occurs on the first paired presentation of prepulse and startle-eliciting stimuli, remains undiminished during sleep despite effects of sleep state on the control reflex (Silverstein, Graham and Calloway, 1980), and shows no evidence of habituation under repetition schedules which do habituate the control blink (Graham and Murray, 1977). It is mediated by a pathway extrinsic to, and more rostral than, the direct acoustic startle path. This indirect path probably includes inferior colliculi (Leitner and Cohen, 1985) and a mixture of crossed and uncrossed inputs different from the direct path because, although the unmodulated reflex is larger with binaural stimuli, a monaural prepulse produces more inhibition than an equally intense, and therefore louder, binaural prepulse (Hoffman and Stitt, 1980; Marsh, Hoffman and Stitt, 1976). The extrinsic inhibition seems to be determined primarily by a change lasting no more than 20–40 ms (Anthony, 1985; Giardina, 1989; Graham and Murray, 1977; but see Dykman and Ison, 1979, for a contrary opinion). Surprisingly for such a low-level effect, prepulse inhibition is not fully mature until near adolescence (Balaban, Anthony and Graham, 1989; Berg *et al.*, 1985; Ornitz *et al.*, 1986). In Chapter 7, Anthony reviews developmental influences on the eyeblink reflex, and provides a brief historical and methodological introduction to the area.

A stimulus change in any modality can produce the effect, and prestimulus and elicitor need not be in the same modality. When they are, refractory effects in the modality-specific portion of the direct path may contribute to reflex attenuation (Balaban, Anthony and Graham, 1985). The temporal course of effects also varies with prestimulus modality (Graham, 1980). For weak to moderately intense auditory prestimuli and auditory elicitors, the most studied combination, inhibition is evident with intrapair ISIs of 16 ms to about 500 ms, and is maximal between 100 and 200 ms. It is greater and longer-lasting with more intense prepulses and is sufficiently sensitive to small changes in intensity, or in duration of a gap, to serve as an alternative to psychophysical methods of estimating acoustic and tactile thresholds (e.g. Blumenthal and Gescheider, 1987; Cranney, Hoffman and Cohen, 1984; Ison and Pinckney, 1983; Reiter and Ison, 1977). In contrast to intensity variations, changes in tone frequency must be considerably larger than the psychophysical difference threshold to affect inhibition (Cranney, Hoffman and Cohen, 1984). Prestimulus effects on reflex amplitude and onset latency are dissociated at short intrapair ISIs; that is, latency is facilitated even though amplitude is inhibited or unaffected. This is consistent with lesion evidence (Leitner, Powers and Hoffman, 1980) for mediation in different paths. Beyond the prepulse inhibition range, a brief prestimulus has no effect when given under passive conditions unless (as discussed in the later section, on the generalized OR) the prestimulus is novel or the nature or timing of the eliciting stimulus is uncertain.

An important question is whether prepulse inhibition plays any role in information processing. Geyer and Braff (1987) suggested that it is a sensory gating mechanism and, in accord with the hypothesis that schizophrenics have a gating mechanism dysfunction, found a relatively weak inhibitory effect in this group. In a similar vein, Graham (1975, 1979) suggested that a mechanism which damped effects of any shortly-following interrupt might prevent disruption in processing the prestimulus for identification. If this were the case, information in the prestimulus should presumably not be degraded by occurrence of a subsequent reflex-eliciting stimulus whose response was attenuated by prepulse inhibition. Although degradation might be expected, given that the paired configuration looks like a backward masking paradigm, a study by Reiter and Ison (1977) found unimpaired prestimulus detection. Furthermore, Perlstein (1989) found that processing of intensity information, as measured by judged magnitude of the prestimulus, was unaffected or even enhanced under conditions producing prepulse inhibition of blink and some transient-detecting ERPs.

Brainstem Potentials

Preattentive processing of transients is also reflected in brainstem potentials recorded from the scalp during the first 10 ms following onset of acoustic stimuli presented at rapid rates (between 5 and 80 per second) and, to distinguish signal from noise, for 2000 or so stimulus repetitions. In the human, the resulting series of six to eight peak deflections originate from overlapping activity in the ascending pathway beginning with the auditory nerve (Picton, Stapells and Campbell, 1981; Hillyard and Picton, 1987). Pathways for monaural stimuli are largely independent up to wave V, the most prominent and latest-maturing deflection. However, wave V achieves adult values at about two years of age (Hecox and Galambos, 1974; Salamy, McKean and Buda, 1975) and, thus, much earlier than prepulse inhibition.

The generator(s) of wave V is not known with certainty. It was originally thought to derive from inferior colliculi, and recordings in the human brain by Hashimoto *et al.* (1981) confirmed this. However, other research suggests that it reflects more caudal activity in fiber tracts and nuclei of the lateral lemnisci (Moller and Jannetta, 1982; Picton, Stapells and Campbell, 1981) or the tegmentum of the pons (Wada and Starr, 1983). Activity of inferior colliculi, as well as thalamic nuclei and tracts, may also be reflected in waves VI–VIII, but are probably best reflected by middle latency components discussed in the following subsection. The question is of interest because inferior colliculi are apparently essential in mediating auditory prepulse inhibition (Leitner and Cohen, 1985).

Picton, Stapells and Campbell (1981) have reviewed findings on the effects of frequency, intensity, rise time and repetition rate. In general, components are non-habituating and do not vary with sleep–wake states or anesthesia. They were not enhanced by small intensity increases and ISI decreases which did affect cortical potentials (Salamy and McKean, 1977), nor did wave V recover or dishabituate to a stimulus change presumed capable of eliciting the generalized OR, that is, 100 ms tones interspersed (between 5 and 11 s) among clicks delivered 16 per second (Rohrbaugh *et al.*, 1987). However, as the authors pointed out, a rapidly-habituating response could have been missed.

The transient-detecting character of brainstem potentials is evident, first, from the fact that they are unaffected by increases in stimulus duration (above 0.5 ms) which do produce marked increases in loudness and lower behavioral thresholds (Gorga *et al.*, 1984; Hecox, Squires and Galambos, 1976). Secondly, a slowing of stimulus rise time that led to wave V latency changes equivalent to a 40 dB intensity decrease, produced less than a 5 dB rise in behavioral threshold (Hecox and Deegan, 1983). Hecox *et al.* concluded that either 'psychological processing' occurs above the brainstem level or 'that it is mediated by brainstem cell populations not involved in the production of the brainstem-evoked response'. They suggested, specifically, that brainstem potentials might be processed by 'short-time constant' neurons.

Middle Latency Potentials

Deflections recorded at 10 ms to about 50 ms after an acoustic stimulus onset require less averaging than brainstem potentials, but have been studied less often, in part, because they are easily contaminated by muscle activity. Like the brainstem potentials, they are relatively stable during sleep and with stimulus rates up to 10 per second, and show a poor response to increases of stimulus rise time (Picton *et al.*, 1974).

Peak deflections at between 10 ms to 20 ms have been associated with activity of inferior colliculi (Hashimoto, 1982). Later deflections at between 25 and 65 ms (Pa/P30, Nb, and Pb/P50/P1), may also have subcortical sources: the Pa/Nb complex disappears with degeneration of medial geniculate, part of the classical specific auditory projection (Woods *et al.*, 1987), while P50 may be generated in the ascending reticular system (Erwin and Buchwald, 1986a,b). Cortical sources, probably at different locations in the supratemporal plane, also contribute to P30 and P50. (See evidence from sequential mapping of potentials, magnetic field recordings, and patients with temporal lobe lesions (e.g. Deiber *et al.*, 1988; Kraus *et al.*, 1982; Pellizone *et al.*, 1987; Reite *et al.*, 1988).)

It is of interest that P30 and P50 might reflect activity in the classical projection and non-specific systems, respectively, because the two potentials do reflect functional differences. In two studies, Perlstein *et al.* (1989) found that weak prestimuli, at 120 or 500 ms ISIs, reduced blink (onset latency, 40–50 ms), P50, and later ERPs, but had no effect on P30. Possible effects of eye movement and blink activity were controlled statistically. In contrast, subjects identified by questionnaire as sensitive to perceptual 'flooding' did *not* show reliable inhibition of blink or P50 with 500 ms ISIs. A series of studies using paired 110 dB clicks reported similar findings. Further, like prepulse inhibition of blink, P50 reduction was very late maturing and was unreliable in schizophrenics (e.g. Freedman, Adler and Waldo, 1987).

Late Transient Evoked Potentials

Obligatory processing of inputs is also reflected in the series of deflections—N1, P2, N2—beginning about 100 ms after stimulus onset. The most prominent deflection is *N1/N100*. It is usually measured from baseline to peak or, mainly in early studies, between N1 and P2 peaks. Näätänen and Picton (1987) reviewed evidence from intracranial and magnetic field recordings, as well as scalp recordings from patients with known lesions (see also Knight *et al.*, 1988), that three different components contribute to the N1 waveform. Two are auditory-specific: component 1, bilaterally maximal over frontocentral scalp, appears to be generated in the supratemporal plane of cortex in or near primary auditory cortex; component 2, the 'T-complex' of Wolpaw and Penry (1975), is diphasic (P100–N130), maximal at midtemporal electrodes, and is probably generated in auditory association cortex in the superior temporal gyrus (see the second part of this chapter). The third component, maximal at vertex and lateral central electrodes, is non-specific; it is elicited by visual and tactile as well as acoustic stimuli. Human intracerebral recordings suggest an origin in the structures, beginning with rostral reticular formation and transmitting through non-specific thalami, that constitute the non-specific sensory projection system (Velasco and Velasco, 1986).

Specific and non-specific components cannot be separated on the basis of the waveforms themselves. However, scalp distribution findings are useful in identifying the T-complex, and magnetic field studies suggest differences between specific component 1 and non-specific component 3 in their functional relations to stimulus intensity and ISI. The component 1 magnetic field appears to reflect only stimulus-evoked activity with a short recovery period and is blind to activity whose recovery is slow. While the magnetic response to 80 dB, 20 ms tones, as well as the electrical response recorded by lateral temporal leads, reaches maximum at ISIs of 4 s between tone repetitions, amplitude of the vertex ERP continues to increase, and its latency to shorten, up to 16 s ISIs (Hari *et al.*, 1982; also see Hari *et al.*, 1987). Magnetic fields reflecting component 1 also fail to increase with stimulus increase above 60 dB

SPL (Hari, in press). Thus, effects due to differences between stimuli above 60 dB or ISIs longer than 4 s are likely due to change in the non-specific component. If only a single intensity or a single ISI is employed, specific and non-specific contributions cannot be separated by ERPs except on the general principle that range is related to sensitivity and the non-specific component may thus be less sensitive between 0 and 60 dB than the specific component for which 0–60 dB is the full range. Similarly, the non-specific component may be relatively more refractory than the specific at ISIs less than 4 s, given that full recovery may take 1–2 minutes. The non-specific component is also implicated when visual and somatosensory stimuli are employed. Studies comparing stimuli in the three modalities, usually equated for subjective magnitude, have found vertex-maximal ERPs at appropriate N1–P2 latencies, that is, somewhat longer for somatosensory and visual, consistent with their slower peripheral transmission.

All N1 components respond to transient onsets and, with stimuli of 0.5 s or more, also to offsets. Their amplitudes decrease with rise times or fall times longer than 30–50 ms and increase with stimulus duration for about the same length of time (Onishi and Davis, 1968), thus showing more temporal integration than the brainstem wave V, and somewhat better correlation with perceived loudness. However, Davis and Zerlin (1966) commented that the mechanisms generating N1–P2 and determining its magnitude 'do not lie on the direct path, so to speak, to psychological sensation but rather on a parallel path with other functions'. Nonetheless, recent work indicates that with ISIs of 460 ms, frequency selectivity of specific component 1, measured by P1–N1, approaches that of psychophysical measures (Näätänen *et al.*, 1988). Further, it appears that the phenomenon of periodity pitch—perception of a missing fundamental—which was not reflected in the electrical potential, tested with 76 dB tones at long ISIs (Butler, 1972), is reflected in the magnetic field at 100 ms (Pantev *et al.*, 1989).

The N1 components also differ from brainstem potentials in maturing somewhat later (Eggermont, 1988) and being much altered during sleep, with N1–P2 attenuated and N2 enhanced (Näätänen and Picton, 1987). Further, a sizable literature (see reviews by Loveless, 1983, Näätänen and Picton, 1987, Picton, Hillyard, and Galambos, 1976) indicates that, unlike the earlier potentials, N1 does decrement with repeated stimulation even when tonic state remains constant as measured by skin conductance level, EEG, or task performance to a different modality stimulus.

The *repetition effects* have included both 'short-term' and 'long-term' habituation, distinguished by whether responses are averaged by serial stimulus position within repeated series or trains (ISIs of 0.5 to about 10 s), or are averaged by train (ISIs of 10 s to about 5 minutes). Rapid, large decrements over one to four averages have been found, as well as small, slow, and linear decrements. In many cases, there is a 'first-stimulus' effect which could be ascribed to the relatively long quiescent interval preceding the first stimulus of a train or session.

Neither of the averaging methods, which include as many as 10 to 60 or more stimulus presentations in a single-subject average, is capable of revealing the rapid habituation within three to about 20 trials that characterizes the generalized ANS–OR. However, several recent studies have obtained ERP and ANS responses under long ISI conditions and have analyzed single trials or few-trial blocks. Simons *et al.* (1987) reported N1 habituation to acoustic stimuli within four single trials or four four-trial blocks in independent studies from two laboratories. Electrodermal responses, recorded simultaneously, showed significant and nearly as rapid habituation; the more linear course of decline in the heart rate decelerative response was not significant. Similarly rapid habituation of single-trial vertex N1 and electrodermal responses to visual stimuli was found by Verbaten *et al.* (1986).

Rate of decrement and shape of the decrementing curve do not, of themselves, distinguish between dual-process and comparator theories because both theories allow for amplifying processes which can slow the course of decrement. Nor do they distinguish between refractoriness and habituation, as the latter is defined by dual-process theory (see earlier). Comparator theories appear better able to account for slower decrementing with variable than fixed ISIs, or with complex relative to simple stimuli, on the grounds that variable and complex conditions require more stimulations to develop an accurate model. Although neither ISI variability nor complexity effects have been unequivocally demonstrated for N1 under passive conditions, effects have been in the direction predicted by comparator theory (Loveless, 1983; Näätänen and Picton, 1987).

As noted above, Simons *et al.* (1987) obtained progressive decrements in both N1 and the electrodermal response to repeated 60 dB tones. Given the low stimulus intensity and the associated cardiac deceleration, these authors interpreted their findings as consistent with a generalized OR. Rust (1977) similarly interpreted findings of significant correlations between N1–P2 habituation and electrodermal and heart-rate habituation to 95 dB tones. However, given the high intensity employed by Rust, it is difficult to exclude the possibility that startle was elicited rather than, or in addition to, an OR. Heart rate changes were not presented in a form which would allow their use in distinguishing between the two types of response.

The question of functional relations between the *non-specific N1 and startle* has been considered in a number of reflex blink studies. Larsson (1956, 1960) described and illustrated, but did not test statistically, similarities which were observed in the relative responsiveness to stimuli of different modalities. He also examined occlusion at short ISIs (300 ms) and sensitization at long ISIs (2–10 s) produced by strong stimuli in one modality on weak stimuli in another modality. Blink and N1 latencies, thresholds, and sensitivity to shock frequency, although showing differences, were judged to be 'of the same order of magnitude'. Larsson concluded that both responses arose in functionally similar systems, whose source was probably the reticular activating system, and that they could be regarded as expressions of an arousal mechanism. Sakano and Pickenhain (1968) reached a similar conclusion based on N1 and blink changes due to pairing neutral or informative warning stimuli with high-intensity stimuli (pistol shot or click). Davis and Heninger (1972) also found parallel changes in sensitization and temporal recovery of N1–P2 and blink to 96 dB noise bursts at ISIs of 4 s or less. However, the magnitudes of response changes were uncorrelated, and blink habituated but N1–P2 did not.

Putnam and Roth (1988; 1990), in an extensive study comparing the effects of stimulus repetition, rise time, and duration on ERPs, blink and heart rate, found that N1 amplitude more closely paralleled effects on blink than did later ERP components. With a fixed ISI of 8.4 s, N1 and blink showed similar decrements over repetitions of 105 dB noise bursts, rise time increases (3 ms to 45 ms in 110 dB, equal-energy tones), and tone duration decreases (90 ms to 3 ms). Simultaneously recorded heart rate suggested that both an OR, reflected in long duration deceleration on the first two trials, and startle, reflected in rapidly habituating acceleration with a short onset latency, were present during the period of N1 and blink habituation. The heart rate response stabilized as a brief, non-habituating deceleration (the transient-detecting response), followed by the long-latency acceleration characteristic of a defense reflex.

The relation of N1 to startle has been of interest in evaluating functional significance of the non-specific component. Näätänen and Picton (1987) proposed that it reflects 'a widespread transient arousal' which may 'facilitate sensory and motor responses to the eliciting stimulus (as well as the associated central integrative processes)'. The fact that cardiac acceleration accompanies startle is consistent with motor facilitation, as is the facilitating effect of relatively high-intensity acoustic prestimuli on the amplitude of subsequently evoked monosynaptic H-reflexes (e.g. Liegeois-Chauvel *et al.*, 1989). However, prestimuli capable of modulating the reflex to a subsequent stimulus not only facilitate mono- and di-synaptic reflexes, but they also inhibit the polysynaptic startle reflex (e.g. Sanes and Ison, 1979).

Thus, terms like 'motor facilitation' and 'arousal' seem too broad for an effect which facilitates some reflexes but inhibits others. An alternative characterization is that the non-specific N1 associated with startle reflects activation of an interrupt system that halts ongoing motor activity but habituates rapidly and shifts from the high-intensity startle system to the transient-detection system following startle habituation (see earlier). Näätänen and Picton (1987) propose a similar separation in distinguishing an arousal process reflected by the non-specific N1 from an attention-triggering process reflected by the specific, supratemporal N1 (component 1). The attention-triggering is viewed as 'making possible or facilitating conscious perception of auditory stimuli' and/or may (1) represent the initial readout of information, and (2) reflect the formation of a memory trace for the eliciting stimulus. As Näätänen (1988) emphasizes, the involuntary trigger must presumably exceed some varying threshold and may produce only a momentary breakthrough if attention is already strongly engaged.

The most important question in the present context is whether or not N1 components show *recovery and dishabituation* to stimulus change in a manner consistent with OR theory but not with an explanation in terms of overlapping elements or extrinsic sensitization. There are many reports of N1 recovery to changes in tone pitch/frequency which reflect gradients of generalization of decrement and which could be due to the degree of overlap among neuronal elements (Näätänen and Picton, 1987). However, the data could not be ascribed to a generalized sensitization process because no evidence has been found, to date, for dishabituation of response to the habituating stimulus; in Simons *et al.* (1987), the simultaneously measured electrodermal response did dishabituate. The same conclusion can be drawn from modality-change findings; that is, recovery to a modality change has been reported but no dishabituation on re-presenting the original modality (Fruhstorfer, 1971).

Interpretation of intensity-change effects on recovery is more complicated. Salamy and McKean (1977) and Simons *et al.* (1987) tested intensity increases, and Butler (1968) and Megela and Teyler (1979) tested both increases and decreases. Recovery was found to increases which ranged across studies from 3 dB to 20 dB but did *not* occur to 16 or 20 dB decreases. In all cases, recovery was tested by comparison with response to the immediately prior habituating stimulus. As discussed earlier, greater response to an intensity increment is predicted both by the 'law of strength', adopted by Sokolov, and by dual-process theory's assumption that more intense stimuli activate more neuronal elements than do less intense stimuli. Enhanced response to intensity decrease would be differentiating unless dual-process theory allowed for elements sensitive to specific intensities. However, a failure to obtain enhancement is not of theoretical significance unless appropriate controls have been employed (Siddle *et al.*, 1983). Comparing response to a low-intensity change stimulus with response to a preceding high-intensity habituating stimulus is biased against finding a change effect, not only by the difference in dynamogenic effects but also by the fact that there is greater generalization of habituation from high to low than from low to high (Thompson *et al.*, 1973).

Interpretation of dishabituation by intensity change is less equivocal. Butler (1968), testing for dishabituation to re-presentation of the habituating stimulus which followed a 20 dB increase or decrease, found no evidence of response enhancement. According to dual-process theory, an intensity increase of this magnitude would be expected to produce sensitization but, as discussed earlier, sensitization might not converge on the intrinsic path at a locus which could influence the N1 generator. Similarly, Picton, Hillyard and Galambos (1976) did not obtain dishabituation of tone-evoked N1 after interpolated electric shocks to the wrist. However, Megela and Teyler (1979), using a design in which position of the change stimulus varied and was, therefore, less predictable, did obtain reliable dishabituation of N1–P2 amplitude, although not N1, following 16 dB acoustic intensity increases and decreases: with visual stimuli, N1 amplitude, but not N1–P2, showed dishabituation to both increases and decreases. Loveless (1983) questioned the identification of components in this study, in part because lateral rather than midline leads were used, and suggested that manipulations affected a later negative component than N1, the mismatch negativity discussed below. It is not clear how dual-process theory could account for dishabituation to intensity decrease whatever the component affected.

Enhanced response to shortening of the ISI, the test recommended by Worden (1973), would also distinguish between dual-process and model-comparison theories. Several studies have found evidence for ERP change to a shortened ISI but the enhanced negativity also appears to occur later than N1. A single study reported enhancement of an N1 whose peak window (85–100 ms) is definitely in the N1 range, but the only evidence given was the ERP curve of one subject (Salamy and McKean, 1977).

Mismatch Negativity (MMN)

The last of the auditory late transient potentials has been divided into an attention-reflecting component, N2b, and a preattentive component, N2a, also named mismatch negativity (MMN) by Näätänen, Gaillard and Mantysalo (1978). Depending on conditions, MMN may overlap in latency with either N100 or N2/N200, but can be separated from both by functional characteristics. Its scalp distribution is more frontal than that of N1 components (e.g. Sams, Alho and Näätänen, 1984), it is often larger at temporal than midline leads (Näätänen *et al.*, 1978), and it appears to be generated, at least in part, by activity in or near primary auditory cortex (e.g. Alho *et al.*, 1986).

The most important difference between MMN and the previously discussed preattentive, obligatory potentials is that MMN is not elicited by occurrence of a stimulus *per se*, but only by a stimulus that differs in some physical characteristic from prior repeated stimuli. Thus, it is a potential associated with detection of mismatch. The passive conditions under which it has been studied include stimulus presentation under ignore instructions, during reading, while performing a primary task, or to the unattended ear during dichotic listening. Amplitude, latency, and duration of the deflection are a function of the degree of change, with amplitude often increasing rapidly to a plateau while latency and duration continue to shorten. Because of an earlier onset with large deviance, it is best visualized when deviance is moderate and the N1 elicited by standards has been completely habituated. It is frequently measured from difference waveforms computed by subtracting the ERP to the habituating (standard) stimulus from the ERP to the change (deviant) stimulus (see, for example, Näätänen, 1988; Figure 4). Difference waves are especially useful when MMN appears as a broad negativity rather than a distinct second peak.

The MMN response also differs from N1 with respect to ISI effects. While N1 increases monotonically to an asymptote as ISI lengthens, MMN disappears with long ISIs. Thus far the longest ISI that has yielded reliable MMN is 4 s (Näätänen *et al.*, 1987a; but see Näätänen's, 1988, citing of Bottcher). Mantysalo and Näätänen (1987) did not find significant MMNs at intervals longer than 1–2 s; three studies reported that significant MMNs at intervals less than 1 s did not differ significantly from, but tended to be larger than, those obtained in the same studies with ISIs between 1 and 4 s (Ford, Roth and Kopell, 1976; Näätänen *et al.*, 1987a; Snyder and Hillyard, 1976). Thus, the decay time for whatever neural representation allows for mismatch detection in the ERP is very brief, of an order of magnitude appropriate for an echoic or initial sensory memory (Cowan, 1988).

The response is sensitive to near-threshold changes in tone frequency. Sams *et al.* (1985b) found that 16 Hz but not 8 Hz change from a 1008 Hz standard elicited a significant MMN under passive conditions; the 8 Hz deviant was still below threshold (44% detection) when it was actively discriminated. Other passive studies have also obtained MMN in response to pitch deviance (e.g. Ford, Roth and Kopell, 1976; Mantysalo and Näätänen, 1987; Squires, Squires and Hillyard, 1975), to a phonemic change (Aaltonen *et al.*, 1987), and to changes in spatial location (Paavilainen *et al.*, 1989). The effect of change cannot be due to long ISIs between deviants because deviants presented without standards, at ISIs obtaining when standards are present, does not elicit MMN (Sams *et al.*, 1985a; Snyder and Hillyard, 1976). Although differential recovery of partially overlapping elements could account for N1 recovery, it is not self-evident how overlapping elements could explain elicitation of a new component. Neither is it obvious how dual-process theory could account for MMN elicitation by a standard immediately following a non-arousing deviant and, thus, itself a change from immediately prior stimulation (Sams, Alho and Näätänen, 1984).

A comparator theory can accomodate the above findings and, unless dual-process theory assumes specific-intensity neurons, is also better able to explain MMN elicitation by intensity decrease (Näätänen *et al.*, 1987b; Snyder and Hillyard, 1976; Squires, Squires and Hillyard, 1975). As illustrated in Näätänen (1988; Figure 1), MMN amplitude increases symmetrically with deviance, whether the change is less or more intense than the standard. Näätänen, Paavilainen and Reinikainen (1989) argue that their finding of MMN in response to deviants of shortened duration (reductions of 50% in tone durations ranging from 25 to 400 ms) makes an even stronger case for a model comparator theory.

A response to shortening of the ISI also suggests a comparison process. Both ISI shortening and stimulus omission have elicited negativity in the MMN range. Klinke, Fruhstorfer and Finkenzeller (1968), using pulses of sinusoidal vibration of the fingertips, found that response to a pulse interspersed during an 860 ms ISI had a significantly enhanced second negative peak at 140–150 ms; omitting a regularly presented pulse led to a small negative deflection at 200–240 ms after the time that stimulus onset had been due. Ford and Hillyard (1981) also found that an early noise burst evoked a late and large negative peak—at 129 ms and $-5.6\ \mu V$ frontally compared with the 111 ms and $-0.4\ \mu V$ peak occurring at the regular ISI. They did not find any consistent potentials immediately following an omitted pulse. In a recent study of ISI shortening, a late, 150 ms negative peak of approximately $-6\ \mu V$ was obtained (Nordby, Roth and Pfefferbaum, 1988a). Because large MMNs were elicited by both pitch and timing deviants, included in the same sequence, it appears that information of both types is available at the time of evocation. A second study (Nordby, Roth and Pfefferbaum, 1988b) tested for response to breaks in alternation of 800 ms and 400 ms ISIs or alternation of 500 Hz and 1000 Hz tones. The change in ISI pattern was not effective but repetition of one pitch, instead of the alternating pitch, did elicit significant MMN—especially convincing evidence that the response was not due to stimulation of fresh elements. There are also reports of recovery of an ANS–OR with change from an alternating to a repeated pattern.

Mismatch negativity can be elicited, therefore, by a number of stimulus change conditions that appear unlikely to activate fresh neuronal elements in a pool made partially refractory, or habituated, by repetition of a standard stimulus. This suggests that MMN might reflect the comparison of current input with the kind of neuronal model of prior stimulation hypothesized as the mechanism of OR elicitation (Sokolov, 1963, 1969). Like the OR, MMN is elicited automatically, occurring even when subjects are engaged in a demanding task involving stimuli in a different modality (Sams *et al.*, 1985b). Furthermore, MMN is responsive to the degree of change in many properties of the auditory stimulus, independent of the direction of change, and including complex patterns such as a change in the succession of stimuli. Neither MMN nor the OR appears to be easily elicited during sleep (Berg, Jackson and Graham, 1975; Paavilainen *et al.*, 1987). However, Csepe, Karmos and Molnar (1987) reported MMN during slow wave sleep in the cat. Also, a study of sleeping humans, instructed to respond with a hand squeeze to the subject's own name among other names, reported more frequent electrodermal responses and K-complexes (presumably including an N2) to the subject's own name (Oswald, 1962).

There are, however, some notable differences between characteristics of the neuronal models inferrable from MMN and OR responses. *First*, the models differ markedly in their rates of decay, from several seconds for MMN to perhaps minutes for ANS components of the OR. The decay time for MMN is compatible with an initial, large-capacity sensory memory, as is suggestive evidence from Aaltonen *et al.* (1987) that the model underlying MMN contains continuous rather than categorical information.

A *second* difference is that, in contrast to the OR model, the model for MMN is auditory-specific. Presumably, if the model underlying the OR depends on or can utilize an early, sensory-specific, rapidly decaying model of change in the auditory environment, similar sensory traces might exist in other modalities and be reflected in scalp-recorded potentials generated in or near the relevant primary sensory cortices. As noted above, Klinke *et al.* (1968) found evidence for an apparent MMN in the somatosensory modality at a latency and electrode site compatible with a generator in primary somatosensory cortex (Hari and Kaukoranta, 1985). Further, unpublished findings cited in Näätänen, Sams and Alho (1986) suggest that an auditory stimulus among somatosensory standards does not elicit an MMN. Mismatch responding in the visual modality under passive conditions has rarely been studied and the few findings are equivocal. Nyman *et al.* (in press; cited by Näätänen, 1988) did not find an MMN to visual deviants at any scalp site (Fz, Cz, Oz). Ford, Pfefferbaum and Kopell (1982), in a visual analog of Ford and Hillyard (1981), delivered light flashes at a 1200 ms ISI on 91% of presentations and interspersed flashes at shorter ISIs (300–450 ms) on 9% of presentations. A negative deflection at 143 ms, appearing at Cz and O_2, was significantly larger at shorter ISIs but was not tested for the passive condition alone. Because latency of the negativity was the same for standard and deviant ISIs, the effect could be ascribed to an enhancement of N1 rather than to a mismatch response. An N2 was also present, equally large at Fz, Cz, and O_2. It was judged not to be an obligatory component because it was greater with an active task; nonetheless, 'a small N2 was elicited by the early flashes even when they were not task relevant'.

A *third* difference is that MMN may be evoked only by rare changes along continuous dimensions and *not* by categorical changes, as in phonetic structure or word meaning (e.g. Aaltonen *et al.*, 1987; Kutas and Hillyard, 1980). Such categorical changes do affect the OR (see earlier), and they do affect later ERPs. Few studies have examined ERPs to categorical acoustic changes under passive conditions, but a broad class of categorical visual changes is reflected in negativity in the 400 ms range when such changes violate expectancies (Hillyard and Picton, 1987). The N400 elicited when an incongruous word violates the semantic expectancies developed as a sentence is read is especially well-documented (Kutas and Hillyard, 1980). These semantic violations apparently do not affect earlier negative ERPs, and expectancy violations regarding physical characteristics (word size) do not elicit N400. Nor did the size change elicit an MMN, a finding relevant to the question of whether a visual MMN exists.

A *fourth* difference is that ANS indices of orienting are elicited by the first stimulus of a series, but the MMN potential may not be. Available evidence is inconclusive because, in practice, up to the first ten trials of each block are often excluded from MMN averages, as in the Nyman *et al.* study cited above. In theory, a first trial might be expected to elicit MMN because MMN is a response to difference from prior stimulation, and onset of a stimulus after a steady-state condition of 'silence' is a large change. On the other hand, if MMN depends on stimulus divergence from a trace or model of recently presented *transient* stimuli, the model would initially be weak or non-existent. It is not easy to answer the question empirically: most studies of response to first stimuli were conducted before investigators became interested in MMN and, thus, amplitude and latency means were reported for windows long enough to include both MMN and N1. Further, if a first stimulus elicits a non-specific N1, a large, broad deflection could obscure smaller components such as the specific N1 and MMN.

A *fifth* difference between MMN and the generalized OR is that the OR to repetition of any non-signal stimulus habituates rapidly (Sokolov, 1963), while MMN habituates very slowly, if at all. However, the database with respect to OR habituation to change stimuli is small and has been obtained under the long-ISI conditions typical of ANS research. Whether an ANS–OR would habituate rapidly under the low-probability, short-ISI conditions used in MMN studies remains an open question.

Thus, a question of particular interest in determining the relation between MMN and the OR is whether or not MMN is associated with ANS components of an OR. That is, does the process reflected by MMN 'provide an attention-switch mechanism' or 'call' for attentional processing when some threshold is reached (Näätänen, 1988), or does it feed information to a later system which, after collating multimodal information and complex relationships among stimuli, issues a call?

Initial efforts to study the ANS–MMN relation have been reported from two laboratories. Verbaten *et al.* (1986), replicated by Kenemans *et al.* (1989), found fast N1 and slow N2 habituation to visual standards and deviants. Like N1, electrodermal response habituation was also rapid to repeated standards but was not measurable to deviants because the response did not recover reliably under passive conditions. Lyytinen and coworkers have published preliminary reports of auditory studies in which ERP, electrodermal activity, and heart rate were simultaneously recorded while subjects performed the visually presented Ravens Matrices test and ignored 74 dB tones, including standards and pitch and rise time deviants, presented every 750 ms. The data suggest that MMN is not necessarily associated with triggering an ANS–OR; that is, MMN was reliably elicited by deviant stimuli that did not elicit electrodermal or heart rate responses (Lyytinen *et al.*, 1987; Lyytinen, Blomberg and Näätänen, in press). Neither ERPs nor ANS responses habituated reliably, as indicated by a gross measure (Lyytinen *et al.*, in press), but averaged waveforms to pitch deviants showed differences in line with those to be expected from past work; that is, ANS responses were reduced after the first third of the trials in a block, but no change was evident in MMN (Näätänen and Lyytinen, 1989; Figure 2).

Summary

For the first 100 ms following onset or offset of stimulation, the obligatory transient-responsive ERPs and reflexly-inhibited blink show modality discrimination but, in comparison with later-occurring perceptual responses, show relatively gross discrimination of changes of intensity and auditory frequency. Exceptions are the excellent frequency discrimination of the supratemporal N1 under very rapid rates of stimulation (Näätänen *et al.*, 1988), and the good intensity discrimination shown by prepulse inhibition of reflex blink. The latter may reflect operation of a gating mechanism that prevents perceptual flooding.

The recovery to changes in physical characteristics could be explained by partially refractory, overlapping elements in a non-specific transient-sensitive generator(s), and is consistent with dual-process theory. The clearest demonstration of recovery seeming to require a comparison process is shown by the negative mismatch response that occurs between 100 and 200 ms in response to deviant auditory stimuli. This preattentive response could reflect a gating mechanism allowing a call for controlled processing and, thus, providing one basis for eliciting the passive attention described by OR theory. However, to accomodate the full range of conditions which elicit the generalized OR, additional mechanisms would be required to explain mismatch comparisons in other sensory modalities, mismatch in categorical information, integration across modalities, and the preservation of information for a longer period than the rapidly decaying MMN trace would permit.

The differences between functional characteristics of the neuronal model inferred from MMN and from ANS orienting responses are consistent with differences in the presumed loci of the models; that is, with a sensory-specific locus for a sensory-specific model, on the one hand, and a locus in an integrational area (e.g. amygdala–hippocampus), on the other hand.

PREATTENTIVE SUSTAINED PROCESSING: REFLEX MODULATION AND EXOGENOUS ERPS

The preattentive processing described in the preceding section is presumably mediated by mechanisms specialized to detect and transmit transient characteristics of stimulation. Although much of ANS and psychophysics research has employed stimuli with steady-state as well as transient characteristics, relatively few psychophysiological studies of reflex modulation or ERPs have been concerned with sustained stimuli. However, the work that has been done suggests that processing of transient and sustained characteristics may be carried out in parallel and may differ in important respects.

Reflex Modulation by Sustained Prestimulation

Unlike transient prestimuli, which have inhibitory effects at onset asynchronies up to about 500 ms, sustained prestimuli produce facilitation of the startle reflex. The facilitation is unlearned and, like the inhibitory effect, does not require that prestimulus and reflex-eliciting stimuli be in the same modality. Because the effect decays rapidly after prestimulus termination, it is best observed when prestimuli persist until onset of the reflex-eliciting stimulus, and when the interval between prestimulus and elicitor outlasts the period of transient-produced inhibition. At short ISIs, the contribution of the sustained-processing mechanism may be evident only in shortened onset latency or lessened inhibition (Graham, 1980; Giardina, 1989).

As would be expected of a modulatory system sensitive to total energy of a stimulus, reflex facilitation is the product of duration and intensity, up to some limit. The facilitation is generally significant with prestimulus durations and onset asynchronies of 2 s (Braff *et al.*, 1978; Geyer and Braff, 1987; Graham, Putnam and Leavitt, 1975; Yamada, Yamasaki and Miyata, 1979; Ornitz *et al.*, 1990) and may peak at about this time in both human subjects (Graham, Strock and Zeigler, 1981) and non-human subjects (Hoffman and Wible, 1969). In the adult human the effect is diminished by 4 s (Graham, Strock and Zeigler, 1981) and absent by 20 s (Putnam, 1975); in non-human subjects it persists through hours of prestimulation (Hoffman, Marsh and Stein, 1969). With duration constant, the facilitation also increases with prestimulus intensity up to moderate levels, but diminishes thereafter (Ison, McAdam and Hammond, 1973; Putnam, 1975; Stitt *et al.*, 1976). It is stronger in infants (Graham, Strock and Zeigler, 1981; Balaban, Anthony and Graham, 1989) and preschool children (Ornitz *et al.*, 1986, 1990) than in adults. Like prestimulus inhibition, modulations of latency and amplitude may be dissociable (Balaban, Anthony and Graham, 1989).

Thus, the system underlying facilitatory reflex modulation is energy-dependent, has a possibly U-shaped relation to intensity, acts cross-modally, and is more persistent in non-human species and stronger in immature than mature humans. These attributes are compatible with a low level 'activation' or arousal system (Graham, 1979; Ison, McAdam and Hammond, 1973) and with the sensitization process of dual-process theory (Groves and Thompson, 1970). In contrast to the midbrain-mediated inhibitory effect, the facilitatory effect is probably mediated at or below the level of a startle center in reticular formation and, thus, acts on the motor rather than the sensory limb of the reflex (Davis *et al.*, 1982). Consistent with preattentive processing, both facilitatory and inhibitory modulations of latency and amplitude can occur in the absence of orienting (Graham, 1975).

Frequency-Following Response

Preattentive processing of sustained auditory stimulation can also be observed in the cochlear microphonic potentials recorded from the periphery by an active electrode within the ear (electrocochleogram) and by far-field neural potentials recorded from the scalp vertex. These far-field potentials consist of a repetitive series of deflections, sometimes roughly sinusoidal, which follow the frequency of clicks at rates up to about 1500 per second, or of sustained sine-waves up to 1500 Hz (e.g. Davis, 1976), and reflect transmission through groups of brainstem cells. Picton, Stapells and Campbell (1981) note that the cells generating the potentials are relatively independent of the cells discharged by stimulus onset. Interest in the response has been mainly limited to its use in audiometry. Within its relatively restricted range, from about 40 dB to 65 dB HL, 'a reasonably close correspondence' has been reported between amplitude of the frequency-following response and two aspects of auditory perceptual experience, loudness and masking (Marsh, Brown and Smith, 1975).

Steady-State Midlatency Responses

Although frequency-following responses are not detected from structures beyond inferior colliculi, steady-state ERPs with an 'apparent latency' in the midlatency range are evoked when stimulus rates produce response overlap, as in the case of the 40 Hz potential, or when a carrier frequency is frequency modulated (FM) or amplitude modulated (AM) at optimal rates (Picton *et al.*, 1985; Stapells *et al.*, 1984). Both AM and FM yield the most consistent ERPs with modulation frequencies between 30 and 50 Hz, but reliable responses are recorded with modulations as low as 5 Hz (Picton *et al.*, 1987). As Picton *et al.* (1987) discuss, a source in polysensory thalamic regions has been suggested, but magnetic fields indicate at least one active source in auditory cortex, tonotopically organized as a function of carrier frequency (Mäkelä and Hari, 1987; Romani, Williamson and Kaufman, 1982).

The ability to respond to modulated auditory stimulation is important because most of the information in speech comes from frequency transitions and changes in stimulus amplitude across time. Thus, there have been studies of both ERP and behavioral thresholds for detecting modulation and for discriminating changes in its rate, direction, and duration. Clynes (1969) briefly reported several surprising characteristics of the ERP response. Although onset of a linear ramp, of increasing or decreasing frequency or amplitude change, elicited an ERP onset response similar to an N1–P2 complex, the response was maximal only after a prior period of constancy, that is, after a period of silence or of constant stimulation lasting at least 300 ms. The onset complex was absent or reduced when modulation changed direction, even when the change was larger than a detected change from constancy to modulation. Clynes also reported that offset of a ramp, even with a duration as long as 1 s, did not elicit a response. Both findings were replicated by Kohn, Lifshitz and Litchfield (1978, 1980). The latter studies also found that transitions yielding small or negligible ERP onset responses were harder to detect behaviorally and yielded highly dispersed reaction times. Although ERPs were recorded under passive listening conditions and behavioral responses under active listening instructions, the measures agreed in showing poor discrimination of modulations not preceded by periods of constant stimulation. Findings of Picton *et al.* (1987) suggest good agreement between perceptual and ERP thresholds (−3% to +2%) for detecting an AM change and insignificantly higher ERP thresholds (0 to 10%) for recognizing FM change.

Another issue is whether AM and FM modulations, as well as the direction of modulation, are processed in separate channels. Psychophysical studies have reported that adaptation to FM and AM stimulation, or to increasing versus decreasing FM, raises thresholds for the same type of modulation (e.g. Gardner and Wilson, 1979; Tansley and Suffield, 1983). Although such findings are usually viewed as evidence for channels tuned to specific sensory properties, Wakefield and Viemeister (1984) suggested a cognitive alternative which depends on subjects changing their internal reference. Evidence from ERP research is sparse. Some evidence exists for greater sensitivity to increasing than decreasing FM, and for quasi-independence of FM and AM modulations (Picton *et al.*, 1987; Ruhm, 1971). A specific adaptation-like effect on magnetic fields has also been reported when pairs of intermittent modulations were both FM or both AM, but not when the type of modulation differed (Mäkelä, Hari and Linnankivi, 1987). Because the source of the response was at the level of supratemporal auditory cortex, the authors interpreted their findings as making a cognitive interpretation less likely.

The preattentive nature of steady-state responses is further supported by a failure to find any effects of attention on steady-state responses when count-deviants and ignore-and-read conditions were compared or during a dichotic listening task that did show attention effects on the late transient potentials (Linden *et al.*, 1987).

Late Sustained Potential

When the response to an auditory stimulus lasting several hundred milliseconds is recorded with a long-time-constant or a DC amplifier, a sustained negative potential can be observed to follow the N1–P2 complex and to persist until stimulus offset. Picton, Woods and Proulx (1978a) estimated that the potential began 120–150 ms after stimulus onset and ended with an offset complex of the same polarities as the onset response. Both sustained and transient potentials were maximal at the vertex, but the latter were more widely distributed in posterior regions. In fact, little or no auditory sustained potential was observed over the occipital region. By contrast, the negative sustained potential to sustained visual stimuli is maximal over a lateral occipital electrode and is minimal at the vertex (Järvilehto, Hari and Sams, 1978; Keidel, 1976). Magnetic studies suggest that the source of the auditory sustained field lies within the Sylvian fissure but is separate from, and anterior to, the source of the magnetic N100 (Hari *et al.*, 1987).

There are a number of functional differences between the transient and sustained potentials. As noted in an earlier section, the amplitude of the late transient N1–P2 potential increases with stimulus duration for only 30–50 ms; in contrast, the sustained potential follows the shape of the stimulus waveform for some seconds (Keidel, 1976). Keidel's Figure 61b illustrates sustained potentials whose amplitudes remained constant throughout rectangular stimuli and did not change with duration increases from 0.5 to 3.5 s. Although Picton, Woods and Proulx (1978b) found reduced amplitudes for longer stimuli (5 s and 9 s), the reduction could be due to the fact that ISI decreased as duration increased.

Transient and sustained responses also differ as a function of stimulus intensity, frequency, and repetition rate. While N1 saturates at relatively low intensities, amplitudes of sustained potentials increase with a nearly linear slope between 10 and 90 dB HL (Keidel, 1976; Picton, Woods and Proulx, 1978b). Picton *et al.* also found a systematic relation between sustained-potential amplitude and tone frequency, with amplitude an inverse function of log-frequency between 250 Hz and 8 kHz. Although N1, too, was smaller at high frequencies, there was little difference among frequencies less than 2 kHz. In contrast, N1 showed much greater frequency specificity of the refractory period than did the sustained potential. In general, sustained potentials were less susceptible to refractory effects, as judged by the relatively small effect of increasing repetition rates from one every 10 s to one every 2 s. However, at a rate, of one per second, Järvilehto, Hari and Sams (1978) obtained a very marked first-stimulus effect on both transient and sustained potentials to trains of 1 s tones or light flashes. The effects were non-specific, that is, maximal at the vertex for both modalities. A first-stimulus effect on the auditory sustained potential did not differ as a function of instructions to attend versus to ignore-and-read (Hari, Sams and Järvilehto, 1979).

An interesting idea is that the transient or sustained character of an adapting stimulus may determine whether it affects the transient or the sustained response to a test stimulus. Picton, Woods and Proulx (1978a) found that interspersing transient clicks among sustained stimuli reduced N1 by a significant 39% but produced only a non-significant 3% reduction in the sustained potential. A converse effect is suggested by findings of David *et al.* (1971); that is, the combination of visual and auditory sustained stimuli reduced both sustained potentials compared with the single-modality potential, but did not affect, or enhanced, the transient N1 response. If this dissociation in effects is replicable, it would indicate that some parallel processing is preserved at least up to early cortical sensory regions.

Sustained potentials can also be distinguished from the slow 'contingent negative variation' (CNV) which is associated with expectancy or uncertainty (Walter *et al.*, 1964). The two waveforms may occur simultaneously, but the *necessary* conditions for eliciting them differ. First, the sustained potential is a sensory response that requires the presence of stimulation sustained longer than 120–150 ms, while CNV can be elicited by any stimulus which serves as a signal, that is, has a contingent relation with information to follow. The necessity of stimulus presence for eliciting a sustained potential has been demonstrated by absence of the potential during equivalent pauses in continuous stimulation (Hari *et al.*, 1987; Picton, Woods and Proulx, 1978a). Picton *et al.* suggested that contrary findings, briefly reported by Järvilehto and Fruhstorfer (1973), might be due to the lack of specific instructions to ignore the auditory stimuli and concentrate on reading. The fact that the scalp distribution of sustained potentials varies depending on stimulus modality and is maximal over the specific sensory region (Järvilehto, Hari and Sams, 1978; Keidel, 1976) is further evidence of its sensory nature.

A second major difference between CNV and sustained potentials is that CNV is presumed to reflect higher-level anticipatory processes. As Putnam (1990) points out, the processes are vaguely defined. Hillyard and Picton (1987) comment that most investigators 'have linked the CNV to intensive aspects of attention (e.g. effort, arousal, expectancy, alertness, or concentration) that may support various specific acts'. Simons (1988) emphasizes the importance of affective processes. Motor preparation, likely to be minimal in passive conditions, is reflected in the *Bereitschaftspotential* which may contribute to the CNV. But however defined, CNV has *not* been described as an automatic, preattentive process which could occur in sleep. Thus, the finding that the auditory sustained potential does occur undiminished in sleep (Picton, Woods and Proulx, 1978a) is important evidence of a basic difference from CNV.

Third, the sustained potential is unaffected by attend instructions, unless stimulus duration is itself the to-be-attended dimension. Picton *et al.* found that when subjects were asked to detect an infrequent intensity change or frequency modulation of 1 s tones, the attended but not the ignored change elicited a significant N2–P3 complex, but no difference in sustained negativity. Only when subjects were required to detect an infrequent longer-duration 1.2 s tone was there additional sustained negativity, presumably due to CNV. The negativity was larger under attend than ignore conditions for both standards and deviants, and the N2–P3 complex was delayed until offset of the deviant, that is, until the requisite information had been delivered.

Summary

The frequency-following, steady-state, and negative sustained potentials in response to auditory stimuli provide information about time-varying changes in stimulus intensity and frequency, and about persistence and shape of the stimulus envelope that is not provided by the transient-sensitive potentials and that appears to be more closely related to perceptual and behavioral responses. Evidence for specific adaptation effects and different generators suggests that sustained and transient characteristics are processed separately at least up to primary sensory cortex. There has been much less research on sustained visual stimuli, but it seems likely that the above generalizations hold for this modality as well. Sustained and transient stimuli also have different effects in modulating reflex startle.

THE GENERALIZED OR: REFLEX MODULATING EFFECTS AND ERP CORRELATES

Our review of preattentive processing identified two ERP components that have been associated with orienting. One, the MMN, is evoked by a variety of types of stimulus change that appear to require a model-comparison process and might, therefore, reflect directly or indirectly an automatic OR trigger. The second, the earlier non-specific N1, does not generally show recovery to the kinds of change requiring model-comparison, but it does habituate rapidly to initial presentations of a stimulus and, in keeping with Näätänen's argument (e.g. 1986) for separate mechanisms producing initial- and change-ORs, might reflect the initial-OR. Loveless (1983) argued that the larger N1 on initial trials of a block is not necessarily due to lessened refractoriness after a longer-than-usual ISI, but could be due to stimulus occurrence at a time that did not match the timing information in a neuronal model. After reviewing evidence for an independent effect of temporal uncertainty on N1 amplitude, he concluded, as do Näätänen and Picton (1987), that two factors—dynamogenic/energizing characteristics of stimuli, and their temporal uncertainty—play the major role in eliciting N1. Because N1 is insensitive to intensity increases lasting beyond about 30 ms, the dynamogenic effect of a high-intensity transient, when eliciting N1 accompanied by rapidly-habituating heart rate acceleration (Putnam and Roth, 1990), is presumably to elicit startle rather than an arousal/defense response or an OR. However, when N1 is elicited by a change in energy pattern occurring 'at a subjectively unexpected time' (Loveless, p.80), it may be functionally related to orienting.

We consider in this section reflex modulation research that demonstrates functional consequences of OR elicitation by uncertainty and novelty. We also consider evidence for relating the generalized OR to ERP activity—the late positive complex, LPC, consisting of P3/P300, and associated slow waves—that may follow an MMN, and that might distinguish between a call for controlled processing and an answer to the call.

Uncertainty, the Generalized OR, and Reflex Modulating Effects

Although the presumed function of the generalized OR is to enhance sensory-perceptual processing, relatively little research has been specifically devoted to a study of the OR's functional consequences. The evidence, much of it indirect and based on active attention conditions, is admirably discussed by Spinks and Siddle (1983). They point out that Sokolov's (1966) model treated the OR as primarily determined by uncertainty or entropy and its consequences led, therefore, to analysis of the information required to reduce the uncertainty. We review, in the following, findings from reflex modulation studies which highlight the importance of uncertainty in eliciting the OR and which contrast with the meagre support obtained for the uncertainty effects of ISI variation noted earlier.

Uncertainty effects on reflex blink emerged serendipitously in a study by Graham, Putnam and Leavitt (1975), intended to replicate reflex modulation effects reported in startle research with rats (e.g. Hoffman and Wible, 1969). Blink-eliciting stimuli were 50 ms noise bursts, occurring alone (9 trials) or preceded by tones at varying ISIs between 200 and 2000 ms (72 trials); the tone prestimuli were either 20 ms long or were sustained until reflex stimulus onset. All prestimuli elicited robust heart rate decelerations that persisted without significant change throughout the 72 prestimulus trials, much longer than previous experience with heart rate deceleration in non-signal situations had led us to expect (e.g. Graham, 1973). The decelerations were followed by an unexpected reflex facilitation under conditions—brief prestimuli and long ISIs—that had not affected the rat reflex. We did replicate the effects that had been seen in rats, namely, a prepulse inhibitory effect at short ISIs and a facilitatory reflex change with sustained prestimuli.

Because heart rate deceleration suggested the presence of an anticipatory OR, we speculated that the varying ISIs produced uncertainty about when a blink-eliciting stimulus would occur. The resulting OR, directed to reducing uncertainty (i.e. extracting information), did not habituate because there was no repetition in the pattern of ISI assignments. Thus, the reflex stimulus continued to be enhanced by attentional processing and, thereby, indirectly speeded and enlarged the reflex response.

To test the hypothesis, three subsequent experiments minimized uncertainty by using only two conditions: a control condition of eliciting-stimulus-alone and a prestimulus condition with a fixed 2000 ms ISI between a brief prestimulus and the eliciting stimulus (see summary in Graham, 1975). None of these experiments yielded a blink magnitude greater in the prestimulus condition than in the control condition, nor, in the two studies in which it was measured, were heart rate decelerations greater than control values. Further, two of the studies also measured slow scalp potentials following the prestimulus without finding evidence of the CNV 'expectancy' potential (see the previous section on preattentive sustained processing). In contrast, an additional two-condition study using sustained prestimuli (Brown, 1975; Experiment 2) yielded the obligatory reflex facilitation that sustained prestimuli had elicited in rats, and evoked an obligatory ERP, the negative sustained potential. The fact that prestimuli again failed to elicit heart rate decelerations greater than control was further evidence that the slow potential was not a CNV.

To replicate the initial uncertainty effects and to test for an associated 'expectancy' potential (i.e. CNV), a second uncertainty experiment included both temporal and event uncertainty, the latter produced by following the brief visual prestimulus with either a blink-eliciting white noise or a 60 dB tone (Bloch, 1972; Experiment 3). Like the first uncertainty experiment, blink was again facilitated in the 2000 ms ISI condition, despite the brief prestimuli. Consistent with the assumption that anticipatory orienting was engaged, prestimuli elicited both persistent heart rate deceleration and CNV.

Thus, the temporal uncertainty with which prestimuli are followed by other stimuli appears to have a potent effect in eliciting an OR and, presumably in consequence, in facilitating the processing of stimuli that might reduce uncertainty. An important question is whether introduction of a novel stimulus, the standard procedure for eliciting a generalized OR, also facilitates the reflex blink elicited by a subsequent stimulus. Bohlin *et al.* (1981) showed that unannounced introduction of brief novel prestimuli (four visual and four auditory), interspersed among 51 tactile prestimuli and nine acoustic-alone controls, did have effects similar to uncertainty. Specifically, heart rate decelerations followed the novel prestimuli, and blinks elicited 2000 ms later were larger on novel than control trials. In line with theoretical ideas of the generalized OR, the effects were modality non-specific, that is, both auditory and visual novels facilitated the auditory reflex.

Bohlin *et al.* (1981) conducted two other experiments, with stimuli and presentation schedules identical to those of the novelty experiment, but with active attention induced by instructions. In one study, subjects judged the duration of blink-eliciting noise bursts that followed the auditory and visual prestimuli and, in another study, focused attention on the 'important' auditory and visual prestimuli so that their biological responses could be tested. A postpublication analysis of blink activity recorded to the prestimuli themselves is relevant here. Although the 65 dB auditory prestimuli, and equally intense visual prestimuli, were below a 50% threshold criterion for eliciting blinks, Figure 3.1 shows non-negligible eyelid activity when attention was actively

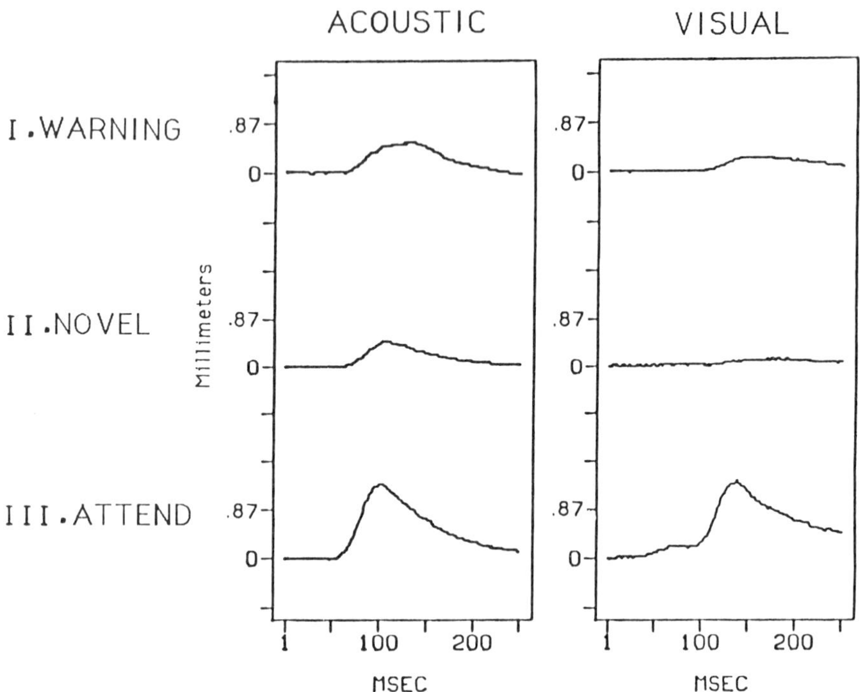

Figure 3.1. Averaged blink reflexes (mm of lid movement) to weak lead stimuli, presented in three experiments that were identical except for instructional set (N = 16 subjects per experiment). In I (Warning) the lead stimuli forewarned of a stimulus whose duration was to be judged; in II (Novel) the lead stimuli were not announced in advance and there was no task; in III (Attend) the only task was to attend to the acoustic and visual lead stimuli: four acoustic (20 ms, 65 dB noise bursts) and four visual (20 ms illumination increases, matched to noise bursts for subjective intensity) were interspersed among 51 electrotactile lead stimuli and nine 104 dB noise bursts in an order counterbalanced across subjects. All lead stimuli were followed in 2 s by the 104 dB noise bursts. These are postpublication analyses of data from experiments described in Bohlin *et al.* (1981).

directed to the prestimuli, by virtue of their being either warning stimuli or the focus of attention. The point of interest is the reliably smaller blink activity elicited by the unannounced novels, indicating that novelty was not detected rapidly enough to affect a reflex response to the novel stimulus itself, even though it enhanced response to a later stimulus.

These studies suggest two differences between passive attention elicited by input that mismatches a model of past stimulation, and active attention directed by instructions and presumably elicited by input that matches primed representations of significant stimuli (Öhman, 1979): (1) a longer latency for effects of passive attention, at least for easily discriminable but low-intensity stimuli; (2) non-selective effects of passive attention as opposed to selective, localized effects of active attention. The reflex modulating effects of active attention are discussed in the second part of this chapter. Also, see Putnam (1990) for a review of the relation between heart rate changes and reflex-modulation under active attending conditions.

The Generalized OR and the Late Positive Complex

Näätänen (1988) has hypothesized that MMN reflects an acoustic-specific but possibly automatic trigger or call for controlled, limited processing. Although the non-habituating MMN cannot itself be considered an OR component, it is frequently followed by a non-specific complex (N2b–P3a) which, it has been suggested, does show the functional characteristics of an OR.

The N2b–P3a complex consists of a 'sharp' negative peak with a latency of about 200 ms and a subsequent positive peak between about 220 and 320 ms for auditory stimuli. A P165–N2b–P3a complex, present under active attention conditions, has also been described but is not considered here (Goodin, Aminoff and Mantle, 1986). It remains uncertain whether or not N2b and P3a are independent components. Squires, Squires and Hillyard (1975) introduced the terms P3a and P3b to distinguish a short-latency P3a, with a frontal–central scalp distribution, from the longer-latency P300 or P3b, often including slow wave positivity, with a parietal–central distribution. They obtained P3a most clearly to acoustic deviants under passive conditions (reading); P3b occurs most clearly under active attention conditions. A principal-components analysis of peaks indicated that the two P3s varied more or less independently from one another and also from N2. A principal-components analysis of ERPs in a similar study (Squires *et al.*, 1977) confirmed N2–P3b separation, but did not find an unequivocal factor for P3a.

A distinction between MMN/N2a and N2b was subsequently made by Renault and Lesevre (1978) and by Näätänen, Simpson and Loveless (1982), and was reviewed in detail by Näätänen and Gaillard (1983). One basis for a distinction is the auditory specificity of MMN as opposed to the modality non-specificity of N2b. Evidence for both specific and non-specific components comes from studies of missing stimuli. The negative ERP to a stimulus deleted from an auditory stream appears to be generated in auditory cortex and, similarly, a deleted visual stimulus elicits a negative ERP with its maximum over parietal–occipital cortex (Renault and Lesevre, 1978; Simson, Vaughan and Ritter, 1976). In both cases, the modality-specific peak is overlapped by a later negativity, the N2b, which peaks in central areas.

The major bases for distinguishing between MMN/N2a and N2b are the joint findings that N2b is associated with active-attention conditions and with a subsequent positive deflection. If any task-related difference in N2 were attributed to N2b on the assumption that MMN is *not* affected by attention, there is, as Näätänen and Gaillard (1983; p.134) point out, a risk of circularity. However, there seems to be good evidence for basing a distinction on the occurrence of subsequent positivity. Näätänen and Gaillard (p.130) state that N2b 'never occurs without the P3a, that is, they form a unitary, inseparable ERP component'. The analogous relationship does not necessarily hold for N2a/MMN; that is, late negativity to unattended or ignored deviants may also be followed by a P3, albeit usually of smaller amplitude (e.g. Sams *et al.*, 1985b). It has been suggested that these instances represent involuntary shifts of attention and are more likely under conditions, such as lowered probability or greater deviance, that make stimuli more salient or obtrusive (Näätänen, Simpson and Loveless, 1982). Näätänen and Gaillard (1983) speculated that MMN accompanied by the N2b–P3a complex, or any late positivity, indicates presence of the classical OR and that MMN not followed by positivity indicates absence of the OR.

Näätänen, Simpson and Loveless (1982) entertained two hypotheses with respect to the nature of the N2b–P3a complex. The first hypothesis was that 'all deviants evoking mismatch negativity generate the complex as its terminus, provided that the stimulus mismatch is detected'. They did not restrict the meaning of 'detecting' to detecting *signals*, but allowed for a momentary breakthrough of attention involving minimal cognitive activity to identify the stimulus as currently irrelevant. The first hypothesis did not propose any 'specific mechanism for passively triggered attention, although the distinction between actively detecting a stimulus and having one's attention caught by it seems subjectively rather clear'. The second hypothesis was that 'occurrence of the complex denotes an involuntary call by preattentive mechanisms for focal attention'. The authors appeared to distinguish between occurrence of a passive, generalized as opposed to an active, localized OR on the basis, respectively, of whether only P3a is found or P3b is also, or instead, present. They noted that Ford, Roth and Kopell (1976) made a similar distinction; the distinction is also in accord with the principal-components analysis of Squires, Squires and Hillyard (1975).

Courchesne and collaborators (Courchesne, 1977; Courchesne, Hillyard and Galambos, 1975) described another positive ERP deflection in response to unrecognizable novel stimuli inserted in a stream of visual stimuli to which subjects were attending. There were four types of slides: a standard stimulus (the digit '2'), rare target stimuli (the digit '4'), and two kinds of rare non-targets which were never repeated—easily recognized patterns such as words or geometric figures, or 'unrecognizable' abstract drawings in color. All deviants elicited post-N2 positivity that was relatively more anterior for non-targets than targets, but only the unrecognizable novels elicited significantly greater frontal than parietal positivity. The authors suggested that the novels' response might not be the same as the P3a described by Squires, Squires and Hillyard (1975) because it was elicited, not just by physical deviance, but by stimuli whose unrecognizability made them difficult to encode or categorize. Whether or not such stimuli receive qualitatively different processing is an interesting question. However, the other grounds for suggesting separate components are less compelling: possible differences in habituation or in the conditions (attended or ignored) required for elicitation have not been adequately assessed and the observed latency and amplitude differences might be ascribable to degree of deviance and to differences between visual and auditory ERPs. In later work, Courchesne *et al.* (1984) identified a centrally maximal positivity with a shorter latency and larger amplitude to auditory novels than to equally rare targets, as did Knight (1984), using an unannounced, simulated dog bark. Knight provided further evidence that the anterior positivity is not the same component as the classical parietal positivity: unlike normal controls, subjects with prefrontal damage showed normal parietal P3s to target stimuli but showed neither an enhanced N2 nor the following frontal–central P3 to novel non-targets.

The basic findings of an anteriorly distributed positivity, with a relatively shorter latency than the classical parietal P3 in response to rare or novel non-target deviants, has been replicated in a number of studies (e.g. Fitzgerald and Picton, 1983; Ford, Roth and Kopell, 1976; Nordby, Roth and Pfefferbaum, 1988a; Picton *et al.*, 1985; Rösler, Hasselmann and Sojka, 1987; Snyder and Hillyard, 1976). However, not all experiments have found that rare, non-target stimuli elicit frontal P3s. Those that do not, report one of two outcomes—either no ERPs are found beyond the obligatory N1–P2 or MMN potentials, or the novel stimuli elicit the parietal P3b positivity associated with task relevance or targets.

Failure to obtain any late positivity could be expected if detected mismatch triggers a call for controlled processing only when a threshold is reached, with factors which increase stimulus salience, such as low probability and large deviance, increasing the likelihood of exceeding threshold. For example, of three studies that measured ERPs to 1000 Hz standards and pitch deviants ($p = 0.10$) while subjects read, two found P3as to a 1500 Hz deviant (Fitzgerald and Picton, 1983; Squires, Squires and Hillyard, 1975), but Sams, Alho and Näätänen (1983) did not obtain P3s to 1250 Hz deviants, nor did Fitzgerald and Picton to a 1050 Hz deviant. Sams *et al.* suggested that another factor may also be important in determining whether threshold is exceeded, namely, capacity allocated to a primary task. Using a demanding word identification task, with payoffs for good performance, Duncan-Johnson and Donchin (1977) found no P3 at all to deviants in an ignored auditory stream, despite a standard-deviant difference (1000 Hz versus 1500 Hz) that was effective in eliciting P3a in the less demanding reading studies.

Emergence of a parietal P3b component in response to non-target deviants may be more common than the absence of any late positivity. Examples of such studies include Ritter, Vaughan and Costa (1968), Roth (1973), Miles *et al.* (1987), and Polich (1987). In each case, the deviance was a very large, easily discriminated difference—octave changes in pitch, change in ear stimulated, change from tone to white noise or vice versa, or change in stimulus modality—and the demands of the primary task were relatively small. Subjects were either reading (Ritter *et al.*), had no primary task except to ignore the stimuli (Roth; Polich), or, in the case of Miles *et al.*, received unannounced novel stimuli among standards and targets delivered at ISIs (12–20 s) long enough for attention to be temporarily diverted. It is reasonable to assume that, without competing demands from a primary task, allocatable resources are readily available for stimulus processing. Hoffman, Simons and Houck (1983) found that highly trained subjects continued to produce substantial P3b well after training in a visual search task had, by all other criteria, produced automatic performance. Thus, if P3a represents a call for processing capacity or resources, the request may be granted (as indexed by P3b) unless the called-for resources are specifically required elsewhere. Note also that the anterior P3a may be present even when rare deviants or novel stimuli give rise primarily to the P3b component. In some cases, both are visible but, as Squires, Squires and Hillyard (1975) pointed out, the relative size of the components differs and may make it impossible to detect a small, early component when it is overlapped by a component many times larger.

The question of particular interest in the present context is whether either P3a or P3b is associated with, or is an index of, the generalized OR measured by ANS components. If either P3 reflects generalized orienting, then, according to the original Sokolov formulation, it would be expected to habituate rapidly under passive, low-demand conditions. However, Öhman's (1979) distinction between a call for controlled processing, reflected in the OR, and an answer to the call, allows for a situation in which an OR elicited by a non-target could fail to habituate or could habituate slowly; namely, under conditions in which the call is not answered, or is answered only sporadically, because resources are engaged in a primary task. Results of a Stenfert Kroese and Siddle (1983) study are consistent with this expectation: electrodermal response to non-target tones delivered during a visual monitoring task were larger, habituated more slowly, and showed less recovery to a stimulus change during high- than during low-demand primary-task conditions.

Data on habituation of P3 under passive conditions are meagre, but suggest that both the frontal P3 and the parietal P3b can decrement relatively rapidly with stimulation repeated at intervals long enough to make refractory effects unlikely. Courchesne, Hillyard and Galambos (1975) found that, with at least 12 s between novel visual stimuli, frontal P3 to the second novel dropped by 50% and, to the third, by 60%, and did not change significantly thereafter. A later study (Courchesne, 1978) showed frontal P3 decreasing 67% between the first and tenth novel stimulus, while parietal positivity increased so that dominance shifted from relatively anterior to relatively posterior positivity. Knight (1984) found a similarly rapid decrease in frontal P3 and a slight shift parietally with repeated presentations of his dog-bark stimulus. There is also evidence that parietal P3b can habituate rapidly under passive conditions. Courchesne, Courchesne and Hillyard (1978) presented easily-recognizable visual non-targets among equally rare targets and frequent standards, with intervals between a given stimulus type averaging about 10–12 s. Both targets and non-targets elicited parietally maximal P3b, but the non-target response decreased progressively by more than 50% of initial amplitude while there was no change in the P3 to targets, even after 40 presentations. For both targets and non-targets, P2 amplitude remained unchanged. Luminance deviants evoked a similarly stable P3b, as targets, and an habituating P3b, as non-targets (Courchesne, 1978).

Thus, both frontal–central and parietal P3 to non-target deviants or novels have shown rapid habituation when presented in an attended stream, while P3 to target stimuli has remained stable. Whether habituation to non-targets would be slowed if the primary task were more demanding has apparently not been assessed. Nor are there data on whether P3a habituates under conditions in which it is not followed by P3b. That is, if P3a is a call for controlled processing and P3b is an answer to the call, then P3a should *not* habituate in situations where the call is unanswered. Verbaten *et al.* (1986), measuring both P3a and P3b in response to a single visual stimulus repeated at relatively long ISIs (6–16 s), obtained habituation of P3b but not of P3a. However, the P3a data are difficult to interpret. It is not clear that P3a ever occurred in the absence of P3b or even that any peaks were observed in the latency range designated for P3a; consequently, the measure may only have indicated an early point in the rise of P3b. Verbaten *et al.* did find that P3b over Cz habituated significantly more slowly (11 trials), than did either the electrodermal response (4.4 trials) or N1 (3.6 trials). Interestingly, the P3 recorded over Oz showed the least habituation of any response and the authors suggested that it might reflect the localized OR.

The Verbaten *et al.* finding of slower P3b than electrodermal habituation should not be accepted as evidence against a P3b association with the generalized OR, given that known OR components have been found to habituate at different rates (as discussed earlier) and that other studies are divided between those finding slower (Becker and Shapiro, 1980) and those finding faster P3b than electrodermal habituation (Rösler, Hasselmann and Sojka, 1987; Simons, 1988). In any case, P3b habituation to non-targets can be called rapid relative to its persistence in response to targets. Further, the P3 elicited by high-intensity non-targets, that should not elicit an OR beyond initial trials, behaves like ANS components of a defense reflex; that is, it is resistant to habituation, increases with stimulus duration, and is associated with persistent heart rate acceleration (Putnam and Roth, 1988, 1990). However, inconsistencies between the recovery of P3 and ANS measures to stimulus change have been reported. Neither Roth *et al.* (1982) nor Simons (1988) found P3 recovery to stimulus changes that did produce recovery of the electrodermal response and, in the Simons study, also recovery of heart rate deceleration. Nonetheless, a substantial literature has linked P3 to the OR both on the grounds that it is sensitive to the kind of complex changes to which an OR is sensitive and because it appears to involve the updating of a model of past stimulation and future expectations (e.g. Donchin, 1981; Donchin *et al.*, 1984; Rohrbaugh, 1984; Roth, 1983).

If the distinction between a call and an answer to the call is meaningful, P3b would be more appropriately associated with the answer, although the two events—call and answer—might occur in such rapid succession as to make a separation difficult in practice. Unfortunately, ANS responses occur too slowly to be aligned in time with ERPs. Further, as Öhman (1979) noted, electrodermal responses may not be discriminating because they may occur both with a call and as a result of the effortful, controlled processing that results if the call is answered. Heart rate might allow identification of a shift from monitoring input, reflected in heart rate deceleration, to searching memory, reflected in heart rate acceleration (see the earlier section on preattentive transient processing). It would still be difficult, however, to separate preattentive transient detection from the call itself because both the automatic transient-detecting response and the OR are associated with deceleration, although the latter is longer-lasting. With sufficient resolution of heart rate timing, the lower and upper temporal limits of input monitoring could be determined, but this would require averaging heart rate across large numbers of subjects during periods (e.g. 100 or 200 ms) short enough to provide the desired resolution (Graham, 1978). Additionally, when there is rapid habituation to change stimuli, only a few trials per subject provide useful information, and data would have to be obtained from enough subjects to yield both reliable ANS and ERP responses.

Three recent studies have reported an initial HR deceleration evoked by both targets and deviants/novels, but a subsequent acceleration only to targets (Miles *et al.*, 1987; Rösler, Hasselmann and Sojka, 1987; Simons *et al.*, 1986). In Simons *et al.*, in which targets and novel stimuli differed in modality, the shift from deceleration to acceleration in response to targets began after 800 ms but, in Miles *et al.*, the divergence in response to a within-modality difference in bandwidth began after 1600 ms.

Interesting differences between the relationship of ERPs to electrodermal response and cardiac acceleration as compared with cardiac deceleration are suggested by ERP data obtained to pitch deviants (during administration of a Ravens Matrices test) and classified in terms of the presence or absence of ANS activity (Näätänen and Lyytinen, 1989; see also the earlier section on preattentive transient processing). Although not tested statistically, electrodermal responses and cardiac accelerations tended to be associated with one another and with a relatively sharp negativity centroparietally, which might be an N2b (Lyytinen, Blomberg and Näätänen, in press; Näätänen and Lyytinen, Figures 2 and 3). However, ANS activity during periods of maximal post-stimulus change did not differ significantly from equal-duration pre-stimulus periods, except for reliable heart rate deceleration between 3 and 4 s following the stimulus (Lyytinen *et al.*).

With respect to late positivity, P3b and/or a slow positive wave tended to be larger when electrodermal activity or cardiac acceleration was present than when ANS responses were absent or heart rate decelerated (Näätänen and Lyytinen, 1989; Figures 3 and 4). The larger slow parietal positivity with cardiac acceleration than with deceleration was significant (Lyytinen, Blomberg and Näätänen, in press). Further, when cardiac deceleration was present, P3 recovered more rapidly after an early peak and showed a broad wave of frontally dominant negativity with peaks at about 300 and 400 ms, perhaps reflecting the 'second look' phenomenon. It is tempting to speculate that prolonged deceleration is associated with a call for processing, accompanied by a P3a, and continued processing of stimulus input. In contrast, cardiac acceleration and electrodermal response may be associated with an answer to the call and an effortful memory search terminated by registrating the stimulus in long-term memory. Alternatively, the late positivity might reflect a defensive response to stimuli interfering with a demanding task (Lyytinen *et al.*; Putnam and Roth, 1990). As Lyytinen (1988) concluded, the results to date suggest that any covariation between ERP and ANS variables 'occurs in a complex form'.

Complex or not, it seems likely that understanding of the organism's response to novelty can be enriched by further research which attempts to disentangle the complexity. Through manipulation of stimulus variables to produce mismatch detection both above and below the threshold for issuing a call, and by manipulation of competing demands for controlled processing in order to vary the probability of, and the rapidity of, a call being answered, it might be possible to assess separately these theoretically interesting processes.

ACTIVE (VOLUNTARY) ATTENTION AND LOCALIZED, SELECTIVE ORIENTING

S.A. HACKLEY AND F.K. GRAHAM

Among the most influential concepts in contemporary psychology is the distinction between mental processes that do, and those that usually do not, require conscious attention. The former processes, variously termed 'controlled' (Schneider and Shiffrin, 1977), 'conscious' (Posner, 1978), or 'effortful' (Kahneman, 1973), involve a temporary sequence of operations under voluntary control of the subject. Controlled processes are used in performing new tasks, dangerous tasks, and tasks in which the relation between stimuli and responses varies inconsistently over time. By contrast, 'automatic' processes involve habitual sequences of operations that develop in situations characterized by highly consistent mappings between stimuli and responses across extended periods of practice. Such processes are reflex-like in that they are fast, they are difficult to suppress, and, because they do not usually draw upon limited attentional resources, they can operate in parallel without mutual interference.

Much research on active attention has been devoted to determining which of the processes engaged by a stimulus are automatic and which are controlled. The long-standing debate between early- versus late-selection theorists may be cast in this framework: the controversy concerns whether perceptual analysis is automatic, with controlled processes beginning only after fully analyzed inputs find representation in short term memory (the late selection view; see, for example, Shiffrin and Grantham, 1974); or whether only relatively low-level analyses are completely automatic (early selection; see, for example, Broadbent, 1958; and review in Johnston and Dark, 1986). This question regarding the lowest level at which attentional control is first realized was articulated for neuroscientists by Lord Adrian in 1954:

> The signals from the sense organs must be treated differently when we attend to them and when we do not, and if we could decide *where* and *how* the divergence arises we should be closer to understanding how the level of consciousness is reached. [italics added]

Adrian mentioned *where* and *how*, but *when* the divergence arises is especially important. It is a goal of psychophysiology, and of the cognitive neurosciences in general, to be able to relate data from three distinct domains—behavior, phenomenology, and physiology. As Michael Posner points out (1978), each of these classes of phenomena is embedded in real-time. Hence, a particularly effective tool for revealing their interrelations is mental chronometry, '...the study of the time course of information processing in the human nervous system' (p. 7). Note the special relevance of a chronometric analysis of active attention for the early-selection/late-selection issue: if the initial divergence in processing of attended and ignored stimuli occurs late in time, after a thorough perceptual analysis has presumably transpired, late-selection theories would be supported. Evidence for a very rapid divergence, by contrast, would tend to support the early-selection view that sensory-perceptual analyses are not fully automatic.

METHODOLOGICAL ISSUES

These questions regarding automatic versus controlled processing, and the *when*, *where*, and *how* of the initial divergence of processing, will be the focus of our review. Because chronometric issues will be stressed, ERP and somatic reflex studies will be emphasized over those employing autonomic measures. Because of their millisecond-by-millisecond temporal resolution, event-related potentials are especially well suited for studies of mental chronometry. Inferences may potentially be made concerning the onset, duration, relative ordering, and simultaneity of distinct stages of mental processing, as illustrated in analyses of passive attention (see the first part of this chapter). If ERPs provided an exhaustive account of time-locked sensory and motor function, there would be little merit in the study of somatic reflexes. However, only a small subset of the electrical activity in the nervous system is manifested as surface-recorded ERPs. In general, ERPs reflect the synchronous activity of graded, postsynaptic potentials in large populations of neurons fortuitously oriented so as to form an 'open field' or, less commonly, compound action potentials in fiber bundles, or glial cell reactions to prior neural activity (e.g. Allison, Wood and McCarthy, 1986). Although only certain, narrowly defined, stimuli and responses are involved in reflex arcs, somatic reflexes offer a useful supplement to ERPs in the study of neural function. The principal advantage of reflexes is that extensive prior research in animals has generated a core of behavioral and neurophysiological knowledge concerning reflexes that may justify strongly reductionistic inferences in humans.

The Hillyard Paradigm

The application of reflex methods to investigate active attention is relatively recent, and has much to gain from methodological innovations introduced by ERP researchers. Foremost among these is the paradigm devised by Hillyard and colleagues for distinguishing selective sensory attention effects from non-selective and non-sensory factors in a task requiring highly focused attention (Hillyard *et al.*, 1973; reviewed by Hillyard and Hansen, 1986). In the prototypical case, a Go/NoGo task is used in which the subject makes a speeded button press to one designated 'target' among four randomly presented stimulus types. The stimuli are presented at a rapid rate, and the four stimulus categories are defined by factorial combination of two levels of a rapidly discriminable attribute and two of a slowly discriminable attribute. For example, the subject might be asked to attend, in alternate blocks of trials, to either the left or the right ear in order to detect rare, slightly longer-duration target stimuli. In this case, ear-of-entry (Location, L) is said to define the to-be-attended (L+) and the to-be-ignored (L−) channels, while tone duration (D), confounded with probability, is said to define the standard (D−) and the deviant (D+) stimuli. To examine the effects of selective attention on time-locked brain potentials, comparisons are made between ERPs to physically identical stimuli under conditions in which the stimulus is either attended to or ignored. The typical finding (see later) is that ERPs to attended tones show relatively enhanced negativity at about the time of the N100 potential, whether the attended tones are targets (L+D+ compared with L−D+), or are standards which merely share the easily discriminable feature with the targets (L+D− versus L−D−). The attention effect for deviants, though, includes a prominent N2–P3b for targets (L+D+) that is not observed for standards in the attended channel (L+D−).

What features of this paradigm are instructive toward designing new ERP and reflex studies in which selective sensory attention effects are to be distinguished from non-selective and non-sensory effects? *First*, multiple evoking stimuli are used. As Hillyard and Picton (1979) point out:

> Since attention refers to the selective aspects of sensory processing, it follows that all experimental demonstrations of attention must measure the responsiveness of the organism to more than one category of stimulus; it is the *differential* response to attended versus unattended stimuli that provides the operational basis for this construct.

It should be noted that a number of reflex studies of active attention have employed only a single category of evoking stimulus. Although these studies are of substantial interest to psychophysiologists, they will not be reviewed here (see reviews by Anthony, 1985, and Putnam, 1990). *Second*, the intensity and quality of stimuli at the receptor are controlled so that receptor orienting maneuvers are not mistaken for attention effects within the central nervous system. Controls for receptor orienting were discussed in the first part of this chapter, but it should be pointed out that controls for middle-ear muscle contractions are especially important in active attention studies where subjects are required to vocalize, as in shadowing tasks, or where intense sounds are used, as in startle research. *Third*, delivery of the different stimulus types is determined randomly, so that systematic anticipatory shifts in general arousal are prevented (Näätänen, 1967). *Fourth*, the same stimuli are repeated in separate runs during which the subject pays attention first to one, then to the other, channel. Such controls for stimulus effects are broadly useful in the study of cognition: balanced comparisons are made across conditions in which stimuli are identical and only the instructionally defined task varies. *Fifth*, comparisons can be made across conditions with equivalent motor requirements. Note that this criterion is concerned with control for reactive postperceptual motor effects; variations in motor activation that could be preset in advance of stimulus identification are controlled for by random stimulus presentation. Note also that the attentional comparison for deviants (L+D+ versus L−D+) does not satisfy the criterion of equivalent motor requirements: subjects are required to respond to targets but not to ignored deviants. *Sixth*, relatively early potentials (e.g. N100) are examined so that, if attention effects are observed, the likelihood that these effects represent a 'selective sensory state' (Näätänen,

1982; p. 629), preset in advance of stimulus arrival, is strengthened. Although later effects may be informative, attention effects on a wave occurring, say, 50 ms later than the mean reaction time, would be more difficult to relate unequivocally to sensory-specific processes.

Methods Using Reflexes

Somatic reflex studies of selective attention exploit the fact that some reflexes have multiple afferent limbs converging on a common central-efferent limb. By comparing the effects of attending or ignoring reflex-eliciting stimuli for reflexes with different afferent limbs, any modulatory effects can be localized either to the preconvergence (sensory-specific) or to the postconvergence (motor-specific) portion of the reflex arc. If rapid onset components are studied and if neuroanatomical evidence is available to define the reflex circuitry, then any sensory-specific modulation could help to localize the initial divergence in processing of attended and ignored stimuli.

An experiment by Hackley and Graham (1987) illustrates this logic in the study of a short-latency brainstem reflex. The experiment also illustrates our efforts to implement the six criteria described above. On each trial, subjects received a visual, neutral warning stimulus followed 1–4 s later by an intense tone pip, capable of eliciting the startle-blink reflex (onset latency, 40–50 ms). The tones were presented unpredictably through the left earphone, right earphone, or both earphones simultaneously (perceived at the midline), and differed in pitch at the three locations. Tone durations were 50 ms on half of the trials and 75 ms on the other trials. Subjects made an unspeeded judgment regarding the duration of all tones in one channel, defined by the easily discriminable location–pitch attributes, and ignored tones in the other channels. The channels designated to-be-attended and to-be-ignored were balanced across six blocks of 15 trials, presented with an intertrial interval of 14–18 s. The startle-blink reflex was measured electromyographically from the upper eyelids of the left and right eyes. Congruent with predictions that attention can produce a preset bias in selected auditory pathways, the latency of the blink was speeded when attention was directed toward the reflex-eliciting tone relative to when it was directed away, that is, toward a different location. This reflex facilitation averaged 1.6 ms and was replicated in two additional groups. The effect was obtained only for lateral, monaural tones. A non-significant trend towards attentional facilitation of magnitude was also observed in lateral conditions. Note that attention effects on the N100 ERP component have also been observed to be larger for lateral tones than for midline tones (Schwent, Snyder and Hillyard, 1976; van Voorhis, Hillyard and Näätänen, unpublished data described in Näätänen, 1988). This may be due to overlap of the attentional focus (i.e. a broad 'spotlight' or gradient of attention, Mangun and Hillyard, 1988) on to adjacent locations: overlap extended on to left and right channels when the midline position was attended, but on to midline only when attention was focused on a lateral channel. (Further implications of these results are considered in the later section, 'Auditory Selective Attention'.)

Of the six methodological criteria described above for distinguishing selective attention effects from non-selective or non-sensory effects, only the fifth—control for reactive motor effects—was not satisfied by the Hackley and Graham (1987) experiment. Ideally, reflexes would be compared across conditions that differ in only one aspect, the internal direction of attention. However, in this experiment, subjects made an unspeeded voluntary response when a tone was presented at the attended location, and made no response on other trials. Could reactive motor effect, consequent to identification of the to-be-attended location and acting on the efferent limb of the reflex arc, have mimicked a selective sensory–attentional effect? For this to occur would require that identification be made and information be fed back to the muscle within 40–50 ms of stimulus onset. There are two reasons, other than time constraints, why a reactive motor explanation lacks cogency. *First*, in a separate experiment using the same design but measuring attention effects on an inhibitory reflex, directing attention towards the eliciting stimulus produced increased inhibition. It seems unlikely that the reactive motor effects would produce facilitation in one experiment, but inhibition in a second, nearly identical experiment. *Second*, no latency difference between attend and ignore conditions was found for the midline stimuli, yet the motor confound was present here as well.

Other Methodological Criteria

Other aspects of the Hillyard paradigm are often considered critical, but these are concerned with the strength of the attentional manipulation rather than with excluding non-selective and non-sensory effects. Rapid delivery rates are recommended (typically 2–4 per second) to ensure that performance is resource-limited; in other words, to ensure that subjects do not have time to attend to irrelevant as well as to relevant stimuli. Systematic manipulation of stimulus presentation rate has confirmed that short ISIs enhance attention effects on auditory ERPs (e.g. Hansen and Hillyard, 1984), and facilitate the phenomenological grouping of tone pips into distinct attended and ignored sources or 'streams' (Bregman and Campbell, 1971). It might seem that such staccato presentation methods would preclude the measurement of reflexes, owing to habituation and refractory effects. However, by using signal averaging techniques to analyze 'microreflexes', reflex-eliciting stimuli may be delivered in rapid streams (Hackley, Woldorff and Hillyard, 1987; discussed in the next section). Methods using rapid presentation rates may provide inherently stronger manipulations of attention than discrete trial paradigms with long

ISIs (cf. Kahneman and Treisman, 1984). Nonetheless, discrete trial methods remain the norm in both reaction-time studies (e.g. Posner, Snyder and Davidson, 1980) and reflex studies of selective attention. The adaptation of ERP methods to the discrete-trial format should facilitate comparison across studies using different measures (e.g. Mangun, Hansen and Hillyard, 1987).

It has also been recommended that only moderate or weak intensities be used, because strong stimuli are difficult to ignore, and may saturate component generators (Hillyard and Picton, 1979; Eason, Oakley and Flowers, 1983). Supporting this recommendation, Schwent, Hillyard and Galambos (1976) found that attention effects on the auditory N100 peak were greater for 20 dB (SL) tone pips than for 60 dB tone pips. Because reflex elicitation is often critically dependent on the use of high stimulus intensities, this might appear to pose a severe problem. However, attention effects were found in the acoustic startle experiment described above (Hackley and Graham, 1987), in which intense (100 dB SPL) stimuli were used. Furthermore, Schwent and colleagues, using a quantitative metanalysis of prior published studies, concluded that the reduction in attention effects with increases in evoking stimulus intensity can be compensated for by using rapid presentation rates. Congruent with this conclusion, Hackley and colleagues (1987) used rapid presentation rates ($M = 4.5$ per second) and were able to obtain large attention effects on the N100 in response to *90 dB* (SL) tones.

These methodological issues are relevant to a wide range of psychophysiological studies of attention. Because the mechanisms and surface manifestations of attention may differ across modalities, we will review studies for the three major modalities separately.

AUDITORY SELECTIVE ATTENTION

According to the original interpretation by Hillyard *et al.* (1973), increased negativity in the region of the N100 peak in the auditory ERP is due to direct modulation of the evoked N100 component, and reflects a 'stimulus set' (Broadbent, 1970) mode of attention. Stimulus set results either in enhanced processing of sensory input that shares a rapidly discriminable physical attribute with target stimuli, or in attenuated processing of sensory input which lacks this channel-defining attribute. Subsequent evidence led Näätänen and colleagues (Näätänen, Gaillard and Mäntysalo, 1978; Näätänen and Michie, 1979) to propose a different interpretation of this effect. Rather than an attentional modulation of the 'exogenous' (obligatory, stimulus-determined) N100 component, the observed effect was interpreted as consisting of superimposition on N100 of an 'endogenous' (optional, task-modifiable) potential produced by different generators. This endogenous component, termed 'processing negativity', is longer-lasting than the N100 deflection itself, and apparently can also be generalized in a reduced form to ignored stimuli

(Alho *et al.*, 1987). Subtracting ERPs to ignored tones from ERPs to attended tones results in a prolonged negativity (the Nd, or 'negative difference' wave) which may be interpreted as the difference in processing negativity between the two conditions (Näätänen, 1988). When rapid, irregular ISIs are used, and the channel-defining attribute is easy to discriminate, the onset latency of Nd is short and it overlaps in time with the exogenous N100 peak. But when stimuli are presented at a fixed, slow rate (less than about 2–3 per second), or when the channel-defining attribute is difficult to discriminate, Nd begins after the N100 peak and, hence, no 'N100 effect' is obtained (Hansen and Hillyard, 1983; Näätänen, Gaillard and Mäntysalo, 1978; Parasuraman, 1980). According to Näätänen (e.g. 1982), processing negativity reflects a comparison process between the incoming stimulus and a rehearsed image of the task-relevant stimulus (i.e. the 'attentional trace'). The comparison process is a gradual one, and processing negativity persists for as long as the progressive stimulus analysis continues to indicate a match with the attentional trace. The similarity between this scheme and Öhman's theory—(1979; discussed in the first part of this chapter) that elicitation of the local orienting reflex is a consequence of match between an incoming stimulus and contents of short-term memory that are primed as important or task-relevant—is striking.

If the evoked, exogenous components of the auditory ERP are not themselves affected by attention, then a late-selection view in which sensory-perceptual processes are fully automatic would seem to be supported. The finding that the mismatch negativity component evoked by rare stimuli in ignored channels is just as large as that evoked in attended channels (reviewed by Näätänen and Gaillard, 1983; Näätänen, 1988) further supports this view. Although not an advocate of late-selection theories of attention, Näätänen (1988; p. 126) states that:

> . . .all auditory stimuli receive a rapid and complete processing of their physical features that is not influenced by attention. Hence, there appears to be no efferent, or top-down, control of this processing, which therefore provides the brain with sensory information of the same quality irrespective of the direction of attention.

Recent evidence, though, is incompatible with a full-automaticity view. Specifically, this evidence indicates that some exogenous auditory processes are modifiable by attention, and that MMN may not be invariant with regard to changes in attentional focus. First we examine data supporting modulation of exogenous processes, then data regarding variation in mismatch negativity in an attentional task.

Reflex Modulation by Attention

The acoustic blink reflex meets the definitional criteria proposed by Donchin, Ritter and McCallum (1978) for an exogenous process: it is present during sleep (Silverstein, Graham and Calloway, 1980), it is evoked by ignored as well as attended stimuli (Silverstein, Graham and Bohlin, 1981), and its absence may provide evidence for neurological deficit (Halliday, 1982). Hence, the finding described above that onset latency of the startle-blink EMG burst varies as a function of the focus of attention (Hackley and Graham, 1987) provides one example of an exogenous potential (myogenic) that varies with attention.

Startle-blink is not the only acoustic reflex influenced by attention. A second experiment by Hackley and Graham (1987) examined attention effects on an inhibitory midbrain reflex, prepulse inhibition (discussed in the first part of this chapter), using a design similar to that described above. However, in this experiment, the left, right, and midline tones were too weak to elicit a blink reflex themselves. Instead, the tone pips served as prepulses to inhibit the blink elicited by a subsequent probe stimulus, a task-irrelevant airpuff delivered to the orbital region. Congruent with the assumption that attention can produce a preset bias in auditory pathways that overlap with the sensory-specific portion of the prepulse inhibition circuit, inhibition was greater for attended tones. Again, the effect held only for lateral, monaural stimuli. Attentional modulation of prepulse inhibition was corroborated in two subsequent experiments in which acoustic reflexes and ERPs were simultaneously recorded (Hackley, Woldorff and Hillyard, 1987).

Modulation of Obligatory ERPs

It has recently been determined that at least one of the exogenous components contributing to the auditory N100 deflection can be directly modulated by attention, congruent with the original interpretation by Hillyard and coworkers (1973) of the 'N100 effect'. As reviewed in the first part of the chapter, Näätänen and Picton (1987) proposed that the N100 wave is generated by three simultaneously active subcomponents: component 1 is generated in supratemporal cortex; component 2, the 'T-complex' (Wolpaw and Penry, 1975), is generated by a radially oriented dipole in or near the superior temporal gyrus, and is biphasic with a positive peak at 100 ms and a negative peak at about 150 ms; and component 3 is maximal at vertex and centrolateral recording sites, and is modality-non-specific.

It is evidence concerning the second component, the T-complex, that further supports the assertion that exogenous auditory processes can be modulated by attention. In a recent experiment examining crossmodal attention effects on this component (Hackley, Woldorff and Hillyard, 1990), subjects were presented with streams of tone pips to the left ear and bright flashes to the right visual field at a rapid rate. In balanced blocks of trials, subjects attended to a designated modality in order to detect and respond to rare, slightly less intense, target stimuli. Physiological recordings of cerebral and brainstem ERPs, blink reflexes, and retinal potentials were obtained. As may be seen in Figure 3.2, a

Tones

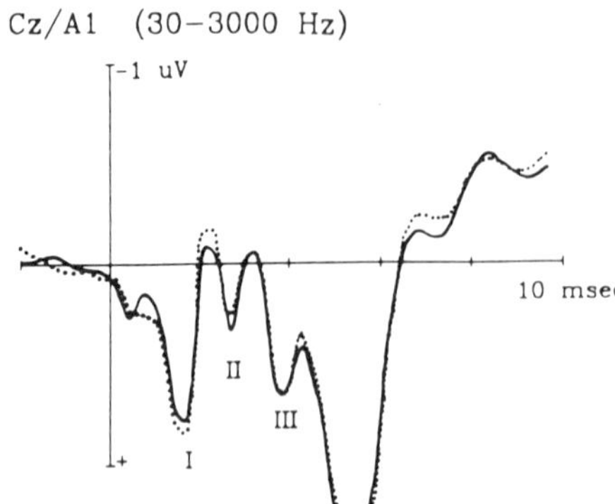

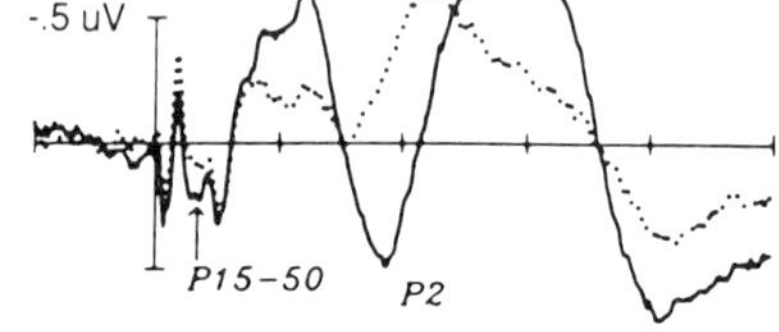

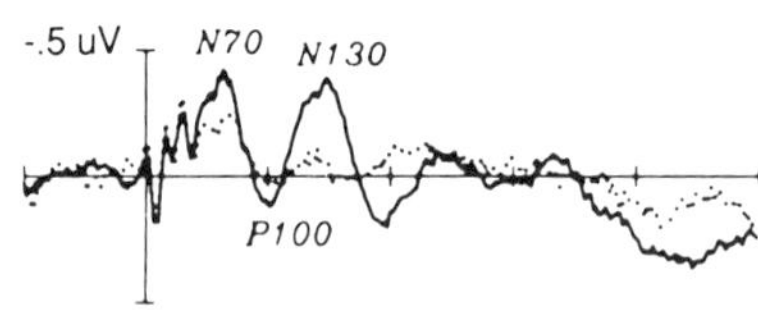

Flashes

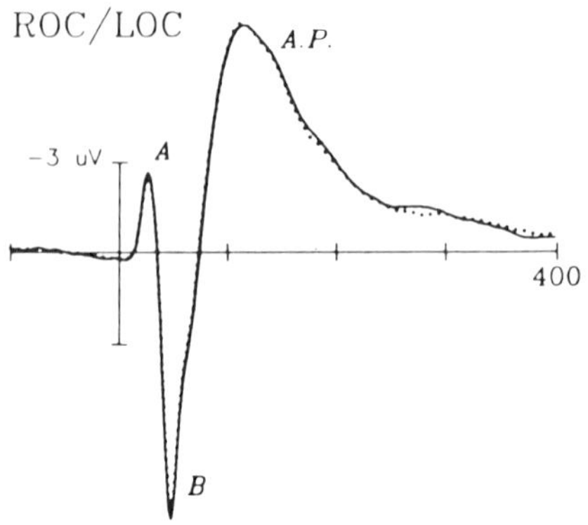

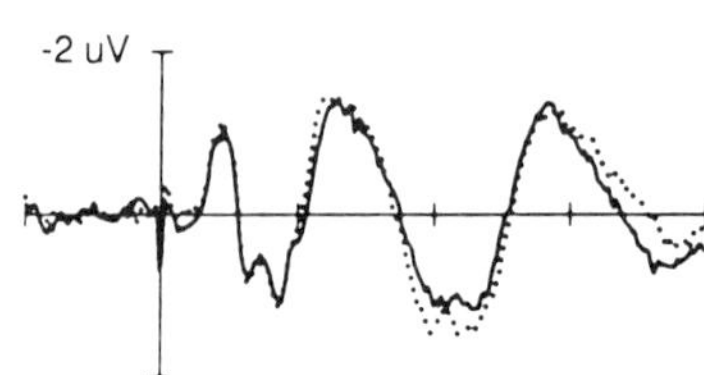

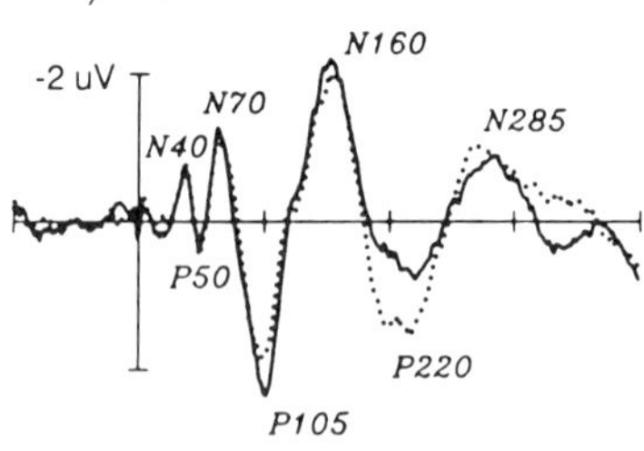

-100 100 200 300 400 500

+

(msec)

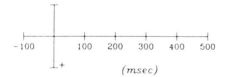

Attend ————

Ignore ··········

T-complex comprising a P100 and an N130 peak was clearly observed at posterior temporal sites ipsilateral to the evoking tone pips. Measures of mean amplitude for the N130 and the earlier N70 were reliably enhanced by attention. The trend towards enhanced positivity at the P100 peak did not reach significance.

Significant enhancement of the negative but not the positive phase of the T-complex was obtained in two other crossmodal attention studies, one in which subjects either discriminated target tone pips or 'played a difficult video game' (Woods, 1990), and one in which subjects either kept a running mental count of target tone pips or read a book (Perrault and Picton, 1984). Enlargement of an N150 deflection may also be clearly seen in the waveforms of Giard *et al.* (1988), who used an intramodal manipulation of attention with slow, fixed ISIs. Using short, variable ISIs, Woldorff (1989) obtained facilitation of the positive (P100) as well as the negative (N135) phase in a dichotic listening task. It would be an extraordinary coincidence if endogenous components produced by different generators happened to be coterminous with the exogenous potentials in each of these experiments.

When very rapid presentation rates (more than four per second) are used and channels are defined by an easily discriminable attribute, the T-complex may not be the only N100 generator that is modulated by attention. A number of such studies have observed attentional enhancement of negativity at the vertex that overlaps in time nearly perfectly with N100 (Hackley, Woldorff and Hillyard, 1987; Woldorff, Hansen and Hillyard, 1987; Woldorff, Hackley and Hillyard, 1989). If one accepts Näätänen and Picton's (1987) three-component theory of the N100, then the frontocentral maximum for this effect and the short ISIs would implicate component 1, the supratemporal generator. Magnetic recordings support this interpretation (Kaufman *et al.*, 1986).

Figure 3.2. Grand average (N=20) evoked potentials to auditory and visual stimuli (left and right panels, respectively) in a crossmodal selective attention task using rapid stimulus presentation rates. The upper tracings demonstrate the invariance of auditory brainstem potentials and retinal potentials. In contrast to these measures of peripheral sensory activity, the cerebral evoked potentials shown in the middle and lower portions of the figure show effects of attention. Significant effects in the auditory modality were obtained for the Pa or P15–50 potential, for the negative phase of the T-complex (comprising P100 and N130), and for N70, N1/early Nd, P2, and N2/late Nd. In the visual modality, significant variation with attention was obtained for P105, P220 (possibly related to suppression of evoked alpha activity), and vertex N115 (not shown). Bandpass was 1–300 Hz for all recordings except the auditory brainstem potentials (30–3000 Hz). The O1′ site was midway between T5 and O1; O2′ was midway between T6 and O2; Nc stands for 'non-cephalic', a potentiometrically balanced pair of electrodes at the base of the neck; and Rm stands for 'right mastoid'; ROC and LOC indicate the right and left outer canthi, respectively. (Adapted from illustrations appearing in Hackley, Woldorff and Hillyard (1990), and reprinted with permission of the authors and publisher.)

Attention Effects on Mismatch Negativity

The findings regarding attentional modulation of putative components 1 and 2 of the N100 converge with evidence summarized above regarding reflexogenic activity. These data are not sufficient, though, to demand rejection of the hypothesis that analysis of the physical features of an auditory stimulus is fully automatic. An exogenous component occurring later in time than the blink reflex and N100—mismatch negativity—is reported to be of equal size and latency whether the evoking stimulus is attended or ignored (Näätänen and Gaillard, 1983). Such invariance might be expected if MMN is consequent to fully automatic stimulus analysis in a path *parallel* to that indexed by N100, startle-blink, and prepulse inhibition. However, recent evidence casts doubt on this claim of invariance.

Woldorff, Hackley and Hillyard (1989) examined the size of MMNs and other potentials in the N200 complex in two dichotic listening experiments which used short, variable ISIs. Deviant stimuli elicited negative waves peaking at around 200 ms which were maximal in amplitude at frontocentral scalp sites and which, at central sites, were larger contralateral to the evoking stimuli. This scalp distribution is similar to that observed in prior studies and is compatible with the modality-specific origin of MMN (N2a), in contradistinction to the non-specific N2b potential. However, this negativity was not invariant with attention. In Experiment 1 (mean ISI = 220 ms), amplitudes averaged 3–4 μV in the attended ear, but in the ignored ear less than 1 μV. In Experiment 2, in which even faster delivery rates were employed (mean ISI = 135 ms), MMN and a subsequent P300 were clearly evident for attended-ear deviants, but were virtually absent for ignored-ear deviants. Such results are readily explained by the assumption that highly focused attention can suppress the response to ignored stimuli. Taken as a whole, these results, and those regarding startle-blink, prepulse inhibition, and the T-complex, are at odds with the hypothesis that auditory processing is fully automatic and that processing of the physical features of a sound is not influenced by attention.

Localizing the Initial Divergence

Having argued that attention can modulate some obligatory evoked processes, we now turn to the question of where and when an attentional influence first occurs in audition. According to the 'peripheral gating' hypothesis, the initial divergence in the processing of attended and ignored stimuli can occur at a level as low as the first synaptic relay or even at the receptor itself. As expressed by one early author (Maudsley, 1876; cited in Ribot, 1896; p. 20), this might be effected 'by a molecular change in the nervous elements, which is propagated either along the sensory nerve to the periphery, or, if not so far, at any rate to the sensory ganglion, the sensibility of which is thereby increased'.

Following the discovery of a centrifugal control system capable in principle of presetting the sensitivity of the cochlear receptors, Hernandez-Peon devised a method for testing the peripheral gating hypothesis. He and his colleagues (e.g. Hernandez-Peon, Scherrer and Jouvet, 1956) recorded auditory evoked potentials from the cochlear nucleus of cats during conditions presumed to be characterized by either greater or lesser attention to the evoking stimuli, and obtained positive results. Although these early studies were roundly criticized for failure to control stimulus and motivational factors (e.g. Worden, 1966), they are important for defining the basic paradigm from which nearly all later electrophysiological studies of active attention have evolved.

Although subsequent animal research has included controls for proximal stimulus intensity (e.g. Oatman and Anderson, 1977) that were lacking in the early work, control for state variables such as arousal, motivation, and motor activation has not been optimal (see the review by Connolly *et al.*, 1989). Most studies examining the possibility of peripheral gating in the auditory modality have used auditory brainstem potentials to index peripheral sensory transmission. Among these, there have been a few reports (Brix, 1984; Lukas, 1980, 1981) of attentional facilitation of either the latency or amplitude of wave I or wave V. These studies have been severely criticized on methodological and theoretical grounds (Connolly *et al.*, 1989; Hillyard *et al.*, 1987). By contrast, the overwhelming majority of studies—thirteen to date—have found that auditory brainstem ERPs and electrocochlear potentials are invariant with attention (Connolly *et al.*, 1989; Davis and Beagley, 1985; Hackley, Woldorff and Hillyard, 1990; Kuk and Abbas, 1989; Lukas, 1982; Michie and Hirschhorn, 1986, cited in Michie *et al.*, 1987; Picton *et al.*, 1978; Picton and Hillyard, 1974; Picton *et al.*, 1971; Picton, Stapells and Campbell, 1981; Rohrbaugh *et al.*, 1987; Woldorff, Hansen and Hillyard, 1987; Woods and Hillyard, 1978). The stability of brainstem ERPs in a crossmodal study of attention is illustrated in Figure 3.2.

The conclusion that the earliest auditory processes are unaffected by attention is supported by converging evidence from reflex psychophysiology. Hackley, Woldorff and Hillyard (1987) examined selective attention effects on the postauricular reflex, which consists of a weak activation of the muscle behind the ear with an onset 8–12 ms after an abrupt sound. The existence of multiple afferent limbs is shown by the fact that action potentials in the muscle behind one ear can be evoked by acoustic stimuli to either ear. Based on the work of Michael Davis and colleagues with rat (e.g. Cassella and Davis, 1986), Hackley and coworkers proposed a circuit for the human postauricular reflex which assumes that convergence of left and right afferent limbs on to the common, central-efferent limb occurs at the paralemniscal zone, near the nuclei of the lateral lemniscus. The paralemniscal zone is the second synapse in a trisynaptic reflex arc which also includes the ventral cochlear nucleus and the medial division of the facial motor nucleus. If attention were to influence sensory transmission in the cochlea or in the cochlear nucleus, it might be expected that directing attention toward or away from the evoking stimuli would alter the latency or size of the postauricular reflex. However, in two experiments employing the Hillyard dichotic listening paradigm, no evidence for an attention effect on the sensory-specific limb of this reflex was obtained.

As described earlier, other brainstem reflexes do show selective attention effects. There are now a number of studies reporting attention effects on either the auditory blink reflex or on prepulse inhibition by acoustic prestimuli (Anthony and Graham, 1983, 1985; Balaban, Anthony and Graham, 1985; Cohen, Cranney and Hoffman, 1983; Hackley and Graham, 1983, 1987; Hackley, Woldorff and Hillyard, 1987). All of these studies used multiple evoking stimuli to compare reflexes with distinct afferent limbs, but the degree to which the other methodological criteria outlined at the start of this part of the chapter were met varied widely. Why do these reflexes show attention effects while the postauricular reflex does not? One possibility lies in the fact that the postauricular reflex and waves I–V are mediated below the level of the inferior colliculi, while at least some pathways involved in the startle and prepulse inhibition reflexes do involve midbrain structures (Holstege *et al.*, 1986; Leitner, Powers and Hoffman, 1979). If the earliest attention effect were at the midbrain level, stability of the postauricular reflex and waves I–V of the auditory brainstem response would be compatible with attention effects on at least some loops of the circuit mediating startle-blink and prepulse inhibition (Hackley, Woldorff and Hillyard, 1987).

The difference in modifiability of these reflexes by attention might also be explained by the relatively longer latencies of startle-blink and prepulse inhibition. If attention first influences auditory processing at cortical levels there would be sufficient time for feedback to the brainstem circuits of these two reflexes. However, the trisynaptic postauricular response has an onset latency (9 ms, Hackley *et al.*, 1987) which is shorter than the time required for auditory information to reach primary auditory cortex (12–14 ms; Celesia, 1976) Hence, its onset could not be affected by feedback from cortex. Recent evidence that primary auditory cortex contributes to audiospinal startle (Liegeois-Chauvel *et al.*, 1989) further qualifies the support of blink reflex studies for a subcortical locus of the earliest effects of attention. Although startle-blink is not so rapid as to rule out a neocortical locus for the initial divergence between the processing of attended and ignored stimuli, it is rapid enough to aid in chronometrically localizing this divergence. The Hackley and Graham (1987) study, described above, found attention effects at around 50 ms, comparable to the earliest effects on the N100 wave (e.g. Hackley, Woldorff and Hillyard, 1987; Woldorff, Hansen and Hillyard, 1987). In a crossmodal attention study, more effective startle stimuli were used, and attention effects on acoustically evoked blinks were obtained at 40–45 ms (Hackley and Graham,

1983). These values underestimate the rapidity of selective attention effects: because modulatory effects were localized to the preconvergence (sensory-specific) portion of the reflex arc, the 40–45 ms value includes the additional time needed for transmission through the central-efferent segment of the arc to the eyelid muscle.

Even earlier attention effects have recently been obtained for a midlatency component of the auditory ERP (Woldorff, Hansen and Hillyard, 1987; cf. Picton *et al.*, 1974, and McCallum *et al.*, 1983). When rapid, irregular, ISIs are used, and channels are defined by easily discriminable attributes, enhanced positivity is observed beginning 15–20 ms after stimulus onset—within a few milliseconds after the initial arrival of acoustic information at cortex. This enhanced positivity is centered around a point in time either synchronous with the Pa deflection, as seen in Figure 3.2 (labeled 'P15–50'; Hackley, Woldorff and Hillyard, 1990), or else just after Pa (Woldorff, Hansen and Hillyard, 1987). Data from lesion studies (Kileny, Paccioretti and Wilson, 1987) and magnetic recording studies (Hari, in press; Hari *et al.*, 1987) suggest that positivity in this latency region arises in or near auditory cortex. An effect at this level in humans is congruent with the results of a well-controlled study in lower primates (Benson and Hienz, 1978) showing modulation by selective attention of evoked unit responses in auditory cortex. The enhanced positivity in humans is relatively prolonged, extending from about 15 to 50 ms after stimulus onset, and does not appear to have an invariant relationship to the morphology of the midlatency ERPs. Consequently, it is not yet clear whether this effect should be considered an example of a modulated obligatory component (i.e. a generator contributing to Pa) or of an endogenous component that is emitted during highly focused attention. To emphasize this current uncertainty, Woldorff and colleagues prefer the term 'P20–50 effect' over the term 'Pa effect' (Hansen and Woldorff, 1989; Woldorff, 1989; Woldorff, Hansen and Hillyard, 1987).

To summarize the auditory psychophysiological data reviewed so far, reflex and ERP studies suggest that the initial divergence in the processing of attended and ignored stimuli occurs above the hindbrain, perhaps in the upper brainstem or in auditory cortex. Chronometric analyses support this conclusion: reflexes and evoked potentials that onset before auditory information has reached the forebrain are not reliably affected by attention. However, beginning as early as 15–20 ms, the nervous system is capable of treating attended and ignored signals differently. Because 15–20 ms is substantially less than the time required for perceptual analysis, as measured by vulnerability to backwards recognition masking (e.g. Foyle and Watson, 1984), these findings are incompatible with the strong version of late selection theory. In contradistinction to the assumptions of late selection theory (e.g. Shiffrin and Grantham, 1974), the psychophysiological data indicate that attention does have an effect on sensory-perceptual processing.

Levels of Automaticity

The central and peripheral psychophysiological data support the concept of multiple levels of automaticity (e.g. Hackley, Woldorff and Hillyard, 1987). Adopting the terminology of Kahneman and Treisman (1984), we can say that the earliest auditory analyses, indexed by brainstem ERPs and the postauricular reflex, are *strongly automatic.* This means that they are neither facilitated by focusing attention on the stimulus nor impaired by diverting attention from it. Intermediate processes, indexed by some midbrain reflexes and by some ERPs in the 15 to 250 ms range, are *partially automatic.* Such processes are obligatory in that they are completed normally even if attention is diverted from the stimulus, but they can be speeded or otherwise facilitated by attention. Finally, the later stimulus-engendered processes, indexed, for example, by the P3b, are *controlled,* in that they occur only if they are allocated limited attentional resources. This trilaminar extension of the traditional automatic–controlled dichotomy maps nicely on to Hillyard, Picton and Regan's (1978; p. 272) extension of the exogenous–endogenous dichotomy for ERPs. Hillyard *et al.* distinguished three categories of ERPs: *exogenous* potentials are obligatory components that are primarily determined by the physical properties of the evoking stimulus; *mesogenous* potentials are also obligatory, but can be influenced by central processing factors as well as by the nature of the stimuli; finally, *endogenous* potentials are not obligatory but rather are emitted in synchrony with a particular cognitive or behavioral process.

The Nature of Selection

Having discussed tentative answers to Adrian's (1954) question regarding 'when' and 'where' the initial divergence in processing of attended and ignored stimuli arises, we turn to the question of 'how' the initial selectivity occurs. According to a recent proposal by Hansen and Woldorff (1989), the pattern of attention effects on auditory ERPs indicates the existence of two different mechanisms of selection. When slow, constant interstimulus intervals are used, or when the channel-defining attribute is difficult to discriminate, only the endogenous Nd distinguishes ERPs elicited by attended and ignored stimuli. By contrast, when rapid, irregular intervals are employed, the effects of attention begin earlier and are more complex, including changes in exogenous components as well as the addition of endogenous components. In such tasks, the Nd potential comprises two subcomponents, the 'early' and 'late' Nd, that can be distinguished by a variety of characteristics, including time course, scalp distribution, and pharmacological sensitivity (reviewed by Hillyard and Hansen, 1986; Hillyard and Picton, 1987). Other manifestations of highly focused attention include effects on the supratemporal and T-complex subcomponents of N100, the very early Pa effect and modulation of prepulse inhibition (Hackley, Woldorff and Hillyard, 1987). Finally, enhanced positivity at around 200 ms is also observed during fast, irregular stimulus presentations (e.g. Hackley *et al.*, 1987, 1990; Woldorff, 1989), and to probe tones superimposed on attended speech messages (e.g. Hink and Hillyard, 1976). Magnetic recordings have revealed a generator contributing to the P200 deflection that is located in supratemporal cortex, but at a site different from that of the N100 subcomponent (Hari *et al.*, 1987). Hansen and Woldorff point out that the short latency of the Pa effect implies that attended and ignored stimuli are differentially processed as a result of an attentional set that is in place prior to stimulus arrival. This set biases perceptual analyses such that ignored stimuli are not as fully processed as attended stimuli.

An influential study by Hansen and Hillyard (1983) using multiattribute stimuli elaborates further on the question of how stimulus selection occurs. Tonal stimuli were presented at moderately fast, irregular ISIs, and varied along three dimensions, location (L), pitch (P), and duration (D). The difficulty with which the two levels of the location and pitch attributes could be discriminated was manipulated across groups of subjects. These two attributes defined the to-be-attended channel (e.g. high-pitched tones in the left ear), while tonal duration distinguished standards from deviants. Subjects pressed a button in response to long-duration deviants in the attended channel (L+P+D+ targets).

The results suggested a hierarchical structure for stimulus selection that is congruent with 'parallel, self-terminating' models of sensory analysis. Consider the group for whom pitch was rapidly and easily discriminable, but location was difficult to discriminate. For these subjects, a large, early Nd distinguished ERPs to tones that did and those that did not share the pitch attribute with the target stimuli, regardless of whether the location of the tone was attended or not. In contrast to this pitch-Nd, a location-Nd was obtained for tones at the attended pitch (L+P+D– minus L–P+D- waveforms), but not for tones at the ignored pitch (L+P–D– minus L–P–D–). Tones satisfying all three dimensions (L+P+D+ targets) elicited a P3b in addition to the location-Nd and the pitch-Nd.

In a study by Okita (1981), the presumed duration of perceptual analysis was experimentally manipulated by requiring subjects to discriminate variation in either the initial or the terminal portion of attended tone pips. Prolongation of the Nd in the latter case supported the inference that the Nd is an index of 'further processing' of selected auditory stimuli. Interpreted in this context, the results of Hansen and Hillyard's study suggest that if a tone is rejected on the basis of a rapidly discriminable attribute, no further analysis along the more difficult dimension takes place. This pattern of results would not be predicted by late-selection theories, which maintain that perceptual analysis proceeds to completion regardless of whether a stimulus is attended or ignored. Neither would these results be predicted by at least one variant of early-selection theory. According to 'feature integration theory' (Treisman and

Gelade, 1980), processing of the various physical dimensions of a stimulus proceeds independently and in parallel. A subsequent process involving focal attention is then required to conjoin these attributes into the unified percept of an object. The assumption that processing of a given stimulus dimension is not influenced by the processing of a separate dimension seems to be contradicted by the results of Hansen and Hillyard (1983).

VISUAL SELECTIVE ATTENTION

Reflex and ERP studies in the visual modality suggest a number of similarities with auditory selective attention. The studies to be reviewed indicate that both endogenous and mesogenous processes are involved in selection; distinct levels of automaticity characterize early, intermediate, and late perceptual analyses; an approximate temporal and neuroanatomical location for the initial divergence in processing of attended and ignored stimuli can be posited; and the hierarchical nature of attribute selection has been described.

Hierarchical Selection

A visual analog of the Hansen and Hillyard (1983) study just described addresses several of these points (Hillyard and Munte, 1984). The stimuli were bar-shaped figures on a computer screen that varied along three dimensions, location (L), color (C), and height (H). The conjunction of location and color defined the to-be-attended channel (L+C+), height distinguished standard (H–) from deviant (H+) stimuli. The discriminability of the location dimension was manipulated across subjects. The overall pattern of results supported the hierarchical structure for selection described by Hansen and Hillyard (1983) for the auditory modality. The target stimuli, which by definition satisfied all three dimensions (L+C+H+), elicited distinct electrophysiological signs of selection for location, for color, and for height. Standard stimuli satisfying the first two dimensions (L+C+H–) elicited signs of selection for both location and color, but lacked the subsequent P3b that reflected identification of target stimuli. For standard stimuli sharing only color (L-C+H–) or only location (L+C–H–) with the target stimuli, the waveforms depended on relative attribute discriminability. Components in the ERP reflecting color selection were more prominent when location was harder to discriminate than color. Evidence for location selection, on the other hand, was distinctly more evident when color was harder than location to discriminate. Thus, a progressive, three-level hierarchy of selection was identified: in the group for whom location was rapidly discriminable, stimuli at the wrong location (L–) were rejected first, then stimuli at the attended location were rejected if they had the wrong color (L+C–); finally, stimuli with the right color and location were rejected if they had the wrong height

(L+C+H−). This left only the stimuli fulfilling all three of the defining criteria for targets and, upon recognition, the voluntary response was released.

Selection by Spatial Location

The Hillyard and Munte (1984) study confirmed earlier evidence (e.g. Harter and Guido, 1980; Harter and Aine, 1984) that the ERP signature for location selection differs from that for color and other attributes. Such differences lend support to the conclusion based on much behavioral research (reviewed by Johnston and Dark, 1986; pp. 49–50), that 'space is special'. The 'special' quality of spatial position is indicated by the fact that location is more effective than other attributes as a cue for guiding selective attention. At central, parietal, and occipital sites in the Hillyard and Munte study, attention to color elicited a broad, apparently endogenous, negativity that lasted from about 150 to 350 ms, and a broad positivity in the 350–500 ms region. At frontal sites a narrower P200 was observed. Potentials similar to the N150–350 have been obtained during selection for other attributes such as size and orientation (reviewed by Harter and Aine, 1984). Such potentials might index further processing of the selected attribute in a manner analogous to the auditory Nd, according to Hillyard and Munte. When location was easily discriminable, spatial selection was indexed by enhancement of a sequence of exogenous potentials over the occipital region, an effect first described in a landmark paper by Eason, Harter and White (1969). All bars flashed to the attended location elicited a sequence of enhanced P120, N170, N265 waves (also referred to as P1, N1, and N2). The N170 peak was larger over the occipital site contralateral to the evoking stimulus and, similarly, the attentional enhancement of this peak was also larger contralaterally. Such distributional and morphological characteristics have led to a general consensus that attention effects in the visual modality can include direct modulation of obligatory potentials (i.e. mesogenous potentials), at least when selection is based on the attribute of spatial location.

Discrete Trial Paradigm

While ERP research on auditory attention has exclusively employed staccato streams of stimuli, at least a few ERP studies have been conducted in the visual modality using the discrete-trial format. Such experiments facilitate comparison with reaction time, somatic reflex, and autonomic studies of attention, where discrete-trial paradigms are the norm (cf. Kahneman and Triesman's, 1984, discussion of 'filtering' versus 'selective-set' paradigms). A particularly influential paradigm was developed by Posner and colleagues (e.g. Posner, Snyder and Davidson, 1980), in which a precue either directs the subject's attention to the correct location of the impending reaction stimulus (valid trials), to the wrong location (invalid trials), or else directs the subject to divide his attention equally among the possible locations (neutral trials). Performance on valid and invalid trials is compared with that for neutral control trials. Facilitation on valid trials, or 'benefits', is ascribed to allocation of limited resources to the attended location. Conversely, 'costs' on invalid trials are attributed to withdrawal of resources from the ignored location. Switching metaphors from economics to optics, it is also said that facilitated processing at the cued location indexes the focus of an attentional 'spotlight' (e.g. Posner and Cohen, 1984). The finding that the movement of attention from fixation to the cued location (in spite of unchanging gaze) is smooth rather than saccadic supports the utility of this metaphor (e.g. Shulman, Remington and McLean, 1979).

The priming of a visuospatial location in this paradigm can be accomplished either by a symbolic precue, such as a foveally presented arrow pointing to the likely stimulus location, or by a peripheral stimulus, such as a brief flash at the primed location. In the former case, costs and benefits develop gradually over a period of about 300 ms following cue onset, and can be diminished by a concurrent task or by an irrelevant, attention-engaging stimulus. Hence, such effects are said to indicate voluntary orienting (reviewed by Muller and Rabbitt, 1989). By contrast, a transient peripheral stimulus engages selective attention automatically, with maximum costs and benefits developing at between 100 and 150 ms but with gradual decay thereafter, and this process is not easily interruptible. These automatic effects occur even if the location of the transient does not predict the position of the subsequent reaction stimulus. Accordingly, this type of attention is described as 'reflexive orienting' (Muller and Rabbitt, 1989). Note, though, that the term 'orienting' is not used here to refer to a non-specific attentional process elicited by novelty; rather, the term refers to the 'localization of an attention system for visual spatial information' (Posner *et al.*, 1988) and would be a transient-detection reflex in the Graham classification described in the first part of this chapter.

One controversy regarding costs and benefits in the reaction time paradigm concerns whether they might reflect postperceptual processes rather than intraperceptual processes. According to Shaw (1984), for example, sensory evidence about the reaction stimulus builds at a constant rate after stimulus onset, as assumed by late-selection theory. As soon as the evidence reaches a criterion level set prior to stimulus arrival, the response is released. If the criterion for stimuli at the cued location is lower than that at the uncued location, the observed variation in reaction latency would result. In contradistinction to this theory, other studies have shown that attentional precues can affect the sensitivity measure, d' (Bashinski and Bacharach, 1980). However, sensitivity and criterion measures do not unambiguously distinguish intra- and extra-perceptual processes because, as Posner points out (1978; p. 131), bias at one level of a complex system affects the input to the next level. More to the point would be direct electrophysiological measurement of sensory-specific processes.

Mangun *et al.* (1987) examined modulation of obligatory components of the visual ERP in a location priming task. Each trial began with a foveally presented arrow that pointed to a position in either the left or the right hemifield. After an 800 ms interval, this precue was followed by a bar-shaped target stimulus either at the cued position ($p = 0.75$, 'valid' trials) or at the uncued position ($p = 0.25$, 'invalid' trials). Consistent with prior research, reaction latencies were shorter on valid trials (566 ms) than on invalid trials (592 ms). More importantly, the ERP data supported the view that the behavioral effect is due, at least in part, to facilitated sensory processing at attended locations. Both P110 (P1) and N170 (N1) were enhanced on valid relative to invalid trials. The scalp topography for the P110 wave supports the assumption that this potential is generated in modality-specific pathways. The early onset of the effect (about 100 ms) also supports an intraperceptual, as opposed to a postperceptual, interpretation. However, it should be noted that perceptual analysis, as measured by vulnerability to backwards recognition masking, can be completed as early as 75 ms for rapidly discriminable visual attributes (Miller and Hackley, submitted). Furthermore, early analysis of easily discriminable attributes can be used to initiate motor preparation prior to complete analysis of other, less discriminable attributes of the same stimulus (Coles, Gratton and Donchin, 1988; Miller and Hackley, submitted; Osman *et al.*, 1988; and discussed later in the section 'Late Selection and the Continuous–Discrete Controversy'). Indeed, the artificiality of the borderline between perceptual and motor processes with regard to selective attention has recently been emphasized by both Näätänen (1988; p. 153) and Eason (Oakley and Eason, 1987).

Attentional Modulation of Reflexes

An earlier study using reflexes also supports the conclusion that obligatory visual processes can be modulated by anticipatory attention (DelPezzo and Hoffman, 1980). The ability of weak visual prestimuli to inhibit the blink reflex to a subsequent (150 ms lead time), task-irrelevant tap to the forehead was compared under two conditions. On half of the trials, the subject was precued as to the location where the prepulse would appear, if it was presented on that trial. On the other half of the trials, no advance information was given as to prepulse location. On one-third of the trials in each cueing condition, no prepulse preceded the reflex-eliciting tap. These 'tap-only' trials served as controls in order to assess the amount of inhibition evoked on 'light-followed-by-tap' trials. The subject's task was to judge whether the near-threshold light was presented and, if so, where. Consistent with attentional modulation of low-level visual pathways, the amount of inhibiton on prepulse trials relative to the tap-alone control trials was greater on precued than on uncued trials. As in the Hackley and Graham (1987) study of auditory prepulse inhibition that was described earlier, the attention effect was obtained only for lateral prepulses. Inhibition by midline prestimuli did not vary with attention.

A weakness in the DelPezzo and Hoffman (1980) design raises the question of whether a non-selective process such as arousal might account for the results. Note that the critical comparison—cued versus uncued—was made across conditions in which task demands were rather different: on uncued trials, subjects had to judge both presence and location of the task stimulus but, on cued trials, only presence versus absence was unknown prior to stimulus delivery. Two aspects of the results make a non-selective explanation implausible: first, inhibition in response to midline prepulses did not differ on cued and uncued trials. If the cue manipulation produced an arousal difference affecting inhibition, foveal as well as peripheral stimuli should have been affected. Second, amplitude of the uninhibited blink on tap-alone control trials apparently did not differ across cueing conditions. If the cued–uncued difference was due to arousal or some similar non-specific process, that process must have affected only the inhibitory circuit, not the circuit for the cutaneous blink reflex itself.

The effect of selective attention on visually evoked blinks has been examined in four crossmodal studies (Anthony and Graham, 1983, 1985; Balaban, Anthony and Graham, 1985; Hackley, Woldorff and Hillyard, 1990). Anthony and Graham compared attention effects on visually and acoustically evoked blinks in parallel experiments on four-month-old infants (1983) and on adults (1985). The modality of attention direction was manipulated across two groups of subjects at each age. Attention was engaged by a 5 s foreground stimulus that was either interesting (slides of smiling faces for the visual group, music-box melodies for the acoustic group) or else dull (blank slides or 1000 Hz tones). Four seconds after the onset of each foreground stimulus, an intense light flash or white noise burst was presented to evoke a reflexive blink. The modality of these probes varied randomly from trial to trial. Significant heart rate decelerations confirmed that the attention of both adults and infants was engaged by the foreground stimuli. For both age groups, blinks were relatively facilitated when the eliciting stimulus was in the same modality as the attention-engaging foreground stimulus, and this effect was larger for interesting than for dull foregrounds. A difference between age groups was observed, such that the attention effect in infants reached significance only for reflex magnitude and, in adults, only for reflex onset latency. Consistent with these differences, a review of the literature has shown that, for adult subjects, attention effects on blink reflex latency are substantially more reliable than on blink magnitude (Hackley and Graham, 1987).

The possibility of undetected shifts in gaze must temper a conclusion that the Anthony and Graham (1983, 1985) results indicate attentional modulation of modality-specific portions of the visual reflex arc. Although fixation on the screen was monitored by an observer and trials with observable shifts were excluded, more precise recordings of ocular movements were not obtained. Thus, small but systematic shifts in gaze might account for variation in the visually evoked reflex. Specifically, few or no shifts during interesting visual foregrounds, occasional small shifts during dull visual foregrounds, and frequent shifts during auditory foregrounds, could have produced the obtained pattern for visual probes; that is, more facilitated visual reflexes during interesting than dull same-modality foregrounds and less visual reflex responsiveness to both interesting and dull different-modality foregrounds. Attentional effects on reflex magnitude for infants and onset latency for adults was replicated in a similar experiment by Balaban, Anthony and Graham (1985) but, again, only observations of gaze were recorded.

A more recent experiment failed to obtain a selective attention effect on visually evoked blinks (Hackley, Woldorff and Hillyard, 1990). However, this study differed in several ways from those that did obtain positive results. Visual and auditory stimuli were presented in rapid streams and, as described in an earlier section, adult subjects attended in balanced blocks of trials to a designated modality in order to respond to rare, weaker intensity targets. Trials in which gaze deviated from the fixation point were automatically rejected, and the stability of averaged evoked retinal potentials verified the constancy of proximal stimulus intensity across attention conditions (see Figure 3.2).

In contrast to all prior studies of which we are aware, no selective attention effect was found for either latency or magnitude of the blink reflex. Because the experiment was designed to investigate subcortical potentials rather than reflexes, conditions were not optimal for corroborating the Anthony and Graham (1985) effect. Only moderately intense stimuli were used, and interstimulus intervals were much shorter than the relative refractory period of the blink reflex. Consequently, the magnitude of the blink 'microreflex' in the grand average waveforms was only 1–2% of a typical voluntary or reflexive blink (100–150 μV with bipolar surface recordings). Thus, at least two alternative interpretations are open for experimental test: either visually evoked blinks are not modulated by attention, and earlier positive reports are due to variation in proximal stimulus intensity, or else highly refractory, near-threshold reflexes are not sensitive to attentionally induced biases in afferent transmission.

Locus of the Initial Divergence

If visually evoked blinks are found to be sensitive to selective attention, the possibility exists of identifying a subcortical locus for this modulation. A number of studies have noted that the visual blink reflex seems to consist of more than one subcomponent (reviewed by Anthony, 1985). The signal-averaging technique employed by Hackley and coworkers in the study just described distinguished four subcomponent bursts, with onset latencies in the grand-average EMG waveform at about 30, 55, 95, and 135 ms. Because the first component begins synchronously with the earliest arrival of thalamic input at primary visual cortex (31 ms, according to Wilson *et al.*, 1983), it must be mediated by a purely subcortical pathway, probably involving the pretectum (Holstege *et al.*, 1986). Like the postauricular reflex in the auditory modality and the R1 blink subcomponent in the tactile modality (discussed later), the rapidity of the 30 ms visual blink component would permit any preset modulatory effects that are subcortical in origin to be distinguished from later effects that could involve cortex.

Attention effects on retinal potentials have been reported by Eason and colleagues (Eason, 1984; Eason, Oakley and Flowers, 1983). In one study (Eason, 1984), subjects attended in balanced blocks of trials to flashes of light 30 degrees to the left or right of fixation, and the electroretinogram was recorded with electrodes at both the inner and outer canthi of the right eye. Both the positive-going B wave and the subsequent negative afterpotential were enhanced in amplitude when attention was directed to the evoking stimulus. Because centrifugal fibers are known to innervate the retina in mammals (Itaya, 1980), the data are consistent with the assumption that a preset bias in retinal function existed at the time of stimulus arrival. However, the B wave occurs relatively late, at 50–60 ms (see Figure 3.2), so the possibility exists that the initial modulation of visual function is at higher levels (cortical or brainstem), with rapid feedback to the ocular region. Because reflex electromyographic potentials can contaminate recordings of the retinal B wave (Hackley, Woldorff and Hillyard, 1990; but see Eason, Flowers and Oakley, 1983), it is conceivable that attentionally modulated, blink reflex activity was mistaken for variation in retinal potentials. The generality of attention effects on electroretinographic deflections is also at issue, because attempts to replicate the effect with different methods have failed, as shown in Figure 3.2 (Hackley, Woldorff and Hillyard, 1990; see also Mangun, Hansen and Hillyard, 1987, in which Eason's methods were followed more closely).

The earliest unequivocal attention effect in the visual modality is enhancement of the occipital P1 (P120) potential (e.g. Eason, Harter and White, 1969; Hillyard and Munte, 1984; Mangun, Hansen and Hillyard, 1987). Recent topographical mapping studies using current density measures indicate that this component, and attentional modulation thereof, originates in lateral, extrastriate visual cortex (S. A. Hillyard, personal communication, 31 Oct. 1989). In the Hackley *et al.* study just described, three deflections that were earlier in time than the P1—the N40, P50, and N70—did not vary during crossmodal attention. Because the P50 and N70 deflections inverted in polarity between the left and right occipital recordings, it is possible that they were generated by a laterally oriented dipole within the longitudinal fissure. Consistent with this possibility, a putative homolog in monkey of the human

N70 is believed to reflect activation of primary visual (striate) cortex (Kraut, Arezzo and Vaughan, 1985). Therefore, these results do not lend support to hypotheses of subcortical modulation of visual transmission (e.g. at the thalamic level; Skinner and Yingling, 1977).

Levels of Automaticity

The results support a tripartite division of visual processes with regard to automaticity, consistent with findings (previously described) in the auditory modality. The early, middle, and late stimulus-engendered processes seem to be fully automatic, partially automatic, and controlled, respectively. Congruent with this, the earliest visually evoked potentials in the brain (N40, P50, and N70) are exogenous; the intermediate potentials (only P105 and P210 in the Hackley *et al.* study, but often N170 and N260 as well) are mesogenous; and the late stimulus-initiated waves (e.g. P3b to weak intensity targets) are endogenous. If purported attentional effects on retinal potentials are substantiated by future research, then the existence of an initial, fully automatic level of analysis would be in doubt.

Summary for Visual Attention

In vision, as in audition, selective attention is reflected by both the modulation of obligatory potentials (i.e. the mesogenous potentials), and the occurrence and modulation of endogenous potentials. The pattern of these effects supports behavioral research in suggesting that selection based on spatial location may be qualitatively different from selection based on color or other physical attributes. So far as is known, modulation of obligatory components is obtained only when attended and ignored stimuli are distinguished by location. As in audition, selection may follow a hierarchical pattern, such that stimuli rejected on the basis of a rapidly discriminable attribute receive no further processing for other, less discriminable features. Another similarity with audition is that three levels of automaticity, reflected in exogenous, mesogenous, and endogenous potentials, have also been identified in vision.

Regarding the chronometric locus of the initial divergence in processing between attended and ignored stimuli, the best estimate is 80–90 ms—the leading edge of the P120 (P1) potential. If attention effects on the retinal B wave or on the earliest visual blink component were established as reliable, this value would be pushed back to 30–60 ms. Assuming that the P1 component is generated in extrastriate cortex, then this represents the best current estimate as to the anatomical locus of the initial divergence. Attentional modulation of visual prepulse inhibition, a midbrain reflex, is compatible with a lower-level locus, but does not demand such an inference. In the single study reporting such an effect (DelPezzo and Hoffman, 1980), attentional effects on inhibition were measured at 150–200 ms after visual stimulus onset; hence, cortical feedback to lower levels cannot be excluded. Confirmation of either the B wave or blink reflex attention effects would also support a locus prior to extrastriate cortex but, again, rapid cortical feedback on to lower levels would have to be ruled out. The extrastriate locus for the initial divergence, and the rapidity of its surface manifestations (80–90 ms), strongly support intraperceptual, early-selection, theories of attention.

SOMATOSENSORY SELECTIVE ATTENTION

The neuroanatomical pathways underlying reflexes and event-related potentials in the somatosensory modality have been elaborated more fully than in the visual and auditory modalities. Following electrical stimulation of the median nerve at the wrist, the transmission of sensory information through peripheral, spinal, brainstem, and cortical pathways can be closely monitored by event-related potentials recorded from surface electrodes (e.g. Allison, Wood and McCarthy, 1986). Similarly, stimulation of the supraorbital nerve near the eyebrow elicits a reflexive blink mediated by a complex circuit that is beginning to be understood on a synapse-by-synapse basis, as illustrated in Figure 3.3 (Holstege *et al.*, 1986). A detailed understanding of the relationship between molar surface potentials and their neuroanatomical substrates allows for the possibility of strong reductionistic inferences by the psychophysiologist. For the study of attention, though, this advantage is offset by two considerations. First, the wealth of information regarding physio-anatomical substrates is not paralleled by studies at the behavioral level that deal with selective attention. In the early years of attention research, most cognitive studies of attention employed auditory stimuli, while in the last decade, vision has become the preferred modality. Only a handful of attention studies have examined selective somatosensory perception (e.g. Shiffrin and Grantham, 1974). A second problem is that control of proximal stimulus intensity is especially difficult with stimuli in this modality. Even with the use of a constant current unit to clamp electrocutaneous stimulation at a fixed level, sensory adaptation, postural changes, self-stimulation of nearby skin sites, and variation in temperature, blood flow, or sweating are all potentially capable of altering stimulus intensity at the receptor or at the first synapse.

ERP Measures of Somatic Attention

Notwithstanding these difficulties, substantial progress has been made in the study of somatosensory selective attention. A recent study by Michie *et al.* (1987) illustrates some representative findings. Electrocutaneous stimuli were delivered to the left and right index fingers at an average rate of one per second. Two intensities, 'weak' and 'strong', were used, with probabilities of

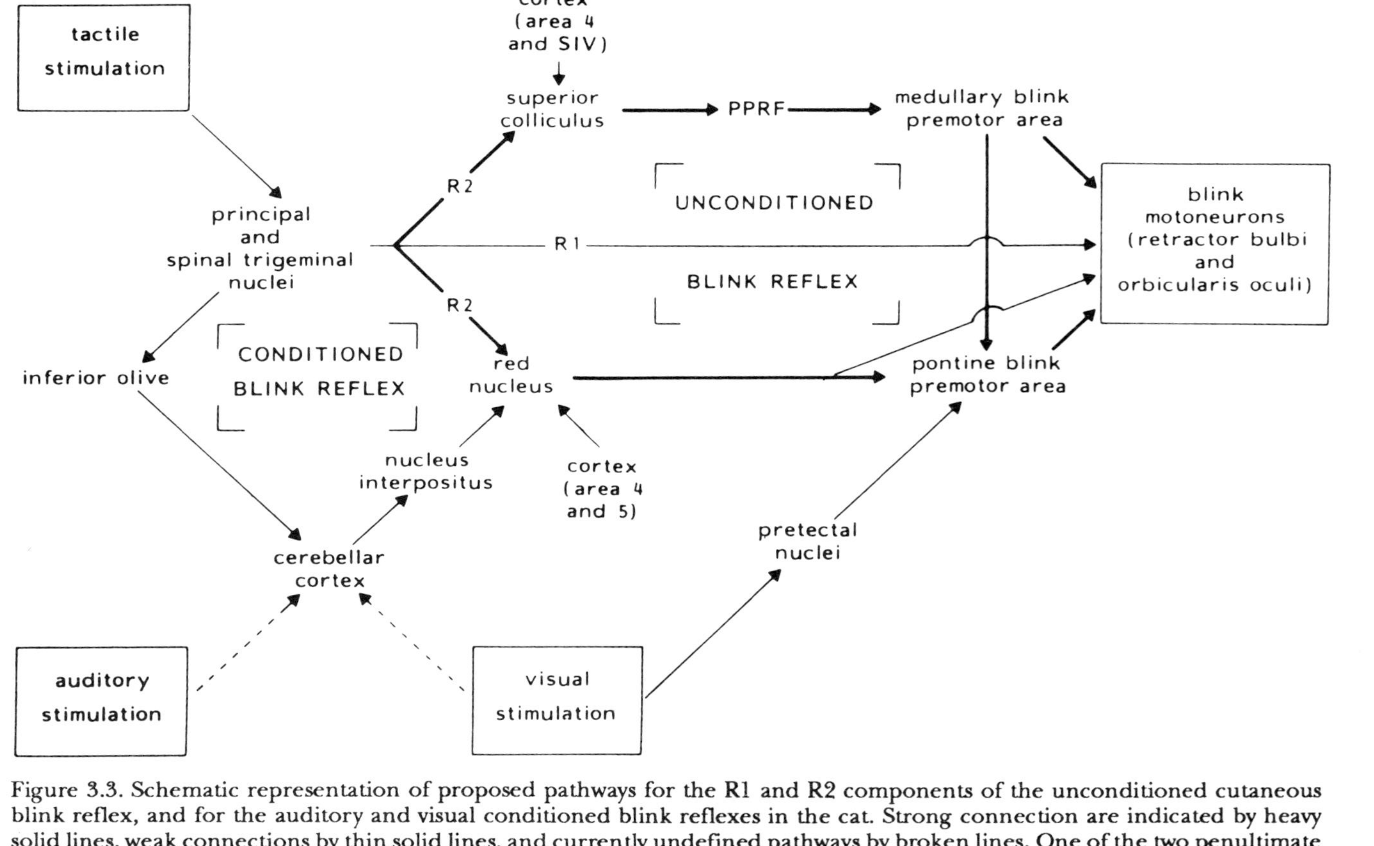

Figure 3.3. Schematic representation of proposed pathways for the R1 and R2 components of the unconditioned cutaneous blink reflex, and for the auditory and visual conditioned blink reflexes in the cat. Strong connection are indicated by heavy solid lines, weak connections by thin solid lines, and currently undefined pathways by broken lines. One of the two penultimate connections for the R2 circuit, the 'medullary blink premotor area', lies in the medial tegmentum at the level of the hypoglossal nucleus. The other, referred to as the 'pontine blink premotor area', is in the ventrolateral pontine area, apparently in or near a region described by Cassella and Davis (1986) as essential for both the tactile whole-body startle and the auditory pinna-flexion (postauricular) reflexes in rat. 'PPRF' stands for 'paramedian pontine reticular formation'. (Reprinted with permission of the authors and publisher from Holstege *et al.* (1986). © Elsevier Science Publishers.)

0.80 (standards) and 0.20 (deviants) varied across blocks of trials. Attention was manipulated across blocks by requiring subjects to count deviant stimuli silently on the index finger of the designated hand (i.e. targets). The digitization rate did not permit the initial cortical (20–30 ms latency) potentials to be distinguished. The earliest potentials that were clearly discernable were P55 and N80 at electrode sites contralateral to the evoking stimulus. The earliest wave that was unambiguously enhanced by attention was the N80 deflection to weak standards, and scalp distribution was consistent with the assumption that at least one of the generators contributing to the N80 deflection was modulated by selective attention. The subsequent P105 and N150 peaks were also affected by attention, but the exact pattern of attention effects varied depending on whether the subject counted the weak or the strong deviant stimuli. Subjects considered counting strong deviants to be the easier task, an observation confirmed by performance measures.

Superimposed on the phasic deflections, Michie *et al.* (1987) observed a prolonged positive displacement of the waveforms for attended relative to unattended stimuli that may have begun as early as 20–35 ms. It persisted undiminished until the end of the recording epoch at 578 ms. In a preliminary report, McCarthy and Wood (1986) described a similar phenomenon. In that study, attended standards elicited a prolonged positivity that was largest at sites ipsilateral to the evoking stimulus, began at about 22 ms, and persisted until the end of the recording epoch (250 ms in this case). Although the onset of this positivity coincided with the presumed initial arrival of information at cortex, the phasic potentials reflecting that arrival were unaffected by attention. Similarly, Desmedt and Robertson (1977) reported the N20 and P45 potentials to be invariant with attention. Two other studies (Desmedt, Huy and Bourget, 1983; Lavine, Buchsbaum and Schechter, 1980) did report task-related changes in a positive deflection at 30–40 ms; however, these studies did not employ designs that permit selective attention effects to be distinguished from non-specific effects.

The prolonged positivity observed by Michie *et al.* (1987) was continuous with a late positive component bearing the distinguishing features of a P3b: it was maximal in amplitude at posterior electrode sites, it was larger for rare deviant stimuli than for standards, it was larger in attended than ignored conditions, and its peak latency was later with the more difficult task of detecting weak, as opposed to strong, targets. This late positivity differed from the prototypical P300, though, in that it was present for non-target and ignored stimuli and varied in amplitude as a function of the physical properties of the eliciting stimulus. Specifically, it was larger for strong than for weak stimuli. These latter attributes suggest that the electric shocks elicited a *mesogenous* P300, similar to that identified by Roth and colleagues for intense auditory stimuli (e.g. Roth, Dorato and Kopell, 1984; cf. Squires, Squires and Hillyard, 1975). The obligatory P300 to intense auditory stimuli habituates slowly, and is sensitive to stimulus intensity and duration but not to rise time; hence, according to Putnam and Roth (1988), it may be functionally related to the defense response in the four-category system of Graham (1979; also see the section 'Distinguishing Characteristics' in the first part of this chapter). Even though the electric shocks used by Michie and colleagues were of relatively weak intensity, all shocks, like loud noises, may have an inherently noxious, obtrusive character. Furthermore, performance, subjective report, and psychophysiological indices of attention were consistent with the assumption that the strong-intensity non-target stimuli were difficult to ignore and, consequently, interfered with task performance in the attend–weak condition.

Reflex Measures of Somatosensory Attention

Attention effects on the blink reflex evoked by cutaneous stimuli have been examined in two crossmodal studies that obtained rather different patterns of results (Cohen, Cranney and Hoffman, 1983; Hackley and Graham, 1983). In the Hackley and Graham study, subjects received, on every trial, an auditory–cutaneous pair of stimuli with simultaneous onsets. Only one member of the pair was an effective blink-eliciting stimulus; the other stimulus was of weak intensity and had a slow rise time. On 83% of the trials, a non-informative warning stimulus preceded the stimulus pair by 3 s; the other trials were unwarned. Attention was manipulated by requiring subjects to judge the duration, 'short' or 'long', of the weak or strong stimulus in counterbalanced halves of the experimental session. As predicted, reflex blinks tended to be larger and faster when attention was directed toward the reflex-eliciting member of the stimulus pair relative to when the weak stimulus was attended. For auditory evoked blinks, facilitation of both magnitude and onset latency reached significance; for cutaneous evoked blinks, attention effects were significant for onset latency only.

In the cutaneous modality, as in the visual modality, the reflex blink comprises multiple components in the electromyogram (Kugelberg, 1952). The earliest component of the cutaneous blink reflex, the disynaptic 'R1', has an onset latency between 10 and 15 ms and usually is observable only in recordings from the eyelid ipsilateral to the evoking stimulus. At 25–35 ms, a bilateral 'R2' component is observed, which is polysynaptic (see Figure 3.3). This bilateral component, recorded from integrated EMG over the eyelid contralateral to the evoking stimulus, was the one analyzed statistically by Hackley and Graham. Averaged, unintegrated EMG waveforms were obtained from the ipsilateral eyelid, but statistical evaluation was not feasible. In the grand-average waveform, it appeared that the earliest evoked myogenic activity (11–14 ms) was unaffected by attention, but that subsequent activity (15 ms and later) might have been enhanced by attention.

Thus, reflexes and event-related potentials support a value at least as early as 20–30 ms for the initial divergence in processing of attended and ignored somatosensory information. This is similar to the proposed divergence for auditory processing, but is some 60 ms earlier than the analogous value for the visual modality. Sensory information first arrives at somatic cortex near the time of the earliest attention effects, but the phasic ERPs reflecting this arrival (N20/P20, P25, P30/N30; Allison, Wood and McCarthy, 1986) are not themselves affected by attention (Desmedt and Robertson, 1977; McCarthy and Wood, 1986). Whether the phasic evoked potentials do not adequately represent the initial cortical processes, because surface potentials provide '*incomplete* and *biased* measures of CNS activity' (Allison *et al.*; italics in original), or whether the initial divergence in processing occurs in a pathway parallel to that generating the early deflections, cannot as yet be determined.

The results of a blink experiment by Cohen and colleagues (1983; Experiment 4) contrast with those of Hackley and Graham (1983). In the Cohen experiment, attention was manipulated by varying subject expectancy for the eliciting stimulus, rather than, as in the Hackley and Graham study, by manipulating task relevance of the stimulus. Subjects in the Cohen study received either an auditory or a cutaneous blink-eliciting stimulus on each trial, and stimulus expectancy was manipulated in two ways. The first method involved temporal expectancy. On half of the trials, subjects presented the stimulus themselves by pressing a button and, on the other half of the trials, the experimenter presented the stimulus. Presumably, subjects would be better able to predict the time of stimulus ocurrence when they controlled delivery themselves. The second manipulation entailed precueing the modality of the impending stimulus on half of the trials in each of the two stimulus delivery conditions. There was no explicit task other than pressing the stimulus-delivery button on half of the trials and watching some slides of artwork and nature scenes that were uncorrelated with the reflex stimuli. Only amplitude of the reflexive blink was measured. The results showed that foreknowledge of either the timing or the modality of the reflex-eliciting stimulus led to smaller, not larger, blinks. Because these results apparently conflict with those obtained from visual precueing studies of reaction time, brain potentials, and prepulse inhibition—all of which found facilitation with valid precues—the Cohen *et al.* results merit close scrutiny. A conclusion that temporal foreknowledge produces reflex inhibition must be qualified by the consideration that a motor confound was inherent in the design. Specifically, subjects made a voluntary movement, pressing the stimulus-delivery button, just prior to receiving the reflex-eliciting stimulus in the self-presentation but not in the experimenter-presentation condition. This is of special concern because it has been shown that the polysynaptic blink reflex is inhibited immediately after a voluntary hand movement (e.g. Sanes, 1984). Hackley and Graham (1983) also obtained an inhibitory effect of warning, unconfounded by differences in motor demands, but the effect was non-selective; that is, it occurred in both the attended and ignored modalities (see also Brown, 1975; Experiment 3). Surprisingly, onset latency and magnitude are modulated in different directions by a neutral warning stimulus that specifies with certainty when the reflex stimulus will occur—warning facilitates latency but inhibits magnitude (reviewed by Hackley and Graham, 1983).

Cohen and colleagues found that modality as well as temporal precueing produced inhibition of reflex magnitude. Although these findings are consistent with the common-sense view that startle is greater for surprising stimuli (Landis and Hunt, 1939), the modality-specific inhibition is clearly not predicted by the theoretical framework developed in this chapter. In the Cohen *et al.* study, the rapidity of the blink reflex and the use of multiple evoking stimuli might seem to necessitate a preset, selective bias in sensory-specific pathways. However, unlike the precueing studies of reaction time by Posner, Snyder and Davidson (1980) or of brain potentials by Mangun, Hansen and Hillyard (1987), stimuli in the Cohen study were never presented in the uncued channel on forewarned trials. In other words, there were no 'invalid precue' trials to permit selective and non-selective processes to be distinguished. If modality precueing alters transmission in the postconvergence segment of the reflex arc, or has a non-specific influence on all sensory-specific pathways, then magnitude inhibition on precued trials could have mimicked a selective sensory effect.

It would be instructive if this experiment were repeated using invalid as well as valid precueing of modality, using a task that explicitly directs attention to the reflex stimuli, and using measures of reflex onset latency as well as magnitude. In an earlier review of the literature (Hackley and Graham, 1987), we found that of seven published studies using adult subjects in which both reflex latency and magnitude were measured, selective attention affected latency in all seven, but magnitude in only one study. Furthermore, because latency is measured at an earlier point in time than peak amplitude, effects on this variable provide stronger evidence for a preset state that prevails at the time of stimulus arrival. The importance of measuring onset latency as well as magnitude is underscored by recent evidence that motor programming of the blink reflex occurs in two stages (Blumenthal and Berg, 1986; Manning and Evinger, 1986): An initial 'trigger' stage determines response probability and the onset portion of the EMG burst, while a subsequent 'amplifier' stage controls the ultimate size and duration of the reflexive movement. In this conception, the trigger stage is relatively more sensitive to rise time (Blumenthal and Berg, 1986), 'short-interval latency facilitation' (Graham and Murray, 1977), and selective attention (Hackley and Graham, 1987). By contrast, the amplifier stage is more sensitive to variation in eliciting stimulus duration (Manning and Evinger, 1986), and to prepulse inhibition, habituation, and learned adaptation to limb load (Evinger and Manning, 1988). The characteristics of trigger and amplifier are compatible with parallel processing by systems specialized for detecting and transmitting, respectively, the transient and sustained characteristics of stimulation (see the two sections on preattentive transient or sustained processing in the first part of this chapter). It is also tempting to speculate that the trigger and amplifier stages are mediated by the two parallel pathways identified by Holstege *et al.* (1986) for the R2 component of the cutaneous blink reflex (Figure 3.3), but little available evidence bears on this question.

Summary for Somatosensory Attention

Although much is known about the neural substrates of the cutaneous blink reflex and the somatosensory event-related potentials, psychological and psychophysiological investigations have not been as numerous for the somatosensory as for the visual and auditory modalities.

Despite the limited number of studies available for review, tentative conclusions can be reached. Initial divergence in the processing of attended and ignored somatic stimuli may be as early as 20–30 ms, roughly synchronous with the arrival of information at primary somatosensory cortex. Nonetheless, the initial cortical responses apparently do not vary with attention. This makes the anatomical location of the initial divergence uncertain, but a subcortical location is probably not required by the available evidence. Whether a hierarchical structure characterizes selection of multiattribute stimuli in the somatosensory modality, as in the visual and auditory modalities, is unknown, but target stimuli can elicit a P3b that is absent or diminished in size for non-targets sharing only one of two attended attributes. As in the other major modalities, somatosensory processing shows three levels of automaticity. The earliest cortical potentials are obligatory and are invariant with attention; hence, they are exogenous. Brain potentials of intermediate latency (such as N80) and the R2 component of the startle-blink reflex are mesogenous, that is to say, they are obligatory but can be modified by attention. Finally, the optional, attentionally dependent potentials such as P3b can be triggered by somatosensory stimuli if task conditions are appropriate. When electric shocks are used as stimuli, a mesogenous P3 can also be evoked, owing to the inherently obtrusive quality of such stimuli.

LATE SELECTION AND THE CONTINUOUS–DISCRETE CONTROVERSY

The psychophysiological evidence of early selective attention effects in the auditory, visual, and somatic modalities stands in direct contradiction to the late-selection view (e.g. Shiffrin and Grantham, 1974) that sensory-perceptual processing is unaffected by attention. Modulation of obligatory, short-latency, sensory-specific activity during highly focused attention demonstrates that the nervous system does treat attended and ignored stimuli differently at an early stage. On the other hand, the strong version of early selection theory (Broadbent, 1958), which maintains that ignored stimuli are completely rejected after a preliminary analysis of physical features, is also not supported. Of special relevance here is the existence of long-latency mesogenous components—potentials that are affected by attention but, nonetheless, are obligatory. Even in highly focused attention tasks, ignored stimuli evoke brain potentials indicating obligatory sensory activity at latencies as great as 200–400 ms (e.g. Hackley, Woldorff and Hillyard, 1990). This is much longer than the time estimated to be required for the analysis of the simple physical features held to underlie early selection. Backward-recognition masking studies suggest that rather complete analysis of easily discriminable attributes can take place within 75–125 ms for visual shape discrimination (Miller and Hackley, submitted) and auditory pitch discrimination (Foyle and Watson, 1984). Furthermore, very easy discriminations of location or of modality may be assumed to require even less time. If the strong version of early selection theory were correct, a straightforward prediction might be that ignored stimuli would evoke exogenous potentials at latencies shorter than around 100 ms, but then no potentials at all beyond that. This assumes, of course, that appreciable delays do not exist between the psychologically relevant sensory analyses and the scalp-recorded potentials that index those operations. Thus, long-latency mesogenous potentials support an interpretation intermediate between the extreme versions of early and late selection theories. One example of such an intermediate theory is Treisman's (1960) theory that ignored stimuli are attenuated rather than completely rejected during early selection.

Semantic Analysis of Ignored Stimuli

A highly influential line of research in autonomic psychophysiology further supports the assertion that ignored stimuli are not gated in an all-or-none fashion after a preliminary physical analysis. In the first of these studies, Corteen and Wood (1972) showed that words that had been previously associated with an electric shock were capable of eliciting an electrodermal response when embedded in the ignored message during a shadowing task. Although the effect was small, it was statistically reliable, and was confirmed in five of six subsequent attempted replications (reviewed by Dawson and Schell, 1982). The most recent of these replications (Dawson and Schell, 1982) incorporated a number of controls to ensure that the effect was not dependent on occasional deviations of attention toward the to-be-ignored ear. When such attention lapses were excluded, the effect was still significant, but only for words presented to the left ear. Consistent with this unexpected laterality effect, positive results were stronger in prior studies in which the test words were presented to the left ear than in those studies that counterbalanced ear assignments (reviewed by Dawson and Schell, 1982).

The small size of such effects merits emphasis. In a review of 12 studies which used a variety of methods to assess processing of ignored verbal material, Kahneman and Treisman (1984) reported that the proportion of stimuli that was apparently processed to the semantic level in these experiments ranged from 2% to 38%, with an average of only 16%. These results seem more congruent with the attenuation form of filter theory (Treisman, 1960) than with the late-selection view that all stimuli receive an automatic analysis to the point of complete representation in short-term memory (e.g. Shiffrin and Grantham, 1974). However, given that analysis to the semantic level can occur, postperceptual (late selection) mechanisms are presumably then involved in controlling access to consciousness, to response systems, and to long-term storage.

The nature of the representation activated in short-term memory for ignored stimuli could be of two logically distinct forms. One possibility is that attenuation of the processing of ignored stimuli results in a graded (continuous) perceptual representation. If so, then the probability and magnitude of the electrodermal response in Dawson and Schell's (1982) study could have been determined by a threshold function relating emotional stimuli in short-term memory to autonomic responding. Alternatively, the attentional filter might work stochastically, with a small proportion of the ignored stimuli receiving full analysis, terminating in complete representation in short-term memory. In this case, these fully analyzed stimuli would have had access to autonomic response mechanisms, but would not have triggered a button press, have entered long-term memory, or have substantially reduced the resources available for shadowing. Although the data of Dawson and Schell do not permit a choice between these hypotheses, they do underscore the relevance of the continuous–discrete issue for attention theory.

Implications of the Continuous–Discrete Issue

One point of relevance is that the notion of graded representation in memory is compatible with early selection theory, but not with the late selection assumption of complete, fully automatic, perceptual analysis of ignored stimuli, as discussed above (we thank Jeff Miller for pointing this out).

A second aspect of the continuous–discrete issue that also has relevance for understanding attention is the question of continuous rather than discrete transmission between distinct but adjacent stages. According to traditional information processing theory (Donders, 1868/1969; Sternberg, 1969), transmission between adjacent stages occurs in a single, discrete step following termination of processing by the earlier stage. It is assumed that stages do not temporally overlap and, consequently, that reaction time can be exhaustively partitioned into the time required for each stage intervening between stimulus and response. By contrast, continuous-transmission theories (e.g. Eriksen and Shultz, 1979) assume that communication between stages occurs continuously, with the output of one stage being transmitted to the next stage gradually, as information becomes available. An intermediate model was proposed by Miller (1982), the 'asynchronous discrete coding model', in which information is transmitted in multiple, discretely coded 'chunks' as soon as they become available for output.

Two implications of the idea of graded transmission can be noted. First, if either continuous or asynchronous–discrete transmission theories are correct, the border between perceptual and postperceptual processes is blurred. For example, if perceptual and response-selection stages partially overlap in time, then purely chronometric techniques will have limited value in distinguishing between early-selection and late-selection effects. This was noted in an earlier section where we reviewed evidence to suggest that the earliest reliable attention effect in the visual modality begins at 80–90 ms, the leading edge of the P1 wave. Because this is longer than the time apparently required for analysis of some easily discriminable visual attributes, transmission to a postperceptual stage such as response selection might already have occurred. Physio-anatomical localization of the generator of the P1 potential to extrastriate visual cortex supports an intraperceptual rather than a postperceptual interpretation, but we cannot be sure that feedback from postperceptual centers is not involved. A stronger case for a purely intraperceptual locus can be made on the basis of the very early (15–25 ms) attention effects in the auditory and somatosensory modalities; however, the difference in force of argument is not categorical, but one of degree.

A second implication of continuous-transmission theory concerns the importance that attaches to psychophysiological analysis of the mechanisms of late selection, as well as early selection, for attention. An example is the 'conflict paradigm' devised to examine the possibility of continuous transmission between perceptual and response-selection stages (Coles, Gratton and Donchin, 1988). In this paradigm, two aspects of stimulus information are arranged so that they vary both with regard to the speed with which they are discriminated and the responses to which they are mapped. The term 'conflict' refers to the fact that, in certain experimental conditions, preliminary and final stimulus information activate different responses. In a study by Miller and Hackley (submitted) which used the paradigm, subjects were required to make a speeded response with the left or right hand depending on the shape of the reaction stimulus (S or T) if the letter was of one size, but to withhold their response if the letter was of another, slightly different size. A backwards-recognition masking study with another group of subjects indicated that shape was rapidly discriminated within 75 ms, but that letter size was slowly perceived, requiring more than 250 ms to reach asymptotic discrimination levels. Response selection/preparation was indexed by lateralization of the readiness potential recorded from scalp sites overlying the hand area of both left and right primary motor cortex. Lateralization of the readiness potential on NoGo trials 250–500 ms after onset of the stimulus suggested that a preliminary analysis of shape had initiated motor preparation, but preparation was aborted when subsequent analyses of size determined that the response should be withheld. With respect to selective attention, the point to be emphasized is this: if motor readiness potentials had not been measured, it would have been unclear whether early- or late-selection mechanisms mediated the selective responding to stimuli of only one size. Because size is an attribute that is capable of mediating early selection (Harter and Previc, 1978), it could not have been predicted, *a priori*, that selective responding in the Miller and Hackley study was mediated by a postperceptual mechanism which aborted an incipient response.

SUMMARY OF CONCLUSIONS

Psychophysiologists using central and peripheral measures have investigated a broad range of topics that fall under the headings of passive and active attention. We have selected a few of these topics that have been studied by both approaches, and have noted in our review a number of consistencies that extend across methodologies.

(1) Qualitatively distinct patterns of central, autonomic, and peripheral nervous system responses support the differentiation of several modality-non-specific reflexes: these include the generalized orienting reflex, triggered by an unexpected change in stimulation; the defense reflex, elicited by high-intensity or noxious stimuli; and the startle reflex, evoked by stimulus onsets that are both sudden and intense. A fourth non-specific reflex, the transient-detecting response, is evoked by low-intensity, abrupt changes in stimulation. The two reflexes elicited by high-intensity stimuli (i.e. startle and defense) evoke short and prolonged heart rate accelerations, respectively, but differ in that startle habituates rapidly. The two reflexes elicited by low- to moderate-intensity stimuli (i.e. transient-detection and orienting) evoke short and prolonged heart rate decelerations, respectively, but differ in that orienting habituates rapidly under passive attention conditions.

(2) The dual-process theory proposed by Thompson and colleagues (e.g. Groves and Thompson, 1970) offers a parsimonious account of stimulus repetition effects for low-level responses such as defense, startle, and modality-specific reflexes, but has difficulty accounting for some phenomena concerning habituation and dishabituation of the OR. A number of effects

on this higher-level reaction are better explained by Sokolov's (e.g. 1963) cognitive theory of the orientation reflex, or by Öhman's (1979) more contemporary articulation of Sokolovian theory. Among the phenomena more easily explicated by a cognitive theory are (a) the non-monotonic relation between intensity and habituation, (b) recovery following a change in pattern, sequence, or word meaning, (c) dishabituation by non-arousing events such as stimulus omission, (d) selective dishabituation—the enhancement, following an interpolated stimulus, of responding to the habituating stimulus but not to other stimuli, and (e) evocation of ERP components in response to change, that is, mismatch negativity and P3, that are not present in the unhabituated response.

(3) Transient and sustained characteristics of inputs appear to be processed preattentively and separately, with at least some separate processing being maintained up to early sensory cortical areas. The sustained processing reflected in ERPs preserves information about time-varying aspects of input intensity and frequency that is closely correlated with psychophysical discrimination and loudness judgments and is not reflected in the transient-sensitive ERPs. The specialized processing of transients may allow for rapid detection of onsets and offsets and may activate gating mechanisms to prevent perceptual flooding by high-intensity stimuli and to call for controlled processing when new information is detected.

(4) The relation of psychophysiological measures to the Sokolov–Öhman theory of orienting is not clear, but evidence supports the following tentative model. Under passive conditions, activity in response to an abrupt high-intensity stimulus may interrupt ongoing processing within 100 ms and elicit a startle reflex, including flexor contractions, heart rate increase, and the non-specific N1. When an abrupt stimulus of any intensity arrives at an unexpected time, or when the stimulus signals uncertain events, it may trigger the generalized ANS–OR, including heart rate decrease and N1. With stimulus repetition, an increasingly accurate model of past stimulation is developed which may be stored both in a crossmodal integrating memory and in specific-modality sensory memories. Delivery of a stimulus deviating from a model along physical or temporal dimensions evokes a specific-modality mismatch negativity in the ERP. If the deviance from expectations exceeds a threshold, a request is automatically issued for additional processing resources. This call is mirrored in N2b–P3a and in ANS–OR components. If the request is granted, sensory processing in general is enhanced and may include further processing of the input, reflected in prolonged heart rate deceleration and perhaps further negativity in the ERP, and/or an effortful search of long-term memory and encoding of the stimulus into memory, reflected in heart rate acceleration and P3b.

(5) Deviance of stimuli from expected categorical rather than dimensional characteristics may be indexed by potentials later than MMN, such as the N400

to violation of semantic expectancy. Under active attention conditions, a call for processing resources may be issued when stimuli match a memory node primed for significance (i.e. task-relevant targets or signals of targets). If the request is granted, the significant stimulus receives enhanced processing by virtue of a maintained set which, for auditory stimuli, is reflected in a prolonged endogenous ERP, the processing negativity.

(6) During optimal conditions of active attention, electrophysiological signs of the divergence in processing of attended and ignored stimuli are evident as early as 15–20 ms for audition, 20–30 ms for somesthesis, and 80–90 ms for vision. For the auditory and somatosensory modalities, these values are a great deal shorter than the estimated time for perceptual analysis. Consequently, such data stand in direct contradiction to the assumption of some late-selection theories of attention that sensory-perceptual analyses are fully automatic and are unaffected by attention. For audition and somesthesis, these values approximate the time that information initially reaches primary sensory cortices; however, the first attention effects for vision occur some 50 ms later than the initial arrival of information at cortex. Findings in regard to the locus of the initial divergence in processing are conflicting, but incontrovertible evidence for a precortical attention effect in humans has yet to be reported.

(7) Event-related potentials and somatic reactions may be categorized as exogenous, mesogenous, or endogenous, consistent with three distinct levels of automaticity: *strongly automatic* processes, indexed by exogenous components, are obligatory and are unaffected by attention; *partially automatic* processes, reflected in mesogenous components, are obligatory, but can be modulated by attention; finally, *controlled* processes, paralleled by endogenous components, are non-obligatory and are dependent on attentional resources. Within the auditory modality, the three categories are exemplified, respectively, by wave I, the T-complex, and P3b, for ERPs. For somatic reactions, examples from the three categories include, respectively, the postauricular reflex, startle-blink reflex, and voluntary speeded reactions.

(8) The issues raised by continuous versus discrete models of human information processing have a number of implications for attention theory. Among these are (a) the incompatibility of graded perceptual representation of ignored stimuli with late-selection theories of attention, and (b) a blurring of the distinction between intraperceptual and extraperceptual processes under the assumption of continuous transmission between stages. Also, a number of studies examining continuous transmission have demonstrated the existence of subthreshold activation of motor processes by to-be-ignored stimuli. Such studies underscore the importance of psychophysiological analysis of postperceptual as well as intraperceptual mechanisms of attentional selection.

ACKNOWLEDGEMENTS

Preparation of this chapter was supported by Research Scientist Award MH21762 amd Research Project Award MH42465 from the National Institute of Mental Health.

We are grateful to Risto Näätänen and Jonathan C. Hansen for helpful commentaries on early versions of the chapter and to Robert F. Simons, Marty Woldorff, Steve Hillyard, and Ron Mangun for many helpful discussions of issues which are considered here.

REFERENCES

Aaltonen, O., Niemi, P., Nyrke, T. and Tuhkanen, M. (1987). Event-related brain potentials and the perception of a phonetic continuum. *Biological Psychology*, **24**, 197–207.

Adrian, E.D. (1954). The physiological basis of perception. In J.F. Delafresnaye (ed.), *Brain Mechanisms and Consciousness*. Oxford: Blackwell, pp. 237–248.

Alho, K., Paavilainen, P., Reinikainen, K., Sams, M. and Näätänen, R. (1986). Separability of different negative components of the event-related brain potential associated with auditory stimulus processing. *Psychophysiology*, **23**, 613–623.

Alho, K., Tottola, K., Reinikainen, K., Sams, M. and Näätänen, R. (1987). Brain mechanism of selective listening reflected by event-related potentials. *Electroencephalography and Clinical Neurophysiology*, **68**, 458–470.

Allison, T., Wood, C.C. and McCarthy, G. (1986). The central nervous system. In M.G.H. Coles, E. Donchin and S.W. Porges (eds), *Psychophysiology: Systems, Processes, and Applications*. New York: Guilford, pp. 5–25.

Anthony, B.J. (1985). In the blink of an eye: implications of reflex modulation for information processing. In P.K. Ackles, J.R. Jennings and M.G.H. Coles (eds), *Advances in Psychophysiology*, vol. 1. Greenwich, CT: JAI Press, pp. 167–218.

Anthony, B.J. and Graham, F.K. (1983). Evidence for sensory-selective set in young infants. *Science*, **220**, 742–744.

Anthony, B.J. and Graham, F.K. (1985). Blink reflex modification by selective attention: evidence for the modulation of 'automatic' processing. *Biological Psychology*, **20**, 43–59.

Balaban, M.T., Anthony, B.J. and Graham, F.K. (1985). Modality-repetition and attentional effects on reflex blinking in infants and adults. *Infant Behavior and Development*, **8**, 443–457.

Balaban, M.T., Anthony, B.J. and Graham, F.K. (1989). Prestimulation effects on blink and cardiac reflexes of 15-month human infants. *Developmental Psychobiology*, **22**(2), 115–127.

Barry, R. (1987). Preliminary processes in orienting response elicitation. In P.K. Ackles, J.R. Jennings and M.G.H. Coles (eds), *Advances in Psychophysiology*, vol. 2. Greenwich, CT: JAI Press, pp. 131–195.

Bashinski, H.S. and Bacharach, V.R. (1980). Enhancement of perceptual sensitivity as the result of selectively attending to spatial locations. *Perception and Psychophysics*, **28**, 241–248.

Becker, D.E. and Shapiro, D. (1980). Directing attention toward stimuli affects the P300 but not the orienting response. *Psychophysiology*, **12**, 385–389.

Benson, D.A. and Heinz, R.D. (1978). Single-unit activity in the auditory cortex of monkeys selectively attending left vs. right ear stimuli. *Brain Research*, **159**, 307–320.
Berg, K.M. (1973). *Elicitation of Acoustic Startle in the Human*. Unpublished doctoral thesis, University of Wisconsin, Madison.
Berg, W.K., Berg, K.M., Harbin, T.J., Davies, M.G., Blumenthal, T.D. and Avendano, A. (1985). Comparisons of blink inhibition in infants, children, and young and old adults. *Psychophysiology*, **22**, 572–573 (abstract).
Berg, K.W., Jackson, J.C. and Graham, F.K. (1975). Tone intensity and rise–decay time effects on cardiac responses during sleep. *Psychophysiology*, **12**, 254–261.
Berlyne, D.E. (1961). Conflict and the orientation reaction. *Journal of Experimental Psychology*, **62**, 476–483.
Berlyne, D.E. (1969). The development of the concept of attention in Psychology. In C.R. Evans and T.B. Mulholland (eds), *Attention in Neurophysiology*. New York: Appleton–Century–Crofts, pp. 1–26.
Bloch, R.M. (1972). *Inhibition and Facilitation Effects of a Prepulse on the Human Blink Response to a Startle Pulse*. Unpublished doctoral dissertation, University of Wisconsin, Madison.
Blumenthal, T.D. and Berg, W.K. (1986). Stimulus rise time, intensity, and bandwidth effects on acoustic startle amplitude and probability. *Psychophysiology*, **23**, 635–641.
Blumenthal, T.D. and Gescheider, G.A. (1987). Modification of the acoustic startle reflex by a tactile prepulse: The effects of stimulus onset asynchrony and prepulse intensity. *Psychophysiology*, **24**, 320–327.
Bohlin, G., Graham, F.K., Silverstein, L.D. and Hackley, S.A. (1981). Cardiac orienting and startle blink modification in novel and signal situations. *Psychophysiology*, **18**, 603–611.
Braff, D., Stone, C., Callaway, E., Geyer, M., Glick, I. and Bali, L. (1978). Prestimulus effects on human startle reflex in normals and schizophrenics. *Psychophysiology*, **15**, 339–343.
Bregman, A.S. and Campbell, J. (1971). Primary auditory stream segregation and perception of order in rapid sequences of tones. *Journal of Experimental Psychology*, **89**, 244–249.
Brix, R. (1984). The influence of attention on the auditory brain stem evoked responses. *Acta Otolaryngology (Stockholm)*, **98**, 89–92.
Broadbent, D.E. (1958). *Perception and Communication*. London: Pergamon.
Broadbent, D.E. (1970). Stimulus set and response set: two kinds of selective attention. In D.I. Mostofsky (ed.), *Attention: Contemporary Theory and Analysis*. New York: Appleton–Century–Crofts, pp. 51–60.
Brown, J.W. (1975). *Contingent Negative Variation and Cardiac Orienting Preceding Startle Modification*. Unpublished doctoral dissertation, University of Wisconsin, Madison.
Buchwald, J.S. and Humphrey, G.L. (1974). An analysis of habituation in the specific sensory systems. In E. Stellar and J.M. Sprague (eds), *Progress in Physiological Psychology*, vol. 5. New York: Academic Press, pp. 1–75.
Burbeck, S.L. and Luce, R.D. (1982). Evidence from auditory simple reaction times for both change and level detectors. *Perception and Psychophysics*, **32**(2), 117–133.
Butler, R.A. (1968). Effect of changes in stimulus frequency and intensity on habituation of the human vertex potential. *Journal of the Acoustical Society of America*, **44**, 945–950.
Butler, R.A. (1972). Frequency specificity of the auditory evoked response to simultaneously and successively presented stimuli. *Electroencephalography and Clinical Neurophysiology*, **33**, 277–282.
Cassella, J.V. and Davis, M. (1986). Neural structures mediating acoustic and tactile

startle reflexes and the acoustically-elicited pinna response in rats: electrolytic and ibotenic acid studies. *Society for Neuroscience Abstracts*, **12**, 1273.

Celesia, G.G. (1976). Organization of auditory cortical areas in man. *Brain*, **99**, 403–414.

Clarkson, M.G. and Clifton, R.K. (1983). Dishabituation of cardiac orienting responses by orienting and startle stimuli. *Psychophysiology*, **20**, 435 (abstract).

Clynes, M. (1969). Dynamics of vertex evoked potentials: the R–M brain function. In E. Donchin and D.B. Lindsley (eds), *Averaged Evoked Potentials*. Washington, DC: NASA, pp. 363–374.

Cohen, M.E., Cranney, J. and Hoffman, H.S. (1983). Motor and cognitive factors in the modification of a reflex. *Perception and Psychophysics*, **34**, 214–220.

Coles, M.G.H. and Duncan-Johnson, C.C. (1975). Cardiac activity and information processing: the effects of stimulus significance, and detection and response requirements. *Journal of Experimental Psychology: Human Perception and Performance*, **1**, 418–428.

Coles, M.G.H., Gratton, G. and Donchin, E. (1988). Detecting early communication: using measures of movement-related potentials to illuminate human information processing. *Biological Psychology*, **26**, 69–89.

Connolly, J.F., Aubry, K., McGillivary, N. and Scott, D.W. (1989). Human brainstem auditory evoked potentials fail to provide evidence of efferent modulation of auditory input during attentional tasks. *Psychophysiology*, **26**, 292–303.

Corteen, R.S. and Wood, B. (1972). Autonomic responses for shock-associated words in an unattended channel. *Journal of Experimental Psychology*, **94**, 308–313.

Courchesne, E. (1977). Event-related brain potentials: a comparison between children and adults. *Science*, **197**, 589–592.

Courchesne, E. (1978). Changes in P3 waves with event repetition: long-term effects on scalp distribution and amplitude. *Electroencephalography and Clinical Neurophysiology*, **45**, 754–766.

Courchesne, E., Courchesne, R.Y. and Hillyard, S.A. (1978). The effect of stimulus deviation on P3 waves to easily recognized stimuli. *Neuropsychologia*, **16**, 189–199.

Courchesne, E., Hillyard, S.A. and Galambos, R. (1975). Stimulus novelty, task relevance and the visual evoked potential in man. *Electroencephalography and Clinical Neurophysiology*, **39**, 131–143.

Courchesne, E., Kilman, B.A., Galambos, R. and Lincoln, A.J. (1984). Autism: processing of novel auditory information assessed by event-related brain potentials. *Electroencephalography and Clinical Neurophysiology*, **59**, 238–248.

Cowan, N. (1988). Evolving conceptions of memory storage, selective attention, and their mutual constraints within the human information-processing system. *Psychological Bulletin*, **104**, 163–191.

Cranney, J., Hoffman, H.S. and Cohen, M.E. (1984). Tonal frequency shifts and gaps in acoustic stimulation as reflex-modifying events. *Perception and Psychophysics*, **35**(2), 165–172.

Csépe, V., Karmos, G. and Molnár, M. (1987). Evoked potential correlates of stimulus deviance during wakefulness and sleep in cat—animal model of mismatch negativity. *Electroencephalography and Clinical Neurophysiology*, **66**, 571–578.

David, E., Finkenzeller, P., Kallert, S. and Keidel, W.D. (1971). Interaction between visually and auditorily evoked DC-potentials in man. In H. Drischel and N. Tiedt (eds), *Biokybernetik*, vol. III. Jena: VEB Gustav Fischer, pp. 228–231.

Davis, A. and Beagley, H. (1985). Acoustic brainstem responses for clinical use: the effect of attention. *Clinical Otolaryngology*, **10**, 311–314.

Davis, H. (1976). Principles of electric response audiometry. *Annals of Otology, Rhinology and Laryngology*, **85**(Suppl. 28). St. Louis: Annals Publishing.

Davis, H. and Zerlin, S. (1966). Acoustic relations of the human vertex potential. *Journal of the Acoustical Society of America*, **39**, 109–116.
Davis, M. and File, S.E. (1984). Intrinsic and extrinsic mechanisms of habituation and sensitization: implications for the design and analysis of experiments. In H.V.S. Peeke, and L. Petrinovich (eds), *Habituation, Sensitization, and Behavior*. Orlando: Academic Press, pp. 287–320.
Davis, M. and Heninger, G.R. (1972). Comparison of response plasticity between the eyeblink and vertex potential in humans. *Electroencephalography and Clinical Neurophysiology*, **33**, 283–293.
Davis, M., Parisi, T., Gendelman, D.S., Tischler, M. and Kehne, J.H. (1982). Habituation and sensitization of startle reflexes elicited electrically from the brainstem. *Science*, **218**, 688–690.
Dawson, M.E., Filion, D.L. and Schell, A.M. (1989). Is elicitation of the autonomic orienting response associated with allocation of processing resources? *Psychophysiology*, **26**, 560–572.
Dawson, M.E. and Schell, A.M. (1982). Electrodermal responses to attended and nonattended significant stimuli during dichotic listening. *Journal of Experimental Psychology: Human Perception and Performance*, **8**, 315–324.
Deiber, M.P., Ibanez, V., Fischer, C., Perrin, F. and Mauguiere, F. (1988). Sequential mapping favours the hypothesis of distinct generators for Na and Pa middle latency auditory evoked potentials. *Electroencephalography and Clinical Neurophysiology*, **71**, 187–197.
DelPezzo, E.M. and Hoffman, H.S. (1980). Attentional factors in the inhibition of a reflex by a visual stimulus. *Science*, **210**, 673–674.
Desmedt, J.E., Huy, N.T. and Bourget, M. (1983). The cognitive P40, N60, and P100 components of somatosensory evoked potentials and the earliest electrical signs of sensory processing in man. *Electroencephalography and Clinical Neurophysiology*, **56**, 272–282.
Desmedt, J.E. and Robertson, D. (1977). Differential enhancement of early and late components of the cerebral somatosensory evoked potentials during forced-paced tasks in man. *Journal of Physiology (London)*, **271**, 761–782.
Donchin, E. (1981). Surprise!. . .Surprise? *Psychophysiology*, **18**, 493–513.
Donchin, E., Heffley, E., Hillyard, S.A., Loveless, N., Maltzman, I., Öhman, A., Rösler, F., Ruchkin, D. and Siddle, D. (1984). Cognition and event-related potentials: The orienting reflex and P300. *Annals of the New York Academy of Sciences*, **425**, 39–57.
Donchin, E., Ritter, W. and McCallum, W.C. (1978). Cognitive psychophysiology: the endogenous componenets of the ERP. In E. Callaway, P. Tueting and S.H. Koslow (eds), *Event-Related Brain Potentials in Man*. New York: Academic Press, pp. 349–441.
Donders, F.C. (1969). On the speed of psychological processes. In W.G. Koster (ed. and trans.), *Attention and Performance*, vol. II. Amsterdam: North-Holland, pp. 412–431. (Original work published 1868).
Duncan-Johnson, C.C. and Donchin, E. (1977). On quantifying surprise: the variation of event-related potentials with subjective probability. *Psychophysiology*, **14**, 456–467.
Dykman, B.M. and Ison, J.R. (1979). Temporal integration of acoustic stimulation obtained in reflex inhibition in rats and humans. *Journal of Comparative and Physiological Psychology*, **93**, 939–945.
Eason, R.G. (1984). Selective attention effects on retinal and forebrain responses in humans: a replication and extension. *Bulletin of the Psychonomic Society*, **22**, 341–344.
Eason, R.G., Flowers, L. and Oakley, M. (1983). Differentiation of retinal and nonretinal contributions to averaged evoked responses obtained with electrodes placed near the

eyes. *Behavior Research Methods and Instrumentation*, **15**, 13–21.
Eason, R.G., Harter, M.R. and White, C.T. (1969). Effects of attention and arousal on visually evoked cortical potentials and reaction time in man. *Physiology and Behavior*, **4**, 283–289.
Eason, R.G., Oakley, M. and Flowers, L. (1983). Central neural influences on the human retina during selective attention. *Physiological Psychology*, **11**, 18–28.
Edwards, D.C. (1975a). Stimulus intensity reduction following habituation. *Psychophysiology*, **12**, 12–14.
Edwards, D.C. (1975b). Within mode quality and intensity changes of habituated stimuli. *Biological Psychology*, **3**, 295–299.
Eggermont, J.J. (1988). On the rate of maturation of sensory evoked potentials. *Electroencephalography and Clinical Neurophysiology*, **70**, 293–305.
Eriksen, C.W. and Schultz, D.W. (1979). Information processing in visual search: a continuous flow model and experimental results. *Perception and Psychophysics*, **25**, 249–263.
Erwin, R. and Buchwald, J.S. (1986a). Midlatency auditory evoked responses: differential effects of sleep in the human. *Electroencephalography and Clinical Neurophysiology*, **65**, 383–392.
Erwin, R. and Buchwald, J.S. (1986b). Midlatency auditory evoked responses: differential recovery cycle characteristics. *Electroencephalography and Clinical Neurophysiology*, **64**, 417–423.
Evinger, C. and Manning, K.A. (1988). A model system for motor learning: adaptive gain control of the blink reflex. *Experimental Brain Research*, **70**, 527–538.
Faber, H.E.L., van der Molen, M.W., Keuss, P.J.G. and Stoffels, E.J. (1986). An OR analysis of the tendency to react toward the stimulus source. *Acta Psychologica*, **61**, 105–115.
Fitzgerald, P.G. and Picton, T.W. (1983). Event-related potentials recorded during the discrimination of improbable stimuli. *Biological Psychology*, **17**, 241–276.
Ford, J.M. and Hillyard, S.A. (1981). Event-related potentials (ERPs) to interruptions of a steady rhythm. *Psychophysiology*, **18**, 322–330.
Ford, J.M., Pfefferbaum, A. and Kopell, B.S. (1982). Event-related potentials to a change of pace in a visual sequence. *Psychophysiology*, **19**, 173–177.
Ford, J.M., Roth, W.T. and Kopell, B.S. (1976). Auditory evoked potentials to unpredicitable shifts in pitch. *Psychophysiology*, **13**, 32–39.
Foyle, D.C. and Watson, C.S. (1984). Stimulus-based versus performance-based measurement of auditory backward recognition masking. *Perception and Psychophysics*, **36**, 515–522.
Freedman, R., Adler, L.E. and Waldo, M. (1987). Gating of the auditory evoked potential in children and adults. *Psychophysiology*, **24**, 223–227.
Fruhstorfer, H. (1971). Habituation and dishabituation of the human vertex response. *Electroencephalography and Clinical Neurophysiology*, **30**, 306–312.
Furedy, J.J. and Ginsberg, S. (1975). Test of an orienting–reaction–recovery account of short-interval autonomic conditioning. *Biological Psychology*, **3**, 121–129.
Gardner, R.B. and Wilson, J.P. (1979). Evidence for direction-specific channels in the processing of frequency modulation. *Journal of the Acoustical Society of America*, **66**, 704–709.
Gersuni, G.V. (1965). Organization of afferent flow and the process of external signal discrimination. *Neuropsychologia*, **3**, 95–109.
Geyer, M.A. and Braff, D.L. (1987). Startle habituation and sensorimotor gating in schizophrenia and related animal models. *Schizophrenia Bulletin*, **13**, 643–668.
Giard, M.H., Perrin, F., Pernier, J. and Peronnet, F. (1988). Several attention-related

waveforms in auditory areas: a topographic study. *Electroencephalography and Clinical Neurophysiology*, **69**, 371–384.

Giardina, B.D. (1989). *Short and Long Time Processing in Mediating Prepulse Inhibition of the Startle Blink Reflex*. Unpublished doctoral dissertation, University of Delaware, Newark.

Ginsberg, S. and Furedy, J.J. (1974). Stimulus repetition, change and assessments of sensitivities of and relationships among an electrodermal and two plethysmographic components of the orienting reaction. *Psychophysiology*, **11**, 35–43.

Goodgold, J. and Eberstein, A. (1977). *Electrodiagnosis of Neuromuscular Diseases*. Baltimore: Williams and Wilkins.

Goodin, D.S., Aminoff, M.J. and Mantle, M.M. (1986). Subclasses of event-related potentials: response-locked and stimulus-locked components. *Annals of Neurology*, **20**, 603–609.

Gorga, M.P., Beauchaine, K.A., Reiland, J.K., Worthington, D.W. and Javel, E. (1984). The effects of stimulus duration on ABR and behavioral thresholds. *Journal of the Acoustical Society of America*, **76**, 616–619.

Graham, F.K. (1973). Habituation and dishabituation of responses innervated by the autonomic nervous system. In H.V.S. Peeke and M.J. Herz (eds), *Habituation: Behavioral Studies and Physiological Substrates*. New York: Academic Press, pp. 163–218.

Graham, F.K. (1975). The more or less startling effects of weak prestimulation. *Psychophysiology*, **12**, 238–248.

Graham, F.K. (1978). Constraints on measuring heart rate and period sequentially through real and cardiac time. *Psychophysiology*, **15**, 492–495.

Graham, F.K. (1979). Distinguishing among orienting, defense, and startle reflexes. In H.D. Kimmel, E.H. van Olst and J.F. Orlebeke (eds), *The Orienting Reflex in Humans*. Hillsdale, NJ: Erlbaum, pp. 137–167.

Graham, F.K. (1980). Control of reflex blink excitability. In R.F. Thompson, L.H. Hicks and V.B. Shvyrkov (eds), *Neural Mechanisms of Goal-Directed Behavior and Learning*. New York: Academic Press, pp. 511–519.

Graham, F.K. (1984). An affair of the heart. In M. Coles, R. Jennings and J. Stern (eds), *Psychophysiology: A Festschrift for John and Beatrice Lacey*. New York: Van Nostrand Reinhold, pp. 171–187.

Graham, F.K. (1989). SPR Award, 1988, for distinguished contributions to psychophysiology: Evgeny Nikolaevich Sokolov. *Psychophysiology*, **26**, 385–391.

Graham, F.K., Anthony, B.J. and Zeigler, B.L. (1983). The orienting response and developmental processes. In D. Siddle (ed.), *Orienting and Habituation: Perspectives in Human Research*. Chichester: Wiley, pp. 371–430.

Graham, F.K. and Jackson, J.C. (1970). Arousal systems and infant heart rate responses. In H.W. Reese and L.P. Lipsitt (eds), *Advances in Child Development and Behavior*, **5**, 59–117.

Graham, F.K. and Murray, G.M. (1977). Discordant effects of weak prestimulation on magnitude and latency of the reflex blink. *Physiological Psychology*, **5**, 108–114.

Graham, F.K., Putnam, L.E. and Leavitt, L.A. (1975). Lead stimulation effects on human cardiac orienting and blink reflexes. *Journal of Experimental Psychology: Human Perception and Performance*, **1**, 161–169.

Graham, F.K., Strock, B.D. and Zeigler, B.L. (1981). Excitatory and inhibitory influences on reflex responsiveness. In W.A. Collins (ed.), *Minnesota Symposia on Child Psychology: Aspects of the Development of Competence*, vol. 14. Hillsdale, NJ: Erlbaum, pp. 1–38.

Groves, P.M. and Thompson, R.F. (1970). A dual-process theory. *Psychological Review*, **77**, 419–450.

Hackley, S.A. and Graham, F.K. (1983). Early selective attention effects on cutaneous

and acoustic blink reflexes. *Physiological Psychology*, **11**, 235–242.
Hackley, S.A. and Graham, F.K. (1987). Effects of attending selectively to the spatial position of reflex-eliciting and reflex-modulating stimuli. *Journal of Experimental Psychology: Human Perception and Performance*, **13**, 411–424.
Hackley, S.A., Woldorff, M. and Hillyard, S.A. (1987). Combined use of microreflexes and event-related brain potentials as measures of auditory selective attention. *Psychophysiology*, **24**, 632–647.
Hackley, S.A., Woldorff, M. and Hillyard, S.A. (1990). Cross-modal selective attention effects on retinal, myogenic, brainstem and cerebral evoked potentials. *Psychophysiology*, **27**, 195–208.
Halliday, A.M. (1982). *Evoked Potentials in Clinical Testing*. New York: Churchill Livingston, pp. 71–120.
Hansen, J.C. and Hillyard, S.A. (1983). Selective attention to multidimensional auditory stimuli. *Journal of Experimental Psychology: Human Perception and Performance*, **9**, 1–19.
Hansen, J.C. and Hillyard, S.A. (1984). Effects of stimulation rate and attribute cueing on event-related potentials during selective auditory attention. *Psychophysiology*, **21**, 394–405.
Hansen, J.C. and Woldorff, M. (1989). Mechanisms of auditory selective attention as revealed by event-related potentials. Paper presented at the Ninth International Conference on Event-Related Potentials of the Brain, EPIC IX, May 28–June 3, 1989; Noordwijk, Netherlands.
Hare, R.D. and Blevings, G. (1975). Conditioned orienting and defensive response. *Psychophysiology*, **12**, 289–297.
Hari, R. (in press). The neuromagnetic method in the study of the human auditory cortex. In F. Grandori, M. Hoke and G.L. Romani (eds), *Advances in Audiology*, vol. 6.
Hari, R., Kaila, K., Katila, T., Tuomisto, T. and Varpula, T. (1982). Interstimulus interval dependence of the auditory vertex response and its magnetic counterpart: implications for their neural generation. *Electroencephalography and Clinical Neurophysiology*, **54**, 561–569.
Hari, R. and Kaukoranta, E. (1985). Neuromagnetic studies of somatosensory system: principles and examples. *Progress in Neurobiology*, **24**, 233–256.
Hari, R., Pelizzone, M., Mäkelä, J.P., Hallstrom, J., Leinonen, L. and Lounasmaa, O.V. (1987). Neuromagnetic responses of the human auditory cortex to on- and offsets of noise bursts. *Audiology*, **26**, 31–43.
Hari, R., Sams, M. and Järvilehto, T. (1979). Auditory evoked transient and sustained potentials in the human EEG. I: Effects of expectation of stimuli. *Psychiatric Research*, **1**, 297–306.
Harter, M.R. and Aine, C.J. (1984). Brain mechanisms of visual selective attention. In R. Parasuraman and D.R. Davies (eds), *Varieties of Attention*. New York: Academic Press, pp. 293–321.
Harter, M.R. and Guido, W. (1980). Attention to pattern orientation: negative cortical potentials, reaction time, and the selection process. *Electroencephalography and Clinical Neurophysiology*, **49**, 461–475.
Harter, M.R. and Previc, F.H. (1978). Size-specific information channels and selective attention: visual evoked potential and behavioral measures. *Electroencephalography and Clinical Neurophysiology*, **45**, 628–640.
Hashimoto, I. (1982). Auditory evoked potentials from the human midbrain: slow brain stem responses. *Electroencephalography and Clinical Neurophysiology*, **53**, 652–657.
Hashimoto, I., Ishiyama, Y., Yoshimoto, T. and Nemoto, S. (1981). Brain-stem auditory-evoked potentials recorded directly from human brain-stem and thalamus. *Brain*, **104**, 841–859.

Hecox, K. and Deegan, D. (1983). Rise–fall time effects on the brainstem auditory evoked response: mechanisms. *Journal of the Acoustical Society of America*, **73**(6), 2109–2116.

Hecox, K. and Galambos, R. (1974). Brainstem auditory evoked responses in human infants. *Annals of Otolaryngology*, **99**, 30–33.

Hecox, K., Squires, N. and Galambos, R. (1976). Brainstem auditory evoked responses in man. I: Effect of stimulus rise–fall time and duration. *Journal of the Acoustical Society of America*, **60**, 1187–1192.

Hernandez-Peon, R., Scherrer, H. and Jouvet, M. (1956). Modification of electrical activity in cochlear nucleus during 'attention' in unanesthetized cats. *Science*, **123**, 331–332.

Hillyard, S.A. and Hansen, J.C. (1986). Attention: electrophysiological approaches. In M.G.H. Coles, E. Donchin and S.W. Porges (eds), *Psychophysiology*. New York: Guilford, pp. 227–243.

Hillyard, S.A., Hink, R.F., Schwent, V.L. and Picton, T.W. (1973). Electrical signs of selective attention in the human brain. *Science*, **182**, 177–180.

Hillyard, S.A. and Munte, T.F. (1984). Selective attention to color and location: an analysis with event-related brain potentials. *Perception and Psychophysics*, **36**, 185–198.

Hillyard, S.A. and Picton, T.W. (1979). Event-related brain potentials and selective information processing in man. In J.E. Desmedt (ed.), *Progress in Clinical Neurophysiology*, vol. 6. Karger: Basel.

Hillyard, S.A. and Picton, T.W. (1987). Electrophysiology of cognition. In F. Plum (ed.), *Handbook of Physiology:* sect. 1, *The Nervous System*, vol. 5, *Higher Function of the Nervous System*, Part 2. USA: American Physiological Society, pp. 519–584.

Hillyard, S.A., Picton, T.W. and Regan, D.M. (1978). Sensation, perception and attention: analysis using ERPs. In E. Callaway, P. Tueting and S. Koslow (eds), *Event-Related Brain Potentials in Man*. New York: Academic Press, pp. 223–321.

Hillyard, S.A., Woldorff, M., Mangun, G.R. and Hansen, J.C. (1987). Mechanisms of early selective attention in auditory and visual modalities. *Electroencephalography and Clinical Neurophysiology*, **39**, 317–324.

Hink, R.F. and Hillyard, S.A. (1976). Auditory evoked potentials during selective listening to dichotic speech messages. *Perception and Psychophysics*, **20**, 236–242.

Hoffman, H.S. and Ison, J.R. (1980). Reflex modification in the domain of startle. I: Some empirical findings and their implication for how the nervous system processes sensory input. *Psychological Review*, **87**, 175–189.

Hoffman, H.S., Marsh, R.R. and Stein, N. (1969). Persistence of backgroud acoustic stimulation in controlling startle. *Journal of Comparative and Physiological Psychology*, **68**, 280–283.

Hoffman, H.S. and Stitt, C.L. (1980). Inhibition of the glabella reflex by monaural and binaural stimulation. *Journal of Experimental Psychology: Human Perception and Performance*, **6**, 769–776.

Hoffman, H.S. and Wible, B.L. (1969). Temporal parameters in startle facilitation by steady background signals. *Journal of the Acoustical Society of America*, **45**, 7–12.

Hoffman, J.E., Simons, R.F. and Houck, M.R. (1983). Event-related potentials during controlled and automatic targets detection. *Psychophysiology*, **20**, 625–632.

Holstege, G., Tan, J., van Ham, J.J. and Graveland, G.A. (1986). Anatomical observations on the afferent projections to the retractor bulbi motoneuronal cell group and other pathways possibly related to the blink reflex in the cat. *Brain Research*, **374**, 321–334.

Houck, R.L. and Mefferd, R.B. (1969). Generalization of GSR habituation to mild stimuli. *Psychophysiology*, **6**, 202–206.

Iacono, W.G. and Lykken, D.T. (1983). The effects of instructions on electrodermal habituation. *Psychophysiology*, **20**, 71–80.

Ison, J.R., McAdam, D.W. and Hammond, G.R. (1973). Latency and amplitude changes in the acoustic startle reflex of the rat produced by variation in auditory prestimulation. *Physiology and Behavior*, **10**, 1035–1039.

Ison, J.R. and Pinckney, L.A. (1983). Reflex inhibition in humans: sensitivity to brief silent periods in white noise. *Perception and Psychophysics*, **34**, 84–88.

Itaya, S.K. (1980). Retinal efferents from the pretectal area in the rat. *Brain Research*, **201**, 436–441.

Jackson, J.C. (1974). Amplitude and habituation of the orienting reflex as a function of stimulus intensity. *Psychophysiology*, **11**, 647–659.

James, W. (1890). *The Principles of Psychology*. New York: Dover.

Järvilehto, T. and Fruhstorfer, H. (1973). Is the sound-evoked DC potential a contingent negative variation? In W.C. McCallum and J.R. Knott (eds), *Event-related Slow Potentials of the Brain: Their Relations to Behavior*. Amsterdam: Elsevier, pp. 105–108.

Järvilehto, T., Hari, R. and Sams, M. (1978). Effect of stimulus repetition of negative sustained potentials elicited by auditory and visual stimuli in the human EEG. *Biological Psychology*, **7**, 1–12.

Jennings, J.R. and Hall, S.W. (1980). Recall, recognition, and rate: memory and the heart. *Psychophysiology*, **17**, 37–46.

Johnston, W.A. and Dark, V.J. (1986). Selective Attention. *Annual Review of Psychology*, **37**, 43–75.

Jonides, J. (1981). Voluntary versus automatic control over the mind's eye. In J. Long and A. Baddeley (eds), *Attention and Performance*, vol. IX. Hillsdale, NJ: Erlbaum, pp. 187–203.

Kahneman, D. (1973). *Attention and Effort*. Englewood Cliffs, NJ: Prentice Hall.

Kahneman, D. and Treisman, A. (1984). Changing views of attention and automaticity. In R. Parasuraman and D.R. Davies (eds), *Varieties of Attention*. New York: Academic Press, pp. 29–61.

Kandel, E.R. (1985). Factors controlling transmitter release. In E.R. Kandel and J.H. Schwartz (eds), *Principles of Neural Science*, 2nd edn. New York: Elsevier, pp. 120–131.

Kaufman, L., Curtis, S., Luber, B. and Williamson, S.J. (1986). Effects of selective attention on auditory and visually evoked fields. *Society for Neuroscience Abstracts*, **12**, 1162.

Keesey, U.T. (1972). Flicker and pattern detection: a comparison of thresholds. *Journal of the Optical Society of America*, **62**, 446–448.

Keidel, W.D. (1976). The physiological background of the electric response audiometry. In W.D. Keidel and W.D. Neff (eds), *The Handbook of Sensory Physiology*: vol. 5, *Auditory System: Clinical and Special Topics*. Berlin: Springer-Verlag, pp. 105–231.

Kenemans, J.L., Verbaten, M.N., Roelofs, J.- W. and Slangen, J.L. (1989). 'Initial-' and 'change-orienting reactions': an analysis based on visual single-trial event-related potentials. *Biological Psychology*, **28**, 199–226.

Kileny, P., Paccioretti, D. and Wilson, A.F. (1987). Effects of cortical lesions on middle-latency auditory evoked responses (MLR). *Electroencephalography and Clinical Neurophysiology*, **66**, 108–120.

Kimmel, H.D., Van Olst, E.H. and Orlebeke, J.F. (eds), (1979). *The Orienting Reflex in Humans*. (Proceedings of an international conference sponsored by the Scientific Affairs Division of the North Atlantic Treaty Organization). New York: Erlbaum.

Klinke, R., Fruhstorfer, H. and Finkenzeller, P. (1968). Evoked responses as a function of external and stored information. *Electroencephalography and Clinical Neurophysiology*, **25**, 119–122.

Knight, R.T. (1984). Decreased response to novel stimuli after prefrontal lesions in man. *Electroencephalography and Clinical Neurophysiology*, 59, 9–20.

Knight, R.T., Scabini, D., Woods, D. L. and Clayworth, C.(1988). The effects of lesions of superior temporal gyrus and inferior parietal lobe on temporal and vertex components of the human AEP. *Electroencephalography and Clinical Neurophysiology*, **70**, 499–509.

Kohn, M., Lifshitz, K. and Litchfield, D. (1978). Averaged evoked potentials and frequency modulation. *Electroencephalography and Clinical Neurophysiology*, **45**, 236–243.

Kohn, M., Lifshitz, K. and Litchfield, D. (1980). Averaged evoked potentials and amplitude modulation. *Electroencephalography and Clinical Neurophysiology*, **50**, 134–140.

Krasne, F.B. (1976). Invertebrate systems as a means of gaining insight into the nature of learning and memory. In M.R. Rosenzweig and E.L. Bennett (eds), *Neural Mechanisms of Learning and Memory*. Cambridge, MA: MIT Press, pp. 401–429.

Kraus, N., Özdamar, Ö., Hier, D. and Stein, L. (1982). Auditory middle latency responses (MLRs) in patients with cortical lesions. *Electroencephalography and Clinical Neurophysiology*, **54**, 275–287.

Kraut, M.A., Arezzo, J.C. and Vaughan, H.G. (1985). Intracortical generators of the flash VEP in monkeys. *Electroencephalography and Clinical Neurophysiology*, **62**, 300–312.

Kugelberg, E. (1952). Facial reflexes. *Brain*, **75**, 385–396.

Kuk, F.K. and Abbas, P.J. (1989). Effects of attention on the auditory evoked potentials recorded from the vertex (ABR) and the promontory (CAP) of human listeners. *Neuropsychologia*, **27**, 665–673.

Kutas, M. and Hillyard, S.A. (1980). Reading senseless sentences: brain potentials reflect semantic incongruity. *Science*, **207**, 203–205.

LaMotte, C. (1977). Distribution of the tract of Lissauer and the dorsal root fibers in the primate spinal cord. *Journal of Comparative Neurology*, **172**, 529–562.

Landis, C. and Hunt, W.A. (1939). *The Startle Pattern*. New York: Farrar and Rinehart.

Larsson, L-E. (1956). The relation between the startle reaction and the non-specific EEG response to sudden stimuli with a discussion on the mechanism of arousal. *Electroencephalography and Clinical Neurophysiology*, **8**, 631–644.

Larsson, L-E. (1960). Sensitization of the startle blink and non-specific electro-encephalographic response. *Electroencephalography and Clinical Neurophysiology*, **12**, 727–733.

Lavine, R.A., Buchsbaum, M.S. and Schechter, G. (1980). Human somatosensory evoked responses: effects of attention and distraction on early components. *Physiological Psychology*, **8**, 405–408.

Leitner, D.S. and Cohen, M.E. (1985). Role of the inferior colliculus in the inhibition of acoustic startle in the rat. *Physiology and Behavior*, **34**, 65–70.

Leitner, D.S., Powers, A.S. and Hoffman, H.S. (1979). The neural system for the inhibition of startle. *Bulletin of the Psychonomic Society*, **14**, 410–412.

Leitner, D.S., Powers, A.S. and Hoffman, H.S. (1980). The neural substrate of the startle response. *Physiology and Behavior*, **25**, 291–297.

Liegeois-Chauvel, C., Morin, C., Musolino, A., Bancaud, J. and Chauvel, P. (1989). Evidence for a contribution of the auditory cortex to a audiospinal facilitation in man. *Brain*, **112**, 375–391.

Linden, R.D., Picton, T.W., Hamel, G. and Campbell, K.B. (1987). Human auditory steady-state evoked potentials during selective attention. *Electroencephalography and Clinical Neurophysiology*, **66**, 145–159.

Livingstone, M. and Hubel, D. (1988). Segregation of form, color, movement, and depth: Anatomy, physiology, and perception. *Science*, **240**, 740–749.

Loveless, N.E. (1983). The orienting response and evoked potentials in man. In D. Siddle (ed.), *Orienting and Habituation: Perspectives in Human Research*. New York: Wiley, pp. 71–108.

Lukas, J.H. (1980). Human auditory attention: the olivocochlear bundle may function as a peripheral filter. *Psychophysiology*, **17**, 444–452.

Lukas, J.H. (1981). The role of efferent inhibition in human auditory attention: an examination of the auditory brainstem potentials. *International Journal of Neuroscience*, **12**, 137–145.

Lukas, J.H. (1982). The effects of attention and voluntary middle ear muscle contractions on the human auditory brainstem potentials. *Psychophysiology*, **19**, 572 (abstract).

Lundberg, A. (1966). Integration in the reflex pathway. In R. Granit (ed.), *Muscular Afferents and Motor Control* (Nobel Symposium I). Stockholm: Almqvist & Wiksell, pp. 275–305.

Lynn, R. (1966). *Attention, Arousal and the Orientation Reaction*. New York: Pergamon.

Lyytinen, H. (1988). Autonomic correlates of mismatch negativity and the nonspecific component of N1 and related ERPs. *Psychophysiology*, **25**, 427 (abstract).

Lyytinen, H., Blomberg, A.-P. and Näätänen, R. (in press). Event-related potentials and autonomic responses to a change in unattended auditory stimuli. *Psychophysiology*.

Lyytinen, H., Näätänen, R., Alho, K., Antervo, A., Blomberg, A.P., Ikonen, T., Leppasaari, T., Paavilainen, P., Reinikainen, K. and Sams, M. (1987). Autonomic concomitants of event-related potentials in the auditory oddball paradigm. *Psychophysiology*, **24**, 600 (abstract).

Magliero, A., Gatchel, R.J. and Lojeski, D. (1981). Skin conductance responses to stimulus 'energy' decreases following habituation. *Psychophysiology*, **18**, 549–558.

Mäkelä, J.P. and Hari, R. (1987). Evidence for cortical origin of the 40 Hz auditory evoked response in man. *Electroencephalography and Clinical Neurophysiology*, **66**, 539–546.

Mäkelä, J.P., Hari, R. and Linnankivi, A. (1987). Different analysis of frequency and amplitude modulations of a continuous tone in the human auditory cortex: a neuromagnetic study. *Hearing Research*, **27**, 257–264.

Mangun, G.R., Hansen, J.C. and Hillyard, S.A. (1987). The spatial orienting of attention: sensory facilitation or response bias? In R. Johnson, J.W. Rohrbaugh and R. Parasuraman (eds), *Current Trends in Event-Related Potential Research* (*EEG* Suppl. 40). Amsterdam: Elsevier, pp. 118–124.

Mangun, G.R. and Hillyard, S.A. (1988). Spatial gradients of visual attention: behavioral and electrophysiological evidence. *Electroencephalography and Clinical Neurophysiology*, **70**, 417–428.

Manning, K.A. and Evinger, C. (1986). Different forms of blinks and their two-stage control. *Experimental Brain Research*, **64**, 579–588.

Mäntysalo, S. and Näätänen, R. (1987). The duration of a neuronal trace of an auditory stimulus as indicated by event-related potentials. *Biological Psychology*, **24**, 183–195.

Marsh, J.T., Brown, W.S. and Smith, J.C. (1975). Far-field recorded frequency-following responses: correlates of low pitch auditory perception in humans. *Electroencephalography and Clinical Neurophysiology*, **38**, 113–119.

Marsh, R.R., Hoffman, H.S. and Stitt, C.L. (1976). Eyeblink inhibition by monaural and binaural stimulation: one ear is better than two. *Science*, **192**, 390–391.

McCallum, W.C., Curry, S.H., Cooper, R., Pocock, P.V. and Papakostopoulos, D. (1983). Brain event-related potentials as indicators of early selective processes in auditory target localization. *Psychophysiology*, **20**, 1–17.

McCarthy, G. and Wood, C.C. (1986). The effects of selective attention on scalp-recorded somatosensory evoked potentials in humans. *Society for Neuroscience Abstracts*, 1448.

Megela, A.L. and Teyler, T.J. (1979). Habituation and the human evoked potential. *Journal of Comparative and Physiological Psychology*, **93**, 1154–1170.

Michie, P.T., Bearpark, H.M., Crawford, J.M. and Glue, L.C.T. (1987). The effects of spatial selective attention on the somatosensory event-related potential. *Psychophysiology*, **24**, 449–463.

Miles, M.A., Perlstein, W.M., Simons, R.F. and Graham, F.K. (1987). ERP and HR components of active and passive orienting in a long-ISI paradigm: anhedonics and normal controls. *Psychophysiology*, **24**, 601 (abstract).

Miller, J.O. (1982). Discrete versus continuous stage models of human information processing: in search of partial output. *Journal of Experimental Psychology: Human Perception and Performance*, **8**, 273–296.

Miller, J.O. and Hackley, S.A. (submitted). Electrophysiological evidence for temporal overlap among contingent mental processes.

Mishkin, M. and Appenzeller, T. (1987). The anatomy of memory. *Scientific American*, **256**(6), 80–89.

Møller, A.R. and Jannetta, P.J. (1982). Evoked potentials from the inferior colliculus in man. *Electroencephalography and Clinical Neurophysiology*, **53**, 612–620.

Müller, H.J. and Rabbitt, P.M.A. (1989). Reflexive and voluntary orienting of visual attention: time course of activation and resistance to interruption. *Journal of Experimental Psychology: Human Perception and Performance*, **15**, 315–330.

Näätänen, R. (1967). Selective attention and evoked potentials. *Annales Academicae Scietiarium Fennicae*, **B151**, 1–226.

Näätänen, R. (1982). Processing negativity: an evoked-potential reflection of selective attention. *Psychological Bulletin*, **92**, 605–640.

Näätänen, R. (1986). The orienting response theory: an integration of informational and energetical aspects of brain function. In R.G.J. Hockey, A.W.K. Gaillard and M. Coles (eds), *Adaptation to Stress and Task Demands: Energetical Aspects of Human Information Processing*. Dortrecht: Martinus Nijhoff, pp. 91–111.

Näätänen, R. (1988). Implication of ERP data for psychological theories of attention. *Biological Psychology*, **26**, 117–163.

Näätänen, R. and Gaillard, A.W.K. (1983). The orienting reflex and the N2 deflection of the event-related potential (ERP). In A.W.K. Gaillard and W. Ritter (eds), *Tutorials in ERP Research: Endogenous Components*. Amsterdam: North-Holland, pp. 119–141.

Näätänen, R., Gaillard, A.W.K. and Mäntysalo, S. (1978). Early selective-attention effect on evoked potential reinterpreted. *Acta Psychologica*, **42**, 313–329.

Näätänen, R. and Lyytinen, H. (1989). Event-related potentials and the orienting response to nonsignal stimuli at fast stimulus rates. In N.W. Bond and D.A.T. Siddle (eds), *Psychobiology: Issues and Applications*, vol. 6 (24th International Congress of Psychology). Amsterdam: Elsevier, pp. 185–197.

Näätänen, R. and Michie, P.T. (1979). Early selective attention effects on the evoked potential: a critical review and reinterpretation. *Biological Psychology*, **8**, 81–136.

Näätänen, R., Paavilainen, P., Alho, K., Reinikainen, K. and Sams, M. (1987a). Interstimulus interval and the mismatch negativity. In C. Barber, T. Blum and R.H. Nodar (eds), *Evoked Potentials*, vol. III. London: Butterworths, pp. 392–397.

Näätänen, R., Paavilainen, P., Alho, K., Reinikainen, K. and Sams, M. (1987b). The mismatch negativity to intensity changes in an auditory stimulus sequence. In R. Johnson, J.W. Rohrbaugh and R. Parasuraman (eds), *Current Research in Event-Related Brain Potentials* (*EEG* Suppl. 40). Amsterdam: Elsevier, pp. 125–131.

Näätänen, R., Paavilainen, P. and Reinikainen, K. (1989). Do event-related potentials to infrequent decrements in duration of auditory stimuli demonstrate a memory trace in man? *Neuroscience Letters*, **107**, 347–352.

Näätänen, R. and Picton, T.W. (1987). The N1 wave of the human electric and magnetic response to sound: A review and an analysis of the component structure. *Psychophysiology*, **24**, 375–425.

Näätänen, R., Sams, M. and Alho, K. (1986). Mismatch negativity: an ERP sign of a cerebral mismatch process. In W.C. McCallum, R. Zappoli and F. Denoth (eds), *Cerebral Psychophysiology: Studies in Event-Related Potentials* (*EEG* Suppl. 38). Amsterdam: Elsevier, pp. 172–178.

Näätänen, R., Sams, M., Alho, K., Paavilainen, P., Reinikainen, K. and Sokolov, E.N. (1988). Frequency and location specificity of the human vertex N1 wave. *Electroencephalography and Clinical Neurophysiology*, **69**, 523–531.

Näätänen, R., Simpson, M. and Loveless, N.E. (1982). Stimulus deviance and evoked potentials. *Biological Psychology*, **14**, 53–98.

Niemi, P. and Näätänen, R. (1981). Foreperiod and simple reaction time. *Psychological Bulletin*, **89**, 133–162.

Nordby, H., Roth, W.T. and Pfefferbaum, A. (1988a). Event-related potentials to time-deviant tones. *Psychophysiology*, **25**, 249–261.

Nordby, H., Roth, W.T. and Pfefferbaum, A. (1988b). Event-related potentials to breaks in sequences of alternating pitches or interstimulus intervals. *Psychophysiology*, **25**, 262–268.

Nyman, G., Alho, K., Laurinen, P., Paavilainen, P., Radil, T., Reinikainen, K., Sams, M. and Näätänen, R. (1990). Mismatch negativity (MMN) for sequences of auditory and visual stimuli: Evidence for a mechanism specific to the auditory modality. *Electroencephalography and Clinical Neurophysiology*, **77**, 436–444.

Oakley, M. and Eason, R.G. (1987). Perceptual and motor set effects on very short-latency components of VERs. *Society for Neuroscience Abstracts*, **13**, 653.

Oatman, L.C. and Anderson, B.W. (1977). Effects of visual attention on tone burst evoked auditory potentials. *Experimental Neurology*, **57**, 200–211.

O'Gorman, J.G. and Lloyd, J.E.M. (1984). Electrodermal orienting to stimulus omission. *Physiological Psychology*, **12**, 147–152.

Öhman, A. (1979). The orienting response, attention, and learning: an information processing perspective. In H.D. Kimmel, E.H. van Olst and J.F. Orlebeke (eds), *The Orienting Reflex in Humans*. Hillsdale, NJ: Erlbaum, pp. 443–472.

Okita, T. (1981). Slow negative shifts of the human event-related potential associated with selective information processing. *Biological Psychology*, **12**, 63–75.

Onishi, S. and Davis, H. (1968). Effects of duration and rise time of tone bursts on evoked V potentials. *Journal of the Acoustical Society of America*, **44**, 582–591.

Ornitz, E.M., Guthrie, D., Kaplan, A.R., Lane, S.J. and Norman, R.J. (1986). Maturation of startle modulation. *Psychophysiology*, **23**, 624–634.

Ornitz, E.M., Guthrie, D., Lane, S.J. and Sugiyama, T. (1990). Maturation of startle facilitation by sustained prestimulation. *Psychophysiology*, **27**, 298–308.

Osman, A., Bashore, T., Coles, M.G.H., Donchin, E. and Meyer, D. E. (1988). A psychophysiological study of response preparation based on partial information. *Psychophysiology*, **25**, 426.

Oswald, I. (1962). Attention and imagery. In I. Oswald, *Sleeping and Waking*. New York: Elsevier.

Paavilainen, P., Cammann, R., Alho, K., Reinikainen, K., Sams, M. and Näätänen, R. (1987). Event-related potentials to pitch change in an auditory stimulus sequence during sleep. In R. Johnson, J.W. Rohrbaugh and R. Parasuraman (eds), *Current*

Research in Event-Related Brain Potentials (*EEG* Suppl. 40). Amsterdam: Elsevier, pp. 246–255.

Paavilainen, P., Karlsson, M.L., Reinikainen, K. and Näätänen, R. (1989). Mismatch negativity to change in spatial location of an auditory stimulus. *Electroencephalography and Clinical Neurophysiology*, **73**, 129–141.

Pantev, C., Hoke, M., Lütkenhöner, B. and Lehnertz, K. (1989). Tonotopic organization of the auditory cortex: pitch versus frequency representation. *Science*, **246**, 486–488.

Parasuraman, R. (1980). Effects of information processing demands on slow negative shift latencies and N100 amplitude in selective and divided attention. *Biological Psychology*, **11**, 217–233.

Pellizone, M., Hari, R., Mäkelä, J.P., Huttunen, J., Ahlfors, S. and Hämäläinen, M. (1987). Cortical origin of middle-latency auditory evoked responses in man. *Neuroscience Letters*, **82**, 303–307.

Perlstein, W.M. (1989). *Evoked-Potential and Magnitude Estimation Concomitants of Prepulse Inhibition of Blink in Control and Psychosis-Prone Subjects*. Unpublished masters thesis, University of Delaware, Newark.

Perlstein, W.M., Fiorito, E., Simons, R.F. and Graham, F.K. (1989). Prestimulation effects on reflex blink and EPs in normal and schizotypal subjects. *Psychophysiology*, **26**, S48.

Perrault, N. and Picton, T.W. (1984). Event-related potentials recorded from the scalp and nasopharynx. I. N1 and P2. *Electroencephalography and Clinical Neurophysiology*, **59**, 177–194.

Picton, T.W., Campbell, K.R., Baribeau-Braun, J. and Proulx, G.B. (1978). The neurophysiology of human attention: a tutorial review. In J. Requin (ed.), *Attention and Performance*, vol. VII. Hillsdale, NJ: Erlbaum, pp. 429–467.

Picton, T.W. and Hillyard, S.A. (1974). Human auditory evoked potentials. II. Effects of attention. *Electroencephalography and Clinical Neurophysiology*, **36**, 191–200.

Picton, T.W., Hillyard, S.A. and Galambos, R. (1976). Habituation and attention in the auditory system. In W.D. Keidel and W.D. Neff (eds), *Handbook of Sensory Physiology:* vol. 5, Pt. 3, *Auditory System: Clinical and Special Topics*. Berlin: Springer-Verlag, pp. 343–389.

Picton, T.W., Hillyard, S.A., Galambos, R. and Schiff, M. (1971). Human auditory attention: a central or peripheral process? *Science*, **173**, 351–353.

Picton, T.W., Hillyard, S.A., Krausz, H.I., Galambos, R. (1974). Human auditory evoked potentials. I: Evaluation of components. *Electroencephalography and Clinical Neurophysiology*, **36**, 179–190.

Picton, T.W., Rodriguez, R.T., Linden, R.D. and Maiste, A.C. (1985). The neurophysiology of human hearing. *Human Communication Canada*, **9**, 127–136.

Picton, T.W., Skinner, C.R., Champagne, S.C., Kellett, A.J.C. and Maiste, A.C. (1987). Potentials evoked by the sinusoidal modulation of the amplitude of frequency of a tone. *Journal of the Acoustical Society of America*, **82**(1), 165–178.

Picton, T.W., Stapells, D.R. and Campbell, K.B. (1981). Auditory evoked potentials from the human cochlea and brainstem. *Journal of Octolaryngology*, **10** (Suppl. 9), 1–41.

Picton, T.W., Woods, D.L. and Proulx, G.B. (1978a). Human auditory sustained potentials. I: The nature of the response. *Electroencephalography and Clinical Neurophysiology*, **45**, 186–197.

Picton, T.W., Woods, D.L. and Proulx, G.B. (1978b). Human auditory sustained potentials. II: Stimulus relationships. *Electroencephalography and Clinical Neurophysiology*, **45**, 198–210.

Polich, J. (1987). Comparison of P300 from a passive tone sequence paradigm and an active discrimination task. *Psychophysiology*, **24**, 41–46.

Posner, M.I. (1978). *Chronometric Explorations of Mind*. Hillsdale, NJ: Erlbaum.

Posner, M.I. and Cohen, Y. (1984). Components of visual orienting. In H. Bouma and D.G. Bowhuis (eds), *Attention and Performance*, vol. X. Hillsdale, NJ: Erlbaum, pp. 531–556.
Posner, M.I., Peterson, S.E., Fox, P.T. and Raichle, M.E. (1988). Localization of cognitive operations in the human brain. *Science*, **240**, 1627–1631.
Posner, M.I., Snyder, C.R.R. and Davidson, B.J. (1980). Attention and the detection of signals. *Journal of Experimental Psychology: General*, **109**, 160–174.
Poulsen, T. (1981). Loudness of tone pulses in a free field. *Journal of the Acoustical Society of America*, **69**, 1786–1790.
Putnam, L.E. (1975). *Mechanisms of Startle Modification by Background Acoustic Stimulation.* Unpublished doctoral dissertation, University of Wisconsin, Madison.
Putnam, L.E. (1990). Great expectations: anticipatory responses of the heart and brain. In J.W. Rohrbaugh, R. Parasuraman and R. Johnson (eds), *Event-Related Brain Potentials: Basic Issues and Applications.* New York: Oxford University Press, pp. 109–129.
Putnam, L.E. and Roth, W.T. (1988). Distinguishing between orienting, defense, and startle: heart rate, event-related potential, and eyeblink responses to intense stimuli. *Psychophysiology*, **25**, 427 (abstract).
Putnam, L.E. and Roth, W.T. (1990). Effects of stimulus repetition, duration, and rise time on startle blink and automatically elicited P300. *Psychophysiology*, **27**, 275–297.
Reite, M., Teale, P., Zimmerman, J., Davis, K. and Whalen, J. (1988). Source location of a 50 msec latency auditory evoked field component. *Electroencephalography and Clinical Neurophysiology*, **70**, 490–498.
Reiter, L.A. and Ison, J.R. (1977). Inhibition of the human eyeblink reflex: An evaluation of the sensitivity of the Wendt–Yerkes method for threshold detection. *Journal of Experimental Psychology: Human Perception and Performance*, **3**, 325–336.
Renault, B. and Lesevre, N. (1978). Topographical study of the emitted potential obtained after omission of an expected visual stimulus. In D.A. Otto (ed.), *Multidisciplinary Perspectives in Event Related Brain Potential Research.* Washington, DC: US Environmental Protection Agency, Report EPA-600/9–77–043, pp. 202–208.
Ribot, T. (1896). *The Psychology of Attention.* Chicago: Open Court.
Ritter, W., Vaughan, H.G. and Costa, L.D. (1968). Orienting and habituation to auditory stimuli: a study of short term changes in average evoked responses. *Electroencephalography and Clinical Neurophysiology*, **25**, 550–556.
Roemer, R.A., Shagass, C. and Teyler, T.J. (1984). Do human evoked potentials habituate? In H.V.S. Peeke and L. Petrinovich (eds), *Habituation, Sensitization, and Behavior*. New York: Academic, pp. 325–344.
Rohrbaugh, J. (1984). The orienting reflex: performance and CNS manifestations. In R. Parasuraman and R. Davies (eds), *Varieties of Attention.* New York: Academic Press, pp. 323–373.
Rohrbaugh, J.W., Varner, J.L., Peters, J.F., Ellingson, R.J., and Eckardt, M.J. (1987). Brainstem auditory evoked potentials are unaltered during the orienting response. In R. Johnson, J.W. Rohrbaugh and R. Parasuraman (eds), *Current Trends in Event-Related Potential Research* (*EEG* Suppl. 40). Amsterdam: Elsevier, pp. 132–137.
Romani, G.L., Williamson, S.J. and Kaufman, L. (1982). Tonotopic organization of the human auditory cortex. *Science*, **216**, 1339–1340.
Rösler, F., Hasselmann, D. and Sojka, B. (1987). Central and peripheral correlates of orienting and habituation. In R. Johnson, J.W. Rohrbaugh and R. Parasuraman (eds), *Current Trends in Event-Related Potential Research* (*EEG* Suppl. 40). New York: Elsevier, pp. 366-372.
Roth, W.T. (1973). Auditory evoked response to unpredictable stimuli. *Psychophysiology*, **10**, 125–138.

Roth, W.T. (1983). A comparison of P300 and skin conductance response. In A.W.K. Gaillard and W. Ritter (eds), *Tutorials in ERP Research: Endogenous Components*. Amsterdam: North-Holland, pp. 177–199.

Roth, W.T., Blowers, G.H., Doyle, C.M. and Kopell, B.S. (1982). Auditory stimulus intensity effects on components of the late positive complex. *Electroencephalography and Clinical Neurophysiology*, **54**, 132–146.

Roth, W.T., Dorato, K.H. and Kopell, B.S. (1984). Intensity and task effects on evoked physiological responses to noise bursts. *Psychophysiology*, **21**, 466–481.

Rousey, C.L. and Reitz, W.E. (1967). Respiratory changes at auditory and visual thresholds. *Psychophysiology*, **3**, 258–281.

Ruhm, H.B. (1971). Directional sensitivity and laterality of electroencephalic responses evoked by acoustic sweep frequencies. *Journal of Auditory Research*, **XI**(1), 9–16.

Rust, J. (1976). Generalization and dishabituation of the orienting response to stimulus of lower intensity. *Psychophysiological Psychology*, **4**, 99–101.

Rust, J. (1977). Habituation and the orienting response in the auditory cortical evoked potential. *Psychophysiology*, **14**, 123–126.

Sakano, N. and Pickenhain, L. (1968). Evoked response and startle blink to strong acoustic stimuli of different signal meaning. *Psychophysiology*, **1**, 1–13.

Salamy, A. and McKean, C.M. (1977). Habituation and dishabituation of cortical and brainstem evoked potentials. *The International Journal of Neuroscience*, **7**, 175–182.

Salamy, A., McKean, C.M. and Buda, F. (1975). Maturational changes in auditory transmissions as reflected in human brainstem potentials. *Brain Research*, **96**, 361–366.

Sams, M., Alho, K. and Näätänen, R. (1983). Sequential effects in the ERP in discriminating two stimuli. *Biological Psychology*, **17**, 41–58.

Sams, M., Alho, K. and Näätänen, R. (1984). Short-term habituation and dishabituation of the mismatch negativity of the ERP. *Psychophysiology*, **21**, 434–441.

Sams, M., Hämäläinen, M., Antervo, A., Kaukoranta, E., Reinikainen, K. and Hari, R. (1985). Cerebral neuromagnetic responses evoked by short auditory stimuli. *Electroencephalography and Clinical Neurophysiology*, **61**, 254–266.

Sams, M., Paavilainen, P., Alho, K. and Näätänen, R. (1985b). Auditory frequency discrimination and event-related potentials. *Electroencephalography and Clinical Neurophysiology*, **62**, 437–448.

Sanes, J.N. (1984). Voluntary movement and excitability of cutaneous eyeblink reflexes. *Psychophysiology*, **21**, 653–664.

Sanes, J.N. and Ison, J.R. (1979). Conditioning auditory stimuli and the cutaneous eyeblink reflex in humans: differential effects according to oligosynaptic or polysynaptic central pathways. *Electroencephalography and Clinical Neurophysiology*, **47**, 546–555.

Schneider, W. and Shiffrin, R. (1977). Controlled and automatic human information processing. I: Detection, search, and attention. *Psychological Review*, **84**, 1–66.

Schwent, V.L., Hillyard, S.A. and Galambos, R. (1976). Selective attention and the auditory vertex potential. II: Effects of signal intensity and masking noise. *Electroencephalography and Clinical Neurophysiology*, **40**, 615–622.

Schwent, V.L., Snyder, E. and Hillyard, S.A. (1976). Auditory evoked potentials during multichannel selective listening: role of pitch and localization cues. *Journal of Experimental Psychology: Human Perception and Performance*, **2**, 313–325.

Shaw, M.L. (1984). Division of attention among spatial locations: a fundamental difference between detection of letters and detection of luminance increments. In H. Bouma and D.G. Bouwhuis (eds), *Attention and Performance*, vol. X. Hillsdale, NJ: Erlbaum, pp. 109–121.

Shiffrin, R.M. and Grantham, D.W. (1974). Can attention be allocated to sensory modalities? *Perception and Psychophysics*, **15**, 460–474.

Shiffrin, R. and Schneider, W. (1977). Controlled and automatic human information processing. II: Perceptual learning, automatic attending, and a general theory. *Psychological Review*, **84**, 127–190.

Shulman, G.L., Remington, R.W. and McLean, J.P. (1979). Moving attention through visual space. *Journal of Experimental Psychology: Human Perception and Performance*, **5**, 522–526.

Siddle, D.A.T. (ed.) (1983). *Orienting and Habituation: Perspectives in Human Research*. New York: Wiley.

Siddle, D.A.T. (1985). Effects of stimulus omission and stimulus change on dishabituation of the skin conductance response. *Journal of Experimental Psychology: Learning, Memory, and Cognition*, **11**, 206–216.

Siddle, D.A.T. and Heron, P.A. (1977). Effects of length of training and amount of tone intensity change on amplitude of autonomic components of the orienting response. *Australian Journal of Psychology*, **29**, 7–16.

Siddle, D.A.T. and Hirschhorn, T. (1986). Effects of stimulus omission and stimulus novelty on dishabituation of the skin conductance response. *Psychophysiology*, **23**, 309–314.

Siddle, D.A.T., Kyriacou, C., Heron, P.A. and Matthews, W.A. (1979). Effects of changes in verbal stimuli on the skin conductance response component of the orienting response. *Psychophysiology*, **16**, 34–40.

Siddle, D.A.T., Remington, B., Kuiack, M. and Haines, E. (1983). Stimulus omission and dishabituation of the skin conductance response. *Psychophysiology*, **20**, 136–145.

Siddle, D., Stephenson, D. and Spinks, J.A. (1983). Elicitation and habituation of the orienting response. In D. Siddle (ed.), *Orienting and Habituation: Perspectives in Human Research*. New York: Wiley, pp. 109–182.

Silverstein, L.D., Graham, F.K. and Bohlin, G. (1981). Selective attention effects on the reflex blink. *Psychophysiology*, **18**, 240–247.

Silverstein, L.D., Graham, F.K. and Calloway, J.M. (1980). Preconditioning and excitability of the human orbicularis oculi reflex as a function of state. *Electroencephalography and Clinical Neurophysiology*, **48**, 406–417.

Simons, R.F. (1988). Event-related slow brain potentials: a perspective from ANS psychophysiology. In P.K. Ackles, J.R. Jennings and M.G.H. Coles (eds), *Advances in Psychophysiology*, vol. 3. Greenwich, CT: JAI Press, pp. 223–267.

Simons, R.F., Balaban, M.T., Macy, M.H. and Graham, F.K. (1986). Heart rate, blink, and ERPs to modality-defined targets and novels. *Psychophysiology*, **23**, 461–462 (abstract).

Simons, R.F., Rockstroh, R., Elbert, T., Fiorito, E., Lutzenberger, W. and Birbaumer, N. (1987). Evocation and habituation of autonomic and event-related potential responses in a nonsignal environment. *Journal of Psychophysiology*, **1**, 45–59.

Simson, R., Vaughan, H.G. and Ritter, W. (1976). The scalp topography of potentials associated with missing visual and auditory stimuli. *Electroencephalography and Clinical Neurophysiology*, **40**, 33–42.

Skinner, J.E. and Yingling, C.D. (1977). Central gating mechanisms that regulate event-related potentials and behavior. *Progress in Clinical Neurophysiology*, **1**, 30–69.

Skolnick, B.E., Walrath, L.C. and Stern, J.A. (1979). Evaluation of temporal vasomotor components of orienting and defensive responses. In H.D. Kimmel, E.H. Van Olst and J.F. Orlebeke (eds), *The Orienting Reflex in Humans*. Hillsdale, NJ: Erlbaum, pp. 269–276.

Snyder, E. and Hillyard, S.A. (1976). Long-latency evoked potentials to irrelevant, deviant stimuli. *Behavioral Psychology*, **16**, 319–331.

Sokolov, E.N. (1960). Neuronal models and the orienting reflex. In M.A.B. Brazier (ed.), *The Central Nervous System and Behavior*. New York: Josiah Macy Jr. Foundation, pp. 187–276.

Sokolov, E.N. (1963). *Perception and the Conditioned Reflex*. New York: Macmillan.

Sokolov, Y.N. (1966). Orienting reflex as information regulator. In A. Leontiev, A. Luria and S. Smirnov (eds), *Psychological Research in the USSR*, vol. 1. Moscow: Progress, pp. 334–360.

Sokolov, E.N. (1969). The modeling properties of the nervous system. In M. Cole and I. Maltzman (eds), *A Handbook of Contemporary Soviet Psychology*. New York: Basic Books, pp. 671–704.

Sokolov, E.N. (1975). The neuronal mechanisms of the orienting reflex. In E.N. Sokolov and O.S. Vinogradova (eds), *The Neuronal Mechanisms of the Orienting Reflex*. Hillsdale, NJ: Erlbaum, pp. 217–235.

Spinks, J.A. and Siddle, D. (1983). The functional significance of the orienting response. In D. Siddle (ed.), *Orienting and Habituation: Perspectives in Human Research*. New York: Wiley, pp. 237–314.

Squires, K.C., Donchin, E., Herning, R.I. and McCarthy, G. (1977). On the influence of task relevance and stimulus probability in event-related-potential components. *Electroencephalography and Clinical Neurophysiology*, **42**, 1–14.

Squires, N.K., Squires, K.C. and Hillyard, S.A. (1975). Two varieties of long-latency positive waves evoked by unpredictable auditory stimuli in man. *Electroencephalography and Clinical Neurophysiology*, **38**, 387–401.

Stapells, D.R., Linden, R.D., Suffield, J.B., Hamel, G. and Picton, T.W. (1984). Human auditory steady state potentials. *Ear Hearing*, **5**, 105–114.

Stenfert Kroese, B. and Siddle, D.A.T. (1983). Effects of attention-demanding task on amplitude and habituation of the electrodermal orienting response. *Psychophysiology*, **20**, 128–135.

Stephenson, D. and Siddle, D.A.T. (1983). Theories of habituation. In D.A.T. Siddle (ed.), *Orienting and Habituation: Perspectives in Human Research*. New York: Wiley, pp. 183–236.

Sternberg, S. (1969). The discovery of processing stages: extensions of Donders' method. In W.G. Koster (ed.), *Attention and Performance*, vol. II. Amsterdam: North-Holland, pp. 276–315.

Stitt, C.L., Hoffman, H.S., Marsh, R.R. and Schwartz, G.M. (1976). Modification of the pigeon's visual startle reaction by the sensory environment. *Journal of Comparative and Physiological Psychology*, **90**, 601–619.

Tansley, B.W. and Suffield, J.B. (1983). Time course of adaptation and recovery of channels selectively sensitive to frequency and amplitude modulation. *Journal of the Acoustical Society of America*, **74**, 765–775.

Thompson, R.F., Berry, S.D., Rinaldi, P.C. and Berger, T.W. (1979). Habituation and the orienting reflex: the dual-process theory revisited. In H.D. Kimmel, E.H. van Olst and J.F. Orlebeke (eds), *The Orienting Reflex in Humans*. Hillsdale, NJ: Erlbaum, pp. 21–60.

Thompson, R.F., Groves, P.M., Teyler, T.J. and Roemer, R.A. (1973). A dual-process theory of habituation: theory and behavior. In H.V.S. Peeke and M.J. Herz (eds), *Habituation. I: Behavioral Studies*. New York: Academic Press, pp. 239–271.

Thompson, R.F. and Spencer, W.A. (1966). Habituation: a model phenomenon for the study of neuronal substrates of behavior. *Psychological Review*, **73**, 16–43.

Treisman, A.M. (1960). Contextual cues in selective listening. *Quarterly Journal of Experimental Psychology*, **12**, 242–248.

Treisman, A.M. and Gelade, G.A. (1980). A feature-integration theory of attention. *Cognitive Psychology*, **12**, 97–136.

Turpin, G. and Siddle, D.A.T. (1983). Effects of stimulus intensity on cardiovascular activity. *Psychophysiology*, **13**, 231–235.

Tursky, B., Schwartz, G.E. and Crider, A. (1970). Differential patterns of heart rate and skin resistance during a digit-transformation task. *Journal of Experimental Psychology*, **83**, 451–457.

Unger, S.M. (1964). Habituation of the vasoconstrictive orienting reaction. *Journal of Experimental Psychology*, **67**, 11–18.

Velasco, M. and Velasco, F. (1986). Subcortical correlates of the somatic, auditory and visual vertex activities. II: Referential EEG responses. *Electroencephalography and Clinical Neurophysiology*, **63**, 62–67.

Verbaten, M.N., Roelofs, J.W., Sjouw, W., Slangen, J.L. (1986). Habituation of early and late visual ERP components and the orienting reaction: the effect of stimulus information. *International Journal of Psychophysiology*, **3**, 287–298.

Voronin, L. G. and Sokolov, E. N. (1960). Cortical mechanisms of the orienting reflex and its relation to the conditioned reflex. In H.H. Jasper and G.D. Smirnov (eds), *The Moscow Colloquium on Electroencephalography of Higher Nervous Activity* (*EEG* Suppl. 13). Amsterdam: Elsevier, pp. 335–344.

Wada, S. and Starr, A. (1983). Generation of auditory brain stem responses (ABRs). III: Effects of lesions of the superior olive, lateral lemniscus and inferior colliculus on the ABR in guinea pig. *Electroencephalography and Clinical Neurophysiology*, **56**, 352–366.

Wagner, A.R. (1976). Priming in STM: an information processing mechanism for self-generated or retrieval-generated depression in performance. In T.J. Tighe and R.N. Leaton (eds), *Habituation: Perspectives from Child Development, Animal Behavior and Neurophysiology*. Hillsdale, NJ: Erlbaum, pp. 95–128.

Wakefield, G.H. and Viemeister, N.F. (1984). Selective adaptation to linear frequency modulated sweeps: evidence for direction specific FM channels? *Journal of the Acoustical Society of America*, **75**, 1588–1592.

Walter, W.G., Cooper, R., Aldrige, V.J., McCallum, W.C. and Winter, A.L. (1964). Contingent negative variation: an electric sign of sensory-motor association and expectancy in the human brain. *Nature*, **203**, 380–384.

Watson, A.R. (1986). Temporal sensitivity. In K.R. Boff, L. Kaufman and J.P. Thomas (eds), *Handbook of Perception and Human Performance*, vol. 1, *Sensory Processes and Perception*. New York: Wiley, pp. 6.1–6.43.

Whitlow, J.W. (1975). Short-term memory in habituation and dishabituation. *Journal of Experimental Psychology: Animal Behavior Processes*, **104**, 189–206.

Wilson, C.L., Babb, T.L., Halgren, E. and Crandall, P.H. (1983). Visual receptive field and response properties of neurons in human temporal lobe and visual pathways. *Brain*, **106**, 473–502.

Woldorff, M.G. (1989). *Auditory Selective Attention in Humans: Analysis of Mechanisms Using Event-Related Brain Potentials*. Doctoral dissertation, University of California, San Diego.

Woldorff, M., Hackley, S.A. and Hillyard, S.A. (1989). Is the mismatch negativity wave of the human auditory ERP independent of attention? *Society for Neuroscience Abstracts*, **15**, 478.

Woldorff, M., Hansen, J.C. and Hillyard, S.A. (1987). Evidence for effects of selective attention in the midlatency range of the human auditory event-related potential. In R. Johnson, J.W. Rohrbaugh and R. Parasuraman (eds), *Current Trends in Event-Related Potential Research* (*EEG* Suppl. 40). Amsterdam: Elsevier, pp. 146–154.

Wolpaw, J.R. and Penry, J.K. (1975). A temporal component of the auditory evoked response. *Electroencephalography and Clinical Neurophysiology*, **39**, 609–620.

Woods, D.L. (1990). The physiological basis of selective attention: implications of event-related potential studies. In R. Johnson, J.W. Rohrbaugh and R. Parasuraman (eds), *Event-Related Brain Potentials: Basic Issues and Applications*. New York: Oxford University Press, pp. 178–209.

Woods, D.L., Clayworth, C.C., Knight, R.T., Simpson, G.V. and Naesser, M.A. (1987). Generators of middle- and long-latency evoked potentials: implications from studies of patients with bitemporal lesions. *Electroencephalography and Clinical Neurophysiology*, **68**, 132–148.

Woods, D.L. and Hillyard, S.A. (1978). Attention at the cocktail party: Brainstem evoked responses reveal no peripheral gating. In D. Otto (ed.), *New Perspectives in Event-Related Potential Research*. Washington, DC: US Government Printing Office, Report EPA-600/9-77-043, pp. 230–233.

Worden, F.G. (1966). Attention and auditory electrophysiology. In E. Stellar and J.M. Sprague (eds), *Progress in Physiological Psychology*. New York: Academic Press, pp. 45–116.

Worden, F.G. (1973). Auditory habituation. In H.V.S. Peeke and M.J. Herz (eds), *Habituation*, vol. 2. New York: Academic Press, pp. 109–137.

Yamada, F., Yamasaki, K. and Miyata, Y. (1979). Lead-stimulation effects on human startle eyeblink recorded by an electrode hookup. *Japanese Psychological Research*, **21**, 174–180.

Yaremko, R.M., Blair, M.W. and Leckert, B.T. (1970). The orienting reflex to changes in a conceptual stimulus dimension. *Psychonomic Science*, **22**, 115–116.

Yaremko, R.M. and Keleman, K. (1972). The orienting reflex and amount and direction of conceptual novelty. *Psychonomic Science*, **27**, 195.

Chapter 4

Preparation for Action

Jean Requin
Cognitive Neuroscience Unit
Laboratory of Functional Neuroscience, CNRS,
13402 Marseille, Cedex 9, France 13402
and
Jasper Brener and Christopher Ring
Department of Psychology, State University of New York,
Stony Brook, NY 11790, USA

ABSTRACT

Preparation for action is examined from both metabolic and neurophysiological perspectives. The relation between behavioral uncertainty and energetic preparation is discussed relative to concepts of attention, motoric plans, and anticipated energy expenditure. Neurophysiological changes during phasic preparation, just prior to movement execution are then discussed in detail.

Handbook of Cognitive Psychophysiology: Central and Autonomic Nervous System Approaches.
Edited by J. R. Jennings and M. G. H. Coles.

INTRODUCTION

THE CONCEPT OF MOTOR PREPARATION

A large number of our gestures, postures and many aspects of our daily behavior do not seem to be designed to reach a behaviorally significant goal immediately, but rather to prepare for a subsequent action, which will make it eventually possible to reach such a goal. Indeed, it seems clear that every overt expression of behavior is the product of a series of antedating processes. The onsets of these processes vary both in their temporal remoteness from the external manifestations of motor activity and in the specificity with which they ready the organism for the particular pattern of muscular activation that is to follow.

As an explanatory concept, 'motor preparation' has a teleological flavor because it insinuates that activity in the present is determined by events in the future. To prepare for future events implies an expectation of these events: an internal representation of what is going to happen. The teleological problem may be overcome by viewing expectations as the memory products of past experiences in similar contexts. Nevertheless, the role attributed to preparation in determining present behavior identifies a conspicuous cognitive facet of this concept. But preparation also has many tangible manifestations that render it responsive to experimental dissection.

It is possible to trace the processes implicated in preparing the organism for a specific action to phylogenetic sources. Certain species such as dogs react to danger by increasing motor activity, whereas others like rabbits and opposums react to similar environmental threats by freezing. These species-characteristic defense responses determine the rate at which members of a species will learn to deal with the defense requirements dictated by a specific set of environmental demands (Bolles, 1970). Thus rabbits will rapidly learn to avoid a noxious stimulus by freezing, whereas dogs will be less successful with this requirement but will rapidly learn to avoid a stimulus by executing a vigorous movement. The notion of a phyletic motor preparedness is encapsulated in the processes of 'Instinctive Drift' (Breland and Breland, 1961). These authors describe the difficulties of training animals to perform acts that are different from those for which they have been phylogenetically prepared. For example, cows cannot be trained to run for food. Like other ruminants, they have been prepared by evolution to stand rather than run when foraging.

In many cases, such preprogrammed motor tendencies are difficult to modify. Nevertheless, the neural mechanisms by which phyletic motor preparedness are realized do admit influence from ontogenetic processes. Sometimes these influences are time-locked to certain stages of development. Thus, by hearing mature members of their species sing (Marler, 1970), birds are prepared to sing a certain song while they are still fledglings. This state of preparedness is maintained throughout the animal's lifetime and expressed for the first time several months after it has been established, when the bird reaches an appropriate state of maturation.

In all but the most primitive species, the motor system is constantly being reprogrammed to meet the changing survival requirements of the environment. Such motor learning defines a fundamental ontogenetic process by which motor activity is prepared. The products of learning are realized in motor programs or plans which thereafter are brought into service when environmental contexts similar to the learning environment are encountered. When specific demands are met in such environments, motor responses are generated according to the learned programs. These encounters activate the final phase of motor preparation in which an appropriate variant of the adaptive response is computed and the effector system is activated. This chapter deals with the latter stages of motor preparation: in particular, the tonic stage of preparation which is activated upon encountering the demand situation and the phasic stage which is activated when a specific demand occurs.

The idea of distinguishing between two functional phases of goal-directed behavior has been emphasized in the ethological description of animal behavior. The first (consummatory) class includes acts which end when a biologically significant goal is reached—such as food consumption or sexual intercourse. The second (appetitive) class includes activities which prepare for the achievement of meaningful actions of the first class. They include such activities as prey foraging and courtship which, for example, in the case of courtship, may precede the consummatory act by periods of weeks.

It is also usually possible to distinguish between the preparatory and target phases of simple activities which may be completed in a period of seconds, such as taking hold of a glass on a table. In this case, the reaching movement of the arm may be described as preparatory to the target movement of grasping the glass. The preparatory phase of this action is quite similar to the reaching movement executed in, for example, picking up a pencil. However, if one observes the moving hand carefully, one can see that the fingers are already positioned to grasp either a glass or a pencil before the reaching movement starts. This prepositioning of the fingers according to the shape of the target to be grasped even before the target is reached identifies a preparatory component of the reaching movement. Moreover, the extension of the arm to reach the glass is accompanied and even preceded by a backward movement of either the trunk or the whole body that compensates for the change in the spatial distribution of body weight, thus making the projection of the center of gravity on to the ground stable. These postural adjustments that anticipate the equilibrium perturbation resulting from voluntary movements form an important aspect of motor preparation (Massion and Dufossé, 1988).

The distinction between the 'preparatory' and 'target' phases of activities is, of course, rather gross and, one may argue, arbitrary in that it may only be useful when isolated segments of behavior, such as those studied in the laboratory, are considered. When a natural stream of behavior is examined, one can say that any part of the behavioral sequence is preparatory to the following one: watching the prey is preparatory to catching it, that is preparatory to eating it, that is preparatory to restoring bodily energy reserves, that is preparatory to starting another similar behavioral sequence, and so on. Therefore, the main issue is not one of separating two different kinds of behavioral activities, that are always intermixed, but of establishing that at any moment a large part of the present activity of an organism is devoted to preparing for subsequent behavior. Such preparatory processes include not only overt movements which any observer can see, but also alterations in the functioning of the nervous system and of the internal organs that are necessary for the expression of the target act. These preparatory processes form the subject of this chapter.

In order for motor activity to meet the demands of a situation, several conditions must be fulfilled. Firstly, the potential survival threats or benefits of the situation must be correctly interpreted. Only when these behavioral implications have been determined can a relevant action be identified and a pattern of muscular activation be composed to meet the specific requirements of the prevailing conditions. Such motor programming processes, which specify the temporal and kinetic features of the forthcoming act, occur immediately prior to muscular activation and continue until the release of the action. Their close temporal proximity to muscular activation may be considered adaptive. Earlier specification of movement features would be beneficial only to the extent that the environment demands invariant responses.

No less important to the execution of effective performance is the regulation of processes concerned with mobilizing and delivering energy to fuel the metabolic needs of the muscular activity. However, unlike the temporokinetic requirements for an effective response which should be precisely calibrated to meet environmental demands, the energetic requirements may be more broadly specified. Their only essential feature is that the levels of energy mobilization and delivery are adequate to support the metabolic demands of effective behavior. Excessive energy mobilization does carry long-term costs, but there are also benefits that accrue from being prepared for unexpected and metabolically-costly demands. Whereas preparing appropriate movement features determines whether or not the forthcoming act will be effective, energetic preparations may be said to serve a permissive function.

Since local oxygen supplies and energy stores are very limited, increases in energy expenditure can only be sustained if the necessary elements of tissue combustion are transported to the implicated tissues. The term 'energy mobilization' is used here to refer to this supply process which involves two main steps: (i) the conversion of bodily energy stores to a usable and transportable form; (ii) increased cardiopulmonary activity to deliver more energy substrates and oxygen to active tissues and carry away and eliminate metabolic byproducts. In many cases these energy mobilization processes are activated prior to the energy expenditure stage and, on occasion, energy mobilization may increase without a subsequent increase in the rate of energy expenditure.

PREPARATION AS THE REDUCTION OF UNCERTAINTY

The notion of 'uncertainty' is useful in interpreting the role of preparation. Whatever the accuracy and extent of our memories, their ability to predict (anticipate) the events for which preparations should be made is limited. The specific timing and features of the future events will remain more or less uncertain until the events themselves occur. Consequently, preparation—defined as the processes by which organisms are readied for perceiving future events and reacting to them—can be broadly considered as a behavioral mechanism for dealing with uncertainty.

For example, experimental data are consistent with the hypothesis that the degree of behavioral uncertainty determines the extent to which energetic preparations are non-specific and excessive in relation to the energy demands of the coping activities that will emerge. This uncertainty is likely to be maximal when the organism encounters a novel situation. Since a coping response has not yet been specified, its energy requirements cannot be estimated. At this early stage of behavioral adaptation, the presumed biological function of energy mobilization is to fuel the processes of generating a behavioral adaptation to the new situation while maintaining an energy reserve for rapid and costly responses that might be demanded. However, with repeated or continued exposure to the situation, the energy mobilization process becomes more attuned to the metabolic requirements of the coping response which emerges. It will be argued here that this progression, which reflects the formulation of actions that are appropriate to the prevailing conditions, and therefore the reduction of behavioral uncertainty, is associated with modulation of activity in pathways which link energy mobilization to striate muscular activity.

In particular, it is proposed that during the initial stages of adapting to a set of environmental contingencies, neural structures responsible for decoding the environmental contingencies and generating appropriate behavior exert a feedforward influence on structures associated with the regulation of energy mobilization. This gives rise to energy mobilization levels that are excessive in relation to energy demand. However, as behavioral uncertainty is resolved and the adaptation to situational demands becomes more precise and automatic, activity in these feedforward pathways wanes and energy mobilization comes to reflect the actual metabolic costs of the behavior. It is suggested that in this mature stage of behavioral adaptation, when uncertainty has reached minimal levels, energy mobilization processes are driven primarily by feedback and autoregulatory processes elicited by the striate muscular adaptation which has emerged (Brener, 1986a).

The effects on energy mobilization of reductions in behavioral uncertainty which result from learning may be examined either longitudinally as subjects acquire a coping response, or cross-sectionally by comparing the energy mobilization responses of subjects who have differential experience (novices and experts) in the performance of a task. It would be expected that highly practiced subjects will exhibit energy mobilization responses that are more precisely attuned to the metabolic requirements associated with meeting task demands than relative novices. Two other experimental paradigms have been used to examine the effects of uncertainty on elements of the energy mobilization response. One of these involves the provision of information to reduce uncertainties that are implicit in the situation; for example, presenting subjects with stimuli that signal the impending occurrence of avoidable electric shocks (Sherwood, Brener and Moncur, 1983; Sherwood *et al.*, 1988). The rationale of this method is that the provision of external information about the times of occurrence of biologically-significant environmental events reduces the burden on the system by limiting preparatory processes to periods when there is a high probability that a response will be required. Therefore the provision of extra information simplifies the process of computing an adequate coping response. A related method is to vary the difficulty of the task (e.g. Turner, 1989): the greater the difficulty, the greater the uncertainty. Both methods would be expected to influence the energy mobilization response in predictable ways and through the pathways that have been mentioned above and are described in greater detail below.

The concept of uncertainty also provides a basis for the reaction time (RT) paradigm which is currently used to study preparatory processes associated with discrete motor acts. The idea here is that, when a subject has to respond as quickly as possible to a stimulus by making a movement, the time to initiate the response is the time necessary to identify the stimulus and to select and program the corresponding movement: in other words, to process information provided by the stimulus. This notion of information is equivalent to that of uncertainty in the sense that to be fully informed means to be fully certain of the required response and to be not informed at all means to be completely uncertain. Chronometric measurement of the processes associated with response production provides information about the subject's state of uncertainty. If one supposes that he knows exactly when the stimulus will occur and what exactly are the stimulus and the corresponding response, he will be able to synchronize his response to the stimulus. In such a case, the RT would theoretically be nil. Conversely, if one supposes that the subject does not know anything about the timing and the significance of the stimulus, he has no reason to do anything when it occurs. In this case, the RT would theoretically be infinitely long. However, these conditions of complete certainty or uncertainty are not realistic. Because of inaccuracies in time estimation and the imperfection of memory, it is not feasible to predict exactly the timing of stimulus presentation and the features of both stimulus and response. Therefore a perfect anticipation of these events is impossible. On the other hand, an entirely naive subject will find some clues in the context of the experimental situation that will provide a basis for anticipating what he will have to do.

The study of preparation for discrete responses relies strongly on chronometric methods. These methods permit inferences to be drawn about the structural and functional features of information processing from experimentally induced changes in RT. Although the rationales and methodological background of this inferential approach cannot be specified and discussed here (see, for instance, Sanders, 1980, and Meyer *et al.*, 1988, for a review), it should be noted that a decisive impulse in the evolution of chronometric analyses of cognition resulted from the development of the 'additive factor method' (Sternberg, 1969). This remains an exceptionally fruitful tool for studying preparatory processes. However, for about ten years, the main assumption underlying this method—that a set of functionally distinct, serially organized, discrete processing stages take place during RT—has been increasingly challenged. On the basis of experimental data provided by chronometric studies, as well as newly-emerging concepts about brain organization as parallel-distributed neuronal networks (Mountcastle, 1978; McClelland and Rumelhart, 1986; Requin, Riehle and Seal, 1988, 1989), information processing models have been proposed which assume overlapping stages between which information can be continuously transmitted (Eriksen and Schultz, 1979; McClelland, 1979; see also Meyer *et al.*, 1984, 1985, and Miller, 1982, 1983). In a clever theoretical paper, Miller (1988) has recently underlined how arbitrary is the dichotomy between the notions of discreteness and continuity in the three meanings associated with these terms: the coding of stage inputs and outputs, the transformation of information within stages, and the timing of information transmission between stages. The notions are essentially relative, depending upon the 'grain size' (the units) of the dimensions on which information quanta are scaled. Furthermore, the current and fashionable shift from serial/discrete to parallel/continuous processing models (a distinction which most often refers only to the information transmission problem) does not appear to be supported convincingly by experimental evidence. Hence, discarding discrete information processing stage models may be considered to be scientifically premature.

In the framework of the RT paradigm, the rationale of studies devoted to preparatory processes is to manipulate the subject's expectancy about the stimulus which is to occur and thus the response to be performed, by providing advance information about these events. This is accomplished by introducing a preparatory signal (S1) which provides prior information about either the timing and/or the features of the expected imperative signal (S2) and associated response (R). From changes in RT, inferences can be made about the processes by which prior information is utilized, first to adjust the timing of preparation to be ready at the right time—that is, to solve the so-called 'time uncertainty' problem—and, second, to make sensory and motor systems more efficient for perceiving S2 and performing R—that is, to solve the so-called 'event uncertainty' problem.

When the preparatory processes presumed to act selectively upon response processing are considered, three main kinds of procedures for providing advance information to the subject are used. In the first one, the differences—whatever they are, but which pre-exist before the experiment—in the strength of the association between stimuli and responses are exploited to vary the subject's expectancy about the response to be made when a given stimulus is presented. This is the rationale of S–R 'compatibility' studies. In the second procedure, either the number of S–R alternatives or the relative frequencies of the S–R alternatives (i.e. the statistical parameters of the distributions of stimuli and responses during a block of trials) are manipulated, so that a subject's expectancy about a given S–R alternative can be changed from block to block during the experiment. This is the rationale used in S and/or R probability studies. In the third procedure, preparatory stimuli (S1) presented on each trial provide information about the response, or some feature(s) of the response to be made, so that a subject's expectancy about this response, or these response feature(s), can be changed from trial to trial. This is the rationale of movement priming or precuing studies.

THE INTERSECTION OF PREPARATION AND ATTENTION

The concept of attention is commonly associated with processes responsible for selecting a particular stimulus, or a specific stimulus feature from the flow of sensory events in the surrounding world. The concept of preparation, on the other hand, is most often identified with the processes which intervene to select a particular response, or a specific response feature, to be performed on the environment. These definitions of the two concepts—which both refer to a similar function of selection, suggesting they have a common adaptative role in goal-directed behavior—reflect the sensory–motor dichotomy which is traditionally imposed on behavioral processes. This somewhat arbitrary division has been reinforced by information processing models which, for analytical purposes, have partitioned the sensorimotor processes involved in the stream of behavior into a series of functionally separable stages. This analytical strategy disregards the behavioral significance of the whole sequence in which the sensory and motor processes are embedded.

The evolution, in recent years, of attentional concepts, especially the swing of the pendulum from attention as an early-selective process to attention as a late-selective process, has contributed to bringing the concepts of attention and preparation closer, thus opening the possibility of linking them in an unified theoretical framework. Kahneman and Treisman (1984), for instance, have pointed out that interest in the behavioral function of selective attention has shifted progressively, during the last 15 years, from perceptual processing to motor processing, a shift related closely to a paradigmatic change. Initially, in the conceptual framework of a limited-capacity model of attention, the so-called 'filtering paradigm' was found to be increasingly unsuccessful in localizing a privileged site for selection in the information processing stage sequence. Following this, in the conceptual framework of unique or multiple attentional processors which would allocate processing 'resources' to different processing stages according to task demands, the so-called 'selective-set paradigm' has emphasized the common functional role played by modulatory processes—wherever they act in the information processing sequence—in adapting the motor output of goal-directed behaviors.

For example, neurophysiological data collected on behaving monkeys have indicated how the objective of performing efficiently an intended action first determines an appropriate motor or 'preparatory' set, which then results in an appropriate sensory or 'attentional' set. The 'enhancement' effect described by Wurtz, Goldberg and Robinson (1980) provides a good illustration of a backward-cascade consequence of goal-directed behavioral demands. The basic finding is that specific stimulus-related neurons of the superficial layers of the superior colliculus yield responses to a visual stimulus presented within their receptive field, these responses being larger when the stimulus is a target for an ocular saccade than when the monkey has to maintain its gaze on the fixation point. Further, it was demonstrated that these changes in activity of stimulus-related neurons are monitored by changes in activity of the eye-movement-related neurons of the deeper layers of the superior colliculus. This finding led Wurtz and his colleagues to interpret the enhancement effect as 'clearly associated with preparation to make eye movements' and forms the ground on which 'premotor' hypotheses of selective attention (e.g. Rizzolatti, 1982) were then proposed. It should be noted that this phenomenon does not occur when a hand movement has to be performed in response to the visual stimulus, confirming that its function is not related to some non-specific activation but is closely restricted to the involvement of the visuo-oculomotor system.

It has been already been mentioned that it is difficult to decide when preparation for a particular action begins within the long-term chaining of behavioral acts. It would be equally difficult to decide when preparation starts in the sequence of stimulus to response processes. Consequently an exhaustive review of preparatory processes would imply logically the integration of a large part of the literature devoted to attentional processes. However, it is not feasible to deal comprehensively with this subject in the present context, and hence this chapter is restricted to the preparatory processes which are unequivocally motor in function. With regard to tonic preparation, this classification is made on biofunctional grounds. Because of their far greater energetic costs, it seems reasonable to associate energy mobilization with preparations for motor rather than perceptual activities: the energy costs of neural processes are negligible. However, this reasoning does not take account of the potential energy costs of motor strategies involved in information gathering which, in certain situations such as food search, may be substantial. In the context of phasic preparation for discrete acts, the discussion centres on processes which intervene during the so-called 'motor' stages of information processing models. This restriction does not deny the growing body of evidence that there exists a functional continuum from perception to action which is potentially very useful for understanding the organization of goal-directed behavior.

MOTOR PREPARATION AND MOTOR PLANNING: IDENTICAL OR DIFFERENT PROCESSES?

Within the boundaries described above, preparation of the motor system for adaptive activity commences when the organism first encounters a novel set of environmental demands. These demands must be decoded in such a way as to identify an appropriate motor response. A plan must be formulated for generating responses that will satisfy the temporal, spatial and intensive demands of the environmental contingencies, and this formulation must be laid down in memory, encoded in such a way that it will be activated when the demand occurs. This process of motor learning will be protracted and falls into the class of what is termed here 'tonic' motor preparation. During motor learning, a plan for adaptive behavior is being formulated in a context in which the behavior is being demanded. Before an adequate response has been formulated, the level of behavioral uncertainty is, by definition, high. This is reflected by variability in motor performance and in its relative ineffectiveness in meeting the environmental requirements. As an adequate response is formulated, success in meeting environmental requirements increases and variability in motor performance declines, reflecting a decrease in uncertainty.

The degree of task difficulty may be said to describe the extent to which behavioral uncertainty may be reduced. A task which is readily learned to total mastery is low in difficulty. When mastered, it may be inferred that there remains little uncertainty regarding the requirements of the task or the features of an adequate response. When this happens, the level of tonic preparation may fall to a low ebb without impairing task performance. However, when success is less than total, higher levels of tonic preparation may aid the formulation of more successful responses and thereby reduce the remaining behavioral uncertainty. Thus it may be said that as the solution of a task is acquired and an appropriate motor plan or program generated, its difficulty decreases and so too does the functional value of tonic preparation. More difficult tasks are more resistant to total solution. They maintain behavioral uncertainty at higher levels and thereby provoke higher levels of tonic preparation. Regardless of the state of tonic preparation, when a specific behavioral demand arises in the situation, an appropriate response for that demand must be calculated and implemented. The processes implicated in this 'phasic' stage of motor preparation are dealt with below.

In the framework of information processing stage models, the concept of motor preparation most often refers to the set of processing operations which intervene after the stimulus is identified and before the response is executed; that is, the selection in memory of the response associated with the stimulus and the planning or programming of the motor output through which the response is expressed (e.g. Rosenbaum, 1983; Meyer *et al.*, 1984). In contrast to this broad sense, motor preparation may be viewed in a more restricted way as a modulatory process, modifying in advance the functional state of the processing systems to be responsible for response selection and planning (e.g. Coles, 1989; Requin, 1980a,b). Apart from the theoretical problems associated with the concept of processing 'stage' (Requin, 1985), these two views of motor preparation imply two different mechanisms by which, in the RT paradigm, manipulating information provided by S1 about either the timing and/or the features of the response triggered by S2, results in changes in RT.

In the first view, some of the processes which are triggered by S2 and which take place during RT when there is no S1 would be triggered by S1 and take place during the S1–S2 interval if S1 was introduced. The effect of motor preparation would result from a tradeoff between similar processes triggered by S1 and by S2. In this *preprocessing* view of motor preparation, to prepare is to process in advance: to preselect and/or to preprogram the required motor activity. What has been done in response to S1 has no longer to be done when S2 is presented, so reducing RT. In the second view, motor preparatory processes act by increasing, during the S1–S2 interval, the efficiency of the processing systems which are responsible for performing the response selection and programming operations triggered by S2 and which take place during RT. In this *presetting* view of preparation, to prepare is to facilitate a subsequent processing: what is done after S1 accelerates what will be done after S2, so reducing RT. The effect of preparation would result from processes, triggered by S1, that are different from those triggered by S2.

This question of whether preparation is mediated by preprocessing or presetting may be explored by appropriate experimental arrangements. Thus, when considering a two-choice RT situation (i.e. in which S1 is not informative) suppose that the two S–R alternatives, *a* and *b*, result in different RTs: for example RT*a* > RT*b*, implying that the processes triggered by S2 are longer for *a* than for *b*. The expected effect of introducing an informative S1 (i.e. announcing the subsequent S2) upon RT*a* and RT*b* will be different according to whether a preprocessing or a presetting mechanism is set into play. If preprocessing occurs, since the processes triggered by S2, which are responsible for the RT difference, no longer take place during RT but between S1 and S2, the difference between RT*a* and RT*b* should disappear. If presetting occurs, since the processes responsible for the RT difference are still triggered by S2, but are facilitated, either equally or differentially during the S1–S2 interval, the difference between RT*a* and RT*b* should either remain the same or be reduced.

Behavioral studies conducted according to this rationale have provided some support for a preprocessing conception of preparation. For instance, it was shown in a choice-RT procedure in which the duration of a key-press response was either cued in advance or not, that the RT difference between long and short uncued responses disappeared when these responses were cued. Similarly, by using the 'movement dimension' precueing technique (Rosenbaum, 1983; 1985), Lépine, Glencross and Requin (1989) have shown that RT differences between the uncued values of movement parameters most often disappeared when these values were precued, thus adding support for the preprocessing model.

However, results provided by recording single-neuron activity in monkeys argue for a hybrid preprocessing/presetting conception of motor preparation. In animals performing spatially-oriented wrist movements in a simplified version of the movement parameter precueing procedure (i.e. in which S1 provided either no information or information about movement direction, movement extent or both parameters), two different kinds of neurons were found in the primary motor (MI) and premotor (PM) cortex (Riehle, 1987; Riehle and Requin, 1989). In the first class of neurons, when S1 did not provide directional information, no change in activity was shown between S1 and S2, but S2 triggered a signal-related burst of activity. When S1 provided directional information, S1 was followed by a progressive increase of discharge frequency, while the S2-related activity decreased, or even disappeared, as if what was processed after S1 had no longer to be processed after S2. These neurons may be thus considered as being involved in the advanced processing of movement direction. In a second class of neurons, a preparation-related change in activity developed between S1 and S2 only when S1 provided prior information about movement direction, while S2 was followed, whatever prior information that S1 provided, by a movement-related burst of activity, whose peaking time was, however, earlier when movement direction was announced by S1. These 'motor' neurons thus appear to be 'preset' during the S1–S2 interval by the neuronal mechanisms responsible for programming movement direction.

The latter example illustrates how physiological measures may assist in discriminating between two information processing models of preparation, and such measures are commonly employed in the study of both tonic and phasic preparatory processes. Indeed, physiological recordings provide the first line of evidence in examining tonic preparation since this state is manifested primarily by alterations in processes which are expressed by alterations in the functioning of the internal organs. For example, assessments of levels of energy mobilization may be made on the basis of concurrent recordings of striate muscular work rates or metabolic rates on the one hand and cardiopulmonary rates on the other. As detailed in the following section, the functioning of the striate muscular apparatus depends on adequate perfusion with oxygenated blood. However, when more oxygenated blood is being delivered to the tissue than is warranted by their rates of activity, it may be inferred that feedforward processes are contributing substantially to the control of cardiopulmonary activity. This inference is based on the assumption that if the energy delivery systems were being driven by feedback from the striate muscular effectors, rates of tissue perfusion would match energetic requirements.

TONIC PREPARATION

STRIATE MUSCULAR ACTIVITY AND ENERGY EXPENDITURE

The striate muscles provide the sole means by which organisms may influence their environments. This effector system, which comprises approximately 50% of the total body mass, consumes a major proportion of the body's energy resources. These energy costs may be minimized by generating striate muscular activities that satisfy behavioral purposes with minimal redundancy. Given the importance of precise regulation of the striate muscles, it is not surprising that the involved processes occupy a substantial fraction of the nervous system's resources.

Variations in striate muscular activity are the most conspicuous source of variations in overall energy expenditure. This energy is liberated by splitting the high-energy phosphate bonds of adenosine triphosphate (ATP) and phosphocreatine (CP). All cellular processes are fueled by ATP which must be rapidly resynthesized using energy transferred from CP. When food substances are degraded, the energy made available cannot be used directly for work, but instead is stored in these phosphate bonds for either immediate or later use. Contraction of the striate muscles is initially supported by the ATP and CP reserves, which need to be immediately replenished by either anaerobic processes (breakdown of glycogen and glucose) or aerobic processes (breakdown of glucose, glycolytic end-products and free fatty acids).

The striate muscles are engaged by the nervous system when the organism is confronted with any demand situation. Responses of the muscles entail not only the specific movements required by environmental demands but also processes which function to support the body frame. These supportive functions are expressed by postural adjustments and increased static muscle tension. During the initial period (0–3 minutes) the muscular activity could be supported entirely by anaerobic metabolism using ATP, CP, glycogen and glucose. However, in order to avoid an 'energy crisis', aerobic degradation pathways for glucose and lipids are also activated. Without the participation of aerobic processes, anaerobic metabolism rapidly leads to the excessive formation of lactic acid. This prevents glycolysis and thereby limits performance. The operation of the aerobic pathways depends critically on appropriate adjustments of cardiopulmonary performance.

From our diet of foods only carbohydrates and fats are normally used to supply energy for work performed by the striate muscles, although amino acids from protein may be utilized for tasks involving protracted and extreme workloads. When an immediate energy supply is required (e.g. at the onset of exercise) carbohydrates can be broken down anaerobically by the processes of glycolysis for glucose present in the circulation and glycogenolysis for glycogen in the liver and muscle. Anaerobic glycolysis produces the byproducts lactic acid and pyruvic acid. In addition, glucose may be broken down aerobically, with pyruvic acid being degraded to CO_2 and H_2, and lactic acid entering the citric acid or Krebs cycle where it is degraded to H and CO_2. The liberation of energy from carbohydrates for ATP resynthesis is approximately 20 times more efficient when the reaction is aerobic than anaerobic. Therefore it would appear to be adaptive to engage aerobic processes as rapidly as possible when physical demands are encountered.

Fat is the major source of stored energy available to the body, and its use is dependent on aerobic metabolism. A small supply of lipids is available in the striate muscle for emergency use, while most is stored in adipose tissue as triglycerides. These triglycerides combine with lipoproteins in the blood plasma, and are broken down during lipolysis into glycerol and free fatty acids (FFA), which is the only form that the striate muscles can use. The mobilization of FFA from adipose tissue is affected by the levels of circulating catecholamines, insulin, and glucose, whereas the extent to which they are available locally to support muscular energy needs is determined by the circulation.

The rate of blood flow to active tissues must be increased to ensure adequate delivery of nutrients and oxygen to the tissues and the removal of metabolic byproducts. This process is supported by adjustments in myocardial and smooth muscle activities to create a resistance pathway which will route a metabolically-appropriate fraction of the cardiac output to the active tissues. At the same time ventilation must increase to eliminate excess CO_2, to restore depleted arterial O_2 levels and to maintain blood pH.

The processes of homeostasis are impressively illustrated by the integration of cardiopulmonary performance with the perfusion needs of the body. It is widely accepted that muscular activity rates are limited by the capacity of the circulation to deliver oxygenated blood to the striate muscular effectors (Astrand and Rodahl, 1986). Over the full aerobic range of muscular workloads, tissues are normally perfused at rates which are appropriate to their metabolic needs. This is illustrated by the strong linear relationship between the rates of cardiovascular and pulmonary activity on the one hand and the rate of striate muscular activity on the other (Astrand and Rodahl, 1986). The relationship is functionally imperative since extremes of striate muscular capacity for energy consumption must be satisfied if behavior is not to be impeded. Under conditions of maximal exercise, this effector system alone burns in excess of ten times more energy per unit time than is required to support the activity of the whole body under resting conditions. The integration of cardiopulmonary activity with striate muscular performance is accomplished by a network of linkages with a striking degree of functional redundancy (Mitchell and Schmidt, 1983). Autoregulatory and reflexive as well as central pathways ensure the high levels of integration in the activities of these effector systems that are required to sustain behavior.

PREPARING FOR ENERGY EXPENDITURE

Numerous studies show that cardiovascular and pulmonary activities increase prior to the onset of exercise and to levels that are related to the cardiopulmonary demands of the forthcoming exercise. For example, Mantysaari, Antila and Peltonen (1988) found that the cardiovascular changes associated with anticipating a light handgrip exercise were similar to those observed during the exercise itself. This led them to conclude that the patterns of central activation associated with anticipated and actual motor activities were also similar. Data from an experiment by Hanson and Tabakin (1964) are also consistent with this hypothesis. They used radiotelemetry to monitor HR at rest, and then before, during and after separate skiing events (downhill race, cross-country race, and 50 m jump). A positive relationship was found between the magnitude of the anticipatory HR and the intensity of the upcoming workload. Thus prior to the cross-country, downhill and jump events, HRs increased 70%, 68% and 62% respectively, while the HRs recorded during the event, which reflect the metabolic costs of the exercise, were 187, 163 and 137 bpm respectively. Similar effects, illustrated in Figure 4.1, were recorded from expert swimmers by Magel, McArdle and Glaser (1969) during preparation for swimming events. They found that anticipatory HRs were greatest for the sprint and lowest for the long-distance events. Brouha and Heath (1943) also found a strong positive relationship between anticipatory HRs and the metabolic costs of a forthcoming activity. The HRs of seated subjects recorded prior to a medical examination, treadmill walking and treadmill running were respectively 73, 84 and 90 bpm. Magel, McArdle and Glaser (1969) hypothesize that such anticipatory cardiac responses result 'from an increase in sympathetic discharge and a diminution of vagal tone due to involvement of the motor cortex preparing the organism for a recognized work task'.

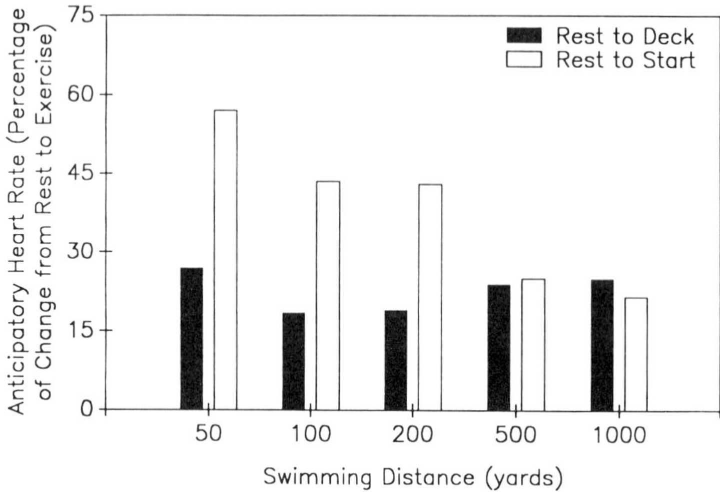

Figure 4.1. Increase in heart rate expressed as a function of the change from rest to exercise (100%) observed while waiting on the deck and immediately before the start of each swimming event. Prior to the start of sprint events (≤200 yards), heart rate rises to a substantial fraction of its exercise value. Based on Magel, McArdle and Glaser (1969).

In order for the anticipatory response to reflect the metabolic costs of the forthcoming motor activity, it is, of course, necessary that the subject be familiar with these costs. On this basis, differences in tonic anticipation are to be expected between experts and novices. This expectation receives confirmation from a study by McArdle, Foglia and Patti (1967). Significant increases in HR in anticipation of running events of different distances were found for both trained and untrained runners. However, as indicated in Figure 4.2, anticipatory HRs in the trained but not the untrained runners were directly related to the average rates of energy expenditure demanded by the forthcoming events, being highest for the 60-yard sprint and lowest for the two-mile race. As suggested earlier, the development of expertise in a task implies a reduction in uncertainty and this is manifested in the present case by the direct relationship found between anticipatory and task levels of cardiopulmonary activity.

The effects of reductions in uncertainty have also been examined by measuring changes in anticipatory heart rates as a function of training. For example, Faulkner (1964) investigated the effect of training on the cardiovascular response to exercise on a cycle ergometer in both athletes and non-athletes. There were no differences between athletes and non-athletes in either the size or the direction of the heart rate conditioning as indexed by difference between the first trial and last trial. However, anticipatory heart

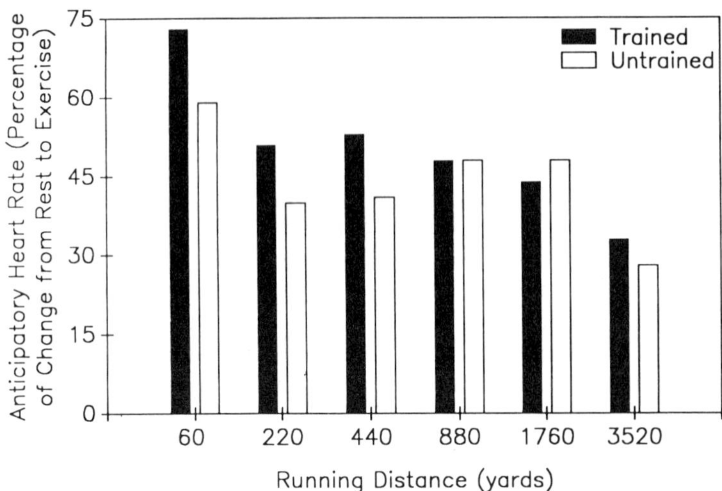

Figure 4.2. Increase in heart rate expressed as a function of the change from rest to exercise (100%) for both trained and untrained individuals before running events of different distances. The anticipatory elevations in heart rate for the 60-yard event which is supported mainly by anaerobic metabolism is approximately double that of the two-mile event. Based on McArdle, Foglia and Patti (1967).

rates (rest–anticipation), expressed as percentages of the difference between resting and exercise levels, declined over trials. Furthermore, this effect was larger for subjects with no prior training (trial 1 = 46%, trial 5 = 22%), than for subjects with previous training (trial 1 = 29%, trial 5 = 16%). Faulkner interpreted the data to mean that 'the height of the anticipatory levels and the amount of overshoot associated with minimal T1 (trial 1) suggests that when subjects cannot recognize any cues in an impending work situation they tend to prepare for a maximal response'. This interpretation is in line with the hypothesis that, as uncertainty wanes, so too does activity in the sympathetic nervous system resulting from a reduction in feedforward control of the energy mobilization response.

Pulmonary ventilation also increases in anticipation of exercise. Tobin *et al.* (1986) investigated whether respiratory changes in anticipation of exercise are due to central command (feedforward control). Similar increases in ventilation found during anticipation of cycling and during the performance of mental arithmetic suggested that increased central ventilatory drive was responsible. If this had been the case, ventilation rate would be expected to exceed metabolic requirements, leading to a decrease in alveolar pCO_2. However, because it was found that the anticipatory augmentation in ventilation was not associated with a depression of end-tidal CO_2 and was accompanied by increases in $\dot{V}O_2$ and cardiac performance, the pulmonary response could not be attributed exclusively to the influence of central processes. Instead, the authors suggest that the changes in ventilation were secondary to changes in the rate of circulation. The assumed mechanism is cardiodynamic hyperpnea (Wasserman, Whipp and Castagnia, 1974) in which increased blood flow delivers more CO_2 to the lungs, stimulating local chemoreceptors which elicit the increased ventilation.

Torelli and Brandi (1964) were able to determine the relative contributions of central, peripheral and reflexive factors in the ventilation response at the onset of treadmill exercise. Subjects performed three consecutive series of trials. First, in the 'conditioning' trials, subjects stood beside the treadmill, were given a warning signal ('3,2,1 ready') followed by a start signal ('go') and jumped on to the treadmill and started walking. Second, in the 'unconditioning' trials, only the warning signal was given, with no exercise. Third, in the 'omission' trials, the warning signal was given, and if no anticipatory response was exhibited, the start signal was presented followed by exercise. During conditioning, pulmonary ventilation increased when the warning signal was presented, peaked soon after exercise onset and then fell slightly to stabilize for the duration of the exercise period. The increase in pulmonary ventilation was mirrored by a decrease in alveolar CO_2, so the earlier hyperventilation cannot be explained by elevated CO_2 levels. It is unlikely that the ventilatory response was mediated either by muscle reflexes (peripheral mechanism) or impulses from the motor cortex (central mechanism) because the response was also exhibited when no start signal was provided and no exercise was performed. The authors proposed that the ventilatory response is governed by a central neural mechanism with two components: a 'conditioned reflex', in which the warning signal has become a conditioned stimulus which elicits the early ventilatory response, and an 'unspecified neural mechanism' which begins at the onset of exercise and lasts for about 20 s, by which time ventilation has come under reflexive control presumably via chemoreceptors sensing blood CO_2 levels.

Patterns of adjustment similar to those evoked by actual and anticipated muscular activity are also recorded in response to emotional or stressful situations. Thus Brod *et al.* (1959) noted that the hemodynamic response to emotional stimuli 'closely resembles the circulatory changes that accompany strenuous muscular exercise (p. 277). Humoral parallels between exercise on the one hand and stress or emotion on the other are also in evidence (e.g. von Euler, 1964). These resemblances support Cannon's characterization of the visceral reactions to psychological challenge as expressions of general motor preparation: the flight or fight response. Energy mobilization attributable to psychogenic sources may be related to the duration of the computation phase required to generate an adequate motor solution to the problem posed by environmental contingencies. Stressful tasks pose difficult problems and, therefore, the computation of an adequate motor solution is protracted.

Viewed in this way, the so-called 'stress response' is a tonic preparatory state which functions to support the rapid emergence and maintenance of coping responses.

It is possible that the cardiovascular and pulmonary reactions observed to psychological challenge are mediated to some extent by reflex pathways triggered by non-specific motor activation. An old but fairly substantial literature indicates that 'mental effort' is accompanied by diffuse increases in muscle tension (e.g. Davis, 1943). Of particular interest are experiments on changes in muscle tension during the course of motor learning. For example, Daniel (1939) found that EMG declined as maze learning progressed and that decreases in muscle tension were associated with error elimination. Duffy (1932) recorded pressure exerted on a dynamograph by each hand during both a tapping task and a discriminative reaction task. The degree of muscular tension generated was correlated with task performance: moderate or low for subjects with superior performance and high tension for subjects with poor performance. Muscle tension was viewed as an expression of a preparatory state accompanying emotional excitation which facilitates performance in terms of both speed and force, so that 'the more strongly motivated the individual or the more difficult the situation which confronts him, the greater would be his muscular tension, or his effort to adjust'. Static muscular contractions create local conditions which strongly stimulate the types III and IV small muscle afferents, thereby causing exaggerated cardiovascular responses (Asmussen, 1981).

The metabolic costs of apparently trivial motor adjustments may be sufficient to elicit systematic alterations in cardiovascular and pulmonary activity. For example, mental arithmetic is frequently employed as a control procedure for the effects of central processes in delineating the effects of physical challenges on cardiovascular and pulmonary adjustments (e.g. Tobin *et al.*, 1986). However in a recent study, Brown, Szabo and Seraganian (1988) found that a substantial portion of the HR elevation recorded during mental arithmetic could be accounted for by the costs of operating the vocal apparatus to speak the solutions. The hypothesis that anticipatory cardiopulmonary responses are actually elicited by the metabolic demands of preliminary striate muscular adjustments gains plausibility from numerous data indicating that 'mental' tasks are associated with significant elevations in metabolic rate (e.g. Benedict and Benedict, 1933). A relevant example is reported by Skubic and Hodgkins (1965) who found that body temperature increased by 0.4 oF above resting levels in the period preceding exercise, this increase representing half of the increase in heat production recorded during the exercise itself. Although this suggests that anticipation is associated with significant increases in muscular activity, there is also a considerable body of evidence suggesting that anticipatory elevations in cardiovascular and pulmonary performance may be driven by central command.

MECHANISMS OF ENERGY MOBILIZATION AND DELIVERY

Rushmer, Smith and Franklin (1960) studied the effects of various experimental protocols in an attempt to simulate the normal cardiovascular response to exercise: an increase in heart rate, systolic and end-diastolic pressures, peak power, rate of change in pressure, and stroke work. It was found that the administration of adrenalin and noradrenalin alone failed to duplicate the exercise response. However, a better correspondence was obtained when tachycardia was superimposed by cardiac pacing. Stimulation of the sympathetic nerves to the heart closely approximated the exercise response, with an increase in heart rate, contractility and arterial pressure. Finally, stimulation of areas of the hypothalamus and subthalamus most accurately reproduced the exercise response.

The hypothalamus receives input from the motor cortex, limbic system and association areas, suggesting that this structure may coordinate the processes by which the cardiovascular response is influenced by higher nervous system activity. Anticipatory changes occurred when the dogs were lifted on to the treadmill or saw the switch in the operator's hand: 'after the animals had become accustomed to the laboratory procedures, the left ventricular responses frequently anticipated the physiologic requirements'. The response declined soon after the onset of exercise, reflecting the operation of reflexive mechanisms coupling the cardiac output with metabolic requirements. Rushmer, Smith and Franklin (1960) found it useful to view the anticipatory response as a conditioned response evoked by situational cues (CS) which have been associated with exercise (US). They concluded that the exercise reponse is a two-part process, with the initial stages predominantly under feedforward control. As exercise proceeds, feedback control becomes dominant.

In the feedforward (neural control) stage, motor cortex sends efference to the effectors producing contraction of striate muscles, and simultaneously stimulates cardiovascular and pulmonary performance via collaterals through the hypothalamus to the cardiovascular and pulmonary control 'centers' in the medulla. The cardiac effects include inhibition of vagal tone and increased sympathetic outflow to the heart, producing tachycardia and increased contractility. They attributed vascular dilation in the implicated muscles to feedforward processes, suggesting that this is a mechanism for increasing blood flow to active muscles. However, this is a contentious issue (Martin, Sutherland and Zbrozyna, 1976). Although some evidence suggests that this response may occur in anticipation of activity (Abrahams, Hilton and Zbrozina, 1960; Eliasson, *et al.*, 1951; Sutherland and Zbrozyna, 1971), other data (Adams *et al.*, 1969) indicates that active vasodilation occurs only when the muscles are contracted and that this is due to the operation of peripheral rather than central factors (Corcondilas, Koroxenidis and Shepherd, 1964).

However, it is not disputed that the nervous system exerts control over the visceral and cutaneous vascular beds in advance of motor activity thereby reducing circulation to these sites and ensuring that an increased supply of oxygenated blood is made available as soon as it is needed. Increases in pulmonary ventilation that are required to effect the necessary gas exchange are implemented mainly by higher ventilation frequencies.

The feedback (reflexive control) stage implicates baroreceptors in the aortic arch and carotid sinus which detect an increase in mean arterial pressure and stimulate heart rate slowing via the baroreflex. When exercise ensues, the gain of the baroreflex is attenuated and receptors in muscle and tendon organs stimulate further augmentations in cardiovascular responses. With increased striate muscular activity, chemoreceptors respond to increasing blood CO_2 levels to link pulmonary ventilation with alveolar CO_2 concentation. The sympathetic nervous system is significantly involved in regulating the energetics of motor performance. Smith and Devito (1984) examined inputs to the intermediolateral cell column of the spinal cord through which the sympathetic nervous system exerts control over the peripheral organs. They concluded that the perifornical region of the lateral hypothalamus regulates input from higher centers including the limbic system and prefrontal cortex, to the autonomic effectors. Of significance to the present discussion is Smith's (1974) observation that stimulation of practically all brain structures which have demonstrable influences on striate muscular activity also produce functionally related alterations in cardiovascular performance. These cardiovascular adjustments are instigated directly and through the influence of the perifornical hypothalamus on several groups of highly interconnected nuclei which also send efferents through the intermediolateral column.

Sympathetic nervous system effects on the cardiovascular and pulmonary effectors are mediated neurally by sympathetic fibers and humorally by circulating catecholamines which are released into the blood stream by the adrenal glands and from the ends of postganglionic sympathetic nerves. In man, circulating norepinephrine originates mainly from sympathetic nerve endings in the myocardium (Peronnet *et al.*, 1981a,b). Sympathetic discharge has numerous effects which, as Cannon (1929) pointed out, clearly represent an energy mobilization response: it functions to increase the delivery of energy, primarily to the striate muscles.

The catecholamines adrenalin and noradrenalin mobilize energy stores by stimulating lypolysis and glycogenolysis. They also cause increases in brochodilation and the vigor and rate of cardiac contraction, producing augmentations in pulmonary gas exchange and in the rate of blood flow. Regional vasoconstriction in the splanchnic, renal and cutaneous circulations diverts blood to the muscles and raises the blood pressure. All these changes, which are essential to the maintenance of elevated levels of energy expenditure, are also found to occur prior to the release of muscular activity. As might be expected, adrenergic blockade decreases the ability of the striate muscles to do work. For example, Hughson, Russell and Marshall (1984) showed that the administration of metoprolol, a selective beta-blocker, reduced the maximum oxygen uptake and the heart rate response to exercise.

Changes in the pattern of hormonal responses in anticipation of psychological tasks have been documented. Frankenhaeuser and Rissler (1970a) observed that anticipation of uncontrollable harmless electric shocks produced significant elevations in adrenalin excretion that were positively correlated with heart rate and blood pressure. In another study (Frankenhaeuser and Rissler, 1970b), experimental but not control subjects were threatened with and received electric shock while performing a choice-RT task. The experimental group showed greater excretion of both adrenalin and noradrenalin. More interestingly, the data revealed a positive correlation between the level of performance, indexed by both the RT speed and the number of errors, and excretion of both adrenalin and noradrenalin. The greater accuracy and speed of subjects with high rates of catecholamine secretion illustrates the adaptive value of the 'emergency response'. Similar hormonal responses have been documented for anticipation of physical exercise. Mason *et al.* (1973) found that during a 20-minute period prior to the onset of sustained exercise (70% $\dot{V}O_2max$) there were significant elevations from baseline in both plasma cortisol levels and plasma noradrenalin levels, although no differences in plasma adrenalin occurred.

PATHWAYS RESPONSIBLE FOR COORDINATING CARDIOVASCULAR AND PULMONARY PERFORMANCE WITH STRIATE MUSCULAR ACTIVITY

Although the sympathetic nervous system is strongly implicated in ensuring an adequate supply of energy to the muscular effectors, the precise mechanisms by which the rate of energy delivery is synchronized with the rate of tissue metabolism has not been fully explained. However, research has identified central, peripheral (reflexive) and local (autoregulatory) pathways by which striate muscular processes may influence the energy delivery system. Activity in each of these pathways may contribute to supporting performance of the motor system. The central pathways are of special interest in analyzing the mechanisms of tonic motor preparation since their influence could account for variations in cardiopulmonary activity which are functionally linked to motor activity but which antedate its overt expression, as when heart rate and ventilation rate increase in anticipation of activity (Tobin *et al.*, 1986). However, additional evidence indicates that the peripheral pathways may also elicit variations in cardiopulmonary activity which are uncorrelated with immediate metabolic demands (Asmussen, 1981). In either case, the contributions of the peripheral pathways must be considered since inferences that anticipatory cardiopulmonary adjustments are attributable to central effects are frequently based on the experimental exclusion of potential peripheral sources of influence.

Autoregulation

Several local mechanisms which function to coordinate cardiovascular and pulmonary activity with current metabolic demands are activated by striate muscular activity. The functional capacity of these processes is illustrated by the observation that the covariation of cardiac output with metabolic rate observed during exercise is not severely compromised by cardiac denervation (Donald and Shepherd, 1963). However, whereas the adjustments in cardiac output are born largely by increases in heart rate in unoperated dogs, animals with denervated hearts adjust cardiac output primarily by increases in stroke volume. This suggests that neural control of cardiac output is exerted primarily through regulation of heart rate. On the other hand, regulation of cardiac output by stroke volume, as seen in the denervated dogs, may be attributed to an autoregulatory property of the heart which determines that stroke volume increases as a function of the end-diastolic volume. This process, described by the Frank–Starling principle, ensures that the cardiac output matches venous return.

The rate of venous return may itself be matched to metabolic requirements through local autoregulatory and mechanical processes that are relatively independent of neurohumoral influence. Thus, the blood vessels adjust their diameters according to the composition of the local blood supply. When the O_2 content of arterial blood is high, blood vessels constrict, and when it is low they dilate (Coleman, Granger and Guyton, 1971). This mechanism serves to decrease the resistance to blood flow of active muscles when the local O_2 supply is relatively depleted. Furthermore, dynamic activity of the striate muscles has a blood-pumping action which contributes to venous return. Veins possess valves that only permit blood to flow towards the heart. Therefore when they are squeezed by the contraction and relaxation of surrounding muscles, blood is forced back to the heart, and venous return is augmented. Pulmonary ventilation also provides the circulation of blood with mechanical assistance. During inspiration, intrathoracic pressure is decreased causing blood to be 'sucked' into the great veins which feed deoxygenated blood to the right atrium. The effectiveness of such local mechanisms in regulating blood flow independently of central mechanisms raises questions regarding the functions of neural processes which are significantly involved in the normal coordination of cardiopulmonary and striate muscular activities.

Reflexes

Muscular activity has mechanical, chemical and thermal consequences which stimulate the afferent limbs of cardiovascular and ventilatory reflexes. Some of these reflexes are of short latency. For example, cardiac acceleration produced by neural feedback from the active muscles can occur within one beat of the instigating muscular contraction (Gelsema, de Groot and Bouman, 1983). A related phenomenon has been reported by Jennings and Wood (1977) who found that response initiation causes suppression of the immediate cardiac deceleration caused by stimulus presentation. At a somewhat longer latency, the exercise pressor reflex which leads to increases in cardiac output and blood pressure is triggered by activity in small muscle afferents (types III and IV). These feedback pathways have been classified as nociceptive and ergoceptive, with the latter being sensitive to metabolic factors (Mitchell and Schmidt, 1983). Within 30 s of the onset of exercise, changes in blood gas composition produced by muscular energy expenditure act on the chemoreceptors of the medulla, the aortic arch and the carotid bodies to bring about reflex augmentations in cardiovascular and pulmonary function. Increases in venous return that are secondary to striate muscular activity stimulate stretch receptors in the right atrium of the heart, causing heart rate to accelerate through the Bainbridge reflex. All these reflexes function to raise perfusion rates to the levels required by muscular activity. Fundamental to sustaining adequate rates of perfusion is the maintenance of blood pressure, and pivotal to the regulation of this cardiovascular variable are the baroceptor reflexes.

The Baroceptor Reflexes

Mechanoreceptors in the heart, blood vessels and lungs activate baroreflexes which are strongly implicated in regulating the circulation. Two baroreflexes can be distinguished on functional and anatomical grounds. The sensory limb of the arterial baroreflex is served by pressure receptors in the carotid sinus and the aortic arch which project through the IXth and Xth cranial nerves to the nucleus tractus solitarii (NTS). Hubbard *et al.* (1988) have shown that the NTS also receives the primary projections from unmyelinated vagal afferents (C-fibers) serving receptors implicated in the cardiopulmonary baroreflex (Seals, 1988). These mechanoreceptors, which are located in the heart, lungs and great veins, respond to increases in cardiac filling pressure (preload), afterload, myocardial contractility and depth of breathing (Marks and Mancia, 1983).

Increased activation of the cardiopulmonary baroreflex raises the level of tonic inhibition of sympathetic outflow, thereby attenuating cardiac activity and lowering vascular resistance. The effective stimuli for eliciting this reflex (increased preload, myocardial contractility and ventilation) are produced by exercise, and it has been suggested (Seals, 1988) that its function may be to buffer excitatory influences produced by exercise reflexes and central command. However, the evidence that the cardiopulmonary baroreflex modulates cardiovascular responses to exercise (Mitchell and Schmidt, 1983) is mixed. For example, Walker *et al.* (1980) did report that when the cardiopulmonary baroreflex was inhibited by the application of lower body negative pressure, vasoconstriction was greatly enhanced in the contralateral limb during isometric contractions of the arm. However, this finding was not confirmed in a similar study by Seals (1988) or in exercising dogs following elimination of the cardiopulmonary vagal afferents (Walgenbach and Donald, 1983). At this time, there is not a strong basis for expecting the cardiopulmonary reflex to be implicated in behaviorally-related alterations in cardiovascular performance.

On the other hand, there is considerable evidence that the aterial baroreflex provides an important mechanism by which central motor processes interact with cardiovascular performance. The primary function of this reflex is to maintain blood pressure at levels that are appropriate to current perfusion requirements. Since these requirements are determined mainly by variations in striate muscular activity, this reflex is strongly implicated in behaviorally-related variations in cardiovascular performance. The circulation is regulated through increased sympathetic outflow when blood pressure falls relative to the prevailing setpoint and by increased parasympathetic outflow when blood pressure rises (Pickering *et al.*, 1972). Sympathetic influences on the heart and blood vessels involve the C1 adrenalin-containing neurons of the rostral ventrolateral medulla. These neurons project to the interomediolateral column of the spinal cord and to the heart and blood vessels through postganglionic sympathetic fibers (Reis and Ledoux, 1987). Increased sympathetic outflow elicits vasoconstriction, augmented heart rate and greater myocardial contractility, which in turn give rise to a compensatory increase in blood pressure. Increases in the activity of the parasympathetic output limb arises in the dorsal motor nucleus and result in reductions in myocardial performance which cause compensatory decreases in blood pressure.

The operating characteristics of the arterial baroreflex have been comprehensively studied. Pickering, Gribbin and Sleight (1972) reported that the responses of the reflex to rising and falling blood pressures are asymmetrical, with the response to falling pressures being only 40% of that found to rising pressures. In rats, the bradycardia produced by rising pressures has been attributed primarily to the parasympathetic system, whereas the sympathetic and parasympathetic systems contribute equally to the tachycardia produced by falling pressures (Stornetta, Guyenet and McCarty, 1987). At rest, the reflex exhibits its greatest sensitivity as measured by δHR/δBP; that is, HR changes more per unit change in arterial blood pressure during rest than in other behavioral states. Although a linear relationship between δHR and δBP has generally been assumed, Head and McCarty (1987) found that the relationship is better described by a sigmoidal function. They calculated that, whereas the parasympathetic system contributed 61% to the HR range covered by the function, the sympathetics contributed only 39%. However, the contribution of the sympathetic division (63%) to the sensitivity of the reflex (as measured by δHR/δBP in the straight part of the sigmoid between the points of inflection) was found to be greater than that of the parasympathetic division.

In reflexological terms, the arterial baroreflex has a long latency. Measuring from the onset of the pressure pulse wave to the immediately following change in HR, Pickering and Davies (1973) estimated the time for the whole reflex loop to be 775 ms, of which 475 ms was the time from activation of the baroceptors to observable changes in heart rate. Borst and Karemaker (1983; see also Borst *et al.*, 1983), who found similar latencies to Pickering and Davies, estimated that central processing of baroceptor afference may require 250 ms. More recently Smith, Stallard and Littler (1986) found reliable inter-individual differences in baroceptor reflex latencies ranging from 650 ms to 2900 ms. Although their study confirmed that reflex sensitivity is inversely related to age (Bristow *et al.*, 1969; Gribbin *et al.*, 1971) and systolic blood pressure, reflex latency was found to be unrelated to these variables or to resting HR.

The sensitivity of the arterial baroreflex is reliably influenced by both physical and psychological demands. During exercise, sensitivity is substantially reduced, thereby permitting blood pressure to rise to the levels required to support higher rates of blood flow (Walgenbach, 1983). Cunningham *et al.* (1972) found that sustained isometric contractions produced a greater decrease in reflex sensitivity than did either dynamic exercise or rhythmic isometric handgrip. Mental arithmetic has also been found to reduce arterial baroreflex sensitivity (Sleight *et al.*, 1978). This effect cannot be simply attributed to 'stress' as indicated in the recent report by Steptoe and Sawada (1989), who replicated Sleight *et al.*'s observation but failed to find a change in reflex sensitivity in response to a cold pressor stress. Because of its demonstrated relationship to behavior, modulation of arterial baroreflex sensitivity emerges as a feasible route for the effects of central motor processes on cardiovascular performance.

Central Pathways

Since the publication of a classic paper by Krogh and Lindhard in 1913, it has been widely accepted that the highest levels of the nervous system are involved in coordinating cardiopulmonary performance with metabolic rate. Smith (1974) and Smith and DeVito (1984) have reviewed evidence showing that brain structures at all levels of the neuroaxis, many of which have a demonstrable influence on striate muscular activity, also produce related changes in cardiovascular performance. These structures would seem likely candidates in the control of preparatory adjustments of the energy mobilization and delivery systems.

Evidence in favor of cardiovascular control by 'central command' processes comes from several *in vivo* studies. For example, Freyschuss (1970) required subjects to respond to a signal with brief isometric contractions of the forearm. Heart rate and blood pressure were recorded as well as EMG from the implicated muscle. While engaged in the task, the active muscle was paralyzed by the local administration of a neuromuscular blocking agent. Although this pharmacological intervention led to a complete suppression of movement and EMG activity in the muscle, the cardiovascular responses to the 'contract' stimulus were exhibited at more than 50% of the magnitude recorded prior to neuromuscular blockade. These observations were interpreted as evidence that the cardiovascular changes were not due to peripheral processes. Similar results were reported in a classic paper by Alam and Smirk (1938) who found the same increases in arterial pressure and heart rate when a deafferented ischemic leg was exercised as when a normal ischemic leg was exercised. However, these data are only suggestive of feedforward control of cardiovascular responses associated with motor activity, since neither the metabolic rates of subjects nor activity in other muscles were monitored. These omissions leave open the possibility that activity in muscles not involved in the task may have elicited the cardiovascular changes through reflex pathways.

In another well-known study of central command, Goodwin, McCloskey and Mitchell (1972) monitored end-tidal pCO_2 and ventilation in addition to blood pressure and heart rate. These investigators required subjects to maintain constant isometric contractions of the biceps or triceps. While executing these maneuvers with the aid of visual feedback, vibratory stimuli were applied to the tendons of either the active muscle or its antagonist. These local stimuli respectively enhanced or inhibited contraction in the involved muscles, thereby requiring an appropriate compensation of the central command to maintain constant performance. In particular, vibration of the agonist of the movement required a decrease in central command, whereas vibration of the antagonist required an increase. In both cases, subjects complied with the instructions and maintained constant levels of muscular work. It was found that cardiopulmonary activity followed central command and not local muscular work rates. Thus, when the antagonists were vibrated, heart rate, blood pressure and ventilation rates increased, whereas when the agonists were vibrated the cardiopulmonary rates fell. Alterations in ventilation rate were compensated by opposite changes in pCO_2, suggesting that metabolic rate remained constant under the different vibration conditions. These results then suggest that the cardiopulmonary changes were influenced by central command.

Strong evidence in favor of the central coupling of cardiopulmonary adjustments with motor outflow comes from an experiment on cats by Eldridge *et al.* (1985). They found that the increases in ventilation and blood pressure associated with locomotion in normal cats was not significantly different from that observed in paralyzed cats while they engaged in 'fictive' locomotion (i.e. locomotory activity in the motor nerves of the legs). Since during fictive locomotion there was no evidence of muscular activity and metabolic rate did not change, it may be inferred that feedback from the locomotory muscles was not involved in generating the cardiopulmonary adjustments. On the basis of brain lesions, these authors concluded that the primary drive for the energy delivery responses emanated from the hypothalamus.

As Mitchell and Schmidt (1983) point out (p.650), it might be expected that the pressor response will be affected by the number of motor units that are centrally activated. This observation is consistent with the report by Schibye *et al.* (1981) that heart rate and blood pressure tend to follow the EMG (reflecting recruitment rate) in the working muscles rather than work rates of the muscles themselves (reflecting peripheral feedback). Congruent observations have also been reported by Mitchell, Reardon and McCloskey (1977) and Mitchell *et al.* (1980), who found that when the percentage effort is held constant (e.g. at 40% of MVC), increases in cardiac pumping action and blood pressure are correlated with the size of the muscle mass activated. However, data presented by Lewis *et al.* (1983; see Figure 4.3) indicates that,

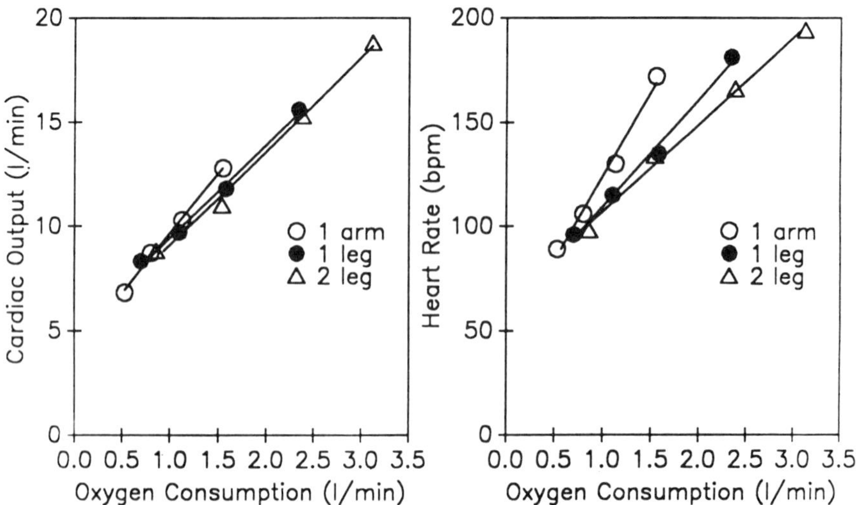

Figure 4.3. Relationships between cardiac output and oxygen consumption (left) and heart rate and oxygen consumption (right) as a function of muscle mass during dynamic exercise. Note that independently of muscle mass, cardiac output is directly proportional to metabolic demand. However, the heart rate contribution to cardiac output is inversely proportional to the muscle mass involved in generating the metabolic load. Based on Lewis *et al.* (1983).

when rates of energy expenditure (as indexed by $\dot{V}O_2$) are held constant, cardiac output is independent of muscle mass, although the magnitude of the heart rate response is inversely related to the size of the implicated muscle mass or directly related to the relative workload for those muscles. Taken together these data suggest that perceived 'effort' as well as absolute recruitment rates contribute significantly to the cardiovascular adjustments seen in exercise.

Other evidence indicates that motor-related processes which are quite remote from muscular activity are reliably associated with elevations in cardiac performance. For example, Rose and Dunn (1964) used radiotelemetry to track the heart rate of spectators during a football game. During the pregame period HR was already elevated (mean 103, range 88–116) and subjects exhibited a sustained tachycardia during the game itself. The magnitude of the HR elevation was related to particular events, such as the punt and punt return, the pass and the long run. As the authors note, it is difficult to determine whether the HR changes seen in spectators are centrally mediated or mediated reflexively by the striate muscular activity in the spectators.

In an experiment which involved no obvious physical activity, Schwartz and Higgins (1971) found comparable HR changes in anticipation of either pressing a key or thinking the word 'stop'. In both cases, the early acceleratory and later deceleratory components of the HR change occurred earlier when a 'fast' response (either pressing or thinking) was required than when a 'slow' response was required. These data, which indicate that the specific form of the anticipatory cardiac response depended upon the same task variables for motor and covert responses, are consistent with the hypothesis that overlapping mediating processes were implicated. Even if the so-called 'covert' response was accompanied by motor subvocalizations, the similar anticipatory (premotor) cardiac responses to the overt and covert tasks may be the product of a common mechanism: modulation of cardiovascular control centers by brain structures of the motor system. Findings that mental practice facilitates subsequent motor performance (Cratty, 1976) also suggests that structures involved in imagining activity overlap with those implicated in motor programming. Perhaps, then, activity in these structures influences cardiovascular performance through the feedforward pathways. However, since metabolic rates were not recorded in these experiments, the possibility that reflexive processes were implicated in their production cannot be discounted.

THE FUNCTIONALITY OF ANTICIPATORY ELEVATIONS IN ENERGY MOBILIZATION AND DELIVERY

In the transition from rest to heavy exercise, the overall rate of energy expenditure may increase by a factor of 20, but blood flow only increases up to six-fold. This apparent mismatch between perfusion requirements and the available blood supply may be of importance to understanding the motor preparatory functions of the energy mobilization response. The blood's oxygen carrying capacity depends primarily on the hemoglobin (Hb4) concentration which ranges between individuals from 14 to 16 g per 100 ml of blood, with each gram of Hb4 able to carry 1.34 ml of O_2. In addition, 0.3 ml of O_2 per 100 ml of blood is dissolved in the plasma. Therefore, in the circulation approximately 19–22 ml of O_2 per 100 ml of blood is available. At rest the arteriovenous oxygen difference δO_2a-v, which reflects the average rate of O_2 usage, is 4–5 ml per 100 ml of blood, and this value increases three-fold to approximately 15 ml per 100 ml of blood during high workloads.

In the case of steady-state exercise (within the aerobic capacity of the individual), the shortfall in blood flow is supported by two mechanisms. Firstly, vascular responses, which define pathways that differ in their resistance to the flow of blood, shunt more blood from the viscera and skin to the striate muscles thereby increasing the proportion of the cardiac output they receive from 15% at rest to 80–85% in exercise. Secondly, exercise produces increases in blood acidity, temperature and CO_2 concentration which shifts the oxyhemoglobin dissociation curve. This 'Bohr' effect causes hemoglobin to yield more O_2 at a given partial pressure of oxygen (pO_2) to the depleted tissues. By these processes, the oxygen requirements of active tissues may be met with relatively modest increases in blood flow rates.

Any inadequacies in the operation of the energy delivery system will restrict the intensity and duration of striate muscular activity. Such a condition arises at the onset of exercise and identifies the functional necessity of an energy mobilization stage of motor preparation. For example, Hales and Ludbrook (1988) note that, whereas the metabolic requirements of tissues increase simultaneously with the onset of their activity, a rise in circulation rates to the levels required to accommodate increased perfusion demands takes several seconds to develop. Depending on the intensity of the activity, the lag is 10–15 s in dogs (Vatner *et al.*, 1972), in rabbits it is about 60 s (Ludbrook and Graham, 1985) and in humans, between 10 and 30 s (McArdle, Foglia and Patti, 1967). These lags in the circulation retard the delivery of oxygen to the active tissues, thereby necessitating the activation of anaerobic metabolism to support the initial stages of activity. The period of insufficient tissue perfusion results in an 'oxygen deficit' which must be repaid with additional cardiopulmonary activity during the period of exercise or when the exercise has ceased. This has been termed the 'oxygen debt'. The extent to which the oxygen debt exceeds the oxygen deficit reflects the degree to which blood flow rates are inadequate in meeting the metabolic requirements of the tissues.

Several processes mediated primarily by the sympathetic nervous system operate to abbreviate the duration of the imbalance between tissue demands and supply. For example, Jackson *et al.* (1961) found that adrenalin levels in astronauts were substantially augmented 82 hours prior to the flight. A similar result was reported by Goodall and Berman (1960) who found that anticipatory catecholamine excretion rates increased in direct relationship to the magnitude of a forthcoming gravitational stress. Research has also indicated that many other elements of the energy mobilization process antedate the onset of motor activity. Thus, prior to the initiation of striate muscular activity, cardiac performance and ventilation increases and blood vessels in non-exercising vascular beds constrict. The onset of muscular contraction is marked by dilation of the vessels in active muscles. These conditions of augmented blood pressure and relatively low resistance to blood flow in the active muscles support the required local increase in circulation before cardiac output has risen to an adequate level.

Therefore on both functional and empirical grounds it would seem reasonable to classify such anticipatory cardiovascular and pulmonary responses as aspects of motor preparation. A common alternative is to interpret these visceral responses as expressions of arousal, activation, anxiety, stress, etc. This seems unsatisfactory on functional grounds since, unlike motor processes, there is no obvious dependency of these cognitive and affective states on cardiovascular and pulmonary changes. Where such interpretations are made, the visceral responses tend to be viewed as byproducts of central processes as in arousal, or as vehicles for the transmission of information as in attention (Lacey and Lacey, 1974) and emotion (Katkin, 1985). On the other hand, analysis of cardiovascular and pulmonary activities within their established physiological roles may enhance understanding of the energetics of motor performance.

DISTURBANCES IN THE RELATIONSHIP BETWEEN CARDIAC PERFORMANCE AND METABOLIC RATE

The direct relationship between cardiac output ($\dot{Q}$) and the rate of metabolism is expressed by the equation: $\dot{V}O_2 = \dot{Q} \times \delta O_2$a-v; that is, the rate of oxygen consumption is equal to the rate of blood flow or cardiac output multiplied by the arteriovenous oxygen difference. Both $\dot{Q}$ and δO_2a-v increase as functions of $\dot{V}O_2$, thereby maintaining an adequate supply of oxygen to the tissues. However, if $\dot{Q}$ increases while $\dot{V}O_2$ is held constant, δO_2a-v will fall to subnormal levels indicating that more oxygen is being circulated to the tissues than is required by the organism's current metabolic rate and a state of excessive perfusion is defined. Such states, in which cardiac performance exceeds metabolic requirements, reflect disturbances of the normal relationship between cardiac and metabolic rates ($\dot{Q}/\dot{V}O_2$) and have been associated here with energy mobilization and motor preparation (Brener, 1986b).

The appropriateness of cardiac performance to metabolic demands is assessed by differences in the $\dot{Q}/\dot{V}O_2$ relationship recorded under conditions of behavioral or psychological challenge on the one hand, and physical exercise on the other. The rationale of this method of assessment rests on the assumption that an 'appropriate' $\dot{Q}/\dot{V}O_2$ relationship will be observed under conditions that involve only physical exercise. Such conditions are, in fact, difficult to realize in convincing terms and experimenters often rely on rough approximations to 'pure' physical demand conditions. Nevertheless, the metabolic 'appropriateness' of cardiac performance is generally assessed by subtracting from measures of cardiac performance obtained under conditions of behavioral challenge, measures obtained during exercise at equivalent metabolic rates (Brener, 1986b). Positive differences reflect a condition of tissue overperfusion and negative values reflect underperfusion. The method is well illustrated in Figure 4.4, taken from a paper by Sherwood *et al.* (1986) who examined cardiovascular and metabolic responses in subjects while they were engaging in exercise, during a cold pressor stress and during a stressful shock avoidance task. The figure also shows that the elevations in $\dot{Q}$ relative to $\dot{V}O_2$ are eliminated by the administration of beta-adrenergic blockade.

Much data concerning variations in the $\dot{Q}/\dot{V}O_2$ relationship come from investigations into the behavioral sources of cardiovascular pathophysiology. Since the early experiments of Grollman (1929) demonstrating that medical students exhibit overperfusion during oral examinations, a considerable body of research has revealed that excessive cardiac activity occurs when individuals are submitted to 'stressful' conditions. Most of the studies have assessed $\dot{Q}/\dot{V}O_2$ using indices of $\dot{Q}$ such as heart rate (HR) and indices of $\dot{V}O_2$ such as activity levels, EMG, CO_2 production and minute ventilation. Such indices may introduce errors in assessing the appropriateness of perfusion rates. For example, although heart rate (HR) is the major determinant of cardiac output ($\dot{Q}$), fluctuations in venous return may influence stroke volume independently of HR, thereby impairing the correlation between HR and $\dot{Q}$. As mentioned earlier, variations in venous return that are independent of $\dot{V}O_2$ occur with alterations in the size of the muscle mass generating the metabolic load (Lewis *et al.*, 1983). The contribution of the muscle pump to the total cardiac output increases as a function of the implicated muscle mass: small, hard-working muscles generate higher cardiac outputs than large, slow-working muscles even when their total metabolic costs are equivalent. Other dimensions of muscular activity also influence the $\dot{Q}/\dot{V}O_2$ relationship. Thus when metabolic rate is controlled, static muscular activity and upper body activity generates higher cardiac outputs than dynamic and lower body activity respectively (Stenberg *et al.*, 1967). Furthermore, measures of motor activity are poorly correlated with $\dot{V}O_2$ under some conditions. For example, Brener, Phillips and Sherwood (1983) and Brener (1987) found that recorded rates of motor activity may increase substantially in the face of declining $\dot{V}O_2$. Many metabolically-costly motor activities, particularly postural adjustments and static muscular activity, are not easily recorded but may contribute significantly to the overall metabolic rate.

In view of these considerations, variations in the relationships between an index of $\dot{Q}$ such as HR and $\dot{V}O_2$ may not provide an adequate basis for inferring

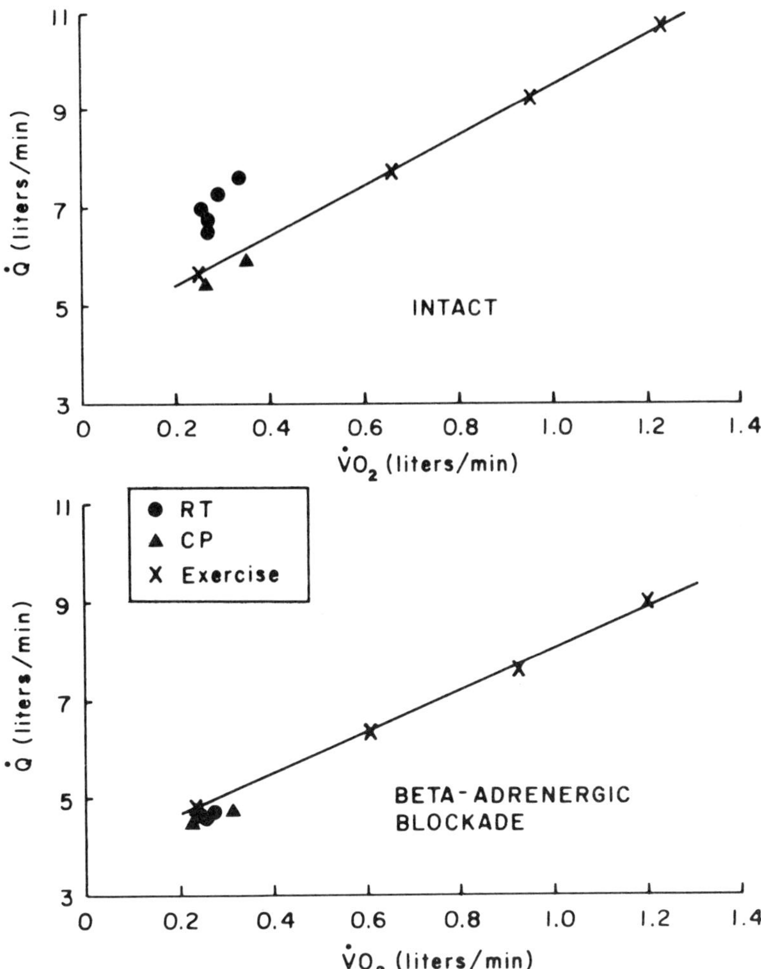

Figure 4.4. The evaluation of tissue overperfusion, indicating a hyperkinetic circulation during behavioral challenges (RT: reaction-time task; CP: cold pressor) shown by positive deviations from the linear relationship between cardiac output and oxygen consumption recorded during dynamic exercise at 25 to 75 watts. Overperfusion during the RT task in the intact condition (top) is prevented by beta-adrenergic blockade (bottom). (Reproduced with permission from Sherwood *et al.* (1986). © Society for Psychophysiological Research.)

the appropriateness of rates of tissue perfusion. They may, nevertheless, provide useful information about the organism's state of motor preparation. As discussed earlier, neurogenic control of the heart is reflected more by HR than by stroke volume (Donald and Shepherd, 1963). Therefore, even if $\dot{Q}$ does not increase, when HR levels exceed predictions based on the organism's prevailing metabolic rate, augmented central drive on the myocardium is implied. However, the use of indices of energy expenditure such as measures of motor performance does raise more serious problems, since such indices may not adequately reflect perfusion requirements and hence will not provide an adequate basis for predicting cardiac performance.

An early demonstration of excessive cardiac activity using an HR/$\dot{V}O_2$ index was reported by Blix, Stromme and Ursin (1974), who found that aircraft pilots exhibited heart rates which were excessive in relation to their concurrent rates of oxygen consumption. Heart rate most exceeded predictions based on metabolic rate when the pilots were involved in difficult flight maneuvers such as landing or taking off. Furthermore the heart rates of novice pilots were more excessive than those of experienced pilots. These observations are consistent with the hypothesis offered earlier, that the greater the behavioral uncertainty (novice pilots, difficult maneuvers), the more prominent were feedforward influences on cardiac performance. A related observation has been reported by Fenz and Epstein (1967) who measured heart rate and respiration before, during and following parachute jumping in experienced and novice parachutists. Both experts and novices exhibited increased cardiopulmonary activity prior to entering the aircraft (i.e. early in the preparatory period). However, once they had boarded the aircraft, cardiopulmonary activity in the experts stabilized, whereas in the novices it continued to rise until the jump had been completed. These observations are consistent with the hypothesis that as behavioral adaptation proceeds and uncertainty is reduced, energy mobilization becomes more attuned to the metabolic requirements of motor performance.

According to Obrist (1981), the condition which most promotes excessive cardiac activity involves 'effortful, active coping'. This concept implies the deployment of motor activity in the solution of a difficult but not intractable problem. If the goal identified by the environmental contingencies (e.g. shock avoidance) is easy to accomplish (e.g. by reaction times of less than 1000 ms), or if it is impossible (e.g. by reaction times of less than 100 ms) or not amenable to a motoric solution (e.g. cold pressor stress), cardiac performance is less elevated. Neither the threat of shock (easy solution), muscular activation (easy solution) nor painful stimulation (cold pressor) can account for the substantial cardiac elevations observed under the 'effortful, active coping' condition. Instead, the critical factor appears to be the extent to which composing a motor response that adequately meets situational requirements draws upon available resources.

A gross distinction may be made between active and passive coping: a laboratory illustration of the former being a stressful reaction time task and the latter, the cold pressor test. In the stressful reaction time task, the subject may make rapid motor responses in order to avoid a painful stimulus. However, in the cold pressor test, no behavioral means is provided for the subject to avoid pain. Experimental comparisons of these two challenges have repeatedly provided evidence supporting the prediction that the $\dot{Q}$ to $\dot{V}O_2$ ratio is significantly higher during stressful reaction time tasks than during cold pressor tests (Obrist, 1981). The most direct evidence comes from an experiment by Sherwood *et al.* (1986) who measured gas exchange as well as a full range of cardiovascular and pulmonary variables while subjects were submitted to the two challenges. They found that the significantly higher $\dot{Q}$ to $\dot{V}O_2$ ratios (indicating overperfusion) recorded during the reaction time task were attributable to greater beta-adrenergic drive on the heart during this task than during the cold pressor test.

Certain environmental contingencies require a more continuous state of preparation (e.g. avoidance of an unpredictable shock) whereas others (e.g. avoidance of a predictable shock) may only require intermittent preparation. In terms of the arguments presented, it would be expected that conditions which require more sustained motor preparation should result in greater disruptions of the normal $\dot{Q}/\dot{V}O_2$ relationship than do conditions which require less preparation. This is because the more sustained the preparation, the more the motor brain will be engaged in computing an adequate response and the more dominant will be feedforward influences in the energy delivery systems. An experiment by Sherwood, Brener and Moncur (1983) examined this hypothesis by using the predictability of an imperative stimulus for shock avoidance to manipulate the extent of motor preparation. In a high-predictability condition, imperative stimuli for rapid high-energy shock-avoidance responses always followed the onset of a 30 s warning stimulus by 5 s, whereas in the low-predictability condition, imperative stimuli could occur at any time during the warning stimulus. In the latter condition, it was also possible for no imperative stimuli or more than one stimulus to occur during the warning stimulus. These conditions were designed to maintain low-predictability animals in a more continuous state of motor preparation than high-predictability animals. In the former condition, subjects had to be ready to make an avoidance response throughout the period that the warning stimulus was present, whereas in the latter condition they needed only to be ready to respond for the first 5 s of each warning stimulus period. Although subjects under both low- and high-predictability conditions exhibited evidence of excessive cardiac activity by the $HR/\dot{V}O_2$ index, this effect was significantly greater in the low-predictability condition. Animals in the two groups exhibited similar rates of shock avoidance, indicating that the effect was not due to rates of aversive stimulation. Further, since the groups did not differ in their recorded rates of motor activity, it seems more likely that the effects of preparation were realized through feedforward influences on cardiac performance than by feedback from the motor system. Thus the data are consistent with the view that more sustained states of motor preparation are associated with more excessive elevations in cardiac performance.

A variant of this paradigm has recently been employed on humans by

Sherwood *et al.* (1988) in a further examination of the effects of preparatory processes on cardiac performance. In this experiment subjects were required to squeeze a hand dynamometer with a high force (90% MVC) or low force (10% MVC) to avoid shock under conditions where the presentation of imperative stimuli were either unpredictable or highly predictable. Significantly greater elevations in HR were recorded in response to the low-predictability and high-force conditions than to high-predictability and low-force conditions respectively. The similar effects on cardiac performance of the physical (force) and 'mental' (predictability) requirements of the task provides additional support for the view that processes which are activated in computing effective motor performance overlap those that are implicated in actual motor performance. It might also be said that the extent of feedforward control on the cardiovascular effects is determined by the degree to which the resources required for task fulfillment tax either the physical or informational capacities of the organism.

It is widely accepted that the motor brain exerts feedforward influences on the cardiopulmonary centers. When such influences are dominant, it may be expected that cardiopulmonary performance will deviate more markedly from metabolic requirements than when feedback influences predominate. In some circumstances, such as at the inception of exercise or in behavioral emergencies, feedforward control of ventilation and circulation serves important adaptive functions by providing a circulatory reserve. However, in many other situations, excessive circulation and ventilation is not only redundant but is potentially pathogenic. Feedback provides online information about perfusion requirements whereas feedforward information provides only an estimate of such requirements. Further, it would seem that estimates of the perfusion requirements of forthcoming activities are exaggerated by difficult or unfamiliar task demands: such demands require much computation to formulate effective coping responses. It seems plausible that the structures and processes which are implicated in computing effective responses provide the sources of feedforward influences on the energy mobilization and delivery systems. An analysis of these processes forms the substance of the following sections of this article. These sections, which deal with the phenomena of phasic preparation for action, describe the sorts of computations which antedate the emergence of adaptive activity and identify the brain processes which are implicated in making these computations.

PHASIC PREPARATION

Several review papers on phasic preparatory processes were published about 10 years ago (Holender, 1980a; Requin, 1978, 1980a,b). Thus, with a few exceptions, in this section we have restricted our citations to publications after 1980.

PREPARING FOR A SPECIFIC RESPONSE

There are two perspectives on how adding physiological measures to behavioral measures may illuminate the processes that are responsible for composing an adaptive action once the command to act has been received. In the reductionistic conception, a knowledge of the functioning of the neuronal network responsible for information processing is considered necessary to fill the explanatory void left by the inferential conception of the chronometric approach. Proponents of this conception explicitly promote a neurophysiology of cognition (e.g. Mountcastle, 1986), an ambitious project which has been encouraged recently by the neoreductionist views of 'neurophilosophers' (Churchland, 1986).

In the second perspective, which is non-reductionist and functionalist, physiological measures are used similarly to behavioral measures, as 'markers' of cognitive processes from which inferences can be drawn about these processes (e.g. Donchin and Coles, 1988). Both sets of indices are thus considered to be outputs from the information processing systems. Proponents of this view employ correlation-based analyses of activity in these systems to infer the cognitive functions of the systems. From their point of view, knowledge of the physiological mechanisms which determine the features of physiological indices is not needed to gain some insight into information processing. Meyer *et al.* (1988), for instance, have recently described the rationales for using ERP measures to draw inferences about information processing within the framework of the chronometric paradigm. Such an approach, by affording a similar status to physiological and performance measures in analyzing brain information processing operations, evades the epistemological problem of the causal relationships between the classes of physiological and behavioral events.

The study of the role that neural structures play in phasic motor preparation was initiated by the discovery of changes in the EEG activity of the human brain during studies conducted in the framework of the RT paradigm. Walter and colleagues (1964) demonstrated a sustained negative change in brain potential between S1 and S2, the so-called 'expectancy wave' or subsequently, 'contingent negative variation' (CNV). Initially investigated in conditions of short (less than 2 s) S1–S2 intervals, the CNV was shown to be loosely related to a number of cognitive factors (cf. Rohrbaugh and Gaillard, 1983, for a review), but not specifically to motor processes. Thus the CNV did not disappear when S2 did not require a motor response. Further, early suggestions that RT could be predicted on the basis of CNV amplitude have been questioned by more recent findings. It was shown later that, provided the S1–S2 interval is long enough (i.e. more than 2 s), the CNV is formed by two successive components which overlap with shorter S1–S2 intervals. The features and scalp distribution, prominent on the frontal areas of the early S1-related component, are similar to those of the late negativity (the '0 wave') which follows a stimulus without warning significance. The late component, which starts about 1 s before S2, was found to be prominent over motor cortical areas contralateral to the movement (Brunia and Vingerhoets, 1980).

Almost at the same time as CNV discovery, Kornhuber and Deecke (1965) showed that the execution of a self-paced repetitive movement was preceded by a slow negative change in brain potential, the so-called 'readiness potential' (RP), starting about 1 s before EMG activity and followed by changes in brain activity closely related to movement execution (see Deecke *et al.*, 1984, for a review). The RP starts over the supplementary motor area (SMA), a finding which was confirmed by Roland *et al.* (1980) through recordings of local changes in brain metabolic activity, and then develops precentrally over the primary motor (MI) and premotor (PM) areas, as well as postcentrally over the somatosensory area (Allison, Wood and McCarthy, 1986; Arrezzo and Vaughan, 1980; Brunia, 1988; Wood and Allison, 1981; see also Hashimoto, Gemba and Sasaki, 1980, in the monkey). This successive activation of the SMA, in which movements are known to be bilaterally represented (see Goldberg, 1986, and Wiesendanger, 1986, for reviews) and then of PM and MI, fit well the scalp distribution of the RP preceding unilateralized movement, which is bilateral during its first half and becomes contralateral during its second half (Brunia and Haagh, 1986; cf. also Libet, Wright and Gleason, 1982).

A recent methodological development in the analysis of preparation-related changes in cerebral potentials is based on the assumption that this small RP component contralateral to the movement side can be extracted from the large bilateral component of the late CNV and/or RP. By first subtracting the between-hemisphere difference in potential recorded from either hemisphere when performing a movement on one side, and then subtracting these hemispheric differences in potential for movements performed on either side, an index of the change in the cerebral potential may be derived. This is the so-called 'lateralized readiness potential' (LRP) which is related specifically to preparation for the side of the movement (Gratton *et al.*, 1988; DeJong *et al.*, 1988).

A more precise description of the physiological mechanisms which underly the changes in brain potential associated with preparation would provide a stronger basis for specifying their functional roles. The use of ERP techniques has enabled the scalp distributions for processes associated with preparation to be broadly mapped. Unfortunately, the low accuracy of the topographical analysis of ERPs, when recorded and analyzed with usual EEG techniques, has led to an accumulation of data which are subject to large individual variation, hard to synthetize and often uninterpretable with regard to underlying brain mechanisms (Rohrbaugh and Gaillard, 1983). However, over the past few years a number of new techniques, based on improved knowledge of the biophysics of the electric fields of the brain (e.g. Nunez, 1981), have been developed for localizing the neural generators of the ERP components recorded from the scalp (e.g. Crammond, MacKay and Murphy, 1985; Scherg, 1989; Lehman and Skrandies, 1984; Perrin, Bertrand and Pernier, 1987). These methods promise to yield information on the anatomical and physiological substrates of preparatory changes in brain potentials.

Following the pioneering work of Hubel (1957) and Jasper, Ricci and Doane (1958), techniques for recording single-neuron activity in behaving animals have become a major method in studying the neural mechanisms of cognitive brain functions (Mountcastle, 1986). Several technical problems associated with the accuracy of specifying anatomical locations, identifying the functional role of individual neurons and determining the temporal relationships between changes in neuronal activity and behavioral events have been progressively solved (Goldberg, 1983; Lemon, 1984). Nevertheless, the interpretation of data provided by single-neuron recordings remains limited for methodological reasons (e.g. Requin, Riehle and Seal, 1989). First, the sequential recording of a sample of neurons, however large, only allows inferences to be drawn about the functions of the brain structure within which these neurons are recorded; that is, to reconstitute the functional properties of a neuronal population from a mosaic of observations distributed in 'behavioral time'. Second, the current recording methods give no direct indication of the dynamic aspects of interneuronal connectivity and, more generally, of the functional cooperation within neuronal populations during a behavioral sequence. However, the recent development of multielectrode, single-neuron recording techniques (e.g. Lurito *et al.*, 1988) promises to further reveal the real time mechanisms of higher brain functions.

Before the ERP and EEG methods had reached their current level of development, most investigations of the preparatory activity of central neural structures in man were attempted by recording changes in the electromyogram (see Duffy, 1962, for a review). Although EMG activity provides information about a small number of spinal motoneurons actually activated during the S1–S2 interval, it cannot reveal subthreshold changes in the excitability of the larger number of still inactivated motoneurons. In order to monitor more subtle excitatory or inhibitory central influences impinging upon spinal motor structures, reflex methods were introduced in the study of motor preparation (Requin, 1965). Following the seminal work of Paillard (1955), the anatomical and physiological background for understanding spinal mechanisms and their supraspinal control, as well as the methodological aspects of spinal reflex testing, have been extensively described (e.g. Bonnet, Requin and Semjen, 1981). Moreover, a significant extension and improvement of this method for investigating the activity of central neural structures has resulted, more recently, from the discovery of the so-called 'long loop' or 'transcortical' reflex techniques (Bonnet and Requin, 1982; Wiesendanger and Miles, 1982). By suddenly stretching a muscle, not only the monosynaptic spinal reflex (M1) is evoked, but also two successive later response components can be electromyographically recorded. They result from the activation of two hierarchically organized reflex loops: the first (M2) almost certainly includes cortical pathways (Cheney and Fetz, 1984), whereas the second (M3) probably includes cerebellar pathways (MacKay and Murphy, 1979). An implication of this neural organization is that M2 (or, better, the difference M2–M1) can be viewed as a specific index of the activity state of cortical structures, and M3 (or, better, the difference M3–M2) as a specific index of the activity state of the set of neural structures, including the cerebellum, which send strong projections to motor cortical areas.

While the rationales of the chronometric paradigm provide a basis for drawing valuable inferences about covert preparatory processes from changes in RT, changes in physiological indices associated with these processes have to be selected on the basis of operational criteria. The timing of physiological changes is the first and most obvious criterion: preparatory processes are supposed to act during the S1–S2 interval and, consequently, their physiological concomitants are expected to occur during this period. However, the problem of delineating precisely the time course of motor preparation and motor action, as either a clear-cut boundary between discrete processes or a gradual transition between continuous processes, remains unsolved. Preparation cannot be considered to end when S2 occurs, but rather at some 'point of no return' after that motor output is irreversibly triggered (Logan and Cowan, 1984; Osman, Kornblum and Meyer, 1986; DeJong *et al.*, in press). The second criterion for labeling physiological changes as preparatory relates to their sensitivity to the informational content of S1. Within the framework of the preparation paradigm, manipulating information provided by S1 about the features of S2 and the associated response is expected to result in parallel changes in RT and physiological measures. The third criterion is that the physiological indices of preparation should predict motor performance. A change in the activity of a physiological system cannot be considered as preparatory if it does not affect the processing that it is supposed to prepare for. This predictive criterion is often missing in neuronal studies of motor preparation. Selecting as preparatory only those physiological processes which met these three criteria of timing, sensitivity to S1 informational content and predictive value for performance would almost certainly result in a drastic reduction of relevant data.

SOLVING THE TIME-UNCERTAINTY PROBLEM: WHEN TO RESPOND

The problem of time uncertainty relates to the nature of the preparatory processes that are activated when an individual is anticipating a behavioral demand to arise at some unspecifiable time in the future. Such a situation is that of a sprinter in his starting blocks waiting for the starting gun, or that of a driver waiting for a green traffic light. The nicely designed experiments presented by Bertelson (1967) and his colleagues (see Alegria, 1980, and Requin, 1978, for reviews) rule out the option of maintaining a perpetual state of preparation *for a specific action*. First, by examining changes in RT when the duration of the S1–S2 interval is progressively reduced, it has been demonstrated that a minimum time of 150 ms is necessary to reach a maximum state of readiness. Second, by requiring subjects to be ready at a given time and occasionally presenting S2 later than expected, it is possible to evaluate the maintenance of preparation by studying the changes in RT as a function of the interval between the expected and the actual times of S2. This maintenance seems to be limited to about 250 ms, after which the state of readiness *for reacting to S2 is dissipated*. Finally, when subjects are required to be ready *to perform the same response* at two successive times, changes in RT according to the interval between these two expected times of S2 reflect the time necessary to be ready again, after having been ready the first time. The time to *re*prepare was found to be about 900 ms.

This set of results is summarized in Figure 4.5, which shows the times necessary to 'prepare', 'de-prepare' and 're-prepare', respectively. They suggest that the processes responsible for expecting events, and preparing for reacting to them, have some inertia and are sensitive to fatigue. It is as if, when expecting to have something to do in the near future, a limited capacity of preparatory 'resources' are available which must be optimally managed. The costs of preparation relative to the limited resources available to support this process is the main constraint on the duration of preparation. This explains why, when facing time uncertainty, it is impossible to be permanently ready

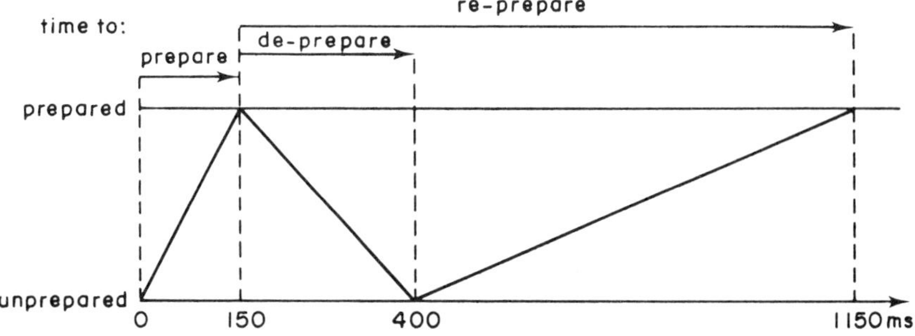

Figure 4.5. Discrete two-step model of preparation (after Algeria, 1974). Diagram of times required to (1) reach a state of preparation from an unprepared state (to prepare), (2) reach an unprepared state from a prepared state (to de-prepare), and (3) reach a prepared state right after having cycled through prepared and unprepared states (to re-prepare). For further explanations see the text.

to execute a specific response. Rather, preparation must be timed by using all information available to be maximally ready at the right time.

This aspect of strategy in solving the time uncertainty problem can be inferred from data published 75 years ago by Woodrow (1914) when studying the effect of the duration of the S1–S2 interval upon RT in two different experimental conditions. In the first ('blocked') condition, the duration of the S1–S2 interval was the same over a block of trials and was then changed from block to block. In the second, ('varied') condition, the different possible durations of the S1–S2 interval were mixed within the same block of trials. In the blocked condition, RT progressively lengthened as the duration of the S1–S2 interval increased. This could be due to a decrease in the subject's accuracy in estimating time elapsed since S1. In the varied condition, the mean RT was greatly increased. In this condition subjects could no longer expect the occurrence of S2 at a particular time, a situation which defines an overall increase in time uncertainty. However, the lengthening of RT as the duration of the S1–S2 interval increased, found in the blocked condition, now disappeared, suggesting that a second factor intervened in the varied condition to cancel the effects of time estimation error.

The factor in question is a conditional probability effect which has been formalized by Durup and Requin (1970; see also Requin, 1978). In their model, the preparation resources are shared equally among the alternative possible times at which S2 could occur. For example, suppose that three possible durations of the S1–S2 interval are equiprobable but randomly used in a series of trials. After some trials, as soon as S1 is presented, the subject knows that there are three possible and successive times when S2 can occur. Provided that intervals between these times are short enough to prohibit, or at least to restrict, successive re-preparation, two strategies are possible. The more risky strategy is to expect S2 to occur at a particular time and, therefore, to prepare only for this time. The more conservative strategy is to expect S2 at all three times, that is to share preparatory resources between them. When these three times of occurrence are equiprobable, this last strategy leads to allocating a third of the available readiness to each of them. However, when the time elapsed since S1 exceeds the shortest possible S1–S2 interval, S2 becomes equally probable after either the medium or the longest possible S1–S2 interval. Now the readiness resource may be split equally between the remaining two alternatives. Finally, if S2 does not occur after the medium S1–S2 interval, it becomes certain that it will occur at the longest interval. Hence, the full readiness resource may be deployed for preparing for this time of occurrence of S2. This leads to the prediction that the level of preparation will increase as a function of the S1–S2 interval in Woodrow's 'varied' condition. This will be manifested by decreasing RT, an effect which opposes and masks the effects of S1–S2 on the time estimation error. Thus, in the 'varied' condition, RT—and by implication preparation—remains more-or-less constant as the S1–S2 interval is varied.

This hypothesis was tested by comparing (a) the effect of altering conditional probability while holding the effects of time estimation constant, with (b) the effects of holding conditional probability constant while varying the time estimation factor.

The method is illustrated in Figure 4.6. First, the accuracy of time estimation is equalized for different durations of the S1–S2 interval by introducing into the varied condition a timer which continuously signals the passage of time, thereby reducing timing uncertainty to a minimum. Second, the conditional probability of S2 is equalized for the different durations of the S1–S2 interval, by appropriately setting the frequencies of these different durations. For example, when there are four equiprobable durations of the S1–S2 interval in a series of trials, the conditional probabilities of S2 to occur at the end of the four possible S1–S2 intervals are 0.25, 0.33, 0.50 and 1.00. However, by appropriately altering the frequencies of the S1–S2 intervals so that they decrease from the shortest to the longest S1–S2 interval, the conditional probabilities of S2 at the end of all the S1–S2 intervals may be held constant ('non-aging' foreperiod distribution). Moreover, combining both these conditions leads to the RT (preparation level) remaining constant as the duration of the S1–S2 interval increases. The same effect is observed when the effects of time estimation and of conditional probability are opposed.

These conditions were investigated in a series of experiments in which level of preparation was monitored by RT and by the changes in the CNV (Besrest and Requin, 1973). As predicted, when the time estimation error was controlled by providing a clock, RT shortened and the amplitude of the CNV progressively increased as the time since S1 increased. However, when a non-aging foreperiod was used without a clock, RT lengthened and brain activity decreased as the duration of the S1–S2 interval increased. The situation in which the conditional probability of S2 increased with the elapsed time but with no clock was compared with the situation in which conditional probability remained constant and a clock was provided. As predicted by the model, changes in RT, as well as in the time course of the CNV, did not differ between these two situations when the S1–S2 interval lengthened (Figure 4.7).

Very similar results were obtained with animals trained in such RT tasks. During these experiments microelectrodes were used to record the activity of neurons in the reticular formation of the midbrain, a neural structure which is considered to be responsible for changes in the activity level of the cerebral cortex. In the condition in which RT shortened as the duration of the S1–S2 interval lengthened, the activity of the neurons recorded in this structure were found to increase (Macar, Lecas and Requin, 1980), thereby providing an index of the increase of the conditional probability of S2.

Note that, in this model, preparation is viewed as a resource distributed in time according to continuously updated, long-term information of the frequency and range of the different foreperiod durations. An alternative

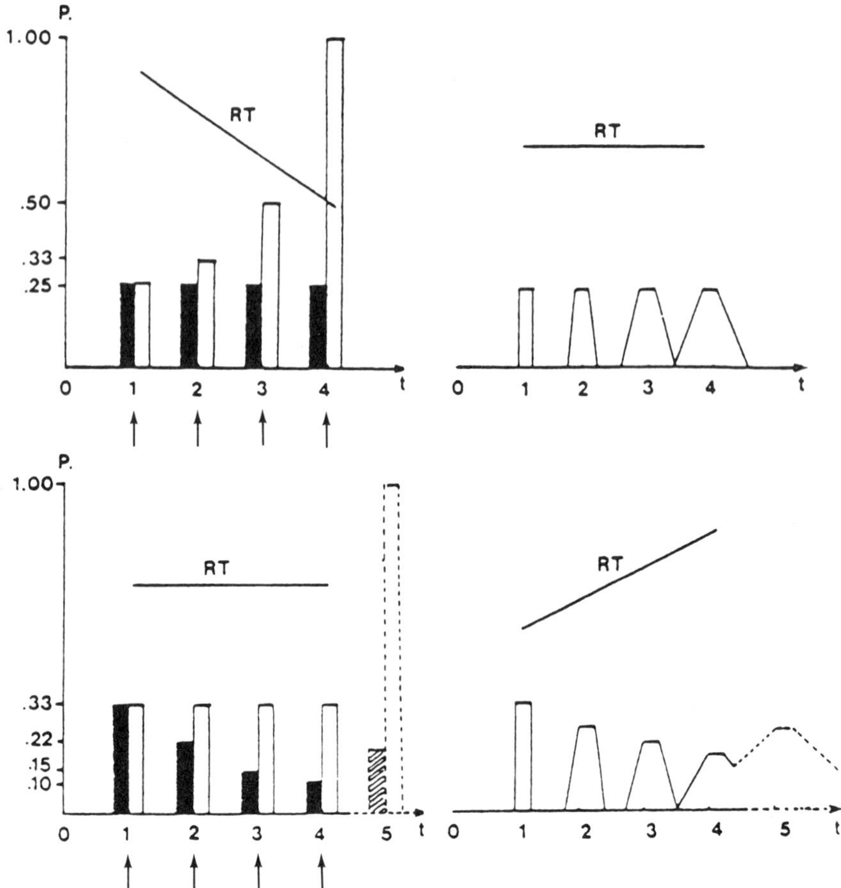

Figure 4.6. A probabilistic model of the time course of preparation in a simple-RT task with a foreperiod of variable duration. *Upper left*: Foreperiod durations with a rectangular frequency distribution (black columns). It is assumed that estimation of the time of occurrence of S2 is reset by a timer at every possible occurrence of S2. Preparation level is therefore a function of the conditional probability of S2 (white columns), which increases with the time elapsed since S1; RT is thus expected to decrease as the foreperiod increases. *Upper right*: When there is no timer, the decrease in time estimation accuracy with increasing foreperiod durations counteracts the simultaneous effects of an increase in the conditional probability of S2. The result is, as expected, that there is no relationship between foreperiod duration and the level of preparation—and thus RT. *Bottom left*: No relationship is expected with a 'non-aging' frequency distribution of foreperiod durations either since this arrangement leads to a rectangular distribution of the conditional probabilities for S2 (at least for a part of this foreperiod distribution). It is assumed that estimation of the time of occurrence of S2 is reset by a timer thereby maintaining time estimation accuracy constant over different foreperiod durations. *Bottom right*: When no timer is provided, the decrease in time estimation accuracy with increasing foreperiod duration is expected to result in a decrease in the preparation level, which in turn leads to an increase in RT. (Reproduced with permission from Requin (1978). © Masson et Cie.)

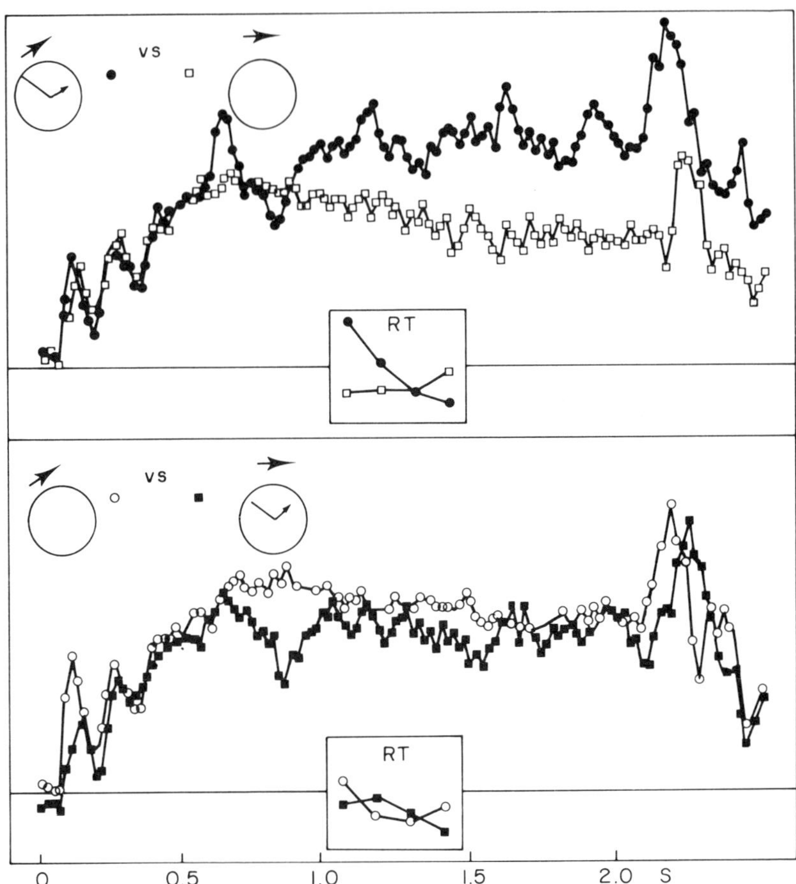

Figure 4.7. Changes in brain potential during the foreperiod of a simple RT task for the four conditions defined in Figure 4.6. In the upper part of the figure the time course of the CNV from S1 to S2 is compared for two conditions: (1) when the conditional probability of S2 (arrow) increases with foreperiod duration and a timer (clock) is used (black circles), and (2) when the conditional probability of S2 remains constant over foreperiod duration and no timer is used (white squares). In the lower part of the figure the time course of the CNV is shown in two conditions: (1) when the conditional probability of S2 increases with foreperiod duration and no timer is used (white circles), and (2) when the conditional probability of S2 remains constant over foreperiod duration and a timer is used (black squares). Corresponding relationships between foreperiod duration and RT are shown in the inserted panels. Averaged data for 10 subjects. (Reproduced with permission from Besrest and Requin (1973). © Academic Press.)

model of the timing of preparation in RT tasks, which entails only two discrete preparatory states (prepared and unprepared), has been proposed on the basis of data indicating that RT depends partly on sequential effects related to foreperiod duration. RTs are shortest when the foreperiod is of the same duration as that of the preceding trial. They increase when the foreperiod is shorter than the preceding one, but not when it is longer (Alegria, 1980). These data were interpreted as evidence for a two-step model based upon the choice of a target-foreperiod. First, the subject automatically repeats the timing of preparation which was, or would have been, successful at the preceding trial. If the passage of time since S1 is longer than expected, he then *re*prepares for a longer foreperiod, which is chosen according to the frequency destribution of foreperiods. This model, which views preparation as 'all-or-none', predicts the same relationship between RT and conditional probability as does the distributed resource model described earlier (Requin, 1978).

As described earlier, two CNV components may be distinguished, an 0-wave which is triggered by S1 and an RP which occurs approximately 1 s before a movement. Where the task requires a movement, the second or later CNV component may be attributed to motor preparatory processes. However, this interpretation is questioned by evidence (e.g. Kutas, 1984) that sustained negativities during the S1–S2 intervals, even of long duration, can be observed without any motor response to S2 (Macar and Besson, 1985; Ruchkin *et al.*, 1986). For instance, in the ERP studies of semantic incongruity (Kutas and Hillyard, 1980), a sustained negativity develops during the silent reading of the sentences ended by the target word. This suggests either that the early negativity triggered by S1 is prolonged until S2, and thus should not be labelled as an 0 wave, or that another negativity, different from the RP, develops before S2. The introduction of this third process might explain how the time interval between S1 and S2 is bridged when long intervals are used. Such a device would seem to be necessary to account for the continuity of information processing in the precueing paradigm, between the occurrence of S1 and the production of a response. With a long foreperiod, motor preparation must be started early enough for the process to peak when S2 is expected. Congruent with this formulation is the hypothesis that there exists a third component of the CNV which is related to time estimation processes taking place during the whole interval.

This hypothesis is supported by data provided by animal (Macar and Vitton, 1979), and human (Macar and Besson, 1985) experiments which demonstrate an important role for time estimation processes in the development of the CNV (Macar, 1977). In these terms, the decrease of the CNV at the end of very long foreperiods (i.e. presumably when the S1–S2 contingency becomes quite weak) could reflect a decreasing accuracy in time estimation. It therefore seems reasonable to propose a three-component conception of the CNV, in which a negativity related specifically to time estimation processes would take place during the S1–S2 interval, bridging the gap between S1 and S2. This negativity would overlap the orienting processes associated with S1 and the readiness potential associated with S2. This would explain how the 0 wave may differ according to S1 information content, as well as how a late negativity may develop when no motor response is required to S2.

Concerning the precise physiological mechanisms involved in the temporal aspects of preparation, some topographical analyses of changes in brain potential indicate that the early CNV component may originate in frontal and, even, prefrontal areas (Rohrbaugh and Gaillard, 1983). As indicated by Brunia and Haagh (1986; see also Brunia, Haagh and Scheirs, 1985), these data are in agreement with the hypothesis that one CNV component could reflect specifically the time contingency between S1 and S2. On the basis of lesion studies the prefrontal areas have been implicated in the temporal aspects of behavioral sequences (cf. Teuber, 1972; Fuster, 1981, 1984). These studies were designed to investigate the role of prefrontal cortex in short-term memory. However, more recent studies conducted with single-neuron recording techniques have provided more specific support for this conception. Data were collected mainly in delayed-response tasks, in which information provided by S1 was to be retained during a delay—sometimes of several seconds duration—so as to perform correctly after S2. These tasks may be viewed as a variation of the preparation paradigm.

Three types of neurons with sustained changes in activity between S1 and S2 were identified in the prefrontal cortex. The first type exhibited changes in activity depending on the physical features of S1 and, thus, were considered as representing short-term storage of information coded in S1. Activity in the second type was modulated in relation to the characteristics of the forthcoming movement, thereby indicating an involvement in response preparation (Niki and Watanabe, 1976). Neurons of the third type exhibited increases in activity during the whole S1–S2 interval. Since these neurons did not respond specifically to S1 or response features, they appeared to express the temporal relationship between S1 and S2 (Fuster, 1985). Although these data are consistent with the three-component CNV hypothesis suggested above, it should be noted that there is no direct evidence for a role of these prefrontal neuronal populations in generating a CNV component which would bridge the temporal gap between S1 and S2.

THE EVENT-UNCERTAINTY PROBLEM: WHAT RESPONSE TO MAKE

Within the framework of the information processing models, choice-RT tasks remain the principal method for studying the effects of event-uncertainty. In the usual choice-RT protocol, different stimuli, associated through a rule with different responses, are randomly presented to the subject so that at the beginning of each trial the next S-R alternative is uncertain. The way in which the stimuli and response sets are circumscribed, as well as the rules that govern which response is to be made to which stimulus, have important ramifications not only for performance but also for the theoretical constructs that will be employed to interpret such performance.

The set of stimuli is either a part or the whole of a stimulus category where the category is defined by one or more dimensions (e.g. light color, tone pitch or intensity, letters, digits, etc.) and individual stimuli are differentiated along the dimensions which define the category. Similarly, the set of responses is either a part or the whole of a motor repertoire defined by one or more dimensions (e.g. movements of either hand, finger presses, letter or digit naming, etc.) and individual responses are differentiated along these dimensions (e.g. side for hands, anatomical or external space for fingers, phonology for letters or digits, etc.).

The amount of difference between stimuli or between responses depends upon the 'distance' between stimuli or between responses along the dimensions which define the stimulus category or the motor repertoire. This distance is the basis on which stimuli or responses are designated, rather arbitrarily, as 'discrete' or 'continuous' events. When the distance is large enough to make the differentiation between stimuli or between responses easy, stimuli or responses have the status of qualitatively different events. This status specifies a class of experimental paradigms in which each event (stimulus and/or response) is viewed 'as a whole': e.g. press the right button when the red light comes on and the left button when the green light comes on. When the distance between stimuli or between responses is small enough to make the differentiation difficult, or at least not trivial, the set of stimuli or the set of responses has the status of only one stimulus or only one response, the features of which may vary quantitatively. This status specifies another class of experimental paradigms in which each event (stimulus and/or response) is considered 'in parts': e.g. when the discriminability of two 'stimuli' is manipulated in reference to one of their attributes, or the similarity of two 'responses' is manipulated in reference to one of their parameters. A conceptual ramification of these methods of differentiating stimuli and responses is reflected by the concepts of 'response selection' which refers to responses as a set of discrete events, and 'motor programming' which refers to movement features as a set of continuous parameters.

Response Selection: Stimulus–Response 'Compatibility' Effects

One of the most robust findings in the experimental analysis of sensorimotor activity is that RT depends on the relationship between S and R. Fitts and his colleagues (Fitts and Seager, 1953; Fitts and Deininger, 1954; see Kornblum, Hasbroucq and Osman, 1990, for a review) have distinguished between two levels at which this 'S–R compatibility' effect acts. In the first, between-set, level there is a match between the dimensions defining the stimulus category and response repertoire, from which the stimulus set and response set are drawn. When stimulus category and response repertoire are both defined by the same dimension (e.g. position in space), RT is shorter than when stimulus category and motor repertoire are defined by different dimensions (e.g. color for the former and letter naming for the latter). In the second, within-set, level there is a pairing between stimuli and responses. When both stimulus category and response repertoire are defined by the same dimension (e.g. spatial location), an ipsilateral pairing (left S/left R, and right S/right R) results in shorter RT than a contralateral pairing (left S/right R and right S/left R).

In a more complex procedure, introduced by Simon and Rudel (1967), two features of the stimuli are independently manipulated: the words 'right' and 'left', and the ear to which they are delivered. Although both features are related to the same stimulus category (space location), one is relevant (the word meaning) and the other is irrelevant (the ear to which the word is presented) for selecting the response (a right or left press). Nevertheless RT is faster for an ipsilateral than for a contralateral pairing between the response location and stimulated ear. However, the current inclusion of the 'Simon effect' within the class of S–R compatibility effects has been challenged recently (Hasbroucq and Guiard, 1991), on the grounds that it may be explained parsimoniously by the spatial incongruity between the two stimulus features when paired contralaterally (the word 'right' delivered to the left ear). This explanation is similar to that proposed to account for the phenomena related to the Stroop effect (Egeth and Blecker, 1969).

Although procedures studying S–R compatibility effects have amassed a considerable body of data, until recently there has been a paucity of theoretical elaborations concerning S–R association processes. This poverty of ideas is quite remarkable, particularly in the absence of any interpretation linking the S–R compatibility effects found at the within-set and between-set levels. The advantage of matching particular stimulus categories and response repertoires, and of a particular pairing between stimuli and responses, were equally but loosely conceptualized in terms of the degree of 'natural tendency', 'naturalness', 'obviousness', 'correspondence', 'congruence' or 'habit strength'. The 'population stereotype' (Fitts, 1959), defined by the proportion of individuals who make the same responses to the same stimuli in the same situation, was the only attempt to provide an empirical measure of the various factors which determine S–R compatibility effects.

The model proposed recently by Kornblum, Hasbroucq and Osman (1990) thus appears to be a decisive step in understanding these effects and S–R association processes, mainly by articulating between and within-set factors. At the core of the model is the concept of 'dimensional overlap' which represents the conceptual similarity between the dimensions which define stimulus categories and response repertoires. Kornblum and his coauthors point out that within-set level effects, resulting from differentially mapping stimuli and responses, appear only when there is some dimensional overlap. Therefore such effects can be considered as a metric of this dimensional overlap. The functional aspect of the model concerning the mechanism by which S–R mapping determines RT, bears upon the automatic activation of the response corresponding to the stimulus. RT is fast when this response is that to be performed and slow when a different response is required, since the activation process must be cancelled and switched to another response. However, Hasbroucq and Guiard (1991) propose an alternative mechanism, under the subject's control, in which the time to select the required response depends upon the time to implement a systematic SR transformation rule. For example, in the Fitts' procedure, RT is shorter for the ipsilateral pairing, which involves only one operation (the assignment of S to R), than for the contralateral pairing, which involves a supplementary operation (the inversion of the S to R assignment) and increases the response selection time.

Whatever the precise mechanism that governs S–R association, whether it is the laws of automatic response activation or the rules of controlled S–R transformation, the framework of the dimensional overlap concept provides a tool to scale the abstract differences between the dimensions which define stimulus categories and response repertoires. This is of theoretical importance insofar as it impinges on questions of how external events are categorized and represented at the cognitive level. Such categorization and structuration, which results from long-term learning (development) and short-term learning (practice), must be viewed as a fundamentally important aspect of motor preparation since it is a determinant of the timing of the first, response-selection process in movement organization.

There have been several studies of S–R compatibility effects in which behavioral and physiological approaches have been combined. By manipulating both stimulus discriminability and S–R compatibility, McCarthy and Donchin (1981) have shown that the latency of the P300 ERP component depends upon the former but not upon the latter factor. Such a dissociation was also found by Magliero *et al.* (1984), thus confirming that P300 latency does not index the timing of the response selection process. This conclusion has, however, been challenged by Ragot (1984) who observed changes in the P300 latency as a function of S–R compatibility. This experiment employed a variation of the Simon procedure, which as already mentioned, probably reveals S–S incongruity effects rather than S–R incompatibility effects. It is surprising that the ERP components which were identified as related specifically to the activity of cortical motor structures have never been examined in the S–R compatibility paradigm. In recent studies based on the Eriksen and Eriksen noise-compatibility paradigm (1974; see also Eriksen *et al.*, 1985), in which conflict between stimulus features results in a competition between responses, Coles and his colleagues (1988) have demonstrated that the 'lateralized readiness potential' (LRP) is a good index of subthreshold activation of inappropriate responses. Similarly, in a between-sides choice-RT condition, correct and incorrect fast response guesses can be detected on the basis of the LRP (Gratton *et al.*, 1988). Moreover, recording of the LRP has provided some insight into the mechanism by which a prepared response could be inhibited successfully before some 'point of no return' (DeJong *et al.*, in press). The problem of S–R compatibility effects which may illuminate the mechanism of response selection could be addressed by examining whether it is possible to detect an early activation of the compatible response in an incompatible S–R pairing.

However, it is doubtful that the motor cortical structures considered to be responsible for generating the RP are the site of the processing operations by which a stimulus is coded to its response. Such an interfacing role can be played only by neuronal networks that incorporate elaborated representations of sensory and motor events, a property which is now attributed to cortical association areas. On the basis of lesion studies, the most sophisticated cognitive functions have been attributed to widespread regions of the neocortex. The posterior parietal cortex has been viewed as responsible for the integration of sensory inputs from different modalities thereby structuring the representation of external and body spaces. Only recently have the implications of this functional localization for the early stages of movement control been realized (Hyvarinen, 1982). Mountcastle and his colleagues (1975) have found that changes in the neuronal activity of this structure were triggered by an object presented in the visual field, provided that the object was a target for forelimb reaching and/or to grasping movement. The functional significance of this 'enhancement' effect, either as motor preparation-related or as sensory attention-related, has led to a debate (Lynch, 1980) which emphasizes the difficulty of delineating the boundary between perception and action at the level of brain mechanisms, a problem that is also prevalent at the level of cognitive analysis. This difficulty is likely to assert itself when modeling an interfacing neural system which is responsible for making connections between perceptual and action representations.

Recent studies conducted with single-neuron recordings have provided some support for such a role (Seal, 1989; see also Andersen, Essick and Siegel, 1987, Seal and Requin, 1987; Requin, Riehle and Seal, 1988). In a series of experiments, the neuronal activity of area 5 was recorded in three conditions: the presentation of a stimulus followed by a movement, the presentation of the stimulus without movement, and the execution of the movement without the preceding stimulus. Three neuronal populations were identified, whose activation timing was sequentially organized. 'Sensory' neurons were active whenever the stimulus was presented, 'sensorimotor' neurons modified their activity when the stimulus was presented and the movement performed, and 'motor' neurons were active whenever the movement was performed. Since the activation of the 'sensorimotor' neurons can be observed only after training, they are good candidates for the 'interfacing' function that the S–R association process requires. The functional features of such neuronal networks during experimental protocols in which S–R compatibility is manipulated would be of interest for detailing the real-time mechanism of response selection.

Response Selection: Stimulus–Response Probability Effects

The large corpus of experimental findings accumulated on the effects upon RT of varying the probability of different S–R alternatives is relevant for understanding the processing operations responsible for response selection. It has been well known since the early fifties (Hick, 1952) that in choice-RT procedures, the RT for a particular S–R alternative increases when either the relative frequency of this S–R alternative within a constant set of S–R alternatives decreases or the number of equiprobable S–R alternatives increases. Since both stimulus frequency and response frequency were manipulated simultaneously, the usual one-to-one S–R mapping choice-RT procedures were inappropriate for determining the locus of the probability effect within processing stages. By introducing many-to-one S–R mapping RT tasks, in which stimulus probability and response probability could be varied independently, an active field of research was initiated (see Holender, 1980a, and Requin, 1980a,b, for reviews). These studies have shown that manipulating either stimulus frequency or response frequency results in RT changes, thus suggesting that not only stimulus processing but also response processing is a target for the probability effect.

Converging, although indirect, arguments have supported this conclusion (see Sanders, 1980, for a review). First, by using the rationale of the additive factor method, the interaction found between response frequency and S–R compatibility, which is considered to act on the response selection process, suggests that this process is also affected by response probability. Second, the S–R probability effects, as with S–R compatibility effects, decrease with practice (Mowbray and Rhoades, 1959). Third, when sequential effects in choice-RT tasks were examined, it was shown that repeating only the response resulted in shorter RTs than alternating only the response. Since the probability of a response being repeated in a series of trials generally increases when response frequency increases, these last data were considered to support the hypothesis that the response probability effect results from a short-term process, such as response priming. Although the alternative explanation (that the response probability effect results from a long-term adjustment of the subject's response expectancy to match the objective response frequency distribution) was rejected, it has been found that these two mechanisms are not mutually exclusive but rather compatible (see Holender, 1980b, for a review).

The few studies in which changes in S–R probability were found to result in changes in the activity of motor systems during the S1–S2 interval have provided direct evidence for both the response processing locus and the preparatory features of the probability effect. The amplitude of the late CNV component was found sensitive to the manipulation of the relative S–R frequency in a choice-RT task (Niemi and Näätänen, 1981). In monkeys trained to perform a visuo-manual pointing-task in a between-hands choice-RT procedure, Lecas, Requin and Vitton (1983) and Lecas *et al.* (1986) have shown that changes in the discharge frequency of MI neurons during the S1–S2 interval were closely related to the changes induced experimentally in the probabilities for either hand to peform the movement. The shortening of RT as S–R probability increased was associated with a decrease of preparatory activity for neurons which were inhibited during movement performance and with an increase in preparatory activity of neurons which were excited during movement performance. Once again, these data do not mean that response probability is processed by MI, but more likely, that this structure is a target for an output from a processing operation located upstream in the neural pathways conveying information to MI. When the proportions of neurons whose activity was sensitive to changes in S–R probability were compared in different cortical areas, it was shown (Requin, Lecas and Vitton, 1990) that the number of probability-related neurons decreased along the neural pathways which connect the posterior parietal cortex to MI, via PM. These data stress again the likely responsibility of the parietal association areas for the earliest response selection processing operation in the initiation of motor action. Note that, in contrast to S–R compatibility-related changes in brain activity, these response probability-related modulations of the central motor pathways seem not to reach the spinal motor apparatus. Requin, Lecas and Bonnet (1984) and Brunia, Haagh and Scheirs (1985) failed to find any effect of varying the probability on the activity of muscles to be involved in movement performance.

Movement Programming: The 'Motor Versus Action' Controversy

> The coordination of leg movements in insects, the song of birds, the control of trotting and pacing in a gaited horse, the rat running the maze, the architect designing a house, and the carpenter sawing a board, present a problem of sequences of action which cannot be explained in terms of successions of external stimuli. (Lashley, 1951)

One can add many other examples of highly skilled human motor activities to Lashley's observations, such as piano playing and typing which are obviously not generated online on the basis of sensory inputs intervening between the elements of the motor sequence. The idea that motor actions are prescribed in some central representation—plan or program—which exists prior to response execution is widely accepted in theories of motor control (Requin, Semjen and Bonnet, 1984; Rosenbaum, 1985; Schmidt, 1982; Sheridan, 1988).

The concept of a motor program is mainly supported by three kinds of experimental evidence. First, studies on deafferented patients or animals have shown that skilled movements can be performed without proprioceptive feedback (Evarts *et al.*, 1971). This phenomenon is considered important enough to be used as a criterion for the identification of motor programs (Keele, 1968; Schmidt, 1982). Second, chronometric analyses have shown that RT for initiating the first element of a movement sequence depends upon the characteristics of the sequences as a whole, such as its length (Henry and Rogers, 1960; Sternberg *et al.*, 1978), the similarity (Semjen and Garcia-Colera, 1986) and the ordering (Semjen, 1984; see also Semjen and Gottsdanker, 1990) of its elements. Third, a number of chronometric and physiological studies, which will be described below, have demonstrated that manipulating the subject's expectancy about the features of a forthcoming movement result in functional changes in the processing systems responsible for performing the movement.

In its early and most influential conception, the motor program was viewed as a set of 'instructions', centrally stored, specifying the spatial and dynamic features of a movement, according to both the initial state of the muscular system and the action goal. After being assembled to construct the program, these instructions would be translated into a set of neural commands addressed to the muscles, that would determine the biomechanical parameters and, thus, the kinematics and dynamics of the movement to be performed. This 'parametric' conception of the motor program structure has been increasingly challenged during the last 15 years from different points of view (e.g. Kelso, 1981).

Firstly, it has been suggested that this view of the motor program is too complex and not flexible enough. The hypothesis that every different movement is controlled by a specific program demands an instructions register of unlimited capacity. Moreover, regulation of the many degrees of freedom associated with even the most simple polyarticular limb movement would require a programming system of enormous computational power. Even if such computational power is granted, it is hard to understand how a motor action that has never been performed before can frequently be performed rather immediately and accurately.

Revised conceptions of motor programming have therefore been proposed to solve these 'memory', 'degrees of freedom' and 'novelty' problems, by proposing a hierarchical organization of the processes responsible for movement control (e.g. Rosenbaum, Kenny and Derr, 1983; Rosenbaum, Inhoff and Gordon, 1984). At the highest levels a limited number of motor schematas or patterns are stored as 'generalized programs' (Schmidt, 1982), 'abstract representations' (Keele, 1981), 'action plans' (Paillard, 1982) or 'movement prototypes' (Rosenbaum, 1983). At this level only the common structure of a large class of movements is specified. The abstract nature of this highest level of movement representation is emphazised in current definitions of the motor program structure. For example, Shaffer (1982) has described the structure as 'a set of grammatical representations of intended actions constructed, by a control system, as a hierarchy of abstractions, terminating in motor output'. Details to complete this schemata would be filled in at lower levels, according to specific contextual requirements.

For instance, in the 'impulse-timing' model of Schmidt (1975), the content of the program would be restricted to the order, temporal structure and force pattern of the sequence of motor events, and would be then completed and adapted to the context in which the movement must be performed, by adding to the protoprogram, 'parameters' such as movement duration and muscles involved. One of the main arguments supporting such a view is summarized by the notion of 'movement invariance'; that is, the common temporal structure and shape of movements performed under quite different neuromuscular constraints. In the so-called 'mass–spring' model (Asatryan and Feldman, 1965), the central motor program disregards the initial location of the limb in space and specifies only its final location in terms of an equilibrium point between forces of the antagonistic muscles involved. In this case, the parameters of the movement trajectory result from the interaction between the spring-like mechanical and physical (mass) properties of the muscles. The maintenance of accurate reaching movements in deafferented monkeys (Bizzi, 1980) and in anesthetized humans (Kelso *et al.*, 1980) when the initial limb position was shifted or the movement trajectory briefly perturbed, favored such a conception of motor control. Although the 'impulse–timing' and 'mass–spring' models lead to rather different predictions, they may be considered as two coexisting modes of motor control, either involved differentially according to movement features such as speed (Bizzi *et al.*, 1982), or even integrated within some hybrid functioning of the control system (Keele, 1981).

A second set of criticisms of the early program concept is that program instructions are conceptualized in terms of the physical and geometrical variables utilized by an observer to describe the kinematics and dynamics of a movement, these variables being unlikely to be those processed by the brain. It is also difficult to conceive of how such program instructions, supposed to be written in a non-motoric language, are translated into motor commands coded in the language of the neuromuscular system. Consequently, there have been many proposals to abandon computer-like models of information flow in the brain and instead to search for the organizing principles which govern motor behavior in terms of natural 'laws' that are assumed to operate in all the living and physical systems. However, this debate is only one manifestation of a more fundamental debate between the cognitive and ecological views of motor control. In the cognitive view, motor activity is determined in a top-down way by some central representation of what has to be done, with the commands for how it should be done being updated continuously on the basis of sensory input. In the 'ecological' view of action, motor activity emerges from and is then shaped by the interaction between the internal (neural and biomechanical) constraints of living systems and the external (physical and, even, cultural) constraints of the environment (Epstein, 1986; Kugler, Kelso and Turvey, 1980; Newell, 1985; Schmidt, 1988; Reed, 1982).

Although proponents of each conception tend to adopt extreme positions in the debate, it is doubtful that either the concept of movement planning or the concept of action constraints will prove to be useless. A more profitable approach may be to reconcile and integrate the two views, thereby generating a model of how constraints are incorporated during development and through learning processes into a flexible representation of motor goals and commands that is able to account for online adaptive regulation of behavioral output.

Movement Programming: Movement Precueing and Priming Studies

In recent years our knowledge of the structure and content of the central representation of movement features has been improved by using the movement 'precueing' and movement 'priming' techniques (see Rosenbaum, 1983, 1985, for reviews). In the framework of an information-processing view of motor control, both these techniques require the assumption that the programming process may be decomposed into operations, each of which has a measurable duration. When information provided to central processing systems about the characteristics of a forthcoming movement is adequately manipulated, the analysis of the resulting changes in RT permits inferences to be made about the duration and timing of the programming operations.

In the precueing technique, a specific movement is demanded by S2 (the respond signal) after partial information about one or several parameter(s) of the forthcoming movement (e.g. direction, extent, limb) has been supplied by S1 (the precue). Insofar as the central programming system is able to utilize such partial information to program the corresponding movement parameter(s), the programming time component of RT will be shortened in comparison with conditions in which no information about movement parameter(s) is given in advance. This shortening is attributed to the programming time(s) for the precued parameter(s) and it may differ according to the movement parameter(s) considered. Further, one can infer that the set of programming operations is serially processed if programming times are additive with the number of precued parameters. Finally, when the RT shortening associated with the precueing of one movement parameter only occurs when another parameter is also simultaneously precued, one can infer that programming process is serially ordered with the latter parameter necessarily being programmed before the former.

In the priming technique (e.g. Rosenbaum and Kornblum, 1982), the preparatory signal or 'prime' supplies the subject with complete target information about movement parameters. However, within a series of trials, the prime is followed either with a high probability by an expected target (a valid prime) or with a low probability by an unexpected target (an invalid prime). Pointing movements toward the expected and unexpected targets can, therefore, differ in one, several or all parameters, according to the spatial locations of both targets. The RT lengthening for pointing movements to an unexpected target is interpreted as the sum of the times necessary to de-program and to re-program movement parameters for which the prime was invalid. The inferences about the timing of programming operations that can be drawn from a comparison of RTs observed in conditions which differ in the number and nature of unprimed parameters, are identical to those provided by the precueing technique.

Two studies using the precueing technique (Rosenbaum, 1980; Goodman and Kelso, 1980) instigated a debate about the generality of a programming process based on assembling separable operations for specifying spatial movement parameters. In Rosenbaum's studies, subjects performed pointing movements toward targets whose spatial location could be described by combining three binary spatial dimensions: side (left or right arm), direction (far from or near to the subject), and distance (long or short). S2 was a colored dot on a display panel, with a one-to-one mapping of colors to targets. S1 supplied the subjects with information about either 0, 1, 2, or 3 movement dimensions and was represented by a set of either 1, 2, or 3 letters, each of them indicating the value of each precued dimension. Based on the RTs observed, Rosenbaum concluded that motor programming is a parametric process in which each movement dimension is independently programmed, with programming times differing between the dimensions.

These conclusions were challenged by Goodman and Kelso (1980; see also Zelaznik and Hahn, 1985) who failed to find any experimental support for a parametric programming process when a spatially 'compatible' arrangement of S1, S2 and targets was used. Consequently, they suggested that changes in RT associated with a precueing of movement parameters resulted from the coding operations required by the 'incompatible' S–R mapping that associated colors with targets and letters with movement parameters. In particular, by translating information provided by the precue into a language suitable to designate the spatial configuration of targets, the subject would be required to translate movements into the artificial 'dimensions' defined by the precues, a factoring process that would not be required by the motor control system when planning actions in more 'natural' conditions. However, by using a spatially 'compatible' S–R code, Bonnet, Stelmach and Requin (1982), Larish and Frekany (1985) and Lépine, Glencross and Requin (1989), in human subjects, as well as Riehle and Requin (1989) in monkeys, have shown significant effects on RT of precueing spatial movement parameters. Moreover, when the priming procedure was used with the same experimental design and apparatus as in the precueing procedure, changes in RT associated with the priming of movement parameters were amplified, in agreement with the hypothesis that the unprimed parameters have to be de-programmed and then re-programmed (Lépine, Glencross and Requin, 1989).

These studies focused on the programming of spatial movement parameters, such as the limb to be involved in performing (right or left arm), the direction of the movement (up or down), and its extent (distance between initial and final positions). It should be noted, however, that at least for ballistic movements, extent could be defined, and may be programmed, in terms of force. This renders the status of this parameter, as a kinematic or dynamic feature of movement control, ambiguous. The fact that the programming time for movement extent has been found to be shorter than for other parameters in many cases, but to be no different in other cases, has provided a basis for the suggestion that, although the motor program concept may be useful in the analysis of movement kinematics, it is of no use in understanding movement dynamics (Kelso, 1984; Newell, in press). However, this conclusion has been questioned both by the provision of more likely explanations of these differences (Lépine, Glencross and Requin, 1989; Riehle and Requin, 1989) and the results of recent experiments. For example, Macar, Vidal and Bonnet (in press; see also Zelaznik and Hahn, 1985; Zelaznik, Shapiro and Carter, 1982) have shown that providing information about the duration of an isometric pressure movement, performed by either the left or right hand, significantly shortened RT, with the amount of shortening depending upon the range of movement durations used. Similarly, Bonnet and MacKay (1989; see also Zelaznik, 1981) have demonstrated that precueing the force which will be opposed against either extension or flexion forearm movements significantly reduced RT.

These results verify the first assumption of the movement precueing and priming technique; that is, it is possible to independently activate the prescriptions (subroutines in the computer metaphor) for different kinematic and dynamic parameters of a movement. The same conclusion about the separability of programming operations was also reached recently by Ghez and his collaborators (Favilla, Hening and Ghez, 1989; Hening, Favilla and Ghez, 1988; Ghez, Hening and Favilla, 1990), by manipulating movement direction and extent in the 'timed-response' paradigm. These results extended early data obtained with similar step-tracking tasks (see Semjen, 1984, for a review). However, the precueing and priming techniques were also designed to provide some insights into the structure of the motor programming process; namely, whether the programming operations for different movement parameters are serially organized.

A serial programming model implies that the programming time component of RT must be an additive function of the number of parameters to be programmed. However, as has been repeatedly pointed out (Goodman and Kelso, 1980; Lépine, Glencross and Requin, 1989; Zelaznik, Shapiro and Carter, 1982), in both the precueing and priming technique, the effects on RT of the number of precued parameters and of the number of S–R alternatives are frequently confounded. In view of this, observations of an additive pattern of RT (e.g. Bonnet, Stelmach and Requin, 1982; Stelmach, Worringham and Strand, 1986) cannot be construed as evidence for a serial programming model. However, data derived from the only RT study to use the precueing technique in monkeys (Riehle and Requin, 1989) does conform well to a serial and hierarchically ordered programming process. The long training provided in this experiment would be expected to have eliminated the effects of the number of S–R alternatives on RT (Mowbray and Rhodes, 1959). Yet, when an appropriate design is used (i.e. when the additivity of programming times can be tested within a set of precueing conditions that do not differ in the number of S–R alternatives), RT data are most often found to be underadditive (Lépine, Glencross and Requin, 1989).

Underadditivity of programming times means that the time to program several movement parameters when they are programmed together is shorter than the sum of the times to program these parameters when they are programmed independently. Observation of underadditivity usually provides a basis for inferring some parallel processing. However, Lépine, Glencross and Requin (1989) have proposed an alternative explanation of underadditivity which is based on the concept of 'dimensional reduction'. When the number of movement parameters to be programmed increases, the number of programming operations is reduced by combining two or more parameters to specify a new parameter. This may be accomplished in the case of direction and extent by specifying the final location of the moving limb, or with direction and force by specifying a linked vector. In principle, such a compound process may apply to any set of physically defined parameters.

These experimental data can be assimilated by a two-stage model of the motor programming process. In the first 'parametric' stage, the subroutines corresponding to the different movement parameters (as they are defined by the experimenter) are selected independently and serially. This explains why providing information about any movement parameter results in an RT shortening and why RT increases as a function of the number of parameters to be programmed. In the second 'compound' stage, these subroutines are assembled by a process which reduces the number of parameters. This explains why RT is not a linear function of the number of parameters to be programmed. In this conception the parameterized subroutines would roughly correspond to the 'representational' aspect of the motor program, while the compound assembling process would correspond to the first step of the translation of program instructions into neuromuscular commands.

CENTRAL PATHWAYS OF MOVEMENT PROGRAMMING

Brain processes related to the programming of movements have received considerable attention during the last ten years. The relevant studies have involved recording motor ERPs in man and have used single-neuron recording techniques in animals trained in sensorimotor tasks. However, until quite recently the human ERP and animal single-unit fields of research have developed quite independently.

The late CNV component was found to be closely related to the features of the motor response (see Rohrbaugh and Gaillard, 1983, for a review). This late component is attenuated and may even disappear when there is no motor response to S2 (Gaillard, 1980). Furthermore, its amplitude is correlated with RT (Brunia and Vingerhoets, 1980). Finally, its scalp distribution over the cortical areas contralateral to the movement depends upon whether the upper or lower limb is involved, in agreement with the somatotopical organization of the motor cortex (Boschert, Hink and Deecke, 1983; Brunia and Vingerhoets, 1980). These topographical and movement-related features of the late CNV component are quite similar to those of the RP for unilateralized movements. The RP distribution over the motor cortex depends upon the limb involved in motor performance (Brunia and van der Bosch, 1984) and its amplitude is related to some of the dynamic movement parameters such as the force to be exerted (Kutas and Donchin, 1980).

Study of the neuronal activity specifically related to the preparation for movement features was initiated by the work of Evarts and his colleagues (see Evarts, 1984, and Evarts, Shimoda and Wise, 1984, for reviews). They developed a prototypic behavioral situation similar to the RT paradigm used with humans, except that animals were not explicitly required to react as rapidly as possible to obtain the reward. Monkeys were trained to pull or to push a handle, by either flexing or extending the forearm. S1 indicated whether a pull or a push was required after S2 which was a perturbation of the handle position either towards or away from the animal. Disregarding its role as S2, the effect of this externally triggered handle displacement was, by either extending or flexing the forearm, either to stretch the biceps and to relax its antagonist, or the inverse. Proprioceptive afferents of the stretched muscle were thus activated, triggering a reflex-like response of the neurons which controlled this muscle and producing a central response at loci conforming to the notion that the somatotopic representation of muscular afferents in the primary motor (MI) cortex overlaps the motor representation (see Evarts, 1981). The effects of S1 upon neuronal activity were sought in changes of unit-resting activity during the S1–S2 interval and/or in unit 'reflex' activity triggered by S2.

First, during the S1–S2 interval, a large number of pyramidal as well as non-pyramidal tract neurons of MI exhibited a change in their resting discharge frequency, with this change depending mainly on the direction of the intended movement. For instance, for a unit controlling biceps activation, when S1 informed the monkey of either a forearm flexion or a forearm extension, either an increase or a decrease in activity respectively was found. Second, a number of units showed transient changes in activity after S2 with these changes being reciprocally related to S1 information for a small proportion of units: the magnitude of the excitatory response to S2 was enhanced when S1 announced that the movement was to be made in the opposite direction to that of the handle displacement and was reduced when S1 indicated a movement in the same direction. Preparatory processes for performing a movement were therefore found to be paralleled by functional changes in neuronal activity of MI. These neuronal responses cannot be attributed solely to non-specific arousal since their features were experimentally controlled by providing the animal with advance information about the muscles to be activated in performing the forthcoming movement. When a particular movement had to be performed, by activating some muscles and relaxing others, the units that controlled the muscles to be activated exhibited an increase in their activity between S1 and S2 and/or an increase in their responsiveness to muscular afferents which were activated by stretching these muscles. In contrast, decreases in activity during the S1–S2 interval and/or reactivity to S2 occurred for units that controlled the muscles to be relaxed during movement performance.

By adapting the movement dimension precueing technique used in human subjects for use in monkeys, these preparation-related changes in the neuronal activity of MI have recently been examined in detail (Riehle, 1987; Riehle and Requin, 1989). While the precueing of movement direction resulted in a large decrease in RT associated with significant changes in neuronal activity between S1 and S2, the precueing of movement extent did not reduce RT and, accordingly, no preparation-related changes in neuronal activity were found. However, when only direction was precued, RT was longer than when both parameters were precued. This result is compatible with a serial, hierarchical model of motor programming in which movement extent could not be specified before movement direction. Accordingly, some neurons were found whose preparation-related changes in activity when both parameters were precued were of greater amplitude than when only movement direction was precued. Furthermore, these changes disappeared almost completely when movement extent was precued as well as when no dimensional information was provided by S1 (Figure 4.8). Although almost all the neurons showing preparation-related changes in activity also showed subsequent execution-related changes in activity, indicating that they were responsible for the control of motor performance, some neurons which exhibited preparation effects were not involved at all in the movement execution process.

Because no trial-by-trial correlation analysis was done, and because no time or accuracy constraints were imposed on the animal, the predictive value for performance efficiency of such specific preparatory changes in the neuronal activity of MI was not demonstrated in these studies. However, the relationships between these preparatory changes in neuronal activity and the speed of the forthcoming movement have been documented by Lecas, Requin and Vitton (1983) and Requin *et al.* (1986) using the between-hands choice-RT procedure, already described. Significant preparatory changes in unit discharge frequency between S1 and S2 were observed in a large proportion of units. Statistically significant trial-by-trial correlations between these changes and associated changes in RT were found when contralateral as well as ipsilateral movements were considered. These changes were most often negatively correlated with RT for units which were excited between S1 and S2, and positively correlated with RT for units which were inhibited. Within the small subset of units that exhibit correlations with RT for both contralateral and ipsilateral movements, more than half exhibited reciprocal correlations (i.e. of inverse sign for either movement).

Therefore, in addition to the function of MI for triggering neuromuscular activation, there is increasing evidence for a sophisticated role of this structure in preparatory processes. First, these processes appear to be highly specific regarding movement features, so that the pattern of preparatory changes in neuronal activity looks like an 'embryo' of the forthcoming execution process, at least when the anatomical distribution of the peripheral effectors is considered. Second, these processes determine, at least in part, the efficiency of the execution process, since changes in neuronal activity during the S1–S2 interval have a high predictive value for RT. These data thus confirm that, besides functioning as a passive motor keyboard, MI is active as a subtle control device adjusting its executive function to the contextual demands and constraints of motor actions.

The role played by MI in programming the set of motor commands addressed to spinal motor structures does not mean, of course, that MI is the only site

---

Figure 4.8. Changes in activity of a neuron in the premotor cortex of a monkey during the performance of a choice RT task in which a preparatory signal (PS) of 1 s duration, followed by a preparatory period (PP) of 1500 ms, provided advance information about various movement parameters. Changes in the frequency of the neuronal discharge starting from 500 ms before the PS up to 1300 ms after the response signal (RS) are shown when the same movement was performed under different conditions of advance information. From top to bottom, the PS provided information about movement direction and extent (complete), about direction only, about extent only, and no information at all (none). In each condition, neuronal activity is shown as a raster display (each horizontal line corresponds to one trial and each point on the line to one impulse) and a peristimulus time histogram (bin width: 40 ms). The duration of the movement is indicated by a black horizontal bar. (Reproduced with permission from Riehle and Requin (1989). © Physiological Society.)

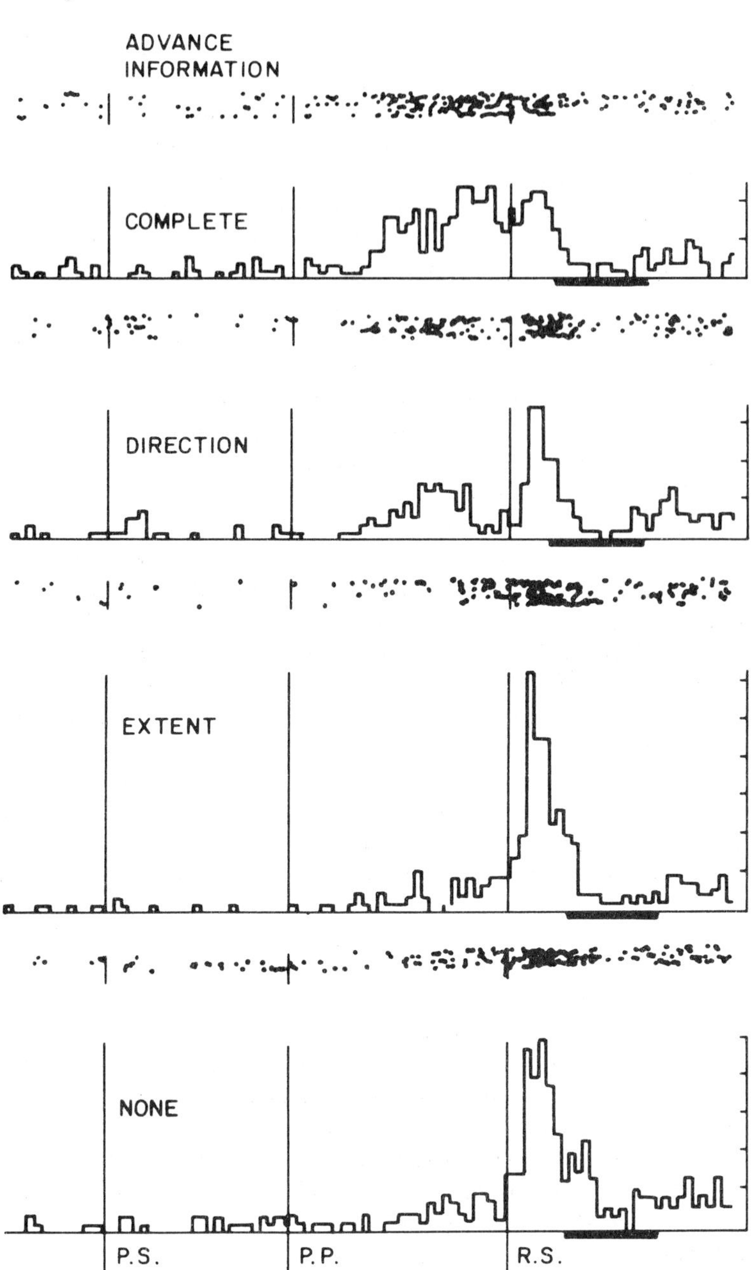
ADVANCE
INFORMATION
COMPLETE
DIRECTION
EXTENT
NONE
P.S.
P.P.
R.S.
1 sec.

where preparation for movement is organized. In accordance with the classical views of the neural pathways involved in motor control (see Paillard, 1982, and Requin, 1980a,b, for reviews), it has been suggested that the cerebellum as well as subcortical structures may be involved in programming processes. By using the same experimental setup as Evarts' MI studies, Strick (1983) found that some of the movement-related neurons of the dentate nucleus, which forms the cerebellar output pathway towards motor cortex, showed differential changes in their 'reflex' responses to muscle stretch according to a prior directional instruction. Furthermore, anatomical and physiological data have pointed recently to the privileged position of the premotor (PM) cortex and supplementary motor area (SMA)—that is, the lateral and medial parts of area 6 respectively—in the modulatory function of the corticospinal commands (Wise and Strick, 1984). Both areas are at an interface between MI, to which they send strong projections, and the prefrontal (PF) and posterior parietal (PP) association areas, from which they receive strong projections. Studies have shown that large populations of PM neurons change their activity between S1 and S2 in a manner dependent upon the information provided by S1 concerning movement direction, but not upon the physical, spatial and temporal features of S1 (Godschalk and Lemon, 1983; Godschalk *et al.*, 1981; Weinrich and Wise, 1982; Wise, 1984, 1985; Wise and Mauritz, 1985; Wise, Weinrich and Mauritz, 1983; 1986). It is important to note that, in all these studies, the predictive value for performance level of changes in neuronal activity was not demonstrated.

The roles played in movement preparation by MI and PM, respectively, have been recently examined by Riehle (1987) and Riehle and Requin (1989). They concluded, from experiments based on the movement dimension precueing technique, that there are quantitative but not qualitative differences between the structures. Movement-related and preparation-related neurons were found to be closely intermixed in both areas, with the proportion of the former decreasing and the proportion of the latter increasing from the central sulcus to the arcuate sulcus. Although the role of the SMA in motor control remains controversial (Goldberg, 1986; Wiesendanger, 1986; Romo and Schultz, 1987), similar results have been obtained in this structure (Tanji, Taniguchi and Saga, 1980; Kurata and Tanji, 1985; Tanji and Kurata, 1982). These experiments confirmed the involvement of the SMA in the early cognitive operations for the elaboration of movement, as suggested by data showing that, in man, just 'thinking about' the execution of a movement, without actually performing it, results in marked changes in metabolic activity focusing on this structure (Roland *et al.*, 1980).

The role of motor cortical areas in programming movement features has been confirmed indirectly by using transcortical reflex techniques in the framework of the movement dimension precueing paradigm. Changes in the amplitude of the late components of the EMG response to muscle stretch were analyzed separately during the S1–S2 interval in a procedure requiring the performance of a wrist movement and when movement direction or movement extent was precued (Bonnet, 1983; Bonnet, Stelmach and Requin, 1984; Bonnet, Requin and Stelmach, in press). It was shown that the specific indexes of the activity of central neural structures were differentially modulated only when movement direction was precued; that is, as a function of whether the stretched muscle was to play an agonist or antagonist role in the forthcoming movement. The late components of the long-loop reflex were found to be consistently larger when the stretched muscle was precued as an agonist than as an antagonist (Figure 4.9). These findings agree closely with those provided by single-neuron recording experiments. Not only do they confirm the role that the set of motor cortical structures and their afferent pathways play in programming spatial movement features, but they also fail again to provide evidence of the neural processes by which dynamic movement features are specified in advance.

Data provided by 20 years of animal as well as human studies converge to illustrate that the neural correlates of motor programming processes are widely distributed throughout brain structures. The relevant data have been identified on the basis of the three criteria of timing, sensitivity to the characteristics of the forthcoming movement, and predictive value for performance. When the features of changes in neuronal activity related to movement parameters are considered, a major difference between data provided by single-neuron recording techniques and those provided by ERP recording techniques emerges. The former have consistently shown preparatory changes in neuronal activity which were associated with spatial parameters (movement direction) but not with the dynamic parameters (movement extent, force or velocity). However, the latter have shown the inverse pattern. Changes in the amplitude of the RP and/or the late CNV component have been found to be affected by dynamic parameters, but not by the spatial characteristics of movement except when broad anatomical differences—such as upper versus lower limb or left versus right body side—were considered.

Such a difference does not exclude that both kinds of physiological indices may express identical processes. Indeed, it fits well with what should be expected according to the anatomofunctional organization of the cortical areas involved in motor control. First, the close intermixing of the neurons responsible for controlling antagonistic muscles, as well as the loss of somatotopic representation in most cortical areas, except MI, implies that any relationship between changes in brain macropotentials and the anatomical features of motor activity may disappear when the simultaneous inhibitory and excitatory preparation-related modulations of large neuronal populations are integrated. Secondly, changes in the activity of a small sample of neurons could fail to provide evidence of the preparatory modulations associated with the programming of dynamic movement parameters since these changes are

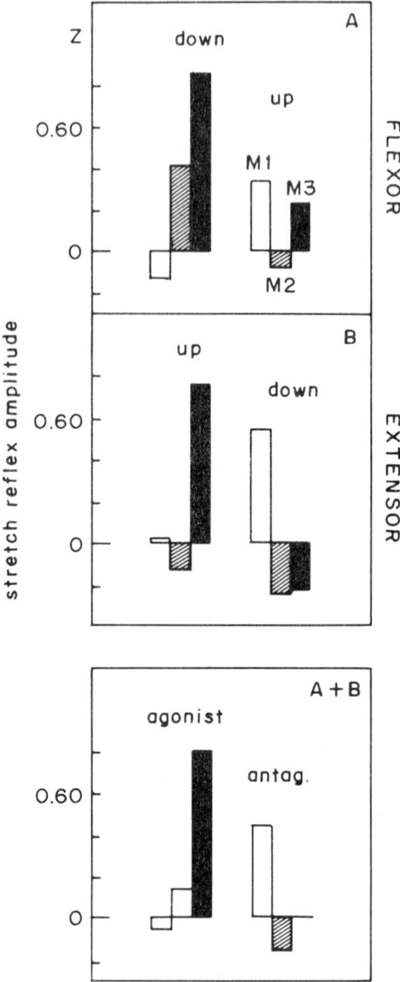

Figure 4.9. Changes in the amplitude of three components (M1, M2 and M3) of the EMG response to a muscle stretch triggered at the end of the foreperiod in a choice RT task in which subjects performed either wrist flexions (down) or extensions (up). The preparatory signal provided either directional information or no information. In panel A the forearm flexor was stretched, in panel B the forearm extensor was stretched; and in panel A + B, EMG responses for both muscles were pooled according to their involvement as either agonist (i.e. down for flexor and up for extensor) or antagonist (i.e. down for extensor and up for flexor). The individual subject's data were transformed into z score, with the 'no information' condition as the reference distribution. These were then averaged over seven subjects. (Reproduced with permission from Bonnet, Requin and Stelmach (in press). © Elsevier Scientific Publishers.)

likely to be expressed more clearly by integrating small, but consistent, changes in the activity of a large set of neurons. Discrepancies between results provided by single-neuron and ERP recording techniques would probably be clarified by coupling both techniques in the same animal experiment. Surprisingly, this has seldom been done (but see Gantchev, 1978, and MacKay and Crammond, in press). When data collected in similar conditions with either methodology are compared (see Figure 4.10), there is little doubt, as emphasized by the recent work of Coles (1989), that such combined experiments may provide a deeper insight into central preparatory processes.

PERIPHERAL EXPRESSION OF MOVEMENT PROGRAMMING

It should be noted that in almost all the single-neuron recording studies conducted on cortical areas, changes in neuronal activity during motor preparation have been observed to occur either without any (Evarts, Shimoda and Wise, 1984; Mauritz and Wise, 1986) or with quite tiny (Lecas *et al.*, 1986; Riehle and Requin, 1989) associated changes in EMG activity. Although this lack of peripheral consequence of preparatory cortical activity has to be taken with caution, since only a limited number of muscles were recorded in animal experiments, these negative findings are in agreement with a number of rather unsuccessful attempts made during the forties and fifties to demonstrate in man that movement performance is preceded by preparatory changes in muscular tension (see Duffy, 1962, for a review). Although authors generally agreed that there was an overall increase in EMG activity before the performance of a motor response, contradictory or inconsistent results were found when the specificity of these EMG increases regarding movement features was considered. Activation was either shown to overspread the whole muscle apparatus or to focus on involved muscles. Similarly, the predictive value for RT of prior muscle tension was found either limited to the muscles to be activated or extending to the other muscles, so that the relationship between changes in EMG activity during the S1–S2 interval and RT has remained unclarified. In an examination of the relationship between peripheral changes and ERP changes during motor preparation, Brunia and Vingerhoets (1980) and Haagh and Brunia (1985) have recently investigated muscular activity in the preparation paradigm. The slight increase of EMG activity that they recorded in a large number of muscles was found to be correlated weakly with RT, but not differentially when agonist versus antagonist muscles were considered.

The use of reflex techniques has made it possible to reveal subtle changes in the functioning of the spinal motor apparatus, which are not expressed in EMG. Changes in spinal reflex pathway reactivity were first examined during a S1–S2 interval of 1 s duration and were found to depend on whether the muscle in which reflexes were evoked was involved in the forthcoming movement

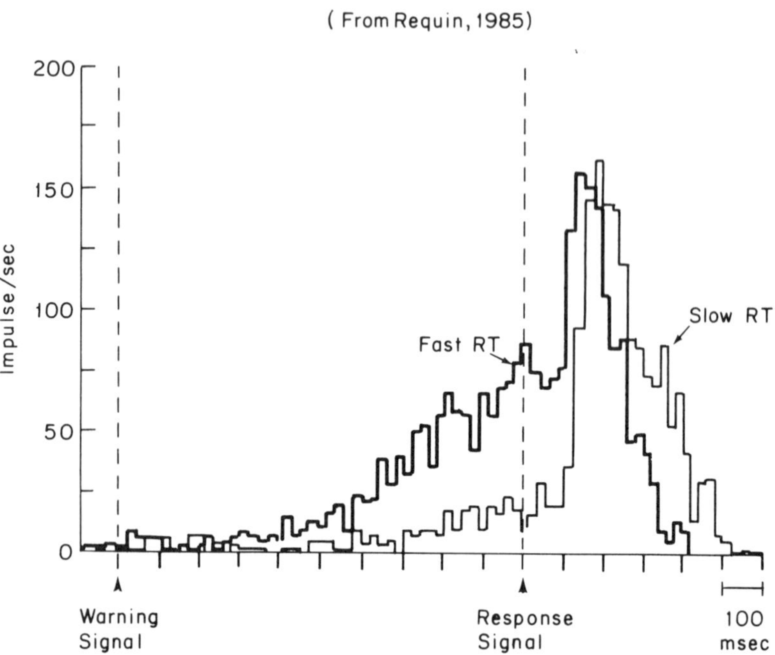

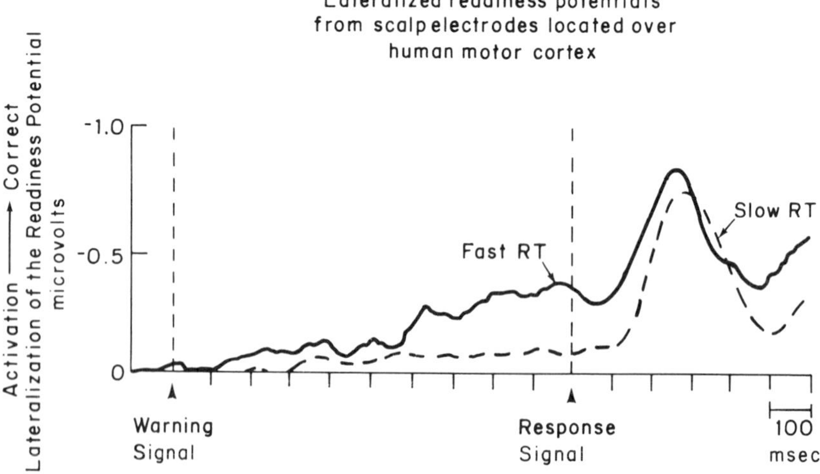

Figure 4.10. Changes in the firing rate of a neuron in monkey motor cortex (upper panel) and in the amplitude of the lateralized readiness potential recorded over human motor cortex (lower panel) in the same simple RT task. For both experiments, the data were ordered according to RT and the physiological data were then averaged separately for fast and slow RTs. Note the relationships, in both figures, between the amplitude of the physiological index, time locked to the response signal, and the time when the movement-related physiological activity peaked. The latter presumably determined RT. (Reproduced with permission from Coles (1989). © Society for Psychophysiological Research.)

(Requin, 1969; Brunia, 1984, see Bonnet, Requin and Semjen, 1981, for a review). A very similar pattern of results was found for electrically (Hoffman: H) and mechanically (Tendinous: T) triggered reflexes. First, reflex amplitude increased in both involved and uninvolved muscles immediately after S1, peaking about 200 ms later. This early increase was found to be an enhancement of the general arousal effect of any stimulus without warning significance, and depended on its intensity. Second, reflex amplitude then evolved differentially until S2, according to the muscle's involvedness in movement performance. While it increased slightly, was maintained or even decreased slightly in an uninvolved muscle, reflex amplitude generally decreased sharply in an involved muscle, falling sometimes to values below the level prior to S1. Subsequent experiments (Figure 4.11) using larger S1–S2 intervals have confirmed this dissociation in the time course of the reactivity of spinal reflex pathways according to the functional involvement of muscles in movement performance (Brunia, 1980, 1984; Brunia, Haagh and Scheirs, 1985; Haagh *et al.*, 1983; Scheirs and Brunia, 1985). However, while the trend to an overall decrease in reflex size previously observed at the end of short (1 s) S1–S2 intervals was shown again to occur about 1 s after S1, it was now followed by a progressive increase in reflex size until S2. These findings suggest that the time course of changes in spinal reflex pathway reactivity triggered by S1 does not adjust to the expected duration of the S1–S2 interval but has its own time constant.

The few studies in which a S1–S2 interval of variable duration has been used (see Requin, 1978) have confirmed that the relative decrease of reflex amplitude in an involved muscle, as compared with an uninvolved muscle, is the main expression of motor preparation at the level of spinal reflex pathways. When subjects were waiting for an unpredictable S1 during a variable interval, a progressive increase of reflex size was found in all muscles. This may be the result of the increase of the conditional probability of S1. When subjects were waiting for an unpredictable S2 during a variable S1–S2 interval, a similar increase of reflex size was shown for an uninvolved muscle, but not for an involved muscle, in which reflex amplitude remained almost stable throughout the S1–S2 interval. Once again, response preparation at the spinal

---

Figure 4.11. Changes in the amplitude of monosynaptic spinal reflexes elicited during the foreperiod of a simple RT task in a muscle that is either involved or not involved in the performance of a movement. Foreperiod duration was 1 s in the upper part of the figure, and 4 s in the lower part. In the left part of the figure, subjects performed a plantar flexion of the left foot, so that the left soleus muscle was involved in the movement and the right soleus muscle was not. In the right part of the figure, subjects performed a plantar flexion of the right foot, so that the involvement of the muscles in the movement was reversed. Changes in reflex amplitude are expressed as a percentage of the control level, i.e. reflexes elicited during the intertrial interval (WS: warning signal; RS: response signal). (Reproduced with permission from Brunia and van der Bosch (1984). © Elsevier Scientific Publishers.)

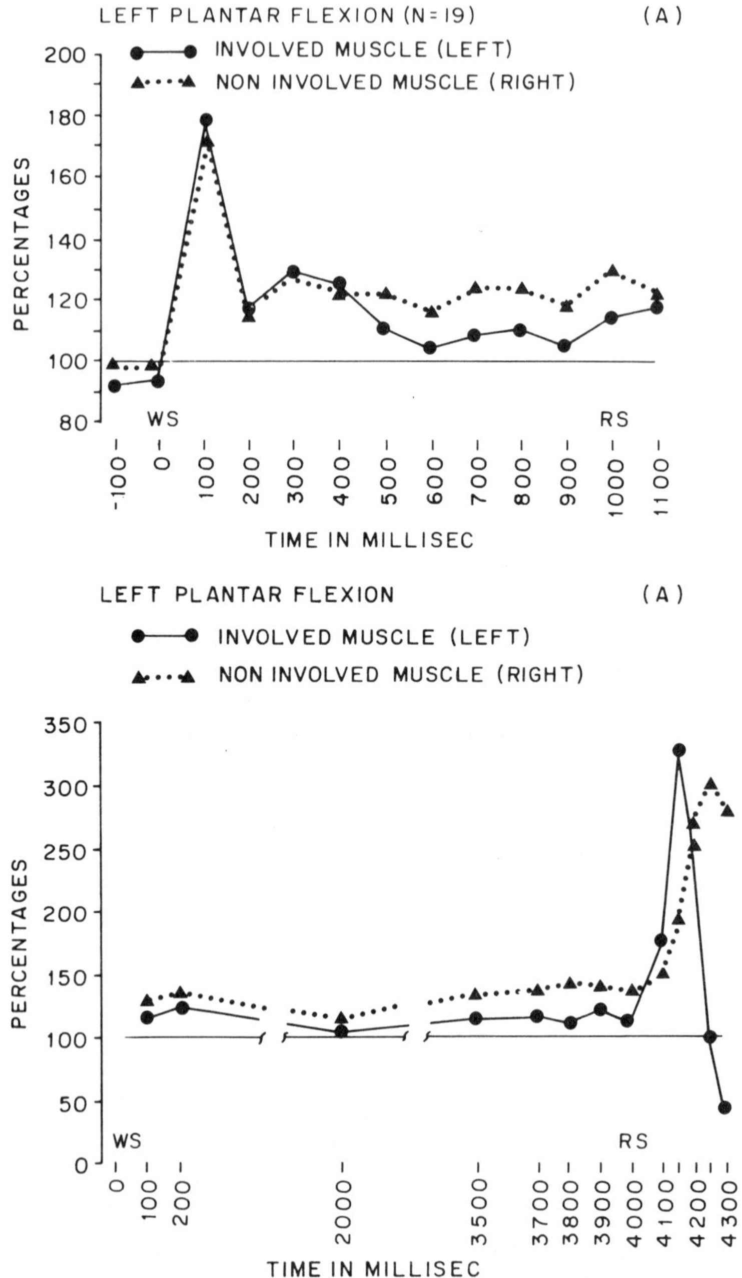

LEFT PLANTAR FLEXION (N=19)
(A)
INVOLVED MUSCLE (LEFT)
NON INVOLVED MUSCLE (RIGHT)
PERCENTAGES
200
180
160
140
120
100
80
WS
RS
-100
0
100
200
300
400
500
600
700
800
900
1000
1100
TIME IN MILLISEC
LEFT PLANTAR FLEXION
(A)
INVOLVED MUSCLE (LEFT)
NON INVOLVED MUSCLE (RIGHT)
PERCENTAGES
350
300
250
200
150
100
50
0
WS
RS
0
100
200
2000
3500
3700
3800
3900
4000
4100
4200
4300
TIME IN MILLISEC

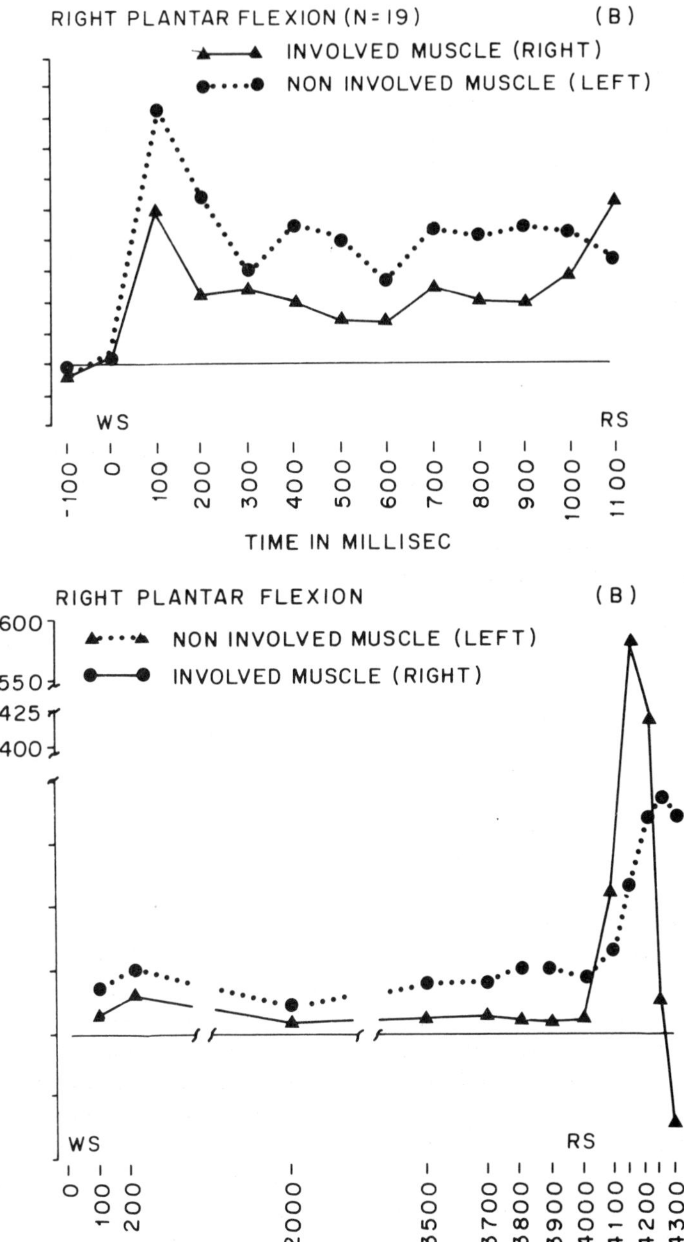
RIGHT PLANTAR FLEXION (N=19)
(B)
INVOLVED MUSCLE (RIGHT)
NON INVOLVED MUSCLE (LEFT)
WS
RS
-100
0
100
200
300
400
500
600
700
800
900
1000
1100
TIME IN MILLISEC
RIGHT PLANTAR FLEXION
(B)
600
550
425
400
NON INVOLVED MUSCLE (LEFT)
INVOLVED MUSCLE (RIGHT)
WS
RS
0
100
200
2000
3500
3700
3800
3900
4000
4100
4200
4300
TIME IN MILLISEC

level appeared to result from some central influence acting upon the spinal structures that control the muscles to be involved in movement performance, to attenuate, cancel or even reverse the non-specific arousal effect triggered by the attentive waiting for a behaviorally significant event. The depth of this depression effect may be expected to depend largely upon the amplitude of the general activation on which it is superimposed (Requin, Lecas and Bonnet, 1984).

However, the specificity of the differential change in spinal reflex pathway reactivity according to muscle involvedness, as well as its predictive value for performance level, were found to be very weak (see Bonnet, Requin and Semjen, 1981, for a review). First, spontaneous changes in reflex amplitude observed at the end of the S1–S2 interval were shown, for involved as well as uninvolved muscles, to be either uncorrelated or weakly correlated with the associated changes in RT. Second, when the features of the muscle 'involvement' in movement execution were manipulated experimentally, no significant changes in reflex amplitude were found. In particular, the function played by the muscle in movement performance, whether it is to be agonist (activated) or antagonist (relaxed), had no effect on the size of spinal reflexes between S1 and S2 (Requin, Lecas and Bonnet, 1984; Brunia, Haagh and Scheirs, 1985). Moreover, changing the force to be developed for performing the movement was found to have a quite weak effect on reflex amplitude, being greater when subjects expected to perform a loaded than an unloaded movement. Taken together, this set of rather negative results suggests that the depression of reflex pathway reactivity in muscles involved in motor performance, as compared with uninvolved muscles, is far from expressing the highly specific preparatory processes that behavioral results imply.

Speculations about the possible physiological mechanisms and functional significance of this inhibitory modulation of spinal reflex pathways have been aimed mainly at explaining the paradoxical finding that spinal motor structures seemed to be less excitable, or actively relaxed, just before being activated by the corticospinal command for movement. This paradox is resolved by viewing the reflex depression not as a manifestation of postsynaptic inhibition of the motoneurons, but rather as an expression of presynaptic inhibition acting upon motoneurons afferents, thereby reducing the excitatory power of the inputs conveyed by these afferents. Convergent, although indirect, arguments have been accumulated supporting the hypothesis that the depression during the S1–S2 interval of monosynaptic, as well as polysynaptic, reflexes elicited in the muscles involved in movement performance is of presynaptic origin (Bonnet, Requin and Scheirs, 1981; Brunia, Haagh and Scheirs, 1985). The functional role of this inhibition of muscular and cutaneous afferents is likely to protect the set of the spinal motor structures involved in any way in movement control against irrelevant inputs of peripheral origin which could either trigger a premature response or disturb the preparatory patterning of these structures. The finding that the reflex depression was less pronounced before ramp movements which are under continuous closed-loop sensory control, than before ballistic movements which are performed in an open-loop mode (Bonnet, 1981), is congruent with this view. Such a transient protective isolation of the motoneurons to be activated would thus reflect an active suspension of the response processes until S2 while maintaining these structures accessible for influences of central origin.

These analyses suggest that H and T reflex amplitudes index the strengths of the inhibitory control mechanisms acting upon motoneuron afferents rather than changes in motoneuron excitability itself. Therefore spinal reflex techniques do not appear to be suitable for examining central influences acting upon peripheral motor structures during preparation. However, results collected with these techniques do not necessarily preclude that such influences could be observed, particularly if motoneuron excitability is investigated by using procedures that avoid the effects of presynaptic inhibition. This may be accomplished by exploiting the transient relaxation of presynaptic inhibitory control that immediately follows activation of spinal reflex pathways triggered either by a previous reflex test or by a brief but loud acoustic stimulus. When the spinal reflex test elicited between S1 and S2 was preceded with a short delay, by such prior motoneuron activation, it was found that the usual depression of spinal reflexes triggered in a muscle involved in movement performance was replaced by a facilitation (Bonnet, Requin and Semjen, 1980, 1981; Semjen and Bonnet, 1982). This suggests that some central activatory influences are acting upon spinal motoneurons during preparation, but are masked in usual reflex testing by presynaptic inhibition. At present, there are no data available showing that this increase of motoneuronal excitability is modulated according to the parameters of the forthcoming movement.

In summarizing studies designed to examine the functional reorganization of spinal motor structures before performing a movement, it must be concluded that there is not a strong basis for claiming that the central command for movement is significantly altered by spinal preparatory set before being transmitted to the muscles. On the contrary, the experimental data provided by studying neuronal activity in motor cortical areas suggests that corticospinal orders are quite fully 'prepared' when activating motoneuron pools and are not subject to restructuring at the spinal level. Thus, although the sophisticated motoneuron and interneuron spinal device is undoubtly responsible for controlling and assisting movement execution, it is doubtful that it is involved in movement planning. Changes observed through reflex studies in excitability, and through EMG studies in the activity of spinal structures during preparation, are mainly non-specific regarding movement features. This is obvious not only for the general arousal effect triggered by S1, but also for the inhibitory mechanisms that seem to spread over all the spinal structures involved in movement control, whatever their precise functional role. Some similarity in the timing of the changes in spinal reactivity and changes in brain potential during the S1–S2 interval (Brunia, 1980; Brunia, Haagh and Scheirs, 1985) suggests a common physiological origin in the ascending and descending effects of activating the reticular formation. However, these changes fail to express the specific features of the motor preparatory processes found when cortical neuronal activity is considered. Not only do these peripheral processes seem to have little to do with motor programming, but the central processes of motor programming appear to have few online consequences at the peripheral level before movement execution starts.

TOWARD AN INTEGRATED ANALYSIS OF TONIC AND PHASIC PREPARATIONS FOR ACTION

The phenomena we have called tonic and phasic preparatory processes have been studied independently by two areas of psychophysiological research. It is not surprising that research into these phenomena developed relatively independently. The study of tonic preparation arose in a cybernetic framework, closely related to the physiology of regulatory systems. On the other hand, the study of phasic preparation arose within an information processing framework, closely related to cognitive psychology and the neurosciences.

These historical and epistemological distinctions may account for three main ways in which the empirical phenomena of tonic and phasic preparation differ. Firstly their timing is different: the time constants and durations associated with tonic preparation are longer than those associated with phasic preparation. Secondly there are differences in the manner in which their specificity is assessed. In tonic preparation, specificity is quantitatively defined, whereas in phasic preparation it is defined qualitatively with respect to the features of the forthcoming action. Finally, the energetic costs of preparation are much larger for tonic than for phasic preparation.

Nevertheless it is clear that the two types of preparatory processes serve a consolidated purpose in preparing the motor system for action; that is, for energy expenditure (tonic preparation) and for generating the specific action to be performed (phasic preparation). This is to be expected on functional grounds since adaptive behavior requires not only that the spatial, temporal and kinetic features of motor activity satisfy the specific requirements of prevailing environmental demands, but also that the metabolic requirements of the behavior be adequately supported.

A relatively simple model in which muscular activity is fueled on the basis of actual demand would require only peripheral linkages between the muscular effectors and the energy delivery systems. In this case, illustrated at (A) in Figure 4.12, motor activation antedates the activation of the energy mobilization and delivery systems: cardiovascular and pulmonary activity and the liberation of energy substrates are driven by feedback generated by striate muscular activity. If this was the case, task-related variations in energy expenditure would always follow the occurrence of task-related muscular activities. However, the adequacy of this model may be questioned on biofunctional as well as empirical grounds. Because of the long response latencies of the energy mobilization and delivery systems, feedback regulation alone would impair performance duration and intensity. Furthermore, the available data provides convincing evidence for the existence of feedforward processes by which tonic preparation may be influenced (see (B) in Figure 4.12). Therefore a model which incorporates both feedback and feedfoward linkages between motor and visceral processes is preferred (see (C) in Figure 4.12).

It has been shown that behavioral uncertainty gives rise both to phasic motor preparation in which an adequate response is formulated, and to tonic preparation in which the energy mobilization and delivery systems are activated. The analysis provided here suggests that tonic preparation is triggered by the processes associated with formulating motor acts that will meet the requirements of the situation. The more demanding are these requirements (and therefore the greater the behavioral uncertainty), the more intense and protracted will be the processes responsible for formulating an adequate response. These planning and programming processes (which include phasic preparation) will, in turn, provide a greater stimulus for the energy mobilization response.

This hypothesis is amenable to further investigation by exploring the temporal and intensive relationships between phasic and tonic motor preparation and by identifying the neural pathways by which the preparatory processes are linked. These issues could be broached by suitably combining the methods described for studying the two types of preparatory processes.

Such an integrative research program should shed light on a central problem associated with psychobiological perspectives on behavior: the interface between the 'low-energy' brain information processing system and the 'high-energy' cardiovascular and muscular metabolic processing system. According to the data summarized here it seems likely that such a linkage is a two-way street involving pathways through which each process may influence the other. For example, the common assumption that behavior tends to maximum efficiency may imply that energetic costs are taken into account in specifying the temporal, kinetic and spatial features of adaptive motor acts. This issue broaches the broader question of how information processing influences the energy efficiency of behavior.

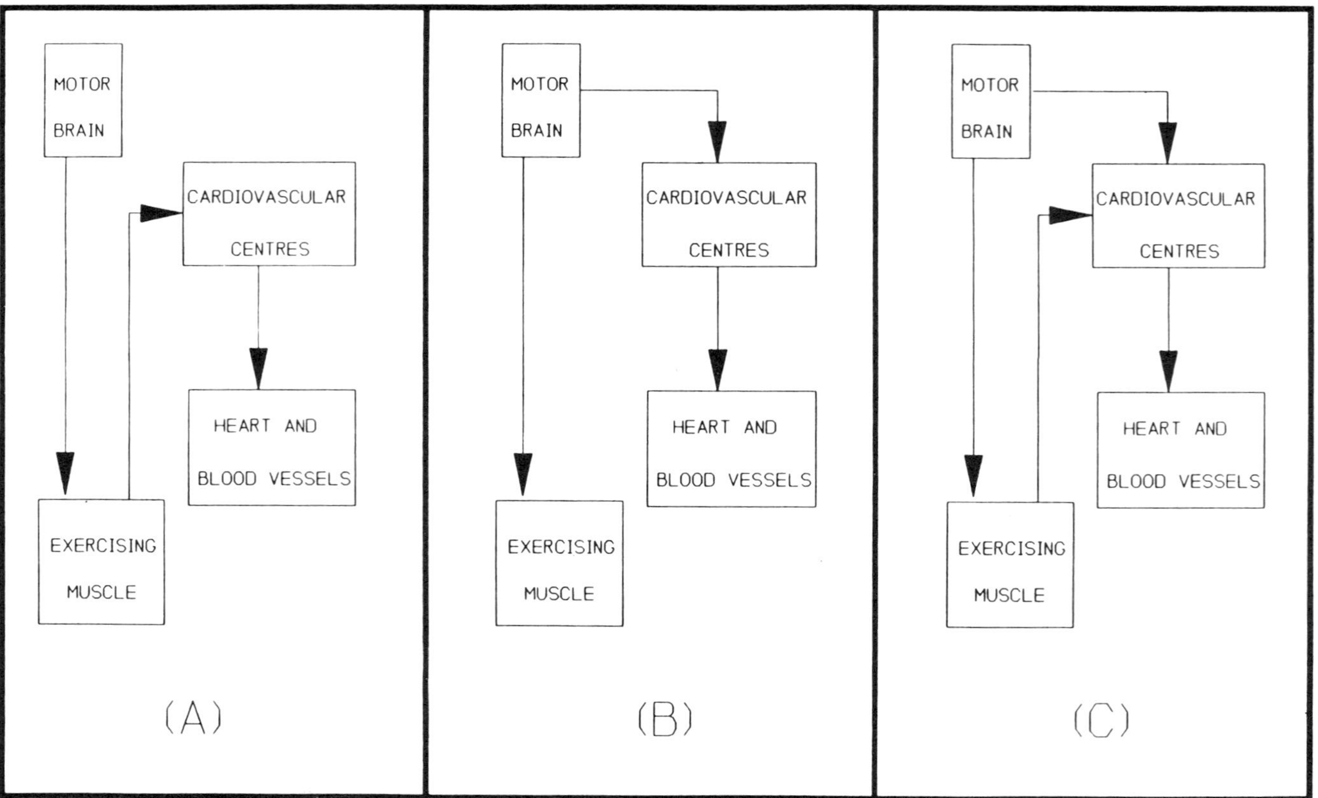

Figure 4.12. Three possible mechanisms controlling the cardiovascular adjustments to exercise: (A) reflexes elicited by striate muscular activity; (B) central command, and (C) a combination of peripheral and central processes. (Reproduced with permission from Mitchell *et al.* (1981). © American Heart Association.)

ACKNOWLEDGEMENTS

Jean Requin has been partly supported by ONR grant N00014-89-J-1557. Jasper Brener has been partly supported by NIH grant 1R01 HL42366 from the National Heart, Lung and Blood Institute.

REFERENCES

Abrahams, V.C., Hilton, S.M. and Zbrozina, A. (1960). Active muscle vasodilation produced by stimulation of the brain stem: its significance in the defense reaction. *Journal of Physiology (London)*, **154**, 491–513.

Adams D.B., Baccelli G., Mancia G. and Zanchetti A. (1969). Cardiovascular changes during naturally elicited fighting behavior in the cat. *American Journal of Psychology*, **216**, 1226–1235.

Alam, M. and Smirk, F.H. (1938). Observations in man on a pulse accelerating reflex from the voluntary muscles of the leg. *Journal of Physiology (London)*, **92**, 167–177.

Alegria, J. (1974). The time course of preparation after a first peak: some constraints of reactivity mechanisms. *Quarterly Journal of Experimental Psychology*, **26**, 622–632.

Alegria, J. (1980). Contrôle stratégique du choix d'un instant pour se préparer â réagir. In J. Requin (ed.), *Anticipation et Comportement*. Paris: Editions du CNRS, pp. 95–105.

Allison, T., Wood, C.C. and McCarthy, G. (1986). The central nervous system. In M.G.H. Coles, E. Donchin and S.W. Porges (eds), *Psychophysiology: Systems, Processes, and Applications*. New York: Guilford Press, pp. 5–25.

Andersen, R.A., Essick, G.K. and Siegel, R.M. (1987). Neurons of area 7 activated by both visual stimuli and oculomotor behavior. *Experimental Brain Research*, **67**, 316–322.

Arezzo, J. and Vaughan, H.G. (1980). Cortical sources and topography of the motor potential and the somato-sensory evoked potential in the monkey. In H.H. Kornhuber and L. Deecke (eds), *Motivation, Motor and Sensory Processes of the Brain*. (*Progress in Brain Research*, vol. 54). Amsterdam: Elsevier, pp. 77–83.

Asatryan, D.G. and Feldman, A.G. (1965). Functional tuning of the nervous system with control of movement or maintenance of a steady posture: mechanographic analysis of the work of the joint on execution of a postural task. *Biophysics*, **10**, 925–935.

Asmussen, E. (1981). Similarities and dissimilarities between static and dynamic exercise. *Circulation Research*, **8** (Suppl.I), 3–10.

Astrand, P. and Rodahl, K. (1986). *Textbook of Work Physiology*. 3rd edn. New York: McGraw-Hill.

Bechbache, R.R., Chow, H.H.K., Duffin, J. and Orsini, E.C. (1979). The effects of hypercapnia, hypoxia, exercise and anxiety on the pattern of breathing in man. *Journal of Physiology*, **293**, 285–300.

Benedict, F.G. and Benedict, C.G. (1933). *Mental Effort in Relation to Gaseous Exchange, Heart Rate and Mechanics of Respiration*. Carnegie Institute of Washington, Publication 446.

Bertelson, P. (1967). The time course of preparation. *Quarterly Journal of Experimental Psychology*, **19**, 272–279.

Besrest, A. and Requin, J. (1973). Development of expectancy wave and the time-course of preparatory set in a simple reaction time task. In S. Kornblum (ed.), *Attention and Performance*, vol. IV. New York: Academic Press, pp. 209–219.

Bizzi, E. (1980). Central and peripheral mechanisms in motor control. In G.E. Stelmach and J. Requin (eds), *Tutorials in Motor Behavior*. Amsterdam: North-Holland.

Bizzi, E., Accornero, N., Chapple, N. and Hogan, N. (1982). Arm trajectory formation in monkeys. *Experimental Brain Research*, **46**, 139–143.

Blix, A.S., Stromme, S.B. and Ursin, H. (1974). Additional heart rate—an indicator of psychological activation. *Aerospace Medicine*, **45**, 1219–1222.

Bolles, R.C. (1970). Species-specific defense reactions and avoidance learning. *Psychological Review*, **77**, 32–48.

Bonnet, M. (1981). Comparison of monosynaptic tendon reflexes during preparation for ballistic of ramp movement. *Electroencephalography and Clinical Neurophysiology*, **51**, 353–362.

Bonnet, M. (1983). Anticipatory changes of long latency stretch responses during preparation for directional hand movements. *Brain Research*, **280**, 51–62.

Bonnet, M. and MacKay, W.A. (1989). Changes in CNV and reaction time related to precueing of direction and force of a forearm movement. *Brain, Behavior and Evolution*, **33**, 147–152.

Bonnet, M. and Requin, J. (1982). Long loop and spinal reflexes in man during preparation for intended directional hand movements. *Journal of Neuroscience*, **2**, 90–96.

Bonnet, M., Requin, J. and Semjen, A. (1980). Intervention d'influences réticulaires dans une réorganisation des structures motrices spinales pendant la préparation au mouvement. In J. Requin (ed.), *Anticipation et Comportement*. Paris: Editions du CNRS, pp. 367–381.

Bonnet, M., Requin, J. and Semjen, A. (1981). Human reflexology and motor preparation. In D. Miller (ed.), *Exercise and Sport Sciences Reviews*, vol. 9. Philadelphia: Franklin Institute Press, pp. 119–157.

Bonnet, M., Requin, J. and Stelmach, G.E. (in press). Changes in electromyographic responses to muscle stretch, related to the programming of movement spatial parameters. *Electroencephalography and Clinical Neurophysiology*.

Bonnet, M., Stelmach, G.E. and Requin, J. (1982). Specification of direction and extent in motor programming. *Bulletin of the Psychonomic Society*, **19**, 31–34.

Bonnet, M., Stelmach, G.E. and Requin, J. (1984). Differential changes in long latency electromyographic responses during motor programming. *Society for Neuroscience Abstracts*, **10**, 185–194.

Borst, C. and Karemaker, J.M. (1983). Time delays in the human baroreceptor reflex. *Journal of the Autonomic Nervous System*, **9**, 399–409.

Borst, C., Karemaker, J.M., Dunning, A.J., Bouman, L.N., Wagner, J. and White, C. (1983). Frequency limitation in the human baroreceptor reflex. *Journal of the Autonomic Nervous System*, **9**, 381–397.

Boschert, J., Hink, R.F. and Deecke, L. (1983). Finger movement versus toe movement—related potentials: further evidence for supplementary motor area (SMA) participation prior to voluntary action. *Experimental Brain Research*, **55**, 73–80.

Breland, K. and Breland, M. (1961). The misbehavior of organisms. *American Psychologist*, **16**, 681–684.

Brener, J. (1986a). Operant reinforcement, feedback and the efficiency of learned motor control. In M.G.H. Coles, E. Donchin and S.W. Porges (eds), *Psychophysiology: Systems, Processes and Applications*. New York: Guilford Press, pp. 309–327.

Brener, J. (1986b). Factors influencing the covariation of heart rate and oxygen consumption. In P. Grossman, K.H.L. Janssen and D. Vaitl (eds), *Cardiorespiratory and Cardiosomatic Psychophysiology*. New York: Plenum Press, pp. 173–190.

Brener, J. (1987). Behavioural energetics: some effects of uncertainty on the mobilization and distribution of energy. *Psychophysiology*, **24**, 499–512.

Brener, J., Phillips, K.C. and Sherwood, A. (1983). Energy expenditure during response-dependent and response-independent food delivery in rats. *Psychophysiology*, **20**, 384–392.

Bristow, J.D., Honour, A.J., Pickering, T.G. and Sleight, P. (1969). Cardiovascular and respiratory changes during sleep in normal and hypertensive subjects. *Cardiovascular Research*, **3**, 476–485.

Brod, F., Fencl, V., Hejl, Z. and Jirka, J. (1959). Circulatory changes underlying blood pressure elevation during acute emotional stress (mental arithmetic) in normal and hypertensive subjects. *Clinical Science*, **18**, 269–279.

Brouha, L. and Heath, C.W. (1943). Resting-pulse and blood-pressure values in relation to physical fitness in young men. *New England Journal of Medicine*, **228**, 473–477.

Brown, T.G., Szabo, A. and Seraganian, P. (1988). Physical versus psychological determinants of heart rate reactivity to mental arithmetic. *Psychophysiology*, **25**, 532–537.

Brunia, C.H.M. (1980). What is wrong with legs in motor preparation ? In H.H. Kornhuber and L. Deecke (eds), *Motivation, Motor and Sensory Processes of the Brain: Electrical Potentials, Behavior and Clinical Use* (*Progress in Brain Research*, vol. 54). Amsterdam: Elsevier, pp. 232–236.

Brunia, C.H.M. (1984). Selective and aselective control of spinal motor structures during preparation for movement. In S. Kornblum and J. Requin (eds), *Preparatory States and Processes*. Hillsdale: Lawrence Erlbaum, pp. 285–302.

Brunia, C.H.M. (1988). Movement and stimulus preceding negativity. *Biological Psychology*, **26**, 165–178.

Brunia, C.H.M. and Haagh, S.A.V.M. (1986). Preparation for action: slow potentials and EMG. In H. Heuer and C. Fromm (eds), *Generation and Modulation of Action Patterns* (*Brain Research*, Series 15). Berlin: Springer-Verlag, pp. 28–40.

Brunia, C.H.M., Haagh, S.A.V.M. and Scheirs, J.G.M. (1985). Waiting to respond: electrophysiological measurements in man during preparation for a movement. In H. Heuer, U. Kleinbeck and K.H. Schmidt (eds), *Motor Behavior: Programming, Control, and Acquisition*. Berlin: Springer, pp. 35–76.

Brunia, C.H.M. and van der Bosch, W.E.J. (1984). Movement-related slow potentials. I: A contrast between finger and foot movements in right-handed subjects. *Electroencephalography and Clinical Neurophysiology*, **57**, 515–527.

Brunia, C.H.M. and Vingerhoets, A.J.J.M. (1980). CNV and EMG preceding a plantar flexion of the foot. *Biological Psychology*, **11**, 181–191.

Cannon, W.B. (1929). *Bodily Changes in Pain, Hunger, Fear and Rage*. New York: D. Appleton.

Cheney, P.D. and Fetz, E.E. (1984). Corticomotoneuronal cells contribute to long-latency stretch reflexes in the rhesus monkey. *Journal of Physiology* (*London*), **349**, 249–272.

Churchland, P.S. (1986). *Neurophilosophy: Toward a Unified Science of Mind/Brain*. Cambridge, MA: MIT Press.

Coleman, T.G., Granger, H.J. and Guyton, A.C. (1971). Whole-body circulatory autoregulation and hypertension. *Circulation Research*, **28–29** (Suppl. 2), 76–81.

Coles, M.G.H. (1989). Modern mind–brain reading: psychophysiology, physiology, and cognition. *Psychophysiology*, **26**, 251–269.

Coles, M.G.H., Gratton, C. and Donchin, E. (1988). Detecting early communication: using measures of movement-related potentials to illuminate human information processing. *Biological Psychology*, **26**, 69–89.

Corcondilas A., Koroxenidid G.T. and Shepard J.T. (1964). Effect of a brief contraction of forearm muscles on forearm blood flow. *Journal of Applied Physiology*, **19**, 142–146.

Crammond, D.J., MacKay, W.A. and Murphy, J.T. (1985). Evoked potentials from passive elbow movements. I. Quantitative spatial and temporal analysis. *Electroencephalography and Clinical Neurophysiology*, **61**, 396–410.

Cratty, B.J. (1976). *Movement Behavior and Motor Learning*. Henry Kimpton.

Cunningham, D.J.C., Petersen, E.S., Peto, R., Pickering, T.G. and Sleight, P. (1972). Comparison of the effect of different types of exercise on the baroreflex regulation of heart rate. *Acta Physiologica Scandinavica*, **86**, 444–455.

Daniel, R.S. (1939). The distribution of muscular action potentials during maze learning. *Journal of Experimental Psychology*, **24**, 621–629.

Davis, R.C. (1943). The genetic development of patterns of voluntary activity. *Journal of Experimental Psychology*, **33**, 471–486.

Deecke, L., Bashore, T., Brunia, C.H.M., Grunewald-Zuberbier, E., Grunewald, G. and Kristeva, R. (1984). Movement-associated potentials and motor control. In R. Karrer, J. Cohen and P. Tueting (eds), *Brain and Information: Event-Related Potentials*. New York: NY Academy of Sciences, pp. 398–428.

DeJong, R., Coles, M.G.H., Gratton, G. and Logan, G.L., (in press). Search of the point of no return. *Journal of Experimental Psychology: HPP*.

DeJong, R., Wierda, M., Mulder, G. and Mulder, L.J.M. (1988). Use of partial information in responding. *Journal of Experimental Psychology: HPP*, **14**, 682–692.

Donald, D.E. and Shepherd, J.T. (1963). Response to exercise in dogs with cardiac denervation. *American Journal of Physiology*, **205**, 393–400.

Donchin, E. and Coles, M.G.H. (1988). On the conceptual foundations of cognitive psychophysiology. *Behavioral and Brain Sciences*, **11**, 406–417.

Duffy, E. (1932). The relation between muscular tension and quality of performance. *American Journal of Psychology*, **44**, 535–546.

Duffy, E. (1962). *Activation and Behavior*. New York: John Wiley.

Durup, H. and Requin, J. (1970). Hypothèses sur le rôle des probabilities conditionnelles du signal d'exécution dans le temps de réaction simple. *Psychologie Française*, **15**, 37–46.

Egeth, H.E. and Blecker, D.L. (1969). Verbal interference in a perceptual comparison task. *Perception and Psychophysics*, **6**, 355–356.

Eldridge, F.L., Millhorn, D.E., Kiley, J.P. and Waldrop, T.G. (1985). Stimulation by central command of locomotion, respiration and circulation during exercise. *Respiration Physiology*, **59**, 313–337.

Eliasson, S., Folkow, B., Lindgren, P. and Uvnas, B. (1951). Activation of sympathetic vasodilator nerves to the skeletal muscles in the cat by hypothalamic stimulation. *Acta Physiologica Scandinavica*, **23**, 333–351.

Epstein, W. (1986). Contrasting conceptions of perception and action. *Acta Psychologica*, **63**, 103–115.

Eriksen, C.W., Coles, M.G.H., Morris, L.R. and O'Hara, W.P. (1985). An electromyographic examination of response competition. *Bulletin of the Psychonomic Society*, **23**, 165–168.

Eriksen, B.A. and Eriksen, C.W. (1974). Effects of noise letters upon the identification of target letter in visual search. *Perception and Psychophysics*, **16**, 143–149.

Eriksen, C.W. and Schultz, D.W. (1979). Information processing in visual search: a continuous flow conception and experimental results. *Perception and Psychophysics*, **25**, 249–263.

Euler, U.S. von (1964). Quantification of stress by catecholamine analysis. *Clinical Pharmacology and Therapeutics*, **5**, 398–404.

Evarts, E.V. (1981). Role of motor cortex in voluntary movements in primates. In V.B.

Brooks (ed.), *Handbook of Physiology*, vol. II, pt 2. Bethesda: American Physiological Society, pp. 1083–1120.

Evarts, E.V. (1984). Neurophysiological approaches to brain mechanisms for preparatory set. In S. Kornblum and J. Requin (eds), *Preparatory States and Processes*. Hillsdale: Lawrence Erlbaum, pp. 137–153.

Evarts, E.V., Bizzi, E., Burke, R.E., Delong, M. and Thach, W.T. (1971). Central control of movement. *Neurosciences Research Program Bulletin*, **9**, no. 1.

Evarts, E.V., Shimoda, Y. and Wise, S.P. (1984). *Neurophysiological Approaches to Higher Brain Functions*. New York: Wiley.

Faulkner, J.A. (1964). Effect of cardiac conditioning on the anticipatory, exercise, and recovery heart rates of young men. *American Journal of Sports Medicine and Physical Fitness*, **4**, 79–86.

Favilla, M., Hening, W. and Ghez, C. (1989). Trajectory control in targeted force impulses. VI: Independent specification of response amplitude and direction. *Experimental Brain Research*, **75**, 280–294.

Fenz, W.D. and Epstein, S. (1967). Gradients of physiological arousal in parachutists as a function of an approaching jump. *Psychosomatic Medicine*, **29**, 33–35.

Fitts, P.M. (1959). *Human Information Handling in Speeded Tasks*. IBM Research Report RC-109.

Fitts, P.M. and Deininger, R.L. (1954). S–R compatibility: correspondence among paired elements within stimulus and response codes. *Journal of Experimental Psychology*, **48**, 483–492.

Fitts, P.M. and Seeger, Ch. M. (1953). S–R compatibility: spatial characteristics of stimulus and response codes. *Journal of Experimental Psychology*, **46**, 199–210.

Frankenhaeuser, M. and Rissler, A. (1970a). Catecholamine output during relaxation and anticipation. *Perceptual and Motor Skills*, **30**, 745–746.

Frankenhaeuser, M. and Rissler, A. (1970b). Effects of punishment on catecholamine release and efficiency of performance. *Psychopharmacologica*, **17**, 378–390.

Freyschuss, U. (1970). Cardiovascular adjustments to somatomotor activation. *Acta Physiologica Scandinavica*, Suppl. 342, 1–60.

Fuster, J.M. (1981). Prefrontal cortex in motor control. In V.B. Brooks (ed.), *Handbook of Physiology*, vol. II, pt 2. Bethesda: American Physiological Society, pp. 1149–1178.

Fuster, J.M. (1984). Behavioral electrophysiology of the prefrontal cortex. *Trends in Neurosciences*, **7**, 408–414.

Fuster, J.M. (1985). The prefrontal cortex, mediator of cross-temporal contingencies. *Human Neurobiology*, **4**, 169–179.

Gaillard, A.W.K. (1980). Cortical correlates of motor preparation. In R.S. Nickerson (ed.), *Attention and Performance*, vol. VIII. Hillsdale: Lawrence Erlbaum, pp. 75–91.

Gantchev, G.N. (1978). Neuronal activity in the sensorimotor cortex of monkey related to the preparation for performing movement. *Activ. Nerv. Sup.* (*Praha*), **20**, 195–202.

Garcia-Colera, A. and Semjen, A. (1988). Distributed planning of movement sequences. *Journal of Motor Behavior*, **20**, 341–367.

Gelsema, A.J., de Groot, G. and Bouman, L.N. (1983). Instantaneous cardiac acceleration in the cat elicited by peripheral nerve stimulation. *Journal of Applied Physiology*, **55**(3), 703–710.

Germana. (1969). Central efferent processes and autonomic–behavioral integration. *Psychophysiology*, **6**, 78–90.

Ghez, C., Hening, W. and Favilla, M. (1990). Initiation and specification of motor response features: parallel interacting channels. In M. Jeannerod (ed.), *Attention and Performance*, vol. XIII. Hillsdale: Lawrence Erlbaum, pp. 265–293.

Godschalk, M. and Lemon, R.N. (1983). Involvement of monkey premotor cortex in the preparation of arm movements. *Experimental Brain Research*, Suppl. 7, 114–119.

Godschalk, M., Lemon, R.N., Nijs, H.G.T. and Kuypers, H.G.J.M. (1981). Behaviour of neurons in monkey peri-arcuate and precentral cortex before and during visually guided arm and hand movements. *Experimental Brain Research*, **44**, 113–116.

Goldberg, G.,(1986). Supplementary motor area structure and function: review and hypotheses. *Behavioral and Brain Sciences*, **8**, 567–615.

Goldberg, M.E. (1983). Studying the neurophysiology of behavior: methods for recording single neurons in awake behaving monkeys. In J.L. Baker and J.F. MacKelvy (eds), *Methods in Cellular Neurobiology*. New York: Wiley, pp. 225–248.

Goodall, McC. and Berman, M.L. (1960). Urinary output of adrenaline, noradrenaline, and 3-methoxy-4-hydroxymandelic acid following centrifugation and anticipation of centrifugation. *Journal of Clinical Investigations*, **39**, 1533–1538.

Goodman, D. and Kelso, J.A.S. (1980). Are movements prepared in parts? Not under compatible (naturalized) conditions. *Journal of Experimental Psychology: General*, **109**, 475–495.

Goodwin, G.M., McCloskey, D.I. and Mitchell, J.H. (1972). Cardiovascular and respiratory responses to changes in central command during isometric exercise at constant muscle tension. *Journal of Physiology*, **226**, 173–190.

Gratton, G., Coles, M.G.H., Sirevaag, E.J., Eriksen, C.W. and Donchin, E. (1988). Pre- and poststimulus activation of response channels: a psychophysiological analysis. *Journal of Experimental Psychology: HPP* **14**, 331–344.

Gribbin, B., Pickering, T.G., Sleight, P. and Peto, R. (1971). Effect of age and high blood pressure in baroreflex sensitivity in man. *Circulation Research*, **29**, 424–431.

Grollman, A. (1929). Physiological variations in the cardiac output of man. *American Journal of Physiology*, **89**, 584–588.

Haagh, S.A.V.M. and Brunia, C.H.M. (1985). Anticipatory response-relevant muscle activity, CNV amplitude and simple reaction time. *Electroencephalography and Clinical Neurophysiology*, **61**, 30–39.

Haagh, S.A.V.M., Spoeltman, W.T.E., Scheirs, J.G.M. and Brunia, C.H.M. (1983). Surface EMG and Achilles tendon reflex amplitudes during a foot movement in a reaction time task. *Biological Psychology*, **17**, 81–96.

Hales, J.R.S. and Ludbrook, J. (1988). Baroreflex participation in redistribution of cardiac output at onset of exercise. *Journal of Applied Physiology*, **64**, 627–634.

Hanson, J.S. and Tabakin, B.S. (1964). Electrocardiographic telemetry in skiers: anticipatory and recovery heart rate during competition. *New England Journal of Medicine*, **271**, 181–185.

Hasbroucq, T. and Guiard, Y. (1991). Irrelevance of the Simon effect to the issue of stimulus–response compatibility: towards a conceptual clarification. *Journal of Experimental Psychology: HPP*, **17**, 246–266.

Hashimoto, S., Gemba, H. and Sasaki, K. (1980). Premovement slow cortical potentials and required muscle force in self-paced hand movements in the monkey. *Brain Research*, **197**, 415–423.

Head, G.A. and McCarty, R. (1987). Vagal and sympathetic components of the heart rate change and gain of the baroreceptor–heart rate reflex in conscious rats. *Journal of the Autonomic Nervous System*, **20**, 203–211.

Hening, W., Favilla, M. and Ghez, C. (1988). Trajectory control in targeted face impulses: gradual specification of response amplitude. *Experimental Brain Research*, **71**, 116–128.

Henry, F.M. and Rogers, D.E. (1960). Increased response latency for complicated movements and a 'memory drum' theory of neuromotor action. *Research Quarterly*, **31**, 448–458.

Hick, W.E. (1952). On the rate of gain of information. *Quarterly Journal of Experimental Psychology*, **4**, 11–26.

Holender, D. (1980a). Le concept de préparation à réagir dans le traitement de l'information. In J. Requin (ed.), *Anticipation et Comportement. Paris: Editions du CNRS*, pp. 29–64.

Holender, D. (1980b). L'effet de répétition dans les tâches de réaction de choix: préparation volontaire ou activation automatique? In J. Requin (ed.), *Anticipation et Comportement*. Paris: Editions du CNRS, pp. 523–542.

Hubbard, J.W., Buchholz, R.A., Reed, K., Nathan, M.A. and Keeton, T.K. (1988). Changes in plasma catecholamines and plasma renin activity during hypotension in conscious rats with lesions of the nucleus tractus solitarii. *Journal of the Autonomic Nervous System*, **22**, 97–106.

Hubel, D.H. (1957). Single unit activity in visual cortex of the unanesthetized cat. *Federation Proceedings*, **16**, 63.

Hughson, R.L., Russell, C.A. and Marshall, M.R. (1984). Effect of metoprolol on cycle and treadmill maximal exercise performance. *Journal of Cardiac Rehabilitation*, **4**, 27–30.

Hyvärinen, J. (1982). *The Parietal Cortex of Monkey and Man*. Berlin: Springer Verlag.

Jackson, C.B., Douglas, W.K., Culver, J.F., Ruff, G., Knoblock, E.C. and Graybiel, A. (1961). Results of preflight and postflight medical examination. In *Proceedings of the Conference on Results of First US Manned Suborbital Space Flight, June 1961.*

Jasper, H., Ricci, G.F. and Doane, B. (1958). Patterns of cortical neurone discharge during conditioned responses in monkeys. In G. Wolstenholme and C. O'Connor (eds), *Neurological Basis of Behaviour*. Boston: Little Brown.

Jennings, J.R. and Wood, C.C. (1977). Cardiac cycle time effects on performance, phasic cardiac responses and their intercorrelation in choice reaction time. *Psychophysiology*, **14**, 297–307.

Kahneman, D. and Treisman, A. (1984). Changing views of attention and automaticity. In R. Parasumaran and D.R. Davies (eds), *Varieties of Attention*. Orlando: Academic Press.

Katkin, E.S. (1985). Blood, sweat and tears: individual differences in autonomic self-perception. *Psychophysiology*, **22**, 125–137.

Keele, S.W. (1981). Behavioural analysis of motor control. In V.B. Brooks (ed.), *Handbook of Physiology*, vol. II, pt 2. Bethesda: American Physiological Society, pp. 1391–1414.

Keele, S.W. (1988). Movement control in skilled motor performance. *Psychological Bulletin*, **70**, 387–403.

Kelso, J.A.S. (1981). Contrasting perspectives on order and regulation in movement. In J. Long and A. Baddeley (eds), *Attention and Performance*, vol. IX. Hillsdale: Lawrence Erlbaum, pp. 437–457.

Kelso, J.A.S. (1984). Considerations from a theory of movement. In E. Donchin (ed.), *Cognitive Psychophysiology: Event-Related Potentials and the Study of Cognition*. Hillsdale: Lawrence Erlbaum, pp. 201–219.

Kelso, J.A.S., Holt, K.G., Kugler, P.N. and Turvey, H.T. (1980). Coordinative structures as dissipative structures: empirical lines of convergence. In G.E. Stelmach and J. Requin (eds), *Tutorials in Motor Behavior*. Amsterdam: North-Holland, pp. 49–70.

Kornblum, S., Hasbroucq, T. and Osman, A. (1990). Dimensional overlap cognitive basis for stimulus–response compatibility: a model and taxonomy. *Psychological Review*, **97**, 253–270.

Kornhuber, H.H. and Deecke, L. (1965). Hirnpotentialänderungen bei Willdürbewegungen und passiven Bewegungen des Menschen: Bereitschaftspotential und reafferente Potentiale. *Pflügers Archiv*, **284**, 1–17.

Krogh, A. and Lindhard, J. (1913). The regulation of respiration and circulation during the initial stages of muscular work. *Journal of Physiology* (*London*), **47**, 112–136.

Kugler, P.N., Kelso, J.A.S. and Turvey, M.T. (1980). On the concept of coordinative structures as dissipative structures: theoretical line. In G.E. Stelmach and J. Requin (ed.), *Tutorials in Motor Behavior*. Amsterdam: North-Holland, pp. 3–48.

Kurata, K. and Tanji, J. (1985). Contrasting neuronal activity in supplementary and precentral motor cortex of monkeys. II: Responses to movement triggering vs nontriggering sensory signals. *Journal of Neurophysiology*, **53**, 142–152.

Kutas, M. (1984). Subcomponents of the contingent negative variation. In E. Donchin (ed.), *Cognitive Psychophysiology: Event-Related Potentials and the Study of Cognition*. Hillsdale: Lawrence Erlbaum, pp. 191–201.

Kutas, M. and Donchin, E. (1980). Preparation to respond as manifested by movement-related brain potentials. *Brain Research*, **202**, 95–115.

Kutas, M. and Hillyard, S. (1980). Reading senseless sentences: brain potentials reflect semantic incongruity. *Science*, **207**, 203–205.

Lacey, B.C. and Lacey, J.I. (1974). Studies of heart rate and other bodily processes in sensorimotor hehavior. In P.A. Obrist, A.H. Black, J. Brener and L.V. Dicara (eds), *Cardiovascular Psychophysiology*. Chicago: Aldine, pp. 538–564.

Larish, D.D. and Frekany, G.A. (1985). Planning and preparing expected and unexpected movements: reexamining the relationships of arm, direction and extent of movement. *Journal of Motor Behavior*, **17**, 168–189.

Lashley, K.S. (1951). The problem of serial order in behavior. In L.A. Jeffress (ed.), *Central Mechanisms in Behavior*. New York: Wiley.

Lecas, J.C., Requin, J., Anger, C. and Vitton, N. (1986). Changes in neuronal activity of the monkey precentral cortex during preparation for movement. *Journal of Neurophysiology*, **56**, 1680–1702.

Lecas, J.C., Requin, J. and Vitton, N. (1983). Anticipatory neuronal activity in the monkey precentral cortex during reaction time foreperiod: preliminary results. *Experimental Brain Research*, Suppl. 7, 120–129.

Lehman, D. and Skrandies, W. (1984). Spatial analysis of evoked potentials in man: a review. *Progress in Neurobiology*, **23**, 227–250.

Lemon, R.N. (1984). Methods for neuronal recording in conscious animals. *IBRO Handbook Series*, vol. 4. New York: Wiley.

Lépine, D., Glencross, D. and Requin, J. (1989). Some experimental evidence for and against a parametric conception of movement programming. *Journal of Experimental Psychology: HPP*, **15**, 347–362.

Lewis, S.J., Taylor, W.F., Graham, R.M., Pettinger, W.A., Schuttte, J.E. and Blomqvist, C.G. (1983). Cardiovascular responses to exercise as functions of absolute and relative work load. *Journal of Applied Physiology*, **54**, 1314–1323.

Libet, B., Wright, E.W. and Gleason, C.A. (1982). Readiness potentials preceding unrestricted 'spontaneous' vs preplanned voluntary acts. *Electroencephalography and Clinical Neurophysiology*, **35**, 369–374.

Logan, G.L. and Cowan, W.B. (1984). On the ability to inhibit thought and action: a theory of an act of control. *Psychological Review*, **91**, 295–327.

Ludbrook, J. and Graham, W.F. (1985). Circulatory responses to onset of exercise: role of arterial and cardiac baroreflexes. *American Journal of Physiology*, **248** (*Heart Circ. Physiol. 17*), H457–H467.

Lurito, J.T., Schwartz, A.B., Petrides, M., Kettner, R.E. and Georgopoulos, A.P. (1988).

Cross correlations between motor cortical cells simultaneously recorded during reaching tasks in the monkey. *Society for Neuroscience Abstracts*, **14**, 342.

Lynch, J.C. (1980). The functional organization of posterior parietal association cortex. *Behavioral Brain Sciences*, **3**, 485–534.

Macar, F. (1977). Signification des variations contingentes négatives dans la dimension temporelle du comportement. *Année Psychologique*, **77**, 439–474.

Macar, F. and Besson, M. (1985). Contingent negative variation in processes of expectancy, preparation and time estimation. *Biological Psychology*, **21**, 293–307.

Macar, F., Lecas, J.C. and Requin, J. (1980). Evolution de l'activité unitaire des formations réticulaires mésencéphaliques chez le chat au cours de la période préparatoire â une réponse motrice simple. In J. Requin (ed.), *Anticipation et Comportement*. Paris: Editions du CNRS, pp. 85–94.

Macar, F., Vidal, F. and Bonnet, M. (in press). Laplacian derivations of CNV in time programming. In *Proceedings of the EPIC IX Meeting, Noordwijk, 1989*.

Macar, F. and Vitton, N. (1979). Contingent negative variation and accuracy of time estimation: a study on cats. *Electroencephalography and Clinical Neurophysiology*, **47**, 213–228.

MacKay, W.A. and Crammond, D.J. (in press). Unit activity related to directed arm reach in cortical area 7a. *Journal of Neuroscience*.

MacKay, W.A. and Murphy, J.T. (1979). Cerebellar influence on proprioceptive control loops. In J. Massion and K. Sasaki (eds), *Cerebrocerebellar Interactions*. Amsterdam: Elsevier, pp. 141–152.

Magel, J.R., McArdle, W.D. and Glaser, R.M. (1969). Telemetered heart rate response to selected competitive swimming events. *Journal of Applied Physiology*, **26**(6), 764–770.

Magliero, A., Bashore, T.R., Coles, M.G.H. and Donchin, E. (1984). On the dependence of P300 latency on stimulus evaluation processes. *Psychophysiology*, **21**, 171–186.

Mantysaari, M.J., Antila, K.J. and Peltonen, T.E. (1988). Circulatory effects of anticipation in a light isometric handgrip test. *Psychophysiology*, **25**, 179–184

Mark, A.L. and Mancia, G. (1983). Cardiopulmonary baroreflexes in humans. In: *Handbook of Physiology, section 2, The Cardiovascular System, vol. 3, Peripheral Circulation and Organ Blood Flow*, pt 2. Bethesda, MD: American Physiological Society, pp. 795–813.

Marler, P. (1970). A comparative approach to vocal learning: song development in white-crowned sparrows. *Journal of Comparative and Physiological Psychology Monograph*, **71**(2), 1–25.

Martin, J., Sutherland, C.J. and Zbrozyna, A.W. (1976). Habituation and conditioning of the defence reactions and their cardiovascular components in cats and dogs. *Pflugers Arch*, **365**, 37–47.

Mason, J.W., Hartley, L.H., Kotchen, T.A., Mougey, E.H., Ricketts, P.T. and Jones, L.G. (1973). Plasma cortisol and norepinephrine responses in anticipation of muscular exercise. *Psychosomatic Medicine*, **35**, 406–414.

Massion, J. and Dufossé, M. (1988). Coordination between posture and movement: why and how? *N.I.P.S.*, **3**, 88–93.

Mauritz, K.H. and Wise, S.P. (1986). Premotor cortex of the rhesus monkey: neuronal activity in anticipation of predictable environmental events. *Experimental Brain Research*, **61**, 229–244.

McArdle, W.D., Foglia, G.F. and Patti, A.V. (1967). Telemetered cardiac response to selected running events. *Journal of Applied Physiology*, **23**(4), 566–570.

McCarthy, G. and Donchin, E. (1981). A metric for thought: a comparison of P300 latency and reaction time. *Science*, **211**, 77–80.

McClelland, J.L. (1979). On the time relations of mental processes: a framework for analyzing processes in cascade. *Psychological Review*, **86**, 287–330.

McClelland, J.L. and Rumelhart, D.E. (1986). *Parallel Distributed Processes*, vols 1 and 2. Cambridge: MIT Press.

Meyer, D.E., Osman, A.M., Irwin, D.E. and Yantis, S. (1988). Modern mental chronometry. *Biological Psychology*, **26**, 3–67.

Meyer, D.E., Yantis, S., Osman, A. and Smith, J.E.K. (1984). Discrete versus continuous models of response preparation: a reaction time analysis. In S. Kornblum and J. Requin (eds), *Preparatory States and Processes*. Hillsdale: Lawrence Erlbaum, pp. 69–94.

Meyer, D.E., Yantis, S., Osman, A.M. and Smith, J.E.K. (1985). Temporal properties of human information processing: tests of discrete vs continuous models. *Cognitive Psychology*, **17**, 445–518.

Miller, J.O. (1982). Discrete versus continuous stage models of human information processing: in search of partial output. *Journal of Experimental Psychology: HPP*, **8**, 273–296.

Miller, J.O. (1983). Can response preparation begin before stimulus recognition finishes? *Journal of Experimental Psychology: HPP*, **9**, 161–182.

Miller, J.O. (1988). Discrete and continuous models of human information processing: theoretical distinctions and empirical results. *Acta Psychologica*, **67**, 191–257.

Mitchell, J.H., Reardon, W.C. and McCloskey, D.I. (1977). Reflex effects on circulation and respiration from contracting skeletal muscle. *American Journal of Physiology*, **233**, H374–H378.

Mitchell, J.H., Payne, F.C., Saltin, B. and Schibye, B. (1980). The role of muscle mass in the cardiovascular response to static contractions. *Journal of Physiology*, **309**, 45–54.

Mitchell, J.H., Payne, F.C., Schibye, B. and Saltin, B. (1981). Responses of arterial blood pressure to static exercise in relation to muscle mass, force development, and electromyographic activity. *Circulation Research*, **48**(Suppl. 1), 70–75.

Mitchell, J.H. and Schmidt, R.F. (1983). Cardiovascular reflex control by afferent fibers from skeletal muscle receptors. In: *Handbook of Physiology*, section 2, *The Cardiovascular System*, vol. 3, *Peripheral Circulation and Organ Blood Flow*, pt 2. Bethesda, MA: American Physiological Society.

Mountcastle, V.B. (1978). An organizing principle for cerebral function: the unit module and the distributed system. In F.O. Schmitt and F.G. Worden (eds), *The Neurosciences*. Fourth Study Program. Cambridge: MIT Press, pp. 21–42.

Mountcastle, V.B. (1986). The neural mechanisms of cognitive functions can now be studied directly. *Trends in Neurosciences*, **9**, 505–508.

Mountcastle, V.B., Lynch, J.C., Georgopoulos, A., Sakata, H. and Acuna, C. (1975). Posterior parietal association cortex of the monkey: command functions for operations within extrapersonal space. *Journal of Neurophysiology*, **38**, 871–908.

Mowbray, G.H. and Rhoades, M.V. (1959). On the reduction of choice reaction times with practice. *Quarterly Journal of Experimental Psychology*, **11**, 16–23.

Newell, K.M. (1985). Coordination, control and skill. In D. Goodman, I. Franks and R.B. Wiberg (eds), *Differing Perspectives in Motor Learning, Memory and Control*. Amsterdam: North-Holland.

Newell, K.M. (in press). Plans and constraints in action. Lecture given at the Neuroscience Movement Conference, Collinwood (Ont., Canada), Nov. 1988.

Niemi, P. and Näätänen, R. (1981). Foreperiod and simple reaction time. *Psychological Bulletin*, **89**, 133–162.

Niki, H. and Watanabe, M. (1976). Prefrontal unit activity and delayed response: Relation to cue location vs direction of response. *Brain Research*, **105**, 79–88.

Nunez, P.L. (1981). *Electric Fields of the Brain*. Oxford: Oxford University Press.

Obrist, P.A. (1981). *Cardiovascular Psychophysiology: a Perspective.* New York: Plenum Press.

Osman, A., Kornblum, S. and Meyer, D.E. (1986). The point of no return in choice reaction time: controlled and ballistic stages of response preparation. *Journal of Experimental Psychology: HPP*, **12**, 243–258.

Paillard, J. (1955). *Réflexes et Régulations d'Origine Proprioceptive chez l'Homme.* Paris: Arnette.

Paillard, J. (1982). Apraxia and neurophysiology of motor control. *Biological Sciences*, **298**, 111–134.

Peronnet, F., Cleroux, J., Perrault, H., Cousineau, D., De Champlain, J. and Nadeau, R. (1981a). Plasma norepinephrine response to exercise before and after training in humans. *Journal of Applied Physiology*, **51**, 812–815.

Peronnet, F., Nadeau, R.A., De Champlain, J., Magraassi, P. and Chatrand, C. (1981b). Exercise plasma catecholamines in dogs: role of adrenals and cardiac nerve endings. *American Journal of Physiology*, **241**, H243–H247.

Perrin, F., Bertrand, O. and Pernier, J. (1987). Scalp current density mapping: value and estimation from potential data. *IEEE Transactions on Biomedical Engineering*, **34**, 283–288.

Pickering, T.G. and Davies, J. (1973). Estimation on the conduction of the baroreceptor-cardiac reflex in man. *Cardiovascular Research*, **7**, 213–219.

Pickering, T.G., Gribbin, B., Petersen, E.S., Cunningham, D.J.C. and Sleight, P. (1972). Effects of autonomic blockade on the baroreflex in man at rest and during exercise. *Circulation Research*, **6**, 177–185.

Pickering, T.G., Gribbin, B. and Sleight, P. (1972). Comparison of the reflex heart rate response to rising and falling arterial pressure in man. *Cardiovascular Research*, **6**, 277–283.

Ragot, R. (1984). Perceptual and motor space representation: an event-related potential study. *Psychophysiology*, **21**, 159–170.

Reed, E.S. (1982). An outline of a theory of action systems. *Journal of Motor Behavior*, **14**, 98–134.

Reis, D.J. and Ledoux, J.E. (1987). Some central neural mechanisms governing resting and behaviorally coupled control of blood pressure. *Circulation*, **76**, I.2–I.9.

Requin, J. (1965). Quelques problèmes théoriques et méthodologiques posés par l'étude psychologique de l'attitude préparatoire à l'action. *Cahiers de Psychologie*, **8**, 101–113.

Requin, J. (1969). Some data on neurophysiological processes involved in the preparatory motor activity to reaction time performance. In W.G. Koster (ed.), *Attention and Performance*, vol. II. Amsterdam: North-Holland, pp. 358–367.

Requin, J. (1978). Spécificité des ajustements préparatoires à l'exécution du programme moteur. In H. Hécaen (ed.), *Du Contrôle Moteur à l'Organisation du Geste.* Paris: Masson, pp. 84–129.

Requin, J. (1980a). Toward a psychobiology of preparation for action. In G.E. Stelmach and J. Requin (eds), *Tutorials in Motor Behavior*. Amsterdam: North-Holland, pp. 373–398.

Requin, J. (1980b). La préparation à l'activité motrice: vers une convergence des problématiques psychologique et neurobiologique. In J. Requin (ed.), *Anticipation et Comportement.* Paris: Editions du CNRS, pp. 261–333.

Requin, J. (1985). Looking forward to moving soon. ante factum selective processes in motor control. In M. Posner and O. Marin (eds), *Attention and Performance*, vol. XI. Hillsdale: Lawrence Erlbaum, pp. 147–167.

Requin, J., Lecas, J.C. and Bonnet, M. (1984). Some experimental evidence for a three-step model of motor preparation. In S. Kornblum and J. Requin (eds), *Preparatory*

States and Processes. Hillsdale: Lawrence Erlbaum, pp. 259–284.

Requin, J., Lecas, J.C. and Vitton, N. (1990). A comparison of preparation-related neuronal activity changes in the prefrontal, premotor, primary motor and posterior parietal areas of the monkey cortex: preliminary results. *Neuroscience Letters*, **111**, 151–156.

Requin, J., Riehle, A. and Seal, J. (1988). Neuronal activity and information processing in motor control: from stages to continuous flow. *Biological Psychology*, **26**, 179–198.

Requin, J., Riehle, A. and Seal, J. (1989). Contribution d'une analyse fonctionnelle de l'activité neuronale à la reconsidération des relations entre structure et fonction dans l'organisation du cortex cérébral. In *Les Modèles Expérimentaux et la Clinique*. (*Collection Confrontations Psychiatriques*, vol. 30). Paris: Specia, pp. 221–251.

Requin, J., Semjen, A. and Bonnet, M. (1984). Bernstein's purposeful brain. In H.T.A. Whiting (ed.), *Human Motor Actions: Bernstein Reassessed*. Amsterdam: North-Holland, pp. 467–504.

Riehle, A. (1987). Changes in neuronal activity of motor cortical areas associated with the coding of spatial parameters of movement. In P. Ellen and C. Blanc-Thinus (eds), *Cognitive Processes and Spatial Orientation in Animal and Man*, vol. 2. Dordrecht: Nijhoff, pp. 146–155.

Riehle, A. and Requin, J. (1989). Monkey primary motor and premotor cortex: single-cell activity related to prior information about direction and extent of an intended movement. *Journal of Neurophysiology*, **61** (3), 534–549.

Rizzolatti, G. (1982). Mechanisms of selective attention in mammals. In J.P. Ewert, R.R. Capranica and D.I. Ingle (eds), *Advances in Vertebrate Neuroethology*. New York: Plenum Press.

Rohrbaugh, J.W. and Gaillard, A.W.K. (1983). Sensory and motor aspects of the contingent negative variation. In A.W.K. Gaillard and W. Ritter (eds), *Tutorials in Event-Related Potential Research: Endogenous Components*. Amsterdam: North-Holland, pp. 269–310.

Roland, P.E., Larsen, B., Lassen, N.A. and Skinhoj, E. (1980). Supplementary motor area and other cortical areas in organization of voluntary movements in man. *Journal of Neurophysiology*, **43**, 118–136.

Romo, R. and Schultz, W. (1987). Neuronal activity preceding self-initiated or externally timed arm movements in area 6 of monkey cortex. *Experimental Brain Research*, **67**, 656–662.

Rose, K.D. and Dunn, F.L. (1964). The heart of the spectator sportsman. *Medical Times*, **92**, 945–951.

Rosenbaum, D.A. (1980). Human movement initiation: specification of arm, direction and extent. *Journal of Experimental Psychology: General*, **109**, 444–474.

Rosenbaum, D.A. (1983). The movement precuing technique; assumptions, applications and extensions. In R.A. Magill (ed.), *Memory and Control in Motor Behavior*. Amsterdam: North-Holland, pp. 231–274.

Rosenbaum, D.A. (1985). Motor programming: a review and scheduling theory. In H. Heuer, U. Kleinbeck and K.H. Schmidt (eds), *Motor Behavior, Programming Control and Acquisition*. Berlin: Springer-Verlag, pp. 1–33.

Rosenbaum, D.A., Inhoff, A.W. and Gordon, A.M. (1984). Choosing between movement sequences: a hierarchical editor model. *Journal of Experimental Psychology: General*, **113**, 372–393.

Rosenbaum, D.A., Kenny, S. and Derr, M.A. (1983). Hierarchical control of rapid movement sequence. *Journal of Experimental Psychology: HPP*, **9**, 86–102.

Rosenbaum, D.A. and Kornblum, S. (1982). A priming method for investigating the selection of motor responses. *Acta Psychologica*, **51**, 223–243.

Ruchkin, D.S., Sutton, S., Mahaffey, D. and Glaser, J. (1986). Terminal CNV in the absence of motor response. *Electroencephalography and Clinical Neurophysiology*, **63**, 445–463.

Rushmer, R.F., Smith, O. and Franklin, D. (1960). Mechanisms of cardiac control in exercise. *Circulation Research*, **7**, 602–627.

Sanders, A.F. (1980). Stage analysis of reaction process. In G.E. Stelmach and J. Requin (eds), *Tutorials in Motor Behavior*. Amsterdam: North-Holland, pp. 331–354.

Scheirs, J.G.M. and Brunia, C.H.M. (1985). Achilles tendon reflexes and surface EMG activity during anticipation of a significant event and preparation for a voluntary movement. *Journal of Motor Behavior*, **17**, 96–109.

Scherg, M. (1989). Fundamentals of dipole source potential analysis. In M. Hoke, F. Grandori and G.L. Romani (eds), *Auditory Evoked Magnetic Fields and Potentials*. Basel: Karger.

Schibye, B., Mitchell, J.H., Payne, F.C. and Saltin, B. (1981). Blood pressure and heart rate response to static exercise in relation to electromyographic activity and force development. *Acta Physiologica Scandinavica*, **113**, 61–66.

Schmidt, R.A. (1975). A schema theory of discrete motor skill learning. *Psychological Review*, **82**, 225–260.

Schmidt, R.A. (1982). *Motor control and learning: a behavioral emphasis*. Champaign: Human Kinetics.

Schmidt, R.A. (1988). Motor and action perspectives in motor behaviour. In O.G. Meijer and K. Roth (eds), *Complex Movement Behavior: The Motor–Action Controversy*. Amsterdam: North-Holland, pp. 3–44.

Schwartz, G.E. and Higgins, J.D. (1971). Cardiac activity to overt and covert activity. *Science*, **173**, 1144–1145.

Seal, J. (1989). Sensory and motor functions of the superior parietal cortex of the monkey as revealed by single neuron recordings. *Brain, Behavior and Evolution*, **33**, 113–117.

Seal, J. and Requin, J. (1987). Sensory to motor transformation within area 5 of the posterior parietal cortex in the monkey. *Society for Neuroscience Abstracts*, **13**(1), 673.

Seals, D.R. (1988). Cardiopulmonary baroreflexes do not modulate exercise-induced sympathoexcitation. *Journal of Applied Physiology*, **64**, 2197–2203.

Semjen, A. (1984). Rapid hand movements in step-tracking: reprogramming of direction and extent. In S. Kornblum and J. Requin (eds), *Preparatory States and Processes*. Hillsdale: Lawrence Erlbaum, pp. 95–118.

Semjen, A. and Bonnet, M. (1982). Interactions d'afférences sensorielles facilitatrices du réflexe H chez l'homme. *Journal de Physiologie*, **78**, 7B.

Semjen, A. and Garcia-Colera, A. (1986). Planning and timing of finger tapping sequences with a stressed element. *Journal of Motor Behavior*, **18**, 287–322.

Semjen, A., Garcia-Colera, A. and Requin, J. (1984). On controlling force and time in rhythmic movement sequences: the effect of stress location. *Annals of the New York Academy of Sciences*, **423**, 168–182.

Semjen, A. and Gottsdanker, R. (1990). Rapid serial movements: relation between the planning of sequential structure and effector selection. In M. Jeannerod (ed.), *Attention and Performance*, vol. XIII. Hillsdale: Lawrence Erlbaum, pp. 409–428.

Shaffer, L.H. (1982). Rhythm and timing in skill. *Psychological Review*, **89**, 102–122.

Sheridan, M.R. (1988). Movement metaphors. In A.M. Colley and J.R. Beech (eds), *Cognition and Action in Skilled Behaviour*. Amsterdam: North-Holland, pp. 157–171.

Sherwood, A., Allen, M.T., Obrist, P.A. and Langer, A.W. (1986). Evaluation of beta-adrenergic influences on cardiovascular and metabolic adjustments to physical and psychological stress. *Psychophysiology*, **23**, 89–104.

Sherwood, A., Allen, M.T., Murrell, D. and Obrist, P.A. (1988). Motor preparation aspects of cardiovascular reactivity to psychomotoor challenge. *International Journal of Psychophysiology*, **6**, 263–272.

Sherwood A., Brener J. and Moncur D. (1983). Information and states of motor readiness: their effects on the covariation of heart rate and energy expenditure. *Psychophysiology*, **20**, 513–529.

Simon, J.R. and Rudell, A.P. (1967). Auditory S–R compatibility: the effect of an irrelevant cue on information processing. *Journal of Applied Psychology*, **51**, 300–304.

Skubic, V. and Hodgkins, J. (1965). Cardiac response to participation in selected individual and dual sports as determined by telemetry. *Research Quarterly*, **36**, 316–325.

Sleight, P., Fox, P., Lopez, R. and Brooks, D.E. (1978). The effect of mental arithmetic on blood pressure variability and baroreflex sensitivity in man. *Clinics in Science of Molecular Medicine*, **55** (Suppl.4), 381s–382s.

Smith, O. (1974). Reflex and central mechanisms involved in control of heart and circulation. *Annual Review of Physiology*, **36**, 93–123.

Smith, O.A. and DeVito, J.L. (1984). Central neural integration for the control of autonomic responses associated with emotion. *Annual Review of Neuroscience*, **7**, 43–65.

Smith, S.A., Stallard, T.J. and Littler, W.A. (1986). Estimation of sinoaortic baroreceptor heart rate reflex sensitivity and latency in man: a new microcomputer assisted method of analysis. *Cardiovaacular Research*, **20**, 877–882.

Stelmach, G.E., Worringham, C.J. and Strand, E.A. (1986). Movement preparation in Parkinson's disease: the use of advance information. *Brain*, **9**, 1179–1194.

Stenberg J., Astrand P.O., Ekblom J. and Saltin B. (1967). Hemodynamic response to work with different muscle groups, sitting and supine. *Journal of Applied Physiology*, **22**, 61–70.

Steptoe, A. and Sawada, Y. (1989). Assessment of baroreceptor function during mental stress and relaxation. *Psychophysiology*, **26**, 140–147.

Sternberg, S. (1969). The discovery of processing stages: extensions of Donder's method. *Acta Psychologica*, **30**, 276–315.

Sternberg, S., Monsell, S., Knoll, R.L. and Wright, C.E. (1978). The latency and duration of rapid movement sequences: comparisons of speech and type writing. In G.E. Stelmach (ed.), *Information Processing in Motor Control and Learning*. New York: Academic Press, pp. 117–152.

Stornetta, R.L., Guyenet, P.G. and McCarty, R.C. (1988). Autonomic nervous system control of heart rate during baroceptor activation in conscious and anesthetized rats. *Journal of the Autonomic Nervous System*, **20**, 121–128.

Strick, P.L. (1983). The influence of motor preparation on the response of cerebellar neurons to limb displacements. *Journal of Neuroscience*, **10**, 2007–2020.

Sutherland, C.J. and Zbrozyna, A.W. (1971). The cardiovascular involvement in the early stages of conditioning of the flexor reflex in dogs. *Journal of Physiology*, **218**, 83–84P.

Tanji, J. and Kurata, K. (1982). Comparison of movement-related activity in two cortical motor areas of primates. *Journal of Neurophysiology*, **48**, 633–653.

Tanji, J., Taniguchi, J. and Saga, T. (1980). Supplementary motor area: neuronal response to motor instructions. *Journal of Neurophysiology*, **44**, 60–68.

Teuber, H.L. (1972). University and diversity of frontal lobe functions. *Acta Neurobiologica Experientia*, **32**, 615–656.

Tobin, M.J., Perez, W., Guenther, S.M., D'Alonzo, G. and Dantzker, D.R. (1986). Breathing pattern and metabolic behavior during anticipation of exercise. *Journal of Applied Physiology*, **60**, 1206–1312.

Torelli, G. and Brandi, G. (1964). The components of nervous regulation of the ventilation. *Journal of Sports Medicine and Physical Fitness*, **4**, 75–78.

Turner, J.R. (1989). Individual differences in heart rate response during behavioral challenge. *Psychophysiology*, **26**, 497–505.

Vatner, S.F., Franklin, D., Higgins, C.B., Patrick, T. and Braunwald, E. (1972). Left ventricular response to severe exertion in untethered dogs. *Journal of Clinical Investigation*, **51**, 3052–3060.

Walgenbach, S.C. and Donald, D.E. (1983). Inhibition by carotid baroreflex of exercise-induced increases in arterial pressure. *Circulation Research*, **52**, 253–262.

Walker, J.L., Abboud, F.M., Mark, A.L. and Thames, M.D. (1980). Interaction of cardiopulmonary and somatic reflexes in humans. *Journal of Clinical Investigation*, **65**, 1491–1497.

Walter, W.G., Cooper, R., Aldridge, V., McCallum, W.C. and Winter, A.L. (1964). Contingent negative variation: an electric sign of sensorimotor association and expectancy in the human brain. *Nature*, **203**, 380–384.

Wasserman, K., Whipp, B.J. and Castagna, J. (1974). Cardiodynamic hyperpnea: secondary to cardiac output increase. *Journal of Applied Psychology*, **34**, 457–464.

Weinrich, M. and Wise, S.P. (1982). The premotor cortex of the monkey. *Journal of Neuroscience*, **2**, 1329–1345.

Wiesendanger, M. (1986). Recent developments in studies of the supplementary motor area of primates. *Review of Physiology, Biochemistry and Pharmacology*, **103**, 1–59.

Wiesendanger, M. and Miles, T.S. (1982). Ascending pathway of low-threshold muscle afferents to the cerebral cortex and its possible role in motor control. *Physiological Review*, **62**, 1234–1270.

Wise, S.P. (1984). The nonprimary motor cortex and its role in the cerebral control of movement. In G.M. Edelman, W.E. Gall and W.M. Cowan (eds), *Dynamic Aspects of Neocortical Function*. New York: Wiley, pp. 525–555.

Wise, S.P. (1985). The primate premotor cortex: past, present, and preparatory. *Annual Review of Neuroscience*, **8**, 1–19.

Wise, S.P. and Mauritz, K.H. (1985). Set-related neuronal activity in the premotor cortex of rhesus monkey: effects of changes in motor set. *Proceedings of the Royal Society of London*, **B223**, 331–354.

Wise, S.P. and Strick, P.L. (1984). Anatomical and physiological organization of the non-primary motor cortex. *Trends in Neurosciences*, **7**, 442–446.

Wise, S.P., Weinrich, M. and Mauritz, K.H. (1983). Motor aspects of cue-related neuronal activty in premotor cortex of the rhesus monkey. *Brain Research*, **260**, 301–305.

Wise, S.P., Weinrich, M. and Mauritz, K.H. (1986). Movement-related activity in the premotor cortex of rhesus macaques. In H.J. Freund, U. Buttner, B. Cohen and J. Noth (eds), *Progress in Brain Research*, vol. 4. Amsterdam: Elsevier, pp. 117–131.

Wood, C.C. and Allison, T. (1981). Interpretation of evoked potentials: a neurophysiological perspective. *Canadian Journal of Psychology*, **35**, 113–135.

Woodrow, H. (1914). The measurement of attention. *Psychological Monographs 17* (whole no. 76).

Wurtz, R.H., Goldberg, M.E. and Robinson, D.L. (1980). Behavioral modulation of visual responses in the monkey: stimulus selection for attention and movement. *Progress in Psychobiology, Physiology and Psychology*, **9**, 43–83.

Zelaznik, H.N. (1981). The effects of force and direction uncertainty on choice reaction time in an isometric force production task. *Journal of Motor Behavior*, **13**, 18–32.

Zelaznik, H. and Hahn, R. (1985). Reaction time methods in the study of motor programming: the precuing of hand, digit, and duration. *Journal of Motor Behavior*, **17**, 190–218.

Zelaznik, H.N., Shapiro, D.C. and Carter, M.C. (1982). The specification of digit and duration during motor programming: a new method of precuing. *Journal of Motor Behavior*, **14**, 57–68.

Chapter 5

Mnemonic Information Processing

ABSTRACT

This divided chapter reviews relationships between autonomic and cortical responses and memory performance. The initial chapter division examines how event processing as indexed by the orienting response relates to item retention. The next chapter focuses on how P300, a particular component of the event related potential, may relate to encoding—particularly of distinctiveness. The final division integrates the autonomic and cortical perspectives.

Memory and Autonomic Activity: The Role of the Orienting Response

David A. T. Siddle
Department of Psychology, University of Tasmania, Hobart, Australia
and
Jeanette S. Packer
School of Behavioural Sciences, Macquarie University, Sydney, Australia

INTRODUCTION

This chapter is concerned with psychophysiology and memory. The present division deals specifically with the relationship between autonomic measures and memory processes and the subsequent division with memory and electrocortical measures.

There are a number of ways in which psychophysiology and memory can be discussed. For example, it is possible to consider the extent to which memory processes have been important in the explanation of psychophysiological phenomena. Although this tactic does not represent the main thrust of our review, the use of memory concepts and processes in the explanation of orienting and habituation has been considered. Alternatively, it is possible to consider the effects of efforts to memorize on autonomic activity. Although there is a considerable literature on the effects of cognitive load on autonomic activity (e.g. Kahneman and Beatty, 1966; Kahneman *et al.*, 1969; Kahneman and Wright, 1971), space considerations preclude a review of this approach. Finally, it is possible to consider psychophysiological measures as indices of important psychological processes and to argue that psychophysiological measures provide insights, which cannot be obtained solely by behavioural measures, into those processes that underlie memory. This is the approach we have adopted.

Our approach presupposes the existence of some unifying conceptual frameworks within which data can be organized. A well-known example is the concept of arousal, and it is perhaps not surprising that there have been a large number of studies aimed at the development of a model of memory in

Handbook of Cognitive Psychophysiology: Central and Autonomic Nervous System Approaches.
Edited by J. R. Jennings and M. G. H. Coles.

which variations in arousal are functionally important (Craik and Blankstein, 1975). There is little point in our restating here the difficulties encountered by arousal models (Craik and Blankstein, 1975; Lacey, 1967). Indeed, we shall argue that many of the findings from studies of memory and arousal are capable of reinterpretation.

Our approach has been to utilize another unifying conceptual framework within the psychophysiological literature, namely the orienting response and its habituation. The proposition we wish to explore is that the orienting response and habituation reflect cognitive processes that are of importance in memory phenomena. More specifically, we wish to argue that orienting reflects the attentional resources allocated to to-be-remembered items and that orienting is thus functionally important in determining memory performance. Thus, we are concerned with phasic changes in autonomic activity and their relationship with memory. The relationship between memory and longer-term tonic changes in autonomic activity has been reviewed recently by Jennings (1986) and will not be discussed here.

THE ORIENTING RESPONSE, HABITUATION, AND INFORMATION PROCESSING

THE ORIENTING RESPONSE AND HABITUATION

Following Sokolov (1963), the orienting response (OR) has been defined in terms of the sensory, autonomic, and electroencephalographic (EEG) changes elicited by novel stimulation of low to moderate intensity. According to Sokolov, the OR is non-specific in that it can be elicited by stimuli in any modality, and is independent of the direction of change in stimulation; that is, it may be elicited by both increases and decreases in stimulation and by both stimulus onset and offset. The most important features of the OR are that it displays an amplitude decrement as a function of repetition (habituation), but may be re-elicited, following habituation, by a change in the habituation stimulus (see also Chapter 1 in this volume).

Sokolov (1963) distinguished between the OR and a number of other reflex systems. For example, the OR is said to enhance perceptual sensitivity whereas the defense reflex is said to be elicited by high-intensity stimuli and to limit the action of the eliciting stimulus. Moreover, the defense reflex is said to differ from the OR in terms of the pattern of cardiovascular reactions (Sokolov, 1963) and in terms of the former's relatively slow rate of habituation (Graham, 1979; but see Cook, 1974, Turpin, 1983, and Turpin and Siddle, 1983). The OR can also be distinguished from the startle reflex. Startle involves a short-latency blink response and cardiac acceleration, whereas orienting involves cardiac deceleration and no blink (Graham, 1979; Turpin and Siddle, 1983).

A good deal is now known about the variables which influence orienting and its habituation (Siddle, Stephenson and Spinks, 1983; Thompson and Spencer, 1966). Variables such as stimulus intensity (Turpin and Siddle, 1983), duration (Spinks and Siddle, 1976), complexity (Fredrikson and Öhman, 1979), interstimulus interval (Gatchel and Lang, 1974), and signal value (Siddle, O'Gorman and Wood, 1979) have been shown to affect within-session habituation. Moreover, the sensitivity of the OR to a change in stimulation following habituation training is well documented (O'Gorman, 1973; Siddle and Spinks, 1979; Siddle, Stephenson and Spinks, 1983). An increase in OR amplitude in response to stimulus change (recovery) has been demonstrated for changes in modality (Furedy and Ginsberg, 1975), tone pitch (Siddle and Heron, 1976), intensity (Edwards, 1975), duration (Magliero, Gatchel and Lojewski, 1981), and word meaning (Siddle *et al.*, 1979). In addition, when paired stimuli are employed, omission of the second element of the pair elicits skin conductance responses at the time of omission (e.g. Siddle, 1985; Siddle, Booth and Packer, 1987) and produces dishabituation when the omitted stimulus is re-presented.

HABITUATION AND MEMORY

The role of memorial processes in the development of habituation has been a continuing theme in theoretical accounts of habituation. For example, Sokolov (1963) proposed that the attributes of iterated stimuli are stored in a 'neuronal model', and that current stimulation is compared with information stored in the neuronal model. Although not discussed explicitly as a memory system, it is clear that, in functional terms, Sokolov's neuronal model resembles what might be termed short-term memory.

More recent theories of habituation have been explicit about the role played by memory systems in mediating habituation. Wagner (1978) has argued that 'unexpected' stimuli are more elaborately processed in a short-term memory store (STS) and that this results in the transfer of more fully consolidated episodic information to a long-term store (LTS). The degree to which a stimulus is expected depends upon the degree to which it is pre-represented or primed in STS. According to Wagner, priming can be self-generated by recent presentations of the stimulus itself, or associatively-generated by retrieval cues. The cues may be explicit, as in the case of a conditioned stimulus priming a representation of an unconditioned stimulus, or they may simply be contextual cues. In the case of contextual priming, associations between contextual cues and the habituation stimulus are said to develop according to the same rules that govern the development of associations between conditioned and unconditioned stimuli. For Wagner's theory, iterated stimulation leads to progressively more effective priming, less processing of the habituation stimulus, and consequently, smaller responses.

In an elaboration of his theory, Wagner (1981) has distinguished between active rehearsal in STS and passive representation in STS. Presentation of an unprimed stimulus is said to involve transition of the stimulus representation from an inactive state in a long-term store to the active rehearsal state in STS, from which it decays, via a passive representation state, to the inactive state. A stimulus will not promote rehearsal if its representation is in either the active rehearsal or the passive representation state in the short-term store. Finally, contextual priming promotes the representation of a stimulus from the inactive state to the passive representation state and not to the active rehearsal state.

Wagner's (1978, 1981) theory was developed to account for more than just habituation of orienting responses. Rather, it is a general theory of the way in which iterated stimulation results in a depression in performance. Öhman's (1979) theory, on the other hand, was formulated to deal specifically with habituation of orienting. Like Wagner, Öhman has utilized the concept of pre-representation or priming in an STS. However, Öhman's theory is explicit in localizing the match/mismatch process as occurring between the result of preattentive processing and the contents of the STS. When preattentive mechanisms fail to identify a stimulus because no matching representation is present in STS, a call for central channel processing is initiated. Autonomic indices of the OR are said to reflect the call for central processing. Thus, Öhman's theory holds that an OR reflects not central channel processing, but the fact that a mismatch has been detected and that a call for processing capacity has occurred. It is possible, according to Öhman's theory, that a call for processing will not be answered because of competing demands on processing capacity. If the call is answered, processing involves the encoding of the stimulus and its context into LTS so that the stimulus can subsequently be contextually primed.

Öhman (1979) has divided STS into two functional units. The first provides working space for central processing and attended items are said to be held in active STS. The second part of STS is said to hold primed items in a passive state. Current stimuli, after pre-attentive processing, are compared with the contents of this part of STS, and unless they are tagged as significant, a match blocks further processing, no call for processing capacity is initiated, and the stimulus is not attended.

It is obvious that the memory-based theories of Wagner (1978, 1981) and Öhman (1979) are quite similar. There are, however, important differences. In a sense, Wagner's theory proposes that the processing of an unexpected stimulus is automatic in the sense that the promotion of a representation of an unprimed event from the inactive state to the active state is obligatory. For Öhman, however, the utilization of processing capacity by unprimed events is not a necessary consequence of the detection of a mismatch. Thus, Öhman's theory holds that the OR reflects a call for processing and not the processing itself.

Whether or not the OR reflects processing *per se* or a call for processing is important for any consideration of the relationship between orienting and memory. Öhman's (1979) identification of the OR with a call for processing allows for a dissociation between orienting and the conscious perception of the eliciting stimulus. Öhman's theorizing was based, in part, on data which appeared to indicate that material presented on an unattended channel elicited skin conductance responses even though subjects failed to perform an instructed response to the critical stimulus (Corteen and Dunn, 1974; Corteen and Wood, 1972). More recently, data from Öhman's laboratory suggest that, after conditioning, certain kinds of stimuli (pictures of angry faces) may be capable of evoking skin conductance responses even when those stimuli are backwardly masked with a stimulus onset asynchrony that precludes the reporting of the nature of the stimulus (Öhman, Dimberg and Esteves, 1989).

However, it can be argued that the OR reflects processing itself, a possibility acknowledged by Öhman. There are a number of methodological problems with the Corteen work, and the effects have proved difficult to replicate (Wardlaw and Kroll, 1976; see also Dawson and Schell, 1982). Moreover, there are other data which indicate that the OR is associated with processing. In a number of studies, Dawson and Siddle have each shown that orienting is accompanied by a slowing of response time to a secondary task probe stimulus presented during the orienting stimulus. For example, Siddle and his colleagues have shown that when secondary task probes are presented during events which elicit orienting (e.g. omission of an expected event or presentation of an unexpected event), reaction time to probes is slowed (e.g. Siddle and Packer, 1987; Packer and Siddle, 1989). Similarly, Dawson *et al.* (1982) have reported that secondary task probe reaction time is slower during a conditioned stimulus that is always followed by an unconditioned stimulus than during a conditioned stimulus that is never followed by an unconditioned stimulus. Dawson, Filion and Schell (1989) have reported that secondary task probe reaction time is slower at the beginning of an habituation series than at the end, and that OR recovery to a change stimulus is accompanied by a dramatic slowing of probe reaction time.

On the other hand, there are data which appear troublesome for our position. First, Jennings, Lawrence and Kasper (1978) employed a serial learning paradigm which was divided into a learning phase and an anticipation phase. During the anticipation phase, words which were perceptually isolated by presentation against a different coloured background were anticipated more accurately than were non-isolated words. During the learning phase, however, reaction time to secondary task probes presented during isolated words was not significantly different from reaction time to probes presented during non-isolated words. It can be argued that if isolated items evoke orienting, reaction time to probes presented during those items will be slowed. However, the isolation effect obtained by Jennings *et al.* appears to have been quite weak, and in fact the effect was evident for words but not for numbers. Indeed, in a second experiment Jennings *et al.* found that perceptual isolation did not influence serial anticipation. Second, Dawson, Filion and Schell (1989) have reported disassociation between electrodermal orienting and secondary tasks reaction time. These authors found that, although stimuli in an attended channel elicited larger electrodermal responses than did stimuli in an unattended channel, reaction time was not slower to probes presented during to-be-attended stimuli than to those presented during to-be-ignored stimuli. Finally, it could be argued that secondary task probe data have been obtained only in situations in which any call for processing was likely to be answered.

In sum, the available data do not permit firm conclusions about whether orienting reflects a call for processing or central channel processing itself (see Chapter 3 of this volume). Nevertheless, as we discuss next, a number of authors have associated orienting with a redistribution of attentional resources, and there appear to be no compelling grounds for rejecting the notion that orienting reflects the processing capacity allocated to an event.

ORIENTING AND ATTENTION

The formulation of memory-based theories of habituation addresses only indirectly the question of the role of the OR in memory performance. A more direct approach to the question requires examination of the functional role the OR might play in information processing.

A relationship between orienting and attention has been implicit in a number of formulations of the functional significance of the OR. Indeed, Pavlov's (1927) original description of the OR as an 'investigatory' or 'what is it?' reflex clearly implied that the OR reflected a redistribution of attention. At a behavioural level, Pavlov noted that the occurrence of an OR coincided with a disruption of conditioned behaviour. A more systematic analysis by Sokolov (1963, 1969) proposed that the OR increases the sensitivity of the perceptual system by increasing the rate at which nervous processes operate and by effecting an increase in the signal-to-noise ratio of neurones for which information is important (Spinks and Siddle, 1983).

Berlyne (1960), Kahneman (1973), and Öhman (1979) have all proposed a relationship between the OR and attention. Berlyne distinguished between the intensive and selective aspects of attention, and although he argued that the OR is primarily related to the former, his theorizing also implies a relationship between orienting and the selective aspects of attention. Thus, Berlyne argued that events which make greater demands on information processing capacity produce larger ORs. Kahneman (1973), too, identified the OR with the allocation of processing resources so that an OR-eliciting stimulus may be processed more intensely. According to Kahneman, the reallocation of processing capacity which accompanies orienting is involuntary. The distinction between voluntary and involuntary shifts in attention has been utilized by Öhman who has argued that an OR elicited by a non-signal stimulus (i.e. a stimulus without task relevance) leads, presumably if the call for processing is answered, to involuntary shifts in attention. Orienting elicited by signal stimuli, on the other hand, is said to result in a voluntary shift in attention. Consistent with the idea that the OR reflects an involuntary shift in attention, Waters, McDonald and Koresko (1977) reported that subjects who were pre-exposed to a to-be-distractor subsequently performed better on mental arithmetic problems in the presence of that distractor than did subjects who were exposed to an experimentally-irrelevant stimulus. On the basis of these data, Waters *et al.* argued that habituation represents a form of 'gating out' of the eliciting stimulus; that is, it results in the removal of the stimulus from attention and further processing.

It is clear that many authors regard the OR as a reflection of changes in the allocation of processing resources. Thus, to the extent that attentional processes are important in memory, we might expect orienting to be functionally related to memory performance. Before reviewing relevant evidence, we will first examine some similarities between theories of habituation and one approach to memory.

MEMORY AND HABITUATION

Although it is perhaps an oversimplification, the processes involved in memory can be divided into encoding processes, storage processes, and retrieval processes. Thus, a feature which distinguishes theories of memory concerns the processing 'stage' on which emphasis is placed. In view of the discussion of the OR and attention, it is perhaps not surprising that our concern is with theories of memory which emphasize the importance of encoding processes.

The 'depth of processing' approach to memory (e.g. Craik and Lockhart, 1972; Lockhart, Craik and Jacoby, 1976) represents an encoding approach which is similar in some respects to the priming theories proposed by Wagner (1978, 1981) and by Öhman (1979). Essentially, Craik and his colleagues (Craik, 1973; Craik and Lockhart, 1972) have argued that, rather than conceptualize memory in terms of a multistore model, a more fruitful approach is to investigate the 'depth' to which an item is processed. According to Craik (1973), greater depth implies more processing which leads to a more durable memory trace. Craik and Lockhart (1972) discussed the processing of a stimulus in terms of a continuum of analyzing operations ranging from the physical and structural features of the stimulus to more elaborate semantic analyses. Some of the initial assertions of the depth-of-processing approach were later modified (Lockhart, Craik and Jacoby, 1976). Thus, semantic and physical analyses are not now seen as lying on the same continuum, but as occupying different domains of processing. According to this formulation, 'depth' can refer to two distinct changes in processing. First, domains might be arranged hierarchically from shallow structural domains to deeper semantic domains. Second, a stimulus can be processed further by the performance of further analyses within one domain.

Although the depth-of-processing approach has been criticized in terms of circularity (Eysenck, 1978; Nelson, 1977) and in terms of conflicting data (e.g. Stein, 1978), the main point here is the similarity between the depth-of-processing approach to memory and priming theories of habituation. For example, the depth-of-processing approach asserts that unexpected stimuli are processed to a deeper level and lead to more durable memory traces than do expected stimuli. Thus, both priming theories and the depth-of-processing approach emphasize that memory traces depend crucially on the way in which an event is encoded, which in turn depends upon the degree to which the stimulus is expected. In their discussion of recall and recognition, Lockhart, Craik and Jacoby (1976) have argued that the initial encoding of a stimulus involves not only the nominal event itself, but also aspects of the context in which that event is presented.

In this way, the context can lead to the construction of expectancies, and if an expected event does occur, 'it can apparently be assimilated by the system with a minimal amount of analysis' (p. 84). In fact, consideration of the role of contextual cueing is important, according to Lockhart, Craik and Jacoby (1976), in distinguishing between recall and recognition:

> In recognition, the stimulus is re-presented and the system has to reconstruct the context; in recall, some aspects of the context are re-presented or referred to and the system has to reconstruct the stimulus. (p. 85)

Thus, Lockhart *et al.* have stressed the importance of contextual cues in determining recall, whereas Wagner (1978) and Öhman (1979) have emphasized the importance of contextual priming in STS in determining responsiveness to a stimulus. The role of contextual cues in determining both recall performance and orienting is an important issue which will be discussed in more detail later. The important point to make here is that there is considerable communality between theories of habituation in which a key role is ascribed to priming and the depth-of-processing approach to memory.

ORIENTING, HABITUATION, AND MEMORY

RELEASE FROM PROACTIVE INHIBITION

Following work by Brown (1958) and by Peterson and Peterson (1959), Keppel and Underwood (1962) demonstrated that, if to-be-recalled items were presented for a short period of time and recall was tested after a retention interval during which rehearsal was prevented by a distractor task, recall performance declined from the first to the third or fourth trial. Moreover, numerous studies (see Wickens, 1970, for a review) have shown that, if the material employed during the first three or four trials shares some common feature, a change in this feature on a shift or change trial results in an improvement in recall on that trial. The decline in recall performance has been referred to as 'the development of proactive inhibition', and improved recall on the shift trial as 'release from proactive inhibition'. It should be noted that we are using 'release from proactive inhibition' in a descriptive sense (cf. Keppel and Underwood, 1962). Although a theoretically neutral description is 'improved recall following attribute shifts' (Tulving and Bower, 1974), the terms 'proactive inhibition' and 'release from proactive inhibition' are used for convenience. One inference that has been drawn from work on release from proactive inhibition is that improved recall on the shift trial indicates that the feature which was changed has been encoded in memory.

The depth-of-processing account of the development of and release from proactive inhibition argues that when examples of the same category are presented repeatedly, subjects come to expect instances of that category so that the encoding of successive items becomes less and less elaborate. Because the shift trial is unexpected, the items are more elaborately processed, leading to a more durable memory trace. An explanation of proactive inhibition in terms of priming theory argues that repetition of items from the same category leads to progressively better priming in STS and to less elaborate processing of the to-be-recalled items. Unprimed items on the shift trial elicit orienting, increased processing, and improved recall. In this connection, it is important to note that habituation does occur, for example, to words from the same taxonomic category (Siddle *et al.*, 1979) and to words which are similarly evaluated on the semantic differential (Grush *et al.*, 1973).

Evidence concerning the relationship between orienting and proactive inhibition phenomena can be adduced from two sources. The first involves studies in which orienting has been measured directly, whereas the second involves studies in which the importance of orienting can be inferred only indirectly. With respect to the direct evidence, only a handful of studies have recorded orienting activity in a standard Brown–Peterson paradigm. Engle (1975) found no evidence that release from proactive inhibition was accompanied by an increase in the amplitude of pupil dilation responses. Yuille and Hare (1980) reported that a shift in taxonomic category produced both improved recall and larger cardiac deceleration, but no increase in either skin conductance response (SCR) amplitude or peripheral vasoconstriction. In contrast, Wilson (1984) reported that improved recall on a shift trial was not paralleled by changes in either SCR magnitude or phasic cardiac activity.

Two studies, however, have reported positive results with the SCR measure of orienting. Magliero, Gatchel and Gorthey (1981) employed a shift in taxonomic category and reported that improved recall on the shift trial was accompanied by an increase in SCR amplitude. Siddle and Stenfert Kroese (1985) also employed a shift in taxonomic category and, in Experiment 1, found that the development of proactive inhibition was accompanied by a decline in the magnitude of SCRs elicited by the to-be-recalled items. A shift in category on trial 5 resulted in both improved recall and an increase in SCR magnitude. These results are shown in Figure 5.1. In Experiment 2, Siddle and Stenfert Kroese demonstrated that both recall performance and SCR magnitude declined more with a short than with a long intertrial interval (see Figure 5.2). The change manipulation used in this experiment involved either an increase or a decrease in the interval between trials 5 and 6. A group exposed to a decrease in intertrial interval displayed a decrement in recall performance, whereas an increase in intertrial interval produced an improvement in recall. These data, which are shown in Figure 5.3, are exactly what is predicted on the basis of priming theory in that a long intertrial interval permits more decay of a representation in STS. Thus, a shift from a short to a long intertrial interval will lead to less effective priming, more elaborate processing, and better recall. A long-to-short change in interstimulus interval, on the other hand, will lead to more effective priming, less processing, and poorer recall. However, the recall results were not accompanied by comparable changes in SCR magnitude. Although the short-to-long manipulation produced an increase in SCR magnitude, there was no change in SCR magnitude in the long-to-short condition.

Although they did not employ a Brown–Peterson paradigm, relevant data were reported by Grush *et al.* (1973). Grush *et al.* exposed subjects to a series of either positively or negatively evaluated words and, on a shift trial, some subjects received a word of the opposite evaluation. Electrodermal activity was monitored throughout, and a free recall test was conducted at the end of the stimulus series. The shift conditions produced significant SCR recovery and an increase in the probability that the shift trial item would be recalled. Moreover, results from the entire series indicated that those words which elicited SCRs tended to be the words which were recalled.

In summary, there appears to be some evidence of a relationship between orienting and memory performance in the Brown–Peterson task. Although not all the evidence is positive, there are data which indicate that at least one variable (intertrial interval) exerts a similar effect on both SCR magnitude and on recall. Moreover, there is evidence, at least with skin conductance, that release from proactive inhibition is accompanied by an increase in SCR magnitude and that increases and decreases in intertrial interval affect recall performance in exactly the manner predicted by priming theories of habituation.

Although they did not measure orienting directly, a number of studies have produced data consistent with an interpretation of proactive inhibition in

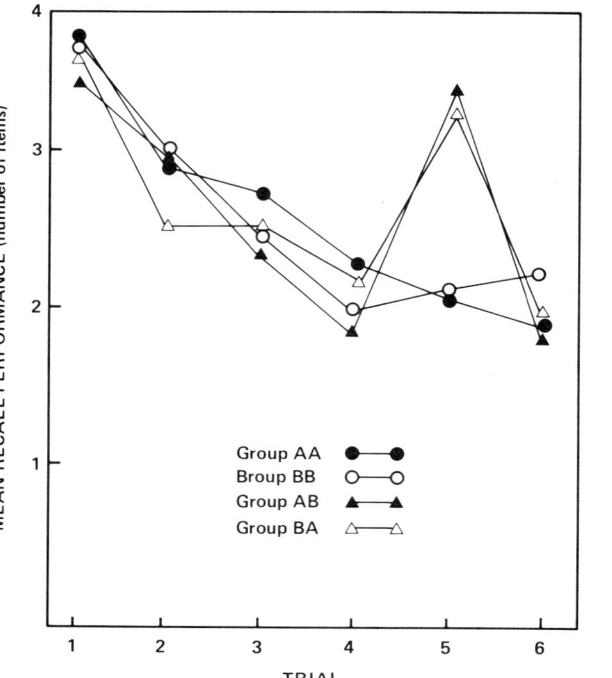

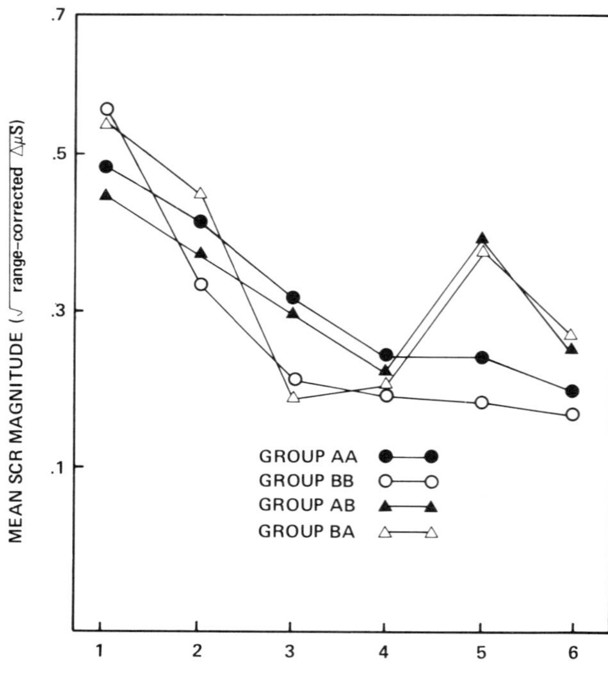

Figure 5.1. Mean recall scores (left panel) and SCR magnitude to to-be-recalled items (right panel) in a Brown–Peterson paradigm. The items to be recalled by Groups AA and BB were animal names and body parts respectively on all six trials. Groups AB and BA received animal names or body parts on trials 1–4 and on trial 6, but were shifted to the alternative category on trial 5. (Reprinted with permission of the publishers from Siddle and Stenfert Kroese (1985). © Society for Psychophysiological Research.)

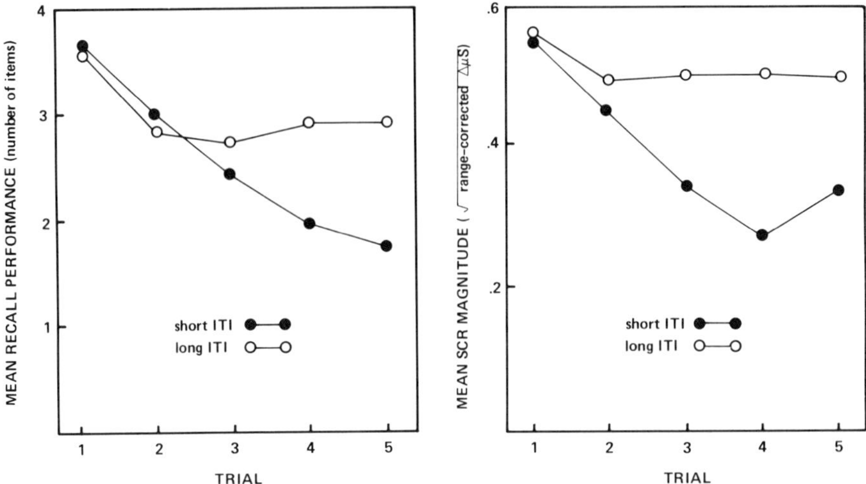

Figure 5.2. Mean recall scores (left panel) and SCR magnitude to to-be-recalled items (right panel) in a Brown–Peterson paradigm. The interval between one recall period and the next memory trial was either 3 s (short intertrial interval) or 83 s (long intertrial interval). (Reprinted with permission of the publishers from Siddle and Stenfert Kroese (1985). © Society for Psychophysiological Research.)

terms of the OR. For example, Loess and Waugh (1967) reported that the development of proactive inhibition was inversely related to intertrial interval, and that, when the intertrial interval was at least 120 s, no proactive inhibition developed. Similarly, Cermak (1970) reported that more proactive inhibition developed with intertrial intervals of 30 s than with intervals of 90 s. Cermak also reported that a change from a short to a long intertrial interval between trials 4 and 5 led to improved recall on trial 5, whereas a decrease in intertrial interval led to a deterioration in recall. We have already noted that Siddle and Stenfert Kroese (1985) found not only that less proactive inhibition developed with a long (83 s) than with a short (3 s) intertrial interval, but that SCR magnitude to to-be-recalled items was greater in the long intertrial interval condition than in the short. Siddle and Stenfert Kroese also replicated Cermak's findings with respect to the effects of change in intertrial interval on recall.

There are other data on release from proactive inhibition which are consistent with an orienting explanation. Cremins and Turvey (1978) reported that an increase in to-be-recalled items duration produced release from proactive inhibition whereas a decrease in to-be-recalled items duration did not. As Cremins and Turvey have noted, an increase in item duration might be expected to produce an OR (Siddle, Stephenson and Spinks, 1983) and thus to enhance the encoding of the to-be-recalled items. A decrease in duration,

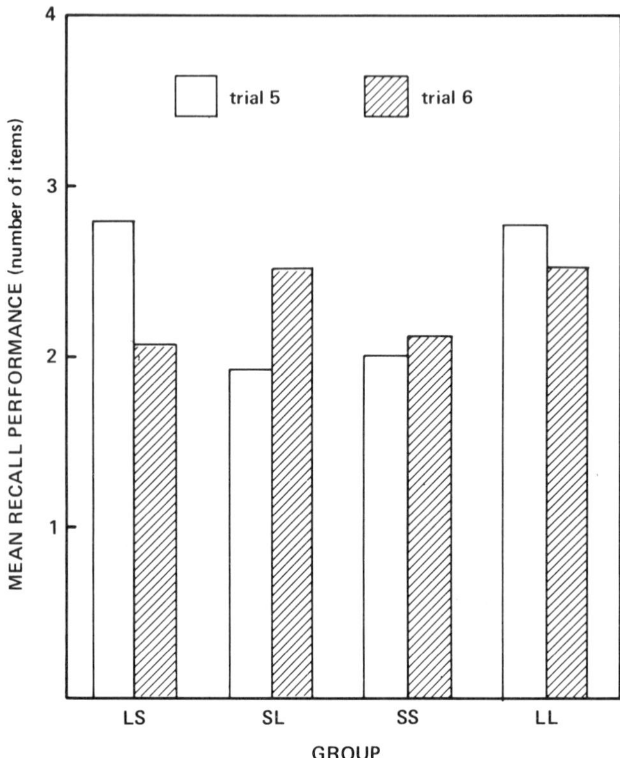

Figure 5.3. Mean recall scores from a Brown–Peterson paradigm in which there were six memory trials. For groups SS and LL, the intertrial intervals were 3 s and 83 s respectively throughout the experiment. The interval between trials 5 and 6 was changed from 83 s to 3 s for group LS. For group SL, the interval between trials 5 and 6 was changed from 3 s to 83 s. (Reprinted with permission of the publishers from Siddle and Stenfert Kroese (1985). © Society for Psychophysiological Research.)

even if it did produce orienting (Siddle, Kyriacou and Heron, 1978), cannot influence the processing of the item whose duration was decreased.

Theoretically important data have been obtained from studies in which the manipulation was a contextual change. For example, Turvey and Egan (1969) manipulated the size of the display area on which to-be-remembered consonant trigrams were presented. Both decreases and increases in display area were employed, and both produced release from proactive inhibition. In terms of an orienting and priming explanation, it can be argued that a contextual change results in less effective priming of to-be-recalled items in STS. Thus, to-be-recalled items are less expected in a changed context, result in more processing and orienting, and are better recalled. A contextual manipulation was also employed by Moscovitch and Winocur (1983) who investigated release from proactive inhibition in aged and young persons. Moscovitch and Winocur first showed that both students and independent elderly people (64–77 years) displayed release from proactive inhibition with a shift in taxonomic category. In a second experiment, both young and aged adults demonstrated release from proactive inhibition with simultaneous changes in both taxonomic category and contextual background. The final experiment demonstrated that a contextual change alone (words printed in red letters on a green background instead of black letters on a white background) produced release from proactive inhibition in a group of institutionalized elderly, but not in a group of young subjects.

ORIENTING AND RECALL

A number of studies have reported that orienting activity during a learning phase predicts subsequent recall of the learned items. Maltzman, Kantor and Langdon (1966) presented subjects with randomly ordered lists of high- and low-arousal words and tested recall immediately, and after an interval of half an hour. The recall test was unwarned. High-arousal items were recalled better than were low-arousal items at both the immediate and delayed recall, and high-arousal words elicited larger SCRs during initial presentation than did low-arousal words. Corteen (1969) employed immediate, 20-minute, and 2-week recall intervals. Mean SCR magnitude during presentation was positively and significantly correlated with recall at all retention intervals, and the correlation increased as a function of interval length. However, it is important to note that Corteen's analysis merely revealed a correlation between SCR responding in general and recall. That is, the relationship between SCR amplitude to any particular word and subsequent recall of that word was not examined.

Warren and Harris (1975) also reported a relationship between orienting and recall, but in this case the relationship was modulated by retention interval. Warren and Harris employed immediate and delayed (45-minute) recall groups, and recorded EEG activity and skin potential during presentation of to-be-recalled lists. Words which elicited an alpha-blocking response were recalled significantly better than no-response words in the immediate recall condition, but there was no difference in the delayed recall condition. Similarly, words which evoked skin potential responses at learning were recalled significantly better than were no-response words in the immediate, but not in the delayed, recall condition. In contrast, Sorgatz and Dannel (1978) reported that, in an intentional memory task, recall of geometric figures which produced large SCRs did not vary between test intervals of 3 and 30 minutes. Items which elicited large SCRs were recalled better than low-SCR items at the delayed, but not the immediate, test. Kaplan, Kaplan and Sampson (1968) examined the relationship between orienting and recall of both words and pictures in an intentional memory task. Although subjects were tested immediately after stimulus presentation and again 30 minutes later, Kaplan *et al.* did not present data separately for each retention interval. When both tests were considered together, there was a direct relationship between SCR at presentation and the probability of correct recall of words. On the other hand, there was no relationship between SCR and the probability of correct recall of pictures. Kaplan *et al.* did, however, demonstrate that SCRs associated with items which were recalled in the second, but not the first, test (reminiscence items) were larger than SCRs associated with items which were recalled in the first, but not the second, test (forgotten items). Interestingly, Sampson (1969) could not replicate these findings when retention interval was manipulated either within or between subjects either in an intentional memory task, as in the original study (Kaplan, Kaplan and Sampson, 1968), or in an incidental memory task. The only reliable finding relating SCR and recall of words or pictures was a positive relationship between SCR and immediate recall of words. However, it should be noted that unlike Kaplan, Kaplan and Sampson (1968), Sampson's (1969) recall tests occurred immediately following presentation and one day later.

More recently, Plouffe and Stelmack (1984) investigated the relationship between orienting and recall of pictures in young and elderly subjects. The study involved two phases. In the first phase, subjects viewed high- and low-frequency line drawings while skin conductance was monitored. Young adults recalled significantly more pictures and displayed larger SCRs than did the elderly. Moreover, pictures that were recalled elicited a greater proportion of SCRs and SCRs of greater magnitude than did pictures that were not recalled. These results were independent of serial position effects. In the second phase, and following recall of the pictures, different groups of subjects received 10 presentations each of a low-frequency picture that had not been presented during the learning phase, a low-frequency picture which had been presented, but which had not been recalled, or a low-frequency picture which had been presented and recalled. The novel picture elicited larger SCRs than did a not-recalled picture, but only on trial 1.

Although concerned with recognition rather than recall, a study by Stelmack, Plouffe and Winogron (1983) has also provided data relevant to the present discussion. In their first experiment, Stelmack *et al.* presented four groups with 10 trials of a high-recognition picture, a high-recognition word, a low-recognition picture, or a low-recognition word while skin conductance was measured. Recognizability of pictures and words was first established with a different sample of subjects. The high-recognition picture group displayed larger SCRs than did the other three groups. In Experiment 2, a sample of subjects who had participated in the original recognition test were assigned to one of four groups on the basis of their performance on the recognition memory test which was performed a week earlier. The subjects in the high-recognition conditions had recognized those words and pictures in the recognition test, whereas subjects in the low-recognition condition had not. The appropriate picture or word was presented 10 times and skin conductance was measured. Pictures and words which were previously recognized elicited smaller SCRs than did pictures and words which were not previously recognized.

The data reported by Stelmack *et al.* contain an apparent contradiction in that high-recognition pictures elicited larger SCRs than did low-recognition pictures in Experiment 1, whereas the reverse was the case in Experiment 2. However, the subjects in Experiment 1 did not take part in the preliminary recognition memory testing. Thus, the participants in Experiment 1 displayed larger SCRs to stimuli defined as highly recognizable in terms of another sample. It could be argued that some attribute of the stimuli (e.g. salience) determined both depth of processing and hence recognition performance in the preliminary study and SCR magnitude in Experiment 1. In Experiment 2 reported by Stelmack *et al.*, the stimuli which elicited the smaller SCRs were those that had been recognized by those same subjects in an earlier recognition test. Thus, it is possible to argue that the smaller responses elicited by previously-recognized items can be interpreted as reflecting the priming of those items in short-term memory.

MEMORY AND AROUSAL: AN OR INTERPRETATION

The majority of studies which have examined the relationship between arousal and memory have considered the effects of phasic changes in arousal as assessed by changes in skin conductance. One paradigm commonly used to examine the effects of phasic changes in arousal on memory is the paired-associate learning task. In one of the first studies, Kleinsmith and Kaplan (1963) gave subjects a single presentation of eight word–digit pairs in which the words were chosen so as to vary in arousal value (e.g. RAPE, SWIM). Subjects were given no indication that there would be a subsequent memory test. Skin resistance measures taken during presentation were used to rank the pairs, for each subject, from low-arousal items which gave rise to small skin resistance changes, to high-arousal items, which elicited large skin resistance changes. Different groups of subjects were then given a retention test after 2, 20, or 45 minutes, one day or one week. Results indicated that high-arousal items showed poor retention in groups given an immediate (2-minute) test, but displayed enhanced retention in groups tested at each of the longer intervals (20 minutes, 45 minutes, one day, and one week). Low-arousal items showed the opposite pattern. Subjects given immediate tests showed good retention of low-arousal items whereas subjects given delayed tests showed poor retention of these items.

According to Kleinsmith and Kaplan (1963), the word–digit association is mediated by reverberating neural circuits. High-arousal levels give rise to an increase in non-specific neural activity which supports reverberation in the neural circuits and thus produces strong long-term memory traces. On the other hand, low levels of arousal give rise to little non-specific neural activity to support reverberation, and consolidation of the long-term memory trace is correspondingly poor. Poor short-term retention of high-arousal items arises from the inaccessibility of the trace while reverberation is taking place (Kleinsmith and Kaplan, 1963), or from reverberation-produced neural fatigue (Pomerantz, Kaplan and Kaplan, 1969). In a subsequent study, Kleinsmith and Kaplan (1964) demonstrated the same effects of arousal on memory using nonsense syllable–digit pairs, and Butter (1970) and Kaplan and Kaplan (1969) replicated the findings with word–digit pairs.

In a further study of paired-associate learning, McLean (1969) examined the relationship between phasic changes in skin conductance and memory in both intentional and incidental learning conditions. In both conditions, 85 dB white noise was presented during the learning session to increase arousal in experimental subjects. Control subjects did not hear the white noise. Skin resistance level was lower for experimental than for control subjects, indicating that, overall, experimental subjects were more highly aroused. However, when the data were analyzed in terms of the SCRs to specific paired associates in the learning phase for both groups considered together, the pattern of results differed according to whether or not subjects expected a memory test. For subjects in the incidental learning condition, low-arousal items which gave rise to only small SCRs were recalled more accurately in groups given an immediate (2-minute) test, whereas high-arousal items which gave rise to large SCRs were recalled more accurately in groups given a delayed (1 day) test. However, there was no evidence of a crossover effect for subjects in the intentional learning condition. Instead, low-arousal associates were recalled more accurately than high-arousal associates in groups given an immediate test. Recall of both low- and high-arousal associates was less accurate in groups given a delayed test. There was no difference in the accuracy of recall of low- and high-arousal associates in the delayed test group.

An explanation for the interaction between arousal and retention interval suggested by Walker and Tarte (1963) and Bower (1967) involves the serial position effect which is commonly observed in studies of memory. Measures of memory indicate that late items show good retention in an immediate test (recency effect—see Craik, 1970), but show poorer retention than early items in a delayed test (primacy effect). At the same time, studies of orienting have shown that items early in a stimulus series give rise to larger SCRs than do later items. When these two sets of data are considered together in the context of the relationship between arousal and memory, it can be seen that it is likely that early items will be considered to be high-arousal items and will show poor retention in an immediate test when compared with later (low-arousal) items. In contrast, early items will show better retention than will later items at longer intervals. This explanation provides a good account of the interaction between arousal and retention interval in the case where arousal is determined on an individual basis (Butter, 1970; Kaplan and Kaplan, 1968; Kleinsmith and Kaplan, 1963, 1964).

This account is also consistent, at least in part, with priming theory. In terms of priming theory, items which give rise to ORs will promote considerable rehearsal in STS. As a result these items will be remembered. Items which do not give rise to ORs, on the other hand, will not be rehearsed and will, therefore, be forgotten. In this way, the difference between high- and low-arousal items at longer retention intervals can be explained in terms of orienting. An explanation in terms of orienting cannot, however, account for the poor short-term retention of high-arousal items.

However, as noted by Craik and Blankstein (1975), any explanation in terms of serial position effects also implies that, when words are chosen as high- and low-arousal on an *a priori* basis, the interaction should not occur. Several studies have used this type of procedure with varying results. As noted earlier, Maltzman, Kantor and Langdon (1966) found that high-arousal words were better recalled at all retention intervals than were low-arousal words. In a study by Walker and Tarte (1963) which used an *a priori* classification of words as high- or low-arousal, the pattern of results was not as clear. When heterogeneous and homogeneous lists of high- and low-arousal words were paired with digits, it was apparent that, although low-arousal items showed poorer retention in groups tested at longer intervals (45 minutes and 1 week), high-arousal items were well-remembered by all groups (2 minutes, 45 minutes, and 1 week). Walker and Tarte (1963) found no difference between retention levels of high- and low-arousal items in groups given an immediate (2-minutes) test. Finally, in an attempt to clarify the nature of any effect due to the method of calculation of arousal levels, Kaplan and Kaplan (1970) reanalyzed data from those of their studies in which they had demonstrated an interaction between individually determined arousal levels and retention interval. The reanalysis was based on an *a priori* measure of arousal. On the basis of these arousal levels, high-arousal meaningful items (Kleinsmith and Kaplan, 1963; Kaplan and Kaplan, 1969) showed good retention at both short and long intervals, whereas for nonsense syllables (Kleinsmith and Kaplan, 1964) the interaction between arousal and retention interval was still evident. These findings suggest that the serial position effect may have contributed to the original findings by Kleinsmith and Kaplan (1963). In a study which set out specifically to examine this possibility, however, Butter (1970) found no evidence of any strong relationship between serial position and SCR.

In summary, although it is possible that some aspects of the interaction between arousal and retention interval may be influenced by serial position, clearly this is not the only factor in operation. In particular, such an explanation cannot account for the influence of the nature of the memory task (incidental of intentional), nor for the variations in results between different types of stimulus material.

DISCUSSION

The data reviewed above seem to provide some evidence that orienting elicited by to-be-remembered material at the time of learning is related to recall of that material. In particular, evidence for the existence of a relationship between orienting and memory has been provided by studies employing the Brown–Peterson and free recall paradigms and studies of arousal and memory. Although there are some contrary data (e.g. Engle, 1975; Wilson, 1984; Yuille and Hare, 1980), three studies (Magliero, Gatchel and Gorthey, 1981; Siddle and Stenfert Kroese, 1985; Grush *et al.*, 1973) have demonstrated that improved recall on the shift trial in the Brown–Peterson paradigm was accompanied by increased orienting. It has also been demonstrated that orienting at the time of learning predicts subsequent memory performance in studies of recall (e.g. Corteen, 1969; Maltzman, Kantor and Langdon, 1966; Plouffe and Stelmack, 1984). In several studies, however, the relationship varied at different retention intervals (e.g. Kaplan, Kaplan and Sampson, 1968; Sampson, 1969; Sorgatz and Dannel, 1978; Warren and Harris, 1975). In a related study of recognition performance, Stelmack, Plouffe and Winogron (1983) showed that pictures which had been recognized previously produced less orienting than previously unrecognized pictures. It appears, however, that the relationship between orienting and memory is not as clear-cut in the case of recall of associative information as in paired-associate learning tasks. In particular, several studies of arousal and memory have shown that orienting at the time of learning is related to enhanced long-term memory for associative information (e.g. Butter, 1970; Kaplan and Kaplan, 1969; Kleinsmith and Kaplan, 1963, 1964; McLean, 1969). However, there are several problems in any attempt to account for the data on arousal and memory in terms of orienting. First, studies have shown that items which do not elicit orienting at learning are well recalled at short intervals, whereas items which do elicit orienting show a reminiscence effect whereby recall improves as the retention interval increases (e.g. Butter, 1970; Kaplan and Kaplan, 1969; Kleinsmith and Kaplan, 1963; McLean, 1969). Second, the relationship is different for intentional versus incidental memory tasks (McLean, 1969).

Several caveats must be added with respect to our thesis concerning a relationship between orienting and memory. First, only a handful of memory phenomena have been discussed, and one might be more confident about the argument if the relationship between orienting and memory had been studied across a wider range of paradigms and phenomena. This is, in part, a reflection of the fact that there is little systematic research on the psychophysiology of memory. Of course, some phenomena which appear to lend themselves to an interpretation in terms of orienting (e.g. the von Restorff or isolation effect) have been omitted deliberately because they are discussed in detail in the next division of this chapter.

A second point which should be made is that, although we have argued for an encoding approach to memory, it is clear that other processes (e.g. storage, retrieval) are also important. For example, there are ample data which indicate that the development of and release from proactive inhibition can reflect retrieval processes (O'Neill, Sutcliffe and Tulving, 1976). This, in turn, raises further important questions. We may ask, for example, whether orienting is always an index of encoding processes in situations in which the importance of such processes has been demonstrated. Moreover, what is the relationship between orienting and memorial processes in situations in which both encoding and retrieval processes have been shown to be important? One possibility is that memory performance is determined jointly by encoding and retrieval processes and that orienting can tell us something about encoding only. Alternatively, one might speculate that orienting at the time of learning is related not only to encoding, but also to the manner and effectiveness with which retrieval processes operate.

Third, it must be acknowledged that the evidence we have adduced in support of the role of the OR in memory performance is largely correlational. Even in situations in which recall of specific words has been examined in relation to the orienting elicited by that word at learning, the nature of the evidence is correlational. One possible way of establishing causal relationships might be to treat orienting as an independent rather than a dependent variable. That is, the hypothesis of a causal relationship between the OR and memory can be established only by manipulation of the OR. The most obvious way to do this is to utilize the fact that the OR displays habituation. Thus, a general maneuver for future research might be to examine the effects of habituation of the OR on memory performance. In the case of proactive inhibition, for example, the interpretation we have offered predicts that prior habituation to the category of to-be-recalled material that is to be used in a Brown–Peterson paradigm will produce relatively poor performance even on trial 1. It also follows that prior habituation followed by some manipulation known to produce dishabituation will restore performance on trial 1 and thus lead to the decrement in performance usually seen in the Brown–Peterson paradigm.

Finally, some comment must be made about the adequacy of the theoretical system we have used in order to explore the psychophysiology of memory. Our analysis is based firmly on priming theories of habituation and on the similarities between priming theory and the depth-of-processing approach to memory. However, it is quite possible that priming theory will not prove to be an adequate account of habituation phenomena. For example, one of the major strengths of priming theory is that it purports to be able to distinguish between short- and long-term habituation at the level of process. That is, long-term habituation is said to be mediated by associatively-generated priming of the habituation stimulus by contextual cues. This proposition leads to the prediction that habituation is context-specific, a prediction that has so far not been supported in either animals (e.g. Marlin and Miller, 1981) or humans literature (Churchill, Remington and Siddle, 1987; Schaafsma, Packer and Siddle, 1989). If context-specificity of habituation cannot be demonstrated, the explanatory power of priming theory will be severly reduced. On the other hand, both recall and recognition of verbal material have been shown to be context-specific (Smith, 1979, 1985, 1986). Notwithstanding these arguments, it is possible to argue that orienting is functionally related to memory performance even if priming theory is ultimately rejected. However, an alternative framework for integrating orienting and memory would then be required.

In his thorough review of memory and psychophysiological activity, Jennings (1986) concluded by stating that 'perhaps the biggest need in the area is for a theoretical framework to replace the concept of general arousal' (p. 306). We have attempted to do this by suggesting a functional relationship between orienting and memory. In this way, we have attempted to provide a theoretical framework for systematic research on the psychophysiology of memory. The validity of this approach, however, must await the verdict of such research.

ACKNOWLEDGEMENT

Preparation of this chapter was facilitated by a grant from the Australian Research Council.

The Use of Event-Related Brain Potentials in the Study of Memory: Is P300 a Measure of Event Distinctiveness?

Emanuel Donchin and Monica Fabiani
Cognitive Psychophysiology Laboratory, University of Illinois at Urbana, Champaign, IL61820, USA

INTRODUCTION

In this part of Chapter 5 we shall illustrate the manner in which psychophysiological measures can contribute to our understanding of human information processing. We examine studies of the relationship between the magnitude of event-related brain potentials (ERPs) and the subsequent recall and recognition of eliciting events. In particular, we shall attempt to show that ERP measures can be used to examine the mechanisms underlying the greater ease with which people recall *distinctive* events.

As will become apparent, our interest here is in the extent to which ERPs can be used to monitor processes which transpire while events are encoded and stored in memory during a standard episodic memory paradigm. In this paradigm, events occur in a *study phase* and their retrievability is tested after a suitable interval. Various attributes of the study and test situation serve as independent variables. Measures of memory performance during the *test phase* of the experiment serve as dependent variables. The ERP recordings provide yet another source of dependent variables which can be analyzed as one examines the outcome of such a memory experiment. It is the thesis of this chapter that the information added by these *psychophysiological* variables enhances the theoretical import of the experiments.

We shall review studies in which the retrieval of information from memory is examined as a function of attributes of the ERP elicited by events occurring during the study (or encoding) phases of memory experiments. This, of course, is not the only domain of memory research in which ERPs can play a role. Several investigators have approached the study of the relationship between memory processes and ERPs by focusing on the ERPs elicited by test probes

---

Handbook of Cognitive Psychophysiology: Central and Autonomic Nervous System Approaches.
Edited by J. R. Jennings and M. G. H. Coles.

during memory retrieval.* These studies investigate how the memory traces are accessed and retrieved, rather than how they are formed or modified. We shall not discuss such studies in the present chapter—see Karis, Fabiani and Donchin (1984, pp. 204–207) for a summary of this literature, and Kutas (1989), for a more extensive review.

The use of ERP-derived measures in the study of memory can be approached from two perspectives. If we take a *psychophysiological perspective*, our studies would be mostly concerned with the testing of theories regarding the functional significance of ERP components. In the context of the study of memory this perspective leads us to form predictions about the relationship between ERP measures and measures of memory retrieval that can be derived from theories of the functional significance of ERP components. If we take a *cognitive perspective*, we are primarily interested in whether it is possible to test theories about the architecture of the mind and its operations by measuring ERPs. That is, within the context of memory experiments, we would be trying to determine if there are predictions about the relationship between ERP measures and subsequent retrieval that can be derived from cognitive theory.

In this chapter we focus on the cognitive perspective and consider the impact that studies of P300 can have on a theory of memory. It is important to note, however, that both the cognitive and the psychophysiological approaches presuppose the existence of a database that allows mapping of psychological constructs on ERP measures. This mapping is not a *construct mapping* but rather what we prefer to call an *algorithmic mapping*.

Construct mapping assumes that there is a direct correspondence between psychological constructs and physiological measures and that psychophysiologists are in the business of identifying physiological activities which are in some way *identical* with psychological constructs. Psychophysiological measures are evaluated in terms of their quality as physiological correlates of psychological processes. Thus, for example, the N100 could be considered in this view as a *correlate of attention*. By the same token, the assertion that the P300 is *related* to memory can be interpreted to mean that P300 is identical with the memory system so that any changes that affect the memory system must be represented by corresponding changes in P300.

Algorithmic mapping refers to a mapping of psychophysiological measures which assumes that *some* of the computational processes which underlie the implementation of various psychological functions may have recordable manifestations which appear in the form of ERP components. We propose that what is manifested by the psychophysiological measures is the computational

---

* In such studies investigators use either recognition paradigms (e.g. Parasuraman and Beatty, 1980; Parasuraman, Richer and Beatty, 1982; Stanny and Elfner, 1980; Warren, 1980) or the Sternberg task (e.g. Adam and Collins, 1978; Ford *et al.*, 1979; Gomer, Spicuzza and O'Donnell, 1976). The focus of these studies tends to be on the latency of the P300 component of the ERP as an index of the duration of stimulus evaluation processes.

process and not the psychological construct. For a detailed discussion of the mapping of ERPs on psychological concepts we refer the reader to Donchin and Coles (1988a), who conclude that:

> (There) is a hierarchy of descriptors of psychological processes, and we claim that ERPs are manifestations of activities related to an elementary level in this hierarchy. Descriptors at the highest level are terms such as motivation, emotion, memory, and learning. . . .we are not trying to correlate a brain wave with a high level psychological process. (p. 358)

This view is also consistent with the idea that broad psychological constructs do not necessarily correspond to unitary neural processes. The proliferation of conceptual frameworks in the memory literature is but one example showing how investigators find that a unifying memory concept is not very fruitful in accounting for data. However, it is true that most of the conceptual segmentation found in the literature is still at a level higher than that at which we place ERP-related processes. This view leads to a research program in which the questions are asked in terms of components of the computational process and where the experimental manipulations must ensure the uniformity of the computational activities across different experimental conditions.* (See also Cacioppo and Tassinary (1990) and Coles, Gratton and Fabiani (in press) for similar discussions of the relationship between physiological signals and psychological constructs.)

It is this concern with the elementary processes manifested by ERP components that leads us to avoid discussions of the association between ERP components and such concepts as *arousal* or *attention*, which are exemplified in a very scholarly manner by Graham and Hackley in Chapter 3. Such concepts appear to us to subsume a vast number of elementary processes, and are unlikely to be useful in explicating the meaning of specific ERP measures. An ERP component cannot, in our view, but be a manifestation of a small subset of the relevant mechanisms.

The utility of ERPs as tools in the study of cognition can be illustrated in a number of different contexts using several different components (for reviews, see Hillyard and Kutas, 1983, Renault *et al.*, 1988). However, in this chapter the discussion will focus on a component commonly labeled P300 (alternately referred to as P3, or P3b), and on the feasibility of using measures of this component to clarify the role of *distinctiveness* in memory. We shall first review studies of the P300. We shall then examine the role which the construct of distinctiveness plays in models of memory. We shall argue that, while the

---

* An example of this approach can be found in the work on the 'lateralized readiness potential' (LRP) (e.g. Coles, Gratton and Donchin, 1988; Gratton *et al.*, 1988). The LRP is not claimed to be identical with response preparation. It is only claimed that it is a necessary component of preparation and that if the experiment is set up in a manner in which preparatory processes occur that are specific to the hand involved in responding, an LRP will be observed.

distinctiveness construct is useful, its definition tends to be circular in the absence of a measure of distinctiveness that is independent of its effect on recall. This leads to the argument that measures of the amplitude of the P300 may serve as measures of distinctiveness and that, by using P300 in this manner, we can examine in some detail the workings of the memory system.

THE P300 COMPONENT*

The P300 is a component of the ERP that can be easily elicited in what has come to be called the *oddball* paradigm. In this paradigm subjects are presented with a series of events each of which can be classified in one of two categories. The subjects are assigned a task whose performance depends, at least in part, on proper classification of the events. The two categories appear in a Bernoulli sequence. In general, one of the two categories occurs much less frequently than the other. Under these circumstances, events in the rarer category tend to elicit a large P300, the amplitude of which is, in general, inversely related to the probability with which the category occurs (Duncan-Johnson and Donchin, 1977). The relationship between P300 amplitude, the probability of the eliciting event, and the relevance of the events to the task the subject is performing is rather complex (for reviews, see Johnson, 1986, 1988).

The P300 component can be elicited with remarkable reliability (Fabiani *et al.*, 1987). Figure 5.4 presents data obtained from 49 different subjects, each participating in an oddball study in which the series of events consisted of a sequence of two letters (H and S), one of which appeared with a probability of 0.20. It can be seen that in each case the ERP elicited by the rare stimuli is characterized by a large positive deflection with a latency of at least 300 ms. This is the P300. The consistency across subjects is rather remarkable even though the inter-subject variability is also quite obvious.

It should be noted that the physical nature of the stimuli used for eliciting the P300 is considerably less important than is the logical structure of the series of events. Figure 5.5, also taken from the Fabiani *et al.* (1987) study of the reliability of P300 measurement, illustrates this point by comparing the P300s elicited, in the same subjects, by various visual and auditory oddball

---

* In this discussion we ignore the often reported observation (e.g. Sutton and Ruchkin, 1984) that more than one positive component may operate concurrently with the P300. For a discussion of conditions under which the multiple-component issue can be ignored with relative impunity, see Donchin and Coles (1988a). A useful review is also presented by Graham and Hackley (this volume). We tend to agree with their conclusion that the so called 'P3a' is essentially the alter-ego of the N200 and hence it is not useful to consider it as a separate component (see also Squires, Squires, and Hillyard, 1976). The 'Slow Wave', on the other hand, may indeed be a source of confusion in studies of P300. But this, as Donchin and Coles (1988a) argue, is a cause for methodological caution, not an argument for despair.

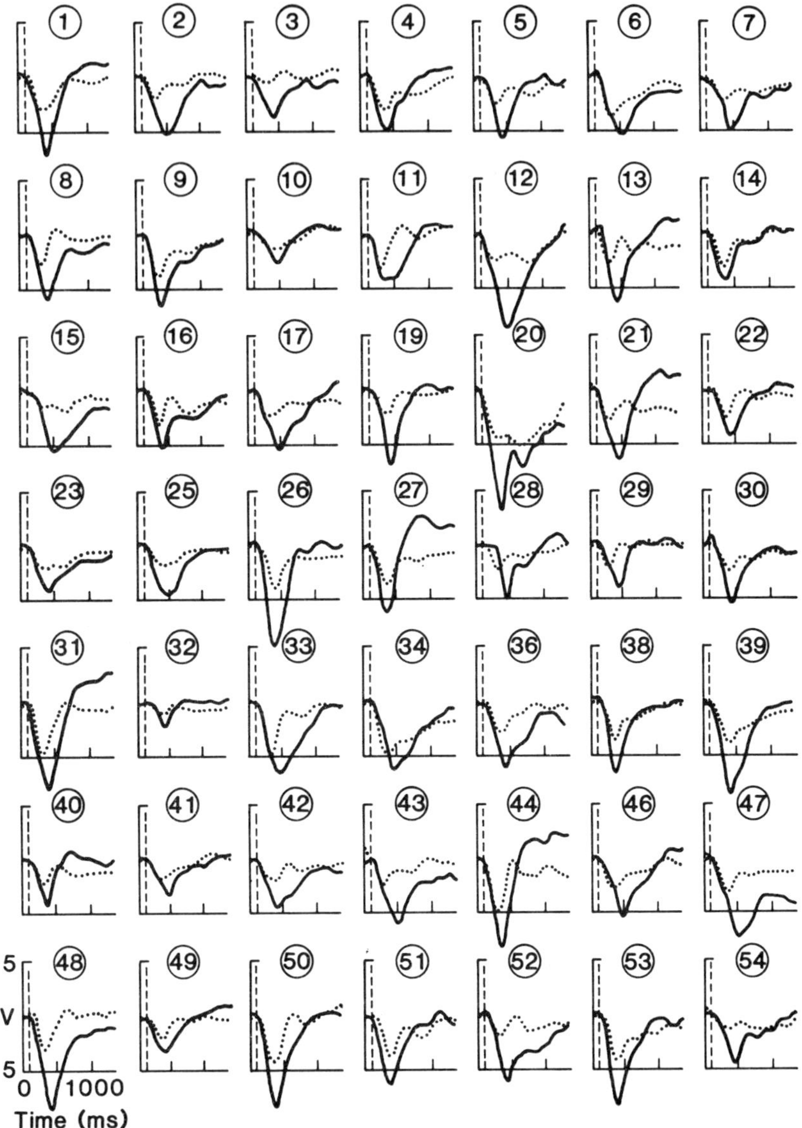

Figure 5.4. Average ERP data obtained in an oddball paradigm from 49 individual subjects. The ERP elicited by the rare stimuli is indicated by a solid line, that elicited by the frequent stimuli is indicated by a dotted line. (Reprinted with permission from Fabiani *et al.* (1987) © JAI Press.)

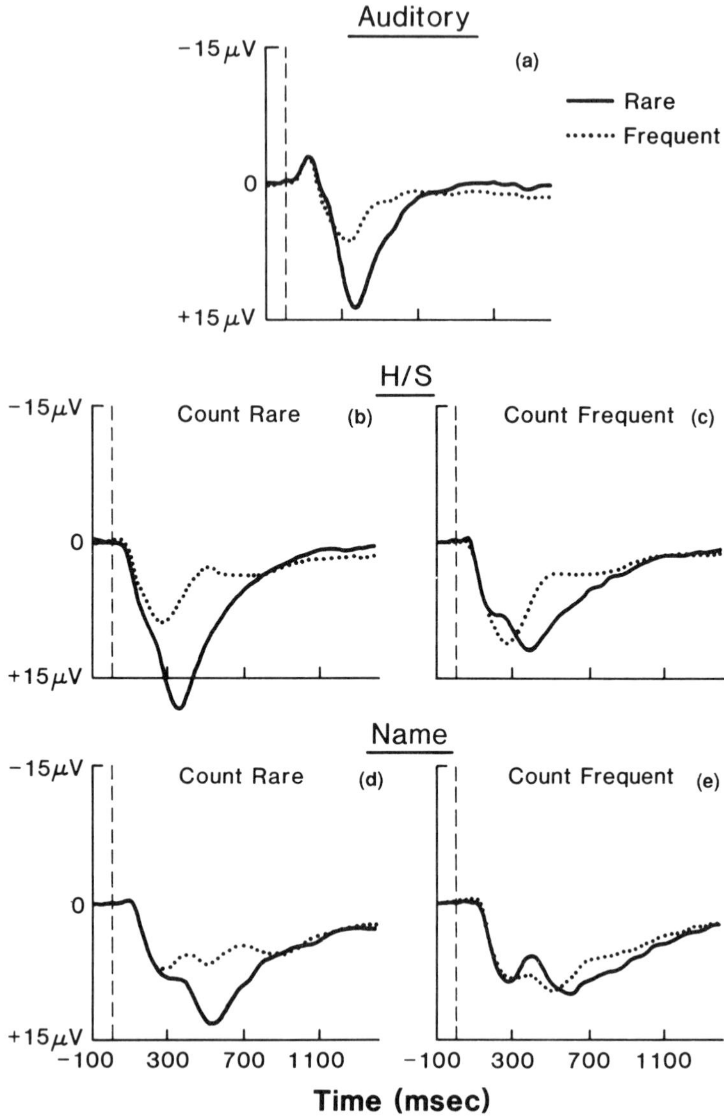

Figure 5.5. Grand average Pz waveforms obtained from the same 49 subjects in five different oddball paradigms: (a) auditory RT task involving pitch discrimination, (b) visual-count rare task involving letter discrimination, (c) visual-count frequent task involving letter discrimination, (d) visual-count rare task involving name gender discrimination, and (e) visual-count frequent task involving name gender discrimination. Rare stimuli (20%) are indicated by a solid line, frequent stimuli (80%) are indicated by a dotted line. (Reprinted with permission from Fabiani *et al.* (1987). © JAI Press.)

paradigms. Figure 5.5(a) shows waveforms from an auditory oddball in which subjects were listening to a series composed of two tones. One of the tones was rare (20%), the other frequent (80%), and the subject's task was to give a discriminating response on the basis of the tone's pitch. Figures 5.5(b)and (c) show waveforms recorded in two visual oddballs in which subjects were presented with a series composed of the letters H and S, with subjects counting the occurrences of the rare (20%) or frequent (80%) letter. Figures 5.5(d) and (e) show waveforms from another visual oddball in which subjects were presented with series of names and were asked to count names of one gender. The P300 component is clearly visible in all these waveforms, even though its latency varies according to task complexity (being shortest for the auditory oddball and longest for the name oddball), and its amplitude is largest for rare and target (counted) stimuli.

During the two decades since Sutton's original description of the P300 (Sutton *et al.*, 1965), we learned much about its *behavior*. Behavior, in this context, refers to changes in the amplitude and latency of P300. It is commonly assumed that the amplitude of P300 can be considered as an index of the *strength* of the underlying psychological process. On the other hand, the latency of P300 is considered to be an index of the *duration* of the processes preceding the one manifested by P300 (perhaps including the duration of the P300 process itself).

The results of many such studies on the P300 lead to the following assertions (for details, see reviews by Donchin, 1981, Donchin, Ritter and McCallum, 1978, Fabiani *et al.*, 1987, Johnson, 1986, 1988, Pritchard, 1981):

(1) A wide range of events can elicit a P300 (Sutton *et al.*, 1965; Sutton *et al.*, 1967; Kutas, McCarthy and Donchin, 1977; Towle, Heuer and Donchin, 1980; Simson, Vaughan and Ritter, 1976).
(2) There is an inverse relationship between the amplitude of P300 and the probability of the eliciting event (Duncan-Johnson and Donchin, 1977; Tueting, Sutton and Zubin, 1970).
(3) Subjective probability (i.e. the subject's perception, on a trial-by-trial basis, of the probability of a stimulus) is a more direct determinant of P300 amplitude than the overall probability of the stimulus in the series (Duncan-Johnson and Donchin, 1982; Johnson and Donchin, 1980; Squires *et al.*, 1976).
(4) All this is true assuming a constant level of task relevance (Duncan-Johnson and Donchin, 1977; Johnson and Donchin, 1978). Thus, variation in P300 amplitude may be due to changes in task relevance and not in stimulus probability.
(5) The amplitude of the P300 is related to the demands that a particular task places on processing resources (Donchin, Kramer and Wickens, 1986). In a dual-task situation, P300 amplitude to primary-task events increases

with increased resource demands, while the P300 elicited by concurrent secondary-task events decreases (Sirevaag *et al.*, 1989).

(6) There may be a general interaction between the amplitude and latency of P300, in that more complex stimuli may take longer to evaluate (longer P300 latency) and the subject may be more uncertain about them (smaller P300 amplitude; Ruchkin, Munson and Sutton, 1982).

Thus, it appears that two important independent variables which control P300 amplitude are the subjective probability associated with, and the task relevance of, the eliciting event. The dependence of P300 amplitude on subjective probability is one of several factors that suggest that this component manifests a process in the chain of information processing transactions performed on novel events. This process appears to be elicited only if the information is relevant and useful to the subject, and appears to have limited capacity. Finally, a P300 appears to be elicited only after a stimulus has been evaluated and categorized.

The information on the antecedent conditions of P300 summarized above led to the formulation of the *context updating* hypothesis which attempts to account for the functional significance of P300 (Donchin, 1981; see also Donchin and Coles, 1988a,b). This hypothesis assumes that the elicitation of a P300 reflects a process involved in the updating of representations in working memory. Rare or unexpected task-relevant events should lead to an updating of the current memory schemas, because only by so doing can an accurate representation of the environment be maintained.

The updating process may involve the *marking* of some attribute of the event that made it *distinctive* with respect to other events. This updating of the memory representation of an event is assumed to facilitate the subsequent recall of the event, by providing valuable retrieval cues, so that the greater the updating that follows an individual event, the higher the probability of later recalling that event; P300 amplitude is assumed to be proportional to the degree of updating of the memory representation of the event. Therefore, as the updating process is supposed to be beneficial to recall, P300 amplitude should also predict the subsequent recall of the eliciting event.

In the following section, we review research concerning the role of event distinctiveness in memory. We also discuss some of the problems inherent in this concept and suggest that measures of the amplitude of P300 may help in solving these problems.

DISTINCTIVENESS IN MEMORY

We use the word *distinctiveness* in the sense that is widely used in the literature. Stimuli are distinctive to the extent that they differ on one or more dimensions from other stimuli that occupy their immediate spatiotemporal neighborhood. In his pioneering paper on 'The distinctiveness of stimuli', Murdock (1960) asserts (after noting the pervasiveness of the concept of distinctiveness in the history of psychology) that 'One difficulty with the concept of distinctiveness is that no generally accepted method of measurement has been developed' (p. 16). The situation has changed but little in the past 30 years.*

Yet, the concept of distinctiveness retains its vitality. Theorists and experimentalists continue to use distinctiveness as an explanatory concept in a wide array of domains. One domain in which this concept is often invoked is the domain of memory research. In fact, the distinctiveness hypothesis has been an influential development that derives from the levels-of-processing account of episodic memory processes (Craik and Lockhart, 1972).

The levels-of-processing approach proposes that the persistence of memory traces is a positive function of depth of processing. Processing which is based on the physical qualities of the stimulus is considered *shallow*, while *deep* processing is based on the abstract, semantic properties of the stimulus. However, Jacoby (1975), among others, reported that physical features of a stimulus are not necessarily forgotten earlier than semantic features. To account for these findings Jacoby and Craik (1979) invoked the critical role of the distinctiveness of an event relative to the other events memorized at the same time. Physical properties of a stimulus that are distinctive (i.e. unique) may leave more persistent traces than semantic features that are common.

The distinctiveness hypothesis, as formulated by Jacoby and Craik, emphasizes:

(1) *The importance of distinctive features in retention.* Distinctive features of an item are those shared by few other items. These features may be semantic or non-semantic, although semantic features are more likely to be shared by fewer other items than will orthographic or phonemic features.
(2) The fact that the encoding of distinctive information depends on the *presence of a less distinctive context.* A specific stimulus is functionally distinct only to the extent that the other stimuli present in the same context do not share with it the distinctive feature. In other words, distinctiveness is not a property of a stimulus *per se* and can thus vary for the same stimulus from one context to another.
(3) The fact that *sensory or non-semantic features are not assumed to decay more rapidly than semantic features.* That is, the effect that distinctive features have on retention is specified in terms of differential *utility*, rather than differential durability.

---

* Murdock did present a method for calculating the *total* distinctiveness in an array of stimuli as well as the percentage of distinctiveness associated with each stimulus in a series. However, this method was restricted to stimuli that vary only in one dimension (i.e. magnitude or intensity) and was applied in the context of an absolute judgment task.

Thus, for example, semantic information may have a positive or negative effect on performance, depending on the extent to which the encoded features are shared by other list items, the extent to which the task required of the subject biases the subject's attention toward these features at encoding, and, finally, the extent to which these features are useful for the task required of the subject at retrieval.

While the distinctiveness hypothesis has had considerable success, the central difficulty identified by Murdock (1960) remains: the concept is largely circular. An examination of studies which invoke distinctiveness reveals that the concept is defined in terms of the operations the investigator executes on the stimuli used in the study. Usually the concept of feature uniqueness is invoked, stimulus arrays are created and the study is run. The degree to which distinctiveness was successfully manipulated is inferred from the outcome of the study. If the manipulation indeed affected measures of memory performance in the predicted direction, the manipulation is deemed to have been successful.

Furthermore, even if one accepts the validity of such an *a priori* definition of distinctiveness, it seems self-evident that distinctiveness is not a property of the stimulus but is rather a property of the *interaction between the subject and the stimulus.* Only if the subject processes the distinctive feature on a specific trial can the stimulus be considered to have been distinctive on that trial. As a consequence, one would assume that distinctiveness *varies in its magnitude from trial to trial*, as a function of the manner in which the input is processed by the subject.

A related problem is that even stimuli that are not considered distinctive on the basis of the experimenter's definition can possess a measure of subjective distinctiveness owing to the manner in which the subject processes them. For example, if a supposedly non-distinctive stimulus happens to be the name of the subject's home town, the subject's own name, or the name of the team's mascot, etc., it is likely to be quite distinctive for that particular subject, even though the experimenter has no control on the features that make it subjectively distinctive.

Finally, distinctiveness is a *relative* rather than an absolute concept, so that stimuli that are distinctive within one context may not be so within another. This can make predictions difficult in many circumstances (for a discussion, see Eysenck, 1979).

A theory of memory that relies on distinctiveness should be able to deal with all these issues. That is, it should be able to predict how the variance in recall would be controlled by the variance in distinctiveness. In the remainder of this part of the chapter we will suggest that, at least under some conditions, it may be possible to assess the subjective distinctiveness of a specific stimulus on a specific trial by measuring the amplitude of the P300 on that trial. Thus, if we accept the distinctiveness hypothesis and we accept the suggestion that the larger the P300 the more distinct was the eliciting event, we should predict that the larger the P300 the more likely is an event to be recalled. Note that we are introducing here a rather novel way of testing the predictions of the distinctiveness hypothesis. If we accept the notion that P300 measures distinctiveness on a trial-by-trial basis, we can ask how the variance in distinctiveness *within* a class of stimuli rendered distinctive by the experimenter's manipulations will correlate with the subject's ability to recall the stimuli.

P300 AS A CANDIDATE MEASURE OF DISTINCTIVENESS

It should be noted that our interest in the relationship between P300 and memory did not derive from an intent to provide a better measure of distinctiveness. The studies reviewed below were initiated from a psychophysiological, rather than a cognitive, stance. In these studies we attempted to account for the functional significance of the P300.

Statements relating to the functional significance of the P300 can be tested by an examination of the predicted consequences of variation in the latency or amplitude of the P300 for the outcome of the interaction between the subject and the environment (Donchin, 1981; Donchin and Coles, 1988a,b). The assumption here is that the subject's behavior is affected by the processing manifested by the P300, and therefore that there will be measurable effects on performance that will be related to the amplitude of the P300 elicited by an event. The 'context updating' hypothesis assumes that the P300 manifests a change in the subject's model of the environment. The consequences of such a change have been examined in two different paradigms. One approach measures the extent to which the subject's strategic choices vary with the amplitude of the P300 elicited by preceding stimuli, as changes in the model of the environment should be reflected in such choices. The other approach investigates the effect that the elicitation of a P300 has on the subsequent retrievability of the eliciting event because of the relationship between the strength, or the form, of the memory traces and the processing of distinct stimuli during encoding.

P300 AND SUBSEQUENT STRATEGIC CHOICES

One of the most critical clues to the functional significance of the P300 came from the recognition that the processing represented by P300 is used in the service of future actions rather than in the execution of the specific responses to the eliciting event (Donchin, 1979; Donchin *et al.*, 1988; Donchin, Ritter and McCallum, 1978; Gratton *et al.*, in press; Munson *et al.*, 1984). Of particular significance in this context are the numerous studies that demonstrate a dissociation between the latency of the P300 and reaction time (Coles *et al.*, 1985; Kutas, McCarthy and Donchin, 1977; Magliero *et al.*, 1984; McCarthy and Donchin, 1981; Ragot, 1984). These studies show that the processing reflected by the P300 is not necessary for the emission of the specific motor response on any trial. That is, the processing leading to the P300 seems to proceed independently of the processes leading to the triggering of the response. It is from this analysis that came the initial indications that the processing manifested by the P300 is concerned with future strategies rather than with immediate response (Donchin, Ritter and McCallum, 1978; Donchin, 1981).

Consistent with this view is the demonstration by Donchin *et al.* (1988) that the subject's changing strategies, as revealed in overt behavior, can be predicted from the P300 response to current events. In this experiment, Donchin *et al.* presented subjects with a series of names, most of which were female names, while a small minority were male names. The subjects were instructed to respond as rapidly as possible, by pressing one of two buttons depending on the gender typically associated with the name. In some blocks of trials female names occurred with an 80% frequency. On such blocks the subjects were biased to press the 'female' button. This response was frequently given even when male names were presented. This erroneous 'female' response to male names tended to be associated with very short reaction times (fast guesses). Donchin *et al.* observed that the latency of P300 on these error trials was about 100 ms longer than P300 latency on other trials. Furthermore, the distribution of P300 latencies for correct trials did not overlap with that of incorrect trials, suggesting that P300 was *actively* delayed in the incorrect trials. This analysis suggests that the increase in P300 latency derived from the subjects' realization (perhaps unconscious) that their response (emitted before a P300 was elicited) had been incorrect. Furthermore, Donchin *et al.* found that the larger the P300 elicited on the error trials, the more accurate and slower the subjects' response on the following trial in which another male name was presented. That is, the amplitude of the P300 after an error predicted the degree to which bias would be reduced in the next error-prone trial.

As another example, Gratton *et al.* (in press) found that the amplitude of the P300 elicited by an informative warning stimulus predicts the degree to which subjects use this information to prepare their responses to the following imperative stimulus. As a third example, Munson *et al.* (1984) recorded ERPs in a prediction paradigm. Subjects were asked to predict, prior to each trial, whether the signal would be the presentation of a click, or the absence of a click. The overall probability of trials in which a click was present and trials in which it was absent was equal. However, trials were presented in a quasi-random sequence, with a weak tendency towards longer runs of the same type of trials. Munson *et al.* (1984) found that the amplitude of P300 was larger at trial *N* when it preceded a prediction that the signal sequence would discontinue at trial $N+1$, than when it preceded the prediction that the sequence would continue.

P300 AND MEMORY: EXPERIMENTS USING THE ODDBALL AND THE VON RESTORFF PARADIGMS

Several studies demonstrated a relationship between the retrieval of an event and the amplitude of the P300 elicited by that event at the time of its initial occurrence. The studies described in this section have employed either the oddball paradigm, or the von Restorff paradigm.

The von Restorff, or isolation, paradigm was developed by a German psychologist of the *Gestalt* school, Hedwig von Restorff, in 1933. In this paradigm, stimuli are presented in sequence for the subject to memorize. One of the stimuli in the sequence differs in some fashion (e.g. size, color, etc.) from the other stimuli. This stimulus is usually recalled better than the other stimuli, and this enhanced recall is called the *von Restorff* or *isolation effect*.

There is an evident similarity between the von Restorff paradigm and the oddball paradigm. In both cases, distinctive (and/or rare) stimuli are presented in the midst of a sequence of homogeneous (frequent) stimuli. These are the stimuli that usually elicit large P300s. It can be hypothesized that the recall variance, in either of these paradigms, should be related to the very factors that are known to elicit and control P300 amplitude.

The Karis, Fabiani and Donchin (1984) Study

As already discussed in the section on P300, the context updating hypothesis led to the prediction that the larger the P300 elicited by a word, the more likely would be its subsequent recall. Karis, Fabiani and Donchin (1984) tested this hypothesis using the von Restorff paradigm. They presented subjects with series of words. In most of the series, one word was *isolated* by changing the size of the characters in which the word was displayed (see Figure 5.6 for an illustration of this paradigm). As already mentioned, isolated items are better recalled than are comparable non-isolated items. In addition, isolated items, being rare and task-relevant, can be expected to elicit large P300s. The ERPs elicited by each word were recorded.

The critical comparisons with respect to the P300/memory relationship were made *within* each type of stimulus. That is, we compared how much variance in the recall of the isolates correlated with variance in P300 amplitude. Thus, ERPs elicited by the isolates were sorted on the basis of their subsequent recall, and the amplitude of P300 was measured separately for recalled and unrecalled isolates. The same comparison was made for stimuli that were not isolated.

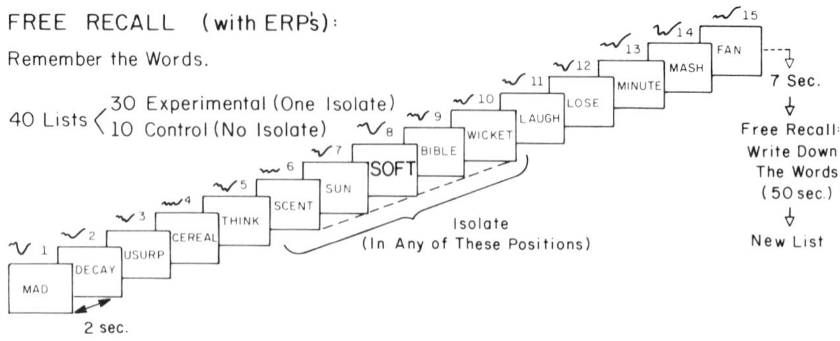

Figure 5.6. The von Restorff paradigm. (Reprinted with permission from Karis, Fabiani and Donchin (1984). © Academic Press.)

It is important to emphasize that we are not merely asserting that the isolates, as a group, will *both* elicit a P300 and be recalled. Such a correlation may be entirely spurious. We are, instead, focusing on the fact that not all isolates are recalled and that not all isolates elicit a P300 of the same amplitude. There is a variance in recall and a variance in P300 amplitude *within* the isolated words, and we are examining the degree to which these two variances are correlated.

Although the results, in general, supported the hypothesis of a relationship between P300 amplitude and subsequent recall, there were strong individual differences, which turned out to depend on the rehearsal strategies used by the subjects. Subjects could be classified in two types: the rote memorizers (who repeated the words over and over) and the elaborators (who formed complex sentences or images to memorize the words). The elaborators recalled more words than did the rote memorizers, but they did not show a von Restorff effect. Rote memorizers were poor at the recall task in general but showed a strong von Restorff effect. In the ERP analyses, the rote memorizers confirmed our general prediction: isolates subsequently recalled elicited larger P300s on their initial presentation, than did isolates that were not recalled. This relationship between recall and P300 amplitude was not observed in elaborators. These results are shown in Figure 5.7 for the isolated words.

It is important to point out that the isolates, on the average, elicited P300s that were consistently larger than those elicited by the non-isolates in all subjects, regardless of their rehearsal strategies. Furthermore, the distribution of the amplitudes of single-trial P300s was the same for both rote memorizers and elaborators. In addition, an N200 component, preceding the P300, was elicited by the isolates in all subjects, even though its amplitude did not predict subsequent recall. Thus, it appears that the initial processing of the stimulus (up to the point at which the P300 was emitted) was similar in the two groups.

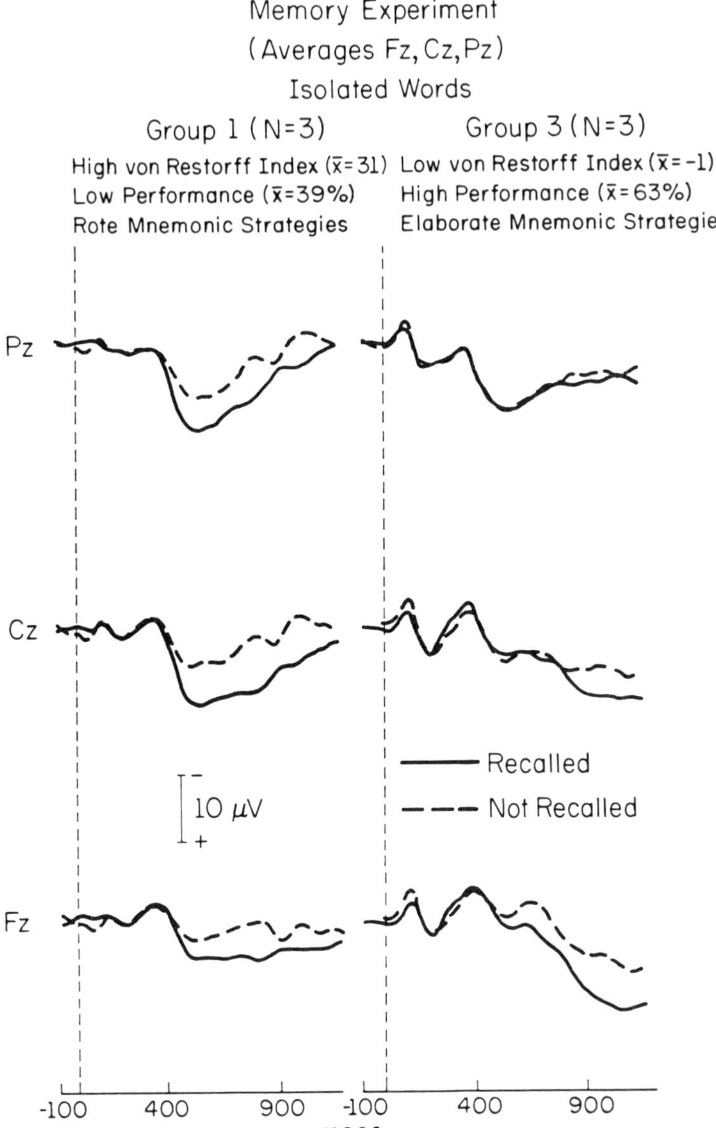

Figure 5.7. Grand average waveforms at Fz, Cz, and Pz, the isolated words sorted on the basis of subsequent recall. Recalled isolates are indicated by a solid line, unrecalled isolates are indicated by a dashed line. The waveforms of the rote memorizers are presented on the left, those of the elaborators on the right. (Reprinted with permission from Karis, Fabiani and Donchin (1984). © Academic Press.)

The differences between the two groups in recall and in its relationship to P300 emerged later, as a consequence of their rehearsal strategies. In this respect, it is noteworthy that the amplitude of a frontal-positive slow wave* was correlated with subsequent recall in the elaborators while it was virtually absent in the rote memorizers, thus suggesting that this component may be related to the degree of elaborative processing.

In the Karis *et al.* study we employed three different memory tests: recognition, immediate free recall, and delayed free recall. We observed a graded relationship between the amplitude of P300 to the isolated words and the subsequent memory performance: isolated words that were neither recognized nor recalled elicited the smallest P300 when first presented. Words that were correctly recognized but not recalled elicited a larger P300 than the previous group. Words that were correctly recognized and recalled only in the immediate free recall test elicited an even larger P300, while the largest P300 of all was elicited by words that were recognized and recalled in both recall tests. Thus, the process manifested by the P300 seems to influence the subjects' performance in immediate and delayed recall as well as in recognition. These results are illustrated in Figure 5.8.

In evaluating these data, we should consider in detail what happens in the von Restorff paradigm. Clearly, isolating a stimulus makes it easier to recall it, at least when rote rehearsal strategies are used. However, not all isolates are recalled. So, obviously, there is some variance in the effect of the isolation on subsequent memory. It is possible to assume that this variance is due to the degree to which the experimenter has succeeded in making every single isolate as perfectly distinct as all other isolates. Possibly, some isolates proved more distinct than others and these are the ones recalled.

Testing this hypothesis requires that we have a measure of the distinctiveness of individual isolates. This is precisely what we assume the P300 provides, based on the knowledge that P300 amplitude varies on a trial-by-trial basis (see the earlier section 'The P300 Component') and that this variation appears to be related to the degree of change imposed on the subject's model of the context. In our studies of the von Restorff phenomenon, we indeed observed that the isolates elicit P300s and that these P300s vary from trial to trial. We also observed that the variance in P300 amplitude within the isolates is correlated with the variance in the subjects' subsequent recall. These findings are consistent with the suggestion that P300 can be used as a measure of *subjective distinctiveness*.

As already mentioned, in the Karis *et al.* study, the degree to which we find a relationship between P300 amplitude and memory varies with the subject's strategy. The following model can be proposed on the basis of this study:

---

* The 'frontal-positive slow wave' was elicited only in elaborators. Its amplitude was largest at the frontal electrode and virtually zero at the parietal electrode, which makes it clearly distinguishable both from P300 and the more typical slow wave (Squires, Squires and Hillyard, 1975). Its peak latency exceeded 900 ms in this study.

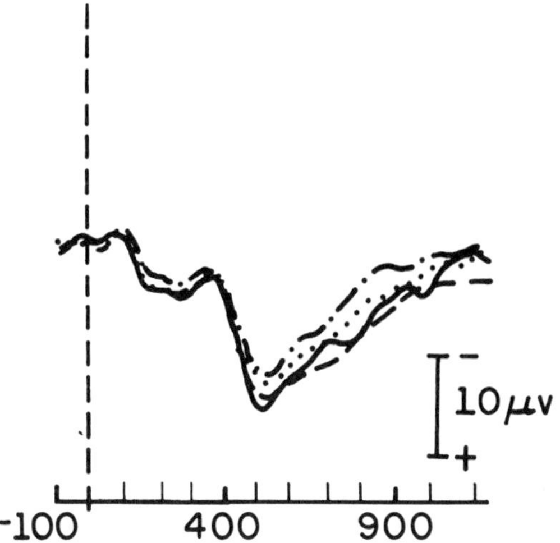

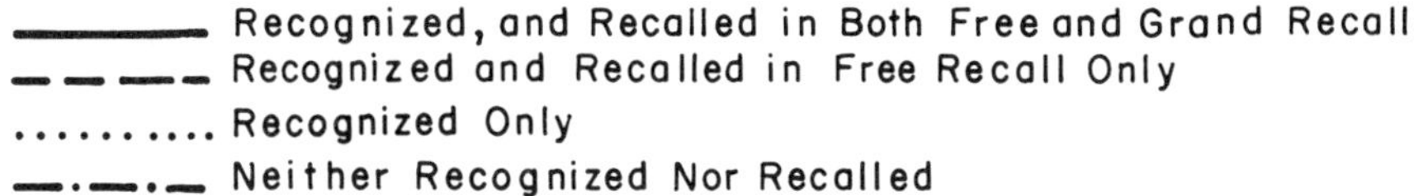

Figure 5.8. Grand average waveforms of the isolated words at Pz. (Reprinted with permission from Karis, Fabiani and Donchin (1984). © Academic Press.)

(1) The distinctive feature(s) of the stimuli trigger the process manifested by P300. This is true for all subjects, regardless of their rehearsal strategies.
(2) The larger the P300 elicited the more the subject reacted to the distinctiveness of the stimulus features. The encoding of events creates representations that are 'marked' in a certain way and this marking is proportional to the amplitude of the P300. 'Marking' in this context merely means that the representations are more likely to be recalled. The marking appears to be specific to the manner in which stimuli are recalled.
(3) At least two levels of representations may be created during the encoding process. A feature-driven (episodic?) representation preserves the features of the encoded events. Subjects who engage in elaboration create a different level of representation in which the attributes of the items that were used in creating the elaborations are emphasized relative to the features associated with the episodic representations. For our purposes it does not matter whether these two levels of representation are viewed as existing as two distinct stores or rather as constituting different access paths into the same store. We do assume that the marking by P300 is unique to

the episodic representation and is lost, or is unavailable, to retrieval from the elaborated representations.

(4) The episodic representations (or the path to these representations) is used by the rote memorizers. Therefore, they are more likely to recall items that elicited a larger P300. Thus, the more distinctive the stimulus, as measured by the P300, the easier it is for rote memorizers to recall. This is evidenced by the fact that the variance from trial to trial in P300 correlates with the subject's ability to recall the items.

(5) The elaborators access the representations in a manner that is insensitive to the effect of the distinctive features as the variance of P300 is not related to recall if the subjects use an elaborative strategy.

To summarize, the data reported by Karis, Fabiani and Donchin (1984) indicated that some early processes distinguish between isolated and non-isolated words. One of these processes consists in the detection of physical deviance, as indexed by the N200, and does not appear to directly influence the subsequent memory of the deviant (isolated) events. The variance of a second process, indexed by the P300, predicts the subsequent memory of the isolated events, when its effects are not overshadowed by further elaborative processing. Both these processes occur within the first 500 ms after stimulus presentation, and are elicited in a similar fashion for all subjects. While the first of these processes is probably largely automatic, the second process, we assume, is related to the subject's use of the distinctiveness of the isolates. In other words, it is related to the subjective distinctiveness of the words. Further processing can determine the extent to which the process indexed by the P300 will influence the retrievability of the eliciting event. This further processing may be manifested, at least in part, by the frontal-positive slow wave.

These two observations are critically dependent on the psychophysiological data. In fact, if only the free recall data were available, it would have not been possible to establish whether or not the elaborators were paying attention to the distinctive (isolated) feature at the moment the isolates were being presented, or whether their lack of a von Restorff effect depended on subsequent processing.

Strategy Manipulation

The analysis of the data of the Karis *et al.* study capitalized, in a *post hoc* manner, on different strategies used by different subjects. To test the hypothesis that the relationship between P300 amplitude and subsequent recall indeed depends on the rehearsal strategy used by the subject, we replicated the von Restorff study described above, but this time we also manipulated the subject's strategy by changing instructions (Fabiani, Karis and Donchin, 1990). Instructions to use rote strategies required the subject to repeat each word as it was presented, while elaborative instructions required the subject to combine words into images, sentences, or stories.

Strategy instructions proved effective in manipulating the performance of the subjects. When instructed to use rote strategies, subjects recalled fewer words, and displayed a larger von Restorff effect, than when they used elaborative strategies. Analyses of the ERPs also supported our predictions. Isolated words elicited larger P300s than non-isolated words, regardless of the instructions given to the subjects. However, when subjects were instructed to use rote strategies, the P300s elicited by words subsequently recalled were significantly larger than those elicited by words which were not subsequently recalled. On the other hand, when subjects were instructed to use elaborative strategies, no relationship was observed between P300 amplitude and subsequent recall, but there was, again, a relationship between recall and the amplitude of a frontal-positive slow wave. This component was also observed in the elaborators of the Karis *et al.* experiment, and may be related to extended processing of the word. The relationship between the P300 elicited by the isolates at encoding and their subsequent recall for the two strategy conditions is shown in Figure 5.9.

In order to determine whether it is the deviant size that facilitates recall when rote strategies are used, we devised a *size recall test*. At the end of the experiment, the subject was presented with a printed list of all the isolates (half of which had been presented under rote instructions and half under elaborative instructions). These isolates were randomly interspersed with an equal number of non-isolated words (half from each strategy instruction). The subject was told to indicate whether or not each word was originally displayed in the larger size. During this test all the words in the list were, of course, printed in the same size font. We reasoned that, if it is the case that the size is a *distinctive* attribute of the memory representation of the word, subjects should have a better memory of the word size when they use rote strategies than when they use elaborative strategies. This was the case: subjects were significantly more accurate in identifying the size of the words first presented to them under rote instructions than under elaborative instructions. They performed at a chance level in identifying the size of words first presented to them under elaborative instructions. It is plausible that under both strategy instructions the size attribute was marked as a distinctive attribute of the word when an isolate appeared (a larger P300 to the isolates than to the non-isolates was observed for all the subjects in all circumstances). However, when the words were memorized under rote instructions, the subjects might have also used the size attribute in their retrieval search, thus rehearsing it. When they were instructed to use elaborative strategies, however, they used stories or images as an aid to retrieval, and did not rehearse the size attribute, thus having a poorer memory for it.

In the following two studies we tested further the validity of our model by

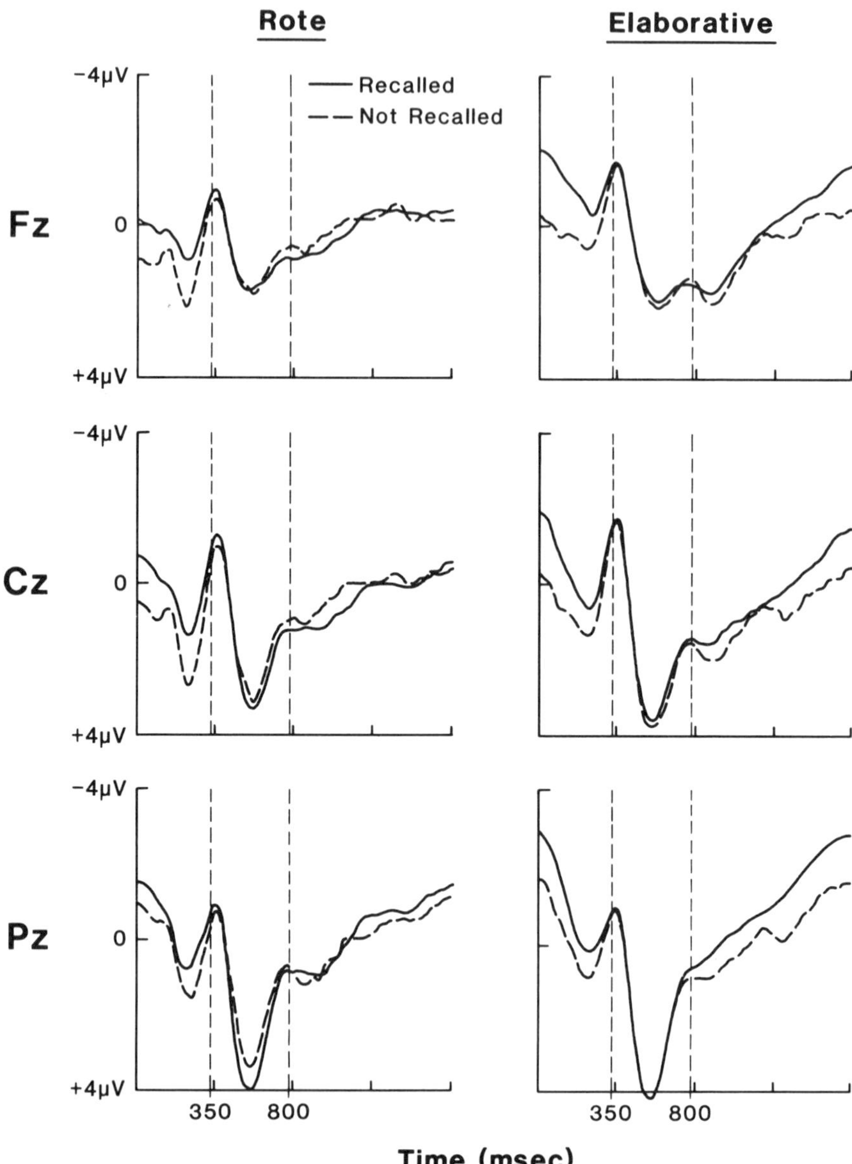

Figure 5.9. Grand average waveforms for all words sorted on the basis of subsequent recall at Fz, Cz, and Pz. The rote instruction condition is presented on the left, the elaborative instruction condition on the right. Solid lines indicate recalled words, dashed lines unrecalled words. The waveforms are latency adjusted. (Reprinted with permission from Fabiani, Karis and Donchin (1990). © Elsevier Scientific Publishers.)

examining the recall/P300 relationship in conditions in which elaborative strategies were not likely to be used. We predicted that, in these cases, the relationship between P300 amplitude and recall would emerge more clearly.

Incidental Free Recall

In this experiment, Fabiani, Karis and Donchin (1986) employed an incidental memory paradigm to reduce the use of rehearsal strategies. Several oddball series were presented in sequence to each of 41 subjects. The probability of the rare events in each oddball task was 0.20, and the stimulus that was rare was counterbalanced across subjects. In each oddball task the subject was presented with a Bernoulli series of events and instructed to count (or to respond to) one of the events. After three oddball tasks, in which the series were composed of tones, and of the letters H and S, subjects were presented with an oddball series created by randomly mixing male and female names, and were instructed to count the names of one gender. The subjects had no reason to expect that they would be asked to recall these names. Therefore, Fabiani *et al.* assumed that they would *not* develop, and use, complex associative rehearsal strategies to facilitate recall. In this situation, the relationship between P300 and recall could be evaluated in the absence of elaborative processes occurring after P300. Our main prediction was that names that were subsequently recalled would have initially elicited larger P300s than names that were not recalled. This prediction was confirmed: Figures 5.10(a) and (b) show rare and frequent names sorted on the basis of subsequent recall for subjects who were instructed to count the rare names and for those instructed to count the frequent names. It can be seen that recalled names, regardless of probability or task relevance, elicit a larger positivity than unrecalled names. In addition, individual differences among subjects were not apparent in this case, and no evidence of the presence of a frontal-positive slow wave was found.

The Von Restorff Effect in Children

Cimbalo, Nowak, and Sodestrom (1981) found that children show very pronounced von Restorff effects. We hypothesized that these enhanced effects may be due, at least in part, to differences in rehearsal strategies. It is plausible that young children may only be able to use rote rehearsal strategies, and that, therefore, they would show clear von Restorff effects and reduced individual differences in the relationship between P300 amplitude and subsequent recall. Therefore, Fabiani *et al.* (in press) replicated the Karis, Fabiani and Donchin (1984) study with 5th-grade children as subjects.

Ten children participated in the study. They were presented with 40 lists of ten words each. Thirty of the lists contained one isolated item, in any position from 4 through 7 (isolated lists). The isolation was achieved by writing the word

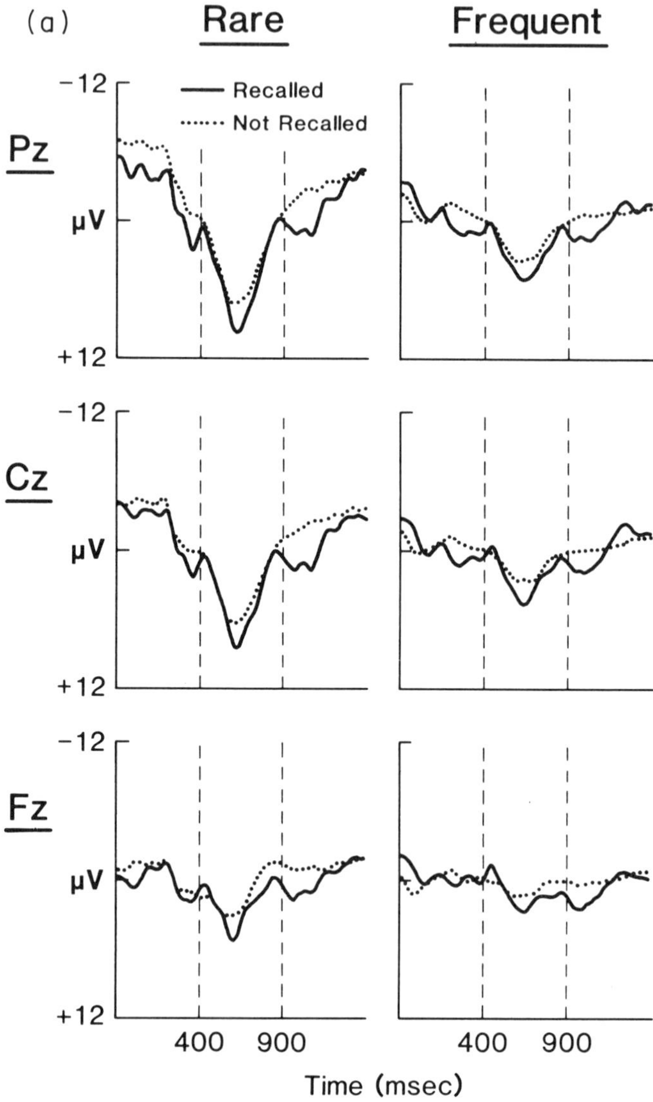

Figure 5.10. Grand average waveforms for rare and frequent names sorted on the basis of subsequent recall (a) for subjects who were instructed to count the rare names, and (b) for those instructed to count the frequent names. Solid lines indicate recalled names, dotted lines unrecalled names. (Reprinted with permission from Fabiani, Karis and Donchin (1986). © Society for Psychophysiological Research.)

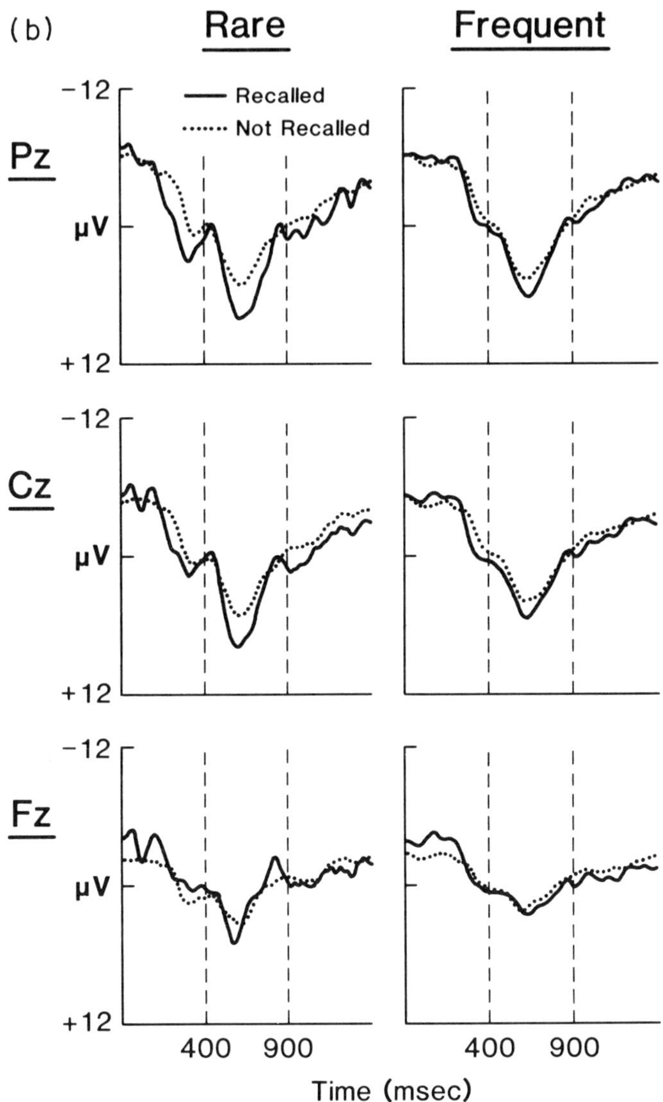

Figure 5.10b.

in a larger-size font. The remaining ten lists did not contain any isolated item (control lists). No word was ever repeated. At the end of each list the subjects were asked to write down all the words they could remember from that list, in any order in which words came to their minds (free recall). At the end of the session, subjects were debriefed about the strategies they used to memorize the words.

All the subjects reported having used rote strategies, and recalled the isolated words better than the non-isolated words (von Restorff effect). The P300s elicited by the isolated words were significantly larger than the P300 elicited by the other words. The amplitude of the P300 at stimulus presentation was larger for words subsequently recalled than for words not recalled. This difference was particularly evident for the isolated words: the grand-average waveform for these words sorted on the basis of their subsequent recall is shown in Figure 5.11.

These data support the claim that children show less pronounced individual differences than adults in their use of rehearsal strategies. As they use mainly rote strategies, the amplitude of P300 at encoding should predict recall for most subjects. This is in fact the case, as for all the subjects but one the amplitude of P300 was larger for isolated words subsequently recalled than for those not recalled.

OTHER STUDIES ON MEMORY AND ERPs

The research reviewed so far supports the claim that the larger the P300 amplitude elicited by a word at encoding, the more likely is the word to be retrieved, at least in those cases in which elaborative strategies do not play an important role. One of the thrusts of this research is that, in order to study the relationship between an ERP component and the processes that lead to improved recall or recognition, it is useful to examine the phenomena under conditions that are likely to maximize the share of the variance related to the psychophysiological relationship being studied. The variance in recall and in recognition is controlled by a vast number of different variables. It is reasonable to assume that only a portion of that variance is controlled by the processes manifested by the P300. Thus, experiments in which the P300/memory relationship is studied within a very general context are not likely to have the necessary sensitivity. The use of the von Restorff paradigm increased the power of the studies reported above because we examined the P300/recall relationship *within* isolates, thus increasing the share of the variance likely to be related to the variance in P300.

In this section, we review research conducted in other laboratories that is also consistent with the claim that the larger the positivity elicited by a word, the more likely is the word to be retrieved. However, in these studies memory paradigms have been utilized that do not capitalize on the use of stimuli for which the P300 is expected to be enhanced; that is, they utilize paradigms in which neither the distinctiveness nor the probability of occurrence of the stimuli to be memorized are manipulated. This research can nevertheless be interpreted in the same framework used for the research described so far, because the memory effect (i.e. the relationship between P300 amplitude and subsequent recall) is not limited to isolated or rare items. This effect

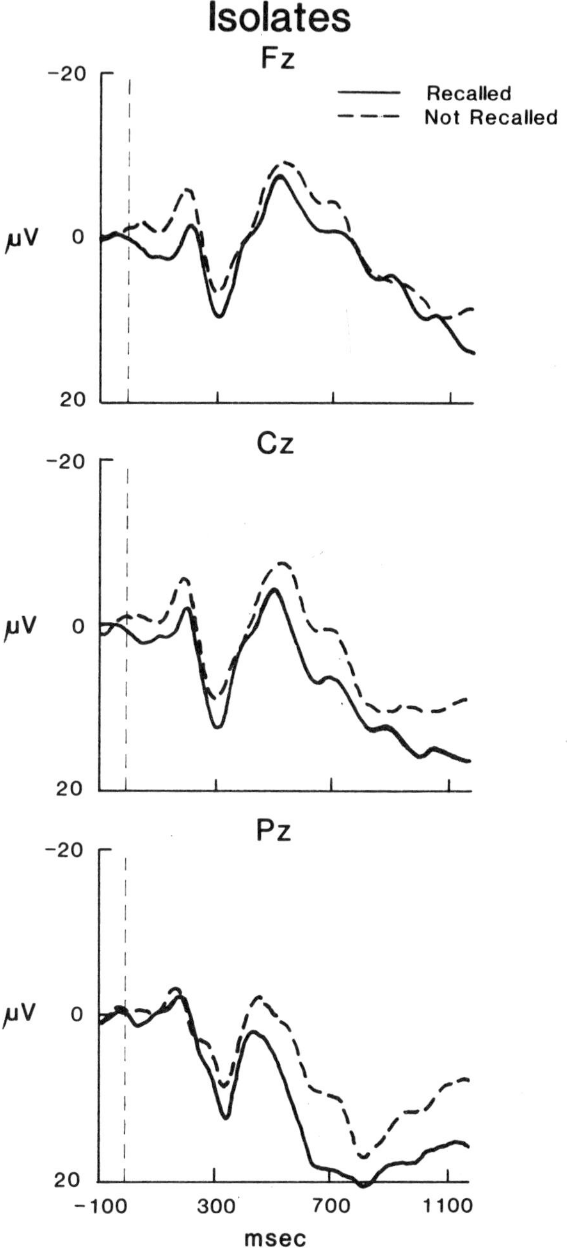

Figure 5.11. Grand average waveform at Fz, Cz, and Pz for isolated words sorted on the basis of their subsequent recall. Solid lines indicated recalled words, dashed lines unrecalled words. (Reprinted with permission from Fabiani *et al.* (1990). © Oxford University Press.)

is also present for the non-isolates and for the frequent items in the oddball experiment, presumably because some of these stimuli can possess a certain measure of 'subjective' distinctiveness, even if the experimenter is not explicitly manipulating it.

A seminal study was conducted by Sanquist *et al.* (1980) who found that larger-amplitude P300s (or late-positive components) were elicited, in a same–different judgment task, by stimuli that were correctly recognized in a subsequent recognition test.

Johnson, Pfefferbaum and Kopell (1985) recorded ERPs in a study-test memory paradigm. They reported that the P300 associated with subsequently recognized words was slightly, but not significantly, larger than that elicited by non-recognized words. They also reported a relationship between the latency of P300 and recognition.

Paller, Kutas and Mayes (1987) recorded ERPs in an incidental memory paradigm in which the subjects were asked to make either a semantic or a non-semantic decision, and were subsequently, and unexpectedly, tested for their recognition or recall of the stimuli. They found that ERPs elicited during the decision task were predictive of subsequent memory performance, because a positive component (late-positive complex) was larger for words subsequently recalled or recognized than to words not recalled or recognized. Similarly, Paller, McCarthy and Wood (1988) recorded ERPs in two semantic judgment tasks, which were followed by a free recall and by a recognition test. ERPs to words later remembered were more positive than those to words later not remembered, even though the memory effect was smaller for recognition than for recall. Neville *et al.* (1986) recorded ERPs to words that were either congruous or incongruous with a preceding sentence in a task in which subjects were asked to judge whether or not the word was congruent with the sentence. They found that the amplitude of a late-positive component (P650) predicted subsequent recognition.

In summary, all these studies indicated that a larger positivity is elicited by words that are recalled or recognized in a subsequent test.

CONCLUSIONS AND OUTLOOK FOR THE FUTURE

The experiments described in the previous section support the hypothesis that the P300 can have an important role in illuminating some of the cognitive processes that accompany stimulus encoding, that are usually opaque to traditional techniques. While the first group of studies conducted in our laboratory has focused on the interaction between distinctiveness and rehearsal strategies in determining the ERP/memory relationship, the other studies have shown that such a relationship is widespread over a variety of different memory paradigms.

The experiments described also suggest that the P300 component of the ERP is invoked when novel and relevant events are presented, and a revision of the subject's internal model of the environment is required. Such a change in the mental representation will help the subsequent recall of the eliciting event when the subjects are precluded from rehearsing or when they use rote rehearsal strategies. When revision of the mental model is not required, P300 is not elicited even by rare and task-relevant events. On the other hand, events belonging to the frequent stimulus category, sometimes do elicit P300s. This may occur when the inter-stimulus interval is long (Heffley, 1981; Fitzgerald and Picton, 1981), and as an effect of the local sequence of stimuli (Squires *et al.*, 1976). In the case of word stimuli, a large P300 may be elicited by non-isolated, but otherwise subjectively distinctive, stimuli. For example, in the case of the incidental memory study, the subject's own name would probably elicit a large P300 even if it is a member of the frequent category. Thus, a relationship between the amplitude of P300 and recall can be observed for non-isolates, or frequent words, to the extent that the recall variance and the P300 variance are related to the same factors.

In this context, P300 can be used to determine whether stimuli that are presumed to be distinctive, are indeed so for a particular subject. Therefore, we suggest that P300 may be used as a measure of the distinctiveness of an event which is independent of its memorability. Note, however, that there could be cases in which distinctive stimuli do not elicit a P300. For example, von Restorff (1933) reported some data concerning the elicitation of a *post hoc* von Restorff effect. In this experiment, subjects were presented with two series of stimuli. The first series was composed of stimuli that were all different from each other. The second series was composed of stimuli belonging to the same class (e.g. all numbers), with the exception of the isolate. The isolated item was presented very early in the series (position 2 or 3). Thus, at the moment the distinctive stimulus was presented to the subject, there was really no reason for the subject to consider it as such, as the sequence became homogeneous only some time subsequent to the presentation of the distinctive stimulus. Thus, to the extent that these data could be replicated, it is possible to hypothesize that a large P300 would not have been elicited by the distinctive stimulus, and that the amplitude of this P300 would not be related to the subsequent recall of the stimulus. However, the subsequent recall of the distinctive stimulus could instead be predicted by the amplitude of the P300 elicited when the subject realizes that the stimulus sequence has become homogeneous (for similar examples, see Johnson and Donchin, 1982).

From these, and related data, we may draw the following conclusions:

(1) It would appear that the ERP does provide a method for monitoring encoding events and that it is possible to illuminate issues in the theory of memory using this approach.

(2) If P300 is indeed related to distinctiveness, then the larger the P300 the better the recall.
(3) It is important to test such hypotheses *within* conditions rather than between conditions. If we conduct a between-conditions study, the differences in recall may be attributed to any of a host of variables that differ between the conditions. We should strive to set up conditions so that as much of the variance in recall can be related to factors that control P300 amplitude.

There are, however, several caveats that need to be considered:

(1) We do not know at this time if the relation between P300 amplitude and memory is correlational or causative.
(2) There are difficult measurement problems in ERPs and it is critical to be sure that the right component is being measured.
(3) We have data that support the use of P300 only if we accept a definition of distinctive feature based on its *low probability*. However, parametric studies are needed that show that if distinctiveness is manipulated (either by increasing the *number* of distinctive features of an item, or by increasing the *intensity* of the distinctive feature on one dimension, you obtain the following: (a) a larger P300, (b) a larger von Restorff effect, and (c) a stronger relationship between P300 and recall (provided that rehearsal strategies are kept constant).
(4) The Orienting Reflex literature appears to bear striking similarities to the issues discussed in this chapter (cf. Siddle and Packer, this volume; Graham and Hackley, this volume). Conditions that facilitate P300 elicitation are also those which are associated with the elicitation of the OR. These issues are reviewed next in a separate commentary.

ACKNOWLEDGMENTS

Preparation of this chapter was facilitated by NINCDS grant #NS24986.

Orienting, P300 and Memory: Commentary

Emanuel Donchin, Monica Fabiani, Janet S. Packer and David A.T. Siddle

In the first division of this chapter, Siddle and Packer reviewed studies in which various autonomic nervous system (ANS) measures were recorded in the context of memory studies. Donchin and Fabiani, in the second part, described studies in which components of the human event-related brain potential (ERP), and in particular P300, were recorded in similar contexts.

The studies reviewed in both divisions use variations of the classic episodic memory paradigm, first described by Ebbinghaus (1885). The general structure of this paradigm is the following. First, there is a study period in which events occur and are encoded by the subject. Psychophysiological measurements are made during and immediately after each event. After an interval, that can vary in duration and in which rehearsal may or may not be allowed, a test period follows, in which memory for the events is tested. At this stage, we obtain a measure or set of measures of memory performance associated with each event.

Both parts of the chapter emphasize the notion that psychophysiological measures provide information about the way in which events are encoded. In particular, the primary theoretical assertion in both is that there are circumstances in which P300 or electrodermal orienting recorded during encoding predict the subsequent memory performance (i.e. the larger the psychophysiological index, the higher the probability that the event will be retrieved in a subsequent memory test).

The two parts of the chapter were written independently. Therefore, it is particularly interesting to note the extent to which they have expressed broadly similar ideas. There are differences, to be sure, but in general we feel that the convergence in ideas is greater than the divergence.

In view of this commonality, it is not surprising that both accounts emphasize the importance of an event characteristic referred to as 'distinctiveness' or 'salience' and employ the depth-of-processing approach as a theoretical framework within which to locate the arguments. That is, the two reviews invoke similar cognitive models to account for memory phenomena, and postulate parallel views of psychophysiological measures as indices of encoding processes within these memory models. However, the two do differ in their interpretation

---

Handbook of Cognitive Psychophysiology: Central and Autonomic Nervous System Approaches.
Edited by J. R. Jennings and M. G. H. Coles.

of the theoretical significance of the psychophysiological measures within this common framework.

For Siddle and Packer the psychophysiological measures are integrated by the concept of the orienting reflex (OR). That is, a theoretical entity called the OR is supposed to be triggered by the events, or by at least some of the events. This entity is manifested by a number of ANS measures. The pattern of these measures serves as an index of the magnitude of the OR and the entire enterprise is then presented as a study of the relationship between the OR and memory.

The theoretical underpinning of the ERP results is somewhat different. The studies described in Donchin and Fabiani's review were driven to a large extent by an attempt to evaluate a theory accounting for the functional significance of the P300 component. Donchin (1981) and Donchin and Coles (1988a,b) have suggested that the P300 is the manifestation of a process that is invoked when a need to update the model of the environment has been recognized by the system. The unifying concept of 'context updating' has been invoked to account for many of the available data on the P300. This theoretical structure, however, is used to account for the psychophysiological data, not for memory phenomena. The context updating model led to the studies reviewed by Donchin and Fabiani because the model predicted that a relationship exists between the amplitude of P300 and the subsequent recall of stimuli (see Donchin, 1981). However, the concept of context updating is not critical for the memory data presented by Donchin and Fabiani. One can also begin with the empirical observation that distinctive items elicit a P300 and that the amplitude of the P300 can be used as an index of distinctiveness. Given that distinctiveness plays an important role in cognitive models of memory, Donchin and Fabiani can predict a relationship between the psychophysiological measures of the event at encoding and the memory for the event, on the basis of theories of distinctiveness developed within the context of cognitive psychology.

Given the formal similarity between the two reviews it is natural to examine the extent to which they are actually concerned with the *same phenomenon*. By that we mean that the same mechanism(s) underlie the relationship between the psychophysiological response to the event and the memory for the event, whether the psychophysiological response recorded is one of the ANS measures, which define the OR, or one of the ERP measures.

This issue begs an important question about the relationship between autonomic orienting and P300. This question has been with us for some time (e.g. Donchin *et al.*, 1984), and has embedded within it a number of other issues. For example, does autonomic orienting reflect a 'call for processing' or processing itself? Although Siddle and Packer have argued that this question cannot at present be answered, Graham and Hackley's model (Chapter 3) proposes, as does Öhman's (1979) theorizing, that autonomic components of the OR reflect a call for processing following the detection of deviance beyond some threshold value. Clearly, this model implies that orienting is an index of *early* encoding processes (such as those reflected by the mismatch negativity; see Näätänen and Gaillard, 1983). On the other hand, theories of the significance of P300 such as Donchin's (1981) 'context updating', Desmedt's (1980, 1981) 'post-decision closure', Grossberg's (1984) 'short-term memory resetting', and Verleger's (1988a,b) 'context closure' seem to imply that P300 occurs *after* some (if not all) of the encoding processing of the stimulus has been completed. A second question concerns the distinction between 'initial' and 'change' ORs. That is, does the OR elicited by the first presentation of a novel stimulus reflect the same process or processes as reflected by the OR elicited by stimulus change following a repetitive stimulus series (e.g. Kenemans *et al.*, 1989). This issue is obviously important in interpreting the results of studies of the OR and release from proactive inhibition in the Brown–Peterson paradigm and of any studies which showed a relationship between orienting and the isolation effect in the von Restorff paradigm.

Thus, the communality between the OR and P300 findings in relation to memory may reflect that the call for processing (reflected by autonomic orienting) for the further encoding of the distinctive features (reflected by P300). A consequence of this view is that measures of the OR and P300 are quite likely to be positively correlated in a number of cases, because if processing of the distinctive features is 'called for' (OR) it is usually executed (P300). However, it follows that it should also be possible to dissociate P300 and OR under appropriate experimental situations.

A concept that may lead to useful dissociations between OR and P300 in the context of memory paradigms is the distinction reported by Graham and Hackley (in Chapter 3) between passive and active attention. As they have noted, autonomic orienting has been most closely identified with passive attention. P300, on the other hand, is only elicited by task-relevant stimuli when they are actively attended (Duncan-Johnson and Donchin, 1977; Hillyard *et al.*, 1973). Unfortunately, the majority of work on orienting and memory and on P300 and memory has involved procedures in which the emphasis was on active attention to input. Clearly, further research on the OR, ERPs, and memory with procedures emphasizing passive attention would be useful. This research should involve stimuli that are isolated on a dimension that is irrelevant to the subject's task (see Fabiani, Buckley and Donchin, 1989, for an implementation of this research strategy in a study on ERPs and memory).

Another dissociation between measures of the OR and P300 may be found in the observation that there are dramatic effects of rehearsal strategies on the relationship between P300 and memory. This suggests that this relationship depends not only on the way the engrams are formed but on the interaction between retrieval methods and the encoding processes. Comparable work has not been carried out with respect to orienting and memory.

A final important issue concerns the extent to which one can conclude that the process reflected by P300 and by autonomic orienting are *causally* related to recall. One research strategy to address this issue might be to treat the psychophysiological measures as independent, rather than dependent, variables. Another, more general, strategy involves the generation and refinement of more detailed models of the significance of the processes manifested by the psychophysiological variables.

REFERENCES

Berlyne, D.E. (1960). *Conflict, Arousal and Curiosity*. New York: McGraw Hill.

Bower, G.H. (1967). Comments on Walker's paper. In D.P. Kimble (ed.), *The Organization of Recall*. New York: Wiley, pp. 210–214.

Brown, J. (1958). Some tests of the decay theory of immediate memory. *Quarterly Journal of Psychology*, **10**, 12–21.

Butter, M.J. (1970). Differential recall of paired-associates as a function of arousal and concreteness-imagery levels. *Journal of Experimental Psychology*, **84**, 252–256.

Cacioppo, J.T. and Tassinary, L.G. (1990). Inferring psychological significance from physiological signals. *American Psychologist*, **45**, 16–28.

Cermak, L.S. (1970). Decay of interference as a function of the intertrial interval in short-term memory. *Journal of Experimental Psychology*, **84**, 499–501.

Churchill, M., Remington, B. and Siddle, D.A.T. (1987). The effects of context on long-term habituation of the orienting response in humans. *Quarterly Journal of Experimental Psychology*, **39B**, 315–338.

Cimbalo, R.S., Nowak, B.I. and Soderstrom, J.A. (1981). The isolation effect in children's short term memory. *Journal of General Psychology*, **105**, 215–223.

Coles, M.G.H., Gratton, G., Bashore, T.R., Eriksen, C.W. and Donchin, E. (1985). A psychophysiological investigation of the continuous flow model of human information processing. *Journal of Experimental Psychology: Human Perception and Performance*, **11**, 529–553.

Coles, M.G.H., Gratton, G. and Donchin, E. (1988). Detecting early communication: using measures of movement-related potentials to illuminate human information processing. *Biological Psychology*, **2**, 69–89.

Coles, M.G.H., Gratton, G. and Fabiani, M. (in press). Event-related potentials. In J.T. Cacioppo, L.G. Tassinary and R.E. Petty (eds), *Tutorials in Psychophysiology: Physical, Social, and Inferential Elements*. Cambridge, MA: Cambridge University Press.

Cook, M.R. (1974). Psychophysiology of peripheral vascular changes. In P.A. Obrist, A.H. Black, J. Brener and L.V. DiCara (eds), *Cardiovascular Psychophysiology: Current Issues in Response Mechanisms, Biofeedback, and Methodology*. Chicago: Aldine, pp. 60–85.

Corteen, R.S. (1969). Skin conductance changes and word recall. *British Journal of Psychology*, **60**, 81–84.

Corteen, R.S. and Dunn, D. (1974). Shock-associated words in a non-attended message: a test for momentary awareness. *Journal of Experimental Psychology*, **102**, 1143–1144.

Corteen, R.S. and Wood, B. (1972). Autonomic responses to shock-associated words in an unattended channel. *Journal of Experimental Psychology*, **94**, 308–313.

Craik, F.I.M. (1970). The fate of primary memory items in free recall. *Journal of Verbal Learning and Verbal Behavior*, **9**, 143–148.

Craik, F.I.M. (1973). A 'Levels of Analysis' view of memory. In P. Pliner, L. Krames and T.M. Alloway (eds), *Communication and Affect: Language and Thought*. London: Academic Press, pp. 45–65.

Craik, F.I.M. and Blankstein, K.R. (1975). Psychophysiology and human memory. In P.H. Venables and I. Martin (eds), *Research in Psychophysiology*. Chichester: Wiley, pp. 388–417.

Craik, F.I.M. and Lockhart, R.S. (1972). Levels of processing: a framework for memory research. *Journal of Verbal Learning and Verbal Behavior*, **11**, 671–684.

Cremins, J.J. and Turvey, M.T. (1978). Release from short-term proactive interference with change in item duration. *Bulletin of Psychonomic Society*, **12**, 25–28.

Dawson, M.E., Filion, D.L. and Schell, A.M. (1989). Is elicitation of the orienting response associated with allocation of processing resources? *Psychophysiology*, **26**, 560–572.

Dawson, M.E. and Schell, A.M. (1982). Electrodermal responses to attended and nonattended significant stimuli during dichotic listening. *Journal of Experimental Psychology: Human Perception and Performance*, **8**, 315–324.

Dawson, M.E., Schell, A.M., Beers, J.R. and Kelly, A. (1982). Allocation of cognitive processing capacity during human autonomic classical conditioning. *Journal of Experimental Psychology: General*, **111**, 273–295.

Desmedt, J.E. (1980). P300 in serial tasks: an essential post-decision closure mechanism. In H.H. Kornhuber and L. Deecke (eds), *Progress in Brain Research*, vol. 54: *Motivation, Motor, and Sensory Processes of the Brain*. Amsterdam, Netherlands: Elsevier/North-Holland, pp. 682–686.

Desmedt, J.E. (1981). Scalp-recorded cerebral event-related potentials in man as point of entry into the analysis of cognitive processes. In F.O. Schmitt, F.G. Worden, G. Adelman and S.D. Dennis (eds), *The organization of Cerebral Cortex*. Cambridge, MA: MIT Press, pp. 441–473.

Donchin, E. (1979). Event-related brain potentials: a tool in the study of human information processing. In H. Begleiter (ed.), *Evoked Potentials and Behavior*. New York: Plenum Press, pp. 13–75.

Donchin, E. (1981). Surprise!. . .Surprise? *Psychophysiology*, **18**, 493–513.

Donchin, E. and Coles, M.G.H. (1988a). Is the P300 component a manifestation of context updating? *Behavioral and Brain Sciences*, **11**, 355–372.

Donchin, E. and Coles, M.G.H. (1988b). On the conceptual foundations of cognitive psychophysiology: a reply to comments. *Behavioral and Brain Sciences*, **11**, 406–417.

Donchin, E. and Fabiani, M. (in press). The use of event-related brain potentials in the study of memory: is P300 a measure of event distinctiveness? In J.R. Jennings and M.G.H. Coles (eds), *Handbook of Cognitive Psychophysiology: Central and Autonomic Nervous System Approaches*. Chichester, UK: Wiley.

Donchin, E., Fabiani, M., Siddle, D.T. and Packer, J.S. (this volume). Integration commentary.

Donchin, E., Gratton, G., Dupree, D. and Coles, M.G.H. (1988). After a rash action: latency and amplitude of the P300 following fast guesses. In G.C. Galbraith, M.L. Klietzman and E. Donchin (eds), *Neurophysiology and Psychophysiology: Experimental and Clinical Applications*. Hillsdale, NJ: Erlbaum, pp. 173–188.

Donchin, E., Heffley, E., Hillyard, S.A., Loveless, N., Maltzman, I., Öhman, A., Rosler, F., Ruchkin, D. and Siddle, D. (1984). Cognition and event-related potentials: II. In R. Karrer, J. Cohen and P. Tueting (eds), *Annals of the New York Academy of Sciences*, vol. 425: *Brain and Information: Event-Related Potentials*. New York: NY Academy of Science, pp. 39–57.

Donchin, E., Kramer, A.F. and Wickens, C. (1986). Applications of event-related brain potentials to problems in engineering psychology. In M.G.H. Coles, E. Donchin and S.W. Porges (eds), *Psychophysiology: Systems, Processes, and Applications*. New York: Guilford Press, pp. 702–718.

Donchin, E., Ritter, W. and McCallum, C. (1978). Cognitive psychophysiology: the endogenous components of the ERP. In E. Callaway, P. Tueting and S. Koslow (eds), *Brain Event-Related Potentials in Man*. New York: Academic Press, pp. 349–441.

Duncan-Johnson, C.C. and Donchin, E. (1977). On quantifying surprise: the variation of event-related potentials with subjective probability. *Psychophysiology*, **14**, 456–467.

Duncan-Johnson, C.C. and Donchin, E. (1982). The P300 component of the event-related brain potential as an index of information processing. *Biological Psychology*, **14**, 1–52.

Ebbinghaus, H. (1885). *Memory: A Contribution to Experimental Psychology*. New York: Columbia University Press.

Edwards, D.C. (1975). Stimulus intensity reduction following habituation. *Psychophysiology*, **12**, 12–14.

Engle, R. (1975). Pupillary measurement and release from proactive inhibition. *Perceptual and Motor Skills*, **41**, 835–842.

Eysenck, M.J. (1978). Levels of processing: a critique. *British Journal of Psychology*, **69**, 157–169.

Eysenck, M.W. (1979). Depth, elaboration, and distinctiveness. In L.S. Cermak and F.I.M. Craik (eds), *Levels of Processing in Human Memory*. Hillsdale, NJ: Lawrence Erlbaum, pp. 89–118.

Fabiani, M., Buckley, J. and Donchin, E. (1989). Are odd things all the same? Semantic distinctiveness, memory, and event-related potentials. *Psychophysiology*, **26**, S22.

Fabiani, M., Gratton, G., Chiarenza, G.A. and Donchin, E. (1990). A psychophysiological investigation of the von Restorff paradigm in children. *Journal of Psychophysiology*, **4**, 15–24.

Fabiani, M., Gratton, G., Karis, D. and Donchin, E. (1987). The definition, identification, and reliability of measurement of the P300 component of the event-related brain potential. In P.K. Ackles, J.R. Jennings and M.G.H. Coles (eds), *Advances in Psychophysiology*. Greenwich, CT: JAI Press, pp. 1–78.

Fabiani, M., Karis, D. and Donchin, E. (1986). P300 and recall in an incidental memory paradigm. *Psychophysiology*, **23**, 298–308.

Fabiani, M., Karis, D. and Donchin, E. (1990). Effects of strategy manipulation in a von Restorff paradigm. *Electroencephalography and Clinical Neurophysiology*, **75**, 22–35.

Fitzgerald, P.G. and Picton, T.W. (1981). Temporal and sequential probability in evoked potential studies. *Canadian Journal of Psychology*, **35**, 188–200.

Fredrikson, M. and Öhman, A. (1979). Heart-rate and electrodermal orienting responses to visual stimuli differing in complexity. *Scandinavian Journal of Psychology*, **20**, 37–41.

Furedy, J.J. and Ginsberg, S. (1975). On the role of orienting reaction recovery in short-interval classical autonomic conditioning. *Biological Psychology*, **5**, 211–219.

Gatchel, R.J. and Lang, P.J. (1974). Accuracy of psychophysical judgments and physiological response amplitude. *Journal of Experimental Psychology*, **98**, 175–183.

Graham, F.K. (1979). Distinguishing among orienting, defense, and startle reflexes. In H.D. Kimmel, E.H. van Olst and J.F. Orlebeke (eds), *The Orienting Reflex in Humans*. Hillsdale, NJ: Erlbaum, pp. 137–167.

Graham, F.K. and Hackley, S.A. (1990). Passive and active attention to input. In J.R. Jennings and M.G.H. Coles (eds), *Psychophysiology of Human Information Processing: An Integration of Central and Autonomic Nervous System Approaches*. Chichester: Wiley.

Graham, F. and Hackley, S. (in press). Active and passive attention to input. In J.R.

Jennings and M.G.H. Coles (eds), *Handbook of Cognitive Psychophysiology: Central and Autonomic Nervous System Approaches*. Chichester: Wiley.

Gratton, G., Bosco, C.M., Kramer, A.F., Wickens, C.D., Coles, M.G.H. and Donchin, E. (in press). Event-related brain potentials as indices of information extraction and response priming. *Electroencephalography and Clinical Neurophysiology*.

Gratton, G., Coles, M.G.H., Sirevaag, E.J., Erikson, C.W. and Donchin, E. (1988). Pre- and post-stimulus activation of response channels: a psychophysiological analysis. *Journal of Experimental Psychology: Human Perception and Performance*, **14**, 331–334.

Grossberg, S. (1984). Some psychophysiological and pharmacological correlates of a developmental, cognitive, and motivational theory. In R. Karrer, J. Cohen and P. Tueting (eds), *Brain and Information: Event Related Potentials*. New York: NY Academy of Science, pp. 58–151.

Grush, J.E., Coles, M.G.H., Ferguson, A.Y. and McGee, G.J. (1973). Habituation, memory, and the evaluative dimension of meaning. *Journal of Research in Personality*, **7**, 189–195.

Heffley, E.F. (1981). Event-related brain potentials in visual monitoring tasks: selective attention, display format, and event frequency. Paper presented at the Eastern Psychological Association annual meeting, New York, April.

Hillyard, S.A., Hink, R.F., Schwent, V.L. and Picton, T.W. (1973). Electrical signs of selective attention in the human brain. *Science*, **182**, 177–180.

Hillyard, S.A. and Kutas, M. (1983). Electrophysiology of cognitive processing. In M.R. Rosenzweig and L.W. Porter (eds), *Annual Review of Psychology*. Palo Alto, CA: Annual Reviews Inc., pp. 33–61.

Jacoby, L.L. (1975). Physical features vs meaning: a difference in decay. *Memory and Cognition*, **3**, 247–251.

Jacoby, L.L. and Craik, F.I.M. (1979). Effects of elaboration of processing at encoding and retrieval: trace distinctiveness and recovery of initial context. In L.S. Cermak and F.I.M. Craik (eds), *Levels of Processing in Human Memory*. Hillsdale, NJ: Lawrence Erlbaum, pp. 1–21.

Jennings, J.R. (1986). Memory, thought, and bodily response. In M.G.H. Coles, E. Donchin and S.W. Porges (eds), *Psychophysiology—Systems, Processes and Applications*. Amsterdam: Elsevier, pp. 290–308.

Jennings, J.R., Lawrence, B.E. and Kasper, P. (1978). Changes in alertness and processing capacity in a serial learning task. *Memory and Cognition*, **6**, 43–53.

Johnson, R. (1986). A triarchic model of P300 amplitude. *Psychophysiology*, **23**, 367–384.

Johnson, R. (1988). The amplitude of the P300 component of the event-related potential: review and synthesis. In P.K. Ackles, J.R. Jennings and M.G.H. Coles. (eds), *Advances in Psychophysiology*, vol. III. Greenwich, CT: JAI Press, pp. 69–138.

Johnson, R. and Donchin, E. (1978). On how P300 amplitude varies with the utility of the eliciting stimuli. *Electroencephalography and clinical Neurophysiology*, **44**, 424–437.

Johnson, R. and Donchin, E. (1980). P300 and stimulus categorization: two plus one is not so different from one plus one. *Psychophysiology*, **17**, 167–178.

Johnson, R. and Donchin, E. (1982). Sequential expectancies and decision making in a changing evnironment: an electrophysiological approach. *Psychophysiology*, **19**, 183–200.

Johnson, R., Pfefferbaum, A. and Kopell, B.S. (1985). P300 and long-term memory: latency predicts recognition time. *Psychophysiology*, **22**, 498–507.

Kahneman, D. (1973). *Attention and Effort*. Englewood Cliffs, NJ: Prentice-Hall.

Kahneman, D. and Beatty, J. (1966). Pupil diameter and load on memory. *Science*, **154**, 1583–1585.

Kahneman, D.M., Tursky, B., Shapiro, D. and Crider, A. (1969). Pupillary, heart rate and skin resistance changes during a mental task. *Journal of Experimental Psychology*, **79**, 164–167.

Kahneman, D. and Wright, P. (1967). Changes of pupil size and rehearsal strategies in a short-term memory task. *Quarterly Journal of Experimental Psychology*, **23**, 187–196.

Kaplan, S. and Kaplan, R. (1968). Arousal and memory: a comment. *Psychonomic Science*, **10**, 291–292.

Kaplan, R. and Kaplan, S. (1969). The arousal–retention interval interaction revisited: the effects of some procedural changes. *Psychonomic Science*, **15**, 84–85.

Kaplan, S. and Kaplan, R. (1970). The interaction of arousal and retention interval: within-subject versus normative GSR. *Psychonomic Science*, **19**, 115–117.

Kaplan, S., Kaplan, R. and Sampson, J.R. (1968). Encoding and arousal factors in free recall of verbal and visual material. *Psychonomic Science*, **12**, 73–74.

Karis, D., Fabiani, M. and Donchin, E. (1984). 'P300' and memory: individual differences in the von Restorff effect. *Cognitive Psychology*, **16**, 177–216.

Kenemans, J.L., Verbaten, M.N., Roelofs, J-W., and Slangen, J.L. (1989). "Initial-" and "change-orienting reactions": An analysis based on visual single-trial event-related potentials. *Biological Psychology*, **28**, 199–226.

Keppel, G. and Underwood, B.J. (1962). Proactive inhibition in short-term retention of single items. *Journal of Verbal Learning and Verbal Behavior*, **1**, 153–161.

Kleinsmith, L.J. and Kaplan, S. (1963). Paired-associate learning as a function of arousal and interpolated activity. *Journal of Experimental Psychology*, **65**, 190–193.

Kleinsmith, L.J. and Kaplan, S. (1964). Interaction of arousal and recall interval in nonsense syllable paired-associate learning. *Journal of Experimental Psychology*, **67**, 124–126.

Kutas, M. (1989). Review of event-related potential studies of memory. In M.S. Gazzaniga (ed.), *Perspectives in Memory Research*. Cambridge, MA: MIT Press, pp. 181–218.

Kutas, M., McCarthy, G. and Donchin, E. (1977). Augmenting mental chronometry: the P300 as a measure of stimulus evaluation time. *Science*, **197**, 792–795.

Lacey, J.I. (1967). Somatic response patterning and stress: some revisions of activation theory. In M.H. Appley and R. Trumbull (eds), *Psychological Stress*. New York: Appleton–Century–Crofts, pp. 14–37.

Lockhart, R.S., Craik, F.I.M. and Jacoby, L. (1976). Depth of processing, recognition and recall. In J. Brown (ed.), *Recognition and Recall*. Chichester: Wiley, pp. 75–102.

Loess, H. and Waugh, N.C. (1967). Short-term memory and intertrial interval. *Journal of Verbal Learning and Verbal Behavior*, **6**, 455–460.

Magliero, A., Bashore, T.R., Coles, M.G.H. and Donchin, E. (1984). On the dependence of P300 latency on stimulus evaluation processes. *Psychophysiology*, **21**, 171–186.

Magliero, A., Gatchel, R.J. and Gorthey, E.M. (1981). The Brown–Peterson paradigm: relationships between short-term recall, final free recall, and electrodermal responding. *Psychophysiology*, **18**, 170 (abstract).

Magliero, A., Gatchel, R.J. and Lojewski, D. (1981). Skin conductance responses to stimulus 'energy' decreases following habituation. *Psychophysiology*, **18**, 549–558.

Maltzman, I., Kantor, W. and Langdon, B. (1966). Immediate and delayed retention, arousal and defensive reflexes. *Psychonomic Science*, **6**, 445–446.

Marlin, N.A. and Miller, R.R. (1981). Associations to contextual stimuli as a determinant of long-term habituation. *Journal of Experimental Psychology: Animal Behavior Processes*, **7**, 313–333.

McCarthy, G. and Donchin, E. (1981). A metric for thought: a comparison of P300 latency and reaction time. *Science*, **211**, 77–80.

McLean, P.D. (1969). Induced arousal and time of recall as determinants of paired-associate recall. *British Journal of Psychology*, **60**, 57–62.

Moscovitch, M. and Winocur, G. (1983). Contextual cues and release from proactive inhibition in young and old people. *Canadian Journal of Psychology*, **37**, 331–344.
Munson, R., Ruchkin, D.S., Ritter, W., Sutton, S. and Squires, N.K. (1984). The relation of P3b to prior events and future behavior. *Biological Psychology*, **19**, 1–29.
Murdock, B.B. (1960). The distinctiveness of stimuli. *Psychological Review*, **67**, 16–31.
Näätänen, R. and Gaillard, A.W.K. (1983). The orienting reflex and the N2 deflection of the event-related potential (ERP). In A.W.K. Gaillard and W. Ritter (eds), *Tutorials in ERP Research: Endogenous Components*. Amsterdam: North-Holland, pp. 119–141.
Nelson, T.O. (1977). Repetition and depth processing. *Journal of Verbal Learning and Verbal Behavior*, **16**, 151–171.
Neville, H.J., Kutas, M., Chesney, G. and Schmidt, A.L. (1986). Event-related brain potentials during initial encoding and recognition memory of congruous and incongruous words. *Journal of Memory and Language*, **25**, 75–92.
O'Gorman, J.G. (1973). Change in stimulus conditions and the orienting response. *Psychophysiology*, **10**, 465–470.
Öhman, A. (1979). The orienting response, attention, and learning: an information processing perspective. In H.D. Kimmel, E.H. van Olst and J.F. Orlebeke (eds), *The Orienting Reflex in Humans*. Hillsdale, NJ: Erlbaum, pp. 443–471.
Öhman, A., Dimberg, U. and Esteves, F. (1989). Preattentive activation of aversive emotions. In T. Archer and L.-G. Nilsson (eds), *Aversion, Avoidance and Anxiety: Perspectives on Aversively Motivated Behavior*. Hillsdale, NJ: Erlbaum, pp. 169–193.
O'Neill, M.E., Sutcliffe, J.A. and Tulving, E. (1976). Retrieval cues and release from proactive inhibition. *American Journal of Psychology*, **89**, 535–543.
Packer, J.S. and Siddle, D.A.T. (1989). Stimulus miscuing, electrodermal activity, and the allocation of processing resources. *Psychophysiology*, **26**, 192–200.
Paller, K.A., Kutas, M. and Mayes, A.R. (1987). Neural correlates of encoding in an incidental learning paradigm. *Electroencephalography and Clinical Neurophysiology*, Suppl. 40, 360–365.
Paller, K.A., McCarthy, G. and Wood, C.C. (1988). ERPs predictive of subsequent recall and recognition performance. *Biological Psychology*, **26**, 269–276.
Pavlov, I.P. (1927). Conditioned reflexes. New York: Dover Publications.
Peterson, L.R. and Peterson, M.J. (1959). Short-term retention of individual verbal items. *Journal of Experimental Psychology*, **58**, 193–198.
Plouffe, L. and Stelmack, R.M. (1984). The electrodermal orienting response and memory: an analysis of age differences in picture recall. *Psychophysiology*, **21**, 191–198.
Pomerantz, J.R., Kaplan, S. and Kaplan, R. (1969). Satiation effects in the perception of single letters. *Perception and Psychophysics*, **6**, 129–132.
Pritchard, W.S. (1981). Psychophysiology of P300. *Psychological Bulletin*, **89**, 506–540.
Ragot, R. (1984). Perceptual and motor space representation: an event-related potential study. *Psychophysiology*, **21**, 159–170.
Renault, B., Kutas, M., Coles, M.G.H. and Gaillard, A.W.K. (eds) (1988). *Event Related Potential Investigations of Cognition*. Amsterdam, Netherlands: North-Holland.
Ruchkin, D.S., Munson, R. and Sutton, S. (1982). P300 and slow wave in a message consisting of two events. *Psychophysiology*, **19**, 629–642.
Sampson, J.R. (1969). Further study of encoding and arousal factors in free recall of verbal and visual material. *Psychonomic Science*, **16**, 221–222.
Sanquist, T.F., Rohrbaugh, J.W., Syndulko, K. and Lindsley, D.B. (1980). Electrocortical signs of levels of processing: perceptual analysis and recognition memory. *Psychophysiology*, **17**, 568–576.
Schaafsma, M.F., Packer, J.S. and Siddle, D.A.T. (1989). The effect of context change

on long-term habituation of the skin conductance response to signal and non-signal stimuli in humans. *Biological Psychology*, **29**, 181–191.

Siddle, D.A.T. (1985). Effects of stimulus omission and stimulus change on dishabituation of the skin conductance response. *Journal of Experimental Psychology: Learning, Memory, and Cognition*, **11**, 206–216.

Siddle, D.A.T., Booth, M.L. and Packer, J.S. (1987). Effects of stimulus preexposure on omission responding and omission-produced dishabituation of the human electrodermal response. *Quarterly Journal of Experimental Psychology*, **39B**, 339–363.

Siddle, D.A.T. and Heron, P.A. (1976). Reliability of electrodermal habituation measures under two conditions of stimulus intensity. *Journal of Research in Personality*, **10**, 195–200.

Siddle, D.A.T., Kyriacou, C. and Heron, P.A. (1978). Effects of change in stimulus duration on amplitude of the electrodermal orienting response. *Physiological Psychology*, **6**, 121–125.

Siddle, D.A.T., Kyriacou, C., Heron, P.A. and Matthews, W.A. (1979). Effects of changes in verbal stimuli on the skin conductance response component of the orienting response. *Psychophysiology*, **16**, 34–40.

Siddle, D.A.T., O'Gorman, J.G. and Wood, L. (1979). Effects of electrodermal lability and stimulus significance on electrodermal response amplitude to stimulus change. *Psychophysiology*, **16**, 520–527.

Siddle, D.A.T. and Packer, J.S. (1987). Stimulus omission and dishabituation of the electrodermal orienting response: the allocation of processing resources. *Psychophysiology*, **24**, 181–190.

Siddle, D.A.T. and Packer, J.S. (in press). Memory and autonomic activity: the role of the orienting response. In J.R. Jennings and M.G.H. Coles (eds), *Handbook of Cognitive Psychophysiology: Central and Autonomic Nervous System Approaches*. Chichester, UK: Wiley.

Siddle, D.A.T. and Spinks, J.A. (1979). Orienting response and information processing: some theoretical and empirical problems. In H.D. Kimmel, E.H. van Olst and J.F. Orlebeke (eds), *The Orienting Reflex in Humans*. Hillsdale, NJ: Erlbaum, pp. 473–498.

Siddle, D.A.T. and Stenfert Kroese, B. (1985). Orienting, habituation, and short-term memory. *Psychophysiology*, **22**, 535–544.

Siddle, D., Stephenson, D. and Spinks, J.A. (1983). Elicitation and habituation of the orienting response. In D. Siddle (ed.), *Orienting and Habituation: Perspectives in Human Research*. Chichester: Wiley, pp. 109–182.

Simson, R., Vaughan, H.G.J. and Ritter, W. (1976). The scalp topography of potentials associated with missing visual and auditory stimuli. *Electroencephalography and Clinical Neurophysiology*, **40**, 33–42.

Sirevaag, E., Kramer, A.F., Coles, M.G.H. and Donchin, E. (1989). Resource reciprocity: an event-related brain potentials analysis. *Acta Psychologica*, **70**, 77–97.

Smith, S.M. (1979). Remembering in and out of context. *Journal of Experimental Psychology: Human Learning and Memory*, **5**, 460–471.

Smith, S.M. (1985). Environmental context and recognition memory reconsidered. *Bulletin of the Psychonomic Society*, **23**, 173–176.

Smith, S.M. (1986). Environmental context-dependent recognition memory using a short-term memory task for input. *Memory and Cognition*, **14**, 347–354.

Sokolov, E.N. (1963). *Perception and the Conditioned Reflex*. Oxford: Pergamon Press.

Sokolov, E.N. (1969). The modeling properties of the nervous system. In M. Cole and I. Maltzman (eds), *A Handbook of Contemporary Soviet Psychology*. New York: Basic Books, pp. 671–704.

Sorgatz, H. and Dannel, W. (1978). Memory and electrodermal activity. *Perceptual and Motor Skills*, **46**, 769–770.

Spinks, J.A. and Siddle, D.A.T. (1976). Effects of stimulus information and stimulus duration on amplitude and habituation of the electrodermal orienting response. *Biological Psychology*, **4**, 29–39.

Spinks, J.A. and Siddle, D. (1983). The functional significance of the orienting reflex. In D. Siddle (ed.), *Orienting and Habituation: Perspectives in Human Research.* Chichester: Wiley, pp. 237–314.

Squires, N.K., Squires, K.C. and Hillyard, S.A. (1975). Two varieties of long-latency positive wave evoked by unpredictable stimuli in man. *Electroencephalography and Clinical Neurophysiology*, **38**, 387–401.

Squires, K.C., Wickens, C., Squires, N.K. and Donchin, E. (1976). The effect of stimulus sequence on the waveform of the cortical event-related potential. *Science*, **193**, 1142–1146.

Stein, B.S. (1978). Depth of processing re-examined: the effects of the precision of encoding and test appropriateness. *Journal of Verbal Learning and Verbal Behavior*, **17**, 165–174.

Stelmack, R.M., Plouffe, L.M. and Winogron, H.W. (1983). Recognition memory and the orienting response: an analysis of the encoding of pictures and words. *Biological Psychology*, **16**, 49–64.

Sutton, S., Braren, M., Zubin, J. and John, E.R. (1965). Evoked-potential correlates of stimulus uncertainty. *Science*, **150**, 1187–1188.

Sutton, S. and Ruchkin, D.S. (1984). The late positive complex: advances and new problems. In J.C.R. Karrer and P. Tueting (eds), *Brain and Information: Event-Related Potentials*. New York: NY Academy of Science, pp. 1–23.

Sutton, S., Tueting, P., Zubin, J. and John, E.R. (1967). Information delivery and the sensory evoked potential. *Science*, **155**, 1436–1439.

Thompson, R.F. and Spencer, W.A. (1966). Habituation: a model phenomenon for the study of neuronal substrates of behaviour. *Psychological Review*, **73**, 16–43.

Towle, V.L., Heuer, D. and Donchin, E. (1980). On indexing attention and learning with event-related potentials. *Psychophysiology*, **17**, 291.

Tueting, P., Sutton, S. and Zubin, J. (1970). Quantitative evoked potential correlates of the probability of events. *Psychophysiology*, **7**, 385–394.

Tulving, E. and Bower, G.H. (1974). The logic of memory representations. In G.H. Bower (ed.), *The psychology of Learning and Motivation.* London: Academic Press, pp. 265–301.

Turpin, G. (1983). Unconditioned reflexes and the autonomic nervous system. In D. Siddle (ed.), *Orienting and Habituation: Perspectives in Human Research.* Chichester: Wiley, pp. 1–70.

Turpin, G. and Siddle, D. (1983). Effects of stimulus intensity on cardiovascular activity. *Psychophysiology*, **20**, 611–624.

Turvey, M.T. and Egan, J. (1969). Contextual change and release from proactive interference in short-term verbal memory. *Journal of Experimental Psychology*, **81**, 396–397.

Verleger, R. (1988a). Event-related potentials and memory: a critique of the context updating hypothesis and an alternative interpretation of P3. *Behavioral and Brain Sciences*, **11**, 341–354.

Verleger, R. (1988b). From epistemology to P3-ology. *Behavioral and Brain Sciences*, **11**, 397–406.

Von Restorff, H. (1933). Über die Wirkung von Bereichsbildungen im Spurenfeld. *Psychologische Forschung*, **18**, 299–342.

Wagner, A.R. (1978). Expectancies and the priming of STM. In S.H. Hulse, H. Fowler and W.K. Honig (eds), *Cognitive Processes in Animal Behavior*. Hillsdale, NJ: Erlbaum, pp. 177–209.

Wagner, A.R. (1981). SOP: a model of automatic memory processing in animal behavior. In N.E. Spear and R.R. Miller (eds), *Information Processing in Animals: Memory Mechanisms*. Hillsdale, NJ: Erlbaum, pp. 5–48.

Walker, E.L. and Tarte, R.D. (1963). Memory storage as a function of arousal and time with homogeneous and heterogeneous lists. *Journal of Verbal Learning and Verbal Behavior*, **2**, 113–119.

Wardlaw, K.A. and Kroll, N.E.A. (1976). Autonomic responses to shock-associated words in a non-attended message: a failure to replicate. *Journal of Experimental Psychology: Human Perception and Performance*, **2**, 357–360.

Warren, L.R. and Harris, L.J. (1975). Arousal and memory: phasic measures of arousal in a free recall task. *Acta Psychologica*, **39**, 303–310.

Waters, W.F., McDonald, D.G. and Koresko, R.L. (1977). Habituation of the orienting response: a gating mechanism subserving selective attention. *Psychophysiology*, **14**, 228–236.

Wickens, D.D. (1970). Encoding categories of words: an empirical approach to meaning. *Psychological Review*, **77**, 1–15.

Wilson, K.G. (1984). Psychophysiological activity and the buildup and release of proactive inhibition in short-term memory. *Psychophysiology*, **21**, 135–142.

Yuille, J.C. and Hare, R.D. (1980). A psychophysiological investigation of short-term memory. *Psychophysiology*, **17**, 423–430.

Chapter 6

Language by Eye:
Behavioral and Psychophysiological Approaches to Reading

Ira Fischler and Gary E. Raney
Department of Psychology, University of Florida, Gainesville, FL 32611, USA

ABSTRACT

Past and potential contributions of physiological measures to the study of language comprehension and reading are surveyed. Autonomic and central nervous system approaches are compared with behavioral measures, with emphasis on eye fixations and event-related brain potentials. The relation of these measures to different levels of analysis of reading is considered.

INTRODUCTION

The purpose of this chapter is to consider how behavioral and physiological measures of performance are contributing to the study of language comprehension. Consistent with the nature of this volume, the focus will be on central and autonomic nervous system measures, although we will first survey some of the major behavioral methods and findings in language and reading research. Our emphasis will also be on central measures, especially those of

Handbook of Cognitive Psychophysiology: Central and Autonomic Nervous System Approaches.
Edited by J. R. Jennings and M. G. H. Coles.

event-related brain potentials, or ERPs. Recent work on the psychophysiology of reading has been dominated by the use of ERPs. These studies have tended to address issues more specifically related to language structure and process, in contrast to more general issues of processing load or individual differences in reading.

The focus will be on comprehension of written language. There have been some attempts to study the psychophysiology of oral and written language *production* (e.g. Deecke *et al.*, 1986), but these have been relatively rare. This parallels in part the emphasis within traditional behavioral psycholinguistics on comprehension rather than production. It also reflects the difficulty of dealing with movement artifacts associated with active speech and writing (see, for example, Brooker and Donald, 1980; Grozinger, Kornhuber and Kriebel, 1975).

The chapter will begin with a brief perspective on language as a complex skill, suggesting the variety of levels of analysis needed to understand language performance. Succeeding sections will be organized around behavioral, autonomic, and central measures of language and reading respectively. In each section, we will assess the particular advantages and limits of each approach, describe some of the contributions made to understanding language and reading by use of those measures, and suggest possible directions for future research.

LANGUAGE, READING AND COGNITION

A VIEW OF LANGUAGE

In the climactic scene of *The Miracle Worker*, a young Helen Keller is overwhelmed when for the first time she grasps the arbitrary but systematic linking of form and meaning, and learns the name for water. The two faces of language are apparent here: its external face, as a means of communication and social interaction; and its internal face, as the mapping of ideas with their sensory–motor representation. In the cognitive sciences, the emphasis has been on the internal, computational side of language, as it has been with other cognitive abilities (Gardner, 1985). The overreaching goal has been to explain how language accomplishes this task. What aspects of language comprehension are 'purely' linguistic, and what aspects reflect mechanisms common to other skills which are recruited for language? How do different languages achieve their similar goals? What are the consequences of acquiring language through signs, rather than speech? How important is individual variation in language processes?

The study of language and reading has played a central role in the study of cognition, from nineteenth century debates about 'imageless thought', to Whorf's (e.g. 1956) hypothesis of linguistic relativity, to Fodor's argument about language as a system of modules relatively isolated from other cognitive 'faculties' (Fodor, 1983). In what has been presented as the first introductory text of Cognitive Science (Stillings *et al.*, 1987), four of the twelve chapters are addressed to aspects of language.

There are good reasons for this dominance. Language is the most distinctive human skill, acquired rapidly and universally across cultures and individuals, and based on apparent neurological specializations. Language is structurally complex and computationally 'rich', and among other cognitive skills, attempts to describe the structure of language have been most explicit and rigorous. Only recently, for example, has the same level of explicitness been brought to the problem of perception (e.g. Marr, 1982).

ATTRIBUTES OF LANGUAGE

A grammar defines a language, by specifying the mapping of physical signs (such as speech sounds), and meaning. In linguistic terms, a grammar consists of four main components: a *phonology* (for spoken languages, at least), which describes the sound patterns of a language and their structure; a *morphology*, which defines how the very small number of phonological patterns combine to form a much larger, but still finite, set of words and affixes ('lexemes', to use Robinson and Moulton's 1985 term); a *syntax*, which describes the rules for combining lexemes into an unbounded number of utterances, wherein relations among lexemes represent relations among ideas and meaning; and a *semantics*, which describes the meaning of utterances. The study of language is most closely linked with that of cognition in the area of *pragmatics*, which is concerned with how linguistic comprehension and production is guided and constrained by general knowledge of the world and of the conventions of communication. It is such knowledge that, for example, produces longer gaze durations on the feminine pronoun in (3) than the masculine when reading the following (from Kerr and Underwood, 1984):

(1) The surgeon examined the X-rays.
(2) It was a bad case.
(3) [He/She] would have to operate immediately.

Language comprehension requires the integrated activity of all these components. Psycholinguistic research can be broadly divided into work addressed to a particular level or component of language, and more ambitious attempts to specify the order in which different levels are active during comprehension, and how these levels interact.

LANGUAGE BY EYE

Over 3000 human languages have been described, some spoken by a billion individuals, and some spoken by a handful. For many of these, there is no written code for the language. When the language is represented graphically, there must be an *orthography*, which describes the relation between graphic and linguistic forms. Reading thus raises some unique psychological questions and problems. In contrast to the ease and uniformity of acquiring a spoken language across individuals and cultures, the learning of written forms of language typically begins later, requires more effort and explicit instruction, and presents special difficulty for about one of every eight children. The difficulty is deeper than the difference between auditory and visual modes for language, since the acquisition of sign languages by the deaf resembles the normal course of auditory language acquisition much more than it does the acquisition of reading skill among hearing children (Bellugi, 1987).

One basic question concerning the relation of reading and listening has been the extent to which different 'routes' are used in accessing the meaning of written words. Early models (e.g. Rubenstein, Lewis and Rubenstein, 1971) saw the problem of reading as the mapping of graphemes to phonemes according to orthographic rules, with comprehension then proceeding as it would during listening. More recent models have stressed a route in which the graphemic string is directly mapped into the lexicon. Reading also differs from listening in the availability of prior material as text is read, and the control by the reader of the rate of progress through the text. The input is different as well: 'utterances' in text are well-formed, longer, and (typically, at least) more highly organized and integrated than is conversationally spoken language. The writer of discourse also has goals that are different from those of a speaker, and writes with a pragmatic understanding of the conditions of reading.

The study of the dynamics of reading, then, involves some issues that are common to spoken language comprehension, and some that are unique to reading. Marshall (1987) has recently argued that the differences between reading and listening to language should not blind us to their common goals and mechanisms; and that 'studies of the 'social' context of reading *qua* cultural invention, transmitted by teaching, should not cause us to lose sight of the biological foundations of visual language' (p. 27).

GLOBAL AND LOCAL MEASURES, MOLAR AND MOLECULAR ISSUES

As with many contemporary approaches to cognitive psychology, there are two broad and complementary perspectives on language and reading. One takes a molar approach, and looks at reading as an integrated activity that results in comprehension of new information. The other approach focuses on a more molecular level, and looks at the moment-by-moment processes and codes that are recruited during that comprehension. At both the behavioral and psychophysiological levels, there is a corresponding broad division of 'global' versus 'local' measures and techniques that are most useful for the molar or molecular perspectives. The most global behavioral measure of comprehension we might imagine is uncued recall—simply asking people what they learned from a text passage (e.g. Owens, Bower and Black, 1979; Thorndyke, 1977). At the other extreme, we might be interested in the effects of a particular syntactic or semantic constraint on ease of processing a single word. For example, Tyler and Marslen-Wilson (1977) asked subjects to provide a continuation for a sentence fragment as quickly as possible, and found that a semantic context and a syntactic cue jointly determined speed of continuation; so that a fragment in which these cues conflicted (e.g. 'If you are trained as a pilot, landing planes *are*...') produced slower responses.

Among central measures, EEG and cerebral blood flow have tended to be used to study more global aspects of reading, such as hemispheric activation in verbal versus spatial tasks, and effects of text difficulty; while event-related potentials (ERPs), with their exquisitely time-locked signatures, have been the measure of choice for a molecular analysis of reading and language. Similarly, autonomic measures such as EMG, heart rate and skin conductance have commonly been used in studies of global function, while measures of pupil size have usually addressed specific molecular questions.

As we survey how particular issues of language and reading have been addressed by these measures, we will note how the 'time grain' of the different measures can provide complementary evidence about global and local levels of analysis.

BEHAVIORAL MEASURES OF READING

GLOBAL MEASURES

Recall of Text

Immediate verbal report of material just read has been widely used as a global measure of comprehension. There are two rather different problems involved in relating free recall of text to comprehension. On the one hand, material can be recalled that is not comprehended. On the other hand, much of text recall is not verbatim, but contains paraphrases, inferences, and other signs that the material has been highly coded (Voss, Tyler and Bisanz, 1982). To deal with the first problem, researchers will sometimes directly ask for paraphrases or summaries of material. Kieras (1978), for example, simply asked subjects to describe the main idea of a prose passage. To deal with the second problem, a large number of scoring methods have been developed that try to capture the *propositional content* of the material recalled. These are generally referred to as 'idea units', and correspond roughly to a simple declarative paraphrase of a fact or relation. The units may be defined intuitively or logically (Cofer, 1941), by use of basic grammatical constructions (Rubin, 1978), or by noting the occurrence of pauses during oral recall (Johnson, 1973). Reliability of scoring by such methods is generally high.

In many cases, the scoring method reflects a particular 'model' of text itself. Such text-structural models have come to dominate global work on comprehension; some of the more influential include those of Kintsch and van Dijk (1978), Meyer (1975), Fredericksen (1975) and Schank and Abelson (1977). Essentially, these models try to make explicit the elemental propositions of a text and how they are related to one another, to determine any implicit inferences that must be made for comprehension, and to describe the overall abstract semantic structure of the passage. Others have emphasized the conventions of what has been called the 'story structure' of narrative prose (e.g. Thorndyke, 1977), and the identification of causal relations among text propositions (e.g. Trabasso, Secco and van den Broek, 1984). Tests of the model may involve differential levels of recall of propositions defined within the theory. A typical result is that propositions which are at a higher or more theme-relevant level in the text structure are recalled more frequently (e.g. Meyer, 1975), and younger or less skilled readers are less sensitive to such text organization (e.g. Dunn, Mathews and Bieger, 1982; Kintsch *et al.*, 1975; Mandler and Johnson, 1977). Another theme of this work has been how semantic and pragmatic knowledge guides and sometimes misguides comprehension and recall (e.g. Owens, Bower and Black, 1979; see Colley, 1987, for a review).

Reading Speed

In contrast to listening, reading in its natural form is a self-paced task. At a global level, then, we can measure the time it takes a person to read a passage under such 'normal' conditions. Not surprisingly, as with many behavioral measures of performance, readers trade off accuracy and speed, with the rate of reading determined by the reader's goals, knowledge of the material, and complexity of text structure. On average, the reading rate for adults is about 250 words per minute, commonly ranging from about 200 to 400 words words per minute as the task and material vary (see Just and Carpenter, 1987, pp. 425–439). Along with comprehension scores, reading rate is among the most widely used measures to differentiate levels of reading skill.

Some studies have suggested that adults tend to read more slowly than they need to, and not to match their rate optimally to the difficulty of the material (see Anderson, 1985, pp. 368–371). This has led to an interest in programs to modestly (e.g. Thomas and Robinson, 1971) or drastically (cf. Taylor, 1965) increase reading speed.

Rather than treat reading rate as a dependent variable, it is possible to manipulate rate and examine its effects on comprehension at a variety of levels. This can be done in a global fashion, by limiting the time available for reading a given passage (e.g. Kieras, 1974). A more constrained method, introduced by Forster (1970), is known as RSVP, for *rapid serial visual presentation*, in which individual words or phrases (cf. Juola, Ward and McNamara, 1982) are presented sequentially in the same spatial location, eliminating the need for eye movements. Comprehension and recall of individual sentences under RSVP conditions can be surprisingly good at rates approaching 1000 words per minute (Fischler and Bloom, 1980; Potter, Kroll and Harris, 1980). In contrast, when short paragraphs are presented, comprehension worsens when RSVP rates exceed that of normal reading (*c.* 200–300 wpm; Potter, Kroll and Harris, 1980). This suggests that the bottleneck in normal reading speed is at a fairly high level of text integration (Potter, 1984).

LOCAL, 'ONLINE' METHODS

Moving to a more molecular level of analysis, we find a great variety of methods that have been developed to study the moment-by-moment processing of written language. Consistent with the information processing framework of much of this work, the response time for some task is the most common dependent measure.

One measure most closely linked to the global methods just described is the time taken to read individual sentences presented sequentially (e.g. Graesser and Riha, 1984), or individual words presented at a subject-paced rate (e.g. Aaronson and Ferres, 1984; Mitchell, 1984). In both cases, the subject's task remains reading for comprehension. Using the sentence-reading method, Keenan, Baillet and Brown (1984) presented subjects with a sequence of related sentences. For example, subjects would see either (4a) or (4b), followed by (5):

(4a) Racing down the hill, Joey fell off his bike.
(4b) Joey went to a neighbor's house to play.
(5) The next day, his body was covered with bruises.

Reading time for sentence (5) was substantially longer (3.2 s versus 2.9 s) when preceded by (4b), where the causal link is much less explicit, than when preceded by (4a). Not surprisingly, reading times are sensitive to a wide range of factors, ranging from lexical (e.g. word frequency; Mitchell and Green, 1978) and syntactic (e.g. negation; Just and Carpenter, 1971) to text-level (e.g. thematic importance of sentences; Cirilo and Foss, 1980). Reviews of studies making use of linear regression techniques to isolate the contributing factors to sentence reading times are presented by Graesser and Riha (1984) and Haberlandt (1984).

At the most local level, word-by-word reading times are similarly affected by perceptual and linguistic aspects of both the current word and of the preceding material. Interestingly, there is less variation in reading times within sentences when subjects are asked to comprehend the sentence as opposed to recalling it (Aaronson and Scarborough, 1976). Mitchell and Green (1978) also found little effect of constraining sentence contexts on reading time for target words, in contrast to studies using less natural procedures (e.g. Fischler and Bloom, 1979; see below); but as with the RSVP technique, contextual effects can be shown if subjects are reading larger units such as paragraphs for comprehension (Mitchell, 1984).

In studies of reading time, whether by sentence or by word, subjects read for comprehension, although the mechanics of the task depend on the level of measurement. In many other online studies of visual language processing, however, the task has little to do with comprehension, but is designed to highlight specific aspects or stages of word processing. The assumption in most cases is that increased complexity, difficulty or processing load at that point will increase response time in the target task.

In most cases, the written material itself—words in isolation or in some context—contains the target items. The most common tasks include decisions about the lexical status of strings (*lexical decision tasks*—e.g. PLACE versus PLAFE; see Scarborough, Cortese and Scarborough, 1977), latency to begin or complete pronunciation of words (e.g. West and Stanovich, 1982), decisions about semantic properties such as the category membership of words (e.g. Rosch, 1975), detection of individual letters or syllables (e.g. Drewnowski and Healy, 1982; Fischler, 1975; McClelland and Rumelhart, 1981), and detection of errors of various sorts intentionally placed in the material (e.g. Healy and Drewnowski, 1983). On the one hand, such tasks can provide specific converging evidence about the particular process affected by, say, frequency of occurrence, syntactic ambiguity or semantic context. On the other hand, these kinds of decisions bear little resemblance to reading for comprehension, and if one is interested in natural reading, the question of task validity must be addressed. In studies of sentence reading, for example, contexts have been shown to strongly influence lexical decisions for words which are meaningful versus anomalous completions of the sentence (e.g. Fischler and Bloom, 1979); but this effect is reduced or absent when the task is to pronounce the final word (e.g. West and Stanovich, 1982) or to read for meaning using the word-by-word technique described above (e.g. Mitchell and Green, 1978).

On the positive side, by careful cross-task comparisons in a variety of contexts, one can develop a toolbox of tasks, so to speak, for subsequent studies. In the case of lexical decision and pronunciation, work by Seidenberg and his colleagues (e.g. Seidenberg *et al.*, 1984) has suggested that pronunciation latency is relatively less sensitive to events following access of the meaning of the target word from memory, while lexical decision may be strongly influenced by such 'post-access' processes. This helps explain the differential effects of sentence contexts on naming and lexical decision described above. Similarly, Seidenberg *et al.* (1984) found that the extent of 'semantic priming' of lexical decisions by individual words associated to the target word (e.g. DOCTOR followed by NURSE; Meyer and Schvaneveldt, 1971) is influenced by the proportion of trials in which related pairs are presented (cf. den Heyer, Briand and Dannenbring, 1983), while pronunciation is not. More recently, Potts, Keenan and Golding (1988) used a contrasting pattern of pronunciation and lexical decision times to words in sentence contexts to argue that, unless an inference is necessary for establishing the cohesiveness of a text passage, it will not be drawn at the time of reading even if it is very plausible.

Embedding such artificial tasks in a primary task of reading for meaning raises other problems, since the additional demands of the monitoring task may intrude on reading and alter the nature of the reading process. In such cases, it is important to include a control condition of reading for meaning without the secondary online task so that the effects of the secondary task on reading can be assessed.

Most of the online methods just described are concerned with specific informational or computational aspects of language processing. There has been some interest, however, in the 'energetic' demands of language comprehension (Hockey, Gaillard and Coles, 1986). One popular technique is the secondary probe reaction-time paradigm (Kerr, 1973; Posner and Boies, 1971). In that paradigm, a primary target task is engaged in, but subjects must concurrently monitor a channel for the occasional occurrence of a probe stimulus, and respond to its occurrence as quickly as possible. As probe RT increases, it is inferred that the primary task at that moment is more demanding of attentional resources.

Britton and his colleagues have used the dual-task probe paradigm extensively to explore capacity demands of reading text. They have found, for example, that reading of text with more complex syntactic structure is more demanding, and that the presence of cues in the text that mark propositional structure and causal relations (e.g. *therefore*; *in contrast*) produced shorter probe reaction times (Britton *et al.*, 1982). A comparison of 'easy' and 'difficult' texts was made by Britton, Westbrook and Holdredge (1978). Difficulty was manipulated by providing clarifying titles for the otherwise obscure texts used by Bransford and Johnson (1972), so that the lexical and syntactic content was controlled. Oddly, the easy text produced *longer* probe RTs. A recent study by Inhoff and Fleming (1989), however, suggested that this counterintuitive finding was due to lack of control over reading times, and a whole-passage presentation method, which allowed subjects to look back over the passages during the probe trials. Inhoff and Fleming used a word-by-word presentation with no regression allowed, and found that for both visual and auditory probe signals, the more difficult texts produced slower probe RTs as well as slower reading rates. They also included a no-probe control condition (see above), and demonstrated no effects of the presence or absence of the probe task.

In summary, a great variety of tasks and methods have been used to study online processes during reading. While they have the potential advantage of converging on very specific processes or stages of influence, collectively they are limited by the inevitable intrusiveness on the natural act of reading for meaning. Nonetheless, a great deal has been learned about how visual, linguistic and conceptual sources of knowledge jointly contribute to the comprehension process. The importance of thematic and pragmatic knowledge in comprehension, the minimal role of phonology in word recognition, the relative autonomy of lexical access, and the joint influence of syntactic and semantic cues in the moment-by-moment processing of text, have all been illuminated by these techniques.

EYE FIXATIONS DURING READING

Spoken language is spread out in time, and the listener must passively await each new segment of speech as it unfolds. Written language, in contrast, is spread out spatially. The reader converts this spatial layout into a temporal one by moving the point of visual fixation—the spot on the page where the 1–2 degree area of the high-resolution fovea is centered—across the text. Subjectively, the movement of the eyes over a page may seem fairly smooth; but in fact eye movements while reading (or inspecting any static scene—see Loftus and Mackworth, 1978) consist of a series of *fixations* that typically last about a quarter of a second, sometimes a bit less and often much longer, interrupted by very rapid *saccades* or jumps from one point of fixation to the next. The saccades last about 15 ms; so overall about 85% of reading time is actually spent with the eyes fixated on some part of the text (Just and Carpenter, 1987; p. 26).

The measurement of these fixations during reading presents a unique source of evidence on the cognitive processes occurring during reading comprehension. Studies of eye fixation provide a bridge of sorts between behavioral and physiological measures of reading. It is a behavioral measure, involving movements of the eye rather than the finger or throat. But it is part of the natural act of reading, rather than an arbitrary task superimposed on, or substituted for, reading, as with many of the other online methods described above. With currently available methods, it can also be obtained quite unobtrusively—another characteristic it shares with psychophysiological recording.

After several halted beginnings, one at the turn of the century (cf. Huey, 1908), and at midcentury (cf. Tinker, 1958), the study of eye fixations was brought back into mainstream cognitive psychology in the 1970s, in work by McConkie and Rayner (e.g. McConkie and Rayner, 1975; Rayner, 1975),

Carpenter and Just (e.g. 1975), and others (see Kennedy, 1987; pp. 169–170). The re-emergence was due to several factors, including (a) the availability of reliable, computer-based methods of recording eye fixations, (b) the ability to analyze these with respect to the particular part of the text being fixated (see, for example, Just and Carpenter, 1987, pp. 58–60, for a description of their system), (c) the development of more psychologically relevant measures of fixation such as the *gaze duration*, in which all fixations given a unit of text (typically a word) are summed (Just and Carpenter, 1980); and (d) the emergence of process-based models of eye movements that considered psycholinguistic as well as perceptual factors in reading text. In the two decades since this re-emergence, eye fixation research has made major contributions to understanding of online reading and language comprehension, and few texts or proceedings on reading lack a chapter on eye movements (e.g. Just and Carpenter, 1984; Rayner and Carroll, 1984; Kennedy, 1987; Underwood, 1985).

The basic assumptions of this research, which have received extensive support, are what Just and Carpenter have called (1) the *immediacy* hypothesis: that readers do as extensive an analysis as possible of the information presented in each fixation, as opposed to postponing interpretation pending further information; and (2) the *eye–mind* hypothesis: that this interpretation occurs while the word is being fixated. These two assumptions allow for the very specific analyses of word gaze duration times to be related to a host of lexical, syntactic and integrative events. A typical observation supporting these assumptions is that the gaze duration time increases linearly with the length of the word being fixated, but is essentially unaffected by the length of words fixated just before or after the target word (Carpenter and Just, 1983).

Much of the basic knowledge about the effective span of information pickup during a fixation comes from work using the *gaze-contingent* paradigm. In these studies, eye fixations on a computer-displayed text are recorded and certain characteristics of the text are altered as a function of the moment-to-moment changes in the point of location. For example, by masking letters at and near the fovea, Rayner *et al.* (1981) showed that reading rate dropped precipitously and numerous errors in word identification occurred when 3–5 letters centered at the point of fixation were masked. In a variation on this method, material *outside* the point of fixation is altered during the saccade which will likely bring the point of fixation to that material. If the fixation on the target material is then longer than in a control condition where there was no change, it is inferred that subjects read some aspects of the material parafoveally. In support of the eye–mind hypothesis, a number of studies have found that, unless visual features of the target material are altered, changes have little effect on the critical gaze durations. For example, Rayner (1975) found that changing between words (e.g. *police* to *palace*) or from a non-word to a word (*pcluce* to *palace*) during the saccade to the target word did not influence fixation time on *palace*. Conversely, McConkie and Rayner (1975) found that removal of spaces between words parafoveally significantly increased fixation times. In general, the gaze-contingent studies show that overall word shape and spaces between letters are detected parafoveally and help determine the location of the next fixation, but the 'span' is limited to perhaps 6–8 letters to the right of fixation and only several letters to the left. The span appears to be somewhat larger for more skilled readers (Underwood, 1986).

Lexical Factors

Fixation times have been shown to be under the control of a number of factors involved in word recognition. Among the most robust of these is the frequency of the word in the language: controlling for length and number of syllables, readers fixate less frequent words longer than more frequent ones, and this effect is not due solely to presentation of rare or very unfamiliar words (Just and Carpenter, 1980; cf. Jastrzemski, 1981). Morphological structure also affects duration time; Lima (1987) compared words consisting of two morphemes—a prefix and a stem (e.g. *revive*)—with 'pseudoprefixed' words (e.g. *rescue*). The pseudoprefixed words received longer fixations. This supported a model of lexical analysis in which prefixes are automatically 'stripped' and both the prefix and stem searched for in lexical memory. The pseudoprefixed words—which were closely matched in length, initial letter cluster and frequency—presumably required longer processing (and fixation) because this initial search failed.

A number of eye movement studies have considered whether the syntactic class of a word influences gaze durations. In general, words from the 'closed' class of words—short words that serve as syntactic markers (e.g. conjunctions, articles, prepositions, auxiliary and copula verbs)—tend to be fixated less frequently and for less time than words from the 'open' class of content words (nouns, pronouns, verbs, adverbs and adjectives), a difference likely due to the contrasting predictability, size and informativeness of the two classes of words. Within the open class, there is a tendency for verbs to receive longer fixations than the subjects or objects of the verbs (O'Regan, 1979). Aside from these overall differences, there is little evidence for differential fixation time among subtler syntactic variables; for example, several studies have failed to show longer fixations to more syntactically complex verbs such as causatives, factives or negatives (Inhoff, 1985; Rayner and Duffy, 1986).

Lexical Ambiguity

An important feature of words in both spoken and written language is that there are more concepts than there are words, and so a large number of words represent multiple concepts. Some of these are *homophones*, and are ambiguous only in speech (e.g. *write* versus *right*); many others are also *homographs* and ambiguous in written form as well (e.g. a *pitcher* of water or of baseballs). Many of these homographs are related in meaning, but for others there is no apparent link between the two meanings. The different meanings of these homographs may have different frequencies of occurrence in the language. Relative frequency can be estimated by production methods. For example, Gorfein, Viviani and Leddo (1982) obtained association norms to over 100 homographs, and derived a dominance score based on the relative frequency of a particular meaning among the responses. Some homographs are strongly biased toward one dominant meaning; *hide* as 'conceal' dominates *hide* as 'animal skin' (0.86 versus 0.14), but others are more 'equibiased', such as *mold*:fungus (0.54) versus *mold*:shape (0.46).

Eye fixation times provide a natural way to ask how the several meanings of homographs are accessed when such words are encountered during reading. In one recent study, Rayner and Duffy (1986) measured eye fixations as subjects read sentences that contained equibiased or biased homographs or control words in the same location. A disambiguating phrase followed the homograph. Examples are given below:

(6) Of course the [*pitcher* or *whiskey*] was often forgotten because it was kept on the back of a high shelf. (equibiased homograph and control).
(7) Last night the [*port* or *wine*] was a great success when she finally served it to her guests. (biased homograph and control).

They found that equibiased homographs were fixated longer than either biased homographs or non-homographic control words. This supported a model of lexical access in which multiple meanings of homographs are elicited automatically, and that during the fixation period, one meaning is rapidly chosen—another example of the immediacy principle. In the case of equibiased meanings, as in (6), both senses are accessed quickly enough so that they may compete during the selection process, increasing gaze durations. For the biased homographs as in (7) above, the dominant meaning is accessed and selected and reading proceeds as if there were only one meaning (cf. Simpson and Burgess, 1985). Consistent with this interpretation, Rayner and Duffy (1986, 1987; cf. Carpenter and Daneman, 1981) found that fixations on the subsequent disambiguating phrase were longest for the biased homographs when the phrase was congruent with the less dominant meaning (as above), requiring a reinterpretation of the prior clause; and next longest for the equibiased homographs, where subjects would choose the wrong interpretation about half the time. When the subsequent phrase was congruent with the dominant meaning, gaze durations were equal to that for the control-word sentence completions.

Context and Word Recognition

Words that are made highly predictable by a preceding context are fixated more briefly than less predictable words (Ehrlich and Rayner, 1981; Zola, 1984). There is evidence that effects of predictability can be observed parafoveally in the preceding fixation; Ehrlich and Rayner (1981), for example, found that predictable words were also fixated less frequently, suggesting a parafoveal decision to skip such words (cf. Balota, Pollatsek and Rayner, 1985). Predictability effects in the form of categorical or associative links between context and target words have also been observed, but these appear to be restricted to cases where the words occur within the same clause, or where the associative link is related to a theme or topic which is maintained across clauses or sentences (Carroll and Slowiaczek, 1986; see below).

Context effects on target word fixation times show that context is being utilized for at least some of the processes occurring during the current fixation; but since those processes include not only lexical access but syntactic, semantic and at least some discourse-level integrative activities, such effects cannot be taken as evidence for the effects of semantic context on lexical access. The studies of homography have been applied to this question: if both meanings of a homograph are automatically accessed in neutral contexts, what happens if the disambiguating context is presented prior to the ambiguity?

Duffy, Morris and Rayner (1988) presented readers with equibiased and biased homographs in sentence contexts during reading. As in Rayner and Duffy (1986, see above), disambiguating information was on some trials presented after the ambiguity; now, however, the disambiguating context could also occur prior to the ambiguity, as in (8):

(8) Because it was kept on the back of a high shelf, the [*pitcher* or *whiskey*] was often forgotten.

Duffy *et al.* (1988) distinguished three models of how the prior context might affect access of the alternate meanings of the homograph. In the *exhaustive access* model, access is unaffected by the prior context, with both meanings automatically activated and the dominant meaning more likely to be accessed first. This model predicts that the gaze durations to homographs will be the same whether the biasing context appears before or after the homograph, with durations to equibiased homographs lengthened relative to either the biased homographs or control target words. At the other extreme, if a constraining context biases access fully, then according to this *selective access* model, all effects of homography will be eliminated in the prior-context condition, since both homographs and control words will have only one meaning elicited. Finally, a *reordered access* model states that the prior context increases the availability, and hence speed of access, of the appropriate meaning without affecting the alternative meaning(s). In this case, the prior context should produce longer gaze durations to the *biased* homographs relative to controls: since the bias in their study was always toward the less dominant meaning, the two meanings would now be more likely to compete during access, and act like the equibiased contexts in the later-context condition. In contrast, the appropriate meaning of the equibiased homographs would now be accessed consistently before the unbiased sense, and so there should be no difference between equibiased homographs and control words in the prior-context condition.

The results for prior context sentences like (8) clearly supported the reordered access model, with the biased homographs fixated longer than either the equibiased homographs or control words, which did not differ in fixation times. Gaze durations in the letter-context condition replicated those described above (Rayner and Duffy, 1986).

These findings converge with those from other recent behavioral studies of how biased and equibiased homographs are differentially affected by a preceding context, including lexical decision (e.g. Swinney, 1979; Onifer and Swinney, 1981) and pronunciation latency (e.g. Seidenberg *et al.*, 1982), and provide some support for relatively more interactive models of how lexical processing and higher-level semantic analysis are coordinated during reading. As Duffy *et al.* (1988) point out, however, there are versions of access models conserving autonomy that deal with contextual effects indirectly through spreading activation within the lexicon (see Seidenberg, 1985).

Syntactic Processes

As a reader scans a passage of text, he or she must apply the rules of syntax to build a structured representation of the propositions in the text. Eye movement studies of syntactic processing have focused on two related issues: whether the syntactic structure is assigned as fully as possible during the current fixation; and the extent to which that assignment is made independently of semantic or pragmatic knowledge or context.

The immediacy of syntactic parsing, like that of lexical processing, has been studied by using ambiguous sentences. Consider the following sentence:

(9) The conductor stood before the audience left the hall.

Just and Carpenter (1980) found that gaze durations to the critical word *left* were increased compared with that in unambiguous control sentences. Apparently, readers choose the syntactically simpler version of the ambiguous phrase, 'The conductor stood before the audience...', according to what Frazier (see Frazier and Rayner, 1982) called the 'minimal attachment' strategy. This syntactic strategy is to attach the new material on to the phrase structure under construction with the smallest possible number of new nodes. In this case, the word *before* is treated as a locative rather than the start of a new relative clause indicating the time of the standing. The strategy in this case leads to what is called a 'garden path' effect. In contrast to the apparent multiplicity of lexical access, it appears that only one syntactic structure is considered, since gaze durations prior to the word that disambiguates the structure show no effect of the presence of an ambiguity. Besides the increased duration at the word *left* in (9), regressive fixations to the source of the ambiguity are often made, as the syntactic relations must be reassigned. Interestingly, the immediacy principle appears again in the sense that readers do not wait until the end of the current clause or sentence to correct the garden path error. Similar results were reported by Frazier and Rayner (1982).

Even if syntactic parsing were immediate, it could be influenced by non-syntactic factors. This question is at the heart of one of the controversies between proponents of modular views of syntax (e.g. Fodor, 1983; Forster, 1979), who argue that syntactic structure is autonomously computed, and those who argue for interactive effects in the operations of the various levels of linguistic analysis (e.g. Thibadeau, Just and Carpenter, 1982; van Dijk and Kintsch, 1983).

Experimental tests of the autonomy issue have involved pitting a syntactic rule or strategy (like the 'minimal attachment' strategy) against semantic or pragmatic cues. In (10a) below, the minimal attachment strategy would lead to the garden path treatment of *defendant* as the agent, and *examined* as a verb of the main clause; but in (10b) the fact that *evidence* is inanimate should lead to treating the entire phrase as a relative clause:

(10a) The defendant examined by the lawyer...
(10b) The evidence examined by the lawyer...

Ferreira and Clifton (1986) found that despite the implausibility of the reading of the non-minimal attachment sentences such as in (10b), the pattern of increases in gaze durations for (10b) versus its control were essentially the same as for the non-biased sentences, as in (10a). Apparently, the syntactic strategy was employed despite the semantic implausibility that potentially was indicated early in the sentence. Ferreira and Clifton (1986) also reported no influence of discourse- or theme-level pragmatic information on application of the minimal attachment strategy when the sentences were embedded in a paragraph.

Such results suggest that at least some syntactic rules or strategies are used autonomously. It remains controversial to what extent this is true of syntactic processes in general. The question of autonomy must concern processing at the level of individual words. The strong version of autonomy is clearly incorrect, since semantic analysis is not delayed until an entire clause is syntactically parsed (cf. Marslen-Wilson and Tyler, 1980; Just and Carpenter, 1987, pp. 187–191).

Integrative Processes

Readers' fixations can reflect across-clause and across-sentence integration of material, establishing the referent of a word, and establishing thematic importance of material. The size of these higher-level effects is, however, small compared with the overall effects of length and familiarity of words. Gaze durations to words which introduce new topics are lengthened, as are those at the ends of sentences; these are points where the need to connect the current material with that of the passage as a whole would seem to be particularly important (Just and Carpenter, 1980).

One of the most studied aspects of text-level integration is the assigning of referents to words. Just and Carpenter (1987) suggest that a failure to comprehend at this referential level is an important cause of what they term 'shallow comprehension', in which 'a reader goes through some of the motions of reading, understanding all of the words in the sentence, but fails to grasp the gist of a text' (p. 218). Identification of a common referent is necessary when words are used anaphorically; that is, where different words are used to refer to the same object or event. Kennedy (1978) varied the ease of anaphoric reference by varying the associative frequency of a target word with its referent, as in (11):

(11) A [*bus* or *tank*] came trundling around the corner. The vehicle nearly flattened a pedestrian.

Fixations were longer to the target word *vehicle* when preceded by the less directly associated word *tank*; apparently, it was harder to understand what vehicle was being referred to when the referent was atypical. Similarly, Just and Carpenter (1978) observed shorter gaze durations to the word *killer* in the following passage when the previous sentence referred explicitly to a murder:

(12) The millionaire [*was murdered* or *died*] on a dark and stormy night. The killer left no clues for the police to trace.

Referent assignment is particularly important when an author uses pronouns extensively. In some cases, the assignment is ambiguous, as in (13):

(13) John told Jim that his car had been stolen.

In general, the greater the distance between a word and its referent, the longer the gaze duration on the word (e.g. Ehrlich and Rayner, 1983). However, if the pronominal referent is important topically and maintained in focus, the distance effects can be reduced or eliminated (cf. Foss, 1982).

The most direct cue to identifying a referent is repetition of the word itself. Schustack, Ehrlich and Rayner (1987) showed again that distance effects on gaze durations are found, which were independent of a priming manipulation in which the target word was sometimes preceded by a strong semantic associate. They suggested that the semantic prime speeded lexical access, while the more recent repetition of the word facilitated its integration into the text structure.

In contrast to word recognition and syntactic parsing, there is stronger evidence that there is 'spillover' of higher-level integrative processes from the point at which the relevant information is fixated, to subsequent fixations. So, for example, Ehrlich and Rayner (1983) found that difficulty of pronoun assignment influenced gaze durations to words after the pronoun itself. They point out that this implies a limit to the eye–mind principle (cf. Masson, 1983).

Summary

The selective review above shows the richness of factors influencing the duration of eye fixations during reading. For the most part, the immediacy and eye–mind principles are maintained, allowing a direct interpretation of these durations as reflecting the ease or difficulty of processing the text at that point. The major shortcoming of the measure, as with other measures of online reading time, is that it does not localize these variations in fixation time to particular stages of processing. Other inferential arguments or convergent measures must be used to do this. For example, Schustack, Ehrlich and Rayner (1987) used additive-factors logic to contrast the effects of pronoun distance and contextual constraint on naming speed versus gaze duration (cf. Ferreira and Clifton, 1986; Experiment 3), and concluded that the effects of pronoun distance occurred only after lexical access.

The rapid sequential visual presentation (RSVP) method described earlier had been considered as a way to improve reading speed, eliminating the need for eye movements. But, as we saw, the need for cross-sentence integration resulted in RSVP methods losing their advantage over normal reading when connected discourse was presented. Kennedy (e.g. 1987) has also shown that knowledge of the spatial location of material on the page can play an important role in integrative processing of text, and that good readers maintain a fairly accurate spatial representation of the text as they read. One method that conserves the spatial information of text, allows for assessment of individual 'fixation' times, but does not require direct recording of fixations, is the 'moving window' technique, where a reader is given manual control over the location of a cursor which moves across a CRT screen, presenting the text only in the location at the cursor, with the remaining text preserved as xx's or dashes. Just and Carpenter (1984) compared the moving window technique to eye movement recordings, and in general found a strong degree of convergence between the two measures, with the main difference being that the overall effect sizes tended to be much greater, in terms of absolute changes in 'fixation' times, with the moving window—presumably owing to the need to coordinate eye movements with the manual response.

PERIPHERAL MEASURES OF READING

In contrast to the behavioral and eye movement measures above, and the central measures to be described below, there has been relatively little use of peripheral physiological measures in the study of language and reading. In discussing what work there is, we will try to indicate how autonomic and other peripheral measures might provide convergent evidence on various aspects of reading. In this section, we will describe several studies using heart rate, skin resistance, electromyography and pupil size during reading. Of these, the former two have been used as more global measures of reading comprehension, while pupil size has served as a more local, online measure of moment-by-moment processing of text.

HEART RATE

John and Beatrice Lacey were the first to suggest that cardiovascular changes may be related to the attentional demands of a task. The Laceys (e.g. Lacey and Lacey, 1974) argued that heart rate deceleration occurred when subjects attended to events in their environment, in other words, during information extraction. In contrast, when engaging in concentrated 'internal' processing and rejecting information from the environment, heart rates increased. This is known as the intake-rejection hypothesis. The proposed mechanism for this effect was baroreceptor feedback (Lacey and Lacey, 1974). In brief, baroreceptors detect changes in blood pressure. The baroreceptors make contact with the brain stem, indirectly influencing the level of activity in both the central and autonomic nervous systems, hence affecting the efficiency of responses to external stimuli.

The physiological mechanism proposed by the Laceys has been criticized on a number of grounds (e.g. Green, 1980; Rentel, Pappas and Pettegrew, 1985). Although no single physiological explanation is supported, the occurrence of heart rate changes during mental activity is not in doubt (Angelotti, Behnke and Carlile, 1973; Green, 1980; Sandman and Walker, 1985).

The specific relationship between heart rate and reading has been the focus of relatively little research. Emphasis has been given to studying the relationship between heart rate and general levels of cognitive activity (Sandman and Walker, 1985) and to the intake of sensory stimuli (Lacey and Lacey, 1977; Walker and Sandman, 1979, 1982). Although some studies have used reading as a primary task (e.g. Angelotti, Behnke and Carlile, 1973; see below), there has been no exploration of specific linguistic or cognitive activities involved in reading using heart rate.

One aspect of reading that can lead to performance differences is the allocation of attention. It has been shown, for example, that comprehension of a text increases at points of attentional focus (Reynolds and Anderson, 1982). Heart rate variation appears to be sensitive to changes in attentional demands and to the onset and offset of attention (Coles and Strayer, 1985; Jennings, 1975; Jennings and Hall, 1980; see Coles, 1984, and Jennings, 1986a, for reviews). For example, Coles (as reported in Coles and Strayer, 1985) studied changes in heart rate during a visual search task. Subjects searched for the letter *b* or *e* in a background matrix composed of the letter *a*. The search for the *e* should be more difficult, thus requiring more attention to be focused upon the environment. Results indicated that search for the *e* was associated with greater heart rate deceleration than for the *b*. This result is consistent with the Laceys' intake-rejection hypothesis.

Jennings (1975) presented subjects with a list of six numbers, which they had to process in varying ways: silent reading of the numbers, storing the numbers in memory, adding numbers to those in the display, adding numbers to those in memory, or discovery of a transformation rule relating two columns of numbers. During the presentation (input) phase, cardiac acceleration occurred. Different patterns of heart rate change occurred across tasks during the performance phase. Whether these results were a factor of memory load or attentional changes was examined in a follow-up study by Jennings and Hall (1980). These authors concluded that the direction of attentional focus—that is, on the intake of information or on the elaboration of information—was related to cardiac acceleration, whereas memory load was not.

In contrast to Jennings and Hall's (1980) results, Aasman, Mulder and Mulder (1987) have shown a relationship between heart rate and memory load. They examined spectral variation in slow wave components (0.10 Hz) of heart rate, whereas Jennings and Hall (1980) examined changes in interbeat intervals. Aasman *et al.* found that the amplitude of the 0.10 Hz component of the signal decreased as memory load increased. Different aspects of cardiac variability may thus be related to different cognitive processes.

Given the sensitivity of heart rate to changes in attentional focus, the use of heart rate variability to study the attentional demands of text would seem promising. Jennings (1986a,b) describes how heart rate studies using dual-task and secondary probe methodologies may be used to assess attentional demands. It seems possible to apply these methods directly to studies of text processing. For example, based on the Laceys' intake-rejection hypothesis one might predict different cardiac reactions to a probe as a function of whether attention is focused more on the intake or elaboration of information. The relationship between heart rate and subsequent memory is also an area needing further refinement.

Angelotti, Behnke and Carlile (1973) used heart rate as a global measure of reading involvement. Heart rate was measured while male seventh-graders read two passages of equal difficulty and during a resting baseline. One passage was a science fiction story, which represented a high-interest topic. The second was a passage from a history book, which represented a low-interest topic. Heart rate was measured using an interval peak method. The highest heart rate reached during successive 12 s intervals was measured and an average was obtained. It was hypothesized that the high-interest passage would generate greater self-involvement, which would lead to a lower heart rate. As predicted, heart rates during the reading of the science fiction passage were significantly lower than for the history passage. Also, heart rates declined from the beginning to the end of the science fiction passage. This effect was reduced for the history passage. The authors concluded that lower heart rates while reading the science fiction passage reflected greater attentional involvement.

Cacioppo (1979) examined the effect of exogenous manipulations of heart rate on reading comprehension and on sentence and argument generation. Cacioppo hypothesized that cardiac acceleration should facilitate the mental elaboration required during the performance of the tasks. Heart rate was increased from 72 to 88 beats per minute (bpm) (using subjects with cardiac pacemakers). Results indicated better performance on the tasks for the 88 bpm condition relative to the 72 bpm condition. These results support the possibility of increased heart rate having a facilitative effect on cognitive processing. Replication of these results has, however, been difficult (see Jennings, 1987b for a review).

In sum, there is substantial evidence that reliable heart rate changes accompany changes in attention. Heart rate has successfully been used as a global (e.g. Angelotti *et al.*) and local (e.g. Jennings) indicator of cognitive processes. Research has also shown that the duration of a cardiac cycle may be influenced by stimuli occurring within that cycle (Coles and Strayer, 1985; Lacey and Lacey, 1977). It is therefore surprising that heart rate has not been conditionalized on small units of text, such as sentences or phrases. When heart rate variation is related to specific aspects of text and quantified over smaller units of time it will provide highly useful information regarding details of language comprehension.

GALVANIC SKIN RESPONSE

Galvanic skin response (GSR) has been sparingly applied as a 'direct' measure of cognitive processing. That is, the GSR is usually associated with a more global energetic construct, such as arousal or anxiety, which is then used to explain some task-related behavioral phenomenon. For example, variation in GSR during the performance of a range of tasks was examined by Lacey *et al.* (1963). The relevant result was that skin conductance (and supposedly arousal) increased during the performance of each of the tasks. This finding supports the notion of the GSR as an indicator of at least some aspects of arousal.

Differences in GSR activity related to specific information processing demands of tasks can also be found. One well-known experiment which related

GSR to memory and arousal was conducted by Kleinsmith and Kaplan (1963). Subjects performed a paired associate learning task comprised of word–number pairs. Some of the pairs contained words such as *rape*, which were chosen to elicit increased arousal. High-arousal items were better recalled after long delays (greater than 45 minutes) than low-arousal items.

Hammond and Jordan (1984) investigated the relationship between the GSR and processing difficulty for a set of verbal and spatial tasks. In one experiment the verbal tasks involved counting the occurrence of a key word within a text (easy condition) and counting the number of words related in meaning to a key word (difficult condition). The spatial tasks included a circle matching test (easy condition) and an arc matching test (difficult condition) which required subjects to match a circle or an arc to a target circle of equal radius. In a second experiment subjects read a page of text from a newspaper (easy text), *Scientific American* (moderately difficult), and from the *Journal of Theoretical Biology* (difficult text). In both experiments skin conductance *decreased* as difficulty increased for both the verbal and spatial tasks. Since GSR is typically thought to increase with increased task difficulty (Edelberg, 1972; Lacey *et al.*, 1963), Hammond and Jordan suggested that the difficult tasks were more 'engaging' for subjects. In any case, the relation between task difficulty, arousal and GSR appears not to be a simple one.

Other recent studies of GSR and information processing in verbal tasks have provided some evidence that GSR activity differentiates relative hemispheric involvement (Fedora and Schopflocher, 1984; Hammond and Jordan, 1984) and the informational value of feedback during learning (e.g. Das-Smaal and De Swart, 1984; De Swart and Das-Smaal, 1979).

None of the above studies, however, was focused directly on reading or language processing, although such application is clearly possible (e.g. Hammond and Jordan, 1984). The temporal resolution of the GSR is typically greater than one second. This discourages its use as a local measure of the most rapidly unfolding events during reading, such as lexical access. But at the level of short phrases and sentences, GSR could provide an important convergent view, especially where affective and emotional apsects of the text are concerned.

ELECTROMYOGRAPHIC MEASURES

The electromyogram, or EMG, is a measure of muscle activity and tension. As with GSR, electromyographic (EMG) measures are most commonly associated with general states of arousal and emotion. Some studies, however, have linked EMG activity with specific aspects of memory (e.g. Bradley, York and Lang, 1989), and speed of cognitive processing (Evans, 1976; Moran and Cleary, 1986).

In general, frontalis (forehead) muscle tension tends to increase during engaging thought. Moran and Cleary (1986) examined the effects of *induced* frontalis tension on cognitive efficiency. They reasoned that since previous research has shown increased discrimination thresholds and reduced cognitive abilities during relaxation, efficiency in a reaction time task should be greatest during relatively higher levels of frontalis tension. To test this, subjects were taught to induce either relatively low, medium, or high levels of frontalis tension. Subjects then performed a four-choice serial reaction time task. Median reaction times decreased as frontalis tension increased. These results suggest that behaviors which increase fontalis tension may also increase cognitive efficiency, at least for simple speeded tasks.

The bulk of the research using electromyographic measures of language processing has examined the effectiveness of EMG biofeedback training as a means of improving scholastic performance. Studies usually involve students with a learning or attentional deficiency, and attempt to enhance performance on a number of scholastic tasks through the use of relaxation training. The results of this research are inconsistent (Denkowski, Denkowski and Omizo, 1983; Sharpley and Rowland, 1986), and its applicability to normal populations unclear.

Other studies have used feedback from EMG recording during reading to train subjects specifically to reduce subvocalization (e.g. Hardyck and Petrinovich, 1970; see Gibson and Levin, 1975, pp. 340–351, and Jennings, 1986b, pp. 302–306 for reviews). Such training can reduce subvocalization, but its effects on comprehension are not impressive. Moreover, the suppression itself is usually not long-lived and is highly sensitive to instructions and to the difficulty of the material. Ninness (1982), however, reports no increase in subvocalization for three individuals $2\frac{1}{2}$ years after treatment. More recent theoretical work on the role of articulatory codes and working memory during reading (e.g. Daneman and Carpenter, 1980) suggest that a blanket suppression of subvocalization during reading could hurt comprehension.

Aside from the series of studies on subvocalization, then, EMG measures of reading have been limited to considerations of global changes in arousal and effort. There is little doubt that certain patterns of covert muscle activity may relate to specific behaviors. For example, EMG patterns recorded during subvocal speech and reading may be similar to the pattern recorded during speech (Jennings, 1986b). After reviewing the literature, Jennings (1986b) concluded that covert motoric changes are only associated with processing efficiency when the task is made difficult. None of the research described above was specifically aimed at studying reading or language processing. As with the GSR, EMG measures may be useful for studying pragmatic aspects of language, such as the influence of emotional statements on physical and cognitive arousal. However, there is no current research using EMG measures to examine specific aspects of language processing such as the effects of syntactic variations on memory or comprehension.

PUPIL SIZE

The utility of pupillary responses as an index of processing load has been demonstrated across a wide range of tasks and paradigms (see, Beatty, 1982, for a review). Changes in pupil size have been shown to reflect differences in processing load during short-term memory tasks, language processing, reasoning or mathematical problems, perceptual tasks, and for tasks requiring selective or sustained attention (Ahern and Beatty, 1981; Beatty, 1982; Beatty and Wagoner, 1978; Metalis and Hess, 1986; Schluroff *et al.*, 1986). Beatty (1982) concluded that pupillary responses meet Kahneman's (1973) criteria for a physiological indicator of processing load; that is, sensitivity to within-task variations, to between-task differences, and to individual differences.

The temporal resolution of pupil size measures makes them well suited for examining local variations in cognitive load. Eye monitoring systems which sample pupil size at a rate of at least 60 Hz have existed since the mid-1970s, so that resolution of the instrument is not a limiting factor. Reliable differences in pupil size as a function of cognitive tasks can be found even though the mean effects are actually quite small, averaging perhaps 0.5 mm. These shifts occur fairly rapidly, giving pupillometry a temporal resolution of one second or less.

Several aspects of written language have been studied using pupillometric measures. Beatty and Wagoner (1978) had subjects perform a letter-matching task (Posner and Mitchell, 1967), in which subjects judged whether pairs of letters were similar or different based either on 'physical' identity (e.g. AA) or 'name' identity (e.g. Aa). Pupil dilation was largest for conditions requiring name matching. Beatty and Wagoner (1978) concluded that this reflected the additional processing required in the name matching condition.

At the lexical level, perception and comprehension of words has been studied by Ahern and Beatty (1981). Word pairs whose semantic relation was easy or difficult to judge, based on psychometric norms, were presented to subjects. The task was to indicate if the words were similar or dissimilar in meaning. Pupil dilations were more than twice as great when processing the more difficult words, again reflecting the increased cognitive load imposed by the difficult word pairs.

Pupillary responses have also been shown to be sensitive to variations in grammatical complexity. For example, Schluroff (1982) auditorally presented subjects with sentences of different length, construction, and content. Sentences which were grammatically more complex were associated with greater pupil dilation. Interestingly, the correlation between grammatical complexity and pupil size was larger than the correlation between the subjects' own ratings of grammatical comprehensibility and pupil size.

Pupillary responses to syntactic ambiguity and complexity were explored by Schluroff *et al.* (1986). Subjects were presented with ambiguous sentences which could be interpreted as verb- or object-oriented. The verb-oriented interpretations represented syntactically more complex sentences. An example used by Schluroff *et al.* is (14).

(14) Peter chased the man on the motor bike. (p. 324)

The object-oriented interpretation is that Peter used the motor bike to chase the man. The verb-oriented interpretation is that Peter chased the man who was on the motor bike. To determine whether verb- or object-oriented interpretations were made, subjects were asked to rephrase each sentence after its reading. Pupil size increased from the beginning to the end of the sentences for readings of both orientations. However, greater pupillary dilations occurred during verb-oriented readings. Differences were maintained during the period in which subjects rephrased the sentences. The authors concluded that larger pupil dilations during the syntactically more complex sentences indicated greater cognitive demands during processing (cf. Ahern and Beatty, 1981).

Wright and Kahneman (1971) demonstrated a relationship between pupillary responses and information search within a sentence. In one condition of their study, subjects were presented with a question, which was followed by a sentence containing the answer. Pupil size was monitored as subjects listened to the sentences. Pupil size increased when the part of the sentence providing the answer to the question was presented. This demonstrates the sensitivity of pupillary responses to local elements of a sentence.

The sensitivities of pupillary responses in these studies indicate their usefulness for investigating a broad range of reading processes. Given that pupillary responses can be localized to a few words within a sentence, it is surprising that pupillary measures are typically used only as a general measure of cognitive load. Applications of pupillometry to more molecular issues of language comprehension are being performed (e.g. Schluroff *et al.*, 1986), but more emphasis needs to be given to such work; comparisons of auditory and visual modes of language would also be useful, since the work on sentence processing to date has used auditory presentation.

THE FUNDUS REFLEX

The fundus reflex refers to the small amount of light reflected back through the lens of the eye. The process used to measure the fundus reflex is called retinoscopy. Retinoscopy involves the projection of a beam of light through the pupil so that a secondary light source is formed on the retina. A portion of the light is reflected off the retina and emerges through the pupil. The amount of light reflected is then measured. Changes of less than 1% can be accurately measured (Kruger, 1975).

A number of properties of the fundus reflex vary depending on the accommodative state of the lens and the state of the retina. The intensity, direction of movement, size, and color of the reflection have all been shown to change depending on the task being performed. Furthermore, these attributes are not independent (Kruger, 1975).

Kruger has conducted a series of studies relating changes in the fundus reflex to changes is cognitive load. In one study Kruger (1975) measured changes in the luminance of the fundus reflex as college students read five texts of varying difficulty levels and while they completed an addition task. Results indicated increased luminance of the fundus reflex relative to a baseline as the task changed from easy to hard reading material and for the addition task. Subjects' comprehension of the material did not appear to be related to changes in the luminance of the reflex. Kruger concluded that changes in the luminance of the reflex were primarily due to changes in accommodation or focus. The possibility that increased pupil size caused the increased luminance was ruled out by including conditions in which pupil changes were restricted through the use of drugs.

Kruger (1980) also found that increasing the cognitive demand of mathematical tasks led to increased luminance of the reflex. This result was attributed to decreases in accommodative lag. He concluded that luminance changes result from a general increase in cognitive load and are not limited to reading.

Kruger (1975) suggests that these luminance changes are another peripheral sign of the orienting response, along with changes in pupil dilation, muscle tone, respiration, heart rate, and galvanic skin response. Consistent with the autonomic nature of accommodation is the finding that luminance changes during reading follow the typical patterns of habituation exhibited by other orienting responses (Kruger, 1975).

The fundus reflex has only been used as a general measure of processing difficulty. The sensitivity of this measure to variations in text structure, such as syntactic complexity, have not been demonstrated. Research based on the fundus reflex supports the conclusion that autonomic changes may be associated with the cognitive demands of a task.

Summary

Of the several peripheral measures discussed, pupil size has been most productively used in the study of reading and language, although even here the number of studies specifically concerned with aspects of language is very limited. With the lowered cost, increasing reliability, and technical ease of use of eye movement and pupillometry systems, we may see a more central role for this peripheral measure of information processing during reading.

In many cases linguistic stimuli and visual presentation are used as pragmatic conveniences to explore more general issues of the energetics of cognition. This appears to be the case for studies using heart rate, GSR, EMG, and the fundus reflex. Applications of heart rate methodologies to reading may prove helpful when the attentional demands of text are at issue. GSR and EMG measures are clearly useful as global indicators of what is typically called arousal. Research using EMG and GSR as measures of specific states during the performance of linguistic tasks has been very limited. The fundus reflex is a relatively new measure and has only been used as a general indicator of cognitive load.

Future research may be enhanced through the use of multiple dependent measures and subsequently relating the activity of each. For example, Sandman and Walker (1985) describe a number of relationships between heart rate and event-related brain potentials, and Coles (1984) has described dissociations between heart rate and measures of somatic activity such as the EMG.

CENTRAL MEASURES OF READING

During the first part of this century, studying the neuropsychology of language and reading was of necessity limited to correlating the behavioral effects of various brain trauma and diseases with gross observations about the location and extent of damage, and with subsequent postmortem pathologies. Animal models and experimental study could provide a metaphor, at best, to the perceptual, linguistic and conceptual skills involved in reading.

It had been known for some time that brain activity was associated with the generation of electrical fields (Caton, 1875). But with the discovery of the electroencephalogram by Hans Berger in 1929, it became possible to observe patterns of brain activity 'online' while a person was engaged in particular tasks. The potential link between the EEG and cognitive activity appears to have been an important factor in Berger's own interest in measuring the brain's electrical activity (Petsche, Pockberger and Rappelsberger, 1986; p.63).

The half century since that discovery has seen a rapid acceleration in the availability of tools for investigating brain activity in a real-time and unobtrusive manner. Among these, event-related brain potentials have by far been most associated with studies of language and reading. Nonetheless, other more recently developed techniques such as regional cerebral blood flow and brain tomography have been brought to bear on questions of language by eye. Following our convention of discussing more molar or global measures first, we will consider these more recent techniques first, which tend to be of broader time grain and targeted to more global states and processes than the EEG measures.

CEREBRAL BLOOD FLOW

It has been demonstrated that the pattern of cerebral blood flow appears to depend on the type of cognitive activity being performed (e.g. Risberg *et al.*, 1975; Roland and Friberg, 1985; Wallesch *et al.*, 1985). As an area of the brain becomes more active, the local metabolic demands increase, leading to increased blood circulation. Increased metabolic activity is taken to reflect increased information processing, or activation, within an area of the brain (Rentel, Pappas and Pettegrew, 1985). However, the specific relationship between increased blood flow, on the one hand, and energy consumption and information processing by an area of the brain on the other, remains controversial (Van den Berg, 1986).

Two primary methods are used to measure regional cerebral blood flow (rCBF). One method is to inject a radioactive tracer into one of the arteries supplying blood to the brain (the intracarotid ^{133}xenon procedure). This procedure supplies the radioactive tracer ^{133}xenon ^{133}Xe) to a single hemisphere. Areas of increased blood flow lead to higher concentrations of ^{133}Xe; the rate of decay is proportional to the amount which has permeated the area. Concentrations of ^{133}Xe are measured using detectors located on the scalp to determine the amount of blood flow to a region (Risberg, 1986). This technique provides a method for single-hemisphere research, but does not allow between-hemisphere comparisons.

A second method for measuring blood flow is to have subjects inhale a radioactive gas (the ^{133}Xe inhalation technique). As with the first method, ^{133}Xe concentration is measured. This method is less invasive and supplies ^{133}Xe to both hemispheres, thus allowing between-hemisphere as well as within-hemisphere comparisons. Furthermore, this method does not have the potential risks and discomfort of an injection in the carotid artery.

Current rCBF methods are capable of isolating changes in blood flow with a spatial resolution of 3–5 cm, although this may soon improve to 10 mm (Risberg, 1986). This degree of resolution matches or surpasses that of other physiological measures, such as event-related brain potentials, and provides the ability to make fine distinctions regarding localization of activity (Risberg, 1986). Furthermore, rCBF systems have been developed which localize activity in three dimensions; however, the resolution of three-dimensional systems is less than for the two-dimensional systems. The temporal resolution of ^{133}Xe systems is approximately one minute (Risberg, 1986). Thus, research is limited to studying processes which may be maintained over extended periods of time. New tracers have been developed which significantly reduce the temporal resolution of rCBF systems. For example, Tulving (1989) reports the use of a gold-based tracer which has a temporal resolution of less than 3 s. This is a dramatic improvement over ^{133}Xe.

In general, rCBF studies support findings regarding the relationship between linguistic performance and hemispheric activity found in research using other techniques. Linguistic tasks result in greater increase in blood flow to the left hemisphere than the right hemisphere, and spatial tasks provide the opposite results (Gur and Reivich, 1980; Jacquy *et al.*, 1977; Risberg *et al.*,

1975). Differences between left hemisphere and right hemisphere activity may be reduced for left-handed individuals and for children (Jacquy *et al.*, 1977) and as task difficulty increases (Wallesch *et al.*, 1985). For example, Jacquy *et al.* (1977) compared rCBF of children (age 6–11) to adults (aged 26–46) during reading. There was an increase in both left- and right-hemisphere activity relative to a resting baseline for right-handed subjects from both age-groups. The adults, however, showed a greater degree of left-hemisphere activation than the children. Left-handed children showed a greater right- than left-hemisphere increase in blood flow.

Patterns of rCBF have been shown to be different for individuals with reading specific disorders such as dyslexia (Hynd *et al.*, 1987), and between adults with normal vision and the blind (Jacquy *et al.*, 1977). For example, Jacquy *et al.* (1977) compared the rCBF of blind adults with a control group with normal vision using the intracarotid ^{133}Xe technique. Blood flow measurements were taken during a resting baseline and while reading fiction. The blind subjects read a braille text and the controls read a normal text. The control group also performed a spatial perception test which required them to locate problems within a picture. For all subjects, both hemispheres were more active during reading than during a baseline period. However, there was for both groups a greater overall increase in left-hemisphere activity, especially in the temporal–parietal area (i.e. Wernicke's area). For the control group there was a large increase in occipital activity. Lastly, the spatial task led to larger right- than left-hemisphere increases in blood flow in the control group.

Studies relating rCBF to reading have only measured global levels of activation. Systems are emerging with increased temporal resolution which should allow researchers to isolate changes in blood flow which occur while processing smaller units of text, such as phrases or words (Risberg, 1986). Regional cerebral blood flow techniques offer a powerful tool for the localization of activity within the brain. When systems with finer temporal resolution are applied to the study of language, this method will no longer be limited to studies of general activation levels.

POSITRON EMISSION TOMOGRAPHY

Positron emission tomography (PET) is a powerful method for localizing areas of metabolic activity within the human brain. To produce a PET image a radioactive tracer is injected into the blood stream. The tracer is carried throughout the brain and the decay process of the tracer is measured. When positron-emitting radionuclides decay, a positively charged particle is released. This particle collides with an electron, which results in the production of a small amount of energy which can be measured by detectors arranged around the skull of a subject (Heiss *et al.*, 1986). By using an appropriate tracer, PET imaging allows mapping of a number of different physiological processes.

Tracers are available which allow measurements of blood flow, blood volume, oxygen consumption, glucose metabolism and transport, protein synthesis, and the activity of dopamine, benzodiazepine, and opiate receptors (Heiss *et al.*, 1986).

PET images have an in-plane resolution of 7–10 mm and represent an object thickness of approximately 10–15 mm (Heiss *et al.*, 1986). Signal averaging methods are now being applied to PET images which produce resolutions near 1 mm (Fox *et al.*, 1988) and allow separation of functional zones with centers as close as 3 mm (Fox *et al.*, 1986). The temporal resolution of PET scans limits its use to tasks which can be continuously performed for approximately one minute.

Recently, PET technology has been applied to issues of cognitive psychology and language comprehension (Petersen *et al.*, 1988; Posner *et al.*, 1988). Petersen *et al.* (1988) used PET scans to measure cerebral blood flow of subjects presented with auditory or visual words. They applied a subtraction method to isolate areas of activity unique to a task. For example, in one condition subjects fixated a visual location (control state) or passively read words (stimulus state). By subtracting the activity present during the control state from the stimulus state, they hoped to isolate areas of the brain active in the stimulus state but not in the control state.

Petersen *et al.* (1988; p. 586) described the differences between the control and stimulus states as representing 'simple sensory input and involuntary word-form processing'. Conditions were developed which represented sensory processing, motor programming and output, and semantic association for both visual and auditory domains. The authors found that stimulus-minus-control differences left relatively few areas of activation, and that these areas were clustered in limited regions of the cortex. One interesting finding was that none of the visual-word processing tasks produced greater-than-control activation in Wernicke's area or in the angular gyrus of the posterior temporal cortex—places where phonological analysis of auditory words is assumed to occur. The authors concluded that this provides evidence for localized areas of processing and supports 'multiple route' models of lexical access, with visually presented words able to contact directly their semantic representation.

Posner *et al.* (1988) review a number of this group's word-processing studies using PET imaging and the stimulus-minus-control logic. Stimulus and control conditions were developed to isolate areas of cerebral activation related to visual, semantic, and phonological processing of words. In the visual condition, for example, subjects looked passively at a set of nouns (stimulus) or a fixation point (control). Areas of activation were predominantly located in the prestriate area of the occipital lobe. Complex naming and semantic activation tasks did not produce any additional posterior activation. Based on this the authors concluded that visual word forms are developed in the occipital lobe.

In the semantic condition, subjects generated and gave uses for concrete nouns (stimulus) or simply repeated the nouns (control). The only areas of activation were in the left frontal lobe. A second semantic task produced similar results. It was concluded that the left frontal lobe supports the type of word associations produced in the generation task.

Posner *et al.* (1988) also note some unpublished data showing that if subjects are asked to judge if two visually presented words rhyme, the phonological areas of the left temporoparietal cortex are now activated. Again, these results support the non-obligatory nature of phonological recoding during reading (see above).

The results of studies using PET imaging support the general finding of increased left hemisphere activation during language processing (Heiss *et al.*, 1986). PET technology has also been used to examine the brain activity of individuals with language disorders, such as aphasia (Metter *et al.*, 1987). PET images provide a clear window for viewing the focus of language impairments. Although the temporal resolution of PET is currently low, applications can be developed for testing specific hypotheses. This is exemplified by the studies of Petersen *et al.* (1988) and Posner *et al.* (1988), both of which examined molecular aspects of word recognition and language processing.

ELECTROENCEPHALOGRAPHY

Until very recently, EEG studies of reading have focused on the search for hemispheric differences in activity as a function of whether the tasks given to subjects were predominantly 'verbal' or 'non-verbal'. The aspect of the EEG that correspondingly received the most attention was the relative amount of 'power' in the EEG in a frequency band around 10 Hz, commonly referred to as *alpha activity* after Berger's terminology. The amount of activity in the various frequency ranges can be derived through visual inspection, through simple filtering, or (most accurately) through spectral analysis based on Fourier transformation. Since increases in relative alpha-activity is associated with a relaxed, restful state—closing the eyes is the most dramatic way to increase alpha—the simple hypothesis was that for right-handers, at least, verbal tasks should be associated with decreases in alpha over left-hemisphere recording sites, and perhaps corresponding increases in homologous right hemisphere activity (e.g. Robbins and McAdam, 1974).

This differential-activation hypothesis received support from a number of studies during the 1970s. For example, Galin and Ornstein (1972) used verbal tasks of writing or mentally composing a letter, and spatial tasks of solving or imagining solving a simple block-design puzzle. Whether or not the tasks required motor output, it was found that the ratio of right- to left-hemisphere power in the alpha band was greater for the verbal tasks, consistent with decreasing alpha in the engaged hemisphere. In an interesting subsequent study, Ornstein *et al.* (1979) found that the content of material being read could influence the asymmetry of alpha; the right/left alpha ratio was greater when subjects read high-imagery stories than when they read fairly abstract, technical material. Other studies reported similar findings as a function of individual differences in training or cognitive style (e.g. Davidson and Schwartz, 1977).

These studies have been criticized on a number of grounds, including failure to control for potential stimulus and motor artifacts, limited range of electrode sites, method of deriving the alpha levels from the EEG, and failure to consider other frequency bands (e.g. Gevins *et al.*, 1979; Petsche *et al.*, 1986). More recent explorations of EEG during various cognitive tasks have continued to report interactions between subjects and tasks in the alpha region, but it is clear that the pattern is not as straightforward as initially thought. There are, for example, several reports of *increases* in relative left-hemisphere alpha activity during ostensibly verbal tasks such as reading (e.g. Dunn, Gould and Singer, 1981, cited in Dunn, 1985; Ehrlichman and Weiner, 1980). Petsche *et al.* (1986) report a very complex set of changes in EEG topography that varied across a series of 'analytic' tasks such as reading for meaning, memorizing text, or doing mental arithmetic; also, their anterior–posterior changes were generally more impressive than the lateral ones.

In view of the difficulties of controlling non-cognitive factors across gross changes in task, it would seem better to focus on more subtle within-task variables and individual differences. The series of studies by Dunn and his colleagues is perhaps the most sophisticated in this regard. Dunn has been interested in how readers of different cognitive style—in particular, those traditionally defined as 'analytic' versus 'holistic'—read text. Using Meyer's (1975) method to describe the hierarchical structure of a series of passages (see the section on 'Global Measures' above), Dunn *et al.* (1981; cited in Dunn, 1985) had college students read passages of expository text (which is typically more complex in structure and content than is narrative text) while EEG was recorded. On the basis of a preliminary EEG session, subjects above the median in amount of alpha—summed over left- and right-hemisphere locations—were classified as holistic, and those below the median, as analytic. For the shorter, less complex passages, there were few differences between the groups; but for the longer, more complex passage, there was an interaction between cognitive style and the 'level' of propositions in the text: for thematically subordinate information (in Meyer's 1975 system), probability of recall did not differ between the groups (0.24 for analytic, 0.20 for holistic), but for higher-level superordinate (Level 1) information, the EEG-defined analytic group recalled significantly more (0.60) than did the holistic group (0.44). Perhaps more impressively, instructions to relax while reading improved recall of superordinate facts by the holistic group (0.49 versus 0.39) but led to *worse* recall for the analytic group (0.52 versus 0.67). The relaxation 'mode' would presumably be more appropriate for the holistic group.

Analysis of EEG recorded during the reading task showed that the median split of subjects during the baseline period was reliable, with analytic subjects continuing to show less overall alpha production. For both groups alpha levels were lower during reading of the most complex passage. A similar interaction between structural importance of information in text and EEG-defined style differences was recently reported for grade school children (Raney, Dunn and Rust, 1989).

The construct of cognitive style has been a controversial one, and the link between it and EEG activity should be considered tentative, especially in view of our lack of understanding of the factors that determine generation of the EEG power spectra. But the work by Dunn is notable in its focus on linguistic and psychological factors during reading, rather than on issues of cortical localization, arousal or the nature of the EEG itself; in its use of explicit models both of cognitive strategies and of text structure; and in the intriguing behavioral differences in text comprehension and recall based on the pattern of EEG. Such work shows that although the temporal grain of the EEG is fairly coarse, it can be used to address very specific issues about language comprehension.

One interesting way in which EEG might be related to text processing, given Dunn's results, would be to compare EEG for reading 'shallowly' versus 'deeply', as described earlier (see the section 'Eye Fixations During Reading'). Analysis of EEG over smaller periods of time would also allow finer-grained comparisons of more momentary shifts in subject state, difficulty of the material, or ease of integration with prior information.

EVENT-RELATED POTENTIALS

Event-related brain potentials, or ERPs, have been widely used as a central nervous system measure of online processing of both written and spoken language. The ERP is obtained by averaging the EEG from a number of trials in a given experimental condition, time-locked to the presentation of a stimulus (or in some cases, other events such as response execution, or even peaks in EEG itself which may be seen on single trials). As with other physiological indices of cognition, ERPs allow observation of psychological activity in the absence of overt responses or arbitrary tasks which may change the nature of language processing. This is not to say that all ERP studies of language have asked subjects simply to read or listen for meaning; on the contrary, many ERP studies in the past decade have used tasks that are as artificial as those common in online behavioral studies of reading (see above), such as monitoring a list of items for non-words or non-letters (e.g. Rugg, 1987) or deciding if a word was an instance of a specified semantic category (e.g. Neville *et al.*, 1987). These manipulations can help specify linguistic and semantic processes in patterns of ERPs as they do in patterns of response latency. But there are several reasons why ERPs are particularly attractive as a window on the dynamics of language processing. First, they can indicate the point in 'real time' at which some variable has its effect. Also, differing patterns of ERPs across several scalp locations can help differentiate the effects of experimental variables that are not separable by behavioral data alone. These topographic patterns in the ERPs can also suggest areas of brain specialization which can then be examined by methods with greater spatial resolution. Finally, the relative insensitivity of the major ERP components related to language and semantic processing to later response selection and execution processes (e.g. Polich and Donchin, 1988) provides a way to analyze the several stages of processing involved in a cognitive task.

Some recent data from our laboratory will help illustrate the several major features of ERPs that will be the focus of the discussion to follow. Subjects were first shown a short videotape which included a number of everyday objects in an apartment, such as a stereo and clock. EEG was recorded from the vertex of the scalp (Cz in the international '10/20' system) as they were then shown a series of two-phrase statements. Some statements described objects from the video, with the first phrase 'cueing' the second, as with (17a):

(17a) Electronics / *stereo*
(17b) Electronics / *television*

Control statements such as (17b) ended in objects not seen in the video. The task was to read both phrases silently, then repeat them aloud together after a delayed cue. The ERP obtained by averaging a large number of trials for each of 14 college students is shown in Figure 6.1. The most obvious feature of the ERPs is the small negative peak and dominant positive peak occurring within the first 200 ms of stimulus presentation. This can be seen to the first phrase (presented at 300 ms into the trial), second phrase (at 2000 ms) and the cue to repeat the statement (at 3500 ms). The *N100* (for negative peak at about 100 ms post-stimulus) and *P200* features are consistently seen in ERPs for visually presented material, and are rarely affected by the task or meaning of the material in ERP studies of language.

Both the studied objects (solid line) and non-studied objects (dotted line) named in the second phrase also produce a sustained positivity extending from about 500 to 1000 ms post-onset (labeled *P600*; likely one of the family of components commonly referred to as 'P300'; see Donchin and Fabiani, Chapter 5 in this volume), followed by a steady negative drift (contingent negative variation, or CNV) in anticipation of making the overt response.

The most interesting feature of the ERPs, in this case, is the striking difference between the two waveforms in the 220–550 ms after onset of the second phrase, peaking at N400. The N400 to non-studied object names is practically eliminated when the first phrase is followed by a studied object. As

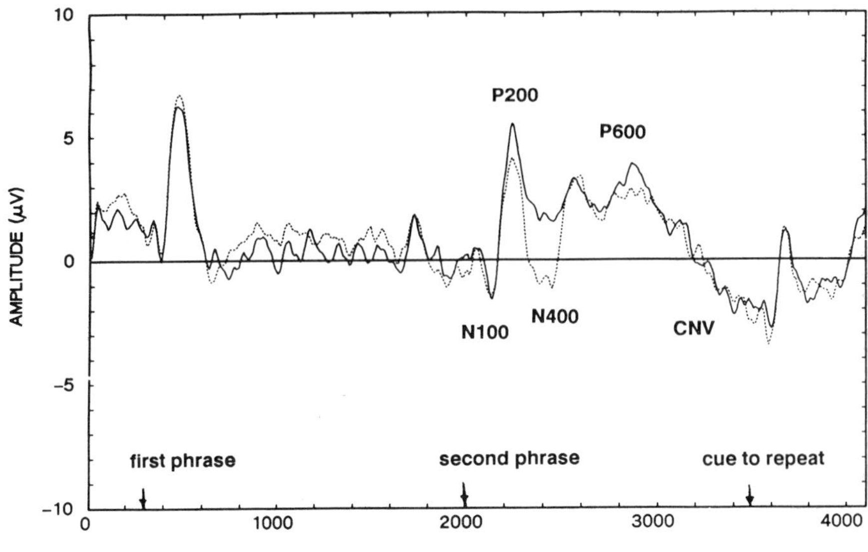

Figure 6.1. Grand averaged ERPs at Cz for statements about studied (solid waveform) and non-studied (dotted waveform) objects following viewing of a videotape (see text). The presentation of the two phrases and cue to repeat them is indicated on the abscissa. Standard labels for the major ERP features are also given.

we will see, this reduction in N400 amplitude to words in predictable contexts has played a central role in studies of language and ERPs.

As with studies of ongoing EEG, much of the initial work on language and ERPs focused on a search for lateral asymmetries as a function of whether the task or materials were 'linguistic' in nature. The disappointing results and increasing recognition of methodological difficulties of this work led to some pessimism about the broader use of ERPs in the study of language dynamics (e.g. Galambos *et al.*, 1975; Picton and Stuss, 1984). But as Kutas and Van Petten (1988) have compellingly argued, a large number of studies have now clearly documented the usefulness of ERPs as indicants of specific linguistic functions. Furthermore, consistent asymmetries can indeed be associated with some of these functions. Although the interest in lateral asymmetries of language continues to be a major part of ERP studies of language (e.g. Kutas, Van Petten and Besson, 1988; Licht *et al.*, 1986), our review will focus on aspects of language and reading less tied to questions of the neurophysiological origin of these functions.

Sublexical Factors

In contrast to the eye movement literature, there has been little work on the effect of physical or visual factors such as length or case of words on word encoding through ERPs. A number of recent studies, however, have been concerned with how orthographic and phonological codes are accessed and integrated in the initial stages of word encoding. Rugg and Nagy (1987) looked for signs of orthographic processing by presenting subjects with orthographically legal (e.g. GRIFE) or non-legal (e.g. EGRFI) non-words. In their first experiment, the task was to count occasional words, so there was no overt response to the non-word stimuli. ERPs to 'legal' non-words that were immediate repetitions of the previous items differed from those of unrepeated non-words by a sustained and topographically widespread positivity beginning about 300 ms post-onset; this *repetition effect* for the non-legal non-words was much smaller and not as temporally sustained. In their second experiment, the task was to detect occasional non-alphabetic characters among the same series of legal and illegal non-words. Despite the non-lexical nature of this task, only the orthographically legal non-words showed a repetition effect in the ERPs; the effect was similar to that found in their first experiment, although somewhat attenuated.

These results suggest that the first presentation of a legal non-word automatically elicits sublexical orthographic codes which are able to 'prime' processing of words that share those codes on a subsequent trial.

Although these results suggest that ERPs are sensitive to orthographic factors in such tasks, the lateness of the repetition effect in the ERPs raises some doubts as to whether it reflects prelexical activity. A comparison of the ERPs on non-repetition trials in the second experiment of Rugg and Nagy (their Figure 2) reveals no consistent differences at any latency. We have suggested (Fischler, 1990) that early components of the ERP may not be sensitive to the prelexical elicitation of orthographic and phonological codes.

A similar conclusion can be drawn about other studies contrasting orthographic and phonological information in words (Kramer and Donchin, 1987; Polich *et al.*, 1983; Rugg, 1984; Rugg and Barrett, 1987). Rugg (1984), for example, had subjects decide if pairs of words or non-words rhymed. He reported the occurrence of a late negative feature (N450) in the ERPs to both words and non-words in the non-rhyming condition. Rugg (1984) suggested that the first item *primed*, by making accessible, the phonological pattern of the rhyming target words, reducing the amount of lexical processing they required and producing a reduced late negativity. Similar patterns in a rhyming task were reported by Polich *et al.* (1983).

Since in Rugg (1984) and Polich *et al.* (1983), the task used was rhyme matching, the occurrence of the late negativity to mismatched pairs could depend on the need intentionally to code this feature of the items. Two more recent studies looked more closely at the role of task and pair similarity in the effects of mismatch on the ERPs. Kramer and Donchin (1987) presented words which matched both in rhyme and orthography (e.g. *match–patch*; their RO condition), only orthographically (XO, e.g. *catch–watch*), only phonologically

(RX, e.g. *blare–stair*) or neither (XX; e.g. *shirt–watch*). For both the rhyme and visual match tasks, a late negative component (N350) was observed that was largest for XX pairs (greatest mismatch) and smallest for RO pairs across tasks. The effect did interact with task, however, since the N350 reduction was not significant when the pair matched phonologically but the task required a visual match RX versus XX). This is consistent with the findings of Rugg (1984) mentioned above, in suggesting that phonological analysis of visually presented words is relatively task-dependent. It is also congruent with recent behavioral studies suggesting that orthographic codes may be elicited relatively automatically when words are spoken, while phonological coding of written words is less obligatory (Tanenhaus, Flanigan and Seidenberg, 1980). These results are in some ways surprising, given the biological and developmental primacy of listening versus reading as forms of language comprehension (but see above). It may be that the automaticity of orthographic analysis is linked to the general dominance of the visual modality over the auditory described by Posner and Nissen (1976).

Reduced late negativity to orthographically similar non-rhyming words during a rhyme-judgement task was also reported by Rugg and Barrett (1987). They observed a strongly right-hemisphere dominant N450 to non-rhyming target words that was delayed, reduced and less asymmetric when the pairs were orthographically similar. The orthographic priming was shown to depend on abstract orthographic features rather than visual similarity, since in their second experiment, neither the behavioral nor ERP pattern was influenced by whether the word pairs were shown in the same case or not.

Rugg and Barrett (1987) went on to show that, while an orthographic priming explanation of the effects of orthography in the rhyme task could deal with the behavioral data, it had difficulty with certain aspects of the ERP results. Their third experiment compared two types of non-rhyming pairs: the previously used orthographically dissimilar pairs (e.g. SPARSE–CREASE), and pairs where the second member had an orthographically similar 'neighbor' that rhymed with the first (e.g. COAST–FROST; with MOST as a neighbor). The 'neighbor' pairs produced the slowest response latencies and a delayed late positive component; however, the N450 to neighbor pairs was identical to that for the non-neighbor pairs. It cannot be the case, then, that the reduction in the N450 component is due strictly to priming of orthographic units of the test word. On the other hand, it is unlikely that a component so strongly lateralized to the right hemisphere reflects only phonological processes, given the lack of right-hemisphere capabilities in such processing (cf. Coltheart, 1983). There is clearly much to be done in specifying the order and interplay of phonological and orthographic events during word recognition. The relative lateness of these components and their sensitivity to task manipulations suggests, on the one hand, that they are part of a postlexical analysis of words; on the other hand, the dissociation of the N450 from overall response time in Rugg and

Barrett's (1987) third experiment suggests that these components are part of the linguistic evaluation of letter strings, rather than early reflections of the difficulty of the arbitrary task assigned to subjects.

To date, these ERP studies of orthographic and phonological processing have been limited to presentation of visual or auditory words to normal hearing subjects in one script. One interesting approach to studying the relation between these codes is the comparison of scripts which differ in how they are mapped on to the phonology of the language (see Henderson, 1982). One comparison of ERPs associated with reading ideographic (hirigana) versus phonetic (kanji) script showed a greater asymmetry for the phonetic script (Hink, Kaga and Suzuki, 1980). Developmental experience also appears to play a role in how visually presented words are processed. Neville, Kutas and Schmidt (1982a,b) compared ERPs to words presented to the left or right of fixation among hearing and deaf adults. Earlier components of the ERPs differentiated the two groups, with an early posterior negativity that was greater contralaterally for hearing but not for deaf subjects. A later negativity (N410) that was largest at the anterior left hemisphere was found for hearing subjects, but not for the deaf, who showed an earlier and less lateralized negativity. A comparison of orthographic and phonological codes with *cheremic* codes in the deaf—sublexical units of hand position, movement and facial expression that determine the meaning of signs (Klima and Bellugi, 1979)—would be an interesting extension of this work, and would help detail the neurological and cognitive specializations that are entailed when language is learned visually.

Lexical Factors

Characteristics of words which have been explored using ERP measures include lexicality, frequency, concreteness of word referents and connotative meaning. Lexicality and frequency can be considered closely linked, since non-words—at least those that conform to the orthography of words—are in one sense just non-familiar words.

If we consider the representation of a word in memory to have at some level an amodal, abstract identity as in Morton's (1969, 1979) popular logogen model, we might expect a unique pattern in the ERPs that mark this convergence. One way to look for such a pattern is to compare ERPs to words versus pseudowords presented out of normal linguistic contexts. In most ERP studies of lexical decision, however, the *lexical status* of the stimulus is confounded with the required response. An exception is in Rugg's (1987) implicit lexical decision, where subjects counted occasional non-words in one experiment, and words in another. A comparison of control words in the first study to control non-words in the second suggests that ERPs to words are less negative as early as 250 ms after stimulus onset. Holcomb and Neville (1990) compared ERPs to words, pseudowords and unpronounceable non-words as part of a semantic priming experiment (see below). For current purposes, the important outcome was that a negativity was observed peaking at around 400 ms after onset that was largest for the pronounceable pseudowords and smallest for the non-words. Holcomb and Neville (1990) suggest that the N400 they observed indicates not lexical access as such, but the search process of the lexicon, with the search terminated earliest for the non-pronounceable items and longest for the pseudowords. The time interval of this search, beginning as early as 200 ms after onset, is roughly consistent with estimates from behavioral studies of the latency of lexical access (cf. Sabol and DeRosa, 1976).

A different approach to the study of lexical access is to compare ERPs to words presented auditorally and visually. Since most of these studies were done as part of explorations of the effects of linguistic contexts on word processing, we will mention these later.

As we have seen, word *frequency* can have substantial effects on performance in a variety of tasks (e.g. Jastrzemski, 1981). These effects often interact with task manipulations, however, and the locus of their effect has remained somewhat controversial (see Balota and Chumbley, 1984, for example). Recently, Smith and Halgren (1988) reported that visual presentation of high-frequency (HF) words resulted in both a larger and earlier P500 than did low-frequency (LF) words. Polich and Donchin (1988) also found that a late positivity was similarly influenced by word frequency, but—in contrast to decision time—was unaffected by the probability of a word versus non-word appearing across blocks of trials. Smith and Halgren (1988) also found an earlier effect of frequency at N430. As would be predicted by the results of Holcomb and Neville (1990), LF words produced a slight but significant increase in the amplitude of the N430.

Collectively, these studies suggest that for visually presented words, a negative-going peak beginning at about 200 ms post-onset and maximal at around 400 ms is the first consistent ERP indicant of the process of lexical access. Interestingly, this component tends to be widespread topographically, observable bilaterally, and largest at central and parietal locations.

The positive effects of word *concreteness* in episodic memory tasks is well documented (see Paivio, 1971), but is much less consistent for semantic tasks (see Kroll and Merves, 1986) and the source of the benefit in episodic tasks has been recently questioned (Schwanenflugel, Harnishfeger and Stowe, 1988).

If, as suggested by the contrasting effects of this variable in episodic and semantic tasks, concreteness is an attribute of words obtained following lexical access which can play a role in its elaborative processing, we might expect that effects of concreteness on ERPs will be fairly late and task-dependent. Several studies have looked at effects of concreteness on ERPs. Paller *et al.* (1988) reported that ERPs to concrete words were more positive than those to abstract words beginning around 300 ms post-onset and extending almost to 1 s. The lateness of the onset of these differences suggests they are linked to the task used by Paller *et al.*, which was to classify the words as to their concreteness.

However, Smith and Halgren (1988) found no effects of concreteness on the ERPs recorded during their lexical decision task (cf. Kroll and Merves, 1986).

The only other attribute of word meaning that has been considered in ERP research has been referred to as '*connotative meaning*', which is closely associated with affective and emotional value of words. Chapman and his colleagues (e.g. Chapman *et al.*, 1980) presented a series of words to subjects and had them rate the connotative meaning on Osgood's Semantic Differential Scale, or simply read the words. In either case, differences in ERP components derived from a principal components analysis differentiated several of the dimensions on Osgood's scale. Words rated as 'active', for example, were distinguished from more passive words in a component with a peak latency of about 350 ms. The early onset of the difference is at least suggestive of a role of connotative attributes in lexical access.

The study of affective and emotional attributes of language in general has been relatively neglected in both behavioral and brain investigations; when linguistic materials are used in studies of emotion, it is more as an incidental convenience to elicit affective responses. There are recent signs, however, of increased interest in how affective knowledge is represented and retrieved (e.g. Greenwald *et al.*, 1988); and a corresponding recognition of the importance of integrating affective and informational aspects of events into models of cognition generally (e.g. Beglieter *et al.*, 1983; Hockey, Gaillard and Coles, 1986; Norman, 1985). It would be valuable in this regard to look more closely at language-specific aspects of the affective dimension of events.

Lexical Ambiguity

Although a number of earlier studies by Brown and his colleagues (e.g. Brown, Marsh and Smith, 1979) compared ERPs to homographs given different biasing contexts (see below), there has been no systematic exploration of ERPs to homographs in isolation. Given the evidence from behavioral and eye fixation studies described above, and the emerging view of the N400 region as reflecting lexical search (see Holcomb and Neville, 1990), we might expect differences between homographs and control words in that region. If, for example, the N400 indicates the degree of search prior to access of at least one entry in the lexicon, then we might expect the results to be similar to that for eye fixations to homographs in neutral contexts, with equibiased homographs giving larger N400s, and biased homographs looking like control words (see the foregoing section on eye fixations during reading).

Context and Word Recognition

ERPs to words in various types of linguistic contexts have been investigated extensively in the past decade. The decade began, in fact, with publication of a seminal report by Kutas and Hillyard (1980b) on ERPs to words in sentence contexts.

Kutas and Hillyard set out to investigate how the late positive component of the ERPs (P300) would be influenced by disruption of linguistic expectancies for words in sentence contexts. The P300 had been associated previously with unexpected or low probability stimulus events. Subjects were asked to read silently and be able to answer questions about a series of short, seven-word sentences presented a word at a time at a central fixation point. Words were shown for 100 ms at a rate of one per second. The final word of the sentence was in some cases a predictable and congruous completion of the sentence (e.g. 'It was his first day at *work*'.), a moderately or strongly incongruous completion (e.g. 'He spread the warm bread with *socks*'.), or a predictable but physically deviant completion, in the form of larger letter size.

The physical deviation of letter size was associated with a classic late positivity (P560); in contrast, the semantic deviation produced a large (*c.* 10 μV), early negative-amplitude feature at about 400 ms post-onset, greatest at the central and parietal sites. The N400 was evident bilaterally, with a tendency to be greater at right hemisphere sites (Kutas and Hillyard, 1980a). There was no significant increase in the later positivity for even the strongly incongruous completions compared with the predictable completions. It was later shown that neither grammatical anomalies within sentences (e.g. 'Ice begins to *grew* around invisible specks...'; Kutas and Hillyard, 1983), nor disruptions of expectancies in non-linguistic but coherent sequences of stimuli such as melodies (Besson and Macar, 1987), resulted in ERPs with the N400 feature. Further evidence for the linguistic nature of the N400 came from studies showing similar effects of contextual incongruity with words presented auditorally rather than visually (McCallum, Farmer and Pocock, 1984; cf. Holcomb and Neville, 1990).

Since Kutas and Hillyard (1980b) always presented the target words at the end of the sentences, it might be thought that the N400 was associated with disrupted processes of syntactic or semantic closure. But an N400 was also found when the incongruity appeared in earlier portions of sentences (Kutas and Hillyard, 1983). Recently, Van Petten and Kutas (1987b) showed that the first two or three words of sentences was sufficient to produce a N400 as large as that observed at the sentences' end.

Kutas and Hillyard (1980a,b) initially suggested that the N400 reflected a reaction to the incongruity of the sentence. But subsequent research has indicated that a similar feature can be obtained in ERPs in a wide variety of circumstances, the common feature of which is that the target word is not predictable from a preceding linguistic context. These studies have been reviewed recently in detail by Kutas and Van Petten (1988) and summarized by Fischler (1990). In this review, we will focus on some of the highlights of this literature that consider the role of incongruity and expectancy, the type of linguistic context (words versus sentences), the kind of knowledge or memory that relates the context and target word, and the extent to which the reduction of N400 with contexts is under a subject's attentional control.

In a series of studies, we have explored whether the kind of knowledge represented by the sentence was important in modulating the N400 component. In each of these studies, subjects were shown a series of sentences in three successive frames or fragments. The final frame was a single word which either fit the sentence context, or was incongruent with it. Across these experiments, the incongruous tests were associated with a large-amplitude N400 that was greatly reduced or absent when the completion was congruent with the context. The congruence could be based on semantic or general knowledge, (e.g. 'A robin / is a / [*bird* or *tool*]'; Fischler *et al.*, 1983), self-referential facts obtained prior to the experiment (e.g. 'My name / is / [*Ira* or *Nate*]'; Fischler *et al.*, 1984), or arbitrary episodic information acquired by subjects in the laboratory prior to ERP testing (e.g. 'Diane / is a / [*lawyer* or *dentist*]'; Fischler *et al.*, 1985).

These studies showed that semantic anomaly was not necessary to obtain an N400, in the sense that in the latter two experiments, the sentences producing the N400s were perfectly sensible, but false for that subject. Similarly, Kutas, Lindamood and Hillyard (1984) reported that words which were unexpected but contextually acceptable completions of sentences (e.g. 'He mailed the letter without a *check*') elicited a typical N400; thus, the amplitude of the N400 was seen as a monotonic, inverse function of the predictability of a word in context, with the semantic anomalies as the least predictable condition.

Sentence Versus Lexical Contexts

It was quickly realized that the contextual constraint reducing N400 need not take the form of a sentence; a short list of words from one semantic category followed by a word from another category will produce an N400 to the final, discrepant word (Harbin, Marsh and Harvey, 1984; Polich, 1985). Kutas (1985) also found similar N400s to words in incongruous sentence contexts and following unrelated single-word primes. In part for this reason, the majority of studies of N400 and linguistic contexts have used single-word contexts that are semantically related or unrelated to the target word (e.g. Bentin, 1987; Boddy, 1986; Holcomb, 1988).

Fischler *et al.* (1983) directly contrasted the contribution of the meaning of the sentence and that of individual words in the sentence to the N400 modulation. We included four types of sentences, as shown here:

(15) A robin is a bird (true, affirmative)
(16) A robin is a tool (false, affirmative)
(17) A robin is not a bird (false, negative)
(18) A robin is not a tool (true, negative)

To the extent that the predictiveness or truth of the sentence proposition as a whole determines the N400 effect, sentences (16) and (17) should be associated with larger N400s. But in fact, strong and equivalent N400s were observed for the sentences in which the subject and predicate were unrelated, i.e. (16) and (18), regardless of the validity of the sentence. This suggests that the overall meaning of the sentence is relatively unimportant in the elicitation of the N400.

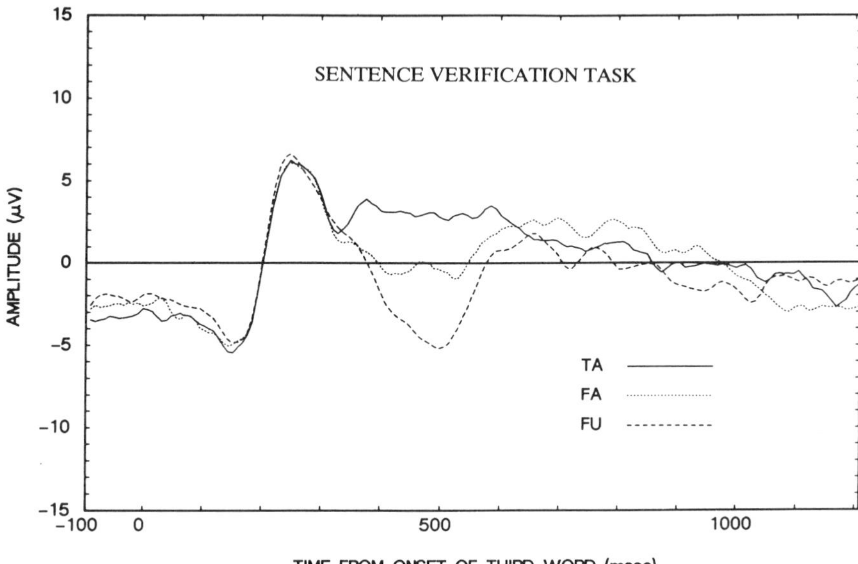

Figure 6.2. Grand averaged ERPs at Cz for the third (final) word of statements in a sentence verification task. TA = true and associated (e.g. 'robins are birds'); FA = false but associated (e.g. 'robins are sparrows'); FU = false and unassociated (e.g. 'robins are wagons').

We subsequently found that if the sentences were all affirmative, sentence validity could affect the size of the N400 reduction to lexical associates; as can be clearly seen in Figure 6.2, the N400 to false sentences like 'Robins are sparrows' (false/associated) was greater than to true sentences like 'Robins are birds' (true/associated) where the pairs were equated for associative strength (Fischler *et al.*, 1985). Still, the influence of lexical association was substantial in spite of the sentence-level task, since false sentences with unassociated terms (e.g. 'Robins are fish'; false/unassociated) produced a significantly larger N400 than did the false/associated sentences.

In contrast, when the task was to judge the relatedness of the two words, no effect of sentence validity can be seen at all (Figure 6.3). The pattern of results suggested that the reduction of N400 in linguistic contexts had little to do with

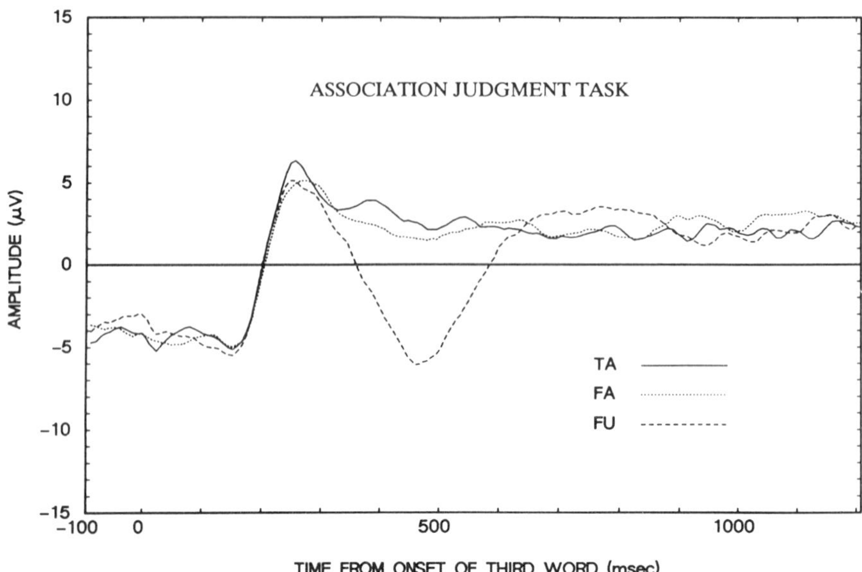

Figure 6.3. Grand averaged ERPs at Cz for the third (final) word of statements in an association judgment task (see text). TA = true and associated; FA = false but associated; FU = false and unassociated.

sentence structure or meaning, and was closely tied to the lexical association of prime and target words. This process appears to most closely resemble the semantic priming between pairs of words described by Meyer and Schvaneveldt (1971) and others (see above). The role of semantic priming within sentence contexts was also demonstrated by Kutas, Lindamood and Hillyard (1984), who found that when a sentence was completed with a word that was an anomalous ending but semantically associated with a predicted ending (e.g. 'The game was called when it started to *umbrella*'), the N400 was significantly reduced.

The similarity of effects of sentence and single-word contexts on the N400, and the suggestion that the sentence-context effects are in fact mediated by a semantic priming mechanism, resembles the pattern obtained in behavioral studies of context effects on pronunciation latency rather than on lexical decision. This pattern has suggested to several researchers (e.g. Bentin, 1987; Holcomb, 1988; Kutas and Van Petten, 1989) that the effects of linguistic contexts on N400 reflects changes in the process of lexical search and access. This would be consistent with the observation of Van Petten and Kutas (1987b), for example, that while low-frequency words at the beginnings of sentences were associated with larger N400 components than were high-frequency words, the effects of frequency interacted with contextual constraint, so that for contextually-appropriate words appearing later in the sentences, the effect of frequency on the ERPs was eliminated.

Attention and Automaticity

A series of recent studies of ERPs and single-word semantic primes have focused on the degree to which the N400 reduction can be obtained automatically. The distinction between processes that are automatic—rapid, difficult to avoid, and not requiring attentional resources—and those that are slower, effortful, and controlled by the subject's strategies and intentions in a given task, has been an important theoretical aspect of the analysis of semantic priming effects (e.g. Neely, 1977), and of cognitive abilities more generally (cf. Posner and Snyder, 1975; Schneider and Shiffrin, 1977). The results of these studies suggest that contextual reduction of N400 has both attentional and automatic components. Bentin (1987), for example, presented word and non-word contextual primes to subjects. On the word-prime trials, they were instructed to generate an antonym associate for the prime (e.g. HOT—*cold*), and indicate whether the following target word was that antonym. This task was intended to maximize the attentional component of priming for the target word. On the non-word-prime trials, they simply made a lexical decision to the target. An N400 to the unprimed (non-antonym) target words was obtained that was unaffected by whether subjects were expecting an antonym (word-prime trials) or merely waiting for the target presentation (non-word-prime trials).

Taking a different approach, Holcomb (1988) compared the ERPs to target words preceded by semantically related or unrelated prime words, or by a neutral fixation field. In an 'attentional' condition, the proportion of trials with related pairs was 50% (see den Heyer, Briand and Dannenbring, 1983) and subjects were encouraged to try to anticipate the target word based on the meaning of the prime. In the 'automatic' condition, the proportion of related pairs was low (12.5%) and subjects were instructed to ignore the prime. In both conditions, unrelated targets produced a significant N400 compared with the related targets, although the size of the difference was significantly reduced in the automatic condition (cf. Rugg, 1987). Interestingly, in the attentional condition, the N400 for unrelated and neutral conditions was equivalent; in contrast, a later positive slow wave was larger and more sustained, and response latency longer, for the unrelated than for the neutral conditions (see Holcomb, 1988; Figure 2). The slow wave and response latency differences were not found in the automatic condition. These latter results are consistent with the idea that inhibition of responses to unexpected events will occur when attention is engaged (cf. Neely, 1977), and provides additional evidence that the priming effects seen in the N400 are relatively automatic.

Kutas (1985) also used a task designed to minimize attentional strategies during presentation of related and unrelated word pairs. In that study, subjects read each word silently, then were shown a target letter, and had to decide if the letter had occurred in either the prime or the target. Despite this non-lexical task (see Henik, Friedrich and Kellogg, 1983), a small but significant N400 was observed to the unrelated target words.

Since automatic priming occurs rapidly, attentional components of priming can be attenuated or eliminated by shortening the time between onset of the priming context and target words (SOA). Kutas (1988) did this by using the RSVP procedure (described earlier) for sentence contexts, presenting words at the rate of 10 per second. The N400 to inappropriate words in context was observed at this rapid rate (cf. Fischler and Bloom, 1980), although it was somewhat smaller than that found at normal reading speeds. Boddy (1985) reduced the SOA between a single-word prime and target words to 200 ms, and observed a significant N400 to words preceded by semantically unrelated primes.

Context, Lexical Ambiguity and the N400

Given that the amplitude of the N400 appears closely associated with the processes of lexical search and access in the above studies, it would seem a natural tool for addressing the issue of autonomy of lexical access. Early studies suggesting that ERPs could indicate differential meanings of homographs in context were reported by Brown and Marsh (e.g. Brown, Marsh and Smith, 1979). More recently, Van Petten and Kutas (1987a) used a wholly visual version of the cross-modal sentence priming paradigm (e.g. Onifer and Swinney, 1981), in which a complete sentence was presented a word at a time in a fixed location. Each word was presented for 200 ms, with a 900 ms SOA between words. Either 16 ms or 700 ms after offset of the last word, a target word was presented which was named as quickly as possible. On critical sentences, the context was congruent with the subordinate sense of a biased homograph, which was the final word of the sentence, as in (19):

(19) The gambler pulled an ace from the bottom of the deck.

The target word was one of three types: related to the contextually appropriate meaning (e.g. *cards*), to the inappropriate meaning (e.g. *ship*), or unrelated to either sense of the homographs (e.g. *parent*). The critical findings involved comparison of the ERPs for the three types of words at the long versus short SOA. At the longer SOA, when the post-access selection process should have been completed, only the context-appropriate target word showed a reduction in the N400, compared with that for the unrelated and the inappropriate target. In contrast, at the short SOA, the ERPs for the inappropriate and the unrelated targets were equivalent until about 500 ms after target onset, at which point the ERP for the inappropriate meaning became somewhat less negative than that for the unrelated target; the contextually appropriate target showed a reduced N400 compared with the other types of targets, beginning at around 300 ms. post-onset.

Van Petten and Kutas (1987a) argued that this pattern of results is evidence against an exhaustive and autonomous model of lexical access, since the context appeared selectively to facilitate access of the subordinate meaning. They suggested that the late emergence of an ERP difference between inappropriate and control conditions at the short SOA could be a sign of 'backward priming', with the target word itself helping to activate the inappropriate sense of the homograph (cf. Glucksberg, Kreuz and Rho, 1986). Alternatively, a *reordered-search* model (see above) might also predict such a late emergence, as the activation of the subordinate meaning would benefit from both lexical and sentence-level priming, but the normally dominant meaning would have only the lexical priming from the homograph. Since equibiased homographs were not presented, the selective access and reordered access models could not be differentiated in the design, as the authors point out.

Given the complex nature of the evidence, and the theoretical importance of the autonomy issue, it is not surprising that controversy continues about lexical access and context in both the ERP literature (e.g. Hammond and Rugg, 1987; Samar and Berent, 1986) and in behavioral studies of reading (e.g. Simpson *et al.*, 1989; West and Stanovich, 1986). But the Van Petten and Kutas (1987a) study is notable as an example of how studies of ERPs and language are approaching the level of specificity until recently only found in studies of gaze duration; and how dissociations between behavioral and physiological data can provide important clues about the dynamics of language function.

Syntactic Factors

As the focus of language processing moves up from sublexical and lexical levels to that of syntax and text-level integration, we find few studies using ERP methods. Some observations can be made about the overall pattern of ERPs during sentence presentation; with word-by-word presentation, there is typically a negative shift (see Fischler *et al.*, 1983; Kutas and Hillyard, 1980b) following the first few words of the sentence which is resolved with a substantial positive rebound following presentation of the final word of the sentence that Friedman *et al.* (1975) related to 'syntactic closure', but that Herning, Jones and Hunt (1987) saw as more generally related to sentence comprehension and integration.

One recent study illustrates the potential use of the N400 component to address issues of syntactic analysis. Garnsey, Tanenhaus and Chapman (1987) tested the immediacy hypothesis for how certain syntactic ambiguities were dealt with. Consider the following sentence:

(20) The mother found out which [*food* or *book*] the child read...

In this context, the word 'read' is syntactically ambiguous, since it could be followed by '...about at school' or 'at school'. If both structures are elicited and maintained until the ambiguity is resolved, then the ERP to the target word *read* should be similar following either *food* or *book*. In fact, an N400 was observed that was larger following the *food* version, suggesting that the structure 'which X the child read' received the same immediate syntactic assignment despite the semantic inconsistency that resulted.

We are not aware of other ERP investigations of syntactic processing that address how specific syntactic rules or strategies are implemented, as has been the case with reaction time and eye fixation studies. The syntactic anomalies used by Kutas and Hillyard (1983) were modest and not theoretically motivated; the syntactic violations used by Samar and Berent (1986) were isolated from sentence contexts (e.g. *the boy* versus *the bring*).

Integrative Processes

A few years ago, the time seemed ripe for application of ERP research to questions of text comprehension (Rugg *et al.*, 1986). But two developments have postponed, at least, any significant efforts in that direction. First was the demonstration that the N400 component was not linked to sentence processing as such, as had been originally suggested by Kutas and Hillyard. The majority of recent studies of N400 and language have used single-word semantic primes. Second was the demonstration of differential patterns among late ERP components recording during a study phase for material later remembered versus forgotten (see Donchin and Fabiani, this volume). This has led to a series of studies manipulating the nature of processing during study, the amount of repetition of material, and the type of memory test (e.g. Neville *et al.*, 1987), with the linguistic nature of the material more or less incidental to the main issue of memory encoding and retrieval.

The fine-grained time resolution of ERPs is no obstacle to the analysis of issues of reading more global than the effects of context on lexical access; the success of eye fixation methods to explore text-level integrative processes demonstrates the value of having an unobtrusive, finely resolved measure of such activity. There may have been a tendency to avoid text-level manipulations because of the apparent need for single-word presentations. But as we have seen earlier, scanning of eyes across the page is not a requirement of reading for comprehension. Alternatively, a recent study by Marton and Szirtes (1988) suggests that meaningful ERPs can be reliably obtained by triggering the averaging to saccades that occur during normal reading. In fact, in their second experiment, such saccade-related potentials (SRPs) to final, semantically anomalous words displayed a negativity that resembled the N400 (ranging from 280 to 460 ms post-onset). Intriguingly, when they had subjects make an overt congruity decision, the negativity to the final anomalous word appeared much earlier (80–310 ms post-onset).

Summary

Of the various CNS measures of mental activity during reading, event-related potentials have in some ways been most successful, in terms of the breadth of issues dealt with, the specificity of questions about how reading proceeds, and the degree to which many of the studies have been motivated by cognitive and linguistic issues, rather than neurological or energetic ones. Much of the work to date has involved validation of the endogenous components observed during tasks which have been defined and developed in the behavioral tradition (Fischler, 1990; Kutas and Van Petten, 1989). As the area matures, more of a balance should be seen between such validating studies, on the one hand, and research using these validated components to address theoretical questions about language and cognition. The study of ambiguity and context by Van Petten and Kutas (1987a) is a good example of the way such a validated ERP component can provide a unique view of a linguistic process.

AN INTEGRATED APPROACH TO READING

Reading is the prototypical cognitive activity: demanding of great effort, depending on exquisitely tuned pattern recognition skills, eliciting spatial, verbal and more abstract codes, engaging the full range of our linguistic abilities, and providing the fabric and substance for thinking and learning. Cognitive psychologists also seem particularly attracted to reading because, to an outside observer, the subject appears to be doing nothing at all.

PHYSIOLOGY, BEHAVIOR, AND THE LEVEL OF ANALYSIS

We have seen how behavioral and psychophysiological studies alike have focused on a few key issues in language comprehension by eye. Molecular studies almost always have taken individual words as the unit of analysis, and explored how sublexical, lexical and contextual factors influence recognition of the word in print. The impact of the modular versus interactive models of word recognition has been striking, and work at this level has been dominated, perhaps more than it should be, by what is in broader view only a small part of reading behavior—the access of a word's meaning from memory. Questions of ambiguity and its resolution, of contextual constraint and expectations, and to some extent of integrative activity during reading, have all been framed in terms of the autonomy-of-access issue.

At a more molar level, the unit of analysis has been the proposition, with the key issue being how the structured knowledge contained in the text and in the reader's head create new knowledge during reading. For the most part, there is not yet a psychophysiology of reading in this sense; work using the major central or autonomic measures we have reviewed either are focused at a molecular level, most notably ERPs and pupil size; or take a rather gross view of reading and consider variables like text difficulty, good versus bad readers, or reading versus some other task; most of the cerebral blood flow and EEG work is at this level. The success of measures of eye fixation as an unobtrusive, high-resolution behavioral index of more global aspects of reading such as text-level integration and the identification of referents in text suggests that the correspondingly fine-grained physiological measures such as ERPs and pupil size could fruitfully be used to explore these more global processes.

AUTONOMIC AND CENTRAL MEASURES OF READING

Autonomic measures are commonly seen as associated with affective or energetic responses of a fairly diffuse nature, both in time and content. Central measures, in contrast, are taken to be a window on more informational, cognitive processes and stages that allow more real-time analysis. Our review shows that for the study of reading, at least, this view is far too simplistic. In the first place, the temporal grain of autonomic measures ranges almost as widely as that of the central measures, with some of the latter (e.g. cerebral blood flow) presently incapable of the sort of temporal grain one can get from pupil size or heart rate shifts. Second, we have seen that studies of autonomic activity during reading rarely concern affective or emotional aspects of the task; rather, the measures commonly serve to indicate transient or more sustained cognitive demands of comprehending text. Conversely, it is striking the extent to which both behavioral and brain measures of the 'informational aspects' of text processing depend on energetic assumptions; for example, eye fixation and reaction time studies of effects of context on lexical ambiguity are both based on the idea that eliciting two words from memory increases the processing demands or difficulty at that point, which requires more time. Latency and amplitude changes in ERP components, and changes in the power of certain EEG frequency bands, are similarly interpreted in energetic terms. It may be that more qualitative aspects of any of these measures will ultimately be shown to be a direct reflection of the content or structure of a task (in our view, topographic patterns in brain activity, be it measured through electrical, metabolic or magnetic means, are the most likely candidates); but at the present time it is clear that our view of reading comes through an energetic lens, whether that lens is focused on autonomic or central activity.

To turn the argument around, even when the interest is in affective aspects of comprehension, central measures of emotion may have much to contribute, as suggested by Chapman's ERP studies of connotative aspects of word meaning. There also are circumstances where central and autonomic measures concurrently recorded provide complementary or convergent evidence on some process. For example, there is growing interest in the use of central measures such as ERPs in polygraphy applications. To the extent that central and autonomic measures reflect different aspects of, say, a subject's knowledge about material he is reading, then combining the signal from these two 'channels' could improve the discriminability of such tests. It would be most interesting to see if integration of a central and autonomic measure of a given process systematically provides more 'gain' than combination of two different measures within central or autonomic systems.

DISSOCIATIONS AMONG MEASURES OF READING

In many cases, as we have seen, various measures of reading provide either redundant or complementary information about specific processes. The really interesting cases, though, are when measures dissociate, with one showing an effect, and the other, either nothing or an effect in the opposite direction. One of the better known examples in ERP studies is the almost complete insensitivity of P300 to response-associated factors such as stimulus–response compatibility (Coles *et al.*, 1985). Similarly, Fischler *et al.* (1985) found that the N400 elicited by false sentence completions was uninfluenced by whether subjects responded correctly, incorrectly, or made no response at all; and Rugg and Barrett (1987) found a dissociation between the effects of type of word pair on response latency and on the amplitude of their N450. Interpretation of these and similar dissociations mark an advance over earlier work, where the question was often whether the psychophysiological index was sensitive or silent to some behaviorally defined process or state. For the most part, we have seen relatively few such dissociations among the various measures of language processes during reading. But as the territory of the various measures begins to overlap more, it is likely that this will change. Rigorous pursuit of such dissociations in the context of explicit theories of reading may be the most direct route to an integrated view of the psychology of language by eye.

REFERENCES

Aaronson, D. and Ferres, S. (1984). The word-by-word reading paradigm: an experimental and theoretical approach. In D.E. Kieras and M.A. Just (eds), *New Methods in Reading Comprehension Research*. Hillsdale, NJ: Erlbaum.

Aaronson, D. and Scarborough, H.S. (1976). Performance theories for sentence coding: some quantitative evidence. *Journal of Experimental Psychology: Human Perception and Performance*, **2**, 56–70.

Aasman, J., Mulder, G. and Mulder, J.M. (1987). Operator effort and the measurement of heart rate variability. *Human Factors*, **29**, 161–170.

Ahern, S. and Beatty, J. (1981). Physiological evidence that demand for processing capacity varies with intelligence. In M. Friedman, J. Das and N. O'Connor (eds), *Intelligence and Learning*. New York: Plenum Press.

Anderson, J.R. (1985). *Cognitive Psychology and its Implications*, 2nd edn. New York: Freeman.

Angelotti, M., Behnke, R.R. and Carlile, L.W. (1973). Heart rate as a measure of reading involvement. *Florida Journal of Educational Research*, **15**, 3–9.

Balota, D.A. and Chumbley, J.I. (1984). Are lexical decisions a good measure of lexical access? The role of word frequency in the neglected decision stage. *Journal of Experimental Psychology: Human Perception and Performance*, **10**, 340–357.

Balota, D.A., Pollatsek, A. and Rayner, K. (1985). The interaction of contextual constraints and parafoveal information in reading. *Cognitive Psychology*, **17**, 364–390.

Beatty, J. (1982). Task-evoked pupillary responses, processing load and the structure of processing resources. *Psychological Bulletin*, **91**, 276–292.

Beatty, J. and Wagoner, B. (1978). Pupillometric signs of brain activation vary with level of cognitive processing. *Science*, **199**, 1216–1218.

Beglieter, H., Projesz, B., Chou, C.L. and Aunon, J.I. (1983). P3 and stimulus incentive value. *Psychophysiology*, **20**, 95–101.

Bellugi, U. (1987). The acquisition of a spatial language. In F. Kessel (ed.), *The Development of Language and Language Researchers: Essays in Honor of Roger Brown*. Hillsdale, NJ: Erlbaum.

Bentin, S. (1987). Event-related potentials, semantic processes and expectancy factors in word recognition. *Brain and Language*, **31**, 308–327.

Besson, M. and Macar, F. (1987). An event-related potential analysis of incongruity in music and other non-linguistic contexts. *Psychophysiology*, **24**, 14–25.

Boddy, J. (1985). Brain event related potentials in the investigation of language processing. In D. Papakostopolous, S. Butler and I. Martin (eds), *Clinical and Experimental Neuropsychophysiology*. Beckenham, England: Croom Helm.

Boddy, J. (1986). Event-related potentials in chronometric analysis of primed word recognition with different stimulus onset asynchronies. *Psychophysiology*, **23**, 232–244.

Bradley, M., York, D. and Lang, P. (1989). Emotion as context in memory. Unpublished manuscript, University of Florida.

Bransford, J.D. and Johnson, M.K. (1972). Contextual prerequisites for understanding: some investigations of comprehension and recall. *Journal of Verbal Learning and Verbal Behavior*, **11**, 717–726.

Britten, B.K., Glynn, S.M., Meyer, B.J.F. and Penland, M.J. (1982). Effects of text structure on use of cognitive capacity during reading. *Journal of Educational Psychology*, **74**, 51–61.

Britten, B.K., Westbrook, R.D. and Holdredge, T.S. (1978). Reading and cognitive capacity usage: effects of text difficulty. *Journal of Experimental Psychology: Human Learning and Memory*, **4**, 582–591.

Brooker, B.H. and Donald, M.W. (1980). Contribution of the speech musculature to apparent human EEG asymmetries prior to vocalization. *Brain and Language*, **9**, 226–245.

Brown, W.S., Marsh, J.T. and Smith, J.C. (1979). Principal component analysis of ERP differences related to the meaning of an ambiguous word. *Electroencephalography and Clinical Neurophysiology*, **46**, 709–714.

Cacioppo, J.T. (1979). Effects of exogenous changes in heart rate on facilitation of thought and resistance to persuasion. *Journal of Personality and Social Psychology*, **37**, 2181–2199.

Carroll, P. and Slowiaczek, M. (1986). Constraints on semantic priming in reading: a fixation time analysis. *Memory and Cognition*, **14**, 509–522.

Carpenter, P.A. and Daneman, M. (1981). Lexical retrieval and error recovery in reading: a model based on eye fixations. *Journal of Verbal Learning and Verbal Behavior*, **20**, 137–160.

Carpenter, P.A. and Just, M.A. (1975). Sentence comprehension: a psycholinguistic processing model of verification. *Psychological Review*, **82**, 45–73.

Carpenter, P.A. and Just, M.A. (1983). What your eyes do while your mind is reading. In K. Rayner (ed.), *Eye Movements in Reading*. New York: Academic Press.

Caton, R. (1875). The electric currents of the brain. *British Medical Journal*, **2**, 278.

Chapman, R.M., McCrary, J.W., Chapman, J.A. and Martin, J.K. (1980). Behavioral and neural analyses of connotative meaning: word classes and rating scales. *Brain and Language*, **11**, 319–339.

Cirilo, R.K. and Foss, D.J. (1980). Text structure and reading time for sentences. *Journal of Verbal Learning and Verbal Behavior*, **19**, 96–109.

Cofer, C.N. (1941). A comparison of logical and verbatim learning of prose passages of different lengths. *American Journal of Psychology*, **54**, 1–21.

Coles, M. G. H. (1984). Heart rate and attention: the intake-rejection hypothesis and beyond. In M.G.H. Coles, J.R. Jennings and J.A. Stern (eds), *Psychophysiological Perspectives: Festschrift for Beatrice and John Lacey*. New York: Van Nostrand Reinhold.

Coles, M.G.H., Gratton, G., Bashore, T.R., Eriksen, C.W. and Donchin, E. (1985). A psychophysiological investigation of the continuous flow model of human information processing. *Journal of Experimental Psychology: Human Perception and Performance*, **11**, 529–553.

Coles, M.G.H. and Strayer, D.L. (1985). The psychophysiology of the cardiac cycle time effect. In J.F. Orlebeke, G., Mulder and L.J.P. van Doornen (eds), *Psychophysiology of Cardiovascular Control*. New York: Plenum Publishing.

Colley, A.M. (1987). Text comprehension. In J.R. Beech and A.M. Colley (eds), *Cognitive Approaches to Reading*. Chichester: Wiley.

Coltheart, M. (1983). The right hemisphere and disorders of reading. In A. W. Young (ed.), *Functions of the Right Cerebral Hemisphere*. London: Academic Press.

Daneman, M. and Carpenter, P.A. (1980). Individual differences in working memory and reading. *Journal of Verbal Learning and Verbal Behavior*, **19**, 450–466.

Das-Smaal, E.A. and De Swart, J.H. (1984). Variation within categories. *Acta Psychologica*, **57**, 165–192.

Davidson, R.J. and Schwartz, G.E. (1977). The influence of musical training on patterns of EEG asymmetry during musical and non-musical self-generation tasks. *Psychophysiology*, **14**, 58–63.

Deecke, L., Kornhuber, H.H., Schrieber, H., Lang, M., Lang., W., Kornhuber, A., Heise, B. and Keidel, M. (1986). Bereitschaftspotential associated with writing and drawing. In W.C. McCallum, R. Zappoli and F. Denoth (eds), *Cerebral Psychophysiology: Studies in Event-Related Potentials* EEG, Suppl. 38). Amsterdam: Elsevier.

Den Heyer, K., Briand, K. and Dannenbring, G. (1983). Strategic factors in a lexical decision task: evidence for automatic and attention-driven processes. *Memory and Cognition*, **11**, 374–381.

Denkowski, K.M., Denkowski, G.C. and Omizo, M.M. (1983). The effects of EMG-assisted relaxation training on the academic performance, locus of control, and self-esteem of hyperactive boys. *Biofeedback and Self Regulation*, **8**, 363–375.

De Swart, J.H. and Das-Smaal, E.A. (1979). Orienting reflex and uncertainty reduction in a concept learning task. In H.D. Kimmel, E.H. van Olst and J.F. Orlebeke (eds), *The Orienting Reflex in Humans*. Hillsdale, NJ: Lawrence Erlbaum Associates.

Drewnowski, A. and Healy, A.F. (1982). Phonetic factors in letter detection: a reevaluation. *Memory and Cognition*, **10**, 145–154.

Duffy, S.A., Morris, R.K. and Rayner, K. (1988). Lexical ambiguity and fixation times in reading. *Journal of Memory and Language*, **27**, 429–446.

Dunn, B. (1985). Bimodal processing and memory from text. In V.M. Rentel, S.A. Corson and B.R. Dunn (eds), *Psychophysiological Aspects of Reading and Learning*. New York: Gordon and Breach.

Dunn, B.R., Mathews, S.R. and Bieger, G.R. (1982). Deviation from hierarchical structure in recall: is there an 'optimal' structure? *Journal of Experimental Child Psychology*, **34**, 371–386.

Edelberg, R. (1972). Electrical activity of the skin: its measurement and uses in psychophysiology. In N.S. Greenfield and R.A. Sternbach (eds), *Handbook of Psychophysiology*. New York: Holt, Rinehart and Winston.

Ehrlich, S.F. and Rayner, K. (1981). Contextual effects on word perception and eye movements during reading. *Journal of Verbal Learning and Verbal Behavior*, **20**, 641–655.

Ehrlich, K. and Rayner, K. (1983). Pronoun assignment and semantic integration during reading: eye movements and immediacy of processing. *Journal of Verbal Learning and Verbal Behavior*, **22**, 75–87.

Ehrlichman, H. and Wiener, M.S. (1980). EEG asymmetry during covert mental activity. *Psychophysiology*, **17**, 228–235.

Evans, D. (1976). The factorial structure of responses to conceptual complexity. *Journal of General Psychology*, **94**, 187–192.

Fedora, O. and Schopflocher, D. (1984). Bilateral electrodermal activity during differential cognitive hemispheric activation. *Psychophysiology*, **21**, 307–311.

Ferreira, F. and Clifton, C. (1986). The independence of syntactic processing. *Journal of Memory and Language*, **25**, 348–368.

Fischler, I. (1975). Detection and identification of words and letters in simulated visual search of word lists. *Memory and Cognition*, **3**, 175–182.

Fischler, I. (1990). Comprehending language with ERPs. In J.W. Rohrbaugh and R. Parasuraman (eds), *Issues in Event-Related Potential Research: Tutorials and Interdisciplinary Vantages*. New York: Oxford University Press.

Fischler, I. and Bloom, P.A. (1979). Automatic and attentional processes in the effects of sentence contexts on word recognition. *Journal of Verbal Learning and Verbal Behavior*, **18**, 1–20.

Fischler, I. and Bloom, P.A. (1980). Rapid processing of the meaning of sentences. *Memory and Cognition*, **8**, 216–225.

Fischler, I., Bloom, P.A., Childers, D.G., Arroyo, A.A. and Perry, N.W. (1984). Brain potentials during sentence verification: late negativity and long-term memory strength. *Neuropsychologia*, **22**, 559–568.

Fischler, I., Bloom, P.A., Childers, D.G., Roucos, S.E. and Perry, N.W. (1983). Brain potentials related to stages of sentence verification. *Psychophysiology*, **20**, 400–409.

Fischler, I., Boaz, T., Childers, D.G. and Perry, N.W. (1985). Lexical and propositional components of priming during sentence comprehension. *Psychophysiology*, **22**, 576 (abstract).

Fischler, I., Childers, D.G., Achariyapaopan, T. and Perry, N.W. (1985). Brain potentials during sentence verification: automatic aspects of comprehension. *Biological Psychology*, **21**, 83–106.

Fodor, J. A. (1983). *Modularity of Mind*. Cambridge, MA: MIT Press.

Forster, K.I. (1970). Visual perception of rapidly presented word sequences of varying complexity. *Perception and Psychophysics*, **8**, 215–221.

Forster, K.I. (1979). Levels of processing and the structure of the language processor. In W.E. Cooper and E.C.T. Walker (eds), *Sentence Processing: Psycholinguistic Studies*

Presented to Merrill Garrett. Hillsdale, NJ: Erlbaum.

Foss, D.J. (1982). A discourse on semantic priming. *Cognitive Psychology*, **14**, 590–607.

Fox, P.T., Mintun, M.A., Raichle, M.E., Miezin, F.M., Allman, J.M. and Van Essen, D.C. (1986). Mapping human visual cortex with positron emission tomography. *Nature*, **323**, 806–809

Fox, P.T., Mintun, M.A., Reiman, E.M. and Raichle, M.E. (1988). Enhanced detection of focal brain responses using intersubject averaging and change-distribution analysis of subtracted PET images. *Journal of Cerebral Blood Flow and Metabolism*, **8**, 642–653.

Frazier, L. and Rayner, K. (1982). Making and correcting errors during sentence comprehension: eye movements in the analysis of structurally ambiguous sentences. *Cognitive Psychology*, **14**, 178–210.

Fredericksen, C.H. (1975). Representing logical and semantic structure of knowledge acquired from discourse. *Cognitive Psychology*, **7**, 371–458.

Friedman, D., Simson, R., Ritter, W. and Rappin, I. (1975). The late positive component (P300) and information processing in sentences. *Electroencephalography and Clinical Neurophysiology*, **38**, 255–262.

Galambos, R., Benson, P., Smith, T.S., Schulman-Galambos, C. and Osier, H. (1975). On hemispheric differences in evoked potentials to speech stimuli. *Electroencephalography and Clinical Neurophysiology*, **39**, 279–283.

Galin, D. and Ornstein, R. (1972). Lateral specialization of cognitive mode: an EEG study. *Psychophysiology*, **9**, 412–418.

Gardner, H. (1985). *The Mind's New Science: A History of the Cognitive Revolution*. New York: Basic Books.

Garnsey, S.M., Tanenhaus, M.K. and Chapman, R.M. (1987). Event related potential measures of parsing in locally structurally ambiguous sentences. *Proceedings of the 4th International Conference on Cognitive Neuroscience*, Paris, June.

Gevins, A.S., Zeitlin, J.C., Doyle, R.E., Schaffer, R.E. and Callaway, E. (1979). EEG patterns during 'cognitive' tasks. II: Analysis of controlled tasks. *Electroencephalography and Clinical Neurophysiology*, **47**, 704–710.

Gibson, E.J. and Levin, H. (1975). *The Psychology of Reading*. Cambridge, MA: MIT Press.

Glucksberg, S., Kreuz, R.J. and Rho, S. (1986). Context can constrain lexical access: implications for models of language comprehension. *Journal of Experimental Psychology: Learning, Memory and Cognition*, **12**, 323–335.

Gorfein, D.S., Viviani, J.M. and Leddo, J. (1982). Norms as a tool for the study of homography. *Memory and Cognition*, **10**, 503–509.

Graesser, A.C. and Riha, J.R. (1984). An application of multiple regression techniques to sentence reading times. In D.E. Kieras and M.A. Just (eds), *New methods in Reading Comprehension Research.* Hillsdale, NJ: Erlbaum.

Green, J. (1980). A review of the Laceys' physiological hypothesis of heart rate change. *Biological Psychology*, **11**, 63–80.

Greenwald, M.K., Bradley, M.M., Hamm, A.O. and Lang, P.J. (1988). Emotion and pictorial stimuli: affective judgments, memory and psychophysiology. *Psychophysiology*, **25**, 451 (abstract).

Grozinger, B., Kornhuber, H.H. and Kriebel, J. (1975). Methodological problems in the investigation of cerebral potentials preceding speech: determining the onset and suppressing artefacts caused by speech. *Neuropsychologia*, **13**, 263–270.

Gur, R.C. and Reivich, M. (1980). Cognitive task effects on hemispheric blood flow in humans: evidence for individual differences in hemispheric activation. *Brain and Language*, **9**, 78–92.

Haberlandt, K. (1984). Components of sentence and word reading times. In D.E. Kieras and M.A. Just (eds), *New Methods in Reading Comprehension Research.* Hillsdale, NJ: Erlbaum.

Hammond, G.R. and Jordan, P.M. (1984). Bilateral electrodermal activity during performance of cognitive tasks of varying difficulty levels. *Physiological Psychology*, **11**, 256–260.

Hammond, K.E. and Rugg, M.D. (1987). Event-related potentials and the processing of lexical ambiguity. In *Proceedings of the 4th International Conference on Cognitive Neuroscience*, Paris, June.

Harbin, T.J., Marsh, G.R. and Harvey, M.T. (1984). Differences in the late components of the event-related potential due to age and to semantic and nonsemantic tasks. *Electroencephalography and Clinical Neurophysiology*, **59**, 489–496.

Hardyck, C.D. and Petronovich, L.F. (1970). Subvocal speech and comprehension level as a function of the difficulty level of reading material. *Journal of Verbal Learning and Verbal Behavior*, **9**, 647–652.

Healy, A.F. and Drewnowski, A. (1983). Investigating the boundaries of reading units: letter detection in misspelled words. *Journal of Experimental Psychology: Human Perception and Performance*, **9**, 413–426.

Heiss, W.D., Herholz, K., Pawlik, G., Wagner, R. and Wienhard, K. (1986). Positron emission tomography in neuropsychology. *Neuropsychologia*, **24**, 141–149.

Henderson, L. (1982). *Orthography and Word Recognition in Reading*. London: Academic Press.

Henik, A., Friedrich, F.J. and Kellogg, W.A. (1983). The dependence of semantic relatedness effects upon prime processing. *Memory and Cognition*, **11**, 366–373.

Herning, R.I., Jones, R.T. and Hunt, J.S. (1987). Speech event related potentials reflect linguistic content and processing level. *Brain and Language*, **30**, 116–129.

Hink, R.F., Kaga, K. and Suzuki, J. (1980). An evoked potential correlate of reading ideographic and phonetic Japanese scripts. *Neuropsychologia*, **18**, 455–464.

Hockey, G.R.J, Gaillard, A.W.K. and Coles, M.G.H. (eds) (1986). *Energetics and Human Information Processing*. Dordrecht, Netherlands: Martinus Nijhoff.

Holcomb, P.J. (1988). Automatic and attentional processing: an event-related potential analysis of semantic priming. *Brain and Language*, **35**, 66–85.

Holcomb, P.J. and Neville, H.J. (1990). Auditory and visual semantic priming in lexical decisions: a comparison using event-related brain potentials. *Language and Cognitive Processes*, **5**, 281–312.

Huey, E.B. (1908). *The Psychology and Pedagogy of Reading*. New York: Macmillan (reprinted by MIT Press, 1968).

Hynd, G.W., Hynd, C.R., Sullivan, H.G. and Kingsbury, T.B. (1987). Regional cerebral blood flow (rCBF) in developmental dyslexia: activation during reading in a surface and deep dyslexic. *Journal of Learning Disabilities*, **20**, 294–300.

Inhoff, A.W. (1985). The effect of activity on lexical retrieval and postlexical processes during eye fixations in reading. *Journal of Psycholinguistic Research*, **14**, 45–56.

Inhoff, A.W. and Fleming, K. (1989). Probe-detection times during the reading of easy and difficult texts. *Journal of Experimental Psychology: Learning, Memory and Cognition*, **15**, 339–351.

Jacquy, J., Noel, P., Segers, A., Huvelle, R., Piraux, A. and Noel, G. (1977). Regional cerebral blood flow in children: a rheoencephalographic study of the modifications induced by reading. *Electroencephalography and Clinical Neurophysiology*, **42**, 691–696.

Jacquy, J., Piraux, A., Jocquet, P., Lhoas, J.P. and Noel, G. (1977). Cerebral blood flow in the adult blind: a rheoencephalographic study of cerebral blood flow changes during braille reading. *Electroencephalography and Clinical Neurophysiology*, **43**, 325–329.

Jastrzemski, J.E. (1981). Multiple meanings, number of related meanings, frequency of occurrence, and the lexicon. *Cognitive Psychology*, **13**, 278–305.

Jennings, J.R. (1975). Information processing and concomitant heart rate changes in the overweight and underweight. *Physiological Psychology*, **3**, 290–296.

Jennings, J.R. (1986a). Bodily changes during attending. In M.G.H. Coles, E. Donchin and S. Porges (eds), *Psychophysiology: Systems, Processes and Applications*. New York: Guilford.

Jennings, J.R. (1986b). Memory, thought, and bodily response. In M.G.H. Coles, E. Donchin and S. Porges (eds), *Psychophysiology: Systems, Processes and Applications*. New York: Guilford.

Jennings, J.R. and Hall, S.W. (1980). Recall, recognition, and rate: memory and the heart. *Psychophysiology*, **17**, 34–46.

Johnson, R.E. (1973). Meaningfulness and the recall of textual prose. *American Educational Research Journal*, **10**, 49–58.

Juola, J.F., Ward, N.J. and McNamara, T. (1982). Visual search and reading of rapid serial presentations of letter strings, words and text. *Journal of Experimental Psychology: General*, **111**, 208–227.

Just, M.A. and Carpenter, P.A. (1971). Comprehension of negation with quantification. *Journal of Verbal Learning and Verbal Behavior*, **10**, 208–227.

Just, M.A. and Carpenter, P.A. (1978). Inference processes during reading: reflections from eye fixations. In J.W. Senders, D.F. Fisher and R.A. Monty (eds), *Eye Movements and the Higher Psychological Functions*. Hillsdale, NJ: Erlbaum.

Just, M.A. and Carpenter, P.A. (1980). A theory of reading: from eye fixations to comprehension. *Psychological Review*, **87**, 329–354.

Just, M.A. and Carpenter, P.A. (1984). Using eye fixations to study reading comprehension. In D.E. Kieras and M.A. Just (eds), *New Methods in Reading Comprehension Research*. Hillsdale, NJ: Erlbaum.

Just, M.A. and Carpenter, P.A. (1987). *The Psychology of Reading and Language Comprehension*. Boston: Allyn and Bacon.

Kahneman, D. (1973). *Attention and Effort*. Englewood Cliffs, NJ: Prentice Hall.

Keenan, J.M., Baillet, S.D. and Brown, P. (1984). The effects of causal cohesion on comprehension and memory. *Journal of Verbal Learning and Verbal Behavior*, **23**, 115–126.

Kennedy, A. (1978). Reading sentences: some observations on the control of eye movements. In G. Underwood (ed.), *Strategies of Information Processing*. London: Academic Press.

Kennedy, A. (1987). Eye movements, reading skill, and the spatial code. In J.R. Beech and A.M. Colley (eds), *Cognitive Approaches to Reading*. Chichester: Wiley.

Kerr, B. (1973). Processing demands during mental operations. *Memory and Cognition*, **1**, 401–412.

Kerr, J.S. and Underwood, G. (1984). Fixation time on anaphoric pronouns decreases with congruity of reference. In A.G. Gale and F. Johnson (eds), *Theoretical and Applied Aspects of Eye Movement Research*. Amsterdam: North-Holland.

Kieras, D.E. (1974). *Analysis of the Effects of Word Properties and Limited Reading Time in a Reading Comprehension and Verification Task*. Unpublished doctoral dissertation, University of Michigan.

Kieras, D.E. (1978). Good and bad structure in simple paragraphs: effects on apparent theme, reading time, and recall. *Journal of Verbal Learning and Verbal Behavior*, **17**, 13–28.

Kintsch, W., Kozminsky, E., Streby, W., McKoon, G. and Keenan, J. (1975). Comprehension and recall of text as a function of content variables. *Journal of Verbal Learning and Verbal Behavior*, **14**, 196–214.

Kintsch, W. and van Dijk, T.A. (1978). Toward a model of text comprehension and production. *Psychological Review*, **85**, 363–394.

Kleinsmith, L.J. and Kaplan, S. (1963). Paired-associate learning as a function of arousal and interpolated interval. *Journal of Experimental Psychology*, **65**, 190–193.

Klima, E.S. and Bellugi, U. (1979). *The Signs of Language*. Cambridge, MA: Harvard University Press.

Kramer, A.F. and Donchin, E. (1987). Brain potentials and indices of orthographic and phonological interaction during word matching. *Journal of Experimental Psychology: Learning, Memory and Cognition*, **13**, 76–86.

Kroll, J.F. and Merves, J.S. (1986). Lexical access for concrete and abstract words. *Journal of Experimental Psychology: Learning, Memory and Cognition*, **12**, 92–107.

Kruger, P.B. (1975). Luminance changes of the fundus reflex. *American Journal of Optometry and Physiological Optics*, **52**, 847–861.

Kruger, P.B. (1980). The effect of cognitive demand on accommodation. *American Journal of Optometry and Physiological Optics*, **57**, 440–445.

Kutas, M. (1985). ERP comparisons of the effects of single word and sentence primes on word processing. *Psychophysiology*, **22**, 575–576 (abstract).

Kutas, M. (1988). Event-related brain potentials (ERPs) elicited during rapid serial visual presentation of congruous and incongruous sentences. In R. Johnson, J. Rohrbaugh and R. Parasuraman (eds), *Current Trends in Brain Potential Research* (EEG Suppl. 40). Amsterdam: Elsevier.

Kutas, M. and Hillyard, S.A. (1980a). Reading between the lines: event-related brain potentials during natural sentence processing. *Brain and Language*, **11**, 354–373.

Kutas, M. and Hillyard, S.A. (1980b). Reading senseless sentences: brain potentials reveal semantic incongruity. *Science*, **207**, 203–205.

Kutas, M. and Hillyard, S.A. (1983). Event-related brain potentials to grammatical errors and semantic anomalies. *Memory and Cognition*, **11**, 539–550.

Kutas, M., Lindamood, T. and Hillyard, S.A. (1984). Word expectancy and event-related potentials during sentence processing. In S. Kornblum and J. Requin (eds), *Preparatory States and Processes*. Hillsdale, NJ: Erlbaum.

Kutas, M. and Van Petten, C. (1988). Event-related brain potential studies of language. In P.K. Ackles, J.R. Jennings and M.G.H. Coles (eds), *Advances in Psychophysiology*. Greenwich, CT: JAI Press.

Kutas, M., Van Petten, C. and Besson, M. (1988). Event-related potential asymmetries during the reading of sentences. *Electroencephalography and Clinical Neurophysiology*, **69**, 218–233.

Lacey, B.C. and Lacey, J.I. (1974). Studies of heart rate and other bodily processes in sensorimotor behavior. In P. Obrist, A. Black, J. Brener and L. DiCara (eds), *Cardiovascular Psychophysiology: Current Issues in Response Mechanisms, Biofeedback and Methodology*. Chicago: Aldine.

Lacey, B.C. and Lacey, J.I. (1977). Change in heart period: a function of sensorimotor event timing within the cardiac cycle. *Physiological Psychology*, **5**, 383–393.

Lacey, J.I., Kagan, J., Lacey, B. and Moss, H.A. (1963). The visceral level: situational determinants and behavioral correlates of autonomic patterns. In P.H. Knapp (ed.), *Expression of the Emotions in Man*. New York: International Universities Press.

Licht, R., Kok, A., Bakker, D.J. and Bouma, A. (1986). The development of lateral event-related potentials (ERPs) related to word naming: a four-year longitudinal study. *Neuropsychologia*, **26**, 327–340.

Lima, S.D. (1987). Morphological analysis in sentence reading. *Journal of Memory and Language*, **26**, 84–99.

Loftus, G.R. and MackWorth, N.H. (1978). Cognitive determinants of fixation location

during picture viewing. *Journal of Experimental Psychology: Human Perception and Performance*, **1**, 103–113.
Mandler, J.M. and Johnson, N.S. (1977). Remembrance of things parsed: story structure and recall. *Cognitive Psychology*, **9**, 111–151.
Marr, D. (1982). *Vision: A Computational Investigation into Human Representation and Processing of Visual Information*. Freeman: New York.
Marshall, J.C. (1987). The cultural and biological context of written languages: their acquisition, deployment and breakdown. In J. Beech and A. Colley (eds), *Cognitive Approaches to Reading*. Wiley: New York.
Marslen-Wilson, W. and Tyler, L.K. (1980). The temporal structure of spoken language understanding. *Cognition*, **8**, 1–71.
Marton, M. and Szirtes, J. (1988). Context effects on saccade-related brain potentials during reading. *Neuropsychologia*, **26**, 453–463.
Masson, M.E. (1983). Conceptual processing of text during skimming and rapid sequential reading. *Memory and Cognition*, **11**, 262–274.
McCallum, W.C., Farmer, S.F. and Pocock, P.K. (1984). The effects of physical and semantic incongruities on auditory event-related potentials. *Electroencephalography and Clinical Neurophysiology*, **59**, 477–488.
McClelland, J.L. and Rumelhart, D.E. (1981). An interactive activation model of context effects in letter perception. 1: An account of basic findings. *Psychological Review*, **86**, 375–407.
McConkie, G.W. and Rayner, K. (1975). The span of the effective stimulus during a fixation in reading. *Perception and Psychophysics*, **17**, 578–587.
Metalis, S.A. and Hess, E.H. (1986). Pupillometric assessment of the readability of two video screen fonts. *Perceptual and Motor Skills*, **62**, 279–282.
Metter, E.J., Kempler, D., Jackson, C.A., Hanson, W.R., Riege, W.H., Camras, L.R., Mazziotta, J.C. and Phelps, M.E. (1987). Cerebellar glucose metabolism in chronic aphasia. *Neurology*, **37**, 1599–1606.
Meyer, B.J.F. (1975). *The Organization of Prose and its Effects upon Memory*. Amsterdam: North-Holland.
Meyer, D.E. and Schvaneveldt, R.W. (1971). Facilitation in recognizing pairs of words: evidence for a dependence between retrieval operations. *Journal of Experimental Psychology*, **90**, 227–234.
Mitchell, D.C. (1984). An evaluation of subject-paced reading tasks and other methods for investigating immediate processes in reading. In D.E. Kieras and M.A. Just (eds), *New Methods in Reading Comprehension Research*. Hillsdale, NJ: Erlbaum.
Mitchell, D.C. and Green, D.W. (1978). The effects of context in immediate processing in reading. *Quarterly Journal of Experimental Psychology*, **30**, 609–636.
Moran, C.C. and Cleary, P.J. (1986). The effects of induced frontalis tension on aspects of cognitive efficiency. *British Journal of Psychology*, **77**, 63–68.
Morton, J. (1969). The interaction of information in word recognition. *Psychological Review*, **76**, 165–178.
Morton, J. (1979). Facilitation in word recognition: experiments causing change in the logogen model. In P.A. Kolers, M.E. Wrolstad and M. Bound (eds), *Processing of Visible Language*. New York: Plenum Press.
Neely, J.H. (1977). Semantic priming and retrieval from lexical memory: roles of inhibitionless spreading activation and limited-capacity attention. *Journal of Experimental Psychology: General*, **106**, 226–254.
Neville, H.J., Kutas, M., Chesney, G. and Schmidt, A.L. (1987). Event-related brain potentials during encoding and recognition memory of congruous and incongruous words. *Journal of Memory and Language*, **25**, 75–92.

Neville, H.J., Kutas, M. and Schmidt, A. (1982a). Event-related potential studies of cerebral specialization during reading. I: Studies of normal adults. *Brain and Language*, **16**, 300–315.

Neville, H.J., Kutas, M. and Schmidt, A. (1982b). Event-related potential studies of cerebral specialization during reading. II: Studies of congenitally deaf adults. *Brain and Language*, **16**, 316–337.

Ninness, C.H. (1982). Two and one-half year follow-up on the effects of elimination of subvocalization with electromyographic feedback. *Behavioral Engineering*, **8**, 5–10.

Norman, D.A. (1985). Twelve issues for cognitive science. In A.M. Aiktenhead and J.M. Slack (eds), *Issues in Cognitive Modelling*. Hillsdale, NJ: Erlbaum.

Onifer, W. and Swinney, D.A. (1981). Accessing lexical ambiguities during sentence comprehension: effects of frequency of meaning and contextual bias. *Memory and Cognition*, **9**, 225–236.

O'Regan, K. (1979). Saccade size in reading: evidence for the linguistic control hypothesis. *Perception and Psychophysics*, **25**, 501–509.

Ornstein, R. Herron, J., Johnstone, J. and Swencionis, C. (1979). Differential right hemisphere involvement in two reading tasks. *Psychophysiology*, **16**, 398–401.

Owens, J., Bower, G.H. and Black, J.B. (1979). The 'soap opera' effect in story recall. *Memory and Cognition*, **7**, 185–191.

Paivio, A. (1971). *Imagery and Verbal Processes*. New York: Holt, Rinehart and Winston.

Paller, K.A., Kutas, M., Simamura, A.P. and Squire, L.R. (1988). Brain responses to concrete and abstract words reflect processes that correlate with later performance on test of recall and stem-completion priming. In R. Johnson, J. Rohrbaugh and R. Parasuraman (eds), *Current Trends in Brain Potential Research* (EEG Suppl. 40). Amsterdam: Elsevier.

Petersen, S.E., Fox, P.T., Posner, M.I., Mintun, M.A. and Raichle, M.E. (1988). Positron emission tomographic studies of the cortical anatomy of single-word processing. *Nature*, **331**, 585–589.

Petsche, H., Pockberger, H. and Rappelsberger, P. (1986). EEG topography and mental performance. In F.H. Duffy (ed.), *Topographic Mapping of Brain Electrical Activity*. Boston: Butterworth.

Picton, T.W. and Stuss, D.T. (1984). Event-related potentials in the study of speech and language: a critical review. In D.N. Caplan, A.R. Lecours and A.M. Smith (eds), *Biological Perspectives on Language*. Cambridge: MIT Press.

Polich, J. (1985). Semantic categorization and event-related potentials. *Brain and Language*, **26**, 304–321.

Polich, J. and Donchin, E. (1988). P300 and the word frequency effect. *Electroencephalography and Clinical Neurophysiology*, **70**, 33–45.

Polich, J.M., McCarthy, G., Wang, W.S. and Donchin, E. (1983). When words collide: orthographic and phonological interference during word processing. *Biological Psychology*, **16**, 155–180.

Posner, M.I. and Boies, S.J. (1971). Components of attention. *Psychological Review*, **78**, 391–408.

Posner, M.I. and Mitchell, R.F. (1967). Chronometric analysis of classification. *Psychological Review*, **74**, 392–409.

Posner, M.I. and Nissen, M.J. (1976). Visual dominance: an information-processing account of its origins and significance. *Psychological Review*, **83**, 157–171.

Posner, M.I., Petersen, S.E., Fox, P.T. and Raichle, M.E. (1988). Localization of cognitive operations in the human brain. *Science*, **240**, 1627–1631.

Posner, M.I. and Snyder, C.R.R. (1975). Facilitation and inhibition in the processing of signals. In P.M.A. Rabbitt and S. Dornic (eds), *Attention and Performance*, vol. V. New York: Academic Press.

Potter, M.C. (1984). Rapid serial visual presentation (RSVP): a method for studying language processing. In D.E. Kieras and M.A. Just (eds), *New Methods in Reading Comprehension Research*. Hillsdale, NJ: Erlbaum.

Potter, M.C., Kroll, J.F. and Harris, C. (1980). Comprehension and memory in rapid sequential reading. In R. Nickerson (ed.), *Attention and Performance*, vol. VIII. Hillsdale, NJ: Erlbaum.

Potts, G.R., Keenan, J.M. and Golding, J.M. (1988). Assessing the occurrence of elaborative inferences: lexical decision versus naming. *Journal of Memory and Language*, **27**, 399–415.

Raney, G.E., Dunn, B.R. and Rust, D.T. (1989). EEG correlates of cognitive style and recall of text in grade school age children. Paper presented at the March meeting of the Southeastern Psychological Association, Washington, DC.

Rayner, K. (1975). The perceptual span and peripheral cues in reading. *Cognitive Psychology*, **7**, 65–81.

Rayner, K. and Carroll, P.J. (1984). Eye movements and reading comprehension. In D.E. Kieras and M.A. Just (eds), *New Methods in Reading Comprehension Research*. Hillsdale, NJ: Erlbaum.

Rayner, K. and Duffy, S.A. (1986). Lexical complexity and fixation times in reading: effects of word frequency, verb complexity, and lexical ambiguity. *Memory and Cognition*, **14**, 191–201.

Rayner, K. and Duffy, S.A. (1987). Eye movements and lexical ambiguity. In J.K. O'Regan and A. Levy-Schoen (eds), *Eye Movements: From Physiology to Cognition*. Amsterdam: North-Holland.

Rayner, K., Inhoff, A.W., Morrison, R.E., Slowiaczek, M.L. and Bertera, J.H. (1981). Masking of foveal and parafoveal vision during eye fixations in reading. *Journal of Experimental Psychology: Human Perception and Performance*, **7**, 167–179.

Rentel, V., Pappas, C. and Pettegrew B. (1985). The utility of psychophysiological measures for reading research. In V.M. Rentel, S.A. Corson and B.R. Dunn (eds), *Psychophysiological Aspects of Reading and Learning*. New York: Gordon and Breach.

Reynolds, R.E. and Anderson, R.C. (1982). Influence of questions on the allocation of attention during reading. *Journal of Educational Psychology*, **74**, 623–632.

Risberg, J. (1986). Regional cerebral blood flow in neuropsychology. *Neuropsychologia*, **24**, 135–140.

Risberg, J., Halsey, J.H., Wills, E.L. and Wilson, E.M. (1975). Hemispheric specialization in normal man studied by bilateral measurements of the regional cerebral blood flow. *Brain*, **98**, 511–524.

Robbins, K.I. and McAdam, D.W. (1974). Interhemispheric alpha asymmetry and imagery mode. *Brain and Language*, **1**, 189–193.

Robinson, G.M. and Moulton, J. (1985). Models for language cognition. In A.W. Ellis (ed.), *Progress in the Psychology of Language*. Hillsdale, NJ: Lawrence Erlbaum, pp. 1–44.

Roland, P.E. and Friberg, L. (1985). Localization of cortical areas activated by thinking. *Journal of Neurophysiology*, **53**, 1219–1243.

Rosch, E.H. (1975). Cognitive representations of semantic categories. *Journal of Experimental Psychology: General*, **104**, 192–233.

Rubenstein, H.H., Lewis, S.S. and Rubenstein, M.A. (1971). Evidence for phonemic recoding in visual word recognition. *Journal of Verbal Learning and Verbal Behavior*, **10**, 645–657.

Rubin, D.C. (1978). A unit analysis of prose memory. *Journal of Verbal Learning and Verbal Behavior*, **17**, 599–620.

Rugg, M.D. (1984). Further study of the electrophysiological correlates of lexical decision. *Brain and Language*, **19**, 142–152.
Rugg, M.D. (1987). Dissociation of semantic priming, word and nonword repetition effects by event-related brain potentials. *Quarterly Journal of Experimental Psychology*, **39A**, 123–148.
Rugg, M.D. and Barrett, S.E. (1987). Event-related potentials and the interaction between orthographic and phonological information in a rhyme-judgment task. *Brain and Language*, **32**, 336–361.
Rugg, M.D., Kok, A., Barrett, G. and Fischler, I. (1986). ERPs associated with language and hemispheric specialization. In W.C. McCallum, R. Zapolli and F. Denoth (eds), *Cerebral Psychophysiology: Studies in Event-Related Potentials* (*EEG* Suppl. 38). Amsterdam: Elsevier.
Rugg, M.D. and Nagy, M.E. (1987). Lexical contribution to nonword repetition effects: evidence from event-related potentials. *Memory and Cognition*, **15**, 473–481.
Sabol, M.A. and DeRosa, D.V. (1976). Semantic encoding of isolated words. *Journal of Experimental Psychology: Human Learning and Memory*, **2**, 58–68.
Samar, V.J. and Berent, G.P. (1986). The syntactic priming effect: evidence for a prelexical locus. *Brain and Language*, **28**, 250–272.
Sandman, C. and Walker, B. (1985). Cardiovascular relationships to attention and thinking. In V.M. Rentel, S.A. Corson and B.R. Dunn (eds), *Psychophysiological Aspects of Reading and Learning*. New York: Gordon and Breach.
Scarborough, D., Cortese, C. and Scarborough, H. (1977). Frequency and repetition effects in lexical memory. *Journal of Experimental Psychology: Human Perception and Performance*, **3**, 1–17.
Schank, R.C. and Abelson, R. (1977). *Scripts, Plans, Goals and Understanding*. Hillsdale, NJ: Lawrence Erlbaum.
Schluroff, M. (1982). Pupil responses to grammatical complexity of sentences. *Brain and Language*, **17**, 133–145.
Schluroff, M., Zimmermann, T.E., Freeman, R.B., Hofmeister, K., Lorscheid, T. and Weber, A. (1986). Pupillary responses to syntactic ambiguity of sentences. *Brain and Language*, **27**, 322–344.
Schneider, W. and Shiffrin, R.M. (1977). Controlled and automatic information processing. I: Detection, search and attention. *Psychological Review*, **84**, 1–66.
Schustack, M.W., Ehrlich, S.F. and Rayner, K. (1987). Local and global sources of contextual facilitation in reading. *Journal of Memory and Language*, **26**, 322–340.
Schwanenflugel, P.J., Harnishfeger, K.P. and Stowe, R.W. (1988). Context availability and lexical decisions for abstract and concrete words. *Journal of Memory and Language*, **27**, 499–520.
Seidenberg, M. (1985). The time course of information activation and utilization in visual words recognition. In D. Besner, T. Waller and G. MacKinnon (eds), *Reading Research: Advances in Theory and Practice*, vol. 3. New York: Academic Press.
Seidenberg, M.S., Tanenhaus, M.K., Leiman, J.M. and Bienkowski, M. (1982). Automatic access of the meanings of ambiguous words in context: some limitations of knowledge-based processing. *Cognitive Psychology*, **14**, 489–537.
Seidenberg, M.S., Waters, G.S., Barnes, M.A. and Tanenhaus, M.K. (1984). Pre- and post-lexical loci of contextual effects on word recognition. *Memory and Cognition*, **12**, 315–328.
Sharpley, C.F. and Rowland, S.E. (1986). Palliative vs direct action stress-reduction procedures as treatments for reading disability. *British Journal of Educational Psychology*, **56**, 40–50.
Simpson, G.B. and Burgess, C. (1985). Activation and selection processes in the

recognition of ambiguous words. *Journal of Experimental Psychology: Human Perception and Performance*, **11**, 28–39.

Simpson, G.B., Peterson, R.R., Casteel, M.A. and Burgess, C. (1989). Lexical and sentence context effects in word recognition. *Journal of Experimental Psychology: Learning, Memory and Cognition*, **15**, 88–97.

Smith, M.E. and Halgren, E. (1988). ERPs during lexical decision: interaction of repetition with concreteness, frequency, and pronounceability. In R. Johnson, J. Rohrbaugh and R. Parasuraman (eds), *Current Trends in Brain Potential Research* (*EEG* Suppl. 40). Amsterdam: Elsevier.

Stillings, N.A., Feinstein, M.H., Garfield, J.L., Rossland, E.L., Rosenbaum, D.A., Weisler, S.E. and Baker-Ward, L. (1987). *Cognitive Science: An Introduction*. Cambridge, MA: MIT Press.

Swinney, D.A. (1979). Lexical access during sentence comprehension: (Re)consideration of context effects. *Journal of Verbal Learning and Verbal Behavior*, **18**, 645–659.

Tanenhaus, M.K., Flanigan, H. and Seidenberg, M.S. (1980). Orthographic and phonological case activation in auditory and visual word recognition. *Memory and Cognition*, **8**, 513–520.

Taylor, S.E. (1965). An evaluation of forty-one trainees who had recently completed the 'Reading Dynamics' program. In E.P. Bliesmer and R.C. Staiger (eds), *Problems, Programs and Projects in College Adult Reading*. Milwaukee, WI: National Reading Conference.

Thibadeau, R., Just, M.A. and Carpenter, P.A. (1982). A model of the time course and content of reading. *Cognitive Science*, **6**, 157–203.

Thomas, E.L. and Robinson, H.A. (1971). *Improving Reading in Every Class: A Sourcebook for Teachers*. Boston: Allyn and Bacon.

Thorndyke, P.W. (1977). Cognitive structures in comprehension and memory of narrative discourse. *Cognitive Psychology*, **9**, 77–110.

Tinker, M.A. (1958). Recent studies of eye movements in reading. *Psychological Bulletin*, **55**, 215–231.

Trabasso, T., Secco, T. and van den Broek, P. (1984). Causal cohesion and story coherence. In H. Mandl, N.L. Stein and T. Trabasso (eds), *Learning and Comprehension of Text*. Hillsdale, NJ: Erlbaum.

Tulving, E. (1989). Remembering and knowing the past. *American Scientist*, **77**, 361–367.

Tyler, R. and Marslen-Wilson, W. (1977). The on-line effects of semantic context on syntactic processing. *Journal of Verbal Learning and Verbal Behavior*, **16**, 683–692.

Underwood, G. (1985). Eye movements during the comprehension of written language. In A.W. Ellis (ed.), *Progress in the Psychology of Language*, vol. 2. Hillsdale, NJ: Erlbaum.

Underwood, G. (1986). The span of letter recognition in good and poor readers. *Reading Research Quarterly*, **21**, 6–19.

Van den Berg, C. (1986). On the relation between energy transformations in the brain and mental activities. In G.R. Hockey, A. Gaillard and M. Coles (eds), *Energetics and Human Information Processing*. Dordrecht, Netherlands: Martinus Nijhoff.

Van Dijk, T.A. and Kintsch, W. (1983). *Strategies of Discourse Comprehension*. New York: Academic Press.

Van Petten, C. and Kutas, M. (1987a). Ambiguous words in context: an event-related potential analysis of the time course of meaning activation. *Journal of Memory and Language*, **26**, 188–208.

Van Petten, C. and Kutas, M. (1987b). Interactions between word frequency and sentence context determine N400 amplitude. In *Proceedings of the 4th International Conference on Cognitive Neuroscience*. Paris, June.

Voss, J.F., Tyler, S.W. and Bisanz, G.L. (1982). Prose comprehension and memory. In C.R. Puff (ed.), *Handbook of Research Methods in Human Memory and Cognition*. New York: Academic Press, pp. 349–393.

Wallesch, C., Henriksen, L., Kornhuber, H. and Paulson, O. (1985). Observations on regional cerebral blood flow in cortical and subcortical structures during language production in normal man. *Brain and Language*, **25**, 224–233.

Walker, B.B. and Sandman, C.A. (1979). Human visual evoked responses are related to heart rate. *Journal of Comparative and Physiological Psychology*, **93**, 717–729.

Walker, B.B. and Sandman, C.A. (1982). Visual evoked potentials change as heart rate and carotid pressure change. *Psychophysiology*, **19**, 520–527.

West, R.F. and Stanovich, K.F. (1982). Source of inhibition in experiments on the effect of sentence context on word recognition. *Journal of Experimental Psychology: Learning, Memory and Cognition*, **8**, 385–399.

West, R.F. and Stanovich, E. (1986). Robust effects of syntactic structure on visual word processing. *Memory and Cognition*, **14**, 104–112.

Whorf, B.L. (1956). A linguistic consideration of thinking in primitive communities. In J.B. Carroll (ed.), *Language, Thought and Reality*. New York: Wiley.

Wright, P. and Kahneman, D. (1971). Evidence for alternative strategies of sentence retention. *Quarterly Journal of Experimental Psychology*, **23**, 197–213.

Zola, D. (1984). Redundancy and word perception during reading. *Perception and Psychophysics*, **36**, 277–284.

Chapter 7

The Development of Information Processing

ABSTRACT

This divided chapter reviews intrinsic and extrinsic mechanisms of startle blink modification, the endogenous event-related potential, and their implications for regulation of information processing and its maturation. Dissociations in effects of transient and sustained stimulation on blink suggest differential development of regulatory systems distinguished by temporal characteristics. Event-related potentials, as well as attentive effects on blink, indicate a selective, developmentally sensitive modulation of sensory–perceptual processing.

Mechanisms of Selective Processing in Development: Evidence from Studies of Reflex Modification

Bruno J. Anthony
Department of Psychiatry, University of Maryland School of Medicine, Baltimore, MD 21201, USA

INTRODUCTION

One of the major characteristics of the nervous system is the extensive filtering that sensory information undergoes as it traverses the analysis system from receptor to cortex. Part of the filtering is a result of intrinsic factors, those associated with characteristics of the sensory path itself. Other filtering mechanisms are extrinsic, involving systems organized at various levels of the nervous system which act to modulate the course of processing within the sensory path.

This part of the chapter reviews work employing a simple reflex, the startle blink, to investigate developmental changes in intrinsic and extrinsic mechanisms of sensory filtering. The use of simple reflexes in the study of behavior has a long and somewhat uneven history (Ison and Hoffman, 1983). Those interested in development have long recognized the value of obligatory responses that can be elicited in much the same fashion and appear in much the same form throughout the lifespan. However, research using reflex measures has been prompted not so much by interest in the responses themselves, but by their plasticity; that is, changes in characteristics of the reflex reflect changes in nervous system function. This notion of reflex plasticity can seem contradictory because of the involuntary and innate characteristics of reflex circuits, suggesting rigid and stereotyped action. However, it is clear that variation in the processing of the reflex-eliciting stimulus or of a stimulus evoking extrinsic modulatory systems should have effects on the characteristics of the motor response. Indeed, although a reflex response is obligatory, characteristics of the response may be altered in specifiable and profound ways.

The startle reflex occurs in a wide range of species and investigation of its plasticity have provided a simple and relatively precise method of measuring

Handbook of Cognitive Psychophysiology: Central and Autonomic Nervous System Approaches.
Edited by J. R. Jennings and M. G. H. Coles.

the impact of a sensory event. This tradition has a long history. In 1905, Yerkes used changes in reflex strength brought about by prior stimulation to study sensory capacities of animals. With an apparatus worthy of Rube Goldberg, Yerkes discovered that frogs could hear by demonstrating that the flexor jerk reflex was modified by a previous acoustic stimulus. In recent years, Howard Hoffman, James Ison and others have carefully charted the effect of prior stimulation on the startle reaction in a wide range of species and have speculated on the implications of this work for understanding central nervous system function (Hoffman and Ison, 1980). In this vein, startle has the potential to link behavioral and physiological processes because of the progress in understanding aspects of the cellular basis of this response. For instance, Davis (e.g. Davis, 1984; Davis *et al.*, 1982) has worked out the circuit controlling the rat's leg flexion reflex as well as identifying possible sites of modification phenomena and their associated neurotransmitters.

Use of the startle reflex to study sensory processing in humans began with systematic investigations in Raymond Dodge's laboratory at Yale (Cohen, Hilgard and Wendt, 1933; Hilgard, 1933; Hilgard and Wendt, 1933). Basic paradigms and parameters of reflex modification were worked out and employed to assess the adequacy of sensory functioning in a wide variety of clinical cases. For instance, Hilgard diagnosed a case of hysterical blindness by showing that a flash of light could modify an acoustically elicited reflex blink which occurred shortly after the flash. Landis and Hunt (1939) provided the first extensive description of developmental changes in startle in their careful observations of the reflex in humans using high-speed photography.

After a hiatus of several decades, the study of startle and its modification in humans was revived by Graham and her colleagues (Graham, 1975). The work was prompted in part by the animal work of Ison and Hoffman. In a variety of species, both inhibitory and facilitatory effects on startle were documented which were precisely tuned to specific aspects of the stimulus environment (e.g. Hoffman and Wible, 1970; Ison and Hammond, 1971; Ison and Leonard, 1971; Stitt *et al.*, 1976). Graham, Putnam and Leavitt (1975) replicated many of the animal phenomena in adult humans using the eyeblink component of startle. K.M. Berg (1973) showed that parameters which characterized effective startle stimuli in animals also optimized the response in humans: a rapid rise in intensity integrated over a short period of time. These data indicated that intrinsic characteristics of the reflex circuit appeared optimal for the processing of fast-rising, transient stimuli. Many modification effects in animals produced by prior stimulation were also present in humans with similar intensity and temporal relationships between the modifying prestimulus and the reflex stimulus, or probe. Properties of the inhibitory and facilitatory effects suggested mediation by low-level extrinsic systems located within the brainstem. Finally, the initial work with humans uncovered a blink modification phenomenon that was not observed in animals but seemed associated with the presence of orienting–attentional processes as indexed by heart rate (HR) deceleration. Subsequent work has confirmed that extrinsic attentive mechanisms, organized at higher levels of the nervous system, can act in an efferent fashion and establish a sensory selective set to influence processing at a level low enough to affect the brainstem mediated startle blink (e.g. Anthony, 1985; Hackley and Graham, 1987).

These investigations of startle and its modification in humans were undertaken with the goal that these simple yet powerful paradigms could be used to understand processing characteristics of relatively inaccessible subjects—in particular, young infants. The present review covers developmental changes in intrinsic, low-level extrinsic, and higher-level extrinsic (attentive) mechanisms of blink modification and their implications for understanding the regulation of sensory processing and its maturation in the developing human. We will emphasize how these paradigms dissociate the effects of processing brief transient stimuli from the effects of processing sustained stimuli and point to differential development of analysis systems which are distinguished by their temporal filtering characteristics. We will also examine the evidence for the presence of a selective attentional system in young infants that can act to filter automatic sensory processing. The initial developmental work was summarized by Graham, Strock and Zeigler (1981); thus the present review concentrates on work completed since that time.

STARTLE BLINK AND ITS MEASUREMENT

BLINK FORM

The startle reflex in humans consists of two components. The first or primary component is an involuntary, general flexion of the musculature which flows in a rostral to caudal sequence. The sequence begins with an eyeblink which is followed by a forward movement of the head and trunk, a widening of the mouth, a tightening of the muscles in the neck, a bending of the elbows, knees and fingers, and a contraction of the abdomen (Landis and Hunt, 1939). A variety of secondary, apparently voluntary, components follow the primary flexion. These appear to be specific avoidance behaviors.

In young infants, the startle reflex occurs coincidentally with the Moro reflex, which is characterized by extension of the arms and fingers, backward extension of the head, and flexion of the legs at the hip and knee. Because of the overlap of these responses, both were considered instances of general 'starting' behaviors or body jerks (Wagner, 1938). In their cinematographic study of startle, Hunt, Clarke and Hunt (1936) demonstrated the existence of a distinct startle pattern, often occurring to the same stimuli that elicited the later-occurring Moro reflex. They showed that the startle pattern emerged within the first six weeks and, as with adults, was typified by flexion of the body, moving from the head to the legs, beginning with the eyeblink.

Blink is not only the most rapid component of startle but also the most reliable, continuing to occur after multiple presentations of the eliciting stimulus. Blink is produced by rapid contraction of the palpebral section of the orbicularis oculi muscle in response to rapidly rising stimulation in any modality. The orbicularis oculi muscle is enervated by motoneurons located in the dorsal division of the facial nucleus of the VIIth nerve. Recent animal work involving lesions, electrical stimulation, and retrograde anatomical tracing techniques has begun to elucidate the pathways responsible for the startle blink. The reflex is organized in subcortical structures, evidenced by the clear flexion reflexes present in decerebrate animals and mesencephalic humans (e.g. Keane, 1979; Szabo and Hazafi, 1965). A number of studies now point to the nucleus reticularis pontis caudalis as the region of the reticular formation critical for the mediation of startle (e.g. Davis *et al.*, 1982; Groves, Wilson and Boyle, 1974; Hammond, 1973). This area has connections to auditory (Davis, 1984), visual (Itoh *et al.*, 1983) and cutaneous (Takada *et al.*, 1984) sensory pathways. Also, lesions to this area abolish both the acoustic and shock-elicited startle response (Leitner, Powers and Hoffman, 1980).

The startle blink is elicited by a rapid increase in the intensity of acoustic, visual, and cutaneous stimuli. However, various characteristics of the response differ depending on the modality of the eliciting stimulus. Acoustic stimulation produces a reliable startle blink with onset latencies ranging between 20 and 80 ms from stimulus onset, depending on stimulus intensity. These values, and all others cited below, are derived from recordings of electromyographic (EMG) activity from orbicularis oculi. The acoustically elicited response consists of a single burst of EMG activity related to movement of the lid. The premotor portion of the acoustic circuit for the rat's flexion reflex has been worked out in detail by Michael Davis and his colleagues (e.g. Davis *et al.*, 1982); however, less is known about the longer-latency blink response in humans. Most likely, this circuit involves the inferior and perhaps superior colliculus (Takmann, Ettlin and Barth, 1982) as well as earlier structures in the acoustic pathway.

Reliable blink reflexes are also elicited by visual stimulation—flashes of light—although latencies are somewhat longer than for acoustic blinks (Mukano *et al.*, 1983; Takmann, Ettlin and Barth, 1982; Yates and Brown, 1981) and more extended in range (Hopf *et al.*, 1973). In addition, visual stimuli can elicit responses with more than one distinct component. We (Anthony and Graham, unpublished data) have observed subjects with an early component, ranging in onset latency between 40 and 70 ms, and a later component with latencies from 95 to 130 ms. Grant (1945) reported the presence of two responses in roughly the same latency range and noted that repeated presentation of stimuli resulted in habituation of the first or alpha response but sensitization of the later response in dark-adapted subjects. More recent work in humans (Mukano *et al.*, 1983) and cats (Hiraoka, Tenjin and Shimamura, 1982) has also reported the presence of two components in the visual blink. The two components may reflect differences in the complexity of circuitry intervening between initial afferent (optic nerve) and final efferent (VIIth nerve) pathways. A direct retinotectal pathway seems likely, given the evidence of unimpaired blink in patients with compromised cortical function (Hill, Cogan and Dodge, 1961; Keane, 1979). Indeed, recent retrograde labeling studies with cats (Itoh *et al.*, 1983; Takada *et al.*, 1984) revealed connections between the pretectal olivary nucleus and the facial nucleus, suggesting these fibers as a link in the visually triggered reflex. A more lengthy pathway, involving the cortex, may produce the second component (Mukano *et al.*, 1983).

Blinks can also be elicited by application of electric current, mechanical taps, and puffs of air to the periorbital region. Examination of orbicularis oculi EMG reveals that, like the visual response, multiple components are elicited by such stimulation. These components are temporally and spatially segregated (Rushworth, 1962), reflecting the difference in complexity of their neural pathways. The first component, labeled R1, is a brief response, occurring ipsilateral to the site of stimulation 10–15 ms following probe onset. Evidence suggests that this component is produced by a circuit containing, at most, one interneuron, possibly located in the lateral reticular formation (Ongerboer deVisser and Moffie, 1979) between the afferent (supraorbital nerve) and efferent (facial nerve) segments (Kimura, 1975; Ongerboer deVisser and Kuypers, 1978). The second component, R2, occurs bilaterally with an onset latency of 20–45 ms and has a more complex, polysynaptic central path. The difference in pathways allows for differential effects on the reactivity of these components to various stimulus manipulations. For instance, R1 is sensitized by repetitive stimulation, while R2 is depressed (e.g. Gregoric, 1973).

BLINK MEASUREMENT

Blink can be measured by a variety of methods. First, lid movement can be sensed mechanically, through connections between the lid and the arm of a potentiometer, or photoelectrically through placement of a photoreflective densitometer in front of the eye (Hoffman, Cohen and English, 1985). Second, blink can be identified and measured in electrooculogram (EOG) recordings. Although this indirect measure appears to provide data comparable with other methods (Clarkson and Berg, 1984), possible difficulties with baseline variation make it a less attractive measurement alternative. Although our early work employed the potentiometric method, we have found a third method—recording the bipolar EMG over orbicularis oculi—the most satisfactory and least intrusive measure for work with infants and children. For this purpose, small, lightweight biopotential electrodes (Silverstein and Graham, 1978) are taped approximately 1 cm apart, as close as possible to the lower lid margin, with the nasal electrode directly below the pupil. For adults, the electrodes can be placed on the upper lid. Direct assessment of the relationship between EMG and potentiometric methods have yielded acceptable within-subject correlations on various blink indices (reported in Graham, Anthony and Zeigler, 1983).

In our work, the raw EMG signal is rectified and integrated and then computer-sampled once per millisecond for either 250 or 500 ms following the blink-eliciting stimulus or probe. Figure 7.1 displays a tracing of an EMG burst corresponding to an acoustically elicited blink and its integrated representation for subjects ranging in age from four months to adulthood. As can be seen, the process of integration overestimates the actual latency of the EMG burst. In our work, single-trial records are computer scored for onset latency, peak latency and peak magnitude (Balaban *et al.*, 1986). In order to distinguish the elicited, reflex blink from spontaneous and voluntary blinks (winks), responses are accepted only if they fall within a restricted latency window following probe onset. For instance, the upper bounds for acceptable onset and peak latencies are 120 and 150 ms, respectively, for acoustic probes with adult subjects. The low rate of spontaneous blinks makes the probability of one falling within the small window of acceptance quite low. Spontaneous blink rates vary from 10 to 15 blinks per minute in adults and from 1 to 5 blinks per minute in infants up to 24 weeks of age (Graham, Strock and Zeigler, 1981; Zametkin, Stevens and Pittman, 1979). Assessment of the minimal reaction time to produce a voluntary blink to a probe has indicated that, at best, it falls in the extreme upper end of the blink scoring window.

The original scoring parameters were developed for use with potentiometrically measured blinks. Certain changes were instituted because of the rougher quality of the integrated EMG-measured blink. Furthermore, the latency windows as well as other scoring parameters are adjusted to compensate for the longer latencies and somewhat elongated form of blinks produced by infants and by visual stimulation. Details of the latter changes can be found in Anthony and Graham (1983). In developmental studies, the longer latency windows are always used in order to keep the nominal probabilities of detecting spontaneous and other non-reflex activity the same for all age-groups.

Reflex and non-reflex blinks can be distinguished by their form and by functional and anatomical features. First, spontaneous blinks tend to be large and brief, while reflex blinks show a more gradual progression to peak amplitude followed by a slower decline. Second, different segments of orbicularis oculi contribute differentially to reflex responses as opposed to other types of blink activity. Gordon (1951) showed that the pretarsal segment, lying close to the ciliary margin of the upper lid, contains motor units which fire at a high frequency (up to 180 impulses per second) but only during rapid activity such as reflex and spontaneous blinks. The preseptal area, located above

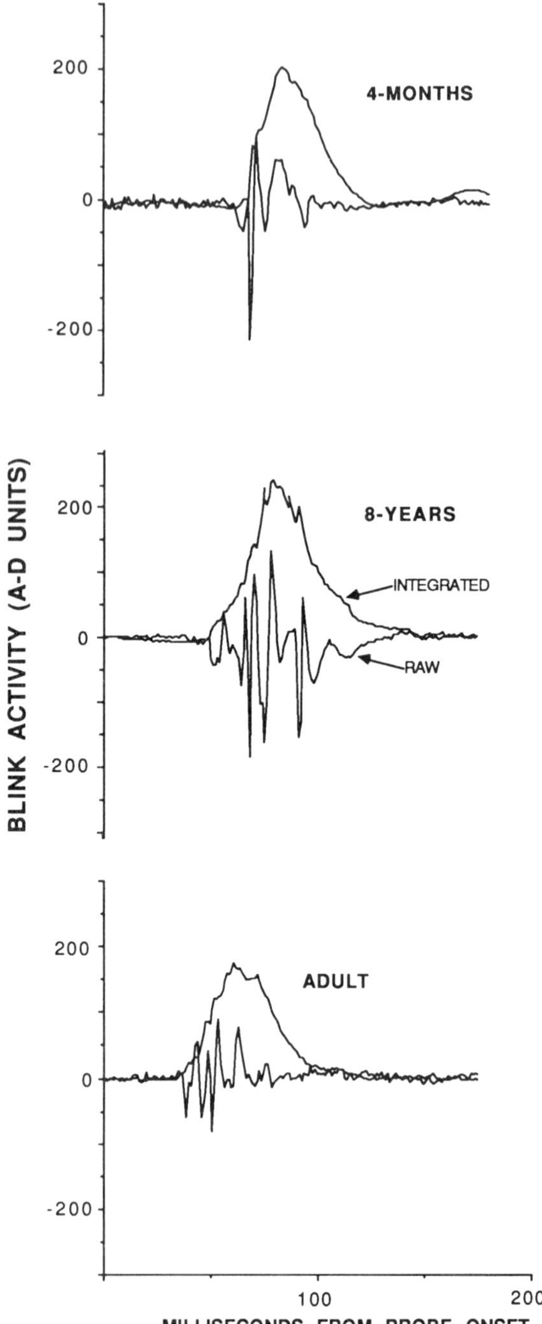

Figure 7.1. Tracings of orbicularis oculi EMG and its integrated representation for 500 ms following the onset of a blink-eliciting burst of white noise (102 dB) in a 4-month-old, 8-year-old, and adult.

the palpebral furrow, contains lower-frequency units involved in both rapid blinks and sustained voluntary contraction. Finally, even slower motor units (e.g. 55 impulses per second), that respond only during voluntary, sustained contraction, have been located exclusively in the orbital section of orbicularis oculi, which relates to the bone surrounding the eye.

This functional analysis is consistent with anatomical evidence, indicating that these different sections of orbicularis oculi contain differential amounts of pale and red muscle fibers. Orbicularis oculi is one of the few muscles in which these fibers are spatially segregated: the pretarsal fibers are largely pale, the preseptal fibers are a mixed group of pale and red, and the orbital section is mainly red muscle. These different muscle types are physiologically appropriate for different types of movement. Pale fibers conduct and contract more quickly, respond best to high frequencies of stimulation, accommodate more quickly, and have shorter after-hyperpolarizations. Also, the motor units have large axons, cell bodies and neuromuscular junctions. These characteristics are appropriate for rapid, phasic movements such as spontaneous and reflex blinks; therefore, it follows that pale muscle should dominate in the portions of orbicularis oculi involved in these movements.

As noted earlier, infants show a lower rate of spontaneous blinking than adults. Given that spontaneous blinks are controlled to a large extent by pale muscle specialized for phasic movement, it may be the case that these phasic systems are not fully functional early in life. In the next section, we present evidence that differential development of fast and slow systems may characterize sensory as well as motor activity.

INTRINSIC MODIFICATION

Sensory filtering can occur because of differences in intrinsic structural characteristics of processing circuits which lead to preferential transmission of selected stimulus features. Identification of such processing channels contributes to the understanding of complex perceptual phenomena. For example, the notion of specific and separable channels based on spatial frequency is well established in the visual system (e.g. N. Graham, Kramer and Haber, 1985), and has provided insight into processes such as masking (e.g. Breitmeyer and Ganz, 1976; Mitov, Vassilev and Manahilov, 1981), motion perception (e.g. Keesey, 1972) and selective attention (Alwitt, 1981). It is becoming increasingly clear that channels may also be defined on the basis of differential sensitivity to temporal aspects of stimulation. This is not surprising given that neuronal elements possess resistance and capacitance. Therefore, time-varying characteristics of stimulation must be critical factors in understanding the efficiency of information transmission in the nervous system. In this vein, elicitation of the startle blink appears to be mediated in large part by neural elements specialized for the processing of fast-rising, brief stimulation. It appears likely that the magnitude of the response may be controlled by parallel elements more sensitive to sustained aspects of the reflex stimulus. As outlined below, this hypothesis is supported by the effects on blink of two critical temporal parameters of the eliciting stimulus—rise time and duration. Furthermore, age differences in these effects suggest a relative immaturity of transient processing systems in early development.

TEMPORAL INFLUENCES

The effects of stimulus *rise time* were first studied by K.M. Berg (1973) who presented 50 ms tones with rise and fall times of 0, 3, 10 or 30 ms to adult subjects. The threshold for eliciting blink was lowest (87 dB) for the stimulus with the instantaneous rise time and increased by about 3 dB with each further lengthening of the rise and fall periods. Confirming results were recently reported by Blumenthal and Berg (1986b). They showed that increasing the rise time (1–25 ms) of similar 1000 Hz 50 ms tones of 95 and 102 dB produced a linearly decreasing probability of response. The amplitude of blink was much less affected by rise time differences than was probability, a finding that will be returned to below.

If the circuit involved in the elicitation of blink is composed of elements differentially sensitive to transient stimulation, then increases in *duration* over a short integrating period should have only minimal influence. Indeed, thresholds for blink vary with stimulus duration but only within a very restricted window. For visual stimuli, Hopf *et al.* (1973) determined that blink thresholds for rapidly rising flashes did decrease with increasing stimulus duration, but only up to 22 ms. Acoustic stimulation has been more extensively studied. In rats, increasing the duration of instantaneously rising stimuli over 8–12 ms did not produce larger startles or lower response thresholds (e.g. Marsh, Hoffman and Stitt, 1973). Similarly, in humans, K.M. Berg (1973) reported that decreases in blink threshold for fast-rising tones with increases in duration reached an asymptote at 16 ms. For white noise stimuli, the threshold function was extended. That is, the stimulus intensity required to elicit a blink 50% of the time decreased as the duration of the noise burst increased to 32 ms. Blumenthal and Berg (1986a) recently found that blink probability rose until white noise duration reached approximately 30 ms. Thus, the period of temporal integration is longer for white noise than for pure tones. In addition, the relative potency of these two types of acoustic stimuli vary with duration. Berg (1973) found that, at short intervals (16 ms), blinks elicited by tones had lower thresholds than those elicited by white noise. The reverse was true for durations over 20 ms (Berg, 1973; Blumenthal and Berg, 1986a).

K.M. Berg (1973) first postulated that the pattern of temporal effects on startle reflects the operation of two neural systems specialized for the transmission of transient and sustained aspects of stimulation. This distinction has been supported by converging psychophysical evidence (e.g. Breitmeyer and Ganz, 1976; Keesey, 1972; Poulson, 1981) and by neurophysiological evidence of differing characteristics of large and small cell types in the somatosensory, auditory, and visual systems (e.g. Enroth-Cugell and Robson, 1966; Gersuni, 1965; Johnson and Lamb, 1981; LaMotte, 1977; Rodieck, 1979). In particular, Gersuni identified short- and long-time-constant neurons at all levels of the auditory system. These neurons differed on several major characteristics. Compared with long-time-constant cells, short-time-constant neurons were more sensitive to stimulus rise time, had lower thresholds for brief energy change, and depended to a greater extent on spatial rather than temporal summation.

Given this notion of distinct and parallel systems with differing time constant characteristics, the processing of brief, fast-rising stimuli would be more adequately carried out by the short-time-constant system. As duration lengthens, the sustained aspects of the stimulus should activate the long-time-constant system which would then contribute to the response. K.M. Berg (1973) suggested that this explained the duration-dependent changes in relative effectiveness of pure tones and noise. Tones provoke a more synchronous neural discharge than does noise and should more adequately stimulate the spatially-summating, short-time-constant system. Increasing duration beyond the brief integrating period would have no further effect on this system but should activate the long-time-constant system. The relatively asynchronous white noise stimuli should be more efficiently transmitted by a temporally-integrating, long-time-constant system.

Distinct actions of transient and sustained portions of stimulation can also be inferred from the independent effects on different blink attributes. As noted before, Blumenthal and Berg (1986a) reported that blink amplitude was less influenced by rise time variations than was blink probability. Also, these same authors (Blumenthal and Berg, 1986b) were able to show a similar dissociation with variations in eliciting-stimulus duration. In this study comparing temporal summation of transient and sustained auditory stimulation, blinks to white noise stimuli of varying duration (3–100 ms) were compared to blinks produced by pairs of 3 ms noise bursts separated by silent intervals equal to the durations of the continuous stimuli. For continuous stimuli, blink latency decreased and blink probability increased with duration, but reached an asymptote at 20 ms. On the other hand, blink amplitude continued to increase as stimulus duration grew to 50 ms. Paired stimuli increased blink amplitude and probability over those values obtained with a single 3 ms noise. However, unlike with continuous stimuli, there was no further increase in blink amplitude for intervals greater than 20 ms. Furthermore, when the interval between noise bursts was greater than 40–45 ms, the paired stimuli were no more effective than a single 3 ms stimulus, indicating that the period in which the effect of transients could be integrated had been exceeded. For latency, paired stimuli did not produce a faster blink than a single stimulus at any interval.

At short intervals, summation of two transients was as effective as summation of higher-energy, continuous stimulation, suggesting that blink to such brief stimuli is determined mainly by a short-time-constant system. At intervals over 40 ms, transient summation no longer occurred and the contribution of the long-time-constant system was observed. However, its effect was only seen on amplitude, the attribute that can more readily reflect the integration of stimulus energy. In accounting for these findings, Blumenthal and Berg (1986a,b) have suggested that probability and amplitude are determined by partially independent processes: a startle 'trigger' and a startle 'amplifier' respectively. The trigger acts to detect a stimulus and initiate the response, while the amplifier modulates the size of the response through integration of energy-determining parameters.

In sum, the effects of temporal variables on blink have supported the existence of independent transient and sustained systems which extract or filter certain aspects of stimulation. This work, along with other evidence (Graham, Anthony and Zeigler, 1983, pp. 389ff; Harbin and Berg, 1983; Poulsen, 1981), estimates the transient integrating period to be approximately 20–40 ms for acoustic stimuli. The next subsection reviews work on blink elicitation which suggests that the transient processing system may be less efficient in young infants.

TEMPORAL INFLUENCES: DEVELOPMENTAL TRENDS

Blinking is more difficult to elicit in young infants than in adults. In newborns, thresholds for acoustic stimulation have been estimated at between 105 and 115 dB (Wedenberg, 1956), far higher than the 85–95 dB levels measured in adults (K.M. Berg, 1973). Similarly high thresholds for newborns have been reported by Ling (1972a,b) and Froding (1960). In older infants (6 weeks to 4 months), Graham, Strock and Zeigler (1981) noted that 50 ms noise bursts, at intensities effective for adults, elicited less reliable blinking. Acoustic blink latencies also tend to be longer in infants by about 15–20 ms (Anthony and Graham, 1985; Anthony, Zeigler and Graham, 1987).

Blinks have been elicited in newborns and older infants by taps to the forehead (Hoffman, Cohen and Anday, 1987; Hoffman, Cohen and English, 1985), puffs of air to the cheek (Anthony and Graham, unpublished data), as well as direct electrical stimulation of the supraorbital nerve (e.g. Vecchierini-Blineau and Guihenene, 1984). As noted earlier, such cutaneous stimulation elicits multiple bursts of activity in the EMG record in adults. Both R1 and R2 components are seen in infants as well, although the thresholds are higher than in adults. The relative ease of elicitation of these components also alters with development. The disynaptic R1 response is present from birth, although thresholds are slightly higher in the first year, and latency decreases rapidly over the first month, coincident with an increase in the conduction velocity of the VIIth nerve (Vecchierini-Blineau and Guihenene, 1984). In contrast, the polysynaptic R2 component, which relates to actual lid movement, is less consistently observed in infancy. Although some have reported a complete absence of this component in young infants (Clay and Ramseyer, 1976; Hopf, Hufschmidt and Stroder, 1965), Vecchierini-Blinieau and Guihenene, paying careful attention to state and other extraneous factors, reported ipsilateral R2s in three-fourths of infants under 8 months and contralateral R2s in two-thirds of these subjects. Compared with the R1 component, the ipsilateral response has a much higher threshold through the first year, and the contralateral threshold continues to be higher until at least 3 years of age. The difference in thresholds for R1 and R2 is reversed in adults. Sanes, Foss and Ison (1982) showed that the minimal electrical stimulus necessary to elicit R1 was always higher than that necessary to elicit R2.

Light flashes are also effective in eliciting blinks in newborns (e.g. Martinus and Papousek, 1970) and older infants (Anthony and Graham, 1983; Anthony, Zeigler and Graham, 1987). However, as with other modalities of stimulation, thresholds are higher in younger subjects (Hopf *et al.*, 1973) and onset latencies are delayed (Anthony and Graham, 1983). These age-related increases in latency are quite striking and far greater than those observed with acoustic stimulation. Figure 7.2 presents blink latencies for several studies which delivered stimuli in both acoustic and visual modalities to the same subjects, either adults or 4-month-old infants. In each study, blink was measured from integrated EMG. Visual blinks were elicited by light flashes and acoustic blinks by white noise between 99 dB and 109 dB or 1 kHz tones at 120 dB. Although paradigms differed across experiments, mean latency values fell within a fairly narrow range for each age. Blinks were faster in adults than in infants for both modalities; however, the age difference was more than four times greater for visual stimuli.

The interaction of age and modality on blink latency, evident in Figure 7.2, could result from a relative immaturity of visual blink pathways in young infants. As noted earlier, although the exact premotor circuits have not been detailed in humans, blinks elicited by both acoustic and visual stimuli require only subcortical structures. However, there is no clear anatomical evidence that the visual pathways are less developed than acoustic pathways at 4 months of age. In fact, based on myelinization data, postnatal maturation is more rapid in the visual system, with the development of cranial nerves and brainstem relays terminating 3–4 months postnatally in both systems (Yakolev and Lecours, 1967).

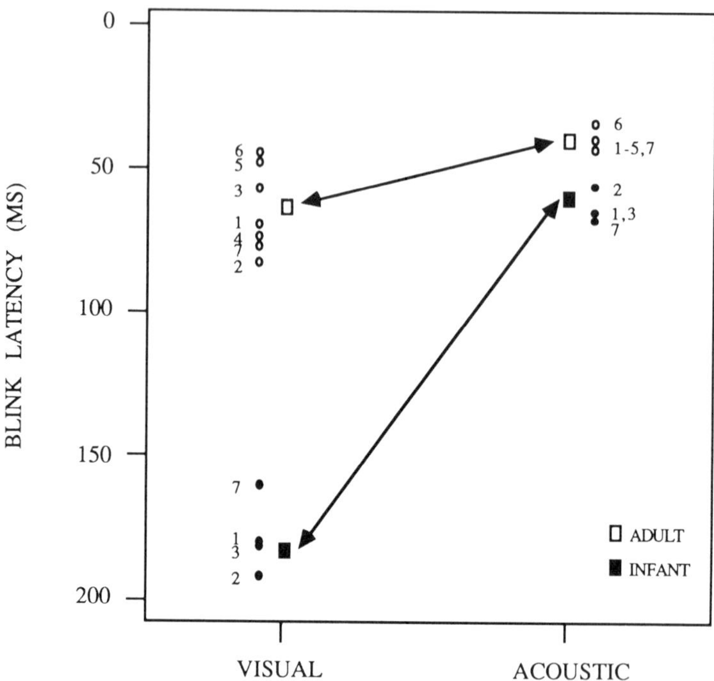

Figure 7.2. Mean latencies of acoustic and visual blink reflexes in seven studies of human adult groups and four studies of 4-month-old infants. See the text. Numbered circles identify the specific studies: (1) Anthony and Graham (1985); (2) Balaban, Anthony and Graham (1985); (3) Zeigler, Anthony and Graham (1981); (4) Zeigler (1982); (5) Yates and Brown (1981); (6) Tackmann, Ettlin and Barth (1982); (7) Anthony, Zeigler and Graham (1987). (Redrawn with permission of John Wiley & Sons Inc.)

It seems likely that differential development of sensory systems cannot account for these age-related changes in the latency difference between visually and acoustically elicited blinks. Instead, these differences, plus the generally increased difficulty of eliciting blinks and their longer latencies in infancy, may result, in part, from developmental differences in the processing of transient as opposed to sustained aspects of stimulation. In previous work, Graham, Strock and Zeigler (1981) suggested that this deficiency results from immaturity in neural systems specialized for the transmission of such stimuli. More specifically, we (Anthony, Zeigler and Graham, 1987) have proposed that the immature transient system may possess a longer time constant which could be expected to have at least three consequences: (1) reduced responsivity to brief stimuli; (2) asymptotic responding at longer stimulus durations; and (3)

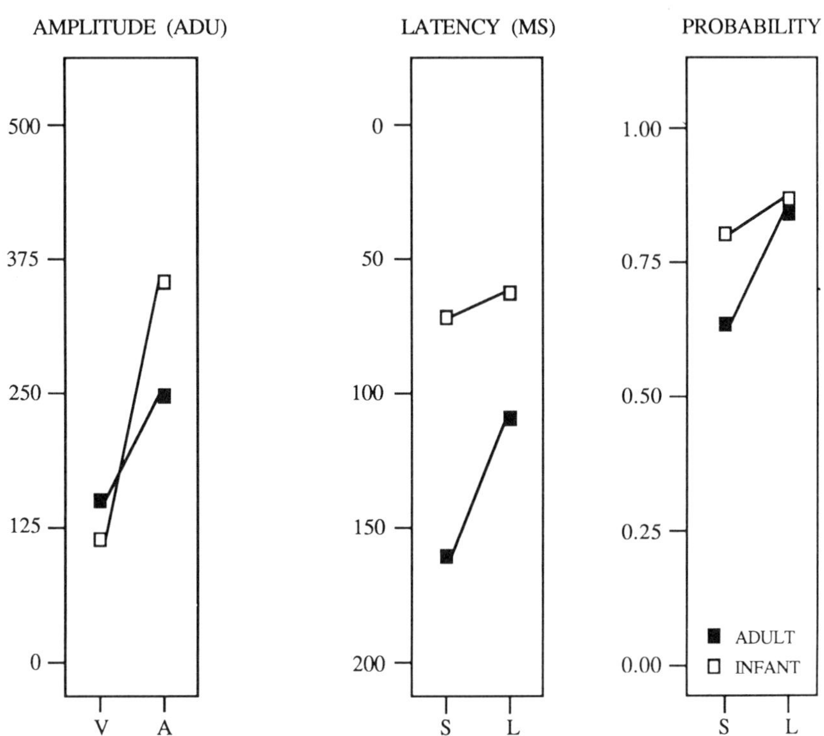

Figure 7.3. Significant interactions of age (adult versus infant) with stimulus variables. (A) Age × modality (visual (V) versus acoustic (A)) effect on blink amplitude; (B) Age × duration (short (S) versus long (L)) on blink latency and elicitation probability. (Redrawn with permission of John Wiley & Sons Inc.)

less facilitation by repeated stimulation. Investigations of the effects on blink of varying the temporal parameters of the eliciting stimulus provide evidence bearing on these predictions.

If the transient system less faithfully reflects rapid change, then brief stimuli should be less effective in the immature organism. Results consistent with this hypothesis were recently collected by Anthony, Zeigler and Graham (1987). The aim of the study was to evaluate two alternative explanations for the far greater difference between the latency of visual and acoustic blinks in young infants than in adults. We tested whether this pattern resulted from developmental differences in the processing of stimuli differing in (a) modality or (b) duration. Previous studies, summarized in Figure 7.2, had confounded these two variables: the acoustic stimuli were between 10 and 50 ms and the visual stimuli were less than 1 ms long. To assess whether infants have difficulty in the processing of brief stimuli or whether they have difficulty in processing visual stimuli, Anthony *et al.* presented blink-eliciting white noise and light flashes at both long (50 ms) and short (1 ms) durations. The major question was what variables would interact with age given orthogonal manipulation of duration and modality. Results from the 16 four-month-olds and 16 adults tested are presented in Figure 7.3. Blink latency and probability showed a clear age × duration interaction: the longer stimulus reduced latency and increased probability to a greater extent in infants than in adults. For latency, the facilitation with longer stimuli was significant for infants (50.5 ms) but not for adults (8.5 ms). An age × modality interaction, such as that portrayed in Figure 7.3 when modality and duration were confounded, was only significant for amplitude. However, the direction of effects was opposite to that predicted by the hypothesis of visual system immaturity. The effect of age on blink size was greater for acoustic than for visual stimulation.

Thus, these results indicate that duration manipulations affected infants and adults differently. Brief stimuli elicited blinks on approximately 25% fewer trials in infants with much slower latencies (nearly 100 ms). Increasing stimulus duration equalized the probability of response in the two age-groups and reduced the latency difference by half. Similar effects of duration were recently reported by Blumenthal and his colleagues using only acoustic stimulation (Blumenthal, Avendano and Berg, 1987; Blumenthal and Berg, 1986a). In newborns, only 50% of noise bursts (100 dB) elicited blinks when the duration was 3 ms, whereas 88% of the bursts were effective when duration was increased to 50 ms. Noise burst intensities were less in adults (95 dB); however, the short stimuli still produced blinks 80% of the time. For the 50 ms stimuli, blink probability was 94%.

Rapid change is critical for eliciting the startle blink. Transient systems are specialized to transduce such rapid change and should be strongly affected by increases in rise time. An immature transient system with a longer time constant should be less affected by such a manipulation. In keeping with this notion, developmental comparisons suggest that increases in rise time have little effect on younger subjects but produce a reduction in the effectiveness of brief stimulation in eliciting blinks in adults. In one study, Blumenthal (1985) found that varying the rise–fall time of 50 ms bursts of white noise from 1 to 10 ms failed to affect blink probabilities in adults or 4- to 6-week-old infants. The lack of an effect of rise time in adults conflicts with previous work (e.g. K.M. Berg, 1973) and, as the author suggests, may result from a ceiling effect: probabilities in adults were above 95% for all rise time conditions. Indeed, when maximal probabilities were less in subsequent experiments which used pure tone stimuli (Blumenthal and Berg, 1986b), a clear linear reduction in the likelihood of response occurred as rise times increased. The failure to find an effect of rise time in infants using white noise stimuli could not be attributed to a reduction in range because blink probabilities were 80% or less. One explanation for the lack of effect in infants is that the transient system is immature and, as a result, does not selectively process fast rise time stimulation. This interpretation is clouded by the lack of an infant study varying the rise time of pure tone stimuli. With these stimulus conditions, it is possible that rise-time effects would be seen in infants as well as adults since, as noted above, pure tones may be more effective in selectively stimulating transient systems. Alterations in stimulus onset that reduce the efficiency of processing by a short-time-constant system may be more faithfully reflected in response to tones.

Besides reduced responsiveness to brief, fast-rising events, a longer time constant should integrate input over longer periods. If the immature transient processing system is characterized by a longer time constant, blink responsivity should asymptote at longer stimulus durations in infants than in adults. Studies by Blumenthal, Avendano and Berg (1987) and Blumenthal and Berg (1986a) tracked the effects of duration on blink probability. Adults and newborns reached approximately the same maximum levels of responding—approximately 94% and 89% respectively. However, the asymptote of the function was reached at a duration of 20 ms for adults and 50 ms for infants.

As a third consequence of a longer time constant for the immature transient system, repeated transients should have less of an effect because of the slower recovery time. In the same Blumenthal studies discussed above, temporal summation functions for continuous stimuli were compared with the functions for paired stimuli separated by intervals equal to that of the continuous stimuli. In adults there was no difference in the effectiveness of continuous and paired stimuli up to an interval of 50 ms. The second transient of the pair produced the same amount of increase in blink as continuous stimulation. In infants, there was a significant effect of stimulus type on all blink measures; paired stimuli were less effective than continuous stimuli at all intervals for amplitude and for all but the 20 ms condition for probability.

Literature on the elicitation of orienting in young infants supports the existence of an early transient-processing deficit at higher levels. In reviewing this work, Graham, Anthony and Zeigler (1983) showed that stimuli sustained for 2 s or more were equally effective in producing heart rate changes in newborns and adults; however, briefer stimuli were either not effective in newborns or needed to be more intense. Also, young infants showed little response to fast-rise-time stimuli except when the onsets were uncontrolled and thus produced a series of high-intensity transients. Event-related potential evidence for a developmental progression in the ability to process transient information is discussed in the final part of this chapter.

This section has reviewed evidence indicating that the initiation of startle blink is mainly controlled by neural elements specialized for the processing of transient aspects of stimulation. The absolute amplitude of blink appears to have relatively greater contributions from an energy-integrating, sustained channel of processing. In young infants, the transient system appears relatively immature, judging from studies showing reduced impact of brief stimuli, the lesser effect of rise time, and a longer integration period. If a transient-processing deficit exists in young infants, it is not surprising that its effects would be most evident in higher-level functions, like orienting, given the general caudal to rostral maturational sequence. However, the effects on the subcortically-mediated blink response are surprising in view of the apparent structural maturity of the neural circuit. These results suggest that, even though low-level pathways are functional at early ages, their efficiency may be far from mature when examined with sensitive indices.

An immaturity in the processing of the transient portions of stimulation in young infants should have consequences for those information control mechanisms dependent on such processing. Conceptualizations of short-time-constant systems derived from neurophysiological investigations (e.g. Eccles, Kostyuk and Schmidt, 1962; Gersuni, 1971) and psychophysical investigations (e.g. Breitmeyer and Ganz,1976) have stressed inhibitory functions which may improve perception through sharpening contrasts or gating of extraneous information. Modification of startle blink by prior stimulation provides a methodology to examine such transient-dependent mechanisms, extrinsic to the blink circuit, as well as those controlled by systems sensitive to sustained input.

EXTRINSIC MODIFICATION: LOW-LEVEL

Activity within sensory pathways is affected not only by intrinsic characteristics of the paths but by influences from extrinsic circuits which act to modify transmission at different points in the processing scheme. The startle blink has been used as a probe to elucidate such extrinsic mechanisms. That is, changes in the size and speed of the reflex are measured and assumed to reflect prevailing processes set in place by prior stimulation or instructions. This section discusses patterns of startle-blink modulation that appear to result from low-level or preattentive regulatory mechanisms. Several features of these blink modification phenomena suggest that they reflect preattentive processes: they are initiated too rapidly to engage higher-level, conscious mechanisms; they are unlearned, occurring on the first pairing of prestimulus and probe (Ison and Ash, 1977) and they occur during sleep and, in adults, are independent of sleep stage (Silverstein, Graham and Calloway, 1980). Temporal parameters of the stimulus situation are critical in differentiating these modification effects.

Before examining developmental trends, the following section briefly reviews the excitatory and inhibitory effects established in adults.

TEMPORAL INFLUENCES

Prestimulation can produce both excitatory and inhibitory effects on startle blink elicited by a shortly-following probe. The direction and extent of modification is highly sensitive to the response characteristic measured, to the lead interval between prestimulus and probe, and to various features of the prestimulus. A critical feature of the prestimulus is whether it is discrete (i.e. brief, 20–50 ms) with offset prior to the onset of the probe, or continuous, lasting until probe onset. Consideration of the different prestimulus effects suggests the operation of parallel excitatory and inhibitory mechanisms, with neural paths differing in complexity and in intrinsic, time-varying characteristics (Anthony, 1985; Graham and Murray, 1977; Hoffman and Ison, 1980).

Excitatory Effects

Blink latency is reduced and/or amplitude is increased when *discrete* prestimuli precede a probe by very short intervals (Blumenthal and Gescheider, 1987; Blumenthal and Levey, 1989; Graham and Murray, 1977) or by no interval at all (Hoffman, Cohen and English, 1985). In the latter study, the size of the blink response to a glabellar tap was increased by a simultaneously presented 50 ms tone. Boelhouwer and colleagues (Boelhouwer *et al.*, in press) reported excitatory effects when a tactile probe actually preceded an acoustic prestimulus. In this case, it must be assumed that the prestimulus reached the startle center at a faster rate than the probe.

Continuous prestimuli produce greater facilitation than discrete prestimuli at a short lead interval of 60 ms (Graham and Murray, 1977). Moreover, unlike discrete prestimuli, they continue to have excitatory effects at longer lead intervals. Absolute facilitation can be masked by concurrent inhibitory influences at lead intervals between approximately 60 and 240 ms (Blumenthal and Levey, 1989); however, the relative facilitation of blink with continuous prestimuli increases during this period (Graham and Murray, 1977). Absolute excitatory effects are again evident at longer intervals. Continuous prestimulation of several seconds produces facilitation of blink latency and amplitude (Graham, Putnam and Leavitt, 1975; Zeigler, 1978), although the effect disappears in humans by 20 s. This excitatory pattern occurs whether the prestimulus and probe are in the same or different modalities and appears to follow an inverted U-shaped relationship with increases in prestimulus intensity (Putnam, 1975).

Prestimulation produces excitatory effects on blink rapidly suggesting that the modification pathway follows a quite direct path to the startle center. In rats, pre-exposure to continuous noise led to equivalent facilitation of startle elicited by acoustic stimuli as by electrical stimulation of the ventral cochlear nucleus pontis caudalis, suggesting that facilitation occurs at or below the level of the startle center (Davis *et al.*, 1982). The fact that excitatory effects are sensitive to prestimulus duration and intensity suggests the operation of a temporally-integrating, 'activation' system mediated by circuits differentially sensitive to sustained aspects of stimulation.

Inhibitory Effects

Startle blink inhibition by prestimulation has been observed with lead intervals of 15–400 ms, suggesting mediation by a less direct pathway than that of the excitatory effects. Any change in stimulation occurring within this interval produces an inhibitory effect on reflex amplitude. This effect has been termed prepulse inhibition (PPI) and, at optimal lead intervals (100–150 ms), can have profound effects; the percentage reduction in blink size can reach 60% (Graham and Murray, 1977). As with excitatory effects, prepulse inhibition occurs whether the modalities of the prepulse and probe are the same or different; however, as amplified in later sections, when the two stimuli are in the same modality, inhibition is greater. This additional reduction in amplitude appears to reflect an intrinsic priming effect which combines with PPI (Balaban, Anthony and Graham, 1985).

Prepulse inhibition competes with the excitatory effects described above. The shortest lead interval which results in inhibition of blink amplitude depends on the modality of the prepulse. For auditory prestimuli, PPI is evident with lead intervals as short as 30 ms. For visual and tactile prestimuli, excitatory effects are sustained for lead intervals of up to 60 ms (Blumenthal and Gescheider, 1987; Graham, 1980; Sanes, 1984) which appears to reflect modality differences in sensory processing time (Boelhouwer *et al.*, in press).

In contrast to the excitatory effects, prepulse inhibition appears mediated solely by the transient portions of the prepulse, although there is some disagreement on this point (Graham, Strock and Zeigler, 1981; Ison, 1978; Dykman and Ison, 1979; see Anthony (1985) for a discussion of this issue). The reduction in blink size occurs no matter what the prepulse event—onset, offset, or qualitative change (e.g. frequency, intensity)—and it is not dependent on the duration of the prestimulation. For instance, Graham and Murray (1977) showed that sustaining a prestimulus for 200 ms prior to a probe did not produce greater inhibition than did a 20 ms discrete prestimulus (Graham and Murray, 1977). Furthermore, transient prestimulus onsets and offsets can apparently summate, producing increased inhibition, provided they are separated by greater than 20–40 ms (Anthony, 1985; Graham and Murray, 1977; Harbin and Berg, 1983).

In sum, the inhibitory and excitatory effects combine to produce the functions relating lead interval duration and reflex modification for discrete and continuous prestimuli. Comparing the modulation produced by onset, offset, or change in frequency of sustained prestimulation at various lead intervals, Stitt *et al.* (1974) concluded that these opposing modification effects were largely independent and additive. The relatively precise temporal relationships suggest that inhibitory and excitatory effects utilize parallel modulatory pathways dependent on transient and sustained aspects of prestimuli, respectively.

TEMPORAL INFLUENCES: DEVELOPMENTAL TRENDS

Developmental trends in the processing of transient and sustained information influence the operation of the low-level extrinsic modification mechanisms described in the previous section. Excitatory effects appear dominant in early development, then may wane over time. In contrast, the inhibitory, low-level filtering mechanisms mediated by transients have a lengthy maturational sequence.

Excitatory Effects

Strong excitatory effects of prestimulation on startle blink are evident from a very early age. Strock (1976) reported a significant reduction in blink onset latency in infants 6–9 weeks old employing acoustic, continuous prestimuli with onsets 30 and 60 ms before the white noise probe. Further, we have shown a striking shortening of blink latency in 15-month-old infants at longer intervals which did not produce facilitatory effects in adults (Balaban, Anthony and Graham, 1989). Discrete acoustic prepulses (25 ms, 1000 Hz tones), occurring 125 or 225 ms prior to a 50 ms, 109 dB noise burst, reduced latency to the probes by about 11 ms or 17% in infants (Table 7.1). Consistent findings of more robust excitatory than inhibitory effects in early development were reported by Ornitz *et al.* (1986). This study used 25 ms, 1000 Hz tones at 75 dB as prestimuli and a 50 ms white noise burst to examine developmental patterns of blink modulation in children of 3, 4, 5, and 8 years and young adults. At 120 ms lead intervals, latency was significantly facilitated in the younger groups but not in the 8-year-olds or adults. This relative ordering of age-groups as a function of latency change remained at a lead interval of 250 ms; however, only the 3-year-olds continued to show significant facilitation. Ornitz *et al.* (1986) also examined modulation of blink with *continuous* prestimuli of 800 ms and 2 s. Under these conditions, the development pattern continued to hold: excitatory effects on blink latency were greatest for the younger subjects with all but the adults showing significant facilitation with a 2000 ms prestimulus.

Table 7.1. Characteristics of the unmodulated reflex blink to 109 dB white noise (S2) and of the blink modulated by weak tone (S1) preceding S2 by 125 or 225 ms.

	Magnitude (ADU)*	Amplitude (ADU)	Latency (ms)
Unpaired S2	179	193	64.3
Paired S1–S2			
125 ms	210	226	54.9
225 ms	229	233	51.6

* ADU = analog-to-digital units.

Excitatory effects on blink *amplitude* are also observed in very early infancy. The augmentation of blink produced by the simultaneous presentation of a brief, weak tone and a reflex-eliciting tap to the forehead (Hoffman, Cohen and English, 1985) is also observed in newborns (Cohen, Hoffman and Anday, 1987). Moreover, this excitatory effect is elicited more easily in infants; whereas blink facilitation was produced by 70 dB tones in newborns, the intensity had to be raised to 90 dB before the effect was seen in adults. With lead intervals at which excitatory effects compete with PPI in adults, prepulses tend to produce increases in blink amplitude relative to control in young infants. Graham, Strock and Zeigler (1981) showed that, with lead intervals of 75 and 175 ms between a discrete acoustic prestimulus and probe, 6- and 9-week-old infants showed 20–30% *facilitation* of blink magnitude. Adults showed strong (50–60%) PPI. This amplitude facilitation was not evident in 4- and 6-month-olds but reappeared, although not at significant levels, at similar intervals in 15-month-olds (see Table 7.1 derived from Balaban, Anthony and Graham, 1989) and 3-year-olds (Ornitz *et al.*, 1986).

The facilitatory effect of continuous stimuli at relatively long intervals has been demonstrated in young infants, and in some cases the effect is stronger than in adults. Graham, Strock and Zeigler (1981) reported a series of studies examining the modification of blink and heart rate by continuous acoustic prestimuli of 1, 2, or 4 s duration. Blink magnitude was facilitated at each lead interval for both adults and 3-month-old infants; however, the peak of the function was somewhat different. The facilitatory effect was always significant for adults but was greatest at the 2 s interval. For infants, reliable increases only occurred with 4 s prestimuli. In the 4 s condition, the average amount of facilitation relative to the control response was 40% and 27% for infants and adults, respectively. In the Ornitz *et al.* (1986) study described above, the facilitatory effect on blink amplitude was actually weaker at older ages. The 3-, 4- and 5-year-olds demonstrated significant facilitation at both of the longer lead intervals, peaking at 2 s. Facilitation was insignificant in young adults and 8-year-old children.

The pattern of dominant excitatory effects at younger ages is also evident in other physiological systems. Graham, Strock and Zeigler (1981) reported that infants showed significant augmentation of cardioacceleratory responses to probes following weak prestimulation sustained for 1-, 2- and 4 s lead intervals, whereas adults showed only slight increases in cardiac responses.

Inhibitory Effects

Unlike the excitatory effects, PPI follows a greatly prolonged and somewhat uneven developmental course. This finding is surprising given the robust nature of this inhibitory effect in animals. Studies have been unable to demonstrate PPI in newborns (Hoffman, Cohen and English, 1985) and the effect is quite weak in early infancy. An earlier review (Graham, Strock and Zeigler, 1981) reported a series of parallel infant and adult studies of the inhibitory effects of transient acoustic prestimulation (25–30 ms) at short lead intervals (75, 175, 225 and 275 ms). The principal finding was relatively weak inhibition by transient stimuli, as opposed to the relatively strong excitatory effects noted above, in 6-, 9- and 16-week-old infants compared with adults. Prepulse intensity had to be raised more than 14 dB for infants to achieve significant blink inhibition; even then, the extent of PPI was far less than in adults. Moreover, infants required lead intervals of about twice the optimal interval for adults; PPI was significant only at a lead interval of 175 and 225 ms for infants in the first six months of life. The heart rate response to the startle probes also showed relatively weaker inhibitory than excitatory effects in infants. Transient prestimuli tended to reduce the acceleratory response to probes in infants, but the effect was less than the facilitatory effect on heart rate produced by lengthy (1–4 s) continuous stimuli. The reverse was true for adults: transient-induced inhibition was more prominent than facilitatory effects.

Subsequent studies have begun to fill in the developmental course of inhibitory effects between infancy and adulthood. Although somewhat sparse, the data do not reflect a continuous increase in PPI with age. Berg and colleagues (Berg and Berg, 1987; Berg *et al.*, 1985) compared PPI in groups of infants, aged 2, 4, and 7 and 18 months of age. Data were derived from a number of studies that used similar stimulus conditions: acoustic prepulses ranging from 20 to 25 ms in duration preceding a 50 ms airpuff probe by lead intervals of 225–260 ms. As in the Graham *et al.* (1981) studies, some reduction in blink was observed in the 2- and 4-month infants, but only 15% or less. By seven months PPI was no stronger. In fact, the majority of infants showed *increased* blink amplitude in the prepulse condition relative to the control condition . A complete lack of PPI was also evident in our study of 15-month-olds discussed above (Balaban, Anthony and Graham, 1989), a finding consistent with the data on 18-month-olds reported by Berg *et al.* (1985). No evidence for PPI was obtained with either a 125 or 225 ms lead interval separating the brief acoustic prepulse and intense white noise burst. The 15-month-olds showed mean differences in the direction of *facilitation* for blink magnitude to paired stimulus conditions relative to the probe-alone condition.

It is somewhat surprising that PPI should be more evident in early than late infancy, although similar types of discontinuities in development have been noted in other contexts (Bever, 1982). However, a recent study (Balaban, Anthony and Graham, 1985) suggests that the weak inhibition seen in young infants may not result from PPI but from a separate type of inhibitory priming process, brought about by the sequential presentation of similar stimuli. In this experiment, blink to auditory (A) and visual (V) reflex-eliciting probes was compared in 32 four-month-old infants and in 32 adults. The probes followed either acoustic or visual prestimuli, resulting in four conditions distinguished by prestimulus/probe modality: A/A, A/V, V/A, and V/V. The 50 ms visual prestimulus was produced by a rapid series of light flashes that achieved a steady-state intensity of approximately one millilambert. The visual probe was a single flash, of approximately one lambert with a duration of less than 500 μs. The acoustic prestimulus was a 43 ms, 1000 Hz tone at 85 dB(A) and the acoustic probe was a 50 ms noise burst at 109 dB(A). These paired stimuli were presented during 5 s foreground stimuli consisting of slides and music-box melodies. The effects of these foreground stimuli are not relevant for the present discussion but will be discussed in connection with higher-level extrinsic effects in a later section.

The results demonstrated a clear repetition effect, supported by an interaction of prestimulus modality and probe modality; same-modality pairs elicited smaller responses than pairs differing in modality. Figure 7.4 illustrates this result by displaying averaged integrated blinks to matching and mismatching stimulus pairs. The effect was highly significant, and approximately the same magnitude, in infants and adults. Same-modality pairs showed a mean reduction, compared with different-modality pairs, of 28.5% for infants and 30% for adults, respectively. A similar inhibitory effect on blink latency was evident in both age-groups but only reached significant levels in adults.

This study suggests that previously reported PPI effects in infants, when same-modality prestimuli and reflex-eliciting stimuli were used, may be completely or partially due to a repetition effect rather than to PPI. The repetition effect appears to reflect a priming, or refractory-like, mechanism, that may occur in the sensory portion of the intrinsic reflex pathway, prior to convergence of information from different modalities (Balaban, Anthony and Graham, 1985; Berg and Berg, 1987).

A similar repetition effect may have contributed to the surprising report by Hoffman and his colleagues (Hoffman, Cohen and Anday, 1987) of a strong inhibitory effect in sleeping or resting neonates. In this study, pairs of blink-eliciting glabellar taps were presented separated by 300, 600, 900, or 1200 ms. Adults showed inhibition at each interstimulus interval and newborns at each

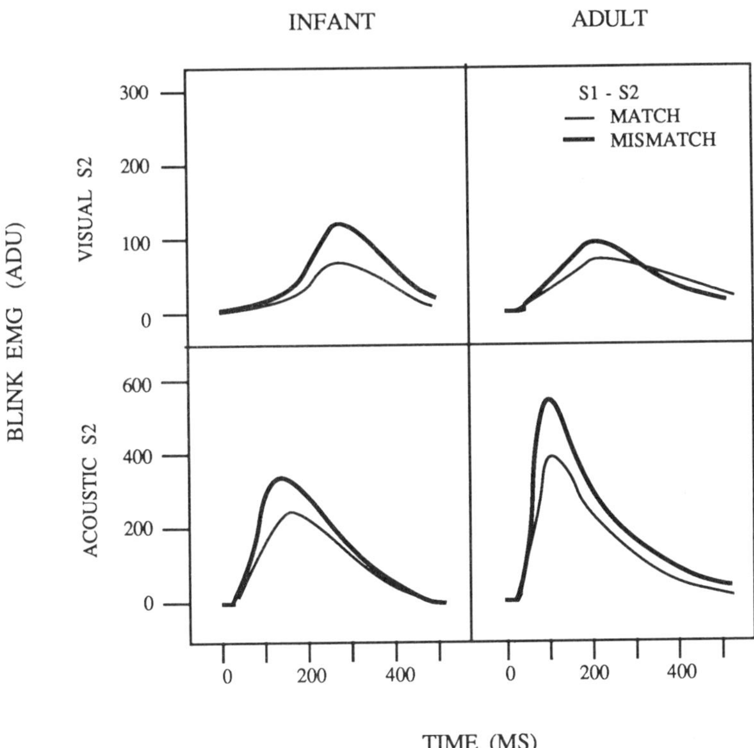

Figure 7.4. Modality-repetition effects of prestimulus (S1) on average integrated blink responses to reflex-eliciting stimuli (S2). ADU = analog-to-digital units. (Redrawn with permission of Ablex Publishing Corp.)

except the 300 ms interval; preterm infants did not demonstrate significant inhibition. In a previous study with neonates, PPI was not evident when a 90 dB, 50 ms tone preceded the glabellar tap by 600 ms (Hoffman, Cohen and English, 1985). Thus, the inhibition obtained by pairing glabellar taps appears linked to a modality-specific mechanism.

Two cross-sectional studies revealed little evidence for significant PPI until after five years of age. Given the preceding discussion of repetition effects, results from the Berg *et al.* (1985) study are particulary important since the prestimulus and probe were of different modalities. As noted above, groups of infants and toddlers (2–18 months) showed inconsistent and weak PPI. In 6- and 9-year-olds, the extent of inhibition was much larger (34%) and significant, although a relatively intense prestimulus was required (84 dB). In adults, profound PPI was elicited by a near-threshold intensity prestimulus. The study by Ornitz and colleagues (Ornitz *et al.*, 1986) was notable for the careful procedures used to ensure similar states of alertness across a wide age-range of 3 years to adulthood. In this study, lead intervals of 120 and 250 ms separated a 1000 Hz, 25 ms, 75 dB prepulse from blink-eliciting white noise bursts. Results showed an initial dip in PPI between 3 and 4 years of age and then a steady increase until mature levels were reached in 8-year-olds.

Summary

Excitatory effects on startle appear dominant in infancy and early childhood. Facilitation of latency and amplitude at brief lead intervals and at longer lead intervals with continuous prestimulation is present very early and appears to decline with age. In contrast, PPI remains weak well into middle childhood. The pattern of PPI maturation appears somewhat discontinuous; the small amount of data suggests reversals within the 6–18 month and 3–5 year periods. Balaban, Anthony and Graham (1989) and Berg and Berg (1987) have suggested that these discontinuities might reflect points of neural reorganization in which the balance between different neural processes may be disturbed by spurts of growth in structures affecting one of these processes but not others. Thus, immature higher centers may actively interfere with the operation of mature lower-level structures. This reasoning was used to account for the precocious appearance of orienting behaviors (Graham *et al.*, 1978) and PPI (Berg and Berg, 1987) in hydraencephalic infants.

The maturity of the reflex augmentation effect, the apparent maturity of the modality-repetition effect, and the relative maturity of facilitation by sustained prestimulation compared with PPI, taken together, suggest that the delayed maturation of PPI is due to a specific immaturity of the extrinsic circuits mediating the effect. However, this lengthy maturational course for PPI is surprising given that the effect seems mediated at relatively low levels of the nervous system. The neural pathway for this effect likely involves systems rostral to those necessary for the startle response itself. It does not appear to involve cortical structures since, in animals, it is seen in decerebrate preparations (Davis and Gendelman, 1977) but is probably mediated in the pontine brainstem or midbrain (Leitner *et al.*, 1981). Recent neuroanatomical investigations implicate a role of the lateral tegmental area of the midbrain, in the area of the cuneiform and ventral parabrachial nuclei. Lesions of this area reduce visual and acoustic PPI but do not affect short-interval excitatory effects (Leitner *et al.*, 1981). It is of interest that the lateral tegmental area of the midbrain reticular formation shows myelination continuing beyond puberty (Yakovlev and Lecours, 1967). Because PPI is dependent on rapid change and not prestimulus duration, the system responsible for the effect likely contains elements specifically sensitive to transient aspects of stimulation. The immaturity of PPI then is consistent with the notion of a transient processing deficit in early development derived from the effects of duration and rise time in the intrinsic reflex pathway.

Immaturity in this low-level filtering mechanism has implications for early sensory–perceptual analyses and for higher-level processing. Before discussing these implications, the next section reviews how higher-level extrinsic processes can act down to modulate the reflex pathway and the PPI pathway.

EXTRINSIC MODIFICATION: HIGHER LEVEL

The extrinsic control systems described in the previous section appear activated by separable, parallel paths specialized to process transient and sustained portions of sensory events. These systems operate at low levels and possess characteristics that imply automatic or preattentive operation at low levels. Blink is also sensitive to the influence of extrinsic control systems organized at higher levels of the nervous system. In this section we briefly review evidence for the modulation of blink by attentional processes in adults. A more extensive treatment can be found in Anthony (1985) and in Chapter 3. We then present recent evidence for the existence of attentive modification of blink in young infants. Finally, we discuss the implications of these selective effects on blink for an understanding of attentive mechanisms and their development.

ATTENTIVE INFLUENCES

The blink reflex is mediated at the brainstem level. However, because structures in the neural circuit have efferent connections from cortical as well as subcortical centers, the reflex can be influenced by higher-level processes. Graham, Putnam and Leavitt (1975) first suggested that blink could be affected by orienting/attentional processes. They reported that the reflex was enhanced when it was elicited during a period of heart rate deceleration. This cardiac response is one of a host of physiological and behavioral changes elicited by a novel change in stimulation or in situations that demand alertness to the environment (e.g. Graham, 1979; Lacey and Lacey, 1970). In the Graham, Putnam and Leavitt (1975) study, a phasic increase in orienting/attentional processes, indexed by heart rate deceleration, was evoked by the onset of a weak tone prestimulus which preceded a blink-eliciting burst of noise on every trial. Attention was elicited because the duration of the lead interval between the tone and noise was varied unpredictably. The intervals ranged between 200 and 2000 ms. Note that these intervals exceed the optimal interval for PPI. On control trials, there was no prestimulus, and heart rate was relatively unchanging for the 2000 ms prior to the occurrence of the reflex stimulus. On prestimulus trials, heart rate decelerated sharply with the onset of the prestimulus and continued to decelerate until reflex-stimulus onset. Furthermore, with foreperiods of 2000 ms, a significant slowing of heart rate was evident at probe onset, and both blink magnitude and latency were facilitated. In contrast, in studies which presented a constant 2000 ms foreperiod (e.g. Bloch, 1972), attention was not increased, judging from the lack of heart rate deceleration during the lead interval, and blink did not differ between control and prestimulus conditions.

A similar association of heart rate deceleration and blink facilitation occurred in other warned paradigms designed to elicit phasic increases in attention. These studies employed a constant foreperiod; however, subjects were required either to judge the duration of, or make a rapid button press to, the reflex stimulus (Bohlin and Graham, 1977; Ison and Ashkenazi, 1980). In each case, anticipatory heart rate deceleration developed within the foreperiod and blink was enhanced compared with the response to the reflex stimulus presented alone. Also, blink was enhanced when a reflex stimulus was inserted during the heart rate orienting produced by presentation of a novel stimulus (Bohlin *et al.*, 1981).

The association between heart rate deceleration and the facilitation of reflex blink suggested that this modification effect was a result of attentional activity mobilized in anticipation of the reflex stimulus. Further work has been aimed at questions concerning the selectivity of this facilitation and the site of these extrinsic modification effects. If attention acted to enhance the processing of the startle probe, then effects should differ depending on whether the probe was in the attended channel or not. Several studies have shown this to be the case (e.g. Anthony, 1981; Hackley and Graham, 1983; Putnam and Meiss, 1980, 1981; Silverstein, Graham and Bohlin, 1981). In these warned paradigms, attention was focused on the auditory or tactile modality, through task manipulations, and acoustic startle probes were inserted either coincidentally with the task stimulus (Bohlin and Graham, 1977; Silverstein, Graham and Bohlin, 1981) or in the foreperiod preceding execution of the task (Anthony, 1981; Bauer, 1982; Putnam and Meiss, 1980, 1981). Control reflex stimuli were introduced without a preceding warning signal. No matter whether the task was a rapid button press or a perceptual judgment, blink magnitude was facilitated only when attention was directed to the acoustic modality. When task demands focused attention on the tactile modality, blink size was either equivalent to control values or was actually inhibited.

In sum, this series of studies supported the hypothesis that differences in the focus of attention, brought about by variation in the modality of expected events, altered the size of the startle blink. However, the exclusive use of an acoustic probe prevented the conclusion that attention was operating on the sensory–perceptual leg of the reflex circuit. Inhibitory effects when attention was directed away from the probe could have resulted from attenuation of auditory transmission by voluntary contraction of the middle ear muscles (Desmedt, LaGrutta and LaGrutta, 1971). Facilitatory effects could have been due to non-specific arousal effects on the motor path. More recent work aimed at separating effects on the sensory and motor limbs of the startle reflex has taken advantage of the fact that blinks can be elicited in more than one modality.

The logic behind this series of studies was outlined by Anthony and Graham (1983). It is based on the fact that blink reflexes, elicited by different modalities of stimulation, have distinct afferent paths but share a common motor pathway. Therefore, differential effects on reflexes in two modalities, occurring when attention is directed to one of those modalities and away from the other, must be localized to preconvergence, sensory-central processing. A study by Hackley and Graham (1983) utilized this approach, although reflex probe modality was varied between subjects. In each of two experiments, subjects received two coincident stimuli, a brief tone burst and an air puff. In Experiment 1, the acoustic stimulus was intense and reflex-eliciting while the tactile stimulus, directed to the back of the hand, was weak. The reverse was true in Experiment 2: the tones were weak and air-puff was blink-eliciting because it was aimed at the periorbital area. Attention was directed by asking subjects to judge the duration of one stimulus in the first half of each experiment and the other in the second half.

The results suggested that attention selectively influenced processing in sensory–perceptual pathways because blink measures varied according to the direction of attention. In Experiment 1, blink magnitude was larger and blink latencies were faster when attention was directed toward the acoustic reflex stimulus than towards the weak tactile stimulus. In contrast, when the modality of the weak and strong stimuli were reversed in Experiment 2, the direction of effects was reversed: attending to the weak acoustic stimulus produced a smaller and slower blink than attending to the tactile, reflex stimulus. Clearly, some alteration in processing occurred before the convergence of tactile and acoustic blink pathways.

Hackley and Graham (1987) employed spatial position instead of modality to define attention and reflex stimulus channels. On each trial, blink-eliciting tones were presented through earphones either to the left ear, the right ear, or to a midline position produced by simultaneous input to both ears. To further distinguish the channels, a specific frequency—either 800, 1800, or 2800 Hz—was associated with each spatial position. Tones were randomly presented at each spatial location, but, on different blocks of trials, subjects were asked to attend to a specific location and to judge the duration of the tones. Again, a selective pattern of blink modification was observed. Small decreases in blink latency were observed when attention was directed toward a lateralized position (either left or right) compared with when attention was directed away from that position. The fact that the effect was greatest for high-frequency tones

(2800 Hz) argues against the involvement of middle ear muscle attenuation, since the latter phenomenon acts mainly on frequencies below 1000–2000 Hz.

In sum, the blink results indicate that attention appears capable of increasing or decreasing the gain of structures in the sensory–perceptual path which are sufficiently low-level to be part of the reflex circuit. The implications of this evidence for *early* selection are discussed in a later section. The next subsection provides data indicating that effects of top-down, selective control can, under certain conditions, occur quite early in development.

ATTENTIVE INFLUENCES: DEVELOPMENTAL TRENDS

The notions of facilitated processing of selected input and, to a lesser extent, inhibited processing of unselected input are at the heart of most definitions of attention. Selective attention is assumed to have been operative if differential processing of simultaneous sources of information can be demonstrated. This has been difficult to establish in infants because of their limited behavioral repertoire. Although attentive or orienting behaviors such as visual fixation, heart rate deceleration, or reduction in heart rate variability can be elicited in newborns and older infants (Graham, Anthony and Zeigler, 1983), little is known about the functional consequences of the process indexed by these behaviors. In other words, can stimulus processing be altered by attention in young infants? Examination of the startle blink reflex elicited by stimulation in two modalities when the reflex stimulus matched or mismatched an attended 'foreground' stimulus has provided relevant data.

One study (Anthony and Graham, 1983, 1985) compared selective effects on blink in adults and 4-month-old infants. At each age, two groups of 16 subjects were distinguished by whether the modality of the attended foregrounds was visual or acoustic. These 5 s foreground stimuli were presented 32 times to adults. Infants completed 28 trials on the average because testing was discontinued if they became fussy or upset. On each trial, a reflex stimulus was delivered 4 s following the onset of the foreground. Equal numbers of visual and acoustic probes were presented, although, on any trial, the modality was unpredictable. Interest value of the foreground stimuli was varied to examine whether selective effects on blink would be greater if attention was more strongly engaged. In the visual group, foregrounds designated as 'interesting' were colored slides of human faces, while the 'dull' foregrounds were blank slides matched in luminance with the colored slides. In the acoustic group, 'interesting' foregrounds were segments of music-box melodies, while 'dull' stimuli were unvarying, 1000 Hz tones.

It was expected that the interesting foregrounds would be intrinsically attention-engaging for infants but not necessarily so for adults. Therefore, instructions were provided to adults which emphasized the importance of maximizing attention to the 'important' interesting foregrounds and ignoring, though still fixating, the dull foregrounds. The HR results suggested that these manipulations were successful in producing an increase in attentive behavior. In both age-groups, significant HR deceleration occurred during the foreground period, peaking at the point of reflex stimulus onset (Figure 7.5). In infants, but not in adults, interesting foregrounds produced more profound deceleration than dull foregrounds.

Given that attention was deployed, the blink data imply a selective influence on low-level sensory pathways in both mature and immature subjects. Figure 7.6 displays averaged evoked blinks in match and mismatch conditions for both infants and adults. Figure 7.7 summarizes the peak magnitude data.

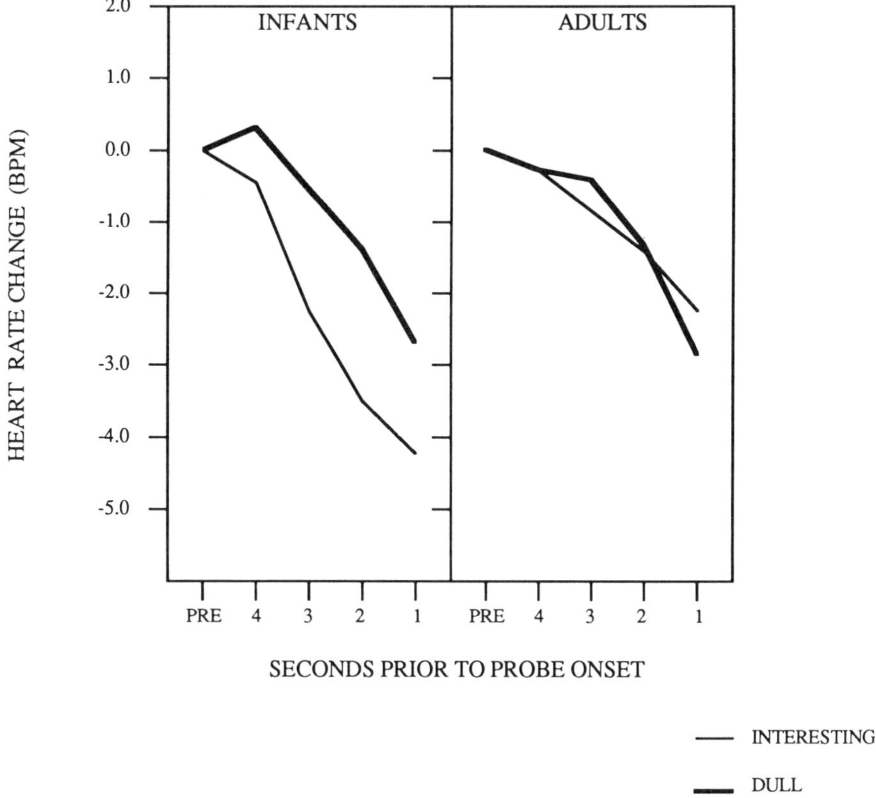

Figure 7.5. Heart rate during the 4 s between foreground and probe onsets, less prestimulus heart rate (PRE) measured during the 1 s prior to foreground onset. Curves for interesting and dull foregrounds are averaged over probe and foreground modality. (Redrawn with permission of Elsevier Science Publishers, B.V.)

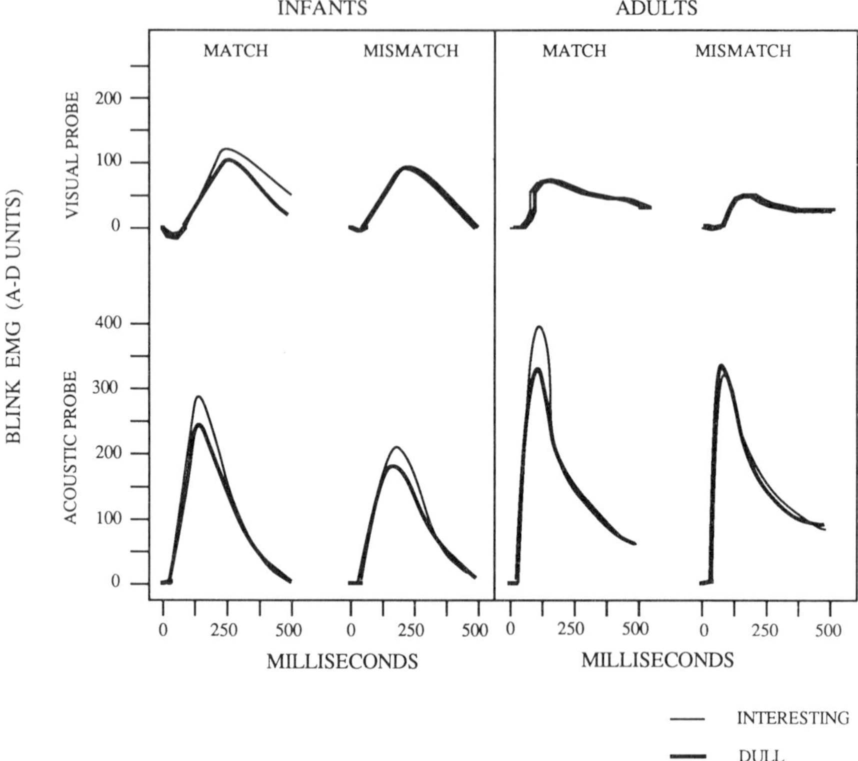

Figure 7.6. Averaged evoked EMG activity in analog-to-digital (A–D) units for 500 ms after the onset of visual and acoustic probes for conditions in which modality of the probe either matched or mismatched the modality of the interesting or dull foreground. (Redrawn with permission of Elsevier Science Publishers, B.V.)

Reflex stimuli produced larger blinks when they matched the modality of the attended foreground than when they did not. Furthermore, the match/mismatch difference was relatively greater for interesting than for dull foregrounds. When analyzed separately for each age-group, both magnitude effects were significant for infants, but the modality-match effect, although evident in the overall means, was not reliable in adults. Blink onset latency showed a pattern of results consistent with the magnitude data. In both age-groups, blinks occurred faster when probe and foreground matched, and the effect was enhanced when the foreground was interesting rather than dull. However, these effects were only statistically reliable in adults.

Presenting both acoustic and visual reflex stimuli in an unpredictable manner in the same experiment strengthens a selective interpretation of the blink modification results in several ways. First, in the Hackley and Graham

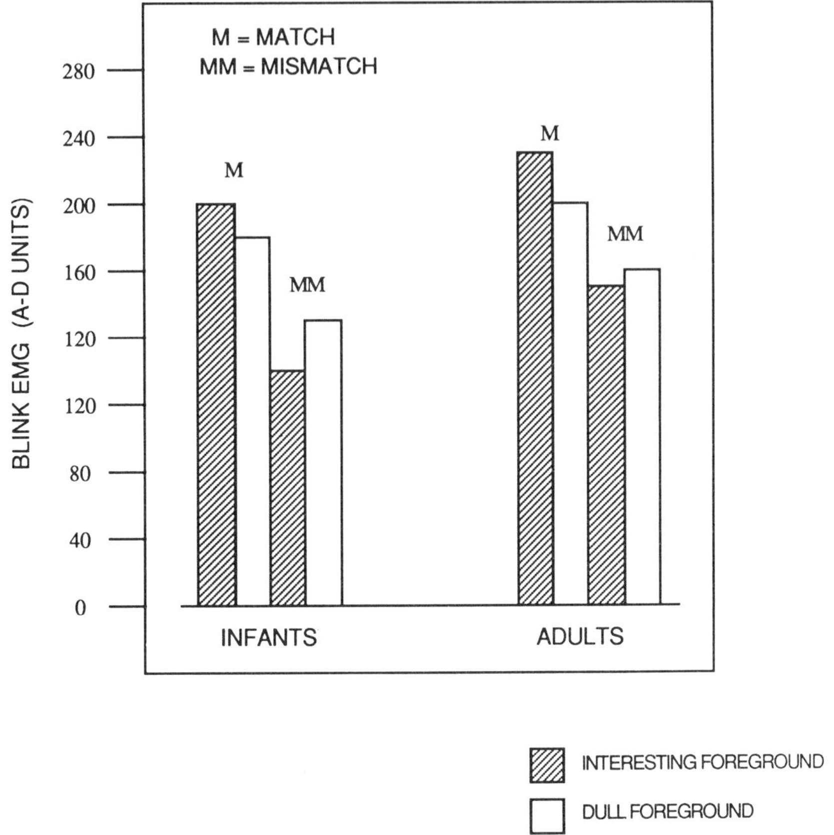

Figure 7.7. Peak magnitude of EMG activity after probe onset where modality of the probe either matched or mismatched the modality of the interesting or dull foreground. (Redrawn with permission of Elsevier Science Publishers, B.V.)

(1983) study, the modality of the reflex stimulus was the same within an experiment. Therefore, it could be argued that the relative blink facilitation, occurring when subjects attended to the reflex stimulus, resulted from increased arousal engendered by this intense stimulus. Second, as pointed out above, the use of reflex stimuli in two modalities argues against explanations of the modification pattern which invoke specific auditory mechanisms or a process, such as general activation, acting on the motor pathway. Finally, a masking effect of foreground stimulation is not a possible explanation because opposite effects would be predicted; that is, the response to a reflex stimulus in the same modality as concurrent foreground stimulation should have been reduced rather than enhanced.

Supporting data for the selective influence of attention on blink have been

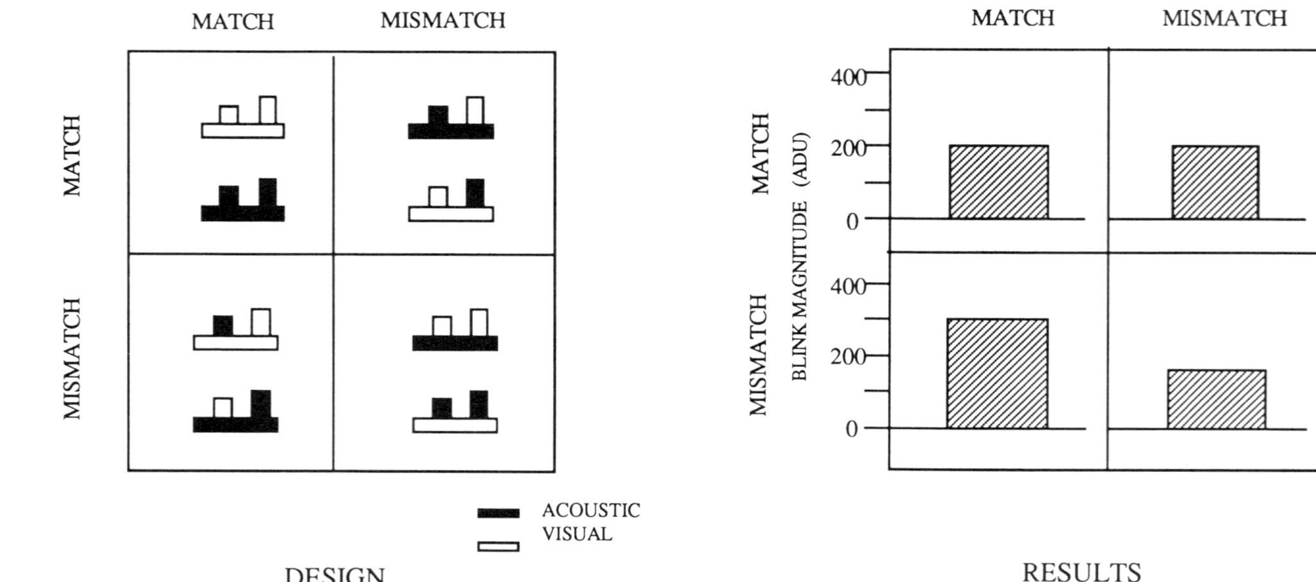

Figure 7.8. Attentional effects on infant blink magnitude in analog-to-digital units (ADU). The design of the experiment is shown on the left. Foreground modality is coded by the horizontal bar, prestimulus (S1) modality by the short vertical bar, and reflex-eliciting stimulus (S2) by the tall vertical bar. The results are shown on the right. The striped bar in each quadrant indicates the average blink magnitude in response to the stimulus conditions described in the corresponding quadrants on the left. (Redrawn with permission of Ablex Publishing Corp.)

obtained in the Balaban, Anthony and Graham (1985) study, described earlier, which also compared adults and 4-month-old infants. The design for this study is presented in Figure 7.8. Foreground and reflex stimuli were identical to those employed by Anthony and Graham (1983, 1985). However, in the Balaban *et al.* study, a brief prestimulus, either visual or acoustic, preceded the reflex stimulus on each trial in order to investigate modality repetition effects on PPI. Thus, in this case, selective attention, elicited by the foregrounds, would be expected to have more complex effects on reflex responsiveness. Prepulse inhibition is enhanced by increased attention to the prestimulus, presumably by facilitating its processing, resulting in a further reduction in blink size (DelPezzo and Hoffman, 1980; Hackley and Graham, 1987). Therefore, when the modalities of the prestimulus and the reflex stimulus are the same, attention to the foreground of that modality should produce opposing effects: enhancement of response to the reflex stimulus and enhancement of the inhibitory effect of the prestimulus. In contrast, when the prestimulus and the reflex stimulus are in different modalities, attention effects should summate. When the foreground matches the reflex stimulus in modality, blink should be facilitated because attention is directed toward the reflex stimulus and away from the inhibiting prestimulus. When the foreground matches the prestimulus, inhibition should be increased because attention is directed away from the reflex stimulus and toward the prestimulus.

As expected, the foregrounds elicited an orienting/attentional process as reflected by a linear heart rate deceleration across the 5 s period of foreground stimulation in both infants and adults. Furthermore, the blink results revealed the separate actions of this attentive process on both prestimulus and the reflex stimulus. This significant interaction of foreground, prestimulus, and the reflex stimulus modalities is evident in Figure 7.8. The upper left and lower right quadrants display average blink magnitude in infants for those conditions in which attention effects should cancel each other. Indeed, there was no difference between blinks elicited by reflex stimuli that mismatched or matched the foreground in modality when the reflex stimulus and prestimulus were both visual or both acoustic. In both cases, the attention effects on the prestimulus and reflex stimulus cancelled each other. However, the match/mismatch difference was significant when the reflex stimulus and prestimulus were different. Comparison of the lower left and upper right quadrants indicates the blink magnitude was greatest when the foreground directed attention toward the modality of the reflex stimulus and away from the modality of the inhibitory prestimulus.

These selective magnitude effects were significant for infants but not for adults. However, like the Anthony and Graham (1983, 1985) study, the reverse was true for blink latency. When the reflex stimulus matched the attended foreground in modality, onset latencies were speeded in adults but not in infants. A different selective effect was observed in infants, however: latencies were slowed when the modality of foreground and prestimulus matched compared with when they did not.

It appears that magnitude and latency may be differentially sensitive to selective effects, and this difference may change with age. In adults, Hackley and Graham (1987) reported that, although relatively constant effects of attention on both measures were obtained across five studies, the latency effect was always reliable, whereas magnitude only reached significance in one case. It is not clear why latency should be less sensitive to selective effects in infants. One possibility involves the relative immaturity of the transient processing system in infants. As outlined in an earlier section, blink latency and probability are largely determined by the transient processing system (Anthony, Zeigler and Graham, 1987; Blumenthal and Berg, 1986a,b). The immaturity of this system might increase variability, obscuring any selective effects. Indeed, estimates of error variance associated with latency modulation is heterogeneous across ages and much greater in infants (Zeigler, 1978). In comparison with onset latency, blink amplitude seems determined to a greater extent by sustained features of the eliciting stimulus. Thus, the relative maturity of the long-time-constant system in infants may contribute to the greater sensitivity of blink magnitude to selective effects.

The pattern of selective influences on blink in early infancy is somewhat surprising given that growth in the ability to voluntarily focus attention represents a major developmental theme through early childhood (e.g. Pick, Frankel and Hess, 1975). However, the circumstances under which selective processing occurs in early development may be restricted. Flexible and planful focusing of attention may be a later developing skill, as evidenced by the results of a recent study comparing attentive effects on blink and heart rate in 5-year-olds and adults (Anthony and Putnam, 1985). On each trial of a warned reaction-time task, acoustic, startle-eliciting probes were presented at one of four points during a 6 s warning interval or at a control position within the intertrial interval. As in the work described earlier, attention was directed away from the acoustic probes by requiring a rapid response to the offset of a tactile warning signal which marked the 6 s warning interval.

In both adults and children, measurement of heart rate change revealed a prominent deceleration during the latter half of the warning interval. This cardiac pattern was taken to indicate the growth of attention in preparation for the tactile respond signal. Coincident with this deceleration, startle blink in adults became increasingly *inhibited*; blink amplitude to the probe presented 0.5 s prior to the end of the warning interval was significantly reduced relative to control levels. The blink modification pattern was exactly opposite in children; their blink amplitude actually *increased* during the warning interval, peaking at the probe position nearest the respond signal.

These results indicate that the attentive process was focused in adults; the effect of stimuli (probes) in an unattended modality was attenuated. The facilitatory trend in children suggests that attention was more generalized, enhancing the processing of information in relevant as well as irrelevant channels. This paradigm differs from that of the infant studies described earlier in several respects; however, a major difference is the more voluntary nature of attentive deployment required in the Anthony and Putnam (1985) study. It is apparent that selective processes can operate in infancy; however, they may require active processing of information in the attended channel to maintain this state. Generating and holding attentive focus in anticipation of an expected event appears to be a later developing skill.

IMPLICATIONS FOR INFORMATION PROCESSING AND DEVELOPMENT

The distinction between intrinsic and extrinsic filtering of input is at the heart of the classic dual-process model of neuronal change outlined by Groves and Thompson (1970). In that model, a stimulus activates two independent but interacting systems: a decremental process (habituation) that occurs in the direct or intrinsic pathway and an incremental sensitization process ('state system') mediated by circuits extrinsic to the direct path. The pattern of blink modification by intrinsic and extrinsic mechanisms extends the dual-process notion and is compatible with 'continuous flow' models of nervous system functioning (e.g. Eriksen and Schultz, 1979; McClelland, 1979; Turvey, 1973). The data suggest that information propagates along parallel, hierarchically organized and interacting paths. These paths may be redundant or they may differ in characteristic ways that lead to *intrinsic* filtering of input. In the proposed model, signals from these separate pathways branch to many relay stations or decision points to activate *extrinsic* systems that influence information processing at various levels or that affect the motor system. The following summarizes the filtering mechanisms revealed by blink modification studies as they extend the basic model proposed by Groves and Thompson. We then outline the implications of the work for the control of information processing and its development.

MODEL OF INTRINSIC AND EXTRINSIC REGULATION

Characteristics of blink elicitation and modification by prestimuli demonstrate several features of intrinsic and extrinsic regulation. First, these results indicate, along with data from other areas, that both intrinsic and extrinsic systems can consist of parallel paths specialized to convey different aspects of stimulation. Stimulus information is selected or filtered in a 'passive' manner by the structural characteristics of the path. The startle blink data delineate one set of such parallel pathways, distinguished by their time-varying characteristics. The action of short-time-constant circuits is reflected by the sensitivity of probability and latency measures to stimulus change occurring within a brief integrating period (<20 ms). Blink amplitude reflects the operation of a longer-time-constant processing system that temporally integrates energy over a more extended period.

The startle data also point up the need to consider the effects of stimuli that do not elicit a behavioral response on transmission along intrinsic pathways. Groves and Thompson (1970) identified a reduction in response resulting from stimulus repetition as the intrinsic mechanism of change, but confined discussion to stimuli that were effective in producing a response. They stated that 'repetition of an *effective* stimulus results in an inferred decremental process in the S–R pathway or an inferred incremental process in excitation of the state system' (p. 441). The blink modification work shows weak prestimuli to have lasting effects in the sensory, reflex path that alter subsequent processing in that path. Same versus different pair effects (Balaban, Anthony and Graham, 1985) revealed that a weak prepulse can act to modify pathway transmission; subsequent intense stimuli traversing the same sensory pathway elicited blinks of longer latency and reduced amplitude compared with blinks elicited by stimuli differing in modality. Similar findings were reported by Zeigler (1982) employing relatively long lead intervals (2 s). Several mechanisms could account for this priming effect, including neuronal refractoriness or higher level match/mismatch effects. Wagner (1976) reports an inhibitory priming effect which he attributes to the prerepresentation of a stimulus in short-term memory. It is interesting to note that Posner (1978) has shown that priming can result in a *facilitation* of response to the second stimulus through pathway activation. Wagner (1981) suggests that the integrity of the second stimulus may determine whether repetition is inhibitory or excitatory; the trace of the priming stimulus enhances subsequent processing of similar stimuli that are weak or degraded but reduces the impact of a more intense stimulus.

In the models of response change proposed by Thompson and others, extrinsic influences are solely excitatory. Blink modification work has identified several such facilitatory effects apparently mediated by sustained aspects of prestimuli. These include a simultaneous augmentation effect; a brief facilitatory effect which appears to compete with PPI and intrinsic refractory effects; and a sustained facilitatory effect prompted by prepulses lasting for several seconds. In each case, these effects are the result of prestimulation of low intensity. However, the most profound extrinsic modulatory effect on blink is inhibitory, initiated by a transient occurring approximately 100 ms prior to the reflex stimulus. This weak stimulus, which can be in a different modality from the reflex stimulus, has latency-priming and amplitude-reducing effects for a short time. Finally, higher-level extrinsic mechanisms of modification can exert either inhibitory or facilitatory influence on blink by altering processing in sensory-central portions of the reflex pathway. Directing attention toward the modality containing the eliciting stimulus acts to selectively facilitate blink. Some evidence suggests that directing attention away from the probe results in blink inhibition.

The patterns of startle elicitation and modification outlined above speak to several issues of information processing. Moreover, differences in these patterns between adults and young infants have implications for the type of sensory stimulation that effectively engages the immature nervous system, and for the action of extrinsic control by systems organized at low and high levels.

IMPLICATIONS OF MODEL

Transient Processing

Comparison of startle elicitation and modification data in adults, infants, and children suggests that systems specialized to transmit transient information may be immature during early development relative to those involved in the processing of sustained aspects of stimulation. In infants, blink was more difficult to elicit by brief stimulation, showed larger effects of stimulus duration increases, and possessed a slower recovery time from repeated stimulation. Similar transient processing difficulties have emerged in work employing other physiological response systems (e.g. Graham, Anthony and Zeigler, 1983). These characteristics suggest that the transient system has a longer time constant in young infants and may show a lengthy developmental course.

It has been pointed out that an understanding of simple sensory processes is critical in order to interpret adequately the development of more complex perceptual phenomena. Changes in the processing of basic parameters of stimulation (e.g. intensity, frequency) have profound impact on the nature of speech perception (e.g. Aslin, Pisoni and Jusczyk, 1983) and visual pattern recognition (Banks and Salapatek, 1983). Although little attention has been paid to temporal aspects of stimulation, the ability to process rapid, transient events may play a crucial role in a variety of perceptual activities. For instance, work on flicker fusion (Regal, 1981) and sound localization (Clifton *et al.*, 1981) imply difficulties in processing brief stimuli in infancy. Also, the ability to detect brief gaps in sound continues to improve with age until about 11 years (Irwin *et al.*, 1985). Some contend that discriminating brief auditory stimuli and stimuli separated by short intervals is important in the development of adequate language abilities. For instance, infants may not be as capable as adults of making fine temporal order discriminations that constitute cues for distinguishing speech sounds (Eilers *et al.*, 1981). Auditory and visual temporal discrimination abilities appear compromised in dysphasic (Tallal and

Stark, 1981) and dyslexic (e.g. DiLollo, Hanson and McIntyre, 1983) children, respectively.

Transient-Based Regulation

Immaturity of short-time-constant systems has implications for extrinsic filtering because transient systems appear adapted for a role in the direction or control of information flow. One aspect of this control is the apparent inhibitory function of fast-conducting systems on processing in sustained pathways. In the visual system, this inhibitory function has been observed in studies of transient Y cells and sustained X cells in the lateral geniculate of the cat (e.g. Singer and Bedworth, 1973) and has been used to explain a variety of phenomena in visual perception including saccadic suppression (Matin, 1974), characteristics of visual persistence (Coltheart, 1980), and metacontrast (Breitmeyer and Ganz, 1976). In the latter effect, sensitivity to a target is decreased by the onset of a spatially contiguous mask *following* target offset. Breitmeyer and Ganz (1976) suggest that onset of the mask, carried over such channels, literally 'catches up' to sustained activity associated with the target and suppresses this activity.

Graham (1975, 1984) has suggested that PPI reflects another type of inhibitory control function linked to the transient system. She views PPI as part of a preattentive mechanism that protects encoding by attenuating the effect of other transient inputs during this brief period of stimulus encoding. In fact, Cohen, Hoffman and Stitt (1981) found evidence for perceptual gating during PPI: adult subjects judged glabellar taps to be less intense when preceded by a weak acoustic prepulse than when presented alone. Furthermore, the amount of inhibition produced by the tap on a subsequent tap was the same regardless of whether the first tap had itself been inhibited by the weak sound. Thus perceptual gating was independent of reflex modification, ruling out the possibility that the attenuation of subsequent input occurs in sensory afferent pathways. The temporal interval sensitive to PPI effects in adults is approximately the same as the interval required for adequate stimulus identification. In studies of backward masking in adults, Massaro (1975) reported that recognition masking occurs when the mask follows the critical stimulus by up to 250 ms. Within this early interval, the occurrence of the mask is disruptive and prevents adequate processing of the initial stimulus.

The prolonged maturation of transient PPI suggests that the encoding period may be more prone to disruption in early development. Although there is scant research on the development of recognition masking, there is some evidence that backward recognition masking intervals are prolonged in infants (Cowan, Suomi and Morse, 1982; Lasky and Spiro, 1980) and, possibly, in children (DiLollo, Arnett and Kruk, 1982). Interestingly, there appears to be a decrease in the effectiveness of these transient-based visual mechanisms in old age (Kline and Schieber, 1981).

If the ability to effectively process transient characteristics of incoming stimuli remains poorly developed, higher-level control functions dependent on such processing may be adversely affected. Research in diverse areas has suggested the importance of such a system for rapid detection of environmental change; for example, Neisser (1979) refers to a transient event as 'initiating a perceptual cycle' (p. 214). A similar distinction has been made by others. For instance, Breitmeyer and Ganz (1976) suggest that rapid analysis of transient information (detection) may cue location and initiate more detailed analysis via channels coding sustained aspects (identification) of stimulation (Breitmeyer and Ganz, 1976). Cohen (1972) emphasizes a similar distinction between the functions of transient and sustained systems in his model of visual attention-getting and attention-holding processes in infancy. He suggests that certain types of sensory information facilitate the initiation of attentive activity including motion and the occurrence of a stimulus in the visual periphery. Both such events are likely to be coded rapidly by transient systems. Finally, a number of researchers have distinguished two HR deceleration responses to non-intense stimulation: a brief deceleration that follows immediately after stimulus onset, and a larger and more prolonged deceleration, peaking many seconds later (Berg and Berg, 1987). Graham (Graham, 1984; Graham, Anthony and Zeigler, 1983) has suggested that the brief deceleration reflects activity in a transient-detection system which may, under appropriate conditions, initiate a sustained, orienting/attentional cycle reflected by the longer-lasting deceleration.

Given the possible importance of transient processing systems in the initiation of attention, it is interesting to speculate that the focus of attentional activity may alter over time. There is evidence to suggest that the transient and sustained processing systems may implement global and focal attention modes, respectively (Alwitt, 1981). Thus, shortly after attention is established, the functional effects on processing may be generalized, resulting from the initiation of a global attentive mode by the transient-detecting system. Selective modification may only occur after the focal attentive mode is engaged through sustained processing. In this context it is interesting to note that the initiation of an alert, attentive state seems to depend on processing in the right hemisphere (e.g. Heilman, Watson and Valenstein, 1985; Posner and Petersen, 1990), which is more sensitive to information processed by transient systems (e.g. low spatial frequencies). Sergent (1982) argues that the right hemisphere is adept at processing early-arriving, preliminary, low-resolution features of stimulation and the left hemisphere at later, high-resolution information. In this fashion, the right hemisphere is seen as 'providing the frame' within which the left hemisphere performs the more discriminating operations possible employing sustained processing systems. Each perceptual cycle provides greater information about the stimulus event. The differential sensitivity of the two hemispheres may lead to a gradual functional lateralization during development. As more complex discrimination becomes possible through the cooperation of the hemispheres, the left hemisphere becomes dominant. As an example, Sergent (1982) cites the shift from left to right visual field superiority in letter recognition once young children are taught to discriminate letters by component features.

If transients serve to facilitate encoding of later occurring information at higher levels, it should be the case that optimally stimulating the immature transient system through the use of slower onsets and/or multiple transients (pulsing) might improve discrimination of stimulus change. Studies of young infants, reviewed by Graham, Anthony and Zeigler (1983), have shown that pulsed presentation of a stimulus is more likely to elicit heart rate deceleration on initial presentations. For instance, Miller and Byrne (1983) found that the HR response of neonates to speech stimuli (the diphthong ai) was greater when the presentation was pulsed and onset was less abrupt. Also, Clarkson and Berg (1983) reported that pulsed presentations improved the ability of newborns to discriminate a change in vowel sound. Finally, Hyson and Rudy (1984) reported that, whereas Pavlovian conditioning with rat pups 12–13 days old using a 2000 Hz tone as a CS was unsuccessful, substituting an intermittent train of clicks for the tone produced learning.

Attentive Regulation

Attention effects on the startle blink indicate that sensory input can be differentially analyzed or filtered at low levels, depending on the focus of concurrent processing demands. Furthermore, this extrinsic mechanism appears operative in infants as young as four months of age. The evidence for attentional effects on the premotor portion of the reflex blink have relevance for a major question in cognitive psychology: can sensory–perceptual processing that occurs 'automatically' be altered without selection by a limited-capacity system (e.g. Duncan, 1980; Johnston and Dark, 1982, 1986). The late-selection position views early perceptual processing as obligatory and unmodifiable; it can run to completion without involvement of conscious processes. The evidence for this position consists of demonstrations that unattended input receives extensive processing (e.g. MacKay, 1973; Posner and Snyder, 1975; Shiffrin and Schneider, 1977). However, semantic processing of irrelevant input does not preclude facilitation of processing on the basis of sensory features. Evidence for differential processing based on attention to sensory features supports an early selection view; however, it requires a measure that is clearly automatic and does not involve a voluntary response, which necessitates the action of a late-selecting, limited-capacity system.

The startle blink meets the major requirements for an automatic response

(LaBerge, 1981). First, it does not demand attention or controlled processing to run to completion; it can be elicited in sleep or after higher brain death. Second, the reflex blink is an obligatory response to an effective stimulus, when relevant boundary conditions are taken into account. Furthermore, the short latency of the reflex makes it difficult to attribute the selective effects on blink to the action of a central processor. Estimates of the time required to complete perceptual analysis of a stimulus, about 200 ms (e.g. Massaro, 1975), are much longer than the onset latency of the startle blink, the point at which consistent selective effects have been measured (Hackley and Graham, 1987). Thus, the blink data indicate that transmission along sensory paths can be modified by attentional processes in force as early as 30 ms after reflex stimulus onset. Consequently, it is unlikely that an attentional response, elicited by the reflex stimulus, could feed back and influence the processing of that stimulus. The importance of the blink results to the early-selection position has been noted in recent reviews of attention (Johnston and Dark, 1986; Shiffrin, 1985). In describing the Anthony and Graham (1983, 1985) studies, Shiffrin (1985) wrote: 'Results like these suggest that there can be some degree of attentive control of automatic processes' (p. 769).

Examination of the co-occurrence of cardiac and blink modification provides a powerful methodology to examine attentive processing in infants and young children. The HR results reviewed in the previous section add to other developmental studies indicating the sensitivity of cardiac change in tracking variation in the intensity of attention (e.g. Porges, 1980; Richards, 1985). The changes in blink size and latency reflect the allocation of attention to a specific sensory channel and the resultant enhanced processing in that channel. The selective effect on blink in 4-month-olds is one of the first demonstrations of a functional effect of attention on stimulus processing in young infants. Furthermore, it provides information on the time course of this effect. It is not known how long it takes for attention to be mobilized and feed back on sensory paths. Porges (e.g. 1980) has suggested that facilitation of information processing only occurs during 'sustained' attention which follows a 5–6 s 'reactive' phase of attention. However, the blink data indicates that attentive effects can be observed as early as 4 s post-stimulus in infants and 2 s in adults (Bohlin *et al.*, 1981; Hackley and Graham, 1983, 1987).

When used as a concurrent indicator of attentive focus, the reflex blink resembles a probe as this term is used in cognitive psychology (Anthony, 1985). That is, a secondary probe task, most commonly simple reaction time, is carried out simultaneously during performance of a primary task. Variation in the efficiency of the secondary task is assumed to reflect changes in the extent of attention allocated to the primary task. Attentive processes in infants have been probed in a similar fashion by Richards (1985, 1987) using shift of visual fixation rather than startle blink. In this 'interrupted stimulus paradigm', infants' attention is drawn to engaging visual stimulation during which time a flashing light, located at the periphery of the visual display, is presented. The latency to shift gaze from the primary stimulus to the interrupting flashing probe is assumed to provide a measure of the extent of attentive focus. Richards has demonstrated a direct relationship between the extent of HR deceleration at the onset time of the interrupting stimulus and the latency to shift gaze.

These shift-of-gaze results seem contradictory to the blink data. Since the attention-engaging and probe stimulus were in the same modality, one might expect that the interrupting stimulus would be more distracting as attention was intensified. However, the opposite direction of response modification associated with HR deceleration points up the differing nature of the blink and shift-of-gaze probes. With reaction-time probes, the effects result from the fact that both primary and secondary tasks demand part of a limited attentive capacity. Increases in attention to one task results in less capacity for performance of the other. Reflexive, saccadic eye movements to peripheral stimulation (the 'visual grasp' reflex) are generated through a system involving the superior colliculus and do not require conscious control. The ability to suppress these reflexive glances and to make more voluntary saccadic shifts seem to involve the prefrontal cortex (Fuster, 1981; Guitton, Buchtel and Douglas, 1985). This type of motor control is characterized by Fuster (1981) as the least automatic and the most dependent on planning and deliberation. Thus, one might expect that increased attentional allocation to the primary visual stimulus would interfere with the high-level decision processes involved in more voluntary gaze shifts, increasing their latency.

In contrast, attention is not required to elicit a startle blink and therefore should not compete for processing resources with concurrent activities. Thus, as Graham, Strock and Zeigler (1981) pointed out: 'The probe does not interfere with what it is designed to measure' (p. 611). The modulation of blink results indirectly from increased allocation of attentional resources to processing in sensory perceptual pathways, not, as Richards (1987) suggests, from the facilitation of an 'automatic attention response' (Shiffrin and Schneider, 1977). Although the reflex stimulus might evoke such a response, the latency of the blink effects are probably too rapid for such a response to feed back and influence processing of the reflex stimulus.

In sum, patterns of startle blink modification and cardiac change have provided evidence for selective attentive effects in infancy under quite specific conditions: shortly after the infant begins to process actively an attention-engaging stimulus. We do not know at what age this mechanism becomes operative. Moreover, we do not know whether selective processes can be established without the presence of concurrent stimulation. Active processing may be required to obtain the modality-specific blink modifications. Presetting the sensory system to facilitate processing of particular expected stimuli may be a later-developing ability (Anthony and Putnam, 1985).

CONCLUDING REMARKS

The behavioral work on the startle reflex and its modification, outlined above, builds on models of basic excitatory and inhibitory systems developed from animal preparations. Reflexive responses are being used extensively as model systems to understand mechanisms by which information is altered as it is processed by the nervous system. As Gluck and Thompson (1987) explain: 'A chief advantage of model systems is that the facts gained from biological and behavioral investigations for a particular preparation are cumulative and tend to have synergistic effects on theory development and research' (p. 176). Invertebrate preparations, in which circuits controlling the reflex consist of a relatively small number of cells, have led to significant progress in understanding neuronal plasticity (e.g. Hawkins and Kandel, 1984; Kandel and Schwartz, 1982). At the same time, more complex vertebrate preparations, such as the startle reflex (Davis and File, 1984), have also shed light on basic properties of change and filtering in the nervous system. One of the advantages of startle is that, since parameters of elicitation and modulation are similar in animals and humans, information from neurobiological analysis on lower organisms can inform theorizing about behavioral phenomena in humans, and vice versa.

Understanding of the regulatory processes involved in startle modification and their development are far from complete. However, present knowledge has now allowed this model system to be used to investigate more complex types of phenomena in both the mature and immature human. For instance, Geyer and Braff (1987) have drawn on the startle work with humans and psychopharmacological work with animals to link mesolimbic dopamine overactivity and sensory gating disturbances identified in schizophrenic patients. Lang and colleagues have recently reported that startle may be a quite sensitive tool for the measurement of normal and pathological states of emotion (Vrana, Spence and Lang, 1988). The finding that blink was modulated by the affective valence of the stimulus context was built, in part, on an understanding of the influences of selective attention on this reflex. This latter work is particularly exciting for it suggests that the startle blink technology may make a major contribution to understanding the relationship between the regulation of emotional and cognitive processes, particularly during development. We are currently exploring this possibility in studies of infants with different temperamental styles and in children with problems of regulation such as attention-deficit hyperactivity disorder and Tourette's disorder.

ACKNOWLEDGEMENTS

This chapter benefited immensely from discussions with Frances K. Graham and Marie T. Balaban who were instrumental in development of the theoretical structure and empirical work presented here.

The chapter was written while the author was with the Laboratory of Psychology and Psychopathology, National Institute of Mental Health.

The Endogenous Scalp-Recorded Brain Potentials and their Relationship to Cognitive Development

David Friedman
Medical Genetics Department,
New York State Psychiatric Institute,
New York City, NY 10032, USA

INTRODUCTION

The discovery of the P300 in 1965 (Sutton *et al.*, 1965) has led to a wealth of findings relating normal brain function and cognitive processes in intact human subjects. This cognitive psychophysiological methodology was soon applied to a host of problems, including psychopathology (in fact, the impetus for the discovery of P300), aging and cognitive development. The application of event-related potentials (ERPs) to cognitive development has lagged behind that in other ERP research areas. However, in recent years, a steadily accumulating research base gives one reason to believe that some ERP components do reflect cognitive processes that undergo developmental change.

The first section of this review explains some of the methodological problems one faces in performing developmental ERP research, and the next very briefly reviews the data that motivated the search for ERP-developmental correlations; that is, the use of the ERP technique in developmentally disabled populations. Following this, the review focuses first on the relatively early work, in which the cognitive ERPs were used to assess developmental changes in infants, children and adolescents; and then on more recent developmental ERP designs and findings using paradigms chosen because task performance was known to follow a developmental course. The strategy used was to attempt to anchor ERP findings in the age-related changes in performance that were expected to appear.

This review deals only with the endogenous or 'cognitive' ERP components. Excellent reviews of the exogenous components and sensory effects on the ERP from a developmental perspective are provided by Klorman, Thompson and Ellingson (1978) and Kurtzberg *et al.* (1984).

Handbook of Cognitive Psychophysiology: Central and Autonomic Nervous System Approaches.
Edited by J. R. Jennings and M. G. H. Coles.

METHODOLOGICAL PROBLEMS

The problems that haunt the cognitive ERP field also plague the developmental area. Component definition, the disentangling of overlapping components, artifact contamination, and fatigue effects, to name just a few, are serious sources of concern in studies using young adult subjects. These can be even more troublesome when recording data from young children. One such difficulty, for example, the equating of task demands across age-groups (see also Kutzberg *et al.*, 1984), may be insoluble. Nevertheless, with careful attention to methodological detail, meaningful ERP data can be recorded, even from infants and very young children. What follows is a very brief description of some of these methodological problems and their possible solutions. The reader is referred to the cited literature for a more detailed treatment.

Artifact contamination is a very large problem in developmental studies, since it is well known that children blink more often than adults (Karrer, 1978; Symmes and Eisengart, 1971). Thus, interpretation of age-related ERP-behavioral effects may be confounded by the reduced (and perhaps biased) sample of behaviorial and ERP trials comprising the average. To avoid severe loss of ERP data, we (Friedman *et al.*, submitted) have recycled trials based on a performance criterion. Although this eliminates the bias of unequal Ns comprising the average among age-groups, it introduces another one—children view more stimulus repetitions than do older subjects. Thus, this problem is difficult to overcome without compromise.

One recent solution is the use of artifact correction, rather than rejection (e.g. Gratton, Coles and Donchin, 1983; Verleger, Gasser and Mocks, 1982). The linear regression between the EOG electrodes and each of the scalp channels is computed and the resulting slope term (i.e. the 'transmission coefficient') is used as the basis for subtracting the proportion of EOG artifact intruding into the EEG. However, this technique is also not without its drawbacks (for an excellent treatment, see Brunia, Mocks and van den Berg-Lenssen, 1989), and these may be exacerbated with children as subjects. Despite its faults, this method is the only one (to date) that can alleviate the even more serious problem of severe loss of trials (and resultant sampling bias) when working with young children in the ERP laboratory.

Equating of task demands is perhaps one of the most difficult issues to deal with effectively, since a task given to an adult may be too easy, while the same task given to a child may be too difficult. One solution which we have instituted is to titrate differences between conditions on a subject-by-subject basis. For example, in studies of selective attention (Berman, Friedman and Cramer, in press), we used a criterion of percentage correct and adjusted the target's duration on an individual basis, resulting in approximately the same distribution of subjects who received targets of the same duration in each age-group, thus roughly equating task difficulty across age-groups.

One of the most interesting, but least well understood, findings in the ERP developmental and aging literature is the age-related shift in scalp distribution for the P300 component. The shift in the distribution of P300 amplitudes across the scalp could reflect an age-related change in the orientation of the generator(s) or a 'real' difference in the site of the intracranial source. The latter could be due to an age-related change in mode of information processing. However, distinguishing between these possibilities will require further advances in our knowledge about the brain generators of the cognition-related components. In Friedman, Putnam and Sutton (1989), for example, components considered to be the classical P300 were recorded in children, young adults and senior citizens, but these 'P300s' had different scalp distributions in the three age-groups. This was the case even after normalizing the data to remove amplitude differences in order to assess shape across the scalp midline (cf. McCarthy and Wood, 1985). The question then arose as to whether the P300s represented the same component, reflecting a similar cognitive function, in the three age-groups. Similarly, Mullis *et al.* (1985) reported age-related changes in the scalp distribution of P300. These data appear in Figure 7.9. As can be seen, P300 was not of large amplitude at frontal sites in their youngest subjects, but as age increased P300 amplitude

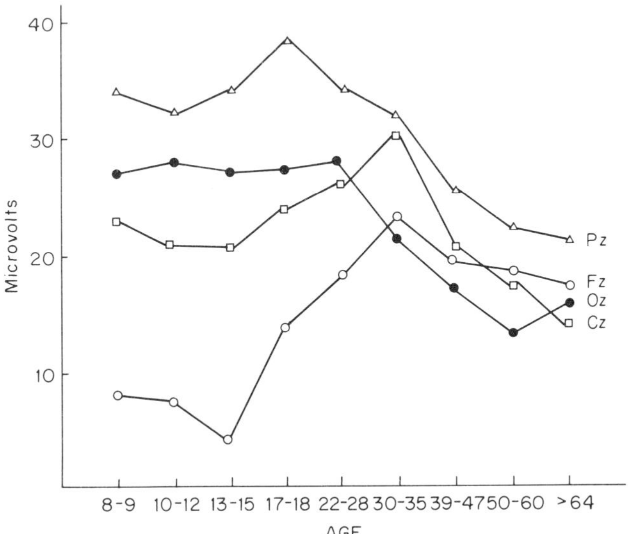

Figure 7.9. Scalp distribution of the P300 component as a function of age from Mullis *et al.* (1985). The P300s were elicited by rare, target stimuli. (Reprinted with permission. © Elsevier Scientific Publishers.)

decreased at posterior sites and increased frontally. These investigators did not scale their data to assess age-related changes in shape across the scalp midline. However, Figure 7.10 depicts the Friedman, Putnam and Sutton (1989) data after normalization and, as can be seen, they show highly similar age-related changes in scalp distibution to those of Mullis *et al.* (1985). Wijker, Molenaar and van der Molen (1989) have also reported essentially identical findings during an oddball task with a younger age-range (8–19 years old). All groups showed the usual rare–frequent P300 effect. Unlike the Friedman *et al.* and Mullis *et al.* data, however, all three of the components they extracted from a principal-components analysis of the data, rather than only P300, showed this frontally-oriented shift in scalp distribution with age. These data begin to suggest an anatomical or physiological effect, since an age-related change in mode of information processing would most likely not affect all

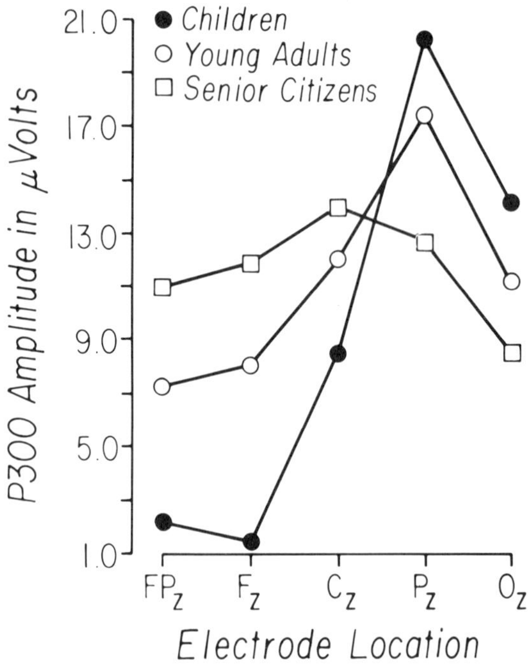

Figure 7.10. Scalp distribution of the P300 component for three age groups, covering approximately the same age range as the Mullis *et al.* data. The ERPs were obtained during the Friedman, Putnam and Sutton (1989) adaptation of Posner's (1978) letter-matching paradigm, using pictorial stimuli. The depicted data have been scaled to remove amplitude differences among the age groups. (Reprinted with permission. © Lawrence Erlbaum Associates.)

components in the ERP sequence. Since this is the only study to report changes in scalp distribution for more than one component, the data are in need of replication.

Our understanding of such changes in scalp distribution could be furthered by uncovering some behavioral correlate of the shift. However, the shift in scalp distribution reported by Friedman, Putnam and Sutton (1989) did not appear to be correlated with age-related changes in performance. Nevertheless, these 'P300s' all behaved similarly in the different age-groups. Similarly, in Mullis *et al.*, their P300 component showed the usual difference between rare and frequent stimuli in all age-groups. Thus, these data suggest that, even though the P300s in these studies may have emanated from different intracranial sources in the different age-groups, their functional roles were similar.

However, more effort needs to be expended to determine if behavioral correlates of these changes in scalp distribution can be found. One step in this direction has recently been reported by Stauder, Molenaar and van der Molen (1989). On the basis of Piagetian conservation tasks, these investigators divided their 5- to 8-year-old children into conservers and non-conservers. An ERP analog of the conservation task was administered, and the results indicated that scalp topography differed more as a function of stage of cognitive development (conserver versus non-conserver) than chronological age. In particular, a P600 (most likely classical P300) was more anteriorly distributed in non-conservers, but parietally focused in conservers. It is not clear from the published abstract, however, whether these investigators scaled the data between conservers or non-conservers or, equally important, between children classified according to age and those same children classified at a given stage of cognitive development. Such assessments would be critical before making the strong interpretation these investigators have suggested. Nevertheless, these data argue for assessing the data in developmental units other than age. One example of such a unit might be mental age.

These data also bear on the problem of component definition. Throughout the remainder of this chapter, the term 'deflection' will be used to refer to a well-defined positive peak or negative trough in the ERP waveform, whereas the term 'component' will refer to electrical activity that is modulated by differences in experimental conditions. In the Friedman *et al.* study discussed above, a clear, well-defined negative deflection at approximately 400 ms post-stimulus was larger in the ERPs to the second of an S1–S2 stimulus package if it mismatched the first ('different') than if it matched ('same'). This negativity could be visualized in both the 'same' and 'different' ERPs of the youngest subjects. In the ERPs of the older subjects, however, a clear negative deflection could not be seen. Rather, the ERPs to 'different' decisions were less positive (or more negative) than those evoked by 'same' judgments, thus suggesting that an underlying negativity, which might be similar to that seen in the youngest

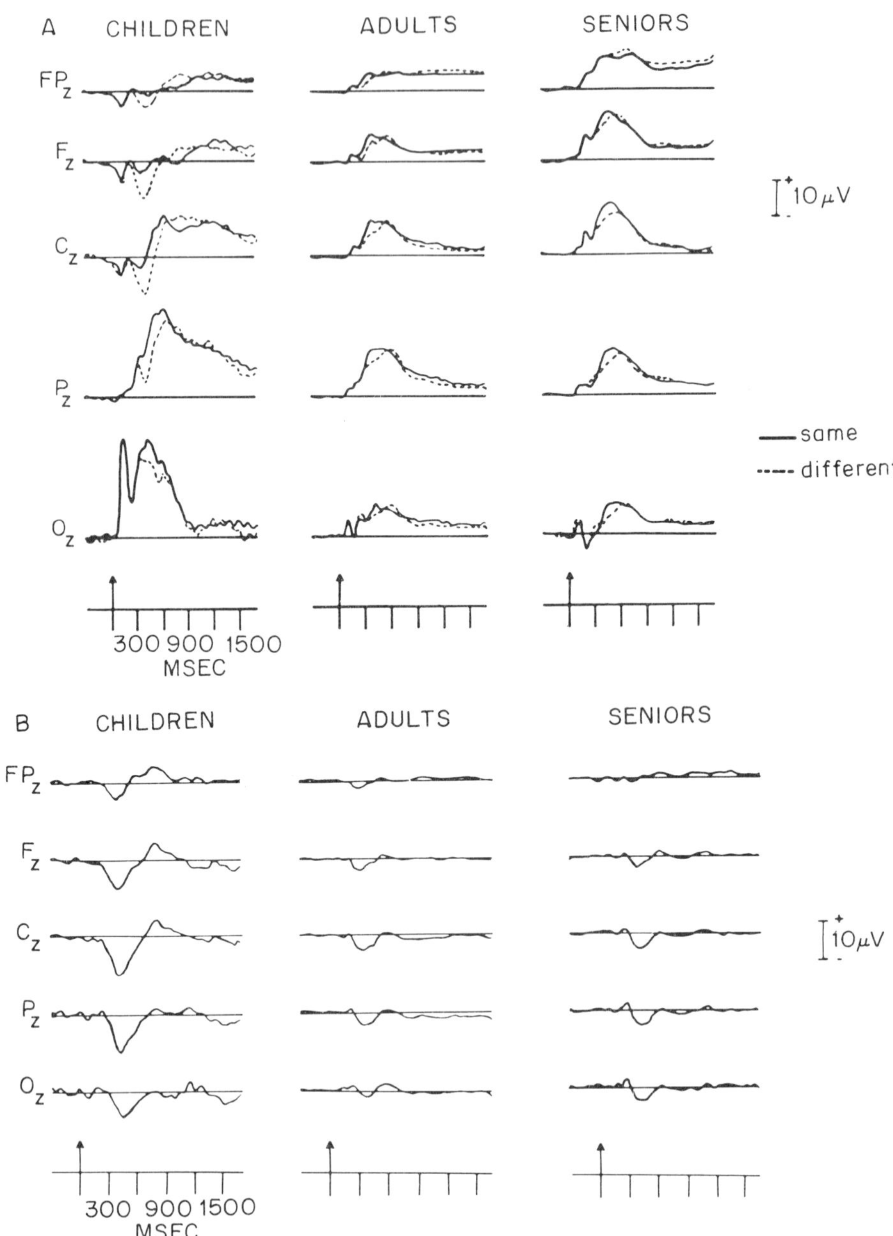

Figure 7.11. Grand mean ERPs, averaged across subjects within each of the three age groups, obtained during the procedure described in Figure 7.10. A. The data are depicted averaged across conditions of the experiment separately for same and different responses. B. Subtraction of the same from the different ERPs depicted in A. (Reprinted with permission. © Lawrence Erlbaum Associates.)

subjects, was responsible for the effect. In fact, in the young adults and senior citizens the negativity could only be discerned by subtraction of the ERPs associated with 'same' judgments from those elicited by 'different' judgments. Figure 7.11 presents the unsubtracted and difference (subtracted) ERPs for all three age-groups. Since this negativity (clearly seen in the difference waveforms) was modulated by the same/different dimension, it is termed a component, and can be seen to occur in the data of all three age-groups. Thus, what initially appeared to be a morphological difference among age-groups (i.e. a clear negative deflection in the ERPs of the youngest subjects, which did not appear to be present in the older subjects' ERPs) turned out to be what we interpreted as the identical component in all three age-groups. Further support for functional similarity of this component across age is depicted in Figure 7.12. After scaling the data, the subtraction negativity can be seen to show highly similar scalp distributions in all age-groups. Had these distinctions not been made, the interpretation of an age-related morphological difference could have been erroneously made.

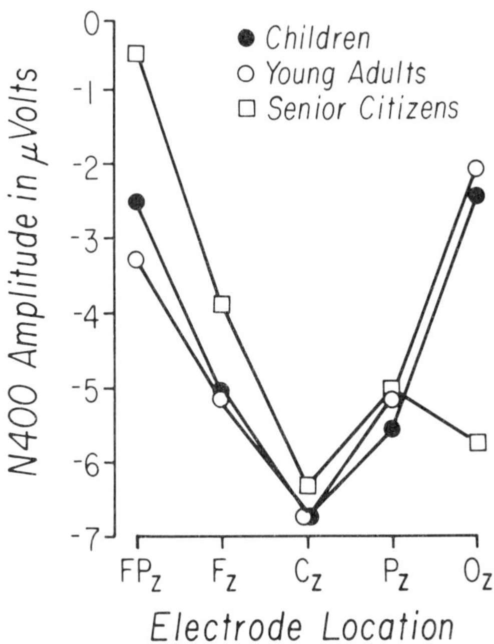

Figure 7.12. Scalp distribution of the Neg400 component from Friedman, Putnam and Sutton (1989) for three age groups, covering approximately the same age range as the Mullis *et al.* data. The ERPs were obtained during the situation described in Figure 7.10. The depicted data have been scaled to remove amplitude differences among the age-groups. (Reprinted with permission. © Lawrence Erlbaum Associates.)

REVIEW OF ERP FINDINGS FROM A DEVELOPMENTAL VANTAGE POINT

STUDIES OF CLINICAL POPULATIONS

Most early normative data came from studies in which ERPs were recorded from normal children serving as controls for samples of children with developmental disabilities, such as autism (e.g. Lelord *et al.*, 1973; Novick, Kurtzburg and Vaughan, 1979; Ornitz *et al.*, 1968), hyperactivity (e.g. Buchsbaum and Wender, 1973; Pricep, Sutton and Hakerem, 1976), and reading disability (e.g. Connors, 1970). Although these data were useful for the light they shed on ERP morphology in children, the focus of these studies was not developmental, the tasks used were not, for the most part, designed to elicit the cognitive waveforms, and only a very restricted range of age-groups was used. Thus, very little information about the functional significance of age-related changes in the cognitive components could be obtained. However, some very recent studies have added significantly to our knowledge concerning developmental effects on ERPs in both normal and abnormal samples (Holcomb, Ackerman and Dykman, 1985, 1986; Stelmack *et al.*, 1988). These will be discussed below, since their methodology is more consistent with recent developmentally-oriented ERP techniques.

ERPS DURING COGNITIVE TASKS IN INFANTS

Despite the difficulties reviewed above, pioneering efforts at recording 'cognitive' ERPs in infants have been accomplished (cf. Courchesne, Ganz and Norcia, 1981; Karrer and Ackles, 1987; Kurtzberg and Vaughan, 1985; Nelson and Salapateck, 1986; Schulman-Galambos and Galambos, 1978). The data from these investigations suggest that large-amplitude negative ('Nc') and positive ('Pc') ERP components respond similarly to negativities and positivities recorded in adults by differentiating 'frequent' from 'infrequent' stimuli in 'oddball' paradigms modified for use with infants. Figure 7.13 presents the ERPs recorded during Courchesne *et al.*'s study. As can be seen in the figure, a large-amplitude negativity (about 900 ms) is followed by a positivity (about 1400 ms), with both of these components larger in response to the infrequent than to the frequent stimuli. These data were replicated and extended by Karrer and Ackles (1987) who showed highly similar ERP components in infants as old as 18 months. A nice feature of the Karrer and Ackles' (1987) design was the collection of behavioral data (i.e. the infant's duration of looking at each stimulus). Significantly more time was spent looking at the 'oddball' than the frequent stimulus. The data suggest that by four months of age, the cognitive processes that enable the recognition of environmentally significant stimuli are already established. Another elegant aspect of the Karrer and Ackles' (1987)

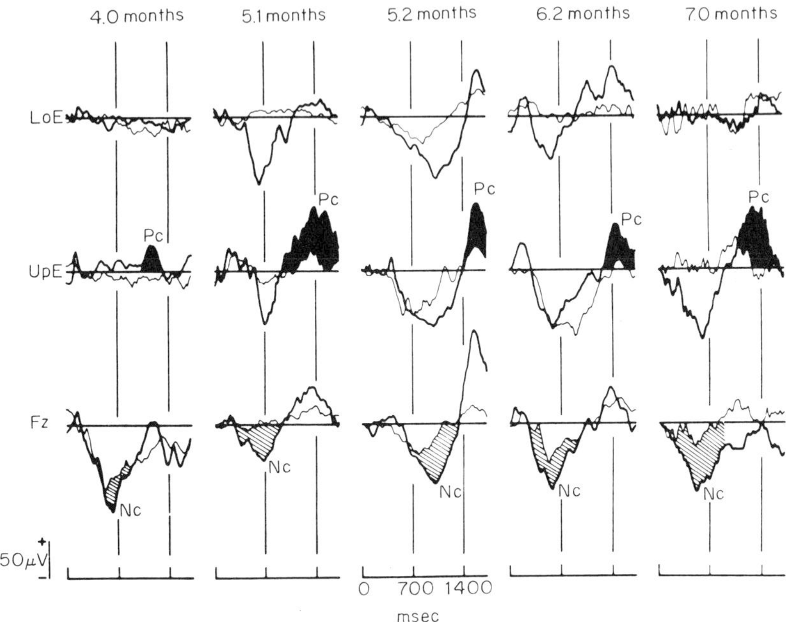

Figure 7.13. Averaged ERPs elicited by frequent faces (thin lines), and rare faces (thick lines) from five infants in the Courchesne *et al.* (1981) study. The ERPs were recorded from infra- (LoE) and supra- (UpE) orbital, as well as frontal scalp (Fz) sites. The Nc and Pc components are indicated by stippling and shading respectively. (Reprinted with permission. © University of Chicago Press.)

study was the use of age-appropriate stimuli—checkerboards versus random shapes for their 6-week-olds; two pictures of adult female faces for their 6-month-olds; and pictures of different exemplars of stuffed animals versus furniture for their 12- and 18-month-olds. Despite the differences in stimuli, the ERPs in all age-groups similarly differentiated the rare and frequent classes of items.

EVIDENCE FOR THE MATURATION OF COGNITIVE ERP PARAMETERS

Although the number of studies reported so far is small, the evidence suggests that the endogenous ERP components do undergo changes related to the development of cognitive skills. This evidence comes from both cross-sectional studies (e.g. Courchesne, 1978, 1983; Goodin *et al.*, 1978; Friedman *et al.*, 1984, 1985, 1988; Kok and Rooijakkers, 1985) and longitudinal studies (e.g. Friedman, Putnam and Sutton, in press; Kurtzberg, Vaughan and Kreutzer, 1979). Differences in cognitive processing mode between age-groups has usually been inferred from the differences in morphology found between age-groups (cf. Courchesne, 1983; Friedman *et al.*, 1983; Kok and Rooijakkers, 1985; for a review, see Kurtzberg *et al.*, 1984). However, as alluded to earlier, morphological differences cannot be the only criterion, since component overlap may mask similarities in component structure between age-groups. Furthermore, a strong test of this hypothesis requires that behavioral performance on the task in question reflect these age-related morphological differences, so that they can be anchored in the behavioral domain.

ERPs During Standard Cognitive Tasks

Kurtzberg, Vaughan and Kreutzer (1979) recorded ERPs in a longitudinal study of ten children whose ages, over the course of the study, ranged from 4 years 6 months to 8 years 6 months. Late positive activity (possibly similar to the P300 or 'P3b') to infrequent chromatic light flashes (i.e. the target) became more distinct with increasing age. Shelburne (1973) recorded visual ERPs from 8- to 12-year-old children during an information delivery paradigm. The amplitude of late positive activity (comprised of P300 and slow wave components) was larger to the letter which delivered information, but the ERPs (presented in his Figure 1) did not contain highly differentiated P300 components, quite possibly owing to variability in stimulus evaluation time in these younger subjects. In fact, mean latency of P300-like activity was longer in these children than it was in adults of a previous study using the same paradigm (Shelburne, 1972).

Goodin *et al.* (1978) recorded ERPs during an auditory oddball paradigm from subjects ranging in age from 6 years to 80 years. These investigators reported no age-related morphological or scalp distribution differences of the endogenous components between young and older subjects. However, the latencies of N200 and P300 decreased rapidly in the 6–15 years age-range, and then increased slowly through old age. Courchesne (1978) reported the same relationship between P300 latency and age for target stimuli over a smaller age-range (6–36). Mullis *et al.* (1985), in a more recent cross-sectional investigation, replicated the latency findings of Goodin *et al.*

In a recent study using the oddball paradigm, Johnson (1989) recorded visual and auditory ERPs from subjects aged 7 years to 20 years. In addition to the usual finding of decreases in P300 latency with increments in age, Johnson reported that the slope of the functions relating age and P300 latency differed for visual and auditory stimuli. Moreover, the scalp distribution of P300 differed between auditory and visual stimuli. However, this latter finding did not appear to interact with development, although Johnson did not directly test this possibility. Taken together, the latency findings and distributional differences led Johnson to conclude that there were independent generators for visual and auditory P300s.

In a series of investigations, Polich and colleagues (Howard and Polich, 1985; Ladish and Polich, 1989; Polich, Ladish and Burns, 1990) have interpreted the changes in P300 latency as reflecting the development of memory span. In all of these studies, P300 latency elicited by auditory oddball stimuli decreased with age. Memory span, measured independently of the P300 recordings, increased with age. When correlated, these two indices produced highly significant and linear relationships. Although the interpretation of Polich *et al.* is quite an interesting one, there are problems with it. Firstly, the memory and ERP data were collected in functionally different sets of trials (see Donchin and Sutton, 1970). Secondly, it is possible that the latency changes reflect something more global than immediate memory; for example, they could reflect changes in a 'general' cognitive skill, as measured by IQ. Thus, correlating an IQ subtest, such as Verbal IQ, may have produced an equally impressive linear relationship. Finally, recent data suggest that P300 is probably not the electrophysiological event that reflects the depositing or updating of a memory. Rather, it appears to be reflected by an overlapping component, that is different (on the basis of scalp distribution) from the P300 (Friedman, 1990a; Paller, Kutas and Mayes, 1987; Paller, McCarthy and Wood, 1988; although, see Donchin and Fabiani, Chapter 5 in this volume). Neverthless, the studies by Polich and colleagues add to the evidence that stimulus evaluation time, as reflected by P300 latency, decreases from childhood through adolescence.

In a very recent experiment, Nelson and Nugent (1990) used the oddball paradigm to investigate children's ERP responses to emotional stimuli. In two different experiments, one 'happy' and one 'sad' face were presented as either the target or non-target stimulus. Probability was crossed with target or non-target status. These investigators reported the usual decrease in P300 latency with increments in age. They also recorded a negativity at 400 ms (N400) which was maximal at the Cz electrode site. This potential did not show any age-related latency changes. While P300 was sensitive to probability, in one experiment N400 was sensitive to the emotional valence of the face, and in the other the probability of the eliciting stimulus. Nelson and Nugent offered an interpretation that their results reflected differences in strategic processing between adults and children, and thus, invoked the updating of memory notion for P300. However, their conclusions are open to question for several reasons. Firstly, it is not clear whether their negativity at 400 ms is an N2 or an N400 (cf. Kutas and Hillyard, 1980), which would affect the way in which one interprets the data. Second, the issue of overlap between N400 and P300 was not dealt with, so that it is difficult to determine which component was affected by the experimental manipulations. Finally, whether it is P300 or an overlapping component that reflects processes that impact on memory performance is currently controversial.

The conclusion to be drawn from the studies reviewed above is that the major difference between the adult and the child is in the latency and not morphology of components reflecting decision time and stimulus evaluation (i.e. N200; P300). In all cases, young children display the slowest motor responses and peak latencies, suggesting quantitative changes in speed of processing, but not qualitative changes in the mode of such processing.

ERPs During More Complex Cognitive Tasks

Classification of objects and events is known to follow a developmental course (e.g. Bruner, Olver and Greenfield, 1966; Inhelder and Piaget, 1964; Rosch *et al.*, 1976), with the data suggesting that age-related changes in classification are characterized by attention to perceptual attributes at young ages and to conceptual attributes at older ages. It was on this basis that Courchesne (1978) attempted to interpret his intriguing finding of the presence of long-latency Nc and Pc waves in young children. In Courchesne's studies (reviewed in Courchesne, 1983), the standard oddball paradigm was used, with one exception—two infrequent events were presented, a novel, uninstructed stimulus (highly abstract and unnameable visual stimuli), and an equally infrequent, target stimulus, to which the subject had to respond. While the targets elicited the usual N200–P300 complex (P300 was recorded with a midline parietal amplitude maximum in all age-groups, 6–36 years of age), the novel stimuli elicited large-amplitude, frontally oriented Nc–Pc complexes that were dramatically larger in children than in adolescents or adults. Since the target stimuli were pre-categorized, whereas the novel stimuli were not, Courchesne (1978) suggested that these morphological differences among age-groups reflected the shift from perceptual to conceptual categorization that has been hypothesized to underly the developmental shift in classificatory behavior.

Several investigators, using a variety of tasks and stimuli, have recorded negative components similar in latency and, to some extent (where more than one electrode was employed), scalp topography to the negativity recorded by Courchesne (1978). Symmes and Eisengart (1971), with 5- to 11-year-old children, recorded a late negative wave (at 500 ms) to colorful depictions of familiar scenes and household objects. In a picture recognition task, with 9- to 13-year-old children, Neville (1977) recorded a late negative wave peaking at 400 ms to line drawings of common objects. Kok and Rooijakkers (1985) demonstrated the presence of negative potentials at about 500 ms in both word reading and picture recognition tasks in children between 5 and 6 years of age. Kok and Roojakker's (1985) negativities were well-formed and of large-amplitude in their children, but were above baseline and seen as negative-going deflections in the adult subjects.

In a study of reading-disabled and control children (7–12 years of age),

Stelmack *et al.* (1988) recorded ERPs during a word recognition paradigm. They found large-amplitude, frontally-oriented negativities at about 400 ms in their reading subjects, which were dramatically reduced in their reading disabled sample. However, the reading error rate in the disabled sample was 58%, but less than 1% in the controls. Since recognition memory for words undoubtedly requires contact with the lexical system to determine if the word had been previously presented or not (see Berman, Friedman and Cramer, 1991, for a discussion), the reduction of N400 in the reading disabled sample is not surprising, and probably indicates their inability to contact a semantic representation of the word.

Holcomb, Ackerman and Dykman (1985, 1986) also reported the presence of negative potentials at about 400 ms post-stimulus elicited by unexpected auditory and visual stimuli in children between the ages of 8 and 11 (serving as normal controls for children with attention deficit and reading disorders). In their 1985 paper, they compared the ERPs elicited by unexpected ASCII symbols (e.g. #) with those elicited by unexpected three-letter words. In their normal control youngsters, the negativity elicited by symbols at approximately 400 ms was larger than that evoked by words at the frontal scalp leads, but was more negative when elicited by words at the posterior scalp leads. Although they termed this component an 'N2' it appears to be more similar to an 'N400' in terms of its latency and posterior distribution when evoked by words.

One of the most consistent interpretations formulated by developmental theorists is that mode of processing changes with age, such that young children rely more on sensory representations, whereas older children and adults rely more on symbolic, semantic representations to encode their experience (e.g. Ackerman, 1981; Bruner, Olver and Greenfield, 1966; Kosslyn, 1978). Thus, it is tempting to speculate that the larger amplitude and more frontal scalp distribution for the negativities evoked by pictorial stimuli compared with those elicited by verbal stimuli (described above) is reflecting this 'sensory' mode of processing. Some additional support, albeit sketchy, comes from a study by Robertson, Mahesan and Campbell (1988), who recorded ERPs in children (8–11), adolescents (14–16) and young adults (20–25) during lexical and object decision tasks. These investigators recorded markedly larger N400s to objects than words in children, but no difference for adolescents and adults. Thus, their data suggest that N400 may be a physiological reflection of a different conceptual representation employed for pictorial objects compared with verbal stimuli. Moreover, their data suggest that, with development, representation in these two systems may become conceptually equivalent (see also our studies of continuous recognition memory reviewed below). However, unlike Holcomb, Ackerman and Dykman (1985) and Berman, Friedman and Cramer (1991), the N400s elicited by words and objects did not appear to have different scalp distributions, detracting from the forcefulness of this interpretation. Moreover, their adult data run counter to that of Berman,

Friedman and Cramer (1991) who did show larger posterior N400s to words than to pictures.

A similar interpretation was made by Kok and Rooijakkers (1985), in which the slow wave was differentially affected by word reading and picture recognition tasks in adults but not in children. On this basis, these authors speculated that their slow wave might reflect pictorial or non-verbal modes of processing by the children in both tasks but, for the adults, verbal versus non-verbal modes in the word and picture recognition tasks respectively.

Several putative functional correlates for these negative waves recorded in children have been suggested, including 'further processing' of stimuli with attention-getting characteristics (Courchesne, 1978), the perception of meaningful stimuli (Symmes and Eisengart, 1971), and the processing of non-verbal information (Neville, 1977). However, these correlates were only loosely tied to the experimental conditions in the above-mentioned studies, and could not be firmly anchored in the behavioral domain. Moreover, with few exceptions, the majority of these investigators did not have sufficient numbers of subjects within each age category to determine if morphology shifted with chronological age.

In adult subjects a negative component at approximately 400 ms, but of scalp distribution somewhat different from the negativities recorded in children (described above), has been shown to be remarkably sensitive to the semantic relationship between a word and the context in which it occurs, whether that context is the sentence (e.g. Kutas and Hillyard, 1980, 1984) or a previously presented prime (Bentin, 1987; Bentin, McCarthy and Wood, 1985; Rugg, 1985). N400 was larger the more anomalous the sentence ending or the more distant the word was from the category of an immediately preceding prime (Kutas and Hillyard, 1989). On this basis, it is tempting to speculate that the negativities (i.e. Nc) recorded in infants and young children may be continuous with those recorded in young and older adults. (Friedman, Putnam and Sutton (1989) and Harbin, Marsh and Harvey (1984) have recorded highly similar negativities in elderly samples.) It could be the case that the large amplitude and frontally oriented scalp distribution of Nc recorded in infants and young children reflect the 'unprimed' nature of the infrequently occurring items. This would be a rather global distinction between stimuli falling into and out of a given class of stimuli—that is, a primitive kind of 'priming', in this case reflecting the discrimination of frequent and infrequent items. We know that as children mature and cognitive skills improve, classes of items that were once undifferentiated become clearly distinguishable (e.g. Rosch, 1976), so that finer and finer classifications can be made, on a semantic basis. Thus, the mode of processing reflected by Nc may be this generalized distinction among large classes of items, whereas the 'N400' recorded from older children and adults would reflect this finer-grained mode of distinguishing among semantic classes. 'N400' could also reflect distinctions made on the basis of other symbolic or conceptual schemata. Sketchy evidence for this continuum comes from the previously described data of Karrer and Ackles (1987; see the section on ERPs during infancy above). However, to test this speculation adequately more age-groups are needed between infancy and 5 years of age (which, to the author's knowledge, is the first age where N400-like components have been recorded; e.g. Kok and Rooijakkers, 1985).

An alternative speculation is also possible. Negativities recorded in infants within the Nc latency range have been interpreted as reflecting recognition memory for previously presented stimuli (e.g. Nelson and Salapatek, 1986)—Nc is smaller to the stimulus that occurs with the greatest frequency and with which the infant is, by inference, the most familiar. In adult subjects, it has been demonstrated that previously presented items show reduced negativity within the 200–600 ms latency range. In contrast to adults, however, it is certainly not clear whether the infant has a true explicit 'recognition' response to those stimuli with which it has become familiar. It has been hypothesized, and the results of several experiments suggest, that recognition performance in adults is mediated by at least two cognitive processes—familiarity and elaboration, a contextual–episodic component. For example, in Mandler's description (1980), recognition is a function of the familiarity of the item and retrieval mechanisms. The former is represented by intra-event integrative processes (e.g. activation), while the latter are assumed to depend upon inter-event elaborative processes. In this schema, activation is a relatively automatic process, occurring whenever a word is presented (for this speculation, it could be any item), and consists of the integration of perceptual and semantic components of an item. By contrast, elaborative processes are necessary to establish links among previously unassociated items and to relate those items to their context. While these processes may not directly map on to infant cognitive skills, recent ERP evidence suggests some categorical (semantic?) processing by one year of age (Karrer and Ackles, 1987). Thus, as others have hypothesized with adults as subjects, the negativity recorded during recognition memory tasks may reflect the familiarity or perceptual fluency component (Smith and Halgren, 1989; but see Rugg and Nagy, 1989). It is thus possible that Nc could also reflect this behavioral process. In both the adult and infant situations, the reduction in negativity to familiar or repeated items would be mediated by this relatively automatic familiarity component. This behavioral process could be inferred to mediate the infant's 'recognition' response without invoking the (conscious) contextual, episodic component. Fagan (1984) has similarly argued for continuity of (automatic) behavioral processes that mediate novelty preference in infants and contribute to later performance on tests of intelligence. Although Fagan's (1984) argument that automatic processes play an important role in intelligent behavior is controversial, he argues quite persuasively in favor of it.

Currently, it is unclear whether these diverse negativities can all be subsumed under the rubric of the 'N400' component that is responsive to semantic distinctions among stimuli (cf. Kutas and Hillyard, 1980, 1989). We raised the issue in previous reports (Friedman *et al.*, 1988; and submitted) that it was not clear whether the negativity we recorded at 400 ms was an N400 (cf. Kutas and Hilyard, 1980) or an N2. Thus, in the remainder of this paper, the term 'Neg400' is used to label negative deflections occurring at around 400 ms recorded by us in our picture-matching and continuous-recognition paradigms, in order to distinguish it from the N400 reported by Kutas and Hillyard (1980).

Taken as a whole, the data described in this section argue for the possibility that developmental changes are reflected in the ERP. Moreover, these ERP changes can be informative as to developmental progressions in information processing, via modulation of component amplitude and/or latency through appropriate experimental manipulation. A discussion of these and other negativities will form a part of the later presentation of data resulting from our normative studies of the cognitive ERPs (e.g. Friedman *et al.*, 1988).

DEVELOPMENTAL FINDINGS USING THE PICTURE-MATCHING PARADIGM

The question of whether or not the ERP might reflect functional changes with a broader span of ages than had been used previously could not be answered by the studies described in the last section. We (Friedman *et al.*, 1983) therefore began to perform pilot experiments to attempt an answer to this question. If inferences as to functional changes could be made, then this would open the door to using the ERP as a diagnostic tool with samples of children characterized by arrests in development. The project which resulted was based on the premise that the ERPs from subjects spanning a wide age-range (from 6 years to adulthood) would reflect the changes in cognitive skill that occur as humans mature. The task initially chosen for this purpose was a pictorial adaptation of Posner's (1978) classic letter-matching paradigm, since performance on that task was known to follow a developmental course. This permitted the possibility that developmental changes in cognitive performance might be paralleled by age-related changes in the ERP waveform.

For example, in tasks similar to Posner's, using behavioral indices only, several investigators (e.g. Ackerman, 1981; Duncan & Kellas, 1978; Hoving, Morin and Konick, 1974; Maisto and Baumeister, 1975; McDermott *et al.*, 1977) have shown a developmental increase in the use of conceptual rather than perceptual encoding with stimuli to be matched, recognized or recalled. In a task very similar to our picture-matching paradigm, Hoving, Morin and Konick (1974) showed that third-grade and older children were able to recognize the conceptual equivalence between pictures and their names, while kindergarten children had difficulty with name but not physical matches. Thus, these behavioral data supported the notion that performance on this kind of hierarchical matching task increased as children matured, and further, that it was likely that mode of processing differed between young and older children and adults. This, in turn, increased our expectation that the ERP might reflect these developmental processing differences.

Our initial cross-sectional studies (Friedman *et al.*, 1988) and short-term longitudinal studies (Friedman, Putnam and Sutton, 1990) using the pictorial adaptation of the Posner paradigm were limited both methodologically (for example, the conditions were always given in the same order), and by the use of a restricted age-range. Thus, we embarked upon cross-sectional and mini-longitudinal replications of these initial studies with methodological improvements and a much wider age-range. These will be detailed below.

For these tasks, we (Friedman *et al.*, submitted and in preparation) used pictures of common objects taken from the Snodgrass and Vanderwart (1980) set of 260 line drawings. Our subjects were required to decide whether two pictures (S1 and S2), presented sequentially with a 2 s ISI, were the same or different on the basis of whether they were physically identical (PID), shared the same name (NID), or were in the same category (CID). Subjects always made a choice 'same' or 'different' delayed response after S2 whose meaning depended on the operative instruction condition in that block of trials. Figure 7.14 presents examples of the two-slide sequences and the appropriate choice responses under each of the three instructional regimes.

For the cross-sectional replication, improvements were instituted by increasing the number of categories the pictures could come from (eight instead of five), thus increasing the number of unique pictures. A wider range of ages was sampled (from 6 years to 39 years, categorized into seven age-groups: 2-year intervals from 6 through 17, and one adult group). The experimental design was completely balanced so that, cross-cutting the instruction conditions, there were six matches and six mismatches between S1 and S2. Moreover, counterbalancing of conditions was instituted. The conditions were given identically to all subjects—PID, NID, CID, CID, NID, PID. This method of counterbalancing had two advantages over more complete counterbalancing schemes: (1) it followed a natural progression from PID to CID for the first three blocks of the experiment, thus minimizing age differences in comprehensibility of the tasks; and (2) it controlled for order effects identically in all subjects.

Cross-Sectional Data

There were 102 subjects in this investigation (Friedman, Sutton and Putnam, 1987; Friedman *et al.*, submitted). The 2-year age-groupings were: 6–7 (N=8),

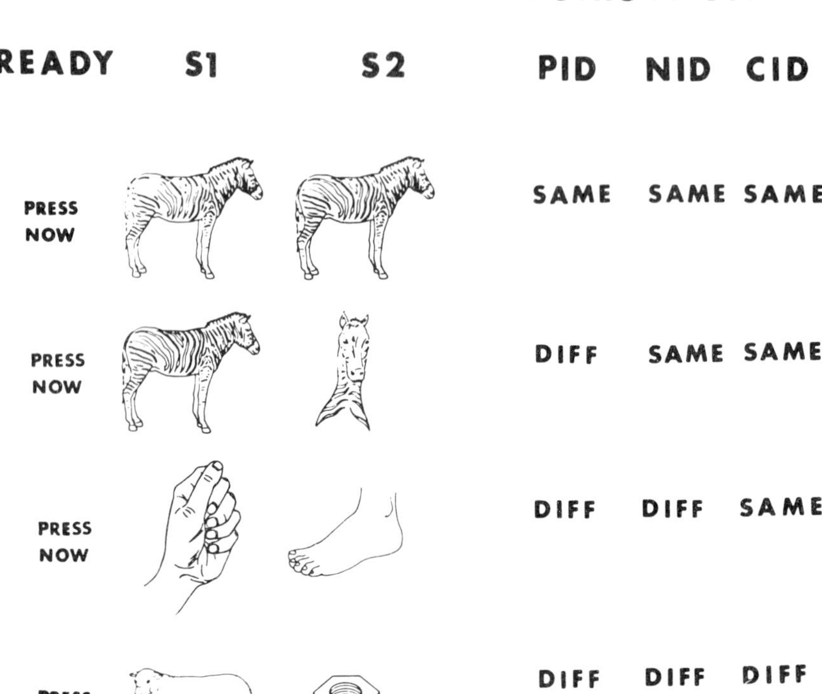

Figure 7.14. Examples of the two-slide sequences and appropriate choice responses under each experimental condition of the Friedman *et al.* Studies discussed in the text. (Reprinted with permission. © Society for Psychophysiological Research.)

8–9 (N=9), 10–11 (N=12), 12–13 (N=18), 14–15 (N=20), 16–17 (N=15), and young adult (N=20; range = 20–38). The matches and mismatches cross-cutting the instruction conditions were categorized according to the number of differences between S1 and S2: for 'same' trials these were 0D = physically identical; 1D = name identical; 2D = category identical. For 'different' trials these were 1D = physically different, but nominally the same; 2D = physically different, nominally different, but in the same category; and 3D = different on all three dimensions. For example, pictures which (a) are physically identical (0D), (b) share the same name but are not physically identical (1D), or (c) share the same category but do not share the same name and are not physically identical (2D), represent three unique match types within the category instruction condition all requiring a response of 'same'. Similarly, reinspection of Figure 7.14 shows that these same comparisons between S1 and S2 within the physical identity instruction condition lead to responses of 'different': pictures which are physically different, but share the same name (1D), physically different with different names, but in the same category (2D), or different on all three dimensions (3D). Thus, the various ways of being 'same' (from 0D to 2D) as well as 'different' (from 1D to 3D) reflect increasing semantic as well as physical distance between S1 and S2.

The main effects of the experimental conditions can be seen in Figure 7.15. This figure depicts the ERPs elicited by correct matches and mismatches (described above), averaged across instruction conditions. For ease of visualization, the data have been averaged across subjects within each of the 2-year age intervals, separately for children (6–11) and adolescents (12–17). As can be seen, for all age-groups there appears to be an effect, between about 250 and 600 ms (i.e. Neg400), that occurs as a function of match or mismatch—the ERPs in that time window become increasingly negative (or less positive) as the number of features on which the S1 and S2 stimuli differ increases.

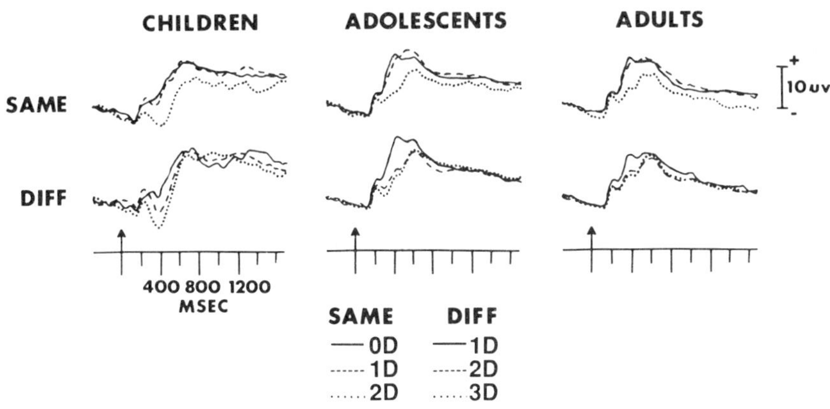

Figure 7.15. Grand mean S2 ERPs averaged across subjects within each age category from Friedman *et al.* (submitted). The data have been averaged across instruction conditions to demonstrate the effect of match/mismatch on the ERPs. Arrows mark stimulus onset, with time lines every 200 ms.

The findings for this negativity can be explained with reference to both the behavioral and ERP priming literature. The manipulation as a function of matching condition involves one of increasing physical as well as semantic distance between S1 and S2. For example, in category identity blocks, although both S1 and S2 are, by definition, in the same category, Neg400 to S2 increased as the number of differences between S1 and S2 increased, or as the degree of semantic relationship between S1 and S2 decreased. A similar explanation can be made for mismatches between S1 and S2. In PID blocks, subjects must generate a response of 'same' whenever the two stimuli are physically identical. In that instance, Neg400 does not appear to be present in the S2 ERP waveform for any age-group (see the ERPs evoked by 0D matches in Figure 7.15—i.e. no differences between S1 and S2). However, for mismatches in physical identity blocks, Neg400 amplitude increased as the degree of relationship between the S1 and S2 stimuli decreased. Even though subjects only had to base their decision on whether the two stimuli were physically different, it is apparent, as evidenced by the increments in Neg400 amplitude, that they also processed the degree of semantic relationship between the S1 and S2 stimuli. The data suggest that an 'automatic spreading activation' (cf. Neely, 1975) mechanism may have been operating regardless of the instruction condition in which the S1 and S2 stimuli occurred. Thus, the S1 stimulus 'primed' the S2 stimulus, such that the closer the semantic relationship (or the greater the number of physical features common to both S1 and S2—see below), the smaller the S2 Neg400.

The most compelling evidence for semantic effects on the Neg400 recorded in the cross-sectional replication comes from the analyses of between-condition match types. For example, 0D matches occur in all three instruction conditions and always require a response of 'same'. These identical matches elicited Neg400 amplitudes that were systematically ordered: category identity (CID) > name identity (NID) > physical identity (PID). Since S1 and S2 in all three cases are physically identical, the fact that the operative instruction modulated Neg400 amplitude strongly suggests the presence of a semantic effect. The fact that children as young as 6 years of age showed these amplitude changes seems to support the notion that the youngest children were able to extract these semantic relationships among stimuli automatically. Moreover, the fact that there were very few interactions of age with the matching conditions of the experiment suggests that the Neg400 we recorded is homologous for all age-groups and that the processes reflected in Neg400, at least for the tasks used here, do not appear to change with experience.

The possibility cannot be ruled out, however, that, although the Neg400 amplitude modulations were similar for all age-groups, the mechanism underlying that modulation may have been different for older and younger subjects. In a series of elegant experiments, Rosch and her colleagues (1976) have shown that basic level categorization (e.g. dogs, cats) is the first learned at a very young age (as young as 3 years), while the ability to categorize at the superordinate level (e.g. dogs and cats are animals) undergoes development with age. Thus, it is possible that the youngest subjects may have performed the matching tasks using visual features at the basic level, while the older subjects may have used the superordinate level. However, distinguishing between these two alternatives is not possible based upon the data generated in these experiments.

The largest differences among the age-groups in this study were in the latencies of both Neg400 and P300. The P300 latency age decrement is a robust phenomenon (e.g. Courchesne, 1978, 1983; Goodin *et al.*, 1978; Friedman *et al.*, 1984, 1985). The age decrement in Neg400 latency has not been previously reported, but is consistent with the P300 latency changes.

To summarize, the results of the cross-sectional replication suggest that similar information processing mechanisms may have been employed by all age-groups in performing these matching tasks (although the possibility of matching on the basis of visual features by the youngest subjects cannot be ruled out). Systematic age differences were found primarily for Neg400 and P300 latencies, which most likely reflect quantitative changes in the speed of information processing.

One issue in developmental investigations is the extent to which changes in behavioral and/or ERP parameters should be attributed to physiological changes accompanying maturation and to what extent to age-related shifts in cognitive abilities (and, to what extent to both). A further problem that arises in interpreting cross-sectional data stems from the fact that age-related variations in both ERP waveform and performance indices could be due to cohort effects (e.g. Baltes, Cornelius and Nesselroade, 1979).

An approach which has been used to tease apart cohort from true age changes is the 'time-sequential' design (Baltes, Cornelius and Nesselroade, 1979; Schaie, 1977) in which two or more cohorts are followed over two or more longitudinal testing sessions. We attempted to use this design to study the ERP and behavioral data in which the children whose initial ERP test session data were described in Friedman *et al.* (1988) were brought back to the laboratory one year following their first testing session (described in Friedman, Putnam and Sutton, 1990), and administered the identical picture-matching tasks. This was primarily a feasability study, to determine the nature and extent of the changes in both ERP and behavioral parameters that might occur over a short time period. In general, when comparing cross-sectional with longitudinal effects in such a design, true age changes are indicated when both cross-sectional and longitudinal data show the same trends. With small samples, as with these data, the longitudinal data might be expected to show stronger effects owing to the smaller within- than between-subject variabilty. Since the longitudinal trends reflect both 'true' age as well as 'familiarity' and/or 'practice' components, whereas the cross-sectional sequences do not, comparisons of these two trends can lead to conclusions as to the presence of 'true' age trends in the data.

Longitudinal Data

Subjects were 19 children (of the original 22 seen at Run 1 and reported in Friedman *et al.*, 1988) whom we were able to retest one year later at Run 2. There were seven 6-year-olds (four male), seven 7-year-olds (six male), and five

8-year-olds (four male) at Run 1, who completed both testing sessions, and thus were 7, 8 and 9 years old respectively at Run 2. Our time-sequential design is schematically illustrated in Table 7.2. Each column in the table represents an independent group of subjects (i.e. the different age cohorts), and each row gives their ages on a given run. Since 'age' as used here is an average for the same subjects across two testing sessions, these are indicated as 6.5, 7.5 and 8.5. Longitudinal run (i.e. the two testing sessions) effects (the row marginals) are assessed by collapsing the data across the three age cohorts, separately for each run, while cross-sectional age effects (the column marginals) averages the data across the two runs, separately for each age cohort. In ANOVAs on these data, the main effect of 'age' compares the data of the three independent groups of subjects (i.e. 6.5, 7.5 and 8.5-year-olds) collapsed across two testing sessions, while the main effect of 'run' compares the data for the two longitudinal testing sessions collapsed across 'age'.

Table 7.2. Schematic of 'age' and 'run' effects.

Age group:	1	2	3	
Run number:				
Main run effect:				
Run 1	6	7	8	(7.0)
Run 2	7	8	9	(8.0)
Main age effect:	(6.5)	(7.5)	(8.5)	

For the vast majority of these data, there were few interactions, for either the ERP or behavioral data, between longitudinal run or cross-sectional age and the matching conditions of the experiment. This suggested, at least for the limited range of ages assessed, that there was no differential age-related *rate* of change over the short one-year period between testing sessions, for the processes reflected in Neg400, P300 or slow wave. Figure 7.16 depicts the Neg400 latency findings for both the longitudinal and cross-sectional comparisons, along with the percentage correct data. As can be seen, for each age cohort, Neg400 latency decreases within subjects from Run 1 to Run 2 (i.e. the repeated testings), while it also decreases between subjects as a function of cross-sectional age (i.e. the independent samples or age cohorts). These data strongly suggest that the Neg400 latency change is a true age change. Similarly, the high degree of correspondence between the longitudinal and cross-sectional functions for percentage correct suggest that it, too, reflects a true age change.

This study showed us that a short-term longitudinal study was feasible and that, other than quantitative shifts in latency, the processes reflected by

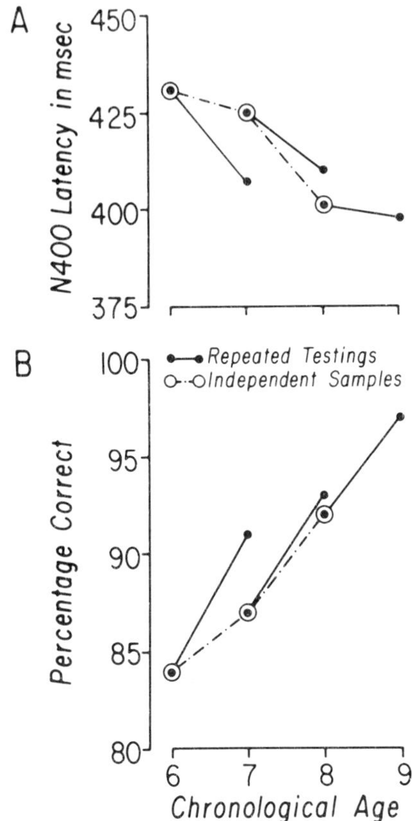

Figure 7.16. Cross-sectional and longitudinal sequences for Neg400 elicited by S1–S2 pairings requiring a response of 'different'; and cross-sectional and longitudinal sequences for percentage correct for the same condition. (Reprinted by permission. © Elsevier Science Publishers B.V.)

Neg400 and P300 appeared to undergo very little change with experience. A mini-longitudinal replication with methodological improvements and many more subjects (Friedman, Sutton and Putnam, 1987; Friedman *et al.*, in preparation)—with 82 of the 102 subjects returning one year after their initial testing session (whose cross-sectional data were described above)—led us to a similar conclusion. Taken as a whole, both the cross-sectional and mini-longitudinal data suggest that the shifts in Neg400 latency reflect a 'true' quantitative speed of processing change with increments in chronological age but, at least for the tasks used here, there is little evidence, in either ERP or behavioral measures, for qualitative change in information processing as age increases.

DEVELOPMENTAL FINDINGS WITH CONTINUOUS-RECOGNITION MEMORY AND SELECTIVE ATTENTION

By and large, the picture-matching experiments failed to produce evidence of ERP components that reflected age-related changes in mode of information processing. Nevertheless, these data served as useful disembarkation points for other studies, in that we had shown that the negativity at 400 ms was modulated similarly by the instruction conditions in all age groups; that is, it was an homologous component for all ages. Further, in showing a lack of 'age' by 'electrode location' interactions after scaling the data to assess shape across the scalp midline, the data suggested that Neg400 appeared to emanate from similar brain tissue in all age-groups.

Thus, these data could serve as important sources of normative information for children with developmental abnormalities. For example, the Neg400 findings could be employed with reading disabled children to determine if they can extract semantic relationships among stimuli, either in natural sentence contexts (cf. Kutas and Hillyard, 1984) or in single-word priming situations (cf. Bentin, McCarthy and Wood, 1985). An overt behavioral response would not be necessary as we (Friedman *et al.*, submitted) as well as others (e.g. Kutas and Hillyard, 1989) have shown that these amplitude modulations can be observed even if the task is incidental to the semantic relationships between stimuli.

CONTINUOUS RECOGNITION MEMORY

Investigations using Sternberg's (1966) paradigm suggest that search processes as reflected in reaction-time slope do not differ between young children and young adults (Hoving, Morin and Konick, 1970; Maisto and Baumeister, 1975), but that the longer reaction times for children are due to slower perceptual and motor processes. Reviewing the area of short-term memory development, Chi (1976) concluded that there is no evidence that either the capacity or the rate of information loss varies with age. Rather, the major changes with age occur in increased encoding efficiency and increased processing speeds. Wickelgren (1975), using the continuous-recognition paradigm, reported that young adults had substantially superior recognition performance to children at all delays between first and second item presentations. However, he concluded that the storage dynamics of both groups, as inferred from the shape of the retention function, were similar.

Several experiments (e.g. Perlmutter, 1980; Ackerman, 1981; Ghatala, Carbonari and Bobele, 1980) support the hypothesis that deficiencies in encoding efficiency in the young child can account for the age-related accuracy differences in recognition memory. For example, Ackerman's (1981, 1985) data point to the child's increased reliance on encoding of the sensory, rather than the semantic, attributes of stimuli, with accuracy suffering as a result. In a major review of this area, Guttentag (1985; see also Kail, 1984) concluded that it is most likely the allocation of processing resources and not encoding efficiency *per se* that accounts for the findings, since, given instructions in correct encoding, young children perform as well as young adults (e.g. Guttentag, 1985). However, without constraints on encoding, children rely more on schematic rather than conceptual stimulus features when encoding for subsequent recognition or recall (Ackerman, 1981).

In a recent series of experiments using the ERP (cf. Friedman, 1990b; Karis, Fabiani and Donchin, 1984; Neville *et al.*, 1986; Paller, McCarthy and Wood, 1987; see also Donchin and Fabiani, Chapter 5 in this volume) it has been demonstrated that the amplitude of P300 and slow wave elicited by to-be-remembered stimuli predicts the accuracy of recall or recognition on second presentation, suggesting that these parameters might provide a measure of encoding or registration of the to-be-remembered item. Both Friedman (1990b) and Paller, McCarthy and Wood (1987) suggested that this 'memory effect' is not directly on P300, but on overlapping slow wave activity (labeled 'Dm' for difference in subsequent memory, by Paller *et al.*).

Further motivation for the use of ERPs during recognition memory is the role that scalp distribution of ERP components might play in understanding developmental changes in processing mode, and in resolving the controversy surrounding the underlying representation of surface forms (see Snodgrass, 1984). For example, suggestive evidence that the youngest subjects employ similar representations for both words and pictures would be obtained if the youngest children produce ERPs which do not differ in scalp distribution or in hemispheric asymmetry between words and pictures, but which do differ for adolescents and adults. Thus, Berman, Friedman and Cramer (1989) studied continuous recognition memory using pictures and their lexical equivalents. Subjects were required to make a choice 'old' or 'new' response on each trial, thus maximally loading the memory system. We added blocks of trials to assess repetition effects where the task requirement was incidental to such repetition, in order to examine any developmental ERP differences related to 'implicit' memory function (Graf and Mandler, 1984). The effects of repetition demonstrated using a direct instruction 'press to old items' has been labeled 'explicit,' while the same effects using encoding tasks that are incidental to such repetition (e.g. 'respond to animal words') has been labeled 'implicit'. The behavioral dissociation of 'implicit' and 'explicit' memory from a developmental perspective is in its infancy, and no other developmental ERP studies exist. The study of how these dissociable memory functions develop is crucial to our understanding of age-related changes in memory function. However, only two such developmental studies exist (Parkin and Streete, 1988; Greenbaum and Graf, 1989), and these were purely behavioral investigations.

Developmental characterization of the processes involved during implicit and explicit memory tasks could eventually prove important in remediation for individuals with developmental disabilities, since information not easily retrieved with conscious effort (i.e. explicit) could be encoded via orienting instructions and tested for retention 'implicitly'.

The effects of repetition on ERPs has been demonstrated in both explicit and implicit situations (see Friedman, 1990a,b, and Rugg and Nagy, 1989, for examples of the former; and Rugg, Furda and Lurist, 1988 for examples of the latter). Generally, the ERPs to 'new' items are characterized by greater negativity between about 250 and 500 ms, whereas those same items when they are 'old' (i.e. repeated) elicit ERPs that display enhanced positivity in that latency range. There is some preliminary evidence that the ERP may be able to differentiate repetition during explicit memory tasks from repetition during implicit tasks (Friedman, 1990b; Rugg, 1987). Moreover, Paller, McCarthy and Wood (1987) reported that the scalp distribution of ERP indices during implicit and explicit memory testing appeared to differ, strengthening the suggestion that the brain mechanisms underlying implicit and explicit memory performance might be distinct.

For both tasks, pictures and words were presented in separate blocks via a Macintosh Plus microcomputer, with a 300 ms duration and 2 s interstimulus interval. Old items followed their first presentation counterparts after lags of 2, 8 or 32 intervening stimuli (equiprobable). During explicit blocks, subjects were asked to identify all 'old' (seen previously in the block) and 'new' (not seen previously) items via speeded choice button-press responses (total of eight blocks; 85 stimuli per block). In order to assess implicit memory, we administered two additional blocks of 85 trials (resulting in a smaller *N* than for explicit blocks) in which items were repeated (separate picture and word blocks with order of these counterbalanced across subjects). For the implicit blocks, stimuli different from those used during explicit conditions were used. The implicit memory task was designed to unconfound the effect of button pressing from the effect of repetition on the ERPs by using an orienting question for both pictures and words that yielded a large proportion of negative responses (e.g. identify 'things that you can read'; e.g. book, magazine). Thus, for the implicit blocks, subjects generated reaction times in response to the instructed items, but these were never any of the items that repeated (see also Rugg, 1987). Following both tasks, all words were shown to the children again in order to ensure that they could, in fact, read them (97% of the words were correctly read; SD = 3.2). There were 14 children (mean age = 9.26; Age 1 in the figures), 13 adolescents (mean age = 14.78; Age 2), and 14 young adults (mean age = 24.56; Age 3) recruited for this study.

Figure 7.17 presents the ERPs for both tasks elicited by the pictures and their lexical equivalents averaged across subjects within each of the three age-groups. Data are depicted separately for old and new items and for the subtraction of new – old ERPs (third column of each task). As can be seen in Figure 7.17, across words and pictures, and for both tasks, new items were associated with greater Neg400s and smaller P300s than old items, replicating previous findings (Berman *et al.*, 1988; Friedman and Sutton, 1987; Neville *et al.*, 1986). This suggests that underlying the old/new effect is a negativity that is similar in all age-groups. This was supported by the fact that, after scaling the data to eliminate amplitude differences among the age-groups, the old/new differences for Neg400 and P300 did not interact with age. Moreover, recent analyses of these data (Berman, Friedman and Cramer, 1990a) suggest that, for all age-groups, the explicit repetition effect modulates two components, a negativity (Neg400) larger to new items, and a subsequent positivity, P300, larger to old items (see also Rugg and Nagy, 1989; Smith and Halgren, 1989). By contrast, the implicit effect appears to modulate only the negativity. This latter point is consistent with the fact that, as can be seen in Figure 7.17, the implicit task resulted in very small or absent P300s.

For the explicit task, the slow wave, which was maximal at the anterior electrodes, and may be synonymous with 'frontal positive slow wave', was larger to new than to old items. Ruchkin and Sutton (1983) have suggested that this activity reflects 'further processing'. Such processing would be required of 'new' items, in order for them to be encoded and stored for subsequent retrieval (see also Friedman, 1990a,b). The fact that all age-groups showed this relationship for the slow wave suggests that this activity may be functionally homologous across this age-range and, if this activity does, in some way, reflect encoding, that the children also engaged in this kind of processing.

As can be seen in Figure 7.17, children showed a larger old/new difference during explicit memory instructions than did adolescents or adults. However, after scaling the data to eliminate amplitude differences among the groups, this 'age' by 'old/new' interaction was no longer significant. As can also be seen, pictures produced larger Neg400s than words at the anterior electrodes, but this effect was much larger for children than for the adolescents or adults. This same effect also occurred during the implicit blocks, was significant after scaling, and suggests developmental differences in the processing of words and pictures that are independent of memory instructions. Thus, these data offer some evidence of developmental differences in the representation of surface forms. Whereas there are clear differences in negative activity between pictures and words (pictures > words) for the children, the magnitudes of these differences are much smaller for the two older groups.

There is also some suggestion in these data that words elicit a greater repetition effect than pictures during implicit blocks (compare the picture and word difference waveforms for the implicit task of Figure 7.17). Although further experimentation would be needed to clarify this finding, the data do suggest that the implicit effects under these conditions differ according to surface form, possibly reflecting differences in the way the memory traces

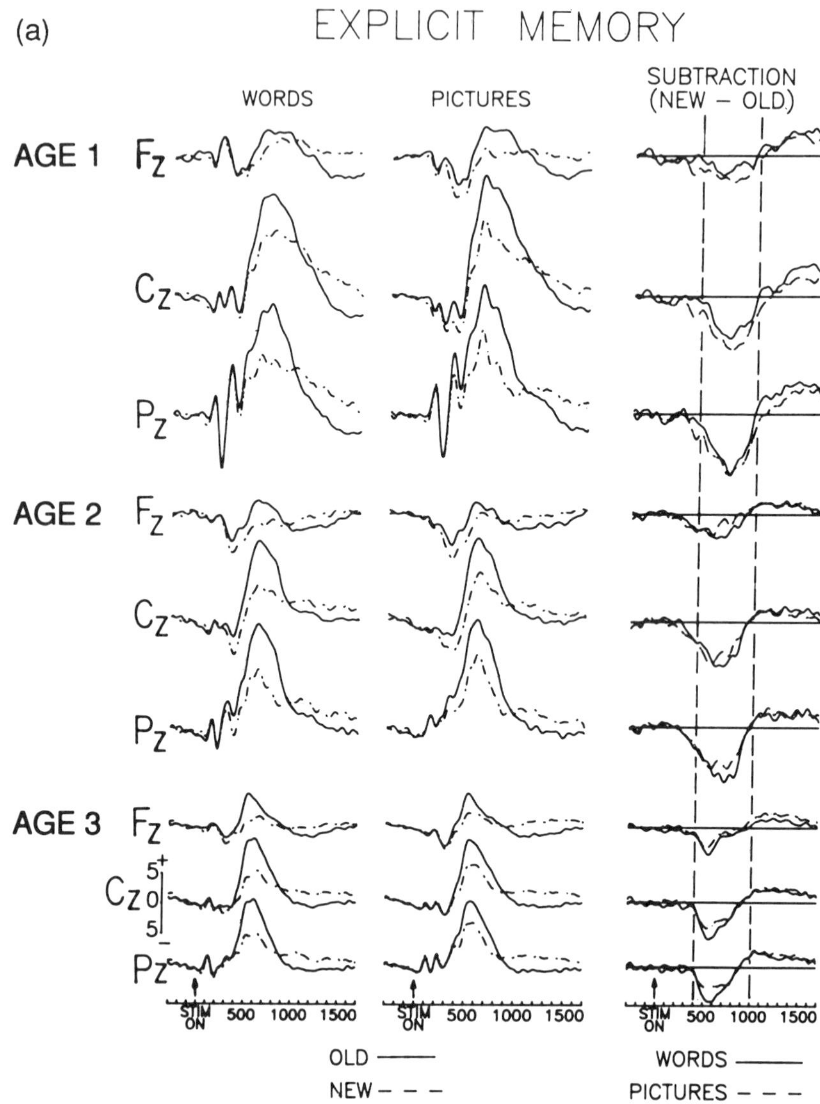

Figure 7.17. (a) Grand mean ERPs averaged across subjects within each age-group elicited by first presentation items (new), and by these same items presented for the second time (old) under explicit memory instructions. (b) Grand mean ERPs averaged across subjects within each age-group elicited by first presentation items (new), and by these same items presented for the second time (old) under implicit memory instructions. The data are from Berman, Friedman and Cramer (1990a). Arrows mark stimulus onset, with time lines every 100 ms. Age 1 = children; Age 2 = adolescents; Age 3 = young adults. (Reprinted with permission. © Elsevier Science Publishers B.V..)

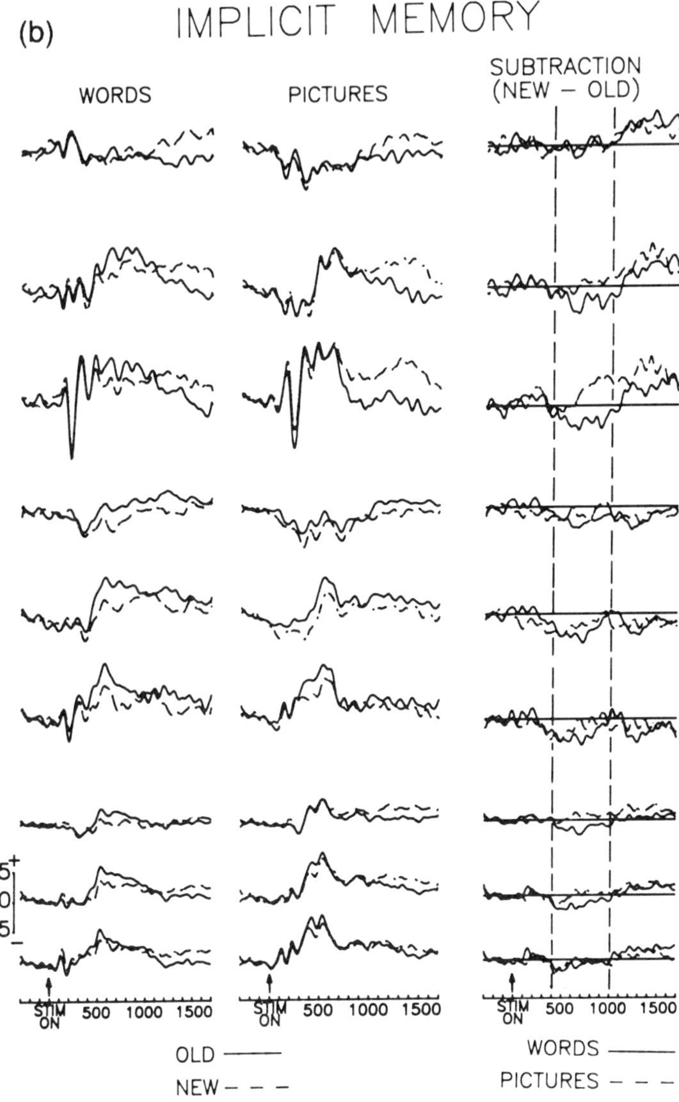

are accessed in the two modalities (see also Snodgrass, 1984). Moreover, for this negativity, words appear to elicit longer duration waveforms than pictures for all groups (although this appears most marked for the children), suggesting greater and more extended activation for words than pictures.

Rugg, Furda and Lurist (1988) have interpreted the presence of N400s to first presentation items in lexical decision and repetition priming experiments as reflecting 'elaborative processes...which act to integrate various attributes of the item, such as its meaning, with its context'. Presumably, a similar mechanism would be required during continuous recognition. Thus, on second presentation, whether in continuous recognition, or lexical decision, or under the current implicit conditions, such integration would not be as detailed, leading to smaller negativities. The fact that children show greater-amplitude Neg400s during explicit conditions suggests that they engage in more of this type of processing in order to produce a response of old or new. The larger Neg400s to pictures than words in children compared with adolescents and adults could be due to the less automatic association between the picture and its name in this age-group. This would necessitate more elaborative processing and/or greater activation on the part of the children, possibly due to translating from a pictorial to a semantic representation, and supporting a picture/word developmental shift in processing mode.

In showing an effect of repetition of a prior event on the ERP without requiring conscious recollection of that event (during the implicit task), these data represent the first demonstration (to the author's knowledge) of 'implicit' effects on ERPs recorded in a developmental study. The data suggest that, for Neg400 and P300, implicit and explicit memory effects are similar in all age-groups. This suggests that, at least by the age of 7 years, processes necessary for both implicit and explicit memory function are in place. This is consistent with a recent report by Parkin and Street (1988), using behavioral data only, that the processes mediating implicit and explicit memory are established by the age of 5 years. No-one has attempted to study implicit memory in infants (but, see Moscovitch, 1985, for an ontogenetic explanation of memory systems similar to the explicit/implicit distinction discussed here; see Greenbaum and Graf, 1989 for very young children). However, the fact that these two memory functions can be dissociated in amnesia (e.g. Graf and Schacter, 1985) as well as in normal aging (e.g. Light and Singh, 1987), suggests that implicit memory may be the oldest from an evolutionary perspective.

SELECTIVE ATTENTION

Studies of attention in children have shown that the ability to perform accurately in divided attention tasks improves with age (e.g. Berlin, 1973; Day, 1980; Hiscock and Kinsbourne, 1980; Smith, Kemler and Aronfried, 1975). However, little is known about the temporal dynamics of either selective or divided attention and their maturation. Seminal experiments in adults using the ERP (Hillyard *et al.*, 1973; see also Chapter 3) had shown that the N100 component of the ERP was sensitive to the selective allocation of attention. Subsequently, Näätänen and Michie (1979) showed that this was due to the development of a slow, endogenous, negative shift or 'processing negativity' ('Nd'—Hansen and Hillyard, 1980) superimposed on the exogenous N100 component. Later experiments by a number of investigators (Hink, Hillyard and Bensen, 1978; Okita, 1979; Parasuraman, 1980) showed that, when the requirement to detect targets in both channels was imposed, the amplitude of the negative shift was intermediate to that elicited by stimuli in the attended and unattended channels during selective attention. The data suggest that the amplitude of 'Nd' reflects the allocation of processing resources (Hillyard and Kutas, 1983). Thus, the selective-attention paradigm seemed a natural one for assessing the ERP and behavioral changes that occur with development. The developmental study that resulted was also carried out with the collaboration of Steven Berman (Berman, Friedman and Cramer, 1990b).

ERPs and RT were recorded during a paradigm where pitch or type of consonant–vowel (CV) syllable (delivered in separate blocks) defined the two channels. Random sequences (1 s interstimulus interval) of two equiprobable tone pips (500 and 1000 Hz; two blocks of 250 trials), or two CVs (all combinations of ba, da, and ga; six blocks of 250 trials) included frequent (90% occurrence) short-duration sounds (100 ms in both attended and unattended channels), and infrequent (10%) sounds of increased duration, which were designated as targets in the instructed 'channel'. Practice trial blocks determined a subject's accuracy at a given target duration. If accuracy was too low, or approached ceiling, the target's duration was adjusted to obtain at least 75% correct detections.

The effect of selective attention on the ERPs was derived by subtracting the ERP associated with the irrelevant standard (the short, 100 ms version of the stimulus when that channel was not attended) from the ERP associated with the relevant standard (the same short-duration stimulus when the channel was attended), resulting in the difference in 'processing negativity' or 'Nd' between channels.

Pre-Subtraction ERPs

The ERP waveforms to relevant CV and pure tone (PT) stimuli at the posterior temporal electrodes are depicted in Figure 7.18. Across age-groups, P300 was larger to PTs than to CVs, and larger over the right than the left hemisphere. However, as can also be seen, the right hemisphere advantage for P300 was restricted to the children. Moreover, these subjects showed larger P300s overlying the right- than the left-hemisphere scalp to both PTs and CVs, whereas adolescents and adults showed a left-hemisphere P300 advantage for CVs only, but no difference for PTs. The fact that the asymmetries reverse for the two older groups and both increase with age (for the CVs), and decrease with age (for the PTs) is suggestive evidence that the ERP asymmetries reflect age-related functional hemispheric differences in the processing of speech and non-speech sounds.

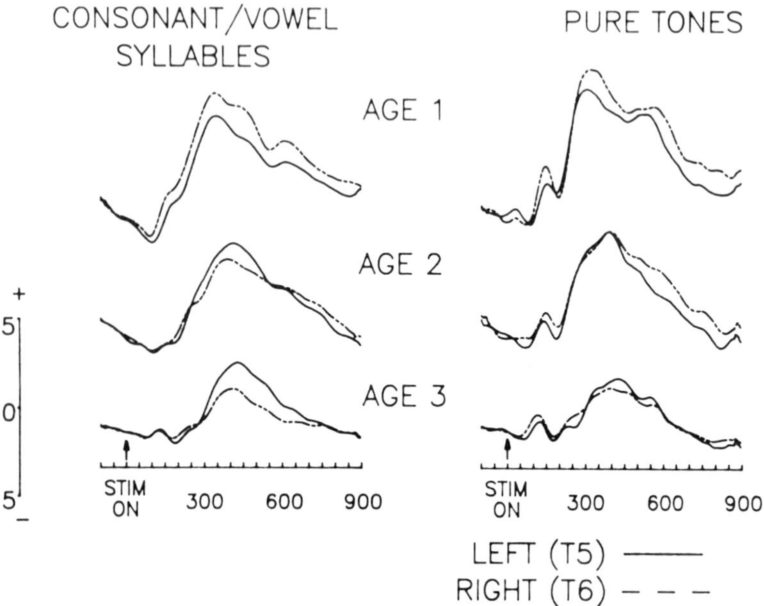

Figure 7.18 Grand mean ERPs averaged across subjects within each age-group elicited by CVs and PTs at the left (T5) and right (T6) temporal scalp electrodes. The data are from Berman, Friedman and Cramer (1990b). Arrows mark stimulus onset, with time lines every 50 ms. Age 1 = children; Age 2 = adolescents; Age 3 = young adults. (Reprinted with permission. © University of Tilburg Press.)

Subtraction ERPs (Processing Negativity or Nd)

The subtraction waveforms are depicted in Figure 7.19 for the CVs and PTs and, as can be seen, were characterized by an early negative deflection (early Nd, measured as the averaged voltage between 0 and 450 ms) and a late negative deflection (late Nd, measured between 450 and 900 ms), both maximal between Fz and Cz. Across age-groups, PTs produced greater early Nd than CVs, with the effects largest at Fz. Our original hypothesis of developmental differences in selective attention was supported by greater early and late Nd components (across CVs and PTs) for the older groups compared with the youngest group. In addition, several analyses of the early Nd suggested developmental differences in the ability to select on the basis of speech sounds, as can be seen at Fz in Figure 7.19. In fact, as can be seen in the figure, the children produce large-amplitude, long-duration negativities in both relevant and irrelevant CV channels, suggesting that processing negativity

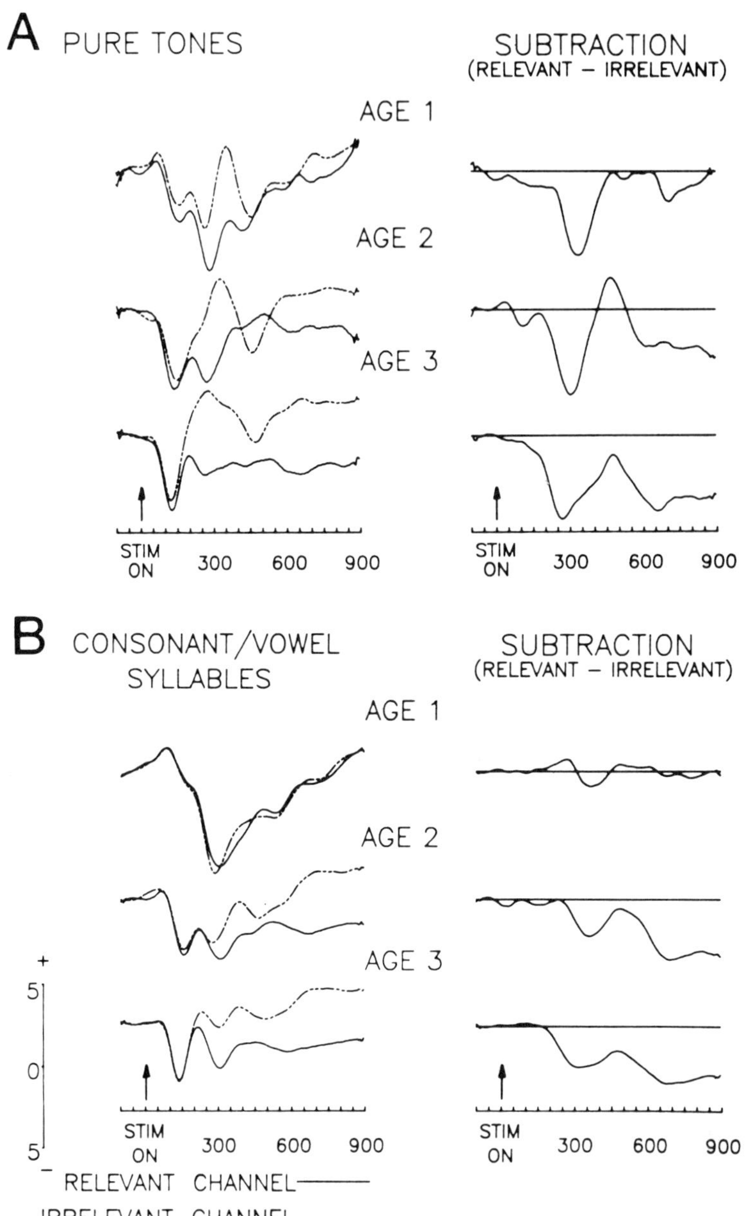

Figure 7.19. Grand mean ERPs averaged across subjects within each age group elicited by PTs (*A*) and CVs (*B*) in the relevant and irrelevant channels. Columns at the right of each panel are the subtraction waveforms, indicating the ERP effect of selective attention. The data are from Berman, Friedman and Cramer (1990b). Arrows mark stimulus onset, with time lines every 50 ms. Age 1 = children; Age 2 = adolescents; Age 3 = young adults. (Reprinted with permission. © University of Tilburg Press.)

was prominent in both channels, resulting in a very small 'Nd' difference waveform. This visually identifiable finding was supported by the statistical analyses—early Nd amplitude increased with age at Fz for CVs, but not for PTs. Additional support came from a comparison of the attended and unattended channels on the pre-subtraction ERPs (averaged voltage in the 200–500 ms window). While the PTs produced larger negative amplitudes in the attended than in the unattended channel in all three age-groups, this was the case for CVs in adults and adolescents, but not the children, indicating no selection by CV for this latter age-group. This effect cannot be viewed as an effect of task difficulty, since the CV task was viewed as *less* difficult than the PT task by all age-groups, including the children (on post-experimental inquiry), and was also less difficult behaviorally. In fact, the children produced greater Nd amplitude in the task that was more difficult for them. This developmental shift in 'processing negativity' (Nd) is the first demonstration of a neurophysiological correlate of the oft-cited inability of young children to direct their attention in a situation where there are two or more competing inputs (e.g. Pick, Christie and Frankel, 1972). Since other data suggest that the amplitude of 'Nd' reflects the allocation of processing resources (Hillyard and Kutas, 1983), these findings suggest that the children allocated resources to both channels (for CVs), with a concomitant decrease in efficiency relative to adolescents and adults, and further suggests developmental differences in selective attention to speech sounds.

OVERVIEW AND DIRECTIONS FOR FUTURE RESEARCH

Although clearly in its infancy, developmental ERP research has yielded some findings that have added to our knowledge concerning cognitive maturation. One of the most consistent of these is the quantitative shift in speed of processing reflected in N200 and P300 latencies indicating, respectively, faster decision and stimulus evaluation times with increments in chronological age. Although more data are clearly necessary to fill in the gap for the ages between about 1 and 5 years, it also appears that the cognitive mechanism responsible for discriminating classes of stimuli of differing probabilities is in place soon after birth.

It is also apparent that some of the components recorded in children are homologs of those recorded in adults. For example, negative components at about 400 ms post-stimulus can be recorded in young children, and appear to be functionally similar from childhood through adulthood. Moreover, the data suggest that this Neg400 component elicited in our picture-matching tasks is generated in similar brain tissue across a wide age-range. P300, although showing different scalp distributions across age, also appears to be homologous across a wide age-range. In showing differences between words and pictures which are larger for younger children, recent findings from our laboratory for a frontally oriented Neg400 component (e.g. Berman, Friedman and Cramer, 1989) suggest that this component may reflect mode-of-processing differences induced by words and pictures (see also Kok and Rooijakkers, 1985). Findings from selective-attention experiments also suggest a developmentally graded change in the processing of speech and non-speech sounds.

The premise that ERP components reflect cognitive development has not been realized fully. In part this is due to the difficulty of developmental ERP research, especially with young children. This has resulted in only a handful of studies specifically designed from a developmental perspective. A second reason results from the constraints imposed on the investigator by the ERP technique itself. The necessity to repeat stimuli, and to tailor those stimuli to elicit ERPs, limits the technique's utility in, for example, some of the tasks that have been used in the investigation of Piagetian-like stages of development. However, the technique is extremely useful (as described above) when developmental research is couched in terms of the maturation of information processing systems. The majority of investigations in the field of adult ERP research on cognition have been guided by the information processing model. This same strategy can and should be applied to developmental ERP research. There are a wealth of developmentally oriented behavioral investigations using tasks that elicit systematic age-related changes in performance. This allows any observed ERP changes to be anchored in behavior. Endogenous event-related brain activity provides a means for the joint study of psychological measures of cognitive operations and electrophysiological measures of brain functioning. Using this strategy means that it should be possible to advance formulations of both psychological and brain function to a greater extent than the study of either domain separately. This potential for illuminating both psychological and brain processes is implicit in the fact that a number of lawful and systematic relationships have been obtained between the amplitude and latency of specific ERP components and behavioral measures (for reviews see Donchin and Coles, 1988, Donchin, Ritter and McCallum, 1978; Ritter, Simson and Vaughan, 1983). However, we have yet to apply the full power and complement of ERP information processing paradigms to the developmental area.

Although the intracranial generators of the cognition-related components are by no means definitively known, there is some evidence that N400- and P300-like potentials may be generated within the medial temporal lobe (e.g. Halgren *et al.*, 1980; Smith, Stapleton and Halgren, 1986; Wood *et al.*, 1984), a brain region known to be intimately involved in memory and learning. In addition, these intracranial potentials have been generated in recognition memory and lexical decision tasks (Smith, 1986). It is also becoming clear that N400- and P300-like potentials are recorded at the scalp when children, adolescents and adults are required to learn and remember a variety of stimuli (e.g. Berman, Friedman and Cramer, 1989; Stelmack *et al.*, 1988). Disruption, by electrical stimulation within one second of stimulus input, of structures in the medial temporal lobe may produce recent memory impairment (Halgren, Wilson and Stapleton, 1985). In addition, the temporal course of the N400- and P300-like potentials in depth as well as at the scalp take place at points in time when the medial temporal lobe is active in memory processes. Moreover, repetition effects during implicit memory conditions also appear to modulate similar late negative and positive components (e.g. Berman, Friedman and Cramer, 1989, 1990a; Kutas and Van Petten, 1988; Rugg, Furda and Lurist, 1988) as those seen during explicit conditions. Since cognitive development depends upon increases in memory function (Kail, 1984), the use of tasks designed to tap all aspects of memory function and their maturation seems especially appropriate for developmental ERP investigations. Thus, studies of repetition and semantic priming, as well as recognition memory, all seem like excellent candidates for developmental study from an ERP vantage point.

ACKNOWLEDGEMENTS

The research reviewed here was supported in part by grant HD14959 from the USPHS and by the New York State Department of Mental Hygiene. The Computer Center at New York State Psychiatric Institute is supported in part by a grant (MH-30906) from the National Institute of Mental Health. Dr Friedman is supported in part by Research Scientist Development Award K02 MH00510. The author thanks Charles L. Brown for computer programming and data reduction, Concetta DiCaria, Marla Hamberger, and Margaret Cramer for aid in the construction of figures. The developmental work reported in this review was greatly furthered by collaborations with Drs Steve Berman, Lois Putnam and Joan G. Snodgrass.

Development of Processing Control Mechanisms: The Interplay of Subcortical and Cortical Components

Bruno J. Anthony
Department of Psychiatry,
University of Maryland School of Medicine,
Baltimore, MD 21201, USA
and
David Friedman
Medical Genetics Department,
New York State Psychiatric Institute,
New York City, NY 10032, USA

INTRODUCTION

In the foregoing reviews we have examined mechanisms involved in the modulation of information as it passes through the nervous system and the maturational changes (or lack of such changes) in these mechanisms. Although similar in theme, the two reviews emphasized control at different levels of stimulus analysis. The first reviewed startle-blink methodology that assessed filtering processes acting within the first 100 ms of sensory analysis. This work pointed up the effects of intrinsic, temporal differences in early processing pathways and elucidated the development of automatic mechanisms such as priming, sensorimotor gating, and arousal. Startle blink is sensitive to selective attention; but only as it operates to influence brainstem processing. The second review, on the other hand, covered changes in event-related potentials (ERPs), occurring more than 100 ms after stimulus onset. Alterations in these cognitive ERPs reflected higher-level processes such as categorization and implicit and explicit memory. In the following sections we try to exploit these seemingly disparate areas of research, and include selected work not covered in our individual reviews, in order to examine one of the key aspects of cognitive development: the integration of high- and low-level components into mature information control systems.

Handbook of Cognitive Psychophysiology: Central and Autonomic Nervous System Approaches.
Edited by J. R. Jennings and M. G. H. Coles.

Most information processing theories now assume that automatic processes and more voluntary control processes go hand in hand, an understanding of one requiring an understanding of the other (e.g. Kahneman & Triesman, 1984; Shiffrin, 1988). For instance, Posner and Peterson (1990) state: 'If there is hope of exploring causal control of brain systems by mental states, it must lie through an understanding of how voluntary control is exerted over more automatic brain systems' (p. 25). In considering developmental trends in certain aspects of information processing, we stress the concept of integrated control systems, incorporating structures at high and low levels. We assume a general gradient of brain maturation from caudal to rostral levels, although progress is not uniform. Some pathways may develop ahead of others in the same cross-section of brain (Gilles, Dooling and Fulchiero, 1976); even adjacent cells in the same nucleus may mature at different rates (Anokhin, 1964). However, we assume that pathways that constitute part of a *system* will follow the gradient (i.e. that high-level portions of the system usually do not mature functionally before lower levels). Thus, more automatic components may exercise dominant control prior to full maturation of higher components of the system. Although this control may bear resemblance to mature function, they may differ in certain characteristics, most notably flexibility. As high, but still immature, components begin to exert influence, control functions may actually be interrupted and disturbed for a period.

PROCESSING EFFICIENCY

One of the most consistent developmental trends emerging from these psychophysiological data is the improvement in processing efficiency with age. Immaturity in nervous system function reflects a variety of factors, including a paucity of active neurons in circuits owing to lack of dendritic growth, slow conduction of impulses resulting from incomplete myelinization of fibers, and less efficient synaptic transmission because of developing properties of the neuronal membrane. These developments are clearly not complete at birth but continue for years postnatally, even into the second decade of life. These changes lead to refinements in sensory–perceptual processing and in its control. The data we have reviewed in the two chapter divisions indicate that this maturation occurs at both high and low levels, progresses at different rates for different types of pathways, and may result in a functional pattern that does not follow a simple caudal to rostral gradient.

The second part of this chapter reported significant decreases in the latency of various cognitive ERP components over a wide range of ages. Consideration of other data suggests that some of this decrease is contributed to by maturation at lower levels. However, caution must be exercised in the interpretation of such data, since there are very few studies of the cognitive ERP components between infancy and early childhood. Thus, a correlative interpretation of such concordances between brainstem auditory evoked responses (BAERs; see below), and the long-latency, endogenous ERPs is difficult to make, because it is based upon an extremely small number of studies that have not examined these changes on a within-subject basis. Nevertheless, for scalp-recorded BAERs, Eggermont and Salamy (1988) described a nonlinear sequence of maturation, consisting of an initial rapid decrease in latency in the first five weeks post-gestation apparently linked to development of the cochlear and early myelinization. This is followed by a longer process occurring over the first three years, attributed to a slower myelinization process (Gilles, Levitan and Dooling, 1983). Significant changes in latency and amplitude are also measured in later portions of the ERP. Exogenous components of the auditory and visual ERPs show substantial latency decreases, particularly in the first years of life. Later components appear to show a more precipitous decline than earlier components (e.g. Ohlrich *et al.*, 1978); however, when infants are studied in the awake state, the extent of this age-related decrease in the latency of later components within the first six months is reduced (Shucard, Shucard and Thomas, 1987).

The latency of the brainstem-mediated blink response also undergoes a lengthy maturational sequence. For acoustically-elicited blinks, significant latency changes continue to at least 8 years of age (Ornitz *et al.*, 1986). The existence of two EMG components in the cutaneous blink response provides a clear example of the developing interaction of different components of a neural circuit. As with other sensory–motor systems, neurons mature in ascending order, beginning with those near the peripheral receptor. Thus, in infants, the elicitation threshold is lower for the early component of the cutaneous response, R1, than the later R2 response (Clay and Ramseyer, 1976; Kimura, Bodensteiner and Yamada, 1977). The afferent and efferent paths for the two components are the same but R2 involves a polysynaptic path extending to the midbrain. Once established, however, the more central circuit becomes predominant, and thresholds are reversed.

Processing efficiency appears to mature at different rates for different types of pathways. A major point of the first part of this chapter was that sensory systems with similar properties are organized into neural channels and represent an intrinsic selection process. Startle-blink research emphasized the distinction between processing channels based on temporal features and the lengthy maturation of the transient system. The recent finding that BAER latency continues to shorten to at least 3 years of age is consistent with this trend since BAERs appear sensitive solely to transient aspects of stimulation.

As yet, little attention has been paid to the possibility that specific components of the transient ERP may reflect processing of specific types of sensory information, although suggestions regarding such relationships have been made for the adult VEP by Harter and Aine (1984). They suggest that the latency of an early negative difference wave distinguishes activity derived from cortical projections of the solely transient tecto-pulvinar-posterior parietal pathway from the geniculo-striate-inferior temporal circuit which subserves more refined pattern perception. In this vein, several findings from work on visual ERPs in infants and children also suggest that different types of retino-cortical fibers mature at different rates. For instance, Sokol and Jones (1979) demonstrated differences in the rate of decrease in VEP latency with age for stimuli of large versus small check size. Also, Moskowitz and Sokol (1980) showed that optimal rates of stimulation to achieve maximal steady-state VEP amplitude varied as a function of age. Kurtzberg *et al.* (1984) indicate that such conduction differences are important to consider when using ERPs to estimate other visual functions, such as spectral sensitivity (e.g. Dobson, 1976).

PRIMING

Priming phenomena, examples of which were examined in both reviews, occur at different levels of processing and represent major sensory–perceptual modulation mechanisms. In a broad sense, priming refers to the differential processing of a stimulus brought about by the prior presentation of a similar as opposed to dissimilar stimulus. It is assumed that neural elements associated with stimulus processing are automatically activated and affect subsequent processing. Paired presentation of a prepulse and startle-eliciting probe demonstrated priming at the brainstem level. A probe elicited smaller and slower blinks when it matched the prepulse in modality than when it did not (Balaban, Anthony and Graham, 1985). The extent of priming on blink did not differ between infants and adults.

Friedman employed ERPs to study the development of priming with more complex stimuli in a pictorial adaptation of sequential letter-matching task (e.g. Posner, 1978). In both cross-sectional and longitudinal designs, children, ranging in age from 6 to 17 years, and adults displayed a negative component (Neg400) to the target stimulus with similar timing (200–600 ms) and scalp topography. When the prime was followed by a matching as opposed to a mismatching target, Neg400 was smaller. Moreover, the amplitude decreased with increasing physical or semantic similarity between the target and the prime. Of most interest, however, was the lack of changes in these effects with age, suggesting that the priming process, reflected in Neg400 amplitude, changes little with experience.

In sum, priming appears operative throughout the nervous system but mechanisms may differ. Different levels of explanations for the smaller responses to matching stimuli have been proposed, including neural refractoriness in sensory specific pathways (Balaban, 1984), non-refractory sensory-specific effects (Näätänen, 1984), and prerepresentation in short-term memory (Wagner, 1981). Faster behavioral responses to stimuli related to a previous prime have been assumed to reflect a spreading, preactivation of processing units (e.g. Neely, 1977). Although priming is assumed to be an automatic process, it appears to be modifiable by influences dependent on higher-level processing. For instance, Friedman reported that the Neg400 to the same physically identical matching stimuli, though always smaller than the mismatching stimulus, varied significantly in amplitude depending on instruction conditions. It was larger when subjects were judging stimuli on the basis of name or category similarity than on the basis of physical similarity.

The small amount of developmental work suggests that automatic priming mechanisms are in place very early in development. Thus, it may be the case that any age-related differences in priming result from a growth in the extent or characteristics of networks automatically activated by stimulation and in higher-level modulatory influences.

TRANSIENT-BASED CONTROL

Different types of processing channels, such as those distinguished by sensitivity to different temporal features of stimulation, are located throughout the sensory projection system; however, it appears that their functions and the information they represent depend on their location in the projection system. The first part of the chapter reviewed work suggesting that the transient system is involved in inhibitory sensory gating at low levels and in an attention-directing function at higher levels.

One of the striking findings evident in the startle work is the lengthy maturation for the low-level, prepulse inhibition (PPI) phenomenon. Adult values are not reached until at least 8 years of age. This result is surprising given the apparent subcortical site of modification; however, a similar developmental sequence is observed in the inhibition of an early component of the auditory ERP by prior stimulation. In a series of studies, Freedman and colleagues have employed a two-stimulus conditioning paradigm in which two intense auditory stimuli are presented at a 500 ms interstimulus interval (e.g. Freedman *et al.*, 1983). The second, stimulus-evoked P50 ERP wave is normally inhibited or gated by the first stimulus in adults. Like PPI, the reduction of P50 is less evident in schizophrenic patients (Braff *et al.*, 1978; Siegal *et al.*, 1984; but see Kathman and Engel, 1990) and has been related to central inhibitory deficits.

Freedman, Adler and Waldo (1987) examined P50 gating in subjects ranging from 18 months to 55 years. Consistent with the general increase in processing efficiency noted above, P50 latency was greater and amplitude less in children, only reaching adult levels in early adolescence. The extent of P50 inhibition to the second stimulus showed an even lengthier developmental course; it was significantly related to age and only showed significant levels in early adulthood.

The P50 paradigm employs two stimuli of the same modality; therefore, modulation could result from changes within the sensory pathway induced by the processing of the first stimulus (i.e. priming). It also seems possible that both P50 and PPI may reflect the action of subcortically mediated extrinsic control which is subject to the influence of higher centers. Integrating information from animal studies, work with clinical groups, and current understanding of monoamine systems, Braff and Geyer (1990) have proposed that the inhibitory control represented by these phenomena reflect a reciprocally acting system involving dopamine activity in prefrontal and mesolimbic areas. This interactional view provides one solution for the rather paradoxical, extended maturational course of these low-level effects. The prefrontal areas follow a lengthy developmental sequence (e.g. Yakovlev and Lecours, 1967). Thus, although circuitry for the subcortical effects may be present and mature at early ages, immature higher centers, involved in the modulation of these functions, may interfere with their automatic operation. Moreover, if immaturity expresses itself as an inconsistent influence, then variability of these low-level processes might be expected. Indeed, the variation in P50 gating was quite a bit higher in children (Freedman, Alder and Waldo, 1987).

Other evidence for the interfering effects of immature, higher centers on transient-based inhibition derives from developmental differences in the expression of PPI as a function of state. In adults, Silverstein, Graham and Calloway (1980) reported that the extent of PPI was similar across sleep and awake states. This is not the case for young infants. In a study of 6- and 9-week-olds, Strock (1981) found significant PPI in quiet sleep, greater than that in the awake state; there was no evidence of PPI in active sleep. One possible explanation of these results is that higher centers exert disruptive modulatory influence on PPI in the awake state and active portions of sleep. During quiet sleep, lower, more mature centers, mediate this inhibitory phenomenon.

Given that the transient system is represented at all levels of the nervous system, the same activity occurring at low levels of the system should be transmitted rapidly to higher centers. There, transients appear to serve a facilitatory rather than inhibitory function. Researchers in a wide range of areas (e.g. Breitmeyer and Ganz, 1976; Graham, Anthony and Zeigler, 1983; Neisser, 1979) have suggested that transients may directly affect encoding by directing attention to the analysis of later-arriving information. In the ERP literature, Harter and Aine (1984) reviewed evidence for the separation of function derived from experiments on visual selective attention. They distinguished an early negativity, linked to the posterior-parietal area, signaling selection of target stimulus location. As noted before, this area receives most of the input from the tecto-pulvinar system which consists of fast-acting, transient cells. Later-occurring changes in the ERP were linked to enhanced processing of features of selected stimuli. These changes were associated with activity in infero-temporal cortex which receives projections from cells that respond to more sustained input in the geniculo-striate system. Little is known about the development of this attention-directing function of transients. However, in keeping with an early deficit in the fast-time-constant system, Anthony (this chapter) reviewed the small amount of psychophysiological evidence indicating the facilitatory effect of multiple transients on discrimination in young infants.

Transient systems may direct attention in a largely automatic fashion. Shiffrin (1988) has suggested that an automatic call for processing must compete with calls elicited by other environmental or internal stimuli and those produced electively. As elaborated further in the following section, the refinement of the allocation of processing resources appears to represent a major developmental trend.

ORIENTING

The orienting reflex (OR) also undergoes an uneven development which appears to reflect the interplay of subcortical and cortical components. In Sokolov's (1963, 1975) view, the OR is elicited through the reticular activating system, influenced by input from ascending afferent paths as well as higher-level, modulatory input from the hippocampus. The afferent pathways form networks which allow particular properties of a stimulus to be encoded with repetition permitting sharpened contrasts and a more fine-tuned 'neuronal model'. In the hippocampus, novelty detectors provide mismatch signals which amplify or inhibit the OR. The importance of higher centers in this response is demonstrated by the inability to elicit the heart rate OR during sleep (Berg, Jackson and Graham, 1975). The cardiac component of the OR, a monophasic deceleration, was difficult to establish in young infants until careful consideration was taken of state. When newborns are unequivocally awake, appropriate stimuli can elicit HR slowing. This directionally distinguishing component has not occurred when newborns are asleep.

The mismatch negativity (MMN) of the ERP, which responds to infrequent changes occurring during a series of frequently presented auditory stimuli, is thought to be an automatic central nervous system component of the OR (Näätänen and Picton, 1987). As with the heart rate OR, the MMN has been recorded from newborns (Alho *et al.*, 1990). These data suggest that the brain mechanisms responsible for *automatically* detecting mismatches between sensory input and a neuronal trace are already in place at birth. However, unlike the cardiac OR data, MMN in the Ahlo *et al.* study was elicited in *sleeping* newborns. At the present time, the significance of this discrepancy is unclear, given the paucity of relevant data. However, even though the generator of the MMN is thought to be primary auditory cortex (Näätänen and Picton, 1987), this ERP component may reflect a preattentive or automatic comparison process that operates during sleep. Modulatory control of the consequences of this comparison may require more conscious processing. For instance, it would be crucial to know whether critical features of the OR reflecting such modulation, such as habituation and dishabituation, also characterize MMN during sleep.

At approximately 6 weeks of age, it is more difficult than earlier to elicit an OR. It has been suggested that this period may represent a maturational transition (Clifton *et al.*, 1981; Graham, Anthony and Zeigler, 1983). At this point, control by subcortical centers may be suppressed temporarily until cortical structures become fully mature. Alternatively, feedback from active but still immature higher structures might be mismatched in timing, and thus disruptive of subcortical activity. By four months, the OR is firmly established and the infant enters a relatively hyper-responsive period. The size of the cardiac OR increases until at least 10 months of age (Berg, 1975).

Some of the ERP components discussed by Friedman appear to share functional properties with the orienting process. Long-latency Nc and Pc waves have been thought to represent an automatic categorization system (Courchesne, 1983; Symmes and Eisengart, 1971) and have been recorded in infants as young as 6 weeks of age. Existing evidence suggests a maturational course for these components broadly similar to that of the OR. Karrer and Ackles (1987) reported that a negative complex, apparently including an Nc wave, was not well defined at 6 weeks but was by 6 months.

Once established, the extent and perseverance of the OR depends to a great extent on the emerging capacity to incorporate stimulus characteristics into the 'neuronal model'. In addition, it appears that the ability to restrict the reflex allocation of attention to novel stimuli develops over time. For instance, Anthony and Putnam (1985) reported that 5-year-old children showed large HR orienting responses to irrelevant startle probes occurring in the warning interval of a reaction time study. Adults appeared to override this rather automatic elicitation of the OR. Similar trends in allocation strategies emerge from a small number of ERP studies. Experiments with older children show changes in processing efficiency with age for positive components possibly linked to the mature P300 (Courchesne, 1983; Friedman, this chapter); however, there were few changes in characteristics that suggested functional processing alterations. In contrast, the frontal Nc component undergoes more major changes. In a study reported by Courchesne (1983), the Nc component elicited by novel stimulation decreased in amplitude with age to the point that by adulthood it was largely replaced or obscured by a fronto-central positive wave. This suggests that children and adults may evaluate novel information quite differently. We suggest that the elicitation of orienting activity by novel unexpected stimuli becomes less 'reflexive' with development as it is modulated by more planful allocation of attentional resources.

SELECTIVE ATTENTION

The development of selective attention was examined in both reviews and also showed rather uneven maturational trends. In the startle-blink work, selective effects on *early* processing were assessed through differences in blink indices when the eliciting stimulus matched or mismatched an attention-engaging foreground stimulus in modality. Under these conditions, infants and adults showed similar patterns of modification. However, older children failed to show selective effects in a paradigm in which attention was directed through instructions rather than captured by engaging stimulation. In the ERP studies reviewed by Friedman, attended and unattended channels were also designated through instructions. In one study (Berman, Friedman and Cramer, 1990), channels were defined by either the pitch or the consonant/vowel constitution of the standard stimuli. Processing negativity (Nd), derived from subtraction of attended and unattended ERPs, was smaller in children than in either adolescents or adults. However, no age differences in Nd were apparent in the pitch condition. The developmental trend was only evident in the consonant/vowel condition. Children produced similar large-amplitude negativities in both relevant and irrelevant channels, indicating a lack of selection for speech sounds.

It is apparent that mechanisms to select incoming stimulation for preferential processing are in place early in development. Various other factors impinge on their operation, however. The results reviewed above suggest possible candidates: the ability to initiate and hold a selective set depends on the ability to process information that defines an attended channel and, possibly, the ability to maintain a selective set without concurrent stimulation. Those with a constructivist view of perception propose that selectivity of perception is an intrinsic aspect of the activity that should be evident at every age. In this view, apparent developmental trends in selectivity do not reflect deficits in specific mechanisms. Rather, they appear because younger children are less engaged in primary tasks because of different interests. According to Neisser (1979), children '. . .can attend closely and continuously to events that genuinely interest them. When they do, their perception should be no less selective than ours' (p. 210). An understanding of developmental changes in 'interest' seems quite complex, however. It appears to involve specification of the types of perceptual information that engage infants and children, the mental structures that process it, and the interaction of components of these structures.

SUMMARY

The work reviewed in this chapter is admittedly a thin slice of psychophysiological work on development. However, this integration has suggested several points that may serve a heuristic purpose. First, as with other rapidly accumulating evidence (e.g. Posner, 1988), the data we covered suggest that mental operations involved in various types of cognitive processing are organized into systems spanning different levels of the central nervous system. Second, components of these systems mature at different rates. However, portions of the mature system can operate independently which appear to lead to apparent discontinuities in development. Third, mature functioning of these systems involves the integration of more automatic portions with higher-level components. The higher-level components are not necessarily critical to the operation of a certain cognitive process, but serve a modulatory function. The development of such functions, sensitive to environmental and internal contingencies, seems to represent one of the major trends in development.

REFERENCES

Ackerman, B.P. (1981). Encoding specificity in the recall of pictures and words in children and adults, *Journal of Experimental Child Psychology*, **31**, 193–211.

Ackerman, B.P. (1985). The effects of specific and categorical orienting on children's incidental and intentional memory for pictures and words. *Journal of Experimental Child Psychology*, **39**, 300–325.

Alho, K., Sainio, N., Sajaniemi, N., Reinikainen, K. and Näätänen, R. (1990). Event-related brain potentials of human newborns to pitch change of an acoustic stimulus. *Electroencephalography and Clinical Neurophysiology*, **77**, 151–155.

Alwitt, L.F. (1981). Two neural mechanisms related to modes of selective attention. *Journal of Experimental Psychology: Human Perception and Performance*, **7**, 324–332.

Anokhin, P.K. (1964). Systemogenesis as a general regulator of brain development. *Progress in Brain Research*, **9**, 54–86.

Anthony, B.J. (1981). *Probe Startle Modification During Heart Rate Deceleration: An Index of Selective Anticipation in Adults and Young Children*. Unpublished doctoral dissertation, Columbia University, New York.

Anthony, B.J. (1985). In the blink of an eye: implications of reflex modification for information processing. In: P.K. Ackles, J.R. Jennings and M.G.H. Coles (eds), *Advances in Psychophysiology*, vol. 1. Greenwich, CT: JAI Press.

Anthony, B.J. and Graham, F.K. (1985). Blink reflex modification by selective attention: evidence for the modulation of 'automatic' processing. *Biological Psychology*, **21**, 43–59.

Anthony, B.J. and Graham, F.K. (1983). Evidence for sensory-selective set in young infants. *Science*, **220**, 742–744.

Anthony, B.J. and Putnam, L.E. (1985). Cardiac and blink reflex concomitants of attentional selectivity: A comparison of adults and young children. *Psychophysiology*, **22**, 508–516.

Anthony, B.J., Zeigler, B.L. and Graham, F.K. (1987). Stimulus duration as an age-dependent factor in reflex blinking. *Developmental Psychobiology*, **20**, 285–297.

Aslin, R.N., Pisoni, D.B. and Jusczyk, P.W. (1983). Auditory development and speech perception in infancy. In: M.M. Haith and J.J. Campos (eds), *Handbook of Child Psychology*, vol. 2. New York: Wiley.

Balaban, M.T. (1984). *Priming and Attentional Effects on the Startle Reflex of Infants and Adults*. Unpublished master's thesis, University of Wisconsin, Madison.

Balaban, M.T., Anthony, B.J. and Graham, F.K. (1989). Prestimulation effects on blink and cardiac reflexes of 15-month human infants. *Developmental Psychobiology*, **22**, 115–127.

Balaban, M.T., Anthony, B.J. and Graham, F.K. (1985). Modality-repetition and attentional effects on reflex blinking in infants and adults. *Infant Behavior and Development*, **8**, 443–457.

Balaban, M., Losito, B., Simons, R.F. and Graham, F.K. (1986). Off-line latency and amplitude scoring of the human reflex eyeblink with Fortran IV (computer program abstract). *Psychophysiology*, **23**, 612.

Baltes, P.B., Cornelius, S.W. and Nesselroade, J.R. (1979) Cohort effects in developmental psychology, in Nesselroade, J.R. and Baltes, P.B. (eds), *Longitudinal Research in the Study of Behavior and Development*. New York: Academic Press, pp. 61–88.

Banks, M.S. and Salapatek, P. (1983). Infant visual perception. In: M.M. Haith and J.J. Campos (eds), *Handbook of Child Psychology*, vol. 2. New York: Wiley.

Bauer, L.O. (1982). Preparatory modification of the polysynaptic eyeblink reflex. *Psychophysiology*, **19**, 550.

Bentin, S. (1987). Event-related potentials, semantic processes, and expectancy factors in word recognition. *Brain and Language*, **31**, 308–327.

Bentin, S., McCarthy, G. and Wood, C.C. (1985). Event-related potentials, lexical decision and semantic priming. *Electroencephalography and Clinical Neurophysiology*, **60**, 343–355.

Berg, K.M. (1973). Elicitation of acoustic startle in the human (Doctoral dissertation, University of Wisconsin, 1973). *Dissertation Abstracts International*, **34**, 5217B–5218B.

Berg, W.K. (1975). Cardiac components of the defense response in infants. *Psychophysiology*, **12**, 244 (abstract).

Berg, W.K. and Berg, K.M. (1987). Psychophysiological development in infancy: state, startle, and attention. In: J. Osofsky (ed.), *Handbook of Infant Development*, 2nd edn. New York: Wiley.

Berg, W.K., Berg, K.M., Harbin, T.J., Davies, M.G., Blumenthal, T.D. and Avendano, A. (1985). Comparisons of blink inhibition in infants, children, and young and old adults. *Psychophysiology*, **22**, 572–573.

Berg, W.K., Jackson, J.C. and Graham, F.K. (1975).Tone intensity and rise–decay time effects on cardiac responses during sleep. *Psychophysiology*, **12**, 254–261.

Berlin, C.I., Hughes, L.F., Lowe-Bell, S.S. and Berlin, H. (1973). Dichotic right ear advantage in children 5–13. *Cortex*, **9**, 394–402.

Berman, S., Friedman, D. and Cramer, M. (1989). ERPs during explicit and implicit memory for pictures and words: a developmental study. *Psychophysiology*, Suppl. 4A, 7 (abstract).

Berman, S., Friedman, D. and Cramer, M. (1990a). A developmental study of event-related potentials to pictures and words during explicit and implicit memory. *International Journal of Psychophysiology*, **10**, 191–197.

Berman, S., Friedman, D. and Cramer, M. (1990b). Age-related changes in processing negativity during selective attention to speech sounds and pure tones. In C. Brunia *et al.* (eds), *Psychophysiological Brain Research.* Tilburg: University of Tilburg Press, pp. 147–151.

Berman, S., Friedman, D. and Cramer, M. (1991). Cognitive brain potential components during continuous recognition memory for words and pictures. *Bulletin of the Psychonomic Society*, **29**, 113–116.

Berman, S., Friedman, D., Cramer, M. and Putnam, L. (1988). Event-related potentials (ERPs) in continuous recognition memory for pictures and words. *Psychophysiology*, **25**, 435 (abstract).

Berman, S., Friedman, D., Hamberger, M. and Snodgrass, J.G. (1989). Name agreement, familiarity and visual complexity norms for 320 line drawings in children and adults. *Behavior Research Methods and Instrumentation*, **21**, 371–382.

Bever, T.G. (ed.) (1982). *Regressions in Mental Development: Basic Phenomena and Theories.* Hillsdale, NJ: Erlbaum.

Bloch, R.M. (1972). *Inhibition and Facilitation Effects of a Prepulse on the Human Blink Response to a Startle Pulse.* Unpublished doctoral thesis, University of Wisconsin, Madison.

Blumenthal, T.D. (1985). *Developmental Differences in the Temporal Summation of Transient and Sustained Auditory Stimuli.* Unpublished doctoral thesis, University of Florida, Gainsville.

Blumenthal, T.D., Avendano, A. and Berg, W.K. (1987). The startle response and auditory temporal summation in neonates. *Journal of Experimental Child Psychology*, **44**, 64–79.

Blumenthal, T.D. and Berg, W.K. (1986a). The startle response as an indicator of temporal summation. *Perception and Psychophysics*, **40**, 62–68.

Blumenthal, T.D. and Berg, W.K. (1986b). Stimulus rise time, intensity, and bandwidth effects on acoustic startle amplitude and probability. *Psychophysiology*, **23**, 62–68.

Blumenthal, T.D. and Gescheider, G.A. (1987). Modification of the acoustic startle reflex by a tactile prepulse: the effects of stimulus onset asynchrony and prepulse intensity. *Psychophysiology*, **3**, 320–327.

Blumenthal, T.D. and Levey, B.J. (1989). Prepulse rise time and startle reflex modification: different effects for discrete and continuous prepulses. *Psychophysiology*, **26**, 158–165.

Boelhouwer, A.J., Teurlings, R.J. and Brunia, C.H.M. (in press). The effect of an acoustic warning stimulus upon the electrically elicited blink reflex in humans. *Psychophysiology.*

Bohlin, G. and Graham, F.K. (1977). Cardiac deceleration and reflex blink facilitation. *Psychophysiology*, **14**, 423–430.

Bohlin, G., Graham, F.K., Silverstein, L.D. and Hackley, S.A. (1981). Cardiac orienting and startle blink modification in novel and signal situations. *Psychophysiology*, **18**, 603–611.

Braff, D.L. and Geyer, M.A. (1990). Sensorimotor gating and schizophrenia. *Archives of General Psychiatry*, **47**, 181–188.

Braff, D., Stone, C., Callaway, E., Geyer, M., Glick, I. and Bali, L. (1978). Prestimulus effects on human startle reflex in normals and schizophrenics. *Psychophysiology*, **15**, 339–343.

Breitmeyer, B.G. and Ganz, L. (1976). Implications of sustained and transient channels for theories of visual pattern masking, saccadic suppression, and information processing. *Psychological Review*, **83**, 1–36.

Bruner, J.S., Olver, R.S. and Greenfield, P.M. (1966). *Studies in Cognitive Growth.* New York: John Wiley.

Brunia, C.H.M., J. Mocks, and van den Berg-Lenssen, M.M.C. (1989). Correcting ocular artifacts in the EEG: a comparison of several methods. *Journal of Psychophysiology*, **3**, 1–50.

Buchsbaum, M. and Wender, P. (1973). Average evoked responses in normal and minimally brain dysfunctioned children treated with amphetamine. *Archives of General Psychiatry*, **29**, 764–770.

Chi, M.T.H. (1976). Short-term memory limitations in children: capacity or processing deficits? *Memory and Cognition*, **4**, 559–572.

Clarkson, M.G. and Berg, W.K. (1984). Bioelectric and potentiometric measure of eyeblink amplitude in reflex modification paradigms. *Psychophysiology*, **21**, 237–241.

Clarkson, M.G. and Berg, W.K. (1983). Cardiac orienting and vowel discrimination in newborns: crucial stimulus parameters of acoustic stimuli. *Child Development*, **54**, 162–171.

Clay, S.A. and Ramseyer, J.C. (1976). The orbicularis occuli reflex. *Neurology (Minneapolis)*, **9**, 892–895.

Clifton, R.K., Morrongiello, B.A., Kulig, J.W. and Dowd, J. (1981). Developmental changes in auditory localization in infancy. In R. Aslin, J. Alberts and M. Petersen (eds), *Audition, Somatic Perception, and the Chemical Senses*, vol. 1. New York: Academic Press.

Clifton, R.K., Morrongiello, B.A., Kulig, J.W. and Dowd, J.M. (1981). Newborns' orientation toward sound: possible implications for cortical development. *Child Development*, **52**, 833–838.

Cohen, L.B. (1972). Attention-getting and attention-holding processes of infant visual preferences. *Child Development*, **43**, 869–879.

Cohen, L.H., Hilgard, E.R. and Wendt, G.R. (1933). Sensitivity to light in a case of hysterical blindness studied by reinforcement-inhibition and conditioning methods. *Yale Journal of Biology and Medicine*, **6**, 61–67.

Cohen, M.E., Hoffman, H.S. and Stitt, C.L. (1981). Sensory magnitude estimation in the context of reflex modification. *Journal of Experimental Psychology: Human Perception and Performance*, **7**, 1363–1370.

Coltheart, M. (1980). Iconic memory and visible persistence. *Perception and Psychophysics*, **27**, 183–228.

Conners, C. (1970). Cortical visual evoked responses in children with learning disorders. *Psychophysiology*, **7**, 418–428.

Courchesne, E. (1978). Neurophysiological correlates of cognitive development: changes in long-latency event-related potentials from childhood to adulthood. *Electroencephalography and Clinical Neurophysiology*, **45**, 468–482.

Courchesne, E. (1983). Cognitive components of the event-related potential: changes associated with development. In A.W.K. Gaillard and W. Ritter (eds), *Tutorials in Event-Related Potential Research: Endogenous Components*. Amsterdam: North-Holland, pp. 329–344.

Courchesne, E., Ganz, L. and Norcia, A.M. (1981). Event-related brain potentials to human faces in infants. *Child Development*, **52**, 804–811.

Cowan, N., Suomi, K. and Morse, P.A. (1982). Echoic storage in infant perception. *Child Development*, **53**, 984–990.

Davis, M. (1984). The mammalian startle response. In: R. Eaton (ed.), *The Neural Basis of Startle Behavior*. New York: Plenum Press.

Davis, M. and File, S.E. (1984). Intrinsic and extrinsic mechanisms of habituation and sensitization: implications for the design and analysis of experiments. In H.V.S. Peeke, and L. Petrinovich (eds), *Habituation, Sensitization, and Behavior*. New York: Academic Press.

Davis, M. and Gendelman, P.M. (1977). Plasticity of the acoustic startle response in the acutely decerebrate rat. *Journal of Comparative and Physiological Psychology*, **91**, 549–563.

Davis, M., Gendelman, D.S., Tischler, H. and Gendelman, P.M. (1982). A primary acoustic startle circuit: lesion and stimulation studies. *Journal of Neuroscience*, **2**, 791–805.

Davis, M., Parisi, T., Gendelman, D.S., Tischler, M. and Kehne, J.H. (1982). Habituation and sensitization of startle reflexes elicited electrically from the brainstem. *Science*, **218**, 688–690.

Day, M.C. (1980). Selective attention by children and adults to pictures specified by color. *Journal of Experimental Child Psychology*, **30**, 277–289.

DelPezzo, E.M. and Hoffman, H.S. (1980). Attentional factors in the inhibition of a reflex by a visual stimulus. *Science*, **210**, 673–674.

Desmedt, J.E., LaGrutta, V. and LaGrutta, G. (1971). Contrasting effects of centrifugal olivo-cochlear inhibition and of middle ear muscle contraction on the response characteristics of the cat's auditory nerve. *Brain Research*, **30**, 375–384.

DiLollo, V., Arnett, J.L. and Kruk, R.V. (1982). Age-related changes in rate of visual information processing. *Journal of Experimental Psychology: Human Perception and Performance*, **7**, 754–769.

DiLollo, V., Hanson, D. and McIntyre, J.S. (1983). Initial stages of visual information processing in dyslexia. *Journal of Experimental Psychology: Human Perception and Performance*, **9**, 932–935.

Dobson, V. (1976). Spectral sensitivity of the 2-month old infant as measured by the visually evoked cortical potential. *Vision Research*, **16**, 367–374.

Donchin, E. and Coles, M.G.H. (1988). Is the P300 component a manifestation of context updating? *Behavioral and Brain Sciences*, **11**, 357–374.

Donchin, E. Ritter, W. and McCallum, C. (1978). Cognitive psychophysiology: the endogenous components of the ERP. In E. Callaway, P. Tueting and S. Koslow (eds), *Event-Related Brain Potentials in Man*. New York: Academic Press, pp. 349–411.

Donchin, E. and Sutton, S. (1970). The 'psychological significance' of evoked responses: a comment on Clark, Butler, and Rosner. *Communications in Behavioral Biology*, **5**, 111–114.

Duncan, J. (1980). The locus of interference in the perception of simultaneous stimuli. *Psychological Review*, **87**, 272–300.

Duncan, E.M. and Kellas, G. (1978). Developmental changes in the internal structure of semantic categories. *Journal of Experimental Child Psychology*, **26**, 328–340.

Dykman, B.M. and Ison, J.R. (1979). Temporal integration of acoustic stimulation obtained in reflex inhibition in rats and humans. *Journal of Comparative and Physiological Psychology*, **43**, 939–945.

Eccles, J.C., Kostyuk, P.G. and Schmidt, R.F. (1962). Presynaptic inhibition of the central actions of flexor reflex afferents. *Journal of Physiology*, **161**, 258–281.

Eggermont, J.J. and Salamy, A. (1988). Maturational time course for the ABR in preterm or full term infants. *Hearing Research*, **33**, 35–48.

Eilers, R.E., Morse, P.A., Gavin, W.J. and Oller, D.K. (1981). Discrimination of voice onset time in infancy. *Journal of the Acoustical Society of America*, **70**, 955–965.

Enroth-Cugell, C. and Robson, J.C. (1966). The contrast sensitivity of retinal ganglion cells of the cat. *Journal of Physiology (London)*, **187**, 517–552.

Ericksen, C.W. and Schultz, D.W. (1979). Information processing in visual search: a continuous flow model and experimental results. *Perception and Psychophysics*, **25**, 249–263.

Fagan, J.F. (1984). The intelligent infant: theoretical implications. *Intelligence*, **8**, 1–9.

Freedman, R., Adler, L.E. and Waldo, M. (1987). Gating of the auditory evoked potential in children and adults. *Psychophysiology*, **24**, 223–227.

Freedman, R., Adler, L.E., Waldo, M., Pachtman, E. and Franks, R.D. (1983). Neurophysiological evidence for a defect in inhibitory pathways in schizophrenia: comparison of medicated and drug-free patients. *Biological Psychiatry*, **18**, 537–552.

Friedman, D. (1990a). Endogenous event-related electrical activity during continuous recognition memory for pictures, *Psychophysiology*, **27**, 136–148.

Friedman, D. (1990b). Event-related brain potentials during continuous recognition memory for words. *Biological Psychology*, **30**, 61–87.

Friedman, D., Boltri, J., Vaughan, H.G. and Erlenmeyer-Kimling, L. (1985). Effects of age and sex on the endogenous brain potentials during two continuous performance tests. *Psychophysiology*, **22**, 440–452.

Friedman, D., Brown, C., Sutton, S. and Putnam, L. (1983). Cognitive potentials in a picture-matching task: comparison of children and adults. In A. Rothenberger (ed.), *Event-Related Potentials in Children: Basic Concepts and Clinical Application*. Amsterdam: North-Holland, pp. 325–336.

Friedman, D., Brown, C., Vaughan, H.G., Cornblatt, B. and Erlenmeyer-Kimling, L. (1984). Cognitive brain potential components in adolescents. *Psychophysiology*, **21**, 83–96.

Friedman, D., Putnam, L. Hamberger, M. and Berman, S. (in preparation). Mini-longitudinal study of the cognitive ERPs in children, adolescents and adults: a replication and extension.

Friedman, D., Putnam, L., Ritter, W., Hamberger, M. and Berman, S. (submitted). A developmental event-related potential study of picture matching: A replication and extension.

Friedman, D., Putnam, L. and Sutton, S. (1990). Longitudinal and cross-sectional comparisons of young children's cognitive ERPs and behavior in a picture-matching task. *International Journal of Psychophysiology*, **8**, 213–221.

Friedman, D., Putnam, L. and Sutton, S.•(1989). Event-related potentials in children, young adults and senior citizens: homologous components and scalp distribution changes. *Developmental Neuropsychology*, **5**, 33–60.

Friedman, D. and Sutton, S. (1987). Event-related potentials during continuous recognition memory. In, R. Johnson, J.W. Rohrbaugh and R. Parasuraman (eds), *Current Research in Event-Related Potentials* (*EEG* Suppl. 40). Amsterdam: Elsevier, pp. 316–321.

Friedman, D., Sutton, S. and Putnam, L. (1987). Cross-sectional, age-related changes in the cognitive ERPs, In Johnson, R., Rohrbaugh, J.W. and Parasuraman, R. (eds), *Current Research in Event-Related Potentials* (*EEG* Suppl. 40). Amsterdam: Elsevier, pp. 596–602.

Friedman, D., Sutton, S., Putnam, L., Brown, C. and Erlenmeyer-Kimling, L. (1988). ERP components in picture matching in children and adults. *Psychophysiology*, **25**, 570–590.

Friedman, D., Vaughan, H.G. and Erlenmeyer-Kimling, L. (1981). Multiple late positive potentials in two visual discrimination tasks, *Psychophysiology*, **18**, 635–649.

Friedman, D., Vaughan, H.G. and Erlenmeyer-Kimling, L. (1978). Stimulus and response related components of the late positive complex in visual discrimination tasks. *Electroencephalography and Clinical Neurophysiology*, **45**, 319–330.

Froding, C.A. (1960). Acoustic investigation of newborn infants. *Acta Oto-Laryngology*, **52**, 31–40.

Fuster, J.M. (1981). Prefrontal cortex in motor control. In V.B. Brooks (ed.), *Handbook of Physiology*: section 1, *The Nervous System*. Bethesda, MD: American Physiological Society.

Gersuni, G.V. (1971). Temporal organization of the auditory function. In G.V. Gersuni (ed.), *Sensory Processes at the Neuronal and Behavioral Levels*. New York: Academic Press.

Gersuni, G.V. (1965). Organization of afferent flow and the process of external signal discrimination. *Neuropsychologia*, **3**, 95–109.

Geyer, M.A. and Braff, D.L. (1987). Startle habituation and sensorimotor gating in schizophrenia and related animal models. *Schizophrenia Bulletin*, **13**, 643–668.

Ghatala, E.S., Carbonari, J.P. and Bobele, L.Z. (1980). Developmental changes in incidental memory as a function of processing level, congruity and repetition. *Journal of Experimental Child Psychology*, **29**, 74–89.

Gilles, F.H., Dooling, E. and Fultchiero, A. (1976). Sequence of myelination in the human fetus. *Transactions of the American Neurological Association*, **101**, 1–3.

Gilles, F.H., Leviton, A. and Dooling, E.O. (1983). *The Developing Human Brain*. Boston: John Wright.

Gluck, M.A. and Thompson, R.F. (1987). Modeling the neural substrates of associative learning and memory: a computational approach. *Psychological Review*, **94**, 176–191.

Goodin, D.C., Squires, K.C., Henderson, B.H. and Starr, A. (1978). Age-related variations in evoked potentials to auditory stimuli in normal human subjects. *Electroencephalography and Clinical Neurophysiology*, **44**, 447–458.

Gordon, G. (1951). Observations upon the movements of the eyelids. *British Journal of Ophthalmology*, **35**, 339–351.

Graf, P. and Mandler, G. (1984). Activation makes words more accessible, but not necessarily more retrievable. *Journal of Verbal Learning and Verbal Behavior*, **23**, 553–568.

Graf, P. and Schacter, D.L. (1985). Implicit and explicit memory for new associations in normal and amnesic subjects. *Journal of Experimental Psychology: Learning, Memory, and Cognition*, **11**, 501–518.

Graham, F.K. (1975). The more or less startling effects of weak prestimulation. *Psychophysiology*, **12**, 238–248.

Graham, F.K. (1979). Distinguishing among orienting, defense, and startle reflexes. In H.D. Kimmel, E.H. van Olst and J.F. Orlebeke (eds), *The Orienting Reflex in Humans: An International Conference Sponsored by the Scientific Affairs Division of the North Atlantic Treaty Organization*. Hillsdale, NJ: Lawrence Erlbaum Associates.

Graham, F.K. (1980). Control of reflex blink excitability. In R.F. Thompson, L.H. Hicks and V.B. Shvyrkov (eds), *Neural Mechanisms of Goal-Directed Behavior and Learning*. New York: Academic Press.

Graham, F.K. (1984). An affair of the heart. In M. Coles, R. Jennings and J. Stern (eds), *Psychophysiology: A Festschrift for John and Beatrice Lacey*. New York: Van Nostrand Reinhold.

Graham, F.K., Anthony, B.J. and Zeigler, B.L. (1983). The orienting response and developmental processes. In D. Siddle (ed.), *Orienting and Habituation: Perspectives in Human Research*. Chichester: John Wiley, pp. 371–430.

Graham, F.K., Leavitt, L.A., Strock, B.D. and Brown, J.W. (1978). Precocious cardiac orienting in a human anencephalic infant. *Science*, **199**, 322–324.

Graham, F.K. and Murray, G.M. (1977). Discordant effects of weak prestimulation on magnitude and latency of the reflex blink. *Physiological Psychology*, **5**, 108–114.

Graham, F.K., Putnam, L.E. and Leavitt, L.A. (1975). Lead stimulation effects on human cardiac orienting and blink reflexes. *Journal of Experimental Psychology: Human Perception and Performance*, **1**, 161–169.

Graham, F.K., Strock, B.D. and Zeigler, B.L. (1981). Excitatory and inhibitory influences on reflex responsiveness. In W.A. Collins (ed.), *Minnesota Symposia on Child Psychology*:

vol 14, *Aspects of the Development of Competence*. Hillsdale, NJ: Lawrence Erlbaum Associates.
Graham, N., Kramer, P. and Haber, N. (1985). Attending to the spatial frequency and spatial position of near-threshold visual patterns. In M.I. Posner and O.S.M. Martin (eds), *Attention and Performance*, vol. XI. Hillsdale, NJ: Lawrence Erlbaum Associates.
Grant, D.A. (1945). A sensitized eyelid reaction related to the conditioned eyelid response. *Journal of Experimental Psychology*, **35**, 393–402.
Gratton, G., Coles, M.G.H. and Donchin, E. (1983). A new method for off-line removal of ocular artifact. *Electroencephalography and Clinical Neurophysiology*, **55**, 468–484.
Greenbaum, J.L. and Graf, P. (1989). Preschool period development of implicit and explicit remembering. *Bulletin of the Psychonomic Society*, **27**, 417–420.
Gregoric, M. (1973). Habituation of the blink reflex: role of selective attention. In J.E. Desmedt (ed.), *New Developments in Electromyography and Clinical Neurophysiology*. Basel: Karger.
Groves, P.M. and Thompson, R.F. (1970). Habituation: a dual process theory. *Psychological Review*, **77**, 419–450.
Groves, P.M., Wilson, C.J. and Boyle, R.D. (1974). Brain stem pathways, cortical modulation, and habituation of the acoustic startle response. *Behavioral Biology*, **10**, 391–418.
Guitton, D., Buchtel, H.A. and Douglas, R.M. (1985). Frontal lobe lesions in man cause difficulties in suppressing reflexive glances and in generating goal-directed saccades. *Experimental Brain Research*, **58**, 455–472.
Guttentag, R.E. (1985). Memory and aging: implications for theories of memory development during childhood, *Developmental Review*, 56–82.
Hackley, S.A. and Graham, F.K. (1983). Early selective attention effects on cutaneous and acoustic blink reflexes. *Physiological Psychology*, **11**, 235–242.
Hackley, S.A. and Graham, F.K. (1987). Effects of attending selectively to the spatial position of reflex-eliciting and reflex-modulating stimuli. *Journal of Experimental Psychology: Human Perception and Performance*, **13**, 411–424.
Halgren, E., Squires, N.K., Wilson, C.L., Rohrbaugh, J.W., Babb, T.L. and Crandall, P.H. (1980). Endogenous potentials generated in the human hippocampal formation and amygdala by infrequent events. *Science*, **210**, 803–805.
Halgren, E., Wilson, C.L. and Stapleton, J.M. (1985). Human medial temporal lobe stimulation disrupts both formation and retrieval of recent memories. *Brain and Cognition*, **4**, 287–295.
Hammond, G.R. (1973). Lesions of pontine and medullary reticular formation and prestimulus inhibition of the acoustic startle reaction in rats. *Physiology and Behavior*, **8**, 535–537.
Hansen, J.C. and Hillyard, S.A. (1980). Endogenous brain potentials associated with selective auditory attention. *Electroencephalography and Clinical Neurophysiology*, **49**, 277–290.
Harbin, T.J. and Berg, W.K. (1983). The effects of age and prestimulus duration upon reflex inhibition. *Psychophysiology*, **20**, 603–610.
Harbin, T.J., Marsh, G.R. and Harvey, M.T. (1984). Differences in the late components of the event-related potential due to age and to semantic and non-semantic tasks. *Electroencephalography and Clinical Neurophysiology*, **59**, 489–496.
Harter, R.M. and Aine, C.J. (1984). Brain mechanisms of visual selective attention. In R. Parasuraman and D.R. Davies (eds), *Varieties of Attention*. Orlando, FL: Academic Press, pp. 293–321.
Hawkins, R.D. and Kandel, E.R. (1984). Is there a cell-biological alphabet for simple forms of learning? *Psychological Review*, **91**, 375–391.

Heilman, K.M., Watson, R.T. and Valenstein, E. (1985). Neglect and related disorders. In K.M. Heilman and E. Valenstein (eds), *Clinical Neuropsychology*. New York: Oxford.

Hilgard, E.R. (1933). Reinforcement and inhibition of eyelid reflexes. *Journal of General Psychology*, **8**, 85–11.

Hilgard, E.R. and Wendt, G.R. (1933). The problem of reflex sensivity of light studied in a case of hemianopsia. *Yale Journal of Biology and Medicine*, **5**, 373–385.

Hill, K., Cogan, D.G. and Dodge, P.R. (1961). Ocular signs associated with hydraencephaly. *American Journal of Ophthalmology*, **51**, 267–275.

Hillyard, S.A., Hink, R.F., Schwent, V.L. and Picton, T.W. (1973). Electrical signs of selective attention in the human brain. *Science*, **182**, 177–180.

Hillyard, S.A. and Kutas, M. (1983). Electrophysiology of cognitive processing. *Annual Review of Psychology*, **34**, 33–61.

Hink, R.F., Hillyard, S.A. and Benson, P.J. (1978). Event-related brain potentials and selective attention to acoustic and phonetic cues. *Biological Psychology*, **6**, 1–6.

Hiraoka, M., Tenjun, T. and Shimamura, M. (1982). The reflex blink to flash of light in cat. *EEG and EMG*, **10**, 233–240.

Hiscock, M. and Kinsbourne, M. (1980). Asymmetries of selective listening and attention switching in children. *Developmental Psychology*, **16**, 70–82.

Holcomb, P.J., Ackerman, P.T. and Dykman, R.A. (1985). Cognitive event-related brain potentials in children with attention and reading disorders. *Psychophysiology*, **22**, 656–667.

Holcomb, P.J., Ackerman, P.T. and Dykman, R.A. (1986). Auditory event-related potentials in attention and reading disabled boys. *International Journal of Psychophysiology*, **3**, 263–273.

Hoffman, H.S., Cohen, M.E. and Anday, E.K. (1987). Inhibition of the eyeblink reflex in the human infant. *Developmental Psychobiology*, **20**, 277–283.

Hoffman, H.S., Cohen, M.E. and English, L.M. (1985). Reflex modification by acoustic signals in newborn infants and in adults. *Journal of Experimental Child Psychology*, **39**, 562–579.

Hoffman, H.S., Cohen, M.E. and Stitt, C.L. (1981). Acoustic augmentation and inhibition of the human eyeblink. *Journal of Experimental Psychology: Human Perception and Performance*, **7**, 1357–1362.

Hoffman, H.S. and Ison, J.R. (1980). Reflex modification in the domain of startle. I. Some empirical findings and their implication for how the nervous system processes sensory input. *Psychological Review*, **87**, 175–189.

Hoffman, H.S. and Wible, B.L. (1970). Role of weak signals in acoustic startle. *Journal of the Acoustical Society of America*, **47**, 489–497.

Hopf, H.C., Bier, J., Breuer, B. and Scheerer, W. (1973). The blink reflex induced by photic stimuli. In J.E. Desmedt (ed.), *New Developments in Electromyography and Clinical Neurophysiology*, vol. 3. Basel: Karger.

Hopf, H.C., Hufschmidt, H.J. and Stroder, J. (1965). Development of the 'trigeminofacial' reflex in infants and children. *Annales Paediatrici*, **204**, 52–64.

Hoving, K.L., Morin, R.E. and Konick, D.S. (1970). Recognition reaction time and size of the memory set: a developmental study. *Psychonomic Science*, **31**, 248–249.

Hoving, K.L., Morin, R.E. and Konick, D.S. (1974). Age-related changes in the effectiveness of name and visual codes in recognition memory. *Journal of Experimental Child Psychology*, **18**, 349–361.

Howard, L. and Polich, J. (1985). P300 latency and memory span development. *Developmental Psychology*, **21**, 283–289.

Hunt, W.A., Clarke, F.M. and Hunt, E.B. (1936). Studies of the startle pattern. IV: Infants. *Journal of Psychology*, **2**, 339–352.

Hyson, R.L. and Rudy, J.W. (1984). Ontogenesis of learning. II: Variation in the rat's reflexive and learned responses to acoustic stimulation. *Developmental Psychobiology*, **17**, 263–283.

Inhelder, B. and Piaget, J. (1964). *The Early Growth of Logic in the Child: Classification and Seriation*. New York: Harper and Row.

Irwin, R.J., Ball, A.K., Kay, N., Stillman, J.A. and Rosser, J. (1985). The development of auditory temporal acuity in children. *Child Development*, **56**, 614–620.

Ison, J.R. (1978). Reflex inhibition and reflex elicitation by acoustic stimuli differing in abruptness of onset and peak intensity. *Animal Learning and Behavior*, **6**, 106–110.

Ison, J.R. and Ash, B. (1977). Effects of experience on stimulus-produced reflex inhibition in the human. *Bulletin of the Psychonomic Society*, **10**, 467–468.

Ison, J.R. and Ashkenazi, B. (1980). Effects of a warning stimulus on reflex elicitation and reflex inhibition. *Psychophysiology*, **17**, 586–591.

Ison, J.R. and Hammond, G.R. (1971). Modification of the startle reflex in the rat by changes in the auditiory and visual environments. *Journal of Comparitive and Physiological Psychology*, **75**, 435–452.

Ison, J.R. and Hoffman, H.S. (1983). Reflex modification in the domain of startle. II: Its context in the history of psychology. *Psychological Bulletin*, **94**, 3–17.

Ison, J.R. and Leonard, D.W. (1971). Effects of auditory stimuli on the amplitude of the nictitating membrane reflex of the rabbit (oryctolagus coniculus). *Journal of Comparitive and Physiological Psychology*, **75**, 157–164.

Itoh, K., Takada, M., Yasui, Y. and Mizuno, N. (1983). A pretectofacial projection in the cat: possible link in the visually triggered blink reflex pathways. *Brain Research*, **274**, 332–335.

Johnson, K.O. and Lamb, G.D. (1981). Neural mechanisms of spatial tactile discrimination: neural patterns evoked by braille-like dot patterns in the monkey. *Journal of Physiology* (London), **310**, 117–144.

Johnson, R. (1989). Developmental evidence for modality-dependent generators: a normative study. *Psychophysiology*, **26**, 651–667.

Johnson, R., Pfefferbaum, A. and Kopell, B.S. (1985). P300 and long-term memory: latency predicts recognition performance. *Psychophysiology*, **22**, 497–507.

Johnston, W.A. and Dark, V.J. (1986). Selective attention. *Annual Review of Psychology*, **37**, 43–75.

Johnston, W.A. and Dark, V.J. (1982). In defense of intraperceptual theories of attention. *Journal of Experimental Psychology: Human Perception and Performance*, **8**, 407–421.

Kahneman, D. and Treisman, A. (1984). Changing views of attention and automaticity. In R. Parasuraman and D.R. Davies (eds), *Varieties of Attention*. Orlando, FL: Academic Press, pp. 29–61.

Kail, R. (1984). *The Development of Memory in Children*, New York: W.H. Freeman.

Kandel, E.R. and Schwartz, J.H. (1982). Molecular biology of learning: modulation of transmitter release. *Science*, **218**, 433–443.

Karis, D., Fabiani, M. and Donchin, E. (1984). 'P300' and memory: individual differences in the von Restorff effect. *Cognitive Psychology*, **16**, 177–216.

Karrer, R. (1978). Development and developmental disorders. In D. Otto (ed.), *Multidisciplinary Perspectives in Event-Related Brain Potential Research*. Washington, DC: US Government Printing Office, Report EPA-600/9–77–043, pp. 291–296.

Karrer, R. and Ackles, P.K. (1987). Visual event-related potentials of infants during a modified oddball procedure. In R. Johnson, J.W. Rohrbaugh and R. Parasuraman (eds), *Current Trends in Event-Related Potential Research* (*EEG* Suppl. 40). Amsterdam: Elsevier, pp. 603–608.

Kathmann, N. and Engel, R.R. (1990). Sensory gating in normals and schizophrenics: a failure to find strong P50 suppression in normals. *Biological Psychiatry*, **27**, 1216–1226.

Keane, J.R. (1979). Blinking to sudden illumination. *Archives of Neurology*, **36**, 52–53.

Keesey, U.T. (1972). Flicker and pattern detection: a comparison of thresholds. *Journal of the Optical Society of America*, **62**, 446–448.

Kimura, J. (1975). Electrically elicited blink reflex in diagnosis of multiple sclerosis. *Brain*, **98**, 413–426.

Kimura J., Bodensteiner, J. and Yamada, T. (1977). Electrically elicited blink reflex in normal neonates. *Archives of Neurology*, **34**, 246–249.

Kline, D.W. and Schieber, F. (1981). Visual aging: a transient/sustained shift? *Perception and Psychophysics*, **29**, 181–182.

Klorman, R., Thompson, L.W. and Ellingson, R.J. (1978). Event-related-brain potentials across the life span. In E. Callaway, P. Tueting and S. Koslow (eds), *Event-Related Brain Potentials in Man*. New York: Academic Press, pp. 511–570.

Kok, A. and Rooijakkers, J.A.J. (1985). Comparison of event-related potentials of young children and adults in a visual recognition and word reading task. *Psychophysiology*, **22**, 11–23.

Kosslyn, S.M. (1978). The representational-development hypothesis. In P.A. Ornstein (ed.), *Memory Development in Children*. Hillsdale, NJ: Lawrence Erlbaum, pp. 157–189.

Kurtzberg, D. and Vaughan, H.G. (1985). Electrophysiologic assessment of auditory and visual function in the newborn. *Clinics in Perinatology*, **12**, 277–299.

Kurtzberg, D., Vaughan, H.G., Courchesne, K.E., Friedman, D.R., Harter, M.R. and Putnam, L.E. (1984). Developmental aspects of event-related potentials. *Annals of the New York Academy of Sciences*, **46**, 300–318.

Kurtzberg, D., Vaughan, H.G. and Kreutzer, J. (1979). Task-related cortical potentials in children. In J. Desmedt (ed.), *Cognitive Components in Cerebral Event-Related Potentials and Selective Attention* (*Progress in Clinical Neurophysiology*, vol. 6). Basel: Karger, pp. 216–223.

Kutas, M. and Hillyard, S.A. (1989). An electrophysiological probe of incidental semantic association. *Journal of Cognitive Neuroscience*, **1**, 38–49.

Kutas, M. and Hillyard, S.A. (1984). Brain potentials during reading reflect word expectancy and semantic association. *Nature*, **307**, 161–163.

Kutas, M. and Hillyard, S.A. (1980). Reading senseless sentences: brain potentials reflect semantic incongruity. *Science*, **207**, 203–205.

Kutas, M., McCarthy, G. and Donchin, E. (1977). Augmenting mental chronometry: the P300 as a measure of stimulus evaluation time. *Science*, **197**, 792–795.

Kutas, M. and C. Van Petten (1988). Event-related brain potential studies of language. In R. Jennings, M.G.H. Coles and P. Ackles (eds), *Advances in Psychophysiology*. Greenwich, CT: JAI Press, pp. 139–187.

LaBerge, D. (1981). Automatic information processing: a review. In: J. Long and A. Baddeley (eds), *Attention and Performance*, vol. IX. Hillsdale, NJ: Lawrence Erlbaum Associates.

Lacey, J.I. and Lacey, B.C. (1970). Some autonomic–central nervous system interrelationships. In: P. Black (ed.), *Physiological Correlates of Emotion*. New York: Academic Press.

Ladish, C. and Polich, J. (1989). P300 and probability in children. *Journal of Experimental Child Psychology*, **48**, 792–795.

LaMotte, C. (1977). Distribution of the tract of Lissauer and the dorsal root fibers in the primate spinal cord. *Journal of Comparitive Neurology*, **172**, 529–562.
Landis, C. and Hunt, W.A. (1939). *The Startle Pattern*. New York: Farrar and Reinhart.
Lasky, R.E. and Spiro, D. (1980). The processing of tachistoscopically presented stimuli by five-month-old infants. *Child Development*, **51**, 1292–1294.
Leitner, D.S. and Cohen, M.E. (1985). Role of the inferior colliculus in the inhibition of acoustic startle in the rat. *Physiological Behavior*, **34**, 65–70.
Leitner, D.S., Powers, A.S. and Hoffman, H.S. (1980). The neural substrate of the startle response. *Physiology and Behavior*, **25**, 291–297.
Leitner, D.S., Powers, A.S., Stitt, C.L. and Hoffman, H.S. (1981). Midbrain reticular formation involvement in the inhibition of acoustic startle. *Physiology and Behavior*, **26**, 259–268.
Lelord, G., Laffont, F., Jusseaume, P. and Stephant, J.L. (1973). Comparative study of conditioning of averaged evoked responses by coupling sound and light in normal and autistic children. *Psychophysiology*, **10**, 415–425.
Light, L.L. and Singh, A. (1987). Implicit and explicit memory in young and older adults. *Journal of Experimental Psychology: Learning, Memory and Cognition*, **13**, 531–541.
Ling, D. (1972a). Response validity in auditory tests of newborn infants. *Laryngoscope*, **82**, 376–380.
Ling, D. (1972b). Acoustic stimulus duration in relation to behavioral responses of newborn infants. *Journal of Speech and Hearing Research*, **15**, 567–571.
MacKay, D.G. (1973). Aspects of the theory of comprehension, memory and attention. *Quarterly Journal of Experimental Psychology*, **25**, 22–40.
Maisto, A. and Baumeister, A.A. (1975). A developmental study of choice reaction time: the effect of two forms of stimulus degradation on encoding. *Journal of Experimental Child Psychology*, **20**, 456–464.
Mandler, G. (1980). Recognizing: the judgement of previous occurrence. *Psychological Review*, **87**, 252–271.
Marsh, R.R., Hoffman, H.S. and Stitt, C.L. (1978). Reflex inhibition audiometry: a new objective procedure. *Acta Otolaryngology*, **85**, 336–341.
Marsh, R.R., Hoffman, H.S. and Stitt, C.L. (1973). Temporal integration in the acoustic startle reflex of the rat. *Journal of Comparitive and Physiological Psychology*, **82**, 507–511.
Martinius, J.W. and Papousek, H. (1970). Response to optic and exteroceptive stimuli in relation to state in the human newborn: habituation of the blink reflex. *Neuropadiatrie*, **1**, 452–460.
Massaro, D.W. (1975). *Experimental Psychology and Information Processing*. Chicago, IL: Rand McNally.
Matin, E. (1974). Saccadic suppression: a review and analysis. *Psychological Bulletin*, **81**, 899–917.
McCarthy, G. and Wood, C.C. (1985). Scalp distributions of event-related potentials: an ambiguity associated with analysis of variance models. *Electroencephalography and Clinical Neurophysiology*, **62**, 203–208.
McClelland, J.L. (1979). On the time relations of mental processes: an examination of systems of processes in cascade. *Psychological Review*, **86**, 287–323.
McDermott, D.A., Young, M.E., Gilford, R.M. and Juola, J.F. (1977). Memory search processes for words and pictures in elementary school children. *Bulletin of the Psychonomic Society*, **10**, 83–84.
Miller, C.L. and Byrne, J.M. (1983). Psychophysiological and behavioral response to auditory stimuli in the newborn. *Infant Behavior and Development*, **6**, 369–389.
Mitov, D., Vassilev, A. and Manahilov, V. (1981). Transient and sustained masking. *Perception and Psychophysics*, **30**, 205–210.

Moscovitch, M. (1985). Memory from infancy to old age: implications for theories of normal and pathological memory. In D.S. Olton, F. Ganzu and S. Corkin (eds), *Memory Dysfunctions: An Integration of Animal and Human Research from Preclinical and Clinical Perspectives* (*Annals of the New York Academy of Sciences*, vol. 444). New York: NY Academy of Sciences, pp. 78–96.

Moskowitz, A. and Sokol, S. (1980). Spatial and temporal interaction of pattern-evoked cortical potentials in human infants. *Vision Research*, **20**, 699–707.

Mukano, K., Aoki, S., Ishikawa, S., Tachibana, S., Harada, H., Hozumi, G. and Saito, E. (1983). Three types of blink reflex evoked by supraorbital nerve, light flash and corneal stimulations. *Japanese Journal of Ophthalmology*, **27**, 261–279.

Mullis, R.J., Holcomb, P.J., Diner, B.C. and Dykman, R.A. (1985). The effects of aging on the P3 component of the visual evoked potential. *Electroencephalography and Clinical Neurophysiology*, **62**, 141–149.

Näätänen, R. (1984). In search of a short duration memory trace of a stimulus in the human brain. In L. Pulkkinen and P. Lyytinen (eds), *Perspectives to Human Action and Personality: Festschrift for Martti Takala*. Jyvaskla: University of Jyvaskla.

Näätänen, R. and Michie, P.T. (1979). Early selective attention effects on the evoked potential: a critical review and reinterpretation. *Biological Psychology*, **8**, 81–136.

Näätänen, R. and Picton, T.W. (1987). The N1 wave of the human electric and magnetic response to sound: a review and an analysis of the component structure. *Psychophysiology*, **24**, 375–425.

Neely, J. (1977). Semantic priming and retrieval from lexical memory: roles of inhibitionless spreading activation and limited-capacity attention. *Journal of Experimental Psychology: General*, **106**, 226–254.

Neisser, U. (1979). The control of information pickup in selective looking. In A. Pick (ed.), *Perception and its Development*. Hillsdale, NJ: Lawrence Erlbaum Associates.

Nelson, C.A. and Nugent, K.M. (1990). Recognition memory and resource allocation as revealed by children's event-related potential responses to happy and angry faces. *Developmental Psychology*, **26**, 171–179.

Nelson, C.A. and Salapatek, P. (1986). Electrophysiological correlates of infant recognition memory. *Child Development*, **57**, 1483–1497.

Neville, H. (1977). Electroencephalographic testing of cerebral specialization in normal and congenitally deaf children. In S.J. Segaloaitz and F.A. Gruber (eds), *Language Development and Neurological Theory*. New York: Academic Press, pp. 121–131.

Neville, H., Kutas, M., Chesney, G. and Schmidt, A.L. (1986). Event-related brain potentials during initial encoding and recognition of congruous and incongruous words. *Journal of Memory and Language*, **25**, 75–92.

Novick, B., Kurtzburg, D. and Vaughan, H.G. (1979). An electrophysiologic indication of defective information storage in childhood autism. *Psychiatry Research*, **1**, 101–108.

Ohlrich, E., Barnet, A.B., Weiss, I.P. and Shanks, B.L. (1978). Auditory evoked potential development in early childhood: a longitudinal study. *Electroencephalography and Clinical Neurophysiology*, **44**, 411–423.

Okita, T. (1979). Event-related potentials and selective attention to auditory stimuli varying in pitch and localization, *Biological Psychology*, **9**, 271–284.

Ongerboer deVisser, B.W. and Kuypers, H.G.J.M. (1978). Late blink reflex changes in lateral medullary lesions. *Brain*, **101**, 285–294.

Ongerboer deVisser, B.W. and Moffie, D. (1979). Effects of brainstem and thalamic lesions on the corneal reflex: an electrophysiological and anatomical study. *Brain*, **102**, 595–608.

Ornitz, E.M., Guthrie, D., Kaplan, A.R., Lane, S.J. and Norman, R.J. (1986). Maturation of startle modulation. *Psychophysiology*, **23**, 624–634.

Ornitz, E.M., Ritvo, E.R., Panman, L.E., Lee, Y.H., Carr, E.M. and Walter, R.D. (1968). The auditory evoked response in normal and autistic children during sleep. *Electroencephalography and Clinical Neurophysiology*, **25**, 221–230.

Otto, D., Benignus, V., Seiple, K., Loiselle, D. and Hatcher, T. (1980). ERPs in young children during sensory conditioning. In H.H. Kornhuber and L. Deeke (eds), *Motivation, Motor and Sensory Processes of the Brain: Electrical Potentials, Behavior and Clinical Use*. Amsterdam: Elsevier, pp. 574–578.

Paller, K.A., Kutas, M. and Mayes, A.R. (1987). Neural correlates of encoding in an incidental learning paradigm. *Electroencephalography and Clinical Neurophysiology*, **67**, 360–371.

Paller, K.A., McCarthy, G. and Wood, C.C. (1987). Brain potentials predictive of later performance on tests of recognition and priming. Presented at the Third Conference on Neurobiology of Learning and Memory, University of California, Irvine, Oct. 14–17.

Paller, K.A., McCarthy, G. and Wood, C.C. (1988). ERPs predictive of subsequent recall and recognition performance. *Biological Psychology*, **26**, 269–276.

Parasuraman, R. (1980). Effects of information processing demands on slow negative shift latencies and N100 amplitude in selective and divided attention, *Biological Psychology*, **11**, 217–233.

Parkin, A.J. and Streete, S. (1988). Implicit and explicit memory in young children and adults. *British Journal of Psychology*, **79**, 361–369.

Perlmutter, M. (1978). What is memory aging the aging of? *Developmental Psychology*, **14**, 330–345.

Perlmutter, M. (1980). A developmental study of semantic elaboration and interpretation of recognition memory, *Journal of Experimental Child Psychology*, **29**, 413–427.

Pick, A.D., Christie, M.D. and Frankel, G.W. (1972). A developmental study of visual selective attention. *Journal of Experimental Child Psychology*, **14**, 165–175.

Pick, A.D., Frankel, G.W. and Hess, V.L. (1975). Childrens' attention: the development of selectivity. In E.M. Hetherington (ed.), *Review of Child Development Research*, vol 5. Chicago, IL: University of Chicago Press.

Polich, J. (1985). Semantic categorization and event-related potentials. *Brain and Language*, **26**, 304–321.

Polich, J., Ladish, C. and Burns, T. (1990). Normal variation of P300 in children: age, memory span, and head size. *International Journal of Psychophysiology*, **9**, 237–248.

Porges, S.W. (1980). Individual differences in attention: a possible physiological substrate. In B.K. Keogh (ed.), *Advances in Special Education*, vol. 2. Greenwich, CT: JAI Press.

Posner, M.I. (1978). *Cronometric Explorations of Mind*. Hillsdale, NJ: Lawrence Erlbaum Associates.

Posner, M.I. (1988). Structures and functions of selective attention. In T. Boll and B. Bryant (eds), *Master Lectures in Clinical Neuropsychology*. Washington, DC: American Psychological Association, pp. 173–202.

Posner, M.I. and Peterson, S.E. (1990). The attention system of the human brain. *Annual Review of Neuroscience*, **13**, 25–42.

Posner, M.I. and Snyder, C.R. (1975). Attention and cognitive control. In R.L. Solso (ed.), *Information Processing and Cognition*. Hillsdale, NJ: Lawrence Erlbaum Associates.

Poulsen, T. (1981). Loudness of tone pulses in a free field. *Journal of the Acoustical Society of America*, **69**, 1786–1790.

Pricep, L., Sutton, S. and Hakerem, G. (1976). Evoked potentials in hyperkinetic and normal children under certainty and uncertainty: a placebo and methylphenidate study. *Psychophysiology*, **13**, 419–428.

Putnam, L.E. (1975). *The Human Startle Reaction: Mechanisms of Modification by Background Acoustic Stimulation.* Unpublished doctoral thesis, University of Wisconsin, Madison.

Putnam, L.E. and Meiss, D.A. (1980). Reflex inhibition during HR deceleration: selective attention or motor interference? *Psychophysiology*, **17**, 324 (abstract).

Putnam, L.E. and Meiss, D.A. (1981). Reflex blink facilitation during cardiac deceleration: Sensory or motor set? *Psychophysiology*, **18**, 173 (abstract).

Regal, D.M. (1981). Development of critical flicker frequency in human infants. *Vision Research*, **21**, 549–555.

Richards, J.E. (1985). The development of sustained visual attention in infants from 14 to 26 weeks of age. *Psychophysiology*, **22**, 409–416.

Richards, J.E. (1987). Infant visual sustained attention and respiratory sinus arrhythmia. *Child Development*, **58**, 488–496.

Ritter, W., Simson, R. and Vaughan, H.G. (1983). Event-related potential correlates of two stages of information processing in physical and semantic discrimination tasks. *Psychophysiology*, **20**, 168–179.

Robertson, A.L., Mahesan, K. and Campbell, K.B. (1988). Developmental differences in event-related potentials during a lexical and object decision task. Paper presented at the Society for Psychophysiological Research, Oct.

Rodieck, R.W. (1979). Visual pathways. *Annual Review of Neuroscience*, **2**, 193–225.

Rosch, E., Mervis, C.B., Gray, W.D., Johnson, D.M. and Boyes-Braem, P. (1976). Basic objects in natural categories. *Cognitive Psychology*, **8**, 382–439.

Ruchkin, D.S. and Sutton, S. (1983). Positive slow wave and P300: association and dissociation. In A.W.K. Gaillard and W. Ritter (eds), *Tutorials in ERP Research: Endogenous Components*. Amsterdam: North-Holland, pp. 233–250.

Rugg, M. (1985). The effects of semantic priming and word repetition on event-related potentials. *Psychophysiology*, **22**, 642–647.

Rugg, M.D. (1987). Dissociation of semantic priming, word and non-word repetition effects by event-related potentials. *Quarterly Journal of Experimental Psychology*, **39A**: 123–148.

Rugg, M.D., Furda, J. and Lurist, M. (1988). The effects of task on the modulation of event-related potentials by word repitition. *Psychophysiology*, **25**, 55–63.

Rugg, M.D. and Nagy, M.E. (1989). Event-related potentials and recognition memory for words. *Electroencephalography and Clinical Neurophysiology*, **72**, 395–406.

Rushworth, G. (1962). Observations on blink reflexes. *Journal of Neurology, Neurosurgery, and Psychiatry*, **25**, 93–108.

Sanes, J.N. (1984). Voluntary movements and excitability of cutaneous eyeblink reflexes. *Psychophysiology*, **21**, 653–654.

Sanes, J.N., Foss, J.A. and Ison, J.R. (1982). Conditions that affect the thresholds of the components of the eyeblink reflex in humans. *Journal of Neurology, Neurosciences, and Psychiatry*, **45**, 543–549.

Schaie, K.W. (1977). Quasi-experimental research designs in the psychology of aging. In J.E. Birren and K.W. Schaie (eds), *Handbook of the Psychology of Aging*. New York: Van Nostrand, pp. 39–58.

Schulman-Galambos, C. and Galambos, R. (1978). Cortical responses from adults and infants to complex visual stimuli. *Electroencephalography and Clinical Neurophysiology*, **45**, 425–435.

Sergent, J. (1982). The cerebral balance of power: competition and cooperation. *Journal of Experimental Psychology: Human Perception and Performance*, **8**, 253–273.

Shelburne, S.A. (1972). Visual evoked responses to word and nonsense syllable stimuli. *Electroencephalography and Clinical Neurophysiology*, **32**, 17–25.

Shelburne, S.A. (1973). Visual evoked responses to language stimuli in normal children. *Electroencephalography and Clinical Neurophysiology*, **34**, 135–143.

Shiffrin, R.M. (1988). Attention. In R.C. Atkinson, R.J. Hernstein, G. Lindsey and R.D. Luce (eds), *Stevens' Handbook of Experimental Psychology*, vol. 2. New York: Wiley.

Shiffrin, R.M. and Schneider, W. (1977). Controlled and automatic human information processing. II: Perceptual learning, automatic attending, and a general theory. *Psychological Review*, **84**, 127–190.

Shucard, D.W., Shucard, J.L. and Thomas, D.G. (1987). Auditory event-related potentials in waking infants and adults: a developmental perspective. *Electroencephalography and Clinical Neurophysiology*, **68**, 303–310.

Siegal, C., Waldo, M., Mizner, G., Adler, L.E. and Freedman, R. (1984). Deficits in sensory gating in schizophrenic patients and their relatives: evidence obtained with auditory evoked responses. *Archives of General Psychiatry*, **41**, 607–612.

Silverstein, L.D. and Graham, F.K. (1978). Eyeblink EMG: a miniature eyelid electrode for recording orbicularis oculi. *Psychophysiology*, **15**, 377–379.

Silverstein, L.D., Graham, F.K. and Bohlin, G. (1981). Selective attention effects on the reflex blink. *Psychophysiology*, **18**, 240–247.

Silverstein, L.D., Graham, F.K. and Calloway, J.M. (1980). Preconditioning and excitability of the human orbicularis oculi reflex as a function of state. *Electroencephalography and Clinical Neurophysiology*, **48**, 406–417.

Singer, W. and Bedworth, N. (1973). Inhibitory interactions between X and Y units in the cat lateral geniculate nucleus. *Brain Research*, **49**, 291–307.

Sinott, J.M., Pisoni, D.B. and Aslin, R.N. (1983). A comparison of pure tone auditory thresholds in human infants and adults. *Infant Behavior and Development*, **6**, 3–17.

Smith, M.E. (1986). Electrophysiology of human memory: scalp and intracranial event-related potentials recorded during recognition judgements and related tasks. Unpublished doctoral dissertation. Ann Arbor: University Microfilms.

Smith, M.E. and Halgren, E. (1989). Dissociation of recognition memory components following temporal lobe lesions. *Journal of Experimental Psychology: Learning, Memory and Cognition*, **15**, 50–60.

Smith, L.B., Kemler, D.G. and Aronfried, J. (1975). Developmental trends in voluntary selective attention: differential effects of source distinctness. *Journal of Experimental Child Psychology*, **20**, 352–362.

Smith, M.E., Stapleton, J.M. and Halgren, E. (1986). Human medial temporal lobe potentials evoked in memory and language tasks. *Electroencephalography and Clinical Neurophysiology*, **63**, 145–159.

Snodgrass, J.G. (1984). Concepts and their surface representations. *Journal of Verbal Learning and Verbal Behavior*, **23**, 3–22.

Snodgrass, J.G. and Vanderwart, M. (1980). A standardized set of 260 pictures: norms for name agreement, image agreement, familiarity, and visual complexity. *Journal of Experimental Psychology: Human Learning and Memory*, **6**, 174–215.

Sokol, S. and Jones, K. (1979). Implicit time of pattern evoked potentials in infants: an index of maturation of spatial vision. *Vision Research*, **19**, 747–755.

Sokolov, E.N. (1963). *Perception and the Conditioned Reflex*. New York: Macmillan.

Sokolov, E.N. (1975). The neuronal mechanisms of the orienting reflex. In E.N. Sokolev and O.S. Vinogradova (eds), *Neuronal Mechanisms of the Orienting Reflex*. Hillsdale, NJ: Erlbaum, pp. 217–235.

Squire, L.R. (1986). Mechanisms of memory. *Science*, **232**, 1612–1619.
Stauder, J.E.A., Molenaar, P.C.M. and van der Molen, M.W. (1989). ERP scalp topography as a function of chronological age and stage of cognitive development. *Psychophysiology*, Suppl. 4A (abstract addendum).
Stelmack, R.M., Saxe, B.J., Noldy-Cullum, N., Campbell, K.B. and Armitage, R. (1988). Recognition memory for words and event-related potentials: a comparison of normal and disabled readers. *Journal of Clinical and Experimental Neuropsychology*, **10**, 185–200.
Sternberg, S. (1966). High speed scanning in human memory. *Science*, **153**, 652–654.
Stitt, C.L., Hoffman, H.S. and Devido, C.J. (1980). Modification of the human glabella reflex by antecedent acoustic stimulation. *Perception and Psychophysics*, **27**, 82–88.
Stitt, C.L., Hoffman, H.S., Marsh, R.R. and Boskoff, K.J. (1974). Modification of the rat's startle reaction by an antecedent change in the acoustic environment. *Journal of Comparitive and Physiological Psychology*, **86**, 826–836.
Stitt, C.L., Hoffman, H.S., Marsh, R.R. and Schwartz, G.M. (1976). Modification of the pigeon's visual startle reaction by the sensory environment. *Journal of Comparitive and Physiological Psychology*, **90**, 601–619.
Strock, B.D. (1981). *Infant Reflex Excitability During Quiet and Active Sleep*. Unpublished doctoral dissertation, University of Wisconsin, Madison.
Strock, B.D. (1976). *Inhibition of Acoustic Startle Response in Six and Nine Week Infants*. Unpublished master's thesis, University of Wisconsin, Madison.
Stuss, D.T., Sarazin, F.F., Leech, E.E. and Picton, T.W. (1983). Event-related potentials during naming and mental rotation. *Electroencephalography and Clinical Neurophysiology*, **56**, 133–146.
Sutton, S., Braren, M., Zubin, J. and John, E.R. (1965). Evoked potential correlates of stimulus uncertainty. *Science*, **150**, 1187–1188.
Symmes, D. and Eisengart, M.A. (1971). Evoked response correlates of meaningful visual stimuli in children. *Psychophysiology*, **8**, 769–778.
Szabo, I. and Hazafi, K. (1965). Elicitability of the acoustic startle reaction after brain stem lesions. *Acta Physiologica, Academy of Science of Hungary*, **27**, 155–165.
Takada, M., Itoh, K., Yasui, Y., Mitani, A., Nomura, S. and Mizuno, N. (1984). Distribution of premotor neurons for orbicularis oculi motoneurons in the cat, with particular reference to possible pathways for blink reflex. *Neuroscience Letters*, **50**, 251–255.
Takmann, W., Ettlin, T. and Barth, R. (1982). Blink reflexes elicited by electrical, acoustic and visual stimuli. I: Normal values and possible anatomical pathways. *European Neurology*, **21**, 210–216.
Tallal, P. and Stark, R.E. (1981). Speech acoustic-cue discrimination abilities of normally developing and language-impaired children. *Journal of the Acoustical Society of America*, **69**, 568–574.
Thompson, R.F. (1986). The neurobiology of learning and memory. *Science*, **233**, 941–947.
Turvey, M.T. (1973). On peripheral and central processes in vision: inferences from an information-processing analysis of masking with patterned stimuli. *Psychological Review*, **80**, 1–52.
Vecchierini-Blineau, M.F. and Guihenene, P. (1984). Maturation of the blink reflex in infants. *European Neurology*, **23**, 449–458.
Verleger, R. Gasser, T. and Mocks, J. (1982). Correction of EOG artifacts in event-related potentials of the EEG: aspects of reliability and validity. *Psychophysiology*, **19**, 472–480.
Vrana, S.R., Spence, E.L. and Lang, P.J. (1988). The startle probe response: a new measure of emotion? *Journal of Abnormal Psychology*, **97**, 487–491.

Wagner, A.R. (1976). Priming in STM: an information-processing mechanism for self-generated or retrieval-generated depression in performance. In: T.J. Tighe and R.N. Leaton (eds), *Habituation: Perspectives from Child Development, Animal Behavior, and Neuropyhsiology*. Hillsdale, NJ: Lawrence Erlbaum Associates.

Wagner, A.R. (1981). SOP: a model of automatic memory processing in animal behavior. In: N.E. Spear and R.R. Miller (eds), *Information Processing in Animals: Memory Mechanisms*. Hillsdale, NJ: Erlbaum.

Wagner, I. F. (1938). The body jerk of the neonate. *Journal of Genetic Psychology*, **52**, 65–77.

Wedenberg, E. (1956). Auditory tests on new-born infants. *Acta Otolaryngologica*, **46**, 446–461.

Wickelgren, W.A. (1975). Age and storage dynamics in continuous recognition memory. *Developmental Psychology*, **11**, 165–169.

Wijker, W., Molenaar, P.C.M. and van der Molen, M.W. (1989). Age-changes in scalp distribution of cognitive event-related potentials elicited in an oddball task. *Journal of Psychophysiology*, **3**, 179–189.

Wood, C.C., McCarthy, G., Squires, N.K., Vaughan, H.G., Woods, D.L. and McCallum, C. (1984). Anatomical and physiological substrates of event-related potentials. In R. Karrer, J. Cohen and P. Tueting (eds), *Brain and Information: Event-Related Potentials*. New York: NY Academy of Sciences, pp. 681–721.

Yakovlev, P.I. and Lecours, A. (1967). The myelogenetic cycles of regional maturation of the brain. In: A. Minkowski (ed.), *Regional Development of the Brain in Early Life*. Philadelphia: F.A. Davis.

Yates, S.K. and Brown, W.F. (1981). Light-stimulus-evoked blink reflex: methods, normal values, relations to other blink reflexes and observations in multiple sclerosis. *Neurology*, **31**, 272–281.

Yerkes, R.M. (1905). The sense of hearing in frogs. *Journal of Comparative Neurology and Psychology*, **15**, 279–304.

Zametkin, A.J., Stevens, J.R. and Pittman, R. (1979). Ontogeny of spontaneous blinking and of habituation of the blink reflex. *Annals of Neurology*, **5**, 453–457.

Zeigler, B.L. (1978). *Acoustic-Startle Modification by Sustained and Transient Components of Long Lead Stimuli in Human Infants and Adults*. Unpublished master's thesis, University of Wisconsin, Madison.

Zeigler, B.L. (1982). *Priming (Match–Mismatch) and Alerting (Modality) Effects on Reflex Startle and Simple Reaction Time*. Unpublished doctoral thesis, University of Wisconsin, Madison.

Zeigler, B.L., Anthony, B.J., and Graham, F.K. (1981). Developmental changes in latency of visual and acoustic blink reflexes. Unpublished data.

Chapter 8

The Aging Information Processing System

ABSTRACT

Aging is accompanied by well-known changes in performance capabilities. This divided chapter examines how changes in sensory, central, and motor processes can be delineated using event-related potential and cardiovascular measures. An introduction notes different approaches to the psychophysiology of aging. An integrative section follows separate discussions of central and autonomic areas.

Introduction

J. Richard Jennings
Department of Psychiatry, University of Pittsburgh, PA 15213, USA
and
Nancy Yovetich
Department of Psychology, University of North Carolina, NC 27510, USA

Why should the psychophysiology of information processing be applied to the study of aging? General reasons for the study of aging abound: the increasing average age of our population, the need to adjust the environment to compensate for aging deficits, and the need to remediate the deficits of aging. Two reasons are more specific, however. First, aging acts as a natural experiment to reveal fragile processes. For example, older individuals may have difficulty searching for an object hidden by distractors in a visual display. Once such a fragility is identified, we can then explore whether this process similarly fails in younger individuals under adverse conditions—for example during fatigue or in the presence of environmental noise. Second, aging is, at least in part, a process of physiological change. Critical physiological bases of information processing may be isolated by relating specific physiological changes with age to concomitant information processing changes. For example, aging in rats seems to cause specific changes in cholinergic receptor mechanisms (Baker *et al.*, 1985). As understanding of the neural and pharmacological circuitry involving these receptors advances, different cholinergic mechanisms might be assessed and related to individual differences in performance among an aging sample. At present, however, our goal must be more modest. The psychophysiology of information processing in the elderly has barely achieved maturity as a field. Thus, the focus of this chapter will be upon whether psychophysiology can provide valuable, differential insights relative to those obtained by performance psychologists.

Few doubt that the aging process slows thought and action. Few, however, can define this aging process. Is aging a 'monolithic' mechanism that uniformly slows processing? Or does age differentially reduce the efficiency of specific processes? A longstanding view within the experimental psychology of human aging is that a uniform slowing in all information processes accounts for

Handbook of Cognitive Psychophysiology: Central and Autonomic Nervous System Approaches.
Edited by J. R. Jennings and M. G. H. Coles.

the observed slowing of thought. The current chapter will critically examine such a view by considering both cortical and autonomic indices of *different* information processes. In general terms we shall ask whether slowing or a malfunction in a particular process or set of processes might explain the change in information processing with age.

In this introduction, following a summary of the general 'slowing' position, a brief history of psychophysiological concepts in the aging area is provided. Mary Schroeder, Richard Lipton, and Walter Ritter then discuss the contribution of measures of brain activity to the assessment of information processing in the elderly. Richard Jennings and Nancy Yovetich then provide a discussion of autonomic responses. A recent model of the relationship between cognitive and energetic processes is presented followed by a review of relevant recent empirical work. Finally, we return to our global question of the general or specific nature of aging deficits and integrate the central and autonomic physiological results.

GENERAL SLOWING THEORY BASED ON PERFORMANCE RESULTS

The work of Salthouse (1985) and Cerella (1985) is representative of the view that aging involves a general slowing of *all* psychological processes. Salthouse (1985) developed this position as follows in his monograph: 'The basic idea in the theory proposed here is that the rate of performing nearly all mental operations slows down with increased age' (Salthouse, 1985, p. 295). His view is based on evidence of the slowing of most processes with age and a careful analysis of the implications of slowing. For example, in the realm of cognitive processes, slowed processes in early stages of processing may disrupt later processes which depend upon timely receipt of information. Such slowing-induced failures might then induce shifts in the strategies of task performance, as well as the performance anxiety frequently observed in the elderly.

Cerella (1985) provided an extensive literature review and comparison of models relating the performance of young and old. The latency of performance across multiple tasks of the old can be plotted against the latency of performance of the young subjects in the same tasks. A classic model of the relation, largely supported by the review, suggests that the latencies of the old are a direct multiplicative function (with the multiplier greater than one) of the latencies of the young. This representation corresponds directly to the Salthouse view in which essentially every process is slowed. Cerella's (1985) review concluded that such a formula did indeed fit the data, but that a better fit was obtained by separate multiplicative factors for sensory–motor and computational slowing. Although both authors are aware of possible exceptions to their views, the literature on response latency changes with age is well captured by their positions. The challenge then becomes to demonstrate a locus of aging effects that is specific (e.g. slowed perceptual analysis) and/or to provide a mechanism for the general slowing. Birren (1974) eloquently stated the contrasting views when he suggested that 'man is not simply a calculator that is slowing down because of an electrical brown-out, but man is a calculator that has some components that decay with time' (p. 810).

EARLY PSYCHOPHYSIOLOGICAL VIEWS OF AGING

Both a general slowing and a specific locus of aging deficit have been explored in the psychophysiology of aging. Among theories anticipating a general slowing of processing are general arousal, neural noise, and cerebral blood flow hypotheses. A specific locus of aging is proposed in Surwillo's alpha gating hypothesis. As we will review, these hypotheses have not found general acceptance, but they provide a useful background for current work on the psychophysiology of information processing in young and old groups. More detailed reviews are available in the two editions of the *Handbook of the Psychology of Aging* (Marsh and Thompson, 1977; Woodruff, 1985).

Textbooks of psychology often suggest that an inverted-U relationship may exist between arousal and performance—as arousal increases, performance first improves but then declines with further increases in arousal (e.g. Easterbrook, 1959; Berlyne, 1960). Arousal is defined as a dimension of general excitation that is evident in self-report, endocrine indices (e.g. catecholamines), central nervous system indices (e.g. EEG frequency), and autonomic nervous system indices (e.g. heart rate). If age is associated with a consistent state of arousal either below or above the optimum for performance, then arousal state would provide an explanation for widespread performance decreases with age. No study to our knowledge has fully tested this hypothesis by attempting to vary both arousal and task requirements parametrically. Age has, however, been frequently shown to alter arousal state. Electroencephalographic and autonomic indices in older individuals typically show lower levels relative to college aged controls (Marsh and Thompson, 1977, Jennings, Brock and Nebes, 1989). Interestingly, indices of catecholamine activity suggest an *overarousal*, which when normalized appears to normalize performance (Eisdorfer, Nowlin and Wilkie, 1970). Thus, the elderly would seem to be overaroused by some indices and underaroused by others. For this reason, although arousal hypotheses have generated some interesting results, general arousal theory may not provide an adequate description of state in the elderly. Furthermore, close examination of arousal–inverted-U results have rather consistently led reviewers to question the validity of the hypothesis (e.g. Näätänen, 1973; Lacey, 1967: Jennings, Brock and Nebes, 1989, 1990; Neiss, 1988).

The cerebral blood flow hypothesis suggests a metabolic explanation for slowing that may also be relevant to any hypothesized increase in neural noise with age. Aging is known to be associated with a stiffening of the vasculature which is frequently associated with atherosclerotic plaque reducing vessel lumen (Lakatta, 1983). Such changes are likely to result in reduced perfusion of brain tissue. Blood flow studies have shown reductions in flow in the aged, particularly in anterior brain regions (e.g. Warren *et al.*, 1985; Gur *et al.*, 1987; Denham *et al.*, 1980). However, the reductions are smaller than those observed with dementia, and responsiveness of blood flow to mental challenge is frequently the same among different age-groups (Warren *et al.*, 1985; Gur *et al.*, 1987). Thus, at present cerebral blood flow changes with age are likely to contribute to performance changes, but cannot be said to account for them.

The neural noise hypothesis incorporates cortical blood flow changes and remains a viable but rather general hypothesis for age changes in performance. The basic idea (Welford, 1965) is that slowing as well as other deficits of age might be due to a combination of slowed conduction in sensory and motor peripheral nerves and central 'noise' due to the reduction of functional cells, increase in random activity, and increased perseveration of signals. These factors would create a low signal-to-noise ratio that would then require a greater integration over time for accurate signal resolution—and ultimately appropriate performance. This hypothesis remains interesting; however, despite advances in neuroscience it remains unclear exactly what neural noise is and how to measure it. Anatomical evidence (Andrew, 1956) as well as biochemical evidence (Carlsson, 1985) suggests specific rather than general changes in anatomical features and biochemical substrates. If so, neural noise should not be conceptualized as being due to diffuse brain changes but rather as due to the failure of certain brain mechanisms. The neural noise hypothesis may form a useful conceptual framework into which knowledge of neuronal changes with age can be integrated.

A specific mechanism of aging changes is expressed in excitability cycle hypotheses based on alpha rhythm changes with age (Woodruff,1985). The alpha rhythm of the EEG is viewed as a timing mechanism for information processing or, more specifically, as the timing for creating a perceptual moment—a sample of the perceptual world that is processed as a unit. Given clear evidence that the frequency of the alpha rhythm slows with age, by equating alpha and excitability cycles, a testable hypothesis can be formed to explain generalized slowing with age. Surwillo (1968) has been a leading advocate of this position. He has reported high correlations between reaction time and alpha frequency across age, but later investigators have observed less striking relationships. Furthermore, attempts to show causal relations between alpha frequency and performance have not been uniformly successful (see the review in Woodruff, 1985).

Our assessment is that none of these theories has succeeded so well that it should determine future research in the psychophysiology of aging. The current lack of a generally accepted psychophysiological view of aging seems to have slowed research in the last few years. Indeed, the growth of the literature in the psychophysiology of aging between the 1977 review of Marsh and Thompson and the 1985 review of Woodruff is rather slight. However, promising beginnings applying recent advances in cognitive and psychophysiology have been made using event-related potentials. Furthermore, the unproductive general arousal approach of autonomic psychophysiology may soon be replaced by an amended conceptual framework that can relate autonomic function to information processing and central nervous system indices. First, however, we shall turn to the research on event-related potentials. The exquisite timing available using this index is an important tool for understanding slowing of sensory as well central processing of information.

Event-Related Potentials in the Study of Aging: Sensory and Psychological Processes

Mary M. Schroeder, R.B. Lipton and W. Ritter*
Departments of Neuroscience and Neurology, Albert Einstein College of Medicine, Bronx, NY 10461, USA

INTRODUCTION

Event-related potentials (ERPs) index electrical changes in the brain time-locked to a particular event, usually a sensory stimulus. Utilized in the context of a reaction-time paradigm, they can provide information about the neural processes associated with perceptual, discriminative, and motor tasks. Since the aged subject's performance is slowed on attention, learning, and memory tasks, ERPs should be useful in exploring the brain mechanisms which underlie cognitive deficits in the elderly.

Certain characteristics of elderly subjects may introduce confounds in ERP studies when elderly ERPs are compared with other age-groups. Age-related changes in the sensory end-organs may affect ERP latency and morphology. If these 'peripheral' effects are not controlled for, age-related alterations may be misinterpreted. Artifacts in the elderly may be unusually prominent. If time-locked to sensory stimuli, ERP averaging may enhance artifacts such as eye movements, blinks and myogenic responses. Inconsistent responses from trial to trial may produce temporal jitter and decrease the amplitude of the ERP component in the average. Components may be difficult to identify because of age-related alterations in latency and topography. In addition, it may be difficult to measure confounding variables which produce ERP alterations. For example, age-related changes in scalp or skull impedance, poor health or medication may have effects which are difficult to take into account.

The distinction between early exogenous and later endogenous components is not as clear as it once was since studies of selective attention and pattern discrimination on young adults have shown very early effects of task relevance. With this qualification, the terms 'endogenous' and 'exogenous' will be used to refer to the manner in which the components are used. While sensory, or

* Also at Department of Psychology, Lehman College.

Handbook of Cognitive Psychophysiology: Central and Autonomic Nervous System Approaches.
Edited by J. R. Jennings and M. G. H. Coles.

exogenous, ERPs are primarily used to assess the functioning of a particular sensory system, the 'cognitive' or endogenous ERP components index psychological processes such as pattern discrimination, stimulus classification, selective attention, and memory. In general, the sensory components are of relatively short latency (<150 ms) and are modality-specific. Their properties are determined by stimulus parameters rather than task requirements. In contrast, the components that index psychological processes are typically of longer latency (>100 ms) and depend more upon task requirements than upon specific stimulus parameters. Generally, these paradigms involve the presentation of at least two stimuli, usually in the same sensory modality; the subject is asked to process and respond to the stimuli differentially (as in a choice reaction-time task), allowing the experimenter to study the pattern of brain electrical activity recorded at the scalp, associated with cognitive processing.

ERP ASSESSMENT OF SENSORY PROCESSES

The exogenous components have found widespread use in the practice of clinical neurology for several reasons. First, they are relatively stable and easily measured. Second, because they assess the integrity of primary sensory pathways they are a logical extension of the bedside clinical examination. Third, they can aid in the localization of lesions within the CNS, and thus have diagnostic utility. Finally, they reveal neurologic dysfunction which might otherwise be undetectable on clinical examination or by using other methodologies.

In the normal elderly, exogenous components have been studied for a variety of reasons. These studies provide essential control data for clinical evaluations of elderly subjects. In addition, they provide a method for assessing and localizing problems in afferent sensory pathways. Finally, in the chronometry of normal aging, they may provide evidence that the primary afferent system is intact, suggesting that delays in later ERP components and reaction time occur from higher-order disturbances of processing.

THE VISUAL SYSTEM

Exogenous visual evoked potentials have traditionally been evaluated using a checkerboard stimulus which reverses in pattern: the black squares of the checkerboard become white while the white squares become black. Brain electrical activity is recorded in response to these alterations in pattern from electrodes positioned over the occipital poles.

Celesia and Daily (1977) studied 75 volunteers ranging in age from 18 to 79. Their pattern-reversal stimulus consisted of 15.5 minute checks presented at a luminance of 10 foot-lamberts. They found that the latency of P100 increased by 2 ms per decade after 20 years of age. The authors suggested that the slowing of the P100 with aging reflects slowed CNS conduction, perhaps due to age-related demyelination.

Subsequent work has confirmed their basic finding but suggested that peripheral problems may partially account for their results. The pupils get smaller as part of the aging process; the pupil diameter of a 70-year-old may be three-quarters of the pupil diameter of a 20-year-old. Smaller pupil size decreases the amount of light reaching the retina. Hawkes and Stowe (1981) studied the effects of pupil size on P100 latency in healthy young adults. They showed that pupillary constriction produced by pilocarpine increased the P100 latency by 4.6 ms on average. Conversely, pupillary dilatation produced by tropicamide decreased the P100 latency by an average of 3.3 ms. In addition, age-related lens opacification may decrease light transmission, further prolonging the P100.

Sokol, Moskowitz and Towle (1981) showed that check size had differential effects on P100 latency at different ages. They studied 125 subjects ranging in age from 13 to 82. All subjects were carefully screened for normal visual acuity. Comparing 12′ and 48′ checks across the adult life-span, they showed that the smaller checks were associated with increased P100 latency with advancing age. The average delay of the P100 was 0.14 ms per year for 48′ checks, and 0.3 ms per year for 12′ checks. They interpreted this finding as an age-related change in the ability of the visual system to process spatial frequency information. Similarly, luminance has differential effects as a function of age (Shaw and Cant, 1980).

Most studies agree that there is little correlation between age and P100 latency in middle adult life (ages 20–50) (Celesia and Daly, 1977; Shaw and Cant, 1980; Sokol, Moskowitz and Towle, 1981). All agree that P100 latency increases with age later in life. In a meticulous study, Allison, Wood and Goff (1983) studied 286 subjects ranging in age from 4 to 95. VEPs were recorded to 50′ full-field checks. They found that P100 latency decreased as a function of age from 4 to 20, was approximately stable from 20 to 60, and increased thereafter.

Several factors may contribute to this age-related increase. These include alterations in pupil size, alterations in luminance at the retina, effects of check size as well as changes in conduction in central visual pathways. Changes in luminance and check size do not abolish age-related differences. At least some of the slowing probably occurs in central visual pathways. Changes in central pathways may include axonal dystrophy, demyelination, neurochemical or vascular changes (Allison *et al.*, 1984).

Since the exogenous components are sensitive to differences in stimulus parameters, changes in the sensory end-organs make it difficult to equate stimulus parameters across the life-span. The changes in pupillary size and lens characteristics account for some of the slowing of the P100 in the visual system. Analogous problems may well occur in the auditory system owing to high-frequency hearing loss and in the somatosensory system owing to age-related changes in cutaneous receptors and in peripheral nerves.

Age-related findings for the brainstem auditory evoked potential (BAEP) and the somatosensory evoked potentials will be reviewed briefly.

BRAINSTEM AUDITORY EVOKED POTENTIALS

Brainstem auditory evoked potentials represent the electrical activity recordable from the scalp associated with the activation of brainstem auditory structures and pathways. Typically, responses to monaural, rapidly presented clicks are recorded from the vertex referenced to mastoids.

In the studies of Allison, Wood and Goff (1983) and Allison *et al.* (1984), 75 dB(SL) clicks were presented monaurally at a rate of 10 per second. Their findings may be summarized as follows:

(1) The peak latency of all components increased with advancing age.
(2) There was a large effect on Wave I which is generated in the acoustic nerve. This increase may well result from presbycusis.
(3) The Wave I to V interval, the most widely used measured of central transmission time, increased as a function of age more rapidly for males than females.

SOMATOSENSORY EVOKED POTENTIALS

Somatosensory evoked potentials are typically elicited by electrically stimulating the median nerve. Recordings reflect the sequential activation of the proximal peripheral nerve, the brachial plexus, the dorsal roots, the dorsal horn of the spinal cord, the dorsal column nuclei and finally somatosensory cortex.

In the studies of Allison *et al.* referred to above, the median nerve was stimulated at a rate of 5 per second using 5 ms pulses. In children, latencies increased with age, presumably paralleling the increase in height and the corresponding increase in the length of the conduction pathway. From the ages of 18 to 95 the N10 increased in latency, reflecting decreasing peripheral nerve conduction velocity. The N10 to the N12a interval actually decreased with age. The N13a to the N20 interval increased, presumably reflecting slowing within the central somatosensory pathways.

ERPS REFLECTING THE TIMING OF COGNITIVE PROCESSES

OVERVIEW

Since some ERP components index neural activity related to task performance, they provide an appealing method for examining changes in information processing with advancing age. Of the components discussed above, only the visual P100 has been studied as an index of cognitive change in the elderly. Until recently the aging literature has focused on the later components, especially P300 (P3) and slow wave (SW). The following sketch of selected components is intended to acquaint the reader with terminology essential to our review of the ERP literature on normal aging (for reviews see Ford and Pfefferbaum, 1980, Smith, Thompson and Michalewski, 1980, Squires *et al.*, 1980, Roth *et al.*, 1984, and Polich, in press).

The P1 is a positive peak that occurs about 110 ms after the onset of visual stimuli, and about 50 ms after auditory stimuli (Simson, Vaughan and Ritter, 1977). Its maximum peak on the scalp is at the occiput for visual stimuli and at the vertex for auditory stimuli. It has been shown to increase in amplitude to a stimulus in the relevant location in visual spatial attention tasks (Harter, Aine and Schroeder, 1982; Hillyard and Munte, 1984). This component has only been reported in one study of aging and visual selective attention (Schroeder and Harter, 1986) where there were selective-attention effects for both young and elderly subjects.

The N1 is a negative peak that occurs at about 160 ms after the onset of visual, and about 100 ms after auditory stimuli (Simson, Vaughan and Ritter, 1977). N1 has the same topography as P1 and, like P1, is sensitive to manipulations of the physical parameters and the task relevance of the evoking stimulus. The N1 component has been shown to increase in latency (0.1 ms per year) over the life-span (Goodin *et al.*, 1978).

The P2 is a positive deflection which occurs at about 245 ms for visual stimuli and 190 ms for auditory stimuli (Simson, Vaughan and Ritter, 1977). Its maximum peak is at the parietal midline for visual stimuli and at the central midline for auditory. Although Beck, Swanson and Dustman (1980) did not shown an increase in P2 latency with age, Pfefferbaum *et al.* (1980b) and Picton *et al.* (1984) did find an age-related increase in the latency of the P2 component. Goodin *et al.* (1978) found a 0.7 ms per year increase in latency of the P2 and a 0.2 ms per year decrease in the amplitude of the N1–P2 peak-to-peak measure, over the life-span.

The endogenous N2, a negative deflection following P2, occurs at about 300–500 ms following visual stimuli and about 200–400 ms after auditory stimuli. The latency of N2 depends on the timing of the discrimination and classification of stimuli (Donchin, Ritter and McCallum, 1978). N2 has been shown to increase in latency with age in some studies, but is not lower in amplitude in aged subjects (Beck, Swanson and Dustman, 1980; Brent, Smith and Michaelewski, 1977; Goodin *et al.*, 1978; Pfefferbaum *et al.*, 1984).

A later endogenous component, the P3, is a positive deflection occurring about 400–600 ms after visual stimuli and about 300–500 ms after an auditory stimulus. It is maximal over the parietal area, with a broader distribution on the scalp than the earlier components (Simson, Vaughan and Ritter, 1977). The latency of P3 has been shown to vary with the timing of completion of stimulus evaluation, or memory updating (see Pritchard, 1981, for a review). In both auditory and visual paradigms, P3 latency is prolonged in older adults. The delay, computed by regression analyses in cross-sectional studies, has been reported as 1.7 ms per year (Pfefferbaum *et al.*, 1984) or 1.8 ms per year (Goodin *et al.*, 1978). In the oldest-old it has been suggested that the increase becomes significantly more rapid (Syndulko *et al.*, 1982). However, manipulations which increase the latency of P3 in young adults sometimes do not increase the latency of P3 for older subjects (discussed below) (Pfefferbaum *et al.*, 1980a; Ford*et al.*, 1982).

Age-related P3 amplitude differences interact with scalp topography. P3 decreases in amplitude over central and parietal areas (Goodin *et al.*, 1978; Tecce *et al.*, 1982; Picton *et al.*, 1984; Mullis *et al.*, 1985; Pfefferbaum and Ford, 1988), and sometimes also increases in amplitude in frontal areas (Pfefferbaum *et al.*, 1980b; Strayer, Wickens and Braune, 1987; Pratt *et al.*, 1989). While the distribution of the raw amplitude of P3 for both young and aged subjects is maximal over the posterior areas, the aged ERP shows a greater uniformity of P3 across scalp locations with age.

Friedman, Hamberger and Putnam (in press) showed that elderly subjects' P3s to targets and novel stimuli were more frontal in topography, compared with middle-aged and young adults. A controversial issue in the ERP literature is whether there are two P3s—an earlier P3a in frontal areas and a later P3b in posterior areas (Squires, Squires and Hillyard, 1975). If these two P3s have separate generators, then as Picton *et al.* (1984) suggested, one or both may be changing differentially with age.

The slow wave (SW) is a long, slow positivity following the posterior P3 and a negativity following the frontal P3, usually interpreted as further processing of the stimulus. The frontal negativity elicited by infrequent targets has been shown to decrease with age (Picton *et al.*, 1984) and older subjects have shown increased SW activity to frequent non-targets (Looren de Jong, Kok and Van Rooy, 1987).

ERP STUDIES OF MEMORY AND AGING

In the Sternberg memory task (Sternberg, 1969) the subject is presented with a set of items followed by a probe. The subject gives a 'yes' response if the probe was contained in the memory set (inset trial) or a 'no' response if the probe was not in the memory set (outset trial). Task difficulty increases as the size of the memory set is increased from one to five items. Reaction-time measures on this task show a longer latency to the probe for larger set sizes. When RT is plotted across set size, the slope (in units of time per item) is interpreted as the time required for memory scanning and the intercept as the time needed for perceptual encoding and response processes.

Anders and Fozard (1973) found that aged subjects had a steeper RT slope on the Sternberg task than young subjects. Based on this finding and the findings of Marsh (1975), Ford *et al.* (1979) proposed that the latency of the P3 component in response to the probe would allow further specification of the slowing of aged subjects. Their inferences are based on the assumption that P3 latency can be used as an index of closure of cognitive processing related to stimulus evaluation that leads to a differential motor response, and that the interval from P3 to RT represents response processing time. Based on these assumptions, Ford *et al.* (1979) proposed that:

(a) The RT intercept represents encoding time plus response time.
(b) The slope of the P3 latency represents memory scanning time per item.
(c) The RT minus P3 interval intercept represents response processing time.
(d) The RT intercept (a) minus the RT – P3 intercept (c) represents encoding time.

This model uses the P3 rather than RT to estimate more precisely the time required to evaluate each item in memory, and to separate encoding and response processes.

In this study the P3 slope (b) indicated that the old did not differ from the young in the time needed to scan each item in memory. The aged were slower at encoding the probe (d) and slower at response processes (c). Fort *et al.* suggested that the slowing with more difficult items at the response end could result from uncertainty in initial stimulus evaluation followed by 'slowness to initiate the response, slowness to move, or in a tendency to re-evaluate items in memory' (p. 457). The failure of P3 to indicate an age-related increase in memory scanning time was the surprising finding. Since there were no group differences in error rate, the P3 in the aged subjects did not appear to be due to 'shallow' processing. Also, the correlation of RT and P3 latency was significant for all four set sizes for the young, but only for set size one for the aged. The authors suggested that the breakdown of the correlation of RT and P3 latencies on difficult tasks may be a subtle indication of cognitive decline.

This study has been followed by several others of ERPs and memory performance on the Sternberg task in the aged, particularly targeting the P3 slope findings. Pfefferbaum *et al.* (1980a) asked if the P3 did not correlate with RT in aged subjects because of variability of the timing of the P3 in each sweep of the EEG (i.e. from trial to trial). If this temporal jitter occurs, then the P3 in the averaged ERP will be reduced in amplitude and the P3 latency measure could be less valid. A trial-by-trial analysis was conducted to evaluate the group differences in P3 latency, and the correlation of P3 with RT. By examining each sweep of EEG with the Woody Filter technique, these authors concluded that the reduction in the P3 amplitude often observed in aged subjects was not due to temporal jitter of the P3 across sweeps. In fact, the younger subjects' P3s increased in amplitude with filtering, indicating more temporal jitter in the young subjects' data. The trial-by-trial analysis of the correlation of P3 to RT in young versus aged subjects also revealed that the young showed a positive correlation and the aged did not. As in the earlier study, RT latency increased more with larger set size for the aged subjects than it did for the young. The latency of the aged subjects' P3 only increased from set size 1 to 2 and then actually decreased slightly from set size 2 to 4. Ford *et al.* (1982) also asked if the finding for P3 slope (Ford *et al.*, 1979; Pfefferbaum *et al.*, 1980a) was due to ceiling effects of P3 latency for the aged subjects. To test this hypothesis, they added a degraded stimulus condition to the standard Sternberg paradigm. Although the P3 was delayed for both groups in the degraded condition, only the young subjects showed a consistent increase in P3 latency with increased set size, as in earlier studies. The older subjects' P3 did not increase in latency from set size 2 to 4. Also, as before, the P3 and RT were correlated for the younger subjects (for non-degraded, inset trials), but not for the older subjects.

Strayer, Wickens and Braune (1987) investigated whether the age-related differences in information processing speed, reflected by the P3 and RT on a Sternberg task, would be affected by manipulations of speed versus accuracy instructions and verbal versus spatial stimuli. Verbal stimuli were letters of the alphabet and spatial stimuli were made up of 14 connected lines. As before, the aged subjects' P3 latency slope across memory set size was not greater than that of the young. In fact, the older subjects showed a significantly smaller effect of set size than the younger subjects. RT was affected by manipulations of speed–accuracy, age, and memory load. As in earlier studies, the RT had a greater memory load slope for the older subjects, but there was no age by speed–accuracy interaction.

Looren de Jong *et al.* (1987) manipulated memory load (two versus four items) in a variation of the Sternberg task designed to study memory and attention in young and aged adults. In the high-memory-load condition the older subjects had smaller P3s than in the easier condition. The RTs were slower for both groups with more items in memory, and the old were slower than the young only in the easier condition. In the high-load condition the aged subjects were actually faster than the young, but had more omission errors.

Pratt *et al.* (1989) compared three types of stimuli in a study of aging on a variation of the Sternberg task. Memory sets were: (1) digits presented visually, (2) digits presented auditorily, and (3) musical notes presented acoustically.

As in previous studies, the latency of RT, but not P3, was delayed more for the aged subjects by larger memory set sizes.

Bashore, Osman and Heffley (1989) approached the problem of slowing in the elderly by performing a meta-analysis on data from speeded reaction-time studies, and a second analysis on reaction time and P3 data from ERP studies of aging. Their method, taken from Cerella (1985), was chosen to distinguish between additive and proportional models of age-related slowing. If slowing is primarily in the peripheral nervous system, slowing in performance will be additive (a fixed increase) across levels of task difficulty. If, however, the slowing is primarily occurring in the central nervous system the increase in latency of performance measures will be proportional to the complexity of the task. The meta-analyses consisted of comparing young and aged group mean reaction times and P3s from a variety of studies. The extent to which the slope of these data points increased from a positive slope of 1.0 determined whether the data were interpreted as reflecting an additive or proportional model. The reaction-time data in both analyses showed an increased slope from 1.0, indicating more centralized slowing for the elderly with more difficult tasks. Since the P3 data, however, did not show a greater slope with task difficulty, they concluded that age differences were not due exclusively to central nervous system factors. There was a constant (or additive) increment for the P3 measures across levels of task difficulty, indicating slowing at an earlier stage of processing. Generally then, these meta-analyses led to conclusions that were consistent with the studies reviewed above, that the RT and P3 data each lead to different interpretations of when and where slowing is occurring.

In summary, the ERP studies of memory on the Sternberg and 'Sternberg-like' tasks have consistently found that the RT, rather than the P3, shows an age-related increase in memory scanning time per item held in memory. It is possible that the absence of a P3 latency slope with difficulty for aged subjects in some of these studies is due to an unknown age-related methodological problem. What is clear, however, is that no study shows a greater slope of P3 latency for elderly subjects than young subjects. If P3 latency is the ERP indicator of relative stimulus evaluation time, then the age-related slowing appears to occur during the encoding of the stimulus (Ford *et al.*, 1979) and during response-related processes (Ford *et al.*, 1979; Pfefferbaum *et al.*, 1980a; Ford *et al.*, 1982; Strayer, Wickens and Braune, 1987). Thus, in contrast to the RT data, the P3 data indicate no increase in memory scanning time associated with normal aging. Consistent with this conclusion, Ford *et al.* (1982) observed that age-related slowing of P3 occurred when the discrimination of the stimulus was made more difficult, rather than when the decision of which way to respond was made more difficult.

A study of memory on the Sternberg task in children and young adults (Harris, 1974) has demonstrated that the slope of memory scanning time does not change on the Sternberg task when comparing ages 8, 16, and 24 years.

The intercept of the slope, however, was shorter in duration with increasing age, indicating a decrease in encoding time and a stable memory scanning time with development to adulthood. These results combined with those of Strayer, Wickens and Braune (1987), Ford *et al.* (1979, 1982) and Pfefferbaum *et al.* (1980a) suggest that memory scanning time on the Sternberg does not change across the life-span, while encoding time shows a U function.

Preliminary data collected in our laboratory support the Ford *et al.* (1979) conclusion that early stimulus encoding processes are slowed in elderly subjects. When a simple auditory oddball Go/NoGo task was compared with a simple RT task it was possible to compare the timing of the NA component in elderly and young subjects. The NA component has been described in visual paradigms (Ritter *et al.*, 1982) and auditory paradigms (Novack *et al.*, in press) where the ERP to the frequent stimulus in a choice RT task is compared with the ERP to the same stimulus in a simple RT task in which the subject is responding in the same way on each trial. The NA has been interpreted as reflecting an early pattern-recognition or stimulus-identification process which precedes and affects the timing of later processes such as stimulus classification (Ritter *et al.*, 1982).

The subjects were seven aged subjects (mean age = 80) and four young (mean age = 33). The auditory oddball consisted of a 1500 Hz stimulus presented 20% of the time (target) and a 500 Hz stimulus presented 80% of the time. The same stimuli were presented in the simple RT condition, but the subjects responded in the same way on every trial. The tones were 100 ms in duration, and 90 dB (SPL).

The ERPs and RTs averaged across subjects in each group are presented in Figure 8.1. The top tracing, superimposing the young normal and elderly ERPs to the 80% frequent tone in the simple response condition, recorded at Fz, shows no delay of N1 for the aged (the darker tracing). The NA subtraction (Fz) immediately below shows an earlier, larger-amplitude peak for the young subjects. The third set of tracings show a small delay in the N2 component (Fz) for the aged (subtraction of ERP to 20% minus ERP to 80%, in the Go/NoGo condition). Below the N2, the P3 delay for the aged subjects is displayed, recorded at the Pz electrode in the Go/NoGo condition. The bottom tracing shows an ogival curve of reaction times for both subjects, also showing a small delay for the aged subjects.

The line graph in Figure 8.2 displays the average peak latencies of these components, showing no age-related delay for the N1 component, but a 25 ms delay for the NA, which accounts for at least 50% of the age-related delay in the later components. Even though the stimuli were all well above threshold, the relationship of individual threshold differences and latency of NA has not been examined. However, if threshold levels were to account for all of the change in NA, then there should have been a group difference in the N1 as well.

Early encoding processes may be delayed owing to age-related central

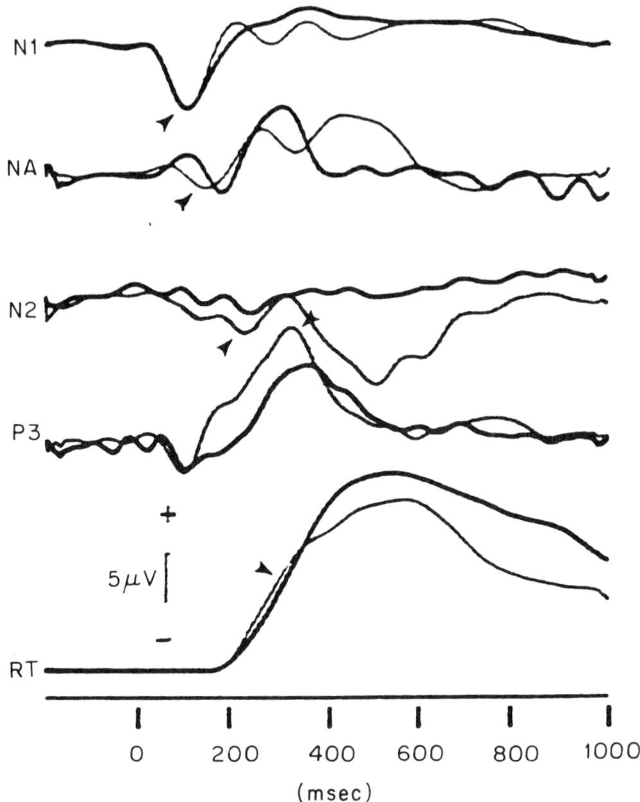

Figure 8.1. Young (thin line) and elderly (thick line) grand mean ERPs and RTs. Arrows indicate components of interest on the young ERP waveform.

nervous system factors. The neural noise hypothesis (Layton, 1975; Welford, 1981) suggested that cognitive processing in the elderly is delayed owing to an increased amount of background noise in the perceptual system, and/or reduced power of the signal to be processed. Using incomplete figures with added visual noise, Cremer and Zeef (1987) provided support for this hypothesis in the normal elderly. Also, Cremer (in preparation) demonstrated that auditory noise had a greater effect on early processing rather than later, in elderly, compared with young subjects. These studies of encoding processes in the normal elderly are consistent with the NA finding presented above, that early processes may be slowed, resulting in delays in later processing.

In the Sternberg memory studies discussed earlier, the increase in response-related processing time has been interpreted as elderly 'conservatism' (Strayer,

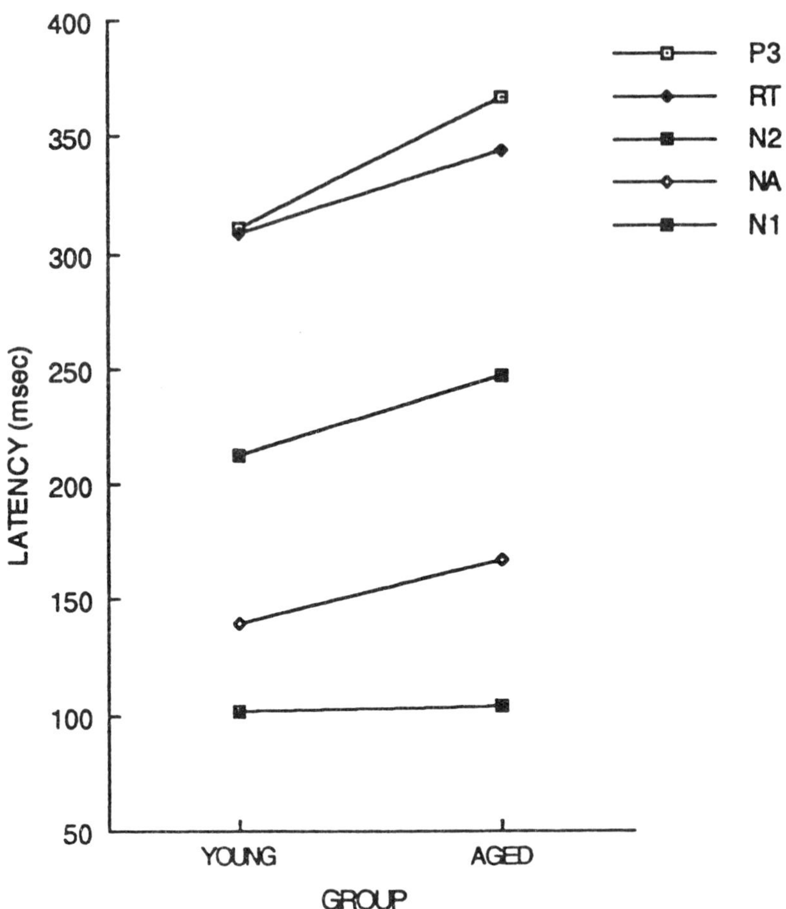

Figure 8.2. Average latencies of each component and RT for young and elderly subjects.

Wickens and Braune, 1987); that is, the aged need more information before responding. If they are less confident (Ford *et al.*, 1979) they may spend time re-evaluating their decision before responding, and take longer to make the response.

It is possible that the aged subjects have slower RTs because difficult tasks use up available resources needed to prepare for the motor response. On simple tasks the elderly may have a slower encoding time (indicated by the Sternberg paradigm studies reviewed above, and the NA findings) which accounts for the slower response time. With increasing task difficulty, however, encoding and memory scanning time may remain stable, with an increasing response time owing to the reduction of available resources needed to prepare for the motor response. Studies by Jennings *et al.* (see pp. 715–717) have found age differences in peripheral vascular change in certain task situations. This age-related reduction in vasoconstriction is interpreted as a reduction in response preparation. Since this age difference occurs only in certain task situations, it could be due to resource limitations in more difficult situations.

The conclusion that memory scanning time does not increase with age is consistent with a series of studies of memory for words by Grober and Buschke (Bushke and Grober, 1986; Grober and Bushke, 1987). These authors found that elderly subjects' free recall is lower than in the young, but when the elderly are given enriched cueing procedures their total recall (free + cued) is no different from that of young subjects. Thus, in the normal elderly, memory is preserved, but processes associated with storing and retrieving the words (e.g. elaboration and attention) are less efficient in the normal elderly.

Recently correlations have been obtained between the amplitude of certain components and memory performance in the young and elderly. Donchin, Miller and Farwell (1986) reported that normal elderly subjects with small P3 amplitudes on simple ERP tasks had significantly lower scores on tests of memory for familiar pairs of digits compared with normal elderly with large P3 amplitudes. Friedman and Hamberger (in press) compared young, middle-aged, and elderly adults on a continuous-recognition task. They found that young and middle-aged adults had a larger positive SW for 'new' items that were remembered later, compared with those that were not remembered. The elderly subjects, however, did not show this amplitude enhancement for items subsequently remembered, suggesting an age-related deficit in the encoding of 'new' stimuli.

ATTENTION AND AGING

It has been proposed that aged subjects display deficits in tasks requiring more cognitive capacity: especially controlled processing (Hoyer and Plude, 1980) and/or divided attention tasks (Craik, 1977). More capacity is needed in controlled processing tasks that vary the response and/or stimulus display so that the same stimuli or class of stimuli are not always associated with the same response. Automatic processes are often sufficient to perform tasks that are highly repetitive and that have a reduced amount of variable response requirement.

An earlier study by Tecce *et al.* (1982) addressed the issue of attentional capacity in the elderly by measuring the CNV rebound of elderly subjects compared with the young. The CNV (contingent negative variation) is a fronto-central long-duration slow negative wave that occurs after a warning stimulus as the subject prepares to respond to the next stimulus. In one condition of the experiment the trials consisted only of a warning stimulus followed by a second stimulus. In a second condition, the trials alternated between a simple task (waiting for an auditory cue to respond) and a dual task (waiting for a cue and monitoring three letters to be remembered). The CNV rebound occurred in the second condition in young adult subjects on the simple task trials. The CNV rebound was the increased amplitude of the CNV on the simple task in Condition 2 compared with Condition 1. The failure of the aged subjects to show this rebound effect was interpreted as an age-related difficulty with switching sets—from a divided-attention task to a simple task.

In studies of selective attention that use reaction-time measures, the efficiency of selective-attention processes is inferred from the degree to which prolonged RTs occur when the number of non-target stimuli are increased. The 'display size effect' is that older subjects, compared with young adults, have more difficulty ignoring irrelevant information as the number of items in the display increases (Layton, 1975; Rabbitt, 1965; Rabbitt, 1980). A series of studies, designed to test whether the aging individual had deficits in 'selective search' for relevant information, or deficits in 'selective filtering' of the irrelevant information (Wright and Elias, 1979; Farkas and Hoyer, 1980; Madden, 1983; Plude and Hoyer, 1986), have shown that searching for targets when the location is unknown is the specific age-related deficit in the display size effect.

In an ERP study of aging and visual search strategies, Looren de Jong *et al.* (1988) manipulated the uncertainty of the location of the target with three experimental conditions—fixed, moving, or random location. In all conditions targets and non-targets were letters, and the possible locations for the target formed a large circle in the middle of the display. The subject's task was to search the display for the target, and then make a finger lift response indicating the presence or absence of the target. In the fixed condition, the target was in the same location in the display on every trial; in the moving condition the target would move one place clockwise from trial to trial; and in the random condition the target location was randomly varied on each trial. Learning of each task was assessed over five blocks of 20 trials. In all conditions the P3 and posterior positive SW were smaller in amplitude in the aged subjects and both groups showed a larger posterior positive SW in the random condition. There was a negative SW at Cz for the aged subjects in the random condition, which was interpreted as an indication of difficulty with the allocation of visual attention resources.

Although the older subjects' RTs and latencies to fixation were slightly slower overall than those of the young, there was no difference in latency of the P3 between the groups, overall or in the more difficult conditions. If P3 is a measure of stimulus evaluation time, this indicates that the search process did not take longer for the elderly subjects, but that they were slower in responding. The similarity between this finding and the series of Sternberg studies reviewed above is interesting: while the amplitude of the P3 is reduced for the aged subjects in all conditions, the P3 latency is not delayed by more difficult search tasks.

A study of visual selective attention and aging that did not have a search component (Schroeder and Harter, in preparation) found that P3 responses to stimuli in relevant locations and RT responses to targets occurred in the old later than in the young. An earlier negativity, N325, was reduced in amplitude to relevant locations for the aged compared with young subjects. Since this task was relatively easy (compared with a Sternberg memory paradigm or a visual search task), it was expected that with practice, the aged ERP relevance effects and RTs would approach those of the young. Over practice trials, however, the young subjects' components (N325 and P3) and RT decreased in latency while the aged subjects' latencies remained the same. This study suggests that the elderly are slower in the neural coding of relevant locations in space, compared with the young, as well as slower in responding to the target stimuli. While the task in this study was easier than the search task described above, the stimuli were smaller and located 10 degrees to the left and right of fixation, compared with the larger stimuli processed in the fovea in the search study reviewed above. The delays of the elderly in the Schroeder and Harter study may be more prominent because the stimuli were more difficult to discriminate, which would indicate differential age-related slowing in encoding processes.

In summary, the ERP studies reviewed here suggest that age-related slowing occurs in early stimulus encoding processes, as well as in later processes. The surprising, but well replicated finding of no increase in P3 latency slope of aged subjects with increased memory load, while the RT increases as expected, suggests that memory scanning time indexed by the P3 in the Sternberg tasks may be relatively stable over the adult life-span. Also, in the visual search task, the ERP latency measures showed no delays for aging subjects, and only the RT increased in the more difficult condition. P3 latency measures, then, have failed to support earlier behavioral studies of the elderly on memory scanning and visual search tasks. We have suggested that the discrepancy between the P3 and RT latency effects of task difficulty in the elderly may be due to age-related capacity reductions, resulting in a slowing of the aged subjects' ability to prepare a motor response. The P3 and SW amplitude reductions reported in elderly subjects on more difficult tasks may be indicants of age-related resource limitations.

ACKNOWLEDGEMENT

This work was supported in part by NIH grants NS19234 and HD10804.

Autonomic Nervous System Indices

J. Richard Jennings
Department of Psychiatry, University of Pittsburgh, PA 15213, USA

and

Nancy Yovetich
Department of Psychology, University of North Carolina, Chapel Hill, NC 27510, USA

INTRODUCTION

Our examination of the event-related potential suggested that in certain task situations some components were slowed more by age than were others. If specific cognitive processes are related to components, then these results question the view that a slowing of *all* central processes is the root of performance changes with age. We have not shown, however, that general slowing or functional changes which influence multiple processes do not occur with age. The autonomic and endocrine systems influence metabolic energy. Thus, changes in these systems might be expected to alter a number of central processes or to influence motivational and emotional processes that then would interact with central processing in influencing performance. As suggested in our introductory section, progress in understanding autonomic and endocrine interactions with central processing may depend on the development of a conceptual scheme which replaces that previously provided by general arousal theory. Our examination of aging and the autonomic psychophysiology of information processing starts by introducing a candidate conceptualization.

A WORKING FRAMEWORK FOR THE PSYCHOPHYSIOLOGY OF AGING

For purposes of organizing our discussion and providing a possible framework for future work in aging, we have developed Figure 8.3. The figure suggests major influences upon psychophysiological responses and incorporates a specific approach to the psychophysiological changes which occur during information processing. This cognitive–energetic approach will be discussed after we review some more general features of the psychophysiological

Handbook of Cognitive Psychophysiology: Central and Autonomic Nervous System Approaches.
Edited by J. R. Jennings and M. G. H. Coles.

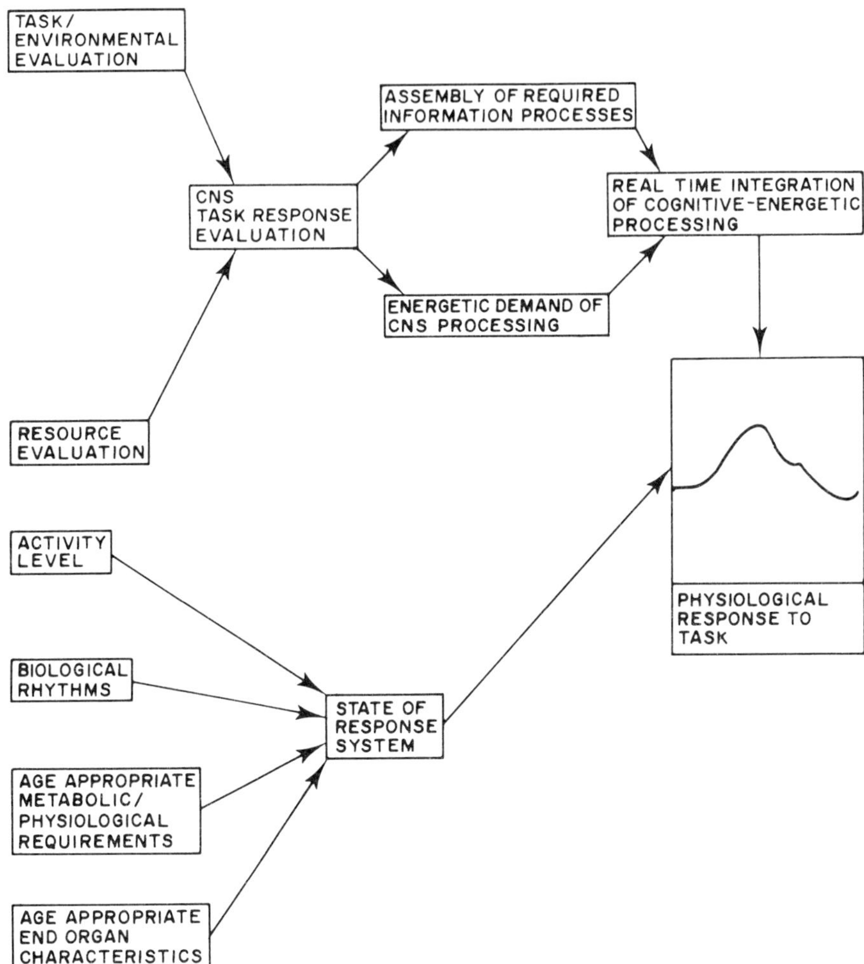

Figure 8.3. Diagram of factors which contribute to physiological responses during information processing. Aging is depicted as influencing the state of the physiological system as well as the assembly of information processes.

responses of the old. Figure 8.3 depicts major factors which contribute to the physiological response to an information processing task. The figure suggests age-related factors in basic physiological functioning and incorporates a temporal sequence for cognitive–energetic integration. The CNS is depicted as continuously monitoring its internal resources and external environment. Recognition of a task is followed by the assembly of relevant information processes and contingent energetic demands. Task processing then elicits both information flow and energetic responses. The observable indices of the energetic response are, however, constrained by the current state of the response system. Transient factors such as activity level and biological rhythms are shown as factors influencing the response system. Age is diagrammed as a factor altering end-organ characteristics (e.g. vessel wall stiffness, sensory transmission) as well as metabolic/physiological functioning (e.g. availability of muscarinic transmitters). The diagram envisions two types of aging effects—one on the state of the response system and one on the assembly of information processes. As we saw in the last part of the chapter, in examining changes in sensory transmission time using event-related potentials, the figure could be expanded to emphasize changes in sensory as well as response systems. Sensory changes, however, would effect the task/environment evaluation (upper left in figure) more directly than the organismic state (bottom diagram). For a psychologist, the state of the response system is less interesting than changes in central processing. A general understanding of basal changes in physiological functioning and changes in overall responsivity is, however, critical to the interpretation of more discrete, process-specific psychophysiological responses. Thus, we turn next to a brief review of changes with age in basal and overall autonomic responsivity to tasks. Through our use of a cognitive–energetic approach we will subsequently ask questions about the information processing of the elderly. Do older individuals assemble and execute information processes that are different from those in younger individuals? Is this evident in altered 'real-time' energetic responses?

AGE DIFFERENCES IN TONIC REACTIONS TO PROCESSING TASKS

Age induces global changes in cardiovascular function and reactivity that we should recognize before examining brief, phasic responses to task events in the young and old. The first type of change is that of basal functioning. This change may alter the physiological capacity for brief reactions and is an alternate explanation for any effects of age on responses to information processing tasks. Between adulthood and old age, basal functioning does indeed change—blood pressure increases, the heart becomes mildly enlarged and less compliant, contraction time is increased, and the ventricles fill more slowly (Lakatta, 1983). These changes are mild, however, and the cardiovascular system remains responsive to physiological and psychological challenges. Functionally, resting and exercising cardiac output are well maintained with age in the absence of coronary artery disease (Walsh, 1987). This functional similarity between age-groups, however, masks some major underlying changes. Endocrine and neural control of the heart and vasculature is largely exerted via adrenergic and cholinergic systems. With age, responsivity to agents stimulating one form of adrenergic receptor (beta-adrenergic) is diminished, as is responsivity to agents stimulating muscarinic receptors—a form of cholinergic receptor (Lakatta, 1983; Pfeifer *et al.*, 1983). Concomitantly, circulating levels of norepinephrine and sometimes epinephrine are elevated in the elderly (Ziegler, Lake and Kopin, 1976; Jennings, Stiller and Brock, 1988). These changes in level may compensate for the reduced sensitivity to beta-adrenergic stimulation and/or for reduced sensitivity of reflex pressor adjustments via the baroreceptors (Lakatta, 1983, Pfeifer *et al.*, 1983).

For the psychophysiologist, some grasp of the relative importance of the aging of basal cardiovascular function can be derived by examining whether pre-task baselines relate to task-induced changes. A brief examination of tonic changes will also suggest whether such responses reflect any general changes in autonomic responsivity with age.

Base to task change correlations do not seem to systematically differ between young and old groups of volunteers. If baseline values constrained the responses of the elderly, correlations between base and change across young and old groups should be substantial, while correlations within groups should fall. Data from two related experiments using young and old men were examined to test this hypothesis (Jennings, Brock and Nebes, 1989; Jennings, Stiller and Brock, 1988).

Average levels during a reaction-time task performed in loud noise were correlated with baseline values collected prior to the performance session. Negative relationships between baseline and change values were consistently observed for heart rate (scored as interbeat interval), pulse transit time, vascular slope and amplitude measures. Correlations across and within the groups were generally of similar magnitude and the young and old showed essentially equivalent correlations within their groups. Table 8.1 shows these results.

Table 8.1. Base to change correlations for young and old averaged across two experiments for cardiac and vascular variables.

	Group		
	Young	Old	Combined
IBI	−0.86	−0.58	−0.61
PTT–thumb	−0.53	−0.61	−0.32
Slope–thumb	−0.68	−0.54	−0.37
PTT–impedance	−0.70	−0.52	−0.36
Slope–impedance	−0.49	−0.64	−0.60
PWV	−0.54	−0.56	−0.50

IBI - inter-beat-interval; PTT = pulse transit time; PWV = pulse wave velocity. Slope refers to the maximum, systolic rise per unit time for either a thumb photoplethysmograph or chest impedance signal. PTT is measured from the r wave of the electrocardiogram to the time of maximum systolic slope for each measure. PWV is the time between impedance and thumb maximum slopes divided into the distance between sites. Correlations were converted to fisher Z scores, averaged, and then re-expressed as correlations.

Despite changes in average functioning between age-groups, the level of functioning does not seem to constrain the reactivity of older volunteers. A similar conclusion was drawn by Rogers *et al.* (1985). They reported that changes in cerebral vasomotor reactions were correlated with baseline blood flow in a sample ranging from 35 to 86 years of age. Reactions to oxygen inhalation, although declining with age, were not, however, explained by these baseline differences.

Overall reactivity may still differ between age-groups despite any absence of constraint by basal functioning. Prior to drawing any inferences of specific deficits related to information processing, we should know whether declines in a responsivity with age occur with all challenges which induce change. In fact, autonomic reactions to both physical and psychological challenges tend to decrease with age. Different response systems do not always show similar changes, however. Dampened responses of both heart rate and pupillary change suggest a consistent decrease in vagally controlled responses (Morris and Thompson, 1969; Jennings, Brock and Nebes, 1990; Pfeifer *et al.*, 1983). Heart rate responses to hand grip and exercise also appear to be damped with age (Sachs, Hamberger and Kaijser, 1985; Fleg, Tzankoff and Lakatta, 1985). Baroreceptor-mediated changes in blood pressure seem to decline, while pressor responses to sustained hand-grip at 30% of maximal voluntary contraction are maintained over age (Vita *et al.*, 1986; Sachs, Hamberger and Kaijser, 1985). Thus, responses to physical challenges appear to show declines in vagal functions, and in some but not all sympathetic functions. Vascular responses may not show the general pattern of decline in responsivity.

Responses to psychological challenge show some similarities to the responses to physical challenges. Heart rate changes are diminished with age in tasks ranging from shock avoidance to orienting to tone stimuli (Gintner, Hollandsworth and Intrieri, 1986; Harbin and Berg, 1983; Garwood, Engel and Capriotti, 1982; Podlesny and Dustman, 1982; Morris and Thompson, 1969). Interestingly, memory tasks seem to yield equal or greater changes in heart rate among old relative to young participants (Powell, Milligan and Furchtgott, 1980; Riege, Cohen and Wallach, 1980; Jennings, Nebes and Yovetich, 1990). In contrast to the heart rate changes, task levels of blood pressure relative to pre-task levels seem similar between age-groups (Jennings, Brock and Nebes, 1989; Gintner, Hollandsworth and Intrieri, 1986) or change is greater in older groups (Powell, Milligan and Furchtgott, 1980; Garwood, Engel and Capriotti, 1982). Relatively increased pressor changes among the old were observed in memory, arithmetic, cold pressor, and exercise tasks, while equivalent responses were observed in perceptual–motor tasks. A series of experiments from our laboratory examined a set of other vascular measures—transit times to chest impedance and thumb vascular signals, pulse wave velocity, and systolic slope of these signals (Jennings, Brock and Nebes, 1989). Generally, base to task changes in these variables were similar for college men and men in their sixties. Despite diversity of tasks and samples, these studies generally suggest declines in tonic heart rate reactivity but maintained vascular reactivity.

A decline in neural receptor functions, less central activation among the old, or less responsive cardiac pacemakers among the old, are suggested by the low tonic heart rate responsivity of the elderly. Definitive evidence is not available to choose among these alternatives, but reviews suggest that reduced muscarinic and beta-adrenergic receptor sensitivity with age are more consistent results than anatomic/physiologic change within the cardiac tissue (Docherty, 1986; Goldberg, Kreider and Roberts, 1984). Assuming an adrenergic mediation, the maintained vascular changes suggest little change or enhanced alpha and beta sympathetic activation, equal or greater central activation, or more responsive vascular tissue. A decrease in central activation—the degree of task involvement of the volunteer—must be presumed to explain cardiac changes; yet, an increase in central activation would be required to explain vascular changes. This inconsistency questions the central activation alternative. Thus, either end-organ or transmitter function seems implicated. Merging the physiological and psychophysiological data suggests that vascular change with age may predominantly be a decline in sensitivity to beta sympathetic activity combined with major anatomic changes in the vasculature (Docherty, 1986; Yin, 1980). The preponderance of evidence suggests that alpha-adrenergic influences on the vasculature may decline less than beta-adrenergic or even remain unaltered with age (Docherty, 1986; Duckles, Carter and Williams, 1985). Owing to major species differences in neural control and the difficulty of such studies, however, definitive interpretation must await further study.

A COGNITIVE–ENERGETIC MODEL FOR INTEGRATING AGE CHANGES IN AUTONOMIC RESPONSE WITH INFORMATION PROCESSING DIFFERENCES

A conceptual approach to interpreting physiological changes during information processing is needed as well as the physiological background we have just discussed. In terms of our framework in Figure 8.3, we are now moving to specify more exactly how the central processing of information may become integrated with autonomic peripheral changes—the upper section of the diagram. We suggest a cognitive–energetic approach. The approach brings together processing capacity approaches to information processing and altered psychophysiological views of the physiological changes during cognitive processing (Hockey, Gaillard and Coles, 1986; and Chapter 2 in this volume). In his seminal monograph Kahneman (1973) discussed attention as arising from a limitation on how much information could be processed at the same time. The limitation was seen as arising from two sources: the anatomical limitations of our sensory and motor systems (e.g. inability to focus the fovea on two widely spaced objects at once) and a limitation on a central processing system. Capacity of the central system was seen as limited by the availability of a single processing resource whose allocation could be monitored using autonomic (pupillary) measures. Different information processing tasks were seen as requiring differing allocations of the processing resource. Kahneman's formulation thus suggested that the same central resource supported different processes. Allocation of this resource induced autonomic change, which in turn was conceived in a unitary fashion consistent with general arousal theory (see Kahneman and Treisman, 1984, for an updated view).

Empirical difficulties with both the unitary conception of processing capacity and of autonomic change have led to modifications of capacity theory. The modifications generally posit more than one type of processing resource and more than one type of arousal. Psychophysiologists have tended to find specific autonomic changes during information processing rather than general arousal changes (e.g. Jennings, 1986a,b; and from a different perspective, Neiss, 1988). Performance psychologists have found that task combinations and task difficulty levels do not yield results uniformly compatible with a single, limited processing resource. Most revisions of capacity theory have been by performance psychologists and these revisions do not link autonomic responses and capacity as closely as Kahneman did. Indeed, resources are often conceived of as processes (e.g. working memory) or as brain space (see Wickens, 1984). These developments are reviewed well in Heemstra (1988) and Wickens (1984). We shall have the space to examine only one view briefly that does provide a clear cognitive–energetic link.

Sanders (e.g. 1981) and Gopher (1986) have proposed a cognitive–energetic model which relates active information processing to different energetic states. Energetic states are divided into arousal, effort, and activation states following Pribram and McGuinness (1975). These states are then mapped into information processing stages identified with reaction-time tasks (e.g. stimulus processing, motor adjustment). A diagram of this model and further discussion may be found in Chapter 1 of this volume. In general the model suggests that neither 'arousal' nor 'performance' is unitary; that is, a single manipulation will not equally influence any measure of either performance or arousal. Varieties of energetic processes map specifically on to varieties of information processes. This then suggests that task variables or physiological changes, such as those occurring during aging, may influence a particular type of information processing because of their effect on the energetic resource. Similarly influences upon the level of cognitive functioning, such as fatigue, emotional involvement, and degree of incentive motivation, can be related to a subset of information processes directly influenced. In short, modulatory influences on the information processing machinery are represented directly.

Intensity adjustments of the information processes are themselves controlled in the model by the evaluation function. The function incorporates feedback to direct the effort mechanism to adjust the energetic relationship between activation and arousal, and thus the energetic support for the different information processes. Well-practiced performance is, however, expected to show rather stable energetic support with a maintained degree and intensity of mapping between the three energetic resources and the specific information processes drawing on them.

The model is a prospectus for research rather than a summary of existing results. Wickens (1984) provides a useful discussion of the methodological difficulties in isolating and describing a resource for a particular task. For the psychophysiologist, a resource once isolated must further be related to a physiological response. If all of this is successful, however, the physiological index has the potential to assess resource allocation within a single task without the cumbersome dual-task/resource operating characteristic methodology used to assess resource allocation behaviorally (see Chapter 2). Steps toward such use of autonomic measures are reviewed in Beatty (1982) and Jennings (1986a,b).

A direct application of the Sanders/Gopher model to changes in heart rate during a complex reaction-time task is provided by van der Molen *et al.* (1987) (see also Chapter 1 in this volume). Utilization of the different information processing stages was varied by manipulating stimulus quality, number of response alternatives, and foreperiod duration. Energetic variables were manipulated using both threat of electric shock and degree of task involvement. Beat-by-beat heart rate indices were the primary dependent variable. The mapping between processing stage and energetic resource (e.g. effort) was assessed from the interactive influences of task and energetic variables upon task-induced heart rate responses. In their results, anticipatory heart rate deceleration initiated a few seconds prior to the expected stimulus was interpreted as due to the action of effort coordinating the arousal and activation resources; while added deceleration immediately prior to the stimulus indicated the allocation of the activation resource.

These conclusions are an interesting illustration of Wickens' (1984) concern that physiological variables may often provide 'scalar' measures of resource allocation. Wickens' model of resources incorporates input modality, internal code, and response-specific resources as well as the stage-related resources of Sanders/Gopher. From this perspective, any task will call upon multiple resources all of which may influence the variance in a physiological output measure (e.g. heart rate). Thus, if the measure is a unidimensional 'scalar' it may only provide an index of a largely unknown combination of resources. The van der Molen *et al.* results suggest that the heart rate deceleration 'scalar' does reflect multiple resources, but that these can be identified if the task demands are reasonably well understood. Note, however, that Wickens and

Sanders would likely disagree on the specific interpretation of the two heart rate results. Wickens (1984) discusses the possibility of a hierarchy of resources that may include some resources more general than the specific resources noted above. Sanders' effort, activation, and arousal resources might be termed such general resources in Wickens' scheme. An interesting possibility is that the general (relatively more energetic) resources might be indexed well by autonomic variables while the specific (relatively more structural, brain space as opposed to energetic) resources might be indexed well by event-related potentials (cf. the preceding section of this chapter, and Chapter 2). Wickens (1984) discusses the use of event-related potentials to index resources allocated early in the processing of complex reaction-time tasks. Strayer, Wickens and Braune (1987) provide an important illustration of the application of this technique to aging. Slowing of specific processes was suggested by their analysis, as already discussed.

Within the aging literature, the possibility of a decline in processing capacity with age has been considered rather closely. Craik (1977) and Craik and Byrd (1983) have reviewed the literature suggesting a decline in general capacity—or as they stated it, 'mental energy'—with increasing age. Such a decline could well account for general slowing, providing a non-specific decline that would yield the overall slowing (see Salthouse, 1985). Older individuals have not, however, uniformly shown evidence of less ability than younger individuals to divide attention (Salthouse and Somberg, 1982). Furthermore, recent evidence from Craik's laboratory suggest that capacity is not acting as a unitary resource when age-groups are compared in memory tasks (Morris, Gick and Craik, 1988; Gick, Craik and Morris, 1988). Thus, within the aging literature as well as the general performance literature, capacity concepts are being scrutinized and revised.

CARDIOVASCULAR ENERGETIC SUPPORT ACROSS AGE

The application of a cognitive–energetic approach to the psychophysiology of aging may be particularly important given our intuition that both energy and cognition change with aging. Little data are available, however. We will only be able to review our own work—which was only imperfectly guided by current cognitive–energetic models. Note that cognitive–energetic interpretations must first take into account overall physiological changes with age in responsivity (see pp. 682–685). For example, presume that an anticipatory activation process induces an energetic response that we measure as a cardiac deceleration. A number of steps may help us show that the cognitive–energetic process is activated less strongly with age. We must first establish that this response occurs in somewhat comparable form in young and old. Task manipulations can then be performed to alter the degree to which the anticipatory process is required. Differential use of this process between age-groups might then be identified from within individual changes in deceleration relative to that in the initial task. If age differences for different manipulations do not preserve the proportional relation observed in the initial tasks, evidence for differential use is inferred. Inferences remain probabilistic, but the assumption of physiologically identical groups is not made. The details of this strategy will be clarified as the empirical work is reviewed.

We have performed a series of experiments comparing young and old men performing simple information processing tasks (Jennings, Brock and Nebes, 1989). Task-related beat-by-beat cardiovascular responses as well as overall base to task changes were examined. The series of experiments was designed (a) to determine whether the general arousal explanation of performance change with age is justified by physiological measures, and (b) to ascertain whether the young and old process tasks differently (i.e. use basic information processes to differing degrees). Beat-by-beat cardiovascular changes were used to infer the evocation of particular information processes, and self-reports attempted to separate changes in information processing strategy with age from changes in the ability to use different processes with age. Initial experiments employed stress–performance paradigms that induce changes in performance, which were previously interpreted as due to the induction of arousal. Subsequent experiments examined processes that appeared to be particularly vulnerable to aging. The strategy of comparing physiological changes induced by information processing both within and between age-groups is particularly important for the later work.

The influence of noise on attention to improbable events was examined in the first experiment. Solely behavioral experiments (e.g. Hockey, 1973) suggest that noise induces a generalized arousal which narrows the focus of attention. This narrowing leads the subject to perform less efficiently on improbable, low-salience aspects of the performance task. Improbable, low-salience events have been created in various ways, but we and Hockey (1973) chose events within the secondary task of a dual-task experiment. In our case volunteers added sequential numbers as a primary task, but also had to watch for lights occurring just before or after the numbers. A speeded reaction to the lights was required but the incentive pay for these reactions was less than that for the arithmetic task. Furthermore, the probability of a particular light array occurring after the number was set extremely low (p=0.05). In noise, responses to this low-frequency light should be relatively slow and inaccurate if the breadth of attention is reduced by any noise-induced arousal. Blood pressure, beat-by-beat measures of heart rate, as well as arterial and peripheral (thumb) pulse timing and amplitude were collected. A common arousal response in these variables should be induced by noise and such responses should be larger in older individuals if arousal is an explanation for performance changes in noise.

In our experiment noise appeared to narrow attention among young and middle-aged volunteers. The proportion of correct responses declined in noise for responses to the low- but not to the high-probability lights. Equating noise with general arousal leads to the conclusion that arousal narrowed attention for these volunteers. All volunteers did indeed report that noise (90 dB(A) pink noise) was mildly arousing. The physiological results, however, failed to support the interpretation that general arousal increased with noise. Heart rate increased slightly, but none of the vascular measures was altered relative to performance in a relative quiet condition (40 dB(A) pink noise).

Old volunteers did not appear over-aroused during task performance. Their performance on the low-probability lights was slowed but more accurate in noise than in quiet, and noise failed to induce larger physiological responses or more extreme self-reports in the old relative to the young. Thus, these results question the notion that changes in arousal account for performance changes due to noise or age.

Vascular changes in noise provided some hints about age differences in performance, but task-induced heart rate changes were not reliably affected by noise. Figure 8.4 shows the pulse transit-time results for noise relative to quiet conditions for the three age-groups in the study. Transit times decrease with neurally-induced constriction and stiffening of the blood vessels. Vasoconstrictive change at either the subclavian (SC) or thumb (TH) site is indicated by a negative difference score. Peripheral (thumb) transit time shortened with the combination of noise and biased probabilities in the young and middle-aged volunteers. Such a change is consistent with enhanced forearm muscular flow in preparation for speeded responses on the likely lights, and is also consistent with the observed relatively high error rates on the low-probability lights among these volunteers. In contrast, the older volunteers showed a lengthening of transit time in the same condition. This suggested a lack of specific preparation and, thus, the slow but relatively accurate responding on low-probability lights of this group. Vascular changes seem to be providing an energetic resource for response preparation that is present in younger, but not older, volunteers.

A second experiment (Jennings, Stiller and Brock, 1988) replicated the noise portion of the first experiment and added measures of endocrine change during noise. The rationale for this experiment was to test the reports of Eisdorfer, Nowlin and Wilkie (1970) that catecholamine changes indicated over-arousal in elderly individuals. By assessing such changes we can directly compare endocrine and electrophysiological indices of arousal. Basal differences in endocrine and electrophysiological results provided some support for general arousal differences between age-groups. However, once again the general arousal explanation of performance was brought into question by the disparity between inconsistent catecholamine reactions to the task–noise combination and consistent cardiovascular reactions. For example, heart rate increased with task engagement, but epinephrine was not

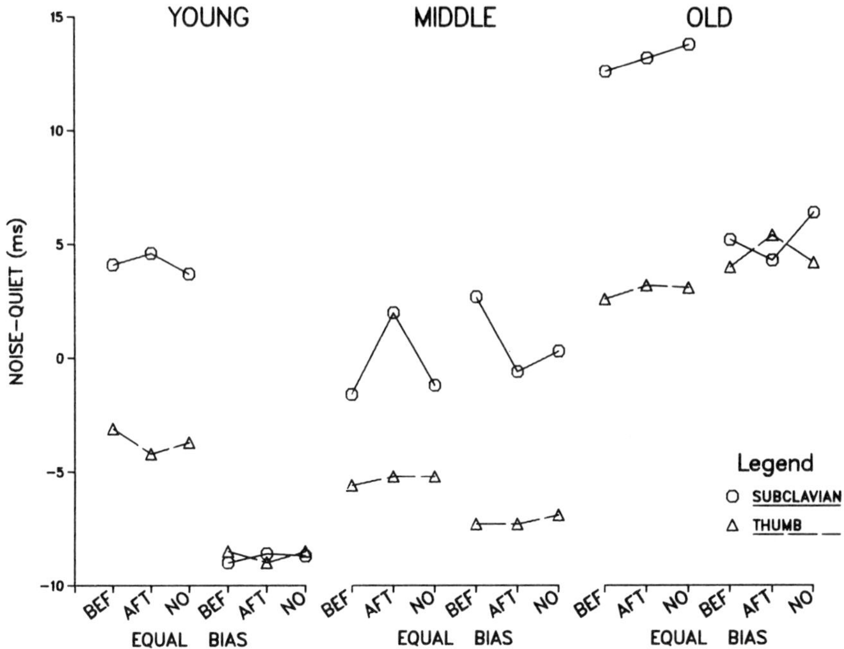

Figure 8.4. Differences between noise and quiet for the vascular pulse transit times from the r-wave to either a site superficial to the subclavian artery or to the thumb. Data are plotted separately for age groups, equal versus biased probability of response signals before or after the integer, and by signal timing or absence of a response signal. (Reproduced with permission. © Beech Hill Publishing.)

significantly altered. Importantly, this disparity occurred in the context of a performance difference: age-groups again responded to the low-probability stimuli differently. Proportion correct data suggested a narrowing of attention in the young but not the old. Vascular changes differed between groups for an impedance slope measure. This measure was, unfortunately, not collected in the prior experiment. Peripheral (thumb) signals did not differ as they had in the previous experiment. Thus, the replication of the cognitive–energetic result was equivocal.

Fortunately, a third look at the relationship between vascular change and probability bias is available from an experiment focusing on age changes in the ability to divide attention between dual tasks (Jennings, Brock and Nebes, 1990). With age, overall information processing capacity may decline (consistent with a general slowing view), a specific capability to divide attention may decline, or specific processes may be altered that are more readily identified when energetic resources are divided among tasks (see the discussions in Craik and Byrd, 1983, and Wickens, 1980). The same dual-task paradigm as in our prior work was used, but noise was not employed. Task emphasis was varied; on some experimental days the reaction-time task rather than the arithmetic task was defined as primary by instructions and payoffs. Within the reaction-time task, probabilities of light arrays again varied. When the reaction-time task was primary, the peripheral vascular differences were clear. Young volunteers vasoconstricted when probabilities were biased, but old volunteers did not. This replication of the result from the first experiment in the series increases our belief that peripheral vascular change provides an energetic resource for response preparation. Furthermore, older men seem less likely than younger men to engage this resource. They are capable of engaging the resource as indicated by their results when probabilities are equal. The remaining question is whether resource limitations or some other factors are inducing older men to show response preparation less readily than younger men.

Other aspects of the results from this experiment support the idea of specific changes in response preparation with age rather than a simple slowing. The timing of the signals for the reaction task had been varied to probe periods of differing resource requirements. Just before the presentation of an integer for the arithmetic task, sums had to be maintained while preparing for the next item; after integer presentation, integration of the new item and maintenance of the new sum was required. Performance, cardiac, and vascular results suggested that the young and old processed the pre-integer RT stimuli differently from the post-integer stimuli. The old tended to perform better in response to the pre-integer stimuli; while the young did better with the post-integer stimuli (as well as performing better overall than the old). The relative depth of cardiac deceleration just prior to the pre- and post-signals was directly related to the performance levels of the young and old. Furthermore, trial-to-trial variability of these cardiac responses was lower in the young than the old, but only after the integer presentation. These results, together with the vascular results, suggest that the young prepared more actively for the stimuli after the integer than did the old. Again we cannot discern the reasons for this, although older volunteers reported a preference for the arithmetic task and may have preferentially devoted capacity to maintaining correct sums. Such a strategy would detract from performance on the stimuli immediately following integer presentation. The evidence does suggest both cardiac and vascular energetic support for a response preparation strategy that differed between age-groups.

Despite these positive results, the manipulation of which task was primary failed to show major effects on either physiological or performance variables. With this dual task, both young and old appeared to divide attention relatively well. Response preparation strategies were identified, but major shifts in attention to one task or the other were not evident in either performance or physiological data. Such changes became evident only when we began to examine memory function in the young and old.

MEMORY AND ENERGETIC SUPPORT ACROSS AGE

Failing memory is a culturally anticipated trait of the elderly. Experimental work has, however, shown that older individuals perform reasonably well on tests of memory for meaningful events in the past, and reasonably well on simple memory span tests (Botwinick, 1980). The clearest deficits appear on rote memory of laboratory generated items. We chose to focus on memory retrieval of previously well-learned associations and on simple memory span. These skills should be relatively well maintained in the elderly, but the energetic resources required for their effective performance might be increased. From a psychophysiological perspective, memory maintenance is associated with cardiac acceleration (Lacey *et al.*, 1963; Jennings and Hall, 1980). Furthermore, memory requirements seem to combine additively with perceptual attention requirements to determine the degree of relative cardiac acceleration/deceleration (Lacey *et al.*, 1963). Thus, memory requirements can be detected in tasks which combine both attention and memory requirements. Conceptually, we anticipated that cardiac acceleration would indicate the commitment of an energetic resource to memory maintenance. Vascular measures were again taken both to identify whether the heart rate changes were vagal or sympathetic and to see if memory resources could be identified with a joint cardiac/vascular response pattern.

The first memory experiment (Jennings, Nebes and Brock, 1988) examined memory retrieval and again counterpoised arousal and specific task resource views. Eysenck (1977) suggested that noise-induced arousal altered the depth of retrieval leading to deficits in associative retrieval relative to performance in quiet conditions. If this were true and the elderly were assumed to be over-aroused, then the elderly should also show a deficit in associative retrieval. Old age and noise combined should be particularly deleterious if arousal mediates the narrowing of retrieval focus in both cases. College-aged men and men over sixty memorized lists of eight one-syllable words. Retrieval of each word was subsequently cued four times each with each of four different types of cues. Two were orthographic cues—the word itself and the first two letters of the word. The other two were associative cues previously shown to the subject—relatively weak associates and strong associates. Cueing took place 5 s after a warning stimulus which named the type of cue (e.g. name or associate). For one experimental day the task was performed in 90 dB(A) pink noise and for the other in relative quiet (50 dB(A)).

Both noise and age influenced associative retrieval errors, but their effects were not synergistic. Age and noise independently induced errors but no interaction was present. Thus, arousal could not be the single factor explaining both kinds of performance deficits. Similarly, mean levels of physiological variables failed to indicate a general arousal increase with noise or with age. Retrieval latency results reflected cue types but did not show age and noise

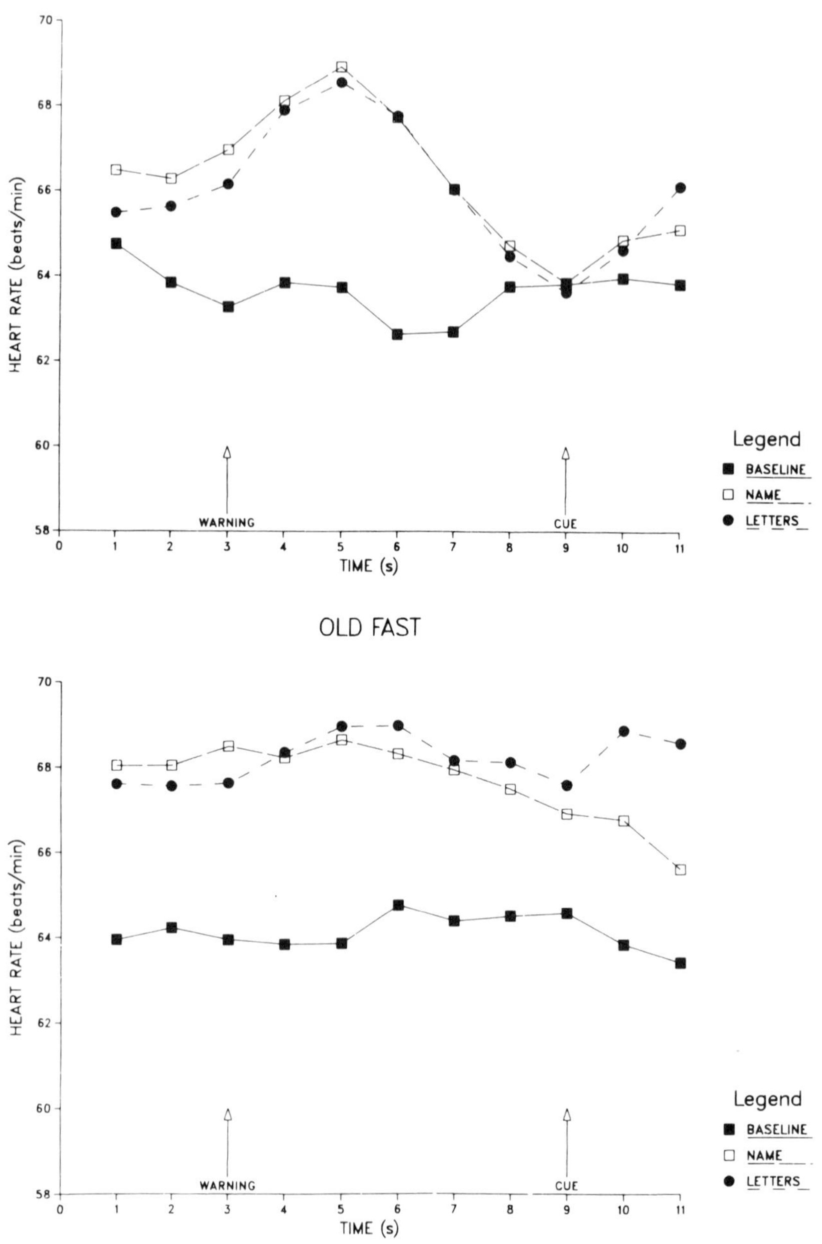

Figure 8.5. Second-by-second heart rate responses to the letter and word cues relative to baseline. The four panels show young and old separately and within each age group those responding relatively rapidly (latency <1140 ms) and relatively slowly (>1140) to the cues. Arrows indicate timing of the warning/prompt and the retrieval cue. (Reprinted with permission. © Society for Psychophysiological Research.)

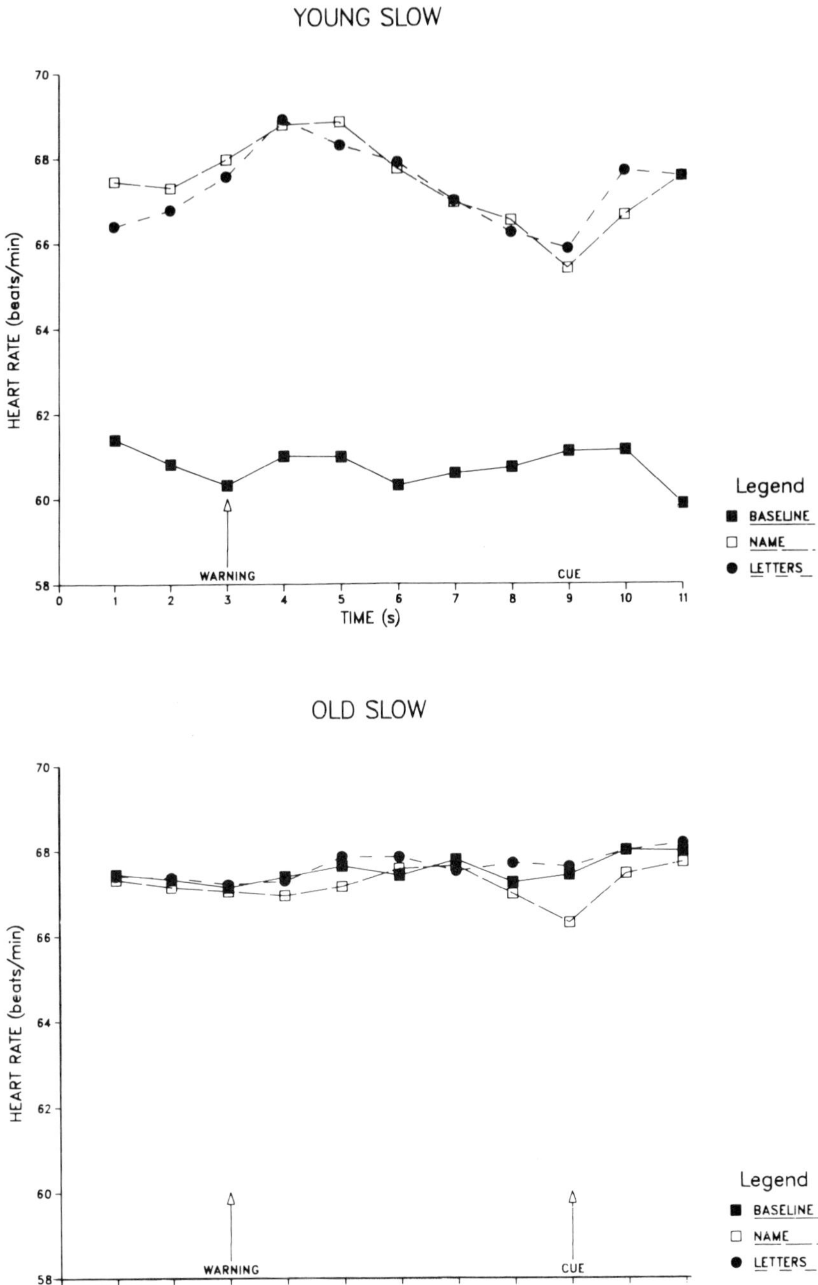

Figure 8.5 (*cont.*)

effects on associative minus orthographic differences. The age difference was, however, borne out in the heart rate results. Heart rate decelerated between the warning and the cue and was altered by cue type—deceleration was less with associative relative to orthographic warning stimuli. Figure 8.5 shows how this response differed between age-groups and within age-groups by level of performance (grouping by above and below median response latency). The results plotted are from the orthographic cue types during noise. Statistical differences were clearest for these data. Differences occurred both in changes relative to baseline and changes between cue types. For the young, good performance is associated with a robust deceleratory response, but little change in level between baseline and task. For the old, good performance is associated with a deceleratory response to both name and letter cues and a moderate change from baseline. The old, relatively poor performers show a striking failure to alter heart rate at all except for a minimal change prior to the 'name' cue. Vascular results suggested that older good performers maintained a peripheral vasoconstriction throughout the task; while younger good performers vasoconstricted only during associative cueing.

The primary conclusion from these results was that general arousal did not relate to performance, but cardiovascular change during task performance did. Moreover, these changes—and perhaps the processing inducing them—differed between young and old. The results also suggested a hypothesis that memory maintenance drew on a resource indicated by cardiac acceleration and peripheral vasoconstriction. The hypothesis was suggested by the results in Figure 8.5. Poor performance was associated with less task-induced deceleration; that is, the acceleratory influence of memory maintenance reduced deceleration related to attention. This could be due to memory rehearsal prior to the cue that followed the 'letter' warning stimulus among performers having difficulty maintaining the list in memory. The differences in this experiment were, however, relatively small and specific to certain cue types. An experiment directly examining memory maintenance was required in order to maintain a resource interpretation for such results.

The second memory experiment (Jennings, Nebes and Yovetich, 1990) explicitly varied memory load and returned to a dual-task paradigm. The results provided good support for the hypothesis that commitment of energetic support for memory was related to cardiac acceleration and peripheral vasoconstriction. The primary task was remembering seven integers presented individually with a 7 s spacing. Results collected during the initial four integers were labeled 'low memory load' and those collected for the remaining integers 'high memory load'. The secondary task was a simple reaction-time task with stimuli occurring 0.5 s either before or after the integer to be remembered. Probability of presentation before or after the integer was varied to examine our response preparation hypothesis when temporal probability but not response probability was varied. (Earlier experiments had varied probability of right or left response being required.) As expected, old and young both performed well on the memory task achieving around 90% correct recall. Secondary-task reaction times appropriately reflected the demand of the primary, memory task. During high-memory-load items, reaction times were longer than during low-memory-load items by 30 ms for the young and 57 ms for the old. Thus, the performance results suggested that memory load required a resource shared with reaction speed; and that this resource was drawn upon more by the old than the young.

The heart rate results (expressed as the time between beats, or interbeat interval) showed a dramatic convergence with the secondary-task results. Figure 8.6 shows the interbeat interval values for the intervals just before, during and after integer presentation for low- and high-memory-load serial positions. The young decelerate prior to and during integer presentation but do so less during high- as opposed to low-memory-load positions. The old show less overall deceleration and a clear overall acceleration during high-

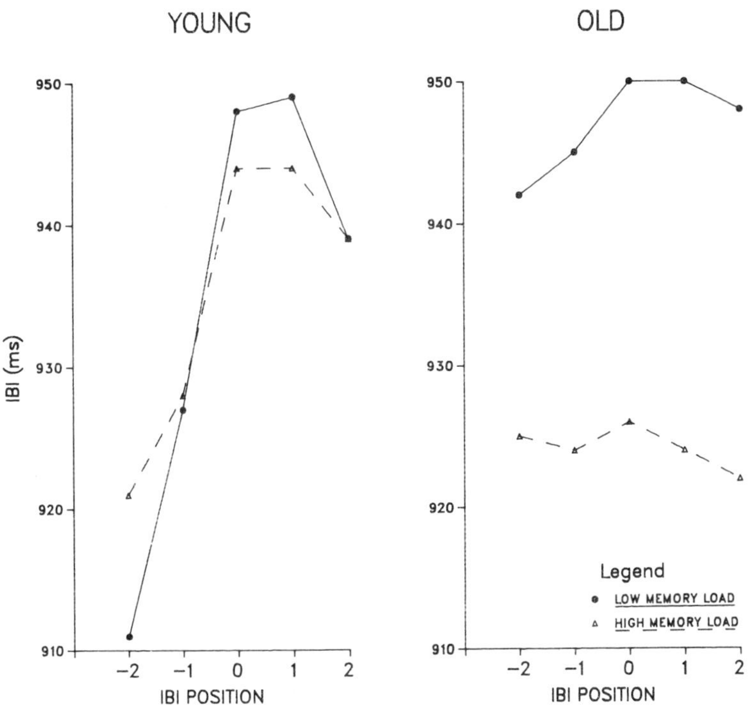

Figure 8.6. Average interbeat interval (IBI) response by young subjects (left) and old subjects (right) throughout integer presentation (at IBI position 0). (Responses during items early in the series—low memload—are compared with those late in the series—high memload). (Reprinted with permission. © American Psychological Association.)

memory-load positions. Note the slight decelerative trend in the low-memory-load positions that disappears for high-memory-load positions. Peripheral vasoconstriction was also increased by memory load, but again the young showed a greater difference in vasoconstriction than the old. Commitment of memory resource seems to be associated with cardiac acceleration and peripheral vasoconstriction. The old show greater cardiac acceleration suggesting a greater requirement for energetic resource, but fail to show greater vascular change. At rest, however, old and young vasculatures are not the same; old vessels may simply be less labile physiologically than young vessels.

Performance variations within age-groups allow us to pursue further our hypothesis of a difference in energetic requirements inducing differences in both heart rate and peripheral vasoconstriction. Figure 8.7 shows the interbeat interval results comparing performance groups within each age-group. Groups were formed by splitting the age-groups at the median of both memory and

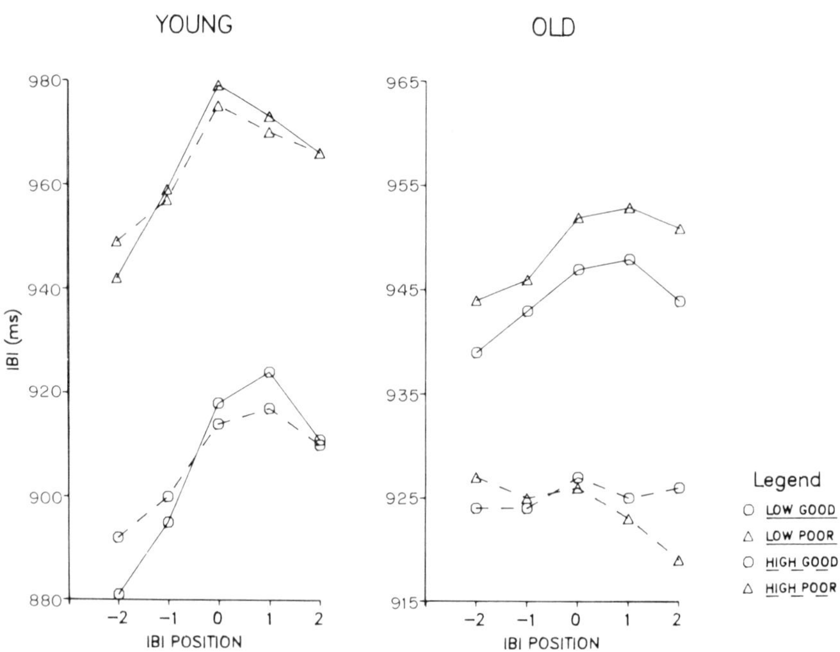

Figure 8.7. Average interbeat interval (IBI) in the young (left panel) and old (right panel) for good performers or poor performers. Interbeat intervals are plotted separately for low and high memory load within each performance group; e.g. Low Good is the response for good performers during low-memory-load items. Responses are centered on integer presentation (IBI position 0). Note the greater scale in the graph for the old. (Reprinted with permission. © American Psychological Association.)

reaction-time performance. The correlation of performance measures permitted a single grouping—young/good (faster than 413 ms of RT, memory proportion correct >0.95); and old/good (faster than 503 ms, proportion correct >0.89). The results again suggest that the young and old achieve good performance via different processes. The young, good performers relative to the young, poor performers show a shorter average interbeat interval but greater phasic cardiac deceleration and a greater average change with memory load. In contrast, the old, good performers relative to the old, poor performers have a comparable average interbeat interval, greater phasic deceleration only during high memory load and less average change with memory load. Interbeat interval levels differed between groups only during performance—not during the baseline period.

As in the prior work, vasoconstriction in the periphery suggested processing differences between age-groups. Young, good performers had less constriction than young, poor performers; while old, good performers had more constriction than old, poor performers.

Further interpretation requires two reasonable assumptions: that physiological function is comparable within age-groups, and that the degree of performance difference between good and poor groups is comparable within age-groups. Given these assumptions, one would expect the same physiological changes between good and poor performers unless the processes used to achieve good performance differed between age-groups or a qualitative change in the linkage of processing and energetic support occurred with age. We would argue that the processing which separates performance groups changes with age. Thus, we must further assume that for both age-groups perceptual detection is linked with anticipatory cardiac deceleration and that memory maintenance is linked with a tonic withdrawal of vagal activation and concomitant alpha sympathetic activation. The processing underlying the performance of the groups can then be inferred from the heart rate and peripheral vascular changes.

Based on the results summarized above and shown in Figure 8.6, we can now arrive at the following interpretive summary. Young, good performers allocate memory resources as needed and allocate resources to perceptual anticipation. Young, poor performers appear to allocate less resource to either memory or perceptual anticipation. Old, good performers (with roughly comparable absolute performance levels to young, poor performers) allocate significant resource to memory maintenance and withdraw resources from perceptual anticipation as memory load increases. Old, poor performers show a similar but amplified pattern—greater resource allocation with memory load and a greater withdrawal of resources from perceptual anticipation. Poor performance in the young seems, at least partially, due to inadequate resource allocation. In the old, relative resource allocation to memory maintenance appears more than adequate, but still insufficient to support the cognitive processing.

The results of the memory experiments suggested that both performance skill and age alter physiological changes during dual-task processing. Taken together, the results provide a reasonable case for a decline in the cognitive processes underlying memory maintenance (inferred from a greater resource requirement). The pattern of changes in physiological indices suggested that the decline was specific to memory processes and not a slowing characteristic of all central processing. Memory processes may, of course, be particularly susceptible to overall slowing; for example, maintenance of a steadily decaying trace will be less effective if renewal processes are uniformly slowed. Such a slowing-induced specific deficit remains specific, however, in a functional sense.

DIRECTIONS FOR EXPLORATION OF THE PSYCHOPHYSIOLOGY OF AGING

A cognitive–energetic approach to the psychophysiology of aging suggests a number of directions for research that have not yet been explored. Two of these will be briefly discussed to illustrate the further implications of the cognitive–energetic approach.

Hypotheses such as those of the Laceys' (e.g. 1978) posit peripheral end-organ changes that alter central nervous system processes via afferent feedback. Aging produces chronic changes in end-organ characteristics that might be expected to alter the energetic support delivered in response to central nervous system commands. Given afferent monitoring of energetic support, one might expect the central nervous system to respond to reduced response to commands by increasing the number and intensity of the commands. This increase in command, up to some limit, will yield similar responses across age-groups in the variable regulated by the central nervous system, but enhanced responses in variables supporting the controlled variable. For example, if blood flow to a muscle is regulated, then heart rate and stroke volume might increase with age as the vasodilative response to central commands becomes less effective. With further aging, such adjustments may no longer be effective, leading to decreases in the controlled response as well. Ultimately, central nervous system strategies may avoid behavioral adjustments which critically require efficient energetic support by the failing end-organ. This conceptual scenario suggests that the psychophysiology of aging might carefully examine psychophysiological and physiological studies which attempt to separate the controlled and controlling adjustments of the cardiovascular system (see Venables, 1984). Additionally, a concurrent examination of EEG/ERP variables might provide some index of central command that increases in appropriate fashion with age. Design-wise, comparisons of older individuals who vary in degree of end-organ change may be a useful strategy. For example, the stiffening and hardening of the vascular wall (atherosclerotic change) with age is endemic but not uniform across the population. Examining individuals with differing degrees of atherosclerosis on a task requiring the energetic support of enhanced blood flow should provide a naturally occurring experiment on variation in central command.

An important, but quite speculative, possibility is that the cognitive deficits of aging result from the progressive deterioration of energetic supports. Thus, if response preparation is supported by anticipatory blood flow shifts to specific muscles, then decline in the capability for vascular adjustment would result in less ability to maintain response preparation. Such an analysis assumes that certain central processes are directly and critically dependent on specific energetic support. The history of the search for peripheral changes which causally regulate central function argues that such an assumption may not be warranted (e.g. Jennings, 1986a). Our physiological system seems to have multiple paths equally capable of maintaining important behaviors. Thus, supportive, energetic changes may be facilitative without being necessary or critical to behavior. With age, however, the number of alternative support paths may be reduced, leading to a greater criticality of remaining energetic supports. Thus, the general goal of linking specific energetic supports with specific cognitive processes supported may be furthered by concurrent examination of young and old samples. Processes requiring significant support in the young become candidates for susceptibility to aging.

ACKNOWLEDGEMENTS

The authors thank the NIH for support of some of the work reported here by grant AG03792.

Kay Brock and Michael Eddy are thanked for their work in technical and laboratory support roles.

Integration

J. Richard Jennings
Department of Psychiatry, University of Pittsburgh, PA 15213, USA
and
Mary M. Schroeder
Department of Neurology, Albert Einstein College of Medicine, Bronx, NY 10461, USA

COGNITIVE AGING FROM AUTONOMIC AND EVENT-RELATED POTENTIAL PERSPECTIVES

This chapter has reviewed psychophysiological results suggesting that changes in information processing due to age are associated with changes in physiological concomitants of that processing. Both autonomic and event-related potential measures have suggested that, depending on task requirements, particular processes are influenced more than others by aging. How can we integrate the information from these two forms of psychophysiological data?

Cortical and autonomic responses provide different views of information processing. The exogeneous event-related potential clearly provides unique information about sensory transmission to the cortex. Autonomic measures are changes in effector systems (heart, skin) that are controlled by the autonomic nervous system. Autonomic afferents, such as from the baroreceptors, have not typically been stimulated or examined in human psychophysiology—and so we know little about age changes in transmission within autonomic afferents. Thus, our information on sensory information processing is confined to the event-related potential work. This work shows, with increasing adult age, small but consistent delays of transmission/processing in the different sensory systems. These delays must be recognized when interpreting delays with age in either autonomic or endogeneous cortical responses: can the increased latency with age be due solely to the peripheral transmission delay? At a less concrete level, we can ask whether the delayed—or possibly distorted—receipt of sensory information in the older individual might be responsible for added

Handbook of Cognitive Psychophysiology: Central and Autonomic Nervous System Approaches.
Edited by J. R. Jennings and M. G. H. Coles.

delays and processing errors in cortical processing. It would be interesting to examine older individuals with no evidence of slowed exogeneous potentials to see if their endogeneous responses and performance in, for example, a memory scanning task were also equivalent to that of younger volunteers. If such relatively peripheral delays were important, then a close examination of early attentional processes in older individuals using reflex and autonomic measures of attention/orienting would be critical (see Chapter 3). These investigations would have to take into account aging of the peripheral response mechanisms as discussed in this chapter for cardiovascular measures, and for startle reflexes by Harbin and Berg (1983).

Peripheral delays of sensory transmission are, however, small relative to changes in endogeneous event-related potentials with age. This, together with analytic performance studies (Welford, 1965), suggests that central processing changes with age are not likely to be totally explained by peripheral transmission/processing delays. Age-related changes in three cognitive processes were identified in our discussion of event-related potentials: encoding, response preparation in difficult tasks, and visual selective attention to points in space. The first two of these also can be examined at least superficially with respect to autonomic changes in these tasks. The selective-attention deficit cannot be examined so specifically. In general, however, autonomic results, as well as perhaps reflex (see Chapters 3 and 7) and eye movement (Chapter 6) results, can be used to examine the 'energetic' or strategic commitment of young and old volunteers to a task. When faced with a selective-attention task, does the older volunteer become as 'involved' as the younger volunteer? Does he/she direct attention in an appropriate fashion to the task in general? The answer to such questions will provide evidence about whether or not task processing of the young and old are truly comparable during the experiment. Analogically, 'energetic' measures can tell us whether the 'context' of the processing is appropriate; while event-related measures can tell us something about whether the 'content' of the processing is appropriate. This use of autonomic, reflex, and cortical measures obviously requires their concurrent collection.

Inferences based on separately collected autonomic and event-related potentials may be (somewhat hesitantly) drawn concerning changes in short-term memory function with age. The event-related potential results suggested that the encoding of memory items and response processes, but not memory scanning time, were influenced by aging. The heart rate results suggested that older volunteers allocated relatively more capacity to the maintenance of memory items than did younger volunteers. As suggested in the ERP review, if capacity is limited for the older subjects, response preparation may be delayed, explaining the delayed reaction times for more difficult memory tasks.

A slowing of response preparation for older subjects was supported on the

Sternberg memory task, albeit very indirectly by the evoked-potential results. The cardiovascular results associated with varying probability of response reviewed earlier may be relevant. Older volunteers appeared to commit fewer resources to preparing for unlikely responses than did young volunteers. Old and young volunteers did not appear to differ in their preparation for likely responses, however. In the memory scanning paradigm, response choice processes are involved but response probability is not usually a variable. Thus, it is not clear that the same response processes are being implicated by the autonomic and event-related potential measures. Both measures do, however, suggest that an examination of response-related processes in the elderly may be worthwhile.

Other results caution us not to trust speculations drawn across studies using different measures. In the area of anticipatory attention, autonomic and event-related potentials have been measured concurrently in young and old individuals. The contingent negative potential and readiness potential (*Bereitschaft* potential) as well as cardiac deceleration occur during the anticipation of a temporally expected signal. Harkins *et al.* (1976) compared the contingent negative potential and heart rate deceleration in a sample of 12 old men. In earlier work, heart rate deceleration but not contingent negative variation had declined with age (e.g. Thompson and Nowlin, 1973). Both heart rate change and contingent negative variation (to a greater degree) were related to response speed, but relations between contingent negative variation and heart rate change were low. Subsequently, Podelesny and Dustman (1982) compared young and old volunteers in a similar task. Their results basically replicated those of Harkins *et al.* (1976) and verified the stability of contingent negative variation—contingent negative variation actually increased slightly with greater age. Their young volunteers showed intercorrelations between contingent negative variation, heart rate deceleration, and reaction speed. Old volunteers did not. Thus, the sparse literature is consistent in showing age trends, but inconsistent in the relationship between cortical, autonomic, and performance measures. It seems likely that cortical and autonomic measures are reflecting different aspects of preparatory processes and that these aspects are influenced differently by age and paradigm. In principle the independence of cortical and autonomic indices—consistently present in the old—should provide greater power than a single index in predicting performance. Practically, a greater understanding of the aging of both measures and how they relate to performance will be required to achieve this predictability. Cortical and autonomic measures of seemingly similar psychological processes may relate differently in young and old volunteers. Subtle task differences may further differentially influence autonomic and cortical measures. Truly integrative experimental design may be required to derive the benefit from different psychophysiological indices.

CONCLUSION: GENERAL SLOWING OR SPECIFIC DEFICITS?

Our discussion started with a general overview of the nature of cognitive aging and a brief look at current views that a slowing of individual central processes may explain the performance deficits of aging. The slowing view is rather well supported using measures of the latency of responses. Latencies are, however, the resultant of a complex sequence of physiological events. Indices of some of these events might be expected to provide a more refined explanation of the locus of the deficits of performance due to age. Our examination of both event-related potential and autonomic (cardiovascular) indices suggested that such might be the case. The event-related potential results suggested deficits in stimulus encoding, response processing, and visual selective attention. The cardiovascular results suggested that certain information processes were supported by particular forms of energetic support—a specific cardiovascular response pattern. With age, the pattern of support changed, suggesting that the related processes—response preparation and memory maintenance—might be particularly influenced by aging.

The question of whether simple slowing explains performance change with age has not been settled. The evidence suggested some specific deficits with age, but precise mechanisms have not been identified. When they are, it remains possible that the primary mechanism might be a slowing that finds expression in the patterned results that have been described. Yet even in this case, the psychophysiological assessment of the processes will have forced a more refined understanding of slowing than that obtainable solely with performance results.

REFERENCES

Allison, T., Hume, A.L., Wood, C.C. and Goff, W.R. (1984). Developmental and aging changes in somatosensory, auditory, and visual evoked potentials. *Electroencephalography and Clinical Neurophysiology*, **58**, 14–24.

Allison, T., Wood, C.C. and Goff, W.R. (1983). Brain stem auditory, pattern-reversal visual, and short-latency somatosensory evoked potentials: latencies in relation to age, sex and brain and body size. *Electroencephalography and Clinical Neurophysiology*, **55**, 619–636.

Anders, T.L. and Fozard, J.L. (1973). Effects of age upon retrieval from primary and secondary memory. *Developmental Psychology*, **9**, 411–416.

Andrew, W. (1956). Structural alterations with aging in the nervous system. *Journal of Chronic Diseases*, **3**, 575–596.

Baker, S.P., Marchand, S., O'Neil, E., Nelson, C.A. and Posner, P. (1985). Age related changes in cardiac muscarinic receptors: decreased ability of the receptor to form a high affinity agonist binding state. *Journal of Gerontology*, **2**, 141–146.

Bashore, T.R., Osman, A. and Heffley, E.F. (1989). Mental slowing in elderly persons: a cognitive psychophysiological analysis. *Psychology and Aging*, **4**(2), 235–244.

Beatty, J. (1982). Task-evoked pupillary responses, processing load, and the structure of processing resources. *Psychological Bulletin*, **91**, 276–292.

Beck, E.C., Swanson, D. and Dustman, R.E. (1980). Long latency components of the visually evoked potential in man: effects of aging. *Experimental Aging Research*, **6**(6), 523–543.

Berlyne, D.E. (1960). *Conflict, Arousal, and Curiosity*. NY: McGraw-Hill.

Birren, J.E. (1974). Translations in gerontology—from lab to life: psychophysiology and speed of response. *American Psychologist*, Nov., 808–815.

Botwinick, J. (1980). *Aging and Behavior*. NY: Springer.

Brent, G.A., Smith, D.B.D. and Michalewski, H.J. (1977). Differences in the evoked potential in young and old subjects during habituation and dishabituation procedures. *Psychophysiology*, **14**, 137–144.

Bushke, H. and Grober, E. (1986). Genuine memory deficits in age-associated memory impairment. *Developmental Neuropsychology*, **2**, 287–307.

Carlson, A. (1985). Neurotransmitter changes in the aging brain. *Danish Medical Bulletin*, **32**(1), 40–43.

Celesia, C.G. and Daly, R.F. (1977). Affect of aging on visual evoked potentials. *Archives of Neurology*, **34**, 403.

Cerella, J. (1985). Information processing rates in the elderly. *Psychological Bulletin*, **98**(1), 67–83.

Craik, F.I.M. (1977). Age differences in human memory. In J.E. Birren and K.W. Schaie (eds), *Handbook of the Psychology of Aging*. NY: Van Nostrand Reinhold.

Craik, F.I.M. and Byrd, M. (1983). Aging and cognitive deficits: the role of attentional resources. In F.I.M. Craik and S. Frehub (eds), *Aging and Cognitive Processes*. NY: Plenum Press.

Cremer, R. (paper in preparation).

Cremer, R. and Zeef, E.J. (1987). What kind of noise increases with age. *Journal of Gerontology*, **42**(5), 515–518.

Denham, M.J., Crawley, J.C.W., Hodkinson, H.M. and Smith, D.S. (1980). Cerebral blood flow and motor nerve conduction velocity in the elderly. In G. Barbagallo-Sangiorgi and A.N. Exton-Smith (eds), *The Aging Brain: Neurological and Mental Disturbances*. New York: Plenum Press.

Docherty, J.R. (1986). Aging and the cardiovascular system. *Journal of Autonomic Pharmacology*, **6**, 77–84.

Donchin, E., Miller, G.A. and Farwell, L.A. (1986). The endogenous components of the event-related potential—a diagnostic tool?. In E. Fliers (ed.), *Progress in Brain Research*, vol. 70. Amsterdam: Elsevier, pp. 86–102.

Donchin, E., Ritter, W. and McCallum, W.C. (1978). Cognitive psychophysiology: the endogenous components of the ERP. In E. Callaway, P. Tueting and S.H. Ksolow (eds), *Event-Related Brain Potentials in Man*. New York: Academic Press, pp. 349–411.

Duckles, S.P., Carter, B.J. and Williams, C.L. (1985). Vascular adrenergic neuroeffector function does not decline in aged rats. *Circulation Research*, **56**, 109–116.

Easterbrook, J.A. (1959). The effect of motion on cue utilization and the organization of behavior. *Psychological Review*, **66**, 183–201.

Eisdorfer, C., Nowlin, J. and Wilkie, F. (1970). Improvement of learning in the aged by modification of autonomic nervous system activity. *Science*, **170**, 1327–1329.

Eysenck, M.W. (1977). *Attention and Arousal*. Berlin: Springer-Verlag.

Farkas, M.S. and Hoyer, W.J. (1980). Processing consequences of perceptual grouping in selective attention. *Journal of Gerontology*, **35**(2), 207–216.

Fleg, J.L., Tzankoff, S.P. and Lakatta, E.G. (1985). Age-related augmentation of plasma catecholamines during dynamic exercise in healthy males. *Journal of Applied Physiology*, **59**, 1033–1039.

Ford, J.M. and Pfefferbaum, A. (1980). The utility of brain potentials in determining age-related changes in central nervous system and cognitive functioning. In L.W. Poon and A.T. Welford (eds), *Aging in the 1980s*. Washington: American Psychological Association.

Ford, J.M., Pfefferbaum, A., Tinkleberg, J.R. and Kopell, B.S. (1982). Effects of perceptual and cognitive difficulty on P3 and reaction time in young and old adults. *Electroencephalography and Clinical Neurophysiology*, **54**, 311–321.

Ford, J.M., Roth, W.T., Mohs, R.C., Hopkins, W.F. and Kopell, B.S. (1979). Event-related potentials recorded from young and old adults during a memory retrieval task. *Electroencephalography and Clinical Neurophysiology*, **47**, 450–459.

Friedman, D. and Hamberger, M. (in press). Event-related potentials during continous recognition memory in young, middle-aged, and elderly adults. Presented at EPIC IX, Noordwijk, Netherlands, June 1989.

Friedman, D., Hamberger, M. and Putman, L. (in press). The 'frontal lobe dysfunction' hypothesis in the elderly: preliminary findings based on evidence from ERPs. Presented at EPIC IX, Noordwijk, Netherlands, June 1989.

Garwood, M., Engel, B.T. and Capriotti, R. (1982). Autonomic nervous system function and aging: response specificity. *Psychophysiology*, **19**(4), 378–385.

Gick, M.L., Craik, F.I.M. and Morris, R.G. (1988). Task complexity and age differences in working memory. *Memory and Cognition*, **16**(4), 353–361.

Gintner, G.G., Hollandsworth, J.G. and Intrieri, R.C. (1986). Age differences in cardiovascular reactivity under active coping conditions. *Psychophysiology*, **23**(1), 113–120.

Goldberg, P.B., Kreider, M.S. and Roberts, J. (1984). Effects of age on the adrenergic cardiac neuroeffector junction. *Life Sciences*, **35**, 2585–2591.

Goodin, D.S. (1986). Event-related (endogenous) potentials. In M.G. Aminoff (ed.), *Electrodiagnosis in Clinical Neurology*. Churchill Livingstone: New York, pp. 575–595.

Goodin, D.S., Squires, K.C., Henderson, B.H. and Star, A. (1978). Age-related variations in evoked potentials to auditory stimuli in normal human subjects. *Electroencephalography and Clinical Neurophysiology*, **44**, 447–458.

Gopher, D. (1986). In defence of resources: on structures, energies, pools and the allocation of attention. In G.R.J. Hockey, A.W.K. Gaillard and M.G.H. Coles (eds), *Energetics and Human Information Processing*. Dordrecht, Netherlands: Martinus Nijhoff, pp. 353–372.

Grober, E. and Buschke, H. (1897). Genuine memory deficits in dementia. *Developmental Neuropsychology*, **3**, 13–36.

Gur, R.C., Gur, R.E., Obrist, W.D., Skolnick, B.E. and Reivich, M. (1987). Age and regional cerebral blood flow at rest and during cognitive activity. *Archives of General Psychiatry*, **44**, 617–621.

Harbin, T.J. and Berg, W.K. (1983). The effects of age and prestimulus duration upon reflex inhibition. *Psychophysiology*, **20**(6), 603–610.

Harkins, S.W., Moss, S.F., Thompson, L.W. and Nowlin, J.B. (1976). Relationship between central and autonomic nervous system activity: correlates of psychomotor performance in elderly men. *Experimental Aging Research*, **2**, 409–423.

Harris, G.J. and Fleer, R.E. (1974). *Journal of Experimental Child Psychology*, **17**, 452–459.

Harter, M.R., Aine, C. and Schroeder, C.E. (1982). Hemispheric differences in the neural processing of stimulus location and type: effects of selective attention on visual evoked potentials. *Neuropsychologia*, **20**, 421–438.

Hawkes, C.M. and Stowe, B. (1981). Pupil size and pattern visual evoked potentials. *Journal of Neurology, Neurosurgery, and Psychiatry*, **44**, 90–91.

Heemstra, M.L. (1988). *Efficiency of Human Information Processing: A Model of Cognitive Energetics*. The Hague, Netherlands: CIP-Gegevens Koninklijke.

Hillyard, S.A. and Munte, T.F. (1984). Selective attention to color and location: an analysis with event-related brain potentials. *Perception and Psychophysics*, *36*(2), 185–198.

Hockey, G.R.J. (1973). Changes in information-selection patterns in multi-source monitoring as a function of induced arousal shifts. *Journal of Experimental Psychology*, **101**, 35–42.

Hockey, R., Gaillard, A. and Coles, M. (1986). *Energetics and Human Information Processing*. Dordrecht, Netherlands: Martinus Nijhoff.

Hoyer, W.J. and Plude, D.J. (1980). Attentional and perceptual processes in the study of cognitive aging. In L.W. Poon (ed.), *Aging in the 1980s*. Washington, DC: American Psychological Association.

Jennings, J.R. (1986a). Bodily changes during attending. In M.G.H. Coles, E. Donchin and S.W. Porges (eds), *Psychophysiology: Systems, Processes, and Applications*. NY: Guilford, pp. 268–289.

Jennings, J.R. (1986b). Memory, thought, and bodily response. In M.G.H. Coles, E. Donchin and S.W. Porges (eds), *Psychophysiology: Systems, Processes and Applications*. NY: Guilford, pp. 290–308.

Jennings, J.R., Brock, K. and Nebes, R. (1989). Aging but not arousal influences the effect of environmental noise on the span of attention. *Experimental Aging Research*, **15**(2), 61–72.

Jennings, J.R., Brock, K. and Nebes, R. (1990). Age and specific processing capacities: a cardiovascular analysis. *Journal of Psychophysiology*, **4**, 51–64.

Jennings, J.R. and Hall, S.W. (1980). Recall, recognition, and rate: memory and the heart. *Psychophysiology*, **17**, 37–46.

Jennings, J.R., Nebes, R. and Brock, K. (1988). Memory retrieval in noise and psychophysiological response in the young and old. *Psychophysiology*, **25**, 633–644.

Jennings, J.R., Nebes, R. and Yovetich, N. (1990). Aging increases the energetic demands of episodic memory: a cardiovascular analysis. *Journal of Experimental Psychology: General*, **119**(1), 77–91.

Jennings, J.R., Stiller, R. and Brock, K. (1988). Are changes in performance with noise and age due to adrenergic arousal? *Psychobiology*, **16**, 270–280.

Kahneman, D. (1973). *Attention and Effort*. Englewood Cliffs, NJ: Prentice-Hall, pp. 1–49.

Kahneman, D. and Treisman, A. (1984). Changing views of attention and automaticity. In R. Parasuraman and D.R. Davies (eds), *Varieties of Attention*. NY: Academic Press, pp. 29–62.

Lacey, J.I. (1967). Somatic response patterning and stress: some revisions of activation theory. In M.H. Appley and P. Trumbull (eds), *Psychological Stress: Issues in Research*. New York: Appleton–Century–Crofts, pp. 14–42.

Lacey, J.I., Kagan, J., Lacey, B.C. and Moss, H.A. (1963). The visceral level: situational determinants and behavioral correlates of autonomic response patterns. In P.H. Knapp (eds), *Expression of the Emotions in Man*. New York: International Universities Press, pp. 161–196.

Lacey, B.E. and Lacey J.I. (1978). Two-way communication between the heart and the brain significant of time within the cardiac cycle. *American Psychologist*, **33**, 99–113.

Lakatta, E.J. (1983). Determinants of cardiovascular performance: modification due to aging. *Journal of Chronic Diseases*, **36**, 15–30.

Layton, B. (1975). Perceptual noise and aging. *Psychological Bulletin*, **82**(6), 875–883.

Looren de Jong, H., Kok, A. and Van Rooy, J. (1987). Electrophysiological indices of visual selection and memory search in young and old adults. In R. Johnson, R. Parasuraman and J.W. Rohrbaugh (eds), *Current Trends in Event-Related Potential Research*. Amsterdam: Elsevier, pp. 341–349.

Looren de Jong, H., Kok, A., Woestenburg, J.C., Logman, C.J.C.M. and Van Rooy, J.C.G.M. (1988). Learning where to look: electrophysiological and behavioral indices of visual search in young and old subjects, *Biological Psychology*, **26**, 277–298.

Madden, D.J. (1983). Differences and similarities in the improvement of controlled search. *Experimental Aging Research*, **8**(2), 22–26.

Marsh, G.R. (1975). Age differences in evoked potential correlates of a memory scanning process. *Experimental Aging Research*, **1**, 3–16.

Marsh, G.R. and Thompson, L.W. (1977). Psychophysiology of aging. In J.E. Birren and K.W. Schaie (eds), *Handbook of the Psychology of Aging*. New York: Van Nostrand, pp. 219–248.

Morris, R.G., Gick, M.L. and Craik, F.I.M. (1988). Processing resources and age differences in working memory. *Memory and Cognition*, **16**(4), 362–366.

Morris, J.D. and Thompson, L.W. (1969). Heart rate changes in a reaction time experiment with young and aged subjects. *Journal of Gerontology*, **24**, 269–277.

Mullis, R.J., Holcomb P.J., Diner, B.C. and Dykman, R.A. (1985). The effects of aging on the P3 component of the visual event-related potential. *Electroencephalography and Clinical Neurophysiology*, **62**, 141–149.

Näätänen, R. (1973). The inverted-U relationship between activation and performance: a critical review. In S. Kornblum (ed.), *Attentional and Performance*, vol. IV. New York: Academic Press, pp. 155–174.

Neiss, R. (1988). Reconceptualizing arousal: psychobiological states in motor performance. *Psychological Bulletin*, **103**, 345–366.

Novack, G., Ritter, W., Vaughan, H.G. and Wiznetzer, M. (in press). Differentiation of negative event-related potentials in an auditory discrimination task. *Electroencephalography and Clinical Neurophysiology*.

Pfefferbaum, A. and Ford, J.M. (1988). ERPs to stimuli requiring response production and inhibition: effects of age, probability and visual noise. *Electroencephalography and Clinical Neurophysiology*, **71**, 55–63.

Pfefferbaum, A., Ford, J.M., Roth, W.T. and Kopell, B.S. (1980a). Age differences in P3–reaction time associations. *Electroencephalography and Clinical Neurophysiology*, **49**, 257–265.

Pfefferbaum, A., Ford, J.M., Roth, W.T. and Kopell, B.S. (1980b). Age-related changes in auditory event-related potentials. *Electroencephalography and Clinical Neurophysiology*, **49**, 266–276.

Pfefferbaum, A., Ford, J.M., Wenegrat, B.G., Roth, W.T. and Kopell, B.S. (1984). Clinical application of the P3 component of event-related potentials. I: Normal aging. *Electroencephalography and Clinical Neurophysiology*, **59**, 85–103.

Pfeifer, M.A., Neinberg, C.R., Cook, D., Best, J.D., Reenan, A. and Halter, J.B. (1983). Differential changes of autonomic nervous system function with age in man. *American Journal of Medicine*, **75**, 249–258.

Picton, T.W., Stuss, D.T., Champagne, S.C. and Nelson, R.F. (1984). The effects of age on human event-related potentials. *Psychophysiology*, **21**(3), 312–325.

Plude, D.J. and Hoyer, W.J. (1986). Age and the selectivity of visual information processing. *Psychology and Aging*, **1**(1), 1–11.

Podlesney, J.A. and Dustman, R.E. (1982). Age effects on heart rate, sustained potential, and PT responses during reaction-time tasks. *Neurobiology of Aging*, **3**, 1–9.

Polich, J. (in press). P300 in the evaluation of aging and dementia. Presented at the aging and dementia symposium, EPIC IX, Noordwijk, Netherlands, June, 1989.

Powell, D.A., Milligan, W.L. and Furchtgott, E. (1980). Peripheral autonomic changes accompanying learning and reaction time performance in older people. *Journal of Gerontology*, **35**(1), 57–65.

Pratt, H., Michaelweski, H.J., Patterson, J.V. and Starr, A. (1989). Brain potentials in a memory scanning task. II: Effects of aging on potentials to the probes. *Electroencephalography and Clinical Neurophysiology*, **72**, 507–517.

Pribram, K.H. and McGuinness, D. (1975). Arousal, activation, and effort in the control of attention. *Psychological Review*, **82**, 116–149.

Pritchard, W.S. (1981). Psychophysiology of P300. *Psychological Bulletin*, **89**(3), 506–540.

Rabbitt, P. (1965). An age decrement in the ability to ignore irrelevant information. *Journal of Gerontology*, **20**, 233–238.

Rabbitt, P. (1980). A fresh look at changes in reaction times in old age. In G. Stein (ed.), *The Psychobiology of Aging: Problems and Perspectives*. Amsterdam: Elsevier North-Holland.

Riege, W.H., Cohen, M.J. and Wallach, H.F. (1980). Autonomic responsivity during recognition memory processing in three age groups. *Experimental Aging Research*, **6**(2), 159–174.

Ritter, W., Simson, R, Vaughan, H.G. and Macht, M. (1982). Manipulation of event-related potential manifestations of information processing stages, *Science*, **218**, 909–911.

Rogers, R.L., Meyer, J.S., Mortel, K.F., Mahurin, R.K. and Thornby, J. (1985). Age-related reductions in cerebral vasomotor reactivity and the law of initial value: a 4-year prospective longitudinal study. *Journal of Cerebral Blood Flow and Metabolism*, **5**, 79–85.

Roth, W.T., Tecce, J.J., Pfefferbaum, A., Rosenbloom, M. and Callaway, E. (1984). ERPs and psychopathology. I: Behavioral process issues. In R. Karrer, J. Cohen and P. Tueting (eds), *Brain and Information: Event-Related Potentials*. New York: NY Academy of Sciences, pp. 496–522.

Sachs, C., Hamberger, B. and Kaijser, L. (1985). Cardiovascular responses and plasma catecholamines in old age. *Clinical Physiology*, **5**, 553–565.

Salthouse, T.A. (1985). *A Theory of Cognitive Aging*. Amsterdam: North-Holland.

Salthouse, T.A. and Somberg, B.L. (1982). Isolating the age deficit in speeded performance. *Journal of Gerontology*, **37**(1), 59–63.

Sanders, A.F. (1981). Stress and human performance: a working model and some applications. In J. Salvendy and M.J. Smith (eds), *Machine Pacing and Occupational Stress*. London: Taylor and Francis, pp. 57–64.

Schroeder, M.M. and Harter, M.R. (1986). Aging and selective attention to color and space: event-related potentials. *Society for Neuroscience Abstracts*, **12**, 492.

Schroeder, M.M. and Harter, M.R. (in preparation). Effects of aging and practice on event-related potentials in a visual selective attention task.

Shaw, N.A. and Cant, B.R. (1980). Age-dependent changes in latency of pattern visual evoked potentials. *Electroencephalography and Clinical Neurophysiology*, **48**, 237–242.

Simson, R, Vaughan, H.G. and Ritter, W. (1977). The scalp topography of potentials in auditory and visual discrimination tasks. *Electroencephalography and Clinical Neurophysiology*, **42**, 528–535.

Smith, D.B.D., Thompson, S.W. and Michalewski, H.J. (1980). Averaged evoked potential research in adult aging: status and prospects. In L.W. Poon and A.T. Welford (eds), *Aging in the 1980s*. Washington: American Psychological Association.

Sokol, N.A., Moskowitz, A. and Towle, V.L. (1981). Age-related changes in latency of visual evoked potentials: influence of check size. *Electroencephalography and Clinical Neurophysiology*, **51**, 559–562.

Squires, K.C., Chippendale, T.J., Wrege, K.S., Goodin, D.S. and Starr, A. (1980). Electrophysiological assessment of mental function in aging and dementia. In L.W. Poon (ed.), *Aging in the 1980s: Selected Contemporary Issues in the Psychology of Aging*. Washington, DC: American Psychological Association, pp. 125–134.

Squires, N.K., Squires, K.C. and Hillyard, S.A. (1975). Two varieties of long-latency positive waves evoked by unpredictable auditory stimuli in man. *Electroencephalography and Clinical Neurophysiology*, **38**, 387–401.

Sternberg, S. (1969). Memory-scanning: mental processes revealed by reaction-time experiments. *American Scientist*, **57**, 421–457.

Strayer, D.L., Wickens, C.D. and Braune, R. (1987). Adult age differences in the speed and capacity of information processing. 2: An electrophysiological approach. *Psychology and Aging*, **2**(2), 99–110.

Surwillo, W.W. (1968). Timing of behavior in senescence and the role of the central nervous system. In G.A. Talland (ed.), *Human Aging and Behavior*. New York: Academic Press, pp. 1–35.

Syndulko, K., Hansch, E.C., Cohen, S.N., Pearce, J.W., Goldberg, Z., Morton, B., Tourtellotee, W.W. and Potvin, A.K. (1982). Long-latency event-related potentials in normal aging and dementia. In J. Courjon, F. Maugiere and M. Revol (eds), *Clinical Applications of Evoked Potentials in Neurology*. Raven Press, New York, pp. 279–285.

Tecce, J.J, Cattanach, L., Yrchik, D.A., Meinbresse, D. and Dessonville, C.L. (1982). CNV rebound and aging. *Electroencephalography and Clinical Neurophysiology*, **54**, 175–186.

Thompson, L.W. and Nowlin, J.B. (1973). Relation of increased attention to central and autonomic nervous system states. In L. Jarvik, C. Eisdorfer and J. Blum (eds), *Intellectual Functioning in Adults: Psychological and Biological Influences*. New York: Springer, pp. 107–124.

van der Molen, M.W., Somsen, R.J.M., Jennings, J.R., Nieuwboer, R.T. and Orlebeke, J.F. (1987). A psychophysiological investigation of cognitive–energetic relations in human information processing: a heart rate/additive factors approach. *Acta Psychologica*, **66**, 251–289.

Vita, G., Princi, P., Calabro, R., Toscano, A., Manna, L. and Messina, C. (1986). Cardiovascular reflex tests: assessment of age-adjusted normal range. *Journal of Neurological Sciences*, **75**, 263–274.

Walsh, R.A. (1987). Cardiovascular effects of the aging process. *American Journal of Medicine*, **82**, 34–40.

Warren, L.R., Butler, R.W., Katholi, C.R. and Halsey, J.H. (1985). Age differences in cerebral blood flow during rest and during mental activation measurements with and without monetary incentive. *Journal of Gerontology*, **40**(1), 53–59.

Welford, A.T. (1965). Performance, biological mechanisms and age: a theoretical sketch. In A.T. Welford and J.E. Birren (eds), *Behavior, Aging, and the Nervous System*. Springfield, IL: Charles C. Thomas, pp. 3–20.

Welford, A.T. (1981). Signal, noise, performance, and age. *Human Factors*, **23**, 97–109.

Wickens, C.D. (1980). The structure of attentional resources. In R.S. Nickerson (ed.), *Attention and Performance*, vol. VIII. Hillsdale, NJ: Lawrence Erlbaum, pp. 239–258.

Wickens, C.D. (1984). Processing resources in attention. In R. Parasuraman and D.R. Davies (eds), *Varieties of Attention*. New York: Academic Press, pp. 63–102.

Woodruff, D.S. (1985). Arousal, sleep, and aging. In J.E. Birren, K.W. Schaie, V. Bengtson, L. Jarvik and T. Salthouse (eds), *Handbook of the Psychology of Aging*. New York: Van Nostrand Reinhold, pp. 261–295.

Wright, L.L. and Elias, J.W. (1979). Age differences in the effects of perceptual noise. *Journal of Gerontology*, **34**, 704–708.

Yin, F.C.P. (1980). The aging vasculature and its effects on the heart. In M.L. Weisfeldt (ed.), *The Aging Heart*. New York: Raven Press.

Ziegler, M.G., Lake, C.R. and Kopin, I.J. (1976). Plasma noradrenaline increases with age. *Nature*, **261**, 333–334.

Index

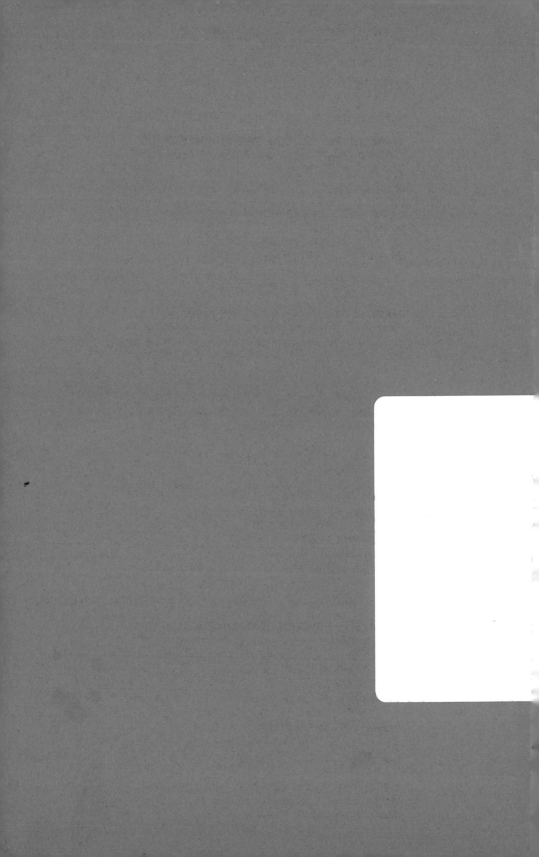